FISHER & LIGHTWOOD'S
LAW OF MORTGAGE

FISHER AND LIGHTWOOD'S

LAW OF MORTGAGE

NINTH EDITION

BY

E. L. G. TYLER, M.A. (Oxon.)

*of Lincoln's Inn and the Northern Circuit, Barrister-at-Law; and
of the Faculty of Law, University of Liverpool*

LONDON
BUTTERWORTHS
1977

ENGLAND:	BUTTERWORTH & CO. (PUBLISHERS) LTD.
	LONDON: 88 Kingsway, WC2B 6AB
AUSTRALIA:	BUTTERWORTHS PTY LTD.
	SYDNEY: 586 Pacific Highway, Chatswood, NSW 2067
	Also at Melbourne, Brisbane, Adelaide and Perth
CANADA:	BUTTERWORTH & CO. (CANADA) LTD.
	TORONTO: 2265 Midland Avenue, Scarborough M1P 4S1
NEW ZEALAND:	BUTTERWORTHS OF NEW ZEALAND LTD.
	WELLINGTON: 26/28 Waring Taylor Street 1
SOUTH AFRICA:	BUTTERWORTH & CO. (SOUTH AFRICA) (PTY) LTD.
	DURBAN: 152/154 Gale Street
USA:	BUTTERWORTH & CO. (PUBLISHERS) INC.
	BOSTON: 19 Cummings Park, Woburn, Mass 01801

©

BUTTERWORTH & CO. (PUBLISHERS) LTD.
1977

ISBN: 0 406 20104 8

Editors of Previous Editions

1856 First Edition   by W. R. FISHER
1868 Second Edition by W. R. FISHER
1876 Third Edition   by W. R. FISHER
1884 Fourth Edition by W. R. FISHER
1897 Fifth Edition   by SIR ARTHUR UNDERHILL
1910 Sixth Edition   by SIR ARTHUR UNDERHILL
                     and ARTHUR COLE
1931 Seventh Edition by J. M. LIGHTWOOD
1969 Eighth Edition by E. L. G. TYLER

Preface to the Ninth Edition

The eighth edition was published in 1969 and kept up to date by supplements in 1971 and 1973. That edition is now out of print, and in any event there has been sufficient development in the law of mortgages to justify a new edition.

The object of the original work was "to explain the nature of the different kinds of securities, the rights and remedies of the persons who make, and of those who are entitled to the benefit of them, and the manner and circumstances attending their discharge". In the last edition I omitted any detailed discussion of pledges and liens (save for the vendor's lien) in order to reduce the size of the book and limit its scope to mortgages and charges in particular, rather than to securities generally, and emphasised the aspects of mortgagee's remedies and discharge. For the present edition I have not attempted to reshape the book. If one was starting afresh the result would no doubt be different. But this is a practitioners' book and what they want is an up-to-date account of the current law and the relevant sources. Sykes' *The Law of Securities* (2nd Edition 1973), published by the Law Book Company Limited in Australia, provides a modern and stimulating general view of the law without the detail of *Fisher and Lightwood* and I have added references to this book where appropriate. I might add that I have continued the policy of the last edition in including, where appropriate, references to Commonwealth decisions.

The major changes in this edition are the chapter on the Consumer Credit Act (written by Mr. Norman Palmer, formerly a colleague of mine at Liverpool and now of the Law Faculty of the University of Tasmania, for whose assistance I am most grateful) and the revised material on the mortgagee's right to possession and duty on selling. In addition there has been a good deal of re-writing throughout to reflect recent decisions and legislation or merely a new emphasis arising out of matters which I have had to consider since the last edition. Good examples of the latter are the binding effect (if any) of a redemption statement and the selling mortgagee's obligation (if any), where appropriate, to account to the mortgagor for interest on the net surplus proceeds of sale.

Finally, I would echo the words of Sir Arthur Underhill and Arthur Cole, editors of the sixth edition (and all the more so since this is a sole effort whereas so many practitioners' books nowadays are team efforts) that I believe that this edition will be found to be accurate and trustworthy, but that if I should be caught tripping, then I must hope that some indulgence may be shown, having regard to the labour and difficulty of editing a work of this kind.

Some readers of the book have in the past been kind enough to write to me on various mortgage points and I have been able to incorporate some of these into this edition. Further help will always be welcomed.

E. L. G. TYLER

14 COOK ST.
LIVERPOOL
April, 1977

Table of Contents

PART II

PARTIES TO MORTGAGES

Contents

PART III

VOID OR IMPERFECT SECURITIES

PART IV

TRANSFER AND DEVOLUTION OF MORTGAGES

PART V

THE MORTGAGEE'S REMEDIES

Contents

xiii

PART VI

PRIORITIES OF MORTGAGES

PART VII

INCIDENCE OF THE MORTGAGE DEBT

PART VIII

DISCHARGE OF THE MORTGAGE

PART IX

ACCOUNTS AND COSTS

PART X

THE OPTION MORTGAGE SCHEME

PART XI

TAXES

APPENDIX

BASIC CONVEYANCING AND
COURT FORMS

INDEX

Table of Statutes

References in this Table to "*Statutes*" are to Halsbury's Statutes
of England (Third Edition) showing the volume and page at which
the annotated text of the Act will be found.

Table of Cases

In the following Table references are given to the English and Empire Digest where a digest of the case will be found.

A

PAGE

PAGE

— 17 —

D

PAGE

PAGE

M

PAGE

PAGE

Q

R

S

PAGE

*e**

U

V

PART I

MORTGAGES AND CHARGES

CHAPTER 1

Mortgages and Other Securities Generally [a]

1—SECURITIES GENERALLY

The nature and kinds of security.—A creditor may be willing to rely solely on his debtor's personal credit for the fulfilment of the latter's contractual obligations. It is likely, however, that he will want something more than a mere contractual remedy against a debtor who defaults (b). This he obtains by taking security. Security is of two kinds, personal and real.

Personal security, or suretyship, consists of the contract of guarantee, whereby the guarantor promises to answer for the obligation of the debtor should the latter default. The effect of personal security is to give the creditor a secondary contractual action against the guarantor should the principal debtor default. The disadvantages of personal security, from the creditor's point of view, are that the efficacy of a guarantee depends on the completeness in the form of the document itself and on the original and continued solvency of the guarantor.

Real security gives the creditor certain rights over property which has been appropriated to meet the debt or other obligation. Its attraction for the creditor is that, if the debtor should become insolvent, the creditor may exercise his rights over the security in priority to the claims of the general creditors. The property may be real or personal.

Real security may be created by contract or may arise by operation of law. In the former case, the security takes the form of mortgage, pledge or charge (c); in the latter it is called a lien (d).

Real securities fall into three classes; first, those by which the creditor obtains proprietary rights over the subject matter of the security but which do not depend on the creditor obtaining possession of such property (e); secondly, those by which the creditor does not obtain proprietary rights over the property, and which depend on him obtaining possession of the property (f); and, thirdly, those which do

---

(a) On guarantee generally, see 3 Halsbury's Laws of England (3rd Edn.), Guarantee.

(b) In some cases, e.g., where the loan is by trustees, security will be *required* by the terms of the trust deed or statute.

(c) But statutory charges do not arise out of agreement. For statutory charges, see p. 164, *infra*. And charges created by will may lack this element of agreement: see Sykes, *The Law of Securities* (2nd Edn.) p. 12.

(d) There is some looseness in the use of the terminology of real securities. In some works the word "lien" includes charges arising out of contract.

(e) *I.e.*, mortgage securities.

(f) *I.e.*, pledge and the possessory lien.

not depend on the creditor obtaining either proprietary rights over or the possession of the property (g).

To each of the kinds of real security is incident a right in the creditor to make the property which is subject to the security answerable for the debt or other obligation, a right in the debtor to redeem the property by paying the debt or performing the obligation, and a liability on the part of the creditor upon such payment or performance to restore the property to the owner.

Mortgage.—A mortgage is a form of security created by contract, conferring an interest in property defeasible (*i.e.* annullable) upon performing the condition of paying a given sum of money, with or without interest, or of performing some other condition (h).   Realty or personalty may be mortgaged.   Mortgages of chattels are generally effected by bills of sale (i).   A mortgage may be either legal or equitable (k).

A charge by way of legal mortgage of land has the same effect as a mortgage (l) without any legal estate being conferred on the mortgagee.

Pledge (m).—A pledge or pawn is a security created by contract and effected by a bailment of a chattel to the creditor to be kept by him until the debt is discharged.   It is incomplete without actual or constructive delivery of the goods to the pledgee.   The general property in the goods remains in the pledgor.

Charge.—A charge is the appropriation of real or personal property for the discharge of a debt or other obligation, without giving the creditor either a general or special property in, or possession of, the subject of the security, *e.g.*, an order upon a third party to apply money in his hands to the discharge of a debt, or a charge on realty for the payment of a specified amount.   The creditor has a right of realisation by judical process in case of non-payment of the debt. Where goods are so appropriated the transaction is called hypothecation (n).   Marine hypothecation may be by way of bottomry or *respondentia* (o).

The charge by way of legal mortgage has been referred to above. Both "mortgage" and "charge" are often loosely used as a generic

---

(g) *I.e.*, charges and non-possessory liens. This threefold classification is given by WILLES, J., in *Halliday* v. *Holgate* (1868), L.R. 3 Exch. 299, at p. 302. On the difficulties of classification and the general nature of security interests, see *Sykes, ubi supra*, Chs. 1 and 24.

(h) The classic description of a mortgage was given by LINDLEY, M.R., in *Santley* v. *Wilde*, [1899] 2 Ch. 474 (C.A.), in the following terms: "A mortgage is a conveyance of land or an assignment of chattels as a security for the payment of a debt or the discharge of some other obligation for which it is given."   And see *London County and Westminster Bank, Ltd.* v. *Tompkins*, [1918] 1 K.B. 515 (C.A.), where the terms "mortgage" and "equitable charge" are discussed.

(i) See Ch. 4, *infra*.

(k) See pp. 5 and 11, *infra*.

(l) Law of Property Act 1925, s. 87 (1). And see p. 25, *infra*.

(m) See, generally, 29 Halsbury's Laws (3rd Edn.,), Pawns and Pledges.

(n) And in most cases the documents used in connection with the transaction will require registration under the Bills of Sale Acts (see Ch. 4, *infra*). The document setting out the terms of a pledge of documents of title is sometimes referred to as a letter of hypothecation, but, nevertheless, the transaction is pledge.

(o) See Ch. 5, *infra*.

term for all species of security (*p*). The mortgage and charge have, indeed, been gradually assimilated, so that today for practical purposes there is little difference between them (*q*), though the fundamental difference in their nature remains.

Lien (*r*).—A lien is a right conferred by law, and not by contract, upon a person to retain possession of, or to have a charge upon, the real or personal property of another, until certain demands are satisfied.

II—MORTGAGES GENERALLY

Legal mortgage.—Subject to the provisions of the Law of Property Act 1925, a legal mortgage is a conveyance or assignment of the whole or part of the estate or interest of the debtor in real or personal property of which he is the legal owner or of some legal estate or interest which he has the power to transfer (*s*). Except in the case of a legal mortgage of land, the absolute assurance of the property is usually subject to a proviso that upon payment of the debt at a certain time the property should be reconveyed. Under the Law of Property Act 1925, a legal mortgage of land must be created by demise for a term of years, or by charge by way of legal mortgage, subject to a provision for cesser on redemption (*t*). The essence of the legal mortgage of land is the vesting of a legal estate in the mortgagee, together with an immediate right of possession (*u*). On payment of the debt at the time fixed, the mortgagor may re-enter (*a*) and is entitled to a reconveyance (*b*).

Mortgages of land before 1926 (*c*).—Pledges of land are found in Anglo-Saxon times and in Domesday Book. In Glanvill (*c.* 1187)

(*p*) Under the Law of Property Act 1925, mortgage includes charges and liens: s. 205 (1) (xvi).

And in the construction of wills "mortgage" includes charge and *vice versa*: see *Re Beirnstein, Barnett* v. *Beirnstein,* [1925] Ch. 12. In the company context especially, mortgage and charge are often used as if there was no difference between them. For a recent example, see *Re Wallis and Simmonds (Builders), Ltd.,* [1975] Q.B. 94; [1974] 1 All E.R. 561.

(*q*) See the Survey of the Land Law of Northern Ireland, 1971, which recommended that the legal charge should be the only form of mortgage: (1971) 35 Conv. (N.S.) 92, 94–95; and Sykes, *The Law of Securities* (2nd Edn.) Chs. 1 and 24; Lawson, *Introduction to the Law of Property,* p. 182.

(*r*) See, generally, 24 Halsbury's Laws (3rd Edn.), Lien, For the unpaid vendors lien and loss thereof, see pp. 166 and 588, *infra.*

(*s*) See the cases referred to in footnote (*h*), *supra.*

(*t*) Law of Property Act 1925, ss. 85, 86 (see pp. 21–23, *infra*). A charge by way of legal mortgage is included in the definition of a legal mortgage: Law of Property Act 1925, s. 205 (1) (xvi); and, although it does not actually create a legal estate, it gives the same powers and remedies as if it did; Law of Property Act 1925, s. 87 (1) (see p. 25, *infra*).

(*u*) But this right to possession in now restricted by statute in certain cases (see p. 326, *infra*).

(*a*) Upon payment the mortgage term becomes a satisfied term and ceases: Law of Property Act 1925, ss. 5 and 116 (see p. 550, *infra*). In this respect the provision for cesser has the same effect as the former condition for defeasance (as to which, see p. 6, *infra*).

(*b*) Notwithstanding the automatic cesser of the mortgage term on payment, the Law of Property Act 1925, provides for the surrender of the term: s. 115 (see, p. 548, *infra*).

(*c*) See, generally, Holdsworth, *History of English Law* (H.E.L.); Pollock and Maitland, *History of English Law* (P. & M.); Turner, *Equity of Redemption*; Plucknett, *Concise History of the Common Law* (5th Edn.), 603–608; (1952), 68 L.Q.R. 317 (J. J. Rabinowitz); (1967), 83 L.Q.R. 229 (J. L. Barton).

the rules relating to gage (or pledge) are dealt with as for movables and then applied by reference to immovables (*d*). Possession would usually be given to the mortgagee (*e*), but he had only a special sort of seisin (*seisina ut de vadio*) which the law did not protect (*f*). Such a pledge was called a mortgage (*mortuum vadium*) when the fruits or rent received did not tend to reduce the debt; it was called a *vivum vadium* when they were so applied (*g*). The property became the mortgagee's on default of repayment on the appointed day, if it was so agreed, or if the mortgagor failed to redeem within a reasonable time after the court had ordered him to do so (*h*).

This form of mortgage of land was succeeded by the one, ever since in use, by which the mortgagee took an ordinary estate in the land entitling him to the usual remedies for recovering possession. In Bracton (*c.* 1257) the mortgagee's estate appears as a term of years capable of being enlarged automatically into the fee simple on default of payment at the end of the term (*i*). Later, when the treatment of estates had become more exact, this elasticity was not permitted. Livery of seisin was essential for the creation of a fee simple, and since there was no livery on the grant of the term a freehold estate would not arise afterwards (*k*). Accordingly it was necessary for the mortgagee to take at once the estate which was to become absolute on non-payment at the time named (*l*). Mortgages might still be made by a lease at a nominal rent (but the mortgagee having no right to the fee) and upon the terms that the mortgagee was to receive the rents and profits of the land in satisfaction of the debt. Alternatively, in the case of freeholds, a mortgage might be made by a conveyance of the land in fee simple, subject to the condition either that the mortgagor might re-enter or that the conveyance should be void if the debt was unpaid by the appointed day (*m*). Under this system the mortgagee did not necessarily go into possession and a new explanation of *mortuum vadium* and *vivum vadium* became necessary (*n*).

In or before the sixteenth century the form of the mortgage by conveyance had changed. The conditions previously mentioned were replaced by the more convenient covenant for re-conveyance by the

---

(*d*) Book X, cc. 6 to 11. See H.E.L., vol. ii, 188 *et seq.*
(*e*) For the influence of the usury laws on mortgages, see H.E.L., vol. viii, 100 *et seq.*
(*f*) H.E.L., vol. iii, 128 *et seq.*; P. & M., vol. ii, 120.
(*g*) Glanvill, Book X, c. 6.
(*h*) Glanvill, Book X, cc. 6 to 8.
(*i*) F. 20. And see P. & M., vol. ii, 121; H.E.L., vol. iii, 129.
(*k*) Littleton (*c.* 1480), Tenures, s. 349; Co. Litt., pp. 216 *et seq.*
(*l*) Litt., s. 333.
(*m*) H.E.L., vol. iii, 129, 130. There were also statutory forms of real security (*e.g.*, under Statutes Merchant and Staple) which were commonly used until the seventeenth century; see H.E.L., vol. iii, 132.
(*n*) Litt., s. 332. This was that the land was dead to the debtor if he did not pay at the appointed day, and the pledge was dead if he did pay. But Coke, in his comment on this, remarks that the mortgage, or *mortuum vadium*, is so called to distinguish it from the *vivum vadium* which he defines in Glanvill's sense (Co. Litt. 205a), though he carries out Littleton's idea by saying that if the creditor's estate is granted only till he has received his debt out of the issue and profits, neither money nor land dieth, or is lost; see also *per* Lord ELDON in *Fenwick* v. *Reed* (1816), 1 Mer. 114, at p. 124. The Usury Act 1545, permitted loans at interest, so that there was no longer any need for rents and profits to be taken in lieu of interest.

mortgagee on repayment by the appointed time (*o*). This form of mortgage by conveyance became the usual form of legal mortgage of freeholds until the provisions of the Law of Property Act 1925 became operative on 1 January, 1926, and it still remains the usual form of legal mortgage in other cases. The alternative form of mortgage by lease continued to be generally used until the early nineteenth century. This form had advantages in that it could be used for a mortgage of both freehold and leasehold land, and, since it created only a chattel interest, on the mortgagee's death this passed to his executors and not to his heir (*p*). It had the disadvantage, however, that a reversion was left in the mortgagor, even if he defaulted. Moreover, there was doubt as to whether the mortgagee could call for the title deeds. Therefore, but for those circumstances where it was particularly useful, as, for example, for raising portions in family settlements (*q*) this form fell into disuse (*r*).

Equity of redemption (*s*).—Whatever form the mortgage took at common law, upon non-payment by the appointed time, the estate of the mortgagee became absolute and irredeemable unless the mortgage provided otherwise (*t*).

In the courts of equity, on the other hand, the mortgagee's estate was subject to a right called the equity of redemption, which arose from the court's consideration that the real object of the transaction was the creation of a security for the debt (*u*). This entitled the mortgagor to redeem (or recover the property), even though he had failed to repay by the appointed time. At first the court would only

---

(*o*) H.E.L., vol. v, 330, 331. The Court of Chancery would grant specific performance of this covenant. Moreover this change simplified proof of title which then depended on execution of the re-conveyance; see *Durham Brothers* v. *Robertson*, [1898] 1 Q.B. 765, at p. 772 (C.A.). Although expressed as a covenant for reconveyance the proviso had the effect of a condition subsequent: see Hazeltine's Preface to Turner, *Equity of Redemption*, pp. xi-xiv.

(*p*) Co. Litt., 204b.

(*q*) The term created did not disturb the limitations of the settlement.

(*r*) As to mortgages of leaseholds immediately prior to 1 January, 1926, see p. 21, *infra*.

It is convenient to mention here two other forms of mortgage now obsolete. Formerly a security was sometimes made in the form of a trust for sale, in case of non-payment of the debt at a certain time. This was in effect a mortgage and redeemable as such; the remedy of the mortgagee being under the trust for sale, instead of by foreclosure, though if the mortgagor commenced an action for redemption and failed to redeem he was foreclased. See also Goode, *Hire-Purchase Law and Practice* (2nd Edn.), p. 552.

A Welsh mortgage was an assurance by which property was conveyed to the creditor without any condition for payment (as distinguished from a personal covenant), but upon the terms that the creditor was to receive the rents and profits in satisfaction of principal and interest or in lieu of interest. Since the assurance was without condition there could be no forfeiture; consequently there was no equity of redemption, which could be the subject of foreclosure. But there was a continuing right of redemption and the mortgagor could redeem at any time.

On both the above, see, further, the earlier editions of this work.

(*s*) See Turner, *Equity of Redemption*; and pp. 8, 519 *infra*.

(*t*) See H.E.L., vol. ii, 336, 579. And the mortgagor was still liable for the debt: see *Kreglinger* v. *New Patagonia Meat and Cold Storage Co., Ltd.*, [1914] A.C. 25, at p. 35 (H.L.), *per* Lord HALDANE.

(*u*) *Sparrow* v. *Hardcastle* (1754), 3 Atk. 798, at p. 805 (H.L.), *per* Lord HARDWICKE; *Seton* v. *Slade* (1802), 7 Ves. 256, *per* Lord ELDON. And the court was, no doubt, anxious to increase its jurisdiction. Moreover there had been a change in the usury laws: see H.E.L., vol. viii, 100 *et seq*.

intervene in cases of special hardship, but by the seventeenth century relief was given as a matter of course (a). At the same time the mortgagee in possession became accountable to the mortgagor for rent (b). The mortgagee was compensated for the special favour shown the mortgagor by the right of foreclosure (c).

Equitable rights became recognised in common law courts by the Judicature Act 1873.

Before 1926, when, by the usual method of freehold mortgage, the fee simple was vested in the mortgagee, the phrase "equity of redemption" was used to denote the equitable interest of the mortgagor (d). In equity the mortgagor was the owner of the land subject to the mortgage (e). Under the present system the legal estate in fee simple remains in the mortgagor, and the phrase denotes the whole interest of the mortgagor in the land (f). The equity of redemption arises as soon as the mortgage is made (g) and should be compared with, but includes, the equitable right to redeem. The latter arises only when the contractual date of redemption has passed (h). The equity of redemption may be disposed of *inter vivos* or by will and passes on intestacy (i). Any attempted restriction on the equity of redemption beyond certain narrow limits is void (k). The equity of redemption may be determined by release (l), lapse of time (m), sale (n) and foreclosure (o).

Legal charge.—As stated above a legal mortgage of land may be made, not only by the creation in the mortgagee of a legal estate, but by a charge expressed to be by way of legal mortgage (p). Under such a mortgage the mortgagee has the same protection, powers and remedies, as if it had been created, by demise, and, save that an actual legal

---

(a) See Turner, pp. 21 *et seq.*; H.E.L., vol. v, 330-332; *Emanuel College* v. *Evans* (1625), 1 Rep. Ch. 18. The Chancellor did not have everything his own way, but an ordinance to limit the right of redemption did not survive the Restoration.

(b) *Holman* v. *Vaux* (c. 1616), Tothill, 133.

(c) First mentioned in *How* v. *Vigures* (1628), 1 Rep. Ch. 32.

(d) See *Casborne* v. *Scarfe* (1737), 1 Atk. 603; *Thornborough* v. *Baker* (1675), 3 Swan. 628, at p. 630.

(e) *Re Wells, Swinburne-Hanham* v. *Howard*, [1933] Ch. 29 (C.A.), at p. 52.

(f) The phrase equity of redemption is used in the Law of Property Act 1925: see s. 115 (1) (b); but, in general, that Act uses the term right of redemption.

The precise nature of the equity of redemption after 1925 is a matter of some controversy. It is said that since the mortgagor now retains a legal estate in the land the equity of redemption, as an equitable estate, must merge in the legal estate. No longer is the equity of redemption an equitable interest but merely a right attached to the mortgagor's legal estate: see 27 Halsbury's Laws (3rd Edn.), 231; *Abigail* v. *Lapin*, [1934] A.C. 491, at p. 501 (P.C.); *British General Insurance Co., Ltd.* v. *A.-G.*, [1945] L.J.N.C.C.R. 113, at pp. 122, 123. The better view is that there is no merger: see Turner, 186, 187; *Re Wells, Swinburne-Hanham* v. *Howard, supra*; and see p. 520, *infra*.

(g) *Kreglinger* v. *New Patagonia Meat and Cold Storage Co., Ltd.*, [1914] A.C. 25, at p. 48 (H.L.).

(h) *Brown* v. *Cole* (1845), 14 Sim. 427.

(i) See p. 520, *infra*.

(k) See p. 522, *infra*.

(l) See p. 525, *infra*.

(m) See p. 564, *infra*.

(n) See p. 359, *infra*.

(o) See p. 382, *infra*.

(p) Law of Property Act 1925, ss. 85 (1), 86 (1), 205 (1) (xvi).

estate is not created, a legal charge does not differ from any ordinary legal mortgage (*q*).

III—SALES WITH RIGHT OF REPURCHASE

Mortgage or absolute conveyance.—When a legal mortgage might be made in the form of an absolute conveyance of the property, it was sometimes doubtful on the terms of the instrument, whether it was really a mortgage or an absolute conveyance. Under the present system of creating legal mortgages of land by demise, this can only happen in a very exceptional case (*r*), though the question may still arise on the assignment of an equitable interest or the disposition of property other than land. While the courts protect a bona fide purchaser (*s*), and will not lightly infer an intention to make a mere security, if none is expressed (*t*), they will give effect to an intention, if proved (*u*), to create a security, and will also take care that a borrower shall not suffer from the omission by fraud, mistake, or accident, of the usual requisites of a mortgage.

An instrument which purports to be an absolute conveyance, may therefore be construed as a mortgage, where, according to the true intention of the parties, it was intended to be regarded as a mortgage (*a*). This will be done where there is parol evidence of the non-execution, erasure, or omission by mistake or fraud of an intended defeasance or proviso for redemption (*b*); if a separate defeasance or agreement for a right of redemption has been made by the mortgagee or his duly authorised agent, either in writing or verbally (*c*); or, if it appears from recitals in, or by inference drawn from, the contents of other instruments, or from the payment of interest or other

---

(*q*) *Ibid.*, s. 87 (1); and see p. 25, *infra*. For the statutory mortgage, see p. 26, *infra*.

(*r*) If the instrument purported to convey the legal fee simple, and was held to be a mortgage, it would operate as a demise: Law of Property Act 1925, s. 85 (2). Similarly, in the case of leasehold, it would operate as a sub-demise: *ibid.*, s. 86 (2); and see *Grangeside Properties, Ltd.* v. *Collingwoods Securities, Ltd.*, [1964] 1 All E.R. 143 (C.A.).

(*s*) *Premier Group, Ltd.* v. *Lidgard*, [1970] N.Z.L.R. 280.

(*t*) *Cotterell* v. *Purchase* (1734), Cas. temp. Talb. 61.

(*u*) *Mayfair London Aank, Ltd.* v. *Workman* (1972), Estates Gazette, 989 (where the security was not proved). The burden of proof is on the party claiming that the apparent absolute conveyance is merely a security.

(*a*) *Douglas* v. *Culverwell* (1862), 4 De G. F. & J. 20; *Re Duke of Marlborough, Davis* v. *Whitehead*, [1894] 2 Ch. 133; *Grangeside Properties, Ltd.* v. *Collingwoods Securities, Ltd.*, *supra*; *Re Kent and Sussex Sawmills, Ltd.*, [1947] Ch. 177; [1946] 2 All E.R. 638; *Scottish and Newcastle Breweries, Ltd.* v. *Liquidator of Rathbourne Hotel Co., Ltd.* 1970 S.L.T. 313; A.S.C.L. 470–471; on mortgages of chattels, see p. 81, *infra*.

(*b*) *Maxwell* v. *Lady Montacute* (1719), Prec. Ch. 526; *England* v. *Codrington* (1758), 1 Eden 169; *A.-G.* v. *Crofts* (1788), 4 Bro. Parl. Cas. 136; *Card* v. *Jaffray* (1805), 2 Sch. & Lef 374.

The Statute of Frauds (see now s.40 Law of Property Act, 1925) would not be allowed to be pleaded to cover what would amount to a fraud, unless perhaps the parties deliberately abstained from putting their meaning into writing; *Re Duke of Marlborough, Davis* v. *Whitehead*, *supra*, distinguishing and commenting on some earlier decisions.

(*c*) *Clench* v. *Witherly* (1678), Cas. temp. Finch, 376; *Manlove* v. *Bale and Bruton* (1688), 2 Vern. 84; *Francklyn* v. *Fern* (1740), Barn. Ch. 30; *Whitfield* v. *Parfitt* (1851), 4 De G. & Sm. 240; *Lincoln* v. *Wright* (1859), 4 De G. & J. 16.

circumstances, that the conveyance was intended to be redeemable (*d*).

Fraudulent or secret conveyance.—If an absolute conveyance is made with a secret defeasance, in order, by concealing the defeasance, to commit a fraud, the defeasance will be void as against an absolute purchaser who had no notice of the fraud (*e*). And if a mortgage has been fraudulently made to appear as an absolute conveyance it will not be corrected at the instance of those concerned in the fraud (*f*).

Mortgage or conveyance with option of repurchase.—Although in certain cases conveyances, apparently absolute, may be construed as mortgages, an absolute conveyance with an agreement for repurchase, or that the conveyance shall be void upon payment of a certain fixed sum at a fixed time, will create a mere right of repurchase to be exercised according to the strict terms of the power (*g*), and not such a right of redemption as is incidental to a mortgage (*h*), unless it is proved that the transaction was in the nature of a mortgage security, and that the grantor and grantee were intended to have mutual and reciprocal rights to insist upon reconveyance of the estate and repayment of the consideration (*i*).

Defeasible purchase of equity of redemption.—The strict compliance with the conditions has been upheld even in transactions relating to securities: where, for instance upon a release by the mortgagor to the mortgagee of the equity of redemption, it had been

---

(*d*) *Maxwell* v. *Lady Mountacute, supra; Cripps* v. *Jee* (1793), 4 Bro. C.C. 472; *Sevier* v. *Greenway* (1815), 19 Ves. 413; *Allenby* v. *Dalton*, (1827), 5 L.J. O.S. K.B. 312; *Barton* v. *Bank of New South Wales* (1890), 15 App. Cas. 379, (considered in *United Dominions Trust, Ltd.,* v. *Beech*, [1972] 1 Lloyd's Rep. 546; *Beattie* v. *Jenkinson*, [1971] 3 All E.R. 495); but see *Tull* v. *Owen* (1840), 4 Y. & C. Ex. 192.

(*e*) *Webber* v. *Farmer* (1718), 4 Bro. Parl. Cas. 170.

(*f*) *Baldwin* v. *Cawthorne* (1812), 19 Ves. 166. A mortgage may be created by a deed duly executed, though it is retained by the debtor without communication with the creditor, unless it is shown that there was fraud in the execution, or that it was delivered as an escrow, and was intended to operate conditionally: *Exton* v. *Scott* (1833), 6 Sim. 31. For escrows, see p. 42, *infra*.

(*g*) See *Thornborough* v. *Baker* (1675), 3 Swans. 628, at p. 631; *Barrell* v. *Sabine* (1684), 1 Vern. 268; *Joy* v. *Birch* (1836), 4 Cl. & F. 57; *Pegg* v. *Wisden* (1852), 16 Beav. 239. Accordingly, where a limited time is fixed for repayment (*Williams* v. *Owen* (1840), 5 My. & Cr. 303; *Acton* v. *Acton* (1704), Prec. Ch. 237; but see *Waters* v. *Mynn* (1850), 14 Jur. 341); or where the agreement for repurchase is to be void on failure in punctual payment of the rent at which the land had been demised to the vendor (*Davis* v. *Thomas* (1831), Russ. & M. 506; *St. John* v. *Wareham* (1635), cited in 3 Swans. at p. 631) repurchase was refused on default in compliance with the condition; and see *Maclaine* v. *Gatty*, [1921] 1 A.C. 376 (H.L.). In the case of a mortgage, the penalty or forfeiture is introduced for the purpose of security only, and, in case of default in payment at the appointed time, the mortgagee is compensated by receiving interest. But in the case of a defeasible purchase, forfeiture is out of the question, the estate being absolutely vested in the grantee; and the power of repurchase, not arising from the nature of the contract, but being a special privilege given to one of the parties without any corresponding right in the other, must be strictly exercised. As to the strict observance of option terms, see also *Hare* v. *Nicoll*, [1966] 2 Q.B. 130 (C.A.); [1966] 1 All E.R. 285. By s. 205 (1) (xvi) of the Law of Property Act 1925, "right of redemption" includes an option to repurchase only if the option in effect creates a right of redemption.

(*h*) *St. John* v. *Wareham, supra; Barrell* v. *Sabine, supra; Ensworth* v. *Griffiths* (1706), 5 Bro. Parl. Cas. 184; *Perry* v. *Meddowcroft* (1841), 4 Beav. 197; *Tapply* v. *Sheather* (1862), 7 L.T. 298; *Manchester, Sheffield and Lincolnshire Rail Co.* v. *North Central Wagon Co.* (1888), 13 App. Cas. 554; *Beckett* v. *Tower Assets Co.*, [1891] 1 Q.B.1, at p. 25.

(*i*) *Goodman* v. *Grierson* (1813), 2 Ball. & B. 274; *Alderson* v. *White* (1857), 2 De G. & J. 97; *Shaw* v. *Jeffery* (1860), 13 Moo, P.C.C. 432. See generally *Coote on Mortgages* (9th Edn.), pp. 27–34. And see *Gurfinkel* v. *Bentley Pty., Ltd.* (1966), 116 C.L.R. 98; *Kreick* v. *Wansbrough* (1973), 35 D.L.R. (3d) 275.

agreed that the mortgagee should reconvey upon repayment to him within a fixed time of the original debt, with the money paid for the release and interest, and the outlay for repairs or improvements (*k*). Similarly, if the creditor agrees to forego part of his debt upon payment of the residue on a fixed day, or to refrain from entering up judgment if an insurance is kept up, in the former case no relief will be given in case of default, but the mortgagee will be entitled to the whole of the original debt, and in the latter the creditor can take advantage of failure in the strict performance of the conditions (*l*).

Test for meaning of instrument.—In every case the question is what, upon a fair construction, is the meaning of the instrument; and the true nature, and not the form of the transaction, is to be regarded (*m*). The inadequacy of the consideration to the value of the property, the taking by the grantee of immediate possession under the conveyance, and the payment by him or by the grantor of the costs of the transaction, or of insurances and other outgoings of the property, will be taken into consideration, but will not be conclusive upon the question whether a doubtful instrument was intended to take effect by way of mortgage or by way of sale (*n*). Circumstances of pressure upon the grantor (as where he is insolvent or represented by the same solicitor as the grantee) will materially influence the court in construing an apparently absolute or conditional sale as a mortgage, where, in the absence of such circumstances, the mere insufficiency of price would be little regarded. Weight will also be given to the circumstance that, in the peculiar position of the grantor, a mortgage might be beneficial to him when a sale would not (*o*).

IV—EQUITABLE MORTGAGES

Generally.—An equitable mortgage is a contract which operates as a security and is enforceable under the equitable jurisdiction of the

---

(*k*) *Ensworth* v. *Griffiths, supra; Gossip* v. *Wright* (1863), 32 L.J. Ch. 648; *Sterne* v. *Beck* (1863), 1 De G. J. & S. 595; *Wallingford* v. *Mutual Society* (1880), 5 App. Cas. 685; *Protector Endowment and Annuity Loan Co.* v. *Grice* (1880), 5 Q.B.D. 592.

(*l*) *Ford* v. *Earl of Chesterfield* (1854), 19 Beav. 428; *Parry* v. *Great Ship Co.* (1863), 4 B. & S. 556; and see *Thompson* v. *Hudson* (1869), L.R. 4 H.L. 1; *Tasburgh* v. *Echlin* (1733), 2 Bro. Parl. Cas. 265; *Ogden* v. *Battams* (1855), 1 Jur. N.S. 791; *King* v. *Bromley* (1709), 2 Eq. Cas. Abr. 595.

(*m*) *Re Watson, Ex parte Official Receiver in Bankpuptcy* (1890) 25 Q.B.D. 27 (C.A.); *Madell* v. *Thomas*, [1891] 1 Q.B. 230 (C.A.); *Salt* v. *Marquess of Northampton*, [1892] A.C. 1 (H.L.); *Bradley* v. *Carritt*, [1903] A.C. 253 (H.L.); *Lewis* v. *Frank Love, Ltd.*, [1961] 1 All E.R. 446; *re Row Dal Construction Pty. Ltd.*, [1966] V.R. 249; *Automobile Association (Canterbury) Inc.* v. *Australasian Secured Deposits, Ltd.*, [1973] 1 N.Z.L.R. 417; *Arnal* v. *Arnal* (1969), 6 D.L.R. (3d) 245.

(*n*) *Thornborough* v. *Baker, supra*, at p. 632; *Davis* v. *Thomas, supra; Williams* v. *Owen, supra; Langton* v. *Horton* (1842), 5 Beav. 9; *Alderson* v. *White, supra; Douglas* v. *Culverwell* (1862), 4 De G. F. & J. 20.

(*o*) *Fee* v. *Cobine* (1847), 11 Ir. Eq. Rep. 406. But it may be shown that the grantor entered into the contract with full knowledge of the consequences; *Bonham* v. *Newcomb* (1681), 1 Vern. 214, 232; *Langton* v. *Horton, supra*.

As to mortgages by way of annuity deed and conditions for cesser of trust limitations, which were formerly, but are no longer, common securities, see previous editions of this work. For a scheme to avoid the effect of the Landlord and Tenant Act 1954, Pt. II involving a legal charge by a would-be landlord to a "friendly" chargee restricting the mortgagor's powers of leasing followed by a lease of the premises which will not be binding on the charge, see Precedents for the Conveyancer, Precedent 5–2.

court. The court carries it into effect either by giving the creditor immediately the appropriate remedies, or by compelling the debtor to execute a security in accordance with the contract (*p*). It is applicable to all property of which a legal mortgage can be made, even where statute provides, as, for example, in the case of ships, a particular method for passing the legal property therein.

An equitable mortgage may be created by general words (*q*) (herein differing from a legal mortgage) and even with regard to future acquired property (*r*).

It is essential that an equitable mortgage be by deed if the mortgagee is to have the power of sale and other powers conferred on a mortgagee by statute (*s*).

Formerly, from the debtor's point of view there was an advantage in an equitable mortgage of land over a legal mortgage, in that an equitable mortgage usually did not appear in the title to the property, and, in some circumstances, there was a stamp duty saving. Now mortgage stamp duty has been abolished (*t*) there is no advantage in an equitable mortgage, other than its informality (but, as stated above, to give the statutory powers it has to be by deed) and a distinct disadvantage in the possible loss of priority if subsequent mortgages are created (*u*).

Equitable mortgages may be divided into two classes, *viz.*: (1) Mortgages by equitable owners of their equitable rights; and (2) the creation by legal owners of equitable rights by way of security.

Mortgages of equitable rights.—Mortgages by equitable owners of their equitable rights usually occur in the case of mortgages of interests by beneficiaries under a trust (*a*). Such a mortgage must either be in writing signed by the mortgagor or his agent authorised in writing or made by will (*b*). Moreover, if the mortgage is not based on valuable consideration, it is essential that it should purport to operate by way of a complete assignment of all the mortgagor's equitable interest; for although equity will give effect to a completed voluntary assignment of equitable rights (*c*), it will not give effect to an incomplete assign-

---

(*p*) *Ashton* v. *Corrigan* (1871), L.R. 13 Eq. 76; *Hermann* v. *Hodges* (1873), L.R. 16 Eq. 18.

(*q*) *William Brandt's Sons & Co.* v. *Dunlop Rubber Co., Ltd.*, [1905] A.C. 454 (H.L.), at p. 462. The ordinary debenture of a limited company is a common example of this.

(*r*) A mortgage of all the mortgagor's "real and personal property whatsoever and wheresoever" is not void for uncertainty, nor as being against public policy, if it is possible at the time when the charge is sought to be enforced to point out the property comprised in it: *Re Clarke, Coombe* v. *Carter* (1887), 36 Ch. D. 348 (C.A.); *Re Turcan* (1888), 40 Ch. D. 5 (C.A.); *Tailby* v. *Official Receiver* (1888), 13 App. Cas. 523 (H.L.); *Re Kelcey, Tyson* v. *Kelcey*, [1899] 2 Ch. 530, at pp. 532-534; and see *Syrett* v. *Egerton*, [1957] 3 All E.R. 331, at pp. 332, 334; cf. *Barker* v. *Barker*, [1952] P. 184 (C.A.); [1952] 1 All E.R. 1128.

(*s*) *I.e.*, under the Law of Property Act 1925, s. 101; see p. 360, *infra*.

(*t*) Finance Act, 1971, s. 64; see the previous edition (at p. 12) for the former position.

(*u*) See, *e.g.*, *McCarthy and Stone, Ltd.* v. *Julian S. Hodge & Co., Ltd.*, [1971] 2 All E.R. 973; *Barclays Bank, Ltd.* v. *Taylor*, [1973] Ch. 63; [1972] 2 All E.R. 752; and (1972), 116 Sol. Jo. 87 (R. L. Harris).

(*a*) Before 1926 a mortgage of an equity of redemption, that is, a mortgage subsequent to a legal mortgage, was an equitable mortgage. As to the transitional provisions of the Law of Property Act, 1925, see pp. 53 *et seq.*, *infra*.

(*b*) Law of Property Act 1925, s. 53 (1) (c).

(*c*) *Kekewich* v. *Manning* (1851), 1 De G.M. & G. 176.

ment or one resting on executory contract only (*d*). The mortgagee should give notice in writing (*e*) to the trustees in whom the legal ownership is in order to preserve his priority (*f*).

Equitable mortgages by legal owners.—Equitable mortgages of the property of legal owners are created by some instrument or act which is insufficient to confer a legal estate or title, but which, being founded on valuable consideration, shows the intention of the parties to create a security, or in other words, evidences a contract to do so (*g*). Formal agreements for mortgages are not common, save in a commercial context (*b*), and in practice the most important type of equitable mortgage is one created by deposit of title deeds, whether with or without a memorandum or other instrument of charge (*i*). Other examples of such mortgages are: a written agreement or covenant to create a security in consideration of a debt due or an advance made (*k*); a document charging property with the debt and containing a declaration by the debtor that he holds the property in trust for the creditor (*l*); an undertaking given in consideration of a loan to hold title deeds to the order of the lender (*m*); an authority for a creditor to sell and retain a debt out of the proceeds (*u*); an assignment of rent (*o*); any written instrument showing the intention of the parties that a security should be thereby created, although it contains no general words of charge, *e.g.*, the appointment of a receiver to receive rents and pay an annuity thereout (*p*); a power of attorney to a creditor to enter up judgment in his favour (*q*), or to receive rents and profits and apply them in payment of interest, or to repay himself out of the surplus proceeds of the sale of property in mortgage to the debtor, or to mortgage the debtor's land for payment of the debt (*r*).

It will be seen from the above examples that an equitable mortgage of land, not being by way of deposit of title deeds, requires to be evidenced

---

(*d*) *Re Earl of Lucan, Hardinge* v. *Cobden* (1890), 45 Ch. D. 470. See p. 105, *infra.*
(*e*) Law of Property Act 1925, s. 137 (3).
(*f*) *Dearle* v. *Hall* (1823–1828), 3 Russ. 1, Law of Property Act 1925, ss. 137, 138. And see p. 463, *infra.* For mortgages of choses in action generally, see Ch. 6, *infra.*
(*g*) See *National Provincial and Union Bank of England* v. *Charnley*, [1924] 1 K.B. 431 at p. 440 (C.A.). For cases where the intention could not be found, see *Travis and Arnold, Ltd.* v. *Burnett*, [1964] Estates Gazette Digest 318; *Georgiades* v. *Edward Wolfe & Co., Ltd.*, [1965] Ch. 487; [1964] 3 All E.R. 433; *Thomas* v. *Rose*, [1968] 3 All E.R. 765.
(*h*) See *Capital Finance Co., Ltd.* v. *Stokes* [1968] 1 All E.R. 577; affd. [1969] 1 Ch. 261 (C.A.); [1968] 3 All E.R. 625.
(*i*) *Russel* v. *Russel* (1783), 1 Bro. C.C. 269. And see pp. 44 *et seq.*, *infra.*
(*k*) *Eyre* v. *M'Dowell* (1861), 9 H.L. Cas. 619; *Parish* v, *Poole*, (1884), 53 L.T. 35; *Re Hurley's Estate*, [1894] 1 I.R. 488; *Capital Finance Co., Ltd.* v. *Stokes, supra.*
(*l*) *London and County Banking Co.* v. *Goddard*, [1897] 1 Ch. 642.
(*m*) *Re Heathstar Properties, Ltd.*, [1966] 1 All E.R. 628.
(*n*) *Re Cook, Ex parte Hodgson* (1821), 1 Gl. & J. 12.
(*o*) *Ex parte Wills* (1790), 1 Ves. Jun. 162; cf. *Re Whitting, Ex parte Hall* (1879), 10 Ch. D. 615 (C.A.).
(*p*) *Cradock* v. *Scottish Provident Institution* (1894), 70 L.T. 718.
(*q*) *Cook* v. *Fowler* (1874), L.R. 7 H.L. 27, at p. 35. See now Administration of Justice Act, 1956, s. 16.
(*r*) *Spooner* v. *Sandilands* (1842), 1 Y. & C. Ch. Cas. 390; *Abbott* v. *Stratten* (1846), 3 Jo. & Lat. 603; *Re Cook, Ex parte Hodgson, supra; Re Parkinson's Estate* (1865), 13 L.T. 26.

in writing (s) or supported by a sufficient act of part performance. An equitable mortgage of personalty, not being of an equitable interest in personalty (t), is not required to be in writing (u).

Specific performance of agreements for mortgages.—Specific performance will not be ordered in respect of a contract to make or take a loan of money, whether or not the loan is to be on security (a), so long as the contract remains executory (b). The parties will be left to their remedies in damages (c).

But specific performance of an enforceable contract to give security will be ordered where the loan has actually been made or the debt or other obligation incurred (d).

Equitable charges.—An equitable charge is created when real or personal property is expressly or constructively made liable, or specially appropriated, to the discharge of a debt or some other obligation. It confers on the chargee a right of realisation by judicial process (e).

V—COLLATERAL SECURITY

Collateral security.—Collateral or additional security may be given by the principal mortgagor himself or by a third party. The most common example of the first type of collateral security is a mortgage of a policy on the life of the principal mortgagor by the principal mortgagor, which is additional to and is to secure the same debt as that secured by the principal mortgage (f). Examples of the second type of collateral security are a guarantee by a third party for the repayment of the principal mortgage debt (g) and a mortgage of land or other property by a third party to secure either a principal debt or his liability under a guarantee (h).

Collateral or additional security has a special meaning in relation to building societies (i).

(s) Law of Property Act 1925, s. 40; *Mounsey* v. *Rankin* (1885), 1 Cab. & El. 496.

(t) Which is required to be in writing, see Law of Property Act 1925, s. 53 (1) (c).

(u) *Tibbits* v. *George* (1836), 5 Ad. & El. 107; *Parish* v. *Poole, supra,* at p. 38; *Brown, Shipley & Co.* v. *Kough* (1885), 29 Ch. D. 848, at p. 854 (C.A.).

(a) See p. 158, *infra. Western Wagon and Property, Co.* v. *West,* [1892] 1 Ch. 271.

(b) *Hunter* v. *Lord Langford* (1828), 2 Mol. 272; *Rogers* v. *Challis* (1859) 27 Beav. 175; *Sichel* v. *Mosenthal* (1862), 30 Beav. 371; *Larios* v. *Bonamy Y Gurety* (1873), L.R. 5 P.C. 346; *South African Territories* v. *Wallington,* [1898] A.C. 309 (H.L.). A contract to take debentures in a limited company is an exception to this rule; see Companies Act 1948, s. 92.

(c) *Astor Properties, Ltd.* v. *Tunbridge Wells Equitable Friendly Society,* [1936] 1 All E.R. 531; *Manchester and Oldham Bank* v. *Cook* (1883), 49 L.T. 674; *Trans Trust S.P.R.L.* v. *Danubian Trading Co., Ltd.,* [1952] 2 Q.B. 297 (C.A.); [1952] 1 All E.R. 970; *Cottrill* v. *Steyning and Littlehampton Building Society,* [1966] 2 All E.R. 295; see Francis, *Mortgages and Securities* (2nd Edn.), Ch. 5; see also *South African Territories* v. *Wallington, supra;* and the text and footnote (h), p. 650, *infra.*

(d) See the cases in footnote (p), p. 12, *supra,* and *Parish* v. *Poole, supra;* and generally *Fry on Specific Performance* (6th Edn.), pp. 24 *et seq.,* and *Beswick* v. *Beswick,* [1968] A.C. 58 (H.L.); [1967] 2 All E.R. 1197; *Loan Investment Corporation of Australasia* v. *Bonner,* [1970] N.Z. L.R. 724 (P.C.), considering, *inter alia, Starkey* v. *Barton,* [1909] 1 Ch. 284 and contracts for sale of land and loan. The distinction is between a genuine sale with loan attached and what is in substance a long-term secured loan.

(e) See p. 158, *infra.*

(f) See p. 108, *infra.*

(g) For form, see Precedent 6 in the Appendix, *infra.*

(h) For forms see 14 Ency. Forms and Precedents (4th Edn.), pp. 399 *et seq.*

(i) See p. 195, *infra.*

The advantage of taking additional real security from a third party to secure the principal debt is that in the event of the principal mortgagor's bankruptcy the collateral security need not go in reduction of proof (*k*).

VI—BORROWING AND EXCHANGE CONTROL

Borrowing control.—The Borrowing (Control and Guarantees) Act 1946 (*l*), empowers the Treasury to make orders for regulating (1) the borrowing of money in Great Britain where the aggregate of the amount of money borrowed under the transaction and of any other amounts so borrowed by the same person in the previous twelve months exceeds £10,000; (2) the raising of money in Great Britain by the issue, whether in Great Britain or elsewhere, by any body corporate, of any shares in that body corporate; (3) the issue for any purpose by any body corporate of any shares in or debentures or other securities of that body corporate, if either the body corporate is incorporated under the law of England or Scotland or the shares, debentures or other securities are or are to be registered in England or Scotland; and (4) the circulation in Great Britain of any offer for subscription, sale or exchange of any shares in or debentures or other securities of any body corporate not incorporated under the law of England or Scotland. These provisions do not apply to the borrowing of money by any person (other than a local authority) in the ordinary course of business from a banker, and they are subject to such exceptions as may be specified (*m*).

Provision is made by the Act for enforcement and penalties (*n*), but the rights of the persons concerned in any transaction are not effected by any contravention of the orders made under the Act (*o*).

Orders have been made imposing the general requirement for Treasury consent to such transactions mentioned above (*p*), but subject to very wide exceptions and exemptions. In particular, consent is not required to a borrowing (*q*) by any person (other than a local authority), if the borrowing is in the ordinary course of his business and is from a person carrying on a banking undertaking (*r*), to a borrowing by a person (other than a local authority) where the money borrowed is repayable on demand or not more than six months after demand and the loan is wholly unsecured (a loan in respect of which a guarantee is given is not unsecured (*s*)) or is secured only by a bill of exchange or a promissory note payable within a specified period (*t*), or to a borrowing by a personal representative in his capacity as such

---

(*k*) See p. 423, *infra*. For the Consumer Credit Act 1974, see p. 146, *infra*.
(*l*) See 16 Halsbury's Statutes (2nd Edn.), 551.
(*m*) Section 1 (1).
(*n*) See Schedule.
(*o*) Section 1 (3).
(*p*) See now Control of Borrowing Order 1958, as amended by the Control of Borrowing (Amendment) Orders 1967 and 1970.
(*q*) For the extended meaning of borrowing, see Control of Borrowing Order 1958, Art. 2.
(*r*) Control of Borrowing Order 1958, Art. 1 (2) (a).
(*s*) *Ibid.*, Art. 1 (3).
(*t*) *Ibid.*, Art. 1 (2) (b).

for the purpose of paying death duties (*u*). There are, moreover, general exemptions, so that consent is not required where the annual limit of borrowing does not exceed £50,000 (*a*), and to any transaction, unless (1) it is affected by or on behalf of a person resident outside the United Kingdom, and is not a transaction consisting of or including the issue of non-sterling securities, or (2) it is effected by a local authority (*b*).

The effect of the latter general exemption in relation to the issue of shares and debentures is that Treasury consent to such issue is not required save in the situations mentioned in (1) and (2) above. But the exemption does not apply to the issue of any securities mentioned in the Trustee Investments Act 1961, Sched. 1, Pt. II, paras. 1–5, unless the approval of the Bank of England on behalf of the Treasury has been obtained, nor to the issue of sterling securities where the amount to be paid is not less than £3 million, unless the timing of it has been similarly approved nor if the transaction is effected by or on behalf of an investment trust which is resident in the Scheduled Territories but outside the United Kingdom (*c*).

Exchange control.—Permission under the Exchange Control Act 1947, is required for any payment (including a loan) made as a consideration for, or in association with, the purchase of land or property (including the payment of deposits on land or property) situated outside the Scheduled Territories (*d*) by a resident of the United Kingdom by any means, whether in sterling or foreign currency, and whether from another resident or from a non-resident (*e*). Permission under the Act is also required for the borrowing of foreign currency by a resident, for example, against a mortgage (*f*).

Except with Treasury permission a security (*g*) may be issued only on a declaration (*h*) signed by or on behalf of the person to whom the security is to be issued, that that person is not resident outside the Scheduled Territories (*d*) and is not acquiring the security as nominee for a person so resident (*k*).

VII—FOREIGN SECURITIES

Mortgage of land situate abroad.—In the case of such land the title to the land is generally governed by the *lex situs* and to perfect his title a mortgagee must comply with the requirements, as to registra-

---

(*u*) *Ibid.*, Art. 1 (2) (e).
(*a*) *Ibid.*, Art. 8 (1).
(*b*) *Ibid.*, Art 8A (1), (3).
(*c*) *Ibid.*, Art. 8A (2), (3). As to control in respect of the issue of shares and other securities, see Arts. 3 and 4.
(*d*) See the Exchange Control (Scheduled Territories) (No. 2) 1972 as amended.
(*e*) Exchange Control Act 1947, ss. 5-7. And see the Bank of England's Notice E.C. (General) 81, para. 1 (a).
(*f*) *Ibid.*, s. 1. And see the Bank of England's Notice E.C. (General) 81, para. 1 (b).
(*g*) *Ibid.*, s. 42 (1), as amended by Finance Act 1968 s. 55; and see also s. 19; and the Exchange Control (Prescribed Secondary Securities) Order 1963.
(*h*) See Exchange Control (Declarations and Evidence) Order 1954, as amended by (Amendment) Order 1968.
(*k*) Exchange Control Act, 1947, s. 8.

tion, etc., of the local law (*l*). But even where the requirements of the local law have not been satisfied an English court may be able to enforce such a mortgage as if it were an effective equitable charge where the mortgagor and mortgagee are within the jurisdiction (*m*); but it will not interfere with rights which have in the meantime been acquired under the foreign law (*n*). For example, a floating charge is not recognised in many foreign countries. But if an English company creates a floating charge over assets situated in such a country it will be a valid equitable security according to English law (*o*).

Locality of debts (*p*).—It is sometimes necessary, particularly for the purpose of ascertaining liability to death duties, to ascertain a specific locality for a debt. A debt, like any other thing in action, has no tangible existence, and strictly has no locality, but for legal purposes it is deemed to possess an attribute of locality, arising from and according to its nature and in this respect there is a distinction between a debt by simple contract and a debt by specialty. The locality of a simple contract debt is the place where the debtor resides, since it is there that the assets to meet it are presumably situate, and it is there that he must be sued if the creditor requires to recover the debt at law. Hence when the creditor has died, duty will be leviable on simple contract debts owing to him according to the residence of the debtor at the time of his death. But a debt secured by an instrument under seal has been regarded as having a corporeal existence by which its locality may be reduced to a certainty; its place is where the instrument happens to be. Hence the incidence of death duties has been determined by the place of the specialty at the creditor's death (*q*).

But the rule that the locality of a simple contract debt is the residence of the debtor is in ordinary cases only an application of the wider principle that "debt or choses in action are generally to be looked upon as situate in the country where they are properly recoverable or can be enforced" (*r*). For if, although the debtor is abroad at the time of

---

(*l*) See Dicey and Morris, *Conflict of Laws* (9th Edn.), pp. 807 *et seq.*; Cheshire's *Private International Law* (9th Edn.), pp. 488, 493.

(*m*) *Mercantile Investment and General Trust Co.* v. *River Plate Trust, Loan and Agency Co.*, [1892] 2 Ch. 303; *Re Anchor Line (Henderson Brothers), Ltd. (No. 2)*, [1937] Ch. 483; [1937] 2 All E.R. 823 (see now Companies (Floating Charges and Receivers) (Scotland) Act, 1972); *Richard West & Partners (Inverness), Ltd.* v. *Dick*, [1969] 2 Ch. 424 (C.A.); [1969] 1 All E.R. 289, 943.

(*n*) *Re Maudslay, Sons and Field, Maudslay* v. *Maudslay, Sons and Field*, [1900] 1 Ch. 602.

(*o*) For the assumed jurisdiction under R.S.C. Ord. 11 in respect of mortgages of property other than land within the jurisdiction, see r.1 (1) (k) in Supreme Court Practice.

(*p*) Dicey and Morris, *Conflict of Laws* (9th Edn.), pp. 506 *et seq.*; Cheshire's *Private International Law* (9th Edn.), pp. 538 *et seq.*; and 592.

(*q*) *A.-G.* v. *Bouwens* (1838), 4 M. & W. 171, at p. 191; *Stamps Commissioner* v. *Hope*, [1891] A.C. 476, at p. 481 (P.C.); *Re Maudslay, Sons and Field, supra*; *New York Life Insurance Co.* v. *Public Trustee*, [1924] 2 Ch. 101 (C.A.); *Re Heibert Wagg & Co., Ltd.*, [1956] Ch. 323; [1956] 1 All E.R. 129. But if the debtor resides in more than one country (e.g., a company with a principal and a branch office in different countries), the debt is situated in the country where the debt is payable: *F. & K. Jabbour* v. *Custodian of Israeli Property*, [1954] 1 All E.R. 145, at p. 152; *Re Russo-Asiatic Bank*, [1934] Ch. 720.

(*r*) Dicey and Morris, *Conflict of Laws* (9th Edn.), p. 506. And see *New York Life Insurance Co.* v. *Public Trustee, supra*, at pp. 109, 119; *National Bank of Greece S.A.* v. *Westminister Bank Executor and Trustee Co. (Channel Islands), Ltd.*, [1971] A.C. 945 (H.L.); [1971] 1 All E.R. 233.

the creditor's death, proceedings can be taken here which will directly result in any order for, and the enforcement of, payment of the debt, then the debt may, at any rate for some purposes, be treated as situate here (s).

Mortgage debts.—A mortgage debt is usually a specialty debt, and in accordance with the rule as to such debts, it is situate where the mortgage deed happens to be. Hence, for the purposes of death duties, it is situate where the mortgage deed is at the death of the mortgagee. But in the case of registered land, this rule is subject to variation, and if the mortgage is registered, and the mortgage deed retained in the registry, the mortgage debt will be regarded as situate at the registry (t).

Shares.—Similarly shares are situate where they can be effectively dealt with. Hence, if they can only pass by registered transfer, they are situate where the registration office is (u).

Securities transferable by delivery.—Where, however, debts are represented by bills of exchange or other marketable securities which are in fact in England and are saleable and transferable there by delivery only with or without endorsement, without its being necessary to do any act out of England in order to render the transfer valid, not only the bills themselves, but also the debts which they represent, are held to be situate in England, and this is so, although the debts are owing by foreigners out of England (a). And similarly, certificates of shares in a foreign company, on which a form of transfer and power of attorney has been endorsed and executed in blank, are treated as situate here, if they are marketable in this country and pass by delivery (b).

Judgment debts.—Judgment debts are assets, for the purposes of jurisdiction, where they are recorded (c).

Proper law of mortgage debt (d).—The proper law will be that chosen by the parties, expressly or by inference. Where an express choice is made, it must have some *bona fide* connection with the contract. An inference will be drawn from, *inter alia*, the form and terminology of the document, the nature and location of the subject matter and the residence of the parties (e).

The proper law of the deed is material to, *inter alia*, the capacity of the parties and its validity (f). More important, perhaps, from a

---

(s) E.g., for the former probate duty: *A.-G.* v. *Sudeley*, [1896] 1 Q.B. 354 at p. 360

(t) *Toronto General Trusts Corporation* v. *R.*, [1919] A.C. 679 (P.C.).

(u) *Brassard* v. *Smith*, [1925] A.C. 371; *R.* v. *Williams*, [1942] A.C. 541 (P.C.); [1942] 2 All E.R. 95. And see *Re Kettle's Gift*, [1968] 3 All E.R. 88.

(a) Dicey and Morris, *Conflict of Laws* (9th Edn.), p. 509; *A.-G.* v. *Bouwens, supra:* *A.-G.* v. *Glendining* (1904), 92 L.T. 87; *Winans* v. *R.*, [1908] 1 K.B. 1022; *Winans* v. *A.-G.*, [1910] A.C. 27 (H.L.).

(b) *Stern* v. *R.*, [1896] 1 Q.B. 211.

(c) *A.-G.* v. *Bouwens, supra*, at p. 191.

(d) Dicey and Morris, *ubi supra*, pp. 721 *et seq.*; Cheshire, *ubi supra*, pp. 201 *et seq.*

(e) *Re Heibert Wagg & Co., Ltd., supra; Keiner* v. *Keiner*, [1952] 1 All E.R. 643.

(f) For a case concerning priorities, to which the *lex fori* applies, see *Todd Shipyards Corporation* v. *Altema Compania Maritima S.A., The Ioannis Daskalelis*, [1974] S.C.R. 1248.

practical point of view is its relevance to the deductibility of tax from payments and interest made under the deed (g).

VIII—MORTGAGES AND TAXATION

See now Ch. 38, *infra*.

IX—CONSUMER CREDIT SECURITIES

See in particular Ch. 9, *infra*, and generally throughout the book, as appropriate.

X—MORTGAGES AND SUPPLEMENTARY BENEFIT

Supplementary benefit generally (h).—The relevant statutory provisions for determining the right to and amount of benefit are contained in Schedule 2 to the Ministry of Social Security Act 1966 (re-named the Supplementary Benefit Act 1966 (i)). Paragraph 13 of the Schedule provides that in addition to the amounts payable under the preceding paragraphs (*i.e.* the normal weekly requirement, etc.), a householder shall receive the amount of the net rent payable (reduced where appropriate where there are sub-tenants, etc.), or such part of that amount as is reasonable in the circumstances (this is called the rent addition or allowance).

Mortgage interest.—Net rent is defined (k) as (a) the rent payable for one week and (b) so much of the outgoings borne by the householder (l) as is attributable to one week including, *inter alia*, such proportion as is for the time being attributable to interest of any sum payable in respect of a mortgage debt or heritable security charged on the house in which the householder resides, or any interest thereon. The rent addition covers only the interest element of the mortgage repayments. Capital repayments are not covered by it (m). If the interest is unreasonably high the excess interest may not be allowed. Interest on a second mortgage may be allowed if, together with the interest under the first mortgage, the amount is reasonable and in line with the local average. A lump sum for arrears of mortgage interest may be payable under the exceptional need provision (n).

(g) See p. 666, *infra*.
(h) See generally (1975) L. A. G. Bulletin 184, 237; (1975) 125 New L.J. 972.
(i) By Social Security Act 1973, s. 99 (18).
(k) By para. 13 (3).
(l) Where a husband has deserted, the wife will usually be the householder under para. 9 (b). It seems that where a divorced woman becomes the owner of the former matrimonial home and wishes to sell it and buy a new house the supplementary benefits authorities will be amenable to the taking out of a new mortgage: see the articles referred to above.
(m) See Supplementary Benefits Handbook, H.M.S.O., 1973, paras. 48–60.
(n) S. 7. See also generally (1977) L. A. G. Bull. 36.

XI—CONTRACTS SUBJECT TO MORTGAGE, ETC.

Generally.—It was formerly not uncommon (*o*) for a contract to purchase land to be made "subject to mortgage", "subject to finance", etc. (*p*). Such conditions are rarely encountered to-day, at least where a formal contract is envisaged, because the purchaser's solicitor would insist on a firm offer from the proposed lender before allowing the purchaser to commit himself by signing the purchase contract (*q*). However, such contracts are quite common in certain Commonwealth countries (*r*).

Certainty.—In any event, unless the condition is sufficiently precise, it will be void for uncertainty. So a condition that the sale was subject to the purchaser obtaining a satisfactory mortgage was held to be too indefinite, thus rendering the condition itself and the whole contract void (*s*). It would seem that if such a condition is to be effective it would be necessary to draft the condition to refer in detail to at least the appropriate time limit on obtaining the finance, the source of the finance and the amount of principal (*t*).

(*o*) The 17th edition of the National Conditions, Condition 9 expressly covered the point.

(*p*) See Farrand, *Contract and Conveyance* (2nd Edn.), pp. 24–25.

(*q*) See *Buckland* v. *Mackesy* (1968), 122 Sol. Jo. 841 (C.A.).

(*r*) See (1967) 8 Univ. of Western Australia L.R.1; (1972) 36 Conv. (N.S.) 317; (1976) 40 Conv. (N.S.) 37 (Brian Coote).

(*s*) *Lee-Parker* v. *Izzet* (*No. 2*), [1972] 2 All E.R. 800. Cf. *Lee-Parker* v. *Izzet*, [1971] 3 All E.R. 1099; *Janmohamed* v. *Hassam* (1976), Times, 10th June; *Brown* v. *Gould*, [1972] Ch. 53, 56–57; and the Commonwealth cases referred to in the above-mentioned articles.

(*t*) (1976) 40 Conv. (N.S.) 37.

CHAPTER 2

Mortgages of Unregistered Land

I—LEGAL MORTGAGES

Legal mortgages of freehold land.—Since 1926 (a) a legal mortgage must be made either by demise for a term of years or by charge by way of legal mortgage. The Law of Property Act 1925, provides:

85.—(1) A mortgage of an estate in fee simple shall only be capable of being effected at law either by a demise for a term of years absolute, subject to a provision for cesser on redemption, or by a charge by deed expressed to be by way of legal mortgage.

Provided that a first mortgagee shall have the same right to possession of documents as if his security included the fee simple.

(2) Any purported conveyance of an estate in fee simple by way of mortgage made after the commencement of this Act shall (to the extent of the estate of the mortgagor) operate as a demise of the land to the mortgagee for a term of years absolute, without impeachment for waste, but subject to cesser on redemption, in manner following, namely:—

(a) A first or only mortgagee shall take a term of three thousand years from the date of the mortgage;

(b) A second or subsequent mortgagee shall take a term (commencing from the date of the mortgage) one day longer than the term vested in the first or other mortgagee whose security ranks immediately before that of such second or subsequent mortgagee;

and, in this subsection, any such purported conveyance as aforesaid includes an absolute conveyance with a deed of defeasance and any other assurance which, but for this sub-section, would operate in effect to vest the fee simple in a mortgagee subject to redemption.

(3) This section applies whether or not the land is registered under the Land Registration Act 1925, or the mortgage is expressed to be made by way of trust for sale (b) or otherwise.

Mortgages of leaseholds before 1926.—Before 1926 a mortgage of leasehold land might be made either by assignment of the term subject to a proviso for redemption, or by way of sub-demise reserving

---

(a) For the position before 1926, see pp. 5 et seq., supra. The reintroduction of mortgages by demise was advocated by Sir Arthur Underhill in his pamphlet *The Line of Least Resistance* (printed as an Appendix to the Fourth Report (1920) of the Acquisition of Land Committee) where the idea is attributed to Mr. C. P. Sanger. The object was to keep the legal estate in the mortgagor, so that on a conveyance subject to the mortgage he should be able to transfer a legal estate and not an equitable interest. The difficulties formerly felt as to term mortgages are expressly provided against in the Law of Property Act 1925: as to the possession of title deeds by ss. 85 (1), 86 (1); and as to sale and foreclosure by ss. 88, 89.

(b) As to mortgage by way of trust for sale, see p. 7, note (r), supra.

to the mortgagor a nominal reversion out of the term (*c*). A mortgage in either form was originally liable to destruction by forfeiture of the term for breach of covenant. Relief against forfeiture was later given by statute (*d*). If the whole term was assigned to the mortgagee, he became liable to be sued by the lessor for the rent and also on the covenants, whether or not he had entered into possession (*e*). Accordingly of the two methods of making leasehold mortgages mentioned above the usual practice was to make the mortgage by sub-demise, since the mortgagee thereby avoided direct liability to the lessor on the covenants in the lease. The sub-demise reserved a nominal reversion of one or more days to the mortgagor (*f*) and the mortgagor declared that he would hold this on trust for the mortgagee. The mortgagee was usually also given power to remove the mortgagor from the trust and to appoint himself or any other person to be trustee in place of the mortgagor. This enabled the mortgagee, when necessity arose, to appoint himself or a purchaser from him to be trustee of the leasehold reversion and vest it by a vesting declaration (*g*).

Leasehold mortgages after 1925.—The Law of Property Act 1925, adopted and made compulsory the method of effecting leasehold mortgages by sub-demise, thereby making the practice analogous to that introduced by the Act for freehold mortgages. The term remains vested in the mortgagor, but, since statutory provision is also made for getting in the nominal reversion when the security has to be realised (*h*), the insertion in the mortgage of a trust of the reversion has become unnecessary. The Law of Property Act 1925 provides:

86.—(1) A mortgage of a term of years absolute shall only be capable of being effected at law either by a sub-demise of the term of years absolute, less one day at least (*i*) than the term vested in the mortgagor, and subject to a provision for cesser on redemption, or by a charge by deed expressed to be by way of legal mortgage; and where a licence to sub-demise by way of mortgage is required, such licence shall not be unreasonably refused:

Provided that a first mortgagee shall have the same right to the possession of documents as if his security had been effected by way of assignment.

(2) Any purported assignment of a term of years absolute by way of mortgage made after the commencement of this Act shall (to the extent of the estate of the mortgagor) operate as a sub-demise of the leasehold land to the mortgagee for a term of years absolute, but subject to cesser on redemption, in manner following, namely:—

(a) The term to be taken by a first or only mortgagee shall be ten days less than the term expressed to be assigned;

(*c*) The sub-demise would be for the term less one or more days. A mortgage by demise for a term concurrent with a term created by a first or other prior mortgage created a legal term: *Re Moore and Hulm's Contract*, [1912] 2 Ch. 105; and see now Law of Property Act 1925, s. 149 (5).

(*d*) See p. 23, *infra*.

(*e*) *Williams* v. *Bosanquet* (1819), 1 Bro. & Bing. 238.

(*f*) See *Bonner* v. *Tottenham and Edmonton Permanent Investment Building Society*, [1899] 1 Q.B. 161 (C.A.).

(*g*) *London and County Banking Co.* v. *Goddard*, [1897] 1 Ch. 642. An earlier device was to appoint the mortgagee the attorney of the mortgagor to convey the nominal reversion, and sometimes mortgages contained both devices.

(*h*) Law of Property Act 1925, s. 89. See p. 378, *infra*.

(*i*) The usual practice is to make the sub-term ten days shorter than the term of the lease. For form, see Precedent 4 in the Appendix, *infra*. Failure to so provide is not fatal. A lease may take effect in reversion upon another lease of the same or greater length: Law of Property Act 1925, s. 149 (5).

(b) The term to be taken by a second or subsequent mortgagee shall be one day longer than the term vested in the first or other mortgagee whose security ranks immediately before that of second or subsequent mortgagee, if the length of the last mentioned term permits, and in any case for a term less by one day at least than the term expressed to be assigned:

and, in this subsection, any such purported assignment as aforesaid includes an absolute assignment with a deed of defeasance and any other assurance which, but for this subsection, would operate to vest the term of the mortgagor in a mortgagee subject to redemption.

(3) This section applies whether or not the land is registered under the Land Registration Act 1925, or the mortgage is made by way of sub-mortgage of a term of years absolute, or is expressed to be by way of trust for sale or otherwise.

Though expressed as an absolute assignment of the term a document intended to be a mortgage operates by way of subdemise (k).

Relief from forfeiture (l).—As previously stated the liability of a mortgagee of leasehold property to lose his security by forfeiture incurred by the mortgagor has been lessened by statute (m). Relief against forfeiture for non-payment of rent can be obtained under the Common Law Procedure Act 1852, ss. 210 to 212, and the Supreme Court of Judicature (Consolidation) Act 1925, s. 46 (previously the Common Law Procedure Act 1860, s. 1 (n)). And by the Law of Property Act 1925, s. 146 (o), a right of entry or forfeiture under any proviso or stipulation in a lease for a breach of any covenant or condition (otherwise than for the payment of rent) in the lease is not enforceable by action or otherwise, unless and until the lessor serves on the lessee the appropriate notice (p) and the lessee fails to remedy the breach, if capable of remedy, or to make reasonable compensation. And if the lessor is proceeding, by action or otherwise, to enforce such a right or entry of forfeiture, the court can grant relief (q).

(k) *Grangeside Properties, Ltd.* v. *Collingwoods Securities, Ltd.*, [1964] 1 All E.R. 143 (C.A.).

(l) See, generally, Hill and Redman's *Landlord and Tenant* (15th Edn.), pp. 526 *et seq.* Where the benefit of a mortgage has become vested in the landlord, the evidence of forfeiture must be unequivocal: *Hone* v. *Daejan Properties, Ltd.* (1976), 120 Sol. Jo. 488 (C.A.). For protection from eviction, see also Rent Act 1965, ss. 31 and 32 (as amended by the Rent Act 1968).

(m) Forfeiture for non-payment of rent might be avoided by the lender paying the rent and adding the amount to the security, see p. 267, *infra.* As to non-repair, the mortgage will usually give the lender the right to enter and repair and to add the cost to the security (see p. 31, *infra*).

(n) The statutes recognise the right to relief for non-payment of rent which exists in equity, the proviso for re-entry being regarded as merely a security for rent: *Howard* v. *Fanshawe*, [1895] 2 Ch. 581, 588. See, generally, *Gill* v. *Lewis*, [1956] 2 Q.B. 1 (C.A.); [1956] 1 All E.R. 844; and *Belgravia Insurance Co., Ltd.* v. *Meah*, [1964] 1 Q.B. 436 (C.A.); [1963] 3 All E.R. 828. And see County Courts Act 1959, s. 191.

(o) Replacing Conveyancing Act 1881, s. 14; Conveyancing and Law of Property Act 1892, ss. 2, 4. For breach of covenant to repair, see *Hill and Redman, ubi supra.*

(p) See *Hill and Redman*, p. 527.

(q) As to restrictions on relief, see s. 146 (8), (9). Section 146 does not affect the law relating to relief in case of non-payment of rent, and it has effect notwithstanding any stipulation to the contrary: sub-ss. (11), (12).

Where a landlord has re-entered peaceably without an order of the court the court's power to grant relief is not statutory but arises from its equitable jurisdiction. There is no time limit for an application under this jurisdiction (save the general principle that equity will not give relief in respect of stale claims) (*r*).

Relief can also be granted to an underlessee (which expression includes a mortgagee by demise and by way of legal charge and anyone entitled to call for such a mortgage (*s*)) when the lessor is claiming to assert his right of entry or forfeiture under the head lease, and in favour of the underlessee the relief extends to non-payment of rent (*t*). An underlessee can also avail himself of the statutory right to relief under the Common Law Procedure Acts (*u*), and there is the distinction that he can apply under these Acts after the lease has been determined by forfeiture (*a*), but under the Law of Property Act 1925, he must apply before the lessor has re-entered (*b*). Under the Common Law Procedure Acts, the mortgagee is entitled to relief on the same terms as the lessee (*c*) and accordingly he can obtain relief if he is willing, within six months after judgment enforcing the forfeiture, to pay all arrears, costs and damages, and to perform all covenants, unless in the meantime third parties have acquired rights which would be thereby infringed (*d*). Relief under the Law of Property Act 1925, may be given upon the underlessee accepting a new lease for a term not exceeding that under his sub-lease (*e*), and upon such other terms as

---

(*r*) *Lovelock* v. *Margo*, [1963] 2 Q.B. 786 (C.A.); [1963] 2 All E.R. 13; *Thatcher* v. *C. H. Pearce & Sons (Contractors), Ltd.*, [1968] 1 W.L.R. 748.

(*s*) *Re Good's Lease*, [1954] 1 All E.R. 275; *Grand Junction Co., Ltd.* v. *Bates*, [1954] 2 Q.B. 160; [1954] 2 All E.R. 385; *Chelsea Estates Investment Trust Co., Ltd.* v. *Marche*, [1955] Ch. 328; [1955] 1 All E.R. 195; *Belgravia Insurance Co., Ltd* v. *Meah, supra* (where the principles applicable to claims by an underlessee or mortgagee by sub-demise are fully dealt with); *Purley Automobile Co.* v. *Aldon Motors* (1968), 112 Sol. Jo. 482 (C.A.).

(*t*) Section 146 (4). Relief of underlessees under sub-s. (4) is not subject to the restrictions on relief in sub-ss. (8), (9): Law of Property (Amendment) Act 1929, s. 1. See *Grangeside Properties, Ltd.* v. *Collingwoods Securities, Ltd., supra*.

(*u*) See *Moore* v. *Smee and Cornish*, [1907] 2 K.B. 8 (C.A.).

(*a*) See *Humphreys* v. *Morten*, [1905] 1 Ch. 739.

(*b*) *Rogers* v. *Rice*, [1892] 2 Ch. 170 (C.A.).

(*c*) *Doe* d. *Whitfield* v. *Roe* (1811), 3 Taunt. 402. A mortgagee may be required to pay the landlord's costs of the proceedings against the tenant: *Egerton* v. *Jones*, [1939] 2 K.B. 702 (C.A.); [1939] 3 All E.R. 889.

(*d*) *Newbolt* v. *Bingham* (1895), 72 L.T. 852 (C.A.); *Howard* v. *Fanshawe, supra*; *Humphreys* v. *Morten, supra*. Note that there is no time limit where the landlord has re-entered peaceably without an order of the court: see the cases referred to in note (*s*), *supra*.

(*e*) *Ewart* v. *Fryer*, [1901] 1 Ch. 499 (C.A.), at p. 515; *Ellerman* v. *Lillywhite* (1923), unreported; see *Factors Sundries, Ltd.* v. *Miller*, [1952] 2 All E.R. 630 (C.A.), at p. 634. Sub-section (4) provides that the court may vest the demised premises in the underlessee for the whole term of the lease or any less term, but the underlessee shall not be entitled to require a lease to be granted to him for any longer term than he had under his original sub-lease. The above cases decided that the latter of these conflicting provisions prevails. And see *Chelsea Estates Investment Trust Co., Ltd.* v. *Marche, supra*, and *Belgravia Insurance Co., Ltd.* v. *Meah, supra*. Such an order in favour of a mortgagee binds the mortgagee directly to the lessor, but the relationship of mortgagor and mortgagee remains nevertheless (*i.e.*, the new lease granted to the mortgagee is a substituted security and is subject to the mortgage: *Chelsea Estates Investment Trust Co., Ltd.* v. *Marche supra*).

to payment of rent, compensation, and otherwise as the court may think fit (*d*).

Surrender.—A surrender of mortgaged leaseholds does not extinguish the mortgagee's interest and the mortgagee will thereupon be entitled to possession (*g*).

Legal charge.—The alternative to creating a legal mortgage by demise of the fee simple or by sub-demise of a term of years is to create it by "a charge by deed expressed to be by way of legal mortgage". Such a charge does not create an actual or notional (*h*) term in the mortgagee, but it puts him in the same position as regards protection, powers and remedies as if a term had been created (*i*). The Law of Property Act 1925, provides:

> **87.**—(1) Where a legal mortgage of land is created by a charge by deed expressed to be by way of legal mortgage (*k*), the mortgagee shall have the same protection, powers and remedies (including the right to take proceedings to obtain possession from the occupiers and the persons in receipt of rents and profits, or any of them) as if:—
>
> (a) where the mortgage is a mortgage of an estate in fee simple, a mortgage term for three thousand years without impeachment of waste had been thereby created in favour of the mortgagee; and
>
> (b) where the mortgage is a mortgage of a term of years absolute, a sub-term less by one day than the term vested in the mortgagor had been thereby created in favour of the mortgagee (*l*).

The chargee of leasehold land may protect his charge by applying for relief against forfeiture as if he were an underlessee (*m*).

(*f*) *Ewart* v. *Fryer, supra; Gray* v. *Bonsall*, [1904] 1 K.B. 601 (C.A.), at p. 604. Where the mortgage is of part of the demised premises relief may be given to the underlessee of the part on terms of his paying the whole of the arrears under the head lease: *Webber* v. *Smith* (1689), 2 Vern. 103; *cf. Chatham Empire Theatre (1955), Ltd.* v. *Ultrans*, [1961] 2 All E.R. 381 (in which *Webber* v. *Smith* was not considered).

(*g*) *Usher's Brewery, Ltd.* v. *P.S. King & Co. (Finance), Ltd.* (1969), 113 Sol. Jo. 815; *E.S. Schwab & Co., Ltd.* v. *McCarthy* (1975), 31 P. & C.R. 196, at p. 209 (C.A.), and see 23 Halsbury's Laws (3rd Edn.), 688–9; *Coote on Mortgages* (9th Edn.), 192–3. See also *London and County (A. and D.), Ltd.* v. *Wilfred Sportsman, Ltd.*, [1971] Ch. 764 (C.A.); [1970] 2 All E.R. 600.

(*h*) *Weg Motors, Ltd.* v. *Hales*, [1962] Ch. 49 (C.A.), at pp. 73, 74, 77; [1961] 3 All E.R. 181, at pp. 190, 192; *Cumberland Court (Brighton) Ltd.* v. *Taylor*, [1964] Ch. 29; [1963] 2 All E.R. 536; *Thompson* v. *Salah*, [1972] 1 All E.R. 530. And see *Edwards* v. *Marshall-Lee* (1975), 119 Sol. Jo. 506. In *Usher's Brewery, Ltd.* v. *P. S. King & Co., (Finance) Ltd., supra*, the legal charge was assumed to create a notional term.

(*i*) *Grand Junction Co., Ltd.* v. *Bates*, [1954] 2 Q.B. 160, at p. 168; [1954] 2 All E.R. 385, at p. 388; *Belgravia Insurance Co., Ltd.* v. *Meah*, [1964] 1 Q.B. 436 (C.A.), at p. 443; [1963] 3 All E.R. 828, at p. 831; *Regent Oil Co., Ltd.* v. *J. A. Gregory (Hatch End), Ltd.*, [1966] Ch. 402 (C.A.), at p. 431; [1965] 3 All E.R. 673, at p. 681. The charge ranks as a legal interest: Law of Property Act 1925, s. 1. (2), (3), (4). In questions of priority it ranks as a legal estate: see *Caunce* v. *Caunce*, [1969] 1 All E.R. 722.

(*k*) It need not be so expressed in a registered charge; see p. 62, *infra*. In the case there mentioned GOFF, J. refrained from saying anything on the point as regards unregistered land. In *Sopher* v. *Mercer*, [1967] C.L.Y. 2543 (Cty. Ct.) it was held that the actual words were not necessary. *Sed quaere.* And see note 14, p. 680, *infra*.

(*l*) Sub-sections (2) and (3) deal with the conversion of mortgages existing on 1 January, 1926, into legal charges upon a declaration in writing to that effect signed by the mortgagee.

(*m*) Law of Property Act 1925, s. 146 (4), see p. 24, *supra*.

Advantages of the legal charge.—The legal charge has certain advantages over the mortgage by demise. The same document may conveniently be used for mortgaging both freeholds and leaseholds. The form of a legal charge is more intelligible to a mortgagor (*n*). Where leasehold property is charged a legal charge probably does not amount to a breach of a covenant in the lease (if any) against subletting (*o*).

There is, however, said to be an objection to the use of the legal charge. A legal charge does not contain a proviso for redemption (*p*). Accordingly it is argued that the mortgagee cannot foreclose, since the date at which the mortgagor's right of redemption and consequently the mortgagee's right to foreclose are to arise is not fixed. However, it is clear from ss. 87, 88 and 89 of the Law of Property Act 1925, that the legal chargee has a right of foreclosure and it can be safely assumed that the right of the legal chargee to foreclose arises on the mortgagor's default in repaying at the date fixed in the covenant for repayment (*q*).

Statutory mortgage.—As a special form of charge by way of legal mortgage, a mortgage of freehold or leasehold land may be made by a deed expressed to be by way of statutory mortgage (*r*). Such a mortgage must be in one of the forms Nos. 1 or 4 in the Fourth Schedule of the Law of Property Act 1925, with such variations and additions, if any, as the circumstances may require. It implies a covenant to pay the mortgage debt with half-yearly interest, and a provision that the mortgagee will, on payment off, discharge the mortgaged property or transfer the benefit of the mortgage as the mortgagor directs (*s*). A statutory mortgage has to be transferred in statutory form. Forms Nos. 2 and 3 are forms of transfer. The statutory mortgage is rarely used today.

Form of mortgage deed.—The mortgage or charge should be made by a separate deed. A combined form of conveyance and mortgage should not be used (*t*). This applies especially where the transaction

---

(*n*) Maitland described the mortgage deed as "one long *supressio veri* and *suggestio falsi*": Maitland, *Equity* (2nd Edn.), p. 182. And see the remarks of Lord MacNaghten in *Samuel* v. *Jarrah Timber and Wood Paving Corporation, Ltd.*, [1904] A.C. 323 (H.L.), at p. 326. For the proposed abolition of the mortgage by demise in Northern Ireland, see note (*q*), p. 5, *supra*.

(*o*) *Gentle* v. *Faulkner*, [1900] 2 Q.B. 267 (C.A.); *Grand Junction Co., Ltd.* v. *Bates*, [1954] 2 Q.B. 160, 168; [1954] 2 All E.R. 385, at p. 388. And see p. 247, *infra*. Where a licence to sub-demise is required, such licence must not be unreasonably refused: Law of Property Act 1925, s. 86 (1); p. 22, *supra*.

(*p*) Not, at least, in the form (Form No. 1) set out in Sched. V of the Law of Property Act 1925. A proviso for redemption is, however, often included in a legal charge.

(*q*) Or, if no date is fixed, on breach of, e.g., the covenant to pay interest: *Twentieth Century Banking Corporation, Ltd.* v. *Wilkinson*, [1976] 3 All E.R. 361.

(*r*) Law of Property Act 1925, s. 117 (1). This is in substitution for s. 26 of the Conveyancing Act 1881.

(*s*) *Ibid.*, s. 117 (2). For joint and several liability and joint benefit, see *ibid.*, s. 119.

(*t*) In such cases there is a danger of the deed being destroyed when the mortgage or charge is discharged.

is one leading to first registration or is of already registered land (*u*).

II—CONTENTS OF MORTGAGE DEED

Covenant for payment. Purpose.—It is usual in a mortgage to insert a covenant to repay the principal sum with interest, on a fixed day, and also to pay interest after default so long as the security shall subsist (*x*). But that is not, nor was it ever, a necessary part of a mortgage which, in itself, implies a loan, and therefore a debt recoverable by action (*a*), and bearing interest even though none is expressly reserved (*b*). In the absence, however, of a covenant or bond, the debt is only a simple contract debt (*c*). The principal secured by the mortgage and the interest thereon are distinct debts, and may be separately recovered (*d*).

If no fixed date for repayment is specified by the mortgage deed the debt is repayable on demand. If a date for repayment is fixed by the mortgage deed—usually six months from the date of the mortgage (*e*)—on default of repayment on the day fixed the mortgagee may

---

(*u*) Because the original deed will be retained in the Land Registry. *Instalment purchase as alternative to mortgage.* It is not uncommon for certain types of property, usually those within an area scheduled for redevelopment within the near future so that a mortgage will not be available, to be sold on the terms that the purchase money shall be payable by instalments. The payment of the instalments should be secured by a mortgage of the property sold. More often there is no immediate conveyance, there being merely an agreement for sale with completion postponed until the purchase money has been paid. The terms of such an agreement are often an amalgam of contract, mortgage and lease terms. See generally (1971) 121 New L.J. 427, 435, 487: (1972) 36 Conv. (N.S.) 325; (1975) 39 Conv. (N.S.) 343 (1976) 126 New L.J. 217; (1976) LAG Bulletin 133; and for the application of the Consumer Credit Act 1974 see (1975) 39 Conv. 112. But so long as there is a genuine sale the purchaser will not be protected by the Rent Acts (see *Dunthorne and Shore* v. *Wiggins*, [1943] 2 All E.R. 678 (C.A.); cf. *Francis Jackson Developments, Ltd.* v, *Stemp*, [1943] 2 All E.R. 601 (C.A.); and see Megarry, *The Rent Acts* (10th Edn.), p. 65) and the Report of the Committee on the Rent Acts 1971, Ch. 15; though for some purposes such an agreement is treated in the same way as a mortgage (see statutory modifications of mortgages, pp. 600 *et seq.*, *infra*).

(*x*) Where appropriate, the provision should deal with the rests, i.e., the intervals at which an account is struck for the purposes of determining interest (see pp. 623 *et seq.*, *infra*). Generally arrears are to be compounded on the same basis: see *Montreal Trust Co.* v. *Hounslow Holdings, Ltd.* (1972), 22 D.L.R. (3d) 503. Personal liability under the covenant may be negatived (where the mortgagors are trustees or personal representatives, see pp. 209 and 213, *infra*) or limited to interest (where the mortgagor is tenant for life, see p. 199, *infra*). And there may be no personal liability where a person charges his own property as collateral security for the debt of another: *Re Midland Bank, Ltd.'s Application*, [1941] Ch. 350; [1941] 2 All E.R. 135. For the covenants implied in a registered charge, see p. 63, *infra*.

(*a*) *Yates* v. *Aston* (1843), 4 Q.B. 182; *Sutton* v. *Sutton* (1882), 22 Ch. D. 511, 515 (C.A.).

(*b*) *Anon.* (1813), 4 Taunt. 876; *Mendl* v. *Smith* (1943), 112 L.J. Ch. 279. But see *Cityland and Property (Holdings), Ltd.* v. *Dabrah*, [1968] Ch. 166; [1967] 2 All E.R. 639. And see p. 561, *infra*.

(*c*) *Ancaster* v. *Mayer* (1785), 1 Bro. C.C. 454, at p. 464; *Quarrell* v. *Beckford* (1816), 1 Mad. 269, at p. 278; *Sutton* v. *Sutton*, *supra*.

(*d*) *Dickenson* v. *Harrison* (1817), 4 Price. 282. It is advisable, in the case of an express covenant, to word it so that the principal and interest are to be construed as two distinct debts, rather than a single debt.

(*e*) By convention, being a reasonably short period before the mortgage is redeemable by the mortgagor and the mortgagee's default powers are exercisable.

pursue his remedies, without having to serve a demand (*f*).

Repayment by instalments.—Many mortgages today provide for repayment of the advance by instalments. Such mortgages may take the form of a covenant to repay at a fixed date, but with a proviso that if the specified instalments are punctually paid the mortgagee will not require payment in any other manner. Alternatively there may be a direct covenant to pay by instalments, with a proviso that in case of default in payment of any instalment the whole debt shall become immediately payable (*g*). The disadvantage of the direct covenant method for the mortgagee is that if he has to exercise his power of sale he will have to prove that the instalments are in arrears (with the fixed date method he merely has to show that that date has passed (*h*)). The disadvantage for the mortgagor is that the form may operate to postpone redemption (*i*).

A provision that the whole loan should become due on default is not bad as a penalty or otherwise (*k*). Provision may be made for the payment by the mortgagor of a commission or fine in the event of an instalment being in arrear (*l*). But where a premium is added to the advance and it is provided that the whole of the premium should also become due on default that is a different matter. Where the premium is substantial the provision may be void as a penalty (*m*).

Covenant not to call in the money.—Unless fraud is proved, there is no objection to an agreement that the debt shall not be called in until a particular time, however long the postponement, and even though a period of six months is fixed for redemption (*n*). If such an agreement is absolute, default in payment of interest pending the day for redemption will not entitle the mortgagee to foreclose (*o*). And if the mortgage provides merely for repayment by instalments, this may prevent the lender calling in the money (*p*). But is, as is usually the case, the covenant is expressed to be conditional on regular payment of interest the right to foreclosure arises on default in such payment (*q*). If "punctual payment" is required, this is construed strictly (*r*). The mere receipt of interest after the due date is not a waiver of the right to sue (*s*), though it is a circumstance to be taken

---

(*f*) See p. 296, *infra*. For forms of covenant to pay, see 14 Ency. Forms and Precedents (4th Edn.), pp. 112 *et seq.*; and Precedent I in the Appendix, *infra*.

(*g*) For forms, see 14 Ency. Forms and Precedents (4th Edn.), 115–117; and Precedent 2 in the Appendix, *infra*. See generally (1972), 122 New L.J. 815, 836.

(*h*) See pp. 360, 687, *infra*.

(*i*) See p. 523, *infra*; and generally, p. 687, *infra*. For early redemption, see p. 522, *infra*.

(*k*) *Sterne* v. *Beck* (1863), 1 De G. J. & Sm. 595; *Wallingford* v. *Mutual Society* (1880), 5 App. Cas. 685 (H.L.); *Protector Endowment and Annuity Loan Co.* v. *Grice* (1880), 5 Q.B.D. 592 (C.A.); *Cityland and Property Holdings, Ltd.* v. *Dabrah*, *supra*.

(*l*) *General Credit and Discount Co.* v. *Glegg* (1883), 22 Ch. D. 549.

(*m*) *Cityland and Property (Holdings), Ltd.* v. *Dabrah*, *supra*. *Wanner* v. *Caruana*, [1974] 2 N.S.W.L.R. 301; and see pp. 528–529, *infra*.

(*n*) See p. 521, *infra*. For form, see proviso in Precedent IA in the Appendix, *infra*.

(*o*) See p. 270, *infra*.

(*p*) See p. 522, *infra*.

(*q*) *Seaton* v. *Twyford* (1870), L.R. 11 Eq. 591; *Tate* v. *Crewdson*, [1938] Ch. 869; [1938] 3 All E.R. 43. And see *Clark* v. *Vile*, [1969] 209 Estates Gazette Digest 169.

(*r*) *Leeds and Hanley Theatre of Varieties* v. *Broadbent*, [1898] 1 Ch. 343 (C.A.); *Maclaine* v. *Gatty*, [1921] 1 A.C. 376 (H.L.).

(*s*) *Keene* v. *Biscoe* (1878), 8 Ch. D. 201; *Re Taafe's Estate* (1864), 14 I. Ch. R. 347.

into account in determining whether there has been a waiver (*t*).

Provisions for punctual payment of interest.—It is a well settled, if not an intelligible rule, that if the mortgagee wishes to stipulate for a higher rate of interest in default of punctual payment he must reserve the higher rate as the interest payable under the mortgage, and provide for its reduction in case of punctual payment (*u*). He cannot effect his object by reserving the lower rate, and making the higher the penalty for non-payment at the appointed time, because, it is said, an agreement of the latter kind, being a penalty, is relievable in equity (*a*).

Rate of interest allowed.—At present, in the case of moneylenders there is a presumption that where the rate of interest exceeds 48 per cent. per annum the interest is excessive (*b*), but the court may nevertheless hold that the interest charged, although not exceeding 48 per cent., is excessive. In due course these provisions will be superseded by provisions in the Consumer Credit Act 1974 of general application, giving the court power to rewrite extortionate credit agreements (*c*). In other cases there is no restriction on the rate of interest which may be charged (*d*). Equity does not reform mortgage transactions because they are unreasonable (*e*). If some other provision in the mortgage relating to the interest could be set aside as an unreasonable collateral advantage, *e.g.*, if all the interest calculated in advance became payable on early redemption, a lower rate of interest might be fixed by the court (*f*). Where no rate of interest is fixed by the parties the court can fix it (*g*).

Variation of interest.—In the absence of express provision in that behalf, the rate of interest cannot be varied though, if the money can be called in, this fact will usually be sufficient to make the borrower agree a variation. Most building society and commercial mortgages provide for variation. This should be subject to some ceiling (otherwise it might be arguable that the power to vary was invalid as unreasonable) or by reference to some external yardstick (such as the Retail Prices Index or the Bank of England's minimum lending rate (*h*)).

(*t*) *Seal* v. *Gimson* (1914) 110 L.T. 583.

(*u*) *Strode* v. *Parker* (1694) 2 Vern. 316. For form, see form in Precedent IA in the Appendix, *infra*. As to the restriction on increasing the rate of interest under the Rent Acts, see p. 277, *infra*. As to companies exempted from the Moneylenders Acts, see p. 235, *infra*.

(*a*) *Wallingford* v. *Mutual Society*, *supra*. And see p. 632, *infra*.

(*b*) Moneylenders Act, 1927, s. 10 (1). And see p. 237, *infra*.

(*c*) See p. 152, *infra*. And note the true cost of borrowing provision (s. 20).

(*d*) See note (*a*), p. 528, *infra*. And compound interest may be agreed: *Clarkson* v. *Henderson* (1880), 14 Ch. D. 348. See p. 528, *infra*. Interest arises on a day to day basis unless otherwise agreed: see p. 627, *infra*.

(*e*) *Knightsbridge Estates Trust Ltd.* v. *Byrne*, [1939] Ch. 441 (C.A.), at p. 457; *per* Green, M.R.; [1938] 4 All E.R. 618, at p. 626.

(*f*) *Cityland and Property (Holdings) Ltd.* v. *Dabrah*, [1968] Ch. 166; [1967] 2 All E.R. 639 (7 per cent. in place of 19 per cent. or, as a premium, 57 per cent.); and see *United Dominions Trust, Ltd.* v. *Thomas* (1976), 120 Sol. Jo. 561.

(*g*) *Re Drax*, [1903] 1 Ch. 781 (C.A.); *Mendl* v. *Smith* (1943), 169 L.T. 153 (5 per cent).

(*h*) See p. 684, *infra*; Wurtzburg and Mills, *Building Society Law* (14th Edn.), pp. 166–168; (1974) 118 S. J. 590; (1975) 119 S.J. 496; for form, see form in *Precedents for the Conveyancer*, p. 355–7. Bank rate and Bank of England minimum lending rate are the same thing: *First National Securities, Ltd.* v. *Onwuegbuzie* (1976), 120 Sol. Jo. 458 (Lambeth County Court).

Classification of legal mortgages of land according to method of repayment (*i*).—Legal mortgages of land are today generally classified according to the method of repayment of the money advanced. There are four principal classes, namely:

(1) Repayment, Annuity or Flat Rate mortgages;
(2) Fixed Instalment mortgages;
(3) Endowment mortgages; and
(4) Standing mortgages.

There is a further class, namely Mixed mortgages, which are a combination of class (1) and either class (3) or (4).

Flat Rate mortgages.—These take the form of repayment by fixed periodical instalments, comprised partly of principal and partly of interest, over a specified period (the term of the mortgage). The amount of the instalments remains the same throughout the term, although the proportion of each instalment which is allocated to principal or interest varies, the amount allocated to principal increasing throughout the period (*k*).

Fixed Instalment mortgages.—Under these a fixed amount of principal is repaid each year of the term of the mortgage together with interest at the appropriate rate on the balance of principal for the time being outstanding. The amount of the instalments therefore varies, decreasing throughout the mortgage term.

Endowment mortgages.—Under these the principal is left outstanding until the end of the term, only the interest thereon being paid during the term. At the end of the term the principal is paid off in a single sum from the proceeds of an endowment policy taken out by the mortgagor on his own life and for a term equal to the term of the mortgage (*l*).

Standing mortgages.—These take a form similar to endowment mortgages insofar as there is no provision for regular repayment of the principal, which is left outstanding until the end of the term, only interest being payable during the term. At the end of the term the principal is repayable.

The demise or charge.—Absolute covenants for title are implied

---

(*i*) This classification is employed in the official guide to the option mortgage scheme (see pp. 657 *et seq.*, *infra.*). And see Wurtzburg and Mills, *ubi supra*, 160. There have been various proposals for new forms of repayment in recent years, i.e., low start mortgages (see (1975) 233 Estates Gazette 457); equitable half mortgage (1975, *The Times*, 22 April); never-never mortgages ((1969) 113 Sol. Jo. 645); and see (1969), 119 New L.J. 327 (Trevor M. Alridge); *Wurtzburg and Mills*, pp. 160–162.

(*k*) This classification should not be confused with *flat rate interest* mortgages, under which interest is calculated as a percentage of the advance over the term and usually added to the advance to form a lump sum (see, *e.g.*, *Cityland and Property (Holdings), Ltd.* v. *Dabrah*, [1968] Ch. 166; [1967] 2 All E.R. 639).

(*l*) Another method of combining mortgage and assurance is that recognised by the Building Societies Act 1962, s. 33, known as the combined scheme. A building society may make a further advance to a borrower to enable payment to be made for a single premium policy on the life of the borrower or his wife, son or daughter, providing for payment of the amount due to the society by the assurance company in the event of the death of the borrower before repayment. See p. 195, *infra*.

by s. 76 of the Law of Property Act 1925, where the mortgagor demises or charges the property as beneficial owner (*m*).

The demise or charge must be of specific realty (*n*).

In the classical form of mortgage after the demise follows the proviso for cesser which provides that if the mortgagor shall on a given day pay to the mortgagee the mortgage debt and interest the mortgage term shall cease (*o*). In the case of a legal charge there may be included a similar proviso that on payment on the given day the mortgagee will discharge the security (*p*). The date for redemption should be the same as the date fixed by the covenant for payment. The proviso for cesser or the proviso for discharge are not essential, since in the former case the term ceases and in the latter case the legal charge is discharged upon payment. But they are inserted, because, by specifying a date for redemption, the end of the legal right of redemption is fixed, and, on default in payment on the date fixed, the right of foreclosure arises (*q*). In the modern form of building society mortgage there is not any express provision for redemption, the mortgage terms or conditions generally allowing repayment at any time on due notice and the right of foreclosure on default by the mortgagor being left to be implied.

Restrictions on the right of redemption are dealt with later (*r*).

Other covenants by the mortgagor (*s*).—After the proviso for cesser follow various covenants by the mortgagor. These may include covenants to repair and to insure or not to insure. There is no statutory obligation on a mortgagor to keep the property in repair. The mortgagor's position as tenant arising by virtue of possession of the mortgaged property with the permission of the mortgagee (*t*) or of an attornment clause (*u*) imposes no obligation upon him to repair. The mortgagee is entitled to have the mortgaged property preserved from deterioration in the hands of the mortgagor or of any other person whose interest is inferior to that of the mortgagee and any moneys expended by him in preserving the property are allowed in

---

(*m*) For the implied covenants, see Law of Property Act 1925, Sched. 2, Pts. III, IV. And see (1964), 28 Conv. (N.S.) 205 (A. M. Prichard.) As to the covenants implied in a statutory mortgage, see p. 26, *supra*. As to the covenants implied in a registered charge, see p. 63, *infra*. As to the necessity for a charge to be expressed to be by way of legal mortgage, see footnote (*k*), p. 25, *supra*.

(*n*) For equitable mortgages of future property, see p. 12, *supra*.

(*o*) See Law of Property Act 1925, ss. 85 (1), 86 (1), *supra*. For forms, see 14 Ency. Forms and Precedents (4th Edn.), 120–123; and Precedents in the Appendix, *infra*.

(*p*) See p. 26, *supra*.

(*q*) See p. 382, *infra*.   (*r*) See pp. 522 *et seq.*, *infra*.

(*s*) If there is age ambiguity as to the construction of the mortgage, it may be construed in the light of the factural background known to the parties at the time of its execution, and of its genesis and purpose objectively viewed; see *Western Bank, Ltd.* v. *Schindler*, [1976] 2 All E.R. 393, 396. Where property is sold subject, to a mortgage, it is usual, particularly where the mortgagee is a building society, for the mortgagee to release the original mortgagor from all future liability under the mortgage and for the purchaser to enter into new covenants with the mortgagee for payment of principal and interest and observance of the covenants in the mortgage. A deed containing such covenants is commonly called a deed of covenant(s). Such a deed may also be executed where the terms of the mortgage, *e.g.*, as to the rate of interest, are varied. As to variation, see p. 43, *infra*. The parties' conduct after execution may be relevant also.

(*t*) See p. 332, *infra*.

(*u*) See p. 34, *infra*.

taking the accounts (*a*). In the absence of express provision difficulty may be experienced by the mortgagee in effecting repairs. Accordingly most mortgages contain a covenant by the mortgagor to keep the property in good repair and to repair on notice from the mortgagee and in case of default to permit the mortgagee to enter and effect repairs without becoming liable as mortgagee in possession (*b*), together with provision for the mortgagor to pay the cost thereof and a charge of such moneys on the mortgaged property (*c*).

As to insurance, where the mortgage is made by deed, the mortgagee has by virtue of the Law of Property Act 1925 (*d*), the following power, to the like extent as if it had been in terms conferred by the mortgage deed but not further:

> A power, at any time after the date of the mortgage deed, to insure and keep insured against loss or damage by fire any building, or any effects or property of an insurable nature, whether affixed to the freehold or not, being or forming part of the property which or an estate or interest wherein is mortgaged, and the premiums paid for any such insurance shall be a charge on the mortgaged property or estate or interest (*e*), in addition to the mortgage money, and with the same priority and with interest at the same rate, as the mortgage money.

By s. 108 (1) of the Law of Property Act 1925:

> The amount of an insurance effected by a mortgagee under this power must not exceed the amount specified in the mortgage deed, or, if no amount is therein specified, two third parts of the amount that would be required, in case of total destruction, to restore the property insured.

And the statutory power cannot be exercised (s. 108 (2)):

> (i) Where there is a declaration in the mortgage deed that no insurance is required.
> (ii) When an insurance is kept by or on behalf of the mortgagor in accordance with the mortgage deed.
> (iii) Where the mortgage deed contains no stipulation respecting insurance, and an insurance is kept up by or on behalf of the mortgagor with the consent of the mortgagee to the amount to which the mortgagee is by the Act authorised to insure.

And further:

> **108.**—(3) All money received on an insurance of mortgaged property against loss or damage by fire or otherwise effected under this Act, or any enactment replaced by this Act, or on an insurance for the maintenance of which the mortgagor is liable under the mortgage deed, shall, if the mortgagee so requires, be applied, by the mortgagor in making good the loss or damage in respect of which the money is received.

(*a*) See p. 267, *infra*.
(*b*) See p. 350, *infra*.
(*c*) For forms, see 14 Ency. Forms and Precedents (4th Edn.), 134, 135; and Precedent 1 in the Appendix, *infra*.
(*d*) Section 101 (1) (ii). This power may be varied or extended by the mortgage deed; and the section applies only if and so far as a contrary intention is not expressed in that deed: sub-ss. (3), (4). The provisions as to insurance in ss. 101, 108, replace, with slight variations, the corresponding provisions of ss. 19, 23, of the Conveyancing Act 1881.
(*e*) The premiums are a charge on the property. They cannot be recovered from the mortgagor as a debt, in the absence of a covenant to pay them.

(4) Without prejudice to any obligation to the contrary imposed by law (*f*), or by special contract, a mortgagee may require that all money received on an insurance of mortgaged property against loss or damage by fire or otherwise effected under this Act, or any enactment replaced by this Act, or on an insurance for the maintenance of which the mortgagor is liable under the mortgage deed, be applied in or towards the discharge of the mortgage money (*g*).

On a joint insurance, if the policy monies are received by one party they cannot be applied by him irrespective of the claims by the other party, and may be ordered to be paid into court (*h*). On the destruction of the security by fire, the right of the mortgagee to the policy money has priority over a garnishee order against the money (*i*).

A prudent mortgagee of property which consists wholly or partly of buildings will of course, notwithstanding the statutory power, take care that his security contains the usual covenant for insurance by the mortgagor and for production of the policy and receipts for premiums, with a provision that the insurance so effected, or any insurance made by the mortgagee under the statutory power, shall be for a specified sum or for the full value of the buildings (*k*). The inclusion of an express covenant to insure by the mortgagor enables the mortgagee, in the case of default by the mortgagor, to recover premiums paid by him (the mortgagee) from the mortgagor as a debt and a breach of the covenant by the mortgagor (*l*). Building society mortgages usually provide that the society shall and the mortgagor shall not insure (*m*).

Other covenants by the mortgagor commonly found in mortgage deeds include a covenant to pay rent and observe covenants (in the case of leasehold land), a covenant to observe the rules of the society (in the case of a building society mortgage), a covenant to observe and perform restrictive covenants to which the land is subject and to

---

(*f*) The Fires Prevention (Metropolis) Act 1774, s. 83, gives persons interested the right to have insurance moneys expended in rebuilding. The Act is of general, and not merely of local, application and applies as between mortgagor and mortgagee: *Sinnott* v. *Bowden*, [1912] 2 Ch. 414; *Portavon Cinema Co., Ltd.* v. *Price and Century Insurance Co., Ltd.*, [1939] 4 All E.R. 601, 607.

(*g*) A mortgagee is not however entitled to the benefit of a further insurance effected by the mortgagor which is independent of the security: *Halifax Building Society* v. *Keighley*, [1931] 2 K.B. 248. Accordingly an express covenant for application of proceeds should include *any* insurance. And see (1953), 103 L. Jo. 230.

Where a capital sum is received by the owner of an asset under a policy of insurance of the risk of any kind of damage or injury to or loss or depreciation of an asset, there is deemed to be a disposal for the purposes of capital gains tax. This general principle does not apply in the case of a non-wasting asset if the sum is wholly applied in restoring the asset. A lease of land becomes a wasting asset when its duration does not exceed 50 years, but, by concession, if the tenant of such a lease applies monies received by him in discharging an obligation to restore the property the monies will not be treated as such a capital sum as previously mentioned: see Finance Act 1965, s. 22 (3) (b), Sched. 6, para. 13 (1) (a), (3), (5); Sched. 8, para. 1 (1), as amended.

These provisions have no application to the receipt of insurance monies *qua* mortgagor or *qua* mortgagee.

(*h*) *Rogers* v. *Grazebrooke* (1842), 12 Sim. 557.　　(*i*) *Sinnott* v. *Bowden, supra*.

(*k*) For forms, see 14 Ency. Forms and Precedents (4th Edn.), 132–134, 416–417; and Precedent 1 in the Appendix, *infra*. For a form of notice to an insurance office by a mortgagee as to his interest in a policy existing at the time of the mortgage, see 2 Ency. Forms and Precedents (4th Edn.), 868.

(*l*) As to the charging of premiums in an account, see p. 32, *supra*.

(*m*) On tied agency provisions, see (1965), 62 L.S. Gaz. 57.

indemnify, a covenant to pay road charges, a covenant to personally occupy the premises, a covenant not to let or assign without consent, a covenant not to alter the premises, a covenant not to obtain a loan or grant creating a charge on the property without consent, a covenant to inform the mortgagee of all notices received, a covenant to observe the provisions of the Town and Country Planning Acts, etc., and, where appropriate, a covenant not to register the title under the Land Registration Act 1925, without the consent of the mortgagee (*n*).

Covenants entered into by the mortgagor are enforceable by the mortgagee and his successors against the mortgagor's successors, since the relationship of mortgagor and mortgagee is in effect that of landlord and tenant (*o*).

Other provisions.—The mortgagee's statutory powers to sell and to appoint a receiver (*p*) are frequently varied (*q*), being commonly made exercisable after a default of a shorter period than that specified in the Law of Property Act 1925, s. 103 (*r*).

A mortgage frequently restricts the mortgagor's powers to grant leases (*s*), for example, by requiring the mortgagee's consent thereto.

The right of consolidation (*t*) is generally reserved.

On a mortgage of one or more of several adjoining properties of the mortgagor it may be appropriate to include appurtenant and adverse rights of way, etc., and an agreement and declaration as to party walls.

Attornment clause (*u*).—This clause is commonly found in mortgages where, as is usually the case in a mortgage of a single private dwellinghouse, the mortgagor is already in possession and is to remain in possession. By the mortgagor attorning tenant to the mortgagee, in other words, acknowledging that he is the tenant of the mortgagee, the relationship of landlord and tenant is created (*a*). Although a

---

(*n*) See 14 Ency. Forms and Precedents (4th Edn.), pp. 147 *et seq.*; and Precedents 1 and 1A in the Appendix, *infra*.

(*o*) See (1966) 82 L.Q.R. 21 (P.V.B.); footnote (*h*), p. 35, *infra*.

(*p*) Law of Property Act 1925, s. 101, see pp. 300, 365, *infra*.

(*q*) The statutory powers apply only so far as a contrary intention is not expressed in the mortgage deed: Law of Property Act 1925, s. 101 (4).

(*r*) See p. 363, *infra*.

(*s*) Law of Property Act 1925, s. 99. See further pp. 341 *et seq.*, *infra*. For restrictions on disposing of the equity without consent see p. 295, *infra*.

(*t*) See p. 510, *infra*.

(*u*) (1966), 30 Conv. N.S. 30 (J. G. Miller); (1969) 22 C.L.P. 129 (E.C. Ryder); Sykes, *The Law of Securities* (2nd Edn.), pp. 71 *et seq.* For a form of attornment, clause, see 14 Ency. Forms and Precedents (4th Edn.), 147; and in Precedent 1A in the Appendix, *infra*.

(*a*) As to the nature of the tenancy, see *Regent Oil Co., Ltd.* v. *J. A. Gregory (Hatch End), Ltd.*, [1966] Ch. 402; [1965] 3 All E.R. 673. But it is not a tenancy within the Rent Acts or Agricultural Holdings Act 1948, see, generally, *Steyning and Littlehampton Building Society* v. *Wilson*, [1951] Ch. 1018; [1951] 2 All E.R. 452; *Alliance Building Society* v. *Pinwill*, [1958] Ch. 788; [1958] 2 All E.R. 408.

The rent reserved under the attornment clause was formerly fixed at an amount equal to the mortgage interest. If so large to be out of all proportion to the value of the estate for use and occupation the inference was that the intention was not to create a tenancy, but a device to give the mortgagee an additional security in case of the mortgagor's bankruptcy. This was a fraud on the bankruptcy law and the mortgagee was not allowed to distrain. Now the rent is nominal: *Woolwich Equitable Building Society* v. *Preston*, [1938] Ch. 129. There is no point in making it other than nominal because any rent received is prima facie applicable to the discharge of principal and interest due: *Re Betts, Ex parte Harrison* (1881), 18 Ch. D. 127, at p. 136 (C.A.).

legal charge does not create a term of years in the mortgagee an attornment clause in a legal charge makes the chargor tenant to the mortgagee (*b*). The tenancy may be a tenancy at will, from year to year, or for the duration of the mortgage according to the terms of the mortgage deed (*b*). Formerly the attornment gave the mortgagee a right to distrain for the rent reserved. Attornment clauses are within the Bills of Sale Act 1878 (*c*), and the mortgagee cannot now distrain, unless the clause has been registered as a bill of sale (*d*). The clause also formerly enabled the mortgagee to obtain a summary judgment for possession *qua* landlord (*e*), a procedure which was not open to a mortgagee (*f*). Now summary judgment is available to a mortgagee independently of attornment (*g*).

In recent years it had been thought that there was no real advantage in including an attornment clause. But it now appears that it may have some use. The inclusion of an attornment clause in a mortgage deed enables restrictive covenants in the deed on the part of the mortgagor to be enforced against the mortgagor's successors in title (*h*).

The tenancy created by an attornment clause is commonly made determinable by re-entry by the mortgagee without notice after default by the mortgagor. The taking of proceedings for possession by the mortgagee is equivalent to re-entry and no notice terminating the tenancy is necessary before proceedings are begun (*i*). But if the attornment clause provides for notice of a particular length proceedings cannot be commenced until such a notice has been given and has expired (*k*). In the case of a mortgage of leasehold property the tenancy created by an attornment clause passes on the assignment of the lease subject to the mortgage (*l*).

An attornment by the mortgagor to a second mortgagee is valid even though he has attorned tenant to the first mortgagee (*m*).

If the clause relates to future acquired property it should be limited to property coming into possession within twenty-one years. A term limited to take effect more than twenty-one years from the date of the instrument purporting to create it and any contract to create such a term is void: Law of Property Act 1925, s. 149 (3).

(*b*) See *Regent Oil Co., Ltd.* v. *J. A. Gregory (Hatch End), Ltd.*, [1966] Ch. at pp. 430, 438; [1965] 3 All E.R. at pp. 678, 683.

(*c*) Section 6. See further p. 81, *supra*. The exemption in s. 189 (1) of the Law of Property Act 1925, is not applicable.

(*d*) *Re Willis, Ex parte Kennedy* (1888), 21 Q.B.D. 384. Although void as a security, the clause still created the relationship of landlord and tenant: *Mumford* v. *Collier* (1890), 25 Q.B.D. 279.

(*e*) Under the Small Tenements Recovery Act 1838; repealed as from 1 October 1972 (S.I. 1972 No. 1161).

(*f*) *Mumford* v. *Collier, supra*; *Kemp* v. *Lester*, [1896] 2 Q.B. 162.

(*g*) R.S.C. Ord. 14, r. 1 (2), Ord. 88; County Courts Act 1959, s. 48.

(*h*) *Regent Oil Co., Ltd.* v. *J. A. Gregory (Hatch End), Ltd., supra*; but see (1965), 81 L.Q.R. 341 (P.V.B.) and (1966), 82 L.Q.R. 21 (P.V.B.).

(*i*) *Woolwich Equitable Building Society* v. *Preston*, [1938] Ch. 129, 131, 132.

(*k*) *Hinckley and Country Building Society* v. *Henny*, [1953] 1 All E.R. 515. The Rent Act 1957, s. 16, requiring four weeks notice to quit, will not apply to an attornment clause, unless, perhaps, the rent is a full rack rent: *Alliance Building Society* v. *Pinwill, supra*.

(*l*) *Regent Oil Co., Ltd.* v. *J. A. Gregory (Hatch End), Ltd., supra*; but see 81 L.Q.R. 341.

(*m*) *Re Kitchin, Ex parte Punnett* (1880), 16 Ch. D. 226 (C.A.).

III—THE EXTENT OF THE SECURITY

Fixtures (*n*).—A legal mortgage of land, whether freehold or leasehold (*o*), comprises whatever is fixed to the land at the time of the mortgage and what is afterwards annexed to the land by the mortgagor (*p*). This applies also to equitable mortgages.

Accretions to the security.—Whatever the mortgagor adds to the property to improve its value is an accretion to the property for the benefit of the mortgagee as also are additions made by a second or subsequent mortgagee (*q*). Where a mortgagor acquires an interest in place of the interest mortgaged the mortgagee will be entitled to it for the purposes of the security.

New leases.—Thus, in the case of a mortgage or charge upon leaseholds, if a new lease or other interest of a like nature is obtained by the mortgagor, either on a forfeiture (by any contrivance or otherwise) of the original lease, or by other means, the owner of the mortgage or charge will have the benefit of the new lease or interest for the purpose of the security (*s*).

On the other hand, if the mortgagee of a term obtains a renewal, the mortgagor will generally have the benefit of the new term, upon redemption; because the term comes from the same root, and is subject to the same equity (*t*).

Enlargement of leases.—Certain long leases may be enlarged into a fee simple (*u*). The fee simple so acquired is subject to all the same covenants, provisions and obligations as the term would have been subject to if it had not been so enlarged (*a*). A mortgage of the term will therefore upon enlargement of the term affect the fee simple so created.

(*n*) For the meaning of fixtures, see p. 74, *infra*.

(*o*) In the case of leasehold land there are three interested parties—the landlord, the mortgagor-tenant and the mortgagee. But the right of the mortgagee to fixtures, both existing and added, and whether removable or not as between landlord and tenant, applies: see footnote (*b*) p. 74, *infra*.

(*p*) See footnote (*c*) p. 74, *infra*.

(*q*) *Maxwell* v. *Ashe* (1752), 1 Bro. C.C. 444, n.; *Landowners West of England and South Wales Land Drainage and Inclosure Co.* v. *Ashford* (1880), 16 Ch. D. 411, 433. And similarly in the case of a mortgage of chattels: *Webster* v. *Power* (1868), L.R. 2 P.C. 69 (sheep). And see *Tucker* v. *Farm and General Investment Trust, Ltd.*, [1966] 2 Q.B. 421 (C.A.); [1966] 2 All E.R. 508 (a hire-purchase case).

(*s*) *Moody* v. *Matthews* (1802), 7 Ves. 174; *Hughes* v. *Howard* (1858), 25 Beav. 575; *Sims* v. *Helling* (1851), 21 L.J. Ch. 76; *Leigh* v. *Burnett* (1885), 29 Ch. D. 231; and see *Re Hill Pottery Co.* (1886), 15 W.R. 97 (claim to additions by execution creditor subject to allowance for labour and costs).

(*t*) *Rakestraw* v. *Brewer* (1729), 2 P. Wms. 511; *Leigh* v. *Burnett, supra*; *Re Biss*, *Biss* v. *Biss*, [1903] 2 Ch. 40 (C.A.), at p. 62.

The rule applies with greater force where the new lease has been obtained by any improper practice: see *Fitzgerald* v. *Rainsford* (1804), 1 Ba. & Be. 37, n. But cf. *Nesbitt* v. *Tredennick* (1808), 1 Ba. & Be. 29.

Where a mortgagee has exercised an option contained in a lease to purchase the freehold, the mortgagor will have the benefit thereof upon redemption: *Nelson* v. *Hannam*, [1943] Ch. 59 (C.A.); [1942] 2 All E.R. 680.

Where a mortgagee obtains a new lease under the Law of Property Act 1925, s. 146 (4) (see p. 24, *supra*), the new lease is a substituted security: *Chelsea Estates Investment Trust Co., Ltd.* v. *Marche*, [1955] Ch. 328; [1955] 1 All E.R. 195.

(*u*) Law of Property Act 1925, s. 153. The provision extends to mortgage terms, where the right of redemption is barred: subs. (3). See, e.g., p. 54, *infra*.

(*a*) *Ibid.*, s. 153 (8).

Leasehold enfranchisement.—The Leasehold Reform Act 1967, entitles tenants of houses held on long leases (*b*) at low rents to acquire the freehold or an extended lease (*c*). Where a tenant, whose interest is in mortgage, acquires the freehold (*d*) the existence of the mortgage will prevent the merger of the enfranchising tenant's leasehold and freehold estates (*e*) and the mortgagee's security will remain the lease. But if the enfranchising tenant and mortgagee agree (and this will often be the case particularly where the mortgagee is making a further advance for the purchase price of the freehold) the freehold estate may be substituted for the leasehold estate as the security and the lease merged in the freehold.

Where a tenant, whose interest is in mortgage, obtains an extended lease (*f*) and the new tenancy takes effect subject to the subsisting charge on the existing tenancy, then if at the time of the execution of the extended lease the mortgagee is entitled to possession of the title deeds relating to the existing tenancy, he is similarly entitled to possession of the title deeds relating to the new tenancy, and the tenant must within one month of the execution of the extended lease deliver it to him, and the instrument creating or evidencing the charge shall apply in the event of the tenant failing to deliver the extended lease as if the obligation to do so were included in the terms of the charge as set out in that instrument (*g*).

Goodwill.—All incidental rights, such as the goodwill of a business carried on upon and inseparably connected with the mortgaged property, and compensation for such goodwill when the property is taken compulsorily, will follow the security (*h*), unless the goodwill is owing to the personal skill of the mortgagor (*i*), or is excluded by the terms of the security (*k*).

(*b*) A mortgage term is excluded (see ss. 1 (2) and 37 (i) (f), unless the term no longer subsists: *Re Fairview Church Street, Bromyard*, [1974] 1 All E.R. 1233; *Re Pettifer's Application* (1974), 231 Estates Gazette 371.

(*c*) For another example of enfranchisement, see the Places of Worship (Enfranchisement) Act 1920, amended by the Act of 1967. Here also a mortgage on the term will affect the fee simple created by enfranchisement: s. 3.

(*d*) See Leasehold Reform Act 1967, ss. 8–13. The tenant acquires the freehold subject to the tenancy and to tenant's incumbrances: s. 8.

(*e*) There can be no merger unless the leasehold and freehold estates are vested in the same person in the same right with no vested estate intervening. See further as to merger, Ch. 32, *infra*. For a protracted correspondence about whether or not there will be a merger where the tenant-mortgagor acquires the freehold reversion, see (1972) 60 L.S. Gaz. 469, 562, 1221 and correspondence in subsequent issues including (1973) 61 L.S. Gaz. 1312.

(*f*) See Leasehold Reform Act 1967, ss. 14–16.

(*g*) Leasehold Reform Act 1967, s. 14 (6). The new lease will generally be subject to the subsisting charge (see the paragraph "New leases", *supra*). It will be so subject in the absence of a provision in the mortgage to the contrary and it is inconceivable to imagine a mortgage containing an exclusion of this rule. The mortgagee will be entitled to the new lease on request under general principles (see "Custody of Deeds", pp. 41 *et seq.*, *infra*) and the above provision goes further by requiring the mortgagor to deliver the new lease.

(*h*) *Chissum* v. *Dewes* (1828), 5 Russ. 29; *King* v. *Midland Rail. Co.* (1868), 17 W.R. 113; *Pile* v. *Pile, Ex parte Lambton* (1876), 3 Ch. D. 36 (C.A.); *Re Kitchin, Ex parte Punnett* (1880), 16 Ch. D. 226 (C.A.). The same rule is not to be applied to the equity of redemption: see *Re Bennett, Clarke* v. *White*, [1899] 1 Ch. 316.

(*i*) *Cooper* v. *Metropolitan Board of Works* (1883), 25 Ch. D. 472 (C.A.).

(*k*) *Whitley* v. *Challis*, [1892] 1 Ch. 64 (C.A.); *Palmer* v. *Barclays Bank, Ltd.* (1971), 23 P. & C.R. 30.

Compensation money.—There are special statutory provisions for the payment of compensation on the compulsory acquisition of mortgaged land (*l*).

Compensation for the licence on the compulsory acquisition of a mortgaged public house belongs to the mortgagee as part of the mortgage security (*m*).

Other rights.—The benefit of some rights relating to the security, *e.g.*, appurtenant easements, will pass automatically with the mortgage of the security. Other rights will have to be expressly assigned by a separate clause or provision in the deed (*n*).

IV—MORTGAGES OF PARTICULAR KINDS OF LAND

Unregistered and registered land.—Mortgages of unregistered land are dealt with in this chapter. The next chapter deals with mortgages of registered land.

Incorporeal hereditaments.—Land includes easements, profits, rentcharges and other incorporeal hereditaments (*o*). Those which can exist at law (*p*) can be the subject of a legal mortgage. Generally, as in the case of easements, a mortgage of the land together with which the right is enjoyed, will include a mortgage of the right. Incorporeal hereditaments, such as manors, commons, rentcharges (*q*), and other property of a like nature existing in gross and apart from the ownership of corporeal property may also be the subject of a mortgage, unless prohibited by law (*r*).

Type of land.—The type of land which forms the security, by which, in this context, is meant whether the land be freehold or leasehold and its use, whether for residential, agricultural or commercial purposes, is of particular relevance to the mortgagee when contemplating a mortgage security and is primarily a matter of valuation (*s*). In this respect leaseholds are a less satisfactory security than freeholds in that the lease may be determined or forfeited (*t*) or surrendered (*u*), and if the term, or the residue of the term, is short the lease is a wasting

---

(*l*) As to which, see p. 535, *infra*. As to claims by a mortgagee under a mortgage created before 1 July 1948, or after 31 December 1954, for compensation, in certain cases, where planning permission is refused or restricted, see Town and Country Planning Act 1971, ss. 162, 163, 178; and for compensation for blight, ss. 193, 201.

(*m*) *Law Guarantee and Trust Society, Ltd.* v. *Mitcham and Cheam Brewery Co., Ltd.*, [1906] 2 Ch. 98.

(*n*) E.g., the benefit of certain covenants, such as road-making covenants (see Wurtzburg and Mills, *Building Society Law* (14th Edn.), pp. 204, 571) and the benefit of a N.H.B.C. agreement (see Luff and Marten, *Guarantees for New Homes*, pp. 134–137; *Marchant* v. *Caswell Redgrave, Ltd.* (1976), 240 Estates Gazette, 127.

(*o*) Law of Property Act 1925, ss. 201 (1), 205 (1) (ix).

(*p*) *Ibid.*, s. 1.

(*q*) For forms of mortgages of rentcharges, see 14 Ency. Forms and Precedents (4th Edn.), pp. 526 *et seq.*

(*r*) As in the case of advowsons, see p. 223, *infra*.

(*s*) As to the importance of planning searches, see Emmet on *Title* (16th Edn.), pp. 984, 985. For restrictions on resale of houses sold by local authorities, see Housing Act 1957, s. 104 and re price condition and right of pre-emption, see p. 306, *infra*.

(*t*) As to relief from forfeiture, see pp. 23–25, *supra*.

(*u*) See p. 25, *supra*.

asset. Some freehold securities, *e.g.*, mines, are also wasting securities, and both freehold and leasehold land may be subject, or become subject, to statutory provisions affecting the mortgagee's security. For example, reference will be made in Ch. 8 to the charge for compensation of the tenant of agricultural land which will take priority to the mortgage (*a*). And where the property is let and the lease is binding on the mortgagee there may be, *e.g.*, restrictions on his right to increase the mortgage rate of interest under the Rent Acts (*b*) or the tenant may be able to acquire the freehold discharged from any mortgage under the Leasehold Reform Act 1967 (*c*).

The use of the land may effect the extent and form of the mortgage and it is intended to deal here very shortly with the mortgage problems which arise out of schemes for dealing with the common parts of flat and estate developments (*d*). Where the stairs, passages, roads, gardens, etc., of a flat or estate development are not transferred with the individual flats or houses there are a number of ways in which these common parts may be dealt with to provide for their maintenance and for contributions to the cost thereof from the owners of parts of the development. The management company scheme, the trust scheme and the deed of covenant scheme will be considered (*e*).

Under the management company scheme the purchaser of a flat, maisonette or house may also be required to take a share in a company which will hold and manage the common parts of the development (*f*). The articles of the company will generally provide that no person may hold such a share unless he is also the owner of a flat or house comprised in the development, and that such a share may only be transferred on a disposition of the flat or house to the purchaser thereof. The agreement for the original sale of the flat or house or the original conveyance or the lease may contain provisions requiring the purchaser on any disposition of the property to transfer his share in the management company to a purchaser of the property. Such a scheme also generally involves a lease by the management company to the flat or house owner of amenity rights over the common parts held by it. Accordingly where such a flat or house is the subject of a mortgage it is imperative that the lease of the amenity rights (if there is a lease) should form part of the security, so that if the mortgagee has to exercise his power of sale of the property he will be able to transfer the rights appurtenant to the property. The share in the management

---

(*a*) See p. 127, *infra*.
(*b*) See p. 276, *infra*.
(*c*) See p. 602, *infra*.
(*d*) For the conveyancing difficulties in relation to freehold flats and maisonettes, and in particular the enforcing of positive covenants, reference should be made to the conveyancing precedent books and George, *The Sale of Flats* (3rd Edn.).; and see *Wurtzburg and Mills, ubi supra*, pp. 146 *et seq.*
(*e*) The form of such schemes may differ from one development to another. All that it is intended to do here is to draw attention to the fact that the security ought perhaps to include more than the individual flat or house.
(*f*) For management company schemes, see George, *The Sale of Flats, ubi supra*, pp. 138 *et seq.*; and precedents (1967), 31 Conv. (N.S., pp. 716 *et seq.*; and *Precedents for the Conveyancer*, forms 5–10.

company should also be included in the security (*g*). Alternatively, the mortgagor should give the mortgagee power of attorney to transfer the share on a sale by the mortgagee. Whilst the enjoyment of the appurtenant easements is not generally conditional upon the holding of a share, without a share a purchaser would have no rights in the management company. However, the articles of the company may provide for a director or other person to be deemed to be the duly appointed attorney of a shareholder who refuses or neglects to transfer his share with power to execute a transfer, so that the failure to include the share in the security may be remedied in this way.

Under the trust scheme the common parts are transferred by the developer to trustees, who will generally be two, three or four of the purchasers of parts of the development, to hold the same upon trusts declared by a trust deed. Those trusts include trusts to maintain the common parts and discharge all liabilities in respect thereof (provision being made for contributions from the owners of the respective parts of the development) and subject thereto to hold the property for the owners of the separate parts of the development (*h*). Whilst the conveyance or lease of each part of the development should include rights over the common parts, a mortgage of such a property should include in the security the benefit of the owner's rights under the trust deed (*i*), thus enabling any purchaser of the property from the mortgagee to enforce the rights thereunder in respect of the maintenance of the common parts.

In the case of a small development it may be convenient for the developer to retain the common parts and the responsibility for the maintenance thereof and provide for a contribution towards the expenses of maintenance from each owner of the respective parts of the development. The developer's obligation to maintain the common parts and the owner's obligation to contribute may be effectively secured by a deed of mutual covenants made between the developer and the owners and the owners between themselves and such a deed may contain a provision that on a disposition by an owner he will require the purchaser or transferee to execute the deed (*k*). On a mortgage of an individual property the security should include the benefit (and the liability) of the covenants in the deed so that should the mortgagee come to sell he will be able to assign the benefit of such covenants. A scheme by way of deed of covenants may also be employed even where the developer does not retain any land.

Finally it may be mentioned that in some modern developments the garages for the respective flats or houses are disposed of separately from the house or flat. Accordingly on taking a mortgage of the house or flat a mortgage of the garage should not be overlooked.

(g) For mortgages of shares, see pp. 109 *et seq.*, *infra*.

(h) For a form of trust scheme, see (1967), 31 Conv. (N.S.), pp. 679 *et seq.*

(i) For mortgages of rights under trusts, see p. 115, *infra*.

(k) For precedents of a deed of mutual covenants, see (1963), 27 Conv. (N.S.), pp. 681 *et seq.*; (1964), 28 Conv. (N.S.), pp. 672 *et seq.* (for where the developer does not retain any land).

V—CUSTODY OF DEEDS

Mortgagee's right to custody of deeds.—A first mortgagee of freehold property has the same right to possession of documents as if his security included the fee simple (*l*). A first mortgagee of leasehold property has the same right to possession of documents as if his security had been effected by assignment (*m*). Failure to take custody of deeds may lead to postponement to other incumbrancers (*n*). As soon as the statutory power of sale has become exercisable the mortgagee can demand to recover from any person, other than a person entitled in priority to himself, all the documents of title which a purchaser under the power of sale would be entitled to recover from him (*o*).

A mortgagee of the beneficial interest of a tenant for life of settled land is not entitled to possession of the documents of title relating to the settled land, nor is the tenant for life required to deliver any such documents to such a mortgagee unless he is also the mortgagee of the whole of the settled land to which such documents relate (*p*). The mortgagee of the life interest has, however, the same rights with respect to such documents as if the tenant for life had given to him a statutory acknowledgment of his right to production and delivery of copies thereof (*p*).

An equitable mortgagee, not having the legal estate, has no right to the deeds, unless the mortgage provides that he shall have such a right. But an equitable mortgagee by deposit of deeds is entitled to retain the deeds until payment or tender of the amount due on his security (*q*), assuming the mortgage is valid.

Production of deeds by mortgagee.—The Law of Property Act 1925, provides:

> **96.**—(1) (*r*) A mortgagor, as long as his right to redeem subsists, shall be entitled from time to time, at reasonable times, on his request, and at his own cost, and on payment of the mortgagee's costs and expenses in this behalf to inspect and make copies or abstracts of or extracts from the documents of title relating to the mortgaged property in the custody or power of the mortgagee (*s*).

The section takes effect notwithstanding any stipulation to the contrary.

(*l*) Law of Property Act 1925, s. 85 (1), proviso. Formerly the mortgagee in fee was entitled to hold the deeds, but the mortgagee by demise had no such right. He therefore had to obtain the deeds at the time of the mortgage or take a covenant for delivery.

(*m*) *Ibid.*, s. 86 (1), proviso.

(*n*) See p. 451, *infra.*

(*o*) Law of Property Act 1925, s. 106 (4).

(*p*) Settled Land Act 1925, s. 111, proviso.

(*q*) See *Re Molton Finance, Ltd.*, [1968] Ch. 325 (C.A.), at p. 333; [1967] 3 All E.R. 843, at p. 845. This right to retain the deeds is not a separate legal or common law lien. Cf. (1970) 33 M.L.R. 131 (J.H.G. Sunnucks). And see p. 48, *infra.*

(*r*) Replacing Conveyancing Act 1881, s. 16. The right to inspect the mortgage deed was established in *Patch* v. *Ward* (1865), L.R. 1 Eq. 436, as an exception to the general rule before the Act of 1881 that the mortgagee could refuse production of the deeds.

(*s*) As to which deeds are in the power of the mortgagee, see *Fenwick* v. *Reed* (1816), 1 Mer. 114 (in possession of solicitor); *Rogers* v. *Rogers* (1842), 6 Jur. 497 (sub-mortgage); *Palmer* v. *Wright* (1846), 10 Beav. 234.

In the case of a partial redemption, where the mortgagee retains the deeds relating to the remainder of his security, he must covenant to produce these deeds or give an acknowledgment for production to the mortgagor (t).

On an action for sale by a subsequent mortgagee against the mortgagor, the prior mortgagee will not be ordered to lodge the deeds in court, if willing to produce them and let copies be taken under this provision (u).

The mortgagee's liability for production is owed to the mortgagor and any person from time to time deriving title under the original mortgagor or entitled to redeem a mortgage, according to this estate, interest or right in the mortgaged property (a). The mortgagee of a beneficial interest of a life tenant of settled land, if he takes the deeds, is liable to produce them for the inspection of remaindermen with a vested, but not with a contingent, interest (b).

Production to mortgagee by tenant for life.—Under the former law the mortgagee of a remainderman who had a vested (but not one who had only a contingent (c)) interest, and whose title was clear and free from reasonable cause of litigation, might sue the tenant for life for production and inspection of the title deeds. If it was suggested that the production was required for an improper purpose, the burden of proving the assertion lay on the person who resisted the production (d). The tenant for life now holds the deeds as estate owner and the remainderman has only an equitable interest. But since he may require the deeds in order to prove his title, it seems that this rule still holds.

VI—DELIVERY OF DEED AS ESCROW

Generally (e).—A deed may be delivered on the condition that it is not to take effect until the happening of some specified event. When the event happens, the deed takes effect as from the date of the original delivery (f).

Mortgage as escrow.—It will rarely happen that a mortgage will be delivered as an escrow. One possible instance, however, is when a builder or developer mortgages a site, the mortgage being made on the basis that the site would be developed. In practice, the terms of the

---

(t) Law of Property Act 1925, s. 64.
(u) *Amstrong* v. *Dickson*, [1911] 1 I.R. 435.
(a) Law of Property Act 1925, s. 205 (1) (xvi).
(b) *Noel* v. *Ward* (1816), 1 Madd. 322; *Pennell* v. *Earl of Dysart* (1859), 27 Beav. 542. Before 1926 the remainderman had a legal estate. Now he has an equitable interest. But the rule probably still applies, although the life tenant has the primary right.
(c) *Noel* v. *Ward, supra.*
(d) *Davis* v. *Earl of Dysart* (1855), 20 Beav. 405.
(e) See generally, *Williams on Title* (4th Edn.), pp. 659–660; *Kingston* v. *Ambrian Investment Co., Ltd.*, [1975] 1 All E.R. 120 (C.A.); *Glessing* v. *Green*, [1975] 2 All E.R. 696 (C.A.). *London Freehold and Leasehold Property Co.* v. *Baron Suffield*, [1897] 2 Ch. 608 (C.A.).
(f) But only for such purposes as are necessary to give efficacy to the transaction: *Security Trust Co.* v. *The Royal Bank of Canada*, [1976] A.C. 503; [1976] 1 All E.R. 381 (P.C.).

mortgage should cover the possibility of development not taking place by allowing the lender to enter and to complete the works himself (*g*). The same applies where the mortgage advance was offered on the terms that the borrower executes certain repairs to the property (*h*). But in the absence of any covenant to execute the works or right of entry in the mortgage, the lender may be able to claim that the mortgage deed was delivered as an escrow, though it will rarely be advantageous to claim the ineffectiveness of the mortgage and repayment of the advance.

VII—VARIATION OF THE MORTGAGE

Generally.—The provisions of a mortgage are frequently varied, *e.g.*, the rate of interest or the length of the mortgage term may be increased when there is a general increase in interest rates (*i*). But a variation can only be effected by agreement between the parties, either initially, so that the mortgage deed contains a provision for variation, or subsequently by mutual agreement between the parties. Without such agreement the mortgage cannot be varied unilaterally, though if there is nothing to restrict the lender from calling the loan in, he will be in a strong bargaining position to enforce a variation. Even where there is a provision for variation, the parties may prefer to completely replace the original mortgage with a new one. Care must be taken not to lose any priority. However, it seems that when, as sometimes happens, an equitable mortgage is replaced by a legal mortgage, there will be no merger if that result is necessary to preserve priority (*k*).

Like any other contract, a mortgage may, as regards its contractual elements, be varied, provided the variation complies with the rules as to variation of contracts (*l*). As regards the proprietary aspects of the mortgage, *e.g.*, the property mortgaged, any variation will require the appropriate disposition, *i.e.*, release or mortgage, or an agreement therefor satisfying the necessary formalities (*m*).

Rescission or variation.—It is a question of the intention of the parties whether a variation rescinds the original contract and produces a new and different contract or merely amends the original contract (*n*). If the former, the original contract will have gone and the new contract must satisfy any necessary requirement of form, *e.g.*, those contained in

---

(*g*) See p. 697, *infra*.

(*h*) This regularly occurs on advances by building societies.

(*i*) On variation of interest, see p. 29, *supra*. Building societies will usually give the borrower the option of extending the mortgage term.

(*k*) *Bank of New Zealand* v. *Farrier-Waimak, Ltd.*, [1964] N.Z.L.R. 9, 19 (citing *Whiteley* v. *Delaney*, [1914] A.C. 132; see p. 596, *infra*); see also *Farrier-Waimak, Ltd.* v. *Bank of New Zealand*, [1965]; A.C. 376; [1964] 3 All E.R. 657 (P.C.); *E.S. Schwab & Co., Ltd.* v. *McCarthy* (1976), 31 P. & C.R. 196.

(*l*) See 9 Halsbury's Laws (4th Edn.), paras. 566 *et seq.*; Cheshire and Fifoot, *Law of Contract* (9th Edn.), pp. 534–540.

(*m*) *I.e.*, s. 40 of the Law of Property Act 1925 or part performance.

(*n*) See *Morris* v. *Baron & Co.*, [1918] A.C.1. (H.L.); *New Hart Builders, Ltd.* v. *Brindley*, [1975] Ch. 342; [1975] 1 All E.R. 1007.

the Moneylenders Acts (o), to be effective. If the latter, and any formalities required are not met, the original mortgage stands(p).

Effecting the variation.—In some cases, the discharge of the original mortgage and its replacement by a new mortgage will be the only course. This will usually be so for moneylenders' mortgages where the formalities, e.g., the signing of the necessary memorandum before the loan, allow of no other method of variation. Where the subject matter of the mortgage is changed, by adding additional property or substituting a different property or taking some property out of the mortgage, the appropriate charge or release will be necessary (q). Between development companies and banks or other institutions the original mortgage is frequently varied as facilities are increased and in this context deeds of consolidation are frequently encountered (r).

Where the terms of a registered charge are varied, the variation must be effected by the appropriate deed (s).

Effect on subsequent incumbrances.—Where the mortgage secures a fixed sum with interest at a fixed rate, a subsequent incumbrancer cannot be affected by an increase of the principal (t) or of the rate of interest. In such a case, where the equity is adequate, the subsequent incumbrancer will usually be willing to allow the increase and there will be a deed of postponement (u). Where the prior mortgage provided for variation (e.g., being security for such sum as shall be owing from time to time, or providing for an increase in the rate of interest) a subsequent incumbrancer takes subject to those terms and the first mortgagee has priority consistently with such terms (a).

VIII—EQUITABLE MORTGAGES

Mortgage by deposit of deeds.—The delivery to the creditor or his agent of deeds or other documents of title with intent to create a security thereon constitutes an equitable mortgage (b). The delivery need not be of the debtor's own deeds, but some third party's (c). The deposit may be with or without a memorandum or other instrument of charge. In practice the deposit is generally accompanied by a memo-

---

(o) *United Dominions Corporation (Jamaica), Ltd.* v. *Shoucair*, [1969] A.C. 340 (P.C.); [1968] 2 All E.R. 904.

(p) *Morris* v, *Baron, supra.*

(q) For forms, see 14 Ency. Forms and Precedents (4th Edn.), pp. 871 *et seq.*

(r) For deeds of consolidation, see p. 511, *infra.*

(s) See p. 64, *infra.*

(t) *Scottish and Newcastle Breweries, Ltd.* v. *Liquidator of Rathbourne Hotel Co., Ltd.* 1970 S.L.T. 313. For further advances, see p. 460, *infra.*

(u) See p. 460, *infra.*

(a) The terms of an equitable mortgage usually provide for the execution of a legal mortgage by the mortgagor when called upon for such by the mortgagee (see p. 50, *infra*). The subsequent legal mortgage may cause the prior equitable mortgage to disappear, by the latter merging in the former (see p. 595, *infra.*). But assuming that the prior equitable mortgage was duly registered or protected on the register, where appropriate, it is not thought that there would be any loss of priority (see p. 43, *supra*).

(b) *Russel* v. *Russel* (1783), 1 Bro. C.C. 269; *Bank of New South Wales* v. *O'Connor* (1889), 14 App. Cas. 273 (P.C.), 282. And see also as to equitable mortgages, pp. 11 *et seq., supra.*

(c) *Re Wallis & Simmonds (Builders), Ltd.*, [1975] Q.B. 94; [1974] 1 All E.R. 561.

randum under seal, thus giving the mortgagee the powers granted by s. 101 of the Law of Property Act 1925 (*d*).

Where there is a memorandum of charge, this will usually contain an agreement to execute a legal mortgage (*e*), and it may contain a power of attorney to execute such a mortgage (*f*). Where there is no memorandum in writing the charge created by the deposit is prima facie unenforceable (*g*), but its validity has long been recognised on the ground that the deposit of deeds implies an agreement to make a mortgage and also operates a part performance (*h*). Consequently actual deposit of the deeds is essential (*i*), and in the absence of actual deposit the security must rest on a document in writing signed by the mortgagor or his authorised agent (*k*).

The charge created by the deposit is contractual, for, although it arises by presumption, it does not arise by operation of law (*l*).

The mortgage may be valid if only some or one of the material documents of title to the property have been deposited (*m*), although a complete title is not thereby shown to the debtor's interest in the property (*n*). It follows that if part of the material documents are deposited with one person, and part with another, each may have a good security (*o*), unless there is evidence of a contrary intention (*p*). An equitable mortgage may be created by deposit of a receipt for purchase money, containing the terms of the agreement for sale, if there are no title deeds or conveyance in the depositor's possession (*q*), or even of a map of the property (*r*), but not by the deposit of an unattested copy of a deed (*s*). An equitable sub-mortgage of an equit-

---

(*d*) *I.e.*, the power to sell and appoint a receiver: see Pt. V, *infra*. Where there is an accompanying document it is a question of construction whether the security is constituted by the deposit or the document: *Hari Sankar Paul* v. *Kedar Nath Saha*, [1939] 2 All E.R. 737 (P.C.). And see *Re White Rose Cottage*, [1965] Ch. 940 (C.A.); [1965] 1 All E.R. 11.

(*e*) An equitable mortgagee by deposit is entitled to call for a legal mortgage, even in the absence of express agreement, unless the right is excluded: *Birch* v. *Ellames and Gorst* (1794), 2 Anst. 427; *Parker* v. *Housefield* (1834), 2 My. & K. 419, 421; and see p. 49, *infra*.

(*f*) See p. 49, *infra* as to form of memorandum.

(*g*) *I.e.*, for want of compliance with s. 40 of the Law of Property Act 1925.

(*h*) *Russel* v. *Russel, supra*; *Burgess* v. *Moxon* (1856), 2 Jur. N.S. 1059; *Re Wallis & Simmonds (Builders), Ltd., supra*.

(*i*) *Re Beavan, Ex parte Coombe* (1819), 4 Madd. 249; *Re Ridge, Ex parte Hallifax* (1842), 2 Mont. D. & De G. 544; *Bank of New South Wales* v. *O'Connor, supra*. Lord ELDON, in *Ex parte Haigh* (1805), 11 Ves. 403, protested against the evasion of the Statute of Frauds but the doctrine came to be well established.

(*k*) *Re Leathes, Ex parte Leathes* (1833), 3 Deac. & C. 112. If there is such a document, the mortgage will be good, even though the documents to be deposited pursuant to it are not executed at its date: *Re Carter and Justins, Ex parte Sheffield Union Banking Co.* (1865), 13 L.T. 477.

(*l*) *Re Wallis & Simmonds (Builders), Ltd., supra*. See (1970) 33 M.L.R. 131 (J.H.G. Sunnucks).

(*m*) *Re Daintry, Ex parte Arkwright* (1864), 3 Mont. D. & De G. 129; *Lacon* v. *Allen* (1856), 3 Drew. 579.

(*n*) *Ex parte Wetherell* (1804), 11 Ves. 398; *Roberts* v. *Croft* (1857), 24 Beav. 223; affd. 2 De G. & J. 1.

(*o*) *Roberts* v. *Croft, supra*.

(*p*) *Re Price, Ex parte Pearse and Prothero* (1820), Buck. 525.

(*q*) *Goodwin* v. *Waghorn* (1835), 4 L.J. Ch. 172.

(*r*) *Simmons* v. *Montague*, [1909] 1 I.R. 87.

(*s*) *Re Borrow, Ex parte Broadbent* (1834), 1 Mont. & A. 635.

able security may be created without a deposit of the memorandum given with the original security (*t*).

Proof of intent to create equitable mortgage.—The intent to create an equitable mortgage by deposit of documents may be established by writing alone, or coupled with parol evidence (*u*), by parol evidence alone (*a*), or by inference arising from the deposit, where the possession of the documents by the holder cannot be otherwise explained (*b*). But an inference that the deposit was made by way of equitable mortgage will not be admitted in contradiction of a written statement (*c*), the terms of which, when it exists will govern the contract, where it is consistent with the security (*d*); nor by reason of the possession by a solicitor of his client's deeds, or against a purchaser who does not enquire into the nature of the possession (*e*); nor where there is no evidence as to the origin of the possession from which a contract may be inferred (*f*). An intention to create an equitable mortgage may be inferred from a delivery of the documents to be held, or a direction to hold them, until the settlement of an account or the execution of a mortgage (*g*), or for the purpose of preparing a legal mortgage for an existing debt (*h*).

Documents remaining in debtor's custody.—Where a document remains in the possession of a debtor, a memorandum annexed to it, purporting to appropriate the proceeds to satisfy the debt, will not generally of itself create a charge (*i*). But a charge may be created where the document is in the actual keeping of the debtor, if it is in the legal custody of the creditor, *e.g.*, where the debtor holds it as his solicitor (*k*), even though the creditor was not aware of the creation of the security (*l*). A verbal direction to a third party who has possession of the deeds to hold for the creditor is not a part performance and will not create an equitable mortgage; but it will be otherwise if there is a written memorandum (*m*).

(*t*) *Re Hildyard, Ex parte Smith* (1842), 2 Mont. D. & De G. 587.

(*u*) *Casberd* v. *A.-G.* (1819), 6 Pr. 411; *Ede* v. *Knowles* (1843), 2 Y. & Coll. C.C. 172; *Burgess* v. *Moxon, supra*; *Re Boulter, Ex parte National Provincial Bank of England* (1876), 4 Ch. D. 241.

(*a*) *Russel* v. *Russel, supra*; *Ex parte Kensington* (1813), 2 Ves. & B. 79; *Ex parte Haigh* (1805), 11 Ves. 403; *Ex parte Mountford* (1808), 14 Ves. 606.

(*b*) *Edge* v. *Worthington* (1786), 1 Cox Eq. Cas. 211; *Ex parte Langston* (1810), 17 Ves. 227; *Re Wallis and Simmonds (Builders), Ltd., supra*.

(*c*) *Ex parte Coombe* (1810), 17 Ves. 369.

(*d*) *Shaw* v. *Foster* (1872), L.R. 5 H.L. 321, at p. 341; *Re White Rose Cottage*, [1965] Ch. 940 (C.A.); [1965] 1 All E.R. 11.

(*e*) *Bozon* v. *Williams* (1829), 3 Y. & J. 150; *Lloyd* v. *Attwood* (1859), 3 De G. & J. 614, 651.

(*f*) *Re Oliver, Ex parte Jones* (1837), 3 Mont. & A. 152, 327; *Chapman* v. *Chapman* (1851), 13 Beav. 308; *Burgess* v. *Moxon, supra*; *Dixon* v. *Muckleston* (1872), 8 Ch. App. 155.

(*g*) *Fenwick* v. *Potts* (1856), 8 De G.M. & G. 506; *Lloyd* v. *Attwood, supra*.

(*h*) *Edge* v. *Worthington, supra*; *Keys* v. *Williams* (1838), 3 Y. & C. Ex. 55. See further as to intent p. 13, *supra*.

(*i*) *Adams* v. *Claxton* (1801), 6 Ves. 226.

(*k*) *Middleton* v. *Pollock, Ex parte Elliott* (1876), 2 Ch. D. 104; *Sharp* v. *Jackson*, [1899] A.C. 419 (H.L.); *Taylor* v. *London and County Banking Co.*, [1901] 2 Ch. 231; *Re Pidcock, Penny* v. *Pidcock* (1907), 51 Sol. Jo. 514.

(*l*) *Re Beetham, Ex parte Broderick* (1887), 18 Q.B.D. 766 (C.A.); *Ex parte Coming* (1803), 9 Ves. 115.

(*m*) *Lloyd* v. *Attwood* (1859), 3 De G. & J. 614. And see p. 156, *infra*.

Property affected by the mortgage.—An equitable mortgage by deposit will prima facie affect the beneficial interest of the mortgagor in all the property comprised in the deposited documents (*n*), including accretions (*o*). But the agreement, if any (which may be explained by other written evidence), will be the measure of the security (*p*), as well with respect to the particular property included in the security (*q*), as to the extent to which the interest of the mortgagor therein is to be affected (*r*). And if the memorandum of deposit refers to deeds which are not shown to have been deposited, and other deeds are deposited, the actual deposit will constitute the security (*s*).

Debt secured by the mortgage.—An equitable mortgage will, prima facie, be a security only for the debt specified in the agreement, and will not include debts previously due from the mortgagor to the mortgagee (*t*). But it may include such debts, if an intention that it should do so appear from the circumstances (*u*). An equitable mortgage by deposit, although accompanied by a written agreement, may either by written or parol evidence (*a*), and also, as it seems, by inference alone arising from possession of the deed (*b*), be extended to further advances, even where changes have occurred in the depositee's firm (*c*). A legal security cannot be extended by such means to subsequent advances made on a parol agreement for a further mortgage, because, it is said, the legal mortgagee holds his mortgage on a contract for conveyance only, and not for deposit (*d*). And it would seem that the leaving of the documents in the custody of each successive firm is constructively a re-deposit (*e*). It cannot, however, be shown by parol that the depositee holds the documents as security both for his own debt and that of another person (*f*), though, if the depositee himself is not a creditor, but a trustee only, he may be shown to hold them for another's benefit (*f*).

(*n*) *Ashton* v. *Dalton* (1846), 2 Coll. 565.

(*o*) *Re Baker, Ex parte Bisdee* (1840), 1 Mont. D. & De G. 333; *Re New, Ex parte Farley* (1841), 1 Mont. D. & De G. 683; *Chissum* v. *Dewes* (1828), 5 Russ. 29; see p. 36, *supra*.

(*p*) *Re Amner, Ex parte Hunt* (1840), 1 Mont. D. & De G. 139; *Re Medley, Ex parte Glyn* (1840), 1 Mont. D. & De G. 29.

(*q*) *Re Leathes, Ex parte Leathes* (1833), 3 Deac. & Ch. 112; *Wylde* v. *Radford* (1863), 33 L.J. Ch. 51.

(*r*) *Pryce* v. *Bury* (1853), 2 Drew. 41. The security will not, as against prior incumbrancers, be extended to property not included in the deposited documents, merely by reason of a false statement by the mortgagor to the mortgagee that such property is included therein: *Jones* v. *Williams* (1857), 24 Beav. 47.

(*s*) *Re Moore, Ex parte Powell* (1842), 6 Jur. 490.

(*t*) *Mountford* v. *Scott* (1823), Turn. & R. 274; *Re Cowdry, Ex parte Martin* (1835), 2 Mont. & A. 243.

(*u*) *Re New, Ex parte Farley, supra; Re Hildyard, Ex parte Smith* (1842), 2 Mont. D. & De G. 587.

(*a*) *Ex parte Whitbread* (1812), 19 Ves. 209; *Re Burkhill, Ex parte Nettleship* (1841), 2 Mont. D. & De G. 124.

(*b*) *James* v. *Rice* (1854), 5 De G.M. & G. 461; see *Barclays Bank Ltd.* v. *Taylor*, [1974] Ch. 137, 140.

(*c*) *Ex parte Kensington* (1813), 2 Ves. & B. 79.

(*d*) *Ex parte Hooper* (1815), 19 Ves. 477. Thus a person who has obtained a legal mortgage may, as to future advances, be in a worse position than an equitable mortgagee.

(*e*) *Ex parte Kensington, supra; Re Gye, Ex parte Smith* (1841), 2 Mont. D. & De G. 314.

(*f*) *Ex parte Whitbread, supra.*

In order to connect a debt of long standing with the possession of the debtor's deeds, the creditor must proceed upon a distinct allegation supported by proper evidence, that they were delivered to him by way of security (g). Nor, if the plaintiff's evidence of the deposit is defective at the hearing, will he be entitled to an inquiry to enable him to establish his security, because a reference will not then be directed upon a matter which involves the very root of the plaintiff's title (h). The rule in bankruptcy also requires that evidence can be given of the intention to effect a security by deposit. The usual order for sale in cases of an equitable mortgage has been refused after the lapse of twelve years from the date of the deposit, there being no memorandum, and the bankrupt being dead (i). But an enquiry will sometimes be directed in bankruptcy as to the circumstances attending a deposit of doubtful effect (k).

Equitable mortgage by deposit and lien mutually exclusive.— When an equitable mortgage or charge is created by deposit of title deeds there is an implied contract that the mortgagee or chargee may retain the deeds until he is paid. This implied contract is part and parcel of the equitable mortgage or charge. It is not a separate legal or common law lien. It has no independent existence apart from the equitable mortgage or charge. And when the mortgage or charge is avoided for non-registration, then everything which is ancillary to it is avoided also, so that the contractual right of retention is avoided too (l).

Agreement to create mortgage (m).—Such an agreement is not enforceable, unless it be in writing, or there is a note or memorandum (n) of the agreement made in writing, signed by the party to be charged therewith or some person thereunto by him lawfully authorised (o), or unless there has been part performance of the agreement (p). The agreement must be for valuable consideration. A voluntary agreement to create a security will not be enforced (q). The money must have been paid (r) or in the case of an antecedent debt there must be an agreement

---

(g) *Chapman* v. *Chapman* (1851), 13 Beav. 308; *Re McMahon, McMahon* v. *McMahon* (1886), 55 L.T. 763.

(h) *Holden* v. *Hearn* (1839), 1 Beav. at p. 456; *Kebell* v. *Philpot* (1838), 7 L.J. Ch. 237.

(i) *Re Oliver, Ex parte Jones* (1837), 3 Mont. & A. 152, 327.

(k) *Re Lindon, Ex parte Clouter* (1843), 7 Jur. 135.

(l) *Re Molton Finance, Ltd.*, [1968] Ch. 325 (C.A.), at pp. 332, 333; [1967] 3 All E.R. 843, at p. 845. And see *Re Wallis and Simmonds* v. *(Builders), Ltd.*, supra. But note (1970) 33 M.L.R. 131.

(m) See p. 13, supra.

(n) *Fenwick* v. *Potts* (1856), 8 De G.M. & G. 506; *Warner* v. *Willington* (1856), 3 Drew. 523; *Liverpool Borough Bank* v. *Eccles* (1859), 4 H. & N. 139; *Fullerton* v. *Provincial Bank of Ireland*, [1903] A.C. 309 (H.L.); *Astor Properties, Ltd.* v. *Tunbridge Wells Friendly Society*, [1936] 1 All E.R. 531.

(o) Law of Property Act 1925, s. 40 (1). See *Mounsey* v. *Rankin* (1885), 1 Cab. & El. 496.

(p) The payment of money (once thought to be an equivocal act: see *Re Whitting, Ex parte Hall* (1879), 10 Ch. D. 615 (C.A.)) may, taken with other matters, be a sufficient act of part performance: see *Steadman* v. *Steadman*, [1974] Q.B. 161; [1974] 2 All E.R. 977 (H.L.); Cheshire and Fifoot, *Law of Contract* (9th Edn.), pp. 198, 199.

(q) See pp. 13, 14, supra.

(r) *Rogers* v. *Challis* (1859), 27 Beav. 175.

to forbear from suing (s). A mere executory agreement to borrow or lend money on mortgage, not intended to create a present security, will not constitute an equitable mortgage, nor will specific performance of such an agreement be ordered (q).

Form of memorandum accompanying deposit (t).—Where the memorandum accompanies a deposit of title deeds it should refer to the deposit and state that the deposit was made to the intent that the property should be equitably charged with the repayment of the monies advanced (u). Express reference should be made that the land is charged with the payment of interest, but an equitable mortgage by deposit of title deeds carries interest even in the absence of such a provision (a). Where the memorandum is under seal (thus giving the mortgagee the statutory power to appoint a receiver and to sell (b)) it should also contain a declaration by the mortgagor that he holds the property on trust for the mortgagee and in addition or alternatively a power of attorney for the mortgagee to convey the property in the name of the mortgagor. It now seems that, even without such power of attorney, the equitable mortgagee, on exercising the statutory power of sale, will be able to convey the legal estate in the mortgaged property (c). The inclusion of the power of attorney makes the lender's position certain on this point (d). Every memorandum should also contain an undertaking by the mortgagor to execute a legal charge when called upon to do so (e), although an equitable mortgagee is entitled to call for a legal mortgage even in the absence of such a provision (f). Upon the execution of such a legal mortgage, it seems that the equitable mortgage continues in existence (for the purposes of priority, etc.), notwithstanding the usual rule of merger of a lower in a higher security (g).

Trust of the legal estate (h).—The purpose of this provision is to enable the mortgagee on exercising the power to sell to vest the legal estate in the mortgaged property in himself or a purchaser. It consists of a declaration by the mortgagor that he holds the mortgaged property in trust for the mortgagee. Properly drafted, it makes the statutory power of appointing new trustees (i) exercisable by the mortgagee and persons deriving title under him and gives the mortgagee and those

---

(s) Or an actual forbearance: *Alliance Bank* v. *Broom* (1864), 2 Dr. & Sm. 289; *Fullerton* v. *Provincial Bank of Ireland, supra.*

(t) For forms, see 14 Ency. Forms and Precedents (4th Edn.), pp. 610 *et seq.*; and Precedents 12 and 13 in the Appendix, *infra.*

(u) As previously mentioned (see p. 48, *supra*), for an equitable mortgage there must be consideration or forbearance.

(a) *Re Drax, Savile* v. *Drax*, [1903] 1 Ch. 781 (C.A.), at pp. 794, 796.

(b) Law of Property Act 1925, s. 101: see pp. 300, 360, *infra.*

(c) See p. 379, *infra.*

(d) Notwithstanding he sells in the name of the mortgagor, he sells as mortgagee and subject to the duty to obtain a proper price (see p. 379, *infra*): *Palmer* v. *Barclays Bank, Ltd.* (1971), 23 P. & C. R. 30.

(e) This undertaking is registrable as a land charge of Class C (iv) under the Land Charges Act 1972, s. 2 (4); see p. 443, *infra.*

(f) See p. 45, *supra.*

(g) See p. 596, *infra.*

(h) *London and County Banking Co.* v. *Goddard*, [1897] 1 Ch. 642.

(i) Trustee Act 1925, s. 36.

deriving title under him power to remove the mortgagor from the trusteeship and to appoint himself or themselves or any of them as trustees. On an appointment of new trustee the legal estate in the mortgaged property will vest in the new trustees (*k*).

A power of attorney by which the mortgagee is appointed to execute the legal mortgage in the name and on behalf of the mortgagor is sometimes included as additional protection for the mortgagee.

Power of attorney (*l*).—This may be included for the same purpose as the trust of the legal estate. The mortgagor irrevocably appoints the mortgagee and the persons deriving title under him the attorney or attorneys of the mortgagor and the persons deriving title under him in his or their name and on his or their behalf to vest the legal estate in the mortgaged property in any purchaser or other person in exercise of the statutory powers conferred on mortgages free and discharged from the mortgagor's right of redemption. Section 4 of the Powers of Attorney Act 1971, provides that where a power is expressed to be irrevocable and is given to secure a proprietary interest of the donee (*m*) or the performance of an obligation owed to the donee, then, so long as the donee has that interest or the obligation remains undischarged, the power shall not be revoked—(i) by the donor without the consent of the donee; nor (ii) by the death, incapacity or bankruptcy of the donor, or, if the donor is a body corporate, by its winding up or dissolution. A power to secure a proprietary interest may be given to the person entitled to the interest and any persons deriving title under him; and these persons shall be duly constituted donees of the power but without prejudice to any right to appoint substitutes given by the power. Where the mortgagee, in exercise of the statutory power of sale, conveys the mortgaged property pursuant to such a power of attorney, it seems that the purchaser will take the property free from subsequent incumbrances as well as the mortgage in respect of which the right of sale is being exercised (*n*).

Undertaking to execute legal mortgage.—The undertaking should be to execute a mortgage in such form and containing such covenants and conditions as the mortgagee shall reasonably require (*o*). This would not entitle the mortgagee to insist on the mortgage including, for example, a reservation of the right of consolidation (*p*). The undertaking should expressly refer to such provisions.

(*k*) *Ibid.*, s. 40.

(*l*) For the law prior to 1 October 1971 and to relevant provisions of the Law of Property Act 1925 see previous editions. As to the possible difficulties on the death of the donor, see *Williams on Title* (3rd Edn.), 393, 394.

(*m*) It is desirable that the power should be expressed to be by way of security in the memorandum; see form, p. 705, *infra*. If this is so then, unless the person dealing with the attorney knows that it was not in fact given by way of security, he is entitled to assume that the power is incapable of revocation except by the appointor acting with the attorney's consent. And so the third person will be treated as having knowledge of the revocation only if he knows that the power has been revoked by the appointor acting with the attorney's consent: see s. 5 (3). For registered land, see p. 68, *infra*.

(*n*) *Re White Rose Cottage*, [1965] Ch. 940 (C.A.); [1965] 1 All E.R. 11. For the effect of the statutory power of sale, see p. 376, *infra*.

(*o*) A covenant for payment of principal and interest is reasonable: *Saunders* v. *Milsome* (1866), L.R. 2 Eq. 573.

(*p*) *Farmer* v. *Pitt*, [1902] 1 Ch. 954.

Form where no deposit.—The intention to create an equitable mortgage must be clear. The instrument should contain a charge on the land of principal and interest. The memorandum should be under seal if the mortgagee is to have the statutory powers and the same requirements and provisions are applicable as where the memorandum accompanies a deposit.

Defective legal mortgage.—A document, which for some defect of form (but which is otherwise valid), fails to take effect as a legal mortgage, will be a good equitable mortgage (*q*). The most common example of this is where land is owned by two persons, usually husband and wife, and the mortgage is made by one of them only. Certain lenders do not investigate title prior to mortgage, so this situation is not uncommon. The effect is to create an equitable mortgage of the mortgagor's beneficial interest (*r*).

Equitable mortgages of registered land.—For these, see pp. 66 *et seq. infra.*

Title against trustee in bankruptcy.—An equitable mortgage or sub-mortgage of property which is within the rules of law concerning property in the reputed ownership of a bankrupt will be valid as against a trustee in bankruptcy of the mortgagor, only when the mortgagee has given such notice and done such other acts as are necessary in like cases to perfect the title of the legal mortgagee (*s*); but as between the contracting parties the equitable mortgage will be valid, although such acts are omitted (*t*).

IX—REGISTRATION OF MORTGAGES

Puisne mortgages and equitable charges.—Provision is made by the Land Charges Act, 1972, for the registration of certain legal and equitable mortgages in the Land Charges Register (*u*). For this purpose a distinction is made between mortgages and charges according as they are protected by a deposit of deeds or not. There may be a succession of legal mortgages, and usually the first mortgagee will hold the deeds. In that case all the other legal mortgages will be puisne mortgages (*a*). Or the deeds may be deposited by way of equitable mortgage. In that case any legal mortgages there may be will be puisne mortgages. For a puisne mortgage is defined to be a "legal mortgage not being a mortgage protected by a deposit of documents relating to the legal

---

(*q*) See *Taylor* v. *Wheeler* (1706), 2 Salk. 449.

(*r*) And see p. 175, *infra*. As to the possibility of the mortgage applying to a beneficial share to which the mortgagor subsequently succeeds, see (1935–36) 9 A.L.J. 431.

(*s*) *Re Daintry, Ex parte Arkwright* (1843), 3 Mont. D. & De G. 129; *Re Sketchley, Ex parte Boulton* (1857), 1 De G. & J. 163.

(*t*) *Cook* v. *Black* (1842), 1 Hare 390.

(*u*) Section 2 (4); p. 442, *infra*. In the case of charges, capable of being registered as land charges, created by a company, registration under the Land Charges Act 1972 is required in addition to registration under the Companies Act, 1948, s. 95 (as to this section, see p. 181, *infra*).

(*a*) Before 1926 a puisne mortgage was a mortgage subsequent to the first mortgage. This, in freehold mortgages, carried the legal estate in fee simple and all subsequent mortgages were equitable.

estate affected" (b). And further, there may be equitable mortgages not protected by deposit of documents. "Protected" in this context means protected by a deposit of deeds at the time of the creation of the mortgage. Such a mortgage does not become registrable if the mortgagee parts with the deeds (c). Thus there are for the purposes of registration four kinds of securities:

(1) Legal mortgages accompanied by title deeds.
(2) Puisne mortgages, *i.e.*, legal mortgages not accompanied by title deeds.
(3) Equitable mortgages accompanied by title deeds.
(4) Equitable mortgages (d) not accompanied by title deeds.

Registration as land charges.—Securities in divisions (1) and (3) above do not require to be registered. It has been suggested that securities in division (3) are registrable as estate contracts (e). An estate contract is a contract by an estate owner to convey or create a legal estate (f), and an equitable mortgage either includes an express agreement to create a legal mortgage or implies such an agreement (g). Although an equitable mortgage accompanied with title deeds is expressly excluded from Class C (iii)—general equitable charge—it is not expressly excluded from Class C (iv)—estate contract. While the argument that a protected equitable mortgage is registrable as an estate contract is logically sound, such a construction would frustrate the policy behind the 1925 legislation which was to exempt all mortgages protected by deposit of deeds from registration (h). It is not the practice of conveyancers to register a protected equitable mortgage as an estate contract unless there is an express agreement to create a legal mortgage.

Securities in division (2) and (4) above require to be registered as land charges in Class C (i)—puisne mortgage—and (iii)—general equitable charge—respectively (i).

Registration of mortgages by companies.—Legal and equitable mortgages by a company must be registered in the Companies Register (k).

Those mortgages capable of registration under the Land Charges Act 1972 must also be registered under the 1972 Act (l).

Registration of mortgages of registered land.—On this, see Ch. 3, *infra.*

(b) Land Charges Act 1972, s. 2 (4), Class C (i). Part of the deeds may be held by one mortgagee and part by another, see p. 443, *infra. Quaere* whether "protected" under the Act means protected by all the deeds; see (1950) 13 M.L.R. 534 (A.D. Hargreaves).
(c) See (1941), 7 C.L.J. 249 (R. E. Megarry). As to the effect of the mortgagee failing to retain the deeds, see p. 452, *infra.*
(d) *I.e.*, equitable mortgages not arising or affecting an interest arising under a trust for sale or a settlement and not included in any other class of land charge: Land Charges Act 1972, s. 2 (4), Class C (iii).
(e) (1930), 69 L.J. News. 227 (J. M. Lightwood); (1941), 7 C.L.J. 250, 251 (R. E. Megarry); (1949), 10 C.L.J. 241 (S. J. Bailey); (1962), 26 Conv. (N.S.) 446–449 (R. G. Rowley).
(f) Land Charges Act 1972, s. 2 (4), Class C (iv). (g) See p. 45, *supra.*
(h) For the arguments against such a construction, see 7 C.L.J. 252.
(i) As to failure to register, see pp. 482 *et seq., infra.*
(k) See p. 181, *infra.*   (l) Land Charges Act 1972, s. 3 (7), (8).

X—TRANSITIONAL PROVISIONS AND COPYHOLD MORTGAGES

Conversion of freehold mortgages into mortgages by demise. —Freehold mortgages and leasehold mortgages by assignment, which were existing immediately before 1 January, 1926, were converted into mortgages by demise and mortgages by sub-demise respectively under the transitional provisions contained in the Law of Property Act 1925, Schedule 1, Part VII and VIII.

As to freehold mortgages a first or only mortgagee took a term of 3,000 years from the commencement of the Act, without impeachment of waste, but subject to a provision for cesser corresponding to his then subsisting right of redemption (*m*). Subsequent mortgagees took in succession terms one day longer than the term taken by the immediately preceding mortgagee. But a sub-mortgagee took a derivative term less by one day than the term of the mortgagee who had created the sub-mortgage. The mortgages being thus converted into terms, the freehold estate in fee simple vested, where the mortgagor was absolutely entitled, in him; where the land was not the subject of absolute ownership, the freehold estate vested in the persons, such as tenant for life, trustees for sale, or personal representatives, who would have been entitled, under the other transitional provisions of the Act, to a conveyance of the fee simple if the mortgage had been paid off at the commencement of the Act, but subject to the mortgage term and the money secured by the mortgage: Part VII.

Conversion of leasehold mortgages by assignment into mortgages by sub-demise.—The provisions of Part VIII with regard to leasehold mortgages by assignment subsisting immediately before 1 January, 1926, are similar. A first or only mortgagee took a sub-term less by ten days than the term assigned to him, but subject to a provision for cesser corresponding to the right of redemption. Subsequent mortgagees took in succession terms one day longer than the term taken by the immediately preceding mortgagee. A sub-mortgagee took a derivative term less by one day than the derivative term of the mortgagee who had created the sub-mortgage. The nominal reversion thus left outstanding vested in the mortgagor, if absolutely entitled, or in the tenant for life, trustees for sale, personal representatives, or other person entitled to the legal estate as in the case of the fee simple (*n*).

The vesting of a nominal reversion.—As previously stated (*o*) under the former system of leasehold mortgages by demise a nominal

---

(*m*) The Law of Property Act 1925 s. 87 (2) provides for the conversion of such a converted mortgage into a legal charge by a written declaration.

(*n*) By Law of Property Act 1922, Sched. XV, perpetually renewable leaseholds were converted into terms of 2,000 years, and by the Law of Property Act 1925, s. 149 (6) (which replaced para. 7 (3) of Sched. XV), leases for lives were converted into leases for ninety years determinable after the death of the original lessee, or of the survivor of the original lessees, by one month's notice on either side. By Part VIII, para. 6, the above provisions were applied to such cases with the substitution of the term created by the statute for the term created by the lease.

(*o*) See pp. 22, 23, *supra*.

reversion was left in the mortgagor and provision was made by the mortgage for getting it in on sale by the mortgagee. This usually took the form of a trust for the mortgagee and his assigns. But since under such trust the mortgagee or a purchaser from him was entitled to call for an assignment of the nominal reversion, the effect under the provisions of the Law of Property Act 1925 (*p*), for getting in automatically legal estates outstanding immediately before 1 January 1926, would have been to get in all the nominal reversions then outstanding.

In the case where the mortgage was an existing mortgage—*i.e.*, where the equity of redemption was subsisting on 1 January, 1926— this would have been opposed to the scheme of the Act, since mortgages by demise would have been converted into mortgages by assignment and these are forbidden (*q*). Hence it was provided by the Law of Property Act 1925, Sched. 1, Pt. II, as follows:

> **7.**—Nothing in this Part of this Schedule shall operate—
> (a) To vest in a mortgagee of a term of years absolute any nominal reversion which is held in trust for him subject to redemption.

Where however the equity of redemption had been extinguished on 1 January, 1926, whether by an assignment by the mortgagee under his power of sale, or by foreclosure, or by operation of the Statutes of Limitation, this did not assist the mortgagee or his successor in title, and the nominal reversion vested in him so that he became an assign of the lease and liable to the covenants contained in it. In order to give him an opportunity of avoiding this liability, the following additional clause was added by the Law of Property (Amendment) Act 1926, to para. 7:

> **7.**—Nothing in this Part of the Schedule shall operate—
> (m) To vest in any person any legal estate affected by any rent, covenants or conditions if, before any proceedings are commenced in respect of the rent, convenants or conditions and before any conveyance of the legal estate or dealing therewith *inter vivos* is effected, he or his personal representatives disclaim it in writing signed by him or them.

Thus a person in whom a nominal reversion has become vested because the equity of redemption was extinguished could get rid of his liability by disclaiming it, provided that he did this before any proceedings to enforce his liability had been commenced, and also before he had assigned the lease (*r*).

There is a nominal reversion under the present system also, but the assignment by the mortgagee under his statutory power of sale passes it to the purchaser (*s*), so that no device for getting it in is required.

(*p*) Law of Property Act 1925, Sched. 1, Pt. II, paras. 3, 6. These provisions applied where, for example, there was a covenant for further assurance of the nominal reversion: *Peachy* v. *Young*, [1929] 1 Ch. 449.

But a mortgagee who under s. 89 (3) of the Law of Property Act 1925 (see p. 503, *infra*), had power to declare a legal estate vested in him was not a person entitled to require the legal estate to be vested in him for the purposes of Sched. 1, Part II, para. 3: *St. Germans (Earl)* v. *Barker*, [1936] 1 All E.R. 849.

(*q*) Law of Property Act 1925, s. 86.

(*r*) *Peachy* v. *Young*, [1929] 1 Ch. 449.

(*s*) Law of Property Act 1925, s. 89.

Land held in undivided shares.—By the Law of Property Act 1925, s. 1 (6), there cannot be a legal estate in an undivided share in land, and though there may be beneficial interests in an undivided share, these take effect behind a trust for sale (*t*). Where immediately before 1 January, 1926, land was held at law or in equity in undivided shares, provision was made by Sched. 1, Pt. IV, of that Act for the vesting of the entirety in trustees on the statutory trusts; namely, on trust to sell and to stand possessed of the net proceeds of sale and of the net rents and profits till sale on trust to give effect to the rights of the persons (including an incumbrancer of a former undivided share or where an incumbrance is not secured by a legal mortgage) interested in the land (*u*).

These words referring to incumbrancers carry out the scheme of the transitional vesting provisions under which incumbrances affecting undivided shares, and incumbrances affecting the entirety which were not under the Law of Property Act 1925 (*a*), or otherwise secured by legal terms, were shifted to the proceeds of sale, and the entirety of the land was vested in the trustees, ascertained for the various cases mentioned in para. 1 of Pt. IV, free from incumbrances. But these incumbrancers were protected by the provision that the statutory trust for sale should not be exercised without their consent, though a purchaser was not concerned to see or inquire whether such consent had been given (*b*).

A mortgagee who immediately before 1 January, 1926, had a legal mortgage on the entirety of the land was not affected by the transitional vesting in trustees, though, as in the case of other legal mortgages, he took a term of years in lieu of his former estate in fee simple (under a freehold mortgage), or a sub-term in lieu of his former term (under a leasehold mortgage by assignment), but this change did not affect priorities (*c*).

The estate of the mortgagee might before 1 January, 1926, be an estate in an undivided share in two cases:

(1)   Where he had taken a legal mortgage of an undivided share.
(2)   Where, under a contributory mortgage, the land had been conveyed to the different mortgagees in undivided shares.

In case (1) the mortgage, being an incumbrance affecting an undivided share, was, as just mentioned, shifted in general to the proceeds of sale; but special provision was made where all the undivided shares in the land were vested in the same mortgagees for securing the same mortgage money, and the rights of redemption affecting the land were the same as might have been subsisting if the entirety had been mortgaged by an owner before the undivided shares were created. In that case, the incumbrance was treated as an incumbrance affecting

---

(*t*) *Ibid.*, s. 34 (1); Settled Land Act 1925, s. 36 (4).
(*u*) Law of Property Act 1925, s. 35.
(*a*) Thus a freehold mortgage on the entirety was by the Act converted into a mortgage by demise for a term of 3,000 years: Sched. 1, Pt. VII, *supra*, and Pt. IV, para. 1 (8).
(*b*) Law of Property Act 1925, Sched. 1, Pt. IV, para. 1 (9).
(*c*) *Ibid.*, para. 1 (8).

the entirety, and the land vested in the mortgagees as joint tenants for a term of 3,000 years, subject to cesser on redemption by the trustees of the entirety (d). Such a mortgage would occur where all the tenants in common had joined in mortgaging the land for one sum of money advanced by several mortgagees, and had conveyed their undivided shares to the mortgagees.

For case (2) no provision was made by the Law of Property Act. Usually a contributory mortgage was made by a grant to the mortgagees as joint tenants, with a provision as to their respective shares in the mortgage money; but occasionally the land was conveyed to the mortgagees in undivided shares. The vesting provisions of Part IV of the First Schedule are not appropriate for mortgagees holding as tenants in common, but since, under the Act, such a holding could not continue, their estate, it may be presumed, became a joint tenancy in accordance with the general scheme of the Act, and the mortgage was then converted into the usual form of contributory mortgage (e).

Transitional provisions common to freehold and leasehold mortgages.—The following further provisions are made by Parts VII and VIII as regards freehold and leasehold mortgages:

(1) The transitional provisions (save where expressly excepted) apply whether or not the land is registered under the Land Registration Act 1925, or the mortgage is made by way of trust for sale or otherwise.

(2) A mortgage affecting a legal estate made before 1926, which is not protected, either by a deposit of documents of title relating to the legal estate or by registration as a land charge, is not, as against a purchaser in good faith without notice thereof, to obtain any benefit by being converted into a legal mortgage, but is, in favour of such purchaser, to be deemed to remain an equitable interest.

But this does not apply to mortgages or charges registered or protected under the Land Registration Act 1925, or to mortgages or charges registered in a local deeds register.

(3) The transitional provisions do not affect priorities or the right of any mortgagee to retain possession of documents, nor affect his title to or rights over any fixtures or chattels personal comprised in the mortgage.

(4) The provisions do not apply unless a right of redemption was subsisting immediately before 1 January, 1926.

Former copyhold mortgages.—A legal mortgage of a copyhold estate was effected by a surrender of the copyhold, subject to a condition that the surrender should be void upon payment of the money at the day fixed; and was perfected by the admittance of the mortgagee. When the copyhold only formed part of the security, the surrender was usually made in pursuance of a covenant to surrender contained in the accompanying mortgage of the freehold or leasehold estate, and the covenants for title in that mortgage were made to extend to the copyholds; or, if there was no such other security, the covenants for payment and title, if made, were contained in a separate deed.

(d) *Ibid.*, Sched. 1, Pt. IV, para. 1 (7).
(e) There would apparently be no restriction on the number of joint tenants, corresponding to the restriction to four under the Law of Property Act 1925, s. 34, and Sched. 1, Pt. IV, para. 1 (2).

Until entry upon the court rolls of the conditional surrender, nothing passed by it; but this having been done, the mortgagee generally abstained from taking admittance until it became necessary or desirable to do so, and in the meantime the fines and fees which would become payable upon his admittance were saved, and he did not become subject to the liabilities incident to copyhold tenancy. His interest, in fact, until admittance, was merely equitable, the surrenderor remaining seised of an estate which was descendible to his heir (even though the lord had accepted rent from the surrenderee), and being liable to the lord both for services and for the purpose of forfeiture.

Upon breach of the condition and admittance of the surrenderee, his estate became absolute; and having already before admittance acquired a good title as against all but the lord, he took upon admittance a title which related back to the date of the surrender; so that he could recover in ejectment against a purchaser who had taken admittance under a later surrender.

Abolition of copyhold tenure.—Under the Property Acts 1922 and 1924, all copyhold land was enfranchised and ceased to be of copyhold or customary tenure, and the enfranchisement had the effect stated in the Twelfth Schedule to the Act of 1922.

Transitional provisions for copyhold mortgages.—The provisions of the Twelfth Schedule which affect mortgages are as follows:

(1) (f) Every mortgage of the copyhold estate in the land shall become a mortgage of the land for a term of years absolute in accordance with the provisions of Part I of this Act (f), and accordingly:

(i) Where at the commencement of this Act a mortgage of the customary estate of inheritance in copyhold land effected by surrender, with or without admission, or by a covenant to surrender, is subsisting, then the mortgagee shall, by virtue of this Act, acquire a legal term of years absolute in the enfranchised land comprised in his mortgage subject to a proviso for cesser corresponding to the right of redemption subsisting under the mortgage;

(ii) Where at the commencement of this Act the copyhold land has been surrendered to the use of a mortgagee, without notice of a previous covenant to surrender contained in another mortgage, that mortgagee shall not be deemed to be a subsequent incumbrancer as respects the last-mentioned mortgage.

In this paragraph the expression 'surrender' includes any other disposition which, when entered on the court rolls, operated as a surrender to the use of any person.

Para. 2 provides that the enfranchisement shall not, except as in the Act mentioned (g), affect the right of any person in the enfranchised land under a mortgage, but the rights continue (subject to the provisions of Part I of the Act) to attach upon the land in the same way as if the freehold had been comprised in the mortgage.

(f) Part I of the Law of Property Act 1922, together with nearly all the remainder of the Act other than the copyhold enfranchisement parts, was repealed and incorporated in the Consolidation Acts of 1925. The reference to Part I of the Act of 1922 must be taken to refer to ss. 85 *et seq.* and Sched. I, Parts VII and VIII, of the Law of Property Act 1925; see particularly Part VII, para. 5.

(g) These savings appear to refer to the provisions of the Act under which the legal estate is shifted, and equitable interests are allowed to be, in certain cases, overreached.

(8) On the enfranchisement of any land by virtue of this Act—

(a) If there is a copyholder in fee (not being a mortgagee) the freehold estate in fee simple shall vest (subject as provided in this schedule) in that person:

(b) If there is no copyholder in fee, the freehold estate in fee simple shall (subject as provided in this schedule) vest in the person who immediately before the commencement of this Act had the best right to be admitted as copyholder in fee, otherwise than as mortgagee, but such person shall (save as hereinafter provided) be personally liable to pay the fines and fees which would have been payable by him on admittance; and if the last person who was admitted as copyholder in fee (being a trustee) has died before the commencement of this Act (whether or not having disposed of the land by will), his personal representative, if any, shall be deemed to have had a better right to be admitted than the devisee or customary heir:

. . .

(f) If the copyholder in fee is a mortgagee, the freehold estate in fee simple shall (subject to the terms of years absolute of any mortgagees) vest in the person entitled to the equity of redemption (h).

Effect of the enfranchisement.—Thus, where immediately before 1 January, 1926, copyhold land was subject to a mortgage of the customary estate of inheritance, whether effected by surrender, with or without admittance, or by a covenant to surrender, it became enfranchised; the freehold estate in fee simple vested in the mortgagor; and the mortgagee took a term of 3,000 years subject to cesser on redemption. Similarly subsequent mortgagees took legal terms. But where an equitable mortgage thus became a legal mortgage, this did not prejudicially affect the priorities existing at the commencement of the Act (i); and similarly where a legal mortgage, such as a mortgage of a life interest, was converted into an equitable mortgage (k).

(h) This sub-paragraph was added by Sched. II of the Law of Property (Amendment) Act 1924.

(i) Law of Property Act 1925, Sched. I, Part II, para. 7 (h).

(k) Ibid., Sched. I, Part I.

CHAPTER 3

Mortgages of Registered Land

Mortgages on first registration.—On completion of the transaction (*a*) leading to first registration (*b*) the application for registration must be lodged by the purchaser, assignee or lessee within two months (*c*). If, as will often be the case, the transaction has been completed by an advance on mortgage, the mortgagee may make the application (*d*). This is what usually happens, for the mortgagee will not want to part with the deeds to allow an application by the mortgagor, and until an application has been made for the registration of the estate, no mortgage relating to that estate can be accepted for registration (*e*).

The procedure on the application is to be found in the registered conveyancing books. Only three points to note will be mentioned here. No fee is payable in respect of a mortgage by an applicant for first registration which accompanies the application (*f*). Care should be taken to see that the blank spaces in the printed mortgage forms have been properly completed and the copies of the mortgage and deed inducing registration duly certified (*g*). Some mortgage forms,

---

(*a*) Generally a conveyance on sale or an assignment on sale of a term having not less than forty years to run or a lease for not less than forty years; see Land Registration Act 1925, s. 123 (1). The transaction may be completed in the usual form for unregistered land. Alternatively the registered land forms—transfer and charge (if any)—may be used, see Land Registration Rules 1925, r. 72. This alternative is particularly useful where several properties are to be transferred, so as to avoid lengthy parcels, and where lengthy recitals would otherwise be necessary. But where the registered land forms are used it must be remembered that there is no title number at that stage and the land must be described by reference to a previous document of title.

(*b*) *I.e.*, a transaction within s. 123 (1) within a compulsory area. Voluntary registration was suspended by the Land Registration Act 1966, s. 1, save for such classes of cases as the registrar may from time to time specify (as to which, see (1967), 31 Conv. (N.S.) 7 and (1977) 121 S.J. 20).

(*c*) If the application is not received by the Registry within the period of two months from the date of the deed inducing registration an extension of time must be sought under s. 123. The application for extension should request that an order be made under that section, give an explanation for the delay, *e.g.*, pressure of work or documents temporarily mislaid, and be accompanied by the fee of £1: Land Registration Fee Order 1976, Schedule para. X.

(*d*) Land Registration Rules 1925, r. 73 (2). See note 10, p. 683, *infra*.

(*e*) Rule 72 (3).

(*f*) Land Registration Fee Order 1976, para. 6 Abatement 1. For where the dealing is subject to a mortgage or charge created previously and the charge does not accompany the application for first registration the fee for the charge is payable under Scale 4, on the amount outstanding thereunder, and an application should be made for substantive registration (rather than mere noting) of such mortgage or charge (if it is a legal mortgage or charge).

(*g*) Indorsed "Certified a true copy" or other such expression and with the firm's name and address and signed by a partner or qualified solicitor employed by the firm: r. 309.

especially local authority mortgage forms and some building society mortgage forms, contain an application to the registrar for a restriction to be entered on the register, for example, that, except under an order of the registrar, no disposition is to be made by the proprietor of the land or in exercise of the power of sale in any charge subsequent to the mortgage containing the application without the consent of the proprietor for the time being of that mortgage. The appropriate fee (*h*) must be paid for such an application for a restriction.

A legal mortgage will be registered with substantive registration (*i*) and on completion of the registration the charge certificate will be returned to the mortgagee with the deeds accompanying the application for first registration. The land certificate is kept at the Registry (*k*).

A person who is obliged to apply for first registration may create a lien on the land equivalent to that created by a deposit of a certificate (*l*) by a Notice of Intended Deposit of the land certificate to the registrar. The notice should be on the printed form (*m*) which must be signed by the borrower (and not by his solicitors). The entry of notice on the register of the intended deposit operates as a caution (*n*). On completion of the registration the land certificate is delivered to the person named in that behalf in the notice (*o*).

An equitable mortgage for which no notice of intended deposit is given will be protected by means of a notice on the register (*p*).

Where there are two or more incumbrances prior to first registration of the land, their relative priorities are not affected by the registration of some or one of them only, or by the order in which such of them as are registered are entered in the register (*q*).

Registered charges.—The Land Registration Act 1925 (*r*), provides:

(*h*) *I.e.*, £1; Land Registration Fee Order 1976, Schedule para. VII (But no fee is payable if the application for the restriction is acompanied by an application for which a fee is payable: *ibid*).

(*i*) *I.e.*, under Land Registration Act 1925, s. 26, which, apparently, applies only to legal mortgages and charges. See p. 61, *infra*.

(*k*) See Land Registration Act 1925, s. 65. Where an official search is obtained by a purchaser (i.e., any person including a lessee or chargee, who in good faith and for valuable consideration acquires or intends to acquire a legal estate in land: Land Registration (Official Searches) Rules 1969, r. 2 (2)) any entries on the, register made during the priority period of 15 days are postponed to the purchasers application, if in order: r. 5; *Smith* v. *Morrison*, [1974] 1 All E.R. 957.

(*l*) As to which, see p. 66, *infra*. A substantive registration and an entry of notice of deposit or intended deposit cannot be made on the same register because, if substantive registration has been effected no deposit will be possible since the land certificate will be lodged in the Registry (Land Registration Act 1925, s. 65) and if there has been a deposit it will not be possible to lodge the land certificate for the purposes of substantive registration. A notice of deposit or intended deposit cannot be entered while another such notice is on the register: Land Registration Rules 1925, r. 243. In such cases registration of a caution or entry of notice should be applied for; see p. 70, *infra*.

(*m*) Form 85 B. No fee is payable: Land Registration Fee Order 1976, para 5 (iv).

(*n*) Land Registration Rules 1925, r. 242 (1). See p. 67, *infra*.

(*o*) Land Registration Rules 1925, r. 242 (2).

(*p*) Under Land Registration Act 1925, s. 49 (1) (c). For the effect of notices, see Land Registration Act 1925, s. 52.

(*q*) Land Registration Rules 1925, r. 160 (2).

(*r*) Which consolidates, with amendments, the Land Transfer Acts 1875 and 1897.

25.—(1) The proprietor (*s*) of any registered land may (*t*) by deed—

    (a) charge the registered land with the payment at an appointed time of any principal sum of money either with or without interest;

    (b) charge the registered land in favour of a building society under the Building Societies Acts 1874 to 1894 (*u*) in accordance with the rules of that society (*a*).

(2) A charge may be in any form provided that—

    (a) the registered land comprised in the charge is described by reference to the register or in any other manner sufficient to enable the registrar to identify the same without reference to any other document (*b*);

    (b) the charge does not refer to any other interest or charge affecting the land which—

        (i) would have priority over the same and is not registered or protected (*c*) on the register,

        (ii) is not an overriding interest (*d*).

(3) Any provision contained in a charge which purports to—

        (i) take away from the proprietor thereof the power of transferring it by registered disposition or of requiring the cessation thereof to be noted on the register; or

        (ii) affect any registered land or charge other than that in respect of which the charge is to be expressly registered,

shall be void (*e*).

Notwithstanding that the above section only requires that the charge be by deed, it seems that an equitable charge may not be the subject of a substantive registration under this section (*f*).

Form and registration of charge.—Thus, subject to the requirements of the above section as to description of the land, and as to exclusion of reference to unregistered or unprotected prior interests, or interests other than overriding interests, the charge can be by deed in any form the mortgagee pleases. A charge on registered land may be made in Form 45 in the Schedule to the Land Registration Rules 1925 (*g*), and commonly is so made in simple cases (*h*). That form contains a number of miscellaneous alternative or additional clauses. Where it is desirable to have express covenants the unregistered form of mortgage or charge with the addition of the Land Registry heading should be used.

(*s*) And persons entitled to be registered (*e.g.*, the proprietor's personal representatives) before they are registered: Land Registration Act 1925, s. 37.

(*t*) Unless prevented from so doing by restriction, inhibition, notice or other entry: see Land Registration Act 1925, s. 69 (4).

(*u*) See now Building Societies Act 1962.

(*a*) It seems that friendly societies and industrial and provident societies are on the same footing as building societies for the purposes of registered charges: see Land Registration Rules 1925, rr. 92, 93 and 152.

(*b*) As to description of registered land, see Land Registration Act 1925, s. 76, and Rules, rr. 272 to 285.

(*c*) By notice, caution, inhibition or restriction.

(*d*) As to overriding interests, see Land Registration Act 1925, ss. 3 (xvi) and 70.

(*e*) But this does not prevent the reservation of a right of consolidation: s. 26 (2); and Land Registration Rules 1925, r. 154.

(*f*) *Re White Rose Cottage*, [1965] Ch. 940 (C.A.), at p. 949, *per* Lord DENNING, M.R.; [1965] 1 All E.R. 11, at p. 14. And this appears to be the Registry practice: [1965] Ch. at p. 954; [1965] 1 All E.R. at p. 17. And see Law Commission Working Paper No. 67 (1976). But *cf.* Wilberforce, J., at [1964] Ch. 490; [1964] 1 All E.R. 173; and see (1966) 19 C.L.P. 26 (E. C. Ryder).

(*g*) Rule 139. Form 45 A is a charge of the whole. Subsequent forms provide for other charges. For a form, see Precedent 5 in the Appendix, *infra*.

(*h*) Building societies either employ a special printed form for registered land or have a standard form for unregistered or registered land with sufficient space for the insertion of the appropriate Land Registry heading.

The charge may be made by a charge by way of legal mortgage or may contain, in the case of freehold land, an express demise, and in the case of leasehold land, an express sub-demise, subject to a provision for cesser on redemption. Otherwise, it will, subject to any provision to the contrary contained in the charge, take effect as a charge by way of legal mortgage (*i*). In the case of registered land the words "by way of legal mortgage" are not required in a legal charge (*k*).

The charge is completed by the registrar entering on the Charges Register the person (*l*) in whose favour it is made as proprietor of the charge and particulars of the charge (*m*). The application for registration of the charge must be on the appropriate form (*n*) and accompanied, in a simple case, by the original charge and a certified copy thereof, the certificate of official search (*o*), the land certificate (*p*), any necessary consent or certificate under a restriction, and a cheque for the fees (*q*). A charge certificate will then be prepared. The basic contents of the charge certificate are prescribed (*r*). The form will vary according to the circumstances. The charge certificate is issued to the chargee (*s*). In all cases the original charge is issued with the charge certificate, the certified copy being filed in the Registry. The requirement, mentioned above, that the land certificate accompany the application causes difficulty when there has been a prior mortgage by deposit of the land certificate. Until registered, the mortgagee will not be able to exercise the statutory powers (*m*). A caution will be the

---

(*i*) Section 27 (1), (2). The introduction of the mortgage by demise into the system of registration of title seems to have been unnecessary. The better course would have been to preserve the registered charge as a statutory charge only, but to have attached to it remedies, including the right to recover possession and to sue on the covenants in leases, incident to ordinary mortgages.

(*k*) *Cityland and Property (Holdings), Ltd.* v. *Dabrah*, [1968] Ch. 166; [1967] 2 All E.R. 639. See also Rules 1925, r. 139, and Act, s. 144 (2).

(*l*) Where a charge is registered in the names of two or more proprietors (whether jointly or in undivided shares) the mortgage term implied or comprised in the charge vests in them as joint tenants and notwithstanding that the money is held in undivided shares, receipts may be given as if the money had been held on a joint account: Land Registration Act 1925, s. 32; Land Registration Rules 1925, r. 146.

(*m*) Land Registration Act 1925, s. 26 (1). Completion takes place as of the day of delivery of the proper documents in the proper order: see Land Registration Rules 1925, r. 83 (2). Until such delivery the charge takes effect in equity only (*Woolwich Equitable Building Society* v. *Marshall*, [1952] Ch. 1, at p. 6; [1951] 2 All E.R. 769, at p. 771; *Grace Rymer Investments, Ltd.* v. *Waite*, [1958] Ch. 831 (C.A.); [1958] 2 All E.R. 777) and, as a minor interest, will be overridden by a registered disposition for valuable consideration: Land Registration Act 1925, s. 101. Until the entry is made the chargee's title is not perfected and he cannot exercise his statutory powers (as to which, see p. 63, *infra*; *Lever Finance, Ltd.* v. *Needleman's Trustee*, [1956] Ch. 375; [1956] 2 All E.R. 378). A prospective purchaser can insist on the mortgagee procuring the registration of himself as proprietor of the charge: Land Registration Act 1925, s. 110 (5).

(*n*) Form A 4 for charge of whole; A 5 for charge of part.

(*o*) For the priority period given by an official search, see footnote (*k*), p. 60, *supra*.

(*p*) Which will be retained in the Land Registry until the charge is cancelled: Land Registration Act 1925, s. 65.

(*q*) Where a charge by the transferee under a transfer for value is delivered with the application to register the transfer, no fee is payable for the registration of the charge: Land Registration Fee Order 1976 para 6. Abatement 2. Otherwise the fee for registration of a charge is on Scale 4: Fee Order Schedule, para. V (4). Where the charge is by a company a certificate that the charge has been registered under the Companies Act must be produced (see p. 185, *infra*).

(*r*) Land Registration Rules 1925, r. 262.

(*s*) Land Registration Act 1925, s. 63.

appropriate means of protecting the mortgage in this case (*t*).

Implied covenants.—The Land Registration Act 1925 (*u*), makes the following provision as to covenants in a registered charge. Where a registered charge is created on any land there is implied on the part of the person being proprietor of such land at the time of the creation of the charge, in the absence of any entry on the register negativing such implication, a covenant with the proprietor for the time being of the charge, to pay the principal sum charged, and interest, if any, thereon at the appointed time and rate, and a covenant, if the principal sum or any part thereof remains unpaid at such appointed time, to pay interest half-yearly at the appointed rate both before and after any judgment in respect of the charge is obtained on so much of the principal sum as for the time being remains unpaid.

Where the land charged is leasehold land, there is also implied in a registered charge, unless there is an entry on the register negativing the implication, a covenant by the proprietor of the land at the time the charge was created, or the persons deriving title under him, to pay the rent and to observe and perform the covenants and conditions contained in the registered lease, and to indemnify the proprietor of the charge, and persons deriving title under him, against any claims, proceedings and expenses in respect thereof (*a*).

Powers of proprietor of charge.—The Land Registration Act 1925, provides:

34.—(1) Subject to any entry on the register to the contrary (*b*), the proprietor (*c*) of a charge shall have and may exercise all the powers conferred by law on the owner of a legal mortgage (*d*).

(2) Subject to any entry to the contrary on the register and subject to the right of any persons appearing on the register to be prior incumbrancers, the proprietor of a charge may, after entry into possession and after having acquired a title under the Limitation Acts, execute a declaration in the prescribed form (*e*), that the right of redemption is barred, and thereupon he shall be entitled, subject to furnishing any evidence which may be prescribed in support thereof (*f*), to be registered as proprietor of the land, with the same consequences as if he had been a purchaser for valuable consideration of the land under the power of sale.

(3) An order for foreclosure shall be completed by the registration of the proprietor of the charge (or such other person as may be named in the foreclosure order absolute for that purpose) as the proprietor of the land, and by the cancellation of the charge and of all incumbrances and entries

---

(*t*) See, generally Law Commission Working Paper No. 67 (1976) for the present position and the proposals for a new scheme for the creation and protection of mortgages of registered land.

(*u*) Section 28. The implied covenants may be modified or negatived: Land Registration Rules 1925, r. 140; and see Form 45 in the Schedule to the Rules. They are in practice often varied. For example, there is no covenant for insurance or repair; and a covenant for payment by trustees is usually restricted (see p. 209, *infra*).

(*a*) For the covenants implied by the use of words "as beneficial owner", see Law of Property Act 1925, s. 76 (1) (C), (D), Sched. 2, Parts III, IV, and Land Registration Rules 1925, r. 76.

(*b*) *E.g.*, a restriction against sub-charging.

(*c*) *Lever Finance, Ltd.* v. *Needleman's Trustee*, [1956] Ch. 375; [1956] 2 All E.R. 378. See footnote (*m*), p. 62, *supra*.

(*d*) As to which, in particular, see Pt. V, *infra*.

(*e*) Form 52, which must bear 50p stamp duty as a deed poll.

(*f*) See Land Registration Rules 1925, r. 149.

inferior thereto; and such registration shall operate in like manner and with the same consequences as if the proprietor of the charge or other person aforesaid had been a purchaser for valuable consideration of the land under a subsisting power of sale (*g*).

(4) A sale by the court or under the power of sale shall operate and be completed by registration in the same manner, as nearly as may be (but subject to any alterations on the register affecting the priority of the charge), as a transfer for valuable consideration by the proprietor of the land at the time of the registration of the charge would have operated or been completed, and, as respects the land transferred, the charge and all incumbrances and entries inferior thereto shall be cancelled (*h*).

(5) Notwithstanding the creation of a term or sub-term, expressly or by implication, under this Act, such transfer shall (subject to any prior incumbrances or other entries on the register) operate to transfer the registered estate, and the mortgage term or sub-term shall become merged, and any purported disposition of or dealing with the mortgage term or sub-term apart from the charge, and any process or act purporting to keep alive that term or sub-term after the cessation of the charge shall be void.

(6) For the purposes of this section an incumbrance or entry on the register shall not be deemed to be inferior to the charge in right of which title is made if the incumbrance or other interest is given the requisite priority by statute or otherwise.

The proprietor of a charge, while in possession, or after a receiver has been appointed, or such receiver on his behalf, has all the powers conferred by ss. 99 and 100 of the Law of Property Act 1925 (*i*), as extended by the instrument of charge or any instrument varying the terms thereof, but subject to any contrary intention expressed in any such instrument, a note of which intention shall, under an application to be made for that purpose, be entered in the register (*k*).

Powers of proprietor of land.—The proprietor of the land, while in possession has all the powers of leasing and of accepting surrenders of leases conferred by ss. 99 and 100 of the Law of Property Act 1925 (*i*), as extended by the instrument of charge or any instrument varying the terms thereof, but subject to any contrary intention expressed in such instrument, a note of which intention shall, under an application to be made for that purpose, be entered on the register(*l*). Subject as aforesaid all dispositions by the proprietor of the land shall, unless the proprietor of the land concurs in the disposition, take effect subject to any charge registered at the time of the disposition (*m*).

Alteration of charges.—The proprietor of a charge may by deed in the prescribed manner alter the terms of the charge, with the consent of the proprietor of the registered land and of the proprietors of all registered charges (if any) of equal or inferior priority affected

---

(*g*) Application for registration is on Form A 4 or A 5, if as to part of the land charged, which must be accompanied by the charge certificate and the order for foreclosure or an office copy thereof: r. 147. The fee for registration is payable under Schedule, para. VI (7) of the Land Registration Fee Order 1976.

(*h*) The sale must be in Form 31: r. 114. The certificate of the charge under which the sale was effected must accompany the application for registration by the purchaser (which should be under application cover A 4 or A 5, if sale of part), together with an office copy of the order for sale where the sale was by order of the court.

(*i*) See pp. 342 *et seq.*, *infra*.

(*k*) Land Registration Rules 1925, r. 141 (2).

(*l*) *Ibid.*, r. 141 (1).

(*m*) *Ibid.*, r. 141 (4).

by the alteration (*n*). The alteration must be completed by the registrar entering it on the register (*o*).

Transfer of registered charges.—The registered proprietor of a charge or person entitled to be registered (*p*) may, in the prescribed manner, transfer the charge to another person as proprietor (*q*). The transfer is completed by the registrar entering on the register the transferee as proprietor of the charge transferred and the transferor is deemed to remain proprietor of the charge until the name of the transferee is entered on the register in respect thereof (*r*). A registered transferee for valuable consideration is not affected by any irregularity or invalidity in the original charge of which he had not notice when it was transferred to him (*s*). On the registration of the transfer, any subsisting mortgage term or sub-term vests in the mortgagee (*t*).

Sub-charges.—For sub-mortgages of registered charges, see p. 262, *infra*.

Transmission of registered charge on death or bankruptcy.— The personal representative of a deceased sole registered proprietor, or of the survivor of two or more joint registered proprietors, and the trustee in bankruptcy of a bankrupt registered proprietor of any charge, is entitled to be registered as the proprietor in the place of the former proprietor (*u*). Such a person may deal with the charge before he is himself registered as proprietor (*a*).

Any person registered in place of a deceased or bankrupt proprietor holds the charge upon the trusts and for the purposes upon and subject to which the same is applicable by law, and subject to any minor interests, subject to which the deceased or bankrupt proprietor held the same; but, save as aforesaid, he is in all respects (and in particular as respects any registered dealings with such land or charge), in the same

---

(*n*) Land Registration Act 1925, s. 31 (1); Land Registration Rules 9125, r. 150. E.g., where on the creation of a subsequent charge, a prior charge is postponed to it. And see p. 66, *infra*. The making of a further advance where the charge so provides is not an alteration of the charge. For further advances, see p. 460, *infra*. For form of application, see 14 Ency. Forms and Precedents (4th Edn.), pp. 875, 876.

(*o*) Land Registration Act 1925, s. 31 (3).

(*p*) *Ibid.*, s. 37.

(*q*) *Ibid.*, s. 33 (1). Land Registration Rules 1925, r. 153. For forms, see 14 Ency. Forms and Precedents (4th Edn.), pp. 761, 771, 799.

(*r*) Land Registration Act 1925, s. 33 (2); and see p. 63, *supra*, note (c).

(*s*) *Ibid.*, s. 33 (3). Nothing in the Consumer Credit Act 1974 affected the transferee who is the proprietor of a registered charge if he had no notice, or derives title through a person who had no notice of any defect in title arising under that Act: s. 117 of the 1974 Act.

(*t*) *Ibid.*, s. 33 (4), (5). Cf. s. 33 with s. 114 of the Law of Property Act 1925 for unregistered land (p. 252, *infra*). In unregistered land the transferee steps into the shoes of the transferor, but in registered land, on registration of the transfer, the transferee is in the same position as a transferee for valuable consideration of the term or subterm. So, by virtue of s. 23 of the Land Registration Act 1925, the transferee may take free of incumbrances and other matters not protected on the register which bound the transferor, *e.g.*, by estoppel, and thereby be in a better position than the transferor. *Quaere* whether the provisions of s. 114 apply to the transfer of registered charges in so far as that section is not inconsistent with ss. 23 and 33: see p. 463, *infra*.

(*u*) Land Registration Act 1925, ss. 41, 42.

(*a*) *Ibid.*, s. 37. Land Registration Rules 1925, r. 170.

position as if he had taken such land or charge under a transfer for valuable consideration (*b*).

On the registration of any transmission of a charge, any subsisting mortgage term or sub-term vests without assignment in the proprietor for the time being of the charge (*c*). The fact of any person having become entitled to any charge in consequence of the death or bankruptcy of any registered proprietor has to be proved in the prescribed manner (*d*).

Priorities of registered charges—Subject to any entry to the contrary on the register, registered charges on the same land, as between themselves, rank according to the order in which they are entered on the register, and not according to the order in which they are created (*e*).

Charge for securing further advances.—When a registered charge is made for securing further advances, the registrar will enter notice of this on the register, and, before making a subsequent entry on the register which would prejudicially affect the priority of any further advance under the charge, he must give notice to the proprietor of the charge of the intended entry. The proprietor of the charge will not be affected, in respect of any further advance, by such a subsequent entry unless the advance is made after the date when the notice ought to have been received in the ordinary course of post (*f*). If the proprietor of the charge suffers loss in relation to a further advance by reason of any failure on the part of the registrar or the post office he is entitled to indemnity, unless the loss arises by reason of the proprietor's omission to amend his address for service on the register (*g*).

But where the proprietor of a charge is under an obligation, noted on the register, to make a further advance, a subsequent registered charge takes effect subject to any further advance made pursuant to the obligation (*h*).

Deposit of certificate.—The proprietor of registered land or of a registered charge may create a lien on the land or charge by deposit of the land or charge certificate. The Land Registration Act 1925 provides:

> **66.**—The proprietor of any registered land or charge may, subject to the overriding interests, if any, to any entry to the contrary on the register, and to any estates, interests, charges, or rights registered or protected on the register at the date of the deposit, create a lien on the registered land or charge by deposit of the land certificate; and such a lien shall, subject as aforesaid, be equivalent to a lien created in the case of unregistered land by the deposit

---

(*b*) *Ibid.*, s. 43.
(*c*) *Ibid.*, s. 44.
(*d*) *Ibid.*, s. 45; Land Registration Rules 1925, rr. 168-185.
(*e*) Land Registration Act 1925, s. 29. See p. 484, *infra*. But see Agricultural Holdings Act 1948, s. 83 (5); Improvement of Land Act 1864, s. 59. And see p. 166, *infra*.
(*f*) *Ibid.*, s. 30 (1). Notice is given by registered post or the recorded delivery service. For the changes proposed by the Land Commission, see Working Paper No. 67 (1976), pp. 66 *et seq.*
(*g*) *Ibid.*, s. 30 (2).
(*h*) *Ibid.*, s. 30 (3), inserted by Law of Property (Amendment) Act 1926, s. 5; *cf.* Law of Property Act 1925, s. 94 (see p. 459, *infra*).

of documents of title or of the mortgage deed by an owner entitled for his own benefit to the registered estate, or a mortgagee beneficially entitled to the mortgage, as the case may be.

The section probably envisages a simple deposit of the certificate without any accompanying documentation. Where a security of this nature is taken, it may be protected by the creditor giving notice (*i*) of deposit to the Land Registry. On receipt of the notice, the registrar enters notice of the deposit in the Charges Register (*k*), and the notice operates as a caution under s. 54 of the Act (*l*). This method of protection has been considered to be appropriate where the deposit does not itself create the security, *e.g.*, where it accompanies a memorandum by way of equitable mortgage (*m*), or even a legal mortgage (*n*).

Where the depositor is a transferee the certificate must first be sent to the Registry for the registration of the transfer before it can be deposited. A notice of *intended* deposit should be given by the depositor in this case (*o*).

The effect of the entry of the notice of deposit or intended deposit is that the creditor is entitled to have notice, and to be heard before any subsequent dealing is registered (*p*). A caution gives protection to the cautioner in that it gives notice of his interest (*q*).

There is no express provision in the Land Registration Act as to priorities where the charges are not registered charges. As the depositee has the land certificate, he can effectively prevent any subsequent charge being registered (since such subsequent chargee could not lodge the certificate with his application (*r*)), and notice of deposit will give him priority to a subsequent equitable charge or interest protected by caution (*s*).

There is no express provision as regards the powers of sale, etc., of other than the proprietor of a registered charge (*t*). A simple depositee under s. 66 would have no power of sale without an order of the Court.

(*i*) Land Registration Rules 1925, r. 239. Notice is given on printed form 85A and is accompanied by the land or charge certificate. No fee is payable: Land Registration Fee Order 1976, para 5 (iv).

(*k*) No notice of deposit or intended deposit may be entered while another such notice is on the register, nor as to part only of the land or charge to which the certificate relates: Land Registration Rules, 1925, r. 243.

(*l*) Land Registration Rules, 1925, r. 239 (4). And so may be warned off: cf. the special caution under s. 106 (*infra*). On the nature of cautionable interests, see (1971) 35 Conv. (N.S.) 21 (S. Robinson).

(*m*) *Re White Rose Cottage*, [1965] Ch. 940 (C.A.), at p. 955, *per* Harman, L. J.; [1965] 1 All E.R. 11 at pp. 14–15. On this case generally, see (1966) 19 Current Legal Problems 26 (E. C. Ryder).

(*n*) *Barclays Bank, Ltd.* v. *Taylor*, [1973] Ch. 63; [1972] 2 All E.R. 752; reversed [1974] Ch. 137 (C.A.); [1973] 1 All E.R. 752.

(*o*) Land Registration Rules 1925, r. 240. Printed form 85C should be used. The notice of intended deposit operates as a caution: r. 242.

(*p*) Land Registration Act 1925, s. 55 and rr. 218, 219, 220.

(*q*) See *Re White Rose Cottage*, [1965] Ch. 940 (C.A.), at pp. 949, 950; [1965] 1 All E.R. 11, at p. 14; *Parkash* v. *Irani Finance, Ltd.*, [1970] Ch. 101; [1969] 1 All E.R. 930.

(*r*) See note (*l*), p. 60, *supra*.

(*s*) *Re White Rose Cottage, infra*; *Barclays Bank, Ltd.* v. *Taylor, supra*, in the Court of Appeal where it seems that the prior unregistered mortgage would have had priority, as the prior minor interest, even without the registration of the notice of deposit. For priorities, see p. 70, *infra*.

(*t*) See p. 63, *supra*.

Accordingly, a deposit should be accompanied by a memorandum under seal or other deed in order to give the depositee the statutory power of sale (*u*). But the power of sale by itself will not be enough to enable the depositee to effect a sale. Section 110 (5) of the Land Registration Act 1925 enables the purchaser of registered land to insist on the vendor's registration as proprietor of the charge under which he is selling or a sale by the proprietor of the land. Accordingly the deeds should be in the form previously mentioned (*a*), incorporating a power of attorney and undertaking to execute a registered charge. The depositee will be able to make a transfer under the power of attorney (*b*).

Mortgages off the register.—A mortgage off the register may be created as follows:

> **106.**—(1) The proprietor of any registered land may, subject to any entry to the contrary on the register, mortgage, by deed or otherwise (*c*), the land or any part thereof in any manner which would have been permissible if the land had not been registered, and with the like effect: Provided that the registered land comprised in the mortgage is described (whether by reference to the register or in any other manner) in such a way as is sufficient to enable the registrar to identify the same without reference to any other document.

Such mortgages may be either unregistered legal mortgages, whether or not with deposit of certificate, or equitable mortgages, whether or not with deposit of certificate.

Until protected by caution or notice mortgages created off the register take effect only in equity and as minor interests will be overridden by a disposition for valuable consideration (*d*).

Protection by caution.—Section 106 of the Land Registration Act 1925, continues:—

> (2) A mortgage made under this section may, if by deed, be protected by a caution in a specially prescribed form (*e*) and in no other way (*f*), and if not by deed, by a caution (*g*).

(*u*) See p. 45, *supra*.

(*a*) See p. 50, *supra*. Where there is a deposit and a memorandum it is a question of construction which creates a security (see *Re White Rose Cottage, supra*), and the method of protection may vary depending upon whether the deposit alone is the security (*i.e.*, only a s. 66 situation) or the memorandum supported by the deposit is the security (protection by notice of deposit, caution or ordinary notice).

(*b*) For production to the Registry of the power of attorney where an instrument is executed by attorney, see Land Registration (Powers of Attorney) Rules 1971 (*inter alia*, if the transaction is completed within 12 months of the power coming into operation, no evidence of non-revocation need be produced to the Registrar).

Alternatively, he could insist on his right to the execution of a registered charge, become registered proprietor and then sell as a registered chargee.

(*c*) There *should* be a deed (thus giving the mortgage the statutory powers) or an instrument including a power of attorney and undertaking: see *supra*.

(*d*) Land Registration Act 1925, ss. 101 (2), 106 (4).

(*e*) Land Registration Rules 1925, r. 223. The caution is entered in the Proprietorship Register. It cannot be warned off: r. 225.

(*f*) *Barclays Bank, Ltd.* v. *Taylor*, [1973] Ch. 63; [1973] 2 All E.R. 752. (The point was not dealt with by the Court of Appeal). That case concerned the practice of banks having a mortgage, whether legal or equitable (with a right to call for a legal mortgage), and deposit of protecting their interests by notice of deposit and thus, in the case of a legal mortgage, saving the borrower the *ad valorem* fee on substantive registration as a registered charge. GOULDING, J., held that where there was a mortgage off the register by deed the only method of protection was the special caution. The decision was contrary to the Land Registry practice and *Re White Rose Cottage, supra*, and criticised

The caution in the specially prescribed form is called a mortgage caution. It may be converted into substantive registration under s. 106 (5) and for that reason the procedure may be limited to legal mortgages (*h*). Until *Barclays Bank, Ltd.* v. *Taylor* (*f*), the procedure was considered obsolescent (*i*) and in the light of the Court of Appeal's decision will, hopefully, remain so. The mortgage cautioner must lodge the land certificate with his application and the fee is the same as for substantive registration. There is, therefore, no advantage in registering a mortgage caution over substantive registration. Ordinary caution is the normal method of protecting equitable mortgages (*k*). It seems that between mortgages or interests protected by caution, priority depends on the order in which the cautions are lodged (*l*).

Protection by registration as land charge.—Section 48 of the Land Registration Act 1925, provides for the registration of notice of a lease and s. 49 provides for the extension of the provisions of the foregoing section to provide for notices of other rights, interests and claims, including land charges until the land charge is registered as a registered charge (*m*). A land charge means a land charge of any class described in s. 2 of the Land Charges Act 1972 or a local land charge (*n*). Accordingly a puisne mortgage (*o*) and general equitable charge (*p*) of registered land may be protected by notice under s. 49 if the land certificate can be produced (*q*). It appears also that an equitable charge protected by deposit of the land certificate (*r*) may also be so protected (*s*).

Where a charge is protected by a notice of this kind it means that every subsequent proprietor or incumbrancer is deemed to be effected with notice of the charge (*t*).

Transfer of protected mortgages.—Transfer is effected in the usual way for unregistered land (*u*). The devolution of the title to the

---

(see, e.g., (1972) 88 L.Q.R. 476 (D. Jackson)), and reversed by the Court of Appeal [1974] Ch. 137; [1973] 1 All E.R. 752 (though the point in question was not expressly dealt with, but the practical effect of that Court's decision is, it is submitted, that the possession of the land certificate will give the depositee all the protection it needs). One way of dealing with s. 106 is to limit it to mortgages made *only* by deed, i.e., without deposit, and where there is a deed and a deposit (whether it be the deposit or the deed which is treated as the security) rely on the authorities referred to above for the effectiveness of a notice of deposit.

(*g*) Under s. 54. Or, if there is no deed, but a deposit, by notice of deposit: *Re White Rose Cottage, supra.*
(*h*) See p. 61, *supra.*
(*i*) See Ruoff & Roper, *Registered Conveyancing* (3rd Edn.), p. 133.
(*k*) Or, where, as will usually be the case, there is a deposit, notice under r. 239; see p. 67, *supra.*
(*l*) See *per* DENNING, M. R., in *Re White Rose Cottage*, [1965] Ch. 940, at p. 949; [1965] 1 All E.R. 11, at p. 14. Subject to the Registrar's direction under r. 220 (3). For priorities, see p. 432, *infra.*
(*m*) The extension was made by r. 190.
(*n*) Land Registration Act 1925, s. 3 (ix), as substituted by Local Land Charges Act 1975, s. 17, Sched. 1.
(*o*) See p. 443, *infra.*
(*p*) See p. 443, *infra.* But see now *Barclays Bank, Ltd.* v. *Taylor, supra.*
(*q*) Land Registration Act 1925, s. 64.
(*r*) As to whether this constitutes an estate contract, see p. 52, *supra.*
(*s*) *Re White Rose Cottage, supra. Sed quaere*, see (1966), 19 Current Legal Problems, pp. 24, 35. The protection may be under s. 49 (1) (*f*) and r. 190 where an equitable charge by deed is protected by deposit: see Hayton, *Registered Land*, see p. 135.
(*t*) Land Registration Act 1925, s. 52.   (*u*) See Ch. 14, *infra.*

mortgage does not appear on the register. If the mortgage is protected by caution a fresh caution should be lodged by the transferee and a withdrawal of the existing caution procured (*a*). No further step is required when the mortgage is noted.

Registered charges of settled land.—The proprietor of settled land which is registered and all other necessary parties, if any, shall, on the request, and at the expense of any person entitled to an estate, interest, or charge conveyed or created for securing money actually raised at the date of such request, charge the land in the prescribed manner with the payment of money so raised, but so long as the estate, interest or charge is capable of being overridden under the Settled Land Act 1925, or the Law of Property Act 1925, no charge can be created or registered (*b*).

Mortgages of equitable interests in registered land.—Such interests are minor interests and as such are not capable of being disposed of by registered dispositions and are capable of being overridden (*c*). Such interests may be disposed of off the register (*d*) and priorities as between minor interests is regulated by the order of priority cautions entered in the Minor Interests Index (*e*).

Floating charge over registered land.—Such a charge may be protected by notice (*f*), provided the land certificate can be produced (*g*) Otherwise it can only be protected by caution (*h*).

Equitable charge of registered land.—Such a charge is a minor interest capable of taking effect in equity only and capable of being overridden by the proprietor of the land unless protected (*c*). It may be protected by caution (*h*).

Second mortgage of registered land (*i*).—If the prior charge has been registered, the land certificate will have been deposited at the Registry (*k*) and a second mortgage, if a legal mortgage (*l*), can be registered and a charge certificate in respect thereof will be issued. For the priorities of registered charges, see p. 66, *supra*. If the prior mortgage was by way of deposit of the land certificate, this will be held by the depositee, and, since the second mortgagee will not be able to deposit the land certificate at the registry (*m*), the second mortgage can only be protected by caution (*n*) or notice (*o*).

(*a*) Under Land Registration Rules 1925, r. 222.
(*b*) Land Registration Act 1925, s. 90. See further, Ruoff and Roper, *Registered Conveyancing* (3rd Edn.), 398–9.
(*c*) *Ibid.*, s. 3 (xv).
(*d*) *Ibid.*, s. 101 (1).
(*e*) *Ibid.*, s. 101 (2); Land Registration Rules 1925, r. 229.
(*f*) Land Registration Act 1925, s. 49 (1) (f); Land Registration Rules 1925, r. 190.
(*g*) Land Registration Act 1925, s. 64. For registration of company charges, see pp. 181 *et seq.*, *infra*.
(*h*) Under Land Registration Act 1925, s. 54.
(*i*) For forms, see 14 Ency. Forms and Precedents (4th Edn.), 198–201.
(*k*) Land Registration Act 1925, s. 65.
(*l*) See p. 61, *supra*.
(*m*) See footnote (*l*) on p. 60.
(*n*) See pp. 62, 63, 67. See p. 68, *supra*, for the problem as to mortgages by deed off the register.
(*o*) Under Land Registration Act 1925, s. 49 (1) (c). This is so, unless the notice is withdrawn by virtue of the provisions of r. 246: see Ruoff and Roper, *Registered Conveyancing* (3rd Edn.), 586–9, 748–9; and (1962), 26 Conv. (N.S.) 169 (H. J. Hartwig).

The effect of protection by notice of deposit or ordinary notice is to give priority to the prior mortgage (*p*). But where the prior mortgage has not been protected by notice there is nothing in the Land Registration Act or Rules to indicate which has priority or whether actual notice is relevant (*q*). It would seem that if a subsequent mortgage is protected before a prior mortgage is protected by notice the subsequent mortgage has priority even where the subsequent mortgagee had actual notice of the prior mortgage.

Discharge of mortgages of registered land.—For this topic, see pp. 553 *et seq., infra.*

Lost charge certificate.—A new land or charge certificate may be issued in place of one lost (*r*). Where it is proved to the satisfaction of the registrar that a certificate has been lost or destroyed, or that it is in the possession of a person out of the jurisdiction of the court or its production cannot be obtained without undue delay or expense, he may issue a new one, after taking such indemnities as he may consider necessary, and after giving such public notice in the *Gazette* and in such local or other newspapers (if any) and in such manner as shall appear to him sufficient in each case (*s*).

(*p*) See pp. 67, 69, *supra.*
(*q*) See *Re White Rose Cottage*, [1964] Ch. 483, at p. 492; [1964] 1 All E.R. 169, at p. 175; reversed, [1965] Ch. 940 (C.A.); [1965] 1 All E.R. 11.
(*r*) Land Registration Act 1925, s. 67.
(*s*) Land Registration Rules 1925, r. 271 (1).

CHAPTER 4

Mortgages of Chattels

I—MORTGAGES OF PERSONAL CHATTELS GENERALLY [(a)]

A—MORTGAGES OF PERSONAL CHATTELS

Generally.—Personal chattels may be the subject of securities, for the validity of which no instrument in writing is necessary (b), and which may be made either by mortgage or by pledge. Mortgages of chattels may be legal or equitable. A legal mortgage of chattels passes the property in the goods to the mortgagee, subject to redemption. Where the goods are already mortgaged or pledged, a second mortgage of them (i.e., of the equity of redemption in them) is as good as it is in the case of land (c). Like other mortgages it may be made subject to a condition; and, unlike the case of a pledge, the possession of the creditor is not necessary for its validity (d). For many years it was considered fraudulent for the debtor to continue in possession of the mortgaged goods, since he was thereby invested with a delusive credit arising out of such possession. It was held in Twyne's Case (e), soon after the passing of the statute against fraudulent deeds and alienations (f), that such possession was within the mischief aimed at by the Act. That rule still holds good in the case of absolute bills of sale, but the continuance of the grantor in possession under a bona fide conditional bill of sale given by way of security only, when consistent with the deed, is no longer regarded as even prima facie evidence of fraud (g).

(a) The second section of this chapter is merely an outline of the law relating to bills of sale. The complicated requirements of the Bills of Sale Acts (failure to observe which may invalidate the bill) make bills of sale unattractive to leanders and the requirements of registration of bills makes them unattractive to borrowers. There are approximately 8,000 registrations annually. Further reference should be made to 4 Halsbury's Laws (4th Edn.), Bills of Sale; Goode, Hire-Purchase Law and Practice (2nd Edn.), Ch. 4; the Report of the Committee on Consumer Credit (Crowther Report) 1971 Cmnd. 4596.

(b) Reeves v. Capper (1838), 5 Bing. N.C. 136; Flory v. Denny (1852), 7 Ex. 581; and see United Forty Pound Loan Club v. Bexton, [1891] 1 Q.B. 28, n. But if the mortgage is in writing it is subject to the statutory provisions affecting bills of sale (unless within an exception thereto), as to which, see infra. Writing will be necessary if the security relates to a regulated agreement under the Consumer Credit Act 1974 (as to which, see 132, infra) and the security is not given by the debtor himself: Consumer Credit Act 1974, s. 105 (6).

(c) Usher & Co. v. Martin (1889), 24 Q.B.D. 272.

(d) Maugham v. Sharpe (1864), 17 C.B. N.S. 443.

(e) (1602), 3 Co. Rep. 80 b.

(d) 13 Eliz. I, c. 5 (1571). Now Law of Property Act 1925, s. 172 (see p. 230, infra).

(g) Pennell v. Dawson (1856), 18 C.B. 355; Hale v. Metropolitan Saloon Omnibus Co. (1859), 28 L.J. Ch. 777.

A mortgage of chattels which is made in writing, is, with certain exceptions (see p. 79, *infra*), the most important of which is when the mortgagor is a company (*h*), subject to the provisions of the Bills of Sale Acts. Certain securities will be subject to the formalities prescribed by the Consumer Credit Act 1974 and regulations made thereunder (*i*).

Provision for possession till default.—A proviso that the mortgagor of goods shall remain in possession till default operates as a re-demise by the mortgagee, who cannot sue for the goods till default has been made, or until the expiration of the time limited, when notice for payment is to be given upon default, and the mortgagor may maintain an action for interference with his possession during the term (see also p. 279, *infra*). Such a proviso, however, will not prevent the mortgagee from exercising an express power to take possession on the happening of other contingencies, though no default has been made. In the case of a bill of sale by way of security the grantee may only take possession on the statutory grounds. The re-demise entitles the mortgagor only to the use of the chattels, and if he or his trustee in bankruptcy sells them during the term, it will be a disclaimer of the tenancy, and the mortgagee or his assignees may sue in respect of the conversion (*k*). There may, however, be an express or implied licence to the mortgagor to deal with the goods in the way of his trade. So long as he does so, a bona fide purchaser from him will be protected. Otherwise, the sale will be bad, despite the bona fides of the purchaser (*l*). If there be an express right to make use of the goods, though a licence to consume such of them as are perishable may be implied, they cannot be sold or otherwise dealt with as if there had been no grant (*m*).

Chattels not yet in existence.—It is not necessary for the validity of a mortgage of chattels that the mortgagor should be aware of their exact nature (*n*). He may even, subject, where appropriate, to the provisions of the Bills of Sale Acts (*o*), create a valid security upon personal property not yet in existence, provided he has an interest, actual or potential, in the source from which the property may arise (*p*).

(*h*) Chattel mortgages by companies are increasingly common: see Goode, *Hire-Purchase Law and Practice* (2nd Edn.), Ch. 4; (1970) 120 New L.J. 1083; (1971) 121 New L.J. 291 (R. W. Ramage).

(*i*) See p. 132, *infra*.

(*k*) *Fenn* v. *Bittleston* (1851), 7 Exch. 152; *Brierly* v. *Kendall* (1852), 17 Q.B. 937.

(*l*) *National Mercantile Bank* v. *Hampson* (1880), 5 Q.B.D. 177; *Payne* v. *Fern* (1881), 6 Q.B.D. 620.

(*m*) *Gale* v. *Burnell* (1845), 7 Q.B. 850.

(*n*) *Re Beattie, Ex parte Kelsall* (1846), De G. 352.

(*o*) Chattels which are not yet in existence do not fall within the category of "personal chattels", as defined in the Bills of Sale Acts, since they are not "capable of complete transfer by delivery": *Brantom* v. *Griffits* (1877), 2 C.P.D. 212 (C.A.); *Thomas* v. *Kelly* (1888), 13 App. Cas. 506 (H.L.), at p. 518, *per* Lord MACNAGHTEN. But see the cases cited in 4 Halsbury's Laws (4th Edn.), para. 610, note 1, especially *Re Reis, Ex parte Clough*, [1904] 2 K.B. 769, 788; also Sykes, *The Law of Securities* (2nd Edn.), pp. 472 et seq.

(*p*) See, *e.g.*, *Langton* v. *Horton* (1842), 1 Hare 549. However, mortgages which are confined to after-acquired chattels and not, therefore, executed under the Bills of Sale Acts, appear to be wholly outside the provisions of the Acts, and to be valid, provided that they conform with the equitable doctrine described *infra*. For the difference between a chattel mortgage and a floating charge, see *Re Zegalski* (1972), 31 D.L.R. (3d), 766.

Incomplete chattels.—An incomplete chattel may be the subject of a security comprising a contract to complete it, and to assign the materials appropriated for its completion, and the chattel when finished (*q*).

Future acquired property.—An assignment of chattels not in the mortgagor's possession at the date of the assignment will, if there is a sufficiently specific (*r*) description of them, operate to transfer an equitable title as soon as the property is acquired by the assignor (*s*). If, however, future acquired chattels are included in a security bill of existing chattels, the validity of such document is affected by s. 9 of the Bills of Sale Act (1878) Amendment Act 1882, which requires every security bill to be made in accordance with the statutory form, and s. 5 of that Act which requires the grantor to be the true owner of the chattels at the time of the execution of the bill. In *Thomas* v. *Kelly* (*t*) it was held that such inclusion avoids the whole bill of sale. But if the reference to future acquired chattels occurs only in the schedule (see p. 89, *infra*), the bill is void only in respect of the future acquired chattels; moreover, the bill is valid even in respect of them as between mortgagor and mortgagee (*u*).

B—EFFECT OF MORTGAGE ON FIXTURES

Fixtures passing by mortgage of land (*a*).—A mortgage of land (*b*) comprises, without express mention, and subject to any contrary intention, all fixtures which at the date of the mortgage are, or at any time afterwards during its continuance may be, annexed to the land (*c*), whether or not they are trade fixtures or removable as between landlord and tenant. Fixtures passing by a mortgage of land will not pass to the trustee in bankruptcy of the mortgagor (*d*).

The general rule is unaffected by the Bills of Sale Acts, except when fixtures are the subject of a separate security distinct from the security in the land. When separately assigned or charged, fixtures

---

(*q*) *Woods* v. *Russell* (1822), 5 B. & Ald. 942; *Reid* v. *Fairbanks* (1853), 13 C.B. 692.

(*r*) As to the meaning of "specific", see *Tailby* v. *Official Receiver* (1888), 13 App. Cas. 523 (H.L.); and *Syrett* v. *Egerton*, [1957] 3 All E.R. 331. See also *King* v. *Greig*, [1931] V.L.R. 413 (re sale of unascertained part of defined whole); *Re Wait*, [1927] 1 Ch. 606 (C.A.).

(*s*) *Holroyd* v. *Marshall* (1862), 10 H.L. Cas. 191. The equitable title relies on the possibility of a decree of specific performance of a contract to assign. See, generally, Sykes, *The Law of Securities* (2nd Edn.), pp. 446–451.

(*t*) See footnote (*o*), *supra*.

(*u*) Bills of Sale Act (1878) Amendment Act 1882, ss. 4, 5, 6.

(*a*) See generally, as to fixtures, 23 Halsbury's Laws (3rd Edn.), pp. 489 *et seq.*; and Megarry and Wade, *The Law of Real Property* (4th Edn.), 711 *et seq.*; and p. 36, *supra*.

(*b*) Whether legal or equitable (see *Re Lusty, Ex parte Lusty* v. *Official Receiver* (1889), 60 L.T. 160), and whether of freeholds or leaseholds (see *Meux* v. *Jacobs* (1875), L.R. 7 H.L. 481; *Southport and West Lancashire Banking Co.* v. *Thompson* (1887), 37 Ch. D. 64 (C.A.)).

(*c*) *Mather* v. *Fraser* (1856), 2 K. & J. 536; *Walmsley* v. *Milne* (1859), 7 C.B. N.S. 115; *Longbottom* v. *Berry* (1869), L.R. 5 Q.B. 123; *Holland* v. *Hodgson* (1872), L.R. 7 C.P. 328; *Smith* v. *Maclure* (1884), 32 W.R. 459; *Reynolds* v. *Ashby & Son*, [1904] A.C. 466 (H.L.); *Ellis* v. *Glover and Hobson*, [1908] 1 K.B. 388 (C.A.); *Vaudeville Electric Cinema* v. *Muriset*, [1923] 2 Ch. 74; *Hulme* v. *Brigham*, [1943] 1 K.B. 152; [1943] 1 All E.R. 204. As to the power of sale in relation to fixtures, see p. 361, *infra*.

(*d*) *Clark* v. *Crownshaw* (1832), 3 B. & Ad. 804.

are "personal chattels" within the Acts (e) though not for other purposes (f); but not, except in the case of trade machinery, when conveyed or assigned together with a freehold or leasehold interest in any land or building to which they are affixed (g).

Where, however, trade fixtures customarily belong to the tenant of the mortgagor, the mortgagee cannot claim them as against the tenant (h). A mortgagor while in possession may permit trade fixtures to be put up and removed, so long as he does not either materially diminish the mortgagee's security, or commit a breach of some express stipulation in the mortgage (i); the right of removal ceases when possession is taken by the mortgagee. But the exception as to trade fixtures in favour of a tenant does not apply in the case of fixtures erected on the mortgaged premises under a hire-purchase agreement on the terms that, until paid for, they shall remain the property of the owner who supplied them. In such cases, if the mortgage is a legal mortgage and the mortgagee had no notice of the hire purchase agreement (k), or the latter was made later than the mortgage, the title of the mortgagee will prevail over that of the owner by virtue of his legal title unless the mortgagee has acquiesced in their removal (l). Where, however, the mortgage is an equitable mortgage, and is given after the hire-purchase agreement, then, even if the mortgagee takes without notice of it, his title is postponed to that of the owner (m).

Before the Bills of Sale Act 1878, a grantee by bill of sale of fixtures annexed to mortgaged premises had no title against the mortgagee (n), and this appears still to be the law (o). A mortgage of land which passes fixtures without mentioning them is not a bill of sale (p).

(e) *Climpson* v. *Coles* (1889), 23 Q.B.D. 465. Agricultural charges on tenants' fixtures are excepted from the Bills of Sale Acts: Agricultural Credits Act 1928, s. 8 (1); Agricultural Marketing Act 1958, s. 15 (5).

(f) *Meux* v. *Jacobs* (1875), L.R. 7 H.L. 481.

(g) Bills of Sale Act 1878, s. 4. See also s. 7. As to personal chattels for the purposes of the Bills of Sale Acts, see p. 82, *infra*.

(h) *Sanders* v. *Davis* (1885), 15 Q.B.D. 218.

(i) *Ellis* v. *Glover and Hobson, Ltd.*, *supra*.

(k) *Re Samuel Allen & Sons, Ltd.*, [1907] 1 Ch. 575. But see footnote (m), *infra*.

(l) *Hobson* v. *Gorringe*, [1897] 1 Ch. 182 (C.A.), distinguishing *Cumberland Union Banking Co.* v. *Maryport Hematite Iron and Steel Co.*, [1892] 1 Ch. 415; *Gough* v. *Wood*, [1894] 1 Q.B. 713 (C.A.); *Reynolds* v. *Ashby & Son, Ltd.*, *supra*; *Lyon & Co.* v. *London City and Midland Bank*, [1903] 2 K.B. 135. But see footnote (m), *infra*.

(m) *Re Samuel Allen & Sons, Ltd.*, [1907] 1 Ch. 575; *Re Morrison, Jones and Taylor, Ltd.*, [1914] 1 Ch. 50 (C.A.).

Where a hire purchase agreement entitles the owner to enter and seize on default, etc., the owner has an equitable interest in the land to which the fixture is attached: *Gough* v. *Wood & Co.*, [1894] 1 Q.B. 713 (C.A.), at p. 722; *Hobson* v. *Gorringe*, [1897] 1 Ch. 182 (C.A.), at p. 192; *Reynolds* v. *Ashby & Son, Ltd.*, *supra*. Such an interest does not appear to be registrable either as a land charge of Class C (iii), s. 4, Land Charges Act 1972—general equitable charge—or under Class C (iv)—estate contract or under Class D (iii)—equitable easement, right or privilege: see *Poster* v. *Slough Estates, Ltd.*, [1969] Ch. 495; [1968] 3 All E.R. 257; *Shiloh Spinners, Ltd.* v. *Harding*, [1973] A.C. 691 (H.L.), [1973] 1 All E.R. 90. See generally (1963), 27 Conv. (N.S.) 30 (A. G. Guest and J. Lever). Nor would the interest seem to be capable of protection under the Land Registration Act 1925. The matter of hire-purchase agreement and fixtures is expressly covered by Australian state legislation.

(n) *Longbottom* v. *Berry* (1869), L.R. 5 Q.B. 123.

(o) *Reynolds* v. *Ashby & Son, Ltd.*, *supra*.

(p) *Meux* v. *Jacobs*, *supra*.

Fixtures not passing.—The general rule as to fixtures is subject to qualifications arising out of the terms of the security. Thus, if two kinds of property are mortgaged, and the fixtures are expressly included in one of them, the principle *expressio unius est exclusio alterius* may exclude the fixtures annexed to the other (*q*). The bare enumeration of specific fixtures in the mortgaged property will not rebut the inference that all fixtures were intended to pass (*r*). Again, if it is the custom of the place that fixed machinery which can be removed without injury to the freehold should be so removed, and it has been treated between the parties as separate from the land and unaffected by the mortgage, such machinery may be held not to pass by a mortgage of the buildings and machinery (*s*).

Loose parts of fixtures.—With any fixture will pass, without any special mention, whatever, though accidentally detached from it, or not of its own nature a fixture, may be essential for the proper employment of the machine or fixed article of which it forms part, even though it is more or less capable of use in a detached state (*t*). The same rule is also applicable in the case of machinery not of a fixed kind (*u*). And on the same principle a mortgage of a ship at sea with its tackle and appurtenances will pass a chronometer then on board belonging to the owner of the ship (*a*).

The separation of chattels from land.—As previously stated fixtures are personal chattels within the Bills of Sale Acts when separately assigned or charged apart from the land (*b*). The problem arose, whether the Bills of Sale Acts should apply when a mortgage of an interest in land specifically mentions fixtures. Section 7 of the Act of 1878 states that fixtures are not to be deemed to be separately mortgaged merely because they are assigned by separate words or that power is given to sever them from the land or building to which they are affixed, without otherwise taking possession of, or dealing with, such land or building, if by the same instrument any freehold or leasehold interest in the land or building to which such fixtures are affixed is also conveyed or assigned to the same persons or person. The effect of ss. 4 and 7 of the 1878 Act is that a mortgage of fixtures is not a bill of sale of personal chattels unless the instrument specifically creates a mortgage of the fixtures apart from the land. The court will examine whether the instrument empowers the mortgagee to realise his security in the fixtures separately from his security in the land (*c*). Of course, a mortgage of fixtures by an instrument dealing with them alone is a bill of sale. If, on its true construction, the security constitutes a mortgage of land and of fixtures separately as

---

(*q*) See, *e.g.*, *Hare* v. *Horton* (1833), 5 B. & Ad. 715. But *quaere* whether this would not be too refined a distinction to be followed now.

(*r*) *Mather* v. *Fraser* (1856), 2 K. & J. 536.

(*s*) *Trappes* v. *Harter* (1833), 2 Cr. & M. 153; *cf. Whitmore* v. *Empson* (1857), 23 Beav. 313.

(*t*) *Place* v. *Fagg* (1829), 4 Man. & Ry. K.B. 277; *Mather* v. *Fraser*, *supra*.

(*u*) *Re Richards, Ex parte Astbury, Ex parte Lloyd's Banking Co.* (1869), 4 Ch. App. 630.

(*a*) *Langton* v. *Horton* (1842), 1 Hare 549.

(*b*) Bills of Sale Act 1878, s. 4.

(*c*) *Re Yates, Batcheldor* v. *Yates* (1888), 38 Ch. D. 112 (C.A.).

chattels, the mortgage of the latter is a bill of sale, and, if not in proper form, is void in respect of the chattels. The mortgagee cannot set up any title to the fixtures on the basis of the mortgage of the land (*d*). In such cases the question is essentially one of construction (*e*). Fixtures may be separately assigned though other goods are assigned with them (*f*).

II—THE EFFECT OF THE BILLS OF SALE ACTS

The Acts.—The registration of bills of sale was introduced by the Bills of Sale Act 1854, and by the Bills of Sale Act 1866, renewal of registration was required every five years. These Acts were repealed, and bills of sale are now regulated by the Bills of Sale Act 1878, called the principal Act, and the Bills of Sale Act (1878) Amendment Act 1882, generally called the amending Act. The Act of 1882 (which relates exclusively to bills of sale given by way of security for money) so completely revolutionised the law of mortgage of personal chattels that, for the purpose of this work, it is really more important than the Act of 1878. The Bills of Sale Act 1890, as amended by the Bills of Sale Act 1891, merely exempted certain commercial hypothecations from the operation of the Acts of 1878 and 1882.

Difference in objects of Acts.—The Bills of Sale Acts 1854 and 1878, were intended to prevent credit being given to people allowed to remain in possession of goods which apparently are theirs, the ownership of which they have surrendered.

As distinct from the "principal" Act of 1878, the purpose of the "amending" Act of 1882 was to prevent needy persons from being entrapped into signing complicated documents which they might often be unable to understand, and so being subjected by their creditors to the enforcement of harsh and unreasonable provisions (*g*). With this object in view, a particular form of words was insisted on, which should plainly express the nature of the contract as to the loan and the security for the loan.

The amending Act, which, so far as is consistent with the tenor thereof, is to be construed as one with the principal Act, does not apply to bills of sale given otherwise than by way of security for the payment of money, limiting, to this extent, the partial repeal of the principal Act.

Two classes of bills of sale have thus been created. The first

---

(*d*) *Johns* v. *Ware*, [1899] 1 Ch. 359.

(*e*) Trade machinery (except fixed motive powers, etc.) is deemed to be personal chattels by s. 5 of the Act of 1878. The courts have not interpreted ss. 4 and 5 of the 1878 Act as excepting trade fixtures from the general rule that fixtures pass with a mortgage of land unless a contrary intention appears. Accordingly for the Acts to apply the mortgage must show an intention that the machinery is to be dealt with separately as chattels or by conferring on the mortgagee an express power to sell the machinery separately: see *Re Yates, Batcheldor* v. *Yates, supra*; *Small* v. *National Provincial Bank of England*, [1894] 1 Ch. 686; *Re Brooke, Brooke* v. *Brooke*, [1894] 2 Ch. 600.

(*f*) *Roberts* v. *Roberts* (1884), 13 Q.B.D. 794.

(*g*) *Manchester, Sheffield and Lincolnshire Rail. Co.* v. *North Central Wagon Co.* (1888), 13 App. Cas. 554 (H.L.), 560.

comprises absolute bills of sale, to which the principal Act continues to apply; and the second comprises bills of sale given to secure the payment of money, with respect to which both Acts are to be construed together.

The operation of the Act of 1882, like that of the Act of 1878, is restricted to bills of sale whereby the holder or grantee has power, either with or without notice, and either immediately or at any future time, to seize or take possession of any personal chattels comprised in or made subject to such bill of sale (*h*).

Bills of Sale Acts affect documents only.—The Bills of Sale Acts affect documents and not transactions (*i*) and they do not apply where the possession of goods passes. Hence pledges (*k*) and liens (*l*), not depending on written documents, are outside the Acts altogether, even when accompanied by collateral instruments regulating the rights of the parties (*i*). They do not require that any transaction shall be put into writing, but they do require that if a transaction is put into writing, and is of a particular character, it shall be registered (*m*). If the real bargain between the parties is reduced into writing, the Bills of Sale Acts apply to the written contract (*n*). If, however, the bargain is complete without any writing, so that the property intended to be dealt with passes independently, the Acts have no application to a document referring to or confirming the transaction (*o*); and the fact that such a document is drawn up, and is not registered, does not invalidate the transaction.

Not every instrument which creates a security on personal chattels for the payment of money necessarily falls within the provisions of the Acts. To bring such an instrument within the Acts it must (1) be a bill of sale within the statutory definition; and (2) relate to personal chattels within the statutory definition. Moreover, the Acts specially exempt certain classes of bills of sale from their operation; and in addition to the statutory exemptions the decisions of the courts have exempted certain other instruments not specially mentioned in the Acts.

Definition of a bill of sale.—A bill of sale has been described as an instrument in writing whereby one transfers to another the property he has in goods or chattels; or as a document given with respect to the transfer of goods or chattels used in cases where possession is not intended to be given (*p*). The Act of 1878 (*q*) declares that the expression "bill of sale" shall, unless there be something in the subject

---

(*h*) Bills of Sale Act 1878, s. 3.
(*i*) *Manchester, Sheffield and Lincolnshire Rail. Co.* v. *North Central Wagon Co.*, *supra.*
(*k*) *Re Hardwick, Ex parte Hubbard* (1886), 17 Q.B.D. 690.
(*l*) *Re Vulcan Ironworks Co.*, [1888] W.N. 37.
(*m*) *United Forty Pound Loan Club* v. *Bexton*, [1891] 1 Q.B. 28, n.
(*n*) *Newlove* v. *Shrewsbury* (1888), 21 Q.B.D. 41 (C.A.).
(*o*) *Ramsay* v. *Margrett*, [1894] 2 Q.B. 18 (C.A.), at p. 23, *per* Lord ESHER, M.R.
(*p*) *Johnson* v. *Diprose*, [1893] 1 Q.B. 512 (C.A.), at p. 515, *per* Lord ESHER, M.R.
(*q*) The term "bill of sale" has the same meaning in the Bills of Sale Act (1878), Amendment Act 1882, except that the latter Act does not apply to bills of sale given otherwise than by way of security for the payment of money.

or context repugnant to such construction, include bills of sale, assignments, transfers, declarations of trust without transfer, inventories of goods with receipt thereto attached, or receipts for purchase-money of goods, and other assurances of personal chattels, and also powers of attorney, authorities, or licences to take possession of personal chattels as security for any debt, and also any agreement, whether intended or not to be followed by the execution of any other instrument by which a right in equity to any personal chattels, or to any charge or security thereon, shall be conferred (*r*).

Documents which are not bills of sale.—The expression "bill of sale" does not include the following: assignments for the benefit of the creditors of the person making or giving the same, marriage settlements, transfers or assignments of any ship or vessel or any share thereof, transfers of goods in the ordinary course of business of any trade or calling, bills of sale of goods in foreign parts or at sea, bills of lading, India warrants, warehousekeepers' certificates, warrants or orders for the delivery of goods, or any other documents used in the ordinary course of business as proof of the possession or control of goods, or authorising or purporting to authorise, either by endorsement or by delivery, the possessor of such document to transfer or receive goods thereby represented (*s*). Nor does the expression include an instrument charging or creating any security on, or declaring trusts of imported goods, given or executed at any time prior to their deposit in a warehouse, factory or store, or to their being re-shipped for export or delivered to a purchaser who did not give or execute the instrument (*t*). But this does not affect the bankruptcy law regarding the division among creditors of goods which, at the commencement of the bankruptcy, were in the possession, order or disposition of the bankrupt in his trade or business by the consent and permission of the true owner under such circumstances that the bankrupt was the reputed owner thereof (*u*).

And s. 17 of the Bills of Sale Act 1882, provides that nothing in that Act shall apply to any debentures issued by any mortgage, loan or other incorporated company, and secured on the capital stock, or goods, chattels and effects of such company. In addition mortgages and charges for the registration of which provision is made by the Companies Acts (*a*) are not within the Bills of Sale Acts (*b*).

An agricultural charge created by a farmer in favour of a bank

---

(*r*) Bills of Sale Act 1878, s. 4. Certain instruments conferring powers of distress are declared to be bills of sale by s. 6; see p. 81, *infra*. (*s*) *Ibid.*, s. 4.

(*t*) Bills of Sale Act 1890, s. 1; Bills of Sale Act 1891, s. 1.

(*u*) Bills of Sale Act 1890, s. 2; Bankruptcy Act 1914, ss. 38 (c), 150 (2). For the bankruptcy law concerning reputed ownership, see pp. 91 *et seq.*, *infra*.

(*a*) See pp. 181 *et seq.*, *infra*.

(*b*) *Re Standard Manufacturing Co.*, [1891] 1 Ch. 627, 645; *Richards* v. *Kidderminster Overseers*, [1896] 2 Ch. 212. A memorandum of deposit of deeds, not containing an agreement for payment of a specific debt, is not a debenture within s. 17: *Topham* v. *Greenside Glazed Fire-brick Co.* (1888), 37 Ch. D. 281. And the charges of societies registered under the Industrial and Provident Societies Act 1965, are excepted from the Acts if an application is made within fourteen days to record the charge at the central office: Industrial and Provident Societies Act 1967, s. 1.

on his farming stock and other agricultural assets is not to be deemed a bill of sale within the meaning of the Bills of Sale Acts (c).

The provisions of the Bills of Sale Act do not apply to mortgages of registered aircraft and stores of spare parts therefor (d).

Instrument must effect the transaction.—An instrument, although within the statutory definition and given by way of security for money, is not necessarily a bill of sale within the Acts unless it was intended by the parties to be a document passing the property in the goods, or giving power to seize them, or to be a record of the transfer (e).

Instrument must be security for a debt.—The Acts do not apply, for instance, to a power for a lessor to re-enter on default in the performance by a builder of his contract, and to take as the lessor's own property the materials on the ground, no security for a debt being thereby created (f). But the lessor may be defeated under the law relating to reputed ownership if he fails to enter before the builder's bankruptcy (g); and a mortgage by a lessee under a building lease providing that all building materials when brought in the premises should be considered as attaching to the land, with power to seize, etc., is void as a bill of sale (h).

Hire purchase agreements not bills of sale.—The Bills of Sale Acts do not extend to an ordinary agreement for the hire or hire-purchase of chattels which, until the stipulated payments have been made, are not the property of the hirer. As the licence to seize (such licences being frequently inserted in hire-purchase agreements), merely empowers the owner to retake possession of his own property, it is not a bill of sale (i). A hire-purchase agreement is, in law, a case of an owner parting temporarily with possession and not of an owner parting with ownership but retaining possession. No security is created on the debtor's goods.

Where, on the other hand, there is a sale of goods passing the immediate property to the purchaser, and a provision for payment by instalments and interest is charged on the unpaid purchase money, the document is a bill of sale (k).

(c) Agricultural Credits Act 1928, ss. 5, 8 (1). See also as to debentures issued by agricultural marketing boards (Agricultural Marketing Act 1958, s. 15 (5)) and by societies registered under the Industrial and Provident Societies Act 1965, which, if registered as agricultural charges, are excluded from the statutory definition of bills of sale (Agricultural Credits Act 1928, s. 14 (1)).

(d) Mortgaging of Aircraft Order 1972 (S.I. 1972 No. 1268) art. 16 (1).

(e) *Marsden* v. *Meadows* (1881), 7 Q.B.D. 80; *Manchester, Sheffield and Lincolnshire Rail. Co.* v. *North Central Wagon Co.* (1888), 13 App. Cas. 554 (H.L.); *Charlesworth* v. *Mills*, [1892] A.C. 231 (H.L.); *Ramsay* v. *Margrett*, [1894] 2 Q.B. 18 (C.A.); *Koppel* v. *Koppel*, [1966] 2 All E.R. 187 (C.A.).

(f) *Brown* v. *Bateman* (1867), L.R. 2 C.P. 272; *Reeves* v. *Barlow* (1884), 12 Q.B.D. 436.

(g) *Re Weibking, Ex parte Ward*, [1902] 1 K.B. 713; *Re Fox, Ex parte Oundle and Thrapston R.D.C.* v. *Trustee*, [1948] Ch. 407; [1948] 1 All E.R. 849.

(h) *Climpson* v. *Coles* (1889), 23 Q.B.D. 465; *Re Hawkins, Ex parte Emerson* (1871), 41 L.J. Bcy. 20; *Re Robertson, Ex parte Crawcour* (1878), 9 Ch. D. 419.

(i) *McEntire* v. *Crossley Bros., Ltd.*, [1895] A.C. 457 (H.L.). For a general discussion of hire-purchase agreements as bills of sale, see (1960), 23 M.L.R. 399, 516 (A. L. Diamond). See re dealer financing *Pacific Motor Auctions Pty., Ltd.* v. *Motor Credits (Hire-Finance), Ltd.*, [1965] A.C. 867 (P.C.); [1965] 2 All E.R. 105.

(k) *Coburn* v. *Collins* (1887), 35 Ch. D. 373.

Substance of transaction.—In deciding whether a document is within the terms of the Acts, the court looks at the substance of the transaction (*l*). Where the documents effecting a transaction are genuine documents and not intended to cloak the true nature of the transaction, the legal rights and obligations flowing from the documents according to their true construction and effect are the substance of the transaction, and, if as a result the transaction is outside the scope of the Acts, the terms of the documents cannot be disregarded in order to bring the transaction within the scope of the Acts (*m*).

The court is, however, entitled to look behind the documents, and if then it appears that the documents are sham documents intended to conceal the fact that the transaction was a loan on security, the documents are within the Acts (*n*).

A hire-purchase agreement will not be allowed to oust the Acts where it is used, together with a sham sale by the borrower to the lender, merely as a cloak to disguise what is really, according to the intent of the parties, a security for a loan (*o*). If a sale is intended to be a genuine transaction, so that the hire-purchase agreement is executed by a person who is in law the true owner of the property, then the transaction cannot be said to be merely a colourable cloak for the mortgage (*p*). But if the real transaction is a loan of money intended to be secured by a sale and hiring agreement the document or documents embodying the arrangement will be within the Acts (*q*). Each case must be determined according to the proper inference to be drawn from the facts (*r*), and, whatever form the transaction may take, the court will decide according to its real substance.

Attornment clauses.—Every attornment, instrument, or agreement, not being a mining lease, whereby a power of distress is given or agreed to be given by way of security for any present, future, or contingent debt or advance, and whereby any rent is reserved or made payable as a mode of providing for the payment of interest on such debt or advance, or otherwise for the purpose of such security only, is deemed to be a bill of sale of any personal chattels which may be seized or taken under such power (*s*). The object of this provision

---

(*l*) *Re Watson, Ex parte Official Receiver in Bankruptcy* (1890), 25 Q.B.D. 27 (C.A.); *Madell* v. *Thomas & Co.*, [1891] 1 Q.B. 230 (C.A.).

(*m*) *Helby* v. *Matthews*, [1895] A.C. 471 (H.L.), at p. 476, *per* Lord HERSCHELL, L.C.; *Staffs Motor Guarantee, Ltd.* v. *British Wagon Co., Ltd.*, [1934] 2 K.B. 305; *Re Lovegrove*, [1935] Ch. 464 (C.A.); *Stoneleigh Finance, Ltd.* v. *Phillips*, [1965] 2 Q.B. 537 (C.A.); [1965] 1 All E.R. 513; *Snook* v. *London and West Riding Investments, Ltd.*, [1967] 2 Q.B. 786 (C.A.); [1967] 1 All E.R. 518.

(*n*) *Re Lovegrove, supra*, at pp. 495, 496, *per* MAUGHAM, L.J.; *Polsky* v. *S. & A. Services, Ltd.*, [1951] 1 All E.R. 185, at p. 189; affd., [1951] 1 All E.R. 1062, n. (C.A.).

(*o*) *Re Walden, Ex parte Odell* (1878), 10 Ch. D. 76 (C.A.); *Maas* v. *Pepper*, [1905] A.C. 102 (H.L.).

(*p*) *Manchester, Sheffield, etc., Rail. Co.* v. *North Central Wagon Co.* (1888), 13 App. Cas. 554.

(*q*) *Maas* v. *Pepper, supra*; *North Central Wagon Finance Co., Ltd.* v. *Brailsford*, [1962] 1 All E.R. 502; *Mercantile Credit Co., Ltd.* v. *Hamblin*, [1965] 2 Q.B. 242 (C.A.); [1964] 3 All E.R. 592.

(*r*) See *Johnson* v. *Rees* (1915), 84 L.J.K.B. 1276. For a general discussion on sham hire-purchase agreements, see Crossley Vaines, *Personal Property* (5th Edn.), pp. 371 *et seq.* and 467 *et seq.*

(*s*) Bills of Sale Act 1878, s. 6.

was to prevent the practice, which had been adopted, in order to avoid registration under the Act of 1854, of making securities upon chattels by assignment or demise of the interest of the debtor in the premises in which the chattels were placed, with a proviso that the premises should be held by the debtor as tenant from year to year at a rent which, with the tenancy itself, should cease upon payment of all moneys recoverable under the security, a power of entry without previous demand being also reserved on default in payment. Before the principal Act came into force, this right of distress could be exercised, not only on the goods of the borrower, but on those of a stranger (*t*). Such a clause is now within s. 6 of the 1878 Act, so as to render any distress under the clause unlawful unless the clause has been registered as a bill of sale. The validity of the clause as regards land is not affected (*u*). It should be noted that the instrument is only "deemed to be" a bill of sale of any personal chattels which may be seized or taken under the power of distress (*a*). It need not, therefore, be in the statutory form, not being in fact a bill of sale, though for the purpose of registration it is treated as one.

Definition of "personal chattels".—The Act of 1882 applies to forms of personalty defined in the 1878 Act, s. 4, as:

> Goods, furniture and other articles capable of complete transfer by delivery, and (when separately assigned or charged) fixtures and growing crops (*b*), but shall not include chattel interests in real estate, nor fixtures (except trade machinery as hereinafter defined), when assigned together with a freehold or leasehold interest in any land or building to which they are affixed, nor growing crops when assigned together with any interest in the land on which they grow, nor shares or interests in the stock, funds or securities of any government, or in the capital or property of incorporated or joint stock companies, nor choses in action (*c*) nor any stock or produce upon any farm or lands which by virtue of any covenant or agreement, or of the custom of the country, ought not to be removed from any farm where the same are at the time of making or giving of such bill of sale.

The description of personal chattels in the principal Act is applicable only for the purpose of the Bills of Sale Acts; it is, for instance, only for the purpose of the Acts that trade machinery is deemed to be personal chattels. The subject matter of bills of sale by way of security is restricted by certain provisions of the Act of 1882 which require, in order that a bill of sale by way of security should have effect against persons other than the grantor, that the personal chattels to which it relates should be capable of specific description, and should be specifically described in the schedule annexed to the bill of sale (*d*),

---

(*t*) *Kearsley* v. *Philips* (1883), 11 Q.B.D. 621.

(*u*) See, *e.g.*, *Mumford* v. *Collier* (1890), 25 Q.B.D. 279 (D.C.).

(*a*) *Green* v. *Marsh*, [1892] 2 Q.B. 330 (C.A.), at p. 335.

(*b*) See *infra*.

(*c*) But note that an absolute assignment of book debts requires registration as if it were an absolute bill of sale, otherwise it is void against the assignor's trustee in bankruptcy as regards any book debts which have not been paid at the commencement of the bankruptcy: Bankruptcy Act 1914, s. 43. And see p. 113, *infra*.

A reversionary interest in chattels is a chose in action, and a mortgage of such an interest does not require to be registered as a bill of sale: *Re Thynne, Thynne* v. *Grey*, [1911] 1 Ch. 282.

(*d*) Bills of Sale Act (1878) Amendment Act 1882, s. 4.

and that the grantor should be the true owner of such personal chattels at the time of its execution (*e*). These provisions are subject to certain exceptions in the case of growing crops, fixtures, plant and trade machinery (*f*).

Crops and trade machinery.—Growing crops become, when severed, personal chattels in the ordinary sense, and an assignment of them requires registration (*g*), unless made in the ordinary course of business (*h*) or contained in an agricultural charge. But crops and ordinary fixtures are not within the Bills of Sale Acts unless they are assigned or charged apart from the land on which they are growing, or to which they are affixed (*i*). They may be separately assigned though other goods are assigned with them (*k*). An assignment of growing crops by separate words, or a power to sever and sell them apart from the land, does not of itself operate as a separate assignment, if by the same instrument any freehold or leasehold interest in the land is also conveyed or assigned to the same person (*l*). If, however, crops which are separately assigned or charged were actually growing at the time when the bill of sale was executed, they are excepted from the provisions of the amending Act, which, as against third parties, avoid a bill of sale given by way of security, in respect of chattels not specifically described in the schedule, or of which the grantor was not the true owner at the time when the bill of sale was executed (*m*).

Trade machinery is, for the purposes of bills of sale, deemed to be personal chattels (*n*). Accordingly, trade machinery cannot ordinarily be made a security for money except by means of a bill of sale complying with the requirements of the Acts. Fixed trade machinery may, however, without express mention, pass as part of mortgaged premises, whether freehold or leasehold, like other fixtures, and if there is no disposition of trade machinery as such, nor any power to sell separately, registration is unnecessary (*o*). But an intention to give a power to sell trade machinery, apart from the premises, may be collected from the whole instrument, even though no express power of separate sale is given, in which case, as regards the trade machinery, the disposition is a bill of sale (*p*).

Conditions for validity of bill of sale (*q*).—The following conditions are essential to the validity of a bill of sale. Breach of any of them makes the instrument void, not merely as against the grantor's creditors, but also as against the grantor himself. In case

---

(*e*) *Ibid.*, s. 5.
(*f*) *Ibid.*, s. 6. And see *infra*.
(*g*) *Re Phillips, Ex parte National Mercantile Bank* (1880), 16 Ch. D. 104.
(*h*) *Stephenson* v. *Thompson*, [1924] 2 K.B. 240.
(*i*) Bills of Sale Act 1878, s. 4.
(*k*) *Roberts* v. *Roberts* (1884), 13 Q.B.D. 794.
(*l*) Bills of Sale Act 1878, s. 7.
(*m*) Bills of Sale Act (1878) Amendment Act 1882, ss. 4, 5, 6.
(*n*) See Bills of Sale Act 1878, s. 5. This section defines trade machinery.
(*o*) *Re Yates, Batcheldor* v. *Yates* (1888), 38 Ch. D. 112 (C.A.).
(*p*) *Small* v. *National Provincial Bank of England*, [1894] 1 Ch. 686.
(*q*) For forms and procedure on execution and registration, see 3 Ency. Forms and Precedents (4th Edn.), Bills of Sale.

of breach of the first two conditions, it is void *in toto*; but on breach of the others, only as to the personal chattels comprised therein.

(1) The bill must be in accordance with the form contained in the Schedule to the Act of 1882 (*r*).

(2) It must be given by way of security for a sum not less than £30 (*s*).

(3) The consideration for which it is given must be truly set forth (*t*).

(4) The execution of it by the grantor must be attested by one or more credible witnesses, not being a party or parties thereto (*a*).

(5) It must be registered within seven clear days after the making or giving of the bill (or, if executed out of England, within seven clear days after the time at which it would, in the ordinary course of post, have arrived in England if posted immediately after its execution) (*b*), or within such extended time as the court may (on being satisfied that the omission to comply with this provision was due to accident or inadvertence) direct (*c*).

On registration the following documents must be produced to, and those numbered (2) and (3) filed in the Filing Department (*d*) of the Central Office at the Royal Courts of Justice, Strand, W.C.2: (1) The bill itself, with every schedule and inventory thereto annexed or therein referred to; (2) a true copy of such bill, schedules and inventory, and of every attestation of the execution thereof; (3) an affidavit of the time of the bill being made or given, and of its due execution and attestation and a description of the residence and occupation of the person making or giving the same, and of every attesting witness; and (4) if the bill is given or made subject to any defeasance or condition or declaration of trust not contained in the body thereof, such defeasance, etc., is to be deemed part of the bill, and must be written on the same paper or parchment before registration, and must be truly set forth in the filed copy, otherwise the registration will be void (*e*).

Finally, such registration must be renewed every five years (*f*).

Compliance with the statutory form—A bill of sale made or given by way of security for the payment of money by the grantor

---

(*r*) Act of 1882, s. 9. It is sufficient if it is in substantial accordance with the form: *Thomas* v. *Kelly* (1888), 13 App. Cas. 506; and see *per* Lord FITZGERALD, at p. 516 as to the object of the form.

(*s*) *Ibid.*, s. 12. See p. 88, *infra*.

(*t*) *Ibid.*, s. 8. See p. 88, *infra*.

(*a*) Act of 1882, ss. 8 and 10.

(*b*) *Ibid.*, s. 8; and Act of 1878, ss. 8, 22.

(*c*) Act of 1878, s. 14; and see R.S.C. Ord. 95, r. 1.

(*d*) *Ibid.*, s. 10 (2).

(*e*) *Ibid.*, s. 10 (3). As to the effect of this, see *Heseltine* v. *Simmons*, [1892] 2 Q.B. 547 (C.A.).

(*f*) *Ibid.*, s. 11. Omission to renew it avoids it even as against the grantor: *Fenton* v. *Blythe* (1890), 25 Q.B.D. 417. There is no power under s. 14 of the Act of 1878 to extend the time for renewed registration: *Re Emery, Ex parte Official Receiver* (1888), 21 Q.B.D. 405.

thereof is void (*g*), unless made in accordance with the form of the Schedule to the amending Act (*h*). This is so even though it purports to be an absolute bill (*i*).

This rule extends to all the instruments which come within the definition of bills of sale in the principal Act given by way of security, but it does not extend to those instruments giving powers of distress which by the principal Act (*k*) are deemed to be bills of sale. Such instruments, although given by way of security, are not required to be in the statutory form (*l*). If an instrument which comes within the description of a bill of sale cannot be reduced to the statutory form any security it purports to give will be void (*m*).

To be in accordance with the statutory form, a bill of sale must be substantially like it. A divergence which purports, by addition or omission, to give an effect greater or less than would result from the use of the form is substantial and material. To be valid, a bill of sale must have the same legal effect as the exact statutory form (*n*). Every word of the statutory form may not be imperative, but a bill of sale must not depart from any characteristic of that form, even where the same legal effect is produced (*o*). Thus the address and description of the attesting witness (*p*) and the description of the grantee (*q*), are material parts of the form, and a bill of sale omitting them will be void. Moreover, nothing must destroy the simplicity which it was one of the objects of the Act to attain; the form was meant for the benefit of plain people, and not experts (*r*). The mere fact, however, that two courts differ as to the proper construction of a bill is not of itself ground for avoiding it under this principle (*s*).

A bill of sale must be complete in itself, and if it has to be read with some collateral agreement it is not in accordance with the statutory form (*t*).

The form requires in the case of a present advance, the grantor's acknowledgement of receipt. It further requires that a fixed sum shall be secured. A bill of sale cannot be given by way of indemnity, the amount ultimately payable being uncertain (*u*), nor can further advances be included (*v*). The amount of interest payable and its time of payment must be certain (*x*). The interest must be stated

---

(*g*) *Thomas* v. *Kelly* (1888), 13 App. Cas. 506, at p. 516, *per* Lord FITZGERALD.
(*h*) See Bills of Sale (1878) Amendment Act 1882, s. 9, and Schedule.
(*i*) *Madell* v. *Thomas & Co.*, [1891] 1 Q.B. 230 (C.A.).
(*k*) Section 6.
(*l*) *Green* v. *Marsh*, [1892] 2 Q.B. 330 (C.A.).
(*m*) *Re Townsend, Ex parte Parsons* (1886), 16 Q.B.D. 532 (C.A.).
(*n*) *Re Barber, Ex parte Stanford* (1886), 17 Q.B.D. 259 (C.A.), where the majority of the court added that the bill must not be calculated reasonably to deceive those for whose benefit the statutory form is provided.
(*o*) *Thomas* v. *Kelly* (1888), 13 App. Cas. 506.
(*p*) *Parsons* v. *Brand, Coulson* v. *Dickson* (1890), 25 Q.B.D. 110 (C.A.).
(*q*) *Altree* v. *Altree*, [1898] 2 Q.B. 267.
(*r*) *Furber* v. *Cobb* (1887), 18 Q.B.D. 494.
(*s*) See, *e.g.*, *Edwards* v. *Marston*, [1891] 1 Q.B. 225.
(*t*) See, *e.g.*, *Stott* v. *Shaw and Lee, Ltd.*, [1928] 2 K.B. 26 (C.A.).
(*u*) *Hughes* v. *Little* (1886), 18 Q.B.D. 32 (C.A.).
(*v*) *Cook* v. *Taylor* (1887), 3 T.L.R. 800.
(*x*) *Attia* v. *Finch* (1904), 91 L.T. 70.

as a rate (*y*) and not as a lump sum (*z*). A provision for payment of interest upon arrears of interest is contrary to the form (*a*) and so is a provision for payment of a bonus (*b*).

A bill of sale must contain an agreement to repay the principal sum at a certain stipulated time or times (*c*), though a time of payment fixed by reference to any known event is not necessarily uncertain. Payment, however, cannot be made to depend on the mere choice or volition of the grantee; thus payment cannot be provided for on demand (*d*), or after demand (*e*). The time for payment must not depend on a contingency (*f*). But a stipulation for payment at a specified time, providing that if the grantor should not commit breaches of the agreements in the bill of sale the grantee should accept payment by given monthly instalments, is in accordance with the form (*g*).

As to the mode of repayment, the general principle seems to be that if the time or times fixed for payment are certain, the manner of payment may be such as the parties agree, provided that the agreement is not misleading or contrary to the provisions of the Acts (*h*).

It is not necessary, though it is permissible, that principal and interest should be repayable together, and it is a question of construction whether the agreement for payment is referable to principal or interest, and which is first payable, or whether principal and interest are to be paid together (*i*).

The statutory form also requires a proviso restricting the grantor's power of seizure to the events specified in s. 7 of the Act of 1882.

Maintenance or defeasance of security.—A note appended to the statutory form expressly authorises the insertion of "terms as to insurance, payment of rent, or otherwise, which the parties may agree to for the maintenance or defeasance of the security". The following covenants and powers have been allowed: covenants to repair and replace (*k*), not to remove the goods without consent (*l*), not to assign or underlet the goods without consent (*m*), and to produce receipts for rent, rates and taxes (*n*); provisions for insurance and application of the insurance money in discharging the debt (*o*),

---

(*y*) But it need not be expressed as a percentage: *Lumley* v. *Simmons* (1887), 34 Ch. D. 698 (C.A.).
(*z*) *Blankenstein* v. *Robertson* (1890), 24 Q.B.D. 543.
(*a*) *Dresser* v. *Townsend* (1886), 81 L.T. Jo. 23.
(*b*) *Myers* v. *Elliott* (1886), 16 Q.B.D. 526 (C.A.).
(*c*) *De Braam* v. *Ford*, [1900] 1 Ch. 142 (C.A.).
(*d*) *Hetherington* v. *Groome* (1884), 13 Q.B.D. 789 (C.A.).
(*e*) *Sibley* v. *Higgs* (1885), 15 Q.B.D. 619.
(*f*) See *Hughes* v. *Little*, *supra*.
(*g*) *Re Coton, Ex parte Payne* (1887), 56 L.T. 571.
(*h*) *Watkins* v. *Evans* (1887), 18 Q.B.D. 386 (C.A.).
(*i*) *Goldstrom* v. *Tallerman* (1886), 18 Q.B.D. 1 (C.A.); *Edwards* v. *Marston*, [1891] 1 Q.B. 225.
See further as to decisions on the statutory form, 4 Halsbury's Laws (4th Edn.), paras. 676 *et seq.*
(*k*) *Furber* v. *Cobb* (1887), 18 Q.B.D. 494 (C.A.).
(*l*) *Re Coton, Ex parte Payne* (1887), 56 L.T. 571.
(*m*) *Seed* v. *Bradley*, [1894] 1 Q.B. 319 (C.A.); *Coates* v. *Moore*, [1903] 2 K.B. 140 (C.A.).
(*n*) *Furber* v. *Cobb*, *supra*; *Cartwright* v. *Regan*, [1895] 1 Q.B. 900.
(*o*) *Neverson* v. *Seymour* (1907), 97 L.T. 788.

power for the creditor, in case of default in insuring or repairing, to enter and insure and repair himself, and to charge all moneys so expended, with interest, on the goods (*p*), and power if the grantee becomes entitled to seize the goods to enter the premises where the goods are (*q*). A covenant for further assurance can be inserted, unless it is too wide (*r*).

A provision for defeasance of the security is one which limits the operation of the bill or stipulates for its discharge on stated events. If such a provision is not contained in the body of the bill it is deemed to be part of the bill and must be written on the same paper or parchment before registration and must be truly set forth in the filed copy, otherwise the registration will be void (*s*).

Power of sale.—The causes for which the grantee may seize the goods are stated in s. 7 of the Act of 1882 (see p. 354, *infra*). On the goods being seized the grantee has an implied power to sell. Consequently the statutory power of sale under s. 101 of the Law of Property Act 1925 (*t*), is not incorporated in bills of sale (*u*). Hence a proviso excluding s. 103 of the Law of Property Act 1925 (*v*) is merely superfluous and does not invalidate the bill, nor does a power to sell goods by private treaty or public auction off the premises (*x*). A provision that the grantee may retain out of the proceeds of sale the costs and expenses incurred in seizing and removing the chattels and his costs in defending and maintaining his rights under the bill, and the expenses of sale is good (*y*). But where such a provision extends generally to costs and expenses incurred in relation to the security, it is too wide and the bill is void (*z*).

Omissions from statutory form.—A bill is invalid which omits the final proviso limiting the creditor's right to seize (*a*), or which omits the name or address or description of the attesting witness (*b*), or the acknowledgement of the receipt of the loan (*c*).

Collateral documents.—It is not possible to avoid the statutory conditions by having a collateral deed containing covenants and provisions which would make the bill void if they formed part of it. In such cases, the two documents must be regarded as one, and the bill at all events will be void (*d*). The collateral document may,

---

(*p*) *Topley* v. *Crosbie* (1888), 20 Q.B.D. 350.
(*q*) *Lumley* v. *Simmons* (1887), 34 Ch. D. 698 (C.A.).
(*r*) *Re Cleaver, Ex parte Rawlings* (1887), 18 Q.B.D. 489.
(*s*) Act of 1878, s. 10 (3). But an agreement subsequent to the bill of sale, and made as a separate transaction, not to enforce the bill so long as certain conditions are complied with, is not a defeasance within s. 10 (3), and the bill is good: *Lester* v. *Hickling*, [1916] 2 K.B. 302.
(*t*) See p. 360, *infra*.
(*u*) *Re Morritt, Ex parte Official Receiver* (1886), 18 Q.B.D. 222 (C.A.); *Calvert* v. *Thomas* (1887), 19 Q.B.D. 204 (C.A.); cf. *Watkins* v. *Evans* (1887), 18 Q.B.D. 386 (C.A.).
(*v*) See p. 363, *infra.*,
(*x*) *Bourne* v. *Wall* (1891), 64 L.T. 530.
(*y*) *Lumley* v. *Simmons, supra; Re Cleaver, Ex parte Rawlings, supra*.
(*z*) *Calvert* v. *Thomas, supra; Macey* v. *Gilbert* (1888), 57 L.J. Q.B. 461.
(*a*) *Thomas* v. *Kelly* (1888), 13 App. Cas. 506 (H.L.).
(*b*) *Blankenstein* v. *Robertson* (1890), 24 Q.B.D. 543.
(*c*) *Davies* v. *Jenkins*, [1900] 1 Q.B. 133; *Burchell* v. *Thompson*, [1920] 2 K.B. 80.
(*d*) *Sharp* v. *McHenry* (1888), 38 Ch. D. 427; *Edwards* v. *Marcus*, [1894] 1 Q.B. 587.

however, be good (e). Where the terms of a bill are varied by a collateral agreement, so that this operates as a defeasance of the security, then, since it is not contained in the bill, the bill is void (f). And a supplemental deed to a bill of sale, whether or not a defeasance, may so vary the bill that it no longer expresses the true interest of the parties, and since the true terms are not in the statutory form, the bill is void (g).

Consideration.—By s. 12 of the 1882 Act a bill of sale by way of security made or given in consideration of any sum under £30 is void. Consideration means the whole consideration received by the grantor for the giving of the instrument (h).

Necessity for correct statement of consideration.—By s. 8 of the 1882 Act the consideration for which a security bill is given must be truly set forth. If the consideration is misstated the bill will be void in respect of the personal chattels comprised therein (i). Such a misstatement does not, however, amount to such a defect of form as to render the bill wholly void (k) and nullify any personal covenant for payment contained in the bill (l).

The real consideration need not be set forth with strict accuracy, but the facts as to the consideration must be stated with substantial accuracy, either as to their legal effect, or as to their mercantile and business effect (m). It is not necessary to set forth any arrangement relating to the mode of its payment to, or application for, the benefit of the borrower. A statement of payment of the consideration to the borrower, at the execution of the deed, is consistent with its application in the payment of a bona fide debt due from him at the time of the transaction, either to the lender himself or to other persons (n). But it must be a debt actually payable at the time, and it must be paid. Therefore it must not be retained for rent or interest, or other debt, which has not yet become due, or which is not paid until after the execution of the deed (o); nor for the costs of preparing and executing the bill, which, though properly payable by the mortgagor, are not due until the completion of the transaction after the execution of the bill (p).

If the consideration is stated as "now paid" there must be a present

---

(e) *Monetary Advance Co.* v. *Cater* (1888), 20 Q.B.D. 785.

(f) *Smith* v. *Whiteman*, [1909] 2 K.B. 437.

(g) *Cornell* v. *May* (1915), 112 L.T. 1085. See 4 Halsbury's Laws (4th Edn.), para. 682.

(h) *London and Provinces Discount Co.* v. *Jones*, [1914] 1 Q.B. 147. The consideration may be past advances. But except to the extent to which the monies have become repayable they cannot be included within the £30 sum for the purposes of s. 12. As to past advances, see *Darlow* v. *Bland*, [1897] 1 Q.B. 125 (C.A.).

(i) Act of 1882, s. 8.

(k) *Ibid.*, s. 9; but a failure to insert any statement of consideration could amount to such a defect.

(l) *Heseltine* v. *Simmons*, [1892] 2 Q.B. 547 (C.A.).

(m) *Credit Co.* v. *Pott* (1880), 6 Q.B.D. 295 (C.A.); and see *Roberts* v. *Roberts* (1884), 13 Q.B.D. 794 (C.A.), where the consideration was very inaccurately, but sufficiently, stated.

(n) *Credit Co.* v. *Pott*, *supra*; *Thomas* v. *Searles*, [1891] 2 Q.B. 408 (C.A.).

(o) *Parsons* v. *Equitable Investment Co., Ltd.*, [1916] 2 Ch. 527 (C.A.).

(p) *Re Cowburn, Ex parte Firth* (1882), 19 Ch. D. 419 (C.A.); *Richardson* v. *Harris* (1889), 22 Q.B.D. 268 (C.A.).

payment in a legal or business sense (*q*).   The expression "now paid" will, however, cover a payment made before execution of the bill, if it was made as part of the transaction (*r*).

Attestation.—The statutory form of bill of sale by way of security requires the execution of the bill to be attested by one or more credible witnesses who must not be a party or parties to the bill (*s*).   The name, address and description of each witness must be inserted (*t*). Failure to comply with these requirements will render the bill wholly void for want of form (*u*).

Schedule.—The bill of sale must incorporate or have annexed to it a schedule containing an inventory of the personal chattels comprised in the bill.   The bill will be effective only in respect of the personal chattels specifically described in the schedule and will be void, except as against the grantor, in respect of any personal chattels not so specifically described (*v*).   Furthermore a bill of sale will be void, except as against the grantor, in respect of any personal chattels specifically described in the schedule thereto of which the grantor was not the true owner at the time of the execution of the bill of sale (*x*).   Growing crops separately assigned or charged, where such crops were actually growing when the bill was executed, and fixtures separately assigned or charged, and plant or trade machinery, where the fixtures, plant, and trade machinery are substituted for the like articles specifically described in the schedule are excepted from the above requirements (*y*).

The declaration in s. 4 that the bill of sale shall have effect only in respect of the personal chattels specifically described in the schedule, is not consistent with the subsequent implication that it shall be good as against the grantor in respect of personal chattels not so specifically described.   But the effect of the section appears to be that the bill of sale will only affect other persons than the grantor in respect of those chattels specifically described, of which the grantor was the true owner at the time of the execution of the bill of sale.   But as to those specifically described, of which he was not then but may afterwards become the true owner, and as to those of which only a general and not a specific description is given, the bill of sale will operate only as against the grantor.

What amounts to specific description.—The scope and object of this requirement for specific description has been described as to facilitate the identification of the articles enumerated in the schedule with those that are to be found in the possession of the mortgagor,

---

(*q*) *E.g.*, within a few hours of the execution of the bill: *Henshall* v. *Widdison* (1923), 130 L.T. 607.   *Cf. Re Spindler, Ex parte Rolph* (1881), 19 Ch. D. 98 (C.A.) (where the money was paid several days afterwards).   Past advances cannot be now paid: *Davies* v. *Jenkins*, [1900] 1 Q.B. 133.

(*r*) *Re Chapman, Ex parte Johnson* (1884), 26 Ch. D. 338 (C.A.); *Re Rouard, Ex parte Trustee* (1916), 85 L.J. K.B. 393.

(*s*) Act of 1882, s. 10.

(*t*) As to forms, see 3 Ency. Forms and Precedents (4th Edn.), Bills of Sale.

(*u*) Act of 1882, s. 9.

(*v*) *Ibid.*, s. 4.

(*x*) *Ibid.*, s. 5.

(*y*) *Ibid.*, s. 6.

that is to say, to render the identification as easy as possible, and to render any dispute as to the intention of the parties as rare as possible, and to shut the door to fraud and controversy, which almost always arise when a general description is used (z). The goods must be described with the particularity usual in an inventory of chattels, in the ordinary business sense of the term (a). Where in the ordinary course goods are frequently replaced or substituted, as in the case of stock of a business, more particularity is required than with articles, such as furniture in a dwellinghouse, which are not changed frequently (b).

True ownership.—With regard to the question whether the grantor was the true owner of the chattels at the execution of the bill, s. 5 of the Act of 1882 avoids (except as against the grantor) (1) bills of sale of future acquired chattels, and (2) bills of sale of chattels in which the grantor has no legal or beneficial interest.

With regard to future acquired chattels, a general assignment of future acquired chattels is absolutely void even as against the grantor, under s. 9 of the Act of 1882, because such an assignment cannot be made in accordance with the statutory form (c). But a bill of sale of specific chattels which in fact do not belong to the grantor at the date of the deed, but of which he subsequently acquires the ownership, would be good as against the grantor by virtue of the doctrine of estoppel. Such an assignment would, however, be void as against the grantor's creditors by virtue of s. 5.

Section 5 does not mean that the grantor must be the absolute or only owner. It is sufficient if the grantor has a partial or equitable ownership. Thus a bill of sale of the equity of redemption in chattels is good (d). A person beneficially interested in chattels is the true owner to the extent of his interest (e), and a bill of sale by a trustee is good, though another person is equitably entitled (f).

How far the security is avoided.—The Acts make a bill of sale void *in toto* where it does not comply with the statutory form (g), and where the consideration is under £30 (h). They make it void only in respect of any personal chattels comprised therein, when the consideration is not truly set forth (i), when it is insufficiently attested (i), when it is not registered (i), and when it is a successive bill of sale, that is, if it is executed within, or on the expiration of, seven days after the execution of a prior unregistered bill of sale, and if it is given for the same or part of the same debt and comprises all or part of the same chattels (k). Further, as against creditors, though not as against

---

(z) *Carpenter* v. *Deen* (1889), 23 Q.B.D. 566 (C.A.), at p. 574, *per* FRY, L.J.
(a) *Witt* v. *Banner* (1887), 20 Q.B.D. 114 (C.A.).
(b) *Davies* v. *Jenkins*, [1900] 1 Q.B. 133; *Herbert's Trustee* v. *Higgins*, [1926] Ch. 794.
(c) *Thomas* v. *Kelly* (1888), 13 App. Cas. 506 (H.L.).
(d) *Thomas* v. *Searles*, [1891] 2 Q.B. 408 (C.A.).
(e) *Re Field, Ex parte Pratt* (1890), 63 L.T. 289.
(f) *Re Sarl, Ex parte Williams*, [1892] 2 Q.B. 591.
(g) Act of 1882, s. 9.
(h) *Ibid.*, s. 12.
(i) *Ibid.*, s. 8.
(k) Act of 1878, s. 9.

the grantor, it is void in respect of chattels which are not specifically described (*l*), or which were not the property of the grantor (*m*) at the execution of the bill.

The registration of a bill of sale is void and the bill is therefore void in respect of the personal chattels comprised therein, if the bill is given subject to an unregistered defeasance, condition or declaration of trust (*n*), or if the registration is not renewed once at least every five years (*o*).

But even where a bill is void *in toto*, this does not mean that the security of which it forms part is void *in toto*. If the security comprises personal chattels and also property which does not fall within that description, and it is possible to sever the security on the personal chattels from the security on the other property, then the security will be void as to the personal chattels but good as to the other property (*p*). But a bill of sale will be bad if it includes in the schedule property other than personal chattels (*q*). Where a bill of sale is void for non-compliance with the statutory form, it is void, not only in respect of the assignment of personal chattels, but also in respect of the personal covenant to pay principal and interest (*r*). But the grantor may be estopped from setting up the invalidity of the bill against the grantee (*s*).

The reputed ownership clause.—Under the Bankruptcy Act 1914, s. 38 (c) (*t*), the property of the bankrupt divisible among his creditors, comprises all goods being, at the commencement of the bankruptcy (*a*), in the possession, order or disposition of the bankrupt, in his trade or business, by the consent and permission of the true owner thereof; provided that things in action (*b*), other than debts

---

(*l*) Act of 1882, s. 4. But note the exception in s. 6.

(*m*) *Ibid.*, s. 5. But note the exception in s. 6.

(*n*) Act of 1878, s. 10 (3).

(*o*) *Ibid.*, s. 11.

(*p*) *E.g.*, where the same instrument comprises a bill of sale of personal chattels and a mortgage of freehold or leasehold property (*Re O'Dwyer* (1886), 19 L.R. Ir. 19), or a bill of sale of personal chattels and also of trade machinery excepted under s. 5 of the Act of 1878 (*Re Burdett, Ex parte Byrne* (1888), 20 Q.B.D. 310 (C.A.)).

(*q*) *Cochrane* v. *Entwistle* (1890), 25 Q.B.D. 116 (C.A.). But the mortgage will be effective as regards the other property.

(*r*) *Davies* v. *Rees* (1886), 17 Q.B.D. 408; *Smith* v. *Whiteman*, [1909] 2 K.B. 437 (C.A.). But the lender may recover his money, with reasonable interest, as money had and received: see *North Central Wagon and Finance Co., Ltd.* v. *Brailsford*, [1962] 1 All E.R. 502. (It is hard to see why, in this case, judgment was given for money had and received, since, when a bill of sale is "void" only for non-registration, the agreement for payment of principal and interest still stands: *Heseltine* v. *Simmons*, [1892] 2 Q.B. 547 (C.A.). *Davies* v. *Rees, supra*, cited in the instant case, is concerned with want of form, an avoiding defect which attracts different considerations from those attaching to non-registration.) In *Bradford Advance Co., Ltd.* v. *Ayers*, [1924] W.N. 152, 5 per cent. per annum was taken as the appropriate rate of interest.

(*s*) *Comitti & Son, Ltd.* v. *Maher* (1905), 94 L.T. 158.

(*t*) Replacing s. 44 of the Bankruptcy Act 1883. A mortgage of a registered aircraft is not affected by the bankruptcy of the mortgagor; Mortgaging of Aircraft Order 1972, art. 15.

(*a*) Namely, the date of the act of bankruptcy: *Re Mackay*, [1915] 2 I.R. 347 (C.A.); *Re Neal, Ex parte Trustee*, [1914] 2 K.B. 910.

(*b*) This exception extends to stocks and shares: *Colonial Bank* v. *Whinney* (1885), 30 Ch. D. 261 (C.A.); reversed on another point (1886), 11 App. Cas. 426; and even if it did not, it would seem that in the case of ordinary traders (other than bankers, brokers, and other financial persons) stocks and shares could scarcely be said to be in

due, or growing due, to him in the course of his trade or business, are not to be deemed goods within the meaning of the clause (c).

It was held before the passing of the Bills of Sale Act 1878 that the reputed ownership clause of the Bankruptcy Act 1869 was not affected by the registration of bills of sale under the Bills of Sale Act 1854, and chattels comprised in a registered bill of sale consequently belonged to the creditors of the maker if they were in his reputed ownership at his bankruptcy (d). But s. 20 of the Act of 1878 provided that chattels comprised in a bill of sale which had been, and continued to be, duly registered under that Act, should not be deemed to be in the possession, order or disposition of the grantor of the bill of sale within the meaning of the Bankruptcy Act 1869. This provision was, however, repealed by s. 15 of the Act of 1882, with regard to bills of sale given by way of security for money (e); and the law as it existed before the Act of 1878 was therefore to this extent restored (f). It is provided by s. 38 A of the Bankruptcy Act 1914, added by the Consumer Credit Act 1974, Sched. 4, para. 6, that goods, *inter alia*, subject to a regulated agreement, under which a bill of sale is given by way of security, shall not be treated as the property of the bankrupt during the period between the service of the default notice and the date on which the notice expires or is earlier complied with (g).

The reputed ownership clause will not operate, unless the bankrupt holds the goods with the consent of the true owner. The latter may, therefore, defeat the title of the trustee by any act which shows a withdrawal of his consent as by making bona fide attempts to get possession before the bankruptcy (h), or by merely demanding the goods with a view to taking possession of them, or giving notice to the sheriff, who has seized under an execution, to withdraw (i).

The possession of a receiver, appointed on behalf of the plaintiff in an action to enforce an agreement to execute a bill of sale, will also take the goods out of the reputed ownership of the defendant (j). But the receiver's possession will not be effectual, unless the proper

---

their possession, order or disposition in the course of their trade or business: *Re Jenkinson, Ex parte Nottingham, etc., Bank* (1885), 15 Q.B.D. 441. And see *Re Collins*, [1925] Ch. 556.

(c) Contingent claims, which may or may not become debts, are not debts within this clause: *Re Fastnedge, Ex parte Kemp* (1874), 9 Ch. App. 383. The equity of redemption of a life policy was held to be "goods and chattels" within the meaning of the Irish Bankrupt and Insolvent Act 1857 (20 & 21 Vict. c. 60), so that where, upon a second mortgage, the second mortgagee had not given notice to the insurance company at the date of the mortgagor's bankruptcy, it was caught by the "reputed ownership" clause: *Re Clancarty*, [1921] 2 I.R. 377.

(d) *Re Fairbrother, Ex parte Harding* (1873), L.R. 15 Eq. 223.

(e) *Swift* v. *Pannell* (1883), 24 Ch. D. 210; *Casson* v. *Churchley* (1884), 53 L.J. Q.B. 335.

(f) *Re Ginger, Ex parte London and Universal Bank*, [1897] 2 Q.B. 461; *Re Weibking, Ex parte Ward*, [1902] 1 K.B. 713; *Hollinshead* v. *Egan, Ltd.*, [1913] A.C. 564 (H.L.). As to when goods are in the reputed ownership of a debtor, see Williams, *Bankruptcy Practice* (18th Edn.), pp. 323 *et seq*.

(g) On the Consumer Credit Act 1974 see pp. 132 *et seq, infra*.

(h) *Re Pulling, Ex parte Harris* (1872), 8 Ch. App. 48; *Re O'Brien, Ex parte Montagu* (1876), 1 Ch. D. 554 (C.A.).

(i) *Smith* v. *Topping* (1833), 5 B. & Ad. 674; *Re Baldwin, Ex parte Foss* (1858), 2 De G. & J. 230; *Re Couston, Ex parte Ward* (1872), 8 Ch. App. 144.

(j) *Taylor* v. *Eckersley* (1877), 5 Ch. D. 740.

certificate that he has complied with the order (if any) requiring him to give the security has been given (k). On the other hand, the mere appointment of a receiver of debts due to the bankrupt in his trade or business, is not of itself sufficient to take them out of the order and disposition clause. In order to protect them, it is necessary to give notice of the assignment to the debtors (l), and this must be done before the act of bankruptcy on which the adjudication is founded (m).

If the holder of the bill of sale allows the goods to remain for an undue period in the hands of the personal representative of the deceased grantor, to be used by him in carrying on the business of the grantor, the goods will be held to be in the reputed ownership of the representative, and will pass to the trustee in his bankruptcy (n).

III—REGISTRATION OF BILLS OF SALE

Registration (o).—Under the Act of 1878 an unregistered bill of sale was void as against execution creditors and against the grantor's trustee in bankruptcy, but not as between grantor and grantee. With regard to bills of sale by way of security, the Act of 1882 renders an unregistered bill of sale void as regards the personal chattels comprised in it (p).

The effect of the registration provisions of the Act of 1882 appears to be that, although seven days are allowed for registration, the necessity for registering the bill of sale cannot, unlike the position under the former Acts, be avoided by taking possession before the expiration of the seven days. Not only does the bill of sale become void as to the chattels for want of registration, but the grantee is prevented by s. 7 of the Act of 1878 from taking possession except by reason of defaults which could hardly occur within the seven days without collusion. Failure to register does not avoid the personal covenant for payment (q).

The mode of registering bills of sale.—The mode of registering both kinds of bills of sale is regulated by the Act of 1878, and is as follows. The bill of sale with every schedule or inventory thereto annexed or therein referred to, and a true copy of such bill and of such schedule or inventory and of every attestation of the execution of such bill of sale together with an affidavit containing the particulars mentioned below must be presented to the registrar (r); and the copy bill of sale and affidavit must be filed with him (s).

(k) *Edwards* v. *Edwards* (1876), 2 Ch. D. 291 (C.A.).

(l) *Rutter* v. *Everett*, [1895] 2 Ch. 872.

(m) *Re Neal, Ex parte Trustee*, [1914] 2 K.B. 910.

(n) *Kitchen* v. *Ibbetson* (1873), L.R. 17 Eq. 46.

(o) For procedure on execution and registration, see 3 Ency. Forms and Precedents (4th Edn.), Bills of Sale. Registration does not of itself constitute notice to third parties: *Joseph* v. *Lyons* (1884), 15 Q.B.D. 280, 286. See 4 Halsbury's Laws (4th Edn.), para. 711. For priorities, see p. 486, *infra*.

(p) Act of 1882, s. 8.

(q) *Heseltine* v. *Simmons*, [1892] 2 Q.B. 547 (C.A.).

(r) The office of registrar is executed by the Master of the Supreme Court, Queen's Bench Division.

(s) Bills of Sale Act 1878, s. 10 (2). As to the copies required for local registration, see the Administration of Justice Act 1925, s. 23 (2). See also *ibid.*, ss. 13 and 22.

What is a sufficient copy.—The copy of the bill of sale, schedule or inventory, and attestation, to be presented to, and filed with, the registrar, must be substantially a true copy, but need not be an exact copy, and clerical or verbal errors (including omission of date and omission of signature of grantor or that of a witness, etc.) do not avoid registration.

Contents of statutory affidavit (*t*).—The affidavit presented to and filed with the registrar must prove the following facts: (1) the due execution and attestation of the bill of sale; (2) the residence and occupation of the grantor, and of every attesting witness; and (3) the true date of the execution of the bill of sale (*u*). The description should be of the grantor's and witnesses' residence and occupation at the time of registering the bill of sale, not at the time of its execution (*v*).

Local registration.—In the case of a bill of sale given by way of security, if the affidavit which is required to accompany the bill when presented for registration describes the residence of the person making or giving the same, or of the person against whom the process is issued, as being in some place outside the London bankruptcy district (*x*), or if the bill describes the chattels enumerated therein as being in some place outside the London bankruptcy district, the registrar, under the principal Act, must forthwith, and within three clear days after registration in the principal registry, and in accordance with the directions prescribed by the rules (*y*), transmit a copy of the bill of sale to the county court registrar in whose district such places are situate, and, if such places are in the district of different registrars, to each such registrar. There must also be presented to the registrar such number of copies of the bill and every schedule and inventory annexed thereto as the registrar may deem necessary for the purpose of local registration (*z*).

Every copy of the bill of sale so transmitted must be filed, kept and indexed by the registrar of the county court in the manner prescribed by the rules (*a*), and any person may search, inspect and make extracts from, and obtain copies of the bill of sale so registered, in the like manner and upon the like terms as to payment or otherwise as near as may be as in the case of bills of sale registered by the registrar under the principal Act.

The provisions for local registration are directory, and the registrar's default in transmitting the copy of the bill of sale to a county court registry does not avoid registration (*b*).

Extension of time for registering.—By s. 14 of the Act of 1878 any judge of the High Court of Justice, or Master of the Supreme Court, on being satisfied that the omission to register a bill of sale,

---

(*t*) For forms, see Queen's Bench Master's Practice Forms, P.F. 177 *et seq.* in Supreme Court Practice 1976, vol. 2, pp. 116 *et seq.*
(*u*) Bills of Sale Act 1878, s. 10 (2).
(*v*) *Button* v. *O'Neill* (1879), 4 C.P.D. 354 (C.A.).
(*x*) See Bankruptcy Act 1914, s. 99, Sched. 3.
(*y*) Bills of Sale (Local Registration) Rules, 1960.
(*z*) Act of 1882, s. 11; Administration of Justice Act 1925, s. 23.
(*a*) Act of 1878, s. 10 (2); Administration of Justice Act 1925, s. 23.
(*b*) *Trinder* v. *Raynor* (1887), 56 L.J.Q.B. 422.

or an affidavit of renewal thereof, within the time prescribed by the Act, or the omission or misstatement of the name, residence or occupation of any person was accidental, or due to inadvertence, may, in his discretion, order such omission or misstatement to be rectified by the insertion in the register of the true name, residence or occupation, or by extending the time for such registration, on such terms and conditions (if any) as to security, notice by advertisement or otherwise, or as to any other matter, as he thinks fit to direct (c). It should be noted that relief is limited to rectification of the register, or extension of time. An order cannot be made for an affidavit to be filed correcting a mistake in the affidavit on registration (d). Such an order will only be granted subject to rights which have already accrued to third persons (e).

Provisions as to keeping and inspecting register.—Provision is made for the keeping of registers in which are entered particulars of registration and renewal of registration of bills of sale, with an index (f). Provision is also made for entering up satisfaction in the register. The register of bills of sale may be inspected either personally or by requisitioning an official search (g) and any person is entitled to have an office copy or extract of any registered bill of sale, and affidavit of execution filed therewith, or copy thereof, and of any affidavit filed therewith, if any, or registered affidavit of renewal, upon payment (h). Any copy of a registered bill of sale, and affidavit purporting to be an office copy thereof, is, in all legal proceedings, admissible as prima facie evidence thereof and of the fact and date of registration as shown thereon (i).

Renewal of registration.—The registration of a bill of sale must be renewed once at least every five years, and if a period of five years elapses from the registration, or renewed registration, of a bill of sale without renewal or further renewal, as the case may be, the registration becomes void. But a renewal of registration does not become necessary by reason only of a transfer or assignment of a bill of sale. The renewal of a registration is effected by filing in the Filing Department an affidavit stating the date of the bill of sale and of the last registration thereof, and the names, residences and occupations of the parties thereto as stated therein, and that the bill of sale is still a subsisting security (k). This affidavit must state the names, residences and occupations of the parties as stated in the bill of sale, even though they are there stated incorrectly; but the correct descriptions may be added. If these requirements of the Act are not complied with, the renewal of registration will be invalid (l). Local registration of

---

(c) See R.S.C. Ord. 95, r. 1, as to application under this section.
(d) *Crew* v. *Cummings* (1888), 21 Q.B.D. 420 (C.A.).
(e) *Crew* v. *Cummings, supra.* And see *Re Parsons, Ex parte Furber*, [1893] 2 Q.B. 122 (C.A.); and p. 185, *infra.*
(f) Bills of Sale Act 1878, s. 12, Sched. B.
(g) Bills of Sale Act (1878) Amendment Act 1882, s. 16.
(h) Bills of Sale Act 1878, s. 16. As to forms and fees, see 3 Ency. Forms and Precedents (4th Edn.), Bills of Sale.
(i) *Ibid.*, s. 16.
(k) *Ibid.*, s. 11.
(l) *Re Morris, Ex parte Webster* (1882), 22 Ch. D. 136 (C.A.).

renewals is effected in the manner required by the amending Act on registering a bill of sale. The court has jurisdiction under s. 14 of the Act of 1878 to extend the time for renewed registration (*m*).

Registration on transfer (*n*).—A transfer or assignment of a registered bill of sale need not be registered (*o*), nor is renewal of registration necessary by reason only of a transfer or assignment of a bill of sale (*p*). A memorandum of charge by the transferee of a bill of sale, given by way of sub-mortgage and accompanied by a deposit of the bill of sale and transfer, need not be registered, even though the transferee afterwards acquires the grantor's equity of redemption (*q*).

(*m*) See 4 Halsbury's Laws (4th Edn.), para. 738; cf. *Re Emery, Ex parte Official Receiver* (1888), 21 Q.B.D. 405.
(*n*) For transfer of bills of sale, see p. 254, *infra*.
(*o*) Bills of Sale Act 1878, s. 10 (but see Moneylenders Act 1927, s. 16).
(*p*) *Ibid.*, s. 11.
(*q*) *Re Parker, Ex parte Turquand* (1885), 14 Q.B.D. 636 (C.A.). For priorities as between two or more holders of bills of sale, see p. 486, *infra*.

CHAPTER 5

Mortgages of Ships and Aircraft

I—SHIPS

Merchant Shipping Act 1894.—British ships do not pass like ordinary chattels by delivery, and the title to them is not proved by possession (a). By the Act of 1894, every British ship must, unless specifically excepted (this includes vessels having a net tonnage not exceeding fifteen tons which are used solely on the rivers or coasts of the United Kingdom and certain fishing vessels having a net tonnage not exceeding thirty tons, in which cases the vessel may be voluntarily registered), be registered; and a registered ship or share of a ship, when disposed of to persons qualified to be owners of British ships, must be transferred by bill of sale. Such a document must be, as nearly as possible, in the prescribed statutory form, and must be produced to the registrar of the ship's port of registry. A registered ship, or any share therein, may be made a security for a loan or other valuable consideration, and the instrument creating the security (called a mortgage) must be in the form mentioned in the First Schedule, or as near thereto as circumstances will permit (b). And the name of the transferee as owner must be entered in the register. The provision relating to the form of the mortgage is, however, directory only, and a mortgage is not invalid by reason of the detailed stipulations of the mortgage being contained in a separate instrument, and not appearing in the mortgage itself (c).

Mortgages are recorded in the order of time in which they are produced to the registrar for registration (d).

If the ship is not registered, a mortgage of it need not be registered either under the Merchant Shipping Act or under the Bills of Sale Acts (see p. 79, *supra*). If the ship is exempt from registration, but is voluntarily registered, the mortgage need not comply with the statutory form nor be registered.

(a) There is no market overt for ships: *per* TURNER, L.J., *Hooper* v. *Gumm* (1867), 2 Ch. App. 282, 290.

(b) See Merchant Shipping Act 1894, ss. 2, 3, 5, 9, 24, 25, 26, 31–38. For forms of mortgage, see Ency. Forms and Precedents (4th Edn.), vol. 2, pp. 863 *et seq.*, vol. 15, pp. 195 *et seq.* and vol. 21, pp. 145 *et seq.* The statutory forms are obtainable from the Government Bookshop.

The mortgagor is deemed to continue the owner of the ship: *ibid.*, s. 34. For priorities of shipping mortgages, see pp. 489 *et seq.*, *infra*.

(c) *The Benwell Tower* (1895), 8 Asp. M.L.C. 13.

(d) Merchant Shipping Act 1894, s. 31. If an owner of the ship is a limited company, the charge must also be registered at the Companies Registry.

Transfer and transmission of registered mortgages.—A registered mortgage of a ship may be transferred in accordance with a statutory form, which is to be registered and endorsed in manner similar to that prescribed in relation to instruments of mortgage (*e*). An agreement to transfer a ship need not be registered, and may be enforced by the registered owner (*f*).

Certificates for mortgaging abroad.—Where the registered owner wishes to mortgage the ship at any place out of the country or possession in which the port of registry is situate, the registrar may grant a certificate enabling him to do so; such a certificate shall be in the form mentioned in the Act. The power must be exercised in conformity with the directions contained in the certificate, and a record of every mortgage made thereunder is to be registered by the endorsement of a record thereof on the certificate by a Registrar or British consular officer (*g*).

Equitable mortgages of ships.—The object of the provisions contained in the Merchant Shipping Act 1894, in relation to transfers and mortgages of ships is merely to provide for legal, as distinguished from equitable, ownership. However, although no notice of any trust can be entered on the register (*h*), the Act nevertheless makes clear provision for the existence of equitable interests in ships (*i*). The court will, moreover, enforce equities between the owner and the mortgagee, and in estimating the rights of the mortgagee will not consider only the registered documents, but all the transactions between the parties relative to the mortgage loan (*k*).

A deposit of a registered mortgage of a ship will create a valid security by way of equitable mortgage (*l*); and an equitable mortgage may also be created by depositing the builder's certificate of an unfurnished ship (*m*).

Notice of equitable mortgages.—Mortgages which are merely equitable do not have priority over or equality with legal mortgages; and their recognition does not introduce the equitable doctrines as to constructive notice into such transactions. A legal mortgagee of a ship does not lose priority, even though he knew, when he made his advance, of an issue of debentures charging some of the mortgagor's ships unless he knew that such debentures charged the ships mortgaged to him (*n*).

Mortgagee not entitled to certificate of registry of ship.—By s. 15, the Act of 1894 provides that the certificate of registry shall be

---

(*e*) *Ibid.*, s. 37.

(*f*) *Batthyany* v. *Bouch* (1881), 4 Asp. M.C. 380. For transmission on death, etc., see ss. 38 and 69. For the discharge of shipping mortgages, see p. 555, *infra*.

(*g*) Merchant Shipping Act 1894, ss. 40–55, 88.

(*h*) *Ibid.*, s. 56.

(*i*) *Ibid.*, s. 57; see *The Byzantion* (1922), 127 L.T. 756.

(*k*) *The Cathcart* (1867), L.R. 1 A. & E. 314.

(*l*) *Lacon* v. *Liffen* (1862), 4 Giff. 75; on appeal (1863), 32 L.J. Ch. 315.

(*m*) *Re Softley, Ex parte Hodgkin* (1875), L.R. 20 Eq. 746. A mortgage of an unregistered and merely equitable interest in a ship cannot itself be registered: *Chasteauneuf* v. *Capeyron* (1882), 7 App. Cas. 127.

(*n*) *Black* v. *Williams*, [1895] 1 Ch. 408; see *Barclay & Co., Ltd.* v. *Poole*, [1907] 2 Ch. 284. Actual knowledge of the equitable mortgage would not prevent the legal mortgagee from obtaining priority, see p. 489, *infra*.

used only for the lawful navigation of the ship, and shall not be subject to detention by reason of any title, lien, charge or interest, which any owner, mortgagee or other person may have or claim in the ship. Pledge of the certificate is illegal, punishable by penalty.

Property passed by the mortgage.—All articles necessary to the navigation of the ship, or to the prosecution of the adventure, pass to the mortgagee under the word "ship", including articles afterwards substituted for them (*o*). But where the cargo belongs to the owner of the ship, it will not, in the absence of any special agreement, pass to the mortgagee (*p*).

Maritime liens, hypothecation and bottomry.—English law recognises maritime liens in respect of bottomry and *respondentia* bonds, salvage of property, seamen's wages and damage.

The master may, in circumstances of unforeseen necessity or distress, pledge the ship and freight to raise the necessary funds for the voyage, by a contract called "bottomry". The contract of bottomry usually took the form of a bond whereby the master states the occasion for resorting to bottomry, and pledges himself, the ship and the freight, and sometimes the cargo, for the repayment of the principal and interest on the safe arrival of the ship at the end of her voyage on such conditions as to risk as may be agreed upon. Where the cargo alone is hypothecated, the instrument is called a *respondentia* bond. Bottomry creates a debt (which is generally treated as only nominal) against the master, but none against the owner (*q*).

Respondentia is the separate hypothecation of the cargo of a ship as security for the repayment of a debt contracted about the necessary cost of transhipping and forwarding the cargo to its destination (*r*).

Bottomry and *respondentia* are obsolete in practice (*s*).

II—AIRCRAFT

Generally.—The Mortgaging of Aircraft Order 1972 (*t*) provides for a register of mortgages of aircraft registered by the Civil Aviation Authority pursuant to s. 8 of the Civil Aviation Act 1949. Registration is voluntary, but since a registered mortgage has priority over an unregistered one (*u*) there is an obvious inducement to register. Mortgages of registered aircraft, which would otherwise require registration under

---

(*o*) *Coltman* v. *Chamberlain* (1890), 25 Q.B.D. 328.

(*p*) *Alexander* v. *Simms* (1854), 18 Beav. 80; affd. 5 De G.M. & G. 57; *Keith* v. *Burrows* (1877), 2 App. Cas. 636.

(*q*) *The Atlas* (1827), 2 Hag. Adm. 48; *The Mary Ann* (1865), L.R. 1 A. & E. at p. 13.

(*r*) *The Atlas, supra.*

(*s*) They are, however, still part of the jurisdiction *in rem* and *in personam* of the Admiralty Court. On maritime liens generally, see further in Halsbury's Laws (4th Edn.), vol. 1 (Admiralty) and (3rd Edn.), 35 (Shipping). Also *British Shipping Laws*, vol. 11, pp. 24 *et seq.*

For remedies of mortgagees under shipping mortgages, see Part V, *infra*, The Mortgagee's Remedies.

(*t*) S.I. 1972 No. 1268 made under s. 16 of the Civil Aviation Act 1968. The order came into force on 1 October 1972.

(*u*) Mortgaging of Aircraft Order 1972, art. 14 (1). See p. 494, *infra*.

the Bills of Sale Acts (*a*) are exempted from those Acts (*b*). Mortgages of unregistered aircraft remain subject to those Acts, where appropriate. Whether or not the mortgage is registered, a mortgage of a registered aircraft made by a company is registrable under s. 95 of the Companies Act 1948 (*c*).

What may be mortgaged.—The 1972 Order confirms that an aircraft registered in the United Kingdom nationality register or such an aircraft together with any store of spare parts for that aircraft may be made security for a loan or other valuable consideration (*d*).

Form of mortgage.—Mortgage of an aircraft is defined (*e*) to include a mortgage which extends to any store of spare parts for that aircraft but does not otherwise include a mortgage created as a floating charge. There is no specified form of mortgage (save for securities created in Scotland (*f*)).

Registration.—Registration is effected by application for registration in the prescribed form (*g*) together with a certified copy of the mortgage and fee (*h*). There is provision for a priority notice where there is intention to register a mortgage (*i*). Where two or more aircraft are the subject of one mortgage, or where the same aircraft is the subject of two or more mortgages, separate applications for registration or priority notice must be made in respect of each aircraft or of each mortgage (*k*). Changes in the registration particulars must be notified by or on behalf of the mortgagee in the prescribed form (*l*). On the discharge of a registered mortgage the mortgagor must notify the Authority in the prescribed form (*m*). The register may be rectified on an order of the High Court (*n*). The Register of Aircraft Mortgages is open to the public on payment of the appropriate fee. Inspection may be made in person (*o*) or by application for a certified copy of the entries in the Register (*p*). Application may also be made for notification as to whether or not there are any relevant entries in the Register (*q*).

An official copy of an entry in the register certified as a true copy by the Authority is admissible in evidence (*r*). Removal of an aircraft from the United Kingdom Nationality Register does not affect the rights of any mortgagee under any registered mortgage and entries

---

(*a*) *Supra*, p. 79.
(*b*) Mortgaging of Aircraft Order 1972, art. 16 (1).
(*c*) *Ibid.*, art. 16 (2), amending s. 95 (2) (*h*). For s. 95, see p. 181, *infra*.
(*d*) Article 3.
(*e*) By art. 2 (2).
(*f*) See Schedule 2.
(*g*) Schedule I, Pt. I.
(*h*) Art. 4. There is transitional provision for registering mortgages made before 1 October 1972 in order to maintain their priority: art. 14 (1).
(*i*) Art. 5. But priority is only given if the contemplated mortgage is made and entered in the register within 14 days of the entry of the priority notice. Days when the office is not open for registration are excluded: art. 14 (3).
(*k*) Art. 6.
(*l*) Art. 8, Sched. 1, Pt. III.
(*m*) Art. 9, Sched. 1, Pt. IV.
(*n*) Art. 10.
(*o*) Art. 11. (1).
(*p*) Art. 11 (2).
(*q*) Art. 11 (3).
(*r*) Art. 11 (4).

shall continue to be made in the register in relation to the mortgage as if the aircraft had not been removed from the register (s).   All persons shall at all times be taken to have express notice of all facts appearing in the register, but the registration of a mortgage shall not be evidence of its validity (t).

Mortgage not affected by bankruptcy.—A registered mortgage is not affected by any act of bankruptcy committed by the mortgagor after the date on which the mortgage is registered, notwithstanding that at the commencement of his bankruptcy the mortgagor had the aircraft in his possession, order or disposition, or was the reputed owner thereof, and the mortgage is to be preferred to any right, claim or interest therein (u) of the other creditors of the bankrupt or any trustee or assignee on their behalf (x).

(s) Art. 12.
(t) Art. 14.
(u) Presumably this means in the aircraft.
(x) Art. 15.

CHAPTER 6

Mortgages of Things in Action

By assignment.—Insurance policies, shares, stocks, book and other debts, equitable interests in land (a) and personalty, and other things in action, legal or equitable, are frequently mortgaged. The Bills of Sale Acts do not apply to mortgages of things in action (b). Save where some special method of disposition is provided by statute, a mortgage of a thing in action is effected by an assignment of the thing. At common law, things in action, with certain exceptions, notably negotiable instruments (c), were incapable of being assigned without the express or implied consent of the holder of the fund to apply it in accordance with the assignment (d), and, therefore, except where particular classes of things in action were made assignable by statute, mortgages of even legal things in action were necessarily purely equitable; equity regarding an assignment of a thing in action as valid, and operating as an agreement to permit the assignee to sue for the thing in action in the name of the assignor (e).

Statutory assignment.—During the course of the nineteenth century the exceptions were extended. Thus, by the Companies Act 1862, shares, stocks, and debentures in public companies were made freely assignable by registered transfer (f). The Judicature Act 1873 (g), introduced a general form of statutory assignment and those provisions are now replaced by the Law of Property Act 1925, which provides:—

136.—(1) Any absolute assignment (h) by writing under the hand of the assignor (not purporting to be by way of charge only (i)) of any debt (j) or

---

(a) These are not strictly things in action, but it is convenient to deal with these here as the same principles apply.

(b) Bills of Sale Act 1878, s. 4.

(c) See *Hopkinson* v. *Forster* (1874), L.R. 19 Eq. 74, at p. 76.

(d) *Lampet's Case* (1612), 10 Co. Rep. 46b, at 48a.

(e) *Crouch* v. *Credit Foncier of England* (1873), L.R. 8 Q.B. 374.

(f) And public funds were made transferable by mere entry in the transfer books at the Bank of England: National Debt Act 1870, s. 22.

(g) Section 25 (6).

(h) There must be an intention to transfer: *Coulls* v. *Bagot's Executor and Trustee Co., Ltd.* (1967), 119 C.L.R. 460.

(i) The mortgage of a debt or thing in action made in the ordinary form of an assignment with a proviso for redemption (express or implied) is an absolute assignment: *Tancred* v. *Delagoa Bay Co.* (1889), 23 Q.B.D. 239 (C.A.); *Hughes* v. *Pump House Hotel Co.*, [1902] 2 K.B. 190 (C.A.). As is also an assignment by way of trust: *Comfort* v. *Betts*, [1891] 1 Q.B. 737 (C.A.). See also *Durham Bros.* v. *Robertson*, [1898] 1 Q.B. 765 (C.A.). As to assignments which were held not to be absolute, see *Durham Bros.* v. *Robertson, supra; Jones* v. *Humphreys*, [1902] 1 K.B. 10.

(j) This does not authorise the legal assignment of part of a debt: *Re Steel Wing*

other legal thing in action (*k*), of which express notice in writing has been given to the debtor, trustee or other person from whom the assignor would have been entitled to claim such debt or thing in action, is effectual in law (subject to equities having priority over the right of the assignee) to pass and transfer from the date of such notice—

(a) the legal right to such debt or thing in action;
(b) all legal and other remedies for the same (*l*); and
(c) the power to give a good discharge for the same without the concurrence of the assignor:

Provided that if the debtor, trustee or other person liable in respect of such debt or thing in action has notice—

(a) that the assignment is disputed by the assignor or any person claiming under him; or
(b) of any other opposing or conflicting claims to such debt or thing in action;

he may, if he thinks fit, either call upon the persons making claim thereto to interplead concerning the same, or pay the debt or other thing in action into court under the provisions of the Trustee Act 1925 (*m*).

(2) This section does not affect the provisions of the Policies of Assurance Act 1867 (*n*).

Notice in writing is essential to enable the assignor to sue in his own name (*o*). It may be given at any time before an action in respect of the chose has begun (*p*). The notice is good if it indicates with sufficient certainty that the assignment has been executed, and the name of the assignee is sufficiently disclosed if there is a reference to the deed of assignment (*q*). If a date is stated, it must be correctly stated (*r*). The notice may be given by either the assignor or the

---

Co., Ltd., [1921] 1 Ch. 349; but cf. *Ramsey* v. *Hartley* (1977), Times, 1st March. But an assignment of part of the debt may be a good equitable assignment: *Walter and Sullivan, Ltd.* v. *J. Murphy & Sons, Ltd.*, [1955] 2 Q.B. 584 (C.A.); [1955] 1 All E.R. 843 and see generally (1959), C.L.J. 99 (J. C. Hall); (1966) 30 Conv. (N.S.) 286 (M. C. Cullity and H. A. J. Ford).

(*k*) Equitable things in actions are within the section: *Re Pain*, [1919] 1 Ch. 38; and see *Torkington* v. *Magee*, [1902] 2 K.B. 427, 430, 431. It is generally considered that the section does not apply to future things in action; but see Sykes, *The Law of Securities* (2nd Edn.), pp. 600–601.

(*l*) Including rights of set-off: *Robbie* (*N. W.*) *& Co., Ltd.* v. *Witney Warehouse Co., Ltd.*, [1963] 3 All E.R. 613 (C.A.). See also *Rother Iron Works, Ltd.* v. *Canterbury Precision Engineers, Ltd.*, [1974] Q.B. 1 (C.A.); [1973] 1 All E.R. 394; *George Baker (Transport), Ltd.* v. *Eynon*, [1974] 1 All E.R. 900 (C.A.); *Security Trust Co.* v. *Royal Bank of Canada*, [1976] A.C. 503; [1976] 1 All E.R. 381 (P.C.); and see *Aluminium Industrie Vaassen BV* v. *Romalpa Aluminium, Ltd.*, [1976] 2 All E.R. 552; *Business Computers, Ltd.* v. *Anglo-African Leasing, Ltd.* (1977), 121 Sol. Jo. 201.

(*m*) Section 63. The county court limit is now £5,000. Less than £500 cannot be paid into the High Court without prior acceptance: see *Practice Direction*, [1976] 1 Lloyd's Rep. 281.

(*n*) See p. 108, *infra*.

(*o*) Law of Property Act 1925, s. 136 (1); and see also s. 137 (3) (p. 474, *infra*) for equitable interests. This is so even if the debtor is unable to read and other means are used to bring the assignment to his attention: *Hockley and Papworth* v. *Goldstein* (1920), 90 L.J. K.B. 111. A payment on account does not estop the debtor from relying on the statutory requirement for notice in writing: *Hockley and Papworth* v. *Goldstein, supra*.

(*p*) *Bateman* v. *Hunt*, [1904] 2 K.B. 530 (C.A.); *Compania Colombiana de Seguros* v. *Pacific Steam Navigation Co.*, [1965] 1 Q.B. 101, at p. 129; [1964] 1 All E.R. 216, at pp. 235, 236.

(*q*) *Denney, Gasquet and Metcalfe* v. *Conklin*, [1913] 3 K.B. 177.

(*r*) *Harrison* (*W. F.*) *& Co., Ltd.* v. *Burke*, [1956] 2 All E.R. 169 (C.A.). This case also suggests that the amount of the debt must be correctly stated. See (1956), 72 L.Q.R. 321 (R.E.M.). But a date need not be stated: *Van Lynn Developments, Ltd.* v. *Pelias Construction Co., Ltd.*, [1969] 1 Q.B. 658 (C.A.); [1968] 3 All E.R. 824.

assignee or their successors in title (s). In the case of joint debtors notice must be given to both (t).

The assignment takes effect on receipt of the notice thereof by or on behalf of the debtor (u).

The priority of assignments is determined by the date of notice under the rule in *Dearle* v. *Hall* as extended by s. 137 (1) of the Law of Property Act 1925 (x).

An assignment which fails to fulfil the requirements of the section may take effect as a good equitable assignment. Equitable assignments are dealt with in the following pages. Two points will be mentioned here. First, the equitable assignee of a legal chose cannot sue in his own name (y). He must either join the assignor as plaintiff, if the latter consents, or, if he does not, as defendant (z). Secondly, quite apart from the statutory notice, it is necessary in all assignments of things in action to give notice of the assignment to the debtor, trustee or other person liable to pay the debt or distribute the fund. This is, first, for the purpose of preventing such person from paying the debt or handing the fund to the assignor; secondly to prevent a subsequent incumbrancer or purchaser without notice of the assignment from gaining priority over it (a); and thirdly, to prevent any equities or further equities arising.

Section 137 preserves the rule governing assignments of things in action other than negotiable instruments (b), namely, that the assignee takes them subject to all equities, whether he has notice of the equities or not (c). Thus an assignee of shares or debentures takes them subject to all equitable claims of the company, such as the company's lien on the shares of its members. But this only extends to cover claims arising before notice of the assignment, and the company cannot, after such notice, create fresh equities (d).

(s) *Bateman* v. *Hunt, supra.*

(t) *Josselson* v. *Borst*, [1938] 1 K.B. 723; [1937] 3 All E.R. 722. For the service of notices, see p. 365, *infra.*

(u) *Holt* v. *Heatherfield Trust, Ltd.*, [1942] 2 K.B. 1; [1942] 1 All E.R. 404.

(x) See pp. 469 *et seq.*, *infra*; (1975) 39 Conv. (N.S.) 261 (Diana M. Kloss). For registration of company charges, see pp. 181 *et seq.*, *infra.*

(y) Nor can the original creditor sue without joining the assignee: *Walter and Sullivan, Ltd.* v. *J. Murphy & Sons, Ltd.*, [1955] 2 Q.B. 584 (C.A.); [1955] 1 All E.R. 843. See *Warner Brothers Records Inc.* v. *Rollgreen, Ltd.*, [1976] Q.B. 430 at p. 435 (C.A.); [1975] 2 All E.R. 105.

(z) *Performing Right Society, Ltd.* v. *London Theatre of Varieties, Ltd.*, [1924] A.C. 1 (H.L.); *Holt* v. *Heatherfield Trust, Ltd., supra.*

(a) *Spencer* v. *Clarke* (1878), 9 Ch. D. 137. For priorities, see pp. 463 *et seq.*, *infra.*

(b) See *London Joint Stock Bank* v. *Simmons*, [1892] A.C. 201 (H.L.); *Lloyds Bank* v. *Swiss Bankverein* (1913), 108 L.T. 143.

(c) See, generally, *Roxburghe* v. *Cox* (1881), 17 Ch. D. 520; *Biggerstaff* v. *Rowatt's Wharf, Ltd.*, [1896] 2 Ch. 93. But the parties may agree to the assignment being without set-off or counter-claim: see *First National Bank of Chicago, Ltd.* v. *Moorgate Properties, Ltd.* (1975), *Times*, 21st October. But a claim to damages for fraud in a contract is not prior to the claim of an assignee of the contract where the debtor is not in a position to rescind the contract: *Stoddart* v. *Union Trust,,Ltd.*, [1912] 1 K.B. 181; *cf.* *Lawrence* v. *Hayes*, [1927] 2 K.B. 111. Upon a claim by mortgagees in possession for rent, the tenant was not allowed to set off a claim for damages on a covenant by the mortgagor, since this claim was not an interest in the land by which the mortgagee was bound: *Reeves* v. *Pope*, [1914] 2 K.B. 284 (C.A.).

(d) *Bradford Banking Co.* v. *Briggs* (1886), 12 App. Cas. 29. And an assignee from a trustee-beneficiary can claim nothing from the trust estate until any default of the trustee has been made good: *Doering* v. *Doering* (1889), 42 Ch. D. 203.

Equitable Assignment. Creation.—An equitable assignment by way of security may be made, for example:

(1) By an agreement between a debtor and his creditor that a specific thing in action which is, or will be, in the hands of or due from a third person and which belongs to the debtor, shall be applied in discharge of the debt (*e*); or

(2) By an order given by the debtor whereby the holder of a fund is directed or authorised to pay it to the creditor (*f*).

The assignment may, generally, be made either by writing or verbally (*g*), no particular words being necessary (*h*), provided that the intention is sufficiently expressed (*i*). An equitable assignment out and out, and an equitable assignment which is intended to operate as a security only, in most respects resemble each other. A mere charge on a fund or debt operates, indeed, as a partial equitable assignment (*k*). But while an equitable assignment which merely gives a charge on property (*l*), and an equitable assignment of property not yet in existence, both require valuable consideration to support them, since they operate by way of contract, an absolute assignment of existing property is effective although voluntary (*m*).

The equitable assignee of a debt is not in the same position as to the obligation of using diligence, as the holder of a bill of exchange or promissory note; but, like a mortgagee in possession, he is chargeable with wilful default (*n*).

Essentials of equitable assignment.—An equitable assignment will not be valid, unless there is an engagement to pay the debt owing by the assignor and to pay it out of a particular fund (*o*), and to the

---

(*e*) *Row* v. *Dawson* (1749), 1 Ves. S. 331; *Brice* v. *Bannister* (1878), 3 Q.B.D. 569; *Palmer* v. *Carey*, [1926] A.C. 703 (P.C).

(*f*) *Row* v. *Dawson*, *supra*; *Burn* v. *Carvalho* (1839), 4 My. & C. 690; *Rodick* v. *Gandell* (1852), 1 De G.M. & G. 763, 777; *Diplock* v. *Hammond* (1854), 5 De G.M. & G. 320; *Palmer* v. *Carey*, *supra*; *Cotton* v. *Heyl*, [1930] 1 Ch. 510; *Re Warren, Ex parte Wheeler* v. *The Trustee in Bankruptcy*, [1938] Ch. 725; [1938] 2 All E.R. 331; *William Brandt's Sons & Co.* v. *Dunlop Rubber Co.*, [1905] A.C. 454 (H.L.).
Such an equitable assignment will not be a bill of exchange: see *Brice* v. *Bannister*, *supra*; *Tibbits* v. *George* (1836), 5 A. & E. 107.

(*g*) *Gurnell* v. *Gardner* (1863), 4 Giff. 626. It was suggested in *Re Richardson, Shillito* v. *Hobson* (1885), 30 Ch.D. 396, that an assignment of a debt had to be effected in writing. As to when writing is required by statute, see p. 115, *infra*.

(*h*) *William Brandt's Sons & Co.* v. *Dunlop Rubber Co.*, *supra*, at p. 462; *Inland Revenue Commissioners* v. *Electric and Musical Industries, Ltd.*, [1949] 1 All E.R. 120, at p. 126.

(*i*) *William Brandt's Sons & Co.* v. *Dunlop Rubber Co.*, *supra*, at p. 462.

(*k*) *Durham Bros.* v. *Robertson*, [1898] 1 Q.B. 765 (C.A.), at p. 769.

(*l*) *Re Earl of Lucan, Hardinge* v. *Cobden* (1890), 45 Ch. D. 470; *Squib* v. *Wyn* (1717), 1 P. Wms. 378.

(*m*) *Squib* v. *Wyn*, *supra*; *Nanney* v. *Morgan* (1887), 37 Ch. D. 346; *German* v. *Yates* (1915), 32 T.L.R. 52; *Re Westerton*, [1919] 2 Ch. 104; *Holt* v. *Heatherfield Trust, Ltd.*, [1942] 2 K.B. 1; [1942] 1 All E.R. 404; *Re McArdle*, [1951] Ch. 669 (C.A.); [1951] 1 All E.R. 905; *Re Wale*, [1956] 3 All E.R. 280. And see (1943), 59 L.Q.R. 58, 208 (R. E. M.); *ibid.*, 129 (H. A. Hollond); (1951), 67 L.Q.R. 295 (R. E. M.); (1955), 33 Can. B.R. 284 (L. A. Sheridan); and the articles referred to in footnote (*j*), p. 102, *supra*.

(*n*) *Glyn* v. *Hood* (1860), 1 De G.F. & J. 334.

(*o*) *Watson* v. *Duke of Wellington* (1830), 1 Russ. & M. 602, 605; *Percival* v. *Dunn* (1885), 29 Ch. D. 128; *Re Gunsbourg, Ex parte Trustee* (1919), 88 L.J. K.B. 479.

person who claims under the assignment (*p*). Therefore the assignment of the benefit of a contract to make a loan, is not good as an equitable assignment, since there is no particular fund bound by the original contract (*q*). But it is not necessary that the exact amount either of the debt to be paid or of that out of which it is directed to be paid, should be ascertained (*r*).

Charge on particular fund must be clear.—The engagement that the particular fund shall be made liable to the debt must be clear (*s*). A letter to the holder of the fund, stating that a particular person is a claimant upon it may be an assignment (*t*); but a promise to pay the debt out of the particular fund is not, if such an arrangement is under the circumstances countermandable (*u*); nor, for the same reason, a direction to apply the fund where no consideration is proved (*x*).

Nor is an assignment created by giving an authority to a person without interest in the debt to receive it though he promises to pay it to the creditor of the person who gives the authority, because such a transaction comprises neither a direction to the person who owes the money, nor a direct agreement between the debtor and the creditor (*y*). If, however, there is a sufficient indication that the supposed assignee is to have the benefit of the fund or thing in action in question, in addition to relying on the credit of the assignor, or, as it is sometimes put, is to be paid "out of the fund" as distinguished from "when the assignor gets the fund", a valid equitable assignment is created, provided that the transaction is for value. The intention must be that the property shall pass (*z*). A cheque is not an equitable assignment of the drawer's balance at his bankers, being in the nature of a bill of exchange (*a*).

Effect of equitable assignment.—We have seen (*b*) that a thing in action was formerly not capable of being assigned at law without the express or implied consent of the holder of the fund to apply it in accordance with the assignment, except in the case of assignments made valid by custom, such as transfers of bills of exchange, or by statute. In equity, however, the assignee of a legal thing in action, that is a thing recoverable in a court of law, could sue under an authority enabling him to sue in the name of the assignor, and the assignee of an equitable thing in action, that is a thing recoverable in a court of equity only, could sue in equity in his own name, pro-

---

(*p*) *Bell* v. *L. & N.W. Ry. Co.* (1852), 15 Beav. 548.
(*q*) *Western Wagon, etc., Co.* v. *West*, [1892] 1 Ch. 271; *May* v. *Lane* (1894), 64 L.J. Q.B. 236 (C.A.).
(*r*) *Riccard* v. *Prichard* (1855), 1 K. & J. 277.
(*s*) *Brown, Shipley & Co.* v. *Kough* (1885), 29 Ch. D. 848 (C.A.).
(*t*) *Re Kent and Sussex Sawmills, Ltd.*, [1947] Ch. 177; [1946] 2 All E.R. 638.
(*u*) *Malcolm* v. *Scott* (1843), 3 Hare 39.
(*x*) *Re Whitting, Ex parte Hall* (1879), 10 Ch. D. 615 (C.A.).
(*y*) *Rodick* v. *Gandell* (1852), 1 De G.M. & G. 763.
(*z*) *Gorringe* v. *Irwell India Rubber, etc., Works* (1886), 34 Ch. D. 128 (C.A.); *Re Casey's Patents, Stewart* v. *Casey*, [1892] 1 Ch. 104 (C.A.).
(*a*) *Hopkinson* v. *Forster* (1874), L.R. 19 Eq. 74.
(*b*) See p. 102, *supra*.

vided he had given notice to the holder of the fund (*c*). Such an assignment would stand, though the assignor became bankrupt, or died before the notice reached the holder of the fund, or could otherwise be acted upon (*d*), since it was effective between assignor and assignee without notice of the holder of the fund (*e*). Nevertheless, notice should be given since notice prevents a subsequent assignee from gaining priority by himself giving notice (*f*), it prevents the holder of the fund from obtaining a good discharge by afterwards paying the fund to the assignor (*g*), and it prevents any or further equities being set up against the assignee. Moreover the giving of notice in writing may give a right to sue at law under s. 136 of the Law of Property Act 1925.

When a debtor has received notice of an equitable assignment of the debt he is bound to pay it to the assignee, although the latter refuses to give him an indemnity. It is no excuse for refusal and payment to the assignor that he has brought an action to which the debtor has no legal defence, for the court will indemnify him by making the wrongful claimant pay the costs. And the fact that, after the assignment, the assignor has become bankrupt, or has made a composition with his creditors, makes no difference (*h*). Where the mortgage is of a fund in court a stop order should be obtained, and this is equivalent to a notice given to the trustees (*i*). Where government stock, or the stock or shares or debentures of any public company are equitably mortgaged a stop notice may be given instead of notice to the company (*k*). Where a debt is a trade debt notice must be given to the debtor. Otherwise in the event of the bankruptcy of the mortgagor the title of the trustee in bankruptcy will prevail (*l*).

Unless by the instrument creating the thing in action it is made assignable by the creditor free from equities between himself and the debtor, the assignee takes subject to rights of set off and otherwise between the debtor and the assignor existing before notice of the assignment (*m*).

(*c*) *Row* v. *Dawson* (1749), 1 Ves. S. 331.

(*d*) *Smith* v. *Everett* (1792), 4 Bro. C.C. 63; *Burn* v. *Carvalho* (1839), 4 My. & Cr. 690; *Gurnell* v. *Gardner* (1863), 4 Giff. 626; *Walker* v. *Bradford Old Bank* (1884), 12 Q.B.D. 511.

(*e*) *Rodick* v. *Gandell, supra; Gorringe* v. *Irwell India Rubber, etc., Works, supra.* Notice is not necessary to complete the title of the assignee: *Ward* v. *Duncombe*, [1893] A.C. 369 (H.L.), at p. 392.

(*f*) *Dearle* v. *Hall* (1828), 3 Russ. 1; *Re Dallas*, [1904] 2 Ch. 385 (C.A.). Where the notice is in respect of an assignment of an equitable interest in real or personal property it must be in writing: Law of Property Act 1925, s. 137 (3); see p. 474, *infra*.

(*g*) *Stocks* v. *Dobson* (1853), 4 De G.M. & G. 11.

(*h*) *Hutchinson* v. *Heyworth* (1838), 9 A. & E. 375; *Jones* v. *Farrell* (1857), 1 De G. & J. 208.

(*i*) *Pinnock* v. *Bailey* (1883), 23 Ch. D. 497; *Montefiore* v. *Guedalla*, [1903] 2 Ch. 26 (C.A.). And see p. 163, *infra*. Express notice should also be given to the trustees.

(*k*) A stop notice was formerly called a notice in lieu of distringas: see, further, p. 112, *infra*. For a form of affidavit and stop notice, see 14 Ency. Forms and Precedents (4th Edn.), 869, 870.

(*l*) *Rutter* v. *Everett*, [1895] 2 Ch. 872; *Re Neal, Ex parte Trustee*, [1914] 2 K.B. 910; *Re Collins*, [1925] Ch. 556. And see Bankruptcy Act 1914, s. 38.

(*m*) See p. 104, *supra*.

.

Mortgages of policies of life insurance (*n*).—Mortgages of life insurance policies are principally effected as collateral security to mortgages of land. Building societies frequently insist on such collateral security. An advantageous mortgage scheme for a person paying income tax at the standard rate on a substantial part of his income is an endowment mortgage (*o*). Under this scheme the principal is left outstanding until the end of the mortgage period and it is then paid off from the proceeds of an endowment policy payable at that time.

Policies of life insurance are assignable either in equity or under the Policies of Assurance Act 1867 (*p*). An equitable assignment of a policy of life insurance is subject to the rules governing equitable assignments generally (*q*). An assignment under the Act of 1867 is a legal assignment subject to certain formalities. If these are observed the assignee can sue in his own name (*r*). The assignment must be in writing, either endorsed on the policy or by a separate instrument in the form given in the Schedule to the Act or to the purpose and effect thereof (*s*), and written notice of the date and purport of the assignment must be given to the insurance company at their principal place of business (*t*). The company must acknowledge receipt of a notice, if requested, and on payment of a fee not exceeding five shillings (*u*). An acknowledgment is conclusive evidence against the company of the receipt of the notice (*u*).

The mortgage takes the form (*x*) of an assignment with a proviso for re-assignment. It commonly includes covenants by the mortgagee not to permit the policy to become void, to pay premiums and produce the receipts therefor to the mortgagee, with power in case of default for the mortgagee to pay premiums and for any such payments to be a charge on the policy (*y*). The mortgage should also provide for a sale (*z*), surrender or exchange of the policy by the mortgagee and other powers.

(*n*) See, generally, MacGillivray and Parkington on *Insurance Law* (6th Edn.), pp. 574 *et seq.* For assignment of policies of marine insurance, see Chalmers' *Marine Insurance Act*, 1906 (8th Edn.), pp. 18, 20.

(*o*) See p. 30, *supra.*

(*p*) The provisions of this Act are not affected by the Law of Property Act 1925, s. 136; *ibid.*, s. 136 (2). The Law of Property Act does, however, offer an alternative method of legal assignment, and if a formal mortgage is made it will generally be made under that Act.

(*q*) See p. 105, *supra.*

(*r*) Section 1. But see the Stamp Act 1891, s. 118.

(*s*) Section 5; *cf. Crossley* v. *City of Glasgow Life Assurance Co.* (1876), 4 Ch. D. 421; *Spencer* v. *Clarke* (1878), 9 Ch. D. 137.

(*t*) Section 3. The policy must specify the places at which notices of assignment may be given: s. 4. For forms of notice, see 14 Ency. Forms and Precedents (4th Edn.), 868. For service of notice, see p. 365, *infra.*

(*u*) Section 6.

(*x*) For forms, see 14 Ency. Forms and Precedents (4th Edn.), pp. 540 *et seq.* For a form of combined mortgage to a building society, see 3 Ency. Forms and Precedents (4th Edn.), p. 741. A mandate conditional on the grantor predeceasing the person to whom it is given is not within the statutory provisions: *Re Williams, Williams* v. *Ball*, [1917] 1 Ch. 1 (C.A.).

(*y*) There will be a right to keep the policy on foot and a charge even if there is no express provision: *Gill* v. *Downing* (1874), L.R. 17 Eq. 316, see pp. 628, 651, *infra.*

(*z*) The statutory power of sale (see p. 360, *infra*) applies to mortgages by deed of policies and other choses in action.

The mortgagee will usually take possession of the policy (*a*). He takes subject to equities (*b*).

If there are several mortgages their priority will be regulated by the order in which notice of the assignments was given (*c*), save that a second mortgagee with notice, whether actual, imputed or constructive (*d*), of a first mortgagee cannot gain priority over the first mortgage by giving notice before the first mortgagee (*e*).

Where a mortgage of a life assurance policy is to be taken as collateral security an assignment is sometimes rendered unnecessary by the creditor taking out a policy on the life of the debtor (*f*). In the absence of express contract, the policy will, on the discharge of the debt, belong to the mortgagor if he pays the premiums, or is with his own knowledge charged with them in account (*g*). In other cases the policy will belong absolutely to the mortgagee (*h*).

Unless the terms of a life policy provide to the contrary the policy will be avoided by the suicide of the insured (*i*). It has not been decided whether, if the policy has been mortgaged, the security is avoided (*k*). Express provision is usually made in the policy for it not to become void in such circumstances against the assignee. Where a policy contains a clause to the effect that it shall be valid notwithstanding the suicide of the assured, a mortgagee, whether legal or equitable, can enforce it against the company in that event, even where the mortgagee could recover the debt from another source, and the company has no claim for indemnity or repayment against the estate of the assured (*l*). And this is so, although the company is itself the mortgagee (*m*).

A legal mortgage of a policy is discharged by re-assignment or receipt (*n*), an equitable mortgage by cancellation. The policy must be returned to the mortgagor or handed over to a subsequent mortgagee, if any. Notice of the discharge should be given to the company (*n*).

Mortgages of shares.—A legal mortgage of shares is effected by a

---

(*a*) *Spencer* v. *Clarke* (1878), 9 Ch. D. 137.

(*b*) *E.g.*, a contract of insurance is a contract *uberrimae fidei*, so that the policy may be avoided by the company if there has not been full disclosure by the insured.

(*c*) Policies of Assurance Act 1867, s. 3.

(*d*) *Re Weniger's Policy*, [1910] 2 Ch. 291; *cf. Re Lake, Ex parte Cavendish*, [1903] 1 K.B. 151.

(*e*) *Newman* v. *Newman* (1885), 28 Ch. D. 674; *Re Wallis, Ex parte Jenks*, [1902] 1 K.B. 719.

(*f*) The policy should not be taken out by the borrower in the name of the creditor because the creditor would have no rights under the policy, not being a party thereto: see *Re Sinclair's Life Policy*, [1938] Ch. 799; [1938] 3 All E.R. 124.

(*g*) *Morland* v. *Isaac* (1855), 20 Beav. 389; *Drysdale* v. *Piggott* (1856), 8 De G.M. & G. 546; *Frems* v. *Brade* (1858), 2 De G. & J. 582; *Bruce* v. *Garden* (1869), 5 Ch. App. 32; *Salt* v. *Marquess of Northampton*, [1892] A.C. 1 (H.L.); and see p. 557, *infra*.

(*h*) *Bruce* v. *Garden, supra*.

(*i*) *Beresford* v. *Royal Insurance Co., Ltd.*, [1938] A.C. 586 (H.L.); [1938] 2 All E.R. 602.

(*k*) *Beresford* v. *Royal Insurance Co., Ltd., supra*, at p. 600. But see *Hardy* v. *Motor Insurers' Bureau*, [1964] 2 Q.B. 745 (C.A.); [1964] 2 All E.R. 742.

(*l*) *Moore* v. *Woolsey* (1854), 4 E. & B. 243; *Solicitors Life Assurance Society* v. *Lamb* (1864), 2 De G.J. & S. 251.

(*m*) *White* v. *British Empire Mutual Life Assurance Co.* (1868), L.R. 7 Eq. 394. And see *Royal London Mutual Insurance Society* v. *Barrett*, [1928] Ch. 411.

(*n*) See p. 556, *infra*.

transfer of the shares to the mortgagee (*o*), subject to an agreement for their re-transfer on repayment of the loan (*p*).

It is not usual to mortgage shares by means of a registered transfer of them, particularly if the shares are not fully paid up, as such a transaction makes the mortgagee a shareholder, and gives him the rights and imposes upon him the liabilities, where they exist, of a shareholder (*q*). A mortgage of shares is most commonly effected by a deposit of the share certificates with the mortgagee accompanied by a memorandum of deposit (*r*). This is not a mere pledge, but affects a true equitable mortgage entitling the mortgagee to foreclosure (*s*). The memorandum usually contains, *inter alia*, a statement that the deposit is by way of security, a covenant for payment of principal and interest, a proviso for redemption, a power for the mortgagee to sell the shares (*t*), a covenant by the mortgagor not to incur a forfeiture, and an undertaking by the mortgagor to execute a registered transfer (*u*).

Sometimes the deposit is accompanied by a form of transfer executed by the mortgagor, but leaving the name of the transferee and the date blank (*v*). This method, however, has the disadvantage that the transfer, if required to be by deed (*x*), cannot be validly completed without re-execution by the mortgagor (*y*), though a person who executes a deed of transfer in blank may be estopped from denying its validity

---

(*o*) The transfer should be for the nominal consideration of 50p. The manner of transfer will be governed by the company's articles of association. But see the Stock Transfer Act 1963, by which, notwithstanding anything to the contrary in any act or instrument relating to particular shares, the transfer of such shares may be under hand and signed by the transferor alone, whose signature need not be attested: ss. 1, 2. Shares are excluded from the definition of personal chattels for the purpose of the Bills of Sale Acts: Bills of Sale Act 1878, s. 4.

(*p*) For forms of agreements, see 14 Ency. Forms and Precedents (4th Edn.), pp. 604 *et seq.* The company is not concerned with the agreement accompanying the transfer: Companies Act 1948, s. 117.

(*q*) Where the shares have been transferred to the mortgagee, a mandatory injunction may be granted to enforce an agreement by him to vote in accordance with the wishes of the mortgagor: *Puddephatt* v. *Leith*, [1916] 1 Ch. 200; *Musselwhite* v. *C. H. Musselwhite & Son, Ltd.*, [1962] Ch. 964, at pp. 981–984; [1962] 1 All E.R. 201, at pp. 206–207.

(*r*) While the mortgagor remains the registered holder of the shares he must vote as the mortgagee directs: *Wise* v. *Landsell*, [1921] 1 Ch. 420.

(*s*) *Harrold* v. *Plenty*, [1901] 2 Ch. 314.

(*t*) There is an implied power to sell on reasonable notice (see p. 359, *infra*) and an express power if the memorandum is under seal (Law of Property Act 1925, s. 101). For foreclosure, see p. 383, *infra*.

(*u*) For forms, see 14 Ency. Forms and Precedents (4th Edn.), pp. 676, 677; and Precedent 15 in the Appendix, *infra*. A mortgage of shares would not, it is submitted, extend to a bonus issue based on the original holding (*cf.* accretions to the security in relation to mortgages of land, p. 36, *supra*). Accordingly the memorandum should contain an express provision extending the security to a bonus issue. Where a rights issue is offered, the mortgagee should consult the borrower. It is submitted that the mortgagee can only disclaim or sell the rights if the borrower refuses to pay the price of the shares or to allow the price to be added to the security (see *Waddell* v. *Hutton* 1911 S.C. 575). It is further submitted that the mortgagee cannot on his own initiative take up the issue and add the shares and the price to the security.

(*v*) See, e.g., *Barclay* v. *Prospect Mortgages, Ltd.*, [1974] 2 All E.R. 672.

(*x*) But see now Stock Transfer Act 1963, under which fully paid up registered securities may, generally, be transferred by instrument under hand, notwithstanding anything to the contrary in the articles.

(*y*) *Powell* v. *London and Provincial Bank*, [1893] 2 Ch. 555 (C.A.); *Ireland* v. *Hart*, [1902] 1 Ch. 522. The principle has been applied to a mortgage of a ship in *Burgis* v. *Constantine*, [1908] 2 K.B. 484.

as against bona fide purchasers from the grantee without notice (z).
But a blank transfer will be effective in the case of shares which are
transferable by writing under hand only (a). Such an instrument,
when filled in, might pass the legal property, for by delivering it to the
mortgagee the mortgagor must be presumed to have authorised him to
act as his agent for the purposes of completing the transfer (b), but this
cannot apply where the transfer is required to be by a deed, which can
only be executed by an agent appointed by instrument under seal (c).
Even in such cases, however, a person dealing with the mortgagee,
ought to make enquiries and cannot claim the benefit of being purchaser
for value without notice, so as to acquire a better right than the person
from whom he received the instrument (d). Accordingly it is usual for
the memorandum to include a provision whereby the mortgagor
appoints the mortgagee his attorney to complete and redeliver the
transfers (e). And, generally, fully paid up registered securities may
since the Stock Transfer Act 1963, be transferred by instrument under
hand, notwithstanding anything to the contrary contained in any
enactment or instrument relating to the shares (f).

Notice of the deposit of share certificates should be given to the
company. This is not for the purpose of priorities for no trust may be
entered on the register of a company (g). Accordingly the rule in
Dearle v. *Hall* (h) does not apply to equitable mortgages of shares (i).
Nevertheless notice is advisable. If the company has notice it will
generally not register another person as owner while there are conflicting
claims (k). Also, while the mortgagee takes the shares subject to all
equitable claims of the company, such as the company's lien on the
shares of its members, this only extends to claims arising before notice
of the mortgage, and the company cannot, after such notice, create
fresh equities (l). Notice is not however, required to protect the
mortgagee of shares against a claim by the mortgagor's trustee in
bankruptcy under the reputed ownership clause (m), since things in
action, including shares (n), other than debts due or growing due to

---

(z) *Earl of Sheffield* v. *London Joint Stock Bank* (1888), 13 App. Cas. 333; *Waterhouse*
v. *Bank of Ireland* (1891), 29 L.R.Ir. 384; *London Joint Stock Bank* v. *Simmonds*,
[1892] A.C. 201 (H.L.); *Fuller* v. *Glyn Mills, Currie & Co.*, [1914] 2 K.B. 168.

(a) *Ortigosa* v. *Brown, Janson & Co.* (1878), 47 L.J. Ch. 168; cf. *France* v. *Clark*
(1884), 26 Ch. D. 257 (C.A.).

(b) *Colonial Bank* v. *Cady* (1890), 15 App. Cas. 267 (H.L.), at p. 286.

(c) *Powell* v. *London and Provincial Bank, supra*, at p. 558. See *Fitch Lovell, Ltd.*
v. *Inland Revenue Commissioners*, [1962] 3 All E.R. 685.

(d) *France* v. *Clark, supra.*

(e) *Hibblewhite* v. *M'Morine* (1840), 6 M. & W. 200; *Société Générale de Paris* v.
Walker (1885), 11 App. Cas. 20 (H.L.); *Re Seymour, Fielding* v. *Seymour*, [1913] 1 Ch.
475 (C.A.).

(f) Sections 1, 2.

(g) Companies Act 1948, s. 117; *Société Générale de Paris* v. *Walker, supra.*

(h) See pp. 463 *et seq., infra.*

(i) Priorities of mortgages of shares are governed by the same rules of priority as
applied to mortgages of land before 1926. As to which, see Part VI, *infra.*

(k) See *Ireland* v. *Hart, supra.*

(l) *Bradford Banking Co., Ltd.* v. *Briggs & Co., Ltd.* (1886), 12 App. Cas. 29 (H.L.);
Mackereth v. *Wigan Coal and Iron Co., Ltd.*, [1916] 2 Ch. 293.

(m) See pp. 91 *et seq., supra.*

(n) *Colonial Bank* v. *Whinney* (1886), 11 App. Cas. 426; *Re Collins*, [1925] Ch. 556.

the bankrupt in the course of his trade or business, are not deemed goods within the meaning of the clause.

The limited effect of notice could be overcome by giving the company a stop notice (the former notice in lieu of distringas (*o*)). This entitles the mortgagee to notice from the company of an application to transfer, and gives the mortgagee an opportunity of obtaining a restraining order or an injunction (*p*). This procedure is, however, rarely used.

Mortgage of partnership share (*q*).—Under the Partnership Act 1890, s. 31, an assignment by a partner of his share in the partnership, either absolute or by way of mortgage, does not, as against the other partners, entitle the assignee during the continuance of the partnership to interfere in the management of the partnership business or affairs (*r*) or to require accounts or inspection of books (*s*). It only entitles the assignee to receive the assignor's share of the profits. But on a dissolution, the assignee is entitled to receive the assignor's share of the assets, and for the purpose of ascertaining the share, he is entitled to an account as from the date of dissolution (*t*). Under s. 33 the partnership may, at the option of the other partners, be dissolved if any partner suffers his share of the partnership property to be charged under the Act, for his separate debt. Such mortgages, therefore, without the consent of the other partner, afford a very unsatisfactory security.

If the mortgage is by deed the mortgagee will have the statutory powers of sale and appointing a receiver (*u*), and, whether by deed or not, may enforce his security by foreclosure (*v*). Notice of the mortgage should be given to the firm.

Mortgage of debts.—Every sub-mortgage involves a mortgage of a debt (*x*). Such a mortgage may be effected by either a legal or equitable assignment of the debt in the manner already mentioned (*y*) with a proviso for redemption (*z*). The mortgage should relieve the mortgagee of any liability should the debt become irrecoverable (*a*).

(*o*) R.S.C. Ord. 50. And see p. 162, *infra*.

(*p*) See *Société Générale de Paris* v. *Tramways Union Co.* (1884), 14 Q.B.D. 424 (C.A.), at p. 453.

(*q*) For forms, see 14 Ency. Forms and Precedents (4th Edn.), pp. 593, 677, 678, 679. A mortgage of a share in a partnership is a mortgage of a chose in action, and is not required to be registered as a bill of sale: *Re Bainbridge, Ex parte Fletcher* (1878), 8 Ch. D. 218. And in a case of bankruptcy, the doctrine of reputed ownership does not apply.

(*r*) See, *e.g.*, *Re Garwood's Trusts, Garwood* v. *Paynter*, [1903] 1 Ch. 236.

(*s*) *Bonnin* v. *Neame*, [1910] 1 Ch. 732.

(*t*) See *Watts* v. *Driscoll*, [1901] 1 Ch. 294 (C.A.).

(*u*) See pp. 359, 301 *infra*.

(*v*) *Whetham* v. *Davey* (1885), 30 Ch. D. 574.

(*x*) See p. 260, *infra*.

(*y*) See p. 102, *supra*. If the assignment is a legal assignment the mortgagee will be able to sue the debtor without joining the mortgagor. The assignee of a judgment debt has the same rights of enforcing the judgment as the assignor had: *Goodman* v. *Robinson* (1886), 18 Q.B.D. 332; *cf. Forster* v. *Baker*, [1910] 2 K.B. 636, at p. 642. An assignee of part of a judgment debt cannot issue execution for the part assigned to him: *Forster* v. *Baker*, *supra*.

(*z*) For forms, see 14 Ency. Forms and Precedents (4th Edn.), pp. 568 *et seq.* and 679 to 682. And see Precedent 10 in the Appendix, *infra*.

(*a*) See *Ex parte Mure* (1788), 2 Cox Eq. Cas. 63; *Williams* v. *Price* (1824) 1 Sim. & St. 581.

There cannot be a legal assignment of a future debt. An assignment of a future debt if made for valuable consideration is treated as a contract to assign (*b*). Accordingly a mortgage of all the book debts due and owing, or which may, during the continuance of the security, become due and owing to the mortgagor, has been held to be sufficiently definite, and to pass the equitable interest in book debts incurred after the assignment, whether in the business carried on by the mortgagor at the time of the assignment or in any other business (*c*). But debts due or growing due in the course of a trade or business are within the reputed ownership clause in bankruptcy (*d*), and when there is a mortgage of such debts, the mortgagee must give notice to the debtor, and take every possible step to obtain possession of the debts. Otherwise in the event of the bankruptcy of the mortgagor the title of the trustee in bankruptcy will prevail (*e*). And a mortgage of payments to become due under contracts entered into by the mortgagor, but not completed at the date of a receiving order made against him, is void against the mortgagor's trustee in bankruptcy (*f*).

Until notice of the mortgage is given to the debtor the assignment is merely equitable (*g*). In the case of a mortgage of book debts the giving of such notice would generally be prejudicial to the mortgagor's credit. Accordingly it will generally be agreed that notice will not be given unless there is default and the mortgage will contain a provision whereby the mortgagor will appoint the mortgagee his attorney to collect the debts (*h*).

In the absence of notice, payment by the debtor to the mortgagor or a release by the mortgagor will be good as against the mortgagee (*i*).

The priority of such mortgages is governed by the date of the receipt by the debtor of notice of the mortgages (*k*).

Profit-sharing loans.—The book debts and goodwill of a business are sometimes mortgaged on the terms of the lender receiving a share of the profits in lieu of interest, or of the interest varying with the profits. Under the Partnership Act 1890 (*l*), such an arrangement, if made under a contract in writing signed by, or on behalf of all parties does not of itself constitute a partnership. But there may be further terms which indicate a partnership, and the substance of the

---

(*b*) *Holroyd* v. *Marshall* (1862), 10 H.L. Cas. 191. And see p. 114, *infra*.

(*c*) *Tailby* v. *Official Receiver* (1888), 13 App. Cas. 523 (H.L.).

(*d*) See p. 91, *supra*. And see also Bankruptcy Act 1914, s. 43 (1), whereby a mortgage by a person engaged in any trade or business of existing or future book debts will be void against his trustee in bankruptcy, as regards any debts not paid at the commencement of the bankruptcy, unless the mortgage has been registered as if it were a bill of sale under the Bills of Sale Act 1878. But this provision does not render void any assignment of book debts due at the date of assignment from specified debtors, or of debts growing due under specified contracts, or any assignment of book debts included in a transfer of business made bona fide and for value, or on any assignment of assets for the benefit of creditors generally.

(*e*) *Rutter* v. *Everett*, [1895] 2 Ch. 872; *Re Neal, Ex parte Trustee*, [1914] 2 K.B. 910.

(*f*) *Re Collins*, [1925] Ch. 556.

(*g*) Law of Property Act 1925, s. 136 (1).

(*h*) See 14 Ency. Forms and Precedents (4th Edn.), 592. And see Precedent 10 in the Appendix, *infra*.

(*i*) *Stocks* v. *Dobson* (1853), 4 De G.M. & G. 11.

(*k*) See pp. 463 *et seq.*, *infra*.

(*l*) Section 2 (3).

transaction will be looked at. If the transaction is in reality a partnership, "no phrasing of it by dextrous draftsmen will avail to avert the legal consequences of the contract, namely, full liability for the debts of the firm" (*m*).

In all such transactions, therefore, there must be a bona fide loan, one necessary ingredient of which is personal liability on the part of the borrower to repay the loan. An arrangement by which the lender is only to be repaid out of the assets of the business can never be a loan, but must be a partnership (*n*). Again, the lender must not take an interest in or share of the capital of the business *in specie*, because thereby he becomes jointly interested in capital and profits, or in other words becomes part owner of (*i.e.*, partner in) the business. Nor must his share of the profits vary in the proportion which his loan may from time to time bear to the rest of the capital, for that shows that he is not lending his money on the security of a definite share of the profits, but is really contributing to a joint speculation, in which he and the other speculators are to take profits *pari passu*. A provision for the return by the lender of a proportion of the profits received by him in one year, in case of subsequent losses, would be an almost certain mark of partnership, for no bona fide lender would submit to such a provision. For the same reason arbitration clauses must be avoided (*o*), and clauses giving the lender a right to interfere or take part in the management of the business. Even a covenant by the borrower to employ the loan exclusively in the business is not to be lightly introduced (*p*).

A lender under such a contract as is mentioned in s. 2 of the Partnership Act 1890, is not entitled to recover anything in respect of his loan or his share of profits in the event of a bankruptcy or insolvency of the borrower until all the claims of the other creditors have been satisfied (*q*). But if he has security he will nevertheless have his rights as a secured creditor (*r*).

Expectancies and future things in action (*s*).—A mortgage of a future thing in action, such as an expectancy under a will, being an assignment for value (*t*) of a future thing in action (*u*), operates as a contract to assign property answering the description of the property mortgaged when it comes into the mortgagor's possession, and passes

---

(*m*) *Adam* v. *Newbigging* (1888), 13 App. Cas. 308 (H.L.). An express declaration that no partnership is to be constituted is not conclusive: *ibid.*, at pp. 313, 316; *Weiner* v. *Harris*, [1910] 1 K.B. 285, 290.

(*n*) *Re Megevand, Ex parte Delhasse* (1878), 7 Ch. D. 511 (C.A.).

(*o*) See *Cox* v. *Hickman* (1860), 8 H.L. Cas. 268; *Syers* v. *Syers* (1876), 1 App. Cas. 174 (H.L.); *Pooley* v. *Driver* (1876), 5 Ch. D. 458; *Re Howard, Ex parte Tennant* (1877), 6 Ch. D. 303 (C.A.); *Davis* v. *Davis*, [1894] 1 Ch. 393; *Re Young, Ex parte Jones*, [1896] 2 Q.B. 484.

(*p*) See *Badeley* v. *Consolidated Bank* (1888), 38 Ch. D. 238 (C.A.). For forms of mortgage avoiding a partnership, see 14 Ency. Forms and Precedents (4th Edn.), pp. 486–490, 560–563, 696–700.

(*q*) Partnership Act 1890, s. 3. And see *Re Abenheim, Ex parte Abenheim* (1913), 109 L.T. 219, at p. 221.

(*r*) *Badeley* v. *Consolidated Bank, supra*.

(*s*) As to future acquired property and bills of sale, see p. 74, *supra*.

(*t*) The assignment is unenforceable if purely voluntary: *Meek* v. *Kettlewell* (1843), 1 Ph. 342.

(*u*) The property must be sufficiently described to be ascertainable: *Tailby* v. *Official Receiver* (1888), 13 App. Cas. 523 (H.L.). And see p. 12, *supra*.

an interest which will attach to the property when acquired (*x*). But until the property is acquired, there is only a liability on a contract, which is provable in the bankruptcy of the mortgagor, and from which he is released by the order of discharge (*y*). An expectant share in the estate of the living person transfers the share and does not impose a mere personal liability which is affected by the bankruptcy of the mortgagor (*z*).

Mortgage of interest in trust funds (*a*).—Such an interest is necessarily equitable. As has already been stated (*b*), it has been held that equitable things in action are within s. 136 of the Law of Property Act 1925, and capable of legal assignment (*c*). However, the generally accepted view is that a mortgage of an equitable interest must be an equitable mortgage (*d*). Nor, generally, is there any need for a statutory assignment, for if the whole interest is assigned the assignee can sue in his own name, without joining the original creditor (*e*).

As to the form of the assignment in such cases the Law of Property Act 1925, provides:

> **53.**—(1) (c) A disposition of an equitable interest or trust subsisting at the time of the disposition, must be in writing, signed by the person disposing of the same, or by his agent thereunto lawfully authorised in writing or by will (*f*).

But such a mortgage is, as a rule, created by a formal deed. And where it is desired to incorporate the statutory power of sale and other powers a deed is essential (*g*). The mortgage takes the form of an assignment of the interest with a proviso for re-assignment on payment of the loan (*h*). In view of the hazardous nature of such securities in such a case the mortgagee will generally insist on the mortgagor effecting a policy of insurance on his own life and mortgaging the policy as collateral security.

Where there are several such mortgages their priority depends upon the rule in *Dearle* v. *Hall*, as extended by the Law of Property Act 1925 (*i*).

The mere giving of notice of the assignment does not constitute the taking of possession of the interest. To do that the notice must also require payment of the income to the mortgagee (*k*). Where the

---

(*x*) *Holroyd* v. *Marshall* (1862), 10 H.L.Cas. 191.

(*y*) *Collyer* v. *Isaacs* (1881), 19 Ch. D. 342; *Wilmot* v. *Alton*, [1897] 1 Q.B. 17; *Bank of Scotland* v. *Macleod*, [1914] A. C. 311 (H.L.).

(*z*) *Re Lind, Industrial Finance Syndicate, Ltd.* v. *Lind*, [1915] 2 Ch. 345 (C.A.). As to the acquisition of expectancies at an undervalue, see the Law of Property Act 1925, s. 174 (p. 233, *infra*). For a form of mortgage of expectancy, see 14 Ency. Forms and Precedents (4th Edn.), 684.

(*a*) For mortgages of equitable interests in registered land, see p. 70, *supra*.

(*b*) See p. 103, *supra*.

(*c*) *Re Pain*, [1919] 1 Ch. 38; *cf. Torkington* v. *Magee*, [1902] 2 K.B. 427, 430, 431.

(*d*) And see the discussion on these cases and others in Marshall's *Assignment of Choses in Action*, pp. 162 *et seq*.

(*e*) *Performing Right Society, Ltd.* v. *London Theatre of Varieties, Ltd.*, [1924] A.C. 1 (H.L.).

(*f*) The section replaces s. 9 of the Statute of Frauds (1677.)   (*g*) See p. 360, *infra*.

(*h*) For forms, see 14 Ency. Forms and Precedents (4th Edn.), pp. 633 *et seq*.

(*i*) See p. 463, *infra*. As to stop orders where the fund is in court, see p. 163, *infra*.

(*k*) *Re Pawson's Settlement, Higgins* v. *Pawson*, [1917] 1 Ch. 541.

interest in a fund is a reversionary one, the trustees may, when the interest falls into possession, pay the whole fund over to the mortgagee (*l*). But they are not bound to do so and they may pay over only so much as suffices to discharge the principal, interest, and costs due on the mortgage (*m*).

Mortgage of patents.—A legal mortgage of letters patent takes the usual form of a mortgage of a chose in action, *i.e.*, a covenant for payment of principal and interest, an assignment of the property with a proviso for redemption, and covenants and provisos applicable to the nature of the property mortgaged (*n*). A mortgagee of a patent cannot sue for an infringement (*o*). No formalities are required for an equitable mortgage. The mortgage should be registered under the Patents Act 1949 (*p*), and the priority of such mortgages is determined by the date of registration.

Where a mortgage of a patent is registered the proprietor of the patent cannot grant effectual licences except with the authority of the mortgagee (*q*). The mortgagee may grant a licence, but he will be liable to account as mortgagee in possession for any royalties received (*r*).

A mortgage of a licence to manufacture a patented invention will take a similar form and may be registered (*s*).

Mortgage of copyright.—A legal mortgage of copyright takes the usual form of a mortgage of a chose in action, *i.e.*, a covenant to pay, an assignment of the copyright (*t*) with a proviso for redemption, and the appropriate covenants and provisions (*u*). A legal assignment of a copyright entitles the assignee to sue for infringements in his own name. An equitable or informal mortgage may be created by agreement, express or implied (*x*). An equitable assignee cannot sue for infringements in his own name, but must make the assignor a party to the action and his rights will be postponed to those of a subsequent assignee, unless such assignee acquired his rights with notice of the prior equitable assignment (*y*). Where there has been a purported assignment of future copyright, then, if on the coming into existence of the copyright, the assignee or a person claiming under him would be entitled to require the copyright to be vested in him, the copyright, on

---

(*l*) *Jones* v. *Farrell* (1857), 1 De G. & J. 208.

(*m*) *Re Bell, Jeffery* v. *Sayles*, [1896] 1 Ch. 1 (C.A.); *Hockey* v. *Western*, [1898] 1 Ch. 350 (C.A.).

(*n*) For forms, see 14 Ency. Forms and Precedents (4th Edn.), pp. 555 *et seq.*

(*o*) *Van Gelder, Apsimon & Co.* v. *Sowerby Bridge United District Flour Society* (1890), 44 Ch. D. 374 (C.A.).

(*p*) Section 74; and see Patents Rules 1958, rr. 127, 130, as to applications for registration.

(*q*) Patents Act 1949, s. 74 (4).

(*r*) *Steers* v. *Rogers*, [1892] 2 Ch. 13 (C.A.); affd., [1893] A.C. 232 (H.L.). For trade marks, see Trade Marks Act 1938, ss. 22, 25.

(*s*) See Patents Rules 1958, r. 127.

(*t*) Copyright is transmissible by assignment: Copyright Act 1956, s. 36 (1). A legal assignment of copyright must be in writing signed by or on behalf of the assignor: *ibid.*, s. 36 (3).

(*u*) For a form, see 14 Ency. Forms and Precedents (4th Edn.), pp. 565–568.

(*x*) *Performing Right Society, Ltd.* v. *London Theatre of Varieties, Ltd.*, [1924] A.C. 1 (H.L.).

(*y*) *Macdonald* v. *Eyles*, [1921] 1 Ch. 631.

its coming into existence, vests in the assignee or his successor in title without further assurance (*z*).

Where the author is the first owner, and his rights to copyright arose before 1 June, 1957, the benefit of an assignment by way of mortgage will endure for twenty-five years only after his death, the copyright for the remainder of its duration then reverting to the estate of the author (*a*).

(*z*) Copyright Act 1956, s. 37.
(*a*) *Ibid.*, Sched. 7, para. 28 (3). For registered designs, see Registered Designs Act 1949, s. 19.

CHAPTER 7

Debentures

Generally (*a*).—A company, although it may, when authorised expressly or impliedly by its constitution (*b*), create ordinary mortgages (*c*), usually borrows on the security of instruments called debentures (*d*). An issue of debentures or debenture stock is in substance a contributory mortgage (*e*) with a large number of contributors. A debenture consists basically of an acknowledgement of indebtedness by the company and charge on the company's property, generally a fixed charge on the company's land and a floating charge on the rest of its undertaking. Debenture stock is of the same nature as ordinary debentures, except that, instead of each debenture securing a definite and generally equal amount, the whole sum secured is treated as a single stock and certificates are issued in respect of multiples of the stock. The great advantage of debenture stock is its divisibility.

The term debenture is usually associated with companies although it is sometimes used in relation to an unincorporated club (*f*) and even an individual (*g*).

Form (*h*).—A single instrument may be a mortgage debenture (*i*), but usually a debenture will be one of a series of short contemporaneous instruments. It is usually, but not necessarily, under the company's

---

(*a*) See 7 Halsbury's Laws (4th Edn.), Companies, paras. 796 *et seq.*; 6 Ency. Forms and Precedents (4th Edn.), Companies, pp. 1097 *et seq.* For registration of company charges, see pp. 181 *et seq., infra.*

(*b*) As to company borrowing powers, see pp. 178 *et seq., infra.*

(*c*) See, *e.g., Knightsbridge Estates Trust, Ltd.* v. *Byrne,* [1940] A.C. 613 (H.L.); [1940] 2 All E.R. 401. Such a mortgage is technically a debenture, but not usually so called.

(*d*) The root meaning of "debenture" is indebtedness, and there may be a debenture which is nothing more than an acknowledgment of indebtedness: see *Lemon* v. *Austin Friars Investment Trust, Ltd.,* [1926] Ch. 1 (C.A.). But, usually, a debenture contains a charge of the property of the company and then it is a mortgage debenture. It is such debentures which are dealt with here. The Companies Act 1948, defines a debenture as including debenture stock, bonds and any other securities of a company whether constituting a charge on the assets of the company or not: s. 455 (1). Debentures of incorporated companies are excepted from the application of the Bills of Sale Acts: Bill of Sale Act (1878) Amendment Act 1882, s. 17.

(*e*) As to which, see footnote (*k*) p. 176, *infra.*

(*f*) *Wylie* v. *Carlyon,* [1922] 1 Ch. 51.

(*g*) As to a charge of future-acquired land by an individual, see text and footnote (*d*), p. 12, *supra.* A charge of chattels by an individual is subject to the Bills of Sale Acts. As to agricultural charges, see p. 128, *infra.*

(*h*) For forms, see 6 Ency. Forms and Precedents (4th Edn.), pp. 1182 *et seq.*; and Precedent 11 in the Appendix, *infra.*

(*i*) *Robson* v. *Smith,* [1895] 2 Ch. 118.

seal (*k*). The ordinary form of debenture contains a covenant by the company to pay a person named or the registered holder (*l*) or sometimes the bearer of the debenture, a sum named on a certain day (*m*) or such earlier day as the debt may become payable under conditions specified in the instrument; a covenant to pay interest in the meantime at the specified rate (*n*); a charge of such payments on the company's undertaking and all its property, present and future, including (sometimes) uncalled capital, or on some specified property (*o*); and a statement that it is issued subject to certain conditions endorsed thereon or otherwise annexed thereto. The conditions provide, for example, that the debenture is one of a series, all of which are to rank *pari passu* as a first (or, as the case may be, a second or third) charge on the property charged without any preference or priority of one over another (*p*); and (very generally) that such charge is to be a "floating security" (*q*). The conditions should also provide that the money secured shall become payable if default is made in payment of interest, or if an order is made, or an effective resolution passed, for the winding up of the company (*r*), and usually include power to appoint a receiver (*s*). They generally also provide in detail for the assignment or transmission of the debenture, sometimes by registered assignment, sometimes by mere delivery (*t*); for meetings of the debenture holders, and for the validity of resolutions passed at such meetings, so as to

---

(*k*) *Lemon* v. *Austin Friars Investment Trust, Ltd., supra.*

(*l*) Where a debenture, not payable to bearer, is issued to a person with his name left blank, the debenture, as such, is void. But where it forms one of a series of debentures secured by a trust deed, the lender will have an equitable security, and can share *pari passu* with the holders of valid debentures in the property comprised in the trust deed: *Re Queensland Land and Coal Co., Davis* v. *Martin*, [1894] 3 Ch. 181.

(*m*) Payment will nevertheless become due on a winding up before that date: *Wallace* v. *Universal Automatic Machines Co.*, [1894] 2 Ch. 547. Where the principal moneys have become immediately payable by reason of a winding up, the company or the guarantors of the loan are entitled to redeem and the debenture holders can only refuse payment if the conditions so provide: *Consolidated Goldfields of South Africa* v. *Simmer and Jack East, Ltd.* (1913), 82 L.J. Ch. 214.

(*n*) A provision that interest shall be paid only out of profits, or that, in addition to interest, the debentures carry a right to share in the profits is uncommon and may have tax disadvantages: see Income and Corporation Taxes Act 1970, s. 233 (d) (iii).

(*o*) An exception of a certain class of assets means assets of the class from time to time, and not only at the date of the debenture: *Imperial Paper Mills of Canada* v. *Quebec Bank* (1913), 83 L.J. P.C. 67. A debenture issued to a member of an unincorporated club by the committee acknowledging the receipt of advances does not create a charge on the assets of the club: *Wylie* v. *Carlyon*, [1922] 1 Ch. 51.

(*p*) As to debentures ranking *pari passu*, see *Re Mersey Rail Co. (No. 1)*, [1895] 2 Ch. 287. Where interest on some debentures has been paid to a later date than on others, the interest will not, in the absence of special provision, be equalised in a winding up, but the principal and interest due to each debenture holder will be calculated, and the assets distributed rateably according to the amounts due: *Re Midland Express, Ltd.*, [1914] 1 Ch. 41.

(*q*) As to floating securities, see p. 121, *infra.*

(*r*) For other specified events upon which the money becomes payable, see, *e.g.*, 6 Ency. Forms and Precedents (4th Edn.), pp. 1106, 1107.

(*s*) As to a receiver, see p. 126, *infra.*

(*t*) For the statutory form of transfer of fully paid up registered securities, see the Stock Transfer Act 1963. A debenture also usually provides for the transfer thereof to be free from equities: see *Re Palmer's Decoration and Furnishing Co.*, [1904] 2 Ch. 743. As to equities, see p. 104, *supra.*

bind a dissentient minority (*u*); the place of payment (*x*); and the service of notices (*y*).

Contrary to the general rule that a mortgage cannot be made irredeemable, it is provided by the Companies Act 1948, s. 89 (*z*), that debentures shall not be invalid by reason only that they are made irredeemable, or redeemable only on the happening of a contingency, however remote (*a*).

As stated above the debenture generally creates a floating charge, but it may also or alternatively create a legal charge or a fixed equitable charge. Where there is power to create a charge and an intention to do so, a good equitable charge will be created notwithstanding any mistake in the attempt to effect it (*b*).

Bearer debentures (*c*).—Debentures payable to bearer are negotiable instruments, so as to pass by delivery free from equities (*d*). Hence the bearer can sue the company in his own name (*e*).

Trust deeds (*f*).—Debentures, though complete in themselves, may also be further secured by a covering trust deed, and such a deed is ordinarily used to secure debenture stock. The advantage of employing a trust deed is to separate the debenture holders from the security holders, *i.e.*, the debenture trustees or trustee (generally a trust corporation). This separation is to the advantage of the company

---

(*u*) Such as a resolution modifying the rights of the debenture holders. Such a power must be exercised bona fide and must not amount to an oppression of the minority: *British American Nickel Corpn., Ltd.* v. *O'Brien, Ltd.*, [1927] A.C. 369 (P.C.). The power given to the court by the Companies Act 1948, s. 206, to sanction schemes between a company and its creditors extends to debenture holders; and the court has jurisdiction to deprive them of their security and to force fully paid up shares on them in lieu thereof, if satisfied that the scheme is fair and equitable, but not otherwise: *Re Alabama, New Orleans, etc., Rail Co.*, [1891] 1 Ch. 213. But except under the provisions of the Act, or under the express conditions of the debentures themselves, no majority of the debenture holders can bind a dissentient minority even where the effect of their dissent is to ruin the securities: *Hay* v. *Swedish and Norwegian Rail. Co.* (1889), 5 T.L.R. 460.

(*x*) See *Fowler* v. *Midland Electric Corpn., etc., Ltd.*, [1917] 1 Ch. 656.

(*y*) If there is no express provision, newspaper advertisement is sufficient: *Mercantile Investment and General Trust Co.* v. *International Co. of Mexico* (1891), [1893] 1 Ch. 484, n. (C.A.).

(*z*) Replacing Companies Act 1929, s. 74. And see s. 455 (1) of the 1948 Act; *Knightsbridge Estates Trust, Ltd.* v. *Byrne*, [1940] A.C. 613 (H.L.); [1940] 2 All E.R. 401.

(*a*) As to the meaning of redeemable and irredeemable debentures, see *Re Joseph Stocks & Co., Ltd.* (1909), [1912] 2 Ch. 134, n. As to the conversion of redeemable into irredeemable debentures, see *Northern Assurance Co., Ltd.* v. *Farnham Breweries, Ltd.*, [1912] 2 Ch. 125. Otherwise the rules as to collateral advantages and clogs on the equity (see pp. 522 *et seq., infra*), apply to debentures.

(*b*) *Re Strand Music Hall Co., Ltd.* (1865), 3 De G.J. & S. 147, 158; *Re Fireproof Doors, Ltd., Umney* v. *Fireproof Doors, Ltd.*, [1916] 2 Ch. 142, 150. A charge on assets situated abroad in a country which does not recognise floating securities may nevertheless be a valid equitable charge according to English law: *Re Anchor Line (Henderson Brothers), Ltd.* (No. 2), [1937] Ch. 483, at p. 487; [1937] 2 All E.R. 823, at p. 827. See now as to floating charges created by an English company over assets in Scotland, the Companies (Floating Charges and Receivers) (Scotland) Act 1972.

(*c*) Bearer debentures may not be issued without Treasury consent and when issued must be deposited with an authorised depository: Exchange Control Act 1947, s. 10.

(*d*) *Edelstein* v. *Schuler & Co.*, [1902] 2 K.B. 144. For equities, see p. 104, *supra*.

(*e*) *Mowatt* v. *Castle Steel and Iron Works Co.* (1886), 34 Ch. D. 58.

(*f*) For forms, see 6 Ency. Forms and Precedents (4th Edn.), pp. 1240 *et seq.*

in that it will only have to deal with the trustees or trustee. If there is a legal mortgage of the company's realty the legal estate thereby created cannot be vested in more than four persons (*g*). Where there are debenture trustees, who will rarely be as many as four, or, as stated, will generally be a trust corporation, the estate can conveniently be vested in them or it. The separation is to the advantage of the debenture holders in that the trustees, who will generally have expert knowledge, can watch over their interests and the taking of any steps to protect the debenture holders' interests is thereby facilitated.

The typical form of trust deed contains a covenant to repay the principal either on a fixed date, or on some earlier date on the happening of certain specified events, or by instalments or by the sinking fund method (*h*); a covenant to pay interest in the meantime at a specified rate; a specific charge of the company's freehold or leasehold property and a floating charge over all the company's other assets; and it will give the trustees rights similar to those which each debenture holder would have in the case of ordinary debentures. The Federation of Stock Exchanges has prescribed certain requirements as to the form of trust deeds, compliance with which is a condition of obtaining a quotation (*i*).

Debenture trustees.—The trustees should have no interest, whether as shareholder or otherwise, which might conflict with their duty as trustees (*k*). The trust deed should provide for remuneration to the trustees (*l*). In the absence of express provision the remuneration is not payable in priority to the claims of stockholders (*m*). Any provision in a debenture trust deed exempting a trustee from or indemnifying him against liability for breach of trust where he fails to show the degree of care and diligence required of him as trustee is void (*n*). But a release is permissible (*o*) and an indemnity provision in force on 1 July, 1948, is not invalidated (*p*).

Floating charge.—Mortgage debentures almost invariably create a floating security (*q*). Such a security is an immediate equitable charge on the assets of the company for the time being, but it remains unattached to any particular property, and leaves the company at liberty to deal with its property in the ordinary course of its business, as it thinks fit, until stopped, either by the appointment of a receiver,

---

(*g*) Law of Property Act 1925, ss. 34, 36; Trustee Act 1925, s. 34 (2).

(*h*) By provision out of the profits of the company (but the tax consequences must be considered: see note (*n*), p. 119, *supra*) or by the company effecting a sinking policy with an insurance company.

(*i*) See 6 Ency. Forms and Precedents (4th Edn.), pp. 1142, 1143.

(*k*) *Re Dorman, Long & Co., Ltd., Re South Durham Steel and Iron Co., Ltd.,* [1934] Ch. 635, at pp. 670, 671.

(*l*) The trustees are entitled to the remuneration provided by the trust deed, notwithstanding the appointment of a receiver: *Re Anglo-Canadian Lands* (1912), *Ltd.,* [1918] 2 Ch. 287; *Re British Consolidated Oil Corpn., Ltd.,* [1919] 2 Ch. 81.

(*m*) *Re Accles, Ltd., Hodgson* v. *Accles, Ltd.* (1902), 51 W.R. 57.

(*n*) Companies Act 1948, s. 88 (1).

(*o*) *Ibid.,* sub-s. (2).

(*p*) *Ibid.,* sub-ss. (3), (4).

(*q*) See *Re Yorkshire Woolcombers Association, Ltd., Houldsworth* v. *Yorkshire Woolmakers Association, Ltd.,* [1903] 2 Ch. 284 (C.A.), at p. 294, *per* ROMER, L.J.; affd, *sub nom. Illingworth* v. *Houldsworth,* [1904] A.C. 355 (H.L.). And see (1960) 23 M.L.R. 630 (R. R. Pennington).

or by a winding up (*r*), or the happening of some agreed event (*s*) when the charge becomes fixed to the assets (*t*) and effective—or, as it is said, crystallises (*u*)—and gives the debenture holder priority over the general creditors (*a*). So long as the security remains a floating security, the property of the company may be dealt with, and even a part thereof sold (*b*) in the ordinary course of business (*c*), as if the security had not been given and any such dealing with a particular property will be binding on the debenture holders, provided that the dealing is completed before the charge ceases to be a floating security (*d*). A purchaser or other mortgagee from the company will require evidence of non-crystallisation. This is generally supplied by a letter to this effect from some officer of the company or the company's solicitor (*e*). Unless prohibited by the conditions of the debentures, this power of disposition extends to the creation of fixed charges (*f*), but not the creation of further general floating securities so as to give these priority (*g*). In fact, it is usual to provide in the deed that no

---

(*r*) *Wallace* v. *Evershed*, [1899] 1 Ch. 891, 894.

(*s*) *Government Stock and Other Securities Investment Co.* v. *Manila Rail. Co.*, [1897] A.C. 81 (H.L.); *Re Florence Land and Public Works Co., Ex parte Moor* (1878), 10 Ch. D. 530 (C.A.). See (1976) 40 Conv. (N.S.) 397 (J. H. Farrar).

(*t*) Including future assets of the description of the assets charged which come into existence after the crystallisation of the charge: *Ferrier* v. *Bottomer* (1972), 46 A.L.J.R. 148.

(*u*) The charge does not crystallise on a demand for payment or on notice by the debenture holder to the company's bank: *Evans* v. *Rival Granite Quarries, Ltd.*, [1910] 2 K.B. 979 (C.A.).

(*a*) *Re Panama, New Zealand, and Australian Royal Mail Co.* (1870), 5 Ch. App. 318; *Hodson* v. *Tea Co.* (1880), 14 Ch. D. 859; *Brunton* v. *Electrical Engineering Corpn.*, [1892] 1 Ch. 434; *English and Scottish Mercantile Investment Co.* v. *Brunton*, [1892] 2 Q.B. 700 (C.A.). On the two theories as to floating charge (i.e., the licence theory and the mortgage of future assets theory) see Pennington's *Company Law* (3rd Edn.), 369 In practice, the makers of floating charges are companies, farmers (see p. 129, *infra*) and registered friendly societies (see p. 131, *infra*) though in principle others could make them. On floating charges and partnerships see [1971] J.B.L. 18 (P. G. Fitzpatrick).

(*b*) *Re Vivian & Co., Metropolitan Bank of England and Wales* v. *Vivian & Co.*, [1900] 2 Ch. 654.

(*c*) But not otherwise than in the ordinary course of business: see *Re Borax Co., Foster* v. *Borax Co.*, [1901] 1 Ch. 326 (C.A.). A sale of all the assets for the purpose of bringing the business to an end will not do, and would not confer a good title on a purchaser with notice of the charge (*Hubbuck* v. *Helms* (1887), 56 L.T. 232), although it would be effectual if he had no notice: *English and Scottish Mercantile Investment Co.* v. *Brunton, supra*.

(*d*) *Robson* v. *Smith*, [1895] 2 Ch. 118, 124. For rights of set-off against the receiver, see *Biggerstaff* v. *Rowatt's Wharf, Ltd.*, [1896] 2 Ch. 93 (C.A.); *N. W. Robbie & Co., Ltd.* v. *Witney Warehouse Co.*, [1963] 3 All E.R. 613 (C.A.); *Rother Iron Works, Ltd.* v. *Canterbury Precision Engineers, Ltd.*, [1973] 1 All E.R. 394 (C.A.); *George Barker (Transport), Ltd.* v. *Eynon*, [1974] 1 All E.R. 900 (C.A.); *Felt and Textiles of New Zealand, Ltd.* v. *R. Hubrich, Ltd.* [1968], N.Z.L.R. 716. And see *Aluminium Industrie Vaassen BV* v. *Romalpa Aluminium, Ltd.*, [1976] 2 All E.R. 552.

(*e*) See *Emmet on Title* (16th Edn.), p. 323, and see the articles there referred to.

(*f*) *Re Florence Land and Public Works Co., supra*; *Re Hamilton's Windsor Ironworks, Ex parte Pitman and Edwards* (1879), 12 Ch. D. 707; *Wheatley* v. *Silkstone and Haigh Moor Coal Co.* (1885), 29 Ch. D. 715; *English and Scottish Mercantile Investment Co.* v. *Brunton*, [1892] 2 Q.B. 700 (C.A.); *Re Valletort Sanitary Steam Laundry Co.*, [1903] 2 Ch. 654. The priority of the subsequent fixed charge (whether legal or equitable) is not affected by notice of the floating charge. But the subsequent mortgagee, to gain priority, would need to obtain the title deeds or register his mortgage under the Land Charges Act 1972, or under the Companies Act 1948. If a specific charge is postponed to a floating charge the doctrine of marshalling (see p. 506, *infra*) will apply.

(*g*) *Re Benjamin Cope & Sons, Ltd.*, [1914] 1 Ch. 800. But where a company has reserved power to charge specified assets, it may create a floating charge on those assets

mortgage or charge ranking *pari passu* with or in priority to the debenture shall be created by the company (*h*). The registration of the charge in the Companies Register will constitute constructive notice of the floating charge to a subsequent mortgagee (*i*). The restriction may be noted amongst the filed particulars of the charge in the Companies Register (though there is no express sanction for this practice under the Companies Act—*cf.* the position under the Companies (Floating Charges and Receivers) (Scotland) Act 1972) and such noting is probably sufficient to give constructive notice of the restriction (*k*). In the case of registered land, if the floating charge is noted (*l*) on the register, the entry will usually refer to the restriction and a subsequent mortgagee will take subject to the noted rights (*m*). The authorities indicate that the subsequent mortgagee would only lose priority if he has actual notice of the restriction (*n*). But the majority of these cases are pre-registration (*o*) and it may be that in the light of the practice of noting the restriction in the Companies Register, referred to above, and the right of the public to inspect registered charges (*p*), the matter would be decided differently by a court to-day (*q*).

Where a company which has issued floating debentures purchases property with money advanced by a person who is to have a charge on the property, the purchase is, in effect, the purchase of an equity of redemption and the charge (*r*) has priority over the debentures (*s*).

The subsequent dealing, in order to confer rights prior to those of the holder of the floating security, need not be a voluntary act on the part of the company. A garnishee order gives no priority in itself (*t*) and the title of a receiver subsequently appointed under a debenture

---

in priority to the general floating charge: *Re Automatic Bottle Makers, Ltd.,* [1926] Ch. 412 (C.A.).

(*h*) For a form of floating charge, see 6 Ency. Forms and Precedents (4th Edn.), 1245 and in subsequent forms.

(*i*) *Wilson* v. *Kelland,* [1910] 2 Ch. 306.

(*k*) Notice of the restriction may also be effected by the registration of a special resolution referring to such a restriction under the Companies Act 1948, s. 143.

(*l*) Under the Land Registration Act 1925, s. 49.

(*m*) Land Registration Act 1925, s. 52.

(*n*) See *English and Scottish Mercantile Investment Co.* v. *Brunton,* [1892] 2 Q.B. 700 (*C.A.*); *Re Castell and Brown, Ltd.,* [1898] 1 Ch. 315; *Re Valletort Sanitary Laundry Co., Ltd., supra; Re Standard Rotary Machine Co.* (1906), 95 L.T. 829; *Wilson* v. *Kelland, supra; G. and T. Earle, Ltd.* v. *Hemsworth Rural District Council* (1928), 44 T.L.R. 605 (C.A.).

(*o*) Registration was introduced by the Companies Act 1900, s. 14.

(*p*) See the Companies Act 1948, s. 426 (1).

(*q*) See generally, Gower, *Company Law* (3rd Edn.), pp. 422–423; *Gore-Brown on Companies* (42nd Edn.), pp. 425–429; (1974) 38 Conv. (N.S.) 315 (J. H. Farrar) Floating Charges and Priorities; cf. Pennington's *Company Law* (3rd Edn.), p. 374; and see Palmer's *Company Law* (22nd Edn.), vol. 1. p. 460.

Section 9 of the European Communities Act 1972 has not affected the point, since the section relates to capacity and authority, not mere contractual commitments; but cf. (1974) 38 Conv. (N.S.) 315, 326; (1975) 125 New L.J. 529 and subsequent correspondence at pp. 1007, 1074.

(*r*) Assuming the chargee has the title deeds or registers.

(*s*) *Re Connolly Brothers, Ltd.* (*No. 2*), *Wood* v. *Connolly Brothers., Ltd.,* [1912] 2 Ch. 25 (C.A.); *Security Trust Co.* v. *The Royal Bank of Canada,* [1976] 1 All E.R. 381 (P.C.).

(*t*) *Cairney* v. *Back,* [1906] 2 K.B. 746. See the discussion on the garnishee point in Sykes, *The Law of Securities* (2nd Edn.), pp. 788–790.

prevails over that of an execution creditor unless the money has been actually paid over under the garnishee order (*u*).

Payments made to the sheriff to get him out of possession have been held to be good as against debenture holders (*a*).

A distress levied by a landlord under a power in a lease, conferred either before the creation of the debentures or while they were still floating, and levied before the debenture ceased to be a floating charge is valid against the debenture holders (*b*).

Creation of floating securities.—The use of the words "floating security" is not essential to the creation of a security of this nature. It has been created by a debenture purporting to bind all the company's "estate property and effects" (*c*). Where the debenture is a charge on specific assets, the words, which are commonly to be found in a floating charge, to the effect that the company is not to be at liberty to create any mortgage or charge in priority to the debentures, do not turn the specific charge into a floating charge (*d*).

Uncalled capital may be charged if the documents of the company so permit, but where a company has by special resolution declared that a part of its capital shall only be capable of being called up for purposes of liquidation, it cannot create a charge on that part (*e*).

Open-end debenture trust deeds.—A debenture trust deed may secure a fixed amount only or may be security also for further advances and may provide for further issues of debentures or debenture stock. An open-end debenture trust deed is used when it is intended that there should be several issues of debenture stock which will rank *pari passu* with the original stock. It is a question of the construction of the principal trust deed whether that deed, in addition to any supplemental deed, secures the further issues or whether they are secured only by the supplemental deed.

Registered land.—On first registration, if the applicant company has issued debentures, this fact must be disclosed on the application form and a certified copy of the trust deed or debenture must accompany the application. If the debenture creates a legal charge this will be registered as a charge (*f*). If it creates a floating charge the trust deed or debenture will be noted in the Charges Register (*g*). Where the land has already been registered, the debenture holder should apply for the registration of the debenture. Where a company is

---

(*u*) *Robson* v. *Smith, supra; Norton* v. *Yates*, [1906] 1 K.B. 112; *Taunton* v. *Sheriff of Warwickshire*, [1895] 2 Ch. 319 (C.A.). The debenture holders have priority even if the debentures were irregularly issued: *Duck* v. *Tower Galvanizing Co.*, [1901] 2 K.B. 314.

(*a*) *Robinson* v. *Burnell's Vienna Bakery Co.*, [1904] 2 K.B. 624; *Heaton and Dugard Ltd.* v. *Cutting Brothers, Ltd.*, [1925] 1 K.B. 655.

(*b*) *Re Roundwood Colliery Co., Ltd.* v. *Roundwood Colliery Co.*, [1891] 1 Ch. 373 (C.A.); *Re Bellaglade, Ltd.*, [1977] 1 All E.R. 319. For priorities, see further Ch. 24, *infra*.

(*c*) *Re Florence Land and Public Works Co.* (1878). 10 Ch. D. 530 (C.A.); *Re Panama, etc., Royal Mail Co.* (1870), 5 Ch. App. 318; *National Provincial Bank of England, Ltd.* v. *United Electric Theatres, Ltd.*, [1916] 1 Ch. 132.

(*d*) *Grigson* v. *Taplin and Co.* (1915), 85 L.J. Ch. 75.

(*e*) *Re Mayfair Property Co., Bartlett* v. *Mayfair Property Co.*, [1898] 2 Ch. 28 (C.A.); *Re Irish Club Co., Ltd.*, [1906] W.N. 127.

(*f*) Under Land Registration Act 1925, s. 26: Land Registration Rules 1925, rr. 72, 160.

(*g*) Under Land Registration Act 1925, s. 49; and see Land Registration Rules 1925, r. 40. A fixed equitable charge is similarly noted. See p. 70, *supra*.

registered as proprietor the registrar is not concerned with any mortgage, charge, debenture, etc., created or issued by the company, whether or not registered under the Companies Act 1948, unless such incumbrance is registered or protected by caution or otherwise under the Land Registration Act 1925 (*h*).

Fraudulent preferences.—Any conveyance, mortgage, delivery of goods, payment, execution or other act relating to property (*i*) made or done by or against a company within six months before the commencement of its winding up which, had it been made or done by or against an individual within six months before the presentation of a bankruptcy petition on which he is adjudged bankrupt, would be deemed in his bankruptcy a fraudulent preference is, in the event of the company being wound up, to be deemed a fraudulent preference of its creditors, and is invalid accordingly (*k*).

The issue of debentures to outsiders in satisfaction of existing debts is not necessarily a fraudulent preference (*l*). But where a person takes debentures to secure an amount due to him, or for which he is a surety, and postpones registration until shortly before the winding up, in order not to injure the company's credit, they may be set aside as a fraudulent preference (*m*).

Floating charge created within twelve months of winding up.— Where a company is being wound up a floating charge on its undertaking or property created (*n*) within twelve months of the commencement of the winding up is, unless it is proved that the company immediately after the creation of the charge was solvent (*o*), invalid, except to the amount of any cash paid to the company (*p*) at the time of (*q*) or subsequently to the creation of, and in consideration for, the charge, together with interest on that amount at the rate of 5 per cent. per annum, or such other rate as may for the time being be prescribed by order of the Treasury (*r*). Only the floating charge is invalidated, the covenant to pay is still valid (*s*). These provisions apply to a floating charge to secure a current account at a bank even though the

---

(*h*) Land Registration Act 1925, s. 60 (1). If a charge by a company, which requires registration, has not been registered in the Companies Register under s. 95 of the Companies Act 1948, or no evidence of such registration is produced to the registrar, a note will be made on the register that the charge is subject to the provisions of that section: Land Registration Rules 1925, r. 145 (2).

(*i*) *Peat* v. *Gresham Trust, Ltd.*, [1934] A.C. 252, at p. 260 (H.L.).

(*k*) Companies Act 1948, s. 320 (1); see p. 228, *infra*.

(*l*) *Re Inns of Court Hotel Co.* (1868), L.R. 6 Eq. 82.

(*m*) *Re Jackson and Bassford, Ltd.*, [1906] 2 Ch. 467.

(*n*) *I.e.*, the date of the execution of the deed: *Transport and General Credit Corpn.* v. *Morgan*, [1939] Ch. 531; [1939] 2 All E.R. 17.

(*o*) *I.e.*, able to pay its debts as they fall due: *Re Patrick and Lyon, Ltd.*, [1933] Ch. 786.

(*p*) The payment must not be illusory: *Re Orleans Motor Co., Ltd.*, [1911] 2 Ch. 41; *Re Destone Fabrics, Ltd.*, [1941] Ch. 319 (C.A.); [1941] 1 All E.R. 545.

(*q*) See *Re Columbian Fireproofing Co., Ltd.*, [1910] 2 Ch. 120 (C.A.); *Re F. and E. Stanton, Ltd.*, [1929] 1 Ch. 180.

(*r*) Companies Act 1948, s. 322 (1). The present rate is 5 per cent.: Companies Winding Up (Floating Charges) (Interest) Order 1952.

(*s*) *Re Parkes Garage (Swadlincote), Ltd.*, [1929] 1 Ch. 139. If the sum secured is repaid before the winding up, the liquidator cannot recover the sum so repaid unless the repayment is set aside as a fraudulent preference.

bank is not obliged to make further advances, and payments made after the creation of such a charge to the company or to third parties or cheques drawn by the company are cash paid to the company and subject to the charge (*t*).

Preferential creditors.—Preferential debts, as set out in s. 319 (5) (b) of the Companies Act 1948, incurred before a floating charge has crystallised (*u*), rank before the claim of debenture holders under the floating charge (*a*).

Remedies of debenture holders (*b*).—Every debenture trust deed should contain provisions for the enforcement of the security without the aid of the court, *e.g.*, by the appointment of a receiver, and, in appropriate cases, the remedies of sale and foreclosure will be available. Apart from such remedies the debenture holders may have remedies available with the aid of the court. Furthermore, a debenture holder whose interest is in arrear, or whose principal is due and unpaid may present a creditor's petition to wind up the company (*c*). But a debenture holder who is only a *cestui que trust* cannot petition to wind up a company (*d*).

Action on covenant.—A debenture holder may sue on the personal covenant, as may the trustees of a trust deed.

Appointment of receiver under trust deed.—A trust deed will usually contain provisions for the appointment by the trustees of a receiver and manager and for the sale of the mortgaged property. And apart from such express provision, where the mortgage is by deed, the statutory power to appoint a receiver will apply (*e*).

Sale and foreclosure.—Where a debenture deed contains a mortgage of specific property the debenture holder has a mortgagee's powers of sale and foreclosure in respect thereof (*f*).

Debenture holders' action.—Where the company is in default as regards principal or interest a debenture holder may bring an action on behalf of all the rest of the debenture holders to realise the security (*d*). The court will give leave to commence or continue such an action as a matter of course, notwithstanding winding up. The writ in the action is indorsed with a claim for a receiver, or a receiver and manager, and immediately after issue of the writ (or contemporaneously with it, by leave) notice of motion for the appointment of a receiver is served (*g*). Frequently it is agreed to treat this motion as the trial of the action and the usual order in a debenture holders' action is taken on the motion (*h*).

(*t*) *Re Yeovil Glove Co., Ltd.*, [1965] Ch. 148 (C.A.); [1964] 2 All E.R. 849.
(*u*) *Re Griffin Hotel Co., Ltd., Joshua Tetley & Son, Ltd.* v. *Griffin Hotel Co., Ltd.*, [1941] Ch. 129; [1940] 4 All E.R. 324.
(*a*) Companies Act 1948, s. 94 (1); *Re Barleycorn Enterprises, Ltd., Mathias and David* v. *Down*, [1970] Ch. 465 (C.A.); [1970] 2 All E.R. 155. As to the liability of the receiver, see *Inland Revenue Commissioners* v. *Goldblatt*, [1972] Ch. 498; [1972] 2 All E.R. 202.
(*b*) See, generally, 7 Halsbury Laws (4th Edn.), paras. 877 *et seq.*
(*c*) Under Companies Act 1948, s. 222 (e), and see s. 223.
(*d*) *Re Dunderland Iron Ore Co., Ltd.*, [1909] 1 Ch. 446.
(*e*) See pp. 300 *et seq., infra.*
(*f*) See pp. 359 *et seq.* and pp. 382 *et seq., infra*, respectively.
(*g*) See generally, 7 Halsbury's Laws (4th Edn.), paras. 917 *et seq.*
(*h*) For forms, 10 Ency. Court Forms (2nd Edn.), pp. 329 *et seq.*

CHAPTER 8

Agricultural Mortgages and Charges

Ordinary mortgages and charges.—The general law of mortgages and bills of sale applies to mortgages and charges of farms and stock (a). With regard to ordinary mortgages and charges of farms and stock there are five special points to note. First, the statutory power of leasing conferred by s. 99 of the Law of Property Act 1925 (b), cannot be excluded by the mortgage deed in the case of a mortgage of agricultural land (c). Secondly, a tenant's charge for compensation at the termination of his tenancy obtained under s. 72 of the Agricultural Holdings Act 1948, ranks in priority to any other charge, however and whenever created (d). Thirdly, a mortgagee who has not taken possession is not entitled to growing crops which have been removed by the mortgagor between the time of demand and recovery of possession, but he has a right to all crops growing on the premises when he takes possession, unless the mortgagor can claim them as emblements under an express contract of tenancy between the mortgagee and himself (e). Fourthly, where an agricultural holding is occupied under a tenancy with the mortgagor not binding on the mortgagee, the occupier is, as against the mortgagee who takes possession, entitled to any compensation which is, or would but for the mortgagee taking possession, be due to the occupier from the mortgagor as respects crops, improvements, tillages, or other matters connected with the holding, whether under the Agricultural Holdings Act 1948, or custom or an agreement authorised by the Act of 1948 (f). If the tenancy is from year to year, or for a term of years, not exceeding twenty-one, at a rack rent, the mortgagee, before he deprives the occupier of possession otherwise than in accordance with the contract of tenancy, must give to the occupier six months' notice in writing of his intention, and, if he so deprives him, compensation is

---

(a) For a form of legal charge of a farm, see 1 Ency. Forms and Precedents (4th Edn.), pp. 633 et seq. For smallholdings, see p. 131, infra. For conditions affecting amalgamated agricultural units and hill lands, see Agriculture Act 1967.

(b) See p. 342, infra.

(c) Agricultural Holdings Act 1948, s. 95, and Sched. 7, para. 2. And see p. 287, infra. Agricultural land includes land used for agriculture, fruit growing, dairy farming and livestock breeding: see Agricultural Holdings Act 1948, s. 1.

(d) Agricultural Holdings Act 1948, s. 83 (5); and see p. 164, infra. See also Improvement of Land Act 1864, s. 59 (p. 206, infra).

(e) Re Skinner, Ex parte Temple and Fishe (1822), 1 Gl. & J. 216; Bagnall v. Villar (1879), 12 Ch. D. 812; Re Phillips, Ex parte National Mercantile Bank (1880), 16 Ch. D. 104 (C.A.). This applies also to an equitable mortgagee: Re Gordon, Ex parte Official Receiver (1889), 61 L.T. 299.

(f) Agricultural Holdings Act 1948, s. 66 (a).

due to the occupier for his crops, and for any expenditure on the land which he has made in the expectation of remaining on the holding for the full term of the contract of tenancy, in so far as any improvement resulting therefrom is not exhausted at the time of his being so deprived (g). A mortgagee is not liable to pay personally any compensation for improvements, but it may be set off against any rent or other sum due from the occupier or charged on the holding (h). Fifthly, it should be noted that the rights of a bank under the form of charge (shortly to be mentioned) known as an agricultural charge which includes growing crops have priority to those of a mortgagee of the farm in respect of the crops, irrespective of the dates of the mortgage and the charge (i). Nevertheless, an ordinary mortgage or charge of a farm should contain a provision that the borrower will not without the consent of the mortgagee include any growing crops in an agricultural charge. A breach of this covenant would bring the statutory power of sale (k) into operation. Having mentioned the agricultural charge, it is now necessary to look at the special types of mortgages and charges available to farmers.

Long term credits.—Part I of the Agricultural Credits Act 1928, provided for the establishment of a corporation for the purpose of making loans on mortgage of agricultural land and of making loans under the Improvement of Land Acts 1864 and 1899 (l). The Agricultural Mortgage Corporation Limited, which is the corporation established under the Act of 1928 (m), may grant on mortgages of agricultural land loans not exceeding two-thirds of the value of the mortgaged property and repayable by equal yearly or half-yearly instalments of capital and interest over a period of sixty years or on such other terms as may be authorised by the corporation's memorandum or articles (n). And such mortgages may be made irredeemable for the period during which instalments are payable (o).

Agricultural charges.—A farmer (p) may by instrument in writing create in favour of a bank (q) an agricultural charge on all or any of the farming stock (r) and other agricultural assets (s) belonging

---

(g) Agricultural Holdings Act 1948, s. 66 (b).

(h) *Ibid.*, s. 74. In view of the fact that the statutory leasing power cannot now be excluded and of the decision in *Pawson* v. *Revell*, [1958] 2 Q.B. 360 (C.A.); [1958] 3 All E.R. 233 (application of s. 152 of the Law of Property Act 1925, to cure defective exercise of the statutory leasing power), s. 66 will rarely apply today.

(i) Agricultural Credits Act 1928, s. 8 (6).   (k) See pp. 360 *et seq.*, *infra*.

(l) As to these Acts, see p. 205, *infra*.

(m) See Part 1 of the Act of 1928 and the Agricultural Mortgage Corporation Acts 1956 and 1958.

(n) Agricultural Credits Act 1928, ss. 1 (1) (a), 2 (3) (c).

(o) Agricultural Credits Act 1932, s. 2. As to the Corporation's power to issue debentures, see *ibid.*, s. 3.

(p) Farmer means any person (not being an incorporated company or society) who as tenant or owner cultivates an agricultural holding for profit: Agricultural Credits Act 1928, s. 5 (7). A tenant may make a charge notwithstanding any contrary provision in the contract of tenancy: *ibid.*, s. 13.

(q) Bank includes any firm, incorporated company or society, carrying on banking business and approved by the Minister of Agriculture, Fisheries and Food: *ibid.*, s. 5 (7).

(r) Farming stock means crops or horticultural produce, whether growing or severed, livestock, vehicles, machinery and plant, and fixtures: *ibid.*, s. 5 (7).

(s) Agricultural assets means a tenant's right to compensation under the Agricultural Holdings Act 1948, for improvements, etc., and any other tenant right: *ibid.*, s. 5 (7).

to him as security for sums advanced or to be advanced to him or paid or to be paid on his behalf under any guarantee by the bank and interest, commission and charges thereon (*t*). An agricultural charge is not a bill of sale within the Bills of Sale Acts 1878 and 1882 (*u*). It has always been exempt from stamp duty (*x*). It must be registered at the Land Registry within seven clear days after execution, otherwise it is void against any person other than the chargor, subject to the power of the High Court to extend the time for registration (*y*). An agricultural charge must be in writing but may be in any form the parties desire (*z*). It may be either a fixed charge or a floating charge or both (*a*). A fixed charge must specify the property charged, but may include in the case of livestock any progeny thereof and in the case of the agricultural plant any plant which may whilst the charge is in force be substituted for the specified plant (*b*). A floating charge covers all farming stock and other agricultural assets from time to time belonging to the farmer (*c*). The sum secured may be either a specified amount or a fluctuating amount advanced on current account (*d*).

Rights of parties under charge.—A fixed charge confers on the bank the right to seize the property on any event specified for the purpose in the charge (*e*), and, after five clear days or such less time as may be allowed by the charge, to sell it (*f*). The proceeds of any sale must be applied in the discharge of the money secured and the costs of seizure and sale, and any surplus must be returned to the chargor.

The farmer is entitled to remain in possession of the property charged and to sell it. Unless otherwise agreed the proceeds of any sale must be paid to the bank to be applied towards the discharge of the sum secured (*g*). The farmer is under the same obligation as to payment to the bank in respect of insurance moneys and compensation for destruction of beasts (*h*). A purchaser from the farmer, and in the case of a sale by auction, the auctioneer, is not concerned to see that the obligations as to payment over to the bank are complied with, notwithstanding that he may be aware of the existence of the

---

(*t*) Agricultural Credits Act 1928, s. 5 (1).
(*u*) *Ibid.*, s. 8 (1).
(*x*) *Ibid.*, s. 8 (8).
(*y*) *Ibid.*. s. 9 as amended by the Land Charges Act 1972, s. 18, Sched. 4, para. 7; Agricultural Credits Regulations 1928.
(*z*) Agricultural Credits Act 1928, s. 5 (6). For a form of agricultural charge, see 1 Ency. Forms and Precedents (4th Edn.), p. 639.
(*a*) *Ibid.*, s. 5 (2).
(*b*) *Ibid.*, s. 5 (3).
(*c*) *Ibid.*, s. 5 (4).
(*d*) *Ibid.*, s. 5 (5).
(*e*) The usual events are breach of covenant to repay, breach of other covenants, death or bankruptcy of the farmer or his making a composition or arrangement with creditors, dissolution of partnership, distress or execution against the property charged, the removal or disposal by the farmer of any of the property charged otherwise than by way of sale in the ordinary way of trading as a farmer.
(*f*) Agricultural Credits Act 1928, s. 6 (1).
(*g*) *Ibid.*, s. 6 (2) (a). A chargor who with intent to defraud fails to pay such sums or removes or suffers to be removed from his holding any property subject to the charge is liable to three years imprisonment: *ibid.*, s. 11.
(*h*) *Ibid.*, s. 6 (2) (b).

charge (*i*). Where any proceeds of sale, which in pursuance of the obligation ought to be paid to the bank, are paid to some other person, nothing in the Act of 1928 confers on the bank a right to recover the proceeds from that other person, unless the bank proves that the other person knew that the proceeds were paid to him in breach of the obligation, but the other person is not deemed to have such knowledge by reason only that he has notice of the charge (*k*).

A floating charge becomes fixed when a receiving order is made against the farmer, on his death or bankruptcy, on the dissolution of a partnership, or upon notice in writing to that effect being given by the bank to the farmer on the happening of any event which by virtue of the charge confers on the bank the right to give such a notice (*l*).

A floating charge gives the bank the same right to receive the proceeds of the sale by the farmer of any assets subject thereto save that it is not necessary for the farmer to pay over such moneys if and so far as they are expended by him in the purchase of farming stock which on purchase becomes subject to the charge (*m*).

Registration of agricultural charges.—An agricultural charge must be registered under the Agricultural Credits Act 1928, at the Land Registry within seven days after execution (*n*), otherwise the charge will be void against any person other than the farmer, subject to the power of the High Court to extend the time for registration (*o*). Provision is made for official searches and inspection of the register (*p*). Registration is deemed to constitute actual notice of the charge and of the fact of such registration to all persons and for all purposes connected with the property charged (*q*). Where, however, a charge in favour of a bank is expressly made for securing a current account or further advances, the bank in relation to such advances is not deemed to have notice of another charge by reason only that it is so registered if it was not registered when the first mentioned charge was created or when the last search, if any, by or on behalf of the bank was made, whichever last happened (*r*). Provision is made for the cancellation of registration on the discharge of a charge and for the rectification of any entry in the register (*s*).

Priority of agricultural charges.—Agricultural charges in relation to one another have priority in accordance with their respective dates of registration (*t*). An agricultural charge creating a fixed charge

---

(*i*) Agricultural Credits Act 1928, s. 6 (3).
(*k*) *Ibid.*, s. 6 (4).
(*l*) *Ibid.*, s. 7 (1). The events specified are usually the same as those giving rise to the right of seizure: see footnote (*e*), *supra*.
(*m*) *Ibid.*, s. 7 (1), proviso (b).
(*n*) Excluding days when the Registry is not open to the public.
(*o*) Agricultural Credits Act 1928, s. 9 (1). Registration is effected by sending a memorandum of the charge in a prescribed form (Form A.C.1) together with the fee, to the Agricultural Credits Superintendent at the Land Charges Registry, Plymouth.
(*p*) *Ibid.*, s. 9; Agricultural Credits Regulations 1928; Agricultural Credits Fees Order 1975. For restrictions on the publication of agricultural charges, see s. 10.
(*q*) *Ibid.*, s. 9 (6).
(*r*) *Ibid.*, s. 9 (8), proviso.
(*s*) Agricultural Credits Regulations 1928, regs. 3, 4, and see Schedule for forms.
(*t*) Agricultural Credits Act 1928, s. 8 (2).

or a bill of sale is void so far as it relates to property subject to a floating charge previously created (*u*). The rights of a bank under an agricultural charge including growing crops have priority to those of a mortgagee of a farm in respect of the crops, irrespective of the dates of the mortgage and charge (*x*). A farmer is not for the purposes of bankruptcy law the reputed owner of farming stock subject to an agricultural charge. But if a charge to secure a sum then owing is made within three months of the presentation of a bankruptcy petition, then, unless it is proved that the farmer was solvent immediately after the execution of the charge, the charge is valid only for advances made after the execution of the charge (*y*). An agricultural charge does not protect the property charged from distress (*z*).

Debentures of agricultural marketing boards.—An agricultural marketing board may create a floating charge on farming stock (*a*) owned by it in favour of a bank (*b*). Such a debenture must be registered in the same way as an agricultural charge.

Debentures of industrial and provident societies.—A debenture issued by an industrial or provident society creating in favour of a bank a floating charge on farming stock may be registered as an agricultural charge and notice of such registered charge must be sent to the central office established under the Friendly Societies Act 1896 (*c*).

Smallholdings.—The main statutory provisions relating to smallholdings are embodied in the Agriculture Act 1970. The Minister may make loans to tenants to provide working capital (*d*). Such loans are unsecured and upon the condition, *inter alia*, that the tenant will not borrow monies from any other source (*e*).

(*u*) Agricultural Credits Act, 1928, s. 8 (3).
(*x*) *Ibid.*, s. 8 (6).
(*y*) Agricultural Credits Act 1928, s. 8 (5).
(*z*) *Ibid.*, s. 8 (7).
(*a*) Farming stock has the same meaning as in the Act of 1928. See footnote (*r*), p. 128, *supra*.
(*b*) Agricultural Marketing Act 1958, s. 15 (5).
(*c*) Agricultural Credits Act 1928, s. 14 (1). Such debentures are also exempted from the provisions of the Industrial and Provident Societies Act 1967; s. 2 (2) of the 1967 Act. By virtue of the 1967 Act an agricultural society may create a floating charge in favour of a lender other than a bank without such charge constituting a bill of sale if the provisions for registration are observed; see p. 79, *supra*.
(*d*) Agriculture Act 1970, s. 53.
(*e*) For forms of agreement for loan, see 1 Ency. Forms and Precedents (4th Edn.) Additional Forms, Allotments and Smallholdings, in Service Binder.

CHAPTER 9

Consumer Credit Securities

I—AGREEMENTS WITHIN THE CONSUMER CREDIT ACT 1974

Introduction.—The Consumer Credit Act represents the most radical and progressive reform ever effected in the fields of security and purchase financing. It emanates (with certain modifications (*a*)) from the report of the Crowther Committee on Consumer Credit (*b*). A whole spectrum of transactions is covered by the Act, including hire purchase, moneylending, running-account (or revolving) credit, consumer hire agreements, pawning and bills of sale (*c*). The Act also affects the law relating to land mortgages (*d*). The present account will concentrate upon providing an abbreviated survey of the Act in its more general aspects; a closer examination of individual provisions will be given elsewhere in the appropriate context. Much of the Act remains (at the time of writing) suspended, and will come into effect piece-meal upon the making of governmental orders (*e*).

The regulated agreement.—The kernel of the Act consists in the notion of a regulated agreement. This is not defined directly, but by means of a series of component definitions which together comprise the elements of the central "regulated" concept. Thus, s. 189 (1) provides that a regulated agreement is a consumer credit agreement, or a consumer hire agreement, other than an exempt agreement. These aspects of the regulated agreement will now be examined in turn.

Consumer credit agreement.—For a transaction to fall within this category it must constitute a personal credit agreement in which

---

(*a*) For instance, the report had recommended the abolition of the legal anatomy of hire-purchase and its replacement by an immediate passing of title to goods acquired under deferred purchasing systems: Cmnd. 4596, paras. 5–21 *et seq*. Cf. the ensuing Government White Paper (Cmnd. 5427, para. 8) which decided in favour of preserving the traditional structure of hire-purchase; and the South Australian Consumer Transactions Act 1972–1973, Div. III, which to a large extent implements the opposite view.

(*b*) Cmnd. 4596 (1971).

(*c*) When fully in force the Act will repeal the following statutes: Pawnbrokers Acts 1872–1960; Moneylenders Acts 1900–1927; Hire Purchase Act 1964; Hire Purchase Act 1965. There is in addition one small amendment to the Bills of Sale Acts: see C.C.A., 1974, Sched. 4, para. 1. See further p. 355, *supra*.

(*d*) Defined by s. 189 (1) of the Acts as including "any security charged on land". The difficulties of this definition are discussed in (1975), 39 Conv. (N.S.) 94, 96–97 (J. E. Adams) and at pp. 136-137, 146-147, *infra*.

(*e*) See s. 192 Sched. 3 to the Act; and S.I. 1975, No. 2123; 1977, No. 325.

the creditor provides the debtor with credit not exceeding £5,000 (*f*). A personal credit agreement is itself defined by s. 8 (1) as an agreement between an individual (*g*)—"the debtor"—and any other person—"the creditor"—by which the creditor provides the debtor with credit of any amount. "Credit" is liberally defined as including a cash loan or any other form of financial accommodation (*g*); and the computation of the £5,000 ceiling is facilitated by a series of specific items which are to be disregarded in assessing whether the financial magnitude of the agreement lifts it beyond the realm of the Act. Thus, down-payments and credit-charges are to be excluded (*h*), as are other items which enter into the total charge for credit (*i*). The financial limits are further amplified by s. 18 of the Act (which permits, in certain circumstances, the sub-division of agreements ostensibly beyond its control into a series of lesser and therefore regulated agreements) and s. 10 (3) which offers guide-lines for the assessment of credit provided under running (or revolving) accounts, irrespective (where necessary) of any stated superior limit which the debtor is in fact unlikely to reach (*j*).

Consumer hire agreements.—These do not strictly involve the provision of credit, since the hirer will generally be paying in advance for the use of a chattel to which he never acquires a full title. However, many hiring agreements now represent a method of long-term disposition and bear a greater resemblance to deferred purchasing systems than to the ordinary bailment of goods. Accordingly, special provision is made to assimilate them within the protection of the Act. Unless qualifying as an exempt agreement, a consumer hire agreement is a regulated agreement within the meaning of the Act (*k*). But for the agreement to constitute a consumer hire agreement several conditions must be fulfilled. It must, of course, involve a bailment of goods (*l*) and the hiring must be to an individual (*m*). Further, the agreement must not be one of hire-purchase; it must be capable of subsisting for more than three months; and it must not require the hirer to make payments exceeding £5,000 (*n*).

Exempt agreements.—An exempt agreement is one specified by

(*f*) Section s. 8 (2): see further s. 8 (3). This is the category of agreement into which those mortgages which are not exempted by s. 16 (*infra*) will fall, although they may (either alternatively or additionally) qualify as a 'security' within the meaning of the special section devoted to securities: *infra* p. 146. Rental purchase schemes (see p. 27, *supra*) within the £5,000 limit, may also fall to be governed by the Act: see (1975) 39 Conv. (N.S.) 94, 112–113.

(*ff*) Which, under s. 189 (1), can extend to partnerships, unincorporated associations and any other form of legal entity which is not a body corporate.

(*g*) Section 9 (1): see further [1975] C.L.J. 79, 84–85 (R. M. Goode).

(*h*) Section 9 (3).

(*i*) Section 9 (4): see the definition of "total" charge for credit in s. 20 (1); and Goode, *loc cit.*, pp. 85–86.

(*j*) See further s. 171 (1); and Examples 5–7 and 9 contained in Sch. 2 to the Act.

(*k*) Section 15 (2).

(*l*) Thus, leaseholds are excluded, as are contracts for the lease of furnished premises where there is no separate rental for the furniture itself: Goode, *The Consumer Credit Act*, 1974, pp. 25, 40; cf. *Pampris* v. *Thanos* (1967), 69 S.R. (N.S.W.) 226. But note that the concept of hire is nowhere defined in the Act.

(*m*) See footnote (*ff*).

(*n*) Section 15 (1) (*a*), (*b*), (*c*).

s. 16. Such agreements do not escape all the provisions of the Act (*o*), but because they are not regulated agreements they are substantially beyond its field of operation. Of particular importance to the present account are ss. 16 (1) and (2). Section 16 (1) provides as follows:

16.—(1) This Act does not regulate a consumer credit agreement where the creditor is a local authority or building society, or a body specified, or of a description specified, in an order made by the Secretary of State, being:—

    (a) an insurance company,
    (b) a friendly society,
    (c) an organisation of employers or organisation of workers,
    (d) a charity,
    (e) a land improvement company, or
    (*f*) a body corporate named or specifically referred to in any public general Act.

This provision is qualified by s. 16 (2) which principally confines the operation of the preceeding sub-section (and therefore the extent of the exemption) to cases where the agreement is *either* a debtor-creditor-supplier agreement financing the purchase of land or the provision of dwellings on any land and is secured by a land-mortgage on that land (*p*) *or* a debtor-creditor agreement secured by any land mortgage (*q*). To understand these limitations, it is necessary to resort to the vocabulary of the Act. A debtor-creditor-supplier agreement is defined by s. 12. It includes the following kinds of agreement. First, a regulated consumer credit agreement designed to finance a transaction between the debtor and the creditor. This transaction need not form part of the regulated consumer credit agreement in order for the latter to qualify as a debtor-creditor-supplier agreement (*r*). Secondly, a regulated consumer credit agreement which is designed to finance a transaction between the debtor and a person ("the supplier") other than the creditor; such agreements qualify as debtor-creditor-supplier agreements *only* if they are made by the creditor under pre-existing arrangements, or in contemplation of future arrangements, between himself and the supplier (*s*). Thirdly, an unrestricted use credit agree-

---

(*o*) The rules as to advertising (see Pt IV of the Act), linked transactions (s. 19 (1)) and extortionate credit bargains (ss. 137–140) continue to apply: see s. 16 (7).

(*p*) Section 16 (2) (*a*).

(*q*) Section 16 (2) (*b*). There is a further possible route to exemption, which has been described as "totally unintelligible": see s. 16 (2) (*c*); Goode, *loc. cit.* p. 88. According to this writer, the sub-section is designed to cover the case " where a building society, pursuant to an arrangement with an insurance company, provides a larger purchase-money advance than it would ordinarily do (*e.g.*, 90 per cent of the price instead of 80 per cent.) against a bond from the insurance company on which payment of the premium charged to the purchaser is financed by the building society as part of the advance."

(*r*) Section 12 (*a*); 11 (1) (*a*).

(*s*) Section 12 (*b*); 11 (1) (*b*). As to the meaning of pre-existing or contemplated future arrangements, see s. 187. Both of the foregoing types of debtor-creditor-supplier agreement qualify as restricted-use credit agreements within the meaning of s. 11 of the Act, and are defined by reference to the notion of a restricted-use credit agreement within that section: see also in this connexion ss. 11 (3) and 11 (4). Section 11 (1) (*c*) also specifies a third type of restricted-use credit agreement, which is not utilised in the definition of a debtor-creditor-supplier agreement. This variety consist of a regulated consumer credit agreement designed to finance any existing indebtedness of the debtor's, whether to the creditor or to any person. Any regulated consumer credit agreement which does not fall within one of the three foregoing categories of restricted-use credit agreement is classed as an "unrestricted-use credit agreement" under s. 11 (2).

ment (*t*) which is made by the creditor under pre-existing arrangements between himself and a person (the "supplier") other than the debtor in the knowledge that the credit is to be used to finance the transaction between the debtor and the supplier (*a*).

A debtor-creditor agreement, on the other hand, corresponds to what the Crowther Committee termed an "unconnected loan". The general feature of such agreements is that they involve the provision of credit by parties other than (i) the supplier of any goods or land intended to be purchased by the advance or (ii) any creditor who acts under pre-existing arrangements (or in contemplation of future arrangements) with the supplier (*b*). More specifically, a debtor-creditor agreement is one which falls within any of the following categories:

> (a) a regulated consumer credit agreement which is made in order to finance a transaction between the debtor and a person (the "supplier") other than the creditor (*c*) and which is not made by the creditor under pre-existing arrangements (or in contemplation of future arrangements) between himself and the supplier (*d*); *or*
> (b) a regulated consumer credit agreement made to refinance any existing indebtedness of the debtor's, whether to the creditor or any other person (*e*); *or*
> (c) an unrestricted use credit agreement (*f*) which is not made by the creditor under pre-existing arrangements between himself and a person (the "supplier") other than the debtor, in the knowledge that the credit is to be used to finance a transaction between the debtor and the supplier (*g*).

The mortgagee who wishes to avail himself of the exempting provisions in s. 16 (1) is therefore confronted by three main difficulties. First, he must qualify as one of the bodies or institutions specified in s. 16 (1) itself. Secondly, he must show that the agreement falls within one of the aforementioned categories; this involves mastering the telescopic glossary of agreements set out in the Act and resolving the inevitable vagueness of such expressions as "under pre-existing" or "in contemplation of future" arrangements (*h*). Thirdly, he must surmount the problems of interpretation inherent in s. 16 (2), arising from the use of such formulae as "land mortgage" and "the provision of dwellings on any land".

It is evident that the ordinary first mortgage taken out by a house purchaser with a local authority or building society will qualify as an exempt agreement, whether or not the relevant amount of credit exceeds £5,000 (*k*). The same is true of the situation where a mortgagor under a building society or local authority mortgage applies to the mortgagee for a further advance to effect improvements to the mortgaged property. In both cases the agreement is a debtor-creditor

---

(*t*) See footnote (s), *supra.*
(*a*) Sections 12 (*c*); 11 (2).
(*b*) Goode, *The Consumer Credit Act*, 1974, p. 36.
(*c*) *I.e.*, a restricted-use credit agreement within the meaning of s. 11 (1) (*b*).
(*d*) Section 13 (*a*).
(*e*) Section 13 (*b*); *i.e.*, a restricted-use credit agreement falling within s. 11 (1) (*c*).
(*f*) See footnote (s), *supra.*
(*g*) Section 13 (*c*).
(*h*) See s. 187 to the Act and Sched. 2, Part II, Examples 8, 16, 21; Guest and Lloyd, *op. cit.*, note to s. 187.
(*k*) Goode, *The Consumer Credit Act*, 1974, pp. 25, 86; but see s. 16 (2) (*c*), discussed in footnote (*q*), *supra.*

agreement secured by a land mortgage and is therefore exempt under s. 16 (2) (b) (*l*).

The foregoing result should follow when the party advancing credit on security of the land is other than an original or first mortgagee.

Most mortgagees do not enter into mortgages under pre-existing arrangements with the "supplier" of the land. However, such arrangements may exist between the mortgagee and a supplier of goods or services at whose suggestion the mortgagor takes out the mortgage. An interesting example of this kind of transaction has been given by one commentator (*m*). Where the owner of a house contracts with a builder for the extension of his property, and at the builder's instigation obtains an advance for the cost of construction from an insurance company (*n*), the identity of any resultant mortgage between the owner and the insurance company as an exempt agreement depends upon two principal questions. The first of these is whether there are any "arrangements" (pre-existing or contemplated) between the builder and the mortgagee. If not, the mortgage is a simple debtor-creditor agreement and falls within the exemption conferred by s. 16 (2) (b). If, however, there are such arrangements, the mortgage becomes a debtor-creditor-supplier agreement and is entitled to exemption only when it finances the purchase of land or the provision of dwellings on land (*o*). It is uncertain whether the extension of existing premises would qualify as a provision of dwellings within the foregoing principle. Possibly the result might depend upon the use for which the extended area is designed, but this criterion would be open to abuse and the intended use itself might change after the agreement has been entered into.

It should be noted that an agreement qualifies as an exempt agreement under s. 16 (2) (a) only when the mortgage in question is secured over the same land as that of which the debtor-creditor-supplier agreement finances the purchase, or as that in relation to which the agreement finances the provision of dwellings. If the mortgage is taken to secure an advance for the purchase of land other than the land upon which the mortgage is secured, or to finance the provision of dwellings upon land other than that which is subject to the mortgage, the agreement is not exempt.

The difficulties of s. 16 (2) are further compounded by the definition of land mortgage contained in s. 189 (1) of the Act. By extending this concept to include "any security charged on land" the Act raises questions as to whether the word security in this context carries the same extensive meaning as the definition of security itself in s. 189 (1). This defines security, "in relation to an actual or prospective consumer credit agreement, or any linked transaction", as "a mortgage, charge, pledge, bond, debenture, indemnity, guarantee, bill, note or other right provided by the debtor or hirer, or at his request (express or implied) to secure the carrying out of the obligations of the debtor or hirer under the agreement". The interrelation between this and the word security

---

(*l*) Adams, *loc. cit.*, p. 99.
(*m*) Adams, *ibid.*
(*n*) It is assumed that the advance does not exceed £5,000.
(*o*) Section 16 (2) (*a*) (i) and (ii).

in the definition of land mortgage is not easy to discern, and it may be that the foregoing definition of security is material only to those cases in which the security, as thus defined, consists of a collateral agreement taken out in support of a primary regulated agreement, and not to these cases in which the "security" and the regulated agreement are one and the same thing (*p*). On balance, however, it is submitted that s. 189 (1) would seem to contemplate both species of mortgage security as within the compass of the statutory concept of security (*q*).

Notwithstanding these difficulties, the combined effect of ss. 16 (1) and (2) and the £5,000 financial ceiling is to take the majority of first mortgages beyond the purview of the Act. It will be noted, however, that banks are not within the categories of institution to whom exemption may be granted. It therefore seems likely that a large number of second mortgages, at least, will fall to be governed by the Consumer Credit Act.

The power to make orders under s. 16 (1) is further amplified by ss. 16 (3) and (4).

Lesser importance, in the context of mortgages, attaches to the remaining classes of exempt agreement, laid down by ss. 16 (5) and (6), but a brief summary is added for completeness. They include: regulated agreements where the number of payments (excluding down-payments) does not exceed the specified number; regulated agreements where the rate of the total charge for credit does not exceed the specified rate (*r*); agreements which enjoy a connection with a country outside the U.K.; and consumer hire agreements involving meters and metering equipment (*s*).

Other categories of agreement.—Transversely to the foregoing classification, the Act describes a number of other categories of agreement for the purposes of particular reforms. Some of these, such as restricted and unrestricted use credit agreements, debtor-creditor agreements and debtor-creditor-supplier agreements, have already been encountered. Other classifications include small agreements (*t*), multiple agreements (*a*) and the concept of the linked transaction (*b*). They will be considered as and when the agreements in question arise.

The content of the Act.—A broad, and admittedly simplistic, division of the reforms effected by the 1974 legislation may be made between its "transactional" provisions (*i.e.*, those which relate *per se* to the rights of the parties and arise from the terms of their agreement) and "non-transactional" provisions (*i.e.*, those which represent controls upon such questions as the method of conducting business and the form of agreements). Although this classification will be adopted in

---

(*p*) Adams, *loc. cit.*, p. 96. Goode, *The Consumer Credit Act, 1974*, p. 24, states that the definition of land mortgage in s. 189 (1) includes rent charges; cf. Adams, *ibid.*
(*q*) See further p. 146, *infra*.
(*r*) *I.e.*, minimum lending rate plus one per cent. or 13 per cent., whichever is the higher.
(*s*) See generally S.I. 1977, No. 326 for exempt agreements.
(*t*) Sections 17 and 189 (1).
(*a*) Sections 18 and 189 (1).
(*b*) Sections 19 and 189 (1); and see Adams, *loc cit.*, 97–99.

the ensuing account, it must be observed that infringement of the non-transactional rules will sometimes produce a fundamental effect upon the enforceability of the agreement itself.

II—NON-TRANSACTIONAL REFORMS

Licensing.—The Act inaugurates an elaborate and revolutionary (c) licensing structure as part of its general policy of control over consumer lending. This structure is contained in Part II and is to be administered by the Director-General of Fair Trading (d). It is expected that its practical implementation will take effect in close association with local weights and measures authorities (e).

Local authorities are exempt from the duty to acquire a licence (f), as are those bodies corporate which are empowered by public general Acts naming them to carry on a business (g). Apart from this, licences are required by all those who carry on a consumer credit business, a consumer hire business or an ancillary credit business (h). Detailed rules as to the types of licence which may be granted, the authority they may confer, the circumstances in which they may be issued, varied, renewed, revoked or suspended, and associated matters are contained in the remainder of Part III (i). Of particular interest is s. 40, which provides that unless the Director-General makes an order to contrary effect, regulated agreements (other than non-commercial agreements (k)) made by an unlicensed creditor or owner are unenforceable against the debtor or hirer (l).

Seeking business.—This area is regulated by Part IV of the Act, which governs such classes of activity as advertisements (m); canvassing (n); quotations (o); compulsory display of information (p) and the conduct of business generally (q).   The relevant sections confine themselves to providing a framework for the operation of the orders

---

(c) Prior to the Act, the main licensing requirements in force were those relating to moneylenders, which operated on a local basis: for criticisms of this see Cmnd. 4596, paras 4.1.11; 6.3.2.

(d) Section 1 (1). See S.I. 1975 No. 2124.

(e) See Goode, [1975] C.L.J. 79, 128.

(f) Section 21 (2).

(g) Section 21 (3).

(h) Section 147 (1). As to the meaning of ancillary credit business, and exceptions to the general definition, see ss. 145, 146.

(i) Sections 22–42. See further S.I. 1976, Nos. 837, 1002; S.I. 1977, No. 325.

(k) See footnote (z), p. 142, infra.

(l) See further Guest and Lloyd, The Consumer Credit Act 1974, note to s. 40.

(m) Sections 43–47. It is important to note that these sections apply to persons who carry on a business whereby they provide credit (to individuals) on the security of land, irrespecitve of whether the operation of such business is confined to the entering into of agreements which are above the £5,000 ceiling or are otherwise exempted from the act under s. 16: see further Goode, The Consumer Credit Act 1974, p. 64. Likewise, s. 50 of the Act (prohibiting the sending of circulars to minors) is not confined to the sending of those circulars which relate to facilities obtainable under regulated agreements.

(n) Sections 48–51.

(o) Section 52.

(p) Section 53.

(q) Section 54.

with which the Act will eventually be supplemented, but there is a considerable degree of specificity as to the scope and method under which such orders shall take effect (*r*).

Entering into agreements.—Again the provisions of the Act are a framework, which will eventually be clad with a detailed range of regulations governing most of the important aspects of the negotiation and conclusion of regulated agreements. However, the impact of these rules upon the validity of the agreement is wider and more immediate. Thus, s. 55 provides that regulations may require specific information to be disclosed in the prescribed manner to a debtor or hirer before the making of the agreement (*s*) and that unless such regulations have been complied with the agreement shall not be deemed to have been properly executed (*t*). Accordingly, it becomes enforceable against a debtor or hirer only by order of the court (*a*).

A slightly different approach is evidenced by s. 60 which empowers the Secretary of State to make regulations concerning the form and content of documents embodying regulated agreements (*b*); the section particularises certain things which the Secretary of State shall ensure are brought to the debtor or hirer's attention by virtue of these regulations (*c*). Compliance with s. 60 (1) may in certain circumstances be waived by the Director upon application by a person conducting a consumer credit or consumer hire business (*d*). There is no specific provision within s. 60 for the civil effects of a failure to conform with that section; but s. 61, which deals with the signing of regulated agreements (*e*), provides that one of the conditions to be fulfilled before the agreement can be deemed to be properly executed (*f*) is that it should be in the form, and be signed in the manner, prescribed by s. 60 (1).

(*r*) See particularly s. 43, which designates the types of advertisement to which Pt. IV. applies.

(*s*) Section 55 (1).

(*t*) Section 55 (2).

(*a*) Section 65 (1). The principles according to which the court's discretion is to be exercised are set out in s. 127 (see p. 150, *infra*). By s. 65 (2), a retaking of goods or lnd to which a regulated agreement relates is an enforcement of the agreement. Cf. *Four-Maids, Ltd.* v. *Dudley Marshall (Properties), Ltd.*, [1957] Ch. 317, 310; [1957] 2 All E.R. 35, 36; *infra*, p. 316.

(*b*) Section 60 (1): see Adams, *loc. cit.*, p. 102 *et seq.*

(*c*) See further s. 60 (2) and, for the possible content of such regulations, Cmnd. 5427 (1973), App. II.

(*d*) Sections. 60 (3), (4).

(*e*) Section. 61 (1) provides as follows:

"A regulated agreement is not properly executed unless—

    (*a*) a document in the prescribed form itself containing all the prescribed terms and conforming to regulations under section 60 (1) is signed in the prescribed manner both by the debtor or hirer and by or on behalf of the creditor or owner, and

    (*b*) the document embodies all the terms of the agreement, other than implied terms, and

    (*c*) the document is, when presented or sent to the debtor or hirer for signature, in such a state that all its terms are readily legible.

And see (1975) 39 *Conv.* (*N.S.*) 94, 104. Under s. 61 (4), where the debtor or hirer is a partnership or other unincorporated body of persons, sub-s. (1) (*a*) shall apply with the substitution of "by or on behalf of the debtor or hirer" for the words " by the debtor or hirer".

(*f*) As to the meaning and effect of "not properly executed", see s. 65; footnote (*a*), *supra*.

Other sections within Part V are more total in their effect and state that their contravention shall render the agreement void. This is the case with s. 59 (1), whereunder an agreement is void "if and to the extent that it purports to bind a person to enter as debtor or hirer into a prospective regulated agreement" (g); and with s. 56 (3) which provides that an agreement is void if and to the extent that it purports in relation to an actual or prospective regulated agreement, *either* to provide that a person acting as, or on behalf of, a negotiator is to be treated as the agent of the debtor or hirer, *or* to relieve a person from liability for acts or omissions of any person acting as or on behalf of a negotiator (h).

Further sections within Part V deal with the duty to give notice of cancellation rights (i) and the duty to supply copies of executed and unexecuted agreements (j).

Withdrawal and cancellation.—When the agreement is still at its negotiating stage, or where it has failed for any other reason to ripen into a contract, the debtor may of course withdraw at any time. Moreover, as we have seen, s. 59 (1) enlarges this entitlement to include even those cases where there has been an agreement to the contrary. The primary consequences of withdrawal are set out in s. 57, which provides that withdrawal may be either written or oral (k) and shall cause the provisions of Part IV to apply not only to the regulated agreement itself but to any linked transaction (l), and to any other

---

(g) Under s. 59 (2) regulations may exempt certain specified agreements from the operation of s. 59 (1).

(h) For the meanings of "antecedent negotiations" and "negotiator" and the circumstances in which a negotiator shall be deemed to be acting as agent for the creditor, see s. 56 (1), (2); for the time at which negotiations are to be deemed to commence, see s. 56 (4).

(i) Section 64; these rights do not, as we shall see *infra*, generally apply to mortgages of land.

(j) Sections 62 and 63. The expressions "executed" and "unexecuted" agreement are defined by s. 189 (1). As to the potential difficulties of implementing these rules in relation to bank mortgages, see Adams, *loc. cit.*, pp. 104–105. The same author points out that the provisions of Part V generally could govern not only those cases in which the mortgagee is an institution which operates a business of providing credit but also those cases in which (for instance) an employer provides house-loans for its staff or a solicitor takes a charge over a client's property as security for costs, unless exempt under s. 16 (5) (see p. 137, *supra*).

(k) Section 57 (2). As to whether a mere posting of the notice of withdrawal would be sufficient, without receipt, to invoke s. 57 (1), see Goode, *op. cit.*, pp. 101–102.

(l) As defined in s. 19. A linked transaction is any transaction, *other than one for the provision of security*, which is entered into by the debtor or hirer under an actual or prospective regulated agreement and, while not forming part of the latter agreement itself, fulfils one of the three following conditions: (a) is entered into in compliance with a term of the principal agreement; (b) is financed, or to be financed, by the principal agreement where that principal agreement is a debtor-creditor-supplier agreement (see *supra*, p. 134); (c) is entered into by the debtor or hirer with a person specified in s. 19 (2), and at the suggestion of such a person, for one of the following purposes: (i) to induce the creditor or owner to enter into the principal agreement; (ii) for another purpose related to the principal agreement; or (iii) where the principal agreement is a restricted-use credit agreement (see *supra*, p. 134), for a purpose related to a transaction financed, or to be financed, by the principal agreement: s. 19 (1). The persons specified by s. 19 (2) are the creditor or owner, or his associate (as defined by ss. 189 (1), 184); a person who in the negotiation of the transaction, is represented by a credit broker (see ss. 189 (1), 145 (2)) who is also a negotiator in antecedent negotiations for the principal agreement; and a person who, at the time the transaction is initiated, knows

thing done in anticipation of the making of the agreement, it as would apply if the agreement had been made and cancelled under s. (69 *m*).

Cancellation is dealt with under ss. 67–73. The right to cancel does not apply to agreements secured on land, restricted-use credit agreements (*n*) to finance the purchase of land, or agreements for bridging loans in connection with the purchase of land (*o*). Taken in conjunction with the exemption of most first mortgages under s. 16, the relevance of these sections to mortgages is therefore slight and they will not be discussed in detail. However, since s. 69 applies by way of statutory analogy to non-cancellable agreements (*p*) it is necessary to examine the consequences enumerated by that section in order to identify the rights of the parties after a withdrawal in accordance with s. 57. A cancellation notice complying with s. 69 operates to cancel the agreement and any linked transaction and to withdraw any offer by the debtor (or hirer) or his relative to enter into a linked transaction (*q*). Further, cancelled agreements are to be treated as if they had never been entered into (*r*). However, where the relevant agreement is a debtor-creditor-supplier agreement financing the doing of work or supply of goods in an emergency, or financing the supply of goods which have become incorporated (*s*) in any land or thing not itself comprised in the agreement or any linked transaction, the effect of cancellation (and thus of withdrawal under s. 57) is less total. In such an event, the cancellation or withdrawal avoids only those provisions of the agreement or any linked transaction as relate to provision of credit, or require the debtor to pay an item in the total charge for credit, or subject the debtor to any obligation other than to pay for the doing of the work or the supply of the goods (*t*).

---

that the principal agreement has been made or contemplates that it might be made. The exclusion from s. 19 of transactions for the provision of security seems, as Adams (1975) 39 *Conv.* (*N.S.*) 94, 98, remarks, to adopt a notion of security in this context as something collateral rather than integral to the regulated agreement: see also Guest and Lloyd, *op. cit.*, note to s. 19, where the example given is that of an indemnity or guarantee. Useful discussions of the concept of a linked transaction are given by Adams and Guest and Lloyd (*loc. cit. supra*) and by Goode, *The Consumer Credit Act, 1974*, Ch. 19. The illustration (no. 11) given in Sch. 2 to the Act is as follows. Y Finance advance £500 to X (an individual) on the terms that he execute a second mortgage on his house in favour of Y Finance and take out a life assurance policy with Y Insurance (an associate of Y Finance within the meaning of s. 184 (3)). This policy is, in accordance with the primary loan agreement, charged to Y Finance as collateral security for the loan. The insurance policy is a linked transaction within the compass of s. 19 (1) (*a*) but the charging of that policy to Y Finance and the mortgage of X's house, being transactions for the provision of security, are not.

(*m*) *Infra*. See further ss. 57 (3) (identifying the parties who shall be deemed to be agents for the creditor or hirer for the purpose of receiving a withdrawal notice) and 57 (4) (s. 57 (1) to apply although the agreement, if made, would not be a cancellable agreement). In relation to s. 57 (3), see further s. 175 (duty of persons deemed to be agents).

(*n*) Defined by ss. 11, 189 (1); see footnote (*s*), p. 134, *supra*.
(*o*) Section 67.
(*p*) Section 57 (4), *supra*.
(*q*) Unless in both cases a linked transaction is exempted by regulation: s. 69 (5).
(*r*) Section 69 (4).
(*s*) By act of the debtor or his relative.
(*t*) Section 69 (2). So if, *e.g.*, the agreement or any linked transaction related to the installation of central heating, the debtor would have to pay the cost of installation but not the credit charges.

Further sections deal with the repayment of money paid by the debtor under a cancelled regulated agreement (*u*); the repayment of credit in like circumstances (*v*); the return of goods acquired by the debtor or hirer under certain kinds of regulated agreement (*w*); and the recovery of goods given by him in part exchange (*x*). Again the consequences specified in these sections shall apply *mutatis mutandis* on the withdrawal by the debtor from a non-cancellable agreement such as a regulated land mortgage. Unfortunately, space does not permit these consequences to be discussed in greater detail (*y*).

Exclusion from Part V.—Certain kinds of agreement, although falling within the general definition of a regulated agreement, are excluded either wholly or in part from the operation of Part V. The primary source of exclusion is s. 74, which provides as follows

74.—(1) This Part (except section 56) does not apply to:—

(a) a non-commercial agreement, (*z*) or
(b) a debtor-creditor (*a*) agreement enabling the debtor to overdraw on a current account, or
(c) a debtor-creditor agreement to finance the making of such payments arising on, or connected with, the death of a person as may be prescribed.

(2) This Part (except sections 55 and 56) does not apply to a small debtor-creditor-supplier agreement (*b*) for restricted-use credit (*c*).

(3) Subsection (1) (b) or (c) applies only where the Director so determines, and such a determination:—

(a) may be made subject to such conditions as the Director thinks fit, and
(b) shall be made only if the Director is of opinion that it is not against the interests of debtors.

(4) If any term of an agreement falling within subsection (1) (b) or (c) or (2) is expressed in writing, regulations under section 60 (1) shall apply to that term (subject to section 60 (3)) as if the agreement were a regulated agreement not falling within subsection (1) (b) or (c) or (2).

This section alone would not operate to exempt the majority of land-mortgages which qualify as regulated agreements from the provisions of Part V. However, the exclusion of such transactions from the rights relating to cancellation (*d*) has precipitated a special provision which grants the debtor or hirer under certain land-mortgage transactions a *locus poenitentiae* comparable to that enjoyed under ss. 67–73. Section 58 (1) provides as follows:

58.—(1) Before sending to the debtor or hirer, for his signature, an unexecuted agreement in a case where the prospective regulated agreement is to be secured on land ("the mortgaged land") the creditor or owner shall give the

---

(*u*) Section 70.
(*v*) Section 71.
(*w*) Section 72.
(*x*) Section 73.
(*y*) See Goode, *op. cit.*, Ch. 8.
(*z*) Defined by s. 189 (1) as "a consumer credit agreement or a consumer hire agreement not made by the creditor or owner in the course of a business carried on by him".
(*a*) Defined by ss. 13 and 189 (1).
(*b*) Defined by ss. 12, 17, 189 (1).
(*c*) Defined by ss. 11 (1), 189 (1).
(*d*) Prompted by the inconvenience which might arise from the registration and almost immediate de-registration of mortgages if they were readily cancellable: Goode, [1975] C.L.J. 79, 99.

debtor or hirer a copy of the unexecuted agreement which contains a notice in the prescribed form indicating the right of the debtor or hirer to withdraw from the prospective agreement and how and when the right is exercisable, together with a copy of any other document referred to in the unexecuted agreement.

Two exceptions are created by virtue of s. 58 (2): neither restricted-use credit agreements to finance the purchase of the mortgaged land, nor agreements for a bridging-loan in connection with the purchase of the mortgaged land or other land, fall within the foregoing provision. Such agreements frequently require the rapid provision of finance and it was felt that the delays necessitated by s. 58 (1) would in many cases be counter-productive. In all other cases, the creditor or owner must, after supplying the copy of the prospective agreement, allow seven days to elapse before sending the unexecuted agreement to the debtor or hirer for his signature (*e*); and he must not during the ensuing consideration period (*f*) approach the debtor or hirer (whether in person or otherwise) except in response to a specific request on the part of the latter after the beginning of the consideration period (*g*). Unless these conditions have been fulfilled, and no notice of withdrawal by the debtor or hirer has been received by the creditor or owner before the sending of the unexecuted agreement (*h*), the agreement is not deemed to have been properly executed (*hh*). The provisions of s. 61 (2) apply in addition to (and not in substitution for) those of s. 61 (1). They represent a powerful and possibly over-protective (*i*) fortification against attempts by lenders to "rail-road" consumers into taking out ill-considered mortgages.

III—TRANSACTIONAL REFORMS

The extent to which the Consumer Credit Act intervenes to protect hirers and debtors from the civil consequences of unbridled freedom of contract is considerable, and almost certainly unprecedented. For instance, it enlarges the liability of a creditor under a debtor-creditor-supplier agreement for breaches of contract or misrepresentations on the part of the supplier (*j*) and strictly circumscribes the courses of

---

(*e*) Section 61 (2) (*b*).

(*f*) The "consideration period" is defined by s. 61 (3) as the period beginning with the giving of the copy under s. 58 (1) and ending *either* at the expiry of seven days after the day on which the unexecuted agreement was sent, *or* on its return by the debtor or hirer after his signature thereto, whichever first occurs.

(*g*) Section 61 (2) (*c*).

(*h*) Section 16 (2) (*d*).

(*hh*) For the effect of this, see ss. 65 and 127 (3) (p. 151, *infra*). But the court may grant relief, see s. 127 (p. 150, *infra*).

(*i*) Cf. Goode, [1975] C.L.J. 79, 100.

(*j*) Section 75 (1); the agreement must be one falling within ss. 12 (*b*) or (*c*) and must not be a non-commercial agreement (s. 75 (3) (*a*)); further s. 75 (1) does not apply to any claim so far as it relates to any single item to which the supplier has attached a cash price not exceeding £30 or more than £10,000 (s. 75 (3) (*b*)). An example of a mortgage which fell within this section, and would therefore render the creditor-mortgagee liable for breaches of contract committed by a supplier of goods or services for the payment of whose charges the mortgage was first taken out, would be that posited on p. 136, *supra*, if pre-existing or contemplated arrangements could be established between the insurance company and the builder.

action which a creditor or owner may legitimately adopt in enforcing a regulated agreement.

Enforcement of agreements.—Where the right to enforce arises other than upon a breach by the debtor or hirer, s. 76 provides as follows:

> **76.**—(1) The creditor or owner is not entitled to enforce a term of a regulated agreement by:—
>
> (a) demanding earlier payment of any sum, or
> (b) recovering possession of any goods or land, or
> (c) treating any right conferred on the debtor or hirer by the agreement as terminated, restricted or deferred,
>
> except by or after giving the debtor or hirer not less than seven days' notice of his intention to do so (*k*).

Notices given under s. 76 (1) must assume the prescribed form in order to be effective (*l*). A breach of the subsection does not prevent a creditor from treating the right to draw on any credit as restricted or deferred, or from taking necessary steps to implement such restriction or deferment (*m*). Moreover, s. 76 (1) may be displaced either by exempting regulations in the case of particular agreements (*n*) and generally when the right of enforcement arises upon a breach by the debtor or hirer (*o*). In such an event the operative provisions are to be found in Part VII (Default and Termination) (*p*). Under s. 87 (1) (*q*) whenever the debtor or hirer is in breach of a regulated agreement, the creditor or owner must serve a "default notice" (*r*) before he can terminate the agreement, demand earlier payment of any sum, repossess goods or land, enforce any security or treat any rights of the debtor or hirer as terminated, restricted or deferred (*s*). Broadly, the notice required is of seven-days duration and must be in writing; but as Professor Goode points out (*t*), the effect of a default notice differs radically from a notice given under s. 76 (*u*) insofar as s. 89 provides that compliance by the debtor or hirer with the action specified by the notice as necessary to remedy the breach, provided such compliance occurs within the stipulated time, means that the breach shall be treated as if it had never occurred (*uu*).

Where the creditor or owner wishes to repossess goods on default, he is further subject to the provisions of s. 90, if the agreement in question is a regulated hire-purchase or conditional sale agreement: this section

---

(*k*) This subsection is qualified to some extent by s. 76 (2), which confines its operations to cases where a period for the duration of the agreement is specified therein, and that period has not ended when the creditor or owner adopts the conduct in question.

(*l*) Section 76 (3).
(*m*) Section 76 (4).
(*n*) Section 76 (5).
(*o*) Section 76 (6).
(*p*) *Infra.*
(*q*) See p. 147, *infra.*
(*r*) For the contents and effect of such notices, see s. 88 (modelled on s. 146 L.P.A. 1925).
(*s*) Sections 87 (2) and (4) correspond substantially with ss. 76 (4) and (5), *supra.*
(*t*) [1975] C.L.J. 79, 108.
(*u*) Or under s. 98 (termination other than by default): *infra.*
(*uu*) Cf. s. 146, *L.P.A.,* 1925; *Scala House & District Property, Ltd.* v. *Forbes*, [1974] Q.B. 575 (C.A.); [1973] 3 All E.R. 308; *supra,* p. 23.

(which is of course of merely marginal interest to mortgages) corresponds substantially to ss. 33–44 of the Hire-Purchase Act 1965, in that it reintroduces the notion of protected goods into the superseding legislation. Recovery contrary to s. 90 involves termination of the agreement, total release of the debtor from liability and the right on his part to recover all sums hitherto paid to the creditor (*v*). A court order is required before creditors under such agreements, or owners under regulated consumer hire-agreements (*w*) may enter premises to take possession of goods subject thereto (*x*); the recovery of possession of land is subject to the same restriction after the debtor is in breach of a regulated conditional sale agreement relating to land (*y*). Failure to obtain a court order may render the creditor or owner liable for breach of statutory duty (*z*). Interest under a regulated consumer credit agreement is not to be increased on default (*a*).

Early payment by debtor.—The Consumer Credit Act acknowledges that debtors or hirers should be entitled, where appropriate, to accelerate their discharge from the agreement or to terminate that agreement before it has run its full course. Accordingly, s. 94 provides for early payment by the debtor under a regulated consumer credit agreement: the debtor is entitled at any time, provided he gives statutory notice to that effect (*b*), to release himself from further liability by immediate discharge of all outstanding commitments under the agreement (*c*). In this event he may be entitled to a rebate (*d*) and either he or any relative of his will generally be discharged from liability under any linked transaction (*e*).

Termination of agreements.—As regards termination by the debtor under a regulated hire-purchase or conditional sale agreement, the provisions of the Act are substantially those embodied in the Hire-Purchase Act 1965 (*f*). Equivalent provision is made for the termination of regulated consumer hire agreements (*g*); and it is further provided that certain persons (*e.g.*, credit-brokers or suppliers, who were the negotiators in antecedent negotiations) shall be deemed to be the agents of the creditor or owner for the purpose of receiving notices of rescission from the debtor or hirer (*h*), although this section does not apply to termination under ss. 99 or 101 or under a right expressly conferred by the agreement (*i*).

Section 98 deals with the termination by the creditor or owner of a regulated agreement, other than upon default by the debtor or hirer, *e.g.*, on the debtor or hirer becoming bankrupt. Here again, no regulated

---

(*v*) Section 91.
(*w*) For the protection of consumer-hirer against repossession, see further s. 132.
(*x*) Section 92 (1).
(*y*) Section 92 (2).
(*z*) Section 92 (3).
(*a*) Section 93.
(*b*) See further s. 94 (2).
(*c*) Section 94 (1).
(*d*) Section 95: the mathematics are to be worked out by regulations.
(*e*) Section 96.
(*f*) H.P. Act 1965, ss. 27, 28; C.C. Act 1974, ss. 99, 100.
(*g*) Section 101; see also s. 132.
(*h*) Section 102 (1).
(*i*) Section 102 (2).

agreement can be lawfully terminated unless the debtor has been given at least seven days notice of the termination (*j*). The notice must be in the prescribed form (*k*) and the section otherwise operates or is excluded in circumstances comparable to ss. 76 and 87 (*l*).

Information and documentation.—Certain information and documents must in specified circumstances be given to debtors and hirers during (or shortly after) the currency of the agreement. Such information includes sums paid and payable under fixed sum (*m*) and running-account (*n*) credit agreements, a break-down of the sums payable under regulated consumer hire agreements (*o*), the amounts required to discharge the debtor's indebtedness under regulated consumer credit agreements (*p*) and statements that the liability of a debtor or hirer under regulated agreements has been discharged (*q*). In most cases a failure to comply will render the agreement unenforceable for the period of default and may, after a certain time, constitute an offence. Further, statements given in connection with the above requirements are generally binding (*r*) unless the court grants relief (*s*).

Other provisions within Part VI deal with the duty of debtors or hirers under regulated agreements to give information about the location of goods (*t*); the appropriation of payments made by debtors or hirers to the same person under two or more regulated agreements (*u*); the variation of regulated agreements (*v*); the debtor's liability for misuse of credit facilities or credit tokens (*w*); and the effect of the death of a hirer or debtor upon a regulated agreement (*x*).

Security.—The rules as to security are contained in Part VIII of the Act. All securities (*y*) in relation to regulated agreements, other than those provided by the debtor or hirer (*z*), must be in writing (*a*), must adopt the prescribed form and must embody the prescribed contents (*b*). Unless these and other formalities are observed (*c*) the security instrument is not properly executed.

With the exception of s. 105, Part VIII would appear to govern both primary and collateral securities. The sections in this Part speak generally in terms of "any security". Section 189 (1) defines security as

---

(*j*) Section 98 (1); this subsection is limited in its operation by s. 98 (2) which imposes *mutatis mutandis* the same restrictions as s. 76 (2) does upon s. 76 (1): *supra*, p. 144.

(*k*) Section 98 (3).

(*l*) See ss. 98 (4), (5), (6).

(*m*) Section 77.

(*n*) Section 78.

(*o*) Section 79.

(*p*) Section 97.

(*q*) Section 103. See also s. 85 (creditor's duty on issue of new credit tokens).

(*r*) Section 172 (1), (2).

(*s*) Section 172 (3).

(*t*) Section 80. This does not apply to non-commercial agreements.

(*u*) Section 81.

(*v*) Section 82.

(*w*) Sections 83 and 84.

(*x*) Section 86.

(*y*) As defined by s. 189 (1); *supra*, p. 136.

(*z*) Section 105 (6): these may, of course, be covered by s. 60: *supra*, p. 139; s. 105 (9).

(*a*) Section 105 (1).

(*b*) Section 105 (2).

(*c*) Section 105 (3); and see s. 105 (5) (copies to sureties).

including "a mortgage . . . provided by the debtor or hirer, or at this request (express or implied) to secure the carrying out of (his) obligations . . . under the agreement". Although the matter is not free from doubt, the definition therefore seems to encompass both the mortgage which is given by way of reinforcement to, and the mortgage which itself constitutes, a regulated agreement (*cc*).

Section 106 allows for the retrospective extinguishment of securities. Whenever a provision of the Act applies s. 106 to any security which has been provided in relation to a regulated agreement, the following consequences shall follow:

(a) the security, so far as it is so provided, shall be treated as never having effect;
(b) any property lodged with the creditor or owner solely for the purposes of the security as so provided shall be returned by him forthwith;
(c) the creditor or owner shall take any necessary action to remove or cancel an entry in any register, so far as the entry relates to the security as so provided; and
(d) any amount received by the creditor or owner on realisation of the security shall, so far as it is referable to the agreement, be repaid to the surety.

These rules are subject, however, to s. 177 (saving for registered charges), which will be considered in due course (*d*). The principal circumstances (*e*) in which a security will be invalidated under s. 106 are: where the court dismisses otherwise than on technical grounds an application to enforce an improperly executed regulated agreement or security (*f*); where the agreement is cancelled under s. 69 (1) or becomes subject to s. 69 (2); or where it is terminated under s. 91 (*g*).

Where there has been a breach of a regulated agreement, no security given in connection therewith can be enforced until a default notice conforming with s. 87 has been given and has duly expired without the breach being remedied (*h*). This provision is not paralleled in s. 76, which deals with non-breach situations (*i*) and is in most other respects a close analogue of s. 87; the nearest s. 76 approaches to the aforementioned provision is a statement that no recovery of possession of goods or land shall occur without service and expiry of the customary seven-day notice. Where, however, the enforcement (or the security) takes some other form, the only prior notification required of the creditor or owner seems to be that set out in the security instrument itself.

Where the regulated agreement is secured by a land-mortgage, however, that mortgage is enforceable only upon an order of the court (*j*). Guest and Lloyd (*k*) characterise this as one of the most important

---

(*cc*) Cf. Hyde, *Trade and Industry*, 8 August 1974, p. 264, and Adams, *loc. cit.*, *supra.*, at p. 109; and see further p. 136, *supra.*

(*d*) *Infra*, p. 154.

(*e*) Goode, [1975] C.L.J. 79, 112; for a fuller list, see Goode, *The Consumer Credit Act, 1974*, p. 138.

(*f*) Sections 113 (3) (c) and 105 (8).

(*g*) Section 113 (3) (a), (b); see further Goode, *The Consumer Credit Act 1974* 13, p. 12.

(*h*) Sections 87 (1) and 88; see also s. 112. The doing of an act by which a floating charge becomes fixed is not enforcement of a security: s. 87 (3).

(*i*) *Supra*, p. 144.

(*j*) Section 126.

(*k*) *The Consumer Credit Act, 1974*, note to s. 126.

provisions of the entire Act, while remarking that no sanction is specifically imposed to cater for its breach. Accordingly, it is thought that a mortgagee who, in contravention of s. 126, obtains vacant possession and exercises a right of sale can pass a good title to the purchaser of the land (*l*). Unless s. 106 applies to the security, the debtor or hirer would appear to be limited to seeking an injunction or to proceeding for the withdrawal of the creditor's licence (*m*).

The redemption and realisation of pawns are dealt with under ss. 116–121 of the Act.

The remainder of Part VIII embraces an assortment of ancillary matters, many of them comparable to provisions in earlier Parts. Thus, there are rules relating to various information requirements (*n*) and a special section (*o*) enabling regulations to be made providing for "any matters relating to the sale or other realisation by the creditor or owner of property over which any right has been provided by way of security in relation to an actual or prospective regulated agreement other than a non-commercial agreement" (*p*). In addition s. 113 makes elaborate provision for ensuring that the Act shall not be evaded by the taking of security and provides that no security provided in relation to an actual or prospective regulated agreement shall be enforced so as to benefit the creditor or owner to a greater extent than would have been the case if the security had not been provided (*q*). The rules by which this policy is implemented are complex and abstruse and space does not permit a detailed discussion. The general drift of s. 113 is to treat securities given in relation to regulated agreements which are subject to some debilitating event, such as termination, cancellation (whether actual or notional (*r*)), or being enforceable only by order of the Court or the Director General, in a manner equivalent to that applied to the regulated agreement itself.

Finally, regard should be paid to the rules relating to negotiable instruments: these are contained in ss. 123–125. The Crowther Committee reported considerable malpractice in the taking of such documents (particularly promissory notes) from consumers under deferred purchasing or work and labour transactions, and s. 123 reflects the restrictive policy now adopted towards these and associated practices:

> **123.**—(1) A creditor or owner shall not take a negotiable instrument, other than a bank note or cheque, in discharge of any sum payable:—

(*l*) See also s. 177 (2) (pp. 154–155). *Quaere* whether the prospective purchaser could legitimately object to the mortgagee's title on the grounds of non-compliance with s. 126.

(*m*) See further, Goode, [1975] C.L.J. 79, 113.

(*n*) See ss. 107 (duty to give information to surety under fixed-sum credit agreement); 108 (duty to give information to surety under running-account credit agreement); 109 (duty to give information to surety under consumer hire agreement); 110 (duty to give information to debtor or hirer under regulated agreements which are non-commercial agreements); 111 (duty to give surety copy of notices despatched under ss. 87 (1), 76 (1) or 98 (1)).

(*o*) Section 112.

(*p*) This section is subject to s. 121, which deals with the realisation of pawns.

(*q*) For a summary of this important section, see Guest and Lloyd, *op. cit.*, note to s. 113.

(*r*) See s. 57; *supra*, p. 140.

(a) by the debtor or hirer under a regulated agreement, or

(b) by any person as surety in relation to the agreement.

(2) The creditor or owner shall not negotiate a cheque taken by him in discharge of a sum payable as mentioned in subsection (1) except to a banker (within the meaning of the Bills of Exchange Act 1882).

(3) The creditor or owner shall not take a negotiable instrument as security for the discharge of any sum payable as mentioned in subsection (1).

(4) A person takes a negotiable instrument as security for the discharge of a sum if the sum is intended to be paid in some other way, and the negotiable instrument is to be presented for payment only if the sum is not paid in that way.

(5) This section does not apply where the regulated agreement is a non-commercial agreement.

(6) The Secretary of State may by order provide that this section shall not apply where the regulated agreement has a connection with a country outside the United Kingdom (s).

Once s. 123 has been contravened in relation to a sum payable as mentioned in s. 123 (1) (a), the agreement under which the sum is payable can be enforced against the debtor or hirer only upon an order of the court (t). A similar restriction on enforcement is imposed in the case of contraventions of s. 123 in relation to sums payable by sureties (u), and the dismissal of any application for an order to enforce such a security (other than a dismissal on technical grounds alone) shall offset the operation of s. 106 (v) and thus retrospectively extinguish the security (w). While nothing in the Act is to affect the right of holders in due course (x), nobody who takes a negotiable instrument contrary to ss. 123 (1) or (3) is to be deemed a holder in due course, or is entitled to enforce the instrument (y). Further, a creditor or owner is bound to indemnify any debtor, hirer or surety against liability to holders in due course when the instrument was originally taken by such creditor or owner contrary to ss. 123 (1) or (3), or taken and executed contrary to s. 123 (2) (z).

IV—ENFORCEMENT OF THE ACT

Part XI of the Consumer Credit Act identifies the persons and institutions charged with its implementation and enforcement (a) and invests these bodies with a formidable array of sanctions and powers. It may be observed that s. 168 contains a "non-fault" defence not dissimilar to that contained in ss. 24 (1) and (2) of the Trade Descrip-

---

(s) Doubt has been expressed as to the meaning of "negotiable instrument" in this section: see Guest and Lloyd, note to s. 123 and Goode *The Consumer Credit Act 1974*. C. 123 n.; [1975] C.L.J. 79, 114 n.; *Crouch* v. *Credit Foncier of England, Ltd.* (1873); L.R. 8 Q.B. 374, at pp. 381, 382.

(t) Section 124 (1).

(u) Section 124 (2). For the definition of surety, see s. 189 (1).

(v) *Supra*, p. 148.

(w) Section 124 (3).

(x) Section 125 (4).

(y) Section 125 (1).

(z) Section 124 (3).

(a) Section 161.

tions Act 1968 and ss. 25 (1) and (2) of the Fair Trading Act 1973 (b).
Certain provisions in Part XI import a transactional effect. Thus,
statements given by creditors or owners under certain of the various
"information" sections (c) are binding upon them (d) subject to any
relief the court considers to be just (e). Any term of a regulated agreement or linked transaction (f) is void insofar as it conflicts with any
provision of the Act (or regulation made thereunder) for the protection
of the debtor or hirer or his relative (g).

V—JUDICIAL CONTROL OF AGREEMENTS (gg)

Part IX generally.—There remains one further (and vitally
important) Part of the Consumer Credit Act which sets out the principles upon which the court may adjust or administer agreements,
and contains wide powers of supervision and intervention. This part
(Part IX) is of unprecedented latitude and specificity. It operates
upon a varying spectrum of agreements through a number of different
media.

Enforcement orders.—It will be recalled that a number of sections
within the Act have the effect, if contravened, of rendering the relevant
agreement unenforceable unless the court orders to the contrary.
Section 127 (1) delineates the circumstances in which this discretionary
power is to be exercised. In the event of an application for an enforcement order under ss. 65 (1) (h), 105 (7) (a) or (b) (i), 111 (2) (j), or 124 (1)
or (2) (k), the application shall be dismissed if and only if the court
considers it just to do so; and in reaching its conclusion the court shall
pay regard to:

(i) prejudice caused to any person by the relevant contravention, and the
degree of culpability involved therein; and
(ii) the powers conferred on the court by ss. 127 (2) and 135 and 136.

Section 127 (2) permits the court, when called upon to grant an
enforcement order, to order an adjustment of the respective liabilities
as an alternative to total enforcement or nullity. The court may, if it
appears just for it to do so, "reduce or discharge any sum payable by

---

(b) Cf. *Tesco Supermarkets, Ltd.*, v. *Nattrass*, [1972] A.C. 153 (H.L.); [1971] 2 All E.R.
E.R. 127; Guest and Lloyd, note to s. 168; *McGuire* v. *Sittingbourne Co-Operative Society,
Ltd.*, (1976), 140 J.P. 306.
(c) Specifically, ss. 77 (1), 78 (1), 79 (1), 107 (1) (c), 108 (1) (c) and 109 (1) (c); also
s. 103 (1) (notice whether customer indebted).
(d) Section 172 (1), (2).
(e) Section 127 (3). See further *infra*, pp. 150–152.
(f) Or any term in any other agreement relating to an actual or prospective regulated
agreement or linked transaction.
(g) Section 173 (1). But note s. 173 (3) which provides that notwithstanding s. 173
(1), an act required to be done only on order of the court or of the Director-General of
Fair Trading may nevertheless be validly done at any time with the consent of the
person to whom it is done: but that the refusal of such consent shall not give rise to any
liability. For criticism of this subsection, see Adams (1975, 39 Conv. (N.S.) 94, 111.
(gg) As to the applicability of the ensuing provisions to "rental purchase" schemes,
see B. M. Hoggett (1975), 39 *Conv.* (N.S.) 343, especially at p. 354; Adams, *loc. cit.*,
supra, pp. 112–113.
(h) Improperly executed agreements.
(i) Improperly executed security instruments.
(j) Failure to serve copy of notice on surety.
(k) Taking a negotiable instrument contrary to s. 123.

the debtor or hirer or any surety so as to compensate him for prejudice suffered as a result of the contravention in question". These powers are supplemented by s. 135, which entitles the court in appropriate circumstances to impose conditions upon (*l*), or suspend (*m*), an order, and by s. 136 which entitles it to vary or amend agreements or security instruments in consequence of a term of its order. Guest and Lloyd suggest that the latter section will be sparingly applied (*n*).

Further conditions are attached to the making of enforcement orders under s. 65 (1). Such an order shall not be made if s. 61 (1) (a) (*o*) has not been complied with; an exception exists where a document containing all the prescribed terms of the agreement has been signed by the hirer, even though the form and contents of the document and the manner in which it was signed did not comply with s. 60 (1) (*p*). Nor shall an order be made pursuant to s. 65 (1) where the agreement is cancellable and (a) a provision of s. 62 or s. 63 was not complied with, and the creditor or owner did not give a copy of the executed agreement, and of any other document referred to in it, to the debtor or hirer before the commencement of the proceedings in which the order is sought, or (b) s. 64 (1) was not complied with (*q*). Section 128 deals with the making of enforcement orders on the death of the debtor or hirer. Under s. 86 (2), a creditor or owner under an unsecured or partly secured regulated agreement may not engage in conduct specified by s. 87 (1) (*r*) by reason only of the death of the debtor or hirer unless he obtains an order of the court. The effect of s. 128 is to prohibit the making of such an order unless the creditor or owner proves that he has been unable to satisfy himself that the present and future obligations of the debtor or hirer under the agreement are likely to be discharged.

Time orders.—Section 129 endows the court with wide powers for the making of time orders, thereby providing for the payment of arrears upon such times and in such quantities as are determined by the court. Section 129 (1) sets out the circumstances in which a time order can be made (*s*), and s. 129 (2) sets out the permitted contents of the order (*t*). This power is further amplified by s. 130.

(*l*) *Viz.*, to make the operation of any term of the order conditional upon the performance of specified acts by any party to the proceedings: s. 135 (1) (a).

(*m*) The suspension may be either until such time as the court subsequently directs, or until the occurrence of a specified act or omission. See further, ss. 135 (2) (suspension of term requiring delivery up of goods) and 135 (4) (suspension or conditional orders in consumer hire agreements).

(*n*) *Op. cit.*, note to s. 136.

(*o*) Which deals with the signing of agreements: see *supra*, p. 139.

(*p*) Section 127 (3); see further s. 127 (5).

(*q*) Section 127 (4).

(*r*) *Supra*, p. 147.

(*s*) Section 129 (1) (a): on an application for an enforcement order; (b) on an application made by a debtor or hirer under this paragraph after service on him of—(i) a default notice, or (ii) a notice under s. 76 (1) or s. 98 (1); (c) in an action brought by a creditor or owner to enforce a regulated agreement or any security, or recover possession of any goods or land to which a regulated agreement relates.

(*t*) Section 129 (2) (a): the payment by the debtor or hirer or any surety of any sum owed under a regulated agreement or a security by such instalments, payable at such times, as the court, having regard to the means of the debtor or hirer and any surety, considers reasonable; (b) the remedying by the debtor or hirer of any breach of a regulated agreement (other than non-payment of money) within such period as the court may specify.

Protection of property pending proceedings.—The court, if invited to do so by the creditor or owner under a regulated agreement, is empowered to make such orders as it thinks just for the protection of any property belonging to the applicant, or of property subject to any security (*u*).

Special powers in relation to hire, hire-purchase and conditional sale agreements.—If they fall within the definition of a regulated agreement, these transactions attract the operation of special powers of the court, set out in ss. 132 (*v*) and 133 (*w*).

Extortionate credit bargains.—Sections 137–140 empower the court to re-open extortionate credit bargains. These sections have been described as the most radical within Part IX of the Act (*x*). They operate by means of distinction between the concepts of "credit-bargain" and "credit agreements". A credit agreement is defined as any agreement between an individual (the "debtor"), and any other person ("the creditor") by which the creditor provides the debtor with credit of any amount (*y*). It follows that the provisions relating to extortionate credit bargains are not subject to the £5,000 limit which is integral to the definition of a regulated agreement, and which applies generally throughout the Act (*z*). Credit bargains are more esoterically defined. Where no transaction, other than the credit agreement, is to be taken into account in computing the total charge for credit "credit-bargain" means the credit agreement itself (*a*). Where one or more other transactions are to be so taken into account, it means the credit agreement and these other transactions collectively (*b*).

The general discretion is stated in s. 137 (1): if the court finds a credit bargain extortionate it may re-open the credit agreement so as to do justice between the parties. Under s. 138 (1) a credit bargain is extortionate *either* if it requires the debtor (or a relative of his) to make unconditional or contingent payments which are grossly extortionate (*c*), *or* if it otherwise grossly contravenes ordinary principles of fair dealing. Among the factors to which regard shall be paid in identifying a credit bargain as extortionate are prevailing contemporary interest rates (*d*), the age, experience, business capacity and health of, and financial pressures confronting, the debtor (*e*), the risk taken by the creditor,

---

(*u*) Section 131.
(*v*) Financial relief for the hirer under a regulated consumer hire agreement.
(*w*) Containing equivalent provisions for cases of hire-purchase and conditional sale. See also s. 134, which caters for evidence of adverse detention in cases of this kind.
(*x*) Goode, [1975] C.L.J. 79, 118.
(*y*) Section 137 (2) (a).
(*z*) Sections 137–140 accordingly apply (*inter alia*) to loans of any amount; exempt agreements; small agreements; non-commercial agreements and all forms of mortgage taken out by individuals. They do not, however, apply to hire-agreements whether qualifying as consumer hire agreements or not. Cf. *Galbraith* v. *Mitchenall Estates, Ltd.*, [1965] 2 Q.B. 473; [1964] 2 All E.R. 653; *Stockloser* v. *Johnson*, [1954] 1 Q.B. 476. [1954] 1 All E.R. 630. It is to be observed that the provisions are retrospective; applying to bargains made both before and after the Act; C.C.A. 1974, Sch. 3, para. 42.
(*a*) Section 137 (2) (b) (i).
(*b*) Section 137 (2) (b) (ii).
(*c*) For discussion as to the probable interpretation of this expression see Guest and Lloyd, *The Consumer Credit Act 1974*, note to s. 138.
(*d*) Section 138 (2) (a); see also s. 138 (5).
(*e*) Section 138 (3) (a), (b).

his relationship with the debtor and the question whether any colourable cash price was quoted (where relevant) for the goods (*f*). These categories are not exclusive, and any other considerations of relevance shall be taken into account (*g*).

Having adumbrated the circumstances in which a credit bargain is to be deemed extortionate, the Act proceeds to set out the methods by which the correlative credit agreement may be re-opened. These are as follows (*h*):

(a) on an application for the purpose made by the debtor or any surety to the High Court, county court of sheriff court; or (*i*)
(b) at the instance of the debtor or a surety in any proceedings to which the debtor and creditor are parties, being proceedings to enforce the credit agreement, any security relating to it, or any linked transaction; or
(c) at the instance of the debtor or a surety in other proceedings in any court where the amount paid or payable under the credit agreement is relevant.

Furthermore, in re-opening the agreement the court may adopt (by order) certain procedures for relieving the debtor or a surety from payment of any sum in excess of that fairly due and reasonable. These are set out in s. 139 (2) and include a direction that accounts to be taken between any persons (*j*); the setting aside of any obligation (in whole or in part) imposed on debtors or sureties by credit bargains or related agreements (*k*); requiring repayments by the creditor (*l*) or the return of security-property to sureties (*m*), and alteration of the terms of credit agreements or of any security instrument (*n*). An order made under s. 139 (2) shall not alter the effect of any judgment (*o*). The court is not precluded from making such an order by the fact that the effect of the order is to place a burden on the creditor in respect of an advantage unfairly enjoyed by another person who is a party to a linked transaction (*p*).

Extensions of ss. 137–139.—Lastly, mention should be made of s. 140 which provides as follows:

140. Where the credit agreement is not a regulated agreement, expressions used in sections 137 to 139 which, apart from this section, apply only to regulated agreements, shall be construed as nearly as may be as if the credit agreement were a regulated agreement."

(*f*) Section 138 (4) (a), (c).
(*g*) Section 138 (2) (c). See the excellent discussion of these factors by Goode, *loc. cit.*, pp. 120–121; and cf. *Cityland and Property (Holdings), Ltd.* v. *Dabrah*, [1968] Ch. 166; [1967] 2 All E.R. 639; *Lloyds Bank, Ltd.* v. *Bundy*, [1975] Q.B. 326; [1974] 3 All E.R. 757; *A. Schroder Music Publishing Co., Ltd.* v. *Macaulay*, [1974] 3 All E.R. 616; [1974] 1 W.L.R. 1308; *Clifford Davis Management, Ltd.* v. *W.E.A. Records, Ltd.*, [1975] 1 All E.R. 237; [1975] 1 W.L.R. 61; (1975) 39 *Conv.* (*N.S*) 67, 210; *infra.*, pp. 227, 528. As to the burden of proof in such proceedings, see Guest and Lloyd, *loc. cit.*, *supra*; Goode, [1975] C.L.J. 79, 121.
(*h*) Section 139 (1).
(*i*) For procedural rules in this connection, see ss. 139 (5), (6), (7).
(*j*) Section 139 (2) (a).
(*k*) Section 139 (2) (b).
(*l*) Section 139 (2) (c).
(*m*) Section 139 (2) (d).
(*n*) Section 139 (2) (e).
(*o*) Section 139 (4).
(*p*) Section 139 (3). See S.I. 1977, No. 325 (appointed day for these provisions is 10th May, 1977).

The object of this provision is to accommodate within ss. 137–139, by way of analogy, certain concepts which are utilised within these sections but which the Act otherwise defines solely in terms of regulated agreements. Since ss. 137–139 are not limited to regulated agreements, s. 140 is necessary in order to permit analogous images of such concepts as the linked transaction to operate within the larger and more specialised sphere of these sections.

VI—ANCILLARY CREDIT BUSINESSES

These are defined by s. 145 and regulated by Part X of the Act. Their relevance to the law of mortgage is oblique rather than immediate and the reader is referred to specialised works (*q*) for further information. However, it should be noted that a regulated agreement made by a debtor or hirer upon introduction by an unlicensed credit-broker (*r*) is enforceable against him only by order of the Director-General of Fair Trading (*s*).

VII—SUPPLEMENTAL PROVISIONS

Part XII of the Act embodies a whole menagerie of supplemental rules, ranging from such matters as the prohibition on disclosure of information about individuals without their consent (*t*), the duty of persons deemed to be agents (*u*) and the service of documents (*v*) to additional amplification of the powers the Secretary of State may exercise by statutory instrument (*w*); clarificatory measures concerning "associates" (*x*), certain multipartite agreements (*y*) and the meaning of pre-existing and future arrangements between creditor and supplier (*z*) and definitions of the novel vocabulary used throughout the Act (*a*). But perhaps the most significant section from the point of view of the present work is s. 177 (*b*), entitled "saving for registered charges". Subsection (I) provides that nothing in the Act is to affect the rights of a proprietor of a registered charge within the meaning of the Land Registration Act, provided that one of two conditions is fulfilled: (i) he became proprietor under a transfer for value without notice of a defect in title arising under the Act, or (ii) he derives title from such a

---

(*q*) Most notably Goode, *The Consumer Credit Act 1974*, Ch. 23.
(*r*) As definied in ss. 145 (2), (3) and (4).
(*s*) Section 149 (1), (2); and for the procedure in making orders, see *ibid.*, sub-ss. (3), (4) and (5).
(*t*) Such information being "obtained under or by virtue of this Act": s. 174 (1). For exceptions see s. 174 (3), (4).
(*u*) Section 175.
(*v*) Section 176. Note that under s. 176 (7), s. 9 of the Administration of Estates Act, 1925 is not to be construed as authorising service on the probate judge.
(*w*) Section 179 and 183.
(*x*) Section 184.
(*y*) Section 185 (agreement with more than one debtor or hirer) and 186 (agreement with more than one creditor or owner).
(*z*) Section 187.
(*a*) Sections 188 and 189.

proprietor (*b*). In addition, s. 177 (3) adds the condition that the proprietor must not carry on a business of debt-collecting for s. 177 (1) to apply (*c*). This saving provision has already occasioned considerable academic criticism. On one level it is said that s. 177 (1) does not go far enough, insofar as it does not apply to the second proprietor or holder of any other form of charge over registered land, or to any transferee of any mortgage over unregistered land (*d*). On another level, the subsection is criticised for a lack of clarity, both in the area of "defects of title", and again in the scope of protection which it purports to confer. Some commentators have contended that the only defect in a mortgagee's title which arises under the Act is that emanating from s. 106 (as applied by ss. 105 (8) and 113 (3),) whereunder the mortgage is treated as never having had effect (*e*). Elsewhere it is questioned whether the unsatisfied necessity to obtain a court order before enforcing an improperly executed mortgage, or the entry into a mortgage by unlicensed professional creditors without enforcement orders, can genuinely be said to constitute or procreate defects in title (*f*). In any event, it would appear that notice of a breach of the Act does not necessarily impart notice of a defect in title, and that a transferee protected by s. 177 (1) may be entitled to enforce the mortgage according to the ordinary law; thus averting, for instance, the operation of s. 126 (requiring a court order before enforcement of a land mortgage securing a regulated agreement) or s. 105 (7) (which likewise requires a court order before an improperly executed security agreement is enforceable against a surety) (*g*).

Further subsections to s. 177 provide that nothing in the Act affects the operation of s. 104 of the Law of Property Act 1925, (*h*) and that where, by virtue of s. 177 (1), a land mortgage is enforced which would otherwise have been unenforceable, the original creditor or owner shall be liable to indemnify the debtor or hirer against any loss suffered by him as a result (*i*).

(*b*) He must also, of course, become registered proprietor of the charge under s. 33 (2) of the Land Registration Act, 1925.

(*c*) This exception has been criticised on the ground that it could imperil "rescue operations" in respect of finance companies, because any mortgage within the Act in which a finance company is mortgagee cannot be taken over by an institution within s. 177 (3) without forfeiting s. 177 (1): J. E. Adams, (1975), 39 *Conv. (N.S.)* 114.

(*d*) Adams, *loc. cit.*, pp. 113–114.

(*e*) Guest and Lloyd, *The Consumer Credit Act 1974*, note to s. 177 (1); they further observe that the primary cases of such a defect arising are those where the court or the Director has refused to make an enforcement order under ss. 40 (2), 65 (1), 105 (1), 124 (1) or 149 (2), or where the court has made a declaration under s. 142 (1), or where a cancellable agreement has been cancelled by the debtor under s. 69 (1). Accordingly it is contended that where the transferee of the mortgage has no notice, actual or constructive, of the making or refusing of the apprpriate order, or of the cancellation of the agreement, the transferee is protected under s. 177 (1).

(*f*) Adams, *loc. cit., supra*, p. 114.

(*g*) Guest and Lloyd, *loc. cit., supra; supra*, p. 146.

(*h*) Section 177 (2). Section 104 provides protection for a purchaser where a mortgagee exercises his power of sale.

(*i*) Section 177 (4).

CHAPTER 10

Charges

I—EQUITABLE CHARGES

Definition.—A charge is a security whereby real or personal property is appropriated for the discharge of a debt or other obligation, but which does not pass either an absolute or a special property in the subject of the security to the creditor, nor any right to possession, but only a right of realisation by judicial process in case of non-payment of the debt (*a*). With the exception of the charge by way of legal mortgage, which has already been dealt with and which is for all intents and purposes equivalent to a legal mortgage and maritime hypothecations, which have also been dealt with already (*b*), charges are enforceable only in equity (*c*).

Equitable charges arise out of agreement between the parties thereto and in that respect differ from statutory charges (*c*) and equitable liens, though the word "lien" is often used to include, not only liens arising by operation of law, but also charges or hypothecations arising out of contract (*d*). A charge, though expressed to be an agreement for a lien, does not confer an actual lien, which is a right given by law. In such cases the rights of the parties are limited by the terms of the express contract (*e*), but, nevertheless, subject to the terms of the contract by which such an agreement is effected, and the special rights thereby created, the rights correspond with such as arise under actual liens. The express stipulation and agreement for a security excludes a lien and limits the rights by the extent of the express contract—*expressum facit cessare tacitum* (*e*).

Creation.—An ordinary charge, *i.e.*, not a maritime hypothecation, may be created

(1) By a charge or direction in a settlement, will, or other instrument, whereby real or personal property (*f*) is expressly

---

(*a*) *Johnson* v. *Shippen* (1703), 2 Ld. Raym. 982; *Stainbank* v. *Fenning* (1851), 11 C.B. 51; *Stainbank* v. *Shepard* (1853), 13 C.B. 418.

(*b*) See pp. 8 and 25, *supra*.

(*c*) As to statutory charges, see p. 164, *infra*.

(*d*) The distinction between lien and charge is especially important for registration under the Companies Act 1948; see *Re Wallis and Simmonds (Builders), Ltd.* [1974] 1 All E.R. 561 and p. 181, *infra*.

(*e*) *Gladstone* v. *Birley* (1817), 2 Mer. 401, at p. 404; *Re Leith's Estate, Chambers* v. *Davidson* (1866), L.R. 1 P.C. 296, at p. 305. See pp. 166–169, *infra*.

(*f*) An agreement to charge property which at the date of the agreement, has been sold, will bind the corresponding interest in the purchase money: *Re Selby, Ex parte Rogers* (1856), 8 De G.M. & G. 271. On the other hand, on the death of the chargor

or constructively made liable or specifically appropriated to
the discharge of a portion, legacy, or other burden, or declared
to be subjected to a lien for securing the same; no debt is
implied, but a right of realisation by judical process is conferred,
and in some cases a power of distress: or

(2) By the appropriation to the discharge of a debt of specific
things in action or chattels, which either are, at the time of
appropriation, or may or will thereafter be in the hands of a
third person.

No special form is required to create a charge (g).

As regards charges of personalty a charge of such as is within the
definition of personal chattels in s. 4 of the Bills of Sale Act 1878,
is a bill of sale and subject to the provisions of the Bills of Sale Acts
1878 and 1882 (h). Amongst the exceptions to the definition of bills
of sale are bills of lading, warrants and orders for delivery of goods,
or any other documents used in the ordinary course of business as
proof of the possession or control of goods, or authorising, either by
indorsement or delivery, the possessor of such document to transfer
or receive the goods. A letter of lien to a bank on goods in the process
of manufacture (i), and a letter of trust to a bank with respect to goods
covered by bills of lading which has been redelivered by the bank for
purposes of sale (k), are within this exception. Section 4 also excludes
transfers of goods in the ordinary course of business of a trade or calling,
but this does not apply to the borrowing of money on mortgage or
special agreement (l). Charges of choses in action are often affected
by an assignment of the property and will then be treated as equitable
mortgages (m). Moreover a mere charge on a fund or debt operates
as a partial equitable assignment (n). But while an absolute
assignment of existing property is effectual though voluntary, an
equitable assignment which merely gives a charge on property requires
valuable consideration to support it (o). The fund upon which the
charge operates must be clear (p).

As regards equitable charges on land the assimilation of mortgages
and charges, which has already been referred to (q), is very clear.

---

the charge will only effect the property of which he died possessed, and not such as
did not belong to him at his death, whether he had it at the date of the obligation or
acquired it afterwards.

(g) *Cradock* v. *Scottish Provident Institution* (1893), 69 L.T. 380; affd. 70 L.T. 718
(C.A.).

(h) See pp. 77 *et seq.*, *supra*. And see *National Provincial and Union Bank of England*
v. *Lindsell*, [1922] 1 K.B. 21.

(i) *Re Hamilton, Young & Co., Ex parte Carter*, [1905] 2 K.B. 772 (C.A.); *Official
Assignee of Madras* v. *Mercantile Bank of India, Ltd.*, [1935] A.C. 53 (P.C.).

(k) *Re David Allester, Ltd.*, [1922] 2 Ch. 211.

(l) *Tennant* v. *Howatson* (1888), 13 App. Cas. 494 (P.C.).
As to letters of hypothecation, see footnote (m), p. 4, *supra*.

(m) As to which, see p. 44, *supra*. For forms of charge, see 14 Ency. Forms and
Precedents (4th Edn.), pp. 677 *et seq.*; and Precedent 14 in the Appendix, *infra*.

(n) *Durham Brothers* v. *Robertson*, [1898] 1 Q.B. 765 (C.A.), at p. 769.

(o) *Re Earl of Lucan, Hardinge* v. *Cobden* (1890), 45 Ch. D. 470. But see Sykes,
The Law of Securities (2nd Edn.), pp. 602–603.

(p) See p. 106, *supra*.

(q) See p. 4, *supra*. And see *Jones* v. *Woodward* (1917), 116 L.T. 378; *London
County and Westminster Bank* v. *Tompkins*, [1918] 1 K.B. 515 (C.A.).

Even an express contract to create a charge has been held to be a contract to make a mortgage and the case to be within the rules of equitable mortgages (*r*). Where a security is intended and the land charged is specified, provided that the instrument by which the charge is effected is not a will (*s*) or a voluntary settlement (*t*), an equitable mortgage will be created (*u*).

But not even a charge will be created where no particular land is mentioned in the agreement; or where the agreement is only for a personal, with power to call for a real, security; or where it otherwise appears to be intended to rely upon the agreement (*x*); or where the agreement is not based on valuable consideration (*y*). The charge must be a present charge of specified property either already in the chargor's possession or such as he may afterwards acquire or derive from a specified source (*z*). An agreement for a future charge is not enforceable if it is voluntary (*a*), but if it is given for value the charge will attach to the chargor's land at the time agreed (*b*).

Remedies of chargee.—Where the charge can be treated as an equitable mortgage the chargee will have the remedies of an equitable mortgagee, namely foreclosure (*c*), sale (where the charge is made by deed (*d*)), possession (*e*), and the right to a receiver, appointed by the chargee himself under the statutory power where the charge is by deed, or by the court in other cases (*f*).

Where the charge cannot be so treated the principal remedies of the chargee are sale and the appointment of a receiver. If the charge is by deed the chargee will have the statutory powers in this respect (*d*). Where the charge is not by deed the chargee must apply to the court for an order for sale (*g*) or for the appointment of a receiver (*h*). But a mere equitable chargee is not entitled to possession (*i*) nor foreclosure (*k*).

Registration of charges.—A charge on land should be registered as a general equitable charge on land charge Class C (iii)—unless it affects an interest arising under a trust for sale or settlement (*l*).

(*r*) See *Ex parte Wills* (1790), 1 Ves. Jun. 162; *Montagu* v. *Earl of Sandwich* (1886) 32 Ch. D. 525.

(*s*) *Re Owen*, [1894] 3 Ch. 220.

(*t*) *Balfe* v. *Lord* (1842), 2 Dr. & Wan. 480; *Re Lloyd*, [1903] 1 Ch. 385 (C.A.).

(*u*) *Cradock* v. *Scottish Provident Institution, supra.* And see the cases in footnote (*q*), *supra.* Cf. *Matthews* v. *Goodday* (1861), 31 L.J. Ch. 282; *Shea* v. *Moore*, [1894] 1 I.R., 158.

(*x*) *Collins* v. *Plummer* (1709), 1 P. Wms. 104; *Berrington* v. *Evans* (1839), 3 Y. & C. Ex. 384.

(*y*) *Re Earl of Lucan, Hardinge* v. *Cobden* (1890), 45 Ch. D. 470.

(*z*) *Metcalfe* v. *Archbishop of York* (1836), 6 Sim. 224; affd. 1 My. & Cr. 547; *Buller* v. *Plunkett* (1860), 1 Johns. & H. 441. And see footnote (*r*), p. 12, *supra.*

(*a*) *Re Earl of Lucan, Hardinge* v. *Cobden, supra.*

(*b*) *Wellesley* v. *Wellesley* (1839), 4 Myl. & Cr. 561.

(*c*) See p. 384, *infra.*

(*d*) Law of Property Act 1925, ss. 101 (1), 205 (1) (xvi). And see p. 379, *infra.*

(*e*) See p. 315, *infra.*

(*f*) See p. 300, *infra.*

(*g*) *Tennant* v. *Trenchard* (1869), L.R. 4 Ch. 537, at p. 542. See p. 384, *infra.*

(*h*) See p. 305, *infra.*

(*i*) *Garfitt* v. *Allen* (1887), 37 Ch. D. 48, 50.

(*k*) *Tennant* v. *Trenchard, supra; Re Lloyd*, [1903] 1 Ch. 385 (C.A.), at p. 404.

(*l*) Land Charges Act 1972, s. 2 (4); and see p. 443, *infra.*

II—JUDGMENTS

Judgments generally.—The distinction between a lien and a mortgage has already been referred to (*m*). A lien is an obligation which by implication of law, and not by express contract, binds real or personal property for the discharge of a debt or other obligation. A judgment does not of itself create any lien or other security interest (*n*).

Charging order on land.—The Administration of Justice Act 1956, abolished writs of elegit and repealed the statutory provision relating to charges on land (*o*). Instead power is given to the High Court and to any county court (*p*), for the purpose of enforcing a judgment or order of those courts respectively for the payment of money to any person, to impose by order a charge on any such land or interest in land of the debtor as may be specified in the order, for securing the payment of monies due or to become due under the judgment or order (*q*). Such an order may be made either absolutely or subject to conditions as to notifying the debtor or as to the time when the charge is enforceable or as to other matters (*r*).

Registration of writs and orders affecting land.—A writ or order affecting land and issued for the purpose of enforcing a judgment should be registered in the register of writs and orders (*s*), or, if the title to the land is registered, should be protected by a caution (*t*). Failure to register as a land charge renders the order void against a purchaser (*u*) of the land for valuable consideration (*a*). As regards registered land a purchaser in good faith and for valuable consideration under a registered disposition will not be affected by any order unless protected as aforesaid (*b*).

Effect of charging order on land.—Subject to the registration or protection of the order such a charge has the like effect and is enforce-

---

(*m*) See pp. 4, 5, *supra*.

(*n*) But note that an order for secured maintenance operates as an equitable charge which will be binding against, *inter alia*, the trustee in bankruptcy of the person ordered to give security: see *Platt* v. *Platt* (1976), 120 Sol. Jo. 199; also *Hyde* v. *Hyde*, [1948] P. 198; [1948] 1 All E.R. 362; (1976) 120 S.J. 459 (M. Steiner).

(*o*) Administration of Justice Act 1956, s. 34; Administration of Justice Act 1965, s. 34 (1), Sched. 2. See, generally, 16 Halsbury's Laws (3rd Edn.), Execution. For a convenient short history of the matter, see The Law Commission Report on Charging Orders (Law Com. No. 74, 1976).

(*p*) It has been held by Croydon County Court in *Merton London Borough* v. *Sammon* (unreported) that a county court has no power to make a charging order on land in respect of a judgment debt created by a judgment of the High Court: see the Law Commission Report, para. 50.

(*q*) Administration of Justice Act 1956, s. 35 (1); County Courts Act 1959, s. 141. The court will not make an order where the debtor is, or is likely to be, insolvent: *Rainbow* v. *Moorgate Properties, Ltd.*, [1975] 2 All E.R. 821 (C.A.); cf. *Burston Finance, Ltd.* v. *Godfrey*, [1976] 2 All E.R. 976 (C.A.). A charge can only be made for an ascertained sum: *A. & M. Records Inc.* v. *Darakdjian*, [1975] 3 All E.R. 983.

(*r*) *Ibid.*, s. 35 (2). See, generally, R.S.C. Ord. 50, r.1. C.C.R. Ord. 25, r.7; 16 Ency. Court Forms (2nd Edn.), Execution.

(*s*) Land Charges Act 1972, s. 6. See p. 442, *infra*.

(*t*) Land Registration Act 1925, s. 59 (1). See *Parkash* v. *Irani Finance, Ltd.*, [1970] 1 Ch 101; [1969] 1 All E.R. 930; *Irani Finance, Ltd.* v. *Singh*, [1971] Ch. at p. 70 (C.A.); [1970] 3 All E.R. 199.

(*u*) This includes a mortgagee: Land Charges Act 1972, s. 20 (8).

(*a*) Land Charges Act 1972, s. 7 (1).

(*b*) Land Registration Act 1925, s. 59 (6).

able in the same courts and in the same manner as an equitable charge created by the debtor under his hand (c).

Priority of charging order on bankruptcy.—A charging order does not of itself give priority over the unsecured creation of the judgment debtor (d), because the obtaining of the order is not completion of execution (e). The judgment creditor must go on to obtain the appointment of a receiver as well to have such priority (d). In practice, the charging order and the appointment of a receiver should be sought by simultaneous applications (f). The Law Commission has recommended the reversal of the effect of the decision in *Overseas Aviation* (g).

Interest in land.—The beneficial interest of a beneficiary under a trust for sale of land cannot be made the subject of a charging order, because by the doctrine of conversion the beneficiary's interest is, technically, an interest in the proceeds of sale of the land (h). However, it has been suggested that a charging order could be made against the beneficiary's interest under a bare trust (i) and where a single judgment in respect of same debt has been obtained against the co-owners of land who hold the legal estate for themselves as joint tenants beneficially, a charging order may be made (k).

Discharge of charging order on land.—There is no express provision in s. 35 of the Administration of Justice Act 1956 for the discharge of charging orders on land (l). This deficiency is mitigated by the provisions as to vacating land charge registrations (m) and the

---

(c) Administration of Justice Act 1956, s. 35 (3). As to the remedies of a chargee, see p. 158, *supra*. Accordingly foreclosure is not an appropriate remedy: see *Daponte* v. *Schubert and Roy Nominees, Ltd.*, [1939] Ch. 958; [1939] 3 All E.R. 495. But see p. 388, *supra*. A charge imposed for the purpose of enforcing a judgment or order of the county court may be enforced in the county court notwithstanding that the amount secured is in excess of the jurisdiction of the county court: *ibid.*, s. 35 (3), proviso.
The interest of a judgment creditor (whether he is with or without notice) in the property of his debtor is subject to every liability under which the debtor holds it: see *Langton* v. *Horton* (1842), 1 Hare 549; *Whitworth* v. *Gaugain* (1844), 3 Hare at p. 427; affd. (1846), 1 Ph. 128; *Abbott* v. *Stratten* (1846), 3 Jo. & Lat. 603; *Eyre* v. *M'Dowell* (1861), 9 H. L. Cas. 619; *Chung Khiaw Bank, Ltd.* v. *United Overseas Bank*, [1970] A.C. 767 (P.C.).
(d) *Re Overseas Aviation Engineering (G.B.), Ltd.*, [1963] Ch. 24 (C.A.); [1962] 3 All E.R. 12. See p. 182, *infra*.
(e) See Companies Act 1948, s. 325; and see *Wilson (D.) (Birmingham) Ltd.* v. *Metropolitan Property Developments, Ltd.*, [1975] 2 All E.R. 814 (C.A.); Bankruptcy Act 1914, s. 40.
(f) See R.S.C. Ord. 50, r. 9. There is no similar rule for county courts, but the same procedure is followed: see County Court Practice 1976, notes to County Courts Act 1959, s. 141.
(g) See Law Commission Report (Law Com. No. 74), paras. 40, 41.
(h) *Irani Finance, Ltd.* v. *Singh*, [1971] Ch. 59 (C.A.); [1970] 3 All E.R. 199. See also as to an interest in land *Elias* v. *Mitchell*, [1972] Ch. 652; [1972] 2 All E.R. 153; *Stevens* v. *Hutchinson*, [1953] Ch. 299; [1953] 1 All E.R. 699; *Cooper* v. *Critchley*, [1955] Ch. 431 (C.A.); (1955) 1 All E.R. 520; *Re a Debtor, Ex parte the Trustee* v. *Solomon*, [1967] Ch. 573; [1966] 3 All E.R. 255; *Re Turner (a bankrupt), Ex parte the Trustee of the bankrupt* v. *Turner*, [1975] 1 All E.R. 5; *Re McCarthy (a bankrupt), Ex parte the trustee of the bankrupt* v. *McCarthy*, [1975] 2 All E.R. 857; *Re a Debtor (No. 24 of 1971), Ex parte Marley* v. *Trustee of Property of Debtor*, [1976] 2 All E.R. 1010; and see (1975), 119 S.J. 582 (J. G. Miller).
(i) Law Commission Report (Law Com. No. 74), para. 72.
(k) *National Westminster Bank, Ltd.* v. *Allen*, [1971] 2 Q.B. 718; [1971] 3 All E.R. 201. See, generally, the discussion in the Law Com. Report, *supra*, Pt. III.
(l) Cf. charging orders on securities and beneficial interests therein: R.S.C. Ord. 50, r.7; C.C.R. Ord. 25, r. 6A (6).
(m) Land Charges Act 1972, ss. 1 (6), 8.

analogous provisions for registered land entries (*n*) and the court may have powers to discharge the order under the Rules and inherent jurisdiction (*o*). The Law Commission has recommended that there should be an express power to discharge charging orders (*p*).

Appointment of receiver by way of equitable execution.—The High Court and a county court may in appropriate circumstances appoint a receiver by way of equitable execution in relation to personal property (*q*) and, since the Administration of Justice Act 1956 (*r*), land and interests therein (*s*). The power may be exercised in relation to an estate or interest in land, whether or not (*t*) a charging order has been imposed on the land, and is in addition to and not in derogation of any power of the court to appoint a receiver in proceedings for enforcing a charge created by a charging order (*u*). The appointment of a receiver does not create a charge on the property (*a*), and is subject to the rights of prior incumbrancers, but the judgment creditor's position is preserved by his being able to obtain an injunction to prevent the property being received by a subsequent assignee to his prejudice (*b*).

Charging orders against stock or shares.—An order charging stock or shares may be made by the divisional court or a judge of the High Court or of a county court, and the proceedings for obtaining the order, and the effect is such as is provided by the Rules of the Supreme Court (*c*) and the County Court Rules (*d*). The order may charge all the interest of the judgment debtor, whether in possession, remainder or reversion, and whether vested or contingent, in Government stock, fund, or annuities or stock in any registered company, and whether standing in his name in his own right or in the name of a person in trust for him and including such property when standing in the name of the Accountant-General (*e*), and the dividends and interest thereon. The order entitles the judgment creditor to all such remedies as he would have been entitled to if the charge had been made in his favour by the judgment debtor, *i.e.*, to take proceedings for sale.

(*n*) Land Registration Act 1925, s. 56 (3); Rules 1925, r. 222 (withdrawal of caution); Rules 1925, rr. 16, 201 (cancellation of notices of land charges).
(*o*) See, generally, the Law Com. Report, Pt. IV.
(*p*) *Ibid.*, para. 101.
(*q*) See, generally, 16 Halsbury's Laws (3rd Edn.), Execution, pp. 104 *et seq.*
(*r*) Section 36 (1).
(*s*) See *Stevens* v. *Hutchinson, supra; cf. Cooper* v. *Critchley, supra.*
(*t*) Accordingly this is the remedy when a charging order cannot be made under the *Irani Finance* (*supra*), principle.
(*u*) Administration of Justice Act 1956, s. 36 (2). See, generally, R.S.C. Ord. 51; C.C.R. Ord. 30.
(*a*) *Re Potts, Ex parte Taylor,* [1893] 1 Q.B. 648 (C.A.), at p. 659; *Re Pearce, Ex parte Official Receiver, The Trustee,* [1919] 1 K.B. 354 (C.A.), at pp. 363, 364; *Giles* v. *Kruyer,* [1921] 3 K.B. 23.
(*b*) *Ideal Bedding Co., Ltd.* v. *Holland,* [1907] 2 Ch. 157, at pp. 169, 170; *Stevens* v. *Hutchinson, supra.*
(*c*) R.S.C. Ord. 50, rr. 2–7, replacing the Judgment Acts 1838 and 1840.
(*d*) County Court Rules, Ord. 2, r. 2A, and Ord. 25, r. 6A. See generally, Law Commission Report on Charging Orders, paras. 78 *et seq.*
(*e*) See *Brereton* v. *Edwards* (1888), 21 Q.B.D. 488 (C.A.).

L.M.—6

But no proceedings may be taken to obtain the benefit of the charge until the expiration of six months from the date of the charging order.

Effect of charging order on shares, etc.—The effect of the order is to make an immediate charge (*f*), but only to the extent to which the debtor himself would have charged the property. The order, therefore, will be inoperative if the debt which it is intended to secure is founded upon an illegal contract (*g*). A charging order can only be obtained in respect of an ascertained sum (*h*).

The priority of the charge holder in the event of the bankruptcy of the debtor (*i*) is uncertain after the *Overseas Aviation case* (*k*).

The property to be charged must be standing in the name of the debtor in his own right (*l*), or in the name of a person in trust for him (*m*). It is not sufficient that he has merely a beneficial interest in the balance of the proceeds of it when sold (*n*).

Charging order on money in court.—The court may for the purpose of enforcing a judgment or order for the payment of an ascertained sum of money to a person by order impose on any interest to which the judgment debtor is beneficially entitled in any money in court identified in the order a charge for receiving payment of the amount due under the judgment or order and interest thereon (*o*).

Charging partnership share.—A writ of execution cannot issue against any partnership property except on a judgment against the firm (*p*), but the court may make an order charging the share of a partner who is a judgment debtor (*q*). The effect of the order is the same as if the partner had executed a document charging his share with the debt (*r*).

Stop notice.—Any person claiming to be beneficially entitled to an interest in any of the following securities, namely any government stock, and any stock of any company registered under any general Act of Parliament, including any such stock standing in the name of the Accountant-General, and any dividend of or interest payable on such stock, other than securities in court, who wishes to be notified of any proposed transfer or payment of those securities, may obtain a stop

---

(*f*) *Montefiore* v. *Behrens* (1865), L.R. 1 Eq. 171; *Re Blakely Ordnance Co., Coates' Case* (1876), 46 L.J. Ch. 367.

(*g*) *Re Onslow's Trusts* (1875), L.R. 20 Eq. 677.

(*h*) *Widgery* v. *Tepper, Hall* v. *Tepper* (1877), 6 Ch. D. 364 (C.A.).

(*i*) *Re Hutchinson* (1885), 16 Q.B.D. 515.

(*k*) See *supra*, Law Com Report, paras 37 *et seq.*

(*l*) Stock in the name of a judgment debtor is not subject to a charging order if it is shown that he is merely a trustee: see *Hawks* v. *McArthur*, [1951] 1 All E.R. 22, As to charging orders against the property of persons of unsound mind, see *Re Leavesley*. [1891] 2 Ch. 1 (C.A.); *Re Plenderleith*, [1893] 3 Ch. 332 (C.A.).

(*m*) *South Western Loan Co.* v. *Robertson* (1881), 8 Q.B.D. 17.

(*n*) *Dixon* v. *Wrench* (1869), L.R. 4 Exch. 154; *cf. Ideal Bedding Co., Ltd.* v. *Holland*, [1907] 2 Ch. 157, at p. 167. And see now *Irani Finance, Ltd.* v. *Singh, supra*, p. 160. See Law Com. Report, paras. 89 *et seq.*

(*o*) *Brereton* v. *Edwards* (1888), 21 Q.B.D. 488 (C.A.); R.S.C. Ord. 50, r. 8.

(*p*) Partnership Act 1890, s. 23 (1).

(*q*) *Ibid.*, s. 23 (2). See R.S.C. Ord. 81, r. 10; C.C.R. Ord. 25, rr. 4, 5.

(*r*) *Ibid.*, s. 23 (2); and see *Brown, Janson & Co.* v. *Hutchinson & Co.*, [1895] 2 Q.B. 126 (C.A.), at p. 131.

notice from the High Court (s). Where a stop notice has been served on the Bank of England or a company, then, so long as the notice is in force, the Bank or company shall not register a transfer of any stock or make a payment of any dividend or interest, being a transfer or payment restrained by the notice, without serving on the person on whose behalf the notice was filed a notice informing him of the request for such transfer or payment (t). But the Bank or company shall not by reason only of the notice refuse to register the transfer or make the payment for longer than eight days after the receipt of the request except under the authority of an order of the court (u).

Order prohibiting transfer, etc. of securities.—The court, on the application of any person claiming to be beneficially entitled to an interest in any government stock or any stock of any company registered under any general Act of Parliament, may by order prohibit the Bank of England or, as the case may be, that company from registering any transfer of such part of that stock as may be specified in the order or from paying any dividend thereof or interest thereon (a).

Stop order on fund in court.—The court, on the application of any person who has a mortgage or charge on the interest of any person in funds in court, or who is a judgment creditor of the person entitled to that interest, may make an order prohibiting the transfer, sale, delivery out, payment or other dealing with such funds, or any part thereof, or the income thereon, without notice to the applicant (b).

Garnishee proceedings.—Where a person (the judgment creditor) has obtained a judgment or order for the payment by some other person (the judgment debtor) of moneys not being a judgment or order for the payment of money into court, and any other person within the jurisidiction (the garnishee) is indebted to the judgment debtor, the court may order the garnishee to pay the judgment creditor the amount of any debt due or accruing due to the judgment debtor from the garnishee, or so much thereof as is sufficient to satisfy that judgment or order and the costs of the garnishee proceedings (c).

The judgment creditor does not become a creditor of the garnishee upon the making of the garnishee order *nisi* (d). Nor does the order,

---

(s) R.S.C. Ord. 50, r. 11. For a form of notice and of the supporting affidavit, see 14 Ency. Forms and Precedents (4th Edn.), pp. 869, 870. The Law Commission has recommended the extension of this procedure: see Report on Charging Orders, paras. 87 *et seq.*

(t) R.S.C. Ord. 50, r. 12 (1).

(u) R.S.C. Ord. 50, r. 12 (2). See further as to stop notices, p. 112, *supra.*

(a) R.S.C. Ord. 50, r. 15 (1). The application is made by motion or summons in the Chancery Division: *ibid.*, r. 15 (2).

(b) R.S.C. Ord. 50, r. 10 (1). The application is made by summons in the cause or matter relating to the funds in court, or, if there is no such cause or matter, by originating summons. See, further, p. 480, *infra*, and as to execution generally, 16 Halsbury's Laws (3rd Edn.), Execution.

(c) R.S.C. Ord. 49, r. 1 (1); as amended by R.S.C. (Amendment) 1976, r. 9 C.C.R. Ord. 27. On garnisheeing banks, see (1976), 126 New L.J. 747. See further as to garnishee proceedings and as they affect surplus proceeds of sale of mortgaged property, p. 375, *infra.*

(d) *Norton* v. *Yates*, [1906] 1 K.B. 112; and see *Re Combined Weighing and Advertising Machine Co.* v. *Automatic Weighing Machine Co.* (1889), 43 Ch. D. 99.

whether nisi or absolute, effect a transfer of the debt to the judgment creditor (e).

III—STATUTORY CHARGES

Generally.—In addition to the charging orders already mentioned in this chapter and the statutory charge created under the Improvement of Land Act 1864, already referred to (f), the following statutory charges may be mentioned:

(1) The charge of a tenant of an agricultural holding for compensation when his landlord has failed to pay the compensation due (g);

(2) The charge of a landlord of an agricultural holding for repayment of the payment of compensation by him to his tenant (h).

Such charges are land charges within the meaning of the Land Charges Act 1972, and where applicable to unregistered land should be registered accordingly (i). If not so registered such a charge will be void against a purchaser for value (j) of the land charged (k). However, it is also provided (l) that tenant's charges (m) shall rank in priority to any other charge, however, and whenever created or arising. A prospective mortgagee of an agricultural holding, which is let, should bear in mind that a charge for compensation in favour of the tenant will have priority to his mortgage.

(3) The charge of a landlord of business premises for repayment of the payment by him to the tenant of compensation for improvements carried out by the tenant or of the cost of executing the work himself (n).

Such a charge is obtained from the Minister of Agriculture, Fisheries and Food and may be registered as a land charge of Class A (o).

Unlike the charge of a landlord of agricultural land mentioned above there is no special provision for the priority of such a charge on business premises and therefore such a charge cannot rank in priority to a mortgage of the premises created before the charge.

(e) See Norton v. Yates, supra; Re Combined Weighing and Advertising Machine Co. supra; Holmes v. Tutton (1855), 5 E. & B. 65; cf. Re Watts, Ex parte Joselyne (1878); 8 Ch. D. 327; see Sykes, The Law of Securities (2nd Edn.), pp. 20–22.

(f) See p. 205, infra.

(g) Agricultural Holdings Act 1948, ss. 72, 73, 74.

(h) Agricultural Holdings Act 1948, s. 82.

(i) Land Charges Act 1972, s. 2 (2), Sched. 2 A; Agricultural Holdings Act 1948, s. 95, Sched. 7, para. 3.

(j) This includes a mortgagee: Law of Property Act 1925, s. 205 (1) (xvi).

(k) Land Charges Act 1972, s. 4 (2).

(l) Agricultural Holdings Act 1948, s. 83 (5).

(m) I.e., those created under ss. 72, 73 and 74 of the Agricultural Holdings Act 1948.

(n) Landlord and Tenant Act 1927, s. 12, Sched. 1, paras. (1), (4); Landlord and Tenant Act 1954, s. 45, Sched. 7, Pt. I.

(o) Landlord and Tenant Act 1927, Sched. 1, para. (7).

(4) Charges in favour of local authorities (*p*) and owners of houses (*q*) in respect of the expense of executing works required to render houses fit for human habitation.

Such a charge is registable as a Class A land charge.

Where a local authority has such a charge it has the same powers and remedies, as if it were a mortgagee by deed having powers of sale and lease, of accepting surrenders of leases and of appointing a receiver (*r*). The charge in favour of an owner takes priority over all existing and future estates, interests and incumbrances, with the exception of other local authority charges (*s*). Where there are several charges they have priority according to their respective dates (*s*).

(5) Charges upon premises of frontagers in favour of local authorities for expenses incurred in making up private streets (*t*).

Such a charge is registrable as a local land charge and, although failure to register no longer affects enforceability of the charge, it will give the purchaser a right to compensation in certain cases (*u*).

For the recovery of expenses charged on premises under s. 181 of the Highways Act 1959, the local authority has all the same powers and remedies under the Law of Property Act 1925, as if it were a mortgagee having powers of sale, of leasing and of appointing a receiver (*a*).

(6) Charges on property recovered or preserved (*b*) for the benefit of legally assisted persons in respect of contributions due from them to the legal aid fund (*c*).

The charge vests in the Law Society which may enforce it in any manner which would have been available if it had been given *inter partes* (*d*); and subject to the provisions of the Land Charges Act 1972, all conveyances and acts done to defeat, or operating to defeat the charge are void as against the Law Society except in the case of a conveyance to a bona fide purchaser for value without notice (*e*).

(7) Charges on property recovered in respect of solicitor's costs (*f*).

(*p*) Housing Act 1957, s. 10 (7).   (*q*) Housing Act 1957, ss. 14 and 15.
(*r*) Housing Act 1957, s. 10 (7).   And see *Paddington Borough Council* v. *Finucane*, [1928] Ch. 567; *Bristol Corpn.* v. *Virgin*, [1928] 2 K.B. 622 (D.C.).
(*s*) Housing Act 1957, s. 15 (1).
(*t*) See, *e.g.*, Highways Act 1959, ss. 181, 190 and 264.
(*u*) Local Land Charges Act 1975, s. 10. But such expenses may also be recoverable from the owner for the time being.
(*a*) Highways Act 1959, s. 181 (3). See *Dennerley* v. *Prestwich Urban District Council*, [1930] 1 K.B. 334 (C.A.); *Payne* v. *Cardiff Rural District Council*, [1932] 1 K.B. 241; *Poole Corporation* v. *Moody*, [1945] K.B. 350 (C.A.); [1945] 1 All E.R. 536.
(*b*) See *Till* v. *Till*, [1974] 1 All E.R. 1096 (C.A.).
(*c*) Legal Aid Act 1974, s. 9 (6); *Cooke* v. *Head* (*No. 2*), [1974] 2 All E.R. 1124 (C.A.). A charge affecting unregistered land is a Class B land charge. For registered land, the charge will be protected by substantive registration: see *Ruoff and Roper*, p. 540.
(*d*) Legal Aid (General) Regulations 1971, r. 19 (1), (2).
(*e*) Legal Aid (General) Regulations 1971, r. 19 (3), (4). For exempted property, see (Amendment No. 2) Regns. 1976.
(*f*) Solicitors Act 1974, s. 73. See generally 36 Halsbury's Laws (3rd Edn.), Solicitors, pp. 184, *et seq.*; and *Currie & Co.* v. *The Law Society*, [1976] 3 All E.R. 832.

Such a charge may give the solicitor priority over a mortgagee, who had notice of the right to claim the order (g).

(8) **Charge of patient's property.** The Mental Health Act 1959, gives a general power of charging the patient's property (h). And the patient's property may be charged as security for money advanced for the permanent improvement or benefit thereof (i).

there are other statutory charges arising in a variety of circumstances (k), the precise nature of which and of the powers thereby conferred on the chargee depends on the terms of the statute conferring the charge.

Where registered land charged.—Where the charge affects registered land and entitles the chargee to enforce it by realisation of the land charged the chargee must be registered as proprietor of the charge before the land can be realised (l). This substantive registration is in addition to registration in the local land charges registry, where appropriate, or of a notice or caution on the register of title (l).

Whilst the priority of registered charges normally depends on the order in which they are entered on the register (m), priority may in the case of certain statutory charges depend on the order of creation (n) and the register will reflect this (o).

IV—VENDOR'S LIEN (p)

Generally.—A vendor has a lien for unpaid purchase-money. Though of an equitable character, the lien was recognised in law as well as in equity. It arises also for the purchase-money of chattels (q), but with this distinction that, in as much as there was not (as a general rule) any lien at law without possession, the vendor of land could have as lien at law for the purchase-money, after he had executed an absolute conveyance, either upon the land or the deeds, which, though

---

(g) *Ridd* v. *Thorne*, [1902] 2 Ch. 344, 349; *Newport* v. *Pougher*, [1937] Ch. 214 (C.A.) at pp. 224, 226; [1937] 1 All E.R. 276, at pp. 283, 285. And see *Wimbourne* v. *Fine*, [1952] Ch. 869; [1952] 2 All E.R. 681.

(h) Mental Health Act 1959, s. 103 (1) (b), replacing specific powers of charging in the Lunacy Act 1890, s. 117 (1).

(i) Mental Health Act 1959, s. 107 (5). Such a charge gives no right of sale or foreclosure during the patient's lifetime. Where the money is advanced out of the patient's general estate the charge should be made in favour of a person as trustee for the patient: s. 107 (5) (a). And see p. 219, *infra*.

(k) See, *e.g.*, Agriculture (Miscellaneous Provisions) Act 1941, ss. 6 and 8 and Sched. III (charge for drainage works); London Building Acts (Amendment) Act 1939, s. 70 (charge for remedying dangerous structure); Weeds Act 1959, s. 3 (3) (charge on land for cost of preventing weeds spreading).

(l) See Ruoff and Roper, *Registered Conveyancing* (3rd Edn.), pp. 541–543.

(m) Land Registration Act 1925, s. 29; see p. 66, *supra*.

(n) See, *e.g.*, Housing Act 1957, s. 15 (1); *Bristol Corpn.* v. *Virgin*, [1928] 2 K.B. 622 (D.C.).

(o) See Land Registration Act 1925, s. 34 (6); Land Registration Rules 1925, rr. 157, 158.

(p) As to liens generally, see 24 Halsbury's Laws (3rd Edn.), Liens, and earlier editions of this work.

(q) See Sale of Goods Act 1893, s. 41. For lien in respect of shares, see *Musselwhite* v. *C. H. Musselwhite & Sons, Ltd.*, [1962] Ch. 964; [1962] 1 All E.R. 201; *Langen and Wind, Ltd.* v. *Bell*, [1972] Ch. 685; [1972] 1 All E.R. 296.

they may actually be in the vendor's possession, belong of right
to the owner of the property. Nor, for the same reason, had the
vendor of chattels any lien for the price after he had parted with
possession of them. But the vendor's right in equity is independent of
possession (*r*) and exists as well after as before conveyance (*s*). This
lien rests upon the plain principle of equity, that he who has obtained
possession of property under a contract for payment of the value, shall
not keep it without payment (*t*).

Cases in which the lien arises.—The vendor's lien exists generally
(the contract not being illegal), in respect of freehold and leasehold
land (*u*), and also in respect of trade machinery (*a*), and, indeed, in
respect of personal property generally other than chattels (*b*). The
lien extends not only to the unpaid price, but also to interest on it
from the time the lien comes into existence (*c*), and whether the
whole or part of the purchase-money is unpaid (*d*), and though a
receipt may have been given for it (*e*), and whether the consideration
is a sum in gross or is payable by instalments (*f*). It binds not only
the purchaser and persons claiming under him as volunteers, but
also persons having equitable interests, and persons claiming under the
original purchaser who acquired the legal estate with notice of the
non-payment of the purchase-money (*g*). And where in the deed the
consideration is expressed to be paid, but is in fact wholly or partly
left unpaid, parol evidence may be given on the part of the purchaser
of the actual transaction, because it is the vendor himself who, by
claiming a lien, is the first to set up an equity against the written
statement in the deed (*h*). The lien extends to money advanced by the
vendor to the purchaser for improvements (*i*).

A vendor's lien may arise where the purchaser fails to perform acts,
the obligation to perform which forms part of the consideration for the
sale (*k*).

(*r*) See *Langen & Wind* v. *Bell, supra.*
(*s*) *Wrout* v. *Dawes* (1858), 25 Beav. 369. The unpaid vendor, does not lose his lien
by remaining in possession in some other capacity *e.g.*, as tenant under a sale and lease
back transaction: *London and Cheshire Insurance Co., Ltd.* v. *Laplagrene Property
Co., Ltd.*, [1971] Ch. 499; [1971] 1 All E.R. 766.
(*t*) *Mackreth* v. *Symmons* (1808), 15 Ves. 329.
(*u*) *Winter* v. *Lord Anson* (1827), 3 Russ. 488.
(*a*) *Re Vulcan Ironworks Co.* (1888), 4 T.L.R. 312.
(*b*) *Davies* v. *Thomas*, [1900] 2 Ch. 462 (C.A.) (share of proceeds of sale of leaseholds);
Re Stucley, Stucley v. *Kekewich, supra* (reversionary interest in a trust fund). For liens
on goods and shares see footnote (*q*) *supra*, are for solicitor's lien on title deeds, see
Caldwell v. *Sumpters*, [1972] Ch. 478 (C.A.); [1972] 1 All E.R. 567; and for liens on
chattels, *e.g.*, innkeeper's lien, carrier's lien, etc., see footnote (*p*), *supra*.
(*c*) *Rose* v. *Watson* (1864), 10 H.L. Cas. 672; *Re Stucley, supra.*
(*d*) *Elliot* v. *Edwards* (1802), 3 Bos. & P. 181.
(*e*) See *London and Cheshire Insurance Co., Ltd.* v. *Laplagrene Property Co. Ltd.*,
supra, for the application of s. 68 of the Law of Property Act 1925 to registered land.
(*f*) See generally Williams' *Vendor and Purchaser* (4th Edn.), vol. ii, pp. 983 *et seq.*;
Sugd. *V. & P.* (14th Edn.), 676.
(*g*) *Elliot* v. *Edwards, supra; Mackreth* v. *Symmons, supra*. This is subject to
registration of the lien as a general equitable charge where appropriate (as to registration,
see *supra*).
(*h*) *Winter* v. *Lord Anson, supra.*
(*i*) *Ex parte Linden* (1841), 1 Mont. D. & De G. 428.
(*k*) *Uziell-Hamilton* v. *Keen* (1971), 22 P & C. R. 655.

It seems that the benefit of the vendor's lien can be transferred, even by parol, to a person in possession of the deeds (l).

And it seems that a vendor who has such a lien is entitled to or to retain the title deeds (m). Where the vendor does not hold the deeds the lien may be registered under the Land Charges Act 1972, as a general equitable charge (n), where the land is unregistered. In the case of registered land, the lien can be protected by notice (o), caution (p) or substantive registration and a charge (q) and if the vendor is in possession his lien is an overriding interest (r).

A vendor's lien upon realty is enforceable by sale once the lien has been established by the court (s). The court may also enforce a lien by appointing a receiver pending sale or by injunction operating to restore possession of the property. The lien of the unpaid vendor also gives him the alternative right to rescind the contract and recover possession (t). But he cannot enforce his lien by foreclosure (u).

Loss of lien.—The lien may never arise because the vendor may take a superior security. This will be the case, for example, where the vendor of property leaves the whole or part of the purchase money outstanding and secured by a mortgage of the property sold (a). The lien may also be lost by waiver (b) or limitation (c).

Liens and invalid mortgages.—By stipulating for and obtaining a valid mortgage or charge the vendor (d) abandons any claim to the unpaid vendor's lien (which, if it had continued to exist would have ranked in priority to any such mortgage or charge granted subsequently), because the vendor has got what he bargained for, namely a mortgage or charge which was valid and enforceable at its inception (e). But if the mortgage or charge was void or unenforceable from the outset, the lien is not lost, for the vendor cannot be taken to have intended to give up his lien except on the basis of acquiring an effective mortgage or charge (f).

(l) *Dryden* v. *Frost* (1838), 3 My. & Cr. 670.

(m) See *Dryden* v. *Frost, supra,* at pp. 672, 673; and see Williams' *V. & P.* (4th Edn.), vol. ii, 987.

(n) See *Uziell-Hamilton* v. *Keen, supra.*

(o) Under Land Registration Act 1925, s. 49 (1) (c).

(p) Land Registration Act 1925, s. 54.

(q) *Ibid.,* s. 26.

(r) *London and Cheshire Insurance Co., Ltd.* v. *Laplagrene Property Co., Ltd., supra.*

(s) For forms, see 28 Ency. Court Forms (2nd Edn.), pp. 77, 78, 81, 82. See *Re Stucley, Stucley* v. *Kekewich, supra.*

(t) *Lysaght* v. *Edwards* (1876), 2 Ch. D. 499 at p. 506.

(u) *Munns* v. *Isle of Wight Rail Co.* (1870), 5 Ch. App. 414; cf. *Hughes* v. *Griffin,* [1969] 1 All E.R. 460 (C.A.), 461.

(a) See *Capital Finance Co. Ltd.* v. *Stokes,* [1969] 1 Ch. 261 (C.A.); [1968] 3 All E.R. 625.

(b) See p. 588, *infra.*

(c) See Limitation Act 1939, s. 18 (1); *Re Stucley, Stucley* v. *Kekewich,* [1906] 1 Ch. 67 (C.A.).

(d) The principle applies also to persons succeeding to the vendor's right: see *supra.*

(e) *Re Molton Finance, Ltd.,* [1968] Ch. 325 (C.A.); [1967] 3 All E.R. 843; *Capital Finance Co., Ltd.* v. *Stokes, supra; Burston Finance, Ltd.* v. *Speirway, Ltd.,* [1974] 3 All E.R. 735; cf. *Coptic, Ltd.* v. *Bailey,* [1972] Ch. 446; [1972] 1 All E.R. 1242. But see (1970) 33 M.L.R. 131.

(f) *Congresbury Motors, Ltd.* v. *Anglo-Belge Finance Co., Ltd.,* [1971] Ch. 81; [1970] 3 All E.R. 385, following, *Thurstan* v. *Nottingham Permanent Benefit Building Society*

This principle applies also to persons, such as mortgagees advancing money for the purchase of the property to be mortgaged, succeeding to the vendor's lien by subrogation and subsequent mortgagees whose advances are used to discharge prior mortgages (g).

[1902] 1 Ch. 1. (C.A.); [1903] A.C. 6 (H.L.); *Greendon Investments* v. *Mills* (1973), 226 Estates Gazette 1957; *Ghana Commercial Bank* v. *Chandiram*, [1960] A.C. 732 (P.C.); [1960] 2 All E.R. 865.

(g) See *Paul* v. *Speirway, Ltd.*, [1976] Ch. 220; [1976] 2 All E.R. 587 (and the lien may be similarly excluded if the intention was simply the creation of an unsecured loan); and generally, the cases mentioned in the previous two footnotes.

CHAPTER 11

Second and Subsequent Mortgages

Form (*a*).—Before 1926 there could be only one legal mortgage of freehold land and all subsequent mortgages of the same land were necessarily equitable (*b*). In the case of leasehold land, where the first mortgage had been made by way of assignment, subsequent mortgages were also necessarily equitable. Where the first mortgage had been made by sub-lease, subsequent legal mortgages might be made by further sub-leases, each generally being longer than the previous one.

Since 1925, as the mortgagor of land retains a legal estate therein, subsequent mortgages may now be legal in all cases. Subsequent legal mortgages are created either by demise or by legal charge. When made by demise each successive mortgage is generally for a term of years one day longer than the previous mortgage (*c*).

The mortgage should recite the mortgagor's title and the state of the prior mortgage debt or debts (*d*). The demise or charge should be made subject to the prior mortgage or mortgages. The statutory power of sale may be made exercisable upon interest under the prior mortgage being in arrear for a specified number of days. The mortgage should also include a power for the mortgagee to settle with prior mortgagees and to redeem their securities and a charge of the costs of so doing upon the mortgaged property (*e*).

Title deeds or registration.—The first mortgagee will usually have the title deeds, but if he does not then the second mortgagee should obtain them. If the first mortgagee does have the deeds, the second legal mortgage should be registered as a land charge (*f*).

(*a*) Trustees should not, it seems, lend on second mortgage, unless expressly authorised to do so, but see p. 210, *infra*. For the restrictions on building societies lending on second mortgage, see p. 196, *infra*.

(*b*) See p. 6, *supra*.

(*c*) See the Law of Property Act 1925, ss. 85 (2) (b), 86 (2) (b). But calculation of the exact appropriate length of the term is not essential: Law of Property Act 1925, s. 149 (5). See p. 21, *supra*.

(*d*) Thus giving the lender a remedy under the covenants for title implied by the mortgagor mortgaging as beneficial owner should a larger sum than that recited be owing.

(*e*) For forms of second mortgage, see 14 Ency. Forms and Precedents (4th Edn.), pp. 191 *et seq.* And see Precedents 16, 17 and 18 in the Appendix, *infra*.

Second equitable mortgages are very rare.

(*f*) Class C (i): Land Charges Act 1972, s. 2 (4). A priority notice should have been lodged at least 15 days prior to completion. If the second mortgage is equitable it should be registered as a general equitable charge (Class C (iii)).

A second mortgagee has the right to inspect and make copies of title deeds in the custody of the first mortgagee (g).

Notice.—On completion the second mortgagee should give notice of the second mortgage to the first mortgagee (h). The purpose of such a notice is to prevent the first mortgagee from making further advances to the mortgagor which will rank in priority to the second mortgagee. It will be seen (i) that although registration as a land charge generally constitutes actual notice (k) a mortgagee under a mortgage made expressly for securing a current account is not deemed to have notice of a mortgage merely by reason that it was registered as a land charge, if it was not so registered at the time when the original mortgage was created, or when the last search (if any) by or on behalf of the mortgagee was made, whichever last happened (l). Furthermore, even though registration does constitute actual notice of the mortgage for the purposes of the second mortgagee being entitled to any surplus proceeds of sale should the first mortgagee exercise his power of sale (m) actual notice ensures that the first mortgagee in fact has notice. And again, the giving of notice to a first mortgagee who has the title deeds will give him no excuse, if, on the discharge of his mortgage, he delivers them to the mortgagor instead of the second mortgagee (n).

Second charge of registered land.—For second charges of registered land, see p. 70, *supra*.

Remedies of second mortgagee.—A second mortgagee has all the remedies of a first mortgagee (o). But save for an action on the personal covenant he will not generally be able to exercise his remedies whilst the first mortgagee is exercising the same remedies. So he cannot take possession if the first mortgagee is already in possession or has appointed a receiver. And if the second mortgagee sells he must sell subject to the first mortgage (p), unless the first mortgagee agrees to join in the conveyance and receive part of the purchase moneys sufficient to discharge his mortgage. Alternatively the second mortgagee could take a transfer of the prior mortgage.

Discharge of second mortgage.—A second mortgage is discharged in the same manner as a first mortgage (q).

Second mortgages generally.—The disadvantages of second mortgages are generally stated to be the risks of tacking (r) and

---

(g) Law of Property Act 1925, ss. 96 (1), 205 (1) (xvi). He will, of course, generally have examined the deeds and the prior mortgage before completion.

(h) For a form of notice, see 14 Ency. Forms and Precedents (4th Edn.), 863; and Precedent 19 in the Appendix, *infra*.

(i) See p. 460, *infra*.

(k) See Law of Property Act 1925, s. 198.

(l) Law of Property Act 1925, s. 94 (2), as amended by the Law of Property (Amendment) Act 1926, s. 7, Sched. As to a spouse's rights of occupation as a subsequent mortgage, see p. 217, *infra*.

(m) See p. 373, *infra*.

(n) Registration of the second mortgage does not for this purpose amount to notice: Law of Property Act 1925, s. 96 (2), added by the Law of Property (Amendment) Act 1926, Sched.

(o) For remedies, see Part v, *infra*. The position of the second mortgagee is dealt with specifically in that part where it differs from that of a first mortgagee.

(p) But see the Law of Property Act 1925, s. 50, p. 559, *infra*.

(q) See Part VIII, *infra*.

(r) See *supra* and pp. 455 *et seq.*, *infra*.

consolidation (s), the absence of the title deeds and the fact that the first mortgagee may sell or foreclose the property. In the ordinary second mortgage of a private dwelling house the first risks are slight and the second mortgagee can protect himself by registering his mortgage as a land charge and giving notice of the mortgage to the first mortgagee (t). The risks attendant on a sale of the property can be minimised by a proper valuation, proper searches, and by ascertaining the amount due under a previous mortgage or mortgages. There is generally a sufficient equity in such a mortgage to enable a second mortgage for an appropriate advance to be taken (u). Foreclosure is rarely employed as a remedy today and the rights of subsequent mortgagees where a prior mortgagee is claiming foreclosure are dealt with subsequently (x).

(s) See pp. 510 et seq., infra.
(t) See supra.
(u) See generally, as to the increase of second mortgages in recent years, the Report of the Committee on the Enforcement of Judgment Debts (Payne Committee) 1969, paras. 1345 et seq.; and the Report of the Committee on Consumer Credit (Crowther Report) 1971, 2. 4. 48–53; 6. 4. 22–25.
(x) See pp. 394 et seq., infra.
As to a further or subsequent security effecting a waiver of a prior security, see Ch. 31, infra.

PART II

PARTIES TO MORTGAGES

CHAPTER 12

Parties to Mortgages

I—ABSOLUTE OWNERS

Absolute owner.—Generally an absolute owner of property, who is not under any incapacity (a) can, in exercise of the power of alienation incident to his ownership (b), mortgage the property (c). But certain property, such as government salaries and the like and permanent maintenance of a woman after divorce, cannot be mortgaged (d).

Co-owners.—Where more persons than one own land they may be beneficially interested in the land either jointly or in common, but in either case the legal estate in the land will be held by not more than four of the co-owners as joint tenants upon trust for sale for the co-owners as joint tenants or tenants in common, as the case may be (e). The co-owners can mortgage the land as being statutory trustees for sale (f). But where the same persons are both the trustees and the beneficiaries there is no need to rely on those powers as they can mortgage by virtue of their beneficial ownership (g).

Where a legal mortgage is made to several persons the legal estate vests in the mortgagees or the first four named as joint tenants upon trust for sale (h). In mortgages to several mortgagees made after 1881 to them jointly or in which the mortgage moneys are expressed to belong to them on a joint account, the mortgage moneys are, as between the mortgagees and the mortgagor, deemed to be and remain moneys belonging to the mortgagees on a joint account, unless a

---

(a) As to infants and mental patients, see pp. 214 *et seq.* and 219 *et seq., infra.*

(b) Co. Litt. 223a. For restrictions on alienation, see p. 247, *infra.*

(c) For forms of mortgage by absolute owners, see 14 Ency. Forms and Precedents (4th Edn.), pp. 165 *et seq.*, and Precedents in the Appendix, *infra.*

(d) See further, p. 246, *infra.*

(e) Law of Property Act 1925, ss. 34, 35, 36; Settled Land Act 1925, s. 36; Trustee Act 1925, s. 34. Where a co-owner is an infant, see Law of Property Act 1925, ss. 1 (6) and 19; Settled Land Act 1925, s. 27 (1), as well as the provisions first mentioned.

(f) For the mortgage powers of trustees for sale, see pp. 207 *et seq., infra.*

(g) For forms of mortgage by co-owners, see 14 Ency. Forms and Precedents (4th Edn.), pp. 209 *et seq.*, and Precedent 1B in the Appendix, *infra.* For mortgages of their beneficial interests, see p. 115, *supra.* A purported mortgage of the property by one co-owner will operate as a mortgage of the mortgagor's beneficial interest (see p. 51, *supra*) and in the case of a beneficial joint tenancy probably severs the joint tenancy (see Megarry & Wade, *The Law of Real Property*, (4th Edn.), 405). As to whether a mortgage by one or more registered proprietors severs the joint tenancy, see (1967) 41 A.L.J. 61.

(h) See the provisions in footnote (e), *supra.*

contrary intention is expressed in the mortgage (*i*). Persons dealing in good faith with several mortgagees may assume, unless the contrary is expressed in the instruments relating to the mortgage, that the mortgagees are entitled to the mortgage moneys on a joint account (*k*).

II—MORTGAGES UNDER POWERS GENERALLY

Powers of limited owners and corporations.—When a person is not the absolute owner of a property, he can only create a security on it to last beyond his own beneficial interest (if any), under some power or authority conferred upon him, either by statute, or by the party beneficially entitled (under power of attorney), or by some will or settlement by which the property was and remains settled. Moreover, in the case of a corporation, unless the instrument by which it was founded, or some statute, either expressly or impliedly authorises a mortgage, it cannot create one.

Power to mortgage.—A power by which it is intended to authorise the raising of money on mortgage should specify the intention. Nevertheless, a mortgage may be made under a general power, such as a power of attorney, the terms of which are sufficiently extensive (*l*).

The donor of a power of doubtful sufficiency may, however, by direction as to its exercise, preclude himself from disputing the validity of a security made under the power (*m*).

Exercise of a power.—The power, even where explicit, must be exercised subject to the general terms of the instrument in which it is contained (*n*). Where a mortgage is made under provision that all mortgages shall be on an equal footing an undue advantage cannot be given to a creditor by a security upon other property belonging to the donees of the power (*o*). A power, whether special or general, must be exercised only for purposes consistent with the object of the

---

(*i*) Law of Property Act 1925, s. 111; and see p. 258, *infra*.

(*k*) Law of Property Act 1925, s. 113 (1) (a); and see p. 255, *infra*. For forms of mortgage to two or more persons, see 14 Ency. Forms and Precedents (4th Edn.), pp. 201 *et seq.*; and Precedent 1C in the Appendix *infra*. A contributory mortgage is a mortgage to several persons who each advance distinct sums (as compared to a mortgage to several trustees advancing money on joint account). In practice a contributory mortgage often takes the form of an ordinary joint account mortgage, the rights of the parties being defined by a declaration of trust in the mortgage or by a separate document. Thus separate covenants for payment of each sum advanced, and separate power of sale, etc., are avoided. For forms of contributory mortgages, see 14 Ency. Forms and Precedents (4th Edn.), pp. 203 *et seq.*

(*l*) *Willis* v. *Palmer* (1859), 7 C.B. (N.S.) 340; see also *Mostyn* v. *Lancaster* (1883), 23 Ch. D. 583. But the general words may be restricted by the particular purpose of the instrument: *Lewis* v. *Ramsdale* (1886), 55 L.T. 179. A general power to sell, assign and transfer is not sufficient to authorise a mortgage: *Australian Auxiliary Steam Clipper Co.* v. *Mounsey* (1858), 4 K. & J. 733; *Jonmenjoy Coondoo* v. *Watson* (1884), 9 App. Cas. 561. One joint tenant cannot grant a power of attorney to another joint tenant to mortgage, etc., as trustees the legal estate vested in them: *Green* v.*Whitehead*, [1930] 1 Ch. 38 (C.A.) (cf. as beneficial owners).

(*m*) *Perry* v. *Holl* (1800), 2 Giff. 138; 2 De G.F. & J. 38; and see *Davies* v. *Bolton & Co.*, [1894] 3 Ch. 678.

(*n*) So that, for example, a corporation, having a general power by statute to mortgage its land, cannot mortgage the land which by the same Act it is bound to sell within a limited time.

(*o*) *De Winton* v. *Brecon Corporation* (1859), 26 Beav. 533.

trust or undertaking for the furtherance of which it was given. Thus, a building society can only exercise its borrowing powers for the legitimate purposes of the society (*p*).

A mortgage purporting to be executed according to, but which is in contravention of, statutory powers, will be good by estoppel in favour of a purchaser for value without notice of the infirmity (*q*).

A mortgage is not invalid only because it is made to secure a debt originally contracted on an improper security, provided it is clear that the mortgage is to secure the money, and not to secure the invalid transaction. A security made in excess of power, but by which an estate passes, will be treated as valid in a foreclosure action, and must be set aside, if at all, by an independent proceeding (*r*).

A special power to mortgage is not inconsistent with the existence of a general right to mortgage property if the donees of the power are not prohibited from so doing, and if they hold the property in a capacity, and mortgage it for purposes, which do not affect the exercise or the objects of the power (*s*).

Upon the principle that in equity whatever is agreed to be done, is done, effect will be given to an intention to create a security where the maker is of capacity to contract the debt, notwithstanding any mistake in the manner of doing it (*t*), or that it was done informally (*u*).

Effect of unauthorised security.—But if the maker of the security is not of capacity to contract the debt, as where borrowing is expressly forbidden or is authorised only subject to the performance of certain conditions, which have not been performed, or within a certain limit which has been exceeded, no debt will arise at law (*x*). But money borrowed or contracted to be paid irregularly on behalf of, but shown to have been bona fide applied in payment of liabilities of, a corporation, may be treated as an equitable debt bearing interest. The principle is either that, as the money was applied in payment of recoverable debts, no addition is made to the liabilities of the corporation, or that the lender should stand by subrogation in the place of the creditor who was paid (*y*). But in the absence of evidence, which must be adduced by the lender, that the money was so applied,

---

(*p*) *Sinclair* v. *Brougham*, [1914] A.C. 398 (H.L.); see also as to improper exercise, *Rigall* v. *Foster* (1853), 18 Jur. 39; *Eland* v. *Baker* (1861), 29 Beav. 137.

(*q*) *Webb* v. *Herne Bay Commissioners* (1870), L.R. 5 Q.B. 642; *Re Romford Canal Co.* (1883), 24 Ch. D. 85.

(*r*) *Scott* v. *Colburn* (1858), 26 Beav. 276.

(*s*) Thus the directors of a company who have power to borrow on mortgage to a certain amount may mortgage the property of the company by debenture or deposit of deeds to secure a past debt (*Re Patent File Co., Ex parte Birmingham Banking Co.* (1870), 6 Ch. App. 83; *Re Inns of Court Hotel Co.* (1868), L.R. 6 Eq. 82; *Re General Provident Assurance Co., Ex parte National Bank* (1872), L.R. 14 Eq. 507), or to secure payment of purchase money (*Seligman* v. *Prince*, [1895] 2 Ch. 617 (C.A.)).

(*t*) *Re Queensland Land and Coal Co., Davis* v. *Martin*, [1894] 3 Ch. 181.

(*u*) *Webb* v. *Herne Bay Commissioners* (1870), L.R. 5 Q.B. 642, at p. 654.

(*x*) *Chambers* v. *Manchester and Milford Rail. Co.* (1864), 10 Jur. N.S. 700; *Re Pooley Hall Colliery Co.* (1869), 18 W.R. 201; *Landowners West of England and South Wales Land Drainage and Inclosure Co.* v. *Ashford* (1880), 16 Ch. D. 411; *Firbank's Executors* v. *Humphreys* (1886), 18 Q.B.D. 54 (C.A.).

(*y*) *Sinclair* v. *Brougham*, [1914] A.C. 398 (H.L.), at p. 441; *cf. Re Wrexham, Mold and Connah's Quay Rail. Co.*, [1899] 1 Ch. 440 (C.A.).

the advance will not be recognised (z). So if a trustee improperly raises money by mortgage, although the security will be void against a mortgagee with notice, the latter may nevertheless be a creditor on the proceeds of the trust property to the extent to which the money lent was properly applied in administration (a).

III—CORPORATIONS

BORROWING POWERS

Distinction between trading and other companies.—The powers of a company formed under the Companies Acts (b) are limited by reference to the objects and purposes specified in the memorandum of association (c), and this principle applies to all companies created by statute for a particular purpose (d). However, in favour of a person dealing with a company in good faith, any transaction, decided on by the directors, must be deemed to be one which is within the capacity of the company, to enter into (e).

Generally an express power to borrow is inserted in the company's memorandum of association. But it is not always essential that powers should be expressly given, and a power of borrowing may be implied from the objects of the company. Thus an ordinary trading or commercial company may borrow money for the purposes of its undertaking, unless positively prohibited (f), and may mortgage its property for the purpose of securing the monies borrowed (g). But

---

(z) *Re National Permanent Benefit Building Society, Ex parte Williamson* (1870), 5 Ch. App. 309; *Blackburn Benefit Building Society* v. *Cunliffe, Brooks & Co.* (1882), 22 Ch. D. 61 (C.A.).

(a) *Devaynes* v. *Robinson* (1857), 24 Beav. 86 (mortgage instead of selling); *Paul* v. *Speirway, Ltd.,* [1976] 2 All E.R. 587. See Goff and Jones, *The Law of Restitution,* pp. 397, 402. As regards mortgages under powers, see p. 209, *infra.*

(b) See generally, 7 Halsbury's Laws (4th Edn.), Companies, paras 796 *et seq.*; Buckley on the *Companies Acts* (13th Edn.), pp. 206 *et seq.* As to the effect of a mortgage by a company struck off the register at the time of the mortgage but subsequently restored to the register, see *Re Boxco, Ltd.,* [1970] Ch. 442; [1970] 2 All E.R. 183.

(c) *Ashbury Railway Carriage and Iron Co.* v. *Riche* (1875), L.R. 7 H.L. 653.

(d) *Baroness Wenlock* v. *River Dee Co.* (1885), 10 App. Cas. 354 (H.L.), at p. 360.
A corporation created by royal charter has, prima facie, the power to do with its property all such acts as an ordinary person can do: *Jenkin* v. *Pharmaceutical Society,* [1921] 1 Ch. 392, 398.
A company incorporated by a special Act of Parliament has the powers conferred by the special Act and the Companies Clauses Consolidation Act 1845, s. 38: see that Act generally and the Companies Clauses Acts 1863 and 1869; 7 Halsbury's Laws (4th Edn.), Companies, paras. 1578 *et seq.*
As to nationalised bodies the borrowing powers of the authority, board, etc., are limited by the statute creating the authority, board, etc.; see *e.g.,* Coal Industry Act 1965 s. 1, amended by Coal Industry Act 1967, s. 1; Electricity Act 1957, s. 15, amended by Electricity Act 1972; Air Corporations Act 1967, s. 7, amended by Air Corporations Act 1969; Transport Act 1962, s. 10, amended by Transport Act 1968, s. 42; Post Office Act 1969, s. 35; Gas Act 1972, ss. 17 *et seq.*; Iron and Steel Act 1975, s. 3.

(e) European Communities Act 1972, s. 9 (1). See 7 Halsbury's Laws (4th Edn.), paras. 701, 799. If there is any doubt about the validity of the transaction, the lender should demand evidence of the director's decision, *e.g.,* a resolution of the board.

(f) *General Auction Estate and Monetary Co.* v. *Smith,* [1891] 3 Ch. 432.

(g) *Howard* v. *Patent Ivory Manufacturing Co.* (1888), 38 Ch. D. 156.
A private company can exercise any borrowing powers immediately on incorporation. A public company cannot exercise any borrowing powers until it is entitled to commence business: see Companies Act 1948, s. 109. For pre-incorporation contracts, see European Communities Act 1972, s. 9 (2); (1973), 89 L.Q.R. 518 (D. D. Prentice).

a non-trading company can borrow only if and when it is expressly authorised to do so (*h*). A company limited by guarantee cannot charge the amounts which the members have undertaken to contribute in the event of a winding up (*i*).

Extent of the powers.—A limited company usually has under its memorandum of association express power to borrow money (*k*) and to secure the repayment thereof in such manner as the company shall think fit (*l*), and by the articles of association the exercise of the power is usually delegated to the directors, generally with a limitation (*m*) on the amount which can be borrowed without the sanction of a general meeting (*n*).

How far mortgagee bound to verify exercise of powers.—Any party to a transaction decided upon by the directors is not bound to inquire as to the capacity of the company to enter into it, or as to any limitation on the powers of the directors under the memorandum or articles of association, and must be presumed to have acted in good faith unless the contrary is proved (*o*). In these circumstances the other party may enforce the transaction. The right of a member to restrain a proposed *ultra vires* contract or a proposed contract in excess of directors' powers is unaffected. Where s. 9 of the European Communities Act 1972 does not apply the mortgagee should bear in mind the following points. If there are restrictions on the amount which may be borrowed, the lender must see that the limit is not exceeded, unless the limit is imposed by the articles and they provide that only express

---

(*h*) *Re Badger, Mansell* v. *Viscount Cobham*, [1905] 1 Ch. 568.

(*i*) *Re Irish Club Co., Ltd.*, [1906] W.N. 127; *cf. Re Mayfair Property Co., Bartlett* v. *Mayfair Property Co.*, [1898] 2 Ch. 28 (C.A.). Nor can reserve capital created under ss. 60 and 64 of the Companies Act 1948, to be charged: *ibid.*

(*k*) A power of borrowing is limited to legitimate purposes: *Re Introductions, Ltd.*, [1970] Ch. 199 (C.A.); [1969] 1 All E.R. 887 (loan for unauthorised business); *cf. Charterbridge Corporation, Ltd.* v. *Lloyds Bank, Ltd.*, [1970] Ch. 62; [1969] 2 All E.R. 1185 (transaction within powers of company and directors can only be impeached if directors abuse power to the knowledge of the other party); and see now footnote (*e*), *supra*. Where a secured loan is deliverately made by way of overdraft that is borrowing: *Brookes & Co.* v. *Blackburn Benefit Society* (1884), 9 App. Cas. 857 (H.L.).

If there is no express power to borrow or only a limited power the memorandum or articles should be altered: see Companies Act 1948, ss. 5, 10.

(*l*) Such a power enables the company to give a mortgage to a surety by way of indemnity, even where the surety is a director of the company: *Re Pyle Works (No. 2)*, [1891] 1 Ch. 173.

(*m*) Such a limitation is to be found in Companies Act 1948, Table A, Part 1, reg. 79. The articles of a company seeking a quotation on a federated stock exchange must contain a restriction on the directors' borrowing powers.

(*n*) For forms, see 5 Ency. Forms and Precedents (4th Edn.), 263, 312, 359, 397, 437–440.

For the power of a company to mortgage its uncalled capital, see, generally, *Newton* v. *Debenture Holders of Anglo-Australian Investment Co.*, [1895] A.C. 244 (P.C.), and the works referred to in footnote (*b*), p. 178, *supra*.

(*o*) European Communities Act 1972, s. 9 (1). Some commentators consider that the provision applies only to acts *ultra vires* the *company* (see, *e.g.*, (1973), 123 New L.J. 312 (A. T. Hirtenstein)). Other commentators take the view that the provision applies also to acts *intra vires* the company, but outside the authority of the *directors* (see *ibid.*, p. 593 (James H. Thompson)). On the latter view the rule in *Royal British Bank* v. *Turquand, infra,* becomes superfluous save for these transactions not decided upon by the directors. For the meaning of a transaction decided upon by the directors, see Pennington's *Company Law* (3rd Edn.), p. 99.

notice of any excess will invalidate the loan (*p*). Where there are no restrictions on the exercise of the borrowing powers conferred by the company's public documents, the lender is not bound to look beyond these (and the register of mortgages and charges at the Companies Registry (*q*)), and, finding that the company is empowered to borrow, may assume that it has done any preliminary acts, such as the passing of resolutions, which its memorandum or articles require (*r*). But where the power expressly provides what shall be evidence of the preliminary acts (*s*), or where the security would, on the face of the articles, be *ultra vires*, unless the power is extended by the share-holders (*t*), the lender must see that what is necessary has been done (*u*).

Where the borrowing powers of directors are limited to a certain amount they cannot borrow beyond that amount so as to bind the company (*a*). If, however, the borrowing, though in excess of their own powers, is not in excess of the powers of the company, the borrowing may be ratified by the company (*b*). And the company may be bound if the borrowing was within the ordinary ambit of the directors' authority (*c*).

Still dealing with those cases where the European Communities Act 1972 does not apply, if a company borrows money in circumstances which render the borrowing *ultra vires* no debt arises either at law or in equity, and the lender cannot recover the money in an action for money had and received (*d*). Where the borrowing powers of a company are limited, any security given for any amount lent to the company beyond the limit is void, even though the limit is subsequently increased (*e*). But where the security is given in respect of a loan which

---

(*p*) *Chapleo* v. *Brunswick Permanent Benefit Building Society* (1881), 6 Q.B.D. 696 (C.A.).

(*q*) As to this, see pp. 181 *et seq., infra.*

(*r*) *Royal British Bank* v. *Turquand* (1856), 6 E. & B. 327. See, further, as to the rule in this case and subsequent cases, Buckley on the *Companies Acts* (13th Edn.), pp. 208 *et seq.*, and 373 *et seq.* And see (1966) 30 Conv. N.S. 123, 160 (R.S. Nock).

The rule applies even where the secretary of the borrowing company knew of the irregularity, he being also secretary of the lending company: *Re Hampshire Land Co.*, [1896] 2 Ch. 743. But where a director of the borrowing company is the lender he will be taken to have notice of non-compliance with internal regulations: *Howard* v. *Patent Ivory Manufacturing Co.* (1888), 38 Ch. D. 156, at p. 170; *cf. Re Fireproof Doors, Ltd.*, [1916] 2 Ch. 142.

The company may also be bound where a director or other agent exceeds his actual authority, but the act is one within the ordinary ambit of the authority of such a person: see the note to the Companies Act 1948, s. 180, in Buckley, *supra*, pp. 373 *et seq.*; and *Freeman and Lockyer* v. *Buckhurst Park Properties (Mangal), Ltd.*, [1964] 2 Q.B. 480 (C.A.); [1964] 1 All E.R. 630; *Hely-Hutchinson* v. *Brayhead, Ltd.*, [1968] 1 Q.B. 549 (C.A.); [1967] 3 All E.R. 70.

(*s*) *Fountaine* v. *Carmarthen Rail. Co.* (1868), L.R. 5 Eq. 316.

(*t*) *Irvine* v. *Union Bank of Australia* (1877), 2 App. Cas. 366 (P.C.).

(*u*) For other exceptions to the rule in *Royal British Bank* v. *Turquand*, see Buckley, *supra*, pp. 373 *et seq.*

(*a*) *Re Pooley Hall Colliery Co.* (1869), 21 L.T. 690. The directors may be personally liable for breach of warranty of authority: *Chapleo* v. *Brunswick Permanent Benefit Building Society, supra; Whitehaven Joint Stock Banking Co.* v. *Read* (1886), 54 L.T. 360 (C.A.).

(*b*) *Irvine* v. *Union Bank of Australia, supra.*   (*c*) See footnote (*r*), *supra.*

(*d*) *Sinclair* v. *Brougham*, [1914] A.C. 398 (H.L.), at p. 426. And see *Re Introductions, Ltd., supra.*

(*e*) *Fountaine* v. *Carmarthen Rail. Co., supra.*

is to be applied in paying off other loans properly made to the company the limit is not exceeded (*f*).

But as previously mentioned (*g*) an *ultra vires* borrowing is not wholly without effect.

Form of mortgage.—A mortgage by a company takes the usual form of mortgage by an absolute owner (*h*). Such mortgages may also include a specific charge of future acquired freehold and leasehold property (*i*) and a floating charge over the company's other assets (*k*). In the case of private companies the mortgagee will often require the directors of the company to guarantee repayment of the advance (*l*).

It is not usually legitimate for one company to charge its property with the debts of another company, *e.g.*, its parent company, though an alteration of the charging company's memorandum will ensure that such a transaction is *intra vires* (*m*).

Registration of company charges.—The Companies Act 1948, provides as follows:

> **95.**—(1) Subject to the provisions of this part of this Act, every charge created (*n*) after the fixed date (*o*) by a company registered in England and being a charge to which this section applies shall, so far as any security on the company's property or undertaking is conferred thereby (*p*), be void against the liquidator and any creditor of the company, unless the prescribed particulars (*q*) of the charge together with the instrument, if any (*r*), by which the charge is created or evidenced, are delivered to or received by the registrar of companies for registration in manner required by this Act within twenty-one days after the date of its creation (*s*), but without prejudice to

---

(*f*) *Re Harris Calculating Machine Co., Sumner* v. *Harris Calculating Machine Co.*, [1914] 1 Ch. 920.

(*g*) See p. 177, *supra.*

(*h*) For forms of mortgage by limited companies, see 2 Ency. Forms and Precedents (4th Edn.), pp. 848-855; 14 Ency. Forms and Precedents (4th Edn.), pp. 289 *et seq.*; and Precedent 11 in the Appendix, *infra.*

(*i*) As to the effect of such a charge, see p. 11, *supra.*

(*k*) See pp. 121, *supra.* For restrictions on mortgage of assets of insurance companies, see Insurance Companies Act 1974, ss. 24, 32.

(*l*) Note that a director who has guaranteed an overdraft of or advance to the company of which he is director may be interested for the purposes of the Companies Act 1948, s. 199, and Table A, Art. 84. See *Victors, Ltd.* v. *Lingard*, [1927] 1 Ch. 323.

(*m*) For a form of mortgage of properties of subsidiary companies to secure loan to holding company, see 14 Ency. Forms and Precedents (4th Edn.), pp. 292 *et seq.*

(*n*) *I.e.*, not arising by operation of law, *e.g.*, a lien: see *London and Cheshire Insurance Co., Ltd.* v. *Laplagrene Property Co., Ltd.*, [1971] Ch. 499; [1971] 1 All E.R. 766; cf. *Re Wallis and Simmonds (Builders), Ltd.*, [1974] 1 All E.R. 561. And compare a charge "created" with acquiring property subject to a charge: p. 184, *infra.*

(*o*) This date is 1 July, 1908, or 1 November, 1929, depending on the type of charge: see Companies Act 1948, s. 95 (10) (b).

(*p*) The charge will still be affective as regards any non-security aspects: *Re J. and D. Contracting Pty., Ltd.*, [1970] Q.W.N. 40.

(*q*) See 6 Ency. Forms and Precedents (4th Edn.), pp. 1345-1349.

(*r*) An oral charge is registrable: *Re F.L.E. Holdings, Ltd.*, [1967] 3 All E.R. 553.

(*s*) The charge is created at the date of execution (*Esberger & Son, Ltd.* v. *Capital and Counties Bank*, [1913] 2 Ch. 366) and, in the case of a trust deed to secure debentures, not when the debentures are issued thereunder (*Transport and General Credit Corpn., Ltd.* v. *Morgan*, [1939] Ch. 531; [1939] 2 All E.R. 17). Where a charge is delivered (*i.e.*, in the technical sense of one of the elements of execution) undated, it is created on the date of delivery. Delivery may be on terms (as an escrow, see p. 42, *supra*) that the deed is not to take effect until the happening of a specified event: see *Re C. L. Nye, Ltd.*, [1971] Ch. 442 (C.A.); [1970] 3 All E.R. 1061; and *Security Trust Co.* v. *The Royal Bank of Canada*, [1976] A.C. 503 (P.C.); [1976] 1 All E.R. 381.

any contract or obligation for repayment of the money thereby secured, and when a charge becomes void under this section the money secured thereby shall immediately become payable.

The types of charge (*t*) which require to be registered are as follows:

A charge for the purpose of securing any issue (*u*) of debentures; a charge on uncalled share capital of the company; a charge created or evidenced by an instrument which, if executed by an individual, would require registration as a bill of sale (*a*); a charge on land, wherever situate, or any interest therein, but not including a charge for any rent or other periodical sum issuing out of land; a charge on book debts of the company (*b*) (not including the deposit for the purpose of securing an advance to the company of a negotiable instrument to secure payment of any book debts of the company); a floating charge on the undertaking or property of the company; a charge on calls made but not paid; a charge on a ship or aircraft (*c*) or any share in a ship; and a charge on goodwill, on a patent or a licence under a patent, on a trademark or on a copyright or a licence under a copyright.

The certificate of the registrar is conclusive that all the required particulars as to registration have been complied with (*d*), even though all the required particulars have not been registered, or have been registered out of time(*e*).

Effect of non-registration.—It is the security only which is void against any creditor and the liquidator of the company for non-registration; the money itself becomes immediately repayable. The security is void against secured creditors of the company, even though they have notice of the unregistered security (*f*). But the security is valid against the company. Accordingly any steps taken by the mortgagee by way of enforcement of his security (*e.g.*, by sale) are

---

(*t*) Companies Act 1948, s. 95 (2), (6). "Charge" includes "mortgage": Companies Act 1948, s. 95 (10) (a). The provisions as to registration of charges cannot be evaded by making what is in fact a mortgage or charge in form an absolute assignment: *Re Kent and Sussex Sawmills, Ltd.*, [1947] Ch. 177; [1946] 2 All E.R. 638 (see p. 9, *supra*). A charging order need not be registered; see *Re Overseas Aviation Engineering (G.B.), Ltd.*, [1963] Ch. 24 (C.A.). For lien, see note (*n*), *supra*.

(*u*) See *Levy* v. *Abercorris Slate and Slab Co.* (1887), 37 Ch. D. 260; *Automobile Association (Canterbury) Inc.* v. *Australian Secured Deposits, Ltd.*, [1973] 1 N.Z.L.R. 417.

(*a*) An instrument does not fall within this head unless it creates or evidences a charge, as well as being an instrument which, if executed by an individual, would require registration as a bill of sale: *Stoneleigh Finance, Ltd.*v. *Phillips*, [1965] 2 Q.B. 537, (C.A.); [1965] 1 All E.R. 513.

(*b*) See *Paul and Frank, Ltd.* v. *Discount Bank (Overseas), Ltd.*, [1967] Ch. 348; [1966] 2 All E.R. 922.

(*c*) See Mortgaging of Aircraft Order 1972, art. 16 (2).

(*d*) Companies Act 1948, s. 98 (2).

(*e*) *Re C. L. Nye, Ltd.*, [1971] Ch. 442 (C.A.); [1970] 3 All E.R. 1061. If a chargee has fraudulently deceived the registrar, a creditor who has thereby suffered loss may be able to take proceedings in *personam: per* RUSSELL, L. J., at [1971] Ch. p. 475; [1970] 3 All E.R. 1073. As to the keeping of the register by the registrar, see Companies Act 1948, s. 98.

(*f*) *Re Monolithic Building Co.*, *Tacon* v. *Monolithic Building Co.*, [1915] 1 Ch. 643 (C.A.); see p. 185, *infra*.

valid and cannot later be upset by a liquidator of the company subsequently appointed (*g*).

The company itself cannot have a cause of action arising out of non-registration (*a*). When a mortgage or charge is avoided as against the liquidator, everything ancillary to it, such as a lien, is also avoided (*b*).

Registration otherwise than under the Companies Act.— Charges of unregistered land (other than floating charges) created by a company on or after 1 January 1970 and which are capable of registration as a land charge should be registered under the Land Charges Act as well as under the Companies Act (*c*).

Registration under the Companies Act does not obviate the necessity for registration or protection of the charge under the Land Registration Act 1925, in so far as the charge relates to land the title to which is registered under that Act (*d*).

Charges on foreign property.—Where a charge is created in the United Kingdom but comprises property situate outside the United Kingdom, the instrument creating or purporting to create the charge may be sent for registration under the provisions of s. 95 outlined above, despite the fact that further proceedings may be necessary to make the charge valid or effectual according to the law of the country in which the property is situate (*e*).

Registration of a series of debentures.—Where a series of debentures containing, or giving by reference to any other instrument, any charge to the benefit of which debenture holders of that series are entitled *pari passu* is created by a company, it is sufficient for the purposes of registration if these are delivered to or received by the registrar within twenty-one days after the execution of the deed containing the charge or, if there is no such deed, after the execution of any debentures of the series, the following particulars:

(a) the total amount secured by the whole series; and

(b) the dates of the resolutions authorising the issue of the series and the date of the covering deed, if any, by which the security is created or defined; and

(c) a general description of the property charged; and

(d) the names of the trustee, if any, for the debenture holders;

together with the deed containing the charge, or if there is no such deed, one of the debentures of the series. Where more than one issue is made of debentures in the series, there must be sent to the registrar for entry in the register particulars of the date and amount

---

(*g*) See *Mercantile Bank of India, Ltd.* v. *Chartered Bank of India, Australia and China and Strauss & Co., Ltd.*, *Chartered Bank of India, etc.* v. *Mercantile Bank of India Ltd., and Strauss & Co., Ltd.*, [1937] 1 All E.R. 231; *Re Row Dal Constructions Pty., Ltd.*, [1966] V.R. 249.

(*a*) *Independent Automatic Sales, Ltd.* v. *Knowles and Foster*, [1962] 3 All E.R. 27.

(*b*) *Re Molton Finance, Ltd.*, [1968] Ch. 325 (C.A.); [1967] 3 All E.R. 843. And see *Capital Finance Co., Ltd.* v. *Stokes*, [1969] 1 Ch. 261 (C.A.); [1968] 3 All E.R. 625; *Re Wallis & Simmonds (Builders), Ltd.*, *supra*; *Burston Finance, Ltd.* v. *Speirway, Ltd.*, [1974] 3 All E.R. 735. For a criticism of the earlier cases, see (1970) 33 M.L.R. 131.

(*c*) Land Charges Act 1972, s. 3 (7), (8) (re-enacting s. 26 of the Law of Property Act 1969, amending s. 10 (5) of the Land Charges Act 1925).

(*d*) See p. 124, *supra*.

(*e*) Companies Act 1948, s. 95 (4).

of each issue, but an omission to do this does not affect the validity of the debentures issued (*f*).

Company's duty to register charges.—It is the duty of a company to send for registration the particulars of every charge created by it, and of every issue of debentures of a series requiring registration (*g*), with the registrar (*h*). The registration of any such charge may, however, be effected on the application of any person interested therein (*h*).

Where a company registered in England acquires any property which is subject to a charge of any such kind as would, if it had been created by the company after the acquisition of the property, have been required to be registered (*i*), the company must cause the prescribed particulars (*k*) of the charge, together with a copy (certified in the prescribed manner (*l*) to be a correct copy) of the instrument, if any, by which the charge was created or is evidenced, to be delivered to the registrar of companies for registration in the manner required (*m*) within twenty-one days after the date on which the acquisition is completed (*n*).

Where property subject to a mortgage is sold and the proceeds are invested in other property which is conveyed to the company, and then mortgaged by the company to the mortgagee, the latter mortgage requires registration (*o*); but the registration of a trust deed securing debenture stock containing specific equitable charges on property is sufficient to cover subsequent legal mortgages of that property to complete the security, and also mortgages of further property substituted under the powers of the deed for property comprised in the original charge (*p*).

(*f*) Companies Act 1948, s. 95 (8). For charges created out of the United Kingdom comprising property situate outside the United Kingdom, see s. 95 (3). For a charge comprising property situate in Scotland or Northern Ireland, see s. 95 (5).

(*g*) *I.e.*, under the Companies Act 1948, s. 95 (2), (4).

(*h*) *Ibid.*, s. 96 (1). Section 96 (3) provides a penalty for non-compliance.

(*i*) *I.e.*, under the Companies Act 1948, s. 95.

(*k*) See 6 Ency. Forms and Precedents (4th Edn.), 1347.

(*l*) *I.e.*, under the seal of the company or under the hand of some other person interested therein otherwise than on behalf of the company: Companies (Forms) Order 1949, art. 4.

(*m*) See Companies Act 1948, s. 98.

(*n*) Companies Act 1948, s. 97 (1). See *Capital Finance Co., Ltd.* v. *Stokes, supra*; *Security Trust Co.* v. *The Royal Bank of Canada*, [1976] A.C. 503 (P.C.); [1976] 1 All E.R. 381. If the property is situate and the charge was created outside Great Britain the time for delivery of particulars etc., is twenty-one days after the date on which the copy could in due course of post, and if despatched with due diligence, have been received in the United Kingdom: *ibid.*, proviso. Section 97 (2) provides for a penalty for non-compliance.

(*o*) *Cornbrook Brewery Co., Ltd.* v. *Law Debenture Corpn., Ltd.*, [1904] 1 Ch. 303 (C.A.); see also *Bristol United Breweries, Ltd.* v. *Abbot*, [1908] 1 Ch. 279, for a situation in which registration would now be required under s. 97 of the Companies Act 1948.

(*p*) *Cunard S.S. Co., Ltd.* v. *Hopwood*, [1908] 2 Ch. 564. This was a case under the Companies Act 1900, s. 14 (4). Section 79 (8) of the Companies Act 1929, and s. 95 (8) of the Companies Act 1948, are similar: but the words "for the purposes of this section" are added. It is doubted, however, whether this addition makes the last named section inapplicable to mortgages of substituted property which would otherwise require registration under the Companies Act 1948, s. 97. In any case, failure to comply with the latter section does not affect the validity of the charge.

For the endorsement of the certificate of registration on debentures issued by the company, see Companies Act 1948, s. 99.

Extension of time for registration and rectification of register.
—The court, on being satisfied that the omission to register a charge
within the time required (*q*), or that the omission or misstatement of
any particular with respect to any such charge or in a memorandum of
satisfaction, was accidental, or due to inadvertence or to some other
sufficient cause, or is not of a nature to prejudice the position of
creditors or shareholders of the company, or that on other grounds
it is just and equitable to grant relief, may, on the application of the
company or any person interested (*r*) and on such terms and conditions
as seem to the court just and expedient, order that the time for
registration be extended, or as the case may be, that the omission or
misstatement be rectified (*s*). The court will not as a rule, on an
application for extension of time for registration, decide the question
whether a charge requires registration (*t*). An order granting an
extension of time for registration is usually made without prejudice
to any rights acquired prior to actual registration (*u*) against the
persons entitled to the mortgage or charge (*a*). Subject to any order the
court may make, the registration out of time renders the charge
valid *ab initio* (*b*).

Registration of charges at company's registered office.—
Provision is made for the keeping by the company at its registered
office of copies of instruments creating charges and of a register of
charges and for the entering therein of all charges specifically affecting
property of the company and all floating charges on the undertaking or
any property of the company (*c*).

Provision is also made for the inspection of such copies and of the
register (*d*).

**Evidence of registration under Companies Act on registration
under Land Registration Act.**—On an application under the Land
Registration Act 1925, to register a charge, which requires to be

---

(*q*) See p. 181, *supra*, as to time within which application should be made.

(*r*) The application is made by summons: see R.S.C. Ord. 102. For form of summons,
see 10 Ency. Court Forms (2nd Edn.), 329.

(*s*) Companies Act 1948, s. 101. This provision does not confer power on the court
to grant interim relief: *Re Heathstar Properties, Ltd.*, [1966] 1 All E.R. 628. Nor to order
the deletion of the whole registration: see *Re C. L. Nye, Ltd.*, [1971] Ch. 442 (C.A.) at
pp. 474, 477; [1870] 3 All E.R. at pp. 1073, 1075.

(*t*) *Re Cunard S.S. Co., Ltd.*, [1908] W.N. 160. See also *Re Heathstar Properties,
Ltd.* (*No.* 2), [1966] 1 All E.R. 1000.

(*u*) *I.e.*, between the end of the 21 days period and actual registration: *Watson* v.
Duff Morgan and Vermont (Holdings), Ltd., [1974] 1 All E.R. 794.

(*a*) For forms of order, see 10A Ency. Court Forms (2nd Edn.), pp. 329 *et seq.* And see
now *Watson* v. *Duff Morgan and Vermont (Holdings), Ltd.*, *supra.*, (1974), 118 Sol. Jo.

(*b*) *Ram Narain* v. *Radha Kishan* (1929), L.R. 57 Ind. App. 762 (P.C.). See now
Watson v. *Duff Morgan and Vermont (Holdings), Ltd.*, *supra* (second debenture created
on same day as that registered late, first had priority); *cf. Re Monolithic Building Co.*,
Tacon v. *Monolithic Building Co.*, [1915] 1 Ch. 643 (second mortgage created after end
of 21 days period, second had priority).

(*c*) Companies Act 1948, ss. 103, 104 (1). Sub-section (2) provides for a penalty for
non-compliance.

(*d*) *Ibid.*, s. 105. A penalty is prescribed if inspection is refused: s. 105 (2); and the
court may by order compel an immediate inspection in relation to a company registered
in England: s. 105 (3).

There is no statutory requirement that a company must keep a register of debenture
holders but provision is made by the Companies Act 1948, for the keeping of such a
register and for inspection of copies of debentures and of the register: ss. 86, 87.

registered under the Companies Act 1948, unless evidence is produced
to the registrar that the charge has been registered under s. 95 of the
Companies Act 1948, a note will be made on the register that the charge
is subject to the provisions of that section (*e*).

Entry of satisfaction or release from charge.—Provision is made
by the Companies Act 1948, for the registrar to enter on the register
a memorandum of satisfaction or of the fact of the release of the
property upon the appropriate evidence thereof (*f*).

LENDING POWERS

Generally.—A company may have an implied power to lend money
and allow credit in the ordinary course of its business and for the
furtherance of the objects of the company. Generally the objects of
the company will include an express power to make advances and that
any money due to the company may be secured by mortgage (*g*).

IV—PUBLIC AUTHORITIES

BORROWING POWERS

Local authorities (*h*).—The power of local authorities to borrow
is generally conferred by statute, but it may be implied (*i*). The
purposes for which money may be borrowed are those for which
the power was granted by the relevant Act or is implied, and under
the Local Government Act 1972 (*k*), a local authority may, with the
consent of the sanctioning authority (*l*), borrow such sums as may be
required for the acquisition of land, for building and for a number of
other statutory purposes (*m*).

A person lending money to a local authority is not bound to inquire
whether the borrowing of the money is or was legal or regular or
whether the money was properly applied and is not prejudiced by any
illegality or irregularity in such matters or by the misapplication or
non-application of any such money (*n*).

Local authorities may, when they borrow money, raise the money,

---

(*e*) Land Registration Rules 1925, r. 145 (2).

(*f*) Section 100. For forms of declaration, see 6 Ency. Forms and Precedents (4th
Edn.), pp. 1333-1337.

For cancellation where the charge is registered or protected under the Land Registration Act 1925, see p. 553, *infra*.

(*g*) As to prohibitions of loans to directors, see Companies Act 1948, s. 190. As to
particulars in accounts of loans, see Companies Act 1948, s. 197. As to loans to assist
purchase of its own or holding company's shares, see Companies Act 1948, s. 54; and
Heald v. *O'Connor*, [1971] 2 All E.R. 1105; *Murray* v. *C. W. Boon*, [1974] 2 W.W.R. 620.
As to these sections generally, see Buckley on the *Companies Act* (13th Edn.), For
moneylenders, see pp. 234–240, *infra*.

(*h*) See 24 Halsbury's Laws (3rd Edn.), Local Government, pp. 560 *et seq.;* 25
Halsbury's Laws (3rd Edn.), London Government, pp. 71 *et seq.;* and Supp.

(*i*) *Baroness Wenlock* v. *River Dee Co.* (1883), 36 Ch. D. 675, n. (C.A.).

(*k*) Section 172, Sched. 13.

(*l*) Generally the Secretary of State for the Environment, save in the case of the
Greater London Council, when the sanctioning authority is the Treasury.

(*m*) For examples of *ultra vires* borrowing, see *A.-G.* v. *West Ham Corpn.*, [1910]
2 Ch. 560; *A.-G.* v. *Oldham Corpn.*, [1936] 2 All E.R. 1022.

(*n*) Local Government Act 1972, Sched. 13, para. 20.

inter alia, by mortgage (*o*), the issue of stock, debentures, or bonds (*p*). The issue of stock or bonds is the most common method of raising money.

All securities created by a local authority rank equally without any priority, subject to any priority existing on 1 June, 1934 (the date of the coming into force of the Local Government Act 1933), or any right to priority conferred by a security created before that date (*q*).

Local authorities may also borrow for specified purposes under general Acts. For example, they may borrow for certain purposes of the Housing Act 1957 (*r*), and for the purposes of the Housing Act 1949 as amended (*s*).

Other public authorities.—For the borrowing powers of the Agricultural Mortgage Corporation Limited, see p. 128, *supra* (*t*).

LENDING POWERS

Local authorities.　Loans for housing purposes generally.— A local authority or county council may (*u*) advance money for the purpose of acquiring, constructing, altering, enlarging, repairing or improving houses, for converting buildings into houses or flats, for acquiring houses for that purpose or for paying off a loan for such purposes (*a*). Before making an advance the local authority must be satisfied that the resultant house will be fit for human habitation, or, in the case of a house to be acquired is or will be made fit (*b*). The amount of the advance must not exceed the value of the mortgaged security in the case of a house or houses (*c*) to be acquired, or, in any other case, the value which it is estimated the mortgaged security will bear when the construction, conversion, alteration, enlargement, repair or improvement has been carried out (*d*). The advance together with

---

(*o*) The form is prescribed by the Local Government (Form of Mortgages and Transfers) Regulations 1974, art. 2. For form, see Ency Forms and Precedents, Service Supp. Additional Forms.

(*p*) Local Government Act 1972, Sched. 13, para. 2.

(*q*) Local Government Act 1972, Sched, 13, para. 11.

(*r*) Section 136 (1).

(*s*) Housing (Financial Provisions) Act 1958; House Purchase and Housing Act 1959; Public Works Loans Act 1964. See further, 19 Halsbury's Laws (3rd Edn.), Housing, pp. 750-752.

(*t*) For the public utility authorities, see footnote (*d*), p. 178, *supra*. For burial boards, see 4 Halsbury's Laws (3rd Edn.), Burial and Cremation, 40; for the National Trust, see 28 Halsbury's Laws (3rd Edn.), Open Spaces, 186; for water authorities, see 39 Halsbury's Laws (3rd Edn.), Waters and Watercourses, 693.

(*u*) Subject to the restraints on local authority lending imposed from time to time for economic reasons.

(*a*) Housing (Financial Provisions) Act 1958, s. 43, as amended by the House Purchase and Housing Act 1959, ss. 3, 31 (2), and Sched. 2 and Local Government Act 1972, s. 37 (2), (3). The borrower's estate in the mortgaged property must be not less than a term of years absolute for a period ten years in excess of the time fixed for repayment: Housing (Financial Provisions) Act 1958, s. 43 (3) (f).

(*b*) *Ibid.*, s. 43 (2).

(*c*) If the effect of the advance is to meet the borrower's housing needs, part may be used otherwise than as a dwelling: *ibid.*, s. 43(5), added by Local Government Act 1974, s. 37 (5).

(*d*) *Ibid.*, s. 43 (3) (b); House Purchase and Housing Act 1959, s. 3 (1). There must be a valuation on behalf of the local authority: Housing (Financial Provisions) Act 1958, s. 43 (3) (e). Except in cases of advances for acquiring houses, the advance may be made by instalments as the works proceed: *ibid.*, s. 43 (3) (d).

interest must be secured by a mortgage on the property (*e*). The mortgage must provide for repayment of the principal either by instalments (of equal or unequal amounts) beginning either on the date of the advance or a later date or at the end of a fixed period (with or without a provision allowing the authority to extend the period) or on the happening of a specified event before the end of that period, and for the payment of instalments of interest throughout the period beginning on the date of the advance and ending when the whole of the principal is repaid. In either case, the balance outstanding is repayable on demand if there is a breach of any of the conditions of the advance and the borrower may repay on any of the usual quarter days, after giving a month's notice of his intention (*f*). Advances may be made in addition to other assistance given by the local authority under any other statutory provisions (*g*).

A local authority or county council may, with the consent of the Secretary of State, and subject to any regulations or conditions he may impose, make loans to housing associations (*h*).

For the acquisition of small dwellings.—Advances to private individuals for houses for their own occupation may be made by local authorities (*i*) under the Small Dwellings Acquisition Acts 1899 to 1923 (*k*). The advance can be made to a resident in any house within the area of the local authority for the purpose of enabling him to acquire the ownership of the house (*l*), or to a person intending to construct a house in which he intends to reside when constructed (*m*). If the market value of the house exceeds £5,000 no advance can be made (*n*). The market value must be ascertained by a valuation made on behalf of the local authority, and the advance must not exceed 90 per cent. of the market value so ascertained (*o*). The advance must be repaid with interest (*p*) within such period not exceeding

---

(*e*) *Ibid.*, s. 43 (3) (a).

(*f*) *Ibid.*, s. 43 (3) (c); as amended by the Local Government Act 1974, s. 37 (4). For forms of mortgage, see 14 Ency. Forms and Precedents (4th Edn.), pp. 320–334, 446–454; Precedents for the Conveyancer, 7–15.

(*g*) *Ibid.*, s. 43 (4). *E.g.*, under the Small Dwellings Acquisition Acts, *infra*, or the Housing Act 1974, ss. 61–64 (improvement grants); on the conditions imposed on an improvement grant, see (1973), 123 N.L.J. 264 (W.L.H. Evans).

(*h*) Housing Act 1957, s. 119. For housing associations, see p. 191, *infra*.

(*i*) See Small Dwellings Acquisition Act 1899, s. 9 (1), (2), for the definition of local authorities for the purposes of the Acts. And see London Government Act 1963, s. 21, Sched. 8, para. 14.

(*k*) This is the collective title of the Small Dwellings Acquisition Act 1899; Part III of the Housing, Town Planning, &c. Act 1919; Part III of the Housing, &c. Act 1923; Housing Act 1949.

(*l*) Small Dwellings Acquisition Act 1899, s. 1 (1). The ownership must be either a fee simple or a term of years of which at least sixty years are unexpired: *ibid.*, s. 10 (2).

(*m*) Added by the Housing, &c. Act 1923, s. 22 (a).

(*n*) See Housing Act 1949, s. 44 (1).

(*o*) Housing, &c. Act 1923, s. 22 (d). An advance in respect of a house in the course of construction may be made by instalments from time to time as the work proceeds, but the total advanced must not at any time exceed 80 per cent. of the value of the work done, including the value of the recipient's interest in the site: Housing Act 1949, s. 44 (2).

(*p*) The rate is one quarter per cent. in excess of the rate on loans to local authorities prevailing one month before the terms of the advance are settled. The rate of interest on such loans is approved by the Treasury from time to time.

thirty years as may be agreed upon (*q*). Repayments may be made either by equal instalments of principal, or by an annuity of principal and interest combined, and payments may be made weekly or at any other periods not exceeding a half-year, as may be agreed (*r*).

Preliminaries to an advance.—Before making the advance the local authority must be satisfied (*s*):

(a) That the applicant for the advance is resident (*t*) or intends to reside (*u*) in the house, and is not already the proprietor within the meaning of the Act of 1899 (*a*) of the house to which the statutory conditions apply; and

(b) that the value of the ownership of the house is sufficient; and

(c) that the title to the ownership is one which an ordinary mortgagee would be willing to accept; and

(d) that the house is in good sanitary condition and good repair; and

(e) that the repayment to the local authority of the advance is secured by an instrument creating a charge by way of legal mortgage or a demise or a sub-demise (*b*) in favour of the local authority, subject to the right of redemption by the applicant, but such instrument shall not contain anything inconsistent with the provisions of the Act.

Conditions during the loan.—During the continuance of the loan the house is held subject to the following conditions (in the Act of 1899 referred to as the statutory conditions) (*c*):

(a) Every sum for the time being due in respect of principal or of interest of the advance shall be punctually paid;

(b) The proprietor of the house shall reside in the house (*d*);

(c) The house shall be kept insured against fire to the satisfaction of the local authority, and the receipts for the premiums produced when required by them;

(d) The house shall be kept in good sanitary condition and in good repair;

(e) The house shall not be used for the sale of intoxicating liquors, or in such manner as to be a nuisance to adjacent houses;

(*q*) Small Dwellings Acquisition Act 1899, s. 1 (2).

(*r*) *Ibid.*, s. 1 (4). After one month's written notice, the proprietor may repay on any of the usual quarter days, the whole of the advance together with interest due, or he may repay part of the advance by £10 or multiples of £10: s. 1 (5).

(*s*) *Ibid.*, s. 2.

(*t*) *Ibid.*, s. 10 (1).

(*u*) *Ibid.*, s. 7.

(*a*) *I.e.*, the purchaser of the ownership, or the person taking the interest of the purchaser by devolution or transfer: *ibid.*, s. 10 (3).

(*b*) *Ibid.*, s. 2 (e); Law of Property (Amendment) Act 1924, Sched. 9, para. 5. For forms of mortgage under the Acts, see 14 Ency. Forms and Precedents (4th Edn.), pp. 334-337, 454-457.

(*c*) *Ibid.*, s. 3 (1). Where the land is registered, the appropriate restriction will be entered automatically.

(*d*) This condition has effect for a period of three years from the date when the advance is made, or from the date on which the house is completed, whichever is the later, but no longer, and compliance with it may at any time be dispensed with: Housing, etc. Act 1923, s. 22 (c).

(f) The local authority shall have power to enter the house by any person, authorised by them in writing for the purpose, at all reasonable times for the purpose of ascertaining whether the statutory conditions are complied with.

A mortgage made under the Acts must not contain anything inconsistent with the provisions of the Acts (*e*).

The proprietor may, with the permission of the local authority (*f*) (which shall not be unreasonably withheld), transfer his interest in the house, but the transfer must be made subject to the statutory conditions (*g*). The mortgagee is personally liable for any sum due in respect of the advance until he ceases to be proprietor by reason of a transfer made in accordance with the Act (*h*). There is a form of statutory receipt to discharge the mortgage provided by the Act of 1919 (*i*). Such a receipt operates as a discharge without any reconveyance, reassignment or release, and it is not liable to stamp duty and must be granted free of cost to the person paying the money, but the right of that person to require the reconveyance, reassignment, surrender, release or transfer to be executed is not affected (*k*).

The realisation of housing mortgages (*l*).—The Act of 1899 provides special modes of realising the mortgage. Where default is made in complying with the statutory conditions as to residence, the local authority may take possession of the house. Where default has been made in any other of the statutory conditions, whether the statutory condition as to residence has been complied with or not, the local authority may either take possession, or order a sale without taking possession (*m*).

In the case of a breach of the conditions for punctual payment, no notice is required before taking possession. In the case of any other condition, the local authority must, previously to taking possession or ordering a sale, give to the proprietor notice in writing calling on him to comply with the condition, and if (1) within 14 days of delivery of the notice, he gives an undertaking in writing to comply with it; and (2) within two months of the delivery of the notice complies therewith, the authority shall not take possession or order a sale (*n*).

Thus the local authority has, in the event of default, the option either to take possession or to sell, except where the default is in compliance with the condition as to residence, and then it can only take possession. The effect of taking possession is that the estate and

---

(*e*) Small Dwellings Acquisition Act 1899, s. 2 (e).

(*f*) This permission is not required for a charge on the proprietor's interest so far as the charge does not affect the rights or powers of the local authority under the Act: *ibid.*, s. 4 (2).

(*g*) *Ibid.*, s. 3 (2).

(*h*) *Ibid.*, s. 4 (1).

(*i*) Housing Town Planning, &c. Act 1919, Sched. 4.

(*k*) *Ibid.*, s. 49 (d); Finance Act 1958, s. 35 (2). For the abolition of mortgage stamp duty, see footnote (*t*), p. 12, *supra*.

(*l*) See further, pp. 330, 376, *infra*.

(*m*) Small Dwellings Acquisition Act 1899, s. 3 (3). Possession may be recovered, whatever the value of the house, in the county court under the County Courts Act 1888; see p. 331, *infra*.

(*n*) *Ibid.*, s. 3 (4). On the bankruptcy of the proprietor, or in the case of his death, the administration of his estate in bankruptcy, the local authority must either take possession or order a sale without taking possession: s. 3 (5).

interest of the proprietor vests in and becomes the property of the local authority, and this being so they may either retain the house under their own management or sell or otherwise dispose of it as they think expedient (*o*). Virtually, however, there is a sale of the house to the local authority, and though they become owners, they have to pay the value of the house. This may be a sum agreed with the proprietor, and in the absence of a sale and in default of agreement, it will be settled by arbitration (*p*). The sum agreed with the proprietor will be the value of the equity of redemption, that is, the value of his interest in the house, less the principal and interest owing on the mortgage. And, similarly, when the value is determined by arbitration, the value so determined will be the value of the mortgagor's interest, less the amount of the advance remaining unpaid and any sum due for interest. From the value so determined, costs of or incidental to the taking possession and sale, including the costs of arbitration (if any), will also be deducted and the balance will be paid to the mortgagor (*q*).

Where the local authority adopt the alternative—allowed except in default as to residence—of sale, the sale must be by auction, and if effective the sum due for interest and principal, and the costs and charges, and expenses of the sale will be deducted and the balance (if any) paid to the proprietor (*r*). But if at the auction the house is not sold for such a sum as will allow for payment of interest and principal, and costs, the local authority may take possession of it, and in this case they are not liable to, nor may (*s*) make any payment to the proprietor (*t*). If subsequently the local authority can sell for a sum in excess of the sums due to it they hold the excess as trustees for the rate-payers and may not pay it to the proprietor (*u*).

Agricultural Mortgage Corporation Limited.—For advances on mortgage by this body, see p. 128, *supra*.

V—HOUSING ASSOCIATIONS

Housing associations (*a*).—A housing association (*b*) is a society, body of trustees or company established for the purpose of, or

---

(*o*) Section 5 (1). For a form of conveyance if the local authority sells, see 17 Ency. Forms and Precedents (3rd Edn.), 387. For the registration procedure on taking possession of registered land, see Land Registration Rules 1925, r. 131.

(*p*) Section 5 (2). The words "in the absence of a sale" appear to assume that the local authority may have sold the house as owners after taking possession. In that case the purchase price will be the value as between the mortgagor and the authority. If there is an arbitration, either the county court judge or an arbitrator appointed by him will be the arbitrator and the Arbitration Act 1950, applies to any such arbitration.

(*q*) Section 5 (4). The costs of sale referred to in sub-s. (4) refer to a sale by the authority after taking possession. Since this determines the value of the house, the costs of the sale should be deducted from the purchase money.

(*r*) Section 6 (1).

(*s*) *Re Brown's Mortgage, Wallasey Corpn.* v. *A.-G.*, [1945] Ch. 166; [1945] 1 All E.R. 397.

(*t*) Section 6 (2). Thus the taking of possession as the result of an abortive auction differs in its incidents from an initial taking of possession, and has the result of vesting the house in the local authority absolutely.

(*u*) *Re Brown's Mortgage, Wallasey Corpn.* v. *A.-G.*, *supra*.; cf. *Re Caunter's Charge*, [1960] Ch. 491; [1959] 3 All E.R. 669. For a form of conveyance after an abortive auction, see 17 Ency. Forms and Precedents (3rd Edn.), 389.

(*a*) As to the history and the various sorts of housing associations, see (1959), 23 Conv. N.S. 3 (J. C. Craddock).   (*b*) This includes a housing society.

amongst whose objects or powers are included those of, constructing, improving or managing, or facilitating or encouraging the construction or improvement of houses or hostels, being a society, body of trustees or company which does not trade for profit or whose constitution or rules prohibit the issue of any capital with interest or dividend exceeding the rate for the time being prescribed by the Treasury, whether with or without differentiation as between share and loan capital (c).

A housing association may be either an industrial and provident society (d), a company registered under the Companies Act 1948 (e), or unincorporated. It may or may not be a charity (f). It may or may not be registered under the Housing Act 1974. The land which it acquires may or may not be grant-aided (g).

The Housing Corporation.—The Housing Corporation, which is a body corporate with perpetual succession and a common seal, was established by Part I of the Housing Act 1964, and its functions extended by the Housing Act 1974. Its objects are to promote and assist the development of registered housing associations and unregistered self-build associations, to facilitate the proper exercise and performance of the functions of such associations, and to publicise their aims and principles, to establish and maintain a register of housing associations (h) and to exercise supervision and control over them, and to undertake the provision of dwellings for letting or sale and of hostels and the management of dwellings or hostels provided by the Corporation (i). It may also provide an advisory service. The Corporation may make loans to housing associations (k).

A registered housing association may not, *inter alia*, mortgage any land, and an unregistered association may not, *inter alia*, mortgage any grant-aided land, except with the consent of the Corporation (l).

Building society advances to housing associations to which the Housing Corporation have made loans.—Where an advance is made by a building society to a housing association on the security of any freehold or leasehold estate by means of a mortgage where (a) immediately before the execution of that mortgage, the Corporation had an interest in the same freehold or leasehold estate under a mortgage entered into by the housing association; and (b) the security represented by the last-mentioned mortgage was, with the agreement of the

---

(c) Housing Act 1957, s. 189 (1), as amended by the Housing Act 1974, Sched. 13, para. 6. The appropriate rates are set out in 19 Halsbury's Laws (3rd Edn.), 703, footnote (s).

(d) See p. 197, *infra*.

(e) See p. 178, *supra*.

(f) See p. 204, *infra*.

(g) See Housing Act 1974, ss. 29–35, Sched. 2.

(h) Housing Act 1974, s. 13. The associations which may be registered are either charities which are not exempt charities and certain industrial and provident societies.

(i) Housing Act 1964, s. 1, as amended by, *inter alia*, Housing Act 1974, s. 1 (1), Sched. I. For the Corporation's borrowing powers, see Housing Act 1974, s. 7.

(k) Housing Act 1974, s. 9.

(l) Housing Act 1974, s. 2 (1). This consent is not required if an association is a registered charity and the disposition requires consent or an order under s. 29 of the Charities Act 1960 (see p. 204, *infra*). By order under s. 2 (6) the Housing Corporation has given consent to any mortgage to a local authority, the Commission for New Towns, development corporations and itself.

Corporation, postponed to the building society's security under the first-mentioned mortgage, such advance shall not constitute a special advance under s. 21 of the Building Societies Act 1962 (*m*). Nor does any advance which under s. 21 (7) of the Building Societies Act 1962, a building society is treated as having made by reason of a transfer

    (i) from one housing association to another, or
    (ii) from one housing association to the Corporation, or
    (iii) from the Corporation to a housing association,

of the mortgagor's interest under a mortgage securing an advance made by that building society, constitute a special advance (*n*).

VI—BUILDING SOCIETIES

GENERALLY (*o*)

Purposes of building societies.—A building society is a society formed for raising, by the subscription of the members, a stock or fund for making advances to members out of the funds of the society upon security by way of mortgage of freehold or leasehold estate (*p*).

Types of building societies.—The usual classification of building societies is into the following classes: (1) unincorporated; (2) incorporated; (3) terminating; and (4) permanent. A terminating or permanent society may be either unincorporated or incorporated.

Unincorporated building societies are extinct (*q*). A terminating society is one which by its rules is to terminate at a fixed date or when a result specified in the rules, is attained (*r*). Few, if any, such societies now exist. Accordingly the vast majority of building societies are incorporated permanent societies.

BORROWING POWERS

Generally.—A building society may borrow money, subject to certain limits and to certain restrictions (*s*), and accordingly may receive deposits or loans at interest to be applied for the purposes of the

---

(*m*) *Ibid.*, s. 8 (1), (2), as amended by Housing Act 1974, s. 130 (2) and Sched. 13, para. 10 (2). And see p. 194, *infra*.

(*n*) *Ibid.*, s. 8 (1), (2). But the total amount of the advances exempted by this section must not exceed 15 per cent. of the total advances made by the building society in the last preceding financial year: *ibid.*, s. 8 (3), (4), (10).

(*o*) See, generally, Wurtzburg and Mills, *Building Society Law* (14th Edn.); Building Societies Act 1962.

(*p*) Building Societies Act 1962, s. 1 (1). The primary object of building societies as stated in the preamble to the Building Societies Act 1836, is to assist its members in obtaining a small landed property. There are two classes of members of a building society, *i.e.*, unadvanced or investing members and advanced or borrowing members.

(*q*) They were all formed under the Building Societies Act 1836, which was repealed, except as regards then existing societies, by the Building Societies Act 1874. Those then existing societies have since been dissolved or incorporated.

(*r*) Building Societies Act 1962, s. 1 (2).

(*s*) *Ibid.*, ss. 12, 13 (commencement of business), 48, 49 (suspension of borrowing powers).

society (*a*). The limits vary according as to whether the society is a permanent or terminating society (*b*). A society may from time to time raise funds by the issue of shares of one or more denominations, either as shares paid up in full or as shares to be paid by periodical or other subscriptions, and with or without accumulating interest (*c*).

A society may mortgage its property for securing authorised loans or deposits. This is not expressly stated in the Act, but provision is made for the form of securities (*d*) and the power to mortgage is to be assumed from this.

Unauthorised borrowing.—A borrowing which is in excess of the limit imposed by the rules (which must not exceed the statutory limit), or which is not for the legitimate purposes of the society, creates no debt or legal obligation to repay the money to the lender (*e*), nor can the lender recover it in an action for money had and received (*f*), though if he can show that it has been used to pay liabilities of the society, he is entitled, on the analogy of subrogation, to have his claim recognised to the extent of such payment (*g*), and he is also entitled to trace his money into the assets of the company and recover it in that way (*h*). And if a building society receives loans or deposits in excess of the statutory limits, the directors of the society receiving the loans or deposits on its behalf will be personally liable for the amount of the excess (*i*).

LENDING POWERS—ADVANCES ON MORTGAGE

Limitation on special advances.—The Act imposes a limitation of the amount of special advances which may be made by a society. A special advance is an advance of one of the following descriptions, *i.e.*, (a) an advance of any amount to a body corporate; (b) an advance of a sum exceeding £20,000 or such other sum as may be prescribed (*k*) to a person other than a body corporate; (c) an advance of any amount to a person other than a body corporate, being a person who, after the advance is made to him, is indebted to the society in amount exceeding £20,000 or such other sum as may be prescribed (*l*). A building society must so conduct its business as to secure that special advances are not made by it except as authorised by the Act (*m*). The Act authorises the making of special advances subject to certain limits on the total amounts which a society may advance in any

---

(*a*) *Ibid.*, s. 39 (1).
(*b*) *Ibid.*, s. 39 (2), (3).
(*c*) *Ibid.*, s. 6.
(*d*) *Ibid.*, s. 41 (1).
(*e*) *Chapleo* v. *Brunswick Building Society* (1881), 6 Q.B.D. 696 (C.A.); *Brooks & Co.* v. *Blackburn Building Society* (1884), 9 App Cas. 857 (H.L.).
(*f*) *Sinclair* v. *Brougham*, [1914] A.C. 398 (H.L.).
(*g*) *Brooks & Co.* v. *Blackburn Building Society*, *supra*.
(*h*) *Sinclair* v. *Brougham*, *supra*.
(*i*) Building Societies Act 1962, s. 40.
(*k*) The limit was raised to its present limit by the Building Societies (Special Advances) Order 1975.
(*l*) Building Societies Act 1962, s. 21 (1). For advances to housing associations, see Housing Act 1964, s. 8 (p. 192, *supra*).
(*m*) Building Societies Act 1962, s. 22 (1).

financial year (*n*). There are provisions for the Chief Registrar to give permission to exceed the ordinary limits (*o*).

Advances.—A borrower may obtain an advance from a building society without holding a share in the society if the rules so provide (*p*). On the other hand a borrower may already be a member of the society subscribing for shares thereof. If the rules require a member to hold shares in the society the loan is made by advancing to the borrower the whole value of the shares in the society for which he has subscribed, the advance being secured by a mortgage.

The security.—The nature of the primary security which may be accepted by a building society is shown by the statutory purpose of a building society, namely to make advances to members out of the funds of the society upon security by way of mortgage of freehold or leasehold estate (*q*). Collateral or additional security may, and often is taken, *e.g.*, by way of guarantee or mortgage of a life insurance policy. In determining the amount of an advance made by a building society to any of its members on the security of freehold or leasehold estate the society may not take into account the value of any additional security except such as is specified in the Third Schedule to the Act (*r*). For the purpose of facilitating the repayment to a building society of an advance made by the society to a member on the security of freehold or leasehold estate the society may make to the borrower, by way of addition to the advance, a further advance of the whole or part of such sum as may be necessary to enable payment to be made of a single premium payable in respect of an appropriate policy of life assurance (*s*).

(*n*) *Ibid.*, s. 22 (2), (3), (4). The limits are based on the proportion that the total amount of special advances bears to the total amount of all advances made by the society. This proportion determines the amount of special advances which may be made in the following financial year. Special advances may not be made in the calendar year in which the society is established: s. 22 (6). There are penalties for exceeding the limits: s. 22 (7). An advance made jointly to two or more persons is taken to be a special advance if an advance of the like amount made under like conditions to any one of those persons would be a special advance: s. 21 (8).

(*o*) For advances on property for letting as houses or flats: s. 23. For special advance to purchaser of mortgaged property from the society selling as mortgagee: s. 24.

(*p*) Building Societies Act 1962, s. 8 (1).

(*q*) Building Societies Act 1962, s. 1 (1). An advance may not be made on the security of the member's shares: *Cullerne* v. *London, etc. Building Society* (1890), 25 Q.B.D. 485 (C.A.).

(*r*) *Ibid.*, s. 26 (1). Additional security means any security for the advance other than a mortgage of freehold or leasehold estate, whether effected by the person to whom the advance is made or by any other person and whether it is a legal or an equitable mortgage: *ibid.*, s. 129 (1). Where a charge on a policy of life assurance is taken as additional security for an advance, the value of the policy is to be assessed at an amount not exceeding the surrender value of the policy at the time when the advance is made: *ibid.*, s. 26 (2). As to the amount of the advance where a guarantee is given in pursuance of a continuing arrangement, see *ibid.*, s. 26 (3). A continuing arrangement is an arrangement made between a building society and another person whereby in contemplation of a series of advances comprising excess advances being made by the society to members for the purpose of their being used in defraying the purchase prices of freehold or leasehold estates, that person undertakes to give to the society a series of guarantees each of which is to secure sums payable to the society in respect of such an advance: *ibid.*, s. 129 (1). See Building Societies (Additional Security) Orders.

(*s*) *Ibid.*, s. 33 (1). This recognises the "combined scheme" of repayment under which a single premium policy is taken out on the life of the borrower, or of his wife or child, providing for the payment by the insurance office to the society on the death

Where a society makes an advance to a member for the purpose of its being used in defraying the purchase price of freehold or leasehold estate and takes any security for the advance from another person (unless the only security taken from the third party is a guarantee not secured by a charge on any property) then, except by leave of the court, no sums are recoverable either by the society or by any other person in respect of such advance or in respect of any security given for such advance, whether by the borrower or otherwise, and no rights are exercisable by virtue of any such security unless, before any contract requiring the borrower to repay the advance is entered into, the society gives the borrower a notice in the prescribed form (t). Where a society fails to give the prescribed notice the court may upon application for such leave or upon an application by the member, re-open the transaction, and make such orders as to the sums which may be recovered in respect of the advance and of any security given therefor, and as to the exercise of any rights conferred by the security, and otherwise, as it considers just (u).

Restrictions on second mortgages.—A building society may not advance money on the security of any freehold or leasehold which is subject to a prior mortgage, other than certain charges in favour of local authorities (*e.g.*, a road-making charge), unless the prior mortgage is in favour of the society (w). An advance made on second mortgage, being prohibited by statute, is irrecoverable, the transaction is void, and the borrower may recover his security (x) (though, in appropriate cases, the society may be able to rely on the doctrine of subrogation (y)). And the security being void the discharge of the prior mortgage does not affect the position. If a building society makes an advance in contravention of the provision, the directors of the society who authorised the advance shall be jointly and severally liable for any loss on the advance occasioned to the society (z).

Form of mortgage (a).—There is no special form of mortgage or charge to a building society. The general law of mortgages applies to

---

of the life assured before the end of the mortgage term of the balance outstanding under the mortgage. The amount of the premium is added to the advance and repaid by means of increased payments of capital and interest combined.

(t) *Ibid.*, s. 28. The form is prescribed by the Building Societies Rules 1962, Sched. 1, Pt. 1, Form 1: see 3 Ency. Forms and Precedents (4th Edn.), 709. The court in relation to a transaction in which the advance has not at any time exceeded £600 means the county court, and in relation to any other transaction, the High Court: Building Societies Act 1962, s. 28 (5).

(u) *Ibid.*, s. 28 (4). See *Re Redgrave, Burnley Building Society* v. *Redgrave*, [1951] W.N. 598.

(w) *Ibid.*, s. 32 (1). See *Portsea Island Building Society* v. *Barclay*, [1895] 2 Ch. 298; *Hayes Bridge Estate* v. *Portman Building Society*, [1936] 2 All E.R. 1400. And *Re Abbotts Park Estate (No. 2)*, [1972] 3 All E.R. 148. Although mortgage usually includes a charge (see p. 4, *supra*) it is submitted that the prior mortgage must be a genuine mortgage or a statutory charge required to be treated or a mortgage.

(x) For the difference between illegal and unauthorised loans, see *Lougher* v. *Molyneux*, [1916] 1 K.B. 718; *Re Coltman, Coltman* v. *Coltman* (1881), 19 Ch. D. 64 (C.A.) (loans under the Loans Societies Act 1840).

(y) See p. 214, *infra*.

(z) *Ibid.*, s. 32 (2).

(a) For forms, see 3 Ency. Forms and Precedents (4th Edn.), pp. 724 *et seq*; (1974), 118 Sol. Jo. 589.

mortgages taken by a building society (*b*).   The usual provisions of a mortgage are dealt with elsewhere (*c*) and in this work reference is made, where appropriate, to any special characteristics in relation to building societies.   The principal difference between a building society mortgage and any other is the incorporation in a building society mortgage of the rules of that society (*d*).   The mortgage usually provides that any alteration of the rules will be binding on the mortgagor.   A society has wide powers to alter its rules (*e*), but any alteration must be such as can reasonably be considered to have been within the contemplation of the members of the society when the contract of membership was made (*f*).   The effect of the incorporation of the rules of the society in the mortgage on the transfer of the mortgage is considered elsewhere (*g*).   The transfer, realisation and discharge of a building society mortgage are also considered elsewhere (*h*).

INVESTMENT OF SURPLUS FUNDS

Mortgages excluded.—Provision is made for the investment of the surplus funds of building societies (*i*).   Mortgages on freehold or leasehold property are not amongst the authorised investments.

VII—INDUSTRIAL AND PROVIDENT SOCIETIES

BORROWING POWERS

Generally.—The rules of the society must provide whether the society may contract loans or receive money on deposit from members or others, and, if so, under what conditions, on what security and to what limits of amount (*k*).   Mortgages and charges of industrial and provident societies do not require registration with the Chief Registrar of Friendly Societies (*l*).   A mortgagee is not bound to inquire as to the authority for the mortgage, and the society's receipt is a good discharge for all moneys arising from such transaction or in connection therewith (*m*).

(*b*) *Provident Permanent Building Society* v. *Greenhill* (1878), 9 Ch. D. 122; *Bell* v. *London and South Western Bank*, [1874] W.N. 10.

(*c*) See pp. 27 *et seq.*, *supra*.

(*d*) For further details as to the special features of building society mortgages, see Wurtzburg and Mills, *Building Society Law* (14th Edn.), pp. 129 *et seq.*, especially pp. 164–165 on the relationship of the society's rules to the mortgage.

(*e*) See *Rosenburg* v. *Northumberland Building Society* (1889), 22 Q.B.D. 373 (C.A.); *Bradbury* v. *Wild*, [1893] 1 Ch. 377.

(*f*) *Hole* v. *Garnsey*, [1930] A.C. 472 (H.L.), at p. 500.

(*g*) See pp. 254-255, *infra*.

(*h*) See pp. 254-255, 370, 552-553, *infra*.

(*i*) Building Societies Act 1962, ss. 58–61; Building Societies (Authorised Investments) Orders.

(*k*) Industrial and Provident Societies Act 1965, s. 1, and Sched. 1.   As to housing associations, see p, 192, *supra*. The Act 1965 consolidates the Industrial and Provident Societies Acts 1893 to 1961.

(*l*) As to debentures issued under the Agricultural Credits Act 1928, see p. 131, *supra*.

(*m*) Industrial and Provident Societies Act 1965, s. 30 (1).

Industrial and provident societies may create charges on their personal chattels free from the provisions of the Bills of Sale Acts, 1878 and 1882, if an application is made within fourteen days to record the charge at the central office established under the Friendly Societies Act 1896 (*n*).

LENDING POWERS

Generally.—The rules of a registered industrial and provident society may provide for advances of money to members (a) on the security of real or personal property or, in Scotland, of heritable estate; or (b) if the society is registered to carry on banking business, in any manner customary in the conduct of such business (*o*). Agricultural, horticultural or forestry societies may make advances to members for agricultural, horticultural or forestry purposes without security (*p*).

Discharge of industrial and provident society mortgage.— Special provision is made for the discharge of mortgages to industrial and provident societies (*q*).

VIII—FRIENDLY SOCIETIES

BORROWING POWERS

Generally.—A registered society or branch may borrow on the mortgage of land and buildings if the rules provide that the society or branch may hold land (*r*).

LENDING POWERS

Generally.—The Friendly Societies Act 1974, makes provision for loans to members out of a separate loan fund (*s*). The trustees of a registered society or branch may, with the consent of the committee or of a majority of the members present and entitled to vote in a general meeting, invest the funds of the society or branch or any part thereof, *inter alia*, upon any security expressly directed by the rules of the society or branch, not being personal security, except as in the Act of 1974 authorised with respect to loans (*t*), and in any investments authorised by law for investment of trust funds (*u*).

(*n*) Industrial and Provident Societies Act 1967, s. 1.
(*o*) Industrial and Provident Societies Act 1965, s. 21. For a form of mortgage, see 14 Ency. Forms and Precedents (4th Edn.), pp. 443–446.
(*p*) *Ibid.*, s. 12.
(*q*) See p. 549, *infra*.
(*r*) Friendly Societies Act 1974, s. 51 implies power to borrow; and see s. 23 (2). The Act was brought into force by the Friendly Societies Act 1974 (Commencement) Order 1975. As to deposits of members, see s. 49. For a form of mortgage by trustees of a working men's club registered under the Friendly Societies Act 1896, see 14 Ency. Forms and Precedents (4th Edn.), pp. 297–298.
(*s*) Section 49. The lending of money to members is not generally a purpose in respect of which a society can be registered, but provision is made for specially authorised societies with that purpose: *ibid.*, s. 7, Sched. 1.
(*t*) Friendly Societies Act 1896, ss. 48, 49.
(*u*) *Ibid.*, s. 46 (1) (d), (e). As to powers of trustees to invest in mortgages, see p. 209, *infra*. For a form of mortgage to trustees of a friendly society, see 14 Ency. Forms and Precedents (4th Edn.), pp. 338–340.

Discharge of friendly society mortgage.—Special provision is made for the discharge of mortgages to friendly societies (*x*).

IX—TENANTS FOR LIFE AND STATUTORY OWNERS

POWER TO MORTGAGE

Mortgages for purposes of the settled estate.—The tenant for life or statutory owner (*y*) has power, by a legal mortgage (*z*), to raise money for certain specified purposes. The Settled Land Act 1925 (*a*), provides as follows:

71.—(1) Where money is required (*b*) for any of the following purposes, namely:

    (i) Discharging an incumbrance (*c*) on the settled land or part thereof;

    (ii) Paying for any improvement authorised by this Act or by the settlement (*d*);

    (iii) Equality of exchange;

    (iv) Redeeming a compensation rentcharge in respect of the extinguishment of manorial incidents and affecting the settled land (*e*) . . .

    (ix) (*f*) Payment of the costs of any transaction authorised by this section or either of the two last preceding sections (*g*);

the tenant for life may raise the money so required, on the security of the settled land, or any part thereof, by a legal mortgage (*z*), and the money so raised shall be capital money for that purpose, and may be paid or applied accordingly (*h*).

Subsequent Acts have added further purposes, namely:

    (1) Satisfying any claim under the Landlord and Tenant Act 1927, for compensation for an improvement (*i*);

(*x*) See p. 549, *infra.*

(*y*) For tenant for life, see Settled Land Act 1925, ss. 19, 20, 117 (1) (xxviii). For a statutory owner, see ss. 23, 26, 117 (1) (xxvi).

(*z*) Or charge by way of legal mortgage: Settled Land Act 1925, s. 117 (1) (xi). And see *ibid.*, s. 72 (1). For forms, see 14 Ency. Forms and Precedents (4th Edn.), pp. 219 *et seq.* The covenant for payment by a tenant for life will usually be limited to interest only. Where a tenant for life executes a mortgage as absolute owner in favour of a mortgagee without notice the charge is void: *Weston* v. *Henshaw*, [1950] Ch. 510; doubted in *Re Morgan's Lease*, [1972] Ch. 1; [1971] 2 All E.R. 235; see (1971) 87 L.Q.R. 338 (D. W. Elliott).

(*a*) Replacing and extending Settled Land Act 1882, s. 18.

(*b*) That is reasonably required having regard to the circumstances of the settled land: *Re Clifford, Scott* v. *Clifford*, [1902] 1 Ch. 87.

(*c*) This includes local charges: *Re Pizzi, Scrivener* v. *Aldridge*, [1907] 1 Ch. 67. Incumbrance in this section does not include any annual sum payable only during a life or lives or during a term of years absolute or determinable: s. 71 (2).

(*d*) For improvements authorised by the Act, see s. 83 and Sched. III. The settlement can confer on the tenant for life the additional or large powers: s. 109.

(*e*) See Law of Property Act 1922, s. 139 (3): Manorial Incidents (Extinguishment) Rules 1925, r. 15; Manorial Incidents (Extinguishment) (Amendment) Rules 1935, r. 2.

(*f*) The purposes specified in (iv), (v), (vii) and (viii) which relate to the extinguishment of manorial incidents and the conversion of perpetually renewable leasehold interests are now spent.

(*g*) That is, s. 69 (shifting incumbrances); s. 70 (varying rate of interest, etc.): *infra*, p. 200.

(*h*) For this purpose it must be paid to the trustees of the settlement: s. 75.

(*i*) Landlord and Tenant Act 1927, s. 13 (2).

(2) Paying a coast protection charge or expenses incurred in carrying out work under a works scheme under the Coast Protection Act 1949 (*k*);

(3) Paying certain expenses and making payments under the Landlord and Tenant Act 1954 (*l*);

(4) Paying certain sums recoverable under the Town and County Planning Act 1971 (*m*);

(5) Paying expenses incurred by a tenant for life or statutory owner in connection with proceedings for enfranchising leaseholds or obtaining extensions of leases under the Leasehold Reform Act 1967, and paying of compensation in connection with the exercise of certain overriding rights of a landlord under that Act (*o*).

Furthermore, the court may direct that any costs, charges, or expenses to be paid out of the property subject to a settlement be raised and paid by means of a legal mortgage of the settled land or any part thereof (*p*).

Shifting incumbrances and varying interest.—Under s. 69 of the Settled Land Act 1925, an incumbrance affecting any part of the settled land (whether capable of being overreached on the exercise by the tenant for life of his powers under the Act or not), may, with the consent of the incumbrancer, be charged on any other part of the settled land, or on capital moneys, whether already charged therewith or not, in exoneration of the first mentioned part, and the tenant for life may by a legal mortgage or otherwise make provision accordingly.

By s. 70 where an incumbrance (*q*) affects any part of the settled land, the tenant for life may, with the consent of the incumbrancer, vary the rate of interest charged and any other provisions of the instrument, if any, creating the incumbrance, and, with the like consent, charge the incumbrance on any other part of the settled land, whether already charged therewith or not, or on capital money, by way of additional security or of consolidation of securities, and by a legal mortgage or otherwise make provision accordingly.

Substituted security.—The Settled Land Act 1925, also provides that land acquired by purchase or in exchange or otherwise under the powers of the Act, may be made a substituted security for any charge from which the settled land or any part thereof has theretofore been released on the occasion and in order to (*r*) the completion of a sale,

---

(*k*) Coast Protection Act 1949, s. 11 (2) (a).
(*l*) Landlord and Tenant Act 1954, Sched. 2, para. 6.
(*m*) Town and County Planning Act 1971, s. 275.
(*o*) Leasehold Reform Act 1967, s. 6 (5), Sched. 2, para. 9 (1).
(*p*) Settled Land Act 1925, ss. 92, 114.
(*q*) Incumbrance in this section includes any annual sum payable during a life or lives or during a term of years absolute or determinable, but in any such case an additional security must be effected so as only to create a charge or security similar to the original charge or security: s. 70 (2).
(*r*) Some word or words are missing in the Act.

exchange or other disposition (s). On land being so acquired, any person who, by the direction of the tenant for life, so conveys it as to subject it to any legal estate or charge by way of legal mortgage, is not concerned to inquire whether or not it it proper that it shall be so subjected (t).

Payment of capital money to trustees.—Since money raised under the statutory powers is capital money it must be paid to not fewer than two persons as trustee of the settlement, unless the trustee is a trust corporation (u). The tenant for life must also give notice to the trustees of his intention to mortgage or charge the land (x). This must be a notice of each specific transaction contemplated (y). But a lender dealing in good faith with the tenant for life is not concerned to inquire concerning the giving of the notice (z).

Overreaching effect of mortgage.—A legal mortgage by the tenant for life under the statutory powers is effectual to give the mortgagee a title free from the limitations of the settlement, and from all estates, interests, and charges subsisting or to arise thereunder, except legal estates and legal charges having priority to the settlement, and such estates and charges created for securing money actually raised at the date of the deed (a).

Additional powers.—The settlement may confer powers to mortgage additional to or larger than the statutory powers and such powers are exercisable by the tenant for life as if they were conferred by the Act (b). The Act contains a general power for the tenant for life to effect any transaction under an order of the court (c).

Restrictions on powers.—The statutory power to mortgage is not capable of restriction (d).

Tenant for life as trustee.—A tenant for life, in exercising any power under the Act, must have regard to the interests of all parties entitled under the settlement, and is, in relation to the exercise of such

---

(s) Settled Land Act 1925, s. 82 (1). But where the charge does not affect the whole of the settled land, the land acquired is not to be subjected, unless it is acquired with the proceeds of sale of the land which was subject to the charge; with a corresponding provision for the case of exchange: *ibid.* For a form of charge by way of substituted security by a tenant for life, see 14 Ency. Forms and Precedents (4th Edn.), pp. 406-408.

(t) *Ibid.*, s. 82 (2).

(u) *Ibid.*, s. 94. It may be applied, *inter alia*, in discharge of incumbrances: s. 73 (1) (ii). Though the advance is paid to the trustees the tenant for life should be the member, when the advance is made by a building society, because he holds the legal estate in the property.

(x) *Ibid.*, s. 101 (1).

(y) *Re Ray's Settled Estates* (1884), 25 Ch. D. 464. Section 101 (2), which allows a general notice in certain cases, does not extend to mortgages.

(z) Section 101 (5).

(a) Section 72 (2).

(b) Settled Land Act 1925, s. 109 (1), (2). And any power conferred on the trustees will be exercisable by the tenant for life as if it were an additional power conferred on him: *ibid.*, s. 108 (2).

(c) *Ibid.*, s. 64; Settled Land and Trustee Acts (Court's General Powers) Act 1943, ss. 1, 2; Emergency Laws (Miscellaneous Provisions) Act 1953, s. 9. And see *Re White-Popham Settled Estates*, [1936] Ch. 725 (C.A.); [1936] 2 All E.R. 1486.

(d) *Ibid.*, ss. 104 (1), (2), 106.

powers by him deemed to be in the position and to have the duties and liabilities of a trustee for those parties (*e*).

Mortgage to tenant for life.—A mortgage or charge of the settled land may be made to the tenant for life. In that case the trustees of the settlement have, in addition to their powers as trustee, all the powers of a tenant for life as to negotiating and completing the transaction (*f*).

Mortgages to give effect to the beneficial interests.—The Settled Land Act 1925, provides:

> **16.**—(1):
>
> (iii) Where—
>> (a) any principal sum is required to be raised on the security of the settled land, by virtue of any trust, or by reason of the exercise of an equitable power affecting the settled land, or by any person or persons who under the settlement is or are entitled or together entitled to or has or have a general power of appointment over the settled land, whether subject to any equitable charges or powers of charging subsisting under the settlement or not; or
>> (b) the settled land is subject to any equitable charge for securing money actually raised and affecting the whole estate the subject of the settlement;
>
> the estate owner shall be bound, if so requested in writing (*g*), to create such legal estate or charge by way of legal mortgage as may be required for raising the money or giving legal effect to the equitable charge (*h*):

But this is subject to the proviso that, so long as the settlement remains subsisting, any legal mortgage so created shall take effect and be expressed to take effect subject to any equitable charges under the settlement which have priority to the interest of the person by or on whose behalf the money is required to be raised, unless the persons entitled to the prior charges consent in writing to the same being postponed, though such consent need not be expressed in the mortgage (*i*).

It is further provided by s. 16 that:

> (2) Where a mortgage or charge is expressed to be made by an estate owner pursuant to this section (*k*), then, in favour of the mortgagee or chargee and persons deriving title under him, the same shall take effect in priority to all the trusts of the settlement and all equitable interests and powers subsisting or to arise under the settlement except those to which it is expressly made subject, and shall so take effect whether the mortgagee or chargee has notice

---

(*e*) *Ibid.*, s. 107 (1). See *Hampden* v. *Earl of Buckinghamshire*, [1893] 2 Ch. 531 (C.A.); *Re Charteris, Charteris* v. *Biddulph*, [1917] 2 Ch. 379; *Re Gladwin's Trust*, [1919] 1 Ch. 232. This provision does not affect the title of a mortgagee, but affects the tenant for life personally with liability as a trustee: *Re Marquis of Ailesbury's Settled Estates*, [1892] 1 Ch. 506 (C.A.), at pp. 535, 536.

(*f*) *Ibid.*, s. 68. For a form, see 14 Ency. Forms and Precedents (4th Edn.), p. 227.

(*g*) Where a tenant for life has power to raise a sum for his own benefit, the request should not be made by himself to himself, but should be made by the person who advances the money: *Re Egerton Settled Estates*, [1926] Ch. 574.

(*h*) Under this provision money can be raised for portions. See also Land Registration Act 1925, s. 90; Land Registration Rules 1925, r. 144.

(*i*) Settled Land Act 1925, s. 16 (1) (iii), proviso. And see Land Registration Rules 1925, r. 156.

(*k*) *N.b.* to have the overreaching effect of this sub-section the mortgage must be expressed to be made pursuant thereto.

of such interests or powers or not, and the mortgagee or chargee shall not be concerned to see that a case has arisen to authorise the mortgage or charge, or that no more money than was wanted was raised (*l*).

A tenant for life, as estate owner, can also create a legal mortgage for the purpose of giving effect to an agreement for a mortgage, or a charge or lien, whether or not arising by operation of law, if the agreement, charge or lien ought to have priority over the settlement (*m*).

Mortgage of land subject to family charges.—The Settled Land Act 1925, extended the meaning of settled land to include, not only the ordinary case of land limited in trust for persons by way of succession but various other cases where land is not vested in some person absolutely and beneficially (*n*). In particular, land is settled land where it is subject to family charges (*o*). In such a case the estate owner can only create a legal mortgage free from the charges if the Settled Land Act procedure as to the appointment of trustees and the execution of a vesting deed are observed (*p*).

By the Law of Property (Amendment) Act 1926, a beneficial owner in fee simple subject to such family charges as would constitute the land settled land may execute a legal mortgage or charge by way of legal mortgage subject to such family charges as if the land had not been settled land and without compliance with the Settled Land Act procedure (*q*).

Mortgage by trustees where tenant for life has ceased to have a substantial interest.—If is shown to the satisfaction of the court that a tenant for life who has by reason of bankruptcy, assignment, incumbrance, or otherwise ceased in the opinion of the court to have a substantial interest in his estate or interest in the settled land or any part thereof, has unreasonably refused to exercise any of the powers conferred on him by the Settled Land Act 1925, or consents to such an order as is hereinafter mentioned, the court may, upon the application of any person interested in the settled land or the part thereof affected, make an order authorising the trustees of the settlement to exercise, in the name and on behalf of the tenant for life, any of the powers of a tenant for life under the Settled Land Act 1925, in relation to the settled land or the part thereof affected, either generally and in such manner and for such period as the court may think fit, or in a particular instance (*r*).

Mortgage of tenant for life's beneficial interest.—For mortgages of beneficial interests in trust funds, see p. 115, *supra*.

(*l*) For a form of mortgage under s. 16, see 14 Ency. Forms and Precedents (4th Edn.), pp. 260 *et seq.*
(*m*) Settled Land Act 1925, s. 16 (4). And see s. 16 (5), (7), for mortgage under order of the court.
(*n*) Section 1 (1).
(*o*) *Ibid.*, s. 1 (1) (v).
(*p*) *Ibid.*, s. 13.
(*q*) Section 1.
(*r*) Settled Land Act 1925, s. 24. See *Re Thornhill's Settlement*, [1940] 4 All E.R. 83; affd., [1941] Ch. 24 (C.A.); [1940] 4 All E.R. 249. A person dealing with the tenant for life is not affected by such an order, unless it is for the time being registered under the Land Charges Act 1972, as an order affecting land: see Land Charges Act 1972, s. 6.

Mortgage of tenant in tail's equitable interest.—Where the tenant in tail is tenant in tail in possession he will generally have the legal estate in the entailed property vested in him as estate owner (s) and as such he will have the power of mortgaging of a tenant for life (t). As regards his equitable interest in entailed lands the tenant in tail has special statutory powers of disposing of such interest (u) apart from the general powers of disposition conferred on limited owners under the Settled Land Act 1925 (x). If the tenant in tail is in possession he may execute by deed a mortgage in the form of a conveyance of his equitable interest in fee simple or any less interest (y). If he is not in possession, unless the mortgage is made with the consent of the protector of the settlement, it will convey to the mortgagee only an equitable interest in the nature of a base fee (z).

Mortgages by charity trustees.—Land vested or to be vested in trustees on or for charitable, ecclesiastical or public trusts or purposes is deemed to be settled land and the trustees of the charity have in reference to the land all the powers conferred by the Settled Land Act 1925, on a tenant for life and trustees (a). But the powers are exercisable subject to such consents or orders, if any, being obtained as would, if the Settled Land Act 1925, had not been passed, have been requisite if the transaction were being effected under an express power conferred by the instrument creating the trust (b).

No land which forms part of the permanent endowment of a charity, or which is or has been occupied for the purpose of the charity, may be mortgaged or charged without an order of the court or the Charity Commissioners (c). A transaction entered into without the requisite consent is void (d), save that a mortgage of land which is or has been occupied for the purposes of the charity, which is made without consent, is valid in favour of a bona fide mortgagee for money or money's worth (e). There are three exceptions to the requirement for consent (f). First a transaction authorised by statute or taking effect thereunder or under a scheme does not require consent (g). Secondly a large number of charitable bodies such as universities, and including industrial and

---

(s) Settled Land Act 1925, ss. 4 (2), 6 (b), 7 (1)–(4), 9 (2), 20 (1) (i), 117 (1) (xxviii). If he is in a position to bar the entail and become absolute owner he will, of course, be able to mortgage as such.

(t) *Supra.*

(u) Under the Fines and Recoveries Act 1833, s. 15. And see Law of Property (Amendment) Act 1924, s. 9, Sched. 9.

(x) By Pt. II (ss. 35–72).

(y) Fines and Recoveries Act 1833, ss. 15, 40. Enrolment was abolished by the Law of Property Act 1925, s. 133 (now repealed spent by Statute Law (Repeals) Act 1969).

(z) For a form of mortgage by a tenant in tail in remainder without consent, see 14 Ency. Forms and Precedents (4th Edn.), pp. 711-714.

(a) Settled Land Act 1925, s. 29 (1).

(b) *Ibid.*, s. 29 (2).

(c) Charities Act 1960, s. 29 (1), (2). The concurrent jurisdiction of the Minister of Education for educational charities was abolished by the Education Act 1973, s. 1 (1), (5).

(d) *Bishop of Bangor* v. *Parry*, [1891] 2 Q.B. 277 and see *Michael Richards Properties, Ltd.* v. *St. Saviour's Parish, Southwark*, [1975] 3 All E.R. 416; (1976) 40 Conv. (N.S.) 173.

(e) Charities Act 1960, s. 29 (2).

(f) *Ibid.*, s. 29 (3), (4).

(g) *Ibid.*, s. 29 (3). And the section does not apply to a disposition of an advowson.

provident societies and friendly societies (or a branch of one), are exempt from the jurisdiction of the Charity Commissioners (*h*). Thirdly a large number of charities, mostly religious charities, are excepted by order of the Charity Commissioners from the full effect of the provisions of the Charities Act 1960, restricting dealing with charity property and are subject only to modified restraint (*c*).

The terms of the charity trust deed may also require the observance of certain conditions before any disposition.

Form of mortgage by charity trustees.—If consent to the mortgage is required and given the consent should be recited. The covenant for repayment should be in the limited form for trustees (*k*), and otherwise the mortgage should be in the form of mortgage by trustees (*l*).

Universities and colleges.—Universities and their colleges are, as corporations and charities, subject to restrictions in dealing with their lands. Oxford, Cambridge and Durham and the colleges therein are no longer subject to the further restrictions imposed by the Universities and College Estates Act 1925 (*m*).

X—MORTGAGES FOR IMPROVEMENTS

Under the Improvement of Land Acts (*n*).—As previously stated (*o*) power to borrow money for improvements is conferred on tenants for life by the Settled Land Act 1925. Powers of improvement had been given to landlowners generally (*p*) by the Improvement of Land Act 1864, and it may still be desirable to make use of the 1864 Act.

The 1864 Act gave in s. 9 a list of improvements which were to be within the Act (*q*) and subsequent Acts (*r*) extended that list. Section 9 of the 1864 Act is in effect superseded, and the improvements which can be dealt with under the 1864 Act are those which are authorised by the Settled Land Act 1925 (*s*), and a number of other

---

(*h*) *Ibid.*, Sched. 2.

(*i*) For regulations, see Charities (Baptist Congregational and Unitarian Churches and Presbyterian Church of England) Regulations 1961; Charities (Methodist Church) Regulations 1961; Charities (Society of Friends, Fellowship of Independent Evangelical Churches and Presbyterian Church of Wales) Regulations 1962; Charities (Church of England) Regulations 1963; Charities (Religious Premises) Regulations 1962.

(*k*) See p. 209, *infra*.

(*l*) For forms of mortgages by charities, see 14 Ency. Forms and Precedents (4th Edn.), pp. 273 *et seq.*

(*m*) See Universities and College Estates Act 1964, especially Sched. 1, Pt. 1, para. 6.

(*n*) See, generally, 23 Halsbury's Laws (3rd Edn.), Land Improvement.

(*o*) See p. 199, *supra*.

(*p*) For the definition of landowner, see Improvement of Land Act 1864, ss. 3, 10, 20, 24, 30.

(*q*) These improvements were of an agricultural nature.

(*r*) Settled Land Act 1882, s. 30; Settled Land Act 1890, s. 13; Housing of the Working Classes Act 1890, s. 74 (1); Housing, Town Planning, &c. Act 1909, s. 7 (1); Law of Property Act 1922, s. 65 (1); Agricultural Credits Act 1923, s. 3 (4).

(*s*) The whole of the Settled Land Acts 1882 to 1890, with the exception of s. 30 of the Act of 1882, were repealed, and their provisions, with the amendments made by the Law of Property Act 1922, and the Law of Property (Amendment) Act 1924, consolidated in the Settled Land Act 1925.

Acts (*t*). The authorised improvements also extend to any operation
incident to or necessary or proper in the execution of the specifically
authorised works, or necessary or proper for carrying into effect any
of the specifically mentioned purposes, or for securing the full benefit
of any of those works or purposes (*u*).

In order that an improvement may be sanctioned it must be shown
that it will effect a permanent increase of the yearly value of the land
exceeding the yearly amount to be charged thereon (*x*).

Charge for improvements.—In the case of improvements to
which the 1864 Act applies the Minister of Agriculture, Fisheries and
Food, when satisfied that the improvements or part thereof have been
properly executed, may execute a charge on the land or some sufficient
part thereof, for the sum, by the provisional, or other sanctioning,
order, expressed to be chargeable (or for a proportional part thereof
if only part of the improvement has been executed), together with
interest, and for the amount which shall have been paid in respect
of the purchase of adjoining lands, or of any easement or right affecting
adjoining lands, with interest (*y*).

Absolute order by way of rent charge.—The charge is created
by an absolute order, and by way of rentcharge, payable half-yearly,
for the term of years fixed by the provisional or other sanctioning
order (*z*). The charge should be registered under the Land Charges Act
1972, as a land charge in Class A (*a*).

Effect and priority of charge.—From the date of the absolute
order, the grantee has a charge upon the lands for the principal money
from time to time remaining undischarged by payment of the rentcharge
with interest at the dates expressed, and with priority over every other
than existing and future charge and incumbrance affecting the lands
or estates and interests, whether created under the powers of any Act
of Parliament or otherwise, except charges under any Act authorising
advances of public money for improvement of land, and charges created
under the 1864 Act, or of prior date created under any other existing
Act authorising the charging of lands with the expense of and incident
to their provements (*b*). In view of the priority given to such rent-

---

(*t*) See Public Health Act 1936, s. 33 (sewage works for agricultural purposes);
Limited Owners Residences Acts 1870 and 1871; Limited Owners Reservoirs and
Water Supply Further Facilities Act 1877; District Councils (Water Supply Facilities)
Act 1897; Improvement of Land Act 1899; Land Drainage Act 1961, s. 44.

(*u*) Settled Land Act 1925, s. 83. (*x*) Improvement of Land Act 1864, s. 25.

(*y*) Improvement of Land Act 1864, s. 49. As to charges for public improvements,
see ss. 57, 58.

(*z*) Improvement of Land Act 1864, s. 51.

(*a*) And note s. 4 (1), (4) of the Land Charges Act 1972, re-enacting the Law of
Property Act 1969, s. 27, which exempted such charges made after the commencement
of the 1969 Act from the provisions of s. 11 of the Land Charges Act 1925, so that they
no longer ranked as mortgages; and if a charge was then already registered building
societies and other bodies might advance money on land subject to such charge. Where
the land is registered the charge is protected by notice under the Land Registration
Act 1925, s. 49 (1) (c): see Land Registration Act 1925, s. 59 (2); Land Registration
Rules 1925, r. 155.

(*b*) Improvement of Land Act 1864, s. 59.

The charge created under the Limited Owners Residences Acts 1870 and 1871, does
not take priority over an incumbrance affecting the land charged at the time when the
charge was created: see s. 9 of the 1871 Act; *Provident Clerks' Mutual Life Assurance
Association* v. *Law Life Assurance Society*, [1897] W.N. 73.

charges in appropriate cases the mortgage should contain a clause prohibiting the obtaining of loans under the Improvement of Land Acts. The person entitled to a rentcharge may assign it to a third party, either absolutely or by way of security (c).

Loans by Agricultural Mortgage Corporation Limited.— Where a loan has been made by the Agricultural Mortgage Corporation Limited (d), for defraying the expenses of an improvement of any kind authorised by Part 1 of the Third Schedule to the Settled Land Act 1925, and the loan is, under the terms of the mortgage securing the loan, repayable by instalments (e), the repayment secured by the mortgage is deemed to constitute an improvement rentcharge which may be redeemed out of capital money, and when so redeemed the tenant for life must maintain and insure the improvement (f).

XI—TRUSTEES

BORROWING POWERS

Power of trustees to mortgage.—Trustees have no power to raise money on mortgage unless they are expressly or implicitly authorised to do so by the instrument creating the trust, or unless power is conferred on them by statute. Trustees empowered to mortgage may also raise the incidental costs by mortgage of the same property (g).

A power for trustees to mortgage has sometimes been implied in a power to sell (h), where an absolute conversion of the land is not necessary for the purpose of effecting the object of the power, such as the raising of money to satisfy a particular charge. But a mortgage cannot, apart from statute, be made under an absolute trust for sale (i). And if the raising of a charge by sale is forbidden, the prohibition extends also to raising it by mortgage, since this may cause the loss of the land by sale or foreclosure (k). A power to mortgage may also be implied from powers of management which necessitate the expenditure of capital (l).

When trustees are empowered to raise money for particular purposes at their absolute discretion, the court will not interfere with their discretion as to the occasion, or the manner of exercising the power, or the refusal to exercise it in any particular manner, though they are bound to effect the general purpose (m).

Statutory powers of mortgaging.—Powers of mortgaging are conferred either on trustees generally or on trustees for sale as follows:

(c) Improvement of Land Act 1864, s. 65. (d) See p. 128, *supra.*
(e) See Agricultural Credits Act 1928, s. 2 (3) (c); Agricultural Credits Act 1932, s. 2.
(f) Agricultural Credits Act 1932, s. 3 (3).
(g) *Armstrong* v. *Armstrong* (1874), L.R. 18 Eq. 541.
(h) *Mills* v. *Banks* (1724), 3 P. Wms. 1; *Stroughill* v. *Anstey* (1852), 1 De G.M. & G. 635.
(i) *Devaynes* v. *Robinson* (1857), 24 Beav. 86. See *Re Suenson-Taylors's Settlement, Moores* v. *Moores*, [1974] 3 All E.R. 397.
(k) *Bennett* v. *Wyndham* (1857), 23 Beav. 521.
(l) *Re Bellinger, Durrell* v. *Bellinger*, [1898] 2 Ch. 534.
(m) *Tempest* v. *Lord Camoys* (1882), 21 Ch. D. 571, distinguished in *Re Courtier, Coles* v. *Courtier* (1886), 34 Ch. D. 136.

Trustee Act, 1925:

16.—(1) Where trustees are authorised by the instrument, if any, creating the trust or by law to pay or apply capital money subject to the trust for any purpose or in any manner, they shall have and shall be deemed always to have had power to raise the money required by sale, conversion, calling in, or mortgage of all or any part of the trust property for the time being in possession.

(2) This section applies notwithstanding anything to the contrary contained in the instrument, if any, creating the trust, but does not apply to trustees of property held for charitable purposes, or to trustees of a settlement for the purposes of the Settled Land Act 1925, not being also statutory owners.

Law of Property Act 1925:

28.—(1) Trustees for sale shall, in relation to land or to manorial incidents and to the proceeds of sale, have all the powers of a tenant for life and the trustees of a settlement under the Settled Land Act 1925 (n), including in relation to the land the powers of management conferred by that Act during a minority (o): and (subject to any express trust to the contrary) all capital money arising under the said powers shall, unless paid or applied for any purpose authorised by the Settled Land Act 1925, be applicable in the same manner as if the money represented proceeds of sale arising under the trust for sale.

The former of these provisions applies, with the exceptions mentioned in sub-s. (2), to trustees generally, and enables them to raise money for any purpose to which, under the trust instrument or by law, capital money can be applied (p). The latter applies only to trustees for sale, and, in the case of a personal settlement, puts them in a position corresponding to that of a tenant for life, and enables them to exercise a tenant for life's statutory power of mortgaging. Both provisions apply to trusts created before as well as those created after 1 January, 1926 (q).

Mortgage at instance of beneficiaries.—The above provisions contemplate that the initiative in raising money is taken by the trustees. It is also provided:

Law of Property Act 1925, s. 3 (r):

(1) (b) (ii) Where, by reason of the exercise of any equitable power or under any trust affecting the proceeds of sale, any principal sum is required to be

---

(n) See ss. 16, 71; pp. 199, 202, *supra.*

(o) See the Settled Land Act 1925, s. 102, p. 215, *infra.* The Law of Property (Amendment) Act 1926, s. 7, Sched., adds at this point— and where by statute settled land is or becomes vested in the trustees of the settlement upon the statutory trusts, such trustees and their successors in office, shall also have all the additional or larger powers (if any) conferred by the settlement on the tenant for life, statutory owner, or trustees of the settlement.

(p) The statutory power does not permit the mortgaging of the trust fund to raise monies for the purchase of further investments: *Re Suenson-Taylor's Settlement, Moores v. Moores, supra.* Where the trustees and the beneficiaries are the same persons the trustees have full power of mortgaging as beneficial owners. And generally the concurrence of all the beneficial owners in a mortgage by trustees makes it unnecessary to have recourse to their statutory powers: Laws of Property Act 1925, s. 3 (1) (b) (ii), *supra.*

(q) Trustee Act 1925, s. 69 (1); Law of Property Act 1925, s. 28 (5).

(r) The object of the section is to provide for the enforcement against the estate owner of equitable interests or powers in or over land. Sub-section (1) (a) makes the like provision for settled land; and sub-s. (1) (c) provides for cases where the estate owner holds neither under a settlement nor as trustee for sale.

See also Law of Property Act 1925, s. 28 (3) (mortgage to provide equality money).

raised . . . then, unless the claim is satisfied out of the net proceeds of sale, the trustees for sale shall (if so requested in writing) be bound to transfer or create such legal estates, to take effect in priority to the trust for sale, as may be required for raising the money by way of legal mortgage. . . .

Here, the initiative is taken by the person entitled to have a principal sum raised.

Form of mortgage (s).—A trustee or other fiduciary owner who mortgages the trust estate does not usually covenant to pay the money borrowed. If there is such a covenant it should be limited to payment only out of money coming into the trustee's hands as trustee (t). However, where the trustees are also the persons beneficially entitled the mortgage will take the same form as a mortgage by an absolute owner and accordingly they will then covenant to pay and demise or charge the property as beneficial owners. Where the trustees are not the same persons as those beneficially entitled the mortgage should contain a provision excluding their personal liability (s), for the demise or charge is in itself sufficient to imply personal liability unless the mortgage negatives it (u). A trustee may not permit the inclusion in the mortgage of a consolidation clause extending to mortgages other than those made by him as trustee (w).

Protection of mortgagee.—In all cases where trustees raise money by mortgage and the mortgage purports to be made under a trust or power vested in them, the mortgagee is not concerned to see that the money is wanted, or that no more than is wanted is raised, or otherwise as to the application thereof (x). Since the mortgage money is capital money, the mortgagee must not pay it to fewer then two trustees, unless the trustee is a trust corporation (y).

LENDING POWERS

Power to lend money on mortgage.—Trustees must either have express power under the trust to lend money on mortgage (z), or rely on the statutory power under the Trustee Investments Act 1961. That Act authorises trustees to invest in mortgages of freehold property in England and Wales or Northern Ireland and of leasehold property in those countries of which the unexpired term at the time of the investment is not less than 60 years and in loans on heritable security in Scotland (a). Mortgages are narrower-range investments requiring

---

(s) For forms of mortgage by trustees, see 14 Ency. Forms and Precedents (4th Edn.), pp. 253 *et seq.*

(t) *Re Robinson's Settlement, Gant* v. *Hobbs,* [1912] 1 Ch. 717 (C.A.), at p. 729; and see p. 294, *infra.* (u) *Yates* v. *Aston* (1843), 4 Q.B. 182.

(w) *Thorne* v. *Thorne,* [1893] 3 Ch. 196; and see *Cruickshank* v. *Duffin* (1872), L.R. 13 Eq. 555.

(x) Trustee Act 1925, s. 17. A mortgagee is not concerned even if he has actual notice that the purpose of the borrowing is unauthorised.

(y) Trustee Act 1925, s. 14.

(z) See generally Lewin on *Trusts* (16th Edn.), pp. 361 *et seq.*

(a) Trustee Investments Act 1961, s. 1 (1), and 1st Sched., Pt. II, para. 13, and Pt. IV, para. 5. For the definition of mortgage, see s. 17 (4), and Trustee Act 1925, s. 58 (7). For the relationship between the 1961 Act and other powers of investment, see Trustee Investments Act 1961, s. 3. And see generally, Lewin, *ubi sup.,* pp. 314 *et seq.*

advice (*a*). The Trustee Act 1925 (*b*), and the 1961 Act (*c*) impose duties on trustees in the exercise of their powers of investing in mortgages (*d*).

Trustees must not lend trust money to one of themselves on mortgage (*e*).

Form of mortgage (*f*).—A mortgage to trustees should generally be a first legal mortgage. The Trustee Investment Act 1961, which authorises trustees to invest in mortgages makes no distinction between the types of mortgage in which trustees may invest (*g*) and it may be that the former restrictions against second, equitable and contributory mortgages no longer apply (*h*).

A mortgage to trustees generally takes the usual form as for a mortgage to a single mortgagee with only those variations necessitated by there being more than one mortgagee. So it is not usual to disclose the trusts, and, indeed, any person dealing in good faith with the mortgagee, or mortgagor if the mortgage has been wholly or partially discharged, is not concerned with any trust at any time affecting the mortgage money (*i*). It is the practice to recite that the mortgage money has been advanced on joint account. This gives no notice of the trusts (*k*) and enables the survivor to give a good receipt for the mortgage money (*l*).

It is not a breach of trust for the trustees to agree to the exclusion of the statutory power of sale (*m*).

XII—PERSONAL REPRESENTATIVES

Power to mortgage personal estate.—An executor or administrator has always had power, by virtue of his office, to raise money, by sale or mortgage of the personal property of the testator, including leaseholds, for payment of debts and other purposes of administration (*n*). The power enables an executor to mortgage even property specifically bequeathed. But it ceases as to property specifically

---

(*a*) See note (*a*), p. 209.
(*b*) Sections 8, 9, 10.
(*c*) Section 6.
(*d*) See, generally, Lewin on *Trusts, ubi sup.*, pp. 314 *et seq.*
(*e*) *Stickney* v. *Sewell* (1835), 1 My. & Cr. 8, 14, 15; *Francis* v. *Francis* (1854), 5 De G.M. & G. 108; *Fletcher* v. *Green* (1864), 33 Beav. 426.
(*f*) For a form of mortgage to trustees, see 14 Ency. Forms and Precedents (4th Edn.), p. 201; and see Precedent 1C in the Appendix, *infra*.
(*g*) *Cf.* Trustee Act 1925, s. 1.
(*h*) See, generally, Lewin on *Trusts, ubi sup.*, 370. Investment in sub-mortgages was permitted: *Smethurst* v. *Hastings* (1885), 30 Ch. D. 490. Trustees could only join in a contributory mortgage if expressly empowered to do so: *Webb* v. *Jonas* (1888), 39 Ch. D. 660; *Re Dive*, [1909] 1 Ch. 328; and *In the Will of MacPherson*, [1963] N.S.W.R. 268.
(*i*) Law of Property Act 1925, s. 113. See p. 255, *infra*.
(*k*) See the cases in footnote (*l*), p. 255, *infra*.
(*l*) Law of Property Act 1925, s. 111. It is not strictly necessary that this recital be made, since in the absence of express provision s. 111 (1) (b) will apply.
(*m*) *Farrar* v. *Barraclough* (1854), 2 Sm. & G. 231.
(*n*) *Mead* v. *Lord Orrery* (1745), 3 Atk. 235; *Scott* v. *Tyler* (1788), 2 Dick. 712; *Vane* v. *Rigden* (1870), 5 Ch. App. 663.

bequeathed as soon as the executors have assented to the bequest, even though the bequest is to the executors themselves as trustees (*o*). A mortgagee from an executor need not have any recital of the purpose for which the money is raised (*p*), and is equally protected whether the mortgage be legal or equitable (*q*). The power of disposition is not affected by a mere administration order, if no receiver has been appointed nor any injunction granted to restrain the personal representative from dealing with the assets (*r*).

When mortgage invalid.—Prima facie, when a personal representative is raising money on the property of the deceased, the presumption is that the money is required to pay debts or for some other purpose of administration (*s*), and if there are no circumstances to raise an inference to the contrary (*t*), and the transaction is consistent with the duty of a personal representative, it will be supported (*u*). But if the nature of the transaction affords intrinsic evidence that the executor is not acting in the execution of his duty, but is committing a breach of trust, as where the mortgage is given to secure a personal debt of the executor, the mortgagee, being a party to the breach of trust, does not hold the property discharged from the trusts, but it remains subject to the requirements of administration just as in the hands of the executor (*x*). And it is the same in the case of an advance made for the private purposes of the executor if notice of the fact is brought home to the mortgagee (*y*). But a mortgage of the estate to secure the private debt of an executor who is beneficially interested will be good to the extent of his beneficial interest, provided the security is effected in terms which show an intention to charge that interest, and not to mortgage in his representative capacity (*z*), though, if the executor is indebted to the estate, the mortgagee will be postponed to the claim of the estate (*a*). If the executor, on borrowing the money, represents that "part of it" is required for executorship purposes the onus of showing how much was so required is on the borrower (*b*).

Power to mortgage real estate.—The Administration of Estates Act 1925, extends over real estate the same powers of disposition which personal representatives had at common law in regard to personal

---

(*o*) *Attenborough* v. *Solomon*, [1913] A.C. 76; *Wise* v. *Whitburn*, [1924] 1 Ch. 460.
(*p*) *Bonney* v. *Ridgard* (1784), 1 Cox Eq. Cas. 145.
(*q*) *Scott* v. *Tyler, supra.*
(*r*) *Berry* v. *Gibbons* (1873), 8 Ch. App. 747; *Re Barrett, Whitaker* v. *Barrett* (1889), 43 Ch. D. 70; Administration of Estates Act 1925, s. 2 (1).
(*s*) *Re Venn and Furze's Contract*, [1894] 2 Ch. 101; *Re Henson, Chester* v. *Henson,* [1908] 2 Ch. 356.
(*t*) *Ricketts* v. *Lewis* (1882), 20 Ch. D. 745.
(*u*) *Nugent* v. *Gifford* (1738), 1 Atk. 463; *Mead* v. *Lord Orrery, supra; Bonney* v. *Ridgard, supra; Scott* v. *Tyler, supra; M'Leod* v. *Drummond* (1810), 17 Ves. 712; *Keane* v. *Robarts* (1819), 4 Madd. 332; *Re Whistler* (1887), 35 Ch. D. 561.
(*x*) *M'Leod* v. *Drummond, supra; Keane* v. *Robarts, supra.*
(*y*) *Bonney* v. *Ridgard, supra; Scott* v. *Tyler, supra; M'Leod* v. *Drummond, supra.* And circumstances of gross negligence on the part of the mortgagee are sufficient to defeat his mortgage, though there is no direct fraud: *Hill* v. *Simpson* (1802), 7 Ves. 152. But the claim to set aside the mortgage will be barred after a great length of time: *Bonney* v. *Ridgard, supra.* (*z*) *Farhall* v. *Farhall* (1871), 7 Ch. App. 123.
(*a*) *Cole* v. *Muddle* (1852), 10 Hare 186.
(*b*) *Carter* v. *Sanders* (1854), 2 Drew. 248.

estate (*c*). This extension is further declared subsequently in that Act
as follows:

> **39.**—(1) In dealing with the real and personal estate of the deceased his
> personal representatives shall, for purposes of administration, or during a
> minority of any beneficiary or the subsistence of any life interest, or until
> the period of distribution arrives, have—
>
> > (i) the same powers and discretions, including power to raise money by
> > mortgage or charge (whether or not by deposit of documents), as a
> > personal representative had before the commencement of this Act,
> > with respect to personal estate vested in him, and such power of
> > raising money by mortgage may in the case of land be exercised by
> > way of legal mortgage (*d*).

Notwithstanding the wide terms of this provision it applies only
while the estate of the deceased remains vested in the personal
representatives as such. It does not apply to an estate which has
become vested in trustees, whether the personal representatives
themselves or other persons (*e*). On a mortgage of real estate all the
personal representatives must concur, or an order of the court must be
obtained, except that where probate is granted to one or some of two
or more persons named as executors, whether or not power is reserved
to the other or others to prove, the mortgage may be made by the
proving executors for the time being (*f*).

Protection of mortgagee.—A conveyance of a legal estate made
after 1925 by a personal representative to a purchaser for money or
money's worth, is not invalidated by reason only that the purchaser
may have notice that all debts, liabilities, etc., have been discharged
or provided for (*g*). A written receipt of a personal representative
for any money payable to him is a sufficient discharge to the person
paying the money, and effectually exonerates him from seeing to the
application or being answerable for any loss or misapplication thereof (*h*)

A mortgagee dealing with a personal representative is not concerned
to see that the money advanced on the mortgage is wanted, or that no
more than is wanted is raised, or otherwise as to the application
thereof (*i*).

(*c*) Section 2 (1). Before the Land Transfer Act 1897, there was no power to mortgage
the deceased's real estate for payment of his debts, unless by his will he created a charge
of debts, which gave the executors a power of sale of the charged property. This gave
rise to difficulties because it was necessary on a sale of the property charged either to
obtain the concurrence of both executors and devisee, or, if a title was taken from a
devisee, for the purchaser to satisfy himself that the debts were paid, or to procure
the executor's authority for payment of the purchase money to the devisee. After that
Act real estate devolved on the deceased's personal representatives and they had over
it the same powers for the purposes of administration as with regard to personal estate.

(*d*) And by para. (ii) personal representatives are given all the powers conferred by
law on trustees for sale. For the mortgage powers of trustees, see p. 207, *supra*. See
also s. 40 (power to raise money to give effect to beneficial interests) and s. 48 (2) as
amended (power to raise sums payable to surviving spouse on intestacy).

(*e*) *Re Trollope's Will Trusts*, [1927] 1 Ch. 596.

(*f*) Administration of Estates Act 1925, s. 2 (2).

(*g*) Administration of Estates Act 1925, s. 36 (8), (11), (12). This applies to a
mortgage and a charge by way of legal mortgage, and purchaser includes a mortgagee:
Administration of Estates Act 1925, s. 55 (1) (iii), (xviii).

(*h*) Trustee Act 1925, ss. 14 (1), 68 (17).

(*i*) Trustee Act 1925, ss. 17, 68 (17).

A mortgagee taking a legal title from a personal representative must see that no memorandum of an assent or of a previous conveyance is indorsed on the grant of probate or letters of administration, and must see that a memorandum of his own mortgage is indorsed (*k*).

Form of mortgage (*l*).—A mortgage made by personal representatives should generally be a first legal mortgage or legal charge (*m*). Personal representatives may grant a building society mortgage for purposes of administration (*n*), but such a mortgage is unusual (*o*). As in the case of a mortgage by trustees (*p*) the usual form of mortgage by personal representatives will contain a limited covenant by the personal representatives for payment, unless they are also beneficiaries. A covenant by the personal representatives as such will not enable the mortgagee to prove against the estate for the debt where the personal representative exceeds his powers (*q*), but the personal representative will be personally liable (*p*).

XIII—PERSONS ACCOUNTABLE FOR DEATH DUTIES

Mortgage for estate duty.—A person authorised or required to pay the estate duty in respect of any property had power to raise the amount of the duty and any interest and expenses properly paid or incurred by him in respect thereof by the sale or mortgage of, or a terminable charge (*r*), on the property or any part thereof (*s*). And a person having a limited interest in the property, who paid the estate duty, was entitled to the like charge as if the duty had been raised by means of a mortgage to him (*t*).

By the Law of Property Act 1925, a personal representative was accountable for all death duties which may become leviable or payable on the death of a deceased owner in respect of land (including settled land) which devolves upon him by virtue of any statute or otherwise; for the purpose of raising the duty and the costs of raising the same, the personal representative has all the powers which are by any statute conferred for raising the duty (*u*).

Mortgage for capital transfer tax.—This provision of the Law of Property Act 1925 is repealed as respects persons dying on or after

---

(*k*) Administration of Estates Act 1925, s. 36 (5), (6).
(*l*) For forms, see 14 Ency. of Forms and Precedents (4th Edn.), pp. 241 *et seq.*
(*m*) And see the Administration of Estates Act 1925, s. 39 (1), p. 212, *supra.*
(*n*) *Cruickshank* v. *Duffin* (1872), L.R. 13 Eq. 555; *Thorne* v. *Thorne*, [1893] 3 Ch. 196.
(*o*) See Wurzburg and Mills, *Building Society Law* (14th Edn.), pp. 130-131.
(*p*) See p. 209, *supra.*
(*q*) *Farhall* v. *Farhall* (1871), 7 Ch. App. 123.
(*r*) As to other terminable charges, see p. 205, *supra.*
(*s*) Finance Act 1894, s. 9 (5). But a tenant for life must keep down interest on charges, and he cannot throw interest on estate duty on the land, unless there are special circumstances showing that it has been properly incurred by him: *Re Earl of Egmont's Settled Estates, Lefroy* v. *Egmont*, [1912] 1 Ch. 251.
(*t*) Here the charge is limited to the duty paid and does not include expenses, though it may include interest demanded by the revenue: *Re Earl Howe's Settled Estates, Earl Howe* v. *Kingscote*, [1903] 2 Ch. 69.
(*u*) Law of Property Act 1925, s. 16 (1), (3).

13 March, 1975 (a). Any person liable, otherwise than as transferor (b) for capital transfer tax has, for the purposes of paying the tax or raising the amount of it when paid, power, whether or not the property is vested in him, to raise the amount of the tax by the sale or mortgage of, or a terminable charge on, the property or any part thereof (c). A person having a limited interest in any property who pays a tax attributable to the value of that property is entitled to the like charge as if the tax attributable had been raised by means of a mortgage to him (d).

Inland Revenue charge.—Unless a land charge in respect of estate duty or capital transfer tax has been registered as a land charge (e), the mortgagee is not required to see to the application of the mortgage money (f).

XIV—INFANTS

BORROWING POWERS

Loans and mortgages void (g).—It is provided by s. 1 of the Infants Relief Act 1874, that all contracts by infants, whether by specialty or simple contract, for the payment of money lent or to be lent, or for goods supplied or to be supplied (other than contracts for necessaries) and all accounts stated with infants are absolutely void (h). By s. 2 no action may be brought against a person on any promise made after coming of age, to pay any debt contracted during infancy, nor upon any ratification when of age, of a contract made during infancy, whether there shall or shall not be any new consideration. And by the Betting and Loans (Infants) Act 1892, s. 5, the principle of the 1874 Act is extended to a new mortgage given by a person who is of age in exchange for a mortgage made during infancy, which he then pays off.

An infant cannot hold a legal estate in land (i) and, therefore, he cannot be a legal mortgagor. An equitable mortgage made by an infant is absolutely void (k), unless the mortgage was made to secure monies lent for the purpose of necessaries, in which case the mortgage is

---

(a) Finance Act 1975, s. 59 (5), Sched. 13.
(b) Or as transferor's spouse to whom the property has been transferred by another transfer: see Finance Act 1975, s. 25 (8).
(c) Finance Act 1975, s. 28 (3).
(d) Finance Act 1975, s. 28 (4).
(e) See Land Charges Act 1972, s. 2 (5) Class D (i); Law of Property Act 1925, ss. 16 (7), 17; Land Registration Act 1925, s. 73 (1); Finance Act 1975, Sched. 4, para 20, 21.
(f) Law of Property Act 1925, s. 17; Finance Act 1975, s. 26.
(g) As to infant's contracts generally, see 21 Halsbury's Laws (3rd Edn.), Infants, pp. 138 et seq. The Family Law Reform Act 1969 reduced the age of majority to 18 (s. 1) and the new age applies for the construction of the expression "infant", etc., in statutory provisions made before the 1969 Act (s. 1 (2)). For the alternative "minor", see s. 11.
(h) The Act does not invalidate contracts into which an infant can validly enter into by statute: see, e.g., footnote (s), infra.
Lodging may be a necessary: Lowe v. Griffith (1835), 1 Scott 458, 460. But the purchase of a house, etc., would rarely, if ever, be a necessary.
(i) Law of Property Act 1925, s. 1 (6). For the effect of a conveyance to an infant, see Law of Property Act 1925, s. 19; Settled Land Act 1925, s. 27 (1).
(k) Nottingham Permanent Benefit Building Society v. Thurstan, [1903] A.C. 6 (H.L.) (where the building society was held to have a lien on the mortgaged property by way of subrogation to the vendor). See pp. 168, 196, supra.

voidable (*l*) and, where the mortgage has been confirmed and further advances made after the mortgagor has attained full age, he will not be allowed to redeem except on payment of the whole of the advance (*m*).

Where an infant is beneficially entitled to any property, the court may direct the trustees to raise money for his maintenance, education or benefit by mortgage of the property (*n*). Personal representatives have powers of mortgaging during the minority of a beneficiary (*o*). Powers of management of an infant's lands are conferred on the trustees appointed for this purpose, or if there are none so appointed then the trustees of the settlement under which the infant is entitled, and these powers may include a power to mortgage (*p*). The court has no jurisdiction to direct a disentailing deed of an infant's estate to be made by way of mortgage even for providing maintenance for the infant (*q*), or to authorise a mortgage of a contingent interest coupled with a policy of assurance on the infant's life (*r*). An infant may be a member of a building society, unless the rules provide otherwise, and may give all necessary receipts, but cannot vote or hold office (*s*).

Method of securing advance for benefit of infant.—As stated above an infant cannot hold a legal estate in land. Where an infant desires to purchase real estate and to raise the money therefor on the security of the property the following procedure is generally adopted. The property should be conveyed to trustees for sale to hold upon the trusts declared by a contemporaneous trust deed. The advance will be made to the trustees who will execute a mortgage or charge of the property in favour of the lender. The trusts upon which the trustees hold the property will be to apply the rents and profits of the property pending sale until the infant attains full age in keeping down the mortgage payments and subject thereto in trust for the infant and upon the infant attaining full age to transfer the property to him (*t*).

(*l*) *Martin* v. *Gale* (1876), 4 Ch. D. 428, 431; *Edwards* v. *Carter*, [1893] A.C. 360 (H.L.). See further Sykes, *The Law of Securities* (2nd Edn.), 37–42.

(*m*) *Gardner* v. *Wainfur* (1920), 89 L.J. Ch. 98.

(*n*) Trustee Act 1925, s. 53. (*o*) Administration of Estates Act 1925, s. 33.

(*p*) Settled Land Act 1925, s. 102. The specified powers do not include a power to mortgage, but the power generally to deal with the land in a proper and due course of management may comprehend such a power. The interest of any principal sum charged on the land is to be kept down out of the income of the land (sub-s. (3)). And see p. 208, *supra*. If the trustees are statutory owners they will have the powers of such. Trustees for sale have these powers of management, even though there is no minority: Law of Property Act 1925, s. 28 (1).

(*q*) *Re Hambrough's Estate, Hambrough* v. *Hambrough*, [1909] 2 Ch. 620.

(*r*) *Cadman* v. *Cadman* (1886), 33 Ch. D. 397.

(*s*) Building Societies Act 1962, s. 9; *Nottingham Permanent Benefit Building Society* v. *Thurstan, supra*.

(*t*) In the case of a husband and a wife, where one is of full age and the other an infant, the one of full age should be one of the trustees. Upon the infant attaining full age he or she may then be appointed a trustee with the other spouse, the third party retiring from the trusts. Alternatively the trustees may, on the infant attaining full age, transfer the property to the husband and wife.

In the event of a transfer to the former infant alone or the former infant and his or her spouse the mortgagee should be joined to release the trustees from the liability under the mortgage and a new covenant entered into by the grantee or grantees. Similarly on the appointment of the former infant as a trustee the mortgagee should release the retiring trustee from the liability under the mortgage and take a new covenant from the new trustee. For forms, see Precedent 8 in the Appendix to the previous edition.

In practice the infant will occupy the property and discharge the mortgage payments. If the infant defaults in making the payments the trustees should execute the trust for sale and discharge the mortgage.

LENDING POWERS

Loans by infants.—It is generally accepted (*u*) that a contract made void by the Infants Relief Act 1874, may be enforced by the infant. Any receipt or acknowledgement given to a building society by a person under eighteen in respect of the payment to him of any sum due in respect of the principal of, or interest on, sums lent by him to the society, is not invalid on the ground that he is under twenty-one (*a*).

Mortgages to infants.—As previously stated (*b*) an infant cannot hold a legal estate in land and therefore cannot be a legal mortgagee of land. An attempt to grant or transfer a legal mortgage or charge to an infant has the effect of an agreement for value to execute a mortgage or transfer when the infant attains his majority and in the meantime to hold the infant's beneficial interest in the mortgage debt in trust (*c*). A grant or transfer made to an infant together with a person of full age operates to vest the legal estate in the person of full age subject to the infant's beneficial interest (*d*). An infant may, however, acquire an interest in property other than a legal estate.

XV—MARRIED WOMEN (*e*)

MATRIMONIAL HOMES ACT 1967 (*f*)

Rights of occupation.—Where one spouse is entitled to occupy a

---

(*u*) But see (1957), 73 L.Q.R. 200–202 (G. H. Treitel); (1958) 74 L.Q.R. 97; 104.
(*a*) Building Societies Act 1962, s. 47, as amended by Family Law Reform Act 1969, s. 1 (3), Sched. 1.
(*b*) See p. 214, *supra*.
(*c*) Law of Property Act 1925, s. 19 (4), (6).
(*d*) Law of Property Act 1925, s. 19 (5), (6).
(*e*) See earlier editions for the development of the separate property of a married woman. A married woman is now capable of acquiring, holding and disposing of any property in all respects as if she were a *femme sole*: see Law Reform (Married Women and Tortfeasors) Act 1935. The only practical difference between male and female mortgagors is that a woman is less likely to be able to obtain a mortgage (but see now the Sex Discrimination Act 1975, s. 29) and where the mortgagor is a woman a surety is commonly insisted upon by the mortgagee. There is no presumption of advancement in respect of such guarantee: see *Re Salisbury-Jones*, [1938] 3 All E.R. 459; *Anson* v. *Anson*, [1953] 1 Q.B. 636; [1953] 1 All E.R. 867. An endowment policy taken out by a husband as collateral security for a mortgage by him self and his wife is not part of settled funds for the purposes of a property adjustment order: *Meldrum* v. *Meldrum*, [1970] 3 All E.R. 1084.
(*f*) For the so-called deserted wife's equity and its rejection (other than as a personal right against the husband), see *National Provincial Bank, Ltd.* v. *Ainsworth*, [1965] A.C. 1175 (H.L.); [1965] 2 All E.R. 472. The 1967 Act raises a number of difficulties (see, *e.g.*, (1968) 32 Conv. (N.S.) 85 (F. R. Crane)), but none specifically in relation to mortgages. It does, however, greatly increase the importance of making a land charges search before completion. Where a property is vested in a husband's sole name his wife may have a beneficial interest therein by virtue of a contribution to the purchase price. As to whether this interest will bind a mortgagee, see *Caunce* v. *Caunce*, [1969] 1 All E.R. 722; *Hodgson* v. *Marks*, [1971] Ch. 892 (C.A.); [1971] 2 All E.R. 684; (1973) 36 M.L.R. 30 (R. H. Maudsley); (1974) 38 Conv. (N.S.) 110 (David J. Hayton). As to whether, where the land is registered, this interest is an overriding interest, see Farrand, *Contract and Conveyance* (2nd Edn.), pp. 197 *et seq*. On the investigation of title by the mortgagee, see the standard conveyancing books and also Fairest, *Mortgages*, Ch. 4.

dwelling house, which is being or has been used as the matrimonial
home, by virtue of any estate or interest or contract or by virtue of
any enactment giving him or her a right to remain in occupation,
and the other spouse is not so entitled, then, subject to the provisions
of the Act, the spouse not so entitled has certain rights, called "rights
of occupation", in the house, namely (a) if in occupation, a right not
to be evicted or excluded from the house or any part of it by the other
spouse, except with the leave of the court, or (b) if not in occupation,
a right with the leave of the court to enter into and occupy the
house (*g*). A spouse who has an equitable interest in a dwelling house or
in the proceeds of sale thereof, but who has no legal estate therein, is
to be treated as not being entitled to occupy the house by virtue of
the interest (*h*).

Rights of occupation as a charge on the house.—The rights of
occupation of a spouse are a charge on the estate or interest of the
other spouse who is entitled to occupy the house by virtue of some
estate or interest, and such charge has the like priority and if it were
an equitable interest created at whichever is the latest of the following
dates, that is to say (a) the date when the spouse so entitled acquired
the estate or interest; (b) the date of the marriage; and (c) the
commencement of the Act (*i*).

Class F land charge.—The Act creates a new class—Class F—of
land charge to cover a charge affecting land by virtue of the Act (*k*).
The charge created by the Act will be void as against a purchaser (*l*)
of the land charged therewith, or of any interest in such land, unless
the land charge is registered in the appropriate register before the
completion of the purchase (*m*). The charge may be registered, where
it arises out of the right not to be evicted, etc., as soon as the spouse
is in occupation (*n*), or, where it arises out of the right to enter and
occupy, even before the court has given leave to enter and occupy (*o*).

Where the title to the legal estate by virtue of which a spouse is
entitled to occupy a dwelling house is registered under the Land
Registration Act 1925, registration of a land charge affecting the
dwelling house by virtue of the 1967 Act shall be effected by registration of a notice or caution under the 1925 Act, and the spouse's
rights of occupation shall not be an overriding interest notwithstanding
the spouse is in actual occupation of the dwelling house (*p*).

Where a spouse's rights of occupation are a charge on the estate or

---

(*g*) Matrimonial Homes Act 1967, s. 1 (1), (8).
(*h*) *Ibid.*, s. 1 (9), added by the Matrimonial Proceedings and Property Act 1970
s. 38.
(*i*) *Ibid.*, s. 2 (1). The commencement date was 1 January, 1968.
(*k*) *Ibid.*, s. 2 (6); the Land Charges Rules 1974.
(*l*) This includes a mortgagee: Land Charges Act 1972, s. 17 (1).
(*m*) *Ibid.*, Sched., para. 3. See *Miles* v. *Bull*, [1969] 1 Q.B. 258; [1968] 3 All E.R. 632;
(*No. 2*), [1969] 3 All E.R. 1585; *Wroth* v. *Tyler*, [1974] Ch. 30; [1973] 1 All E.R. 897.
(*n*) See *Miles* v. *Bull*, *supra*.
(*o*) See *Watts* v. *Waller*, [1973] 1 Q.B. 153 (C.A.); [1972] 3 All E.R. 257.
(*p*) *Ibid.*, s. 2 (7); Land Registration (Matrimonial Homes) Rules 1967. The application for registration of a notice or caution is made on Form 99.

interest of the other spouse, and that estate or interest is the subject of a mortgage within the meaning of the Law of Property Act 1925, then if, after the date of creation of the mortgage the charge is registered as a land charge, the charge shall, for the purposes of s. 94 of that Act (which regulates the rights of mortgagees to make further advances ranking in priority to subsequent mortgages) be deemed to be a mortgage subsequent in date to the first-mentioned mortgage (*q*).

Release of rights of occupation and postponement of priority of charge.—A spouse entitled to rights of occupation may by a release in writing release those rights or release them as respects part only of the dwelling house affected by them (*r*). The registration of the charge may be cancelled by the spouse entitled to rights of occupation (*s*) and where a contract is made for the sale of the house or for the grant of a lease thereof the rights shall be deemed to have been released on the delivery to the purchaser or lessee or his solicitor on completion of an application by the spouse entitled to the charge for cancellation of the registration of the charge or the lodging of such an application at the Land Registry, whichever first occurs (*t*). A spouse entitled to a charge may agree in writing that any other charge on, or interest in, that estate or interest shall rank in priority to the charge to which that spouse is entitled (*u*). Where a prospective mortgagee ascertains that a Class F land charge is registered (*a*), he should therefore require the spouse entitled to the charge to release the rights (and apply for the cancellation of the registration) or postpone the priority of the charge.

Payments under mortgages by spouse entitled to rights of occupation.—Where a spouse is entitled to rights of occupation, any payment or tender made or other thing done by that spouse in or towards satisfaction of the liability of the spouse in respect of, *inter alia*, mortgage payments shall whether or not it was made or done in pursuance of an order of the court (*b*) be as good as if made or done by the other spouse, and, in respect of mortgage payments, the person to whom the payment is made may treat it as having been made by the other spouse, but that shall not affect any claim of the spouse making the payment against the other spouse to an interest in the house by virtue of the payment (*c*).

(*q*) Matrimonial Homes Act 1967, s. 2 (8).

(*r*) *Ibid.*, s. 6 (1). For a form of release, see Precedent 27 in the Appendix, *infra*. Otherwise the charge is ended by the death of the other spouse or the termination of the marriage: *ibid.*, s. 2 (2).

(*s*) Land Charges Act 1972, s. 16 (1); Land Charges Rules 1974; Land Charges (Matrimonial Homes) Rules 1967.

(*t*) Matrimonial Homes Act 1967, s. 6 (2).

(*u*) *Ibid.*, s. 6 (3). For a form, see Precedent 7 in the Appendix, *infra*.

(*a*) Or a priority notice lodged in respect of the charge to arise on completion.

(*b*) The court is the High Court or the county court and in the latter case notwithstanding that the amount of the net annual value for rating of the dwellinghouse or otherwise the jurisdiction would not but for the Act be exercisable by the county court: s. 1 (6).

(*c*) Matrimonial Homes Act 1967, s. 1 (5). A spouse exercising the right under this section is not entitled to be joined as a defendant in possession proceedings against the mortgage by the mortgagee: *Hastings and Thanet Building Society* v. *Goddard*, [1970] 3 All E.R. 954 (C.A.); see (1974) 118 Sol. Jo. 554; p. 324, *infra*.

XVI—MENTAL PATIENTS (d)

Capacity to contract.—A contract made with a person who was apparently of sound mind, but who in fact was suffering at the time of the contract from such mental disorder as rendered him incapable of entering into the contract, is voidable (e). If the contract is to be avoided the person or persons denying its validity must prove that the person alleged to be mentally disordered at the time of the contract was so disordered and that the other party was aware or ought to have been aware of that fact (f). A contract made by a person mentally disordered during a lucid interval is binding upon him, whether or not the other party knew of his intermittent incapacity (g).

Capacity of disposition.—The deed of a person suffering from such mental disorder as to render him incapable of understanding the effect of the deed is void (h). A deed made by a mentally disordered person during a lucid interval, the nature and effect of which he understood (i), is binding upon him, unless a receiver has been appointed for him (k).

Mortgages on behalf of persons mentally disordered.— Part VIII of the Mental Health Act 1959, confers the modern statutory jurisdiction for the management of the property and affairs of mental patients (l). Without prejudice to the general functions of the judge (m) he may, *inter alia*, make orders or give directions and authorities for the charging of the patient's property (n).

Where the judge has ordered, directed or authorised the expenditure of money for the carrying out of permanent improvements on, or otherwise for the permanent benefit of any property of the patient, he may order that the whole or any part of the money expended or to be expended shall be a charge upon the property whether with or without interest at a specified rate, provided that no right of sale or foreclosure during the patient's lifetime is conferred thereby (o). The charge may be made in favour of such person as may be just and in particular, where the money charged is paid out of the patient's general estate, in favour of a person as trustee for the patient (p). Where an order has been made charging property with the cost of permanent improvements, the order may also provide for excluding or restricting

---

(d) See generally, 29 Halsbury's Laws (3rd Edn.), Persons Mentally Disordered.

(e) *Molton* v. *Camroux* (1848), 2 Exch. 487; affd. (1849), 4 Exch. 17; *Imperial Loan Co., Ltd.* v. *Stone*, [1892] 1 Q.B. 599 (C.A.).

(f) *York Glass Co., Ltd.* v. *Jubb* (1925), 134 L.T. 36 (C.A.); *Broughton* v. *Snook*, [1938] Ch. 505; [1938] 1 All E.R. 411.

(g) *Selby* v. *Jackson* (1844), 6 Beav. 192.

(h) *Price* v. *Berrington* (1849), 7 Hare 394, 402.

(i) *Towart* v. *Sellers* (1817), 5 Dow. 231 (H.L.).

(k) See *Re Marshall, Marshall* v. *Whateley*, [1920] 1 Ch. 284.

(l) Replacing s. 117 of the Lunacy Act 1890, supplemented by s. 22 of the Law of Property Act 1925.

(m) See Mental Health Act 1959, s. 100. The authority to mortgage will generally be an order of the Court of Protection.

(n) Mental Health Act 1959, s. 103 (1) (b).

(o) Mental Health Act 1959, s. 107 (5). See *A.-G.* v. *Marquis of Ailesbury* (1887), 12 App. Cas. 672 (H.L.).; *Re Gist*, [1904] 1 Ch. 398.

(p) Mental Health Act 1959, s. 107 (5) (a).

the provisions for preservation of the interests of other persons in the patient's property (q).

The mortgage in such cases will be made by the patient's receiver, or, if he has none, some person authorised in that behalf pursuant to the order of the court and it must be settled and approved by the court (r).

Loans on behalf of mental patients.—The court has in the past authorised the committee or receiver of a person of unsound mind to lend the patient's money upon mortgage (s).

Where the patient is tenant for life of settled land money may be raised out of the patient's free estate on the security of the settled land. The authority of the Court of Protection is required only for the receiver to raise the money and in this case the receiver will not be the mortgagor (t).

XVII—BANKRUPTS

Mortgages by bankrupts (u).—When a person is adjudicated a bankrupt his property, with certain exceptions, passes to his trustee in bankruptcy, so that the bankrupt cannot mortgage such property or redeem it if already mortgaged (a). But the bankrupt may mortgage the excepted property which remains vested in him (b) and property acquired after his bankruptcy, if the trustee has not intervened to exercise his right thereto (c).

A mortgage by a bankrupt will be effective against his trustee in favour of the mortgagee acting in good faith without notice of an available act of bankruptcy where the receiving order or bankruptcy petition has not been registered pursuant to the Land Charges Act 1972 (d), where the mortgage is of an equitable chose in action and the trustee has not perfected his title by notice (e), and where the trustee has stood by and allowed the mortgagee to advance his money on the supposition that the bankrupt could dispose of the property (f).

Mortgages by trustee in bankruptcy.—The trustee in bankruptcy, with the consent of the committee of inspection, may mortgage part of the property of the bankrupt which has passed to him under

---

(q) Mental Health Act 1959, s. 107 (5) (b). And see p. 166, *supra*.

(r) Court of Protection Rules 1960, rr. 84, 85. For forms of mortgage on behalf of mentally disordered persons, see 14 Ency. Forms and Precedents (4th Edn), 285-288.

(s) *Re Ridgeways* (1825), Hog. 309.

(t) The mortgage will be made by the trustees of the settlement in the name and on behalf of the patient under the Settled Land Act 1925, s. 68 (see p. 202). The receiver will of course be a party to the mortgage as mortgagee.

(u) For aircraft mortgages, see p. 99, *supra*.

(a) Bankruptcy Act 1914, ss. 18, 53. For transactions effected before the date of the receiving order, see p. 229, *infra*.

(b) *Bird* v. *Philpott*, [1900] 1 Ch. 822.

(c) *Cohen* v. *Mitchell* (1890), 25 Q.B.D. 262; Bankruptcy Act 1914, s. 47.

(d) Land Charges Act 1972, ss. 6, 7, 8 (17).

(e) *Stuart* v. *Cockerell* (1869), L. R. Eq. 607; *Palmer* v. *Locke* (1881), 18 Ch. D. 381 (C.A.).

(f) *Troughton* v. *Gitley* (1766), Ambl. 630; *Tucker* v. *Hernaman* (1853), 4 De G.M. & G. 395.

the bankruptcy for the purpose of raising money for the payment of the bankrupt's debts (*g*).

XVIII—AGENTS

Authority of agent to mortgage.—As a general rule, an agent who is placed in temporary control of his principal's property has no authority to pledge or mortgage it. Thus a solicitor cannot, without authority (express or to be implied from strong circumstances) do anything to prejudice the estate or interest of his client (*h*).

Where a principal hands his title deeds to an agent to raise a specific sum, and the agent uses them for the purpose of raising a larger sum, the principal will not be able to redeem without paying the entire sum for which they were pledged. For the authority to pledge in fact existed and the pledgee was not aware of the limitation on it (*i*).

Exceptions to the rule in so far as it relates to goods and documents of title thereto and to negotiable instruments have arisen from necessity and by the custom of trade (*k*).

XIX—PARTNERS

BORROWING POWERS

Agency of partners (*l*).—The Partnership Act 1890, provides that every partner is an agent of the firm and his other partners for the purpose of the business of the partnership; and the acts of any partner who does any act for carrying on in the usual way business of the kind carried on by the firm of which he is a member bind the firm and his partners, unless the partner so acting has in fact no authority to act for the firm in the particular matter, and the person with whom he is dealing either knows that he has no authority, or does not know or believe him to be a partner (*m*).

General power to mortgage personal property.—Accordingly one of several partners may make a security affecting the personal property of the partnership for a loan or debt contracted for the ordinary purposes of the undertaking, where there is no notice of fraud or want of authority (*n*). This power continues after the dissolution of the partnership, for the purposes of winding up its affairs, and of completing contracts entered into during its continuance (*o*). The partnership will not be bound by a security given by one of the firm to a person who knowingly makes advances for extraordinary

---

(*g*) Bankruptcy Act 1914, s. 56 (5). For a form of mortgage by a trustee in bankruptcy, see 14 Ency. Forms and Precedents (4th Edn.), pp. 701-704.

(*h*) *Cory* v. *Eyre* (1863), 1 De G.J. & S. at p. 168.

(*i*) *Brocklesby* v. *Temperance Permanent Building Society*, [1895] A.C. 173 (H.L.).

(*k*) See the Factors Act 1889, and the powers of bankers to pledge customers' negotiable instruments and stockbrokers to pledge customers' negotiable securities.

(*l*) Only ordinary partners are dealt with here. A limited partner does not have power to bind the firm: Limited Partnerships Act 1907, s. 6 (1).

(*m*) Section 5.

(*n*) *Re Litherland, Ex parte Howden* (1842), 2 Mont. D. & De G. 574.

(*o*) *Butchart* v. *Dresser* (1853), 4 De G.M. & G. 542; *Re Bourne, Bourne* v. *Bourne*, [1906] 2 Ch. 427 (C.A.).

purposes, such as raising additional capital for payment of the share of a deceased partner, or making new arrangements for carrying on the business (*p*). And *a fortiori*, one member of the firm cannot bind the others by a security for the payment of his separate debt, unless the creditor can prove a direct assent by the other partners, or circumstances from which such assent may reasonably be inferred. The presumption is, that such a security was known by the creditor to have been given without the authority of the firm, and he takes the onus of proving the authority (*q*). If such a security is made by a partner knowing his firm is insolvent it is a fraud on the creditors of the firm and an act of bankruptcy (*r*).

Mortgage of real property.—Where partners hold the legal estate in freehold or leasehold property, they necessarily hold it as joint tenants (*s*). A single partner cannot give a legal mortgage on the property without express authority given under seal so to do (*t*). But where the mortgage does not require to be effected by deed or for instance, in the case of an equitable mortgage made by deposit of the deeds, whether with or without a memorandum in writing, it seems that the same rule applies as in the case of any other transaction entered into by a partner on behalf of the firm, and the mortgage is valid and binds the firm, provided it is effected for carrying on in the usual way business of the kind carried on by the firm (*a*). And after the death of a partner, the surviving partners have power to mortgage the partnership property, whether real or personal, to secure a partnership debt, and such mortgage takes priority over the lien of the personal representatives of the deceased partners on the partnership assets (*b*).

Mortgage of partnership share.—An assignment by a partner of his share in the partnership, either absolute or by way of mortgage, does not, as against the other partners, entitle the assignee during the continuance of the partnership to interfere in the management of the partnership business or affairs (*c*), or to require accounts or inspection of books (*d*). It only entitles the assignee to receive the partner's share of profits (*e*). But on the dissolution the assignee is entitled to receive the assignor's share of the assets, and for the purpose of ascertaining the share, he is entitled to an account as from the date of dissolution (*f*). If any partner suffers his share of the partnership property to be charged under the Partnership Act 1890, for his separate debt, the partnership may, at the option of the other partners, be dissolved (*g*).

(*p*) *Fisher* v. *Tayler* (1843), 2 Hare 218.
(*q*) *Snaith* v. *Burridge* (1812), 4 Taunt, 684; *Leverson* v. *Lane* (1862), 13 C.B. N.S. 278.
(*r*) *Re Douglas, Ex parte Snowball* (1872), 7 Ch. App. 534, at p. 542.
(*s*) Law of Property Act 1925, ss. 34, 36; Settled Land Act 1925, s. 36 (4).
(*t*) *Steiglitz* v. *Egginton* (1815), 1 Holt N.P. 141.
(*a*) Partnership Act 1890, s. 5: see p. 221, *supra.*
(*b*) *Re Bourne, Bourne* v. *Bourne,* [1906] 2 Ch. 427.
(*c*) See, *e.g., Re Garwood's Trusts, Garwood* v. *Paynter,* [1903] 1 Ch. 236.
(*d*) *Bonnin* v. *Neame,* [1910] 1 Ch. 732.
(*e*) Partnership Act 1890, s. 31. See p. 112, *supra.*
(*f*) *Watts* v. *Driscoll,* [1901] 1 Ch. 294 (C.A.).
(*g*) Partnership Act 1890, s. 33.

LENDING POWERS

Partner's power to lend on mortgage.—A partner has authority to lend the moneys of the firm on mortgage, when such a transaction is part of the ordinary business of the firm (*h*).

XX—MORTGAGES OF ECCLESIASTICAL PROPERTY

Powers to mortgage ecclesiastical property.—In addition to the powers conferred by the Improvement of Land Act 1864 (*i*), mortgages of glebe land may be made by incumbents under the Clergy Residences Repair Act 1776, and the Acts by which that Act has been amended and extended, for the purpose of providing or repairing parsonage houses (*k*).

Since mortgages of ecclesiastical property are generally made to the Church Commissioners, who will supply all the necessary forms, nothing further will be said of them here.

Advowson.—An advowson cannot now be mortgaged (*l*).

(*h*) *Re Land Credit Co. of Ireland, Weikersheim's Case* (1873), 8 Ch. App. 831; *Niemann* v. *Niemann* (1889), 43 Ch. D. 198 (C.A.).

(*i*) See p. 205, *supra*. Where the land is held in right of any church, chapel, or other ecclesiastical benefice, the consent of the patron and of the bishop is essential: Improvement of Land Act 1864, s. 20; and see Improvement of Land (Ecclesiastical Benefices) Act 1884.

(*k*) See generally, 14 Halsbury's Laws (4th Edn.), paras. 1146–1152.

By the Glebe Exchange Act 1815, powers were given to incumbents to purchase additional land for the glebe, and, for that purpose, to make limited mortgages of the profits of the benefice.

Provisions for raising money for dilapidations are contained in the Ecclesiastical Dilapidations Measures 1923 to 1951.

(*l*) Benefices Act 1898, ss. 1 (1) (b), 7; Benefices Act 1898 (Amendment) Measure 1923, s. 4.

PART III

VOID OR IMPERFECT SECURITIES

CHAPTER 13

Void or Imperfect Securities

I—SECURITIES VOID AGAINST THIRD PARTIES

A—GENERALLY

Classification.—As already stated (pp. 83 *et seq.*, *supra*) securities on personal chattels may be void (*a*) by reason of non-compliance with the provisions of the Bills of Sale Acts, and such securities, and also securities on things in action, may become ineffective against the mortgagor's trustee in bankruptcy, where the mortgagor is a trader and the chattels or things in action are in his reputed ownership (*b*). But in addition to these special statutory dangers, there are others of a more general nature arising (1) under the provisions of the Bankruptcy Act 1914; and (2) in consequence of the statutory provisions against fraudulent dispositions.

B—SECURITIES VOID IN BANKRUPTCY

Avoidance of settlements (*c*).—With regard to the avoidance of settlements made when insolvency is existent or probable, the Bankruptcy Act 1914, provides:

42.—(1) Any settlement of property (*d*), not being a settlement made before and in consideration of marriage (*e*), or made in favour of a purchaser (*f*) or incumbrancer in good faith and for valuable consideration (*g*), or a settlement made on or for the wife or children of the settlor of property which has accrued to the settlor after marriage in right of his wife, shall, if the settlor becomes bankrupt within two years after the date of the settlement, be void against the trustee in bankruptcy, and shall, if the settlor becomes bankrupt at any subsequent time within ten years after the date of the settlement, be void against the trustee in bankruptcy, unless the parties claiming under the settlement can prove that the settlor was, at the time of making the settlement,

---

(*a*) A security which is not *malum in se*, but is only prohibited, is not necessarily void for all purposes, but only so far as it is expressly forbidden. Thus a security which is, by statute, void as a charge may be good for other purposes: see *Re Richardson, Ex parte Jones* (1832), 2 Cr. & J. 513; *cf. Wynne* v. *Robinson* (1830), 4 Bli. N.S. 27.

(*b*) See p. 91, *supra*.

(*c*) See further, Underhill, *Law relating to Trusts and Trustees* (12th Edn.), pp. 144 *et seq.*

(*d*) That is, any conveyance or transfer of property: sub-s. (4); and s. 167 for the definition of property.

(*e*) See *Re Densham*, [1975] 3 All E.R. 726; (1975) 119 Sol. Jo. 582 (J. G. Miller).

(*f*) That is, a buyer in the ordinary sense; not a purchaser in the legal sense: *Re Pumfrey, Ex parte Hillman* (1879), 10 Ch. D. 622 (C.A.); and *Re Windle*, [1975] 3 All E.R. 987.

(*g*) *Re Windle, supra*.

able to pay all his debts without the aid of the property comprised in the settlement, and that the interest of the settlor in such property passed to the trustee of the settlement on the execution thereof.

Although the Act only purports to avoid the settlements specified against the trustee in bankruptcy, yet it does not put that trustee in the place of the grantee whose settlement is made void, and, therefore, where the settlor has made a subsequent mortgage of the property for value, the rights of the mortgagee are not merely preserved but accelerated (*h*).

This provision does not contain any express proviso in favour of bona fide purchasers, but they are in fact protected, since the settlement is voidable only. If there has been a sale or mortgage before the trustee in bankruptcy has taken steps to avoid it, the purchaser or mortgagee without notice of an available act of bankruptcy, gets a title against him (*i*), even though the purchase or mortgage is subsequent to the act of bankruptcy (*k*). Knowledge of the voluntary settlement does not destroy the purchaser's bona fides (*l*).

Settlements of future property.—It is further provided:

42.—(2) Any covenant or contract made by any person (hereinafter called the settlor) in consideration of his or her marriage, either for the future payment of money for the benefit of the settlor's wife or husband or children, or for the future settlement on or for the settlor's wife or husband or children, of property wherein the settlor had not at the date of the marriage any estate or interest, whether vested or contingent, in possession or remainder, and not being money or property in right of the settlor's wife or husband shall, if the settlor is adjudged bankrupt and the covenant or contract has not been executed at the date of the commencement of his bankruptcy, be void against the trustee in bankruptcy.

There is a reservation of the beneficiaries' rights to prove in the bankruptcy, but any claim to dividend is postponed until creditors for valuable consideration in money or money's worth have been satisfied (*m*).

Fraudulent preference.—With respect to dispositions which constitute a fraudulent preference, the Bankruptcy Act 1914, provides:

44.—(1) Every conveyance or transfer of property, or charge thereon made . . . by any person unable to pay his debts as they become due out of his own money in favour of any creditor, or of any person in trust for any creditor, with a view of giving such creditor, or any surety or guarantor for the debt due to such creditor (*n*), a preference over the other creditors, shall, if the person making . . . the same is adjudged bankrupt on a bankruptcy petition presented within [six] (*o*) months after the date of making the same,

---

(*h*) *Sanguinetti* v. *Stuckey's Banking Co.*, [1895] 1 Ch. 176.
(*i*) *Re Carter & Kenderdine's Contract*, [1897] 1 Ch. 776 (C.A.).
(*k*) *Re Hart*, [1912] 3 K.B. 6 (C.A.), explained in *Re Gunsbourg*, [1920] 2 K.B. 426 (C.A.). For registration of writs and orders, see p. 442, *infra*. As to when that bankruptcy commences, see Bankruptcy Act 1914, s. 37.
(*l*) *Re Brall, Ex parte Norton*, [1893] 2 Q.B. 381.
(*m*) A secured maintenance order cannot be attacked under this provision: see the cases in footnote (*n*), p. 159, *supra*.
(*n*) See *Re Conley, Ex parte Trustee* v. *Lloyds Bank, Ltd.*, [1938] 2 All E.R. 127 (C.A.); and Companies Act 1948, s. 321 (as to liability of surety).
For fraudulent preferences by limited companies and the avoidance of floating charges created within twelve months of winding up, see p. 125, *supra*.
(*o*) As amended by Companies Act 1947, *s*. 115.

be deemed fradulent and void as against the trustee in bankruptcy (*p*).

(2) This section shall not affect the rights of any person making title in good faith and for valuable consideration through or under a creditor of the bankrupt.

Preference as the dominant motive.—Under this provision two matters must be proved in order to establish that conveyance is void against the trustee in bankruptcy: (1) that the grantor was insolvent, and (2) that the grantor's object was to prefer a creditor.   Preference implies that a conveyance was voluntary (*q*). The burden of proof of both these points is on the trustee who seeks to set aside the conveyance, so that he must not only show insolvency, but also that the conveyance was made by the bankrupt with a view to prefer the particular creditor (*r*).   In respect to preference the question is whether the desire to prefer the creditor was the dominant motive of the debtor in making the conveyance (*s*). If other motives were present to his mind, it is necessary to show that it was really the desire to prefer which actuated him (*t*).   If the creditor has pressed for payment or security, the yielding to his demand may not be a fraudulent preference (*u*).   Nor will the subsequent execution of a security for money advanced on an absolute promise to give the security be a fraudulent preference (*a*).   An agreement to execute the security when required will, it seems, be good (*b*), unless the postponement was merely for the purpose of saving the debtor's credit (*c*).   The payment at maturity of a bill of exchange given in the ordinary course of business is not a fraudulent preference, notwithstanding that the debtor knew of his insolvency when the bill was given (*d*).   The circumstance that the creditor is the solicitor of the debtor, does not affect the question of fraudulent preference, except so far as it gives facilities for disguising a voluntary transaction under an appearance of demand and submission (*e*).

Securities without notice of bankruptcy.—Subject to the foregoing provisions the Bankruptcy Act 1914, does not invalidate

---

(*p*) For joinder of a guarantor, see *Re Idenden, Ex parte Trustee* v. *Bateman & Co., Ltd.*, [1970] 2 All E.R. 387.

(*q*) *Sharp* v. *Jackson*, [1899] A.C. 419 (H.L.).

(*r*) *Re Cohen*, [1924] 2 Ch. 515; *Peat* v. *Gresham Trust, Ltd.*, [1934] A.C. 252 (H.L.); *Re William Hall (Contractors), Ltd.*, [1967] 2 All E.R. 1150.

(*s*) *Re M. Kushler, Ltd.*, [1943] Ch. 248; [1943] 2 All E.R. 22 (C.A.).   The question more usually arises on a payment to the creditor, than a conveyance to him.

(*t*) *Re Bell, Ex parte Official Receiver* (1892), 10 Morr. 15.

(*u*) *Peat* v. *Gresham Trust, Ltd.*, *supra; Re Cutts*, [1956] 2 All E.R. 537 (C.A.). The mere demand of payment may be sufficient: *Re Walker, Ex parte Topham* (1873), 8 Ch. App. 614.   The pressure must be real pressure and operate on the debtor's mind: *Re Bell, Ex parte Official Receiver, supra; Re Ramsay, Ex parte Deacon*, [1913] 2 K.B. 80. A threat of proceedings when the debtor is on the eve of bankruptcy is not real pressure: *Re Cooper, Ex parte Hall* (1882), 19 Ch. D. 580.   And where the transaction is fraudulent in its inception, it is immaterial that the payments are made under pressure: *Re Wrigley, Ex parte Reader* (1875), L.R. 20 Eq. 763.

(*a*) *Hermoux* v. *Harbord* (1898), 14 T.L.R. 243; *Bulteel and Colmore* v. *Parker and Bulteel's Trustee* (1916), 32 T.L.R. 661.

(*b*) *Re Barker, Ex parte Kilner* (1879), 13 Ch. D. 245.

(*c*) *Re Tunstall, Ex parte Burton* (1879), 13 Ch. D. 102.

(*d*) *Re Clay & Sons, Ex parte Trustee* (1895), 3 Mans. 31; *cf. Re Eaton & Co., Ex parte Viney*, [1897] 2 Q.B. 16.

(*e*) *Johnson* v. *Fesemeyer* (1858), 3 De G. & J. 13.

any conveyance or assignment by, or any contract, dealing or transaction by, or with, the bankrupt for valuable consideration, provided:

    (i) it takes place before the date of the receiving order; and

    (ii) that the person dealing with the bankrupt had not, at the time of the transaction, notice of an available act of bankruptcy committed by the bankrupt before that time (*f*).

But where a mortgagee takes with such notice and a receiving order is made within three months after such act of bankruptcy his security will be void (*g*).

After-acquired property of bankrupt.—The Act does not invalidate a bona fide transaction for value with an undischarged bankrupt in respect of after-acquired property, whether real or personal, even with notice of the bankruptcy, unless the trustee has intervened, and any estate or interest in such property which, by virtue of the Bankruptcy Act, is vested in the trustee determines and passes in such manner and to such extent as may be required for giving effect to the transaction (*h*). For this purpose notice of the bankruptcy is immaterial.

C—FRAUDULENT DISPOSITIONS

Conveyances in fraud of creditors (*i*).—The Law of Property Act 1925 (*k*), provides:

    172.—(1) Save as provided by this section, every conveyance (*l*) of property (*m*), made whether before or after the commencement of this Act, with intent to defraud creditors, is voidable, at the instance of any person thereby prejudiced.

    (2) This section does not affect the operation of a disentailing assurance, or the law of bankruptcy for the time being in force.

    (3) This section does not extend to any estate or interest in property conveyed for valuable consideration and in good faith or upon good consideration and in good faith to any person not having, at the time of the conveyance, notice of the intent to defraud creditors.

Fraudulent intent.—A fraudulent intention on the part of the grantor may be inferred from various circumstances. His indebtedness at the time of the transaction is an important consideration, though not absolutely decisive on the validity of the conveyance, for there may be insolvency without fraud, and the deed may be good though the grantor is indebted (*n*). The mere fact that the conveyance (or

---

(*f*) Bankruptcy Act 1914, s. 45. The transaction must be bona fide: *Re Simms*, [1930] 2 Ch. 22.

(*g*) *Re O'Shea's Settlement, Courage* v. *O'Shea*, [1895] 1 Ch. 325.

(*h*) Bankruptcy Act 1914, s. 47.

(*i*) See, further, Underhill *op. cit.*, pp. 149 *et seq.* For the jurisdiction to set aside transactions to prevent relief in divorce proceedings, see Matrimonial Causes Act 1973, s. 37. And see *Cadogan* v. *Cadogan*, [1977] 1 All E.R. 200.

(*k*) Replacing the statute of 1571, 13 Eliz. I, c. 5.

(*l*) This includes a mortgage: Law of Property Act 1925, s. 205 (1) (ii). As to whether the transaction must be in writing, see *Rye* v. *Rye*, [1962] A.C. 496 (H.L.); [1962] 1 All E.R. 146; and *cf. Re Eicholz*, [1959] Ch. 708; [1959] 1 All E.R. 166.

(*m*) *I.e.*, anything in action, and any interest in real or personal property: Law of Property Act 1925, s. 205 (1) (xx).

(*n*) See *Re Holland, Gregg* v. *Holland*, [1902] 2 Ch. 360 (C.A.).

mortgage) is voluntary is not conclusive evidence of an intention to defeat or delay creditors within the section (*o*).

As a general rule the transaction will be void if it appears that there was an intention to defeat or delay the creditors, though no actual delay was caused; or if the debtor knew that delay would be the consequence of the transaction (*p*). There will be a prima facie inference of such an intention where the settlement is voluntary, and the plaintiff was a creditor at its date, if the effect of it was to take from the grantor's property an amount without which his debts can not be paid (*q*). So too where a mortgagor granted a lease to his wife after the mortgagee had commenced proceedings for possession, the transaction was made with intent to defraud (*r*). The insolvency of the grantor shortly after the date of the conveyance will throw upon those who uphold it the burden of showing that the grantor was in a position to make it (*s*). But when the conveyance is for valuable consideration, evidence must be given of circumstances which show an intention to defeat or delay creditors (*t*).

The intention which will avoid the conveyance must be an intention to defeat or delay creditors generally. A deed of assignment made in good faith in favour of a creditor is not invalid by reason of its being made with the express intention of defeating other particular creditor or creditors (*u*). But the question is always whether, looking at the whole of the circumstances surrounding the execution of the conveyance, it was in fact executed with the intent to defeat or delay creditors (*a*).

Retention of possession.—A settlement of the whole of the settlor's property, or of the whole of his property with certain exceptions, is not void in the absence of an intention to defraud his creditors (*b*). Though possession and reputed ownership by the debtor of chattels after an alleged absolute assignment by him, or after they have been taken in execution by a creditor, was from an early period treated as a badge or as evidence of fraud, because possession is the chief test of the ownership of chattels and by means of it the debtor acquires a

---

(*o*) See *Re Wise, Ex parte Mercer* (1866), 17 Q.B.D. 290 (C.A.); *Godfrey* v. *Poole* (1888), 13 App. Cas. 497 (P.C.); *Lloyds Bank, Ltd.* v. *Marcan*, [1973] 3 All E.R. 754 (C.A.) (a dishonest intention is required; cf. Pennycuick, V-C, at [1973] 2 All E.R. 359 generally on the history of the section). See (1975) 91 L.Q.R. 86.

(*p*) *Townsend* v. *Westacott* (1840), 2 Beav. 340; *Thompson* v. *Webster* (1859), 4 Drew. 628; *French* v. *French* (1855), 6 De G.M. & G. 95; *Holmes* v. *Penney* (1856), 3 K. & J. 90.

(*q*) *Freeman* v. *Pope* (1870), 5 Ch. App. 538; *Ideal Bedding Co., Ltd.* v. *Holland,* [1907] 2 Ch. 157. As to avoidance by creditors subsequent to the settlement, see *Spirett* v. *Willows* (1864), 3 De G.J. & S. 293.

(*r*) *Lloyds Bank, Ltd.* v. *Marcan, supra.*

(*s*) *Crossley* v. *Elworthy* (1871), L.R. 12 Eq. 158; *Mackay* v. *Douglas* (1872), L.R. 14 Eq. 106.

(*t*) *Freeman* v. *Pope, supra; Re Bamford, Ex parte Games* (1879), 12 Ch. D. 314 (C.A.); *Re Johnson, Golden* v. *Gillam* (1881), 20 Ch. D. 389; affd. (1882), 51 L.J. Ch. 503 (C.A.).

(*u*) *Glegg* v. *Bromley*, [1912] 3 K.B. 474; see *Alton* v. *Harrison* (1869), 4 Ch. App. 622. (*a*) *Re Holland, Gregg* v. *Holland*, [1902] 2 Ch. 360 (C.A.).; see *Re Wise, Ex parte Mercer* (1886), 17 Q.B.D. 290 (C.A.).

(*b*) *Cadogan* v. *Kennett* (1776), 2 Cowp. 432; *Re Reis, Ex parte Clough*, [1904] 2 K.B. 769 (C.A.); on app. *sub nom. Clough* v. *Samuel*, [1905] A.C. 442 (H.L.).

credit to which his real circumstances do not entitle him (*c*), it is not so where retention of the chattels was consistent with the nature of the transaction (*d*). The inference of fraud arises also in relation to real estate, where the grantor retains possession of the title deeds. But there is no such inference, as to both real estate and chattels, where, the transaction being a mortgage, the mortgagor remains in possession. For this is usual in mortgages (*e*). And if a mortgage deed is duly executed and delivered, the mere retainer of it by the mortgagor without fraud will not affect is validity (*f*).

It is unnecessary that an assignment of chattels should be followed by possession in order to make it valid against the assignor himself, or against his creditors who are cognizant of and take part in the arrangement under which it is made, or which proceeds upon the assumption of its validity; or against strangers (*g*).

Conveyances in fraud of subsequent purchasers.—The Law of Property Act 1925 (*h*), provides:

173.—(1) Every disposition of land (*i*) made with intent to defraud a subsequent purchaser is voidable at the instance of that purchaser.

(2) For the purposes of this section, no voluntary disposition, whenever made, shall be deemed to have been made with intent to defraud by reason only that a subsequent conveyance for valuable consideration was made, if such subsequent conveyance was made after 28 June, 1893.

Thus, to avoid a settlement, conveyance or security under this provision, actual intent to defeat or defraud subsequent purchaser is essential (*k*).

II—SECURITIES OF AN OPPRESSIVE NATURE

A—CLOGGING THE EQUITY (*l*)

Clogging the equity.—From the doctrine of the courts of equity, that a mere security for a debt cannot be forfeited for non-payment on the stipulated day, was deduced the corollary, that, not only should no stipulation to the contrary in or contemporaneously with the mortgage (*m*) be valid, but that any attempt to clog or fetter the right of redemption by a provision which would encumber the property, or give the mortgagee any beneficial interest in it after redemption, should be equally void. As regards collateral advantages it is now settled, contrary to the older cases, that in certain circumstances such stipulations are permissible. This matter is dealt with subsequently (*l*) in relation to redemption.

(*c*) *Twyne's Case* (1602), 3 Co. Rep. 80b.
(*d*) *Cadogan* v. *Kennett, supra.*
(*e*) *Martindale* v. *Booth* (1832), 3 B. & Ad. 498.
(*f*) *Exton* v. *Scott* (1833), 6 Sim. 31.
(*g*) *Steel* v. *Brown* (1808), 1 Taunt. 381; *Robinson* v. *M'Donnell* (1818), 2 B. & Ald. 134. As to a stranger afterwards becoming a creditor, see *Holmes* v. *Penney* (1856), 3 K. & J. 90, 100.
(*h*) Reproducing the Voluntary Conveyances Act 1893.
(*i*) *Cf.* s. 172 which applies to all property.
(*k*) *Moore* v. *Kelly*, [1918] 1 I.R. 169.
(*l*) See further, pp. 522 *et seq. infra.*
(*m*) See *Reeve* v. *Lisle*, [1902] A.C. 461 (H.L.), where an agreement made subsequently to the mortgage giving the mortgagee an option to purchase was upheld.

B—SECURITIES BY EXPECTANT HEIRS (*n*)

Securities granted by expectant heirs and reversioners.—The court will in the exercise of its equitable jurisdiction interfere in regard to securities taken from expectant heirs or reversioners, or persons in great straights for money, especially if in weak health (*o*). In this, courts of equity have gone far beyond the original principle of protecting young and improvident persons, whose expectations made them subject to impositions (*p*). In so much that, in case of inadequate consideration, a mortgage will be reduced to a security for the actual advance, with interest at the rate of £5 per cent. per annum (*q*), although the expectant heir with whom the transaction was made, was of full, and even of mature age, and was independently advised, and understood the nature of the bargain. And the onus of showing that the transaction was reasonable and provident is thrown on the mortgagee, not of the showing the contrary upon the mortgagor (*r*).

Inequitable sale treated as a mortgage.—Where the transaction takes the form of a sale, the conveyance will be directed to stand as a security for the amount actually found due, with interest, and in ordinary cases with costs, on the footing of a mortgage (*s*). A security under the like circumstances will be ordered to stand for the sums actually advanced to, or for the benefit of, the owner of the expectancy. But where the case is tainted with fraud and misrepresentation, and it is not shown that the money was applied for the plaintiff's benefit, the security may be set aside unconditionally (*t*).

Statutory protection for dealings with reversions.—Subject, however, to the jurisdiction of the court as regards unconscionable bargains, mere undervalue is not a ground for setting aside the acquisition of a reversionary interest. Thus the Law of Property Act 1925, provides:

174.—(1) No acquisition made in good faith, without fraud or unfair dealing, of any reversionary interest in real or personal property for money or money's worth, is liable to be opened or set aside merely on the ground of undervalue.

In this subsection "reversionary interest" includes an expectancy or possibility.

(2) This section does not affect the jurisdiction of the court to set aside or modify unconscionable bargains.

This is a re-enactment of the Sales of Reversions Act 1867, and sub-s. (2) incorporates the restriction placed by the courts on that Act (*u*). The provision is carefully limited to purchases made in good

---

(*n*) See further, Withers on *Reversions* (2nd Edn.), pp. 401 *et seq.*
(*o*) See *Croft* v. *Graham* (1863), 2 De G.J. & S. 155.
(*p*) See remarks of Lord HARDWICKE, L.C., in *Walmesley* v. *Booth* (1741), 2 Atk. 25.
(*q*) *Croft* v. *Graham, supra; Miller* v. *Cook* (1870), L.R. 10 Eq. 641; *Tyler* v. *Yates* (1871), 6 Ch. App. 665; *Beynon* v. *Cook* (1875), 10 Ch. App. 389.
(*r*) *Davis* v. *Duke of Marlborough* (1819), 2 Swans. 108, at p. 139; *Emmet* v. *Tottenham* (1865), 12 L.T. 838; *King* (J.), *Ltd.* v. *Hay Currie* (1911), 28 T.L.R. 10.
(*s*) *Davis* v. *Duke of Marlborough, supra; Douglas* v. *Culverwell* (1862), 4 De G.F. & J. 20.
(*t*) *Smith* v. *Kay* (1859), 7 H.L. Cas. 750.
(*u*) *Earl of Aylesford* v. *Morris* (1873), 8 Ch. App. 484.

faith and without fraud or unfair dealing, and leaves undervalue still a material element in cases in which it is not the sole equitable ground for relief (*a*). The jursidiction of the court was not affected by the repeal of the usury laws (*b*), and an exorbitant rate of interest agreed to be paid by a young and needy man on the security of an indefeasible reversionary interest shows unfair dealing (*c*). But the doctrine does not apply to mere cases of a high rate of interest, where extraordinary risk is incurred. This justifies the taking of a security for interest beyond the usual rate, and even for a much larger principal sum than was really lent, the surplus being treated as a bonus (*d*). And the doctrine does not apply to the ordinary case of a loan by a money-lender (*e*).

C—MONEYLENDING SECURITIES (*f*)

Relief against moneylending securities.—Relief against money-lending securities is granted in certain circumstances under the Moneylenders Acts 1900 to 1927 (*g*). The Act of 1900 provides as follows:

> **1.**—(1) Where proceedings are taken in any court by a moneylender for the recovery of any money lent after the commencement of this Act (*h*), or the enforcement of any agreement or security made after the commencement of this Act, in respect of money lent either before or after the commencement of this Act;
>
> And there is evidence which satisfies the court that the interest charged in respect of the sum actually lent is excessive, or that the amounts charged for expenses, inquiries, fines, bonus, premiums, renewals, or any other charges are excessive (*i*);
>
> And that, in either case, the transaction is harsh and unconscionable, or is otherwise such that a court of equity would give relief;
>
> The court may reopen the transaction, and take an account between the moneylender and the person sued;
>
> And may, notwithstanding any statement or settlement of account, or any agreement purporting to close previous dealings and create a new obligation, reopen any account already taken between them;
>
> And relieve the person sued from payment of any sum in excess of the sum adjudged by the court to be fairly due in respect of such principal, interest and charges, as the court, having regard to the risk and all the circumstances, may adjudge to be reasonable;

(*a*) *Brenchley* v. *Higgins* (1900), 70 L.J. Ch. 788.

(*b*) *Croft* v. *Graham, supra; Miller* v. *Cook, supra.*

(*c*) *Tyler* v. *Yates, supra.* In such a case the charge will stand as security only for the sums actually advanced and interest at 5 per cent. per annum: *ibid.; Beynon* v. *Cook, supra;* and cases in note (*b*), *supra.*

(*d*) *Potter* v. *Edwards* (1857), 26 L.J. Ch. 468; *Mainland* v. *Upjohn* (1889), 41 Ch. D. 126; see now *Cityland and Property (Holdings), Ltd.* v. *Dabrah,* [1968] Ch. 166; [1967] 2 All E.R. 639.

(*e*) *Gordon* v. *Fowler* (1901), 17 T.L.R. 243.

(*f*) The Consumer Credit Act 1974, s. 192 (3) (b) and 5th Sched. provides for the re-peal of the Moneylenders Acts but the relevant order effecting the repeal and bringing the provisions of the 1974 into effect has not yet been made. On the 1974 Act, see Ch. 9, *supra.*

(*g*) The Moneylenders Act 1911, was repealed by the Act of 1927 and substituted provisions made by the later Act. The section is set out above in paragraphs for clearness.

(*h*) *I.e.,* 1 November, 1900.

(*i*) But an agreement for the payment by the borrower of any sum on account of costs charges or expenses incidental to or relating to the negotiations for or granting of the loan or proposed loan is illegal and any money so paid is recoverable: s. 12 of Act of 1927.

And if any such excess has been paid, or allowed in account by the debtor, may order the creditor to repay it; and may set aside either wholly or in part, or revise, or alter, any security given or agreement made in respect of money lent by the moneylender;
And if the moneylender has parted with the security may order him to indemnify the borrower or other person sued.

Meaning of moneylender.—Section 6 of the Act of 1900 provides that the expression includes every person whose business is that of moneylending, or who advertises, or announces, or holds himself out in any way as carrying on that business (*k*), but does not include (*l*):

(a) any pawnbroker in respect of business carried on by him in accordance with the provisions of the Acts for the time being in force in relation to pawnbrokers (*m*); or

(b) any registered society within the meaning of the Friendly Societies Act 1974 (*n*), or any society registered or having rules certified under that Act, or the Loan Societies Act 1840, or under the Building Societies Acts (*o*); or

(c) any body corporate incorporated or empowered by a special Act to lend money in accordance with that special Act; or

(d) any person bona fide carrying on the business of banking (*p*) or insurance or bona fide carrying on any business not having for its primary object the lending of money in the course of which and for the purposes whereof he lends money (*q*); or

(e) any body corporate for the time being exempted from the Moneylenders Acts 1900 to 1927, by order of the Board of Trade made and published pursuant to regulations of the Board of Trade (*r*).

Moneylenders' licences and certificates.—A moneylender is required to take out an annual excise licence which is granted only to

---

(*k*) System and continuity in moneylending transactions must be proved: *Kirkwood* v. *Gadd*, [1910] A.C. 422 (H.L.), at pp. 423, 431. See generally Goode, *Hire-Purchase Law and Practice* (2nd Edn.), Ch. 5; 15 Ency. Forms and Precedents (4th Edn.), Moneylending. Also *Skelton Finance Co., Ltd.,* v. *Lawrence* (1976), 120 Sol. Jo. 147 (two isolated transactions with strangers, not moneylending); *Fahey* v. *MSD Speirs, Ltd.,* [1975] 1 N.Z.L.R. 240 (P.C.). As to the documents in respect of which discovery may be ordered, see *Marshall* v. *Goulston Discount (Northern), Ltd.,* [1967] Ch. 72 (C.A.); [1966] 3 All E.R. 994; *Coni* v. *Robertson,* [1969] 2 All E.R. 609.

(*l*) The burden of proof is on the person whose business is that of moneylending to bring himself within one of the exceptions: *United Dominions Trust, Ltd.* v. *Kirkwood,* [1966] 2 Q.B. 431 (C.A.); [1966] 1 All E.R. 968.

(*m*) The Pawnbrokers Acts of 1872 and 1922, as amended by the Pawnbrokers Act 1960. These will be repealed by the Consumer Credit Act 1974.

(*n*) See p. 198, *supra.*

(*o*) See p. 193, *supra.*

(*p*) For the characteristics of banking, see *United Dominions Trust, Ltd.* v. *Kirkwood, supra.* A Board of Trade's certificate that a person is carrying on the business of banking is conclusive evidence of that fact for the purpose of defining moneylender: Companies Act 1967, s. 123. But a bank may be able to establish its status without a certificate. The clearing banks for example, have not applied for certificates, but their status is indisputable. See further Goode, *ubi sup.,* pp. 105–6.

(*q*) See *Premor, Ltd.* v. *Shaw Bros.,* [1964] 2 All E.R. 583 (C.A.). Accordingly a property dealer who grants second mortgages to purchasers of his properties is a moneylender, but exempted: *Halsall* v. *Egbunike* (1963), Estates Gazette Digest, 458.

(*r*) Since the rate of interest currently charged must generally not be more than a true rate of 12½ per cent. this exemption for companies is largely illusory: see Goode, *ubi sup.,* p. 109.

a person who holds a justices' or metropolitan stipendiary magistrate's certificate (s). The certificate must show the moneylender's true name and the name under which, and the address at which, he is authorised by the certificate to carry on business (t). The licence requires to be taken out annually and it must be in force at the time of the transaction in respect of which proceedings are taken (u).

Illegality of transactions in breach of restrictions.—If a moneylender in entering into any transaction contravenes any of the statutory restrictions on the carrying on of a moneylending business or is guilty of any contravention of the requirements relating to moneylenders' licences not only will he be subject to penalties but also the transaction will be void and can confer no rights (x). The moneylender cannot maintain any action to recover the money lent and the borrower is entitled to recover any securities which he has given to the moneylender (a). Also, when a loan has been made knowingly to discharge a loan which was wholly or partially illegal, the loan will be irrecoverable and the security unenforceable (b). But where the money borrowed was used to acquire the mortgaged property (c), and the mortgage is void initially, the moneylender will be entitled, by subrogation, to a lien on the property for so much of the advance as was paid towards the purchase price.

Recovery of securities.—Where the transaction is void, as just stated, the borrower may recover his securities although the moneylender cannot recover the advance. The borrower will be entitled to the appropriate declaration (d) and delivery up of the security; and although the latter depends on the equitable jurisdiction of the court, the borrower will not, it seems, be put on terms of doing equity himself and repaying the money advanced (e).

Circumstances in which relief granted.—Where the interest exceeds the rate of 48 per cent. per annum the court must, unless the contrary is proved, presume that the interest is excessive, and that the transaction is harsh and unconscionable (i.e., the burden of proof that

---

(s) Moneylenders Act 1927, s. 2.

(t) Moneylenders Act 1927, s. 2 (3). And see this sub-section as to the names permitted for this purpose.

(u) Ibid., ss. 1 (1), (3) (b). As to description in documentation, see London and Harrogate Securities, Ltd. v. Pitts, [1976] 2 All E.R. 184.

(x) Cornelius v. Phillips, [1918] A.C. 199 (H.L.).

(a) Bonnard v. Dott, [1906] 1 Ch. 740 (C.A.); Whiteman v. Sadler, [1910] A.C. 514 (H.L.); Re Robinson, Clarkson v. Robinson, [1911] 1 Ch. 230; Re Robinson's Settlement, Gant v. Hobbs, [1912] 1 Ch. 717, (C.A.); Cook v. Greendon Investments (1969), 113 Sol. Jo. 35. For the binding effect of a compromise admitting the legality of a transaction, see Binder v. Alachouzos, [1972] 2 Q.B. 151 (C.A.); [1972] 2 All E.R. 189.

(b) Spector v. Ageda, [1973] Ch. 30; [1971] 3 All E.R. 417.

(c) Congresbury Motors, Ltd. v. Anglo-Belge Finance Co., Ltd., [1971] 1 Ch. 81 (C.A.); [1971] 3 All E.R. 385; Greendon Investments v. Mills (1973), 226 Estates Gazette 1957; aliter, where the mortgage is initially valid, but becomes subsequently invalid: see Burston Finance, Ltd. v. Speirway, [1974] 3 All E.R. 735, not following Coptic, Ltd. v. Bailey, [1972] 1 Ch. 446; [1972] 1 All E.R. 1242; and see p. 183, supra.

(d) Chapman v. Michaelson, [1909] 1 Ch. 238 (C.A.).

(e) Kasumu v. Baba-Egbe, [1956] A.C. 539 (P.C.); [1956] 3 All E.R. 266; Barclay v. Prospect Mortgages, Ltd., supra; cf. Lodge v. Union Investment Co., [1907] 1 Ch. 300. See 15 Ency. Forms and Precedents (4th Edn.), p. 29, note 5. As to the right to a lien, see supra.

the interest is not excessive is on the lender (*f*), but the court may nevertheless hold that the interest charged, although not exceeding 48 per cent., is excessive (*g*). The court will grant relief from payment in excess of the sum adjudged by the court to be fairly due in respect of principal and interest, and, if any such excess has been paid or allowed in account, may direct the moneylender to repay it (*h*). A secured advance has been held to be in a different position from an unsecured advance, and a rate of interest will be more readily regarded as excessive (*i*). And interest may be excessive in view of the borrower's financial position (*k*). A moneylender cannot have compound interest, and a contract for a loan by a moneylender is illegal in so far as it provides directly or indirectly for the payment of compound interest, or for the rate or amount of interest being increased on default in payment, but simple interest can be charged during default (*l*).

The phrases that the transaction is harsh and unconscionable, or is otherwise such that a court of equity would grant relief in s. 1 of the Money-lenders Act 1900, are alternative, so that if the transaction is harsh and unconscionable, it need not be of such a nature that apart from the Act, a court of equity would grant relief (*f*).

There may be circumstances to justify the reopening of the transaction, although there has been no deception or pressure by the moneylender (*g*). But in the absence of active malpractice, deception, or unfair pressure, dealings voluntarily settled will not be reopened after the lapse of years (*h*).

Power to close contract.—Without prejudice to the powers of the court under s. 1 of the Act of 1900, the Act of 1927 provides that if at a time when proceedings are taken by a moneylender in respect of default in payment of a sum due under the contract, any further amount is outstanding but not yet due, the court may determine the contract, and order the principal outstanding to be paid with such interest as the court may allow (*i*).

Form of moneylenders' contracts.—The Act of 1927 provides:

6.—(1) No contract for the repayment by a borrower of money lent to him or to any agent on his behalf by a moneylender after the commencement of this Act or for the payment by him of interest on money so lent, and no security given by the borrower (*j*) or by any such agent as aforesaid (*k*) in respect of any such contract, shall be enforceable, unless a note or memorandum in

---

(*f*) *Reading Trust, Ltd.* v. *Spero, Spero* v. *Reading Trust, Ltd.*, [1930] 1 K.B. 492 (C.A.).
(*g*) Moneylenders Act 1927, s. 10 (1).
(*h*) Moneylenders Act 1927, s. 1 (1), *supra.* For instances of what is harsh and unconscionable, see *Bonnard* v. *Dott, supra; Carringtons, Ltd.* v. *Smith*, [1906] 1 K.B. 79; *Lancashire Loans, Ltd.* v. *Black*, [1934] 1 K.B. 380 (C.A.).
(*i*) *Kruse* v. *Seeley*, [1924] 1 Ch. 136; *Verner-Jeffreys* v. *Pinto*, [1929] 1 Ch. 401 (C.A.).
(*k*) *Oakes* v. *Green* (1907), 23 T.L.R. 560; *Stirling* v. *Musgrave* (1913), 29 T.L.R. 333.
(*l*) Moneylenders Act 1927, s. 7. See *Spector* v. *Ageda, supra.* For the statutory rules for calculating the interest where this is not expressed in terms of a rate per cent., see *ibid.*, Sched. 1.
(*f*) *Samuel* v. *Newbold*, [1906] A.C. 461 (H.L.).
(*g*) *Kerman* v. *Wainewright* (1916), 32 T.L.R. 295 (C.A.).
(*h*) *Stone* v. *Hamilton*, [1918] 2 I.R. 192; and see *Cohen* v. *Jonesco*, [1926] 2 K.B. 1.
(*i*) Section 13 (2).
(*j*) Or a third person: *Barclay* v. *Prospect Mortgages, Ltd., supra.*
(*k*) To the lender: *Argo Caribbean Group, Ltd.* v. *Lewis*, [1976] 2 Lloyds' Rep. 289 (C.A.).

writing of the contract (*l*) be made and signed personally by the borrower, and unless a copy thereof (*m*) be delivered or sent to the borrower (*n*) within seven days of the making of the contract; and no such contract or security shall be enforceable if it is proved that the note or memorandum aforesaid was not signed by the borrower before the money was lent, or before the security was given, as the case may be.

(2) The note or memorandum aforesaid shall contain all the terms of the contract (*o*), and in particular shall show the date on which the loan is made (*p*), the amount of the principal of the loan (*q*), and, either the interest charged on the loan expressed in terms of a rate per cent. per annum (*r*), or the rate per cent. per annum represented by the interest charged as calculated in accordance with the provisions of the First Schedule to this Act (*s*).

Although breach of this provision does not make the security void, but only not enforceable (*t*) the borrower will be entitled to the appropriate declaration and the return of the security without any payment to the lender (*u*).

Limitation of action.—Proceedings by a moneylender for the recovery of money lent by him or for the enforcement of any security must be commenced before the expiration of twelve months from the date on which the cause of action accrued (*a*). The period may be renewed by an acknowledgement in writing of the amount due and a written undertaking to pay that amount (*b*), and in the case of instalments time does not begin to run until the last instalment is due (*c*).

(*l*) Several documents may make up the note or memorandum: see *Reading Trust, Ltd.* v. *Spero*, [1930] 1 K.B. 492 (C.A.), at pp. 505, 507; *Tooke* v. *Bennett & Co., Ltd.*, [1940] 1 K.B. 150; [1939] 4 All E.R. 200. For the mortgage deed as a note or memorandum, see *Congresbury Motors, Ltd.* v. *Anglo-Belge Finance Co., Ltd.*, *supra*.

(*m*) And of all documents referred to in the contract: *Edgware Trust, Ltd.* v. *Lawrence*, [1961] 3 All E.R. 141.

(*n*) And to all joint borrowers: *J. W. Grahame (English Financiers), Ltd.* v. *Ingram*, [1955] 2 All E.R. 320.

(*o*) *I.e.*, those affecting or imposing liability. The place of repayment need not be stated: *Reading Trust, Ltd.* v. *Spero*, [1930] K.B. 492 (C.A.); *Congresbury Motors, Ltd.* v. *Anglo-Belge Finance Co., Ltd.*, *supra* (dates material). And as to what constitutes a term of the contract, see *Re 22 Albion Street, Westminster, Hanyet Securities, Ltd.* v. *Mallett*, [1968] 2 All E.R. 960 (C.A.). The memorandum will be bad if it does not include a provision in an accompanying legal charge which makes the borrower's liability more onerous then would otherwise appear from the memorandum itself: *Holiday Credits, Ltd.* v. *Erol* (1975), 119 Sol. Jo. 368.

(*p*) *Gaskell, Ltd.* v. *Askwith* (1928), 45 T.L.R. 566 (C.A.).

(*q*) *I.e.*, the amount actually lent: s. 15 (1); see *Dunn Trust, Ltd.* v. *Feetham*, [1936] 1 K.B. 22 (C.A.); *Hoare* v. *Adam Smith (London), Ltd.*, [1938] 4 All E.R. 283.

(*r*) *London and Harrogate Securities, Ltd.* v. *Pitts*, [1976] 2 All E.R. 184 (C.A.) (omission of words "per annum" did not invalidate the contract); cf. *Provincial and Northern Finance, Ltd.* v. *Grant* (1976) 120 S.J. 834 (C.A.); *Directloans, Ltd.* v. *Cracknell* (1975), *Times*, 18 April (amount of interest inaccurately stated, contract invalid).

(*s*) *Askinex, Ltd.* v. *Green*, [1969] 1 Q.B. 272 (C.A.); [1967] 1 All E.R. 65. See further, as to form and generally, Meston, *Law relating to Moneylenders* (5th Edn.), Ch. 8. As to an unenforceable variation of form, see *United Dominions Corporation (Jamaica), Ltd.* v. *Shoucair*, [1969] A.C. 340 (P.C.); [1968] 2 All E.R. 904; *Congresbury Motors, Ltd.* v. *Anglo-Belge Finance Co., Ltd.*, *supra*; *Spector* v. *Ageda*, *supra*.

(*t*) Either by action or extra-judicially: see *Barclay* v. *Prospect Mortgages. Ltd.*, *supra*.

(*u*) *Cohen* v. *J. Lester, Ltd.*, [1939] 1 K.B. 504; [1938] 4 All E.R. 188; *Barclay* v. *Prospect Mortgages, Ltd.*, *supra*. And see p. 236, *supra*.

(*a*) Moneylenders Act 1927, s. 13 (1). And see the section for disabilities, etc.

(*b*) *Ibid.*, s. 13 (1), proviso (a).

(*c*) *Ibid.*, s. 13 (1), proviso (b). But where the contract provides that on default of payment of an instalment the whole shall or may become due, time runs from the date of the default: *Harry Smith, Ltd.* v. *Craig*, 1938 S.C. 620; *Wotherspoon* v. *M'Intosh*, 1953 S.L.T. (Sh. Ct.) 50. See (1971) 121 New L.J. 725 (B. L. Nathan) and also *Lakshmijit* v. *Sherani*, [1974] A.C. 605 (P.C.); [1973] 3 All E.R. 737.

A moneylender whose rights of action are barred is not entitled to any surplus of the proceeds of the sale of the mortgaged property by a prior mortgagee (*d*).

Bona fide assignees for value.—The prima facie result of a moneylending security being void is that it is void for all purposes, and an assignee of the security, is in no better position than the original holder (*e*). The Act of 1927 (*f*) requires that on an assignment of such a security the assignor (whether the moneylender or a person to whom the debt has previously been assigned) must, under a heavy penalty, give to the assignee notice in writing that the debt or security is effected by the operation of the Act of 1927, and the provisions of the Act will continue to apply notwithstanding the assignment; but under section 17 (1) this is subject as follows:

Provided that—
(a) Notwithstanding anything in this Act—
    (i) any agreement with, or security taken by, a moneylender in respect of money lent by him after the commencement of this Act shall be valid in favour of any bona fide assignee or holder for value without notice of any defect due to the operation of this Act and of any person deriving title under him; and
    (ii) any payment of transfer of money or property made bona fide by any person whether acting in a fiduciary capacity or otherwise, on the faith of the validity of any such agreement or security, without notice of any such defect shall, in favour of that person, be as valid as it would have been if the agreement or security had been valid; and
    (iii) the provisions of this Act limiting the time for proceedings in respect of any such money lent shall not apply to any proceedings in respect of any such agreement or security commenced by a bona fide assignee or holder for value without notice that the agreement or security was affected by the operation of this Act, or by any person deriving title under him,
but in every such case the moneylender shall be liable to indemnify the borrower or any other person who is prejudiced by the virtue of this section; and nothing in this proviso shall render valid an agreement or security in favour of, or apply to proceedings commenced by, an assignee or holder for value who is himself a moneylender; and
(b) for the purposes of this Act and of the Moneylenders Act 1900, the provisions of s. 199 of the Law of Property Act 1925 (*g*), shall apply as if the expression "purchaser" included a person making any such payment or transfer as aforesaid.

Registered land.—On registration of a charge in favour of a moneylender the applicant's solicitor must certify that the provisions of the Moneylenders Acts have been observed and that the chargee holds a moneylender's excise licence (*h*). In the absence of this certificate the registrar may refuse to register the charge. In addition, the applicant's solicitors must satisfy the registrar that a note or memorandum in writing of the contract was duly made and delivered. In the absence of this latter evidence the charge will be registered but with a restriction

---

(*d*) *Matthews* (*C. & M.*), *Ltd.* v. *Marsden Building Society*, [1951] Ch. 758 (C.A.). And see *Orakpo* v. *Manson Investments, Ltd.*, [1977] 1 All E.R. 666 (C.A.).
(*e*) *Re Robinson, Clarkson* v. *Robinson*, [1911] 1 Ch. 230.
(*f*) Sections 16, 17.
(*g*) Which places restrictions in favour of a purchaser on the doctrine of constructive notice. See p. 435, *infra*.
(*h*) See generally, Ruoff & Roper, *Registered Conveyancing* (3rd Edn.), pp. 539–540.

preventing the registration of a transfer of the property on the exercise of the lender's power of sale unless the statutory provisions as to the form of the contract have in fact been complied with.

D—CONSUMER CREDIT SECURITIES

Unenforceable agreements and securities, reopening extortionate credit bargains etc.—See, generally, Ch. 9, *supra*.

E—SECURITIES MADE UNDER UNDUE INFLUENCE

Fiduciary relationship.—Assurances for which there was an inadequate or no consideration, and between the parties to which such a fiduciary or other relation existed, that the maker of the security might be assumed to have been misled, unable to form a correct judgment, or under the influence of the person in whose favour it was made, are liable to be set aside by the court (*i*), or to be treated only as securities for so much money as can be proved to have been advanced, with interest at a reasonable rate.

When, therefore, an inadequate consideration (which alone gives no right to relief (*k*)), is given to a person who is of weak intellect; or is subject to the influence which arises out of the relation of parent and child (*l*), guardian and ward (*m*) or fiancés (*n*); in a transaction with the person under whose influence he is or is supposed to be (*o*), *e.g.*, between bank and customer (*p*); or who, by reason of superior knowledge of the property or other circumstances, is likely to have an advantage over him; he is entitled, as against the grantee and the volunteers claiming under the grantee, and all other persons who claim with notice of the equity or of the circumstances under which it arose (*q*), to be relieved from the consequences. And it is for the other party to show that the grantor had such professional advice (though not necessarily from another solicitor than the solicitor who acted for the

---

(*i*) Where the grantor commences proceedings to have the transaction set aside he must do so within a reasonable time of the influence ceasing: *Allcard* v. *Skinner* (1887), 36 Ch. D. 145 (C.A.); *Bullock* v. *Lloyds Bank, Ltd.*, [1955] Ch. 317; [1954] 3 All E.R. 726.

(*k*) *Harrison* v. *Guest* (1860), 8 H.L. Cas. 481. See, generally, [1973] 24 N.I.L.Q. 171 (R. G. Lawson); (1971) 121 New L.J. 1159 (J. G. Ross-Martyn); (1976) 39 M.L.R. 369 (S. M. Waddams).

(*l*) *Espey* v. *Lake* (1852), 10 Hare 260; *Bainbrigge* v. *Browne* (1881), 18 Ch. D. 188. The presumption continues after the child's marriage and for a time after attaining majority: see *Bainbrigge* v. *Browne*, *supra*; *Lancashire Loans, Ltd.* v. *Black*, [1934] 1 K.B. 380; *Re Pauling's Settlement Trusts*, [1964] Ch. 303, at p. 337; [1963] 3 All E.R. 1, at p. 10.

(*m*) Even though the actual relation may be at an end: *Hylton* v. *Hylton* (1754), 2 Ves. S. 547.

(*n*) *Re Lloyds Bank, Ltd.*, [1931] 1 Ch. 289; *Zamet* v. *Hyman*, [1961] 3 All E.R. 933.

(*o*) *I.e.*, religious, medical or other advisers: see *Allcard* v. *Skinner*, *supra*; *Inche Noriah* v. *Shaik Allie Bin Omar*, [1929] A.C. 127 (P.C.); *Tufton* v. *Sperni*, [1952] 2 T.L.R. 516; see, generally, *Snell, Equity* (27th Edn.), pp. 546 *et seq.*

(*p*) *Lloyds Bank, Ltd.* v. *Bundy*, [1975] Q.B. 326; [1974] 3 All E.R. 757 (C.A.); *McKenzie* v. *Bank of Montreal* (1975), 55 D.L.R. (3d) 641.

(*q*) *Bainbrigge* v. *Browne*, *supra*; *De Witte* v. *Addison* (1899), 80 L.T. 207; *Inche Noriah* v. *Shaik Allie Bin Omar*, *supra*.

grantee (*r*), as to enable him to exercise a proper judgment (*s*), and that he was not misled by artifice or contrivance (*t*).

On the other hand, in cases of undue influence depending not on relationship, but on express influence or threats, the onus of proof lies on the plaintiff (*u*).

Express influence.—Where there is no fiduciary relationship influence must be proved by the person alleging it (*a*). There is no presumption of undue influence between husband and wife (*b*) and proof of express influence is necessary if the transaction is to be avoided.

Securities obtained by threats.—The court may also grant relief when the security has been obtained from the mortgagor by threats (*c*).

F—SECURITIES TO SOLICITORS

No advantage must be taken.—A security given to a solicitor by his client is subject to the principles applied in cases of undue influence; partly, because of the personal influence of the solicitor over his client, and partly because of the solicitor's knowledge of his client's property and value. Hence if a solicitor purchases, or obtains a benefit, from his client, the solicitor is bound to show that he has taken no advantage of his professional position, but has given every information and advice, and has protected his client's interests in the same manner as if he had dealt with a stranger. In default of such proof the deed will only stand as a security for the amount found to be due (*d*). And a gift or a security for a gift pending the relation is subject to the same principles (*e*). An assignment by a client to his solicitor of a bare right to sue is good when it is made by way of security (*f*).

Conditions for validity of security.—For a security given by a client to his solicitor to be valid, it is necessary that the money secured shall have been advanced, or shall otherwise be actually due (*g*); that the amount, if not ascertained at the time, shall be capable of being ascertained (the onus of the inquiry being on the solicitor); and that

---

(*r*) *Inche Noriah* v. *Shaik Allie Bin Omar, supra.*

(*s*) *Allcard* v. *Skinner, supra*, at p. 171; *Inche Noriah* v. *Shaik Allie Bin Omar, supra*, at p. 135; *Zamet* v. *Hyman, supra*; *Lloyds Bank, Ltd.* v. *Bundy, supra.*

(*t*) The existence of which any false recital or suggestion in the security will tend to show: *Baker* v. *Bradley* (1855), 7 De G.M. & G. 597.

(*u*) See *Williams* v. *Bayley* (1866), L.R. 1 H.L. 200, where a mortgage executed by a father to prevent the prosecution of his son by the mortgagee was set aside.

(*a*) *Howes* v. *Bishop*, [1909] 2 K.B. 390 (C.A.); *Bank of Montreal* v. *Stuart*, [1911] A.C. 120 (P.C.); *Mackenzie* v. *Royal Bank of Canada*, [1934] A.C. 468 (P.C.).

(*b*) See *Bank of Montreal* v. *Stuart, supra* (influence); *Mackenzie* v. *Royal Bank of Canada* (no influence).

(*c*) On duress, see *Barton* v. *Armstrong*, [1976] A.C. 104 (P.C.); [1975] 2 All E.R. 465. On drunkeness, see *Peeters* v. *Schimanski*, [1975] 2 N.Z.L.R. 328.

(*d*) *Tomson* v. *Judge* (1855), 3 Drew. 306; *Wright* v. *Carter*, [1903] 1 Ch. 27 (C.A.); *Demarara Bauxite Co., Ltd.* v. *Hubbard*, [1923] A.C. 675 (P.C.); *McMaster* v. *Byrne*, [1952] 1 All E.R. 1362 (P.C.).

(*e*) *Liles* v. *Terry*, [1895] 2 Q.B. 679; *Wright* v. *Carter, supra*. But, in the absence of *mala fides*, trifling gifts are not within this rule: *Rhodes* v. *Bate* (1866), 1 Ch. App. 252.

(*f*) *Wood* v. *Downes* (1811), 18 Ves. 120; *Anderson* v. *Radcliffe* (1858), E.B. & E. 806: affd. (1860), 29 L.J. Q.B. 128.

(*g*) *Nelson* v. *Booth* (1857), 27 L.J. Ch. 110.

there are no unusual provisions by which the client may be injurea or kept in the solicitor's hands (*h*). If any greater advantage is given to the solicitor than the law would give him (such as interest on his costs), the client must first have been informed of his rights (*i*).

The security may be for costs or advances, the amount of which has not been fixed, or where bills for the costs have not been delivered; and the amount due on such securities for costs will be ascertained by taxation (*k*). Though a solicitor cannot commence an action for his charges until a month after his bill of costs has been delivered (*l*), this does not prevent his enforcing a security for his costs though no bill has been delivered (*m*). A solicitor may take security for his future charges and disbursements, to be ascertained by taxation or otherwise (*n*).

Security must not be oppressive.—Where the debt is bona fide, the security will not be invalid because it was made under pressure from the solicitor (*o*). If the mortgage is oppressive in form, as by an unreasonable postponement of the time for redemption, the mortgagor will have the general rights of a mortgagor (*p*) and where there has been a concealment or misrepresentation in obtaining or framing the security, the mortgage will be valid only for so much as, on taking the accounts, shall appear to be actually due (*q*). So, where the power of sale omitted the usual conditions precedent to its exercise, the solicitor mortgagee was not allowed to sell, even when interest was three months in arrears, the solicitor not having explained the omission to the client (*r*).

Where a mortgagee, being a solicitor for the mortgagor, neglects his duty towards him as by omitting to register the mortgage when it requires registration by statute—he will not be allowed to avail himself of it, even though it is not avoided by the non-registration (*s*).

Loss of lien.—If a solicitor takes a security for his costs, this is, in the absence of evidence of a contrary intention, an abandonment

---

(*h*) *Cockburn* v. *Edwards* (1881), 18 Ch. D. 449 (C.A.); but where the mortgage is to secure costs it may include special provisions: *Pooley's Trustee* v. *Whetham* (1886), 33 Ch. D. 111 (C.A.). And see Law Society's Digest, Opinions Nos. 352 to 364.

(*i*) *Lyddon* v. *Moss* (1859), 4 De G. & J. 104.

(*k*) An agreement to give security for costs to be ascertained by taxation is not required to be in writing: *Jonesco* v. *Evening Standard Co.*, [1932] 2 K.B. 340 (C.A.).

(*l*) Solicitors Act 1974, s. 69 (1).

(*m*) *Thomas* v. *Cross* (1864), 11 L.T. 430.

(*n*) Solicitors Act 1974, ss. 56 (6) (non-contentious matters), 65 (1) (contentious matters). For a form of mortgage to solicitors to secure costs owing and to be incurred, see 14 Ency. Forms and Precedents (4th Edn.), pp. 309-311.

(*o*) *Johnson* v. *Fesenmeyer* (1858), 25 Beav. 88; *Pearson* v. *Benson* (1860), 28 Beav. 598.

(*p*) See p. 522, *infra*.

(*q*) *Cowdry* v. *Day* (1859), 1 Giff. 316.

(*r*) *Cockburn* v. *Edwards* (1881), 18 Ch. D. 449 (C.A.); *Cradock* v. *Rogers* (1884), 53 L.J. Ch. 968; affd., [1885] W.N. 134 (C.A.).

(*s*) *Re Patent Bread Machinery Co., Ex parte Valpy and Chaplin* (1872), 7 Ch. App. 289. For negligence in relation to mortgages, see *Whiteman* v. *Hawkins* (1878), 4 C.P.D. 13 (failure to call for production of title deeds and consequent non-disclosure of prior equitable mortgage); *Cooper* v. *Stephenson* (1852), 16 Jur. 424 (failure to search in bankruptcy); *Bean* v. *Wade* (1885), Cab. & El. 519; on app. 2 T.L.R. 157 (C.A.) (failure to give notice of mortgage).

of his lien (*t*). But the fact of his taking a security on the documents, by way of securing an advance, does not prejudice his lien (*u*).

III—MISREPRESENTATION AND MISTAKE

Misrepresentation (*a*).—A person who is induced to advance money on account of a misrepresentation may be entitled to have the security set aside (*b*). This will generally (*c*) be so whether the misrepresentation is fraudulent (*d*) or innocent (*e*). And such person may also or alternatively be entitled to damages (*f*).

Mistake.—In certain situations, where a person has mistakenly signed a document which turns out to be radically different from that which the signor thought he was signing, the document will be set aside. The defence of the person who signed the document to any action on the document is *non est factum* (*g*). The doctrine will only rarely be established by a person of full capacity. Although it is not confined to the blind and illiterate, any extension of the scope of the plea will be kept within narrow limits. In particular it is unlikely that the plea will be available to a person who signed a document without informing himself of its meaning (*h*). The distinction formerly drawn

---

(*t*) *Re Taylor, Stileman and Underwood*, [1891] 1 Ch. 590 (C.A.); *Re Douglas Norman and Co.*, [1898] 1 Ch. 199. See p. 168, *supra*.

(*u*) *Re Harvey's Estate* (1886), 17 L.R. Ir. 165.

(*a*) As to warranties by building societies, see Building Societies Act 1962, s. 30 (warranty that purchase price is reasonable. But this may be negatived by notice in the prescribed form). If a person having a financial interest in the disposition of property makes a representation that the making of an advance by a building society is an implied assurance that the property is sufficient security for the advance, then without prejudice to any other remedy, he will be liable to a fine, unless he had reasonable grounds for believing the representation to be true: Building Societies Act 1962, s. 31.

(*b*) See generally, 26 Halsbury's Laws (3rd Edn.), pp. 856 *et seq.* and Supp.

(*c*) There can be no rescission where innocent third parties have acquired rights in the property.

(*d*) *Lee* v. *Angus* (1866), 15 L.T. 380. See *Bloomfield* v. *Blake* (1833), 6 C. & P. 75; *Lake* v. *Brutton* (1856), 8 De G.M. & G. 440 (untrue misrepresentation that representor liable as representee's surety).

(*e*) Before the Misrepresentation Act 1967, there could be no rescission for an innocent misrepresentation not forming part of the contract once the contract was completed by conveyance or execution (the rule in *Seddon* v. *North Eastern Salt Co., Ltd.*, [1905] 1 Ch. 326). Section 1 of the 1967 Act removes this bar. But damages may be awarded in lieu of rescission in this situation: Misrepresentation Act 1967, s. 2 (2). Where the innocent misrepresentation forms part of the contract the representee is also now entitled to rescission, see Mispresentation Act 1967, s. 1, in addition to his common law rights for a breach of contract. For a comment on these provisions, see (1967), 30 M.L.R. 369 (P. S. Atiyah and G. H. Treitel); and see Cheshire and Fifoot, *Law of Contract* (9th Edn.), pp. 262 *et seq.*

(*f*) Damages are available for fraudulent misrepresentation and for innocent misrepresentation where the misrepresentation forms part of the contract. And by s. 2 (1) of the Misrepresentation Act 1967, damages are now available for an innocent misrepresentation not forming part of the contract, unless the representor can prove that he had reasonable ground to believe and did believe that the facts represented were true.

(*g*) See generally, 9 Halsbury's Laws (4th Edn.), para. 284; Cheshire and Fifoot, *Law of Contract* (9th Edn.), pp. 237 *et seq*; *Saunders* v. *Anglia Building Society*, [1971] A.C. 1004 (H.L.); [1970] 3 All E.R. 691.

(*h*) The party raising the plea must have acted with reasonable care. Carelessness or negligence will preclude him from later pleading *non est factum*. But this is not an instance of negligence operating by way of estoppel: see generally *Saunders* v. *Anglia Building Society*, *supra; United Dominions Trust, Ltd.* v. *Western*, [1976] Q.B. 513 (C.A.); [1975] 3 All E.R. 1017 (document incomplete when signed).

between the character and the contents of the document has been rejected (*i*). For the plea to succeed there must be a radical (fundamental, serious or very substantial) difference between what the party signing signed and what he thought he was signing.

Rectification.—The mortgage may be rectified where its terms fail to record the common intention of the parties (*k*). In the absence of mutual mistake, the deed will only be rectified on the ground of inequitable conduct (*l*).

IV—FORGERIES (*m*)

Generally.—A forged mortgage will generally be of no effect. For what it is worth, there may be a right of action against the recipient of the money for the money advanced and, in appropriate cases, the payer may be able to rely on estoppel against the true owner (because of his conduct) (*n*), or a lien on the deeds of the property (*o*). Registration does not give validity to a forged document (*p*), though an innocent third party may be entitled to indemnity where the register is rectified because a document was forged (*q*).

Husband and wife cases.—It not uncommonly happens that where a husband and wife are co-owners of property the husband will raise a loan on the property without telling his wife and forging her signature. The mortgage is usually a second or subsequent mortgage where the lender does not bother to investigage title. (If such a lender took the trouble to investigate the title, a comparison of the relevant signatures on the disposition to the would-be borrowers and a first mortgage with those on the letter of acceptance would often disclose the true position). Where there is such a forgery, the mortgage will operate as a mortgage of the husband's beneficial interest (*r*), but the legal title and the wife's beneficial interest will remain unaffected by the mortgage. It may be that, in appropriate cases, *e.g.*, where the wife was party to the earlier negotiations, she may be estopped from relying on the forgery and in some cases the husband may be deemed to have acted as agent for both himself and his wife, so that the mortgage could be treated as an effective equitable mortgage or equitable charge by both of them. And where the money has been used to purchase property, or for a permanent and substantial improvement to property, if the mortgage

---

(*i*) See *Saunders* v. *Anglia Building Society, supra.*

(*k*) See *Vaudeville Electric Cinema, Ltd.* v. *Muriset*, [1923] 2 Ch. 74, at p. 80; also *Coote on Mortgages*, (9th Edn.), p. 84; and generally Snell, *Equity* (27th Edn.), 610–619.

(*l*) *Riverlate Properties, Ltd.* v. *Paul*, [1975] Ch. 133 (C.A.); [1974] 2 All E.R. 656; *Leighton* v. *Parton*, [1976] 1 N.Z.L.R. 165.

(*m*) See Wurtzburg & Mills, *Building Society Law* (14th Edn.), pp. 222–223; (1975) 119 Sol. Jo. 690 (W. A. Greene).

(*n*) See *Re Cooper, Cooper* v. *Vesey* (1882), 20 Ch. D. 611 (C.A.); *Re De Leeuw, Jakens* v. *Central Advance and Discount Corporation, Ltd.*, [1922] 2 Ch. 540.

(*o*) *E.g.*, if the monies are used on the property.

(*p*) *Re Cooper, supra* (registration in the Middlesex Deeds Registry).

(*q*) See Land Registration Act 1925, s. 83 (4).

(*r*) *Taylor* v. *Wheeler* (1706), 2 Salk. 449; see also p. 175, *supra*. There may be a remedy available against a witness who knew or ought to have known of the forgery on the ground of warranty that the wife had signed when clearly she had not.

is ineffective, the lender may be able to claim a lien or equitable charge over the property purchased or improved (*s*).

V—UNLAWFUL CONSIDERATION

A—IMMORAL OR ILLEGAL CONSIDERATION

Generally.—A mortgage which is given in respect of a debt or other obligation arising out of an illegal transaction is not enforceable by a party who was also a party to the illegal transaction and who would be unable to enforce that transaction (*t*). The security is tainted by the illegality of the original transaction (*u*). So too where the mortgage secures a loan to discharge an illegal transaction (*a*). But a party to a security may be able to enforce his rights thereunder if at the time of the execution of the security he had no knowledge of the illegality of the original transaction (*b*). Where the original transaction is not wholly unenforceable, the security will be unenforceable only in so far as it is related to or connected with the original transaction; if, for example, there are distinct considerations, it may be possible to sever the considerations (*c*).

B—GAMING TRANSACTIONS

Gaming securities.—Under the Gaming Act 1835, s. 1, every note, bill or mortgage, the whole or part of the consideration for which is money or other valuables won by gaming, or playing at or betting on any games, or for the repayment of money knowingly lent for such gaming or betting, or at the time or place of such play, to any person gaming or betting, is deemed to have been made for an illegal consideration (*d*).

Wagering securities.—Under the Gaming Act 1845, s. 18, all contracts or agreements by way of gaming and wagering are null and void and no action may be brought or entertained in any court of law or equity for recovering any sum of money or valuable thing alleged to be won upon any wager, or which has been deposited in the hands of any person to abide the event on which any wager has been made. The effect of this provision was only to make a contract which is within it void, but not to make it illegal, so that money paid for one who lost a

---

(*s*) See p. 168, *supra*.

(*t*) *Fisher* v. *Bridges* (1854), 3 E. & B. 642. For illegal constracts, see 9 Halsbury's Laws (4th Edn.), paras. 429 *et seq*; Cheshire and Fifoot, *Law of Contract*, (9th Edn.), Ch. 4. See also *Selangor United Rubber Estates, Ltd.* v. *Cradock* (*No. 3*), [1968] 2 All E.R. 1073, at p. 1149 *et seq*; *Heald* v. *O'Connor*, [1971] 2 All E.R. 1105; *Patterson* v. *Roden* (1972), 223 Estates Gazette 945; *Sidmay* v. *Wehttam Investments* (1967), 61 D.L.R. (2d) 358; *Williams* v. *Fleetwood Holidays, Ltd.* (1974), 41 D.L.R. (3d) 636.

(*u*) *Cannan* v. *Bryce* (1819), 3 B. & Ald. 179.

(*a*) *Spector* v. *Ageda*, [1973] Ch. 30; [1971] 3 All E.R. 417, considering *Fisher* v. *Bridges*, *supra*, and *Cannan* v. *Bryce*, *supra*.

(*b*) *Cannan* v. *Bryce*, *supra*; *Spector* v. *Ageda*, *supra*, at pp. 45 and 427.

(*c*) *Sheehy* v. *Sheehy*, [1901] 1 I.R. 239; see *Robinson* v. *Marsh*, [1921] 2 K.B. 640. See also on illegal transactions, *Shackell* v. *Rosier* (1836), 2 Bing. N.C. 634; *Willyams* v. *Bullmore* (1863), 33 L.J. Ch. 461; *Re Onslow's Trusts* (1875), L.R. 20 Eq. 677; *Herman* v. *Jeuchner* (1885), 15 Q.B.D. 561; *Moulis* v. *Owen*, [1907] 1 K.B. (C.A.), at p. 753.

(*d*) As to the loan itself, see *Carlton Hall Club, Ltd.* v. *Laurence*, [1929] 2 K.B. 153; cf. *C.H.T., Ltd.* v. *Ward*, [1965] 2 Q.B. 63 (C.A.), at p. 86; (1963) 3 All E.R. 835, at pp. 842, 843; Gaming Act 1968, s. 16.

wager, at his request was recoverable. But by the Gaming Act 1892, losses paid by an agent are not recoverable from the principal (*e*).

Loan for payment of bets.—And if a loan is made by a lender to a borrower under an agreement that bets should be paid out of the loan, any security for the repayment of the loan will be bad (*f*). But such a security will be good if the borrower can dispose of money lent as he pleases (*g*).

V—SECURITIES AFFECTED BY THE NATURE OF THE SECURITY

A—PUBLIC PAY AND PENSIONS

Public offices.—A public office is deemed to be a position of public trust and the sale or other assurance of such offices is, even apart from statute (*h*) by which such assurances are declared to be void, contrary to public policy (*i*).

Officers' pensions and pay.—The assignment of the pay or half-pay of public officers is contrary to public policy (*k*). This applies to officers in the Armed Forces (*l*), civil servants (*m*), etc. But to come within the rule the pay must come out of national and not out of local funds (*n*).

And by statute the alienation of naval, military and air pensions (*o*) and the pensions of many other people, such as police officers, firemen, school teachers, etc., is prohibited (*p*). But pensions given entirely as compensation for past services are assignable (*q*), unless this is prohibited by the statute under which they are paid (*r*).

B—PROPERTY FORBIDDEN TO BE INCUMBERED

Restraint on alienation.—Property cannot be given to a person beneficially with a proviso that he shall not have the power of alienating or incumbering it. Such a proviso would be repugnant to the gift and void (*s*).

(*e*) Section 1.
(*f*) *Hill* v. *Fox* (1859), 4 H. & N. 359; *MacDonald* v. *Green*, [1951] 1 K.B. 594 (C.A.).
(*g*) *Re O'Shea*, [1911] 2 K.B. 981 (C.A.), at pp. 987-988; *MacDonald* v. *Green, supra*, at pp. 605, 606.
(*h*) See Sale of Offices Act 1551; Sale of Offices Act 1809; Criminal Law Act 1974, s. 1.
(*i*) *Stackpole* v. *Earle* (1761), 2 Wils. 133.
(*k*) *Flarty* v. *Odlum* (1790), 3 Term Rep. 681; *Stone* v. *Lidderdale* (1795), 2 Anst. 533. A mortgage of the profits of a college fellowship is not contrary to public policy: *Feistel* v. *King's College, Cambridge* (1847), 10 Beav. 491; *cf. Berkeley* v. *King's College, Cambridge* (1830), 10 Beav. 602.
(*l*) *Stone* v. *Lidderdale, supra*.
(*m*) See *Lucas* v. *Lucas*, [1943] P. 68; [1943] 2 All E.R. 110.
(*n*) *Re Mirams*, [1891] 1 Q.B. 594.
(*o*) See Army Act 1955, s. 203; Air Force Act 1955, s. 203; Naval and Marine Pay and Pensions Act 1865, s. 4.
(*p*) As is alienation of the old age pension. See generally, 6 Halsbury's Laws (4th Edn.), para. 84.
(*q*) *Willcox* v. *Terrell* (1878), 3 Ex. D. 323.
(*r*) *E.g.*, under the Army Act 1955, s. 203. See *Crowe* v. *Price* (1889), 22 Q.B.D. 429. Maintenance is not assignable unless secured: see 6 Halsbury's Laws (4th Edn.), para. 85. Nor are national insurance benefits, child benefits, etc., alienable (see under the respective Acts providing for the benefit). As to family allowance as security, see *R.* v. *Curr*, [1967] 1 All E.R. 478 (C.A.).
(*s*) See Megarry and Wade, *The Law of Real Property* (4th Edn.), pp. 78-81. And note *Caldy Manor Estate, Ltd.* v. *Farrell*, [1974] 3 All E.R., 753; but *cf. In the Estate of Leahy*, [1975] 1 N.S.W.L.R. 246.

Forfeiture on alienation.—Although a person cannot be restrained from alienating property which is his, property may be settled in trust for him until he alienates or incumbers it, or attempts to do so, or becomes bankrupt or the like, and then in trust other person or class of persons (*t*). But a person cannot settle his own property so as to confer on himself an interest determinable on his own bankruptcy, and if he becomes bankrupt, the forfeiture clause is void against his trustee in bankruptcy (*u*). However, a clause defeating the settlor's interest takes effect in the event of voluntary alienation (*a*).

When forfeiture is incurred.—Where the prohibition extends to an attempt to incumber, forfeiture is only operative if the act would, but for the prohibition, have the effect of an assignment or security upon the property.   An offer to give a security will not create a forfeiture, much less the expression of a desire to create an incumbrance, and the taking of advice as to the power to do so (*b*).

Restraints on alienation in leases.—Restraints on alienation in respect of leasehold property are frequently imposed by a covenant in the lease against sub-letting, assigning or parting with the property (*c*). Such a covenant is broken by a mortgage by sub-demise (*d*); but not by a deposit of the lease by way of equitable mortgage, the object of the covenant being only to restrain the alienation of the legal interest (*e*). Similarly a mortgage by way of legal charge is probably not a breach of a covenant against sub-letting, etc. (*f*).

But where the covenant is against "charging" the property any mortgage or charge, including a floating charge (*g*), will be a breach of such covenant.

(*t*) "Protective trusts" received statutory recognition in the Trustee Act 1925, s. 33, but this does not validate trusts which apart from this recognition would be invalid: sub-s. (3).

(*u*) See *Mackintosh* v. *Pogose*, [1895] 1 Ch. 505; *Re Brewer's Settlement, Morton* v. *Blackmore*, [1896] 2 Ch. 503; *Re Burroughs-Fowler*, [1916] 2 Ch. 251.

(*a*) *Brooke* v. *Pearson* (1859), 27 Beav. 181.   And it has been held that it takes effect in the event of voluntary alienation at the instance of a particular creditor: *Re Detmold, Detmold* v. *Detmold* (1889), 40 Ch. D. 585.   But notwithstanding the decision, it appears still open to contend that the settlement is void as a fraud upon creditors: *Re Holland, Gregg* v. *Holland*, [1902] 2 Ch. 360.

(*b*) *Graham* v. *Lee* (1857), 23 Beav. 388; *Jones* v. *Wyse* (1838), 2 Keen 285.   And as to "attempting" to assign, see *Re Porter*, [1892] 3 Ch. 481; *Re Tancred's Settlement*, [1903] 1 Ch. 715.

(*c*) The covenant is usually a covenant not to assign, etc., without the consent of the lessor, such consent not to be unreasonably withheld, and this qualification is implied by the Landlord and Tenant Act 1927, s. 19. And s. 86 (1) of the Law of Property Act 1925 provides that where a licence to sub-demise by way of mortgage is required, consent is not to be unreasonably withheld (Presumably this means "required by the terms of the lease"). As to whether the taking of possession by the mortgagee is a breach of a covenant not to part with possession, see p. 317, *infra*.

(*d*) *Sergeant* v. *Nash, Field & Co.*, [1903] 2 K.B. 304 (C.A.).

(*e*) *Doe d. Pitt* v. *Hogg* (1824), 4 Dow. & Ry. K.B. 226, 229; *Ex parte Drake* (1841), 1 Mont. D. & De G. 539.   A covenant against assigning is not broken by a mortgage by sub-demise: *Crusoe d. Blencowe* v. *Bugby* (1771), 3 Wils 234; *Grove* v. *Portal*, [1902] 1 Ch. 727.

(*f*) *Gentle* v. *Faulkner*, [1900] 2 Q.B. 267 (C.A.). *Grand Junction Co., Ltd.* v. *Bates* [1954] 2 Q.B. 160 at p. 168; [1954] 2 All E.R. 385, at p. 388, on the basis that no term is created. See p. 26, *supra*.

(*g*) See *Fell* v. *Charity Lands Official Trustee*, [1898] 2 Ch. 44.

PART IV

TRANSFER AND
DEVOLUTION OF
MORTGAGES

CHAPTER 14

Transfer and Devolution of Mortgages

I—TRANSFER

Concurrence of mortgagor.—A mortgagee is entitled to transfer his security (*a*) either absolutely or by way of sub-mortgage, and with or without the concurrence of the mortgagor. It is, however, always desirable that the latter should be a party (*b*), because, in his absence, the transferee is bound by the state of accounts between the mortgagor and the transferor (*c*), whatever may have been the representations of the latter to the transferee, and though he has no notice of the discharge of any part of the debt (*d*). As the amount of the debt and not the nature of the estate—which is only the security for it—is the relevant consideration, the possession by the transferee of the legal estate does not strengthen his position (*e*). Where, however, the mortgagor has enabled the transferor to deceive the transferee for instance, by allowing it to be stated in the mortgage deed that a larger sum was advanced than was actually the case, he will be estopped from denying it as against the transferee (*f*). Arrears of interest will be capitalised where the transfer is made with the concurrence of the mortgagor (*g*). The transferee steps into the shoes of the transferor and he cannot stand in a better position than the transferor (*h*). He is bound by such

---

(*a*) *Re Tahiti Cotton Co., Ex parte Sargent* (1874), L.R. 17 Eq. 273, 279; *France* v. *Clark* (1883), 22 Ch. D. 830; (1884), 26 Ch. D. 257 (C.A.). But after a mortgagee has been in possession he will remain liable even after a transfer, unless that transfer is by the direction of the court: see p. 349, *infra*.

(*b*) Where he is a party he usually enters into a new covenant for payment of the mortgage debt and interest with the transferee, although the transferee will have a right to sue under the Law of Property Act 1925, s. 114 (1) (b), *infra*. The advantage of the new covenant is that it starts time running for the purposes of the Limitation Act 1939 (see p. 280, *infra*). A new covenant which is inconsistent with the covenant in the original covenant extinguishes the latter. A fresh covenant for payment at a new date with corresponding proviso for redemption amounts to a new mortgage: *Bolton* v. *Buckenham*, [1891] 1 Q.B. 278 (C.A.). A surety should also join in any new covenant: *Bolton* v. *Buckenham*, *supra*. When the mortgagor has not created further incumbrances the transfer may also contain a new demise or charge thus implying new covenants for title (as to which, see p. 31, *supra*).

(*c*) *De Lisle* v. *Union Bank of Scotland*, [1914] 1 Ch. 22 (C.A.); *Parker* v. *Jackson*, [1936] 2 All E.R. 281.

(*d*) See p. 618, *infra*.

(*e*) *Chambers* v. *Goldwin* (1804), 9 Ves. 254.

(*f*) *Bickerton* v. *Walker* (1885), 31 Ch. D. 151; *Powell* v. *Browne* (1907), 97 L.T. 854.

(*g*) See p. 631, *infra*. But a transfer does not without express provision therefore pass the right to arrears of rent: *Salmon* v. *Dean* (1851), 3 Mac. & G. 344.

(*h*) *Ashenhurst* v. *James* (1745), 3 Atk. 270.

equities and accounts as would bind the transferor (*i*). The transferee is also in no better position than the mortgagee, when the mortgage deed is absolutely void from the beginning, although he took for valuable consideration and without notice of the fraud. But where the security was originally only voidable, it may become valid in the hands of such a transferee (*k*). A so-called mortgagee who knows his deed is absolutely void, *e.g.*, where it is a forgery, is liable to the transferee unless he discloses the fact (*l*).

Form of transfer (*m*).—The transfer of a mortgage consists of the assignment of the debt and the conveyance of the mortgagee's estate which is the security for the debt. Formerly these two parts of the transfer were separate. Thus it was usual in the deed of transfer first to assign the debt absolutely and then to convey the property subject to the equity of redemption.

The separate assignment of the debt and the mortgagee's estate was rendered unnecessary by the Law of Property Act 1925, under which a deed merely purporting to transfer the mortgage has the effect of transferring at once the debt, the securities for the debt, and the estate of the mortgagee. Thus the Act provides:

> **114.**—(1) A deed executed by a mortgagee purporting to transfer his mortgage or the benefit thereof shall, unless a contrary intention is therein expressed, and subject to any provisions therein contained, operate to transfer to the transferee—
>
> (a) The right to demand, sue for, recover and give receipts for, the mortgage money or the unpaid part thereof, and the interest then due, if any, and thenceforth to become due thereon; and
>
> (b) the benefit of all securities for the same, and the benefit of and the right to sue on all covenants with the mortgagee, and the right to exercise all powers of the mortgagee; and
>
> (c) all the estate and interest in the mortgaged property then vested in the mortgagee subject to redemption or cesser, but as to such estate and interest subject to the right of redemption then subsisting.
>
> (2) In this section "transferee" includes his personal representatives and assigns.
>
> (3) A transfer of mortgage may be made in the form contained in the Third Schedule of this Act with such variations and additions, if any, as the circumstances may require.
>
> (4) This section applies, whether the mortgage transferred was made before or after the commencement of this Act, but applies only to transfers made after the commencement of this Act.
>
> (5) This section does not extend to a transfer of a bill of sale of chattels by way of security.

Necessity for deed.—Apart from the requirement of a deed to get the benefit of the above section, a deed is necessary in the case of

---

(*i*) *Earl of Macclesfield* v. *Fitton* (1683), 1 Vern. 168; *Matthew* v. *Wallwyn* (1798), 4 Ves. 118; *Williams* v. *Sorrell* (1799), 4 Ves. 389; *Turner* v. *Smith*, [1901] 1 Ch. 213.

(*k*) See *Judd* v. *Green* (1875), 45 L.J. Ch. 108; *Nant-y-glo and Blaina Ironworks Co.* v. *Tamplin* (1876), 35 L.T. 125; cf. 27 Halsbury's Laws (3rd Edn.), pp. 267, 268.

(*l*) *Marnham* v. *Weaver* (1899), 80 L.T. 412.

(*m*) See 14 Ency. Forms and Precedents (4th Edn.), pp. 755 *et seq.*; and Precedents 20 to 23 in the Appendix, *infra*.
It may be a question of construction as to whether a purported transfer is a transfer or some other transaction: *Re White Rose Cottage*, [1965] Ch. 940 (C.A.); [1965] 1 All E.R. 11. As to the costs of transfer, see p. 651, *infra*. For transfers of registered charges on registered land, see p. 65, *supra*.

a legal mortgage, otherwise the legal estate will remain in the transferor (*n*) and in the case of the mortgage of an equitable interest in either land or personalty the transfer must be in writing (*o*). Even in the case of an equitable mortgage the right to sue at law for the debt transferred can only be transferred by writing under the hand of the transferor accompanied by notice to the debtor (*p*). Where the transfer is a voluntary transfer, all formalities necessary for the complete transfer of the mortgage at law must be complied with, otherwise the transfer will be an incomplete gift and void, even where the deeds have been handed over (*q*). Where, however, there has been valuable consideration for the transfer, the fact that legal formalities have not been complied with will be immaterial, as between transferor and transferee, inasmuch as equity in such cases treats the transaction as an agreement to make over the benefit of the mortgage which will be enforced.

Transfer of equitable mortgage by deposit.—This is effected by delivery of the deeds to the transferee, either with or without a memorandum (*r*).

Transfer of statutory mortgage.—A transfer of a statutory mortgage may be made by a deed expressed to be by way of statutory transfer of mortgage in either of the three forms (Nos. 2, 3 and 4) given in the Fourth Schedule to the Law of Property Act 1925, with the variations adapted to the particular case (*s*). A transfer in any of these forms vests in the person to whom the benefit of the mortgage is expressed to be transferred, the right to demand, sue for, recover, and give receipts for the mortgage money or the unpaid part thereof, and the interest due and to become due, and the benefit of all securities for the same, and the benefit of and the right to sue on all covenants with, and to exercise all powers of the mortgagee. And all the term and interest, if any, subject to redemption, of the mortgagee in the mortgaged lands vests in the transferee, subject to redemption (*t*).

Transfer by endorsed receipt.—Where by the receipt the money appears to have been paid by a person who is not entitled to the immediate equity of redemption, the receipt operates as if the benefit of the mortgage had by deed been transferred to him, unless it is otherwise expressly provided or unless the mortgage is paid off out of capital money, or other money in the hands of a personal representative or trustee properly applicable for the discharge of the mortgage, and it is not expressly provided that the receipt is to operate as a transfer (*u*).

(*n*) Law of Property Act 1925, s. 52 (1).
(*o*) Law of Property Act 1925, s. 53 (1) (c).
(*p*) Law of Property Act 1925, s. 136. See p. 102, *supra*.
(*q*) *Re Richardson, Shillito* v. *Hobson* (1885), 30 Ch. D. 396 (C.A.).
(*r*) *Brocklesby* v. *Temperance Building Society*, [1895] A.C. 173 (H.L.), at pp. 182, 183. But writing is required for a voluntary transfer: see *Re Richardson, Shillito* v. *Hobson*, *supra*, and Law of Property Act 1925, s. 53 (1) (c). And see the equitable rights of person paying off mortgage debt, p. 256, *infra*.
(*s*) Law of Property Act 1925, s. 118.
(*t*) As to the covenants implied, see s.118; as to when the covenants in the case of joint mortgagors are joint and several, see s. 119.
(*u*) Law of Property Act 1925, s. 115 (2); see p. 548, *infra*.

Transfer in lieu of discharge.—A mortgagor, and a subsequent incumbrancer, is entitled to require a mortgagee to transfer the mortgage to a third party instead of re-conveying or surrendering (v).

Transfer of registered charges.—As to transfer of registered charges, see p. 65, *supra*.

Transfer of sub-mortgages.—As to transfer of sub-mortgages, see p. 263, *infra*.

Transfer of registered mortgages of ships.—As to transfer of registered mortgages of ships, see p. 98, *supra*.

Transfer of bills of sale.—The provisions of the Law of Property Act 1925, s. 114, do not apply to a transfer of a security bill of sale (w). A registered bill of sale can be transferred so as to constitute a valid security in favour of the transferee. The transfer need not be registered (x) and a renewal of registration does not become necessary by reason only of the transfer or assignment (y). The transfer is usually effected by deed (z). An equitable assignment by delivery of the bill is possible (a). If the bill is unregistered, the transfer, in order to create an effective security, requires the same formalities as an original bill of sale (b).

Transfer of part of mortgage.—Since the mortgagee's remedies by sale, foreclosure, etc., are indivisible, a transfer of part of a mortgage debt can only be effected (1) by the mortgagee declaring himself a trustee for the transferee of so much of the debt as is intended to be assigned, or (2) by transferring the whole debt to a trustee for both mortgagee and partial assignee, or (3) by the joinder of the mortgagor and the consequent severance of the mortgage into two separate mortgages each with its own powers of sale, etc. In any of these three cases the deed must state whether the amounts respectively retained by the mortgagee and assigned to the assignee are to rank *pari passu*, or whether one is to rank in priority to the other (c).

Transfer of building society mortgages.—In the case of a building society mortgage, the special relation existing between the mortgagor as a member of the society, and the society, and the special form of the mortgage, prevent the mortgage from being transferable like an ordinary mortgage, and even if there are indications in the mortgage that it is intended to be transferable, such as the definition of the "society" so as to include its "successors and assigns" (d), yet, unless special provision is made, or the mortgagor consents, a transfer

---

(v) Law of Property Act 1925, s. 95; and see pp. 546, *infra*. These provisions do not apply in the case of a mortgagee of land being or having been in possession: s. 95 (3).

(w) Law of Property Act 1925, s. 114 (5).

(x) Unless the terms are varied: Bills of Sale Act 1878, s. 10; and see *Marshall and Snelgrove, Ltd.* v. *Gower*, [1923] 1 K.B. 356.

(y) Bills of Sale Act 1878, s. 11.

(z) For forms, see 3 Ency. Forms and Precedents (4th Edn.), pp. 80, 81.

(a) *Re Parker, Ex parte Turquand* (1885), 14 Q.B.D. 636.

(b) *Jarvis* v. *Jarvis* (1893), 63 L.J. Ch. 10.

(c) For forms, see 14 Ency. Forms and Precedents (4th Edn.), 784, 805. And see p. 260, *infra*.

(d) *Sun Building Society* v. *Western Suburban and Harrow Road Building Society*, [1920] 2 Ch. 144, 157.

will not be possible (*e*). Without special provision or the mortgagor's concurrence it may be that the society can only assign the mortgage debt (*f*). Even if a transfer is possible the transferee may not be able to exercise the power of sale (*g*), and will not be in the same position as the society for the purpose of exercising the mortgagee's rights generally (*h*). But this difficulty can be met by making special provision in the mortgage defining the rights of a transferee (*i*).

Transfer of trust mortgages.—In the case of a mortgage to trustees, it is the usual and convenient practice to take and transfer the mortgage without disclosing the trusts, and in particular, on the appointment of new trustees, the transfer to the new trustees is made by a separate deed. Where no trust is disclosed, and all that appears is that the mortgage money has been advanced on a joint account (*k*), this gives no notice of a trust (*l*). Formerly where a trust was disclosed in the course of examination of title, the purchaser had to satisfy himself that the trustee had been properly appointed (*m*). The following provision of the Law of Property Act 1925, now relieves him of the inquiry:

113.—(1) A person dealing in good faith with a mortgagee, or with the mortgagor if the mortgage has been wholly or partially discharged, released or postponed, shall not be concerned with any trust at any time affecting the mortgage money or the income thereof, whether or not he has notice of the trust (*n*), and may assume unless the contrary is expressly stated in the instruments relating to the mortgage—

   (a) that the mortgagees (if more than one) are or were entitled to the mortgage money on a joint account (*o*); and

   (b) that the mortgagee has or had power to give valid receipts for the purchase money or mortgage money and the income thereof (including any arrears of interest) and to release or postpone the priority of the mortgage debt or any part thereof or to deal with the same or the mortgaged property or any part thereof;

without investigating the equitable title to the mortgage debt or the appointment or discharge of trustees in reference thereto.

(2) This section applies to mortgages made before or after the commencement of this Act, but only as respects dealings effected after such commencement.

(3) This section does not affect the liability of any person in whom the mortgage debt is vested for the purpose of any trust to give effect to that trust.

(*e*) But a transfer may be made under a union or transfer of engagements between societies and the mortgagor will be bound by the rules of the united or transferee society, see Building Societies Act 1962, ss. 18-20.

(*f*) *Re Rumney and Smith*, [1897] 2 Ch. 351 (C.A.), at p. 359.

(*g*) *Re Rumney and Smith, supra.*

(*h*) *Sun Building Society* v. *Western Suburban and Harrow Road Building Society*, [1921] 2 Ch. 438, 459, 467 (C.A.).

(*i*) See 3 Ency. Forms and Precedents (4th Edn.), 731, 732.

(*k*) See p. 175, *supra.*

(*l*) *Re Harman and Uxbridge and Rickmansworth Rail Co.* (1883), 24 Ch. D. 720; *Re Balen and Shepherds' Contract*, [1924] 2 Ch. 365.

(*m*) *Re Blaiberg and Abrahams' Contract*, [1899] 2 Ch. 340.

(*n*) The Law of Property Act 1925, s. 112 provides that the fact that a transfer bears only a 10s. stamp, although the ad valorem stamp would exceed that sum, does not give notice of a trust. Stamp duty payable under the heading "Mortgage, Bonds, etc." was abolished by Finance Act 1971, s. 64.

(*o*) Consequently the survivor can give a valid receipt for the mortgage money: s. 111.

Transfer on appointment of new trustee.—On an appointment of new trustee the trust property in many cases automatically vests in the new and continuing trustees under the provisions of s. 40 of the Trustee Act 1925. However land conveyed by way of mortgage for securing money subject to a trust (except land conveyed on trust for securing debentures or debenture stock) is excluded from the operation of this section (*p*). But the mortgage debt itself is not so excluded. It is convenient on the appointment of new trustee for the mortgage debt to be excluded from the implied vesting declaration and transferred together with the mortgaged land by a separate transfer of the benefit of the mortgage.

Transfer of collateral securities.—Collateral securities must be expressly assigned (*q*); they do not pass under general words giving the transferee the benefit of the mortgage security.

Notice of transfer.—Notice of the transfer should be given to the mortgagor by the transferee so that payment of the mortgage interest will be made to him. After notice the mortgagor will only get a good discharge of the mortgage by paying the transferee (*r*). Where the transfer takes the form of an express assignment of the mortgage debt, if the assignment is to be legal, notice must be given (*s*). If the mortgage is of an equitable interest in settled land, capital money or securities representing capital money, notice should be given to the trustees of the settlement: if the mortgage is of an equitable interest in the proceeds of the sale of land, to the trustees for sale; or where the mortgage is of an equitable interest in land, to the estate owner of the land (*t*). If the mortgage is of an equitable interest in land or personalty the notice should be in writing (*u*). In other cases the notice should be in the form required by the mortgage deed (*x*), or, in the absence of express provision, in the statutory form (*y*).

Effect of transfer.—The rights of the transferee upon a transfer of the mortgage or the benefit thereof are set out in s. 114 of the Law of Property Act 1925 (*z*).

Equitable rights of person paying off mortgage debt.—Although there has been no actual transfer, a person who advances money for the purpose of paying off the mortgage, and whose money is so applied, becomes an equitable assignee of the mortgage and is entitled to have it kept alive for his benefit (*a*).

(*p*) Trustee Act 1925, s. 40 (4) (a). For forms of such transfer, see Precedent 22 in the Appendix, *infra*; and 14 Ency. Forms and Precedents (4th Edn.), 764, 765.

(*q*) For notice to insurance offices, see. p. 108, *supra*.

(*r*) *Dixon* v. *Winch*, [1900] 1 Ch. 736; *Turner* v. *Smith*, [1901] 1 Ch. 213.

(*s*) Law of Property Act 1925, s. 136; see p. 102, *supra*.

(*t*) Law of Property Act 1925, s. 137 (2). The provisions of the Law of Property Act 1925, s. 113 (*supra*), have no effect on priorities: *Beddoes* v. *Shaw*, [1937] Ch. 81.

(*u*) *Ibid.*, s. 137 (3). And see pp. 471, 474 *infra*.

(*x*) For forms, see 14 Ency. Forms and Precedents (4th Edn.), 861, and Precedent 23 in the Appendix, *infra*.

(*y*) Law of Property Act 1925, s. 196. See p. 365, *infra*.

(*z*) See p. 252, *supra*. See also ss. 106 (1), 205 (1) (xvi). As to the effect of a transfer on an order for possession, see *Chung Kwok Hotel Co., Ltd.* v. *Field*, [1960] 3 All E.R. 143.

(*a*) *Chetwynd* v. *Allen*, [1899] 1 Ch. 353; *Butler* v. *Rice*, [1910] 2 Ch. 277; *Ghana Commercial Bank* v. *Chandiram*, [1960] A.C. 732 (P.C.), at pp. 744, 745; [1960] 2 All E.R. 865, at pp. 807, 871. And Ch. 32, *infra*.

II—DEVOLUTION OF MORTGAGES ON DEATH OR BANKRUPTCY OF MORTGAGEE

Devolution on death.—Previously to the Conveyancing Act 1881, the mortgagee's interest in mortgaged land, in the absence of testamentary disposition by the mortgagee, devolved upon his death on his heir or his personal representative, depending on whether it was freehold or leasehold respectively. But since the interest of the mortgagee lay substantially in the money, the mortgage debt went as part of his personal estate (*b*), and, in the case of a mortgage of freehold land the heir was regarded as a trustee thereof for the personal representative (*c*). This separation of the land from the money was avoided in practice by inserting in wills a general devise of mortgaged properties to the executors (*d*). It was provided by s. 30 of the Conveyancing Act 1881, that mortgaged freehold should, notwithstanding any testamentary disposition, devolve on the personal representative as if it were a chattel real vesting in him. Thereupon the devise of mortgaged properties became unnecessary, and mortgaged freeholds devolved (as mortgaged leaseholds did) with the mortgage debt on the personal representatives. After the Land Transfer Act 1897 (*e*), all property, whether real or personal, vested in the personal representatives in the same way as leaseholds had previously thereto. The provisions of the Acts of 1881 and 1897 are now replaced as to deaths after 1925 by those of the Administration of Estates Act 1925 (*f*).

If the mortgage has been specifically bequeathed, then the executors, when they are ready to assent, will vest both the debt and the mortgage term (if any) in the beneficiary (*g*). Otherwise the mortgage will be disposed of as part of the residuary personalty. On intestacy (*h*) the mortgage will be subject to the statutory trust for sale (*i*), and dealt with according to the statutory provisions (*k*).

The personal representatives for the time being are deemed to be the heirs and assigns of the mortgagee within the meaning of all trusts

---

(*b*) *Thornborough* v. *Baker* (1675), 1 Cas. in Ch. 283; 3 Swans. 628, 630.

(*c*) *Re Loveridge, Drayton* v. *Loveridge*, [1902] 2 Ch. 859.

(*d*) See further the earlier editions of this work. Note that a specific devise of the debt carries the land: *Silberschildt* v. *Schiott* (1814), 3 Ves. & B. 45; *Renvoize* v. *Cooper* (1822), 6 Madd. 371; and a specific devise of the land by a mortgagee in possession passes also the mortgage debt: *Re Carter, Dodds* v. *Pearson*, [1900] 1 Ch. 801.

(*e*) Section 1 (1).

(*f*) Sections 1 (1), 3 (1) (ii).

(*g*) Usually this is done by transfer. For forms, see 14 Ency. Forms and Precedents (4th Edn.), 765, and Precedent 21 in the Appendix, *infra*.

A personal representative may assent to the vesting of any estate or interest in land: Administration of Estates Act 1925, s. 36 (1). An executor may assent at common law to the vesting of personalty, and on an assent of the mortgage term or charge the debt may pass also: see *Re Carter, supra*. But a beneficiary can only sue for the debt in his own name if the assent operates as a transfer under s. 114 of the Law of Property Act 1925 (p. 252, *supra*) or as an assignment under s. 136 of that Act (p. 102, *supra*).

(*h*) The doctrine of assent does not, apart from statute, apply to intestacy. So a transfer is needed to pass the debt. See footnote (*g*), *supra*.

(*i*) Administration of Estates Act 1925, s. 33.

(*k*) See Administration of Estates Act 1925, as amended by the Intestates' Estates Act 1952, and the Family Provision Act 1966.

and powers (*l*), and can therefore exercise all powers conferred on the mortgagee, his heirs and assigns in mortgages made before 1926. As the definition of mortgagee includes any person from time to time deriving title under the original mortgagee (*m*), the personal representatives can exercise the statutory powers of the mortgagee.

Death of one of several mortgagees.—Where there are several mortgagees the mortgage deed will usually either expressly state that they advanced money on a joint account, or this will be implied under the Law of Property Act 1925:

111—(1) Where—

  (a) in a mortgage, or an obligation for payment of money, or a transfer of a mortgage or of such an obligation, the sum, or any part of the sum, advanced or owing is expressed to be advanced by or owing to more persons than one out of money, or as money, belonging to them on a joint account; or

  (b) a mortgage, or such an obligation, or such a transfer is made to more persons than one, jointly;

the mortgage money, or other money or money's worth, for the time being due to those persons on the mortgage or obligation, shall, as between them and the mortgagor or obligor, be deemed to be and remain money or money's worth belonging to those persons on a joint account; and the receipt in writing of the survivors or last survivor of them, or of the personal representative of the last survivor, shall be a complete discharge for all money or money's worth for the time being due, notwithstanding any notice to the payer of a severance of the joint account.

  (2) This section applies if and so far as a contrary intention is not expressed in the mortgage, obligation, or transfer, and has effect subject to the terms of the mortgage, obligation, or transfer, and to the provision therein contained.

  (3) This section applies to any mortgage, obligation, or transfer made after the thirty-first day of December, eighteen hundred and eighty-one.

But such a provision (which is intended to facilitate the discharge of the mortgage) does not by itself affect the rights of the mortgagees *inter se* (*n*), and, accordingly, as between the mortgagees themselves, on the death of one of several mortgagees his personal representatives are prima facie entitled to his share or interest in the mortgaged property.

Bankruptcy.—On the bankruptcy of the mortgagee, all his interest in the property vests in his trustee (*o*), and the trustee can exercise his remedies under the mortgage, including the right to sue for foreclosure (*p*).

Death and bankruptcy of proprietors of registered charge.— This is dealt with at p. 65, *supra*.

Dissolution of company mortgagee.—On the dissolution of a company all property and rights whatsoever vested in or held on trust for the company immediately before its dissolution (including leasehold

---

(*l*) *Ibid.*, s. 1 (2), reproducing s. 30 (1) of the Conveyancing Act 1881.
(*m*) Law of Property Act 1925, s. 205 (1) (xvi).
(*n*) *Re Jackson, Smith* v. *Sibthorpe* (1887), 34 Ch. D. 732.
(*o*) Bankruptcy Act 1914, ss. 18, 53.　(*p*) *Waddell* v. *Toleman* (1878), 9 Ch. D. 212.

property, but not including property held on trust for any other person), is deemed to be *bona vacantia* and belongs to the Crown, or to the Duchy of Lancaster, or the Duke of Cornwall for the time being, as the case may be (*q*).

(*q*) Companies Act 1948, s. 354, reproducing s. 296 of the Companies Act 1929. See, generally, Buckley on the *Companies Acts* (13th Edn.), 703; and Ing, *Bona Vacantia*, Pt. III. And see *Re Wells, Swimburne-Hanham* v. *Howard*, [1933] Ch. 29 (C.A.); *Re Strathblaine Estates, Ltd.*, [1948] Ch. 228; [1948] 1 All E.R. 162.

CHAPTER 15

Sub-Mortgages

Generally (*a*).—A sub-mortgage is a mortgage of a mortgage. A sub-mortgage for £600 of a mortgage for £1,000 consists in substance of a covenant to pay £600 and interest, and a transfer of the mortgage for £1,000, subject to redemption on payment of £600 and interest. A mortgagee has, by implication of law, the right to mortgage his security without an express agreement to that effect (*b*).

A sub-mortgage is the best way of effecting a transfer of part of a debt (*c*).

Form of sub-mortgage (*d*).—Before 1926 the transfer was effected, as in the case of any other transfer of the mortgage, by an assignment of the debt and a conveyance or assignment of the property (*e*). Thus the sub-mortgage consisted, taking the example given above, of (a) a covenant to pay £600 and interest; (b) an assignment of the debt of £1,000 subject to redemption on payment of £600 and interest; and (c) a conveyance or assignment of the mortgaged property subject to the subsisting right of redemption on payment of £1,000 and interest under the mortgage and also subject to redemption on payment of £600 and interest under the sub-mortgage. This is still the method today where the principal mortgage is a charge by way of legal mortgage, or where it is equitable, although in these cases advantage can probably be taken of s. 114 of the Law of Property Act 1925 (*f*), to avoid expressing (b) and (c) above separately, so that the sub-mortgage can be effected by (1) a covenant to pay £600 and interest; and (2) a transfer of the benefit of the mortgage for £1,000 subject to redemption on payment of £600 and interest.

But where the mortgage is a legal mortgage by demise, neither of these methods is now available, since the sub-mortgagor has a term of years absolute, and can only mortgage this by sub-demise or legal

---

(*a*) (1948), 12 Conv. (N.S.) 171 (H. Woodhouse).
(*b*) *Re Tahiti Cotton Co., Ex parte Sargent* (1874), L.R. 17 Eq. 273; *France* v. *Clark* (1884), 26 Ch. D. 257 (C.A.).
(*c*) See p. 254, *supra.*
(*d*) See 14 Ency. Forms and Precedents (4th Edn.), pp. 774 *et seq.* And see also forms of transfer, pp. 252, 253, *supra.*
(*e*) See p. 252, *supra.* For the conversion of sub-mortgages made before 1926 by conveyance or assignment into terms one day shorter than that held by the sub-mortgagor, see Law of Property Act 1925, 1st Sched., Pts. VII, para. 4, VIII, para. 4.
(*f*) See p. 252, *supra.* It may be that s. 114 is restricted to a transfer under which a transferee will become absolutely entitled to the mortgage debt and, indeed, the practice is for there to be an express transfer of the debt; see the forms referred to in footnote (*d*), *supra.*

charge (g). Hence the sub-mortgage must consist of three clauses as under the old practice, namely (1) a covenant to pay £600 and interest; (2) an assignment of £1,000 subject to redemption under the sub-mortgage; and (3) a sub-demise (or a legal charge) of the mortgaged premises subject to redemption under the sub-mortgage (h).

A sub-mortgage of several properties should not be effected by a single deed, as such a deed would be brought onto the title of each mortgagor. A sub-mortgage of each mortgage may be made and each sub-mortgage should contain a provision allowing consolidation. Alternatively each mortgage may be transferred accompanied by a collateral deed by way of sub-mortgage, regulating the rights of sub-mortgagor and sub-mortgagee between themselves (i).

An equitable sub-mortgage may be made by deposit of the mortgage deed or, where the principal mortgage is an equitable mortgage, by redeposit of the deposited title deed or deeds (k), with or without an accompanying memorandum.

As the sub-mortgagee is in the position of transferee of the mortgage debt, he takes subject to equities (l), and notice of the sub-mortgage should be given to the mortgagor to prevent fresh equities, which arise after the sub-mortgage, being enforceable against him (m). If the mortgage is of an equitable interest notice in writing of the sub-mortgage should be given to the trustees (n).

Effect of sub-mortgage.—The effect of a formal sub-mortgage is to put the sub-mortgagee in the position of the transferee of the principal mortgage (o). He may exercise rights under the principal mortgage or under the sub-mortgage. He may exercise the power of sale under the principal mortgage, on default being made thereunder, and in that case he extinguishes both the right of redemption under that mortgage and the right of redemption under the sub-mortgage and can dispose of the fee simple or lease under ss. 88 (5) and 89 (5) of the Law of Property Act 1925 (p), or he may exercise the power of sale under the sub-mortgage on default being made thereunder and sell the mortgage debt and the security for that debt (q). If the

---

(g) Law of Property Act 1925, s. 86; see p. 22, *supra*. Although the effect of the statutory transfer under s. 114 is the same, *i.e.*, it operates as a sub-demise: *ibid.*, sub-s. (2). But it is undesirable to leave it to this provision to cure an inaccuracy in drafting.

(h) The sub-mortgage term is made subject to redemption under the sub-mortgage only; the reversion of the sub-mortgage term, *i.e.*, the mortgage term, is outstanding, and it is this that is subject to the right of redemption under the mortgage.

(i) For form, see 14 Ency. Forms and Precedents (4th Edn.), 781.

(k) *Re Hildyard, Ex parte Smith* (1842), 2 Mont. D. & De G. 587. An equitable sub-mortgage of a bill of sale need not be registered: *Re Parker, Ex parte Turquand* (1885), 14 Q.B.D. 636 (C.A.); and see p. 96, *supra*.

(l) *De Lisle* v. *Union Bank of Scotland*, [1914] 1 Ch. 22 (C.A.); *Parker* v. *Jackson*, [1936] 2 All E.R. 281.

(m) *Reeve* v. *Whitmore, Martin* v. *Whitmore* (1863), 4 De G.J. & Sm. 1, 19; *Bateman* v. *Hunt*, [1904] 2 K.B. 530 (C.A.). At the same time, or, preferably, before completion, the mortgagor should be asked to confirm the amount due under the principal mortgage.

(n) Law of Property Act 1925, ss. 136, 137. See p. 112, *supra*.

(o) See p. 256, *supra*.

(p) See pp. 378 *et seq.*, *infra*.

(q) Formerly a doubt appears to have existed as to whether a sub-mortgagee could exercise an express power of sale contained in the principal mortgage: *Cruse* v. *Nowell* (1856), 25 L.J. Ch. 709. But it seems clear that if (as in most well-drawn powers and

sub-mortgagee receives the principal mortgage money he must reconvey to the principal mortgagor (*r*) and, after satisfying his own debt he must account to the sub-mortgagor for the surplus (*s*). If he realises the security by exercising the power of sale under the principal mortgage, he must set aside the amount due thereunder and pay the surplus to the mortgagor; and out of the amount so set aside he will retain the sub-mortgage debt and pay the remainder to the mortgagee (*s*). Since the mortgagee is liable to the sub-mortgagee for the debt due to the latter he can require him to sue for the mortgage debt (*t*). But every well-drawn sub-mortgage should contain a provision that the sub-mortgagee shall be under no obligation to take steps to enforce the security and shall not be liable for any loss arising from any omission on his part to take any such steps.

Sub-charges of registered charge.—A proprietor of a registered charge may charge the mortgage debt with the payment of money in the same manner as a proprietor of the land may charge the land, and such charges are referred to as sub-charges (*u*). The sub-charge must be completed by registration (*x*). The sub-chargee will then be entered as a proprietor of the sub-charge and be issued with a sub-charge certificate (*y*). The proprietor of the sub-charge has, subject to any entry to the contrary in the register, the same powers of disposition, in relation to the land, as if he had been registered as proprietor of the principal charge (*z*). A sub-charge is required to be completed, transferred, and discharged in the same form and manner as a charge (*a*). Subject to any entry in the register to the contrary, (1) a sub-charge, as against the person creating it, implies the same covenants and, as against that person and all persons over whose interests the charge confers power, confer the same powers and have the same effect as a charge, and (2) registered sub-charges on the same charge or incumbrance, as between themselves, rank accordingly to the order in which they are entered on the register and not according to the order in which they are created (*b*).

An equitable sub-charge may be created by deposit of the charge certificate (*c*). Application should be made for a notice of the deposit

---

as in the case of the statutory power) the power is expressly made exercisable by any person entitled to give a receipt for the mortgage debt, the sub-mortgagee would be capable of exercising it. And see *Re Burrell, Burrell* v. *Smith* (1870), L.R. 7 Eq. 399.

An informal sub-mortgage, whose sub-mortgage is not by deed, will generally have to seek an order for sale from the court. For the power of sale of an equitable mortgagee, see p. 379, *infra*.

(*r*) For the sub-mortgagee's power to execute a vacating receipt, see 12 Conv. (N.S.), at pp. 177-179.

(*s*) Law of Property Act 1925, ss. 105, 107 (2); see p. 373, *infra*.

(*t*) Cf. *Gurney* v. *Seppings* (1846), 2 Ph. 40.

(*u*) Land Registration Act 1925, s. 36; Land Registration Rules 1925, r. 163 (1). For a form of sub-charge (there is no prescribed form), see 14 Ency. Forms and Precedents (4th Edn.), pp. 780, 781.

(*x*) Land Registration Rules 1925, r. 164 (1). Application should be made on Form A4 accompanied by the sub-charge, a certified copy thereof, and the charge certificate (r. 165).

(*y*) Land Registration Rules 1925, r. 166.

(*z*) *Ibid.*, r. 163 (2).

(*a*) *Ibid.*, r. 164 (1).

(*b*) *Ibid.*, r 164 (2).

(*c*) Land Registration Act 1925, s. 66.

to be entered in the Charges Register of the registered chargee's title (*d*).

Transfer of sub-mortgage (*e*).—A transfer of a sub-mortgage formerly consisted of:

(a) an assignment of the covenant (using the example above) to pay £600 and interest;

(b) an assignment of the debt of £1,000 subject to redemption under the sub-mortgage; and

(c) a conveyance of the mortgaged property subject to redemption under the mortgage and the sub-mortgage.

Where now the principal mortgage is a charge by way of legal mortgage or an equitable mortgage, this conveyance would be an assignment of the benefit of the legal charge or equitable mortgage. Where it is a legal mortgage by demise the conveyance would be an assignment of the sub-mortgage term subject to the redemption under the sub-mortgage. But whether the sub-mortgage is a security on an equitable mortgage or a legal charge, or is a security on a legal mortgage by demise, it is now sufficient to rely on s. 114 of the Law of Property Act 1925 (*f*), and simply to transfer the benefit of the sub-mortgage (*g*). Notice of the transfer should be given to the sub-mortgagor and the principal mortgagor (*h*).

Discharge of sub-mortgage (*i*).—A legal sub-mortgage is generally discharged by a statutory receipt (*k*). It has been suggested that a statutory receipt may be inappropriate, because in such a receipt a covenant by the mortgagee is implied that he has not incumbered (*l*). Moreover the re-assignment of the debt is involved (*m*). Nevertheless the practice is to use a statutory receipt, where appropriate. If the mortgagee insists on a re-assignment, and reconveyance or, where there has been a sub-demise, re-assignment and surrender, his wishes should be deferred to.

An informal sub-mortgage may be discharged by re-delivery if there is no accompanying document, or where there is an accompanying document by re-delivery and cancellation (*n*).

Notice of the discharge should be given to the mortgagor under the principal mortgage.

(*d*) Application is made on Form 85A. For notice of deposit, and intended deposit, see p. 67, *supra.*

(*e*) As to transfer of sub-charges, see transfer of charges, p. 65, *supra.*

(*f*) See p. 252, *supra.*

(*g*) For forms of transfer of sub-mortgage, see 14 Ency. Forms and Precedents (4th Edn.), pp. 786-788.

(*h*) See p. 256, *supra.* And see Ch. 14 as to transfers generally.

(*i*) As to discharge of sub-charges, see discharge of charges, p. 554, *infra.* As to discharge of the principal mortgage by the sub-mortgagee, see p. 262, *supra.*

(*k*) As to which, see p. 548, *infra.*

(*l*) Law of Property Act 1925, s. 115 (6).

(*m*) As to whether or not a statutory receipt should be used for a thing in action, see pp. 555, 556, *infra.*

(*n*) Or by receipt. For the discharge of equitable mortgages generally, see p. 551, *infra.*

PART V

THE MORTGAGEE'S REMEDIES

CHAPTER 16

The Mortgagee's Remedies

I—THE EXERCISE OF THE REMEDIES

A—PROTECTION OF THE SECURITY

Preservation of the mortgaged property.—From the time of lending his money, the mortgagee, whether he is in or out of possession, is entitled to have the mortgaged property preserved from deterioration in the hands of the mortgagor or of any other person whose interest is inferior to that of the mortgagee. Instances of acts to preserve the mortgaged property are the payment of rent to prevent forfeiture, the payment of a premium to keep a policy on foot (a) and the taking of possession to prevent vandalism (b). Thus, the mortgagee may not only obtain the restraint of such acts as mining under buildings, so as to endanger their stability (c), but, if he shows that the security will be made insufficient, he may restrain acts which lessen its value. These may consist of the removal of valuable fixtures (d), or the cutting of timber (e). Similarly, a debenture holder may obtain the appointment of a receiver before the debentures fall due, if the company's assets are endangered, e.g., by threatened executions by unsecured creditors (f). And on the same principle the Admiralty Division will order the arrest of a mortgaged ship before the debt falls due if the mortgagor is using her for a purpose likely to injure the security (g).

Where the property is compulsorily acquired notice to treat must be served on the mortgagee as well as on the mortgagor and provision made for the mortgagee's interest (h). If the mortgaged property comprises licensed premises, the mortgagee may take part in proceedings to obtain a renewal of the licence (i).

(a) See p. 639, 651 infra.
(b) Western Bank, Ltd. v. Schindler, [1976] 2 All E.R. 393, at p. 396.
(c) Dugdale v. Robertson (1857), 3 K. & J. 695.
(d) Ackroyd v. Mitchell (1860), 3 L.T. 236; Gough v. Wood & Co., [1894] 1 Q.B. 713 (C.A.); Huddersfield Banking Co., Ltd. v. Henry Lister & Son, Ltd., [1895] 2 Ch. 273 (C.A.); Ellis v. Glover and Hobson, Ltd., [1908] 1 K.B. 388 (C.A.).
(e) Usborne v. Usborne (1740), 1 Dick. 75; Hampton v. Hodges (1803), 8 Ves. 105; Hippesley v. Spencer (1820), 5 Madd. 422; Humphreys v. Harrison (1820), 1 Jac. & W. 581; King v. Smith (1843), 2 Hare, at p. 243; Simmins v. Shirley (1877), 6 Ch. D. 173; Harper v. Aplin (1886), 54 L.T. 383.
(f) Wildy v. Mid-Hants Rail. Co. (1868), 16 W.R. 409; Re Carshalton Park Estate, Ltd., Graham v. Carshalton Park Estate, Ltd., [1908] 2 Ch. 62; Higginson v. German Athenaeum, Ltd. (1916), 32 T.L.R. 277.
(g) The Blanche (1887), 58 L.T. 592.
(h) See further, p. 536, infra.
(i) Garrett v. St. Marylebone, Middlesex Justices (1884), 12 Q.B.D. 620.

The mortgagee's right to the preservation of the security has also
been asserted by restraining the trustees of a turnpike road from
reducing the tolls which formed the subject of the mortgage (*j*). A
judgment creditor has been restrained, at the suit of the prior mortgagee, even before the mortgage debt has become due, from taking
possession of the property under the legal right acquired by the former
elegit (*k*). On the same principle, where a company mortgaged a call
upon its shareholders, and, before it was received, made another call,
it could not prejudice the mortgagees by getting in the second call at
the expense of the first (*l*). The principle is also applied where the
security itself is the subject of litigation. The liquidator of a company
has, therefore, been restrained, at the suit of a person who claimed a
lien for unpaid purchase money, from selling part of the property, the
destruction or removal of which would have affected the plaintiff's
interest (*m*).

Not only may the mortgagor be restrained from the sort of conduct
above mentioned, but he may also be liable as mortgagor in possession
as the tenant of the mortgagee (*n*).

Completion of security.—The mortgagee may also at any time,
until the arrival of the day of payment fixed in a redemption action,
compel the creation in his favour of a legal estate, or otherwise for the
perfecting of his security (*o*). And for the purpose of enforcing his
security upon the interest of his mortgagor in an agreement, the
mortgagee, may sue for specific performance of the agreement (*p*).

As against third parties.—The mortgagee is entitled, as against
third parties, to protect his own or the mortgagor's title to the
mortgaged property (*q*).

B—ENFORCEMENT OF THE SECURITY

The mortgagee's remedies.—The mortgagee's remedies for the
recovery of the debt are either against the mortgagor personally, or
by enforcement of the security (*r*). The remedy against the mortgagor
personally is by an action for the debt. Usually the mortgage contains
a covenant for payment, and the action is on the covenant. As just
stated, the mortgagee is entitled to preservation of the security, and
in general, he is entitled to enter into possession immediately upon the
execution of the mortgage. In the latter case he may obtain repayment
out of the rents and profits. Or, without entering into possession, he
can appoint a receiver. Realisation of the security is effected by sale,
or the mortgagee may by foreclosure, deprive the mortgagor of his

---

(*j*) *Lord Crewe* v. *Edleston* (1857), 3 Jur. N.S. 128, 1061; 1 De G. & J. 93.
(*k*) *Legg* v. *Mathieson* (1860), 2 Giff. 71; *Wildy* v. *Mid-Hants Rail. Co.*, *supra*. As to
elegit, see p. 159, *supra*.
(*l*) *Re Humber Ironworks Co.* (1868), 16 W.R. 474, 667.
(*m*) *Blakely* v. *Dent* (1867), 15 W.R. 663.
(*n*) See p. 333, *infra*. As to repairs, see p. 31, *supra*, and p. 351, *infra*.
(*o*) Even after notice or tender, if improper notice or insufficient notice is given:
Grugeon v. *Gerrard* (1840), 4 Y. & C. Ex 119; *Malone* v. *Geraghty* (1843), 3 Dru. & War.
239; see also *Sporle* v. *Whayman* (1855), 20 Beav. 607.
(*p*) *Browne* v. *London Necropolis, etc. Co.* (1857), 6 W.R. 188.
(*q*) For costs of litigation, see p. 649, *infra*.
(*r*) For the meaning of "enforcement" of the security, see pp. 277, 316 *infra*.

equity of redemption, and himself become the owner of the property. Thus the mortgagee's remedies are: (1) action on the debt; (2) appointment of a receiver; (3) possession; (4) sale; and (5) foreclosure.

The remedies by action for the debt, or by a receiver, or by sale, or by foreclosure do not arise until the debt has become due and there has been default in payment; and even then the remedies by a receiver and by sale are subject to restrictions (s). As to foreclosure, it should be noticed that the mortgagor has two rights of redemption. Until the day fixed for payment arrives, he has a legal right of redemption, and, where there is an express proviso for redemption, of this he cannot be deprived (t). But on default in payment at that day his legal right to redeem ceases and thenceforth his right of redemption is only equitable. Foreclosure consists in depriving the mortgagor of this equitable right (u). Sale may be ordered by the court in lieu of foreclosure (v).

The date for legal redemption.—In the classical form of mortgage the date for redemption is specified in the proviso for redemption— usually six months from the date of the mortgage and the same date as the date fixed by the covenant for payment. On default in payment at the end of the period, the right of foreclosure arises. But a later date may be agreed upon, with consequent postponement of foreclosure. And the effect is the same where, although the period of six months is fixed for redemption, there is a stipulation that the money shall not be called in until a later date. Such a postponement is not subject to the same restriction as a postponement of the right to redeem (w), for the mortgagee does not require the same protection as the mortgagor. There is, therefore, no objection to an agreement that the debt shall not be called in during the lifetime of any particular person (x), and unless fraud is proved, no objection probably would be made to a postponement whatever its length. In the modern form of instalment mortgage there is generally no provision for redemption, but it seems to be accepted that the right of foreclosure nevertheless arises when the mortgage monies become due, on default or otherwise (t).

If the postponement is contained in the proviso for redemption, and this is expressed so that there is a right to redeem on payment of principal at a distant date with interest in the meantime, the failure to pay interest periodically does not accelerate the right to foreclosure; and this is so, even where there is a covenant to pay interest periodically, for the proviso for redemption is treated as independent of the covenant (y). But it is otherwise where the condition for periodical payment is contained in the proviso itself; where, for example, the proviso is for redemption on payment of principal with interest

---

(s) See p. 363, *infra.*
(t) *Twentieth Century Banking Corporation, Ltd.* v. *Wilkinson,* [1976] 3 All E.R. 361.
(u) The mortgagee thereupon acquires a new title as owner; see *Heath* v. *Pugh* (1881), 6 Q.B.D. 345 (C.A.); on appeal *sub nom. Pugh* v. *Heath* (1882), 7 App. Cas. 235 (H.L.).
(v) See p. 385, *infra.*
(w) See p. 522, *infra.*
(x) *Bonham* v. *Newcomb* (1684), 1 Vern. 232.
(y) *Re Turner, Turner* v. *Spencer* (1894), 43 W.R. 153; *Williams* v. *Morgan,* [1906] 1 Ch. 804.

half-yearly in the meantime, or on payment of principal and interest in accordance with the covenant for payment (z).

Covenant not to call in the money.—A similar distinction arises where a proviso for early redemption in the usual form is accompanied by a covenant that the money shall not be called in until a later date (a). If the covenant is absolute, default in payment of interest pending the day for redemption will not entitle the mortgagee to foreclose (b). But if, as is usually the case, the covenant is expressed to be conditional on regular payment of interest, the right to foreclose arises on default in such payment (c).

If "punctual" payment is required, this word is construed strictly (d). The mere receipt of interest after the due date is not a waiver of the right to sue (e), though it is a circumstance to be taken into account in determining whether there has been a waiver (f).

A covenant not to call in the money also affects the right to sue in respect of any moneys to which the mortgagee becomes entitled in that character (g), but not in respect of injury to the security (h).

Exercise of remedies.—As soon as the mortgagor has made default (i) in payment of the mortgage debt (k)—that is, where a time for payment is fixed, by non-payment on that day; or where no time is fixed, by non-payment on demand (l)—or, where the mortgage so provides, there is some other breach of the terms thereof, the mortgagee is entitled to pursue any or all of his remedies against the debtor, or his assets, or the incumbered estate (m), subject as regards the appointment of a receiver, and the power of sale to the restrictions imposed by the mortgage deed, if the powers are conferred by that deed, or by statute, if they are statutory. For contrary to the general rule,

---

(z) *Burrowes* v. *Molloy* (1845), 2 Jo. & Lat. 521, at p. 526; *Edwards* v. *Martin* (1856), 25 L.J. Ch. 284; *Kidderminster Mutual Benefit Building Society* v. *Haddock*, [1936] W.N. 158; *Twentieth Century Banking Corporation, Ltd.* v. *Wilkinson, supra*. And see *Mohamedali Jaffer Karachiwalla* v. *Noorally Rattanshi Rajan Nanji*, [1959] A.C. 518 (P.C.); [1959] 1 All E.R. 137.

(a) It has been held that such a covenant by the second mortgagee prevents him from redeeming the first mortgage, because he cannot bring the mortgagor before the court: *Ramsbottom* v. *Wallis* (1835), 5 L.J. Ch. 92. But this seems to be straining a technicality too far.

(b) *Burrowes* v. *Molloy, supra*.

(c) *Stanhope* v. *Manners* (1763), 2 Eden 197; *Seaton* v. *Twyford* (1870), L. R. 11 Eq. 591. For a form, see clause in Precedent 1A in the Appendix, *infra*.

(d) *Leeds and Hanley Theatre of Varieties* v. *Broadbent*, [1898] 1 Ch. 343 (C.A.); *Maclaine* v. *Gatty*, [1921] 1 A.C. 376 (H.L.).

(e) *Keene* v. *Biscoe* (1878), 8 Ch. D. 201.

(f) *Seal* v. *Gimson* (1914), 110 L.T. 583.

(g) *Burrowes* v. *Molloy, supra*.

(h) *Dugdale* v. *Robertson* (1857), 3 K. & J. 695.

(i) *Bonham* v. *Newcomb* (1684), 1 Vern. 232. It was allowed to be shown by parol evidence, that an omission to pay did not amount to default within the meaning of the deed, the consent of the person entitled to payment to enlarge the time, though made without consideration, being held to show that there was no default: *Albert* v. *Grosvenor Investment Co.* (1867), L.R. 3 Q.B. 123. But in *Williams* v. *Stern* (1879), 5 Q.B.D. 409, the Court of Appeal held that a consent so given was no evidence of waiver of the mortgagee's rights to take possession at any time.

(k) *Burrowes* v. *Molloy, supra;* *Wilkes* v. *Saunion* (1877), 7 Ch. D. 188.

(l) Cas. & Op. II, 51; Glanv. Lib. 10, c. 8. For implied demand, see *The Halcyon Skies (No. 2)* (1976), 120 Sol. Jo. 502.

(m) *Lockhart* v. *Hardy* (1846), 9 Beav. 349; *Paynter* v. *Carew* (1854), Kay, App. xxxvi; *Palmer* v. *Hendrie* (1859), 27 Beav. 349, 351.

that a person liable to be sued is not to be harassed by a multiplicity of actions, it is the right of the mortgagee, or other secured creditor, so long as any part of the debt remained unpaid (*n*) to pursue any or all of his remedies at the same time. Hence he may at the same time sue for payment on the covenant to pay principal and interest, for possession of the mortgaged property and for foreclosure, and he can combine these claims in the same action. A mortgagee who has sold the property under his power of sale can sue the mortgagor for any deficiency (*o*). And the same applies where the sale is a sale by the court (*p*). A mortgagee who has taken possession may appoint a receiver (*q*). But, nevertheless, after obtaining a judgment nisi for foreclosure, he cannot sell without the leave of the court before the judgment is made absolute (*r*). And if after foreclosure absolute the mortgagee sues on the personal covenant, this will open the foreclosure (*s*).

And since a mortgagee is entitled to pursue all his remedies, the court will not interfere with his action on the covenant, on the ground that a contract, still incomplete, has been made by him to sell the mortgaged property for a larger sum than is due on the mortgage (*t*); nor with his right to recover possession, because, after contracting to sell, he has brought an action on the covenant, and has compromised it on payment of a sum of money by another person whom the original mortgagee afterwards redeemed for the purpose of completing his contract for sale (*u*); nor interfere with his proceedings by reason of an order made in another action in his absence (*x*).

A prior incumbrancer may also bring an action after a judgment has been obtained in another action by the owner of a later charge; for he is not bound to come in under that judgment at the risk of losing his rights by the suspension of the proceedings in the later incumbrancer's action (*y*).

Administration action.—The mortgagee, whether his security is legal or equitable, may also proceed against the assets of the deceased mortgagor (*z*), or he may prove in an administration action for his debt, less the value which he sets upon his security, or may apply for a sale with liberty to prove for his deficiency (*a*). A mortgagee is even

---

(*n*) But if he had been paid all that he claimed in an action, he could not sue in equity for a further sum unclaimed by mistake in the action: *Darlow* v. *Cooper* (1865), 34 Beav. 281. Nor can a building society who have in error given the usual statutory receipt: *Harvey* v. *Municipal Building Society* (1884), 26 Ch. D. 273; p. 553, *infra*.

(*o*) *Rudge* v. *Richens* (1873), L.R. 8 C.P. 358.

(*p*) *Gordon Grant & Co., Ltd.* v. *Boos*, [1926] A.C. 781 (P.C.).

(*q*) *Refuge Assurance Co., Ltd.* v. *Pearlberg*, [1938] Ch. 687; [1938] 3 All E.R. 231.

(*r*) *Stevens* v. *Theatres, Ltd.*, [1903] 1 Ch. 857. See p. 362, *infra*.

(*s*) *Perry* v. *Barker* (1806), 13 Ves. 198. See p. 407, *infra*.

(*t*) *Willes* v. *Levett* (1847), 1 De G. & Sm. 392.

(*u*) *Davies* v. *Williams* (1843), 7 Jur. 663. (*x*) *Crowle* v. *Russell* (1878), 4 C.P.D. 186.

(*y*) *Arnold* v. *Bainbrigge* (1860), 2 De G.F. & J. 92.

(*z*) *King* v. *Smith* (1843), 2 Hare 239. Formerly the mortgagee had to sue on behalf of himself and all other creditors. This is no longer so: *Re James, James* v. *Jones*, [1911] 2 Ch. 348.

(*a*) Administration of Estates Act 1925, Sched. 1, para. 2, replacing Judicature Act 1875, s. 10. If after the mortgagee has valued his security, the property is sold at his instance, and realises less than the valuation, he cannot prove for more than the deficiency as originally estimated: *Re Hopkins, Williams* v. *Hopkins* (1881), 18 Ch. D. 370 (C.A.).

allowed to prove as a creditor, in an action for administration of the
mortgagor's estate, after obtaining an order of foreclosure, and
contracting to sell the property; but upon the terms of rescinding the
contract and reconveying (*b*).

II—RESTRICTIONS ON SUING

A—RESTRAINT OF PROCEEDINGS IN GENERAL

Where action would be inequitable.—In certain cases, incumbrancers will be restrained from pursuing one or more of their
remedies (*c*). Thus a mortgagee's action for possession has been
stayed (on security being given to redeem) on the ground of entangled
accounts, where an action for an account was also pending against the
mortgagee, and it was considered beneficial to all parties to keep the
possession in suspense in the meantime (*d*). And the owner of property
subject to a charge, upon paying the amount of it with interest into
court in an action to raise the charge, has been protected by injunction
from proceedings by the mortgagee of the charge to obtain possession
of the land (*e*).

The mortgagee may also be prevented from using his remedies if he
has neglected to furnish a proper account, and has refused a proper and
sufficient tender (*f*).

Where mortgagee cannot return the security.—If a creditor
holding security sues for his debt, he must on payment of the debt
return the security, and if, having improperly made away with it, he
cannot return it, he cannot have judgment for the debt (*g*). A mortgagee has been restrained from proceeding on his collateral security,
where, the title deeds being out of his power, he is unable effectually
to reconvey the estate, the amount due being directed to be ascertained
and paid into the bank, there to remain until the title deeds would be
secured, and a reconveyance had (*h*). So, a mortgagee who has foreclosed one mortgage, and afterwards sold the property comprised in it
(though he sold it fairly) for less than was due, will not be allowed to
proceed on his collateral securities, the sale having made it impracticable for the foreclosure to be reopened (*i*); and the same result follows
where a mortgagee, having transferred the mortgage without the
collateral securities, afterwards proceeds to sue the mortgagor on the

---

(*b*) And the proof will be limited in such a case to the amount recoverable under the
mortgage covenant, and therefore will not include the costs of the foreclosure action:
Haynes v. *Haynes* (1857), 3 Jur. N.S. 504. As to the mortgagee's rights in the mortgagor's bankruptcy, see Ch. 23, *infra*.
For the remedy of debenture holders of public utility companies, see p. 307, *infra*.
(*c*) As to restraining sale, see p. 367, *infra*.
(*d*) *Booth* v. *Booth* (1742), 2 Atk. 343.
(*e*) *Duncombe* v. *Greenacre* (1860), 28 Beav. 472.
(*f*) *Herries* v. *Griffiths* (1854), 2 W.R. 72.
(*g*) *Ellis & Co.'s Trustee* v. *Dixon-Johnson*, [1925] A.C. 489 (H.L.).
(*h*) *Schoole* v. *Sall* (1803), 1 Sch. & Lef. 176.
(*i*) *Lockhart* v. *Hardy* (1846), 9 Beav. 349.

latter (*k*). But a mortgagee who has sold the property under his power of sale can sue the mortgagor for the deficiency, since the sale was a proper dealing with the security (*l*).

Incumbrancer not bound to pursue simplest remedy.—An incumbrancer is not generally prevented from using such remedies as are open to him, on the ground that he has easier mode of relief, or on the ground of interference with the rights of other persons claiming under the same security (though this may be a ground for staying execution (*m*)), unless the pursuit of the remedy in question would be contrary to the spirit and intention of the contract, and in breach of good faith (*n*).

Conditional agreement not to sue.—Where a collateral agreement has been entered into that the security shall not be enforced if the debtor observes certain conditions, the creditor will not be prevented from enforcing the security if the debtor has failed to observe such conditions (*o*). Thus a mortgagee was not restrained from exercising his remedy under a mortgage, on the ground of an agreement that it should contain a clause postponing the mortgagee's right to call in the money, where a corresponding condition for punctual payment of interest had not been observed by the mortgagor (*p*).

Rights of third parties.—The mortgagee will be restrained from doing acts in disregard of the rights of third persons which are superior to his own (*q*). And he will be compelled to respect rights which have been acquired by third persons from the mortgagor since the date of the security, if he has done acts which amount to an acknowledgement of such rights, or if the security was taken with the knowledge that the granting of such rights was incident to the purposes to which the property was devoted (*r*).

The mortgagee will not be allowed to cause unnecessary injury to the property, as by cutting timber, when the security is not shown to be defective (*s*).

Staying proceedings on payment or tender.—The court will stay

---

(*k*) *Walker* v. *Jones* (1866), L.R. 1 P.C. 50. Similarly, if the mortgagee joins with the transferee of the equity of redemption in a sale, and allows the transferee to receive the purchase money, the mortgagee, since he is no longer able to reconvey the estate will not be allowed to sue the mortgagor on his covenant to pay: *Palmer* v. *Hendrie* (1859), 27 Beav. 349.

(*l*) *Rudge* v. *Richens* (1873), L.R. 8 C.P. 358; *Gordon Grant & Co.* v. *Boos*, [1926] A.C. 781 (P.C.); *Coast Realities, Ltd.* v. *Nolan* (1972), 20 D.L.R. (3d) 96.

(*m*) *Bolckow* v. *Herne Bay Pier Co.* (1852), 1 E. & B. 75.

(*n*) *Sherborn* v. *Tollemache* (1863), 13 C.B. N.S. 742. And there would be similar impropriety in an action by a mortgagee on his security after proving for his whole debt, when the estate was to be divided as in bankruptcy: *Kingsford* v. *Swinford* (1859), 4 Drew. 705.

(*o*) *Parry* v. *Great Ship Co.* (1863), 4 B. & S. 556.

(*p*) *Seaton* v. *Simpson*, [1870] W.N. 261.

(*q*) A mortgagee of a ship has been restrained from so dealing with her as to prevent the performance of a charter party of which he had notice: *De Mattos* v. *Gibson* (1859), 4 De G. & J. 276; *Lord Strathcona S.S. Co., Ltd.* v. *Dominion Coal Co., Ltd.*, [1926] A.C. 108 (P.C.); *cf. Port Line, Ltd.* v. *Ben Line Steamers, Ltd.*, [1958] 2 Q.B. 146; [1958] 1 All E.R. 787.

(*r*) *Mold* v. *Wheatcroft* (1859), 27 Beav. 510. As to modification of the relationship of mortgagor and mortgagee by a subsequent contract between them, see *Drummond* v. *Pigou* (1835), 2 My. & K. 168; *Feehan* v. *Mandeville* (1891), 28 L.R. Ir. 90.

(*s*) *Withrington* v. *Banks* (1725), 25 E.R. 205.

proceedings, under its inherent powers, upon payment or tender by a defendant incumbrancer to the plaintiff (who is always liable to be paid off) of his principal, interest, and costs, and upon bringing into court a sum sufficient to cover the costs of the other defendants, so far as the plaintiff is liable to them, until the amount has been ascertained (*t*). But the court will refuse to make such an order, where it would affect the interests of the other defendants, by interfering with questions as to priorities of the incumbrances; or with the order of the court made in another action relating to the same securities. Though even in such a case it will anticipate the order at the hearing by directing inquiries as to the priorities of, and the amounts due to, the incumbrancers, and if proper, by directing a sale (*u*).

The court can also, under its inherent powers, make such an order before the hearing as it might have made at the hearing (*x*), *viz.* for accounts and for foreclosure in default of payment on a given day (*y*).

B—UNDER THE BANKRUPTCY LAW

Power of the bankruptcy court.—The Bankruptcy Act 1914, contains the following provisions with respect to proceedings after bankruptcy. The court (*a*) may, at any time after the presentation of a bankruptcy petition, stay any action, execution or other legal process against the property or person of the debtor; and any court in which proceedings are pending against a debtor may, on proof of the presentation of a petition, either stay the proceedings or allow them to continue on such terms as it may think just (*b*). Further the court has power to decide all questions of priorities, and all other questions, whether of law or fact, which may arise in any case of bankruptcy coming within the cognizance of the court, or which the court may deem it expedient or necessary to decide, for the purpose of doing complete justice or making a complete distribution of property in any such case (*c*).

But the right of a secured creditor to realise or otherwise deal with his security is unaffected by the presentation of a bankruptcy petition or the making of a receiving order (*d*).

The exercise of the powers.—The court has restrained the exercise by secured creditors of their legal rights contrary to the provisions of the bankruptcy law, or to equitable considerations (*e*). It has stopped an action of foreclosure by a mortgagee, commenced after the trustee

---

(*t*) See form of order in *France* v. *Cowper*, [1871] W.N. 76.

(*u*) *Paine* v. *Edwards* (1862), 6 L.T. N.S. 600.

(*x*) *Aberdeen* v. *Chitty* (1839), 3 Y. & C. Ex. at p. 382.

(*y*) Or for a stay with a proviso that on default of payment it should be deemed that no order had been made on the application: *Jones* v. *Tinney* (1845), Kay, App. xlv.

(*a*) *I.e.*, the court having jurisdiction in bankruptcy: s. 167; and see s. 96 (1), (2).

(*b*) Section 9. And see s. 7 as to the effect of a receiving order.

(*c*) Section 105. But this jurisdiction is not to be exercised by the county court for the purpose of adjudicating upon any claim, not arising out of the bankruptcy, which might before the Act have been enforced in the High Court, unless the parties consent, or the subject matter of the dispute does not exceed £200.

(*d*) Section 7 (2).

(*e*) *Re Chidley* , *Re Lennard* (1875), 1 Ch. D. 177 (C.A.).

had made an advantageous contract for the sale of the estate, ordering him to concur in the sale and to give up his deed on payment into court of the full amount which he claimed (*f*). It has prevented the creditor from suing the trustee on an alleged bill of sale, the validity of which was disputed by the trustee (*g*). But it has refused to intervene in an action by a mortgagee which involved questions not affecting the administration of the estate in bankruptcy (*h*); or to interfere with the rights of an execution creditor who had seized the goods before the petition for bankruptcy (*i*). And in general it will not restrain a mortgagee or other secured creditor in the exercise of his legal remedies (*k*).

C—UNDER THE COMPANIES ACT 1948

Powers in winding up.—The Companies Act 1948, contains the following provisions with respect to proceedings against a company in liquidation. At any time after the presentation of a winding-up petition, and before a winding-up order has been made, the company or any creditor or contributory may, where any action or proceeding against the company is pending in the High Court or Court of Appeal, apply to the court in which the action or proceeding is pending for a stay of proceedings therein, and where any other action or proceeding is pending against the company apply to the court having jurisdiction to wind up the company, to restrain further proceedings in the action or proceeding. The court to which application is so made may, as the case may be, stay or restrain the proceedings accordingly on such terms as it thinks fit (*l*).

When a winding-up order has been made or a provisional liquidator has been appointed no action or proceeding is, except by leave of the court (*i.e.*, the winding up court) and subject to such terms as the court may impose, to be proceeded with or commenced against the company (*m*).

Any attachment, sequestration, distress or execution put in force against the estate or effects of the company after the commencement of the winding-up is void to all intents (*n*).

Exercise of the powers.—The court will not interfere with the rights of a mortgagee by withholding from him leave under s. 231 to proceed with an action after a winding-up order, or by preventing him from proceeding to realise his security, without special ground, or without offering him all that he is entitled to. Generally the court is unwilling to interfere with the legal rights of mortgagees, and hardly

---

(*f*) *Re Woods, Ex parte Ditton* (1876), 1 Ch. D. 557 (C.A.).
(*g*) *Re Sparke, Ex parte Cohen* (1871), 7 Ch. App. 20.
(*h*) *Re Taylor and Rumboll, Ex parte Rumboll* (1871), 6 Ch. App. 842.
(*i*) *Re Hall, Ex parte Rocke* (1871), 6 Ch. App. 795.
(*k*) *Re Wherly, Ex parte Hirst* (1879), 11 Ch. D. 278. See *Re Evelyn, Ex parte General Public Works, etc., Co., Ltd.*, [1894] 2 Q.B. 302. And see p. 380, *infra*.
(*l*) Section 226. And see ss. 396 (companies registered under Part VIII of the 1948 Act), 402 (unregistered companies).
(*m*) Section 231. And see ss. 397 (companies registered under Part VIII), and 403 (unregistered companies).
(*n*) Section 228.

ever does so without requiring payment into court of, or other security for, the mortgage debt (o).

D—UNDER THE RENT ACT 1968 (p)

Mortgages created on or after 8 December, 1965.—The Rent Act 1968, does not apply, so far as it restricts the rights and remedies of a mortgagee, to a mortgage created on or after 8 December, 1965 (q).

Controlled mortgages.—Restrictions are imposed on mortgagees under controlled mortgages (r). A controlled mortage is one which had the 1965 Act not been passed, would have been a mortgage to which the Increase of Rent and Mortgage Interest (Restrictions) Act 1920, would have applied (whether by virtue of the modifications of that Act effected by Schedule 1 of the Rent and Mortgage Restrictions Act 1939, or otherwise) (s). Where the dwelling-house is subject to old rent control—*i.e.*, a dwelling-house controlled before 2 September, 1939—the Act applies only to a mortgage (t) thereof created before 2 July, 1920. Where the house became subject to control on or after 2 September, 1939, the Act would appear to apply to a mortgage thereof whenever created.

The Act applies only to legal mortgages (u). It does not apply to any mortgage comprising one or more dwelling-houses to which the Act applies and other land, if the rateable value of such dwelling-houses is less than one-tenth of the rateable value of the whole of the mortgaged land (x).

Where the Act does apply, so long as interest at the permitted rate is paid, and is not more than twenty-one days in arrear, and the

---

(o) *Re David Lloyd & Co., Lloyd v. David Lloyd & Co.* (1877), 6 Ch. D. 339 (C.A.); *Re Longdendale Cotton Spinning Co.* (1878), 8 Ch. D. 150; *Re Henry Pound Son and Hutchins* (1889), 42 Ch. D. 402 (C.A.); *Re Joshua Stubbs, Ltd., Barney v. Joshua Stubbs, Ltd.*, [1891] 1 Ch. 475 (C.A.); *Strong v. Carlyle Press*, [1893] 1 Ch. 268 (C.A.); *The Zafiro*, [1960] P. 1; [1959] 2 All E.R. 537. And see p. 381, *infra*.

(p) As amended by the Rent Act 1974.

(q) Rent Act 1968, s. 93 (1). There are three exceptions for later mortgages, *i.e.*, (1) where a long tenancy has been converted into a regulated tenancy under the Leasehold Reform Act 1967 s. 39, the relevant date is the 28 November 1967; (2) where a furnished tenancy was converted into a regulated furnished tenancy under the Rent Act 1974, the relevant date is the 14th August 1974 (Rent Act 1974, Sched. 1, para. 10); and (3) where a tenancy became a regulated tenancy under the Counter-Inflation Act 1973. See further Hill and Redman's *Law of Landlord and Tenant* (16th Edn.), p. 1029.

(r) Rent Act 1968, s. 96.

(s) Rent Act 1968, s. 93 (2). For the dwelling-houses to which the 1920 and 1939 Acts apply, see the Act of 1920, s. 12 (2), (7). And see, generally, Megarry, *The Rent Acts*, pp. 481 *et seq.*

(t) "Mortgage" includes a charge on registered land: Rent Act 1968, s. 99 (b).

(u) The 1920 Act, s. 12 (4) (b), which excludes an equitable charge by deposit of title deeds or otherwise. This extends to an equitable charge created by writing without deposit of deeds (*Jones v. Woodward* (1917), 116 L.T. 378) and also to a bank charge with an undertaking to execute a legal mortgage when required (*London County and Westminster Bank, Ltd. v. Tompkins*, [1918] 1 K.B. 515 (C.A.)).

(x) The 1920 Act, s. 12 (4) (a). Where the rateable value of the dwelling-houses is more than one-tenth of the rateable value of the whole of the mortgaged property the mortgagee may apportion the principal between the dwelling-houses to which the Act does or does not apply: Rent Act 1968, s. 97 (1). There are no restrictions on the rights and remedies of the mortgagee in respect of the part apportioned to the houses to which the Act does not apply: *Coutts & Co. v. Duntroon Investment Corpn., Ltd.*, [1958] 1 All E.R. 51.

mortgagor performs his covenants other than for payment of principal, and keeps the property in a proper state of repair (*y*), and pays interest and instalments of principal recoverable under prior incumbrances, the mortgagee cannot call in his mortgage or take any steps for exercising any right of foreclosure or sale, or for otherwise enforcing the security or for recovering the principal money thereby secured (*z*). If the mortgagor fails to comply with any one of these conditions he loses the protection of the Act (*a*). However, if the mortgagee satisfies the county court that greater hardship would be caused if these restrictions continued to apply to the mortgage than if they were removed or modified, the court may by order allow him to exercise such of those rights and remedies as may be specified in the order on such terms as may be so specified (*b*). The restrictions do not apply where the principal money is repayable in periodical instalments extending over a term of not less than ten years from the creation of the mortgage (*c*), nor do they affect a power of sale exercisable by a mortgagee who was a mortgagee in possession, in the case of a house subject to old control, on 25 March, 1920, or, in the case of a house subject to 1939 control, on 1 September, 1939, or in cases where the mortgagor consents to the exercise of a mortgage power; and in the case of a mortgage of a leasehold interest, the court may authorise the mortgagee to call in and enforce the same, if it is satisfied that the security is seriously diminishing in value or is otherwise in jeopardy, and that for that reason it is reasonable that the mortgage should be called in and enforced (*d*).

The Act also imposes restrictions on the increase of interest payable under a mortgage to which it applies (*e*). Where the dwelling-house is subject to old control the permitted increase is an amount not exceeding 1 per cent. per annum above the standard rate or so as to exceed $6\frac{1}{2}$ per cent. per annum; in the case of 1939 control there is no permitted increase above the standard rate. In the case of houses subject to old control, the standard rate of interest is, where the mortgage was in force on 3 August, 1914, the rate payable on that date, or, where the mortgage was created between that date and 2 July, 1920, the original rate (*e*); in the case of houses subject to 1939 control, the standard rate is, where the mortgage was in force on 1 September, 1939, the rate payable on that date, or, where the mortgage was created after that date, the original rate (*f*). Where the rate of interest under a mortgage made in 1929 depended on the

---

(*y*) This depends on the general condition of the property at the date of the mortgage. It is sufficient if that condition is maintained: *Woodifield* v. *Bond*, [1922] 2 Ch. 40.

(*z*) Rent Act 1968, s. 96 (1), Sched. 12, Pt. II. See *Welby* v. *Parker*, [1916] 2 Ch. 1 (C.A.); *Martin* v. *Watson and Egan*, [1919] 2 I.R. 534; *London County and Westminster Bank, Ltd.* v. *Tompkins, supra*; and see p. 268, *infra*.

(*a*) And subsequent compliance does not revive the protection thereby given: *Evans* v. *Horner*, [1925] Ch. 177; *Nichols* v. *Walters*, [1953] 2 All E.R. 1516 (C.A.).

(*b*) Rent Act 1968, s. 96 (2). Such an order may be varied or revoked: sub-s. (3).

(*c*) *I.e.*, most building society mortgages: Rent Act 1968, Sched. 12, Pt. II, para. 6 (1).

(*d*) Rent Act 1968, Sched. 12, Pt. II, paras. 5 (2), 6 (2), 7.

(*e*) Rent Act 1968, Sched. 12, Pt. I.

(*f*) Rent Act 1968, Sched. 12, Pt. I. The Act gives no indication as to how the increase is to be effected: see Megarry, *ubi supra*, at p. 492.

rate of income tax, the standard rate of interest was fixed according to the rate of tax payable on 1 September, 1939 (g). If, in a mortgage of a dwelling-house subject to 1939 control, the rate of interest is expressed as an amount which will after deduction of income tax yield a certain percentage, no increase in the rate of interest based on an increase in the rate of income tax is recoverable in so far as the increased rate exceeds the standard rate (g).

Regulated mortgages.—If the mortgage was created before 8 December, 1965, and is a mortgage comprising or including a dwelling-house subject to a regulated tenancy (h) binding on the mortgagee, the Rent Act 1968, imposes certain restrictions on or variations of the rights of the mortgagee. If the rate of interest payable under such a mortgage has been increased, or if there has been registered in respect of any dwelling-house comprised in the mortgaged property a rent lower than that payable immediately before such registration, or if the mortgagee (not being a mortgagee in possession on 8 December, 1965) calls in or takes any steps to enforce his security, and if the court (i) is satisfied that by reason thereof and also by reason of the provisions of the Act the mortgagor would suffer severe financial hardship (k) unless given relief, then it may make such order varying the terms of the mortgage or imposing limits or conditions on the exercise of his rights by the mortgagee as may seem appropriate (l). Mortgages created after 8 December, 1965, are not affected by these provisions (m).

Where the mortgaged property comprises a dwelling-house or dwelling-houses subject to a regulated tenancy or regulated tenancies and other land these provisions only apply if, on the appropriate day (n), the rateable value or the aggregate of the rateable values of such dwelling-house or dwelling-houses was not less than one-tenth of the rateable value of the whole of the land comprised in the mortgaged property (o).

The mortgagor must make application to the court within twenty-one days, or such longer time as the court may allow, of the event giving rise to the right to apply (p). The mortgagor has no right to apply if he is in breach of any of his covenants (other than a covenant for repayment of principal otherwise than by instalments) (q).

If the mortgaged property includes other land as well as a dwelling-house or dwelling-houses subject to a regulated tenancy or regulated tenancies, then, if on any such application of a mortgagor as is mentioned above the court makes such an order it may also, if the

---

(g) *Warrilow* v. *Ward*, [1942] Ch. 257; [1942] 1 All E.R. 366.
(h) As to regulated tenancies, see Rent Act 1968, s. 7 (2). And see Megarry, *The Rent Acts* (10th Edn.).
(i) The court is the county court except where an application is made in pursuance of any step taken by the mortgagee in another court when it is that other court: s. 95 (6).
(k) On this, see Megarry, *ubi supra*, at p. 494.
(l) Section 95 (1), (2). Such an order may be revoked or varied: s. 95 (5).
(m) Rent Act 1968, s. 93 (1).
(n) See Rent Act 1968, s. 6 (3).
(o) Section 94 (2) (a).
(p) Section 95 (1).
(q) Section 94 (2) (b).

mortgagee so requests, make provision for apportioning the money secured by the mortgage between the other land and the dwelling-house or dwelling-houses, whereupon the mortgage is to have effect as two separate mortgages of the apportioned parts (*r*).

Protection of civil interests.—Restrictions are imposed by the Reserve and Auxiliary Forces (Protection of Civil Interests) Act 1951, and Rules 1951, on mortgage remedies against persons called up or volunteers for certain naval, military or air service, or doing work or training as conscientious objectors (*s*).

E—UNDER THE CONSUMER CREDIT ACT 1974 (*t*)

Land mortgages.—A land mortgage securing a regulated agreement is enforceable (so far as provided in relation to the agreement) on an order of the court only (*u*).

Generally.—Before a creditor can become entitled, by reason of any breach by the debtor or hirer of a regulated agreement, to recover possession of any goods or land or enforce any security (*a*), he must serve a default notice on the debtor or hirer (*b*). The default notice must be in the prescribed form (*c*) and specify (a) the nature of the alleged breach; (b) if the breach is capable of remedy, what action is required to remedy it and the date before which that action is to be taken; and (c) if the breach is not capable of remedy, the sum (if any) required to be paid as compensation for the breach, and the date before which it is to be paid. The date specified must not be less than seven days after the date of service of the default notice. The default notice must contain information in the prescribed terms about the consequences of failure to comply with it (*d*). If a security is not expressed in writing or a security instrument is improperly executed (*e*), the security (so far as provided in relation to a regulated agreement) is enforceable against the surety on an order of the court only (*f*). If an application for such an order is dismissed (except on technical grounds only), the security will be ineffective (*g*). A security, provided in relation to a regulated agreement, cannot be enforced so as to benefit the creditor or owner to an extent greater than would be the case if the agreement had been with security (*h*).

(*r*) Section 95 (3), (4).
(*s*) As this jurisdiction is not relevant at the present time, reference should be made to the previous edition for further details.
(*t*) See, generally, Ch. 9, *supra.*
(*u*) Consumer Credit Act, 1974, s. 126. The court means the county court: s. 189 (1).
(*a*) The doing of an act by which a floating charge becomes fixed is not enforcement of a security: *ibid.*, s. 87 (3).
(*b*) *Ibid.* s. 87 (1).
(*c*) No form has been prescribed at the date of writing.
(*d*) Consumer Credit Act, 1974, s. 88 (1), (2), (4).
(*e*) See p. 146, *supra.*
(*f*) Consumer Credit Act, 1974, s. 105 (7).
(*g*) *Ibid.*, s. 105 (8). For the consequences of inefficacy, see s. 106 (p. 147, *supra*); for the saving for certain transferees of registered charges and purchasers from mortgagees selling under the statutory power, see s. 177 (p. 154, *supra.*).
(*h*) *Ibid.*, s. 113 (1).

III—LIMITATION OF ACTIONS

A—ACTIONS ON THE COVENANT FOR PAYMENT

Period of limitation.—The Limitation Act 1939 (*i*), provides:

2.—(1) The following actions shall not be brought after the expiration of six years from the date on which the cause of action accrued, that is to say:—
(a) actions founded on simple contract . . .
(3) An action upon a specialty shall not be brought after the expiration of twelve years from the date on which the cause of action accrued:
Provided that this subsection shall not affect any action for which a shorter period of limitation is prescribed by any other provision of this Act (*k*).

Accordingly, subject to the proviso set out above, an action on the mortgagor's covenant for payment of the principal money secured by the mortgage may not be brought after twelve years from the date when the cause of action accrued (*l*), if the mortgage is by deed, or after six years if the mortgage is not by deed (*m*).

The remedies on the contract and against the land have their separate periods (*n*).

B—ACTIONS TO RECOVER MONEY CHARGED ON PROPERTY: (i) PRINCIPAL

Period of limitation.—The Act provides:

18.—(1) No action shall be brought to recover any principal sum of money secured by a mortgage or other charge on property, whether real or personal (*o*), or to recover proceeds of sale of land (*p*), after the expiration of twelve years from the date when the right to receive the money accrued.
(4) Nothing in this section shall apply to a foreclosure action in respect of mortgaged land, but the provisions of this Act relating to actions to recover land (*q*) shall apply to such an action.

What is money charged on land.—Money is charged upon land when the land can only be enjoyed subject to its payment, even though there is no direct remedy against the land itself (*r*). The charge may be one imposed by statute (*s*). There must be land on which the charge can take effect.

(*i*) See, generally, 24 Halsbury's Laws (3rd Edn.), Limitation of Actions; Preston and Newsom, *Limitation of Actions* (3rd Edn.). References hereafter to the Act mean the Limitation Act 1939, and references to a section, without more, mean a section of that Act. For moneylenders, see p. 238, *supra*.

(*k*) See, *e.g.*, s. 18 (5), p. 281, *infra*.

(*l*) As to when the right of action arises, see p. 296, *infra*.

(*m*) The Act contains general and particular provisions suspending the running of time and effecting a fresh accrual of a right of action: see pp. 285 *et seq.*, *infra*.

(*n*) *London and Midland Bank, Ltd.* v. *Mitchell*, [1899] 2 Ch. 161.

(*o*) There had previously been no statutory provision for personalty. Ships are excluded from s. 18 by sub-s. (6) thereof and accordingly a mortgagee of a ship does not lose his right to enforce his security against the ship by lapse of time.

(*p*) The proceeds of sale of land are land for the purposes of the Act: s. 31 (1). As to the effect, if any, of the expression, see Preston and Newsom, *ubi sup.*, at p. 155.

(*q*) *I.e.*, ss. 4-6: see p. 283, *infra*.

(*r*) *Payne* v. *Esdaile* (1888), 13 App. Cas. 613.

(*s*) *Hornsey Local Board* v. *Monarch Investment Building Society* (1889), 24 Q.B.D. 1 (C.A.); *Poole Corpn.* v. *Moody*, [1945] 1 K.B. 350 (C.A.); [1945] 1 All E.R. 536.

The action on the covenant has been held to be an action to recover money charged on land (*t*), even when the covenant is contained in a separate deed (*u*).

Date from which time runs.—Time begins to run from the date when the right to receive the money accrued (*a*). The right to receive probably means the same as the expression "a present right to receive" used in the Real Property Limitation Act 1874 (*b*). A present right to receive is an immediate right without waiting for the happening of any future event (*c*). Where there is a present right time runs notwithstanding there may be no means of immediately enforcing it (*d*). The requirement that notice shall be given before suing does not postpone the running of time (*e*). The right to receive any principal sum of money secured by a mortgage or other charge is not deemed to accrue so long as the mortgaged property comprises any future interest or any life insurance policy which has not matured or been determined (*f*).

C—ACTIONS TO RECOVER MONEY CHARGED ON PROPERTY:

(ii) ARREARS

Period of limitation.—The Act provides:

18.—(5) No action to recover arrears of interest payable in respect of any sum of money secured by a mortgage or other charge or payable in respect of proceeds of the sale of land, or to recover damages in respect of such arrears (*g*) shall be brought after the expiration of six years from the date on which the interest became due:

Provided that—

(a) where a prior mortgagee or other incumbrancer has been in possession of the property charged, and an action is brought within one year of the discontinuance of such possession by the subsequent incumbrancer, he may recover by that action all the arrears of interest which fell due during the period of possession by the prior incumbrancer or damages in respect thereof, notwithstanding that the period exceeded six years;

(b) where the property subject to the mortgage or charge comprises any future interest or life insurance policy and it is a term of the mortgage or charge that arrears of interest shall be treated as part of the principal sum of money secured by the mortgage or charge (*h*), interest shall not be deemed to become due before the right to receive the principal sum of money has accrued or is deemed to have accrued.

(*t*) *Sutton* v. *Sutton* (1882), 22 Ch. D. 511 (C.A.). If this is so, s. 18 (3) (see *supra*) applies to an action on the personal covenant.

(*u*) *Re Powers* (1885), 30 Ch. D. 291 (C.A.), at p. 297.

(*a*) Section 18 (1); *Cotterell* v. *Price*, [1960] 3 All E.R. 315, see p. 296, *infra.*

(*b*) In s. 8 of that Act.

(*c*) *Farran* v. *Beresford* (1842), 10 Cl. & F. 319, 334.

(*d*) *Hornsey Local Board* v. *Monarch Building Society, supra; Dennerley* v. *Prestwich U.D.C.*, [1930] 1 K.B. 334 (C.A.).

(*e*) *Hervey* v. *Wynn* (1905), 22 T.L.R. 93.

(*f*) Section 18 (3).

(*g*) Where there is no covenant for payment of interest arrears are given by way of damages: *Mellersh* v. *Brown* (1890), 45 Ch. D. 225.

(*h*) For capitalisation of interest, see p. 630, *infra.*

Different effect in foreclosure of mortgage of land and redemption.—An action for foreclosure of a mortgage of land is excluded from s. 18 (*i*). Accordingly the account taken in such an action will be of the whole of the arrears, though the mortgagee's claim against the mortgagor personally would be limited to six years (*k*).

And in a redemption action, the mortgagee is not seeking to recover his mortgage debt and interest, and there is no limit to the arrears which the mortgagor must pay as a condition of redeeming (*l*).

The mortgagee's right of retention.—In other cases, too, the mortgagee can get the whole of the arrears. Where, for instance, he has sold the mortgaged property under his power of sale and has the proceeds in his hands (*m*). Where the money is in court on behalf of all parties interested, the mortgagee, if he petitions for payment out, is restricted to six years of interest (*n*). But if the mortgagor petitions, he is only allowed the balance after the mortgagee has received his principal and full arrears of interest (*o*). If, however, the mortgage debt is barred and the mortgagee's title extinguished, the mortgagee cannot rely on this doctrine to claim either principal or interest (*p*).

If the mortgagee sells after being in possession of the mortgaged land for twelve years he may keep the whole of the proceeds of sale, for the title of the mortgagor and those claiming under him is barred (*q*).

Receipt of rents by mortgagee's receiver.—A receiver appointed by the mortgagee under the statutory power (*r*), is the agent of the mortgagor (*s*). Hence, in applying rents and profits received by him in payment of the interest accruing due he cannot pay interest which is statute barred; nor if he pays the rents and profits to the mortgagee, can the mortgagee appropriate thereto arrears of interest which are barred. In such circumstances the doctrine of retaining full arrears does not apply (*t*).

Trust of surplus sale moneys.—A first mortgagee who has sold the mortgaged property under his statutory power of sale is under a statutory obligation (*u*) to hand the surplus sale moneys, remaining after satisfying his own claim, to the second mortgagee, who can then exercise the rights of retention. He is not entitled to pay the second mortgagee his principal and six years' arrears of interest only, and hand

---

(*i*) Section 18 (4).

(*k*) See Preston and Newsom, *ubi sup.*, at p. 165.

(*l*) *Dingle* v. *Coppen*, [1899] 1 Ch. 726; *Holmes* v. *Cowcher*, [1970] 1 All E.R. 1224. And the same applies where the mortgagee has instituted proceedings for foreclosure and the mortgagor counterclaims for redemption.

(*m*) *Edmunds* v. *Waugh* (1866), L.R. 1 Eq. 418; *Banner* v. *Berridge* (1881), 18 Ch. D. 254; *Holmes* v. *Cowcher*, *supra*.

(*n*) *Re Stead's Mortgaged Estates* (1876), 2 Ch. D. 713; *Re Owen Lewis' Estate*, [1903] 1 I.R. 348. But see *Matthews (C. & M.), Ltd.* v. *Marsden Building Society*, [1951] Ch. 758, at pp. 768–769. [1951] 1 All E.R. 1053, at p. 1059.

(*o*) *Re Lloyd*, [1903] 1 Ch. 385 (C.A.).

(*p*) *Re Hazeldine's Trusts*, [1908] 1 Ch. 34 (C.A.).

(*q*) *Young* v. *Clarey*, [1948] Ch. 191; [1948] 1 All E.R. 197.

(*r*) See the Law of Property Act 1925, s. 101 (1) (iii), p. 301, *infra*.

(*s*) *Ibid.*, s. 109 (2). See p. 301, *infra*.

(*t*) *Hibernian Bank* v. *Yourell (No. 2)*, [1919] 1 I.R. 310.

(*u*) By virtue of the Law of Property Act 1925, s. 105. See p. 373, *infra*.

the remainder to the mortgagor or a third mortgagee. And a summons by the second mortgagee to have his rights determined is in substance an action for the execution of the trusts of the surplus proceeds (*a*), and not an action for the recovery of interest in respect of money secured by a mortgage or charge (*b*).

D—FORECLOSURE

Period of limitation.—The provisions of the Limitation Act 1939, relating to actions to recover land (*c*) apply to a foreclosure action in respect of mortgaged land (*d*). Accordingly no such foreclosure action may be brought after the expiration of twelve years from the date on which the right of action accrued (*e*). Foreclosure actions in respect of mortgaged personalty are barred after twelve years from the date on which the right to foreclosure accrued (*f*).

Date from which time runs.—Time commences to run upon default in payment at the date fixed for redemption (*g*), or, where the principal is payable on demand and, on a proper construction of the terms of the mortgage, the sum is not recoverable until it has been demanded, from the demand (*h*). Where the mortgagee has been in possession of the mortgaged property after the right of action has accrued the right is deemed not to have accrued until the mortgagee has been dispossessed or has discontinued his possession (*i*).

Future interests in personalty.—The right to foreclose in respect of mortgaged personalty is deemed not to accrue so long as the mortgaged property comprises any future interest or any life insurance policy which has not matured or been determined (*k*).

Future interests in land.—The right to recover any land shall, in a case where the estate or interest claimed was an estate or interest in reversion or remainder or any other future estate or interest and no person has taken possession of the land by virtue of the estate or interest claimed, be deemed to have accrued on the date on which the estate or interest fell into possession by the determination of the preceding estate or interest (*l*). If the person entitled to the preceding estate or interest, not being a term of years absolute, was not in possession of the land on the date of the determination thereof, no action shall be brought by the person entitled to the succeeding estate

---

(*a*) *Re Thomson's Mortgage Trusts, Thomson* v. *Bruty*, [1920] 1 Ch. 508.
(*b*) *I.e.*, not an action within the Limitation Act 1939, s. 18 (5).
(*c*) *I.e.*, ss. 4–6.
(*d*) Section 18 (4). Foreclosure in respect of mortgaged land is excluded from s. 18.
(*e*) Section 4 (3). Longer periods are prescribed for actions by the Crown or any spiritual or eleemosynary corporation sole.
(*f*) Section 18 (2).
(*g*) *Samuel Johnson & Sons, Ltd.* v. *Brock*, [1907] 2 Ch. 533, at p. 536; *Purnell* v. *Roche*, [1927] 2 Ch. 142.
(*h*) At least where the security is collateral: *Lloyds Bank, Ltd.* v. *Margolis*, [1954] 1 All E.R. 734, at pp. 737, 738; and see *Re Brown's Estate, Brown* v. *Brown*, [1893] 2 Ch. 300, and *Wakefield and Barnsley Union Bank, Ltd.* v. *Yates*, [1916] 1 Ch. 452 (C.A.). See p. 296, *infra.*
(*i*) See s. 5 (1) (land) and s. 18 (2), proviso (personalty).
(*k*) Section 18 (3).
(*l*) Section 6 (1).

or interest after the expiration of twelve years from the date on which the right of action accrued to the person entitled to the preceding estate or interest, or six years from the date on which the right of action accrued to the person entitled to the succeeding estate or interest, whichever period last expires (m).

Whether the above stated provisions apply to an action to foreclose a mortgage of a future interest in land is questionable (n). It has been held at first instance that where the remedy is foreclosure time does not run until the interest falls into possession (o). On the other hand it was subsequently held by the Court of Appeal that where the mortgagee has a right of foreclosure his estate is not turned into a future estate with the consequent postponement of the time for bringing foreclosure (p). It would appear, therefore, that s. 6 does not apply to an action for foreclosure of a mortgage of a future interest in land.

Effect of payment of interest.—There is a fresh accrual of the right of action where interest or part of the principal is paid (q). But a payment made after the statutory period has expired does not revive the mortgagee's right (r).

Successive mortgages.—Where there are two successive mortgages, and no payment is made by the second mortgagee, time runs against him (s); and this is so even though the first mortgagee is in possession (t).

Where stranger in possession.—Where a stranger is in possession of the land, so that time is running in his favour as against both mortgagor and mortgagee, payment of interest by the mortgagor keeps alive the right of the mortgagee (u). This is so where the mortgage was created before the adverse possession began (s). But if at the date of the mortgage time was already running against the mortgagor, payment of interest does not operate under the Act to give the mortgagee a new right of entry and so stop time running (a).

E—POSSESSION

Period of limitation.—The provisions of the Act relating to

(m) Section 6 (2).

(n) See Preston and Newsom, ubi sup., at pp. 110-114.

(o) Hugill v. Wilkinson (1888), 38 Ch. D. 480. A foreclosure action, being an action to recover land, had the benefit, where the mortgaged property was a future interest in land, of s. 2 of the Real Property Limitation Act 1874, which postponed the running of time until the interest fell into possession.

(p) Wakefield and Barnsley Union Bank, Ltd. v. Yates, [1916] 1 Ch. 452 (C.A.), where Hugill v. Wilkinson was referred to without disapproval. And see Re Witham, [1922] 2 Ch. 413.

(q) Section 23.

(r) Sanders v. Sanders (1881), 19 Ch. D. 373 (C.A.); Nicholson v. England, [1926] 2 K.B. 93 (D.C.).

(s) Kibble v. Fairthorne, [1895] 1 Ch. 219.

(t) Johnson (Samuel) & Sons, Ltd.v. Brock, [1907] 2 Ch. 533. In Re Bermingham's Estate (1870), 5 I.R. Eq. 147, it was considered that on the first mortgagee taking possession, the second mortgagee ceased to have a right of entry, and his interest became for the purpose of Limitation Acts a future interest. But he can enter if he pays off the first mortgagee, and in any case he has an immediate right of foreclosure.

(u) Section 23 (1) (b); Doe d. Palmer v. Eyre (1851), 17 Q.B. 366; Ludbrook v. Ludbrook, [1901] 2 K.B. 96 (C.A.).

(a) Thornton v. France, [1897] 2 Q.B. 143 (C.A.).

actions to recover land apply to an action for possession (*b*). Accordingly the right of a mortgagee to enter upon the mortgaged land or to bring an action for possession will be barred twelve years after the right has accrued (*c*).

Date from which time runs.—Since a legal mortgagee prima facie has a right of entry on the execution of the mortgage, time prima facie begins to run from the execution of the mortgage. But if the mortgagee's right to possession is qualified, time begins to run from default in payment on the date fixed for payment. This will be so where there is a provision that the mortgage shall not be called in until the expiration of a given term and that until default in payment it shall be lawful for the mortgagor peaceably to enjoy and receive the rents. This amounts to a re-demise by the mortgagee to the mortgagor during the term fixed (*d*).

An equitable mortgagee has no right to possession without an order of the court, unless his mortgage expressly gives him such a right (*e*).

Foreclosure gives new title.—An order absolute for foreclosure vests in the mortgagee a new right to the land and accordingly the mortgagee's right to possession, he having obtained such an order, accrues on the date of the order (*f*).

F—PART PAYMENT AND ACKNOWLEDGEMENT (*g*)

Generally.—Where there has accrued any right of action (including a foreclosure action) to recover land or any right of a mortgagee of personal property to bring a foreclosure action in respect of the property, and (a) the person in possession of the land or personal property acknowledges the title of the person to whom the right of action has accrued, or (b) in the case of a foreclosure or other action by a mortgagee, the person in possession of the mortgaged property or the person liable for the mortgage debt makes any payment in respect thereof, whether of principal or interest, the right is deemed to have accrued on and not before the date of the acknowledgement or payment (*h*).

Where any right of action has accrued to recover any debt or other liquidated pecuniary claim and the person liable or accountable therefor acknowledges the claim or makes any payment in respect thereof, the right is deemed to have accrued on and not before the date of the acknowledgement or the last payment: provided that a payment of a part of the rent or interest due at any time shall not extend the period for claiming the remainder then due, but any

---

(*b*) Sections 4–6.
(*c*) See *Wright* v. *Pepin*, [1954] 2 All E.R. 52; *Cotterell* v. *Price*, [1960] 3 All E.R. 315. This is, of course, only where there had been no acknowledgement, part payment, etc.; as to which, see *infra*.
(*d*) *Wilkinson* v. *Hall* (1837), 3 Bing. N.C. 508. See p. 333, *infra*.
(*e*) See p. 315, *infra*.
(*f*) *Heath* v. *Pugh* (1881), 6 Q.B.D. 345 (C.A.); on app. (1882), 7 App. Cas. 235 (H.L.).
(*g*) See, generally, 24 Halsbury's Laws (3rd Edn.), *Limitation of Actions*, pp. 297 *et seq.*; Preston and Newsom, *Limitation of Actions* (3rd Edn.), Ch. VIII.
(*h*) Limitation Act 1939, s. 23 (1).

payment of interest shall be treated as a payment in respect of the principal debt (*i*).

Person who may pay.—In the case of foreclosure or other action by a mortgagee the payment to be effective must be made by the person in possession of the mortgaged land or personal property or by the person liable for the mortgage debt (*k*). In the case of an action on the personal covenant the payment must be made by the person liable or accountable for the mortgage debt (*l*).

Payment of rent by a tenant of the mortgaged property in pursuance of a notice by the mortgagee will not preserve the debt (*m*). A mere voluntary payment by a third person will not suffice (*n*). Payment by a person interested to pay will suffice (*o*). A payment by a person entitled to pay, such as a surety, is effective (*p*); so is payment by a person, *e.g.*, a trustee (*q*), bound to pay as between himself and the mortgagor (*r*). Payment by a devisee for life of interest on the testator's specialty debt will keep alive the right of action against the remainderman (*s*). And payment of interest in respect of a simple contract debt of the testator by a tenant for life keeps the debt alive against the remaindermen (*t*).

Payment by agent.—Payment may be made by an agent (*u*), but where agency is set up, it must be shown that the agency was continuing at the time of payment (*a*). A tenant is not the implied agent of the mortgagor to make acknowledgements or payments to the mortgagee (*b*). A receiver appointed by the court (*c*), or by the mortgagee under the power conferred on him by the mortgage (*d*) or by statute (*e*), is treated as the agent of the person liable to pay, and payment by him is effectual. On the other hand, the realisation, after the expiration of the twelve years, of a policy of assurance which forms a collateral security is not a part payment of principal or interest so as to revive a title to land which the Act has previously extinguished (*f*). Nor is there an effective payment when a beneficiary mortgages his interest in a trust fund and the trustees make a payment to the mortgagee (*g*).

(*i*) Section 23 (4).   (*k*) Section 23 (1) (b).
(*l*) Section 23 (4).
(*m*) *Harlock* v. *Ashberry* (1882), 19 Ch. D. 539.
(*n*) *Chinnery* v. *Evans* (1864), 11 H.L. Cas. 115; *Harlock* v. *Ashberry, supra; Newbould* v. *Smith* (1889), 14 App. Cas. 423. Not even where it is paid by the third party to conceal his own fraud: *Thorne* v. *Heard*, [1895] A.C. 495 (H.L.).
(*o*) *Roddam* v. *Morley* (1856), 1 De G. & J. 1.
(*p*) *Lewin* v. *Wilson* (1880), 11 App. Cas. 639.
(*q*) *Alston* v. *Mineard* (1906), 51 Sol. Jo. 132.
(*r*) *Bradshaw* v. *Widdrington*, [1902] 2 Ch. 430.
(*s*) *Roddam* v. *Morley, supra; Barclay* v. *Owen* (1889), 60 L.T. 220.
(*t*) *Re Hollingshead* (1888), 37 Ch. D. 651; *Re Chant*, [1905] 2 Ch. 225.
(*u*) *E.g.*, a solicitor with authority to make an acknowledgement: *Wright* v. *Pepin*, [1954] 2 All E.R. 52.
(*a*) *Newbould* v. *Smith, supra.*
(*b*) *Harlock* v. *Ashberry, supra.* But a payment by a tenant to the mortgagee on the mortgagor's express instructions will make him an agent.
(*c*) *Chinnery* v. *Evans, supra.*
(*d*) *Re Hale*, [1899] 2 Ch. 107 (C.A.).
(*e*) Law of Property Act 1925, ss. 101 (1) (iii), 109 (2).
(*f*) *Re Clifden* (*Lord*), *Annaly* v. *Agar-Ellis*, [1900] 1 Ch. 774.
(*g*) *Re Edward's Will Trusts*, [1937] Ch. 553; [1937] 3 All E.R. 58.

Where a mortgagor has assigned the equity of redemption and the assignee has paid interest on the mortgage, he has been held to be the agent of the mortgagor with like result (*h*). On the other hand, although the mortgagor has parted with the equity of redemption, payment by him will still be effectual to keep alive the mortgage against the land (*i*).

Nature of acknowledgement.—To be effective an acknowledgement must be in writing and signed by the person making it (*k*). There must be an admission made to the person entitled to make the demand or his agent, with a view, on the part of the person acknowledging, of making himself liable to the demand (*l*), or an admission, whether express or implied (*m*), of the title of the person to whom it is made or of the person whose agent the latter is (*n*).

Who may make acknowledgement.—In the case of an action against the security the acknowledgement to be effective must be made by the person in possession of the mortgaged property (*o*). In the case of an action on the personal covenant it must be made by the person liable or accountable for the debt (*p*). The acknowledgement may also be made by the agent of the person by whom it is required to be made (*q*). The acknowledgement will also be sufficient if made by a trustee of the estate, whether he is devisee in trust for the debtor (*r*), or a trustee appointed by the court (*s*).

Where an acknowledgement is made by a person who fills a double character, as that of executor and beneficial devisee of the debtor, it is a general acknowledgment, and will not be applied to one character more than to the other, and the interest of the person making it as beneficial devisee will be affected (*t*). But if he is executor of one debtor, and is also a debtor individually, in respect of the same debt, an act done by him which he was bound to do in his individual character, and which amounts to an acknowledgement, will not prima facie be considered to have been done as executor (*u*). He fills the place of two persons, and the first question is, by whom the promise was made, and not what is the extent or effect of it.

Joint obligations.—Part payment by one co-debtor binds all

(*h*) *Forsyth* v. *Bristowe* (1853), 8 Ex. 716; *Dibb* v. *Walker*, [1893] 2 Ch. 429. It is no longer necessary to treat him as such; see s. 23 (1) (b).
(*i*) *Chinnery* v. *Evans, supra; Bradshaw* v. *Widdrington, supra.* The contrary seems to have been assumed by the Court of Appeal in *Newbould* v. *Smith* (1886), 33 Ch. D. 127. The House of Lords reserved their opinion on this point (1889), 14 App. Cas. 423.
(*k*) Section 24 (1).
(*l*) *Wright* v. *Pepin, supra.* See *Good* v. *Parry*, [1963] 2 Q.B. 418 (C.A.); [1963] 2 All E.R. 59; *Dungate* v. *Dungate*, [1965] 3 All E.R. 393 (C.A.). See, further, Preston and Newsom, *op. cit.*, pp. 229–233.
(*m*) See *Edginton* v. *Clark*, [1964] 1 Q.B. 367 (C.A.); [1963] 3 All E.R. 468.
(*n*) Section 24 (2). See *Re Gee & Co. (Woolwich), Ltd.*, [1975] Ch. 52; [1974] 1 All E.R. 1149 (balance sheet).
(*o*) Section 23 (1) (a).
(*p*) Section 23 (4); and see p. 285, *supra.*
(*q*) Section 24 (2); and see *Re Lloyd*, [1911] 1 Ir.R. 153.
(*r*) *St. John* v. *Boughton* (1838), 9 Sim. 219.
(*s*) *Toft* v. *Stephenson* (1851), 1 De G.M. & G. 28.
(*t*) *Fordham* v. *Wallis* (1853), 10 Hare, 217.
(*u*) *Thompson* v. *Waithman* (1856), 3 Drew. 628.

persons liable in respect of the debt (*x*). An acknowledgement by one co-debtor binds only the person making it and his successors (*y*).

A payment by one of two mortgagors who covenant jointly and severally to pay the mortgage debt prevents time running in favour of the other mortgagor (*z*).

A surety is a person liable in respect of the debt (*a*) which he has guaranteed and a payment of interest by the principal debtor makes the cause of action accrue afresh against the surety (*b*). Payment of interest by the surety makes the cause of action accrue afresh against the principal debtor (*c*).

Effect of payment and acknowledgement.—An acknowledgement of the title to land or mortgaged personalty by any person in possession thereof binds all other persons in possession during the ensuing period of limitation (*d*). A payment in respect of a mortgage debt by the mortgagor or any person in possession of the mortgaged property shall, so far as any right of the mortgagee to foreclose or otherwise to recover the property is concerned, bind all other persons in possession of the mortgaged property during the ensuing period of limitation (*e*).

At the expiration of the period prescribed by the Act for any person to bring an action to recover land the title of that person to the land is extinguished (*f*). Accordingly a payment or acknowledgement made after the expiration of the period of limitation does not revive the right of the mortgagee of land against the security (*g*). But there is no corresponding provision in the Act extinguishing the title of the mortgagee of personalty (*h*).

An acknowledgement of any debt or other liquidated pecuniary claim binds the acknowledgor and his successors (*i*) but not any other person (*k*). A payment made in respect of any debt or other liquidated pecuniary claim binds all persons liable in respect thereof (*l*).

Acknowledgements and part payments made after the period of limitation has expired are effective where, although the remedy is barred (*m*), the debt is not extinguished. Thus the remedy on the

---

(*x*) Section 25 (6), but see qualification in proviso thereto.

(*y*) Section 25 (5), and see proviso.

(*z*) *Baillie* v. *Irwin*, [1897] 2 I.R. 614; and see *Re Earl Kingston's Estate*, [1869] 3 I.R. 485.

(*a*) Within s. 25 (6).

(*b*) *Re Powers, Lindsell* v. *Phillips* (1885), 30 Ch. D. 291 (C.A.); *Re Frisby, Allison* v. *Frisby* (1889), 43 Ch. D. 106 (C. A.).

(*c*) *Re Seager's Estate, Seager* v. *Aston* (1857), 26 L.J. Ch. 809.

(*d*) Section 25 (1).

(*e*) Section 25 (2).

(*f*) Section 16. See *Lewis* v. *Plunket*, [1937] Ch. 306; [1937] 1 All E.R. 530. The mortgagor is then entitled to recover the mortgage and other title deeds. A second mortgagee whose rights against the mortgagor are barred cannot claim to redeem a prior incumbrancer: *Cotterell* v. *Price*, [1960] 3 All E.R. 315.

(*g*) *Sanders* v. *Sanders* (1881), 19 Ch. D. 373 (C.A.); *Kibble* v. *Fairthorne*, [1895] 1 Ch. 219; *Nicholson* v. *England*, [1926] 2 K.B. 93 (D.C.).

(*h*) Notwithstanding s. 3, dealing with conversion of chattels and the extinction of title thereto.

(*i*) "Successor" is defined by s. 25 (8).

(*k*) Section 25 (5).

(*l*) Section 25 (6). *E.g.*, sureties, see *Re Powers, Lindsell* v. *Phillips* (1885), 30 Ch. D. 291 (C.A.).

(*m*) *Re Frisby, Allison* v. *Frisby* (1889), 43 Ch. D. 106 (C.A.). Under s. 12.

personal covenant may be revived by a subsequent acknowledgement or payment (*n*). But an acknowledgement made after the period of limitation does not bind any successor (*i*) on whom the liability devolves on the determination of a preceding estate or interest in property under a settlement taking effect before the date of the acknowledgement (*o*). And a payment made after the expiration of the period of limitation does not bind any person other than the person making the payment and his successors (*i*), and does not bind any successor (*i*) on whom the liability devolves on the determination of a preceding estate or interest in property under a settlement taking effect before the date of the payment (*p*).

An acknowledgement by one of several personal representatives of any claim to the personal estate of a deceased person, or to any share or interest therein, or a payment by one of several personal representatives in respect of any such claim binds the estate of the deceased person (*q*).

Constructive payment of interest.—Where the mortgagee is himself entitled to the rents of the mortgaged property—*e.g.*, if he is tenant for life of the equity of redemption—time does not run against the mortgage title. Since it is his duty as owner in possession of the land to keep down the interest, he is deemed to pay himself the interest out of the rents and profits, and this is a sufficient payment to prevent time running (*r*). And this principle of constructive payment applies whenever there is in substance the same hand to receive the income and to pay the interest (*s*). It applies, therefore, where the same person is beneficially entitled as tenant for life to the land and the charge, notwithstanding that the land and the charge are vested in different sets of trustees (*t*) and also where a wife is mortgagee of her husband's property (*u*). But where the owner of the charge is the owner of only a share in the proceeds of sale of the land under a trust for sale affecting the entirety of the land there is no constructive payment to keep the charge alive against the land (*x*).

Where a tenant for life of land pays off a charge on the land the presumption is that he intends to keep it alive for his own benefit (*y*), and since it is thus saved from merger, it is also, as just stated, saved from extinction under the Act. But while this is so as regards the charge on the land—since the tenant for life is presumed to pay himself the interest on the charge—it is not so as regards personal remedies for the charge unless the tenant for life is under a legal liability to pay the interest. Thus, where under a settlement A was tenant for life of

---

(*n*) *Re Clifden (Lord)*, [1900] I Ch. 774.
(*o*) Section 25 (5), proviso.
(*p*) Section 25 (6), proviso.
(*q*) Section 25 (7).
(*r*) *Burrell* v. *Earl of Egremont* (1844), 7 Beav. 205; *Re Drax, Savile* v. *Drax*, [1903] I Ch. 781 (C.A.); but see *Carbery (Lord)* v. *Preston* (1850), 13 Ir. Eq. R. 455.
(*s*) *Hodgson* v. *Salt*, [1936] I All E.R. 95.
(*t*) *Topham* v. *Booth* (1887), 35 Ch. D. 607.
(*u*) *Re Hawes, Re Burchell, Burchell* v. *Hawes* (1892), 62 L.J. Ch. 463; *Re Dixon, Heynes* v. *Dixon*, [1900] 2 Ch. 561 (C.A.).
(*x*) *Re Finnegan's Estate*, [1906] I Ir. R. 370.
(*y*) See p. 592, *infra*.

money secured by a covenant of the settlor and charged on his land, and the settlor devised the land to A, the constructive payment of interest, while it saved the charge on the land, did not keep alive the remedy on the covenant (*z*). Nor does the principle of constructive payment apply unless there is an actual charge on the land (*a*).

<h2 style="text-align:center">G—DISABILITY (*b*)</h2>

Generally.—A person is deemed to be under a disability while he is an infant or a person of unsound mind (*c*). If on the date when any right of action accrued for which a period of limitation is prescribed by the Act, the person to whom it accrued was under a disability (*d*), the action may be brought at any time before the expiration of six years from the date when the person ceased to be under a disability or died, whichever event first occurred, notwithstanding that the period of limitation has expired (*e*).

If at the time when one disability ceases another disability has already supervened, time does not begin to run until the latter disability ceases (*f*). But when a right of action which has accrued to a person under a disability accrues, on the death of that person while still under a disability, to another person under a disability, no further extension of time is allowed by reason of the disability of the the second person (*g*).

Recovery of land and money charged thereon.—No action to recover land or money charged on land shall be brought by virtue of the section extending the limitation period in the case of disability (*h*) by any person after the expiration of thirty years from the date on which the right of action accrued to that person or some person through whom he claims (*i*).

<h2 style="text-align:center">H—FRAUD AND MISTAKE (*k*)</h2>

Generally.—Where, in the case of any action for which a period of limitation is prescribed by the Act, either—(a) the action is based upon the fraud (*l*) of the defendant or his agent (*m*) or of any person through whom he claims or his agent, or (b) the right of action is

---

(*z*) *Re England, Steward* v. *England*, [1895] 2 Ch. 820 (C.A.).

(*a*) *Re Allen, Bassett* v. *Allen*, [1898] 2 Ch. 499.

(*b*) See, generally, 24 Halsbury's Laws (3rd Edn.), Limitation of Actions, pp. 293 *et seq.*; Preston and Newson, *op. cit.*, Ch. VII.

(*c*) Section 31 (2); Mental Health Act 1959, Sched. 7. The other disability mentioned in s. 31 no longer applies: Criminal Justice Act 1948, s. 70 (1).

(*d*) *I.e.*, the person to whom the right of action has accrued must be under a disability at the date of the accrual of the right of action. There is no extension if he subsequently becomes disabled. And see s. 22, proviso (a), whereby the section shall not affect any case where the right of action first accrued to some person (not under a disability) through whom the person under a disability claims.

(*e*) Section 22.

(*f*) *Borrows* v. *Ellison* (1871), L.R. 6 Ex. 128.

(*g*) Section 22, proviso (b).

(*h*) *I.e.*, s. 22.

(*i*) Section 22, proviso (c).

(*k*) See, generally, 24 Halsbury's Laws (3rd Edn.), Limitation of Actions, pp. 316 *et seq.*; Preston and Newsom, *op. cit.*, Ch. IX.

(*l*) *Beaman* v. *A.R.T.S., Ltd.*, [1949] 1 K.B. 550 (C.A.), at p. 558; [1949] 1 All E.R. 465, at p. 467; *Clark* v. *Woor*, [1965] 2 All E.R. 353, at pp. 355, 356.

(*m*) *Thorne* v. *Heard*, [1894] 1 Ch. 599 (C.A.).

concealed by the fraud (*n*) of any such person as aforesaid, or (c) the action is for relief from the consequences of a mistake (*o*), the period of limitation does not begin to run until the plaintiff has discovered the fraud or the mistake, as the case may be, or could with reasonable diligence have discovered it (*p*). But these provisions do not enable any action to be brought to recover, or enforce any charge against, or set aside any transaction affecting, any property which—(i) in the case of fraud, has been purchased for valuable consideration by a person who was not a party to the fraud and did not at the time of its purchase know or have reason to believe that any fraud had been committed, or (ii) in the case of mistake, has been purchased for valuable consideration, subsequently to the transaction in which the mistake was made, by a person who did not know or have reason to believe that the mistake had been made (*q*).

IV—PROOF OF THE SECURITY

Proof of execution.—The mortgagee can have no relief, unless the mortgage deed or security is admitted or proved (*r*).

Like other instruments, in the establishing of which proof of the handwriting of the person subscribing is necessary, the mortgage may be proved at the hearing—where its execution is not controverted, though its validity may be in question (*s*)—either *viva voce*, or by affidavit when the evidence is taken in that form. But it cannot be proved as an exhibit at the hearing if it is impeached for fraud, especially if one of the attesting witnesses is alleged to have been concerned in the fraud by which the execution of the deed was obtained (*t*). Where the execution and the payment of the consideration are contested by a person who is not a party to the deed, it must be proved by the witness, though the mortgagor admits its execution, in order that there may be an opportunity for cross-examination (*u*).

If the security is attested by one witness only, who afterwards becomes entitled to the mortgage, proof of his handwriting, by a third person, will be sufficient evidence of the execution of the security (*x*).

Lost document.—In the case of the loss of the security it may be established by secondary evidence, *e.g.*, copy, draft, offer, payment book, etc. (*y*), and by proof of its existence as a security (*z*).

(*n*) *Petre* v. *Petre* (1853), 1 Drew, 371, 397; *Eddis* v. *Chichester Constable*, [1969] 2 Ch. 345 (C.A.); [1969] 2 All E.R. 912; *King* v. *Victor Parsons & Co.*, [1973] 1 All E.R. 206 (C.A.).

(*o*) *Re Jones' Estate*, [1914] 1 Ir. R. 188; *Phillips-Higgins* v. *Harper*, [1954] 1 Q.B. 411, 420 (C.A.); [1954] 2 All E.R. 51, n.

(*p*) Section 26.

(*q*) Section 26, proviso.

(*r*) *Jacobs* v. *Richards* (1854), 18 Beav. 300.

(*s*) *Booth* v. *Creswicke* (1844), 8 Jur. N.S. 323.

(*t*) *Hitchcock* v. *Carew* (1853), Kay, App. xiv.

(*u*) *Leigh* v. *Lloyd* (1865), 35 Beav. 455.

(*x*) *Inman* v. *Parsons* (1819), 4 Mad. 271.

(*y*) A statutory declaration as to the lost security should be made as soon as possible after the loss is discovered, whether proceedings are pending or not. For a form of statutory declaration in respect of lost title deeds, see 7 Ency. of Forms and Precedents (4th Edn.), pp. 582 *et seq.*

(*z*) *Abington* v. *Green* (1866), 14 W.R. 852; *Heath* v. *Crealock* (1874), 10 Ch. App. 22 (C.A.).

Payment of consideration.—The payment of the advance need not generally be proved, unless the fact is put in issue on the pleadings, the security being sufficient evidence of such payment (*a*). But a person claiming to be transferee of an equitable mortgage, must not only prove payment of the debt, but that it was his own money, or that he was to stand in the place of the original mortgagee (*b*). In the case of a security given by a client to his solicitor, strict evidence of the payment of the money may be required (*c*), though ordinarily receipts are admitted as prima facie evidence of advances. Where, however, the security is for the balance found due on a settled account, the solicitor must be prepared with evidence that the client was not under pressure or undue influence, and that the account was stated upon the production of books or other proper evidence, and under circumstances which enabled the client to judge of the result of the transactions between himself and the solicitor (*d*); and where the security does not express the real nature of the transaction, it must also be supported by extrinsic evidence (*e*). Where there is room for the exercise of undue influence, the mortgagee must show that the transaction was fair and not procured by false representation. But this is only as between the parties giving and taking the benefit of the transaction, for no such duty is cast upon a purchaser of the security for valuable consideration, not privy to the fraud (*f*).

Validity of the security.—Where from the circumstances under which the mortgage was executed (*g*), or for other reasons, there are doubts whether it ever subsisted as a mortgage, its validity may be ascertained by the court, or an inquiry may be directed; and similarly, where the security is not proved on the one side or admitted on the other (*h*).

If a mortgage is made without notice of the mortgagor's mental disability, and the advance is duly made (as to which, if there are any suspicious circumstances, the court will direct an inquiry) the security will be ordered to stand for the amount advanced, though it is admitted at the hearing that the mortgagor was at the date of the execution of the mortgage of unsound mind (*i*). It is immaterial in such cases whether the action is by the mortgagee for foreclosure, or by persons claiming under the mortgagor to set aside the deed (*k*). And where an illegal agreement has been added to a security, an order for foreclosure may be made upon non-payment of what shall be found due on the original mortgage, if general relief is asked for, though

---

(*a*) *Minot* v. *Eaton* (1826), 4 L.J. O.S. Ch. 134. As to the effect of a receipt, see note 7 to Precedent 1 in the Appendix, *infra.*

(*b*) *Pandoorung, etc.* v. *Balkrishen, etc.* (1838), 2 Moo. Indian App. 60.

(*c*) *Lawless* v. *Mansfield* (1841), 1 Dru. & War. 557, 605; and see *Carter* v. *Palmer* (1842), 1 Dru. & Wal. 722.

(*d*) *Judd* v. *Ollard* (1859), 5 Jur. N.S. 755; *Davies* v. *Parry* (1859), 1 Giff. 174; *Morgan* v. *Higgins* (1859), 1 Giff. 270.

(*e*) *Per* Lord ELDON in *Lewes* v. *Morgan* (1817), 5 Pr. at p. 143.

(*f*) *Cobbett* v. *Brock* (1855), 20 Beav. 524.

(*g*) *Melland* v. *Gray* (1843), 2 Y. & C.C.C. 199; *Wynne* v. *Styan* (1847), 2 Ph. 303.

(*h*) *Guardner* v. *Boucher* (1850), 13 Beav. 68.

(*i*) *Kirkwall* v. *Flight* (1855), 3 W.R. 529; *Campbell* v. *Hooper* (1855), 3 Sm. & G. 153.

(*k*) *Campbell* v. *Hooper, supra.*

the action will be dismissed, so far as it seeks relief founded on the illegal agreement (*l*). If an action to deliver up securities on account of fraud, and for further relief, fails, the court does not order redemption (*m*).

Proof of subsequent incumbrances.—In a foreclosure action by the first mortgagee, if he proves the subsequent incumbrances, he may at once have an order for redemption or foreclosure against the owners of them, according to their priorities. But if the subsequent incumbrances are not proved or admitted, or if their priorities are disputed, the course is to direct an inquiry upon these questions (*n*). And there will be no order, until the securities have been established, and the priorities of the respective incumbrances ascertained (*o*), for the incumbrancers cannot be excluded or postponed, without a declaration of their rights by the judgment.

(*l*) *Powney* v. *Blomberg* (1844), 14 Sim. 179.
(*m*) *Johnson* v. *Fesenmeyer* (1858), 25 Beav. 88; on app. 3 De G. & J. 13.
(*n*) *Guardner* v. *Boucher, supra.*
(*o*) *Duberly* v. *Day* (1851), 14 Beav. 9.

CHAPTER 17

The Personal Remedy

Action on the covenant to pay.—Every mortgage implies a loan, and every loan implies a debt, for which the borrower is personally liable, though he has entered into neither bond nor covenant for payment of it. But the debt is of the nature of simple contract only, unless there is a bond or an express or implied covenant to give it the character of specialty (*a*). The principal secured by the mortgage, and the interest thereon, are distinct debts, and may be separately recovered (*b*). Upon the breach of an absolute covenant for payment of the debt on a certain day, the mortgagee (*c*) may maintain an action on the covenant, whether the covenantor is principal (*d*) or surety (*e*), unless the qualified form of the covenant implies that there is no personal contract for repayment, upon which an action can be brought, *e.g.*, where the covenantor, borrowing in the character of a trustee, covenants for repayment only out of money coming to his hands as trustees (*f*) or where a person merely agrees to charge his property as collateral security for the debt of another (*g*). The action on the covenant is only for principal and interest and any other sums which the mortgagor has covenanted to pay, not for expenses incurred by

---

(*a*) *Meynell* v. *Howard* (1696), Prec. Ch. 61; *King* v. *King* (1735), 3 P. Wms. 358; *Sutton* v. *Sutton* (1882), 22 Ch. D. 511 (C.A.). The limitation period will be different where there is a covenant (12 years) and where there is no covenant (6 years).

(*b*) *Dickenson* v. *Harrison* (1817), 4 Pr. 282.

(*c*) And those claiming under him by devolution on death (see Administration of Estates Act 1925, s. 26 (1)) or alienation *inter vivos*. In the latter case the right to sue on the covenant vests in the transferee on his giving notice in writing of the transfer to the mortgagor. If the requirements of s. 136 of the Law of Property Act 1925, are fulfilled the transferee can sue in his own name; otherwise he must join the original mortgagee.

Where the mortgagees are trustees the right of action is in the trustees, unless it appears that the beneficiaries were to have the benefit of the contract of mortgage: *Gandy* v. *Gandy* (1885), 30 Ch. D. 57 (C.A.). The same applies to debenture trustees.

(*d*) The mortgagor cannot, without the mortgagee's consent, relieve himself of his liability under the covenant by transferring the equity of redemption: see p. 295, *infra*; and *West Bromwich Building Society* v. *Bullock*, [1936] 1 All E.R. 887.

(*e*) *Evans* v. *Jones* (1839), 5 M. & W. 295.

(*f*) *Mathew* v. *Blackmore* (1857), 1 H. & N. 762; *Re Robinson's Settlement*, [1912] 1 Ch. 717. But where there is an absolute covenant for payment, a clause excluding personal liability is repugnant and therefore void: *Watling* v. *Lewis*, [1911] 1 Ch. 414; *Re Tewkesbury Gas Co.*, [1912] 1 Ch. 1 (C.A.). And where, although the covenant is absolute in form, the mortgage was really given to secure the balance of a current account, that fact may be proved and only so much as is due on the account can then be recovered: *Trench* v. *Doran* (1887), 20 L.R. Ir. 338.

(*g*) *Re Midland Bank, Ltd.'s Application*, [1941] Ch. 350; *sub nom. Franklin* v. *Midland Bank, Ltd.*, [1941] 2 All E.R. 135.

the mortgagee outside the covenant, though he may be entitled to these in a redemption or foreclosure action.

Implied covenant.—A covenant for payment will be implied by an admission of the debt coupled with an agreement to execute a security which would create a speciality debt (*h*), or even by a mere admission of liability in a deed, provided an intention to enter into an engagement to pay appears on the face of the deed; but it is otherwise where the acknowledgement appears to have been made solely for a collateral purpose, as by way of recital in an appointment of new trustee (*i*).

Assignment of equity of redemption (*j*).—The burden of the covenant for payment does not run with the equity of redemption, and therefore the mortgagee cannot sue the assignee of that equity either for principal or interest (*k*) nor prove for them in his bankruptcy (*l*). But the assignee is liable to indemnify the mortgagor (*m*) and usually the assignment contains an express proviso to this effect (*n*); the express covenant then excludes implied liability (*o*). The benefit of the covenant of indemnity is not assignable (*p*). The assignee may make himself directly liable by entering into a fresh covenant with the mortgagee (*q*), but such liability is not implied from the mere payment of interest (*r*).

While on assignment the mortagor ceases to be entitled to redeem, his right to do so revives if he is sued for the mortgage debt. He is then in effect, a surety for the assignee, and he may redeem notwithstanding that the assignee has created fresh charges in favour of the mortgagee (*s*).

Recovery of insurance premiums.—Where the mortgagor of a policy of insurance, the insurers being the mortgagees, covenants with them to keep up the policy, or in default that the insurers may pay

---

(*h*) *Saunders* v. *Milsome* (1866), L.R. 2 Eq. 573.

(*i*) *Courtney* v. *Taylor* (1843), 6 Man. & Gr. 851; *Jackson* v. *North Eastern Rail Co.* (1877), 7 Ch. D. 573. Where the mortgage contains no covenant for payment the mortgagee may sue for the debt, if the security is collateral to it, and was not taken in satisfaction of an existing debt: *Yates* v. *Aston* (1843), 4 Q.B. 182. But if it was so taken, the contract will have merged in the security which is of a higher nature; as (under like circumstances) the remedy on simple contract will merge in a bond or covenant: *Price* v. *Moulton* (1851), 10 C.B. 561; and see p. 595, *infra*.

(*j*) And see p. 520, *infra*.

(*k*) The mortgagor remains liable: *Hall* v. *Heward* (1886), 32 Ch. D. 430 (C.A.); and see *Foster* v. *Woolvett* (1963), 39 D.L.R. (2d) 532. But liability under a running account is limited to the amount outstanding at the date when the mortgagee had notice of the change of ownership. Accordingly, the purchaser of the equity of redemption in a farm was liable for the price of goods supplied after that date and not the original mortgagor: *Edwards* v. *Ottawa Valley Grain Products, Ltd.* (1970), 11 D.L.R. (3d) 137. For a conveyance where a husband's interest in the mortgaged property is transferred under s. 24 of the Matrimonial Causes Act 1973, see Precedent 8 in the Appendix, *infra*.

(*l*) *Re Errington, Ex parte Mason*, [1894] 1 Q.B. 11.

(*m*) *Waring* v. *Ward* (1802), 7 Ves. 332; *Simpson* v. *Forrester* (1973), 47 A.L.J.R. 149. And this liability survives assignment: *Re Windle, Ex parte Trustee of Bankrupt* v. *Windle*, [1975] 3 All E.R. 987, at p. 995. So the survivor of joint tenants must indemnify the estate of the deceased joint tenant.

(*n*) See 15 Ency. Forms and Precedents (3rd Edn), pp. 487 *et seq*.

(*o*) *Mills* v. *United Counties Bank, Ltd.*, [1912] 1 Ch. 231 (C.A.).

(*p*) *Rendall* v. *Morphew* (1914), 84 L.J. Ch. 517; but see *British Union and National Insurance Co.* v. *Rawson*, [1916] 2 Ch. 476 (C.A.).

(*q*) *Shore* v. *Shore* (1847), 2 Ph. 378. See *Esso Petroleum Co., Ltd.* v. *Alstonbridge Properties, Ltd.*, [1975] 3 All E.R. 358.

(*r*) *Re Errington, supra*.

(*s*) *Kinnaird* v. *Trollope* (1888), 39 Ch. D. 636. And see p. 530, *infra*.

and add the premiums to the mortgage debt, but there is no covenant to repay them the premiums, the mortgagees, in an action against the mortgagor for breach of the covenant to keep up the policy, are entitled only to nominal damages, the addition of the premiums to the debt being the remedy provided. But under a covenant to repay, the amount paid would be given as damages (*t*).

When the right of action accrues.—This depends on the form of the covenant (*u*). Where it fixes a date for repayment the right of action arises upon non-payment on that date (*x*). Where the covenant is to pay on or after a certain date the mortgagee cannot sue until after a demand for payment has been made (*y*). If the principal is payable on demand, and there is no provision, express or implied, for notice to be given, the right of action accrues on the execution of the mortgage (*z*), unless the covenant is collateral, *e.g.*, to secure the debt of another or to secure a current account between the covenantor and the covenantee, when demand must first be made (*a*). And for an instalment mortgage a demand is necessary before the right of action accrues, because of the change in the nature of the debtor's obligation from instalments to lump sum (*b*). If the covenant provides, expressly or impliedly, for notice to be given, actual demand in writing must be made before the right of action arises (*c*), and any other condition prescribed as a preliminary to suing on the covenant must be observed (*d*). The notice given must be sufficient to allow the mortgagor a reasonable time to obtain the money (*e*). Any mode of service is sufficient which brings home to the mortgagor the fact that the demand has been made (*f*). A notice is still an effective demand even if it overstates the amount due (*g*) and the true amount due is recoverable.

(*t*) *Browne* v. *Price* (1858), 4 C.B.N.S. 598. It has been held that a covenant "not to do or suffer anything whereby the policy may become voidable or void" is not broken by the mortgagor allowing the insurance company to take over a fully paid-up policy at surrender value: *Sapio* v. *Hackney* (1907), 51 Sol. Jo. 428.

(*u*) As to the form of the covenant, see p. 27, *supra*. As to instalment mortgages, see p. 28, *supra*.

(*x*) *Bolton* v. *Buckenham*, [1891] 1 Q.B. 278 (C.A.). And the mortgagee cannot sue before that date or exercise the power of sale: *Twentieth Century Banking Corporation, Ltd.* v. *Wilkinson*, [1976] 3 All E.R. 361.

(*y*) *Re Tewkesbury Gas Co.*, [1911] 2 Ch. 279; *affirmed* [1912] 1 Ch. 1 (C.A.). For an example of implied demand, see *The Halcyon Skies (No. 2)* (1976), 120 Sol. Jo. 502.

(*z*) *Evans* v. *Jones* (1839), 5 M. & W. 295; *Re Brown's Estate, Brown* v. *Brown*, [1893] 2 Ch. 300, at p. 304; *Esso Petroleum Co., Ltd.* v. *Alstonbridge Properties, Ltd.*, [1975] 3 All E.R. 358.

(*a*) *Re Brown's Estate, supra*; *Lloyds Bank, Ltd.* v. *Margolis*, [1954] 1 All E.R. 734.

(*b*) *Esso Petroleum Co., Ltd.* v. *Alstonbridge Properties, Ltd., supra*; and *Murphy* v. *Lawrence*, [1960] N.Z.L.R. 772.

(*c*) *Lloyds Bank, Ltd.* v. *Margolis, supra*. The issue of proceedings does not constitute a demand: *Esso Petroleum Co., Ltd.* v. *Alstonbridge Properties, Ltd., supra*.

(*d*) *Rogers & Co.* v. *British and Colonial Colliery Supply Assocation* (1898), 68 L.J. Q.B. 14.

(*e*) *Brighty* v. *Norton* (1862), 3 B. & S. 305; *Massey* v. *Sladden* (1868), L.R. 4 Exch. 13; *Fitzgerald's Trustees* v. *Mellersh*, [1892] 1 Ch. 385, at p. 390; *Cripps (Pharmaceuticals), Ltd.* v. *Wickenden*, [1973] 2 All E.R. 606.

(*f*) *Worthington & Co., Ltd.* v. *Abbott*, [1910] 1 Ch. 588.

(*g*) *Fox* v. *Jolly*, [1916] 1 A.C. 1 (H.L.); *Campbell* v. *Commercial Banking Co. of Sydney* (1879), 40 L.T. 137 (P.C.); *Clyde Properties, Ltd.* v. *Tasker*, [1970] N.Z.L.R. 754; *Stanley* v. *Auckland Co-operative Terminating Building Society*, [1973] 2 N.Z.L.R. 673. For the effect of a vacating receipt made for the wrong amount, see p. 553, *infra*. For the binding effect of statements given under the Consumer Credit Act, 1974, see s. 172 of that Act and p. 146, *supra*.

Loss of the right of action (h).—The right to sue on the covenant may be lost where the mortgagee cannot reconvey the mortgaged property. A mortgagee will be restrained from suing on the covenant if, by his own conduct (i), he cannot hand back the title deeds, because he has parted with the mortgaged property (j) or for any other reason (k). This principle applies also to personalty. So where shares had been deposited as security with a broker and he wrongfully sells them he cannot sue for the balance due (l).

A mortgagee who has foreclosed and subsequently sold the property is precluded from suing on the covenant (m). But a mortgagee who has sold the property under his power of sale (n) or under an order of the court (o) can sue the mortgagee for the deficiency, since the sale was a proper dealing with the security. The right to sue is not prejudiced by the covenantee submitting to a judgment for foreclosure at the suit of a prior mortgagee (p). An action on the covenant after foreclosure reopens the foreclosure (q).

Procedure (r).—The action may be brought in the Chancery Division (s) or the county court where the latter has jurisdiction (t).

Chancery Division.—The plaintiff has a choice between originating

---

(h) And see p. 280, supra.

(i) He is not prevented from suing if his inability to restore the property is due to the intervention of a third party as in the case of a forfeiture of leasehold property by the lessor, not due to the mortgagee's default: Re Burrell, Burrell v. Smith (1869), L.R. 7 Eq. 399.

(j) Walker v. Jones (1866), L.R. 1 P.C. 50. E.g., because a solicitor had a lien on the property.

(k) Schoole v. Sall (1803), 1 Sch. & Lef. 176.

(l) Ellis & Co's Trustee v. Dixon-Johnson, [1925] A.C. 489, (H.L.). Though if the shares are readily purchaseable their money value may be substituted and the mortgagee then entitled to sue on the covenant.

(m) Lockhart v. Hardy (1846), 9 Beav. 349; Palmer v. Hendrie (1859), 27 Beav. 349; Walker v. Jones, supra; Rushton v. Industrial Development Bank (1973), 34 D.L.R. (3d) 582 (S.C. of Can.).

(n) Rudge v. Richens (1873), L.R. 8 C.P. 358; Re McHenry, McDermot v. Boyd, Barker's Claim, [1894] 3 Ch. 290 (C.A.).

(o) Gordon Grant & Co. v. Boos, [1926] A.C. 781 (P.C.).

(p) Worthington v. Abbott, [1910] 1 Ch. 588.

(q) Perry v. Barker (1806), 13 Ves. 198.

(r) See, generally, 28 Ency. Court Forms (2nd Edn.), Mortgages.

(s) See R.S.C. Ord. 88, r. 2, which applies to any action for payment of moneys secured by a mortgage of real or leasehold property. Where a debt formerly secured by a mortgage is no longer so secured, because, for example, a first mortgagee has exercised his power of sale and sold the mortgaged property without there being sufficient surplus proceeds of sale to discharge the second mortgage, Ord. 88 does not apply: Newnham v. Brown, [1966] 2 All E.R. 229 (C.A.); overruling CROSS, J., at [1966] 1 All E.R. 281. See also Samuel Keller (Holdings), Ltd. v. Martins Bank, Ltd., [1970] 3 All E.R. 950 (C.A.).

Quaere whether where there is, for example, a mortgage and a promissory note in respect of the same sum (see p. 596, infra), an action on the promissory note must be commenced in the Chancery Division, rather than the Queen's Bench Division. It is submitted that the action can be commenced in the Queen's Bench Division (see p. 596, infra). Similarly an action against a guarantor (alone) of a mortgage debt can, it is submitted, be commenced in the Queen's Bench Division though it is for the same sum as that secured by the mortgage. And see 20 Court Forms (1973 re-issue) p. 214. For moneylenders' actions, see R.S.C. Ord. 83. Where a guarantor is being sued Ord. 14 procedure may be appropriate; for a case where the defendant was given leave to defend, see Stock and Trade Facilities, Ltd. v. Foley Plastics Manufacturing Co., Ltd. (1975), 119 Sol. Jo. 440.

(t) County Courts Act 1959, s. 39. See p. 298, infra. For possession actions, see p. 319, infra.

summons and writ (*u*). Generally the action will be commenced by originating summons (*x*), and the claim will usually be coupled with other relief, *e.g.*, a claim for foreclosure (*y*).

In every case the plaintiff's right to the order sought must be established. There is no right to an order merely because the defendant fails to appear (*z*). The affidavit supporting the summons must exhibit a true copy of the mortgage or charge, and the original mortgage or charge or the charge certificate must be produced at the hearing (*a*). The affidavit must prove that the money is due and payable and give particulars of the amount of the advance, the amount of the repayments, the amount of any interest or instalments in arrear at the date of the issue of the summons and at the date of the affidavit and the amount remaining due under the mortgage (*b*). Where the plaintiff's claim includes a claim for interest to judgment, the affidavit must state the amount of a day's interest (*c*). The affidavit should set out full particulars of the mortgage (whether by demise, sub-demise, charge or deposit), including the date thereof, parties, rate of interest, etc., any relevant covenants or stipulations (*e.g.*, as to notices or demands to be made) and all transfers and devolutions.

If the defendant enters an appearance an appointment to hear the summons must be taken out and the requisite documents lodged and notice of the appointment served on the defendant (*d*). If the defendant fails to appear, not less than four clear days before the day fixed for the first hearing of the summons the plaintiff must serve on the defendant a copy of the notice of appointment for the hearing and a copy of the affidavit in support of the summons (*e*).

A master or district registrar will generally hear the summons, but he may in certain circumstances adjourn the matter to the judge (*f*). Whenever an order for payment is made the costs will be in accordance with the table of fixed costs in respect of money claims in force in the High Court (*g*), subject to the master's discretion in special circumstances to direct taxation or to assess or fix costs (*h*).

County court.—The mortgagee may claim for payment of principal

---

(*u*) Procedure by writ is suitable where there is a substantial dispute as to fact or an issue of fraud. If the plaintiff proceeds by writ where he could have proceeded by summons any additional costs incurred will not be allowed. See p. 322, *infra*.

(*x*) And only that procedure is considered here. As to when discovery will be ordered in an action commenced by orginating summons, see *Coni* v. *Robertson*, [1969] 2 All E.R. 609.

(*y*) For forms, see 28 Ency. Court Forms (2nd Edn.), pp. 49 *et seq.* But for possession see p. 320, *infra*.

(*z*) For non-appearance by a defendant, see R.S.C. Ord. 88, r. 5.

(*a*) R.S.C. Ord. 88, r. 6 (2).

(*b*) R.S.C. Ord. 88, r. 6 (6), (3). For computer produced evidence, see R.S.C. Ord. 38, rr. 20 *et seq.*

(*c*) R.S.C. Ord. 88, r. 6 (7). In practice this requirement is not insisted upon and the plaintiff's solicitor is normally directed to bring a computation of interest into chambers.

(*d*) R.S.C. Ord. 88, r. 4.

(*e*) R.S.C. Ord. 88, r. 5 (2); and see (5) and (6).

(*f*) And a party to the proceedings may apply to have the matter adjourned to the judge. See generally, the notes to R.S.C. Ord. 32, r. 14, in the Supreme Court Practice.

(*g*) R.S.C. Ord. 62, Appendix 3.

(*h*) See note (*i*), p. 644, *infra*.

and interest in the county court (*i*) where the sum claimed does not exceed £2,000 (*k*) or for any sum, where there is also a claim for possession and the net annual value for rating of the property does not exceed the county court limit (*l*). Where a plaintiff claims payment of principal money and interest secured by a mortgage or charge, he must state in his particulars of claim (1) the date of the mortgage, (2) the amount of the principal money lent, (3) the amount remaining due and unpaid in respect of (a) principal and (b) interest, and (4) what proceedings, if any, the plaintiff has taken against the defendant in respect of the property mortgaged or charged, and whether he has obtained possession of the property (*m*).

(*i*) The court for the district in which the land or any part thereof is situate: C.C.R. Ord. 2, r. 2 (d). For other property, the court for the district in which the defendant resides, etc: Ord. 21 r. 1 (1).

(*k*) County Courts Act 1959, s. 39; County Courts Jurisdiction Order 1977.

(*l*) Administration of Justice Act 1970, s. 38 (1); see p. 320, *infra*.

(*m*) C.C.R. Ord. 7, r. 7 (1). For forms of particulars of claim and further procedure, see 28 Ency. Court Forms (2nd Edn.), pp. 146, 147 and precedents of particulars and affidavit in the Appendix, *infra*.

As to costs of proceedings in the High Court which might have been brought in the county court, see footnote (*i*), p. 644, *infra*.

CHAPTER 18

The Appointment of a Receiver [(a)]

I—THE APPOINTMENT OF A RECEIVER BY THE MORTGAGEE

Advantage of appointing receiver.—A receiver appointed by the mortgagee is the agent of the mortgagor and one appointed by the court is an officer of the court. Accordingly in neither case is the mortgagee liable for wilful default as he would be if he pursued the alternative remedy of taking possession himself (b).

Express and statutory powers of appointment.—The mortgage sometimes contains an appointment of, or a power for the mortgagee to appoint a person to be, a receiver, or receiver and manager, of the mortgaged property in order to secure to the mortgagee the payment of his interest out of the rents and profits (c). The Trustees, Mortgagees, etc., Powers Act 1860 (d), gave statutory powers for such appointment. The clauses of that Act containing those powers (ss. 11–30) were repealed by the Conveyancing Act 1881, with the proviso, that the repeal should not affect the validity or invalidity, or any operation, effect, or consequence of any instrument executed or made, or of anything done or suffered before the commencement of the Act (31 December, 1881), or any action, proceeding or thing then pending or uncompleted, and provisions with respect to the appointment of receivers were contained in that Act (ss. 19 (1) (iii), 20, 24). Those provisions were replaced by corresponding provisions of the Law of Property Act 1925, which are as follows:

> **101.**—(1) A mortgagee (e), where the mortgage is made by deed, shall, by virtue of this Act, have the following powers, to the like extent as if they had been conferred by the mortgage deed, but not further (namely):

(a) The consideration of the persons who may be appointed receivers, the allowances to receivers, their liabilities, the passing of accounts, and the payment of their balances and final discharge, being matters common to all receiverships are not dealt with here. On these matters, see 32 Halsbury's Laws (3rd Edn.), Receivers. Note that a body corporate may not be appointed receiver of the property of a company: Companies Act 1948, s. 366; and see *Portman Building Society* v. *Gallwey*, [1955] 1 All E.R. 227.

(b) As to the liability of a mortgagee in possession, see pp. 348 *et seq., infra*. But, as the receiver appointed by the mortgagee is the agent of the mortgagor, his possession cannot be adverse to the mortgagor: *Re Hale, Lilley* v. *Foad*, [1899] 2 Ch. 107 (C.A.).

(c) For express powers of appointment, see 14 Ency. Forms and Precedents (4th Edn.), pp. 148, 149 and 885–886; and Precedents 11 and 29 in the Appendix, *infra*.

(d) Lord Cranworth's Act.

(e) Including a chargee by way of legal mortgage and a person from time to time deriving title under the original mortgagee: s. 205 (1) (xvi).

(iii) A power, when the mortgage money has become due, to appoint a receiver of the income of the mortgaged property, or any part thereof; or, if the mortgaged property consists of an interest in income, or of a rentcharge or an annual or other periodical sum, a receiver of that property or any part thereof (*f*).

The provisions of the section may be varied or extended by the mortgage deed (*g*), and, as so varied or extended, will, as far as may be, operate as if the variations or extensions were contained in the Act (sub-s. (3)). The section applies only if and as far as a contrary intention is not expressed in the mortgage deed, and has effect subject to the terms and provisions of that deed (sub-s. (4)). The section applies, as regards receivers, where the mortgage was executed after 31 December, 1881.

109.—(1) A mortgagee entitled to appoint a receiver under the power in that behalf conferred by this Act shall not appoint a receiver until he has become entitled to exercise the power of sale conferred by this Act (*h*), but may then, by writing under his hand, appoint such person as he thinks fit to be receiver.

(2) A receiver appointed under the powers conferred by this Act, or any enactment replaced by this Act, shall be deemed to be agent of the mortgagor (*i*); and the mortgagor shall be solely responsible for the receiver's acts or defaults unless the mortgage deed otherwise provides (*k*).

(3) The receiver shall have power to demand and recover all the income of which he is appointed receiver, by action, distress, or otherwise, in the name either of the mortgagor or of the mortgagee, to the full extent of the estate or interest which the mortgagor could dispose of, and to give effectual receipts accordingly for the same, and to exercise any powers which may have been delegated to him by the mortgagee pursuant to this Act.

(4) A person paying money to the receiver shall not be concerned to inquire whether any case has happened to authorise the receiver to act.

(5) The receiver may be removed, and a new receiver may be appointed, from time to time by the mortgagee by writing under his hand.

(6) The receiver shall be entitled to retain out of any money received by him, for his remuneration, and in satisfaction of all costs, charges, and

---

(*f*) For forms of appointment, see 14 Ency. Forms and Precedents (4th Edn.), pp. 886–894. As to when the appointment takes affect, see *Cripps* (*Pharmaceuticals*), *Ltd.* v. *Wickenden*, [1973] 2 All E.R. 606. The power is exercisable notwithstanding the mortgagee has gone into possession: *Refuge Assurance Co., Ltd.* v. *Pearlberg*, [1938] Ch. 687; [1938] 2 All E.R. 231. In the case of a registered charge the power is not exercisable until the charge is registered: *Lever Finance Co., Ltd.* v. *Needleman's Property Trustee*, [1956] Ch. 375; [1956] 2 All E.R. 378. As to when the mortgage money is due, see footnote (*q*), p. 360, *infra*.

(*g*) As to forms, see 14 Ency. Forms and Precedents (4th Edn.), pp. 138–140 (these relate to the power of sale).

(*h*) Section 103, quoted at p. 363, *infra*. As to interest being in arrear when the mortgagee is in possession, see *Wrigley* v. *Gill*, [1906] 1 Ch. 165, at p. 172 (C.A.); p. 363, *infra*.

(*i*) Including any person from time to time deriving title under the original mortgagor, or entitled to redeem the mortgage: s. 205 (1) (xvi). As to the position of a receiver under the statute, see *White* v. *Metcalf*, [1903] 2 Ch. 567.

(*k*) See *Hibernian Bank* v. *Yourell* (No. 2), [1919] 1 Ir. R. 310; *Leicester Permanent Building Society* v. *Butt*, [1943] Ch. 308; [1943] 2 All E.R. 523; *Portman Building Society* v. *Gallwey*, [1955] 1 All E.R. 227. To what extent this applies to a receiver appointed by debenture holders, where the debenture or debenture trust deed incorporates the statutory provisions will depend on the extent and terms of the incorporation see p. 303, *infra*).

As to the date from which a receiver appointed by a second mortgagee must account to a receiver subsequently appointed by a first mortgagee, see *Re Belbridge Property Trust, Ltd., Swale Estates, Ltd.* v. *Belbridge Property Trust, Ltd.*, [1941] Ch. 304; [1941] 2 All E.R. 48.

expenses incurred by him as receiver, a commission at such rate, not exceeding five per centum on the gross amount of all money received, as is specified in his appointment, and if no rate is so specified, then at the rate of five per centum on that gross amount, or at such other rate as the court thinks fit to allow, on application made by him for that purpose (*l*).

(7) The receiver shall, if so directed in writing by the mortgagee, insure to the extent, if any, to which the mortgagee might have insured and keep insured against loss or damage by fire, out of the money received by him, any building, effects, or property comprised in the mortgage, whether affixed to the freehold or not, being of an insurable nature.

(8) The receiver shall apply all money received by him as follows, namely:
  (i) In discharge of all rents, taxes, rates (*m*), and outgoings whatever affecting the mortgaged property; and
  (ii) In keeping down all annual sums or other payments, and the interest on all principal sums, having priority to the mortgage in right whereof he is receiver; and
  (iii) In payment of his commission, and of the premiums on fire, life, or other insurances, if any, properly payable under the mortgage deed or under the Act, and the cost of executing necessary or proper repairs directed in writing by the mortgagee (*n*); and
  (iv) In payment of all interest accruing due in respect of any principal money due under the mortgage (*o*); and
  (v) In or towards discharge of the principal money if so directed in writing by the mortgagee;

and shall pay the residue, if any, of the money received by him to the person who, but for the possession of the receiver, would have been entitled to receive the income of which he is appointed receiver, or who is otherwise entitled to the mortgaged property.

Receiver is agent of the mortgagor.—The receiver is the agent of the mortgagor (*p*), as well where he is appointed by the parties as under the Act. Where a person is appointed to receive the profits of the estate on behalf of the mortgagee, and the mortgagor is afterwards allowed to receive them, the mortgagee's rights are not affected, except as to later incumbrancers of whose claim he had notice (*q*). The appointment does not bar the right of the mortgagee to sue for

---

(*l*) It is doubtful whether, as has been suggested, the rate can be increased by a provision in the mortgage under the provisions of s. 101 (3). Accordingly it is better to expressly provide for the appointment of a receiver in the mortgage deed, rather than to rely on the statutory power, and to include a provision for remuneration in accordance with a professional scale. See Precedents in the Appendix. Note Companies Act 1948, s. 371 whereunder a liquidator may apply to the court to fix the rate of remuneration and an order made thereunder may prevail over the terms of the mortgage deed of the appointment.

(*m*) See *Liverpool Corpn.* v. *Hope*, [1938] 1 K.B. 751 (C.A.); [1938] 1 All E.R. 492.

(*n*) *White* v. *Metcalf*, [1903] 2 Ch. 567.

(*o*) This extends to arrears of interest due at the time of the appointment of the receiver, and not merely to interest accruing due afterwards: *National Bank* v. *Kenny*, [1898] 1 I.R. 197. Consent to the alteration of the order of the application of the surplus may be inferred from the facts: *Yourell* v. *Hibernian Bank*, [1918] A.C. 372 (H.L.).

(*p*) Under the Act, see Law of Property Act 1925, s. 109 (2), *supra;* under an express appointment, see *Lord Kensington* v. *Bouverie* (1855), 7 De G.M. & G. 134; *Jefferys* v. *Dickson* (1866), 1 Ch. App. 183; *Law* v. *Glenn* (1867), L.R. 2 Ch. 634, 641; *Re Joyce, Ex parte Warren* (1875), 10 Ch. App. 222. See, generally, *Gaskell* v. *Gosling* [1896], 1 Q.B. 669 (C.A.), at p. 692. *Visbord* v. *Taxation Commissioner*, [1943] A.L.R. 153. For a receiver appointed by debenture holders, see p. 303, *infra*. A receiver appointed by the court (see p. 304, *infra*) is an officer of the court.

(*q*) *Juggeewun-das-Keeka Shah* v. *Ramdas Brijbookun-das* (1841), 2 Moo. Ind. App. 487.

the debt (*r*). The mortgagee may appoint a receiver even where he has himself already gone into possession of the mortgaged property (*s*).

The receipt of rent by a receiver who is the agent of the mortgagor does not create a tenancy by estoppel binding on the mortgagee, but if the receiver is the agent of the mortgagee the demand and receipt of rent by such a receiver is an unequivocal recognition of the existence of a tenancy, but not necessarily of a tenancy on the terms of any lease under which the tenant holds the premises (*t*).

A receiver appointed under the Act to receive rents must not be interfered with by the mortgagor, and any attempt to do so (*e.g.*, by distraining on the tenants) will be restrained (*u*).

A receiver, who, although originally appointed by the mortgagee, is subsequently appointed by the court, ceases to be agent of the mortgagor (*v*).

The death of the mortgagor does not operate as a revocation of the power to appoint a receiver (*w*). The receiver may be permitted to sue in the name of the mortgagor's personal representatives on giving indemnity (*x*).

A receiver appointed by trustees or debenture holders is their agent, unless the debenture deed provides otherwise. Section 109 (2) of the Law of Property Act 1925, *supra*, applies only when the receiver is appointed to receive income under the power conferred by that Act and it does not apply to a receiver invested with the wider powers usually conferred by a debenture (*y*).

Powers of receiver.—A receiver appointed under the statutory power has the powers set out above (*z*). He is not entitled to grant leases without the sanction of the court (*a*), unless the mortgagee has delegated to him (the mortgagee's) leasing powers (*b*). A receiver appointed under an express power has only the powers conferred on him by his appointment, and in the absence of express provision as to remuneration, will be entitled to a proper remuneration as a *quantum meruit* (*c*). A receiver appointed to do a thing has an incidental power to do what is necessary to effect that object (*d*).

A receiver appointed by debenture holders usually has a power of sale under the debenture. But, unless there is a specific legal charge, when the debenture holders can sell under the statutory power of

---

(*r*) *Lynde* v. *Waithman*, [1895] 2 Q.B. 180.

(*s*) *Refuge Assurance Co., Ltd.* v. *Pearlberg*, [1938] Ch. 687 (C.A.); [1938] 3 All E.R. 231.

(*t*) *Lever Finance Co. Ltd.* v. *Needleman's Property Trustee*, [1956] Ch. 375; [1956] 2 All E.R. 378; *Chatsworth Properties, Ltd.* v. *Effiom*, [1971] 1 All E.R. 604 (C.A.); *Baring Brothers & Co., Ltd.* v. *Hovermarine, Ltd.* (1971), 219 Estates Gazette 1450. See (1976) 120 S. J. 496 (Henry E. Markson).

(*u*) *Bayly* v. *Went* (1884), 51 L.T. 764.

(*v*) *Hand* v. *Blow*, [1901] 2 Ch. 721 (C.A.), at p. 732. *Cf. Lever Finance Co., Ltd.* v. *Needleman's Property Trustee, supra*.

(*w*) *Re Hale, Lilley* v. *Foad*, [1899] 2 Ch. 107 (C.A.)., at p. 117.

(*x*) *Fairholme and Palliser* v. *Kennedy* (1890), 24 L.R. Ir. 498.

(*y*) *Re Vimbos, Ltd.*, [1900] 1 Ch. 470; *Deyes* v. *Word*, [1911] 1 K.B. 806 (C.A.).

(*z*) *I.e.*, under s. 109 of the Law of Property Act 1925.

(*a*) *Re Cripps*, [1946] Ch. 265.

(*b*) Law of Property Act 1925, ss. 99 (19), 100 (13), 109 (3).

(*c*) *Re Vimbos, Ltd., supra.*

(*d*) *M. Wheeler & Co., Ltd.* v. *Warren*, [1928] Ch. 840 (C.A.).

sale (e) (or the receiver as their agent), on a sale by a receiver the mortgaging company will have to be a party, as the property will remain vested in it. Accordingly the debenture should appoint the debenture holders (or their receiver) attorneys of the company (f). Often, of course, the company will be in liquidation and the liquidator will be able to assist in the sale (g).

II—APPOINTMENT OF A RECEIVER BY THE COURT

Power of court to appoint receiver (h).—The statutory power of a mortgagee to appoint a receiver has made this jurisdiction one that is rarely exercised today. Under certain circumstances and on the application of some or one of the parties interested in the mortgaged property, but not a stranger (i), the court will appoint a receiver, whose duty it is to get in and take charge of any outstanding parts, and the rents and profits, and to see to the management of the mortgaged property, applying the monies received according to the directions of the court, and accounting to the court for such application.

The application for a receiver may be made to the court by any party to an action by summons or motion or where necessary *ex parte* on affidavit (j).

Security.—The receiver is required to give security (by himself and two or more sureties (k)) duly to account for what he shall receive on account of rents and profits for the receipt of which he is appointed, or to be answerable for what he shall receive in respect of the personal estate which he is to get in, and to account for and pay the same respectively as the court shall direct. The court will not generally dispense with sureties, even by consent of the parties interested (l).

The receiver is not legally clothed with, or able to perform the duties of, his office until it is certified that his security has been completed, so until that time no contempt is committed by interfering with the property (m). But frequently the receiver is permitted to act at once, before completing his security, on the applicant undertaking to be responsible for him.

Purpose of appointment.—The appointment, which is a matter of discretion to be governed by the whole circumstances of the case (n), is made in the first place for the protection of the estate. It does not

---

(e) See pp. 360, 380 *infra*.
(f) For forms, see Ency. Forms and Precedents (4th Edn)., vol. 2, p. 873; vol. 6 p. 1193.
(g) For form, see 19 Ency. Forms and Precedents (4th Edn.), p. 1138. See, generally, *Williams on Title* (4th Edn.), pp. 226, 227.
(h) Under the Supreme Court of Judicature (Consolidation) Act 1925, s. 45; see p. 305, *infra*.
(i) *A.-G.* v. *Day* (1817), 2 Mad. 246.
(j) R.S.C. Ord. 30, r. 1. See generally, the Supreme Court Practice under R.S.C. Ord. 30. And see C.C.R. Ord. 30.
(k) R.S.C. Ord. 30, r. 2.
(l) *Manners* v. *Furze* (1847), 11 Beav. 30; *Tylee* v. *Tylee* (1853), 17 Beav. 583; and see *Bainbrigge* v. *Blair* (1841), 3 Beav. 421.
(m) *Edwards* v. *Edwards* (1876), 2 Ch. D. 291.
(n) *Owen* v. *Homan* (1851), 3 Mac. & G. 378, at p. 412; *Greville* v. *Fleming* (1845), 2 Jo. & Lat. 335.

affect the ultimate rights of the parties to the action. Even where a receiver is appointed in an administration action the appointment is also for the benefit of the mortgagees if they avail themselves of it (*o*).

Receiver in debenture holders' action.—The receiver in a debenture holders' action on giving notice to the tenants is entitled to rent in arrear (*p*). There being no liquidation of the company, the appointment does not affect the contracts of the company, and therefore questions arising under the contracts must be determined on the footing that they are valid, notwithstanding that the receiver has purported to cancel them (*q*). And a receiver and manager will not be authorised to repudiate contracts where this will damage the goodwill, which it is his duty to preserve (*r*). But the court will not sanction the borrowing of money to complete the contract, where the completion will produce no profit, direct or indirect (*s*).

For and against whom the receiver may be appointed. In favour of legal mortgagee.—Before the Judicature Act 1873, the court could not generally (*t*) appoint a receiver in favour of a legal mortgagee, the general right of the legal mortgagee against the income of the mortgaged property being to take possession. The Judicature Act 1873 (*u*), now replaced by the Judicature Act 1925 (*x*), enabled the court to appoint a receiver when it should appear just or convenient, and such appointments are as freely made, if the appointment of a receiver of receiver is desirable, as they have always been where the mortgagee has only an equitable interest (*y*). The court will make an appointment, even although the mortgagee might himself appoint a receiver out of court under an express or the statutory power (*z*), and where an action is pending, a judicial appointment is preferable (*a*). The appointment may be made, even where the plaintiff is mortgagee in possession, and has surplus rents (*b*). But the court will not, as a rule, assist a mortgagee in possession to get rid of his liabilities by appointing a receiver (*c*). The same considerations apply to second and subsequent mortgages and, of course, legal charges.

In favour of equitable mortgagee.—An equitable mortgagee is generally entitled to a receiver (*d*), provided the court is satisfied of the existence of the equitable right in the applicant (*e*).

(*o*) *Bainbrigge* v. *Blair, supra; Gresley* v. *Adderley* (1818), 1 Swans. 573.
(*p*) *Re Ind, Coope & Co., Ltd., Fisher* v. *Ind, Coope & Co.,* [1911] 2 Ch. 223.
(*q*) *Parsons* v. *Sovereign Bank of Canada,* [1913] A.C. 160.
(*r*) *Re Newdigate Colliery, Ltd., Newdegate* v. *Newdegate Colliery, Ltd.,* [1912] 1 Ch. 468 (C.A.).
(*s*) *Re Thames Ironworks, etc., Co., Farrer* v. *Thames Ironworks, etc., Co.* (1912), 106 L.T. 674; *Re Great Cobar, Ltd., Beeson* v. *Great Cobar, Ltd.,* [1915] 1 Ch. 682.
(*t*) It would, however, to avoid danger to the security, or where there was difficulty in exercising the usual remedy.
(*u*) Section 25 (8).
(*x*) Section 45.
(*y*) *Truman* v. *Redgrave* (1881), 18 Ch. D. 547.
(*z*) Law of Property Act 1925, s. 101; see p. 300, *supra.*
(*a*) *Tillett* v. *Nixon* (1883), 25 Ch. D. 238.
(*b*) *Mason* v. *Westoby* (1886), 32 Ch. D. 206.
(*c*) *Re Prytherch, Prytherch* v. *Williams* (1889), 42 Ch. D. 590.
(*d*) *Berney* v. *Sewell* (1820), 1 Jac. & W. 647. So too a chargee.
(*e*) *Davis* v. *Duke of Marlborough* (1819), 2 Swans. 108, 138; *Greville* v. *Fleming, supra.*

The appointment may be made for the purpose of keeping down the interest, even though the applicant is unable at the time to enforce the usual mortgagee's remedies, *e.g.*, if he has covenanted not to call in the mortgage debt during a certain time (*f*).

Appointment is without prejudice to prior incumbrancer.— The right of an equitable mortgagee to the appointment of a receiver was formerly subject to the general principle that the appointment was made without prejudice to the rights of the prior legal incumbrancer (*g*). The same principle probably now applies to successive legal mortgages, so that the appointment of a receiver at the instance of a later incumbrancer, whether legal or equitable, is without prejudice to the rights of prior incumbrancers. Hence where a prior mortgagee is not in possession, the appointment is made subject to his right to take possession (*h*). The prior mortgagee can take possession without the leave of the court, though application for leave is usually made (*i*), and notify the tenants to pay their rents to him (*k*). If, however, the order contains no express reservation of the prior mortgagee's rights, he must obtain leave before going into possession (*l*).

Where prior mortgagee in possession.—But when a prior mortgagee is in possession a receiver will not be appointed, so long as anything remains due to him (*m*). In order to save his possession, he must be able to swear that something (however small, it seems, may be the amount) is due to him upon his security (*n*). If he can do so, no receiver will be appointed against him, and the only course is to pay him off according to his own statement of his debt (*o*). But if he refuses to accept what is due, or admits that he is paid off, or if he will not swear that something is due, the court will appoint a receiver (*m*). It being the mortgagee's business so to keep his accounts that he may know whether anything is due, the incomplete state of his accounts will not help him, though time may be given to make an affidavit of the debt (*p*).

The mortgagee must, it seems, swear that some definite sum is due. It is not enough for him to state, in general terms, his belief that when the accounts are taken some particular sum, and parts of other sums will be found due, without supporting the statement by accounts which will serve to test its truth (*q*).

(*f*) *Burrowes* v. *Molloy* (1845), 2 Jo. & Lat. 521. And see p. 270, *supra*.
(*g*) *Davis* v. *Duke of Marlborough, supra; Berney* v. *Sewell, supra.*
(*h*) *Cadogan* v. *Lyric Theatre, Ltd.*, [1894] 3 Ch. 338 (C.A.).
(*i*) *Preston* v. *Tunbridge Wells Opera House, Ltd.*, [1903] 2 Ch. 323.
(*k*) *Underhay* v. *Read* (1887), 20 Q.B.D. 209 (C.A.), at p. 219; *Engel* v. *South Metropolitan Brewing and Bottling Co.*, [1891] W.N. 31.
(*l*) *Re Henry Pound, Son, and Hutchins, Ltd.* (1889), 42 Ch. D. 402 (C.A.), at p. 422.
(*m*) *Berney* v. *Sewell, supra.*
(*n*) *Quarrell* v. *Beckford* (1807), 13 Ves. 377; *Berney* v. *Sewell, supra.*
(*o*) *Berney* v. *Sewell, supra; Rowe* v. *Wood* (1822), 2 Jac. & W. 553. An incumbrancer who is in possession, not in that character, but as tenant, cannot set up his possession as tenant as a reason against the appointment of a receiver: *Archdeacon* v. *Bowes* (1796), 3 Anst. 752.
(*p*) *Codrington* v. *Parker* (1810), 16 Ves. 469; *Hiles* v. *Moore* (1852), 15 Beav. 175. It has been intimated that where by reason of the negligent mode of keeping the accounts, neither party can ascertain what is due, the court may assume that nothing is due: *Codrington* v. *Parker, supra.*
(*q*) *Hiles* v. *Moore, supra;* and see *Rowe* v. *Wood, supra.*

Of what property a receiver may be appointed.—A receiver may generally be appointed over any property, real or personal, which may be taken in execution (*r*) (on the analogy of which remedy the mortgagee's right to a receiver is founded (*s*)). Where the property consists of payments, such as tolls, a receiver may be appointed because the payments are fixed (*t*). But if they have still to be assessed there can be no receiver. If the payments are made out of a fund, as might be the case where the property was a pension (*u*), the fund out which the payments are made must be certain (*x*).

Holders of debentures of companies formed for carrying out public undertakings, such as waterworks and the like, are entitled to the appointment of a receiver, this being the only remedy open, the right of sale or foreclosure having been in the public interest denied (*y*). The appointment of a receiver does not supersede the statutory powers where an undertaking is carried on under statutory powers (*z*).

A receiver may be appointed over property of a personal kind, as well as over the rents and profits of realty, which is outside the United Kingdom, if the owner is within the jurisdiction (*a*).

When manager appointed.—A receiver of the property of a limited company can be appointed at the instance of debenture holders or other secured creditors, but a manager is only appointed where the security includes the business of the company, and then only for the purpose of selling the business as a going concern (*b*). A receiver and manager of mines may be appointed at the instance of a mortgagee, even although the business was not expressly mortgaged, because of the peculiar nature of the property, a mine being considered in this respect to be in the nature of a trade (*c*).

When the appointment may be made.—The mortgagee may apply for the appointment of a receiver where the mortgagor breaks any of his obligations (*d*), or the security is in jeopardy (*e*) or derelict. A receiver will not be appointed unless an action is pending (*f*). For the purpose of this rule, proceedings on originating summons constitute an action (*g*).

(*r*) *Hope* v. *Croydon and Norwood Tramways Co.* (1887), 34 Ch. D. 730.
(*s*) *Davis* v. *Duke of Marlborough, supra*, at p. 83.
(*t*) *Lord Crewe* v. *Edleston* (1857), 1 De G. & J. 93; *De Winton* v. *Brecon Corporation* (1859), 26 Beav. 533.
(*u*) Which may be lawfully assigned.
(*x*) *Cooper* v. *Reilly* (1829), 2 Sim. 560.
(*y*) *Blaker* v. *Herts and Essex Waterworks Co.* (1889), 41 Ch. D. 399.
(*z*) *Marshall* v. *South Staffordshire Tramways Co.*, [1895] 2 Ch. 36 (C.A.).
(*a*) *Mercantile Investment and General Trust Co.* v. *River Plate Trust, Loan, and Agency Co.*, [1892] 2 Ch. 303.
(*b*) *Whitley* v. *Challis*, [1892] 1 Ch. 64 (C.A.), at pp. 69, 70. As to the distinction between a receiver and manager, see *Re Manchester and Milford Rail. Co.* (1880), 14 Ch. D. 645 (C.A.), at p. 653; and as to the duties of a receiver and manager in regard to contracts made by the company, see *Re Newdigate Colliery, Ltd.*, [1912] 1 Ch. 468 (C.A.).
(*c*) *Strong* v. *Carlyle Press*, [1893] 1 Ch. 268 (C.A.).
(*d*) *Stevens* v. *Lord* (1838), 2 Jur. 92. And see *Re Carshalton Park Estate, Ltd., Graham* v. *Carshalton Park Estate, Ltd.*, [1908] 2 Ch. 62.
(*e*) *Higginson* v. *German Athenaeum, Ltd.* (1916), 32 T.L.R. 277.
(*f*) *Ex parte Mountfort* (1809), 15 Ves. 445; *Taylor* v. *Emerson* (1843), 6 L. R. Eq. 224; and see *Gasson and Hallaghan, Ltd.* v. *Jell*, [1940] Ch. 248.
(*g*) *Re Fawsitt, Galland* v. *Burton* (1885), 30 Ch. D. 231 (C.A.).

After the action has been commenced, a receiver may be appointed, either at the hearing or by interlocutory order (h) (which may be either before or af\er final judgment (i)); and even before appearance of the owner of the equity of redemption, if, but not unless, from the state of the security, or other urgent circumstances an immediate appointment is necessary (k).

The appointment has also been made before service of the writ, where the residence of an absconding defendant was unknown (l), and where he was out of the jurisdiction (m).

A receiver may be appointed at the hearing, though such relief was not sought, if the facts are sufficient to justify the appointment (n). It may also be done after judgment (o) in cases of urgency, without any supplemental action (p), e.g., where a person not a party to an action had been so long in possession without accounting, that there was danger of his acquiring a title by adverse possession (q). And a similar result will follow if it appears that the circumstances would, at the hearing, have entitled the party to a receiver (r). But not, it seems, after judgment, where no subsequent circumstances have made it necessary for the protection of the estate or otherwise (s). The appointment will not be made after foreclosure absolute, even where the mortgagor remains in possession pending the settlement of the proper form of conveyance (t).

The authority of the receiver. Expenditure.—It is a general rule that the receiver should do no act which may involve the estate in expense without the sanction of the court (u). Therefore he cannot of his own authority enter into contracts relating to the property. If he does so, he is not acting as agent of either party so as to bind them, and is personally liable (x). He must observe strictly the terms of his appointment and not incur liability on his own responsibility, and then go to the court for sanction (y). Questions as to whether or not an expenditure by the receiver was for the benefit of the property and

---

(h) *Campbell* v. *Lloyds, etc. Bank Ltd.*, (1889), [1891] 1 Ch. 136, n.; expl. in *Whitley* v. *Challis, supra; County of Gloucester Bank* v. *Rudry, Merthyr, etc., Colliery Co.*, [1895] 1 Ch. 629 (C.A.).

(i) *Smith* v. *Cowell* (1880), 6 Q.B.D. 75; *Anglo-Italian Bank* v. *Davies* (1878), 9 Ch. D. 275 (C.A.).

(k) *Taylor* v. *Eckersley* (1876), 2 Ch. D. 302.

(l) *Pitcher* v. *Helliar* (1781), 2 Dick. 580; *Dowling* v. *Hudson* (1851), 14 Beav. 423.

(m) But absence beyond the jurisdiction is not by itself a reason for appointing a receiver before service of the writ, since an order may be made for service out of the jurisdiction.

(n) *Osborne* v. *Harvey* (1841), 1 Y. & C.C.C. 116; but see *Wright* v. *Vernon* (1855), 3 Drew. 112.

(o) See the cases in footnote (i), *supra*.

(p) *Thomas* v. *Davies* (1847), 11 Beav. 29; *Wright* v. *Vernon, supra*.

(q) *Thomas* v. *Davies, supra;* and see *Hiles* v. *Moore* (1852), 15 Beav. 175.

(r) *A.-G.* v. *Galway Corporation* (1829), 1 Mol. 95, 105; *Harris* v. *Shee* (1844), 6 Ir. Eq. R. 543.

(s) *Wright* v. *Vernon, supra*.

(t) *Wills* v. *Luff* (1888), 38 Ch. D. 197; see also *Pedwell* v. *Wright* (1972), 23 D.L.R. (3d) 198.

(u) *A.-G.* v. *Vigor* (1805), 11 Ves. 563.

(x) *Burt* v. *Bull*, [1895] 1 Q.B. 276 (C.A.); and see *Re Ernest Hawkins & Co., Ltd. Brieba* v. *Ernest Hawkins & Co., Ltd.* (1915), 31 T.L.R. 247.

(y) *Re Wood Green and Hornsey Steam Laundry, Ltd., Trenchard* v. *Wood Green and Hornsey Steam Laundry, Ltd.*, [1918] 1 Ch. 423.

the parties interested therein are considered in chambers and the necessary expenditure is authorised there (*z*).

A receiver being an officer of the court appointed on behalf of all parties, the person at whose instance he is appointed is not (in the absence of express undertaking) liable for his debts (*a*).

In case of emergency, where it is necessary for the preservation of the property, the court has jurisdiction to authorise a receiver to raise money by mortgage of the property, even where all parties are not before the court, as in the case of a debenture holders' action (*b*). But although the court has jurisdiction by this or other means to authorise expenditure for preventing the property being deteriorated, *e.g.*, for keeping on a business as a going concern, yet, where all parties interested are not before the court, it will not do so, unless the expenditure is very urgent and is not merely speculative (*c*).

Litigation.—A receiver should not *ex mero motu* bring an action for possession (*d*). Nor is it proper for him to defend actions brought against him in respect of the estate, without the sanction of the court; especially if they arise out of acts improperly done by the receiver of his own authority; and if he is unsuccessful, he will not be allowed the costs of such actions (*e*). But if he succeeds without putting the estate to the expense of an application, which he might have made for his own security, he has the same right to be indemnified as if he had applied to the court (*f*).

Letting.—Any necessary directions for the receiver to manage and let will be given in chambers. The receiver ought not to let without the consent of the court (*g*).

Applications against receiver by strangers to action.—A motion to restrain a receiver from doing acts not within his authority, will be dismissed with costs if made by persons who are strangers to the action (*h*), *e.g.*, tenants of the mortgaged property. Nor can a stranger to an action generally obtain, on summons or motion, payment of money in the hands of the receiver, although it may be justly due to him, and the receiver may have funds in hand applicable to payment (*i*).

Receiver's right to and liability for rents (*j*).—The receiver is entitled to receive all rents in arrear at the date of his appointment (*k*), and a person, who admits a sum of money to be due from him to the

---

(*z*) As to repairs, see *Re Graham, Graham* v. *Noakes,* [1895] 1 Ch. 66.
(*a*) *Gosling* v. *Gaskell,* [1897] A.C. 575 (H.L.), where, however, the receiver was appointed by the mortgagees.
(*b*) *Greenwood* v. *Algeçiras (Gibraltar) Rail. Co.,* [1894] 2 Ch. 205.
(*c*) *Securities and Properties Corpn., Ltd.* v. *Brighton Alhambra, Ltd.* (1893), 62 L.J. Ch. 566.
(*d*) *Wynne* v. *Lord Newborough* (1790), 3 Bro. C.C. 88.
(*e*) *Swaby* v. *Dickon* (1833), 5 Sim. 629.
(*f*) *Bristowe* v. *Needham* (1847), 2 Ph. 190.
(*g*) *Wynne* v. *Lord Newborough, supra; Swaby* v. *Dickon, supra.*
(*h*) *Wynne* v. *Lord Newborough, supra.*
(*i*) *Brocklebank* v. *East London Rail. Co* (1879), 12 Ch. D. 839.
(*j*) For receipt of rent by the receiver creating a fresh tenancy binding on the mortgagee, see p. 339, *infra.*
(*k*) *Codrington* v. *Johnstone* (1838), 1 Beav. 520.

estate, may not dispute the receiver's right to collect it (*l*). But the receiver may not claim rent from a person who, being in possession of the estate, has been ordered to pay an occupation rent, in respect of any period prior to such order. It is only from the date of the order that his tenancy and liability to payment of rent commences (*m*).

When the receiver is informed that the defendant has interfered with the rents, he should move for an attachment (*n*). The interference of the owner with the rents does not exempt the receiver from being charged with the whole amount, but he must discharge himself by showing what the owner received, or hindered him from getting (*o*).

Where money comes into the hands of a receiver, appointed in a foreclosure action at the instance of the plaintiff, and no particular directions have been given for its application, it belongs in the first instance to the plaintiff, who will be entitled to receive it on the dismissal of the action (*p*). In sequestration, if incumbrancers come in for examination *pro interesse suo*, and obtain a certificate that they are prior mortgagees, they are entitled to have possession from the sequestrators, and to have the rents and profits, which have been received by the latter, applied in payment of their mortgage debt, after paying the sequestrator's costs, and the costs of the application (*q*).

There is no privity of estate or contract between a landlord and the debenture holders or receiver where the demised premises are included in a floating charge, and the landlord is not entitled to occupation rent out of the proceeds of goods sold by the receiver while in occupation (*r*). The receiver is not liable for rent even when he has not complied with terms on which the lessor's judgment for rent and possession has been stayed (*s*).

It seems that a receiver may distrain, at his own discretion, for rent which has accrued within the year, but if more than a year's rent is behind, the order of the court should be obtained (*t*). The regular course is to make the tenants attorn (*u*) to the receiver, in whose name (*x*) the distress may then be made, and a direction that they shall attorn is usually contained in the order appointing the receiver (*y*). The attornment creates a tenancy by estoppel between the tenant and

---

(*l*) *Wood* v. *Hitchings* (1840), 2 Beav. 289.

(*m*) *Lloyd* v. *Mason* (1845), 2 My. & Cr. 487.

(*n*) It is sufficient if he swears that he had the information from the tenants and that he believes it: *Anon.* (1824), 2 Mol. 499.

(*o*) *Hamilton* v. *Lighton* (1810), 2 Mol. 499.

(*p*) *Paynter* v. *Carew* (1854), 23 L.J. Ch. 596; *Wright* v. *Mitchell* (1811), 18 Ves. 293; *Re Hoare, Hoare* v. *Owen*, [1892] 3 Ch. 94.

(*q*) *Walker* v. *Bell* (1816), 2 Mad. 21; *Re Hoare, supra; Preston* v. *Tunbridge Wells Opera House, Ltd.*, [1903] 2 Ch. 323.

(*r*) *Re J. W. Abbott & Co., Abbott* v. *J. W. Abbott & Co.* (1913), 30 T.L.R. 13.

(*s*) *Re Westminster Motor Garage Co., Boyers* v. *Westminster Motor Garage Co.* (1914), 84 L.J. Ch. 753.

(*t*) *Brandon* v. *Brandon* (1821), 5 Mad. 473.

(*u*) See p. 34, *supra*.

(*x*) Rather than in the name of the mortgagor.

(*y*) Dan. Ch. Pr. (8th Edn.), 1476; for form of order, see Seton (7th Edn.), pp. 725, 762. And see *Hobhouse* v. *Hollcombe* (1848), 2 De G. & Sm. 208 (where tenants properly oppose a motion to enforce the direction).

the receiver only, and none between the tenant and the mort-gagor (z).

Receiver's right to apply to the court.—Except in cases of necessity, the receiver ought not to originate any proceedings in an action. If an application to the court becomes necessary, the receiver should apply to the party having the carriage of the order, who is the proper person to bring any difficulty before the court (a); and if, after he has done so, no application is made, or no proper means are taken to relieve the receiver from his difficulty, he may apply himself, and will then be entitled to his costs. There are, however, cases in which receivers have applied to the court without any objection having been made (b).

If a party to an action is appointed a receiver he does not lose his privileges as a party and may apply to the court as if he did not hold office (c) And in some cases it is necessary that the receiver should join in the proceedings (d).

The receiver's right to possession.—The receiver being appointed and completing his security—or immediately on appointment if he is allowed to act at once—is entitled to possession and receipt of the rents of the property to which his appointment extends (e), subject to the rights of a prior incumbrancer who is in possession (f).

Where the person in possession refuses to deliver possession to the receiver, it is not necessary in the first instance to make him a party to the action by reason of its not appearing what is the nature of his interest. But the common direction being that the tenants shall attorn, the court treats the person in possession as a tenant; the proper course is to apply that he may attorn, and the motion will be allowed to stand over, that he may inform the court whether he is tenant or not. But unless he shows the contrary, it will be assumed, it seems, that he is tenant, and he will be ordered to attorn accordingly. Where the person in possession does not hold as a tenant, the court will order that possession be given to the receiver (g), and, if it is refused, the receiver will be put into possession by the ordinary process of the court (h).

Where the mortgagor is in possession, and the order does not direct him to attorn, the liability to pay rent commences from demand by

---

(z) *Evans* v. *Mathias* (1857), 7 E. & B. 590.
(a) *Windschuegl* v. *Irish Polishes, Ltd.*, [1914] 1 I.R. 33.
(b) *Mills* v. *Fry* (1815), Coop. G. 107; *Wickens* v. *Townshend* (1830), 1 Russ. & Myl 361; *Shaw* v. *Rhodes* (1826), 2 Russ. 539.
(c) *Scott* v. *Platel* (1847), 2 Ph. 229.
(d) *Chater* v. *Maclean* (1855), 3 W.R. 261.
(e) The order of appointment must be so distinct on the face of it that it may be known of what property the receiver is in possession: see *Crow* v. *Wood* (1850), 13 Beav. 271. The appointment should be over the rents of the particular property, and should be followed by a direction to the owner to deliver possession, or that the tenants should attorn: *Davis* v. *Duke of Marlborough* (1819), 2 Swans. at p. 116.
(f) If there are two receivers, both acting under the authority of the court, one of them ought not to take possession against the other; but he, or those at whose instance he was appointed, should seek the directions of the court: *Ward* v. *Swift* (1848), 6 Hare 309.
(g) *Davis* v. *Duke of Marlborough, supra*, at p. 116.
(h) See *Wyman* v. *Knight* (1888), 39 Ch. D. 165.

the receiver (*i*). Where the order directs him to attorn at a rent, or at a rent to be fixed in chambers, the liability commences from the date of the order (*k*).

The possession of the receiver is the possession of the court (*l*), without whose authority no one may interfere with the receiver, or with property of which he has taken or has been directed to take, possession (*m*), by any proceedings, whether of an ordinary kind or authorised by statute (*n*). Even a libel on the business carried on by a receiver and manager is a contempt (*o*). Where, however, the receiver is expressly appointed subject to the rights of prior incumbrancers, a prior incumbrancer may exercise his rights without the leave of the court (*p*). But a first mortgagee is not entitled to rents collected by a receiver prior to his application to take possession (*q*).

Whether the claimant knew, or not, of the appointment of a receiver, or however clear may be his title, he will be restrained from prosecuting his claim if he has not first obtained the leave of the court (*r*), and, if he has commenced proceedings without leave he may be obliged to discontinue them, and with leave of the court to commence *de novo* (*s*).

Committal for contempt.—The court uses its powers of committal sparingly, and only when it is necessary to vindicate its authority. It will not sanction a motion to commit a person for disturbing a receiver's possession, when it is made long after the act complained of, and not for the protection of the receiver's possession, but to compel payment of his expenses after the question relating to the possession is settled. The proper course is to make such a direct application for the costs as is warranted by the circumstances (*t*).

Leave to prosecute claim.—The court may give leave to a person who claims an interest in real or personal property paramount to that of the receiver, or of a sequestrator, to bring an action, or to come in and be examined *pro interesse suo*; or an inquiry may be directed as to the claimant's interest in the property (*u*). And if he has already brought an action, or otherwise interfered with the receiver's possession without leave of the court, the order which restrains these acts wil also give him leave, or direct him to be examined *pro interesse suo*,

---

(*i*) *Yorkshire Banking Co.* v. *Mullan* (1887), 35 Ch. D. 125.

(*k*) *Re Burchnall, Walter* v. *Burchnall* [1893], W.N. 171.

(*l*) *Russell* v. *East Anglian Rail. Co.* (1850), 3 Mac. & G. 104.

(*m*) *Ames* v. *Trustees of Birkenhead Docks* (1855), 20 Beav. 332.

(*n*) See *Angel* v. *Smith* (1804), 9 Ves. 335; *Evelyn* v. *Lewis* (1844), 3 Hare 472; *Tink* v. *Rundle* (1847), 10 Beav. 318; *Hawkins* v. *Gathercole* (1855), 1 Drew, 12; *De Winton* v. *Brecon Corporation* (1860), 28 Beav. 200.

(*o*) *Whadcoat* v. *Shropshire Rail. Co.* (1893), 9 T.L.R. 589.

(*p*) *Underhay* v. *Read* (1887), 20 Q.B.D. 209, 218; *Engel* v. *South Metropolitan Brewing and Bottling Co.*, [1891] W.N. 31.

(*q*) *Re Metropolitan Amalgamated Estates, Ltd., Fairweather* v. *The Co.*, [1912] 2 Ch. 497. As to the first mortgagee obtaining possession against the receiver, see p. 261, *supra*.

(*r*) *Evelyn* v. *Lewis, supra*.

(*s*) *Lees* v. *Waring* (1825), 1 Hog. 216; *Potts* v. *Warwick and Birmingham Canal Navigation Co.* (1853), Kay 142 (lessor restrained from proceeding to enforce a forfeiture without the leave of the court).

(*t*) *Ward* v. *Swift* (1848), 6 Hare 309.

(*u*) *Angel* v. *Smith* (1804), 9 Ves. 335; *Walker* v. *Bell* (1816), 2 Mad. 21; *Re Henry Pound, Son and Hutchins* (1889), 42 Ch. D. 402; *Lane* v. *Capsey* (1891), 3 Ch. 411.

the plaintiff in the action being directed to exhibit interrogatories for that purpose (*x*).

The application for leave to proceed notwithstanding the receiver's possession, or to come in for examination *pro interesse suo* is generally made by motion (*y*) in the Chancery Division and is usually framed in the alternative that the receiver pay the amount of the claimant's demand, or that the latter be allowed to proceed.

(*x*) *Johnes* v. *Claughton* (1822), Jac. 573.
(*y*) See *Angel* v. *Smith, supra; Potts* v. *Warwick and Birmingham Canal Navigation Co., supra.*

CHAPTER 19

The Mortgagee's Right to Possession

I—MORTGAGEE'S RIGHT TO POSSESSION OF LAND

Mortgagee's right of entry.—After the execution of the mortgage, the mortgagor is usually allowed to retain possession of the property, until, upon default in payment of interest, the mortgagee finds it necessary to use the remedies given him by the security. A right to retain possession is sometimes specially secured to the mortgagor (*a*). Where the advance is repayable by instalments the mortgage deed sometimes provides that the mortgagee will not be entitled to possession until default (*b*). In the absence of any such provision (*c*) and subject to the statutory restrictions (*d*), the legal mortgagee may enter into possession immediately after the execution of the mortgage by virtue of the estate thereby vested in him (*e*). This also applies to a

---

(*a*) The wording of the implied statutory covenants for title in Sched. II, Part III, of the Law of Property Act 1925, seems to assume that such a right is given. The right may also be secured by an attornment clause (as to which, see p. 34, *supra*, and p. 334 *infra*), or by the mortgagor becoming tenant of the mortgagee (see p. 333, *infra*).

(*b*) And see p. 28, *supra*. Such a provision may be implied: *Birmingham Citizens Permanent Building Society* v. *Caunt*, [1962] Ch. 883, at p. 890; [1962] 1 All E.R. 163, at p. 168; *Esso Petroleum Co., Ltd.* v. *Alstonbridge Properties, Ltd.*, [1975] 3 All E.R. 358, at p. 367.

(*c*) If there is any restriction an injunction restraining the mortgagee from taking possession contrary thereto will be granted: *Doe d. Parsley* v. *Day* (1842), 2 Q.B. 147. And the right is, of course, only exercisable so long as an action to enforce it may be brought: see *Wright* v. *Pepin*, [1954] 2 All E.R. 52.

(*d*) Administration of Justice Act 1970, s. 36 as amended (p. 326, *infra*); Rent Act (p. 276, *supra*).

(*e*) *Doe d. Roylance* v. *Lightfoot* (1841), 8 M. & W. 553; *Four-Maids, Ltd.* v. *Dudley Marshall (Properties), Ltd.*, [1957] Ch. 317; [1957] 2 All E.R. 35; *Western Bank, Ltd.* v. *Schindler*, [1976] 2 All E.R. 393 (C.A.) See, generally, (1961) 25 Conv. (N.S.) 278 (B. Rudden); (1969) 22 Current Legal Problems 129 (E. C. Ryder); (1970) 120 New L. J. 808, 829 (the editor). As to mortgages under the Small Dwellings Acquisition Acts, see p. 330 *infra*; *Alnwick R.D.C.* v. *Taylor*, [1966] Ch. 355; [1966] 1 All E.R. 899.

Section 95 (4) of the Law of Property Act 1925, provides that nothing in the Act affects prejudicially the right of mortgagee of land, whether or not his charge is secured by a legal term of years absolute, to take possession of the land.

A second or subsequent mortgagee is similarly entitled to possession, except as against prior mortgagees.

A guarantor of a mortgage debt who has paid off the debt and to whom the benefit of the mortgage has been transferred is entitled to possession of the mortgaged property: *Spector* v. *Applefield Properties, Ltd.* (1968), 206 Estates Gazette 537.

The assignment of rights under a mortgage to a sub-mortgagee does not destroy the right of the head mortgagee to go into possession: *Owen* v. *Cornell* (1967), 203 Estates Gazette 29.

legal charge (*f*) and to a registered charge (*g*). Accordingly the mortgagor may remain in possession only until possession is demanded by the mortgagee or he is ordered to give up possession, and he is not liable to pay any occupation rent until such demand or order has been made (*h*).

Equitable mortgagee.—An equitable mortgagee, having no estate vested in him, is usually said to have no right (*i*) to possession against the mortgagor, (in the absence of express provision giving him such a right (*k*)), without an order of the court (*l*) or the permission of the mortgagor (*m*). But this appears to be inconsistent with general principles and there is some authority to the contrary (*n*). Very often, the equitable mortgagee will be able to call for a legal mortgage (*o*) and so take possession as legal mortgagee. Whilst, to-day, possession is rarely taken under *any* mortgage without an order of the court (*p*), the existence or non-existence of such a right is of some significance, because, if there is a right, on an application to the court an order for possession is a matter of course, subject to the powers of adjournment, etc., (where they apply) (*q*).

When the right arises.—As stated above, unless there is a provision to the contrary, and subject to the statutory restrictions, the right to possession arises on the execution of the mortgage, and, unless the contrary is expressed or can be implied, is not dependent on default by the mortgagor (*r*). Where the right of entry is to arise only on default on payment on demand, a reasonable time must be given to the mortgagor to comply with the demand before the right is exercised (*s*); and if the demand is made by an agent the mortgagor must be given a reasonable time to ascertain if the agent is duly authorised to receive

---

(*f*) Law of Property Act 1925, s. 87 (1).
(*g*) Land Registration Act 1925, s. 34 (1); *Cityland and Property (Holdings), Ltd.* v. *Dabrah,* [1968] Ch. 166, at pp. 171, 172; [1967] 2 All E.R. 693, at pp. 649, 641.
(*h*) *Heath* v. *Pugh* (1881), 6 Q.B.D. 345 (C.A.) at p. 359; affd. *sub. nom. Pugh* v. *Heath* (1882), 7 App. Cas. 235 (H.L.); *Yorkshire Banking Co.* v. *Mullan* (1887), 35 Ch. D. 125.
(*i*) In the sense of an actively enforceable right (see *Sykes,* below) as opposed to a right to defend possession if taken extra-judicially. In the latter case the equitable mortgagee could rely on the doctrine of *Walsh* v. *Lonsdale* (1882), 21 Ch. D. 9 (C.A.).
(*k*) *Ocean Accident and Guarantee Corporation.* v. *Ilford Gas Co.,* [1905] 2 K.B. 493 (C.A.); see also *Mercantile Credits, Ltd.* v. *Archbold,* [1970] Q.W.N. 9.
(*l*) *Barclays Bank, Ltd.* v. *Bird,* [1954] Ch. 274; [1954] 1 All E.R. 449. An equitable mortgagee may claim possession without any other relief: *ibid.* He certainly has no right to the rents from the mortgagor's tenants without an order of the court: *Finck* v. *Tranter,* [1905] 1 K.B. 427 (but if rent is paid to him he is entitled to keep it). And see the articles referred to in footnote (*n*), *infra.*
(*m*) *Re Postle, Ex parte Bignold* (1834), 4 Deac. & Ch. 259.
(*n*) See *Re Postle, Ex parte Bignold, supra; Re Gordon Ex parte Official Receiver* (1889), 61 L.T. 299; *Ocean Accident Guarantee Corporation* v. *Ilford Gas Co., supra;* Spencer v. Mason (1931), 75 Sol. Jo. 295. And also (1954), 70 L.Q.R. 161 (R.E.M.); (1955), 71 L.Q.R. 204 (H.W.R. Wade); Megarry & Wade, *The Law of Real Property* (4th Edn.), pp. 923–924; Sykes, *The Law of Securities* (2nd Edn.), pp. 125–126; Francis, *Mortgages and Securities* (2nd Edn.), pp. 127–128.
(*o*) See p. 45, *supra.*
(*p*) See p. 319, *infra.*
(*q*) See p. 326, *infra.* As previously mentioned (see Ch. 18, *supra*) an equitable mortgagee may be able to appoint a receiver or apply to the court to appoint one.
(*r*) *Western Bank, Ltd.* v. *Schindler,* [1976] 2 All E.R. 393 (C.A.).
(*s*) *Toms* v. *Wilson* (1863), 4 B. & S. 455.

the money (*t*). An action for possession alone is simply an action for the recovery of land (*u*) and is not proceedings for enforcing the mortgage (*a*).

Exercise of the right.—Where the mortgagor is in possession (and he is not a tenant of the mortgagee (*b*)), or a tenant of the mortgagor, whose tenancy is not binding on the mortgagee (*c*), is in possession, the right is exercised by taking physical possession of the land, if that can be done peaceably (*d*), or by bringing an action for possession (*e*). The mortgagee need not give notice either before entering (*f*), or commencing proceedings (*g*).

If a tenant of the mortgagor, whose tenancy is binding on the mortgagee (*h*), is in possession, the right is exercised by notice to the tenant to pay the rent to the mortgagee (*i*).

If a receiver appointed by the court is in possession, and the rights of prior incumbrancers have not been preserved (*k*), the mortgagee wishing to go into possession must apply in the action in which the receiver was appointed for the discharge of the receiver (*l*), or for leave to bring an action for the recovery of the land (*m*). If the rights of prior incumbrancers are preserved, as they usually will be, the mortgagee is entitled to possession as against the receiver and accordingly should give the tenant notice to pay rent to him (*u*).

Mortgagor cannot set up *jus tertii*.—Since no one is allowed to dispute a title which he himself has granted, the mortgagor cannot set up as against his mortgagee the title of a third person, even though such third person may have a right to receive possession (*o*).

Estoppel.—Where a mortgage contains a recital that the mortgagor is seised in fee simple this operates as an estoppel in favour of the mortgagee, and if the mortgagor, having then only an equitable interest, *e.g.* under a contract to purchase, subsequently acquires the legal estate, this will feed the estoppel, and the mortgagee's estate will become legal (*p*). But in the absence of such precise averment the mortgagee will not obtain the legal estate, and the mortgagor can create

---

(*t*) *Moore* v. *Shelley* (1883), 8 App. Cas. 285 (P.C.); *Cripps (Pharmaceuticals), Ltd.* v. *Wickenden*, [1973] 2 All E.R. 606.
(*u*) See p. 320, *infra*.
(*a*) *Esso Petroleum Co., Ltd.* v. *Alstonbridge Properties, Ltd.*, [1975] 3 All E.R. 358, at p. 365; *Western Bank, Ltd.* v. *Schindler, supra;* cf. *Martin* v. *Watson and Egan*, [1919] 2 I.R. 534. Mortgages sometimes refer to the lender being able to enforce the mortgage or security on default, etc.
(*b*) See p. 333, *infra*.
(*c*) See p. 338, *infra*. As to the rights of occupation of a spouse, see p. 216, *supra*.
(*d*) See p. 317, *infra*.
(*e*) See p. 319, *infra*.
(*f*) *Birch* v. *Wright* (1786), 1 Term Rep. 378, 383.
(*g*) *Jolly* v. *Arbuthnot* (1859), 4 De G. & J. 224, 236.
(*h*) See p. 339, *infra*.
(*i*) *Horlock* v. *Smith* (1842), 6 Jur. 478; *Davies* v. *Law Mutual Building Society* (1971), 219 Estates Gazette 309. For form, see 14 Ency, Forms and Precedents (4th Edn.), 867.
(*k*) See p. 306, *supra*.
(*l*) *Thomas* v. *Brigstocke* (1827), 4 Russ. 64; *Searle* v. *Choat* (1884), 25 Ch. D. 723 (C.A.); see p. 312, *supra*.
(*m*) *Doe d. Roby* v. *Maisey* (1828), 8 B. & C. 767.
(*n*) *Underhay* v. *Read* (1887), 20 Q.B.D. 209 (C.A.), at p. 219.
(*o*) *Doe d. Bristowe* v. *Pegge* (1785), 1 Term Rep. 758, n.
(*p*) *Doe d. Christmas* v. *Oliver* (1829), 10 B. & C. 181. Cf. *Heath* v. *Crealock* (1874), 10 Ch. App. 22; *Onward Building Society* v. *Smithson*, [1893] 1 Ch. 1.

a legal estate in favour of a subsequent mortgagee, so that, if such subsequent mortgagee took without notice (*q*), he will have priority (*r*).

Taking actual possession.—Possession must be taken peaceably. If the entry is forcible the mortgagee may be liable to prosecution under the criminal law (*s*). But the mortgagor will have no civil remedy against the mortgagee (*t*). An entry is forcible not only in violence done to the person, but also in respect to any other violence in the manner of entry, as by breaking open the doors of a house (*u*). Entry may be made against a trespasser (*a*).

Consequently, save where the mortgagor consents to the mortgagee taking actual possession, the occasions where a physical taking of possession is possible will be rare. It will generally only be possible where the mortgagor has totally abandoned the premises.

Covenants against parting with possession.—Leases often contain a covenant by the tenant against sub-letting, assigning or parting with possession of the demised property, such covenant being either absolute or qualified by the requirement of consent (*b*). Where the covenant is qualified, the position on an assignment on sale by the mortgagee is covered by a part of s. 89 (1) of the Law of Property Act 1925. This provides that where a licence to assign is required on a sale by a mortgagee, such licence shall not be unreasonably refused (*c*). It is submitted that a parting of possession by the mortgagor arising on the sale of the property by the mortgagee with such licence is not a breach of a covenant against parting with possession. Where the mortgagee himself takes possession prior to a sale (as will usually be the case) or for a longer period it is submitted that the landlord cannot complain, where the mortgage is valid against him, *i.e.*, if by sub-demise and licence was given or by legal charge (*d*). For, if the mortgage itself is valid against him, *a fortiori*, any power exercisable thereunder.

The position may be the same for an absolute covenant. It is not certain precisely what the part of s. 89 referred to above is intended to cover. There are three possibilities. First, it may be referring to a covenant in the lease which expressly requires a licence to assign on a sale by a mortgagee. This is unlikely. Leases rarely, if ever, have or have had such a provision. Secondly, it may be referring to the situation where there is a qualified covenant in the lease against assignment, etc. Thirdly, it may be referring to the situation where, as a matter of fact, rather than the terms of any covenant, licence is required. This latter

---

(*q*) Registration under the Land Charges Act 1972, constitutes notice: Law of Property Act 1925, s. 198 (1); and see p. 442, *infra*.

(*r*) *Right* d. *Jefferys* v. *Bucknell* (1831), 2 B. & Ad. 278.

(*s*) Forcible Entry Acts 1381, 1391, 1429, 1588 and 1623. For proposals for reform, see Criminal Law Bill 1977.

(*t*) *Beddall* v. *Maitland* (1881), 17 Ch. D. 174; *Hemmings* v. *Stoke Poges Golf Club*, [1920] 1 K.B. 720 (C.A.); *Aglionby* v. *Cohen*, [1955] 1 Q.B. 558; [1955] 1 All E.R. 785; *McPhail* v. *Persons (names unknown)*, [1973] 3 All E.R. 393, at p. 398.

(*u*) *Hemmings* v. *Stoke Poges Golf Club*, *supra*.

(*a*) *Scott* v. *Matthew Brown & Co.* (1884), 51 L.T. 746. But see p. 323, *infra*.

(*b*) See pp. 26, 247, *supra*.

(*c*) See p. 247 footnote (*c*), *supra*.

(*d*) It is assumed that a legal charge in itself cannot be a breach of the covenant: see pp. 26, 247, *supra*.

construction would include the case where there was an absolute covenant. It is submitted that this third construction is not correct, since to hold that it was correct would mean that where there was an absolute covenant and there had been a mortgage, without the landlord's approval he could be forced to accept a new tenant by virtue of the exercise of the mortgagee's power of sale. It is submitted that the second alternative is the correct construction. This means that, where there is an absolute covenant, an assignment on sale by a mortgagee by demise will involve a breach of the covenant. So too a legal charge, for, although the charge itself may be effective against the landlord (e), the assignment and parting with possession to the purchaser from the chargee will be a breach. As regards the mortgagee's own possession, if the mortgage itself is in breach of covenant, a *fortiori*, the taking of possession by the mortgagee (f).

Sometimes an absolute covenant is qualified only to allow mortgaging. In that case the mortgagee's own possession and the assignment to and possession of a purchaser from the mortgagee, are, it is submitted, unobjectionable. By allowing the mortgage, the landlord allows all that the mortgage entails. The matter is, it is submitted, one of estoppel or implied licence (g). Furthermore, it is well established that there is no breach of a covenant against assignment, etc., unless the disposition is voluntary, and, where the mortgage is valid against the landlord, it can be argued that any potential breach of covenant occurring through the exercise of the mortgagee's powers for enforcing the security is a result of an involuntary disposition or act by the mortgagor-tenant (h).

Possession.—Where the mortgagee has taken actual possession this possession is beyond doubt and he thereby assumes the liabilities of a mortgagee in possession (i). Entry on to part of the mortgaged property, where it has a defined area or is a unit, will be regarded as entry on the whole (k), but the mortgagee may limit his possession to part (l). The mortgagee's intention is also clear when he gives notice to the mortgagor's tenants to pay rent to him or his agent, as this is equivalent to taking possession (m). In other cases the position

---

(e) See pp. 26, 247, *supra*.

(f) If the legal charge is not a breach (see p. 26, *supra*.) it can be argued that the mortgagee's own possession is also not in breach.

(g) See Wolstenholme and Cherry's *Conveyancing Statutes* (13th Edn.), p. 182 (repeating the statement in earlier editions) for support for this view, but no reasons are given there.

(h) But see *Re Wright, Ex parte Landau* v. *The Trustee*, [1949] Ch. 729; [1949] 2 All E.R. 605.

(i) As to which, see p. 348, *infra*.

(k) *Low Moor Co.* v. *Stanley Coal Co., Ltd.* (1876), 34 L.T. 186 (C.A.); *Lord Advocate* v. *Young* (1887), 12 App. Cas. 544 (H.L.), 556.

(l) *Soar* v. *Dalby* (1852), 15 Beav. 156; *Simmins* v. *Shirley* (1877), 6 Ch. D. 173.

(m) As to acts which amount to taking possession, see *Noyes* v. *Pollock* (1886), 32 Ch. D. 53; *Kirby* v. *Cowderoy*, [1912] A.C. 599 (P.C.); *Davies* v. *Law Mutual Building Society* (1971), 219 Estates Gazette 309. The mere demand for rent without obtaining payment is not sufficient: *Ward* v. *Carttar* (1865), L.R. 1 Eq. 29. Notice to a tenant not to pay rent to the mortgagor suffices: *Heales* v. *M'Murray* (1846), 23 Beav. 401.

In the case of a mortgage by assignment of an interest in personalty, giving notice to the trustees is not equivalent to going into possession, unless the notice also requires payment of income to the mortgagee: *Re Pawson's Settlement, Higgins* v. *Pawson*, [1917] 1 Ch. 541. See p. 357, *infra*.

might not be so clear. The mere fact that the mortgagee is in receipt of the rents does not necessarily make him accountable as a mortgagee in possession. The question depends on whether he has taken out of the mortgagor's hands the power and duty of managing the mortgaged property and dealing with the tenants (*n*). Merely to receive from the mortgagor's agent a sum equal to the rents which the agent has to collect, while the agent has not served on the tenants any notice on behalf of the mortgagee is not enough to render the mortgagee chargeable as a mortgagee in possession (*o*). Where a receiver appointed by the court is discharged and thereafter pays the rents to the mortgagee, his possession will be treated, as from his discharge, as the possession of the mortgagee (*p*).

A mortgagee who is in possession of the mortgaged property will not be liable to account as mortgagee in possession unless he entered as mortgagee, and the court will not treat possession as being held by the mortgagee as such unless it is satisfied that he took possession in his capacity of mortgagee without reasonable grounds for believing himself to hold in another capacity (*q*).

Once a mortgagee has taken possession as such and thereby assumed the liabilities of a mortgagee in possession he cannot easily give up possession and will remain liable even after he has transferred the mortgage, unless the transfer is by order of the court (*r*). While he is not prevented from appointing a receiver under an express or the statutory power (*s*), in the absence of special circumstances the court will not assist him to give up possession (*t*).

Because of this liability a mortgagee will not generally want to take possession, and, if it is a question of intercepting rents, he will do better to appoint a receiver, who will be the agent of the mortgagor (*u*). But a mortgagee exercising an express or statutory power of sale (*a*) will want to sell the mortgaged property with vacant possession. The mortgagor or other person in possession will not normally voluntarily give up possession and an order of the court will therefore generally be required (*b*).

Possession action: County court (*c*).—Where the mortgaged property comprises or includes a dwelling-house (*d*), proceedings for

---

(*n*) *Noyes* v. *Pollock, supra; Mexborough Urban District Council* v. *Harrison,* [1964] 2 All E.R. 109.
(*o*) *Noyes* v. *Pollock, supra.*
(*p*) *Horlock* v. *Smith* (1842), 11 L.J. Ch. 157.
(*q*) *Gaskell* v. *Gosling,* [1896] 1 Q.B. 669, 691; *Vacuum Oil Co., Ltd.* v. *Ellis,* [1914] 1 K.B. 693; *Re Colnbrook Chemical and Explosives Co., A.-G.* v. *Colnbrook Chemical and Explosives Co.,* [1923] 2 Ch. 289.
(*r*) *Hall* v. *Heward* (1886), 32 Ch. D. 430 (C.A.).
(*s*) See p. 300, *supra.*
(*t*) *Refuge Assurance Co., Ltd.* v. *Pearlberg,* [1938] Ch. 687 (C.A.); [1938] 3 All E.R. 231.
(*u*) See p. 302, *supra.*
(*a*) See p. 359, *infra.*
(*b*) See, *e.g., Hughes* v. *Waite,* [1957] 1 All E.R. 603, at p. 604.
(*c*) See 28 Ency. Court Forms (2nd Edn.), Mortgages, and Supplement.
(*d*) Dwelling-house includes any building or part thereof which is used as a dwelling: Administration of Justice Act 1970, s. 39 (1). The fact that part of the premises is used as a shop or office or for a business, trade or profession does not prevent the dwelling-house from being a dwelling-house for the purposes of the relevant provision: s. 39 (2).

possession must, generally, be commenced in the county court (e). The exceptions to this general rule are for property in the Greater London area and where the net annual value for rating is above the county court limit (f). For controlled and regulated mortgages (g) and those made under the Small Dwellings Acquisition Acts (h) the appropriate court is again the county court. Where a dwelling-house is not involved, the plaintiff has a choice between the county court, subject to the usual county court limits (i) and the High Court. Further, the provision for the exclusive jurisdiction of the county court does not apply to an action for foreclosure or sale in which a claim for possession is also made (k). But the action for foreclosure or sale must be a genuine one for that relief and the claim for foreclosure or sale not merely added as a colourable device to take the proceedings outside the county court's exclusive jurisdiction (l). It is commonplace to claim payment, possession, foreclosure or sale and other relief in the same proceedings (m), but the mere claim for foreclosure or sale does not make the action one for foreclosure or sale. The test is what is the plaintiff genuinely seeking (n).

Where there is a claim for payment and possession of a dwelling-house, the county court has exclusive jurisdiction (if the net annual value is within its jurisdiction and the mortgaged property is not in the Greater London area) notwithstanding that the money claim exceeds the county court limits (o). An action for possession is an action for the recovery of land (p).

(e) Administration of Justice Act 1970, s. 37 (1). The section follows a recommendation of the Committee on the Enforcement of Judgment Debts (the Payne Committee) set out in their Report (1969 Cmnd. 3909).

(f) *Ibid.*, s. 37 (1). The jurisdiction is given by the County Courts Act 1959, s. 48 (actions for the recovery of land). The current limit is £1,000: Administration of Justice Act 1973, s. 6, Sched. 2.

(g) See pp. 276, 278, *supra.*

(h) See p. 330, *infra.*

(i) *I.e.*, County Courts Act 1959, s. 48; Administration of Justice Act 1973, s. 6, Sched. 2.

(k) Administration of Justice Act 1970, s. 37 (2).

(l) *Trustees of Manchester Unity Life Insurance Collecting Society* v. *Sadler*, [1974] 2 All E.R. 410; cf. *Lord Marples of Wallasey* v. *Holmes* (1975), 31 P. & C.R. 94.

(m) See p. 719, *infra.*

(n) *Trustees of Manchester Unity Life Insurance Collecting Society* v. *Sadler*, *supra.* Whether the matter be heard in the county court or the High Court the court will have the powers of adjournment, etc., given by the Administration of Justice Act 1970 (see p. 326, *infra*), if it is a possession action. The reason for trying to get the action into the High Court is the assumption that the High Court will be less favourable to the mortgagor than the county court with its Rent Acts experience, see the editor's article on the 1970 Act in (1970) 120 New L.J. 808, 829. The Administration of Justice Act 1973 has made the matter less important. Section 8 (3) of that Act extends the powers under s. 36 of the 1970 Act to an action for foreclosure (with or without a claim for possession), save that the powers to suspend an order, etc., under s. 36 (2) (b) of the 1970 Act shall apply only in relation to any claim for possession. One would hope, of course, that a judge or master or registrar in the High Court would not be so lenient to a mortgagor as a county court judge or registrar, so a claim for foreclosure to get the matter into the High Court is still worth considering. There is nothing in the 1973 Act to extend the s. 36 powers to an action for an order for sale where possession is also sought.

(o) Administration of Justice Act 1970, s. 38 (1).

(p) *R.* v. *Judge Dutton Briant, Ex parte Abbey National Building Society*, [1957] 2 Q.B. 497, at p. 498; [1957] 2 All E.R. 625; *West Penwith Rural District Council* v. *Gunnell*, [1968] 2 All E.R. 1005 (C.A.); *Esso Petroleum Co., Ltd.* v. *Alstonbridge Properties, Ltd.*, [1975] 3 All E.R. 358, at p. 365; cf. *Redditch Building Society* v. *Roberts*, [1940] Ch. 415 (C.A.), at p. 420; [1940] 1 All E.R. 342, at p. 345.

The appropriate county court is the one for the district in which the land is situated (*q*). The principles as to the choice of defendents are the same as that for the High Court and this is dealt with in the next section (*r*). In any matter not expressly provided for by or in pursuance of the County Courts Act 1959, the general principles of practice in the High Court may be adopted and applied (*s*).

Where a person claims possession of any property forming a security for the payment to him of any principal money or interest, he must state in his particulars: (i) the date of the mortgage or charge; and (ii) whether or not the property consists of or includes a dwelling-house within the meaning of Part IV of the Administration of Justice Act 1970; and (iii) the state of account between the plaintiff and the defendant, with details of (a) the amount of the advance, (b) the sums payable from time to time under or in connection with the mortgage or charge, (c) the amount of any such sums in arrears, and (d) the amount remaining due under the mortgage or charge; and (iv) what proceedings (if any) the plaintiff has taken against the defendant in respect of the principal money or interest (*t*).

Unless the court orders otherwise, evidence in support of or in opposition to the plaintiff's claim may be given by affidavit (*u*). Institutional lenders will often want to make use of this provision. In the usual case, the mortgagee should give the mortgagor notice of his intention to use an affidavit, together with a copy of the affidavit not less than five clear days before the hearing. The mortgagor may object to the use of affidavits (*a*). A statement contained in a document produced by a computer is, subject to rules of court, admissible as evidence of any fact stated of which direct oral evidence would be admissible, if it is shown that certain conditions are satisfied in relation to the statement and the computer in question (*b*).

The registrar of a county court may hear and determine any action in which the mortgagee under a mortgage of land claims possession of the mortgaged land (*c*). Subject thereto, the usual county court procedure is applicable.

In the landlord and tenant context the county court has always had power to adjourn any application (*d*), or to postpone an order (*e*) (but

---

(*q*) County Court Rules 1936, Order, 2, r. 2. In the case of a charging order the appropriate court is the one in which the order imposing the charge was made: Order 2, r. 2A (and see p. 159, *supra.*).
(*r*) See p. 323, *infra.*
(*s*) County Courts Act 1959, s. 103.
(*t*) County Court Rules 1936, Ord. 7, r. 7 (2). For form, see Precedent 33 in the Appendix, *infra.* For moneylenders, see Ord. 7, r. 6.
(*u*) County Court Rules 1936, Ord. 20, rr 4–6.
(*a*) Ord. 20, r. 5. The Payne Committee recommended the use of affidavit evidence in mortgage possession cases; see Report, para. 1408.
(*b*) Civil Evidence Act 1968, s. 5; C.C.R. Ord. 20, rr 20–29 and 32.
(*c*) Administration of Justice Act 1970, s. 38 (3).
(*d*) County Courts Act 1959, s. 35; C.C.R. Ord. 13, r. 4 (1).
(*e*) *Sheffield Corporation* v. *Luxford*, [1929] 2 K.B. 180; see *Department of the Environment* v. *James*, [1972] 3 All E.R. 629, at p. 631; *McPhail* v. *Persons (names unknown)*, [1973] 3 All E.R. 393 (C.A.), pp. 398–399.

the postponement will not generally be for longer than one month (*f*), but it is doubtful whether these powers applied in the mortgage context (*g*). Now, however, since the Administration of Justice Act 1970, the court has additional powers of adjournment, etc., in actions by a mortgagee for possession of a dwelling-house. These powers are considered subsequently (*h*).

Chancery Division (*i*).—As mentioned in the previous section, most possession actions in respect of a dwelling-house must be commenced in the county court and what is, in essence, a possession action will be treated as such, notwithstanding the relief claimed includes foreclosure or other relief. Subject thereto, proceedings for possession may be commenced in the High Court (*k*).

Before proceedings are commenced it should be confirmed that the right to possession has arisen and any necessary notice given (*l*). Mortgage actions (*m*) are assigned to the Chancery Division (*n*). Proceedings may be commenced by summons or writ. Summons is the appropriate method where the matter is simple and the facts are not substantially in dispute (*o*). If summons is the appropriate procedure, the mortgagee will not be allowed the extra costs of an action commenced by writ (*p*).

(*f*) See *Sheffield Corporation*. v. *Luxford, supra*, at p. 186; *Jones* v. *Savery*, [1951] 1 All E.R. 820 (C.A.); *Air Ministry* v. *Harris*, [1951] 2 All E.R. 862 (C.A.); see notes to s. 48 in The County Court Practice. For stay of execution pending appeal, see *Sewing Machines Rentals, Ltd.* v. *Wilson*, [1975] 3 All E.R. 553 (C.A.). Note the point remarked on in that case that interest does not run on a county court judgment (but, usually, the mortgage will provide for interest after judgment, see pp. 596, 680, *infra*), unless the debt does not carry interest: see p. 627, *infra*.

(*g*) See *Department for the Environment* v. *James, supra; McPhail* v. *Persons (names unknown), supra*. For the High Court powers, see p. 325, *infra*.

(*h*) Page 326, *infra*. For costs, see p. 326, *infra*.

(*i*) See 28 Ency. Court Forms (2nd Edn.), Mortgages, and Supplement; Supreme Court Practice under Order 88.

(*k*) An originating summons asking only for possession which is subject to the exclusive jurisdiction of the county court cannot be amended to give the High Court jurisdiction, but can be transferred to the county court: *Corbiere Properties, Ltd.* v. *Taylor* (1971), 23 P. & C.R. 289; *Manchester Unity Life Insurance Collecting Society Trustees* v. *Sadler*, [1974] 2 All E.R. 410.

(*l*) *E.g.*, notice to quit might be necessary if the mortgagor had attorned tenant, depending on the wording of the clause (see p. 34, *supra*.). Possession should not be sought before the power of sale has arisen. Usually possession is merely a preliminary to a sale and in that case, because of the liability imposed on a mortgagee in possession (see p. 348, *infra*), there is no point in having an order for possession before the power of sale has arisen. A subsequent mortgagee, intending to apply for possession, should give notice of intention to any prior mortgagee. There used to be a Practice Direction ([1968] 1 All E.R. 752) requiring this but it has been cancelled (*Practice Direction*, [1970] 1 All E.R. 671). Nevertheless the practice of informing any prior mortgagee is a useful one. Often the subsequent mortgagee will want to take a transfer of any prior mortgage: see p. 171, *supra*.

(*m*) *I.e.*, any action in which there is a claim for (a) payment of moneys secured by a mortgage of any real or leasehold property (see p. 294, *supra*) or (b) delivery of possession (whether before or after foreclosure) to the mortgagee of any such property by the mortgagor or by any other person who is or is alleged to be in possession of the property. For foreclosure, redemption, etc., actions, see Supreme Court of Judicature (Consolidation) Act 1925, s. 56 (1), as well as Ord. 88, r. 1.

(*n*) R.S.C. Ord. 88, r. 2.

(*o*) R.S.C. Ord. 5. And see *Re Giles, Real and Personal Assurance Co.* v. *Michell* (1890), 43 Ch. D. 391 (C.A.).

(*p*) *Barr* v. *Harding* (1887), 36 W.R. 216.

If the action is to be commenced in a district registry, the mortgaged property must be situated in the district of the registry. There is an exception for the Liverpool and Manchester district registries (*q*). The only persons who need be made defendants, other than the mortgagor, are persons having an independent right to remain in occupation (*r*), *e.g.*, a tenant of the mortgagor (even where it is uncertain whether or not his tenancy is binding on the mortgagee (*s*)), although it will often be advisable to join every person who may assert a claim. As to the latter class, a spouse of the mortgagor is the usual claimant or potential claimant. But such a person is not entitled to be joined merely because he or she is the spouse of the mortgagor (*t*). The occupying spouse should be joined if her claim is known to the mortgagee before proceedings are commenced (*u*). Generally speaking, the mortgagor for the time being (*a*) should always be joined, *a fortiori*, if he (or she) is in occupation. If there are several mortgagors, they should all be joined, but, if they are not all in occupation and it is not possible to effect service (personal or substituted) on any or all of those not in occupation, only those in occupation and the others on whom service can be effected without difficulty, need be served (*b*). As will now be apparent the problem is not merely one as to parties but also one of service. Moreover, on the hearing of the originating summons the master or district registrar may order that additional persons be joined and served (though this will usually be when a non-party has asserted a claim after the proceedings have been commenced and has applied to be joined, in which case there should be no difficulty about service). Furthermore, though a person may not need to be joined as defendant, there will be situations when it will be advisable to give notice of the proceedings to non-parties (*c*) thus enabling them to apply to be joined and, again, the master or district registrar may order that notice of the proceedings be given to such persons. If the mortgagor is not in occupation and service (personal or substituted) cannot be effected on him at all (*d*) or without difficulty (*e*), any person in occupation should be made defendant, or, at least, be given notice of

(*q*) R.S.C. Ord. 88, r. 3.
(*r*) *Brighton and Shoreham Building Society* v. *Hollingdale*, [1965] 1 All E.R. 540.
(*s*) For tenancies binding on the mortgagee, see p. 339, *infra*. A former tenant cannot be evicted from premises to which the Rent Acts apply without an order of the county court: Rent Act 1965, s. 32; Rent Act 1968, Sched. 15; see also 31 of the 1965 Act. But nothing in the Rent Acts affect the jurisdiction of the High Court in respect of a claim to possession by a mortgagee against a former tenant of the premises whose tenancy is not binding on the mortgagee: Rent Act 1965, s. 35 (3); and see *Bolton Building Society* v. *Cobb*, [1965] 3 All E.R. 814. In *Midland Bank, Ltd.* v. *Monobond* [1971] Estates Gazette Digest 673 was doubted whether the summary procedure under R.S.C. Ord. 113 could be used to evict "tenants" of a mortgagor letting without consent; *London Goldhawk Building Society* v. *Eminer* (1977), Times, 9th February; and see (1976) 126 New L. J. 1193.
(*t*) *Brighton and Shoreham Building Society* v. *Hollingdale, supra; Hastings and Thanet Building Society* v. *Goddard*, [1970] 3 All E.R. 954 (C.A.).
(*h*) For married women, etc., see further p. 216, *supra*.
(*a*) After the original mortgagor has parted with the property, he should not be a defendant in respect of a claim for possession: *Esso Petroleum Co., Ltd.* v. *Alstonbridge Properties, Ltd.*, [1975] 3 All E.R. 358.
(*b*) *Alliance Building Society* v. *Yap*, [1962] 3 All E.R. 6, n.
(*c*) Especially persons in occupation.
(*d*) *E.g.*, he is dead and no personal representative has yet been appointed.
(*e*) *E.g.*, he has emigrated and his whereabouts cannot easily be ascertained.

the proceedings (*f*) and an order for possession can be made against such a defendant (*g*). If there is no one in occupation, the mortgagor must be made defendant and an order for substituted service sought (*h*).

Where the mortgagor is bankrupt, his trustee in bankruptcy should not be joined as defendant, unless the court otherwise directs (*i*). Where a person has not been joined who should have been, the order for possession may be set aside, but only as against such person (*k*). A wife who had registered a Class F land charge (*l*) after the mortgage was not entitled to an order that the execution of a warrant for possession following an order for possession against her husband be stayed and that she be joined as defendant in the proceedings, notwithstanding that under the Matrimonial Homes Act 1967, s. 1 (5) she had the right to pay the arrears (*m*). But where such a spouse asserts that she is in a position to redeem the mortgage or take over the obligations of the mortgage under s. 1 (5), she ought to be joined. However, there is no obligation on the mortgagee to make any inquiries before proceedings are commenced as to the existence of a spouse or her prospects. It is for the spouse to assert her claim (*n*).

Assuming that the proceedings are commenced by originating summons, the property must be sufficiently described in the originating summons so that as adequate description will be carried forward into any possession order made and any subsequent writ of possession (*o*). The summons must be supported by an affidavit. The affidavit must contain similar particulars as those required where the claim is for payment (*p*). In addition, the affidavit must show the circumstances under which the right to possession arises (*q*) and give particulars of every person who, to the best of the plaintiff's knowledge, is in possession

---

(*f*) *Leicester Permanent Building Society* v. *Shearley*, [1951] Ch. 90; [1950] 2 All E.R. 738; *Taylor* v. *Ellis*, [1960] Ch. 368; [1960] 1 All E.R. 549 (occupier claiming to be tenant, but tenancy not binding on mortgagee); and see *McPhail* v. *Persons (names unknown)*, [1973] 3 All E.R. 393 (C.A.), at p. 397.

(*g*) *Alliance Building Society* v. *Shave*, [1952] Ch. 581; [1952] 1 All E.R. 1033; *Esso Petroleum Co., Ltd.* v. *Alstonbridge Properties, Ltd.*, [1975] 3 All E.R. 358, at p. 365. See also *Barclays Bank, Ltd.* v. *Kiley*, [1961] 2 All E.R. 849 (in this case the mortgagor was dead and no personal representatives had been constituted). Where the only defendant is the mortgagor and he dies after proceedings have commenced but before the hearing, any occupants should be joined as defendants and the proceedings pursued against them. So too where such a mortgagor dies after the order had been made but before it has been served. Proceedings could be continued against the deceased mortgagor's estate on application under R.S.C. Ord. 15, r. 6A, but this will delay proceedings and the better course is to add the occupants. If there are none, proceedings will have to be continued against the estate or, if the mortgagee is prepared so to do, physical possession could be taken without continuing the proceedings.

(*h*) It will be possible to take actual physical possession in these circumstances, but mortgagees, especially institutional lenders, are often reluctant to do this: see p. 317, *supra*.

(*i*) *Alliance Building Society* v. *Shave, supra*.

(*k*) *Brighton and Shoreham Building Society* v. *Hollingdale, supra*.

(*l*) See p. 217, *supra*.

(*m*) See *Hastings and Thanet Building Society* v. *Goddard*, [1970] 3 All E.R. 954 (C.A.); (1971) 35 Conv. (N.S.) 48; (1974) 118 S.J. 554; see p. 218, *supra*.

(*n*) See further on defendants, the notes to R.S.C. Ord. 88 in the Supreme Court Practice.

(*o*) See *Thynne* v. *Sarl*, [1891] 2 Ch. 79.

(*p*) See p. 299, *supra*. Where the plaintiff is a moneylender the matters set out in Ord. 83 must also be observed.

(*q*) R.S.C. Ord. 88, r. 3.

of the mortgaged property (*r*). If the mortgagor claims a tenancy, other than a tenancy at will between himself and the mortgagee, the affidavit must show how and when the tenancy was determined and, if by service of notice, when the notice was duly served (*s*).

The hearing (*t*) will generally be before the master, or, where the summons is issued out of a district registry, the district registrar. As indicated above, he may order further parties to be joined or notified of the proceedings, and may require further evidence to be filed. If a point of law or principle is involved, the summons will usually be adjourned into court.

The statutory power of adjournment, etc., where a dwelling-house is involved is dealt with below. Subject to this, the court has no jurisdiction to stand the application over generally, whether on terms of keeping up payments or paying arrears, unless the mortgagee agrees. The only adjournment which may be ordered is one for a short time to afford the mortgagor a chance of paying off the mortgage in full, or otherwise satisfying the mortgagee; but this will not be done if there is no reasonable prospect of this occurring (*u*). However, if there is a *bone fide* defence, such as that the plaintiff is a moneylender and the requirements of the Moneylenders Acts have not been satisfied (*a*), or any default has been waived (*b*) or there be some estoppel which can be raised against the mortgagee (*c*) or counterclaim or set-off arising out of the mortgage (*d*), the master or registrar will adjourn the matter into court (*e*).

(*r*) *Ibid.*, r. 4.
(*s*) *Ibid.*, r. 5. For a form of affidavit, see Precedent in the Appendix, *infra*.
(*t*) For the preliminaries, *i.e.*, documents to be lodged on taking appointment for hearing (r. 4), non-appearance by defendant (r. 5 and Ord. 25), judgment in default in writ action (r. 7).
(*u*) *Birmingham Citizens Permanent Building Society* v. *Caunt*, [1962] Ch. 883; [1962] 1 All E.R. 163; *Royal Trust Co. of Canada* v. *Markham*, [1975] 3 All E.R. 433 (C.A.). For the previous position, see (1961) 77 L.Q.R. 351-2 (Master Ball).
R.S.C. Ord. 45, r. 11, does not confer on the court any power to grant a stay of execution of an order for possession: *London Permanent Benefit Building Society.*, v. *De Baer*, [1969] 1 Ch. 321; [1968] 1 All E.R. 372. Although this case and the *Birmingham Citizens* case are prior to the introduction of the statutory power of adjournment etc., there seems to be no reason why they are not still applicable to cases outside the scope of the statutory provisions.
(*a*) See p. 237, *supra*, for these Acts; *Lidco Investments, Ltd.* v. *Hale*, [1971] *Estates Gazette Digest.* 169; *Royal Trust Co. of Canada* v. *Markham*, *supra*.
(*b*) *Hughes* v. *Birks* [1958] *Estates Gazette Digest* 341; *Ushers Brewery* v. *Alvo Club Holdings, Ltd.* (1970), 213 Estate Gazette 1537.
(*c*) See *Manson Finance* v. *Oliso-Emosingoit*, [1975] C.L.Y. 273 (repairs-defendant should have been allowed to answer affidavit).
(*d*) Even an admitted liquidated claim which exceeds the mortgage does not *per se* discharge the mortgage and is no reason for adjourning the application: *Samuel Keller (Holdings), Ltd.* v. *Martins Bank, Ltd.*, [1970] 3 All E.R. 950 (C.A.). See also *Inglis* v. *Commonwealth Trading Bank of Australia* (1972), 126 C.L.R. 161. But where the amount due under the mortgage is determined by some other transaction between the parties, *e.g.*, where the mortgage is to secure the amount owing from time to time for goods supplied by the mortgagee to the mortgagor, the possession claim may be adjourned, if the mortgagor has a cross-claim for goods supplied to the mortgagee.
(*e*) For other instances (besides those cases mentioned elsewhere in this section) where attempts to obtain adjournments failed, see *Threlfalls, Chesters, Ltd.* v. *Clark* [1962] *Estates Gazette Digest* 456; *Clark* v. *Vile*, [1969] *Estates Gazette Digest* 169; *De Borman* v. *Makkofaides*, [1971] *Estates Gazette Digest* 909; *Patterson* v. *Roden* (1972), 223 Estates Gazette 945.

Any party dissatisfied with the order or proposed order of the master or registrar has the right to have the matter adjourned to the judge (*f*). Where a mortgagee is seeking to enforce his security and persons not party to the mortgage claim to be entitled in possession to or to remain in possession of the mortgaged property, if any party is dissatisfied with a decision of the master, the latter should adjourn the summons into court (*g*). The usual order for possession is for delivery up of possession within 28 days after service (*h*). A writ of possession issues as of right on proof of service and non-compliance (*i*). No order for costs is usually made, the plaintiff being left to add the costs to his security. Leave to issue execution on a suspended order for possession must not be given without allowing the defendant an opportunity to be heard (*k*).

Additional powers of adjournment, etc.—Whether the action is brought in the High Court or the county court, the Administration of Justice Act 1970, as amended, gives the court certain powers to adjourn the proceedings, stay the order or postpone the date for delivery of possession. The Act provides:

36.—(1) Where the mortgagee under a mortgage of land which consists of or includes a dwelling-house brings an action in which he claims possession of the mortgaged property, not being an action for foreclosure in which a claim for possession of the mortgaged property is also made, the court may exercise any of the powers conferred on it by subsection (2) below if it appears to the court that in the event of its exercising the power the mortgagor is likely to be able within a reasonable period to pay any sums due under the mortgage or to remedy a default consisting of a breach of any other obligation arising under or by virtue of the mortgage.

(2) The court—

    (a) may adjourn the proceedings, or

    (b) on giving judgment, or making an order, for delivery of possession of the mortgaged property, or at any time before the execution of such judgment or order, may—

        (i) stay or suspend execution of the judgment or order, or

        (ii) postpone the date for delivery of possession,

for such period or periods as the court thinks reasonable.

(3) Any such adjournment, stay, suspension or postponement as is referred to in subsection (2) above may be made subject to such conditions with regard to payment by the mortgagor of any sum secured by the mortgage or the remedying of any default as the court thinks fit.

(4) The court may from time to time vary or revoke any condition imposed by virtue of this section (*l*).

(*f*) *Birmingham Citizens Permanent Building Society* v. *Caunt, supra.*

(*g*) *District Bank, Ltd.* v. *Webb*, [1958] 1 All E.R. 126; *Practice Note*, [1958] 1 All E.R. 128.

(*h*) *Barclays Bank, Ltd.* v. *Bird*, [1954] Ch. 274, at p. 282; [1954] 1 All E.R. 449, at p. 453; *Four-Maids, Ltd.* v. *Dudley Marshall (Properties), Ltd.*, [1957] Ch. 317; [1957] 2 All E.R. 35; *London Permanent Benefit Building Society* v. *De Baer, supra.*

(*i*) And if the mortgagor afterwards gets back into possession a writ of restitution (R.S.C. Ord. 46 r. 3) or, more rarely, committal for contempt should be sought: *Alliance Building Society* v. *Austen*, [1951] 2 All E.R. 1068.

(*k*) See *Fleet Mortgage and Investment Co., Ltd.* v. *Lower Maisonette, 46 Eaton Place, Ltd.*, [1972] 2 All E.R. 737; *Practice Direction*, [1972] 1 All E.R. 576.

(*l*) This section follows (in most respects) a recommendation of the Payne Committee (Report of the Committee on the Enforcement of Judgment Debts 1969, Cmnd. 3909, pp. 355 *et seq.*). From their Report it seems clear that the recommendation intended a return to the position before *Birmingham Citizens Permanent Building Society* v. *Caunt, supra*, as understood by the masters and registrars, *i.e.*, that they had power to adjourn

The saving for a foreclosure action in which a claim for possession is also made in sub-s. (1) above has been modified by the Administration of Justice Act 1973, s. 8, which applies only to mortgages where the mortgagor is entitled or is to be permitted to pay the principal sum secured by instalments or otherwise to defer payment of it in whole or part, *e.g.*, an endowment mortgage (*m*), but provision is made for earlier payment in the event of any default by the mortgagor or of a demand by the mortgagee or otherwise (*n*). For such instalment mortgages, s. 36 is applied to a foreclosure action (with or without a claim for possession) as if there was a claim only for possession, except that s. 36 (2) (b) shall apply only in relation to any claim for possession (*o*). The effect of this amendment appears to be that, if the only claim is for foreclosure, the only statutory power is adjournment, whereas if the claim is for foreclosure and possession there is power to adjourn the foreclosure claim and to adjourn the possession claim or stay or postpone, etc., any order for possession.

A foreclosure action in respect of a mortgage, which is not an instalment mortgage, and thereby within s. 8 of the Administration of Justice Act 1973, is outside the s. 36 powers. Following the 1970 Act a good many mortgagees changed their procedures on default by the borrower and claimed foreclosure rather than possession simpliciter. As appears hereafter (*p*) a claimant for foreclosure need not also claim possession. Delivery of possession will generally be ordered as part of the foreclosure order, even though possession is not expressly sought in the relief claimed in the foreclosure action. A foreclosure action was a way around the powers of adjournment, etc., in the 1970 Act and, save for instalment mortgages which are now caught by the 1973 Act, still is. The meaning of "an action for foreclosure" is therefore of some importance (*q*). Moreover, as we have seen (*r*), an action for foreclosure or sale, even where possession is expressly claimed, is excluded from s. 37 of the 1970 Act (exclusive jurisdiction of the county court). As for s. 37, so for s. 36 the foreclosure must not be a disguise for what in reality is a claim for payment and/or possession (*s*). If the plaintiff has claimed foreclosure in his summons and pursues his remedy of foreclosure at the hearing (in which case his evidence will be somewhat different from that on a claim for possession simpliciter (*t*)) the

---

to allow the mortgagor to solve his financial difficulties on terms of paying off arrears, etc. (see (1961) 77 L.Q.R. 351, 352 (Master Ball) and the articles referred to in footnote (*e*), p. 314, *supra*.). The section is designed to give the mortgagor an opportunity to make good his default if there is a reasonable prospect that he can do so. The section came into force on 1 February 1971: Administration of Justice Act 1970 (Commencement No. 3) Order 1970. In the application of this section to Northern Ireland, "the court" means a judge of the High Court in Northern Ireland, and in subsection (1) the words from "not being" to "made" shall be omitted: s. 36 (6).

(*m*) See p. 30, *supra*.
(*n*) See p. 328, *infra*.
(*o*) Administration of Justice Act 1973, s. 8 (3).
(*p*) See p. 396, *infra*.
(*q*) See generally on the point the editor's article in (1970) 120 New L.J. 808, 829.
(*r*) See p. 320, *supra*.
(*s*) *Manchester Unity Life Insurance Collecting Society Trustees* v. *Sadler*, [1974] 2 All E.R. 410.
(*t*) See p. 396, *infra*.

action will be a foreclosure action and s. 36 will not apply (*u*) (unless the mortgage is an instalment mortgage brought within s. 36 by the 1973 Act).

Another point on s. 36 (1) has already been solved. That is the reference to "any sums due under the mortgage". This could mean that the powers are exercisable (but, of course, will not necessarily be exercised) if the mortgagor can pay off any sum or sums, however small, due under the mortgage, for example, where the whole of the mortgage monies have become due, say £4,000, if the mortgagor could pay off £100 or £10 or £1. Alternatively, "any sums due under the mortgage" could mean "*the* sum or sums due under the mortgage". On this latter view the powers are only exercisable if the mortgagor is likely to be able within a reasonable time to pay off the whole of the principal etc. If that is so the section does not take the matter beyond *Caunt's* case (*a*), save perhaps to give the mortgagor a longer period to find the monies or arrange a transfer (*q*). Both constructions have been upheld (*b*). But the conflict is now only of historical interest, since the Administration of Justice Act 1973 has restored what was presumably the original intention. The 1973 Act provides:

> **8.**—(1) Where by a mortgage of land which consists of or includes a dwelling-house, or by any agreement between the mortgagee under such a mortgage and the mortgagor, the mortgagor is entitled or is to be permitted to pay the principal sum secured by instalments or otherwise to defer payment of it in whole or in part, but provision is also made for earlier payment in the event of any default by the mortgagor or of a demand by the mortgagee or otherwise, then for purposes of s. 36 of the Administration of Justice Act 1970 (under which a court has power to delay giving a mortgagee possession of the mortgaged property so as to allow the mortgagor a reasonable time to pay any sums due under the mortgage) a court may treat as due under the mortgage on account of the principal sum secured and of interest on it only such amounts as the mortgagor would have expected to be required to pay if there has been no such provision for earlier payment.
>
> (2) A court shall not exercise by virtue of sub-s. (1) above the powers conferred by s. 36 of the Administration of Justice Act 1970 unless it appears to the court not only that the mortgagor is likely to be able within a reasonable period to pay any amounts regarded (in accordance with sub-s. (1) above) as due on account of the principal sum secured, together with the interest on those amounts, but also that he is likely to be able by the end of that period to pay any further amounts that he would have expected to be required to pay by then on account of that sum and of interest on it if there has been no such provision as is referred to in sub-s. (1) above for earlier payment (*c*).

The effect of these provisions is as follows. Section 8 of the 1973 Act applies to instalment mortgages and all other mortgages where the payment of the whole or part of the principal is deferred (*e.g.*, an endowment mortgage (*d*)), but provision is also made for earlier repayment on default by the mortgagor or demand by the mortgagee.

(*u*) See *Lord Marples of Wallasey* v. *Holmes* (1976), 31 P. & C.R. 94.
(*a*) See p. 325, *supra*.
(*b*) *Halifax Building Society* v. *Clark*, [1973] Ch. 307; [1973] 2 All E.R. 33 (in favour of the latter view); cf. *First Middlesbrough Trading and Mortgage Co., Ltd.* v. *Cunningham* (1974), 28 P. & C.R. 69 (C.A.) (in favour of the former view).
(*c*) Section 8 came into force on 18 May, 1974: s. 20 (1), (b) of the 1973 Act.
(*d*) See p. 30, *supra*.

In these cases the court may treat as due under the mortgage, on account of the principal sum secured and of interest on it, only such amounts as the mortgagor would have expected to be required to pay if there had been no such provision for earlier payment (s. 8 (1)). A court shall not exercise the powers conferred by s. 36 of the 1970 Act unless it appears to the court, not only that the mortgagor is likely to be able within a reasonable period to pay any amounts regarded (under s. 8 (1)) as due on account of the principal sum secured, together with interest thereon, but also that he is likely to be able, by the end of that period, to pay any further amounts that he would have expected to be required to pay by then (s. 8 (2)). The effect of these new provisions is to reverse *Halifax Building Society* v. *Clark* (e) and to permit the court to adjourn proceedings, suspend the order, etc., under s. 36 in the case of an instalment mortgage if the mortgagor is likely to be able within a reasonable period to pay off arrears of instalments *and* also keep up current instalments meanwhile.

Notwithstanding the amendments in the 1973 Act s. 36 continues to cause difficulties. What is "likely" and how long is "a reasonable period"? Is the reasonableness to be considered from the mortgagor's position or the mortgagee's? If the powers are exercised, how long is "a reasonable period" under sub-section (2)?

"Likelihood" is a question of fact to be determined by the judge on the evidence before him (f). If the mortgagor has a purchaser immediately in view or has signed a contract for sale and the price will cover the monies due under the mortgage, the condition will be satisfied and there is a good case for adjourning the application (g). The fact that the mortgagor is unemployed at the time of the hearing is not fatal for him, since his mortgage repayments may be met by the Social Security authorities (h). As regards "a reasonable period", a period of five years has been mentioned (i) but in the case of an instalment mortgage there is some argument for linking the period of suspension to the residue of the term of the mortgage. It can be said that so long as the lender is likely to be paid all that is due by the end of the term he really has no complaint. It is submitted that the reasonableness has to be considered from the point of view of both parties. On identical figures what is reasonable between a borrower and an institutional lender may be unreasonable between a borrower and, *e.g.*, a private individual who has sold his house to the borrower and taken a mortgage back. The reasonable period in sub-s. (2) will, presumably, usually be the same period as that for sub-s. (1).

As between adjournment and the other powers, it is submitted that

---

(e) *Supra.* For criticism of that decision, see (1973) 89 L.Q.R. 171 P.V.B.; (1973) 37 Conv. (N.S.) 133, 213.

(f) *Royal Trust Co. of Canada* v. *Markham*, [1975] 3 All E.R. 433 (C.A.), at p. 438; *Western Bank, Ltd.* v. *Schindler*, [1976] 2 All E.R. 393 (C.A.).

(g) *Royal Trust Co. of Canada* v. *Markham, supra; Western Bank, Ltd.* v. *Schindler, supra.*

(h) See p. 19, *supra.*

(i) See (1971), 69 L.S. Gaz. 268 (P. H. Wareham) and letters at pp. 377, 427 where it is suggested that a county court judge had been directed that five years was a reasonable period.

adjournment (other than for further evidence, etc.) is only appropriate in such cases as that mentioned above of a prospective sale by the mortgagor. Otherwise a possession order should be made and suspended. The suspension must be for a fixed period. There is no jurisdiction to suspend indefinitely (*k*).

The meaning of the expression in sub-s. (2) (b) "before the execution of any such judgment or order" is uncertain. Does this mean that the powers in sub-s. (2) (b) are excluded as soon as execution is commenced or only when execution is completed? The latter view is probably the correct one. The question is unlikely to be of much practical significance, since the mortgagor is likely to have had his say before any order has been made and an unconditional order will only be made where his financial position is so hopeless that he is unlikely to require the assistance of the court at the last moment.

A point of particular importance is whether or not the court can exercise its powers when the defendant mortgagor has not asked it to do so. Often the defendant will not file any evidence on which the court can reach a view, and in this case it will not be able to exercise any of the additional powers (*l*). But there may be enough of the background in the plaintiff's evidence to enable the court to make a suspended order. There is no burden of proof imposed by the relevant sections one way or the other. It is for the court to decide whether or not to exercise the additional powers on such evidence as it has before it.

It seems that the additional powers can be exercised by the court whether or not there is default by the mortgagor under the mortgage of the dwelling-house (*m*).

Action for possession under Small Dwellings Acquisition Acts (*n*).—Where a local authority takes possession of a house, all the estate, right, interest and claim of the proprietor in or to the house vest in and become the property of the local authority, and that authority may retain the house under their own management or sell or otherwise dispose of it as they think expedient (*o*). The effect of this provision is that the taking of possession by a local authority operates as an immediate and irrevocable foreclosure of the proprietor's interest, subject only to his right, if the property is sold, to payment of a sum representing the excess, if any, of the value of his interest over the balance due under the mortgage (*p*). This provision is unlike anything to be found in the general law (*q*).

Where the local authority are entitled under the Acts to take

---

(*k*) *Royal Trust Co. of Canada* v. *Markham*, *supra*.

(*l*) *Royal Trust Co. of Canada* v. *Markham*, *supra*.

(*m*) See *Western Bank, Ltd.* v. *Schindler*, [1976] 2 All E.R. 393 (C.A.); Goff, L.J., dissenting at p. 409. (In that case there was default only under a collateral mortgage of a policy).

(*n*) As to these, see pp. 188–191 *supra*.

(*o*) Small Dwellings Acquisition Act 1899, s. 5 (1). And see *Mexborough U.D.C.* v. *Harrison*, [1964] 2 All E.R. 109.

(*p*) *Ibid.*, s. 5 (2).

(*q*) See, generally, *Alnwick R.D.C.* v. *Taylor*, [1966] Ch. 355, at p. 361; [1966] 1 All E.R. 899. Note that there is no equivalent of ss. 88 and 89 of the Law of Property Act 1925 (pp. 377–379, *infra*) extinguishing subsequent mortgages. For this reason authorities are advised to proceed by way of foreclosure proper.

possession of a house, possession may (*r*) be recovered under the County Courts Act 1888 (*s*) as if the local authority were landlord and the mortgagor the tenant (*t*). The effect of this provision is that if the arrears have been paid off by the time of the hearing of the action no order for possession can be made (*u*).

Furniture on the premises.—Where the mortgagee takes possession either by taking physical possession or under an order of the court questions may arise as to his rights and duties in respect of the mortgagor's (or his tenant's) chattels left on the premises. Where the mortgagee takes possession under an order of the court the order for possession means vacant possession (*x*). If furniture and other effects are left on the premises the mortgagee may obtain an order for the removal of the goods (*a*). If the mortgagor fails to obey such an order he may be committed or attached for contempt. Alternatively, if an order for payment under the personal covenant is obtained and not satisfied, execution may be levied against the furniture. This may be in conjunction with taking possession or separately from it.

It is submitted that the mortgagee who goes into possession without an order of the court (such cases, as has been stated, will be rare) has the same right to vacant possession and accordingly is entitled to an order for removal.

The position is rather more difficult where the owner of the chattels is not to be found, or has died and there are no personal representatives. There are three possible courses of action in this situation. The presence of the chattels on the premises constitutes a trespass to the mortgagee's possession, which he is entitled to take steps to end. But to turn furniture out on to the street is not really a practical solution. The mortgagee could arrange for the property to be stored. It is doubtful whether expenses of removal and storage could be properly added to the mortgage debt (*b*). If there is or will be an outstanding balance of the proceeds of sale of the premises, the storage expenses could, it is submitted, be paid out of these where the balance has not been paid into court (*c*), and if and when the mortgagor appears the balance should only be handed over on terms that the expenses were a proper deduction. But if the proceeds of sale of the premises will not satisfy what is due to the mortgagee who is selling, there is no reason, it is submitted, why he should incur an expense which he will not be able to recoup and in this case (but this case only) the mortgagee would probably be justified in selling the furniture and putting the proceeds on deposit account (*d*).

(*r*) *Quaere*, must be recovered: see *Alnwick R.D.C.* v. *Taylor, supra.*
(*s*) Section 139. See County Courts Act 1959, ss. 48, 191.
(*t*) Small Dwellings Acquisition Act 1899, s. 5 (5).
(*u*) *Alnwick R.D.C.* v. *Taylor, supra.*
(*x*) *Norwich Union Insurance Society* v. *Preston*, [1957] 2 All E.R. 428.
(*a*) See *Norwich Union Insurance Society* v. *Preston, supra;* for a form of order, see Ency. Court Forms (2nd Edn.), Supplement, vol. 28, p. 142.
(*b*) As to those expenses which may be, see p. 639, *infra.*
(*c*) Under s. 63 of the Trustee Act 1925. See p. 374, *infra.*
(*d*) These difficulties may be provided for by the terms of the mortgage deed, but unless carefully drawn such a provision may infringe the Bills of Sale Acts. For form, see proviso (4), p. 682, *infra.*

A mortgagee who has taken possession is not obliged to look after chattels left on the premises pending their removal (*e*).

II—MORTGAGOR IN OCCUPATION

Mortgagor or tenant in occupation.—In considering the mortgagee's right to possession the occupation of the mortgaged premises by the mortgagor or a tenant under a lease made before or after the mortgage is relevant as to whether the mortgagee's right is exercisable at all, and, if it is, as to who should be made a defendant to the proceedings for possession.

Relation of mortgagee and mortgagor (*f*).—The relation of mortgagee and the mortgagor where the mortgagor is in occupation has been the subject of much discussion, less from any real question as to the relative rights of the parties, than from the embarrassment which led one learned judge to declare, that it was very dangerous to define the precise relation in which the mortgagor and mortgagee stand to each other in any other terms than those very words (*g*); another, that one is much at a loss as to the proper term in which to describe the relation (*h*); and a third, that it is sufficient to call them mortgagor and mortgagee, without having recourse to any other description of men or to what they are most like: their rights, powers and interests being as well settled as any in the law (*i*).

It will, therefore, be sufficient to say that the mortgagor in possession, under such circumstances, is not, as he is sometimes called, tenant at will to the mortgagee. He is not, like a tenant at will (*j*), entitled to the crops growing on the land at the end of the tenancy (*k*), and he may be ejected without notice or demand for possession (*l*). Nor is he the mortgagee's bailiff or receiver, because he is not obliged to account to him for rents (*m*). He has, however, been called a tenant at will *quodam modo* (*n*), and he has also been said to be a tenant *by*, as distinguished from tenant *at*, sufferance (*o*). But these definitions barely mark, without explaining, the distinctions which they imply. The likeness of the mortgagor's interest to that of a tenant at sufferance is so far correct, that it agrees with his position as one who comes in by right, and holds over without right (*p*).

(*e*) See *Jones* v. *Foley*, [1891] 1 Q.B. 730.
(*f*) See (1969) 22 Current Legal Problems, 129 (E. C. Ryder).
(*g*) *Doe d. Higginbotham* v. *Barton* (1840), 11 A. & E. 307, at p. 314.
(*h*) *Doe d. Jones* v. *Williams* (1836), 5 A. & E. at p. 297.
(*i*) *Birch* v. *Wright* (1786), 1 Term. Rep., at p. 383.
(*j*) See *Ex parte Temple* (1822), 1 G. & J. 216, where the mortgagor was held entitled to the crops as tenant at will by express contract.
(*k*) *Re Gordon, Ex parte Official Receiver* (1889), 61 L.T. 299.
(*l*) *Birch* v. *Wright, supra; Doe d. Roby* v. *Maisey* (1828), 8 B. & C. 767.
(*m*) *Birch* v. *Wright, supra.*
(*n*) Per Lord MANSFIELD, *Moss* v. *Gallimore* (1779), 1 Doug. K.B. 279, at p. 282. See R.S.C. Ord. 88, r. 6 (5), which supposes the relationship to be that of tenancy at will.
(*o*) See also *Keech* v. *Hall* (1778), 1 Doug. K.B. 21, and *Moore* v. *Shelley* (1883), 8 App. Cas. 285.
(*p*) *Thunder d. Weaver* v. *Belcher* (1803), 3 East, 449; *Doe d. Roby* v. *Maisey, supra; Bagnall* v. *Villar* (1879), 12 Ch. D. 812; *Heath* v. *Pugh* (1881), 6 Q.B.D. 345, 359.

Accordingly the mortgagor in possession may be described as one who, having parted with his immediate estate, remains in possession at the pleasure and consistently with the right of the grantee, exercising the ordinary rights of property, including the rights of receiving rents for his own use (*q*), of being able to bring actions in respect of the mortgaged property against anyone save the mortgagee (*r*) and to grant leases subject to certain restrictions (*s*), yet liable at the option of the mortgagee to be treated either as a tenant or as a trespasser, in the one character to be sued for injuring the reversion (*t*), in the other to be ejected without notice, demand for possession, or claim to rents in arrear or accruing or to the growing crops (*u*).

Effect of the Limitation Act.—Under the Limitation Act 1939, a mortgagee's right to bring an action for possession is barred after twelve years from the date when repayment became due and his title to the land is extinguished (*w*). It is not considered that the provisions in the 1939 Act relating to tenancies at will (the effect of which is that a landlord's title is extinguished after thirteen years (*x*)) apply to a mortgagor in possession *qua* mortgagor, though it is of interest to note that s. 7 of the Real Property Limitation Act 1833, which these provisions replaced, expressly provided that a mortgagor was not to be deemed a tenant at will to the mortgagee within the meaning of that section.

Creation of tenancy in mortgagor (*y*).—The mortgagor may become tenant to the mortgagee either by virtue of a provision in the mortgage qualifying the mortgagee's prima facie right to possession or under an attornment clause. Thus a tenancy arises where there is a provision that the mortgage shall not be called in until the expiration of a given term, and that until default in payment it shall be lawful for the mortgagor peaceably to enjoy and receive the rents (*z*). This amounts to a re-demise by the mortgagee to the mortgagor during the term fixed. The result is not the same where the covenant is, that the mortgagee may enter after default, which is held not to imply that the mortgagor may remain in possession until default, but only to leave the mortgagee up to that time to rest upon his title under the mortgage, and afterwards to give him also the benefit of the covenant (*a*). While the words used imply some right to possession in the mortgagor, they will not amount to a re-demise to him, unless, as in *Wilkinson* v. *Hall* (*b*), some certain time is fixed during which the mortgagor is to

---

(*q*) *Moss* v. *Gallimore, supra; Rogers* v. *Humphreys* (1835), 4 A. & E. 299; *Re Ind, Coope & Co., Ltd., Fisher* v. *Ind, Coope & Co.* [1911] 2 Ch. 223.

(*r*) *Sellick* v. *Smith* (1826), 11 Moo. C.P. 459; Law of Property Act 1925, s. 98. And see p. 336, *infra.*

(*s*) Law of Property Act 1925, s. 99. And see p. 342, *infra.*

(*t*) *King* v. *Smith* (1843), 2 Hare, 239; *Bagnall* v. *Villar* (1879), 12 Ch. D. 812.

(*u*) *Doe d. Roby* v. *Maisey, supra; Doe d. Griffith* v. *Mayo* (1828), 7 L.J. (O.S.) K.B. 84; *Jolly* v. *Arbuthnot* (1859), 4 De G. & J. 224; *Re Gordon, Ex parte Official Receiver, supra.*

(*w*) See p. 285, *supra.*

(*x*) Section 9 (1).

(*y*) See (1969) 22 Current Legal Problems 129.

(*z*) *Wilkinson* v. *Hall* (1837), 3 Bing. N.C. 508.

(*a*) *Doe d. Roylance* v. *Lightfoot* (1841), 8 M. & W. 553.

(*b*) See footnote (*z*), *supra.*

hold (c); so that no demise is created by a covenant that the mortgagee shall not sell or lease without a month's notice demanding payment and default thereon. And although a tenancy may be created by sufficient words in the mortgage deed, it will not be allowed where the effect would be inconsistent with the general object of the deed (d).

Where the mortgagor is tenant to the mortgagee the nature of the tenancy will depend upon the language and intention of the deed. The reservation of a yearly rent will not necessarily create a tenancy from year to year. A covenant for quiet enjoyment by the mortgagor, as tenant at will to the mortgagee, on payment of a yearly rent, will create only a tenancy at will at a yearly rent, though coupled with a proviso that no possession shall be taken till the expiration of twelve months after notice of such intention to the mortgagor, no certain term being thereby created (e). And an agreement by the mortgagor to become tenant during the will and pleasure of the mortgagee at a rent payable on certain days in every year, will also create a tenancy at will, with rent payable at the rate of so much a year (f). The same effect has been said to be produced by a power for the mortgagee to enter at any time without notice, although the tenancy was nominally created for a term of years (g).

Where the mortgagor is tenant at will he cannot determine the tenancy by transferring his interest to another, without notice to the mortgagee (h), but the death of the mortgagor determines it and his successor is not tenant to the mortgagee (i). And it seems that a tenancy at will which existed before the mortgage will not be determined by the mortgage (k).

Attornment.—A tenancy is also created where the mortgagor, being in occupation, attorns tenant to the mortgagee. The nature and purpose of an attornment clause have already been dealt with (l). It is sufficient to state here that the tenancy created, while artificial in some respects, e.g., it is not a tenancy protected by the Rent Acts, may nevertheless have a use and it is in any case commonly inserted in mortgage deeds. The type of tenancy created will depend on the terms of the mortgage deed.

Ejectment notwithstanding tenancy.—Notwithstanding the existence of apt words for the creation of a tenancy the mortgagee may retain his ordinary power of ejectment *qua* mortgagee, if his ordinary rights are reserved (m). When the mortgagee, having covenanted not to take possession until default is made, seeks possession before

---

(c) *Doe d. Parsley* v. *Day* (1842), 2 Q.B. 147; and see *Clowes* v. *Hughes* (1870), L. R. 5 Exch. 160.

(d) *Walker* v. *Giles* (1848), 6 C.B. 662; *Pinhorn* v. *Souster* (1853), 8 Ex. 763; *Thorn* v. *Croft* (1866), L.R. 3 Eq. 193.

(e) *Doe d. Dixie* v. *Davies* (1851), 7 Exch. 89.

(f) *Doe d. Bastow* v. *Cox* (1847), 11 Q.B. 122.

(g) *Morton* v. *Woods* (1869), L.R. 4 Q.B. 293; but see *Re Threlfall, Ex parte Queen's Benefit Building Society* (1880), 16 Ch. D. 274.

(h) *Pinhorn* v. *Souster, supra.*

(i) *Scobie* v. *Collins*, [1895] 1 Q.B. 375.

(k) *Doe d. Goody* v. *Carter* (1847), 9 Q.B. 863.

(l) See p. 34, *supra.*

(m) *Doe d. Garrod* v. *Olley* (1840), 12 A. & E. 481; *Doe d. Snell* v. *Tom* (1843), 4 Q.B. 615.

default it is possible that an order for delivery of possession might be
refused to the mortgagee on the ground that his covenant operated to
estop him from asserting his legal right to possession. If the court
considered that the mortgagee was, in spite of his covenant, still entitled
to possession, the mortgagor would presumably be entitled to damages
for breach of covenant (*n*).

Liability of mortgagor in possession.—While in possession the
mortgagor may not diminish the security so as to make it insufficient.
Waste, for example, by felling timber or pulling down a house, or other
conduct which would prejudice the security, will be restrained by
injunction (*o*).

III—TENANCY BEFORE THE MORTGAGE

Reversion vests in the mortgagee.—A lease by the mortgagor
made before the mortgage is binding on the mortgagee (*p*). Under
former freehold mortgages the entire reversion in the land subject to
the lease passed to the mortgagee, and with it the right to receive the
future rents, and the other rights incident to the estate which
theretofore belonged to the mortgagor (*q*). The position remains the
same now that the mortgage is made by demise or legal charge, for the
mortgage operates as a concurrent lease and carries the reversion upon
the existing term with the rights (*r*) and the liabilities incident thereto (*s*).
The tenant may nevertheless safely pay the rent to the mortgagor,
provided it is rent due and not a payment in anticipation on account
of rent (*t*), so long as he is allowed by the mortgagee to receive it, for
although the assurance is effective as to the mortgagee's rights against
the tenant, without an attornment by the latter, the tenant is not
prejudiced by payment of the rent to the mortgagor, nor does he
thereby incur liability for breach of any covenant for non-payment of
rent before notice of the mortgage (*u*). But if he pays rent to the
mortgagor after notice to pay to the mortgagee and is afterwards
compelled to pay the latter, the payment, being voluntary, cannot

---

(*n*) *Doe d. Parlsey* v. *Day* (1842), 2 Q.B. 147.
(*o*) See p. 267, *supra*.
(*p*) *Moss* v. *Gallimore* (1779), 1 Doug. K.B. 279, at p. 283. Where a tenancy is binding
on a mortgagee he is an owner for the purpose of the Rent Act 1965, s. 32 (protection
from eviction without due process of law): see *Bolton Building Society* v. *Cobb*, [1965]
3 All E.R. 814.
(*q*) *Rogers* v. *Humphreys* (1835), 4 A. & E. 299, 314; *Trent* v. *Hunt* (1853), 9 Exch. 14.
Arrears of rent do not pass without express words: *Salmon* v. *Dean* (1851), 3 Mac. & G.
344.
(*r*) *Neale* v. *Mackenzie* (1836), 1 M. & W. 747; *Harmer* v. *Bean* (1853), 3 Car. & K.
307. See Law of Property Act 1925, s. 141, p. 336, *infra*.
(*s*) Law of Property Act 1925, s. 142 (1), replacing 32 Hen. 8, c. 34 (1540) (Grantees
of Reversions), s. 2, and the Conveyancing Act 1881, s. 11 (1).
(*t*) *De Nicholls* v. *Saunders* (1870), L.R. 5 C.P. 589; *Cook* v. *Guerra* (1872), L.R. 7 C.P.
132. But if at the time of the mortgage he has paid rent in a lump sum in advance
under an arrangement with the mortgagor, this binds the mortgagee, since he should
inquire as to the terms on which the tenant holds: *Green* v. *Rheinberg* (1911), 104 L.T.
149; *Grace Rymer Investments, Ltd.* v. *Waite*, [1958] Ch. 831 (C.A.), at p. 847; [1958]
2 All E.R. 777, at pp. 781, 782.
(*u*) Law of Property Act 1925, s. 151 (1).

afterwards be recovered from the mortgagor (*x*). If the mortgagee goes into possession and gives notice to the tenant, the tenant cannot set off against the rent a personal claim he has against the mortgagor (*y*). If the mortgagor himself is in possession of the mortgaged property under a lease made to him before the mortgage, he is not estopped from setting up the lease merely because in a conveyance of the legal estate in fee simple of the mortgaged property it was recited that he was seised in unincumbered fee simple in possession (*z*).

Mortgagor's right to sue.—Before the mortgagee has taken possession, the mortgagor has a statutory right to sue in his own name for possession or damages for trespass. The Law of Property Act 1925, provides as follows:

> **98.**—(1) (*a*) A mortgagor for the time being entitled to the possession or receipt of the rents and profits of any land, as to which the mortgagee has not given notice of his intention to take possession or to enter into the receipt of the rents and profits thereof, may sue for such possession, or for the recovery of such rents or profits, or to prevent or recover damages in respect of any trespass or other wrong relative thereto, in his own name only, unless the cause of action arises upon a lease or other contract made by him jointly with another person.
>
> (2) This section does not prejudice the power of a mortgagor independently of this section to take proceedings in his own name only, either in right of any legal estate vested in him or otherwise.
>
> (3) This section applies whether the mortgage was made before or after the commencement of this Act.

This provision, however, only means that, so long as the mortgagor is allowed to remain in possession, he may recover the rents, and as against trespassers may recover possession or obtain an injunction without joining the mortgagee (*b*). It does not mean that he can do things which might prejudicially affect the mortgagee's interests. Thus, it does not enable him to forfeit a lease under a power of the re-entry for a breach of covenant (*c*), or to enforce a right which would involve the taking of accounts in which the mortgagee is interested (*d*). If in any such case the mortgagee refuses to be a plaintiff, he may be made a defendant; but in that case, it seems, the mortgagor must offer to redeem (*e*).

The above provision does not enable the mortgagor to sue on the covenants in the lease, but he can do so under s. 141 of the Law of Property Act 1925, which entitles him to enforce the covenants so long as he is in receipt of the income of the land leased. Rent reserved by a lease and the benefit of every covenant or provision therein contained, having reference to the subject matter thereof, and on the lessee's part to be observed or performed, and every condition of

---

(*x*) *Higgs* v. *Scott* (1849), 7 C.B. 63.
(*y*) *Reeves* v. *Pope*, [1914] 2 K.B. 284.
(*z*) *District Bank, Ltd.* v. *Webb*, [1958] 1 All E.R. 126.
(*a*) This replaces s. 25 (5) of the Judicature Act 1873.
(*b*) *Fairclough* v. *Marshall* (1878), 4 Ex. D. 37.
(*c*) *Matthews* v. *Usher*, [1900] 2 Q.B. 535; see *Molyneux* v. *Richard*, [1906] 1 Ch. 34.
(*d*) *Van Gelder, Apsimon & Co.* v. *Sowerby Bridge United District Flour Society* (1890), 44 Ch. D. 374 (C.A.), at p. 392.
(*e*) See *Hughes* v. *Cook* (1865), 34 Beav. 407.

re-entry and other condition therein contained, is annexed and incident to and goes with the reversionary estate in the land, or in any part thereof, immediately expectant on the term granted by the lease, notwithstanding severance of that reversionary estate, and without prejudice to any liability affecting a covenantor or his estate (*f*). Any such rent, covenant or provision is capable of being recovered, received, enforced, and taken advantage of, by the person from time to time entitled to the income of the whole or any part, as the case may require, of the land leased (*g*). Where that person becomes entitled by conveyance or otherwise, such rent, covenant or provision may be recovered, received, enforced or taken advantage of by him, notwithstanding that he becomes so entitled after the condition of re-entry or forfeiture has become enforceable; but this sub-section does not render enforceable any condition of re-entry or other condition waived or released before such person becomes entitled as aforesaid (*h*). Section 141 of the Law of Property Act 1925, applies to leases made before or after the commencement of that Act, but does not affect the operation of (a) any severance of the reversionary estate; or (b) any acquisition by conveyance or otherwise of the right to receive or enforce any rent, covenant, or provision; effected before the commencement of the Act (*i*).

Notice of mortgage to tenant.—If the mortgagee takes possession or gives notice (*k*) to the tenant holding under a tenancy prior to the mortgage, his title relates back to the date when his right first accrued. Thus, he can sue a trespasser for a trespass committed before he took possession (*l*); and he becomes entitled to and may distrain or sue for, the rent in arrear since the mortgage, and also for that which subsequently accrues (*m*); and this is so whether the tenant holds under a lease, or from year to year. And he may sue a tenant, claiming under an agreement for a lease made by the mortgagor, for use and occupation (*n*); and he may do so though, after the mortgage, the terms of the holding have, by agreement between the tenant and the mortgagor, been varied so as to increase the rent, such an agreement being considered not to alter the relative positions of the mortgagee and the tenant, but to be adopted by the former as the act of an agent,

---

(*f*) Section 141 (1). The reference in the sub-section to the severance of the reversionary estate suggests that the provision was aimed primarily at the difficulties formerly caused by such severance. But while this is one effect, the sub-section is not restricted to cases of severance and it enables a mortgagor in possession to sue in his own name on the covenants in the lease whether the lease is by deed or not, and whether made before or after the commencement of the Act: see *Turner* v. *Walsh*, [1909] 2 K.B. 484 (C.A.).

(*g*) *Ibid.*, sub-s. (2). Sub-sections (1) and (2) reproduce s. 10 (1) of the Conveyancing Act 1881, with the addition at the end of sub-s. (1) of the words "and without prejudice to any liability affecting a covenantor or his estate". Like provision, but somewhat restricted, was made by the Grantees of Reversions 1540. These earlier Acts are repealed.

(*h*) *Ibid.*, sub-s. (3). This reproduces s. 2 of the Conveyancing Act 1911.

(*i*) *Ibid.*, sub-s. (4).

(*k*) He cannot charge as mortgagee's costs for the expense of drafting more than one notice, however many tenants there may be: *Re Tweedie* (1908), 53 Sol. Jo. 118.

(*l*) *Ocean Accident and Guarantee Corpn.* v. *Ilford Gas Co.*, [1905] 2 K.B. 493 (C.A.).

(*m*) *Moss* v. *Gallimore* (1779), 1 Doug. K.B. 279.

(*n*) *Rawson* v. *Eicke* (1837), 7 A. & E. 451.

and to entitle him to recover the additional as well as the original rent (*o*). The mortgagor, after the mortgagee has taken possession, has no remedy against the tenant in respect of rent alleged to be due from him (*p*), even where the mortgagee has refused to apply for it (*q*). In the latter case, his only remedy is against the mortgagee on taking the accounts.

Rent of furnished house.—As to property to which the mortgagee has no claim (as furniture in a mortgaged house, which has become vested in the mortgagor's assignees in bankruptcy), if the tenant of a house and furniture, after notice from the mortgagee pays him the whole rent, then the tenant may be sued again for the use of the furniture in which the mortgagee had no interest; for either the rent may be apportioned, or, upon the entry of the mortgagee, a new agreement may be inferred, for the letting of the different kinds of property at several rents (*r*).

Leases granted by prospective purchasers.—If a person purports to grant a lease of land in which he has no legal estate he is estopped from repudiating the tenancy. If the lessor later acquires the legal estate in the land, the estoppel is fed and the tenancy becomes a legal tenancy. This matter is dealt with subsequently (*s*)

IV—TENANCY AFTER THE MORTGAGE

Lease by mortgagor.—The mortgagor, being unable to confer upon another a greater right than he himself possesses, his tenant claiming under a lease made after the mortgage, without the privity of the mortgagee, was, and in cases outside s. 99 of the Law of Property Act 1925 (*t*), still remains—like his lessor, liable to be ejected (*u*) without notice, and he has no remedy except against the mortgagor (*x*).

(*o*) *Burrowes* v. *Gradin* (1843), 1 Dowl. & L. 213.
(*p*) *Underhay* v. *Read* (1887), 36 W.R. 75, affd. 36 W.R. 298, and 20 Q.B.D. 209.
(*q*) *Salmon* v. *Dean* (1849), 14 Jur. 235; see, on app. (1851), 3 Mac. & G. 344.
(*r*) *Salmon* v. *Matthews* (1841), 8 M. & W. 827; see *Hoare (Charles) & Co.* v. *Hove Bungalows, Ltd.* (1912), 56 Sol. Jo. 686.
(*s*) See p. 340, *infra*.   (*t*) See p. 342, *infra*.
(*u*) See, *e.g.*, *Dudley and District Benefit Building Society* v. *Emerson*, [1949] Ch. 707 (C.A.); [1949] 2 All E.R. 252; *Parker* v. *Braithwaite*, [1952] 2 All E.R. 837; *Taylor* v. *Ellis*, [1960] Ch. 368; [1960] 1 All E.R. 549; *Stroud Building Society* v. *Delamont*, [1960] 1 All E.R. 749; *Baring Brothers & Co., Ltd.* v. *Hovermarine, Ltd.* (1971), 219 Estates Gazette 1450. Unless he redeems the mortgage: *Barclay's Bank, Ltd.* v. *Stasek*, [1957] Ch. 28; [1956] 2 All E.R. 439.
(*x*) *Keech* v. *Hall* (1778), 1 Doug. K.B. 21; *Rogers* v. *Humphreys* (1835), 4 A. & F. 299; *Trent* v. *Hunt* (1853), 9 Exch. 14. *United Starr-Bowkett Co-operative Building Society (No. 11), Ltd.* v. *Clyne* (1967), 68 S.R. N.S.W. 331, 338. Such a lease is binding on the mortgagor by estoppel: *Cuthbertson* v. *Irving* (1859), 4 H. & N. 742; but see *Lewis & Son, Ltd.* v. *Morelli*, [1948] 2 All E.R. 1021 (C.A.), and the tenant is estopped from disputing the mortgagor's title. The mortgagor's power to grant a lease binding between himself and the tenant is not affected by the statutory leasing provisions (as to which, see p. 341, *infra*): *Iron Trades Employers Insurance Association, Ltd.* v. *Union Land and House Investors, Ltd.*, [1937] Ch. 313; [1937] 1 All E.R. 481. A tenant under such a lease does not obtain the benefit of the Rent Acts: *Dudley and District Benefit Building Society* v. *Emerson, supra*; whether a statutory tenant can claim the protection of the Acts was left open; *Bolton Building Society* v. *Cobb*, [1965] 3 All E.R. 814; *Jessamine Investment Co.* v. *Schwartz*, [1976] 3 All E.R. 521 (C.A.); *Moore Properties (Ilford), Ltd.* v. *McKeon*, [1977] 1 All E.R. 262. Such a lessee is entitled to redeem the mortgage: *Tarn* v. *Turner* (1888), 57 L.J. Ch. 452; affd. 39 Ch. D. 456 (C.A.).

There are, however, two cases in which the tenancy will be effective against the mortgagee, namely if he treats the tenant as his own and in the case of a mortgage of agricultural land.

New tenancy under mortgagee.—The mortgagee may treat the mortgagor's tenant as his own. Until the relation of landlord and tenant has been established between the mortgagee and the occupier the mortgagee cannot distrain or bring an action for rent and he is not entitled to arrears of rent due at the date of his taking possession (*y*). But if the mortgagee recognises the occupier as his own tenant, he cannot afterwards treat him as a trespasser (*z*).

Neither a mere notice to the tenant, requiring him to pay rent to the mortgagee, without an attornment or other evidence of consent by the tenant, nor an authority to him from the mortgagor to pay rent to the mortgagee, though communicated to and acted upon by the tenant, would make him the tenant of the mortgagee, or entitle the latter to distrain for the subsequent rent (*a*); and a subsequent attornment by the tenant would not set up the mortgagee's title by relation from the time at which a previous notice was given (*b*). Nor was the change of tenancy established only by proof of payment of interest, as such, by the person in possession of the land (*c*). But it was held to be effected if the mortgagee, or his agent, called on the mortgagor's tenant to pay, and he actually paid, the interest of the mortgagee instead of rent to the mortgagor (*d*). Actual payment of rent to the mortgagee will create a tenancy between the tenant and the mortgagee (*e*). Such tenancy will usually be a yearly or periodic one and not necessarily on the terms of the old tenancy (*f*).

Estoppel in favour of mortgagor.—Although the lease made after the mortgage was thus void against the mortgagee, yet, since the tenant would not dispute his landlord's title, the lease was good against the mortgagor until the mortgagee interfered (*g*). And the tenant's

---

(*y*) See the cases referred to in footnote (*c*), p. 348, *infra*.

(*z*) *Birch* v. *Wright* (1786), 1 Term. Rep. 378. For the effect of the recognition is not to set up the lease made by the mortgagor, but to create a new tenancy: *Corbett* v. *Plowden* (1884), 25 Ch. D. 678 (C.A.), 681, 682. Where the tenancy of a dwelling-house is effective against the mortgagee, s. 32 of the Rent Act 1965, may apply: see p. 335, *supra*, footnote (*p*).

(*a*) *Evans* v. *Elliot* (1838), 9 A. & E. 342; *Towerson* v. *Jackson*, [1891] 2 Q.B. 484 (C.A.).

(*b*) *Evans* v. *Elliot, supra.*

(*c*) *Doe d. Rogers* v. *Cadwallader* (1831), 2 B. & Ad. 473.

(*d*) *Doe d. Whitaker* v. *Hales* (1831), 7 Bing. 322. As to evidence of the recognition of the tenancy, see *Keech* v. *Hall* (1778), 1 Dougl. 21; *Smith* v. *Eggington* (1874), L.R. 9 C.P. 145. As to a lease contemporaneously with the mortgage, see *Rogers* v. *Humphreys* (1835), 4 A. & E. 299. And see *Kitchen's Trustee* v. *Madders*, [1949] Ch. 588; [1949] 2 All E.R. 54.

(*e*) *Keith* v. *R. Gancia & Co., Ltd.*, [1904] 1 Ch. 774 (C.A.); *Parker* v. *Braithwaite*, [1952] 2 All E.R. 837; *Stroud Building Society* v. *Delamont*, [1960] 1 All E.R. 749; *Chatsworth Properties, Ltd.* v. *Effiom*, [1971] 1 All E.R. 604 (C.A.); *Baring Brothers & Co., Ltd.* v. *Hovermarine, Ltd.* (1971), 219 Estates Gazette 1450. See (1976) 120 S.J. 497 (Henry E. Markson).

(*f*) *Keith* v. *R. Gancia & Co., Ltd., supra.*

(*g*) *Trent* v. *Hunt* (1853), 9 Exch. 14. After the mortgagee has obtained payment of the rent, the tenant, in defending himself against a subsequent action by the mortgagor, was still not allowed to deny the mortgagor's title. He must admit it and then show that it had been determined and that he had been compelled to make the payment to the mortgagee: *Underhay* v. *Read* (1887), 20 Q.B.D. 209 (C.A.).

interest by estoppel might be converted into a lease in interest by the consent of the mortgagee; so that a purchaser from the mortgagor, making a conveyance in which the mortgagee concurred, would have a remedy against the lessee on his covenants (h). The mortgagor's interest by estoppel also passed by descent to his heir, and by purchase to an assignee who might sue the tenant on the covenants in the lease (i). But there was no estoppel where the lease disclosed that the land was mortgaged, and that the lessor had only an equity of redemption. The lessee's covenants were then only in gross and could not be sued upon by the assignee of the mortgagor (k).

Mortgages of agricultural land.—As previously stated (l) the statutory powers of leasing (m) cannot be excluded in the case of a mortgage of agricultural land made after 1 March, 1948 (n). Accordingly a mortgagee of agricultural land can now make leases after the mortgage which will be binding on the mortgagee. In the case of mortgages of agricultural land created before that date, where the mortgagor has made a lease, from year to year or for a fixed term not exceeding twenty-one years, at a rack rent, which is not binding on the mortgagee, the mortgagee must normally give the tenant six months' written notice before he deprives him of possession (o). And the tenant, on being deprived of possession by the mortgagee, is entitled to compensation for crops and for expenditure on any unexhausted improvement made in the expectation of remaining for the full term of the tenancy. Any sum due to the tenant for compensation may be withheld from the rent payable by him, and, if not withheld, made a charge on the land, but cannot be recovered from the mortgagee personally (p).

Feeding the estoppel (q).—It not uncommonly happens that a purchaser of land after contract, but before completion, will purport to grant a lease of the land he has agreed to purchase. This creates a tenancy by estoppel. The "lessor" is estopped from repudiating the tenancy and the "tenant" is estopped from denying its existence (r). On completion the estoppel created by the grant is fed by the legal interest acquired by the purchaser on conveyance and the tenancy becomes a legal tenancy (s).

(h) *Webb* v. *Austin* (1844), 7 Man. & G. 701.

(i) *Cuthbertson* v. *Irving* (1860), 4 H. & N. 742.

(k) *Pargeter* v. *Harris* (1845), 7 Q.B. 708; *Saunders* v. *Merryweather* (1865), 3 H. & C. 902. But *cf. Morton* v. *Woods* (1869), L. R. 4 Q.B. 293, at p. 303, referring to *Jolly* v. *Arbuthnot* (1859), 4 De G. & J. 224.

(l) See p. 127, *supra*.

(m) See p. 360, *infra*.

(n) Agricultural Holdings Act 1948, s. 95, Sched. 7, para. 2.

(o) *Ibid.*, s. 66.

(p) *Ibid.*, s. 74. See generally, Ch. 10, *supra*.

(q) See generally, (1964) 80 L.Q.R. 370 (A. M. Prichard).

(r) See *Cuthbertson* v. *Irving* (1859), 4 H. & N. 742; *Iron Trades Employers Insurance Association, Ltd.* v. *Union Land and House Investors, Ltd.*, [1937] Ch. 313; [1937] 1 All E.R. 481. See p. 339, *supra*.

(s) *Webb* v. *Austin* (1844), 7 Man. & G. 701, 724. For a scheme to avoid the possibility of a tenant gaining priority to the mortgagee, see 14 Ency. Forms and Precedents (4th Edn.), pp. 388–390 (demise to lender by vendor by the direction of the purchaser followed by conveyance by the vendor to the purchaser). See also (1954).

Where the purchase is made with the assistance of an advance on mortgage, although the conveyance and mortgage may, and often will, be executed simultaneously, there are two separate transactions (*t*). The conveyance must precede the mortgage for a short period of time, for the purchaser-mortgagor must have the legal estate vested in him free from the mortgage for the mortgage to be effective. This moment of time is sufficient to feed the estoppel created by the grant of the tenancy, with the result that the lease is binding on the mortgagee even if the mortgage excludes the statutory power of leasing. This doctrine applies where there has been a valid grant (*u*) at a time when the purchaser-mortgagor has some interest in the property (*x*). The doctrine does not seem to apply where both the mortgage and the tenancy have been granted before completion (*y*).

But the tenant may lose priority to the mortgagee if he is party to any deception or defrauding of the mortgagee (*z*).

The position is similar in the case of registered land, save that in that case the mortgagee is also bound where a tenant has taken possession under an agreement for a lease, because on completion the tenant's interest constitutes an overriding interest (*a*) to which the mortgage is subject (*b*).

Statutory power of leasing.—The inconvenience, in the absence of express provision in the deed (*c*), of neither the mortgagor nor the mortgagee alone being able to make a lease which would be valid against the other, was remedied by s.18 of the Conveyancing Act 1881, which is now replaced by s. 99 of the Law of Property Act 1925. The section provides that, if and so far as a contrary intention is not expressed in the mortgage deed, or otherwise in writing, and subject to the terms

---

18 Conv. (N.S.) 723. And *cf.* (1957), 101 Sol. Jo. 438, 439, 822-824 (L.H.E.) (where reliance is placed on the transfer to the mortgagee of the vendor's lien (as to the vendor's lien, see p. 166, *supra*, and as to the loss of the lien, see p. 590, *infra*)). The safest course, but one practically impossible, is to inspect the premises before completion. For a form of warranty by the mortgagor that he is in personal occupation, see Hallett's *Conveyancing Precedents*, 608 and the note thereto.

(*t*) *Church of England Building Society* v. *Piskor*, [1954] Ch. 553 (C.A.); [1954] 2 All E.R. 85; *Grace Rymer Investments, Ltd.* v. *Waite*, [1958] Ch. 831 (C.A.); [1958] 2 All E.R. 777; *Capital Finance Co., Ltd.* v. *Stokes*, [1969] Ch. 261 (C.A.); [1968] 3 All E.R. 625; *Security Trust Co.* v. *Royal Bank of Canada*, [1976] A.C. 503; [1976] 1 All E.R. 381 (P.C.).

(*u*) An agreement for a lease will only bind the mortgagee in these circumstances if registered as an estate contract under the Land Charges Act 1972: see *Universal Permanent Building Society* v. *Cooke*, [1952] Ch. 95 (C.A.), at p. 104; [1951] 2 All E.R. 893, at p. 898. See also *Coventry Permanent Economic Building Society* v. *Jones*, [1951] 1 All E.R. 901.

(*x*) *Hughes* v. *Waite*, [1957] 1 All E.R. 603; *City Permanent Building Society* v. *Miller*, [1952] Ch. 840 (C.A.); [1952] 2 All E.R. 621. And see *Grace Rymer Investments, Ltd.* v. *Waite, supra*.

(*y*) *Rust* v. *Goodale*, [1957] Ch. 33; [1956] 3 All E.R. 373. At least where the mortgage precedes the tenancy and the tenant has notice, by registration, of the mortgage. And see (1956), 20 Conv. (N.S.) 444 (F. R. Crane).

(*z*) See *Church of England Building Society* v. *Piskor*, [1954] Ch. 553 (C.A.), at pp. 559, 560, 561; [1954] 2 All E.R. 85, at pp. 88, 89.

(*a*) Land Registration Act 1925, ss. 20 (1), 70 (1) (g).

(*b*) *Grace Rymer Investments, Ltd.* v. *Waite, supra*. And see *Webb* v. *Pollmount, Ltd.*, [1966] Ch. 584; [1966] 1 All E.R. 481.

(*c*) *Carpenter* v. *Parker* (1857), 3 C.B. (N.S.) 206.

of the deed or of any such writing, and the provisions therein contained (d), leases may be made as follows:

99.—(1) A mortgagor (e) of land while in possession (f) shall, as against every incumbrancer, have power to make from time to time any such lease of the mortgaged land, or any part thereof (g), as is by this section authorised.

(2) A mortgagee of land while in possession (h) shall, as against all prior incumbrancers, if any, and as against the mortgagor, have power to make from time to time any such lease as aforesaid (i).

(3) The leases which the section authorises are—

> (i) agricultural or occupation (j) leases for any term not exceeding twenty-one years, or, in the case of a mortgage made after the commencement of this Act, fifty years; and

> (ii) building leases (k) for any term not exceeding ninety-nine years, or, in the case of a mortgage made after the commencement of this Act, nine hundred and ninety-nine years.

(4) Every person making a lease under this section may execute and do all assurances and things necessary or proper in that behalf.

(5) Every such lease shall be made to take effect in possession not later than twelve months after its date.

(6) Every such lease shall reserve the best rent that can reasonably be obtained, regard being had to the circumstances of the case (l), but without any fine being taken (m).

(d) Section 99 (13). But the statutory power cannot be modified or excluded in a mortgage of agricultural land made after 1 March, 1948: Agricultural Holdings Act 1948, 7th Sched., para. 2. Nor can it be modified or excluded so as to prevent the carrying out of an order for a grant of a new tenancy of business premises: Landlord and Tenant Act 1954, Part II, s. 36 (4). A clause excluding the statutory leasing powers does not deprive the mortgagor of his power of creating a lease valid as between himself and the tenant by estoppel: *Iron Trades Employers Insurance Association, Ltd.* v. *Union Land and House Investors, Ltd.,* [1937] Ch. 313; [1937] 1 All E.R. 481; *Rust* v. *Goodale,* [1957] Ch. 33; [1957] 3 All E.R. 373; *Bolton Building Society* v. *Cobb,* [1965] 3 All E.R. 814. A mortgagor who has bound himself not to exercise the statutory power of leasing cannot authorise a second mortgagee to do so. Section 99 does not confer on a mortgagee rights which the mortgagor does not himself have: see *Julian S. Hodge & Co., Ltd.* v. *St. Helen's Credit, Ltd.* (1965), Estates Gazette Digest 143.

(e) For the purposes of this and the next section only "mortgagor" does not include an "incumbrancer" deriving title under the original mortgagor (sub-s. (18) and s. 100 (12), that is, a subsequent incumbrancer: *cf.* s. 205 (1) (xvi)).

(f) A prospective purchaser, who is also a prospective mortgagor, is not in possession: *Hughes* v. *Waite,* [1957] 1 All E.R. 603.

(g) *Rhodes* v. *Dalby,* [1971] 2 All E.R. 1144, was a case where a part of premises was involved.

(h) This includes in receipt of rents and profits: Law of Property Act 1925, s. 205 (1) (xix). If the mortgagor is in possession he has the statutory powers (unless they are excluded) to the exclusion of the mortgagee and *vice versa*: see *Meah* v. *Mouskos,* [1964] 2 Q.B. 23 (C.A.), at p. 40; [1963] 3 All E.R. 908, at p. 914.

(i) A mortgagee (which expression includes a legal chargee: Law of Property Act 1925, s. 205 (1) (xvi)) who has appointed a receiver under his statutory powers can exercise the powers of leasing as if he were in possession; and may by writing delegate any of the powers to the receiver: sub-s. (19). Leases may be granted under the statute in the name of the estate owner: s. 8 (1). A legal chargee has no legal estate in the mortgaged property and must grant a lease under s. 8. The immediate reversion on such a lease is in the chargor, not the chargee: see *Weg Motors, Ltd.* v. *Hales,* [1961] Ch. 176, at pp. 194, 195; [1960] 3 All E.R. 762, at pp. 771, 772; affd., [1962] Ch. 49 (C.A.); [1961] 3 All E.R. 181.

(j) The inclusion in the lease of chattels and sporting rights over other land comprised in the mortgage, but not in the lease, does not take a lease out of the description of "an occupation lease": *Brown* v. *Peto,* [1900] 2 Q.B. 653.

(k) *I.e.,* the lessee must be obliged to erect, improve or repair buildings on the land within five years. As to building leases, see sub-ss. (9), (10).

(l) *Coutts & Co.* v. *Somerville,* [1935] Ch. 438.

(m) The rent must be paid annually or oftener. A lump sum for future years will not do: *Municipal Permanent Investment Building Society* v. *Smith* (1888), 22 Q.B.D. 70

(7) Every such lease shall contain a covenant by the lessee for payment of the rent, and a condition of re-entry on the rent not being paid within a time therein specified not exceeding thirty days (*n*).

(8) A counterpart of every such lease shall be executed by the lessee and delivered to the lessor, of which execution and delivery the execution of the lease by the lessor shall, in favour of the lessee and all persons deriving title under him, be sufficient evidence (*o*).

Where a lease fails to comply with the above terms, if it was made in good faith and the lessee has entered thereunder, it takes effect in equity as a contract for the grant, at the request of the lessee, of a valid lease of like effect as the invalid lease, subject to such variations as may be necessary in order to comply with the terms of the power (*p*).

The mortgagor and mortgagee may, by agreement in writing, whether or not contained in the mortgage deed, reserve to or confer on either party, or both, any further or other powers of leasing or having reference to leasing, but without prejudice to the rights of other mortgagees, and these will be exercisable, so far as may be, as if they were conferred by the Act (*q*).

Restrictions on or exclusion of statutory powers.—In practice, the mortgagor's powers of leasing under the section are generally restricted or excluded by the mortgage deed (*r*). If not excluded, it is usual that the consent of the mortgagee is required before the statutory

---

(C.A.); *Green* v. *Rheinberg* (1911), 104 L.T. 149 (C.A.); *Rust* v. *Goodale*, [1957] Ch. 33; [1956] 3 All E.R. 373; *Hughes* v. *Waite*, [1957] 1 All E.R. 603; *Grace Rymer Investments, Ltd.* v. *Waite*, [1958] Ch. 831 (C.A.); [1958] 2 All E.R. 777. *Quaere* whether the rent can be left to be fixed by a valuer later: *Lloyds Bank, Ltd.* v. *Marcan*, [1973] 3 All E.R. 745, at p. 761.

(*n*) It seems that a condition of re-entry is not required in the case of an oral tenancy agreement. See *Rhodes* v. *Dalby*, [1971] 2 All E.R. 1144; *cf. Pawson* v. *Revell*, [1958] 2 Q.B. 360 (C.A.); [1958] 3 All E.R. 233. And see Wolstenholme and Cherry, *Conveyancing Statutes* (13th Edn.), vol. 1, p. 198.

(*o*) In the case of a lease by the mortgagor, he shall, within one month after making the lease deliver to the mortgagee, or, where there are more than one, to the mortgagee first in priority, a counterpart of the lease duly executed by the lessee, but the lessee shall not be concerned to see that this is complied with: sub-s. (11). The provision that the lessee shall not be concerned to see that the provision for delivery of the counterpart lease is complied with applies also to a lease granted under an extended statutory power: *Public Trustee* v. *Lawrence*, [1912] 1 Ch. 789. Failure to deliver a counterpart to the mortgagee does not invalidate the lease, although it would cause the statutory power of the sale to become immediately exercisable: *Public Trustee* v. *Lawrence, supra*. The provisions of the section referring to a lease shall be construed to extend and apply, as far as circumstances admit, to any letting, and to an agreement whether in writing or not for leasing or letting: sub-s. (17); but the provision as to a counterpart lease does not apply to an oral tenancy: *Rhodes* v. *Dalby, supra; cf. Pawson* v. *Revell, supra*.

(*p*) Law of Property Act 1925, s. 152 (1). See *Pawson* v. *Revell, supra; Rhodes* v. *Dalby, supra*; (1971), 87 L.Q.R. 338 (D. W. Elliott).

(*q*) Sub-section (14).

(*r*) It is so common that the Northern Ireland Land Law Working Party (see p. 5, note (*q*), *supra*) proposed that any new provision in N.I. should be to the effect that any lease granted by the mortgagor would not be binding on the mortgagee unless made with his consent. The exclusion of the mortgagor's powers are more important since the Lease-hold Reform Act 1967. It is also particularly important in the case of building leases. Without a check on the statutory powers there would be nothing to prevent a reckless mortgagor from making the security valueless by granting building leases to persons of insufficient means and throwing the property upon the mortgagee's hands covered with half-finished buildings. For forms of modification of the statutory power, see 14 Ency. Forms and Precedents (4th Edn.), pp. 141 *et seq.*; and Precedent 1, *infra*. As to the extent of the restriction, see *Westbourne Park Building Society* v. *Levermore*, [1955] C.L.Y. 1703.

powers are exercised (s). If the mortgage permits the mortgagor to exercise the statutory leasing powers with the consent of the mortgagee, the onus is on the lessee to prove that the mortgagee gave his consent (t). If the mortgage deed provides that an intending lessee shall not be concerned to inquire as to such consent the mortgagee is estopped from denying the lease was made with his consent (u). Furthermore, if a lease is made without consent and the mortgagee then accepts the lessee as his own, the lease will be binding on him (v). Besides restricting or excluding the statutory powers it is not uncommon for the deed to expressly exclude all powers of leasing, though, of course, leases not made under statutory or express powers would not generally be binding on the mortgagee anyway, or for the mortgagor to covenant not to grant any lease without the mortgagee's consent. And the clause is usually extended to cover any parting with possession (w).

Extension of statutory powers.—The statutory powers are only exercisable by a mortgagee when he is in possession (x). Accordingly the mortgage deed may provide not only that the statutory powers of leasing shall not be exercisable by the mortgagor, but that such powers may be exercised by the mortgagee without going into possession (y).

The statutory leasing powers are fairly restrictive, in particular they do not permit the taking of premiums (z). In suitable cases, as in the mortgage of a building development, the mortgagee's powers of leasing should be extended so as to enable him to grant leases at ground rents taking a premium (a).

Registered land and charges.—The proprietor of the land, while in possession, has all the powers of leasing and of accepting surrenders of leases conferred by ss. 99 and 100 of the Law of Property Act 1925, as extended by the instrument of charge or any instrument varying the terms thereof, but subject to any contrary intention expressed in any such instrument, a note of which intention shall, under an application to be made for that purpose, be entered in the register (b).

The proprietor of the charge, while in possession, or after a receiver has been appointed, or such receiver on his behalf, has all the powers

---

(s) And if consent is not obtained there will be a breach of the terms of the mortgage. Where there is a provision that the statutory power shall not be exercised without the mortgagee's consent and the mortgagor leases without consent such lease is a lease outside the statute and there is therefore no breach of the above-mentioned provision: *Iron Trades Employers Insurance Association, Ltd.* v. *Union Land and House Investors, Ltd., supra* (unless, as is usually the case nowadays, the mortgage expressly makes it a breach). And this is not a defective exercise of the statutory power which the Law of Property Act 1925, s. 152, *supra*, will cure.

(t) *Taylor* v. *Ellis,* [1960] Ch. 368; [1960] 1 All E.R. 549.

(u) *Lever Finance, Ltd.* v. *Needleman's Property Trustee,* [1956] Ch. 375; [1956] 2 All E.R. 378.

(v) *Stroud Building Society* v. *Delamont,* [1960] 1 All E.R. 749. See p. 339, *supra*.

(w) In *Rhodes* v. *Dalby, supra*, a "gentleman's agreement" was not a letting and therefore no breach.

(x) Law of Property Act 1925, s. 99 (2), *supra*.

(y) See 14 Ency. Forms and Precedents (4th Edn.), 142.

(z) See s. 99 (6), *supra*.

(a) See clause in Precedent 1A, p. 684 in the Appendix, *infra*.

(b) Land Registration Rules 1925, r. 141 (1). Land Registration Act 1925, s. 34 (1).

conferred by the above-mentioned sections (as extended as aforesaid), but subject to any contrary intention expressed as aforesaid, a note of which intention shall, under an application to be made for that purpose, be entered in the register (c).

Subject as aforesaid all dispositions by the proprietor of the land authorised by ss. 18 and 21 of the Land Registration Act 1925 (d), shall, unless the proprietor of the charge concurs in the disposition, take effect subject to any charge registered at the time of the disposition (e).

Effect of leases under statutory powers.—A lease granted under s. 99 of the Law of Property Act 1925, has the same effect as if both mortgagor and mortgagee were parties to it, so that if a mortgagor grants such a lease the assignees of the mortgagee cannot obstruct the lessee's lights (f). On the same ground the mortgagee (on default being made by the mortgagor) becomes lessor, and may enforce payment of the rent and performance and observance of the covenants (g). A lease under the statutory power is not invalidated by reason of its containing an option for determination or renewal, but it is invalidated as against the mortgagee by the inclusion of other land not comprised in the mortgage at a single rent (h).

Leases by mortgagor and mortgagee together.—Where the lease is not granted under the statutory or some other power of leasing, both mortgagor and mortgagee should concur, and then, in the case of a mortgage by demise, it will operate as a demise by the mortgagee and a confirmation by the mortgagor (i), and, in the case of a charge by way of legal mortgage, as a demise by the mortgagor and a confirmation by the mortgagee. To make the lessee's covenants run with the reversion, they should be with the owner of the immediate reversion, that is with the mortgagee in the case of a mortgage by demise, but, it would seem, with the mortgagor in the case of a charge by way of legal mortgage (j).

Surrender of lease.—Under the Law of Property Act 1925 (k), a mortgagor or mortgagee in possession may accept a surrender of a lease to enable another lease to be granted (l). The Act provides:

(c) *Ibid.*, r. 141 (2).
(d) Section 18 (powers of disposition of registered freeholds); s. 21 (powers of disposition of registered leaseholds).
(e) Land Registration Rules 1925, r. 141 (4). Rule 141 has effect without prejudice to s. 104 of the Land Registration Act 1925 (protection of leases granted under statutory powers by persons other than registered proprietor and restriction on power): r. 141 (5).
(f) *Wilson* v. *Queen's Club*, [1891] 3 Ch. 522; *Turner* v. *Walsh*, [1909] 2 K.B. 484 (C.A.).
(g) *Municipal, etc., Building Society* v. *Smith* (1888), 22 Q.B.D. 70 (C.A.).
(h) *King* v. *Bird*, [1909] 1 K.B. 837; *cf. Dundas* v. *Vavasour* (1895), 39 Sol. Jo. 656.
(i) *Doe d. Barney* v. *Adams* (1832), 2 Cr. & J. 232. For a form of lease by a concurring mortgagor and mortgagee, see 12 Ency. Forms and Precedents (4th Edn.), pp. 1219–1221.
(j) *Webb* v. *Russell* (1789), 3 Term. Rep. 393.
(k) A surrender of a lease granted under the statutory power could not before the Conveyancing Act 1911, be made to the mortgagor without the joinder of the mortgagee: *Robbins* v. *Whyte*, [1906] 1 K.B. 125. Section 100 of the Law of Property Act 1925, replaces s. 3 of the Conveyancing Act 1911.
(l) *Barclays Bank, Ltd.* v. *Stasek*, [1957] Ch. 28; [1956] 3 All E.R. 439; 73 L.Q.R. 14 (R.E.M.). As to the effect on a surrender of an invalid fresh grant, see *Rhyl U.D.C.* v. *Rhyl Amusements*, [1959] 1 All E.R. 257, at pp. 267, 268.

100.—(1) For the purpose only of enabling a lease authorised under the last preceding section, or under any agreement made pursuant to that section, or by the mortgage deed (in this section referred to as an authorised lease) to be granted, a mortgagor of land while in possession shall, as against every incumbrancer, have, by virtue of this Act, power to accept from time to time a surrender of any lease of the mortgaged land or any part thereof comprised in the lease, with or without an exception of or in respect of all or any of the mines and minerals therein, and, on a surrender of the lease so far as it comprises part only of the land or mines and minerals leased, the rent may be apportioned.

(2) For the same purpose, a mortgagee of land while in possession shall, as against all prior or other incumbrancers, if any, and as against the mortgagor, have, by virtue of this Act, power to accept from time to time any such surrender as aforesaid.

(5) (*m*) No surrender shall, by virtue of this section, be rendered valid unless:—

    (a) An authorised lease is granted of the whole of the land or mines and minerals comprised in the surrender to take effect in possession immediately or within one month after the date of the surrender; and

    (b) The term certain or other interest granted by the new lease is not less in duration than the unexpired term or interest which would have been subsisting under the original lease if that lease had not been surrendered; and

    (c) Where the whole of the land mines and minerals originally leased has been surrendered, the rent reserved by the new lease is not less than the rent which would have been payable under the original lease if it had not been surrendered; or where part only of the land or mines and minerals has been surrendered, the aggregate rents respectively remaining payable or reserved under the original lease and the new lease are not less than the rent which would have been payable under the original lease if no partial surrender had been accepted.

(7) (*n*) This section applies only if and so far as a contrary intention is not expressed by the mortgagor and mortgagee in the mortgage deed, or otherwise in writing, and shall have effect subject to the terms of the mortgage deed or of any such writing and to the provisions therein contained.

(10) (*o*) The mortgagor and mortgagee may, by agreement in writing, whether or not contained in the mortgage deed, reserve or confer on the mortgagor or mortgagee, or both, any further or other powers relating to the surrender of leases; and any further or other powers so conferred or reserved shall be exercisable, as far as may be, as if they were conferred by this Act, and with all the like incidents, effects and consequences:

Provided that the powers so reserved or conferred shall not prejudicially affect the rights of any mortgagee interested under any other mortgage subsisting at the date of the agreement, unless that mortgagee joins in or adopts the agreement.

(*m*) Sub-section (3) deals with variation of the lease on a surrender of part and provides that the value of the lessee's interest shall be taken into account in determining the rent and covenants under the new lease. Sub-section (4) provides that if a consideration is given for the surrender, the consent of prior incumbrancers is required.

(*n*) Sub-section (6) provides that a contract to make or accept a surrender may be enforced by or against every person on whom the surrender, if completed, would be binding.

(*o*) Sub-section (8) applies the section to mortgages made after 31 December, 1911, but the provisions of the section may by agreement in writing made after that date between mortgagor and mortgagee be applied to a mortgage made before that date, without prejudice to the interests of persons not parties to or adopting such agreement. Sub-section (9) extends the provisions of the section to any letting and agreement for a lease.

(12) (*p*) For the purpose of this section "mortgagor" does not include an incumbrancer deriving title under the original mortgagor (*q*).

(13) The powers of accepting surrenders conferred by this section shall, after a receiver of the income of the mortgaged property or any part thereof has been appointed by the mortgagee, under the statutory power, and so long as the receiver acts, be exercisable by such mortgagee instead of by the mortgagor, as respects any land affected by the receivership, in like manner as if such mortgagee were in possession of the land; and the mortgagee may, by writing, delegate any of such powers to the receiver.

V—MORTGAGEE IN POSSESSION

A—RIGHTS OF MORTGAGEE IN POSSESSION

Rents and profits.—The mortgagee in possession as such is entitled to the rents and profits of the mortgaged property by virtue of the legal or equitable ownership which the mortgage confers on him (*r*).

Where the tenancy was created before the mortgage or is otherwise binding on the mortgagee, he will take possession by giving notice to the tenant requesting payment of the rent to himself (*s*), and thereafter he will be entitled to the rents and profits accruing. He may demand payment of all arrears of rent due at the date of his taking possession (*t*), and may claim an increased rent, although the variation effecting the increase had been agreed between the mortgagor and the tenant after the mortgage (*u*). Where rent has been paid in advance to the mortgagor the mortgagee on going into possession may demand payment over again (*x*), unless the payment was made before the mortgage, in which case the payment binds the mortgagee since he should inquire as to the terms on which the tenant holds (*y*). The tenant cannot set off against the rent claimed by the mortgagee in possession a personal claim he had against the mortgagor (*z*).

Where the tenancy is not binding on the mortgagee, as previously stated (*a*), a new tenancy may be created under the mortgagee. Even if this does not occur, after notice from the mortgagee the tenant should pay the rent to the mortgagee, since the mortgagee will in any case be entitled to an equivalent amount as mesne profits (*b*). But the

---

(*p*) Sub-section (11) provides that the statutory powers do not authorise a surrender which could not have been accepted by the mortgagor with the concurrence of all the incumbrancers before 1 January, 1912.

(*q*) A subsequent mortgagee who exercises the statutory powers of leasing and accepting surrenders of leases exercises the powers as mortgagee and not because he derives title under the mortgagor. See note (*f*), p. 345, *supra*.

(*r*) *Cockburn* v. *Edwards* (1881), 18 Ch. D. 449 (C.A.), at p. 457. See Law of Property Act 1925, s. 141 (p. 336, *supra*). Although a legal chargee has no term reversionary to that of the lessee he is in the same position as a mortgagee by demise (see p. 25, *supra*).

(*s*) See pp. 337, 339, *supra*.

(*t*) *Moss* v. *Gallimore* (1779), 1 Doug. K.B. 279; *Rogers* v. *Humphreys* (1835), 4 A. & E. 299, 314.

(*u*) *Burrowes* v. *Gradin* (1843), 1 Dow. & L. 213.

(*x*) *Reeves* v. *Pope*, [1914] 2 K.B. 284 (C.A.).

(*y*) *De Nicholls* v. *Saunders* (1870), L.R. 5 C.P. 589.

(*z*) *Green* v. *Rheinberg* (1911), 104 L.T. 149 (C.A.).

(*a*) See p. 339, *supra*.

(*b*) *Ocean Accident and Guarantee Corpn.* v. *Ilford Gas Co.*, [1905] 2 K.B. 493 (C.A.).

mortgagee is not entitled to arrears of rent under such a tenancy due
at the date of his taking possession (c).

Carrying on of business.—Where the mortgaged property includes
a business carried on upon mortgaged premises the mortgagee in
possession is entitled to carry on the business with a view to a sale (d).
The terms of the mortgage in such a case should provide for this
eventuality (e).

Leasing.—A mortgagee of land while in possession has the same
statutory power of leasing and of accepting surrenders of leases as
a mortgagor in possession (f). Such a lease by a mortgagee in
possession binds all prior incumbrances and the mortgagor himself (g).
A mortgagee who has appointed a receiver has, while the receiver is
acting, the same powers, and may delegate the power of leasing to the
receiver (h).

Application of receipts.—Receipts should be applied in discharging
outgoings and in paying the interest due under the mortgage. Any
surplus may be applied in partial discharge of the principal. But the
mortgagee is not bound to accept payment by driblets (i) and he may,
if he prefers, hand over the surplus to the mortgagor.

B—LIABILITIES OF MORTGAGEE IN POSSESSION

To account.—A mortgagee who as such goes into possession of the
mortgaged property is bound to account to the mortgagor. The
account usually directed against the mortgagee in possession is of
what he has, or without wilful default might have received from the
time of his taking possession. The mortgagee who takes possession of
the mortgaged property is required to be diligent in realising the
amount due on the mortgage, so that the property may be re-delivered
to the mortgagor (k). The rule applies whether the possession be of
land, tangible property, or of a business (l).

(c) *Corbett* v. *Plowden* (1884), 25 Ch. D. 678; *Kitchen's Trustee* v. *Madders*, [1950]
Ch. 134 (C.A.); [1949] 2 All E.R. 1079.

(d) *Cook* v. *Thomas* (1876), 24 W.R. 427; *County of Gloucester Bank* v. *Rudry Merthyr
Colliery Co.*, [1895] 1 Ch. 629. As to his position, see *Chaplin* v. *Young* (1864), 33
Beav. 330. Because of the liability of the mortgagee in possession (*supra*), it will usually
be more convenient to appoint a receiver who will be agent of the mortgagor (see p. 302,
supra); see generally (1976), 120 S.J. 497.

(e) See 14 Ency. Forms and Precedents (4th Edn.), 699.

(f) Law of Property Act 1925, ss. 99 (2), 100 (2). See pp. 342, 346 *supra*. If the
mortgagor's statutory power of leasing has been excluded a second mortgagee in possession will not have the statutory powers. Sub-section (13) of s. 99 applies as much to
sub-s. (2) as to (1): *Julian S. Hodge & Co., Ltd.* v. *St. Helen's Credit, Ltd.* (1965), Estates
Gazette Digest 143.

(g) Law of Property Act 1925, s. 99 (2). But for the purposes of s. 99 "mortgagor"
does not include an incumbrancer deriving title under the original mortgagor:
sub-s. (18).

(h) Law of Property Act 1925, s. 99 (19).

(i) *Nelson* v. *Booth* (1858), 3 De G. & J. 119, 122; *Wrigley* v. *Gill*, [1905] 1 Ch. 241,
at p. 254; affd., [1906] 1 Ch. 165. As to accounts in respect of the surplus, see pp. 620,
621, *infra*.

(k) *Lord Kensington* v. *Bouverie* (1855), 7 De G.M. & G. 134, 157; *Langton* v. *Waite*
(1869), 4 Ch. App. 402.

(l) *Williams* v. *Price* (1824), 1 Sim. & St. 581; *Chaplin* v. *Young* (1864), 33 Beav.
330; *Bompas* v. *King* (1886), 33 Ch. D. 279 (C.A.).

The mortgagee is liable to account for the rents and other profits during his possession, and if he goes into and remains in occupation himself he is liable to pay an occupation rent (*m*). But he is not liable to account for any notional rent if his possession is only for the purposes of sale within a reasonable time. His liability to account includes the receipts of any person whom the mortgagee has put into possession without a just title, and in derogation of the rights of the mortgagor (*n*). If the mortgagee in possession has sold the property, he will be liable to account for the proceeds of sale received by him, or which without wilful default he might have received. But if no special case is made (*o*), there will be no inquiry into the propriety of the sale or the adequacy of the price.

The mortgagee's liability to account extends in favour of all those who are interested in the equity of redemption. After receiving notice of a later mortgage (*p*) the mortgagee in possession becomes liable to account to the later incumbrancer for so much of the surplus rent as he has paid to the mortgagor or his representatives.

The mortgagee in possession cannot by any dealing with the estate discharge himself of his liability to account (*q*), and he will remain liable after a transfer of the mortgage unless the transfer is made with the consent of the court or the concurrence of the mortgagor (*r*).

Amount of rent to be accounted for.—Where a mortgagee enters into receipt of rents he accounts at the rate of the rent reserved (*s*). Where he enters into actual possession, it has been said that he will be charged with the utmost value the lands are proved to be worth (*t*). But this liability is limited by the circumstances of the case, and he will not usually be required to account for more than he has received, unless it is proved that, but for his gross default, mismanagement or fraud, he might have received more (*u*). This may be evidenced by his refusal or removal of a satisfactory tenant, who offered or paid a certain rent (*x*), or his making an improper use of his security, by allowing

---

(*m*) *Marriott* v. *Anchor Reversionary Co.* (1861), 3 De G.F. & J. 177, 193. Unless from its ruinous state, or for any other reason, the property is incapable of making a return: *Marshall* v. *Cave* (1824), 3 L.J. O.S. Ch. 57; *Fyfe* v. *Smith*, [1975] 2 N.S.W.L.R. 408. And see p. 621, *infra.*

(*n*) *National Bank of Australasia* v. *United Hand-in-Hand and Band of Hope Co.* (1879), 4 App. Cas. 391 (P.C.).

(*o*) *Mayer* v. *Murray* (1878), 8 Ch. D. 424; *Farrar* v. *Farrars, Ltd.* (1888), 40 Ch. D. 395. And see p. 367, *infra.*

(*p*) *Parker* v. *Calcraft* (1821), 6 Mad. 11.

(*q*) *Hinde* v. *Blake* (1841), 11 L.J. Ch. 26; *Re Prytherch* (1889), 42 Ch. D. 590. Nor, in the absence of special circumstances, will the court assist him to give up possession by appointing a receiver: *County of Gloucester Bank* v. *Rudry Merthyr Colliery Co.*, [1895] 1 Ch. 629. But he may relieve himself by appointing a receiver under an express or the statutory power: *Refuge Assurance Co., Ltd.* v. *Pearlberg*, [1938] Ch. 687; [1938] 3 All E.R. 231 (C.A.).

(*r*) *Hall* v. *Heward* (1886), 32 Ch. D. 430 (C.A.). And see p. 618, *infra.*

(*s*) *Lord Trimleston* v. *Hamill* (1810), 1 Ba. & Be. 377, 385; *Metcalf* v. *Campion* (1828), 1 Mol. 238.

(*t*) *Lord Trimleston* v. *Hamill, supra.*

(*u*) *Hughes* v. *Williams* (1806), 12 Ves. 493; *Wragg* v. *Denham* (1836), 2 Y. & C. Ex. 117. If there is included in a lease by the mortgagee land not mortgaged to him, but to another who concurred in the lease, there will be an apportionment: *Harryman* v. *Collins* (1854), 18 Beav. 11.

(*x*) *Noyes* v. *Pollock* (1886), 32 Ch. D. 53, 61; *White* v. *City of London Brewery Co.* (1889), 42 Ch. D. 237 (C.A.).

the mortgagor himself to take the profits to the prejudice of his other creditors, or where he is bankrupt, his trustee (y). But in these cases the proof must be distinct. The mortgagor is not allowed to bring in the mortgagee, and ask him how much rent he could have got when in possession, nor to involve him in a minute inquiry, whether some person was ready, unknown to him, to have given a greater rent. The mortgagee may be excused for refusing a higher offer from a credit-worthy person, where, for example, the tenant in possession is in arrears, and by removing him the arrears might have been lost. It is the duty of the mortgagor, if he has the opportunity, to give notice to the mortgagee, that the mortgaged property can be made, and to assist him in making it, more productive. If the mortgagor fails to do this and stands by, making no objection to the mortgagee's conduct, he cannot afterwards charge him with mismanagement (z). An act to prevent the letting will not be chargeable as wilful default if the mortgagor was a party to it (a).

Mortgagees of a public house with a covenant that all beer should be purchased from them are, if they take possession, liable to account for such rent as they might have received if the house were let as a free (as distinguished from a tied) house. But they are not liable to account for profits made by them by selling beer on the premises (b).

Where the mortgagee employs an agent to collect the rents, he must account for all the rents received by that agent, and not merely for what the agent has paid to him (c).

Liability for waste, etc.—A mortgagee in possession is not liable for waste (d). But he will not be allowed to cause unnecessary injury to the security when the security is not shown to be defective (e). If, without special authority, he opens mines or quarries he will be charged with his receipts, and will not be allowed the costs of severing the minerals or other expenses. For the mortgagee has no right to speculate at the mortgagor's expense and such an act is a sale of part of the inheritance (f). But he may work mines already opened (g) (but he is not obliged to advance more money on them (h)), and he has statutory power to cut and sell timber and other trees ripe for cutting, and not planted or left standing for shelter or ornament (i).

(y) *Loftus* v. *Swift* (1806), 2 Sch. & Lef. 642, at p. 656.

(z) *Hughes* v. *Williams, supra*; *Metcalf* v. *Campion, supra*; *Brandon* v. *Brandon* (1862), 10 W.R. 287.

(a) *Lord Trimleston* v. *Hamill, supra*; *Metcalf* v. *Campion, supra*.

(b) *White* v. *City of London Brewery Co., supra.* Similarly, a co-owner of a patent who takes a mortgage of his co-owner's share is not bound to bring his profits into account as mortgagee in possession: *Steers* v. *Rogers*, [1893] A.C. 232 (H.L.).

(c) *Noyes* v. *Pollock, supra*.

(d) Law of Property Act 1925, ss. 85 (2), 86 (2), 87 (1), 1st Sched., Pt. VII, paras. 1, 2.

(e) *Withrington* v. *Banks* (1725), 25 E.R. 205. He may be prevented from so doing by injunction or by being deprived of possession: *Hanson* v. *Derby* (1700), 2 Vern. 392.

(f) *Hughes* v. *Williams* (1806), 12 Ves. 493; *Thorneycroft* v. *Crockett* (1848), 16 Sim. 445.

(g) *Elias* v. *Snowdon Slate Quarries Co.* (1879), 4 App. Cas. 454.

(h) *Rowe* v. *Wood* (1822), 2 Jac. & W. 553.

(i) Law of Property Act 1925, s. 101 (1) (iv). This power may be varied or excluded by the mortgage deed: s. 101 (3), (4).

But a mortgagee with an insufficient security may cut timber and open new mines, and may lease or work abandoned mines, and will only be liable to account for the profits or royalty, and not for the value of the minerals raised or the damage caused to the surface (*j*).

If the mortgagee is expressly authorised to work mines he will be allowed the expenses incurred in doing so, with interest (*k*). Where there is a mortgage of a business as a going concern, the mortgagee may carry on the business with a view to a sale (*l*), and is entitled to be recouped for losses (not attributable to negligence) out of the proceeds of sale of the business (*m*).

The mortgagee is entitled to add to the security reasonable and proper expenses incurred in preserving the property pending sale or otherwise, *e.g.*, the cost of protecting the premises against vandals (*n*).

Maintenance of the property: Repairs.—The mortgagee in possession is not judged by the degree of care which a man is supposed to take of his own property. He need not rebuild ruinous premises (*o*), and will not be charged with deterioration of the property arising from ordinary decay by lapse of time. He will be allowed the cost of proper and necessary repairs (*p*), and he ought to do such repairs as can be paid for out of the balance of the rents after his interest has been paid (*q*), though he need not increase his debt by laying out large sums beyond the rents (*o*).

If buildings are incomplete, or have become unfit for use, he may complete them or pull them down and rebuild (*r*). The rebuilding or repairing may be done in an improved manner, and more substantially than before (*r*), so long as the work be done providently, and that no new or expensive buildings be erected for purposes different from those for which the former buildings were used (*s*).

This right of the mortgagee is founded on the principle that the mortgagor, whose right to redeem is only equitable, must repay all that is equitably due.

The mortgagee should not enter into possession merely for the sake of effecting repairs, because, if he goes into possession, he becomes liable on the footing of wilful default. If the property is income-producing his better course is to appoint a receiver and direct him to effect repairs. The well-drafted mortgage will generally contain a covenant by the mortgagor to repair, with power for the mortgagee to enter and effect repairs in case of default and in effecting repairs under this provision the mortgagee will not be a mortgagee in possession. But such a pro-

---

(*j*) *Millett* v. *Davey* (1862), 31 Beav. 470.

(*k*) *Norton* v. *Cooper* (1854), 25 L.J. Ch. 121.

(*l*) See p. 348, *supra*.

(*m*) *Bompas* v. *King* (1886), 33 Ch. D. 279 (C.A.).

(*n*) See p. 267, *supra*, and p. 639, *infra*.

(*o*) *Moore* v. *Painter* (1842), 6 Jur. 903.

(*p*) *Sandon* v. *Hooper* (1843), 6 Beav. 246; affd. 14 L.J. Ch. 120.

(*q*) *Richards* v. *Morgan* (1753), 4 Y. & C. Ex. (App.) 570; *Moore* v. *Painter*, *supra*; *Tipton Green Colliery Co.* v. *Tipton Moat Colliery Co.* (1877), 7 Ch. D. 192.

(*r*) *Marshall* v. *Cave* (1824), 3 L.J. (O.S.) Ch. 57.

(*s*) *Moore* v. *Painter*, *supra*; *Jortin* v. *South Eastern Rail. Co.* (1854), 2 Sm. & G. 48; reversed on other points (*sub nom. South Eastern Rail. Co.* v. *Jortin* (1857), 6 H.L.C. 425).

vision only covers the execution of necessary and proper repairs. Otherwise the mortgagee will be liable as mortgagee in possession. The terms of the mortgage should contain a covenant by the mortgagor to pay the cost of repairs effected by the mortgagee and a charge of such costs on the mortgaged property (t).

Mortgagee's liability for negligence.—The mortgagee will be liable to the mortgagor for gross or wilful negligence resulting in damage to the mortgaged property arising out of his possession of the mortgaged property (u). This will be so, for example, if mortgaged mines are flooded by improper working (v), or mortgaged chattels are injured by negligent removal (w). The mortgagee will be liable for loss due to alterations injurious to the value of the property, such as the pulling down of cottages on an estate or the cutting of timber. In such a case he will be charged with the value thereof with interest, or be liable to pay such rent as would otherwise have been received (x). And the same applies if, being in possession under a mortgage of unfinished leasehold buildings, he neither sells the property nor completes the building, and so the leases are forfeited (y). He will also be liable if, after an order for possession has been made in his favour, he fails to take reasonable steps to protect the premises, e.g., against vandals, and damage to the premises ensues (z). As to liability to persons other than the mortgagor, the mortgagee in possession will be subject to liability for loss or injury through nuisance, dis-repair, etc., as any other person who has control of property (a).

Improvements.—Though the mortgagee may, under appropriate circumstances, make improvements, these must always be reasonable, having regard to nature and value of the security (b). The mortgagee should inform the mortgagor as soon as possible of the necessity or the intention to incur extraordinary expenses. If he does so, and the mortgagor agrees expressly, or by acts which show consent or acquiescence, the mortgagee need not show that the outlay was reasonable. If the mortgagor does nothing, he will not be charged with an unreasonable outlay, merely because he has notice. Nor, on the other hand, will the mortgagee lose his right to repayment for want of giving notice, if the improvement was reasonable and beneficial. If the property has been sold, the mortgagee will have a stronger claim than in a redemption action, and will be repaid whatever is

---

(t) See p. 32, supra.
(u) Russel v. Smithies (1792), 1 Anst. 96.
(v) Taylor v. Mostyn (1886), 33 Ch. D. 226 (C.A.).
(w) Johnson v. Diprose, [1893] 1 Q.B. 512 (C.A.).
(x) Wragg v. Denham (1836), 2 Y. & C. Ex. 117; Sandon v. Hooper, supra; Batchelor v. Middleton (1848), 6 Hare, 75.
(y) Perry v. Walker (1855), 24 L.J. Ch. 319; Taylor v. Mostyn, supra.
The mortgagee of a debt is liable for its loss, if it becomes irrecoverable through his wilful default: Williams v. Price (1824), 1 Sim. & St. 581. But the mortgagee in possession is not obliged to incur the cost and risk of defending doubtful rights in respect of the mortgaged property: Cocks v. Gray (1857), 1 Giff. 77.
(z) For allowance for outgoings, see p. 353, infra.
(a) For liability to third parties in nuisance and negligence, see (1954) 98 S.J. 377.
(b) See Sandon v. Hooper, supra.

shown to have been added to the selling value of the property by the expenditure (c).

Outgoings.—The mortgagee will be allowed what he has expended in preserving the security, *e.g.* rent, where the security is leasehold, and the cost of preserving the property from deterioration (d). He will be allowed the amount of compensation payable to an outgoing tenant (e) and the cost of renewing a lease, even though there is no covenant by the mortgagee to renew (f). All such monies will be added to the principal debt and, like it, carry interest.

The mortgagee in possession is treated as owner for the purposes of various statutes (g). Any liability in respect of the premises arising as such will be allowable.

But where such sums are laid out by a subsequent mortgagee in possession, they will not be allowed as against a first mortgagee (h).

No allowance for personal trouble.—The mortgagee in possession is generally not allowed anything for personal care or trouble in receiving rents, even though he might have appointed a receiver (i). Upon taking possession he becomes quasi-owner of the property, and, being in uncontrolled management without power of interference by the mortgagor, unless some act is done which calls for the interference of the court, no allowances are made to him, either directly or indirectly in respect of his personal trouble (j). Previously this rule prevailed even where there was an express agreement between mortgagor and mortgagee that a commission should be allowed to the mortgagee. Now the general principles applicable to collateral advantages apply to such an agreement (k). A solicitor-mortgagee may charge remuneration, whether or not there is an agreement for remuneration (l). The mortgagee will be allowed the expenses of a sale of the mortgaged property or part of it (m). A commission will be allowed only if it constitutes a valid collateral advantage (n).

(c) *Shepard* v. *Jones* (1882), 21 Ch. D. 469; *Matzner* v. *Clyde Securities, Ltd.*, [1975] 2 N.S.W.L.R. 293. As to estimating the value of improvements to buildings, see *Robinson* v. *Ridley* (1821), 6 Mad. 2.

(d) *Burrowes* v. *Molloy* (1845), 2 Jo. & Lat. 521; *Brandon* v. *Brandon* (1862), 10 W.R. 287. With regard to the mortgages of ships outgoings are not allowed unless incurred with the sanction of the court: *The Fair Haven* (1866), L.R. 1 A. & E. 67.

(e) *Oxenham* v. *Ellis* (1854), 18 Beav. 593.

(f) *Woolley* v. *Drage* (1795), 2 Anst. 551. But he cannot compel the mortgagor to renew.

(g) *E.g.*, for notices under the Highways Acts: *Maguire* v. *Leigh-on-Sea Urban District Council* (1906), 95 L.T. 319; under the Public Health Act 1936: *Davies* v. *Law Mutual Building Society* (1971), 219 Estates Gazette 309; for the rating surcharge under s. 17A and B of the General Rate Act 1967: *Banister* v. *Islington London Borough Council* (1972), 71 L.G.R. 239 (see (1976) 40 Conv. (N.S.) 222).

(h) *Landowners, etc., Drainage and Inclosure Co.* v. *Ashford* (1880), 16 Ch. D. 411.

(i) *Bonithon* v. *Hockmore* (1685), 1 Vern. 316; *Nicholson* v. *Tutin* (*No.* 2) (1857), 3 K. & J. 159.

(j) *Cholmondeley* v. *Clinton* (1820), 2 Jac. & W. 1, 184, 191; *Leith* v. *Irvine* (1833), 1 Myl. & K. 277; *Robertson* v. *Norris* (1857), 1 Giff. 421.

(k) See p. 526, *infra*. Even before the change of policy introduced by *Biggs* v. *Hoddinott* ([1898] 2 Ch. 307 (C.A.)), it was recognised that some such agreements might be binding: *Eyre* v. *Hughes* (1876), 2 Ch. D. 148.

(l) Solicitors Act 1974, s. 58.

(m) *Farrer* v. *Lacy, Hartland & Co.* (1885), 31 Ch. D. 42 (C.A.).

(n) See p. 528, *infra*; and see *Browne* v. *Ryan*, [1901] 2 I.R. 653. The general prohibition extends to the partnership of which the mortgagee is a member: *Matthison*

Agent's salary.—If the mortgagee in possession manages the property by his agent or employees he may charge for the agent's or employees' salary (*o*).

C—LIMITATION

Possession by mortgagee.—When a mortgagee has been in possession of the mortgaged land as mortgagee, and not in any other character, for twelve years, he will thereby extinguish the title of the mortgagor or any person claiming through him (*p*). And the title of a subsequent mortgagee is extinguished with that of the mortgagor through whom he claims. The time required to extinguish the title of the mortgagor may be extended in the case of disability, acknowledgement, part payment, fraud or mistake (*q*).

Where a proprietor of a charge has acquired a title under the Limitation Act 1939, he can execute a declaration in the prescribed form (*r*) that the right of redemption is barred. Subject to furnishing evidence in support of his application (*s*), he will then be entitled to be registered as proprietor of the land with the same consequences (*t*) as if he had been a purchaser for valuable consideration of the land under the power of sale (*u*). This right is only exercisable subject to any entry to the contrary on the register and subject to the right of any person appearing on the register to be a prior incumbrancer (*u*).

For enlargement of mortgage terms and vesting declarations where the land is not registered, see p. 567, *infra*.

VI—MORTGAGEE'S RIGHT TO POSSESSION OF OTHER PROPERTY

Bills of Sale Act 1882.—By s. 7 of the Bills of Sale Act (1878) Amendment Act 1882, personal chattels comprised in a bill of sale may not be seized or taken possession of by the grantee for any other than the following causes:

(1) If the grantor shall make default in payment of the sum or sums of money thereby secured, at the time therein provided for payment, or in the performance of any covenant or agreement contained in the bill of sale and necessary for maintaining the security;

(2) If the grantor shall become a bankrupt, or suffer the said goods, or any of them to be distrained for rent, rates or taxes;

(3) If the grantor shall fraudulently either remove or suffer the said goods, or any of them, to be removed from the premises;

---

v. *Clarke* (1854), 3 Drew 3; *Furber* v. *Cobb* (1887), 18 Q.B.D. 494, 509. The rule is otherwise where the mortgage is employed to sell by the court: *Arnold* v. *Garner* (1847), 2 Ph. 231.

(*o*) *Union Bank of London* v. *Ingram* (1880), 16 Ch. D. 53 (C.A.). The mortgagee may agree with the mortgagor for the appointment of a receiver to be paid by the latter, or may appoint one under the statutory power (p. 300, *supra*).

(*p*) Limitation Act 1939, ss. 12, 16. As to registered land, see Land Registration Act 1925, ss. 34 (2), 75. And see *Young* v. *Clarey*, [1948] Ch. 191; [1948] 1 All E.R. 197.

(*q*) See pp. 564 *et seq.*, *infra*.

(*r*) Land Registration Rules 1925, r. 149 (1), Sched., Form 52.

(*s*) *Ibid.*, r. 149 (2), (3).

(*t*) Land Registration Act 1925, s. 34 (4).

(*u*) *Ibid.*, s. 34 (2).

(4) If the grantor shall not (without reasonable excuse) upon demand in writing by the grantee, produce to him his last receipts for rent, rates and taxes;

(5) If execution shall have been levied against the goods of the grantor under any judgment at law:

Provided that the grantor may within five days from the seizure or taking possession of any chattels on account of any of the above-mentioned causes, apply to the High Court, or to a Judge thereof in chambers, and such Court or Judge, if satisfied that by payment of money or otherwise the said cause of seizure no longer exists, may restrain the grantee from removing or selling the said chattels, or may make such other order as may seem just (*x*).

The five excepted cases are strictly construed. Thus, where a mortgagor has not in fact paid his rent which, although a few days overdue had not been demanded, he does not fall within exception (4) by omitting to produce the receipt (*y*). The power of the court, on seizure, to order delivery up of possession on payment of principal, interest and costs, depends on whether the seizure has been made for the purpose of realising, or only for the purpose of protecting the security. In the former case, delivery up will be ordered under the general rule that a mortgagee who takes steps to realise is estopped from declining to receive payment (*y*). In the latter, if the date of payment has not arrived, redemption will not be forced on the mortgagee (*z*).

Consumer credit agreements.—Paragraph (1) of s. 7 of the Bills of Sale Act (1878) Amendment Act 1882 (*a*) does not apply to a default relating to a bill of sale given by way of security for the payment of money under a regulated agreement under the Consumer Credit Act 1974 to which the need for a default notice (*b*) applies: (i) unless the debtor or hirer has failed to take the action specified in the notice within the specified period; or (ii) if, by virtue of s. 89 of the 1974 Act, the default is to be treated as not having occurred (*c*). Where para. 1 of the 1882 Act does apply in relation to a bill of sale such is mentioned above the proviso to s. 7 of the 1882 Act the county court shall be substituted for the High Court therein (*d*).

Rights of mortgagee against third parties.—The mortgagee of personal chattels may sue third parties in respect of them, if, when the cause of action accrued, he had a right to immediate possession. Apart from the Act of 1882 this right was complete, if there was an assignment to the mortgagee not qualified by any clause which gave the mortgagor a right to continue in possession until default in payment on demand, nor limited as to the right of possession until some other future time which had not arrived when the goods were taken by a

---

(*x*) As to the effect of provisions in the bill which conflict with the above restrictions on seizure, see p. 87, *supra*.

(*y*) *Ex parte Cotton* (1883), 11 Q.B.D. 301; *Ex parte Wickens*, [1898] 1 Q.B. 543.

(*z*) *Ex parte Ellis*, [1898] 2 Q.B. 79.

(*a*) P. 354, *supra*.

(*b*) See s. 87 of the Act: p. 144, *supra*. And see s. 129 of the Act for time orders (p. 151, *supra*.).

(*c*) Bills of Sale Act 1878 (Amendment) Act 1882, s. 7A (1) added by the Consumer Credit Act 1974, Sched. 4, para. 1.

(*d*) S. 7A (2).

third person (*e*). What the effect of the statute is in this respect seems never to have been decided. But it is apprehended that as it takes away, without any qualification, the right of possession of the mortgagee except in the five specified cases, the rights of the mortgagee against third parties must be affected in precisely the same way as if s. 7 were set out in the mortgage. Where the sheriff has taken possession of the goods and interpleads, he will as a rule be ordered to withdraw unless the judgment creditor is willing to redeem (*f*).

The mortgagee may also recover against a bailee, to whom the chattel was delivered by the mortgagor before the mortgage. Accordingly, after demand by the mortgagee, the bailee is justified in refusing to re-deliver the chattel to the mortgagor, notwithstanding his contract to do so made before his position was changed by the mortgage (*g*).

Use of mortgaged ship by mortgagee.—The Merchant Shipping Act 1894, provides that the mortgagee shall not by reason of his mortgage acquire, nor the mortgagor lose, the character of owner, except so far as may be necessary for making the ship or share available for the payment of the mortgage debt (*h*).

The first duty of the mortgagee of a ship who takes possession is to sell, but he is not bound to do so at a sacrifice. If he cannot reasonably or prudently sell, he will be justified, in the exercise of the sound discretion of a prudent owner, in employing the ship. But he has not the unlimited right to send her to any distance, and to employ her for an indefinite time at the mortgagor's cost for repairs, wages, insurance, and other disbursements and risks, and at the risk of involving her in speculative adventures (*i*). A mortgagee may properly refuse to enter into a charter party for the employment of the ship in a voyage of a speculative character.

By the mortgagor.—The mortgagor, on the other hand, while the mortgagee allows him to retain possession (and in the absence of express contract the mortgagor is entitled to possession until the debt is payable, unless the ship is being so dealt with so as to impair the security (*k*)), has full liberty to deal with the ship, so far as he can do so consistently with the sufficiency of the security. And the mortgagee, so long as he does not interfere, will be held to have acquiesced in all proper engagements for her use which have been made by the mortgagor. The mortgagor may enter into such contracts as are

---

(*e*) *Wheeler* v. *Montefiore* (1841), 2 Q.B. 133. Where the mortgagor has wrongfully sold the property, the mortgagee may sue the purchaser, unless the latter is protected by sale in market overt or under the Factors Act 1889, or the Sale of Goods Act 1893: *Cooper* v. *Willomatt* (1845), 1 C.B. 672.

(*f*) *Stern* v. *Tegner*, [1898] 1 Q.B. 37.

(*g*) *European and Australian Royal Mail Co.* v. *Royal Mail Steam Packet Co.* (1861), 30 L.J.C.P. 247.

(*h*) Section 34; *The St. George*, [1926] P. 217.

(*i*) *European and Australian Royal Mail Co.* v. *Royal Mail Steam Packet Co.*, supra. As to damages for loss of profit where a mortgagee is restrained from using the ship, see *De Mattos* v. *Gibson* (1860), 1 John & H. 79; but on that case see now *Port Line, Ltd.* v. *Ben Line Steamers, Ltd.*, [1958] 2 Q.B. 146; [1958] 1 All E.R. 787.

(*k*) *The Blanche* (1887), 58 L.T. 592; *The Heather Bell*, [1901] P. 272 (C.A.).

proper to give him the full benefit of the ownership, and by which he may earn the means of discharging the mortgage debt (*l*), and the mortgagee cannot interfere with such a contract, without showing that it will materially prejudice his security (*m*). And so that the ship may also be a source of profit to the mortgagee himself when he takes possession, the mortgagor may do all that is proper to keep the ship in an effective condition, and for such repairs as are made by his direction when in possession, the shipwright may enforce his possessory lien against the mortgagee (*n*). But in contracts for repair the mortgagor in possession does not have authority to pledge the mortgagee's credit by reason of the relationship of mortgagor and mortgagee (*o*).

If, however, the mortgagee can show that the acts of the mortgagor will injure his security, the statutory provision that the mortgagor shall retain the character of owner (which in fact is said to have been for the benefit of the mortgagee) will cease to operate (*p*). The mortgagee, on taking possession may require payment to himself of the fruits of any contract for the use of the ship which has been made by the mortgagor. But as the right to receive the earnings of the ship, whether freight or passage money, does not pass to him by way of assignment of the freight (unless it is specially assigned as incident to the ownership of the vessel), he must take possession, or assert his right by some corresponding act, such as requiring payment from the charterer before the mortgagor has received the produce (*q*). Even in the hands of the mortgagee, the produce is liable for the expenses of the voyage in which it was earned (*r*). The mortgagee, whether in possession or not, is not liable for necessaries supplied to the ship, unless they were ordered by his agent or upon his credit (*s*). Nor does the lien created by s. 22 of the Judicature Act 1925 (*t*), take priority to his claims, unless, apparently, he had expended money by leave of the court (*u*). If the mortgagee has paid expenses for which the ship was liable in order to obtain possession of her, he may recover them from the person by whose neglect to pay them the ship became liable (*a*).

Taking possession under mortgages of choses in action.—In the case of a mortgage of an interest in a trust fund mere notice to the trustees of the assignment is not in itself equivalent to taking possession of the interest. Possession is taken by the mortgagee giving the

---

(*l*) *Collins* v. *Lamport* (1864), 34 L.J. Ch. 196; *Keith* v. *Burrows* (1877), 2 App. Cas. 636 (H.L.).
(*m*) *The Blanche, supra.*
(*n*) *Williams* v. *Allsup* (1861), 10 C.B. (N.S.) 417; *The Skipwith* (1864), 10 Jur. N.S. 445.
(*o*) *Tyne Dock Engineering Co., Ltd.* v. *Royal Bank of Scotland* 1974 S.L.T. 57.
(*p*) *Law Guarantee and Trust Society* v. *Russian Bank for Foreign Trade*, [1905] 1 K.B. 815 (C.A.).
(*q*) *Wilson* v. *Wilson* (1872), L.R. 14 Eq. 32; *Keith* v. *Burrows, supra.* And see *Beynon* v. *Godden* (1878), 3 Ex. D. 263 (C.A.). And p. 493, *infra.*
(*r*) *Alexander* v. *Simms* (1854), 18 Beav. 80; affd. 5 De G.M. & G. 57.
(*s*) *The Troubador* (1866), L.R. 1 A. & E. 302; *El Argentino*, [1909] P. 236.
(*t*) Replacing ss. 4 and 5 of the Admiralty Court Act 1861.
(*u*) *The Lyons* (1887), 57 L.T. 818.
(*a*) *Johnson* v. *Royal Mail Steam Packet Co.* (1867), L.R. 3 C.P. 38.

trustees notice to pay over the income to him (b).   Where a mortgaged reversionary interest falls into possession the mortgagee is not entitled to receive the whole of the mortgagor's interest, but only so much as suffices to discharge the principal, interest, and costs due on the mortgage (c).

The mortgagor of a patent can sue for infringement without joining the mortgagee even where the latter is registered as assignee (d).

(b) *Re Pawson's Settlement, Higgins* v. *Pawson,* [1917] 1 Ch. 541.
(c) *Hockey* v. *Western,* [1898] 1 Ch. 350 (C.A.).
(d) *Van Gelder, Apsimon & Co.* v. *Sowerby Bridge United Flour Society* (1890), 44 Ch. D. 374 (C.A.).

CHAPTER 20

The Mortgagee's Power of Sale

Liability of property to be sold.—The property comprised in the security may become liable to be sold for the purpose of discharging the debt either by the creditor himself or by judicial process; and in the former case either under a power which the law annexes to his security as a legal incident thereof, or under an express or statutory power.

Mortgages of chattels and choses in action.—The mortgagee of a personal chattel (when possession has been delivered to him (a)), of stocks and shares, of a policy of insurance, or other thing in action, has an implied power of sale as a legal incident of his security (b). This right is exercisable on non-payment on the day fixed for payment, or, where no day has been fixed, after a proper demand and notice (c) and the lapse of a reasonable time (d). The mortgagee of chattels, who sells either under a special or implied power, is bound to account for the proceeds, to pay over to the owner the surplus purchase-money beyond his demand and the necessary charges and expenses, and to return any unsold part of the security to the debtor. If the mortgagee attempts to dispose of the money so as to prejudice any person entitled to receive it, he may be ordered to pay it into court, and a receiver may be appointed of the proceeds of any part of the property which may remain unsold (e). The mortgagor's right of redemption ceases on a contract to sell made after the power of sale has arisen (f).

Express power of sale.—A right in the mortgagee to sell may be created by the insertion in the mortgage of an express power of sale (g).

(a) *Re Morritt, Ex parte Official Receiver* (1886), 18 Q.B.D. 222 (C.A.). See p. 354, *supra*.

(b) *Wilson* v. *Tooker* (1714), 5 Bro. P.C. 193; *Lockwood* v. *Ewer* (1742), 2 Atk. 303; *Kemp* v. *Westbrook* (1749), 1 Ves. Sen. 278; *Re Morritt, Ex parte Official Receiver, supra*. As to sale by mortgagees of stocks and shares, see *Stubbs* v. *Slater*, [1910] 1 Ch. 632 (C.A.).

(c) *France* v. *Clark* (1883), 22 Ch. D. 830; affd. 26 Ch. D. 257 (C.A.); *Re Morritt, Ex parte Official Receiver, supra*.

A mistake as to the amount does not invalidate the notice: *Stubbs* v. *Slater, supra*; and see *Harrold* v. *Plenty*, [1901] 2 Ch. 314. See also p. 364, *infra*.

If shares are sold without notice the mortgagor is entitled to set off the value of the shares on the day preceding the date of the master's certificate in an action on the account: see *Ellis & Co.'s Trustee* v. *Dixon-Johnson*, [1925] A.C. 489 (H.L.).

(d) *Deverges* v. *Sandeman, Clark & Co.*, [1902] 1 Ch. 579 (C.A.); *cf. Re Harrison and Ingram, Ex parte Whinney*, [1905] 54 W.R. 203.

(e) *Wilson* v. *Tooker, supra*.

(f) *The Ningchow* (1916), 31 T.L.R. 470. And see footnote (i), p. 370, *infra*.

(g) Such a power became common at the beginning of the 19th century: *Stevens* v. *Theatres, Ltd.*, [1903] 1 Ch. 857, 860. As to the former mortgages by trust for sale, see p. 7, *supra*.

Provision is usually made that the power shall not be exercised until the expiration of notice to the mortgagor, so that he may have a further opportunity of paying off the debt. Though such a provision is not essential, and sometimes non-payment on demand is the only preliminary, it has been said that a power to sell without notice is of an oppressive character (*h*).

An express power of sale is not affected by an arrangement subsequently made between mortgagee and mortgagor for the management of the property (*i*). It is not extinguished by an ineffective attempt to exercise it (*k*). The effect of the exercise of the power is the same as the effect of the exercise of the statutory power of sale.

Statutory power of sale.—But reliance is usually placed on the statutory power of sale, though this may be modified (*l*), and an express power is now rarely inserted in mortgages. By the Law of Property Act 1925, s. 101 (1) (*m*) it is provided that a mortgagee (*n*), where the mortgage is made by deed (*o*), shall, by virtue of the Act, have to the same extent as if the power had been in terms conferred by the mortgage deed (*p*)—

> (i) A power, when the mortgage money has become due (*q*), to sell, or to concur with any other person in selling, the mortgaged property, or any part thereof, either subject to prior charges or not, and either together or in lots, by public auction or by private contract (*r*), subject to such

---

(*h*) *Miller* v. *Cook* (1870), L.R. 10 Eq. 641. Hence it is a breach of duty by a solicitor, who becomes the mortgagee to his client, to omit a stipulation for notice in an express power of sale, without taking care that the client has a full explanation of the circumstances: *Cockburn* v. *Edwards* (1881), 18 Ch. D. 449 (C.A.). But this does not apply to a mortgage for securing money presently payable, for payment of which the solicitor is giving time: *Pooley's Trustee* v. *Whetham* (1886), 33 Ch. D. 111 (C.A.).

(*i*) *E.g.*, under which a receiver is to grant leases, but is to permit the mortgagor to receive the rents till default: *King* v. *Heenan* (1853), 3 De G.M. & G. 890.

(*k*) *Henderson* v. *Astwood*, [1894] A.C. 150, 162 (P.C.).

(*l*) Law of Property Act 1925, s. 101 (3). For forms, see 14 Ency. Forms and Precedents (4th Edn.), 138–140, and the subsequent general forms; and Precedents 1 and 1A in the Appendix, *infra*.

(*m*) Replacing Conveyancing Act 1881, s. 19 (which itself replaced Lord Cranworth's Act 1860).

(*n*) The power is applicable to a registered chargee; see Land Registration Act 1925, s. 34 (1) (p. 63, *supra*) and *Lever Finance, Ltd.* v. *Needleman's Property Trustee*, [1956] Ch. 375; [1956] 2 All E.R. 378.
Where there was before 1926 a mortgage of an undivided share of land, the statutory power applies to the corresponding share of the proceeds of sale under the statutory trusts: Law of Property Act 1925, s. 102.

(*o*) The power applies to any mortgage of any property made by deed, save those to which the Bills of Sale Acts apply (see p. 87, *supra*) and to debentures issued by a statutory public utility company: *Blaker* v. *Herts and Essex Waterworks Co.* (1889), 41 Ch. D. 399; and see *Deyes* v. *Wood*, [1911] 1 K.B. 806 (C.A.), at p. 818.

(*p*) But it applies only so far as a contrary intention is not expressed therein: Law of Property Act 1925, s. 101 (4). The mere fact that the mortgage contains an express power exercisable at a future date does not show a contrary situation so as to negative the earlier exercise of the statutory power: *Life Interest, etc., Corpn.* v. *Hand-in-Hand Fire and Life Insurance Society*, [1898] 2 Ch. 230.

(*q*) *I.e.*, when the legal date for redemption (if any) has passed, and thereafter, if the debt is repayable by instalments, as soon as each instalment becomes due; where there is a direct covenant for repayment by instalments (see p. 28, *supra*), as soon as each instalment becomes due. See *Payne* v. *Cardiff R.D.C.*, [1932] 1 K.B. 241. The power may be excluded before a specified date: see *Twentieth Century Banking Corpn., Ltd.* v. *Wilkinson*, [1976] 3 All E.R. 361. In which case the mortgagee may be able to claim a judicial sale.

(*r*) *Williams* v. *Wellingborough Borough Council*, [1975] 3 All E.R. 462 (C.A.) (a retaking by the council under a right of pre-emption is not either).

conditions respecting title or evidence of title, or other matter (s), as the mortgagee thinks fit, with power to vary any contract for sale, and to buy in at an auction, or rescind any contract for sale, and to re-sell, without being answerable for any loss occasioned thereby (t).

An express power of sale may be extended by reference to a collateral security, e.g., a mortgage of an insurance policy, to property comprised in that security (u). But the statutory power being only applicable where the mortgage is by deed, it seems doubtful whether it will extend to such collateral security made by writing only, unless there is an agreement that it shall be incorporated (a). Where there is a collateral security by a mortgage by a person other than the mortgagor the exercise of the power of sale may involve between the principal mortgagor and the third party the operation of the doctrine of contribution.

Incidental powers.—Where the mortgage deed was executed after 31 December, 1911, the statutory power of sale includes power to impose restrictive covenants on the land, to grant or reserve easements, and to sell the surface and the mines separately (b). These powers (c) are conferred by s. 101 (2) of the Law of Property Act 1925, in the following terms:

(i) A power to impose or reserve or make binding, as far as the law permits, by covenant, condition, or otherwise, on the unsold part of the mortgaged property or any part thereof, or on the purchaser and any property sold, any restriction or reservation with respect to building on or other user of land, or with respect to mines and minerals, or for the purpose of the more beneficial working thereof, or with respect to any other thing:

(ii) A power to sell the mortgaged property, or any part thereof, or all or any mines and minerals apart from the surface:—

    (a) With or without a grant or reservation of rights of way, rights of water, easements, rights and privileges for or connected with building or other purposes in relation to the property remaining in mortgage or any part thereof, or to any property sold: and

---

(s) See *Property and Bloodstock, Ltd.* v. *Emerton*, [1968] Ch. 94 (C.A.), at pp. 117–118, 122; [1967] 3 All E.R. 321, at pp. 328, 331. The reference to "other matter" would not, it is submitted, permit an instalment sale of the property. For this, there should be express provision: see Precedent 1A in the Appendix, *infra*. The mortgagee could of course grant a new mortgage to the purchaser, but the mortgagee would have to account to the original mortgagor for the price. Where the mortgage permits an instalment sale the mortgagee is bound to account for the instalments as they are received not the whole purchase price: *Wright* v. *N.Z. Farmers Co-operative Association of Canterbury Ltd.*, [1939] A.C. 439 (P.C.); [1939] 2 All E.R. 701.

(t) Apart from such a provision a power of sale is not extinguished by an abortive attempt to sell: *Henderson* v. *Astwood, supra*.

(u) *Ashworth* v. *Mounsey* (1853), 2 C.L.R. 418.

(a) *Re Thomson and Holt* (1890), 44 Ch. D. 492, 499.

(b) The statutory power extends to fixtures (Law of Property Act 1925, ss. 88 (4), 89 (4)). But there is no power to sell timber or fixtures apart from the land: *Cholmeley* v. *Paxton* (1825), 3 Bing. 207; *Re Yates* (1888), 38 Ch. D. 112 (C.A.); *Hunter* v. *Hunter*, [1936] A.C. 222 (H.L.), 248, 249; *Kay's Leasing Corporation, Pty., Ltd.* v. *C.S.R. Provident Fund Nominees*, [1962] V.R. 429. For forms of conveyance under the statutory power of sale, see 19 Ency. Forms and Precedents (4th Edn.), pp. 1339 *et seq.* and 1639 *et seq.*

(c) These powers were first conferred by s. 4 of the Conveyancing Act 1911, which came into force on 1 January, 1912, and accordingly, while in general the statutory powers apply to mortgages executed after 31 December, 1881 (see Law of Property Act 1925, s. 101 (5)), these powers are restricted, as above stated, to mortgages executed after 31 December, 1911.

(b) With or without an exception or reservation of all or any of the mines and minerals in or under the mortgaged property, and with or without a grant or reservation of powers of working, way-leaves, or rights of way, rights of water and drainage and other powers, easements, rights, and privileges for or connected with mining purposes in relation to the property remaining unsold or any part thereof, or to any property sold: and

(c) With or without covenants by the purchaser to expend money on the land sold.

Before the Conveyancing Act 1911, there was power to sell the surface and minerals separately only with the leave of the court, and the requirement of leave is preserved as to mortgages made before 1 January, 1912 (*d*).

Further points on the statutory power.—The power of sale is effectively exercised as soon as there is a contract for sale of the mortgaged property (*e*). The extent and effect of the exercise of the power of sale is dealt with subsequently (*f*). The power is to sell the mortgaged property or any part thereof (*g*). Where there are several properties included in the mortgage, the mortgagee is entitled to sell all of them, notwithstanding the sale of one or more only would raise sufficient to discharge the mortgage. Where the property is subject to a right of pre-emption (*h*) this will affect the value of the security to the mortgagee. If the right is enforceable there is nothing more the mortgagee can do than offer the property to the person with the benefit of the right (*i*), or, possibly, foreclose, rather than sell.

The power of sale does not affect the right of foreclosure (*k*). The mortgagee is not answerable for any involuntary loss happening in the exercise of the statutory power of sale or where the mortgage was executed after 31 December, 1911, of any power or provision in the mortgage deed (*l*). At any time after the power of sale has become exercisable, the person entitled to exercise it may demand and recover from any person (other than a person having in the mortgaged property an estate, interest or right in priority to the mortgage), all the deeds and documents relating to the property or to the title thereto, which a purchaser under the power of sale would be entitled to demand and recover from him (*m*).

(*d*) And see Law of Property Act 1925, s. 92; *Re Hirst's Mortgage* (1890), 45 Ch. D. 263.

(*e*) *Waring* (*Lord*) v. *London and Manchester Assurance Co., Ltd.,* [1935] Ch. 310; *Property and Bloodstock, Ltd.* v. *Emerton,* [1968] Ch. 94 (C.A.); [1967] 3 All E.R. 321.

(*f*) See p. 377, *infra.*

(*g*) See s. 101 (1) (i), *supra.*

(*h*) Which has been duly registered as an estate contract or, if over registered land, protected.

(*i*) *First National Securities Ltd.* v. *Chiltern District Council* [1975] 2 All E.R. 766. See Wurtzburg and Mills, *Building Society Law* (14th Edn.), pp. 211–212 (dealing with former council houses, etc.); (1973) 117 Sol. Jo. 41, 168, 208, 308. On sales of council houses, see (1976), 120 Sol. Jo. 126.

(*k*) Law of Property Act 1925, s. 106 (2). This is in accordance with the law as to express powers of sale: *Wayne* v. *Hanham* (1851), 9 Hare 62. But after order *nisi* and pending foreclosure absolute, the mortgagee cannot sell without the leave of the court: *Stevens* v. *Theatres, Ltd.,* [1903] 1 Ch. 857. See pp. 407, 408, *infra.*

(*l*) *Ibid.,* s. 106 (3). The first part of this clause reproduces s. 21 (6) of the Conveyancing Act 1881. The latter part reproduces an amendment made by the Act of 1911.

(*m*) *Ibid.,* s. 106 (4).

Devolution of the statutory power.—The statutory power of sale is exercisable by persons deriving title under the original mortgagee (*n*), and this appears to be sufficient to ensure the devolution of the power. But it is also provided that it shall be exercisable by any person for the time being entitled to receive and give a good discharge for the purchase money (*o*). An express power is exercisable only by the persons who are designated for that purpose by the power (*p*). In the rare cases where an express power is given, it is sufficient to make it exercisable by persons deriving title under the mortgagee (*q*). A transferee can take advantage of a right to sell forthwith existing at the date of the transfer (*r*).

When statutory power arises and is exercisable.—A power of sale arises, where the power is the statutory power, if the mortgage was made by deed and the mortgage money has become due (*s*), or where the power is express, after due notice or the happening of some specified event. With regard to the time when the statutory power can be exercised, it is provided by the Law of Property Act 1925:

103.—A mortgagee shall not exercise the power of sale conferred by this Act unless and until—

    (i) Notice requiring payment of the mortgage money has been served on the mortgagor or one of two or more mortgagors, and default has been made in payment of the mortgage money, or of part thereof, for three months after such service (*t*); or

    (ii) Some interest under the mortgage is in arrear and unpaid for two months after becoming due (*u*); or

    (iii) There has been a breach of some provision contained in the mortgage deed or in this Act (*a*), or in an enactment replaced by this Act, and on the part of the mortgagor, or of some person concurring in making the mortgage, to be observed or performed, other than and besides a covenant for payment of the mortgage money or interest thereon (*b*).

(*n*) *Ibid.*, s. 205 (1) (xvi).

(*o*) *Ibid.*, s. 106 (1). But this does not confer the power of sale on an agent with a power of attorney to receive and give a good discharge for the purchase money: *Re Dowson and Jenkins's Contract*, [1904] 2 Ch. 219 (C.A.).

(*p*) *Re Crunden and Meux's Contract*, [1909] 1 Ch. 690, at p. 695.

(*q*) An assign of a mortgagee cannot sell under an express power unless the power is expressed to be given to the mortgagee and his assigns: *Re Rumney and Smith*, [1897] 2 Ch. 351 (C.A.).

(*r*) *Bailey* v. *Barnes*, [1894] 1 Ch. 25 (C.A.), at p. 32.

(*s*) See p. 360, *supra.*

(*t*) *I.e.*, after actual service, not after the time fixed by the notice for payment: *Barker* v. *Illingworth*, [1908] 2 Ch. 20.

(*u*) This includes an instalment expressed to be for principal and interest combined: *Walsh* v. *Derrick* (1903), 19 T.L.R. 209 (C.A.); *Payne* v. *Cardiff R.D.C.*, [1932] 1 K.B. 241. A capitalisation clause may make this inapplicable: see *Davy* v. *Turner* (1970), 114 Sol. Jo. 884.

Where a mortgagee has gone into possession and has received rents to an amount sufficient to keep down the interest, he cannot be allowed to say that interest is in arrear: *Cockburn* v. *Edwards* (1881), 18 Ch. D. 449 (C.A.), at pp. 456, 463; *Wrigley* v. *Gill*, [1906] 1 Ch. 165 (C.A.).

(*a*) *E.g.*, failure to fulfill the requirements for the statutory power of leasing: *Public Trustee* v. *Lawrence*, [1912] Ch. 789.

(*b*) Where the statutory or express power to sell or appoint a receiver is exercisable by reason of the mortgagor's bankruptcy, it is not to be exercised without the leave of the court: Law of Property Act 1925, s. 110 (1); *Re Huddersfield Building Society*, [1940] W.N. 247. As to other restrictions, under the Rent Act, etc., see pp. 272 *et seq.*, *supra*. As to estoppel, see *Braithwaite* v. *Winwood*, [1960] 3 All E.R. 642. As to where the default has been put right, see *Hughes* v. *Birks*, [1958] Estates Gazette Digest 341.

These restrictions on the exercise of the statutory power may be, and commonly are, modified or excluded (c).

Right of sale as between successive incumbrancers.—Where there are successive mortgages, the first mortgagee can exercise his power of sale without the concurrence of the subsequent mortgagees, although he will have to account to them for the surplus (if any) of the purchase money (d). Where a first mortgagee, after making preliminary arrangements (but without a binding contract) for an advantageous sale of the property, bought up the interest of the second mortgagee at a reduced sum the court refused to set aside the sale (e). A second or subsequent mortgagee may sell subject to the first or prior mortgages (f). Alternatively he may sell free of prior incumbrances by arranging for them to be discharged out of the proceeds of sale. In the latter case, the concurrence of the prior mortgagees or application to the court to allow payment into court (g) is necessary.

Notice.—The second ground, *i.e.*, that some interest is in arrear and unpaid for two months after becoming due, is the one usually relied on and, accordingly, a notice requiring payment is then not required. "Mortgagor" includes, unless the context otherwise requires, any person deriving title under the original mortgagor or entitled to redeem a mortgage according to his estate interest or right in the mortgaged property (h). It has been held that a subsequent mortgagee should be served where an express power required notice to the mortgagor or his assigns. But it was doubted whether notice must also be given to the mortgagor (i). The wording of s. 103 (i), *supra*, is somewhat different and it seems proper to give the notice to the mortgagor and at least the first subsequent incumbrancer (k). A subsequent assent to the sale by an interested person, and an agreement by him to join in the conveyance, will operate as a waiver of the notice (l).

If in an express power the length of notice is not specified, a reasonable notice must be given. Notice to pay on the day on which notice is given is not reasonable (m).

Form of notice.—The object of the notice is to guard the rights of the mortgagor, and if this object is substantially attained, the court will not, as against a bona fide purchaser, minutely criticise the exact

---

(c) See footnote (l), p. 360, *supra*.
(d) See p. 373, *infra*. As to notice requiring payment, see *supra*. In practice a first mortgagee will often give a second mortgagee an opportunity of taking a transfer of the first mortgage.
(e) *Dolman* v. *Nokes* (1855), 22 Beav. 402.
(f) See *Manser* v. *Dix* (1857), 8 De G.M. & G. 703.
(g) Under Law of Property Act 1925, s. 50; see p. 559, *infra*.
(h) Law of Property Act 1925, s. 205 (1) (xvi). If the mortgagor is dead, the notice should be served on his personal representatives as long as the equity of redemption remains in them: *Gill* v. *Newton* (1866), 14 W.R. 490.
(i) *Hoole* v. *Smith* (1881), 17 Ch. D. 434.
(k) See Wolstenholme and Cherry's *Conveyancing Statutes* (13th Edn.), vol. 1, p. 211. To ascertain the subsequent incumbrancers search should be made for mortgages registered under the Land Charges Act 1972.
(l) *Selwyn* v. *Garfit* (1888), 38 Ch. D. 273 (C.A.); *Re Thompson and Holt* (1890), 44 Ch. D. 492; but see *Forster* v. *Hoggart* (1850), 15 Q.B. 155.
(m) *Massey* v. *Sladden* (1868), L.R. 4 Ex. 13. As to notice where the mortgage is an equitable mortgage of stocks and shares, see *Stubbs* v. *Slater*, [1910] 1 Ch. 632 (C.A.).

terms of the notice. A notice is not bad if it overstated the principal (*n*). A sale, nor made until the expiration of the proper interval after the service or delivery of the notice has been held good, though the notice declared the intention to sell when that interval had elapsed from its date (*o*). An agreement for sale may be made before the expiration of the notice, if the agreement is conditional upon the power becoming exercisable and if the price is then proper (*p*).

Under the statutory power, the notice may be in the form of demand for immediate payment, with an intimation that if the money is not paid before the expiration of three months from the date of service, the mortgagee will proceed to sell (*q*). But it is equally effective if it is a notice to pay at the end of that period (*r*).

If after the demand, the sale is stopped on receipt of a cheque for the amount due under the mortgage, but the cheque is afterwards dishonoured, the right of sale and the running of the notice having been only suspended, revive, and the power may be exercised without giving a new notice (*s*).

Service of notice.—The service of notice under the Law of Property Act 1925, is regulated by s. 196 of that Act (*t*):

(1) The notice must be in writing.

(2) The notice is sufficient, although only addressed to the mortgagor by that designation without his name, or generally to the person interested without any name, and notwithstanding that any person to be affected by the notice is absent, under disability (*u*), unborn or unascertained (*a*).

(3) The notice is sufficiently served if it is left at the last-known place of abode or business of the mortgagor (*b*), or is affixed or left for him on the mortgaged premises (*c*).

(4) It is also sufficiently served if sent by registered post, and if not returned through the post as undelivered (*d*).

Once a notice has been given it cannot be withdrawn without the consent of the mortgagor (*e*).

(*n*) *Clyde Properties, Ltd.* v. *Tasker*, [1970] N.Z.L.R. 754; see p. 296, *supra.*
(*o*) *Metters* v. *Brown* (1863), 33 L.J. Ch. 97.
(*p*) *Major* v. *Ward* (1847), 5 Hare 598, 604; *Farrar* v. *Farrars, Ltd.* (1888), 40 Ch. D. 395 (C.A.), at p. 412.
(*q*) For form, see 14 Ency. Forms and Precedents (4th Edn.), pp. 863, 864; and Precedent 30 in the Appendix, *infra.*
(*r*) *Barker* v. *Illingworth*, [1908] 2 Ch. 20.
(*s*) *Wood* v. *Murton* (1877), 47 L.J. Q.B. 191.
(*t*) The provisions of the section extend to notices under instruments coming into operation after 1925, unless a contrary intention appears; but not to notices in court proceedings: sub-ss. (5), (6).
(*u*) *Tracey* v. *Lawrence* (1854), 2 Drew. 403 (infancy); *Robertson* v. *Lockie* (1846), 15 L.J. Ch. 379 (mental incapacity).
(*a*) But this does not seem to cover the case where there is no person in existence on whom notice could be served, *e.g.*, where the mortgagor has died intestate, and no administrator has been appointed: *Parkinson* v. *Hanbury* (1860), 1 Dr. & Sm. 143; on appeal (1865), 2 De G.J. & S. 450; affd. (1867), L.R. 2 H.L. 1.
(*b*) *Cannon Brewery Co., Ltd.* v. *Signal Press, Ltd.* (1928), 139 L.T. 384.
(*c*) It is sufficient to fix it to the door of the residence: *Major* v. *Ward, supra.*
(*d*) It is also sufficiently served if sent by recorded delivery service: Recorded Delivery Service Act 1962, s. 1; and see *Re 88 Berkeley Road N.W. 9, Rickwood* v. *Turnsek*, [1971] Ch. 648; [1971] 1 All E.R. 254.
(*e*) *Santley* v. *Wilde*, [1899] 1 Ch. 747; reversed on a different point, [1899] 2 Ch. 474 (C.A.).

A mortgagee is entitled to add to the security the costs incurred in the preparation and service of all proper notices (*f*).

Protection of purchaser.—Unless excused by the terms of the power, or of the conditions of sale, the mortgagee is bound to obtain for the purchaser proper evidence of the facts which entitle him to exercise the power. His unsupported statutory declaration, being the evidence of an interested person, will not be sufficient for the purpose. Formerly it was the practice to insert in mortgages a clause expressly protecting the purchaser against irregularities in the exercise of the power. However nowadays, usually, all that the purchaser will be concerned about will be whether or not the power of sale has arisen (*h*) (and the mortgage deed will usually indicate this), and he will not be concerned to inquire whether the power of sale had become exercisable (*i*), for, in the case of a sale under the statutory power, the purchaser is protected by the following provision of the Law of Property Act 1925 (*k*):

104.—(2) Where a conveyance is made in exercise of the power of sale conferred by this Act, or any enactment replaced by the Act, the title of the purchaser shall not be impeachable on the ground—

(a) that no case had arisen to authorise the sale; or
(b) that due notice was not given; or
(c) where the mortgage is made after the commencement of this Act, that leave of the court, when so required, was not obtained (*l*); or
(d) whether the mortgage was made before or after such commencement, that the power was otherwise improperly or irregularly exercised; and a purchaser is not, either before or on conveyance (*m*), concerned to see or inquire whether a case has arisen to authorise the sale, or due notice has been given, or the power is otherwise properly and regularly exercised; but any person damnified by an unauthorised, or improper, or irregular exercise of the power shall have his remedy in damages against the person exercising the power.

(3) A conveyance on sale by a mortgage, made after the commencement of this Act, shall be deemed to have been made in exercise of the power of sale conferred by this Act unless a contrary intention appears (*n*).

(*f*) As to mortgagee's right to costs, see pp. 649 *et seq.*, *infra.*

(*g*) *Hobson* v. *Bell* (1839), 2 Beav. 17; *Re Edwards and Rudkin to Green* (1888), 58 L.T. 789. A covenant by the mortgagor that he will join in the sale is for the benefit of the mortgagee only, and the purchaser cannot require such concurrence: *Corder* v. *Morgan* (1811), 18 Ves. 344.

(*h*) See p. 360, *supra.*

(*i*) See p. 363, *supra.*

(*k*) Replacing s. 21 (2) of the Conveyancing Act 1881. Under a similar express provision, it was held that a sale to a bona fide purchaser without notice was good, though the security, had been satisfied: *Dicker* v. *Angerstein* (1876), 3 Ch. D. 600.

(*l*) Accordingly the purchaser is not concerned to see whether the Rent Acts apply to the property. This was not in the Conveyancing Acts 1881 to 1911. Irregularities had arisen through a failure to obtain orders giving leave to sell under the Courts (Emergency Powers) Acts 1914 to 1919, and the Increase of Rent and Mortgage Interest (Restrictions) Act 1920, s. 7: see *Anchor Trust Co.* v. *Bell*, [1926] Ch. 805.

(*m*) These words reproduce the amendment made by the Conveyancing Act 1911 s. 5 (1), in order to get over *Life Interest and Reversionary Securities Corporation* v. *Hand-in-Hand Fire and Life Insurance Society*, [1898] 2 Ch. 230, where it was held that the vendor could not rely on the Conveyancing Act 1881, s. 21 (2), as precluding inquiry by the purchaser before conveyance. And see *Holohan* v. *Friends Provident and Century Life Office*, [1966] I.R.1; *Forsythe* v. *Blundell* (1973), 129 C.L.R. 477, at p. 502.

(*n*) See *Re White Rose Cottage*, [1965] Ch. 940 (C.A.); [1965] 1 All E.R. 11. Under the Conveyancing Act 1881 s. 21 (2), the conveyance in order that the purchaser might get the protection of the statute, had to be made "in professed exercise of the power of sale". This is no longer necessary.

The section does not provide, as was usual in express powers of sale, that a purchaser shall not be affected by knowledge that the notice required by the power has not been given. Since he is not protected by a mere provision that he shall not be bound to ascertain or inquire into the propriety of the sale, he is, notwithstanding the above provision, liable to have the sale set aside if he took with actual or constructive notice of an irregularity, such as failure to give proper notice (*o*). Similarly, if it appears that the time for exercising the power has not arrived, the sale is bad (*p*). But, subject to the point about constructive notice, just mentioned, since enquiries might lead to the mortgagee having notice of an irregularity, it is probably better for him to refrain from enquiring.

Stopping the sale.—The power of sale is given to the mortgagee for his own benefit, to enable him the better to realise his debt (*q*). The court may interfere with the exercise of the power at the instance of those interested in the proceeds of sale (*r*). But the court will not interfere merely to prevent its exercise contrary to the wishes of the mortgagor, or even (except on terms of payment of the mortgage debt), it has been said (*s*), because the mortgagee is seeking some collateral object and not merely the payment of his debt. For the mortgagee is not a trustee of the power for the mortgagor (*t*), and the court will not inquire into his motives for exercising it (*u*). So the mortgagee may consult his own convenience as regards the time of the sale (*a*). But, while the mortgagee may look to his own interests, he must pay some regard to the interests of the mortgagor. Where their interests conflict, he is not entitled to act in a manner which sacrifices the interests of the mortgagor (*b*).

The duty of the mortgagee in respect of the sale itself was, formerly,

---

(*o*) *Jenkins* v. *Jones* (1860), 2 Giff. 99, at p. 108; *Parkinson* v. *Hanbury* (1860) 1 Dr. & Sm. 143 (this point was not considered on appeal); *Bailey* v. *Barnes*, [1894] 1 Ch. 25 (C.A.); *Holohan* v. *Friends Provident and Century Life Office, supra.* Cf. *Prichard* v. *Wilson* (1864), 10 Jur. N.S. 330 (express power that the only remedy for irregularity was to be damages against the mortgagee). Notwithstanding *Bailey* v. *Barnes* it has been suggested that the protection is only lost by actual, and not constructive, notice, or, alternatively, that the purchaser, so long as the power of sale has arisen, will always get a good title and the mortgagor will be left to his remedy in damages against the mortgagee; see the discussion in Fairest, *Mortgages*, pp. 66–67; Sykes, *The Law of Securities* (2nd Edn.), p. 95; and see (1976) 73 L.S. Gaz. 654 (H. E. Markson).

(*p*) *Selwyn* v. *Garfit* (1888), 38 Ch. D. 273 (C.A.).

(*q*) See, *e. g.*, *Warner* v. *Jacob* (1882), 20 Ch. D. 220, 234; *Farrar* v. *Farrars. Ltd.* (1888), 40 Ch. D. 395 at p. 398; *Palmer* v. *Barclays Bank, Ltd.* (1971), 23 P. & C.R. 30; *Lake Apartments, Ltd.* v. *Bootwala* (1973), 37 D.L.R. (3d) 523; *Forsyth* v. *Blundell* (1973), 129 C.L.R. 477, at pp. 483, 494.

(*r*) *Jarrett* v. *Barclays Bank, Ltd.*, [1947] Ch. 187. (C.A.); [1947] 1 All E.R. 72; and see *Clark* v. *National Mutual Life Association of Australasia, Ltd.*, [1966] N.Z.L.R. 196.

(*s*) *Nash* v. *Eads* (1880), 25 Sol. Jo. 85 (C.A.), *per* SIR GEORGE JESSELL; and see *Belton* v. *Bass, Ratcliffe and Gretton*, [1922] 2 Ch. 449, at pp. 465–466.

(*t*) *Cuckmere Brick Co., Ltd.* v. *Mutual Finance, Ltd.*, [1971] Ch. 949 (C.A.), at pp. 965, 969; [1971] 2 All E.R. 633 at pp. 643, 746; and see p. 368, *infra.* See generally Waters, *The Constructive Trust*, Ch. III. As to building societies, see p. 370, *infra.*

(*u*) See *Belton* v. *Bass, Ratcliffe and Gretton, Ltd., supra*, 465.

(*a*) *Reliance Permanent Building Society* v. *Harwood-Stamper*, [1944] Ch. 362, at p. 372, per Vaisey, J.; [1944] 2 All E.R. 75, at p. 80; *Cuckmere Brick Co.*, v. *Mutual Finance, Ltd., supra*, at pp. 965, 969; 644, 646.

(*b*) *Forsyth* v. *Blundell* (1973), 129 C.L.R. 477, at p. 494 *per* WALSH, J., And see p. 368, *infra.*

generally put on the basis of good faith alone (c). There were dicta
that something more was required of the selling mortgagee besides
absence of bad faith, namely that he was also under a duty to take
reasonable care to obtain whatever was the true market value of the
mortgaged property at the moment he chose to sell it (d). Whether or
not there was really any conflict between these two tests (which is to be
doubted, since, as it has been said, to take reasonable precautions to
obtain a proper price is but a part of the duty to act in good faith (e)) it
is now clearly established that a mortgagee, when exercising his power
of sale, owes a duty to the mortgagor (f) to take reasonable care to
obtain a proper price (g). The burden of proof is on the mortgagor to
prove breach of this duty by the mortgagee (h). The same duty is owed
whether the sale be a statutory one, an express one or under a power of
attorney (i).

Therefore, when selling tenanted property, which would realise a
much higher price with vacant possession, the mortgagee should, in
appropriate cases, attempt to obtain vacant possession (k). Where
commercial premises are involved the sale should generally include any
goodwill (l) and licences (m). All material planning permissions known
to the mortgagee should be advertised in good time before the sale (n).
To accept less in a private sale than a prospective purchaser, with
means, has indicated he would bid at the proposed auction may be a
breach of the mortgagee's duty. The mortgagee has to balance a higher
offer, which is not firm, against a lower firm offer which will be withdrawn if not accepted within a specified period (o). The disclosure of a
reserve price to an intending purchaser may be a breach of the mortgagee's duty (p). Often, however, an alleged undervalue will merely be

---

(c) Kennedy v. De Trafford, [1897] A.C. 180 (H.L.). See generally Cuckmere Brick
Co., Ltd. v. Mutual Finance, Ltd., [1971] Ch. 949 (C.A.); [1971] 2 All E.R. 633.
(d) Wolff v. Vanderzee (1869), 20 L.T. 353; National Bank of Australasia v. United
Hand-in-Hand and Band of Hope Co. (1879), 4 App. Cas. 391 (P.C.); Tomlin v. Luce
(1889), 41 Ch. D. 573; on appeal, 43 Ch. D. 191 (C.A.); McHugh v. Union Bank of Canada,
[1913] A.C. 299 (P.C.).
(e) Forsyth v. Blundell (1973), 129 C.L.R. 477 (H.C. of A.), at p. 481.
(f) And equally, it is submitted, to any other mortgagees; see Midland Bank, Ltd.
v. Joliman Finance, Ltd. (1967), Estates Gazette Digest 612 (second mortgagee against
selling first mortgagee). and see Alliance Acceptance Co., Ltd. v. Graham [1974–75] 10
S.A.S.R. 220 (S.A.S.C.) (third mortgagee obtained injunction restraining sale).
(g) Cuckmere Brick Co., Ltd. v. Mutual Finance, Ltd., supra. SALMON, L.J. preferred
"true market value". See also Holohan v. Friends Provident and Century Life Office,
supra; Forsyth v. Blundell, supra; Alexandre v. New Zealand Breweries, Ltd., [1974]
1 N.Z.L.R. 497; Gulf and Fraser Fishermen's Union v. Calm C Fish, Ltd., [1975] 1
Lloyd's Rep. 188 (B.C. C.A.). Francis Mortgages and Securities (2nd Edn.), p. 99 speaks
of a hardening attitude to the mortgagee over the past century.
(h) Haddington Island Quarry Co., Ltd. v. Huson, [1911] A.C. 727 (P.C.).
(i) For a sale under power of attorney, see Alexandre v. New Zealand Breweries,
Ltd., supra. The same duty applies to a receiver appointed by debenture-holders:
Kernohan Estates, Ltd. v. Boyd, [1967] N.I. 27.
(k) Holohan v. Friends Provident and Century Life Office, supra.
(l) Palmer v. Barclays Bank, Ltd. (1971), 23 P. & C.R. 30.
(m) Alexandre v. New Zealand Breweries, Ltd., supra.
(n) Cuckmere Brick Co., Ltd. v. Mutual Finance, Ltd., supra; Alexandre v. New Zealand Breweries, Ltd., supra; Palmer v. Barclays Bank, Ltd., supra.
(o) Forsyth v. Blundell, supra; Midland Bank, Ltd., v. Joliman Finance, Ltd., supra.
(p) Barns v. Queensland National Bank, Ltd. (1906), 3 C.L.R. 925, 944.

the difference in the opinions of several valuers (*q*). The mortgagee can safely accept the highest bid for a properly described and advertised property at a properly publicised auction (*r*).

A mortgagee does not relieve himself of his duty by placing the sale in the hands of reputable agents (*s*).

It is quite clear that the mortgagee will not generally fulfil his duty by selling the property at a sum sufficient to pay off the mortgage. A threat to do so was often made in the past (*t*), but this was always wrong. In view of the sufficient equity in the property required by most mortgagees, a sale at just above the sum to discharge the mortgage will be looked at carefully by the court, but this is not to say that there may be occasions when that sum is the proper price or true market value.

Assuming that the mortgagee is otherwise acting properly, the mortgage will not be restrained from exercising his power of sale because the amount due is in dispute (*u*). But he will be restrained if, before there is a contract for the sale of the mortgaged property (*a*), the mortgagor tenders to the mortgagee or pays into court the amount claimed to be due (*b*); that is, the amount which the mortgagee claimed to be due to him for principal, interest and costs (*c*) (unless on the face of the mortgage, the claim is excessive (*d*), when the amount less such excess must be tendered or paid) or, where notice is required, if due notice has not been given (*e*). The mortgagee will be restrained if

---

(*q*) *Cottenham Park Developments, Ltd.* v. *Cohen* (1967), Estates Gazette Digest 315; *Sinfield* v. *Sweet*, [1967] 3 All E.R. 479; *Pallant* v. *Porter* (1972), 233 Estates Gazette 391; *Waltham Forest London Borough* v. *Webb* (1974), 232 Estates Gazette 461; *Johnson* v. *Ribbins* (1975), 235 Estates Gazette 757.

(*r*) *Cuckmere Brick Co., Ltd.* v. *Mutual Finance, Ltd., supra, per* SALMON, L.J., at p. 965 and 643 respectively.

(*s*) See *per* CROSS, L.J., in *Cuckmere Brick Co., Ltd.* v. *Mutual Finance, Ltd.*, at p. 973 and 649 respectively; see also (not so firmly) SALMON, L.J., at pp. 969 and 646 and CAIRNS, L.J., at pp. 980, 655.

(*t*) See, *e.g.*, *Midland Bank, Ltd.* v. *Joliman Finance, Ltd., supra.*

(*u*) *Gill* v. *Newton* (1866), 14 W.R. 490. Although, where the mortgagor is a company, the presentation of a winding-up petition is not in general a ground for stopping the sale, an interim injunction may be granted where the mortgagee had himself presented the petition: see *Re Cambrian Mining Co., Ltd., Ex parte Fell* (1881), 50 L.J. Ch. 836.

(*a*) *Waring (Lord)* v. *London and Manchester Assurance Co., Ltd.*, [1935] Ch. 310; *Property and Bloodstock, Ltd.* v. *Emerton*, [1968] Ch. 94 (C.A.); [1967] 3 All E.R. 321. And in some jurisdictions, at any time before conveyance: see *Camp-Wee-Gee-Wa for Boys, Ltd.* v. *Clark* (1971), 23 D.L.R. (3d) 158; *Re Hal Wright Motor Sales, Ltd. and Industrial Development Bank* (1975), 8 O.R. (2d) 76.

(*b*) *Jones* v. *Matthie*; *Warner* v. *Jacob, supra*; *Duke* v. *Robson*, [1973] 1 All E.R. 481; *Inglis* v. *Commonwealth Trading Bank of Australia* (1972), 126 C.L.R. 161 (H.C. of A.). It seems that a mortgagor need not offer to redeem where the mortgagee is not exercising his powers of sale *bona fide: Murad* v. *National Provincial Bank* (1966), 198 Estates Gazette 117. Payment into court may be a condition of granting an injunction restraining the sale: see *United Builders Pty., Ltd.* v. *The Commercial Banking Co. of Sydney, Ltd.*, [1975] Qd. R. 357; *Henry Roach Petroleum Pty., Ltd.* v. *Credit House (Vic.) Pty., Ltd.*, [1976] V.R. 309.

(*c*) *Hill* v. *Kirkwood* (1880), 28 W.R. 358; *Hickson* v. *Darlow* (1883), 23 Ch. D. 690 (C.A.); *Macleod* v. *Jones* (1883), 24 Ch. D. 289 (C.A.). A tender at the sale of principal and interest, though without costs, has been held to be sufficient: *Jenkins* v. *Jones* (1860), 2 Giff. 99.

(*d*) *Hickson* v. *Darlow, supra; cf. Deverges* v. *Sandeman, Clark & Co.*, [1902] 1 Ch 579 (C.A.). And where the mortgagee was, at the time of the mortgage, the mortgagor's solicitor, the court fixed the sum which if considered would cover the advance: *Macleod* v. *Jones, supra.*

(*e*) This seems to be so, since want of notice is a ground for setting aside the sale, where the purchaser is aware of the defect: *Selwyn* v. *Garfit*, see p. 367, *supra*. Though

a subsequent incumbrancer has brought an action to redeem and his right to do so has been denied (*f*).

If the mortgagee has exercised his powers improperly, and the purchaser has knowledge of the facts, the purchaser cannot obtain a right superior to the right of the mortgagor. The mortgagee and the purchaser may then both be restrained from completing the sale (*g*). And the same applies even where, at the date of the contract, the purchaser was unaware of the impropriety of the sale (*h*).

If the mortgagor has, in exercise of his power of sale, entered into a contract for the sale of the property, the court will not, upon tender of the money due under the mortgage, interfere to stop the completion of the sale by conveyance unless the sale is improper (*i*).

Where the mortgagee is a building society, however, it must, in exercising any power of sale, obtain the best price reasonably obtainable (*k*). It has been said, therefore, that a building society, unlike an ordinary mortgagee, is in the position of a fiduciary vendor (*l*). But, in view of what had been said above about the duty of the mortgagee (*m*) there would appear to be little practical difference between building societies and other mortgagees.

Mortgagee may not purchase.—The mortgagee "cannot sell to himself either alone or with others, or to a trustee for himself, nor to any one employed by him to conduct the sale" (*n*), unless the sale is made by the court, and he has obtained leave to bid (*o*). "For a sale by a person to himself is no sale at all, and a power of sale does not authorise the donee of the power to take the property subject to it at a price fixed by himself, even though such price be the full value" (*n*). The same rule applies to any officer of the mortgagee or the solicitor or other agent who is acting for the mortgagee in the matter

---

it has been held that, unless the right to sell is vested in a trustee, whose duty binds him to give notice to both parties, the court will not generally stop the sale on the ground that the required notice had not been given, but will leave the mortgagor to bring an action to impeach the sale, and to give notice to the purchaser that he has done so: *Anon.* (1821), 6 Madd. 10.

(*f*) *Rhodes* v. *Buckland* (1852), 16 Beav. 212.

(*g*) *Forsyth* v. *Blundell* (1973), 129 C.L.R. 477, at p. 497.

(*h*) *Forsyth* v. *Blundell, supra*, at pp. 497–499.

(*i*) *Waring* (*Lord*) v. *London and Manchester Assurance Co. Ltd., supra; Property and Bloodstock, Ltd.* v. *Emerton*, [1968] Ch. 94 (C.A.); [1967] 3 All E.R. 321; *Duke* v. *Robson*, [1973] All E.R. 481.

(*k*) Building Societies Act 1962, s. 36, replacing s. 10 of the Building Societies Act 1939.

(*l*) *Reliance Permanent Building Society* v. *Harwood-Stamper*, [1944] Ch. 362; [1944] 2 All E.R. 75; and see *Cottrill* v. *Steyning and Littlehampton Building Society*, [1966] 2 All E.R. 296, n.

(*m*) *Cuckmere Brick Co., Ltd.* v. *Mutual Finance, Ltd., supra.*

(*n*) *Farrar* v. *Farrars, Ltd.* (1888), 40 Ch. D. 395, at p. 409; *Martinson* v. *Clowes* (1882), 21 Ch. D. 857; on appeal (1885), 52 L.T. 706 (C.A.); *Hodson* v. *Deans*, [1903] 2 Ch. 647.

(*o*) *Downes* v. *Grazebrook* (1817), 3 Mer. 200; *National Bank of Australasia* v. *United Hand-in-Hand, etc., Co.* (1879), 4 App. Cas. 391 (P.C.); *Farrar* v. *Farrars, Ltd., supra; Williams* v. *Wellingborough Borough Council*, [1975] 3 All E.R. 462 (C.A.).

If the mortgagee is a trustee, he will not have leave to bid if the beneficiary objects, unless attempts to sell to others have failed: *Tennant* v. *Trenchard* (1869), L.R. 4 Ch. 537. A way around the rule stated above may be to obtain a money judgment on the personal covenant and then purchase the property on a sale on the execution of that judgment: *Simpson* v. *Forrester* (1973), 47 A.L.J.R. 149; (1972), 46 A.L.J. 469; (1973) 47 A.L.J. 544 (Ross Barber).

of the sale (*p*) or a servant of the mortgagee (*q*), but not to the solicitor who acted in the matter of the mortgage, but not in the matter of the sale (*r*). The rule does not apply to an execution creditor (*s*).

A sale by a person to a corporation of which he is a member is not, either in form or in substance, a sale by a person to himself (*t*). Nevertheless, such a sale might be restrained or set aside or ignored (*u*) on the ground that the mortgagee had not acted bona fide (*a*).

The mortgagor himself may purchase as may one of several co-mortgagors (*b*). And a later mortgagee may do so, provided he has not used his position as mortgagee to get an undue advantage or has otherwise acted mala fides (*c*).

The sale.—If only authorised to sell by public auction, the mortgagee without statutory power could not sell privately. But where either mode of sale is permitted, a private sale, even without advertisement, is good, provided it is made bona fide and for a fair price (*d*). Where the sale is to be by private treaty, it is preferable to put the matter in the hands of competent agents. If the sale is to be effected by the mortgagee himself, at least a proper valuation should be obtained. If the sale is to be by auction, it is usual and proper, though probably not essential, to fix a reserve price.

The mortgagee should avoid the use of unnecessarily stringent conditions of sale. Conditions commonly used by conveyancers are, as a general rule, safe for mortgagees, who will not, however, be restrained from adding such further conditions, adapted to the state of the title, as may be reasonably used in the disposal of his property by a prudent owner, anxious to protect himself against the risk and expense of litigation; a risk which is as much for the benefit of the mortgagor as of the mortgagee to avoid, and the proper avoidance of which outweighs the possible diminution in the number and value of the biddings which may be caused by the conditions (*e*).

The mortgagee should be careful as to the description of the property in the particulars, for if, by reason of a misdescription, compensation has to be allowed to the purchaser, the vendor will be liable to a subsequent incumbrancer (and to the mortgagor), not necessarily for

---

(*p*) *Martinson* v. *Clowes, supra*; *Parnell* v. *Tyler* (1833), 2 L.J. Ch. 195 (solicitor's clerk); *Hodson* v. *Deans, supra*.

(*q*) *Sewell* v. *Agricultural Bank of Western Australia* (1930), 44 C.L.R. 104.

(*r*) *Nutt* v. *Easton*, [1899] 1 Ch. 873; affd. on another point, [1900] 1 Ch. 29 (C.A.).

(*s*) *Stratford* v. *Twynam* (1822), Jac. 418. See footnote (*o*), p. 370, *supra*.

(*t*) *Farrar* v. *Farrars, Ltd., supra*, at p. 409.

(*u*) See *Henderson* v. *Astwood*, [1894] A.C. 150 (P.C.).

(*a*) *Farrar* v. *Farrars, Ltd., supra*; *Hodson* v. *Deans, supra*.

(*b*) *Kennedy* v. *De Trafford*, [1897] A.C. 180 (H.L.); followed in *Re Nunes and District Registrar for the District of Winnipeg* (1972), 21 D.L.R. (3d) 97.

(*c*) *Parkinson* v. *Hanbury* (1860), 1 Dr. & Sm. 143; *Shaw* v. *Bunny* (1864), 33 Beav. 494; affd. (1865), 2 De G.J. & Sm. 468; *Kirkwood* v. *Thompson* (1865), 2 Hem. & M. 392; *Flower & Sons* v. *Pritchard* (1908), 53 Sol. Jo. 178.

(*d*) *Davey* v. *Durrant* (1857), 1 De G. & J. 535.

(*e*) *Hobson* v. *Bell* (1839), 2 Beav. 17; *Kershaw* v. *Kalow* (1855), 1 Jur. (N.S.) 974; *Falkner Equitable Reversionary Society* (1858), 4 Drew. 352. See *Cragg* v. *Alexander*, [1867] W.N. 305, as to improper conditions on sale of a reversion. And see generally as to conditions on the exercise of the statutory power, Law of Property Act 1925, s. 101 (1) (i), p. 361, *supra*.

the sum paid as compensation, but for the difference between the price paid and the price which would have been obtained if the mistake had not been made (*f*).

A mortgagee, who is selling, need not consult the mortgagor nor subsequent incumbrancers, and although he elects to keep them informed of the progress of negotiations, he does not thereby limit his freedom of action (*g*).

A mortgagee who has contracted to sell, but before the land has become vested in the purchaser has rescinded, and who later sells at a lower price, is only accountable for the purchase money received (*h*).

A mortgagee or his auctioneer may accept the purchaser's cheque for the deposit, and if it is dishonoured, the mortgagee is not liable for the costs of an abortive sale, but may add them to his security (*i*).

Mortgagees may join in selling together different properties, or different interests in the same property, where it is clearly beneficial to do so. But they must see that the purchase money is properly apportioned by their own valuers before the completion of the purchase (*k*).

The property may be sold upon the terms that part or even the whole of the purchase money shall remain on mortgage, where the mortgagee takes the risk and charges himself in account with the mortgagor with the whole purchase money (*l*).

With respect to the receipt by the mortgagee of the purchase money, the Law of Property Act 1925, provides that the receipt in writing of a mortgagee (*m*), shall be a sufficient discharge for any money arising under the power of sale conferred by the Act, or any money or securities comprised in his mortgage, or arising thereunder; and a person paying or transferring the same to the mortgagee shall not be concerned to inquire whether any money remains due under the mortgage (*n*).

Setting the sale aside.—The protection of the purchaser has been dealt with above (*o*). In those cases where the purchaser is not so protected, because he has notice, actual or constructive, of the impropriety in the sale, the mortgagor can have the sale set aside, if he seeks relief promptly (*p*). Alternatively, the conveyance may be treated as

---

(*f*) *Wolff* v. *Vanderzee* (1869), 17 W.R. 547; *Tomlin* v. *Luce* (1889), 43 Ch. D. 191 (C.A.).

(*g*) *G. Merel & Co., Ltd.* v. *Barclays Bank* (1963), 107 Sol. Jo. 542.

(*h*) *Wright* v. *New Zealand Farmers Co-operative Association of Canterbury, Ltd.*, [1939] A.C. 439 (P.C.) (assuming the rescission was proper).

(*i*) *Farrer* v. *Lacy, Hartland & Co.* (1885), 25 Ch. D. 636; affd. 31 Ch. D. 42 (C.A.).

(*k*) *Hiatt* v. *Hillman* (1871), 19 W.R. 694; *Re Cooper and Allen's Contract* (1876), 4 Ch. D. 802.

(*l*) *Davey* v. *Durrant, supra*; *Thurlow* v. *Mackeson* (1868), L.R. 4 Q.B. 97; *Farrar* v. *Farrars, Ltd.* (1888), 40 Ch. D. 395 (C.A.); *Kennedy* v. *De Trafford*, [1897] A.C. 180 (H.L.); *Belton* v. *Bass, Ratcliffe and Gretton, Ltd.*, [1922] 2 Ch. 449.

(*m*) Where first and second mortgagees have power to sell and give receipts, they may concur in the sale, the one giving a receipt for so much of the purchase money as will discharge his debt, and the other for the balance: *M'Carogher* v. *Whieldon* (1864), 34 Beav. 107.

(*n*) Section 107 (1).

(*o*) Page 366, *supra*.

(*p*) *Nutt* v. *Easton*, [1900] 1 Ch. 29 (C.A.); *Belton* v. *Bass, Ratcliffe and Gretton, Ltd.* [1922] 2 Ch. 449.

operating only on a transfer of the mortgage and of the debt secured by it, and not as a transfer of the mortgagor's interest (*q*).

The mortgagor's claim to impeach a sale by the mortgagee being a mere equity, it will be defeated by a purchaser for value of any interest, legal or equitable, without notice of the irregularity (*r*).

Application of purchase-money.—A sale (*s*) destroys the equity of redemption in the mortgaged property, and constitutes the mortgagee exercising the power of sale a trustee of the surplus proceeds of sale, if any, for the persons interested according to their priorities (*t*). The order of application of any surplus under an exercise of the statutory power is set out in the Law of Property Act 1925, as follows:

> **105.**—The money which is received by the mortgagee, arising from the sale (*u*), after discharge of prior incumbrances to which the sale is not made subject, if any, or after payment into court under this Act of a sum to meet any prior incumbrance (*x*), shall be held by him in trust to be applied by him, first, in payment of all costs, charges, and expenses properly incurred by him as incident to the sale or any attempted sale (*a*), or otherwise; and secondly, in discharge of the mortgage money, interest (*b*), and costs, and other money, if any, due under the mortgage; and the residue of the money so received shall be paid to the person entitled to the mortgaged property, or authorised to give receipts for the proceeds of the sale thereof (*c*).

Where there are subsequent incumbrancers (*d*), it has been held that the surplus proceeds should be paid to the incumbrancer next in order (*e*), and if the first mortgagee has notice (*f*) of any subsequent

---

(*q*) See *Selwyn* v. *Garfit* (1888), 38 Ch. D. 273 (C.A.); *Latec Investments, Ltd.* v. *Hotel Terrigal Pty., Ltd.* (1965), 113 C.L.R. 265, 274–5; considered in *Forsyth* v. *Blundell*, *supra*.   (*r*) *Latec Investments, Ltd.* v. *Hotel Terrigal Pty., Ltd.*, *supra*.

(*s*) As does a binding contract for sale: *Waring* (*Lord*) v. *London and Manchester Assurance Co., Ltd.*, [1935] Ch. 310; *Property and Bloodstock, Ltd.* v. *Emerton*, [1968] Ch. 94 (C.A.); [1967] 3 All E.R. 321; *Duke* v. *Robson*, [1973] 1 All E.R. 481.

(*t*) *S.E. Rail. Co.* v. *Jortin* (1857), 6 H.L.C. 425; *Rajah Kishendatt Ram* v. *Rajah Mumtaz Ali Khan* (1879), L.R. 6 Ind. App. 145 (P.C.); and see Law of Property Act 1925, s. 105, *supra*, Waters, *The Constructive Trust*, pp. 203 *et seq.*

(*u*) The direction as to application of the proceeds of sale applies, with an adaptation as to costs, to other money received by a mortgagee, *e.g.*, the proceeds of sale arising on a sale under an express power of sale: Law of Property Act 1925, s. 107 (2).

(*x*) Under the Law of Property Act 1925, s. 50; see p. 559,*infra*.

(*a*) *Matzner* v. *Clyde Securities, Ltd.*, [1975] 2 N.S.W.L.R. 293.

(*b*) *Quaere* whether early repayment discount (see p. 522, *infra*) should be allowed.

(*c*) These words seem to be incorrect, the person entitled to the property at the time of division of the surplus being in strictness the purchaser, and the person authorised to give receipts for the proceeds of sale being the mortgagee who exercises the power, but practically the meaning is clear. The surplus is to be paid to the subsequent incumbrancer, if any, or to the mortgagor or his successors in title.

(*d*) With enforceable claims: *Matthews* (*C. & M.*), *Ltd.* v. *Marsden Building Society*, [1951] Ch. 758 (C.A.); [1951] 1 All E.R. 1053. *E.g.*, a bank claiming under a lien: *Greendon Investments* v. *Mills* (1973), 226 Estates Gazette 1957.

(*e*) *Re Thomson's Mortgage Trusts*, [1920] 1 Ch. 508. But EVE, J., admitted that the matter was not free from doubt. The alternative is that the selling mortgagee distributes the surplus between those entitled (see as to mortgages of reversions, p. 375, *infra*). But this will involve the selling mortgagee in the state of accounts between each subsequent mortgagee and the mortgagor. It is submitted that the proper course for the selling mortgagee is, as in *Re Thomson's Mortgage Trusts, supra*, it was held he was obliged to do, namely to pay over the surplus to the next incumbrancer. But see *Matthews* (*C. & M.*), *Ltd.* v. *Marsden Building Society, supra*.

(*f*) *E.g.*, by registration in the Land Charges Register: Law of Property Act 1925, s. 198 (1). For constructive notice, see Law of Property Act 1925, s. 199 (1). A registered chargee who is selling should search the register of title. Actual notice should be given by a second or subsequent mortgagee: see p. 171, *supra*.

incumbrance, he is liable to any subsequent incumbrancer if he pays the proceeds to the mortgagor (*g*).

The solicitor of the selling mortgagee, who pays over proceeds to the mortgagor, against whom there is a well-founded claim to be met to the knowledge of the solicitor (*h*), may be liable to the creditor as constructive trustee. Liability depends on receipt or dealing with the proceeds with knowledge of the claim and of his client's intention not to meet the claim or assisting in the disposal of the monies with such knowledge (*i*).

If, by a mistake, the mortgagee pays over to a subsequent incumbrancer or to the mortgagor more than he should have, he may claim repayment (*k*).

Where there are no subsequent incumbrancers the surplus must be paid over to the mortgagor (*l*) or other person entitled to the equity of redemption, or if the equity of redemption is held upon trust for sale to the trustees (*m*) or, in cases of difficulty, into court (*n*).

If there is a dispute as to whether or not there is a subsequent incumbrance, *e.g.*, where the mortgagor contests the validity of the second mortgage, the surplus should be paid into court, or, if so requested, put on deposit pending a settlement of the dispute (*o*). If the rights of the mortgagor and his successors have become statute-barred, the mortgagee may keep the surplus (*p*).

If a mortgagor unsuccessfully impeaches a sale by a first mortgagee, the latter is not allowed to add the costs of defending such action to his mortgage debt as against a second mortgagee (*q*).

If the proceeds of sale are not sufficient to satisfy his debt, the mortgagee can sue the mortgagor on the personal covenant for the deficiency (*r*).

The mortgagee of a reversionary interest is not entitled to receive the

---

(*g*) *West London Commercial Bank* v. *Reliance Permanent Building Society* (1885), 29 Ch. D. 954 (C.A.), at p. 962. This liability is not dependent on the registration of the subsequent mortgage. For the costs of payment over, see footnote (*k*), p. 648, *infra*.

(*h*) *E.g.*, where the mortgagor is a husband and his wife with whom he is at odds, clearly has a claim to a share in the house. Or where a subsequent mortgage is ineffective for some reason, but there is clearly a good money claim against the mortgagor.

(*i*) See *Carl-Zeiss-Stiftung* v. *Herbert Smith & Co.* (*No.* 2), [1969] 2 Ch. 276; [1969] 2 All E.R. 367; *Lake* v. *Bayliss*, [1974] 2 All E.R. 1114; and generally, (1975) 39 Conv. (N.S.) 162, pp. 172 *et seq.* (A. J. Hawkins).

(*k*) *Weld-Blundell* v. *Synott*, [1940] 2 K.B. 107; [1940] 2 All E.R. 580.

(*l*) Where the mortgagor has by his will given his realty and personalty to different persons and has died questions may arise as to who is entitled to the surplus proceeds of sale. If the sale took place during the mortgagor's life the surplus goes as personalty (*Re Grange, Chadwick* v. *Grange*, [1907] 2 Ch. 20); after his death, as realty.

(*m*) The money is capital money and must be paid to not fewer than two trustees or to a trust corporation: Law of Property Act 1925, ss. 27 (2), 28 (1); Trustee Act 1925, s. 14.

(*n*) *Re Walhampton Estate* (1884), 26 Ch. D. 391; Trustee Act 1925, s. 63. See R.S.C. Ord. 92, r. 2; C.C.R. Ord. 39 (where the amount does not exceed £5,000). Prior permission is required to pay not more than £500 into the High Court: *Practice Direction*, [1976] 1 Lloyd's Rep. 281.

(*o*) For a dispute as to the entitlement of surplus proceeds of sale see *Samuel Keller (Holdings), Ltd.* v. *Martins Bank, Ltd.*, [1970] 3 All E.R. 950 (C.A.).

(*p*) *Young* v. *Clarey*, [1948] Ch. 191; [1948] 1 All E.R. 197.

(*q*) *Re Smith's Mortgage, Harrison* v. *Edwards*, [1931] 2 Ch. 168.

(*r*) The rule that a mortgagee disables himself from suing for the debt by putting it out of his power to reconvey does not apply to a sale under a power given by the mortgage: *Re McHenry, Barker's Claim*, [1894] 3 Ch. 290.

whole of the mortgagor's interest when it falls in, but only so much as to discharge the principal, interest and costs due on the mortgage (s).

Where a building society exercises a power of sale it must, within twenty-eight days of the sale, send to the mortgagor certain particulars relating to the sale (t).

Surplus purchase money and particular subsequent incumbrancers.—The position where trustees for sale are entitled to the surplus has already been stated (u). And it is submitted that the same will apply where, for example, although the mortgage was properly made by the husband alone, the property being held in his name alone, the court has subsequently declared (a) that the beneficial interest in the mortgaged property is held by the husband and his wife as tenants in common (b). Where the mortgaged land is settled land, any surplus, as capital money, must be paid to not fewer than two trustees or a trust corporation (c). A properly protected execution creditor with a charging order is in the same position as an equitable mortgagee (d) and, accordingly, the mortgagee who has exercised the power of sale may insist on paying over the whole balance to such a person where there is no intermediate incumbrance. Where a garnishee order *nisi* has been obtained against the mortgagee, by a judgment creditor of the mortgagor and there are no intermediate mortgages, any surplus will be bound by the order (e). If there are intermediate mortgages or charges, the order will usually have been made subject to the rights thereunder (f), and, in any event, the order cannot give the judgment creditor priority over such incumbrances (g). And under an order absolute the debt is subject to all rights attaching to it in the hands of the garnishee (h). The surplus in the hands of a mortgagee who has realised his security cannot be attached by a garnishee order against the mortgagor obtained by a judgment creditor of a subsequent mortgagee before the sale (i). It is necessary to obtain a garnishee order after the sale against the first mortgagee. A mortgagor's interest in surplus proceeds of sale following a sale of the mortgaged property by

---

(s) *Re Bell, Jeffrey* v. *Sayles*, [1896] 1 Ch. 1 (C.A.); *Hockey* v. *Western*, [1898] 1 Ch. 350 (C.A.); *Re Lloyd, Lloyd* v. *Lloyd*, [1903] 1 Ch. 385 (C.A.), at p. 403.

(t) Building Societies Act 1962, ss. 36 (1) (b), (3), (4), 123 (2).

(u) P. 374, *supra*.

(a) *E.g.*, upon an application under s. 17 of the Married Women's Property Act, 1882.

(b) Accordingly it will be necessary for another trustee to be appointed to receive the monies: see (1967) 31 Conv. (N.S.) 259 (R. E. Poole). The mortgage in this case would seem to be valid; see *Re Morgan's Lease, Jones* v. *Norseowicz*, [1972] Ch. 1; [1971] 2 All E.R. 235, doubting *Weston* v. *Henshaw*, [1950] Ch. 510 (unauthorised mortgage by tenant for life as absolute owner invalidated by s. 18 of the Settled Land Act 1925. There is no corresponding provision under the Law of Property Act 1925). See further (1969) 33 Conv. (N.S.) 240 (J. F. Garner).

(c) Or into court: Settled Land Act 1925, s. 18 (1) (b), (c).

(d) Administration of Justice Act 1956, s. 35 (3). See p. 159, *supra*.

(e) Even if the surplus exceeds the judgment debt, unless the order is restricted to such amount as will satisfy the judgment debt: *Joachimson* v. *Swiss Bank Corpn.*, [1921] 3 K.B. 110 (C.A.), at p. 121. And see p. 163, *supra*.

(f) R.S.C. Ord. 49, r. 6.

(g) *Badeley* v. *Consolidated Bank* (1888), 38 Ch. D. 238 (C.A.). *Cf. Vacuum Oil Co., Ltd.* v. *Ellis*, [1914] 1 K.B. 693 (C.A.).

(h) *Norton* v. *Yates*, [1906] 1 K.B. 112, 121.

(i) *Chatterton* v. *Watney* (1881), 17 Ch. D. 259 (C.A.).

the mortgagee under his statutory power of sale is an equitable chose in action and is included in the mortgagor's personal estate, so that if the mortgagor's personal estate is subject to a writ of sequestration the interest is subject to the writ. The mortgagee is bound to pay over the surplus proceeds to the sequestrators and does not need the protection of a specific court order before paying over the surplus (*k*).

The trust of the surplus.—Section 105 of the Law of Property Act 1925, declares trusts of the proceeds of sale and such trusts used sometimes to be declared by the mortgage deed itself (*l*). The trust under s. 105 of the Law of Property Act 1925 arises as soon as the proceeds of sale are received. As regards the mortgagor, however, an express trust, and, it is submitted, the statutory trust, applies only to the surplus and cannot be enforced by him for any other purpose (*m*). And where a clause in the mortgage deed merely declares that the mortgagee shall apply the purchase money as above stated, or where under statute (*n*) there is no special provision for the application of the purchase money, a constructive trust arises, and the mortgagee becomes a constructive trustee of the surplus as soon as it is shown that there is a surplus(*o*). Whether the trust is statutory, express or constructive, time will not run against the person or persons entitled to the surplus, if the selling mortgagee retains the surplus or converts it to his own use (*p*).

Interest after sale.—Upon the sale being completed, interest ceases to run against the mortgagor (*q*). The mortgagee is then allowed a reasonable time to do his sums to ascertain any surplus (*r*). A period of 28 days will, generally, be adequate for this purpose. Thereafter interest will run on the surplus. This has been stated to be a matter of the court's discretion, rather than entitlement, but the practice is to allow interest in most cases (*s*). The old cases refer to interest at 4 per cent. per annum (*t*), but, probably, now the appropriate rate is obtainable on deposit accounts with banks or building societies (*u*).

Effect of conveyance, etc.—Under the Conveyancing Act 1881 (*a*),

---

(*k*) *Bucknell* v. *Bucknell*, [1969] 2 All E.R. 998.

(*l*) *Gouthwaite* v. *Rippon* (1839), 8 L.J. Ch. 139.

(*m*) *Banner* v. *Berridge* (1881), 18 Ch. D. 254; *Warner* v. *Jacob* (1882), 20 Ch. D. 220.

(*n*) *E.g.*, the Merchant Shipping Act 1894, s. 35, and see *The Benwell Tower* (1895), 72 L.T. 664; the Small Dwellings Acquisition Act 1899, s. 6 (2), and see *Re Brown's Mortgage, Wallasey Corporation* v. *A.-G.* [1945] Ch. 166; [1945] 1 All E.R. 397; *cf. Re Caunter's Charge, Bishop* v. *Southgate Corporation* [1960] Ch. 491; [1959] 3 All E.R. 669.

(*o*) *Banner* v. *Berridge, supra; Charles* v. *Jones* (1887), 35 Ch. D. 544.

(*p*) Limitation Act 1939, s. 19 (1) (b). See also *Thorne* v. *Heard*, [1895] A.C. 495, (H.L.).

(*q*) *West* v. *Diprose*, [1900] 1 Ch. 337, at p. 340.

(*r*) The appropriate searches (see p. 373, *supra.*) should have been made previously and the amount due under the mortgage easily obtainable, since details will have been required in any possession proceedings. Usually the only outstanding matters will be the fees and disbursements of the sale itself.

(*s*) See *Eley* v. *Read, supra; cf. Mathison* v. *Clark* (1855), 25 L.J. Ch. 29.

(*t*) *Eley* v. *Read* (1897), 76 L.T. 39 (C.A.), at p. 40, per LORD ESHER, M. R.; affd. sub. nom. *Read* v. *Eley* (1899), 80 L.T. 369 (H.L.).

(*u*) See, generally, *Coote on Mortgages* (9th Edn.), vol. 2, p. 945. And p. 628, *infra*.

(*a*) Section 21 (1). The 1881 Act repealed the Trustees and Mortgagees etc., Powers Act 1860 (Lord Cranworth's Act). Under Lord Cranworth's Act the mortgagee on exercising his power of sale was empowered by s. 15 to convey the mortgaged property for all the estate and interest which the mortgagor on creating the mortgage had power

the mortgagee could only convey the property sold for such estate and interest in the property as was the subject of the mortgage. Thus, the equitable mortgagee of freehold could not convey the legal estate, and the mortgagee of leaseholds by demise could not assign the nominal reversion (*b*). Hence, if it was desired to give an equitable mortgagee of freeholds power to convey the legal estate, the mortgage had to contain a power of attorney to convey the legal estate. In the case of leaseholds, a mortgage by sub-demise included either a power of attorney to assign the nominal reversion, or a declaration of trust of that reversion. Frequently both provisions were inserted, and in its final form the declaration of trust contained a power for the mortgagee to remove the mortgagor from the trusteeship and appoint a new trustee (*c*). Thus on a sale he could vest the legal estate in the purchaser as trustee for himself.

Now a mortgagee exercising the power of sale conferred by the Law of Property Act 1925, has power, by deed, to convey the property sold, for such estate and interest therein *as he is by the Act authorised to sell or convey* (*d*) or may be the subject of the mortgage, freed from all estates, interests, and rights to which the mortgage has priority (*e*), but subject to all estates, interests, and rights which have priority to the mortgage (*f*).

The Law of Property Act 1925, empowers the mortgagee by demise to convey not only the mortgage term but, in freehold mortgages, the fee simple; and in leasehold mortgages, the nominal reversion. Thus as regards freehold mortgages, the Act provides:

> **88.**—(1) Where an estate in fee simple has been mortgaged by the creation of a term of years absolute limited thereout or by a charge by way of legal mortgage and the mortgagee sells under his statutory or express power of sale—
>
>   (a) the conveyance by him shall operate to vest in the purchaser the fee simple in the land conveyed subject to any legal mortgage having priority to the mortgage in right of which the sale is made and to any money thereby secured and thereupon;
>
>   (b) the mortgage term or the charge by way of legal mortgage and any subsequent mortgage term or charges shall merge or be extinguished as respects the land conveyed;
>
> and such conveyance may, as respects the fee simple, be made in the name of the estate owner in whom it is vested (*g*).

---

to dispose of. Thus an equitable mortgagee by deed could convey the legal estate (*Re Solomon and Meagher's Contract* (1889), 40 Ch. D. 508); and a mortgagee of leaseholds by demise could assign the leasehold reversion (*Hiatt* v. *Hillman* (1871), 25 L.T. 55). The 1860 Act still applies to mortgages made after 28 August, 1860, and before 1882, which did not contain an express power of sale.

(*b*) *Re Hodson and Howes' Contract* (1887), 35 Ch. D. 668 (C.A.).

(*c*) *London and County Banking Co.* v. *Goddard*, [1897] 1 Ch. 642.

(*d*) Italics supplied. *Cf.* the wording in the 1881 Act, *supra*.

(*e*) *Duke* v. *Robson*, [1973] 1 All E.R. 481.

(*f*) Law of Property Act 1925, s. 104 (1). As to the effect of the conveyance on equitable interests, see s. 2 (2) (i), (iii); and as to implied covenants for title, s. 76 (1) (F).

(*g*) Where the mortgage includes fixtures or personal chattels the statutory power of sale extends to the absolute or other interest therein affected by the charge: sub-s. (4). But the fixtures cannot be sold apart from the land: *Re Yates, Batcheldor* v. *Yates* (1888), 38 Ch. D. 112 (C.A.); see p. 361, *supra*.

The section applies to a mortgage whether created before or after the commencement of the Act, and to a mortgage term created by the Act, but does not operate to confer

Hence, whether the mortgage was made by demise or by a charge by way of legal mortgage, the purchaser obtains the fee simple free from the mortgage term or the charge, and this is the effect whether the mortgagee conveys in his own name or in the name of the mortgagor. The conveyance will be subject to any prior legal mortgage—whether it was by demise or legal charge—but it extinguishes all subsequent mortgage terms and legal charges, as well as the mortgagor's equity of redemption (*h*).

The following provision applies to a sub-mortgage of freeholds by demise:

88.—(5) In the case of a sub-mortgage by sub-demise of a long term (less a nominal period) itself limited out of an estate in fee simple, the foregoing provisions of this section, shall operate as if the derivative term, if any, created by the sub-mortgage had been limited out of the fee simple, and so as to enlarge the principal term and extinguish the derivative term created by the sub-mortgage as aforesaid, and to enable the sub-mortgagee to convey the fee simple or acquire it by foreclosure, enlargement or otherwise as aforesaid.

This assumes that the sub-mortgagee is exercising the power of sale conferred by the head mortgage, and the effect is that the head term is enlarged into the fee simple, and the derivative term is extinguished. Hence the purchaser takes the fee simple free both from the head mortgage term and the sub-mortgage term.

As regards leasehold mortgages:

89.—(1) Where a term of years absolute has been mortgaged by the creation of another term of years absolute limited thereout or by a charge by way of legal mortgage, and the mortgagee sells under his statutory or express power of sale—

(a) the conveyance by him shall operate to convey to the purchaser not only the mortgage term, if any, but also (unless expressly excepted with the leave of the court) the leasehold reversion affected by the mortgage, subject to any legal mortgage having priority to the mortgage in right of which the sale is made and to any money thereby secured, and thereupon

(b) the mortgage term, or the charge by way of legal mortgage and any subsequent mortgage term or charge shall merge in such leasehold reversion or be extinguished unless excepted as aforesaid:

and such conveyance may, as respects the leasehold reversion, be made in the name of the estate owner in whom it is vested.

Where a licence to assign is required on a sale by a mortgagee, such licence shall not be unreasonably refused (*i*).

Thus a mortgagee of leaseholds by sub-demise can vest in the purchaser both the mortgage sub-term and the nominal reversion, and the mortgage term thereupon merges in the nominal reversion, and

---

a better title to the fee simple than would have been acquired if the same had been conveyed by the mortgage (being a valid mortgage), and the restrictions imposed by the Act in regard to the effect and creation of mortgages were not in force, and all prior mortgages (if any), not being merely equitable charges, had been created by demise or by charge by way of legal mortgage: sub-s. (6). As to a sale of registered land, see Land Registration Act 1925, s. 34 (4); p. 64, *supra*.

(*h*) The provision in s. 4 (1) of the Matrimonial Homes Act 1967, that a contract for sale of a dwelling house effected by a charge of the spouse under the Act which has been registered in accordance with s. 2 (6) and (7) include a term requiring cancellation of the registration before completion.

(*i*) See p. 317, *supra*.

the conveyance operates as an assignment of the lease. This can be prevented if the court allows the nominal reversion to be excepted from the operation of the conveyance, and in that case only the mortgage sub-term will pass (*k*).

The section takes effect without prejudice to any prior incumbrance or trust affecting the original term, and it does not apply where the mortgage term does not comprise the whole of the land included in the leasehold reversion unless the rent (if any) payable in respect of that reversion has been apportioned as respects the land affected, or the rent is of no money value or no rent is reserved, and unless the lessee's covenants and the conditions (if any) have been apportioned either expressly or by implication, as respects the land affected. For this purpose it is sufficient that there has been an equitable apportionment, that is, an apportionment made by agreement between the owners of the several parts of the premises, but without the consent of the lessor (*l*).

A further provision defines the effect of the conveyance under a sub-mortgage of leaseholds:

89.—(5) In the case of sub-mortgage by demise of a term (less a nominal period) itself limited out of a leasehold reversion, the foregoing provisions of this section shall operate as if the derivative term created by the sub-mortgage had been limited out of the leasehold reversion, and so as (subject as aforesaid) to merge the principal mortgage term therein as well as the derivative term created by the sub-mortgage and to enable the sub-mortgagee to convey the leasehold reversion or acquire it by foreclosure, vesting or otherwise as aforesaid.

This differs from the technical effect of a conveyance by a sub-mortgage of freeholds. The head mortgage term is not enlarged into the original term and the derivative term then extinguished, but both the head and derivative mortgage terms are merged in the original term. But the effect in each case is identical—the purchaser obtains the whold estate of which the mortgagor could dispose (*m*).

Sale by equitable mortgagee.—An equitable mortgagee, where the mortgage is made by deed, may be able to convey the legal estate in the property. It has been held, in a decision under the Conveyancing Act 1881 (*n*), that the equitable mortgagee can only convey his equitable interest (*o*). But dicta in a more recent case, relying on a difference in wording between the 1881 Act and the 1925 Act noted above (*n*),

---

(*k*) The Act does not suggest the grounds on which the nominal reversion should be excepted. The object would be to prevent the purchaser becoming liable on the covenants in the lease and these might in certain circumstances be so onerous as to justify the intervention of the court.

(*l*) Law of Property Act 1925, s. 89 (6), as amended by Law of Property (Amendment) Act 1926, Schedule. Section 89 (4) corresponds to s. 88 (4) as to fixtures and personal chattels, and, with the additions mentioned in the text, s. 89 (6) corresponds with s. 88 (6).

(*m*) The provision above mentioned, that the statutory power of sale shall include the power of selling the fee simple or the leasehold reversion (s. 101 (6)), is complementary to the provisions as to conveyance.

(*n*) See p. 377, *supra.*

(*o*) *Re Hodson and Howes' Contract, supra.*

suggest that the equitable mortgagee can convey the legal estate (*p*). Because of the uncertainty on the point, it is necessary to extend the equitable mortgagee's power of sale by the terms of the deed using the devices mentioned above (*q*), of a power of attorney to convey the legal estate (*r*) or declaration of trust of the legal estate. In the case of an equitable mortgage by deposit of title deeds without any accompanying document the mortgagee, if he wishes to sell, must apply to the court (*s*).

The equitable mortgagee, whether selling under the statutory power or a power of attorney, owes the same duty as the legal mortgagee (*t*).

Sale by proprietor of registered charge.—The powers of the proprietor of a charge have already been noticed (*u*). Subject to an entry on the register to the contrary, the proprietor has all the powers of a legal mortgagee (*a*). But he only has these powers when he has been registered as the proprietor (*b*). The Land Registration Act provides for the completion of the sale by registration and the cancellation of the charge (*c*).

Sale by receiver (*d*).—A receiver may sell, either as delegate of the mortgagee (*e*) or under an express power of sale in the mortgage. In the latter case, the mortgagor will have to convey the property, unless the receiver is given power of attorney to execute deeds in the name of the mortgagor (*f*). When the mortgagor becomes bankrupt, his trustee will have to join in any sale by the receiver in the absence of a power of attorney. On a mortgagor-company going into liquidation, the same principles apply. In a compulsory winding up, any disposition of the company's property after the commencement of the winding up is void,

---

(*p*) *Re White Rose Cottage*, [1965] Ch. 940 (C.A.), at p. 951, *per* LORD DENNING, M.R.; [1965] 1 All E.R. 11, at p. 15. And see *per* WILBERFORCE, J., at [1964] Ch. 483, at pp. 494–496; [1964] 1 All E.R. 169, at pp. 176–177. These statements to the contrary are *obiter*, for the conveyance was not construed as an exercise of the mortgagor's power of sale, but as a transfer by the mortgagor with the mortgagee's concurrence. HARMAN, L.J., relied on the power of attorney for the conveyance of the legal estate: [1965] Ch. at p. 956; [1965] 1 All E.R. at p. 18.

(*q*) See p. 49, *supra.*

(*r*) The sale can be made under the power of attorney without the formality of a legal charge being first called for: *Re White Rose Cottage*, [1965] Ch. 940, at pp. 955–956; [1965] 1 All E.R. 11, at p. 18.

(*s*) Under s. 91 (2) of the Law of Property Act 1925; see p. 385, *infra.* If the court orders a sale it may vest a legal term of years in the mortgagee so that he can sell as if he were a legal mortgagee: s. 90, Law of Property Act 1925.

(*t*) See *Palmer* v. *Barclays Bank, Ltd.* (1971), 23 P. & C.R. 30.

(*u*) See p. 63, *supra.*

(*a*) Land Registration Act 1925, s. 34 (1).

(*b*) *Lever Finance, Ltd.* v. *Needleman's Trustee*, [1956] Ch. 375; [1956] 2 All E.R. 378. There is a difficulty when a second mortgagee of registered land following a mortgage by deposit sells. A purchaser can insist upon him procuring his registration as proprietor of the charge, but this will require the co-operation of the depositee of the land certificate; see Land Registration Act 1925, s. 110 (5): the alternative suggested by that sub-section of procuring a disposition from the proprietor of the land should be avoided (see *Re White Rose Cottage, supra.*).

(*c*) Land Registration Act 1925, s. 34 (4). And for the merger of any mortgage term: sub-s. (5).

(*d*) And see p. 303, *supra.*

(*e*) Law of Property Act 1925, s. 109 (3); p. 301, *supra.*

(*f*) For forms, see 19 Ency. Forms and Precedents (4th Edn.), p. 1138; and generally *Williams on Title* (4th Edn.), pp. 226, 227.

unless the court orders otherwise (*g*). It seems to be generally accepted that a sale under a mortgage does not fall within this provision, the object of which is to prevent the dissipation of the company's assets. The relevant disposition, in such case, is the mortgage, which precedes the winding up, not the sale thereunder (*h*).

Shipping mortgagee's power of sale.—The Merchant Shipping Act 1894, empowers every registered mortgagee absolutely to dispose of the ship or share in respect of which he is registered and to give effectual receipts for the purchase money. But if there are more persons than one registered as mortgagees of the same ship or share, no subsequent mortgagee can, except under the order of some court capable of taking cognisance of such matters, sell such ship or share without the concurrence of every prior mortgagee (*i*). The first step taken by the mortgagee will often be the arrest of the ship and the order ultimately sought will be appraisement and sale (*k*). The sale is usually by the direction of the court, but in exceptional cases the court might permit the mortgagee to sell (*l*). A court sale in Admiralty proceedings *in rem* transfers the mortgagee's contractual or statutory rights to the proceeds of sale in court (*m*). The mortgagee owes the same duty of care as mentioned above (*n*). The Act, as has already been noticed (*o*), contains no express direction as to the disposal of the purchase money. On the principles already stated the selling mortgagee holds any surplus for subsequent mortgagees (if any) and the owner.

(*g*) Companies Act 1948, ss. 227, 313.

(*h*) See *Kerr on Receivers* (14th Edn.), p. 322; footnote (*o*), p. 276, *supra*. The liquidator will have to join in the conveyance in the absence of a power of attorney; for form, see 19 Ency. Forms and Precedents (4th Edn.), p. 1150; and see generally *Williams on Title* (4th Edn.), pp. 226, 227.

(*i*) Section 35. For damages for improper sale after tender of debt, see *Fletcher and Campbell* v. *City Marine Finance*, [1968] 2 Lloyd's Rep. 520. For an order for sale, see *The Basildon*, [1967] 2 Lloyd's Rep. 134.

(*k*) See, generally, *British Shipping Laws*, vol. 1.

(*l*) See *The Monmouth Coast* (1922), 12 Ll. L. Rep. 22.

(*m*) *The Queen of the South*, [1968] 1 Lloyd's Rep. 182, at p. 192.

(*n*) See, *Gulf and Fraser Fishermen's Union* v. *Calm C Fish, Ltd.*, [1975] 1 Lloyd's Rep. 189 (B.C.C.A.).

(*o*) See p. 373, *supra*.

CHAPTER 21

Foreclosure and Judicial Sale

Foreclosure generally (*a*).—Upon non-payment of the debt when due (*b*), or earlier default (*c*), or, where no date is fixed for payment, after demand or notice (*d*), and notwithstanding that the mortgagee may have a power of sale (*e*), the mortgagee may commence an action asking that the equity of redemption of the mortgagor and all persons claiming through him, including subsequent incumbrancers, may be extinguished, so as to vest the mortgaged property absolutely in the mortgagee. Such an action is called a foreclosure action, and the relief sought foreclosure. and if the relief is granted, the mortgage is said to be foreclosed. As an alternative to foreclosure, or, where foreclosure is not available as the sole remedy, the court may order a sale of the property (*f*). Foreclosure was formerly a mortgagee's primary remedy, but it is rarely sought or granted today (*g*). The vast majority of mortgages made today are building society mortgages, under which the society will have a power of sale and the only relief it will want to seek from the court will be an order for possession, so that it can sell with vacant possession. A building society would not want to have the property vested in itself. However, foreclosure is still an appropriate remedy in the case of an equitable mortgage by deposit of title deeds unaccompanied by any deed or document, thereby giving a power of sale (*h*). But whenever foreclosure is sought, if there are other incumbrancers interested in the property or if the value of the property exceeds the mortgage debt, the court will, if requested, usually order a sale, rather than foreclosure (*i*).

Unlike the remedy by sale under a power of sale, there can generally (*j*)

(*a*) And see Ch. 22, *infra*. For the periods of limitation applicable to foreclosure actions, see p. 283, *supra*.

(*b*) *I.e.*, upon default under the proviso for redemption, as to which, see p. 31, *supra*; and see p. 28, *supra*, Covenant not to call in the money.

(*c*) *E.g.*, breach of convenant to pay interest: *Twentieth Century Banking Corporation, Ltd.* v. *Wilkinson*, [1976] 3 All E.R. 361.

(*d*) See pp. 269, 296, *supra*.

(*e*) *Wayne* v. *Hanham* (1851), 9 Hare 62; *Hutton* v. *Sealy* (1858), 27 L.J. Ch. 263.

(*f*) *Moore* v. *Morton*, [1886] W.N. 196; and see pp. 384 *et seq.*, *infra*.

(*g*) The general public still often thinks of the mortgagee's remedies in terms of foreclosure, see, *e.g.*, *Alliance Perpetual Building Society* v. *Belrum Investments, Ltd.*, [1957] 1 All E.R. 635.

(*h*) See p. 45, *supra*.

(*i*) See pp. 385 *et seq.*, *infra*.

(*j*) For cases of foreclosure without judicial order, note Small Dwellings Acquisition Act 1899, under which the taking of possession operates as a summary foreclosure: *Mexborough U.D.C.* v. *Harrison*, [1964] 2 All E.R. 109; and see p. 330, *supra*. And dismissal of an action for redemption is equivalent to foreclosure: *Cholmley* v. *Countess of Oxford* (1741), 2 Atk. 267; and see p. 569, *infra*.

be no foreclosure except by judicial order (*k*) in an action to which the mortgagor must be a defendant, however remote his chance of redeeming may be (*l*), and, except by consent, it will not be granted until an account is taken of what is owing on the mortgage for principal, interest, and costs of the action (*m*), and until default is made for a certain period after the balance on such account has been ascertained. Any special matter affecting the account, such as a valuation of a security in bankruptcy, ought to be pleaded and noticed in the judgment (*n*). The usual period allowed for redemption after the account has been taken is six months, but where the action is not merely against the mortgagor, but also against subsequent incumbrancers, and the subsequent incumbrancers appear and ask for successive periods of redemption and there is no question of priority between them (but not otherwise (*o*)), they will be allowed such successive periods (*p*), the party first entitled to redeem being allowed six months, and each of the others successive periods of three months more (*q*). During the period allowed for redemption a mortgagee can only exercise his power of sale by leave of the court (*r*).

On the day fixed and at the place named in the Master's certificate, some person attends on behalf of the mortgagee, and if the principal, interest, and costs are not paid to him, a final order is applied for on summons founded on an affidavit of non-payment. The order obtained on this summons is called an order absolute, and, subject to certain rights of opening the foreclosure (*s*) hereinafter referred to (*t*), it extinguishes the equity of redemption and gives the property to the mortgagee absolutely and beneficially. It is immaterial that the person who attends on behalf of the mortgagee to receive payment of the debt is not furnished with a power of attorney, if no one in point of fact attends on behalf of the mortgagor to pay (*u*).

The procedure on foreclosure is dealt with in Ch. 22, *infra*. Foreclosure is not confined to mortgages of land. It is applicable to mortgages of chattels (*x*) and of shares and other things in action (*y*).

(*k*) *Re Farnol, Eadès, Irvine & Co.*, [1915] 1 Ch. 22, 24.

(*l*) *Moore* v. *Morton, supra.*

(*m*) If the mortgagee claims costs, charges, and expenses beyond his costs of action, he must make out a special case for them at the hearing: *Bolingbroke* v. *Hinde* (1884), 25 Ch. D. 795.

(*n*) *Sanguinetti* v. *Stuckey's Banking Co.* (*No. 2*), [1896] 1 Ch. 502.

(*o*) *Platt* v. *Mendel* (1884), 27 Ch. D. 246; *Doble* v. *Manley* (1885), 28 Ch. D. 664.

(*p*) *Platt* v. *Mendel, supra.* But each case has to be judged on its merits, and sometimes an additional three months is allowed to the second person, and a further three months to all the others: *Smithett* v. *Hesketh* (1890), 44 Ch. D. 161.

(*q*) See p. 399, *infra.*

(*r*) *Stevens* v. *Theatres, Ltd.*, [1903] 1 Ch. 857; *Marshall* v. *Miles* (1971), 13 D.L.R. (3d) 158; cf. *Petranick* v. *Dale* (1973), 33 D.L.R. (3d) 389 (where the foreclosure order had not been entered up).

(*s*) In order to entitle a mortgagor to open a foreclosure the security must be ample (*Thornhill* v. *Manning* (1851), 1 Sim. N.S. 451), and there must be immediate payment of interest and costs (*Coombe* v. *Stewart* (1851), 13 Beav. 111).

(*t*) See p. 405, *infra.*

(*u*) *Cox* v. *Watson* (1877), 7 Ch. D. 196; *King* v. *Hough*, [1895] W.N. 60.

(*x*) *Harrison* v. *Hart* (1726), 2 Eq. Cas. Abr. 6; *Tancred* v. *Potts* (1749), 2 Fonbl. Eq. 261, n.

(*y*) *General Credit and Discount Co.* v. *Glegg* (1883), 22 Ch. D. 549; *Harrold* v. *Plenty*, [1901] 2 Ch. 314; *Stubbs* v. *Slater*, [1910] 1 Ch. 632 (C.A.).

The right to foreclosure exists, although the mortgagee has recovered part of the debt, so long as he has not been fully paid (z). But if, after foreclosure absolute, he proceeds for personal payment, the effect is to re-open the foreclosure (a).

When foreclosure available: Under formal mortgage.—The strict right of the legal mortgagee is foreclosure, and, independently of statute (b), he has no general right to a sale (c), although in certain cases (d), he is entitled to that relief. Where there are successive mortgages, each legal mortgagee has a right to foreclosure and to get in the legal estate of the mortgagor, subject only to prior mortgages (e). A proprietor of a registered charge has all the powers of a legal mortgagee (f).

Under equitable mortgage.—Although a mortgagee has not taken a formal mortgage, but only a charge, yet if this is accompanied by an agreement, express or implied, on the part of the mortgagor to execute a legal mortgage, there is a right to foreclosure. Hence the depositee of title deeds is entitled to foreclosure, where the deposit is accompanied by an agreement to execute a legal mortgage (g). And the right is available even where there is a simple deposit or memorandum without an agreement to execute a mortgage (h), unless the terms of the agreement exclude the right to a legal mortgage (i). For the deposit is of itself evidence of an agreement to make a legal security, which the court will carry into effect against the mortgagor or any who claim under him with actual or constructive notice of the deposit (k).

Under equitable charge.—But an equitable chargee cannot foreclose, because there is in his case no agreement to make a legal security nor any estate in him (l).

Sale apart from statute.—Where a charge gave a right of foreclosure on the ground that it implied an agreement to execute a legal mortgage, the remedy was prima facie restricted to foreclosure (m), but if it was a mere charge without such agreement, then the remedy was sale (n). If, however, the agreement was to execute a legal

---

(z) A foreclosure will not, however, be made in respect of interest only: *Drought* v. *Redford* (1827), 1 Moll. 572.

(a) *Lockhart* v. *Hardy* (1846), 9 Beav. 349; *Palmer* v. *Hendrie* (1859), 27 Beav. 349. There can be no foreclosure against the Crown: see *Hancock* v. *A.-G.* (1864), 33 L.J. Ch. 661.

(b) See p. 385, *infra*.

(c) *Tipping* v. *Power* (1842), 1 Hare 405.

(d) See *supra*.

(e) And when before 1926 second and subsequent mortgages took the form of assignments of the equity of redemption and were only equitable the right was the same.

(f) Land Registration Act 1925, s. 34 (1); and see p. 63, *supra*.

(g) *Perry* v. *Keane*, *Perry* v. *Partridge* (1836), 6 L.J. Ch. 67; *Cox* v. *Toole* (1855), 20 Beav. 145; *Underwood* v. *Joyce* (1861), 7 Jur. N.S. 566.

(h) *Pryce* v. *Bury* (1854), L.R. 16 Eq. 153, n.; *Redmayne* v. *Forster* (1866), L.R. 2 Eq. 467; *James* v. *James* (1873), L.R. 16 Eq. 153.

(i) *Sporle* v. *Whayman* (1855), 20 Beav. 607.

(k) *Birch* v. *Ellames* (1794), 2 Anst. 427; *Ex parte Wright* (1812), 19 Ves. 255; *Parker* v. *Housefield* (1834), 2 Myl. & K. 419.

(l) *Re Owen*, [1894] 3 Ch. 220; *Shea* v. *Moore*, [1894] 1 I.R. 158; *Tennant* v. *Trenchard* (1869), 4 Ch. App. 537, 542.

(m) *Pryce* v. *Bury* (1853), 2 Drew. 41. But there had previously frequently been decisions allowing sale as an alternative; see, *e.g.*, *King* v. *Leach* (1842), 2 Hare 57.

(n) See the cases referred to in footnote (l), *supra*. But debenture holders are entitled to foreclosure: *Sadler* v. *Worley*, [1894] 2 Ch. 170.

mortgage with a power of sale, then the court might order sale as an alternative remedy (*o*), and now that all mortgages by deed give a power of sale, it may be said that wherever there is an agreement, express or implied, to execute a legal mortgage, the mortgagee has the remedies of foreclosure and of sale (*p*).

There were other cases in which, for special reasons connected with the subject matter of the security, sale was the proper remedy. Thus it seems, that the legal or equitable mortgagee had a general right to a sale where the security was, or was thought to be, scanty or deficient (*q*). The mortgagee of a reversion was entitled to a sale on account of the unproductive nature of the security (*r*), but he was also entitled to foreclosure (*s*).

Sale under the Law of Property Act 1925.—Jurisdiction to order a sale in a foreclosure action was first conferred by s. 48 of the Court of Chancery Procedure Act 1852 (*t*). That section was repealed by the Conveyancing Act 1881, which by s. 25 made similar provision, and it also allowed the plaintiff in a redemption action to have an order for sale. Section 25 is reproduced in the first five sub-sections of s. 91 of the Law of Property Act 1925:

91.—(1) Any person entitled to redeem mortgaged property may have a judgment or order for sale instead of for redemption in an action brought by him either for redemption alone, or for sale or redemption in the alternative.

(2) In any action, whether for foreclosure, or for redemption, or for sale, or for the raising and payment in any manner of mortgage money the court (*u*), on the request of the mortgagee, or of any person interested either in the mortgage money or in the right of redemption (*a*), and, notithstanding that—

(a) any other person dissents; or

(b) the mortgagee or any person so interested does not appear in the action;

and without allowing any time for redemption or for payment of any mortgage money, may direct a sale of the mortgaged property, on such terms as it thinks fit, including the deposit in court of a reasonable sum fixed by the court to meet the expenses of sale and to secure performance of the terms.

(3) But, in an action brought by a person interested in the right of redemption and seeking a sale, the court may, on the application of any defendant, direct the plaintiff to give such security for costs as the court thinks fit, and may give the conduct of the sale to any defendant, and may give such directions as it thinks fit respecting the costs of the defendants or any of them.

(*o*) *Lister* v. *Turner* (1846), 5 Hare 281. Seton (7th Edn.), 1976.

(*p*) As to waiver by the mortgagee of his right to the legal security and a claim to sale under the charge, see *Kennard* v. *Futvoye* (1860), 2 Giff. 81; *Matthews* v. *Goodday* (1861), 8 Jur. (N.S.) 90.

(*q*) *Dashwood* v. *Bithazey* (1729), Mos. 196; *Earl of Kinnoul* v. *Money* (1767), 3 Swanst. 202, n. And see *Daniel* v. *Skipwith* (1787), 2 Bro. C.C. 155.

(*r*) *How* v. *Vigures* (1628), 1 Rep. Ch. 32.

(*s*) *Slade* v. *Rigg* (1843), 3 Hare 35; *Wayne* v. *Hanham* (1851), 9 Hare 62.

And sale is the proper remedy, rather than foreclosure, when the mortgagee is in conflicting positions, as where he becomes executor of the mortgagor or trustee of the mortgaged property: *Lucas* v. *Seale* (1740), 2 Atk. 56; *Tennant* v. *Trenchard* (1869), 4 Ch. App. 537.

(*t*) This has the restrictive words "instead of foreclosure" which have been omitted n the subsequent statutes.

(*u*) See Law of Property Act 1925, s. 203 (3).

(*a*) See *Rhymney Valley District Council* v. *Pontygwindy Housing Association, Ltd.* (1976) 73 Law Soc. Gaz. R. 32.

(4) In any case within this section the court may, if it thinks fit, direct a sale without previously determining the priorities of incumbrancers (*b*).

(5) This section applies to actions brought either before or after the commencement of this Act.

(6) In this section "mortgaged property" includes the estate or interest which a mortgagee would have had the power to convey if the statutory power of sale were applicable (*c*).

(7) For the purposes of this section the court may, in favour of a purchaser, make a vesting order conveying the mortgaged property, or appoint a person to do so, subject or not to any incumbrance, as the court may think fit; or, in the case of an equitable mortgage, may create and vest a mortgage term in the mortgagee to enable him to carry out the sale as if the mortgage had been made by way of legal mortgage (*d*).

The Act also makes special provision for the realisation of equitable mortgages by the court:

90.—(1) Where an order for sale is made by the court in reference to an equitable mortgage on land (not secured by a legal term of years absolute or by a charge by way of legal mortgage) the court may, in favour of a purchaser, make a vesting order conveying the land or may appoint a person to convey the land or create and vest in the mortgagee a legal term of years absolute to enable him to carry out the sale, as the case may require, in like manner as if the mortgage had been created by deed by way of legal mortgage pursuance to this Act, but without prejudice to any incumbrance having priority to the equitable mortgage unless the incumbrancer consents to the sale.

Exercise of statutory jurisdiction.—The statute gives no absolute right to the parties to require a sale, but only empowers the court to direct it (*e*). The order for a sale may be made on an interlocutory application before trial (*f*), or at any time before foreclosure absolute (*g*). It is no objection to the order that the mortgagee has a power of sale which has become exercisable (*h*). The court has a discretion in exercising its power, and it exercises it with a view to the general benefit of the persons interested without injury to any of them. Where there is a reasonable equity in the property, the court will prefer a sale to foreclosure, as it will usually be unwilling to give the mortgagee a windfall profit (*i*). Evidence of value must be given (*k*), and provided that the first mortgagee is secured against loss (*l*), the mortgagor or subsequent mortgagees should have the chance of obtain-

---

(*b*) But the order may be accompanied by an inquiry as to priorities: see *Paine* v. *Edwards* (1862), 6 L.T. N.S. 600.

(*c*) This sub-section was introduced so that a sale might have the same conveyancing effect as a sale by the mortgagee under his power of sale: see Law of Property Act 1925, ss. 88, 89 (as to which, see pp. 377 *et seq., supra*).

(*d*) This provision applies to an equitable mortgage, whether accompanied by an agreement to execute a legal mortgage or not: *Oldham* v. *Stringer* (1884), 33 W.R. 251.

(*e*) *Brewer* v. *Square*, [1892] 2 Ch. 111; cf. *Clarke* v. *Pannell* (1884), 29 Sol. Jo. 147.

(*f*) *Woolley* v. *Colman* (1882), 21 Ch. D. 169.

(*g*) *Union Bank of London* v. *Ingram* (1882), 20 Ch. D. 463 (C.A.); *Weston* v. *Davidson*, [1882] W.N. 28; *Industrial Development Bank* v. *Lees* (1971), 14 D.L.R. (3d) 612. But if only foreclosure has been claimed and the mortgagor does not appear, sale will not be ordered unless he has had notice of the mortgagee's intention to ask for a sale in lieu of foreclosure: *South Western District Bank* v. *Turner* (1882), 31 W.R. 113

(*h*) *Brewer* v. *Square, supra.*

(*i*) See, *e.g.*, *Twentieth Century Banking Corpn., Ltd.* v. *Wilkinson; Rhymney Valley District Council* v. *Pontygwindy Housing Association, Ltd.* (1976) 73 Law Soc. Gaz. 32.

(*k*) *Smithett* v. *Hesketh* (1890), 44 Ch. D. 161, 163.

(*l*) *Hurst* v. *Hurst* (1852), 16 Beav. 372.

ing the surplus likely to be realised upon a sale. Consequently a sale may be ordered on the terms of the subsequent mortgagee or the mortgagor asking for it paying into court a sum sufficient to secure the first mortgagee against loss (*m*), and such terms will be required where the security is deficient, and the mortgagor's expectation of a surplus is based only on a speculative rise in value (*n*). Where the mortgaged property was in several places, and could not be sold as a whole, and some part was more valuable than others, the risk of selling merely the most valuable part, and leaving the mortgagee saddled with the worthless part, was a good reason for refusing a sale requested by the second mortgagee (*o*). Where the security is deficient, and it is not for the benefit of either party that the expense of a sale or attempted sale should be incurred, a sale will not be ordered (*p*). Nor will a sale be ordered where vacant possession of the property cannot be given (*q*). An immediate sale will not usually be directed, but the order will provide that the sale shall not take place until three months from the Master's certificate as to the amount due, so as to give the mortgagor an opportunity of redeeming (*r*), especially if there is evidence of the solvency of the mortgagor (*s*). But where the property is small and the security deficient, an immediate sale may be ordered (*t*). An order for sale may be postponed for a short time to give interested persons, *e.g.*, tenants of the mortgaged property, who were not parties to the proceedings, a chance to redeem (*u*).

The conduct of the sale will usually be given to the mortgagor since it is to his interest to obtain as high a price as possible (*a*), and when this is done, he need not in general give security for the costs of the sale since he will himself be liable for them (*b*). A sale may be made out of court, but the reserve price must be fixed in chambers and the purchase money paid into court (*c*).

(*m*) *Norman* v. *Beaumont*, [1893] W.N. 45. A sale has been refused where the defendant requesting it would not give security: *Cripps* v. *Wood* (1882), 51 L.J. Ch. 584.

(*n*) *Hurst* v. *Hurst, supra*; *Merchant Banking Co. of London* v. *London and Hanseatic Bank* (1886), 55 L.J. Ch. 479.

(*o*) *Provident Clerks' Mutual, etc., Association* v. *Lewis* (1892), 62 L.J. Ch. 89.

(*p*) *Lloyds Bank, Ltd.* v. *Colston* (1912), 106 L.T. 420.

(*q*) *Silsby* v. *Holliman*, [1955] Ch. 552; [1955] 2 All E.R. 373 (mortgagee statutory tenant).

(*r*) *Green* v. *Biggs* (1885), 52 L.T. 680; *Jones* v. *Harris*, [1887] W.N. 10. The order will, in a suitable case, be limited to the sale of so much of the property as will be sufficient to satisfy the amount due: *Wade* v. *Wilson* (1882), 22 Ch. D. 235. For forms of order, see 28 Ency. Court Forms (2nd Edn.), pp. 110 *et seq.*; Seton (7th Edn.),vol. 3.

(*s*) *Hopkinson* v. *Miers* (1889), 34 Sol. Jo. 128.

(*t*) *Oldham* v. *Stringer* (1884), 33 W.R. 251; *Williams* v. *Owen* (1883), 27 Sol. Jo. 256; or a short interval may be fixed: *Charlewood* v. *Hammer* (1884), 28 Sol. Jo. 710.

(*u*) *Rhymney Valley District Council* v. *Pontygwindy Housing Association, Ltd.*, [1976] L.S. Gaz. 32.

(*a*) *Davies* v. *Wright* (1886), 32 Ch. D. 220; *Christy* v. *Van Tromp*, [1886] W.N. 111. If not to him, then to the mortgagee last in priority: *Norman* v. *Beaumont, supra*. But the first mortgagee may be given the conduct: *Re Jordan* (1884), 13 Q.B.D. 228; *Hewitt* v. *Nanson* (1858), 28 L.J. Ch. 49.

(*b*) *Davies* v. *Wright, supra*; but the court may require this to be done: *Brewer* v. *Square, supra*. For estate agents' and auctioneers' remuneration, see *Practice Direction*, [1972] 3 All E.R. 256.

(*c*) *Woolley* v. *Colman, supra*; *Davies* v. *Wright, supra*; *Brewer* v. *Square, supra*. The reserve price should, if the mortgagee does not consent to the sale, be fixed at a

The party having the conduct of the sale is not responsible for the fraud of other parties to the action who act as or engage "puffers" (d).

An order for sale does not prevent the creditor pursuing his other remedies, e.g., presenting and prosecuting a bankruptcy petition against the mortgagor (e).

Sale may be ordered where it is the proper remedy, or, under the Law of Property Act 1925, though foreclosure only is sought, and though there is no right to foreclosure. But, except under the statutory powers of the court, no sale can be made of mortgaged property as against a mortgagee with a paramount title, save with his express consent (f). Otherwise the sale can only be subject to his mortgage. The course is to direct a sale, free from the mortgagee's security if he concurs, but subject to it if he does not. If he is a party to the action, he will be required at once to consent or refuse (g).

Registered land.—In the case of a registered charge under the Land Registration Act 1925, the registered proprietor of the charge has all the powers conferred by law on a legal mortgagee, and he is entitled to foreclosure or sale of the land charged in the same manner and under the same circumstances in and under which he might enforce the same if the land had been demised to him by way of mortgage, subject to a proviso for cesser on payment of the money at the appointed time (h).

Charging orders (i).—An order absolute against stock or shares confers on the judgment creditor the same remedies as if the judgment debtor had made a valid and effective charge for the judgment debt and interest thereon in favour of the judgment creditor, but no proceedings can be taken until the expiration of six months from the date of the order nisi (k). When this period has elapsed, the unpaid judgment creditor can take proceedings to secure a sale of the charged property (l). A properly protected charging order on land under the Administration of Justice Act 1956 (m), has the like effect and is enforceable in the same courts and the same manner as an equitable charge created by a debtor under his hand (n).

---

sum sufficient, if practicable, to cover the amount due to him: *Woolley* v. *Colman*, supra. As to sales by order of court, see R.S.C. Ord. 31; and *Cumberland Union Banking Co.* v. *Maryport Hematite Iron and Steel Co.*, [1892] 1 Ch. 92. As to form of conveyance on such a sale, see 19 Ency. Forms and Precedents (4th Edn.), 1447.

(d) *Union Bank* v. *Munster* (1887), 37 Ch. D. 51.

(e) *Re Kelday, Ex parte Meston* (1888), 36 W.R. 585.

(f) *Wickenden* v. *Rayson* (1855), 6 De G.M. & G. 210. As to the interest which will be allowed to the mortgagee, see *Re Fowler, Bishop* v. *Fowler* (1922), 128 L.T. 620.

(g) *Jenkin* v. *Row* (1851), 5 De G. & Sm. 107.

(h) Section 34 (1). The section provides expressly for the completion of an order for foreclosure by the registration of the proprietor of the charge as the proprietor of the land: sub-s. (3); and see sub-s. (4) as to the completion on the register of a sale by the court.

(i) See pp. 159 et seq., supra.

(k) R.S.C. Ord. 50, r. 6 (3), (4); C.C.R. Ord. 25, r. (6)A (3), (5).

(l) *Daponte* v. *Schubert and Roy Nominees, Ltd.*, [1939] Ch. 958; [1939] 3 All E.R. 495. *Quaere* whether foreclosure is available: see *Hosack* v. *Robins*, [1917] 1 Ch. 332, 336; *Dalston Development Pty., Ltd.* v. *Dean*, [1967] W.A.R. 176, at pp. 178–179.

(m) See p. 159, supra.

(n) Administration of Justice Act 1956, s. 35 (3).

Maritime securities.—The Admiralty Division of the High Court has power in all cases of salvage, damages, necessaries, wages, or bottomry, to order the sale of the ship against which the proceeding is carried on, unless the demands of the successful plaintiff are satisfied (*o*). A sale is not ordered at the instance of a bottomry bondholder, until the court is satisfied by perusal of the bond that is duly executed, and with maritime risk. Upon the sale of a ship by order of the court, for the satisfaction of bottomry or other claims, the title is complete without any delivery of the register.

(*o*)   *The Tremont* (1841), 1 W. Rob. 163.   See p. 380, *supra.*

CHAPTER 22

Action for Foreclosure [a]

I—FORM OF PROCEEDINGS

Originating summons or writ.—A foreclosure action is commenced either by originating summons or writ in the Chancery Division (b), or, where the amount owing in respect of the mortgage does not exceed £5,000 in the county court of the district where the mortgaged property is situate (c). The provision giving the county court exclusive jurisdiction in certain possession actions and how this cannot be avoided by a claim for foreclosure, which is not genuine, has already been considered (d).

Foreclosure actions by different plaintiffs in respect of different mortgages made by the same mortgagor can be consolidated (e).

II—PARTIES TO THE ACTION

A—PERSONS INTERESTED IN THE SECURITY

The holder of the security.—The person in whom the legal interest in the security becomes vested whether originally by the mortgage (f), or by assignment (g), and though he is only a trustee for the persons

---

(a) See, generally, Marriott and Dunn, *Practice in Mortgage Actions in Ontario* (3rd Edn.). In Canada foreclosure remains a principal remedy. According to the Report of the Committee on the Enforcement of Judgment Debts (the Payne Committee), 1969 Cmnd. 1309, para. 1360, there had been a revival in the popularity of foreclosure as a remedy. The Administration of Justice Act 1970 as extended by the Administration of Justice Act 1973 (see p. 319, *supra*), has undoubtedly made foreclosure a more popular remedy. But, although there are cases when foreclosure is ordered (*e.g.*, where there would be a deficiency on a sale and see, *e.g.*, *Lord Marples of Wallasey* v. *Holmes* (1975), 31 P. & C.R. 94), the Court is usually reluctant to make a foreclosure order where the result would be a windfall profit for the mortgagee. The remedy has been replaced in the Republic of Ireland by judicial sale, and its abolition here would be no great loss.

(b) Supreme Court of Judicature (Consolidation) Act 1925, s. 56 (1); R.S.C. Ord. 88. The principles effecting the choice of originating summons or writ are considered at p. 322, *supra*. For transfer from the High Court to the county court, see County Courts Act 1959, s. 54.

(c) County Courts Act 1959, s. 52, as amended by the Administration of Justice Act 1970; C.C.R. Ord. 2, r. 2 (c), (d). The jurisdiction of the county court may be extended by a agreement: *ibid.*, s. 53. The amount owing referred to above means the amount owing at the time of commencing proceedings: *Shields etc., Building Society* v. *Richards* (1901), 84 L.T. 587. As to costs of proceeding in the High Court which might have been taken in the county court, see footnote (*i*), p. 644, *infra*.

(d) See p. 320, *supra*.

(e) R.S.C. Ord. 4, r. 10; *Holden* v. *Silkstone and Dodworth Coal and Iron Co.* (1881), 30 W.R. 98.

(f) *Wood* v. *Williams* (1819), 4 Mad. 186.

(g) *Wetherell* v. *Collins* (1818), 3 Mad. 255. And the original mortgagee must be joined in an action by a sub-mortgagee: *Norrish* v. *Marshall* (1821), 5 Mad. 475.

entitled to the mortgage money (*h*), is a necessary party to an action for foreclosure (*i*). Such a person is a necessary party because a reconveyance will be required should the mortgagor redeem (*k*) and in case of a judgment for foreclosure, because the legal interest is to be protected by the judgment (*l*). A transferee of a mortgage may bring the action (*m*), but he is subject to the state of the accounts between the mortgagor and the mortgagee at the date of the transfer, and also to any equities then existing in favour of the mortgagor (*n*).

Personal representatives.—On the death of the mortgagee, without having transferred the mortgage, and on the death of a transferee, the debt and security devolve upon his personal representatives, who can institute foreclosure proceedings until they have transferred the mortgage to a beneficiary or a transferee for value (*o*)).

Co-mortgagees.—Where there are co-mortgagees (*p*) they may institute proceedings jointly, or, if some are unwilling to be joined as plaintiffs, or have done some act precluding them from suing in that capacity, one can sue by himself, provided he makes all the others defendants (*q*). A mortgagee entitled to part only of the mortgage money cannot sue alone and obtain foreclosure of a corresponding part of the mortgaged property (*r*).

Subsequent incumbrancers.—The second or other later incumbrancers may foreclose the mortgagor and those subsequent, without joining the incumbrancers prior to themselves; for the latter can suffer no damage. The subsequent mortgagees, it is true, are left without the opportunity of redeeming all who are prior to themselves in the same action; but this, however inconvenient, is not thought to be unjust towards those who, lending money upon incumbered estates, have a full knowledge of the state of the security (*s*).

(*h*) A trustee of the legal estate in the security having no adverse rights may properly be, and to save expenses to the mortgagor, ought to be, a co-plaintiff: *Smith* v. *Chichester* (1842). 2 Dru. & War. 393, at p. 404; unless he refuses, or is likely to refuse, and then he should be made a defendant: *Browne* v. *Lockhart* (1840), 10 Sim. 420.

(*i*) *Bartle* v. *Wilkin* (1836), 8 Sim. 238; *Smith* v. *Chichester, supra*.

(*k*) See form of foreclosure order, p. 396 *infra*.

(*l*) The rule is not affected by the present automatic effect of a receipt on the discharge of the mortgage.

(*m*) *Platt* v. *Mendel* (1884), 27 Ch. D. 246, at p. 247.

(*n*) See p. 251, *supra*.

(*o*) See p. 257, *supra*. As to representation by trustees and personal representatives, see p. 572, *infra*.

(*p*) As to co-mortgagees, see p. 175, *supra*.

(*q*) *Davenport* v. *James* (1847), 7 Hare 249; *Remer* v. *Stokes* (1856), 4 W.R. 730; *Luke* v. *South Kensington Hotel Co.* (1879), 11 Ch. D. 121 (C.A.). Unless the advance is made on a joint account, the mortgagees are tenants in common of the mortgage money, and on the death of one, his representatives are necessary parties: *Vickers* v. *Cowell* (1839), 1 Beav. 529.

(*r*) *Palmer* v. *Earl of Carlisle* (1823), 1 Sim. & St. 423.

(*s*) *Rose* v. *Page* (1829), 2 Sim. 471; *Briscoe* v. *Kenrick* (1832), 1 L.J. Ch. 116; *Richards* v. *Cooper* (1842), 5 Beav. 304; and see *Slade* v. *Rigg* (1843), 3 Hare 35. Under special circumstances however, it may be necessary for the second mortgagee to join the first. Thus where A, the tenant for life, being entitled to a charge on the estate for £20,000 mortgaged the charge to B, for £14,000, and then, with other property to C for £20,000, and after C's death, the next tenant for life claimed to split the £20,000 and redeem C on payment of such a sum as was due on account of the £6,000, it was held that B was a necessary party, since he was interested in the amount comprised in C's security: *Lord Kensington* v. *Bouverie* (1852), 16 Beav. 194; in H.L. (1859), 7 H.L.C. 557.

Nor are the owners of prior incumbrances necessary parties to actions for sale of the estate by subsequent creditors, the sale being made subject to those incumbrances (*t*). And a judgment creditor may proceed against a receiver and the owner of the estate, for satisfaction out of surplus rents by a former judgment directed to be paid to the owner, without making prior incumbrancers parties (*u*).

B—PERSONS INTERESTED IN THE EQUITY OF REDEMPTION

Owner of equity of redemption.—The judgment in a foreclosure action gives to all persons interested in the equity of redemption the opportunity of redeeming. In default of their doing so they are foreclosed. Hence all such persons must be parties, or be sufficiently represented by persons who are parties (*a*). The mortgagor himself while owner, or the owner for the time being, of the equity, or, if the equity of redemption is held jointly, all the joint owners must be parties. And where a second mortgagee sues to redeem the first mortgagee, the mortgagor is a necessary party, since on redemption the action will become a foreclosure action against him (*b*).

The original mortgagor is not a necessary party to an action for foreclosure between a sub-mortgagee and sub-mortgagor (*c*). But where a sub-mortgagee seeks to foreclose the original mortgagor the original mortgagee must be joined (*d*).

Collateral securities.—The mortgagor of another property as a collateral security is a necessary party to an action for foreclosure against the principal mortgagor by virtue of his right to redeem, and thereby to prevent his own estate from being burdened to a greater amount that the estate of his principal is insufficient to satisfy (*e*). But the surety is not a necessary party, where he is bound by a personal covenant only, unless he has paid off part of the debt (*f*).

(*t*) *Delabere* v. *Norwood* (1786), 3 Swans. 144, n.; *Parker* v. *Fuller* (1830), 1 Russ. & Myl. 656.

(*u*) *Lewis* v. *Lord Zouche* (1828), 2 Sim. 388. If a receiver of the general proceeds of the estate is asked for, the presence of the prior incumbrancers is necessary, since there is an interference with their interests: *Gibbon* v. *Strathmore* (1841), cited Calvert on *Parties in Suits in Equity* (2nd Edn. 1847), 16, unless, of course, the order is to be without prejudice to the prior incumbrancers. And in an action by later incumbrancers against a receiver appointed by the prior incumbrancers, and the mortgagor who had covenanted to keep down the incumbrances according to their priorities, the prior incumbrancers had to be joined: *Ford* v. *Rackham* (1853), 17 Beav. 485; and see *Re Lord Annaly, Crawford* v. *Annaly* (1891), 27 L.R. Ir. 523.

(*a*) *Tylee* v. *Webb* (1843), 6 Beav. 552, at p. 557; *Gedye* v. *Matson* (1858), 25 Beav. 310; *Caddick* v. *Cook* (1863), 32 Beav. 70; *Griffith* v. *Pound* (1890), 45 Ch. D. 553, at p. 567.

As to foreclosure where there are rights of contribution and indemnity between co-mortgagors, see *Gee* v. *Liddle*, [1913] 2 Ch. 62.

(*b*) See p. 572, *infra*.

(*c*) See 3 Seton's *Judgments and Orders* (7th Edn.), 2011.

(*d*) *Hobart* v. *Abbot* (1731), 2 P. Wms. 643.

(*e*) *Stokes* v. *Clendon* (1790), 3 Swans. 150, n.; *Gee* v. *Liddell*, [1913] 2 Ch. 62; *Re a Debtor* (*No. 24 of 1971*), *Ex parte Marley* v. *Trustee of Property of Debtor*, [1976] 2 All E.R. 1010; *Re Thompson* (1976), 8 A.L.R. 479. And similarly, where a mortgage of the estate of a married woman is in effect a security for the husband's debt (as to which, see p. 445), he is a necessary party: see *Hill* v. *Edmonds* (1852), 5 De G. & Sm. 603.

(*f*) *Newton* v. *Earl of Egmont* (1831), 4 Sim. 574; *Gedye* v. *Matson* (1858), *supra*.

Trustee in bankruptcy.—The official receiver, or trustee under the bankruptcy of the mortgagor, is the proper party to actions in respect of his interest, and the bankrupt will be bound by a judgment against him (g). But if the trustee absolutely disclaims and states that he is ready to have the equity released, and that all the estate had been distributed, he should not be brought to the hearing; otherwise if, by the disclaimer, he admits having an interest in the estate (h). If the mortgagor has parted with his interest before the bankruptcy, the trustee should not be joined. Hence he should not be joined in respect of an estate of which the equity of redemption was settled by the mortgagor for valuable consideration before his bankruptcy (i).

Personal representatives and trustees.—On the death of the mortgagor, or, where the equity of redemption has been transferred, the transferee, the mortgaged property devolves upon his personal representatives, who are necessary parties, unless the property has by assent or conveyance by the personal representatives become vested in some other person (k). The personal representatives must be parties if the mortgagee is asking for a sale of the property and the security is deficient (l).

Trustees, executors and administrators sufficiently represent the trust estate, or the estate under administration, and if this includes the equity of redemption it is generally unnecessary to join any of the beneficiaries as defendants (m).

Settlement of equity of redemption.—In such case the fee simple subject to the mortgage term is vested in the tenant for life, or, where there is no tenant for life or the tenant for life is an infant, in the statutory owners, who hold on trust for all persons beneficially entitled. It will, therefore, be sufficient to bring the holder of the legal estate before the court in the first instance, and, if necessary, directions for adding other parties will be given (n).

(g) Bankruptcy Act 1914, ss. 53, 56. Hence the mortgagor should not be made a party: see *Kerrick* v. *Saffery* (1835), 7 Sim. 317; not even if charges of fraud or other charges are made which are not particularly directed to matters on which relief is sought: *Lloyd* v. *Lander* (1821), 5 Mad. 282.

(h) *Thompson* v. *Kendall* (1840), 9 Sim. 397; *Collins* v. *Shirley* (1830), 1 Russ. & Myl. 638; see *Melbourne Banking Corpn.* v. *Brougham* (1879), 4 App. Cas. 156 (P.C.). And a bankrupt cannot appeal even though a right of redemption has been given him by the judgment, and it is alleged that there is a surplus: *Re Leadbitter* (1878), 10 Ch. D. 388 (C.A.); *Re Austin, Ex parte Sheffield* (1879), 10 Ch. D. 434 (C.A.); and see *Re A Debtor, Ex parte Debtor* v. *Dodwell (Trustee)*, [1949] Ch. 236; [1949] 1 All E.R. 510.

(i) *Steele* v. *Maunder* (1844), 1 Coll. 535.
If the mortgagee has valued his security, the trustee can redeem at the valuation and the order must show this: *Knowles* v. *Dibbs* (1889), 37 W.R. 378. The form of the order allows for an amendment of proof: *Hayes and Harlington U.D.C.* v. *Williams' Trustee* [1936] Ch. 315.

(k) Administration of Estates Act 1925, ss. 1 (1), 3; see p. 257, *supra*. In a case where the mortgagor's personal representative would be a necessary party and there is no such person in existence, the court may proceed in his absence or appoint some person to represent the estate for all the purposes of the action: R.S.C. Ord. 15, r. 15; and for proceedings against estates, see Ord. 15, r. 6A.

(l) See *Daniel* v. *Skipwith* (1787), 2 Bro. C.C. 155.

(m) R.S.C. Ord. 15, r. 14; see p. 572, *infra*. As the same applies to trustees for creditors and debenture trustees where the debentures are secured by a trust deed. For death and bankruptcy in the course of proceedings, see p. 411, *infra*.

(n) See p. 572, *infra*.

Subsequent incumbrancers.—The first (*o*), or any subsequent (*p*) mortgagee or incumbrancer, whether of a legal (*q*), or equitable (*r*) estate, who commences an action for foreclosure or sale (*s*), must make every incumbrancer, whose security is subsequent to his own, a party to the action, in order that their successive rights of redemption may be preserved, and that they may be able to protect their interests on the taking of the accounts (*t*).

But the converse proposition does not hold good, and as a prior mortgagee cannot be affected by the foreclosure action of a subsequent incumbrancer, he is not a proper or necessary party to it (*u*).

Severance of title to property.—If two properties are mortgaged, and the mortgagor afterwards mortgages the equity of redemption of one of them to a second mortgagee, and sells that of the other to a third person, the original mortgagee in foreclosing must bring forward both the second mortgagee and the purchaser; for he cannot foreclose either of the properties alone, each being equally liable to the debt. It is also incumbent on the mortgagee, where the equity of redemption has been sold in lots, to proceed against all the purchasers (*a*). The rule is the same where the mortgagee holds securities upon distinct properties, and even for distinct debts of the mortgagor (where there is a right to consolidate), whether the securities are by the same or by different instruments (*b*).

Judgment creditors.—The rule that subsequent incumbrancers are necessary parties applies to a judgment creditor who has obtained a charging order on the land of the debtor, which has been duly registered in the Register of Writs and Orders (*c*).

Notice received pending the action.—If, pending the action, the

---

(*o*) *Adams* v. *Paynter* (1844), 1 Coll. 530; *Tylee* v. *Webb* (1843), 6 Beav. 552. And, generally, persons interested in the entire equity of redemption, not being *cestuis que trust* who are represented by a trustee, are necessary parties. Thus partners of the mortgagor, who have a right of pre-emption over his mortgaged share, are necessary parties to an action to foreclose the security: *Redmayne* v. *Forster* (1866), L.R. 2 Eq. 467.

(*p*) *Johnson* v. *Holdsworth* (1850), 1 Sim. N.S. 106.

(*q*) *Adams* v. *Paynter, supra.*

(*r*) *Tylee* v. *Webb, supra.*

(*s*) *Burgess* v. *Sturges* (1851), 14 Beav. 440; *Ormsby* v. *Thorpe* (1808), 2 Mol. 503.

(*t*) See *Graves* v. *Wright* (1842), cited in 1 Dru. & War. 193. Where debentures are a second charge and are not secured by a trust deed, it is necessary in an action by the first mortgagee to enforce his security, for all debenture holders to be defendants, or for an order to be made that one or more shall represent the class: *Wallace* v. *Evershed*, [1899] 1 Ch. 891. A representation order is made under R.S.C. Ord. 15, r. 12. In *Griffith* v. *Pound* (1890), 45 Ch. D. 553, and *Westminster Bank, Ltd.* v. *Residential Properties Improvement Co., Ltd.*, [1938] Ch. 639; [1938] 2 All E.R. 374, it was held that all the debenture holders must be joined: *cf. Re Wilcox & Co.*, *Hilder* v. *Wilcox & Co.*, [1903] W.N. 64. If there are trustees the trustees will be made parties: *Cox* v. *Dublin City Distillery Co., Ltd. (No. 3)*, [1917] 1 I.R. 203 (C.A.).

(*u*) *Rose* v. *Page* (1829), 2 Sim. 471; *Slade* v. *Rigg* (1843), 3 Hare 35, 38.

(*a*) *Peto* v. *Hammond* (1860), 29 Beav. 91. As to an allegation by the purchaser that he is assignee for valuable consideration without notice of the mortgage, see *Payne* v. *Compton* (1837), 2 Y. & C. Ex. 457; and see *Hall* v. *Heward* (1886), 32 Ch. D. 430 (C.A.).

(*b*) *Ireson* v. *Denn* (1796), 2 Cox Eq. Cas. 425; and see *Payne* v. *Compton, supra*. The above paragraph was quoted in *Rushton* v. *Industrial Development Bank* (1973), 34 D.L.R. (3d) 582 (S.C. of Can.).

(*c*) *Earl of Cork* v. *Russell* (1871), L.R. 13 Eq. 210. For charging orders, see p. 159, *supra*.

plaintiff receives notice of a subsequent incumbrance, the owner thereof should be added as a defendant (*d*). But where the plaintiff does not have notice, it may be stated, but (from the imperfect character of the early reports) with caution:

(1) That if the plaintiff obtains his judgment without having received notice, the judgment will bind the subsequent incumbrancer as to the accounts, if taken bona fide, but not his right of redemption (*e*). He may, however, be joined even after judgment is pronounced (*f*).

(2) But collusion or other fraud will give the subsequent incumbrancer a right to open the accounts also, upon his stating particular errors (see p. 611, *infra*); but not a right to unravel them upon general charges of fraud and collusion, if the fraud and collusion are denied (*g*). And the fraudulent or vexatious conduct of the mortgagor, if he should create subsequent incumbrances with the view of shielding himself from foreclosure, will excuse the mortgagee from making the owners of such securities parties to the action (*h*).

III—THE PLEADINGS

The relief sought.—Where the mortgagee is suing for foreclosure only, the claim is that an account may be taken of what is due to him on the mortgage, which must be specifically described, for principal, interest and costs, and that the mortgage may be enforced by foreclosure (*i*). Where registered land is mortgaged the summons should refer to the contemporaneous instrument of charge (*k*), but there is no need to ask for rectification of the register, nor should the summons be entitled in the matter of the Land Registration Act (*l*). It is usual to ask for sale in the alternative to foreclosure but though foreclosure only is claimed, the court may direct a sale (*m*). Payment under the covenant for payment may be claimed and in default of payment foreclosure or sale (*n*).

If the mortgagee is in possession, he will ask for an account of rents

---

(*d*) See *Moser* v. *Marsden*, [1892] 1 Ch. 487 (C.A.), at p. 490.

(*e*) *Cockes* v. *Sherman* (1676), Freem. Ch. 13; and *semble* in *Lomax* v. *Hide* (1690), 2 Vern. 185; and *Godfrey* v. *Chadwell* (1707), 2 Vern. 601. But *Morret* v. *Westerne* (1710), 2 Vern. 663, seems *contra* as to accounts. In *Greswold* v. *Marsham* (1685), 2 Ch. Ca. 170, a judgment creditor was held to be bound, because he had not given notice of his incumbrance.

(*f*) *Keith* v. *Butcher* (1884), 25 Ch. D. 750; *Re Parbola, Ltd., Blackburn* v. *Parbola, Ltd.*, [1909] 2 Ch. 437, following *Campbell* v. *Holyland* (1877), 7 Ch. D. 166.

(*g*) *Needler* v. *Deeble* (1677), 1 Ch. Ca. 299; *Cockes* v. *Sherman, supra*.

(*h*) *Yates* v. *Hambly* (1742), 2 Atk. 237; and see *Smith* v. *Chichester* (1842), 2 Dru. & W. 393, at p. 404.

(*i*) For forms, generally, see 28 Ency. Court Forms (2nd Edn.), Mortgages.

(*k*) *Weymouth* v. *Davis*, [1908] 2 Ch. 169.

(*l*) *Practice Note*, [1932] W.N. 6. As to foreclosure of registered charges, see p. 388, *supra*.

(*m*) Law of Property Act 1925, s. 91. See p. 385, *supra*.

(*n*) *Dymond* v. *Croft* (1876), 3 Ch. D. 512; *Farrer* v. *Lacy, Hartland & Co.* (1885), 31 Ch. D. 42 (C.A.).

and profits received (*o*) and for the allowance of any special expenses (*p*). If he is not in possession, he may claim delivery of possession (*q*), but this is not necessary. An action for foreclosure includes a claim for possession, and delivery of possession may be ordered as against the mortgagor though not included amongst the relief sought (*r*), notwithstanding that the mortgagor does not appear (*s*). It will not, however, be ordered *ex parte* where not asked for by the summons (*t*). An order for possession may be made after foreclosure absolute (*u*), although not asked for by the summons (*a*).

Where the mortgage is an equitable mortgage by deposit the mortgagee may claim in the first instance that he is entitled to be considered as being a legal mortgagee (*b*).

Matters to be proved.—The affidavit in support of the originating summons, or, where the action is commenced by writ, the statement of claim must contain the following matters: full particulars of the mortgage (*c*), and the circumstances, including the date, the sum or sums (including further advances) secured, the rate of interest, the amount due, the proviso for redemption or cesser, and any relevant covenants or stipulations; all transfers and devolutions; and all material facts, such as taking of possession by the mortgagee or the appointment of a receiver (*d*). If possession is claimed the mortgaged property should be sufficiently described in order that a writ of possession may be completed so as to enable the sheriff to identify the property (*e*).

IV—THE JUDGMENT

A—THE NATURE AND FORM OF THE JUDGMENT

General form of judgment (*f*).—In an action for foreclosure or sale the judgment is prefaced by a declaration that the security is valid; where this has been in dispute (*g*). It declares, where necessary, the rights and priorities as well of the several incumbrancers as of any person who has a paramount claim on the property (*h*); and after providing for other incidental matters, it directs that the accounts be

---

(*o*) See p. 619, *infra.*

(*p*) See p. 649, *infra.*

(*q*) For the difference between a genuine foreclosure action and a disguised possession action, see p. 320, *supra.*

(*r*) *Manchester and Liverpool Bank* v. *Parkinson* (1889), 68 L.T. 258.

(*s*) *Salt* v. *Edgar* (1886), 54 L.T. 374.

(*t*) *Le Bas* v. *Grant* (1895), 64 L.J. Ch. 368.

(*u*) *Keith* v. *Day* (1888), 39 Ch. D. 452 (C.A.).

(*a*) *Jenkins* v. *Ridgley* (1893), 41 W.R. 585.

(*b*) *Marshall* v. *Shrewsbury* (1875), 10 Ch. App. 250, at p. 254.

(*c*) In the case of registered land the charge certificate must be produced.

(*d*) Affidavits of due execution of mortgages or charges are no longer required on applications for foreclosure nisi unless the court directs otherwise: *Practice Direction,* [1969] 2 All E.R. 639. And see generally as to evidence *The Supreme Court Practice* 1976, 88/2—8/27.

(*e*) *Thynne* v. *Sarl*, [1891] 2 Ch. 79.

(*f*) For forms of order, see 28 Ency. Forms and Precedents (2nd Edn.), Mortgages.

(*g*) *Holmes* v. *Turner* (1843), 7 Hare 367, n. and form; *Faulkner* v. *Daniel* (1843), 3 Hare 199, establishing judgment debt: *Carlon* v. *Farlar* (1845), 8 Beav. 526.

(*h*) *Jones* v. *Griffith* (1845), 2 Coll. 207.

taken (*i*), and where necessary, that rests be made against a mortgagee in possession (*k*), and that the sum due from him on account of his receipts be applied in payment first of interest and then of principal (*l*). To the amount due to each mortgagee in respect of his own debt, are added all sums which may have been paid for the redemption of preceding incumbrancers, or to which he may be declared to be entitled for improvements (*m*), or for payments in respect of or for the protection of his security, or of the property (*n*).

The mortgagor, when an order for personal payment has been claimed against him, will then be ordered to pay the debt to the mortgagee within a limited time, usually six months from the date of the master's certificate (*a*), and upon his doing so, the mortgagee will be ordered to reconvey to the mortgagor, when a conveyance is necessary, and to deliver to him all deeds and documents relating to the property (*p*). The same course is followed as to any other person entitled to redeem, but who is not liable to an order for personal payment, upon payment of the sum found due from him.

In either case, on non-payment by the person who was ordered, or was declared to be at liberty to pay, he is directed to be foreclosed whether the mortgage is legal or equitable; with the addition, in the case of an equitable mortgage, that a conveyance is to be executed by the mortgagor to the mortgagee (*q*). But if he is plaintiff in an action for redemption, his action will be dismissed, and this will have the effect of foreclosure (*r*).

Price of redemption.—Whether the action be one for foreclosure

---

(*i*) For form of foreclosure judgment by consent without account, see *Boydell* v. *Manby* (1842), 9 Hare App. liii. For accounts, see pp. 612 *et seq.*, *infra*.

(*k*) See p. 623, *infra*.

(*l*) See *Thorneycroft* v. *Crockett* (1848), 2 H.L.C. 239. And see p. 543, *infra*. As to form where a receiver has been in receipt of rents and profits, see *Simmons* v. *Blandy*, [1897] 1 Ch. 19.

(*m*) See p. 352, *supra*.

(*n*) See p. 353, *supra*.

(*o*) *Platt* v. *Mendel* (1884), 27 Ch. D. 246. If the mortgagor is entitled to a set-off, the court may give him the benefit of his set-off, and, upon payment by him into court of the principal and interest, the foreclosure may be suspended until both accounts have been taken: *Dodd* v. *Lydall* (1842), 1 Hare 333.

Where the mortgage debt is payable by instalments, the order will direct payment of the amount certified to be already due, and will declare, if necessary, that the mortgagee has a charge in respect of the unpaid instalments; and will give him liberty to apply in chambers for the purpose of giving effect to it: *Greenough* v. *Littler* (1880), 15 Ch. D. 93; *Nives* v. *Nives* (1880), 15 Ch. D. 649.

(*p*) To avoid unnecessary expense in the preparation of documents for reconveyance should the mortgagor fail to redeem the order must provide (1) that the mortgagor must give seven days' clear notice of his intention to attend and redeem, and (2) if no such notice is given but the mortgagor in fact attends at the appointed time and place then at the option of the mortgagee the time for redemption must be extended for one week: *Practice Directions*, [1955] 1 All E.R. 30.

(*q*) See *Dymond* v. *Croft* (1876), 3 Ch. D. 512; *Greenough* v. *Littler*, *supra*; *Lees* v. *Fisher* (1882), 22 Ch. D. 283. But it seems that if, for any reason, the judgment to account, instead of being made in the usual manner, proceeds upon the undertaking of the mortgagor to pay what shall be found due, the mortgagee, relying upon this undertaking, cannot avail himself of the right to foreclose if default is made in the payment: *Dunstan* v. *Patterson* (1847), 2 Ph. 341. As to the order where, in an action by a mortgagee of shares in a company to enforce his security, the company unsuccessfully disputes the security on the ground that the shares have been forfeited for non-payment of calls, see *Watson* v. *Eales* (1857), 23 Beav. 294.

(*r*) See p. 578, *infra*.

by the mortgagee or for redemption by the mortgagor (*s*), the price of redemption is the same (*t*). Each party, according as he may be plaintiff or defendant, may be subject to particular equities arising out of these characters, but no distinction is made, as to the course and order of redemption, between an action in which the owner is seeking to clear his estate from incumbrances, and one in which the first (*u*), or a subsequent (*a*) mortgagee is seeking to get possession of the estate in satisfaction of his debt. And though the mortgagee submits to depart from the common form of the judgment in one particular (as if it directs an account, and then reserves further consideration, instead of the usual order for payment or foreclosure), yet he retains his right to have the further order made in the usual form (*b*).

Delivery up of deeds.—The order further provides that on a receipt under Law of Property Act 1925, s. 115, the deeds shall be delivered up. And where the person redeeming is a later mortgagee and the judgment is for personal payment by the mortgagor, the plaintiff mortgagee will also be directed to assign the benefit of the judgment to the redeeming party, with liberty to enforce it in the name of the plaintiff upon giving him a sufficient indemnity (*c*). If the mortgagee is in possession, it is also proper to add (*d*), that he shall deliver possession of the mortgaged estate.

The judgment finally directs that, in default of payment, the person to whom the right to redeem was given shall be foreclosed, and, if possession is claimed (*e*), that the mortgagor shall forthwith deliver possession to the mortgagee.

Equitable mortgage.—Where the security is equitable, the mortgagee upon redemption is ordered to deliver up all deeds, etc., in his custody relating to the estate, to the person redeeming; but in case of non-payment, the party making default is ordered to convey or surrender to the mortgagee, free from incumbrances (*f*); and in default of compliance, a vesting order will be made (*g*); or if a sale is directed, the proceeds are ordered to be paid to the credit of the action,

---

(*s*) See p. 568, *infra*.

(*t*) *Du Vigier* v. *Lee* (1843), 2 Hare 326; *Watts* v. *Symes* (1851), 1 De G.M. & G. 240.

(*u*) *Barnes* v. *Fox*, Seton (7th Edn.), p. 1907.

(*a*) *Jackson* v. *Brettall*, Seton (7th Edn.), p. 1908.

(*b*) *Dunstan* v. *Patterson*, *supra*. See observations, *Watts* v. *Symes*, *supra*, at p. 242.

(*c*) *Greenough* v. *Littler* (1880), 15 Ch. D. 93.

(*d*) *Yates* v. *Hambly* (1742), 2 Atk. 360; *Arthur* v. *Higgs* (1856), and *Evans* v. *Kinsey* (1855), Seton (7th Edn.), 1887. As to the practice where the mortgagee refuses a proper tender, see *Bank of New South Wales* v. *O'Connor* (1889), 14 App. Cas. 273 (P.C.), at p. 283.

(*e*) *Wood* v. *Wheater* (1882), 22 Ch. D. 281. The court has jurisdiction to order possession even where it is not asked by the writ, pleadings, or originating summons: *Salt* v. *Edgar* (1886), 54 L.T. 374. See p. 395, *supra*; and p. 413, *infra*.

(*f*) *Holmes* v. *Turner* (1843), 7 Hare 367, n.; *Footner* v. *Sturgis* (1852), 5 De G. & Sm. 736; *Pryce* v. *Bury* (1853), 2 Drew. 11. Where the estate has already been sold by the mortgagee under his power of sale, see *Re Smith's Mortgage Account* (1861), 9 W.R. 799. Where the mortgagor was a company, and it had been dissolved before conveyance, a vesting order could be obtained: *Re Nos. 56* and *58, Albert Rd., Norwood*, [1916] 1 Ch. 289. See now Law of Property Act 1925, s. 181; *Re Wells, Swinburne-Hanham* v. *Howard*, [1933] Ch. 29 (C.A.); *Re Strathblaine Estates, Ltd.*, [1948] Ch. 228; [1948] 1 All E.R. 162.

(*g*) As to vesting orders, see p. 560, *infra*.

to be applied as the judgment directs, or, if no directions are given, there is liberty to apply (*h*).

Successive mortgages.—Where there are successive mortgages, the judgment proceeds upon the principle that the second mortgagee, as the first assignee of the equity of redemption, fills the place and acquires the rights of the mortgagor (*i*); and he has, therefore, the first right to redeem, upon payment of what is due to the first mortgagee; but, in default of payment, he is foreclosed.

The second mortgagee being thus removed out of the way, an account is taken of the first mortgagee's subsequent interest and costs, and upon payment thereof, with the amount originally found due, the third mortgagee may redeem him, and in default he in turn is foreclosed (*k*); and this process is carried on as to all the successive incumbrancers, until the mortgagor or ultimate owner of the equity of redemption alone remains, when he may in like manner redeem, and in default stands foreclosed; and then the property remains to the first mortgagee, free from all incumbrances.

And where there are several incumbrancers, and the mortgagor's action for redemption is dismissed (which is generally equivalent to foreclosure (*l*)), the last incumbrancer becomes *quasi* mortgagor, and the others become first and subsequent incumbrancers according to their priorities (*m*).

Effect of redemption.—It has been thus far assumed, that none of the successive incumbrancers have exercised their rights of redemption. But the judgment provides for the exercise of these rights, by directing that, in case the second mortgagee shall redeem the first, an account shall be taken of what is due to the person so redeeming on his own security, and for what he shall have paid the first mortgagee, with interest thereon (*n*), and costs; and upon payment of the aggregate of these sums, the third mortgagee has liberty to redeem the second, in default of which he is foreclosed according to the process first pointed out; and a further account having been taken of what is due to the second mortgagee in respect of his own debt, and of his payments, the next incumbrancer, or, if there is none, the mortgagor will be at liberty to redeem.

But if the third mortgagee shall have redeemed the second, an account is taken of what is due to the third, in respect of his security, and of what he has paid; and he may be redeemed by the next

---

(*h*) A vesting order may be made in favour of the purchaser, or the court may create and vest in the mortgagee a legal term of years to enable him to carry out the sale: Law of Property Act 1925, s. 90.

(*i*) Thus, in taking the account the second mortgagee may assert such equity as the mortgagor himself might have to exclude any particular item: *Mainland* v. *Upjohn* (1889), 41 Ch. D. 126.

(*k*) In *Bingham* v. *King* (1866), 14 W.R. 414, a later mortgagee, who verified the amount of his debt by affidavit, obtained an order for payment, without taking a formal account, out of surplus proceeds of sale paid in by the first mortgagee; creditors, however, being allowed time to dispute the account.

(*l*) See p. 578, *infra*.

(*m*) *Cottingham* v. *Earl of Shrewsbury* (1843), 3 Hare 627. As to whether successive periods for redeeming will be allowed to the successive incumbrancers, or whether one time only will be limited for redemption, see p. 401, *infra*.

(*n*) See p. 631, *infra*.

incumbrancer, or by the ultimate owner of the equity of redemption.

Finally, upon non-payment to the last person to be redeemed of what he shall have paid to the prior incumbrancers, and of his own principal, interest, and costs, the owner of the equity himself stands absolutely foreclosed, and the property, as before, remains in the hands of such one of the incumbrancers as has cleared off the rest, free from all the debts which affected it (*o*).

Mortgage by surety.—Where a principal debtor and a surety has each mortgaged his property, the judgment is so framed as to give the surety the full benefit of his rights against the property of the principal debtor. And the right of redemption being given to both, it is ordered that if the money is paid by the principal debtor, the properties shall be conveyed to their respective owners; but if by the surety, both properties are conveyed to him, and he, of course, holds that which belongs to his principal, subject to redemption by him. If neither principal nor surety redeems, the equities of both their properties are foreclosed (*p*).

But as no relief will be given against a surety beyond the express terms of his contract, his mortgage of a reversionary interest will not be subject either to sale or foreclosure, if its operation is limited to the application of the proceeds when it falls into possession (*q*).

Judgment in respect of a sub-mortgage.—Where a security is a sub-mortgage, W being the mortgagor, H the mortgagee, and K the sub-mortgagee, and a foreclosure action is brought by K against H and W, the judgment directs an account of what is due to H, and then of what is due to K. Upon payment to K of the sum due to him, not exceeding the sum due to H, and on payment of any residue to H, each will give a statutory receipt. In case of default W is foreclosed, and then, after the computation of subsequent interest and costs due to K, and payment to him of the whole amount due to him by H, he will give a statutory receipt. In default H will be foreclosed (*r*).

Mixed mortgages.—Where the mortgage is of land, and there is

(*o*) As to costs where an intermediate mortgagee redeems the first, who also holds a later mortgage, see *Mutual Life Assurance Society* v. *Langley* (1886), 32 Ch. D. 460 (C.A.). As to an action by a later mortgagee of two estates, subject to separate mortgages, see *Pelly* v. *Wathen* (1849), 7 Hare 351–363; on app. (1851), 1 De G.M. & G. 16; *Hallett* v. *Furze* (1885), 31 Ch. D. 312. For a curious case of mixed specific performance, foreclosure, and partition, see *Davies* v. *Davies* (1860), 6 Jur. N.S. 1320.

(*p*) *Beckett* v. *Micklethwaite* (1821), 6 Mad. 199; Seton (7th Edn.), 2088. See *Aldworth* v. *Robinson* (1840), 2 Beav. 287, which also provides for redemption as between the principal and the surety.

For an order where a wife and husband had mortgaged her estates for the husband's debts, and, after a second security on the whole property to another incumbrancer, the husband became insolvent, see *Hill* v. *Edmonds* (1852), 5 De G. & Sm. 603. The estate of the husband or wife, as the case may be, will be indemnified out of the estate of the other of them for whose benefit the money was raised: *Wilkinson* v. *Beale* (1823), 1 L.J. O.S. Ch. 89; *Gray* v. *Dowman* (1858), 27 L.J. Ch. 702.

For form of decree where mortgagee had a mortgage of property belonging to A and B for money advanced to them in different proportions, and another mortgage of the separate property of A, and of his interest in the joint property, to secure his separate debt, see *Higgins* v. *Frankis* (1846), 10 Jur. 328.

(*q*) *Stamford, etc., Banking Co.* v. *Ball* (1862), 4 De G.F. & J. 310.

(*r*) Seton (7th Edn.), 2009; and see pp. 2010, 2011. Directions to give statutory receipts have been substituted above for the former directions to convey.

also a simple assignment of stock or other personal chattels (*s*), or of a policy of assurance, the proper order is for sale of the chattel security in the first instance, and then for foreclosure in respect of the deficiency; lest by taking the land first, the foreclosure should be opened by the subsequent sale of the policy (*t*).

B—THE TIME ALLOWED FOR PAYMENT

Six months allowed to mortgagor.—It is the practice to allow the mortgagor six months for payment, the period being reckoned from the date of the master's certificate fixing the amount of the debt (*u*). The master's certificate must nominate as the place of redemption the office of the mortgagee's solicitors if it be within five miles of the Royal Courts of Justice or such other place as may be agreed between the parties and recorded in the order or certificate. In all other cases the place of redemption shall be recorded as Room 136 of the Royal Courts of Justice (*a*). The equitable, as well as the legal, mortgagee has a right to this time under the ordinary process of the court, whether the judgment is for foreclosure or sale (*b*). But under the statutory jurisdiction to order a sale, less than six months may be given, or an immediate sale may be directed.

Successive periods for payment.—Where there are later incumbrancers the right to redeem is exercisable by them in succession, and ultimately by the mortgagor. Formerly it was the practice to give the

---

(*s*) For forms of judgment on mortgages of stock and chattels, see Seton (7th Edn.), 1923 *et seq.*; and on a mortgage by one of the partners in a mine where the other partners have a right of pre-emption, see *Redmayne* v. *Forster* (1866), L.R. 2 Eq. 467. For judgment on a mortgage of a pension, see *James* v. *Ellis* [1870] W.N. 269; 24 L.T. 12; Seton (7th Edn.), 1925.

(*t*) But where the assignment of the policy is followed by provisions which indicate that the mortgagee shall have the benefit of the policy moneys, foreclosure only may be ordered: *Dyson* v. *Morris* (1842), 1 Hare 413; though this would be liable to be opened, if the mortgagee should afterwards resort to the moneys to become payable on the policy (which he was allowed to retain for that purpose) to cover the amount for which the estate might be insufficient. Hence, where a mortgage of a policy or other future thing in action is made as a collateral security, no provisions should be inserted which may affect the mortgagee's right to an immediate sale of the thing in action, and thereby abridge the remedy against the primary security also. And see p. 406, *infra*.

And as to bringing the value of the collateral security into account, see *De Lisle* v. *Union Bank of Scotland*, [1914] 1 Ch. 22 (C.A.).

(*u*) *Platt* v. *Mendel* (1884), 27 Ch. D. 246, 248.

(*a*) *Practice Directions*, [1955] 1 All E.R. 30 (the room has been charged since 1955).

(*b*) *Parker* v. *Housefield* (1834), 2 My. & K. 419; *Price* v. *Carver* (1837), 3 My. & Cr. 157, 163; *King* v. *Leach* (1842), 2 Hare 57; *Lister* v. *Turner* (1846), 5 Hare 281, 293; *Lloyd* v. *Whittey* (1853), 17 Jur. 754. And although the security is given for a debt which does not carry interest: *Meller* v. *Woods* (1836), 1 Keen 16. A judgment creditor when he has obtained a charging order on land under the Administration of Justice Act 1956, is in the position of an equitable mortgagee (*supra*, p. 159) and the judgment debtor has the usual six months.

Whether the Bankruptcy Court can order foreclosure has been questioned. If it can, the period of six months is proper to be allowed although the trustee has no assets except the equity of redemption: *Re Hart, Ex parte Fletcher* (1878), 9 Ch. D. 381; (1879), 10 Ch. D. 610. Probably it has no such jurisdiction. The proper course is for the mortgagee to bring a foreclosure action in the Chancery Division. See p. 415, *infra*.

The direction for "payment within six months after the date of the certificate", being matter which would have been inserted by the registrar as part of a usual order, may be added by way of correction of the judgment, on motion: *Bird* v. *Heath* (1848), 6 Hare 236; see R.S.C. Ord. 20, r. 11.

incumbrancers successive periods within which to redeem; six months
for the first, and successive periods of three months each for those
subsequent to the first (c); and apparently a final three months after
the last incumbrancer's time for payment was allowed to the mortgagor (d). But this rule was not applied in certain cases, and as to
those to which it was applied, it is either obsolete, or it is applied only
under special circumstances.

Cases where only a single period was allowed.—The rule did
not, and does not now apply where there are several judgment creditors
entitled to a charge on land, and they were allowed only a single period
of three months, as if their judgments formed one incumbrance only (e).
And only one period of redemption was allowed where several
incumbrances were created on the same day (f); where persons entitled
to redeem claimed under the same instrument, although, as in the case of
tenant for life and remainderman, their periods of enjoyment were
different (g); and for any other good cause shown, such as the existence
of a very small margin for subsequent incumbrancers (h).

Present practice.—And even where the rule allowing successive
periods for redemption would formerly have been applied it is now
obsolete in two cases, namely, where there are questions of priority
between the later incumbrancers and where some or all of them do
not appear. Where there are questions of priority, the successive
periods could not be assigned without determining these questions,
and that is a matter in which the plaintiff, the first mortgagee, is not
interested. It is therefore unnecessary to determine it in his action,
and the order allows only one period of redemption without prejudice
to the order of the later incumbrancers amongst themselves (i).
Similarly, where some or all of the defendants to a foreclosure action
do not appear at the hearing, only one period for redemption is allowed,
since to give successive periods would be to fix their priorities in their
absence (k).

(c) See *Titley* v. *Davies* (1743), 2 Y. & C.C.C. 399; *Beevor* v. *Luck* (1867), L.R. 4 Eq.
537; *Lewis* v. *Aberdare and Plymouth Co.* (1884), 53 L.J. Ch. 741.

(d) Seton (7th Edn.), 1907; although the mortgagor should not, by incumbering
the equity of redemption, obtain a further right to redeem: *Platt* v. *Mendel, ubi supra,*
at p. 248.

(e) *Radcliff* v. *Salmon* (1852), 4 De G. & Sm. 526; *Stead* v. *Banks* (1851), 5 De G. & Sm.
560; *Bates* v. *Hillcoat* (1852), 16 Beav. 139.

(f) *Long* v. *Storie* (1854), 23 L.J. Ch. 200.

(g) *Beevor* v. *Luck, supra.* And only one period was allowed to members of a
building society, to whom an estate purchased by their trustees had been allotted:
Peto v. *Hammond* (1861), 30 Beav. 495; and see *Loveday* v. *Chapman* (1875), 32 L.T.
689.

(h) *Cripps* v. *Wood* (1882), 51 L.J. Ch. 584.

(i) *Bartlett* v. *Rees* (1871), L.R. 12 Eq. 395; *General Credit and Discount Co.* v. *Glegg*
(1883), 22 Ch. D. 549; *Lewis* v. *Aberdare and Plymouth Co., supra*; *Tufdnell* v. *Nicholls*
(1887), 56 L.T. 152.

In case more than one of several persons entitled to redeem at the same time should
be then prepared to redeem, liberty is given to apply to the court without giving notice
to the plaintiff, and without prejudice to any question as to the rights of the defendants
as between themselves: see forms of judgment, in *Edwards* v. *Martin* (1858), 28 L.J. Ch.
49; *Bartlett* v. *Rees, supra.* See *Biddulph* v. *Billiter St. Offices Co.* (1895), 72 L.T. 834,
applying *Jennings* v. *Jordan* (1881), 6 App. Cas. 698 (H.L.), at p. 711.

(k) *Doble* v. *Manley* (1885), 28 Ch. D. 664. This is done whether the statement of
claim alleges that the defendants are entitled, or only claim to be entitled, to charges
upon the property: *ibid.*; *Smithett* v. *Hesketh* (1890), 44 Ch. D. 161, 164.

And even where no questions of priority arise and all the defendants are before the court the practice now is to fix only one period for redemption (*l*); but this will be departed from and successive periods allowed under special circumstances, and the onus lies on the subsequent incumbrancers to prove that they are entitled to this indulgence (*m*).

C—ENLARGING THE TIME FOR PAYMENT AND OPENING THE FORECLOSURE

Relaxation as to time of payment.—The enforcement of the strict terms of that part of the judgment in a foreclosure action, which directs absolute foreclosure upon non-payment of the redemption money on a certain day, is in the discretion of the court, which may relieve against it either by a postponement of that day, or by an opening of the foreclosure after the day has been allowed to pass without payment (*n*). The application is made by summons by the person entitled to redeem (*o*), or it may be made at the hearing of a special application by the mortgagee to make the foreclosure absolute (*p*).

Relaxation usually only in foreclosure.—It is only in a foreclosure action, as a general rule, and not in an action for redemption (*q*), that this indulgence is granted; because, in the latter case, the mortgagor comes to the court for relief, professing that his money is ready; but, in a foreclosure action, he redeems by compulsion (*r*).

Several enlargements may be granted.—Upon good cause shown, the court does not stop at a single enlargement in a foreclosure action. Relief has been given three, and even four times in succession; and this, although the time fixed by previous orders of enlargement has been thereby expressed to be peremptory, and even though the mortgagor has undertaken, by signing the registrar's book, not to ask for any further time (*s*).

The period granted upon the first application is usually six months, and it does not appear that any longer time has been granted at once. The like period has also been given on a subsequent application, but the period has then varied from five to three months according to the circumstances.

Reasons for enlargement.—But the time is not enlarged as of course, even upon the first application. Some reason—though a very

---

(*l*) *Smith* v. *Olding* (1884), 25 Ch. D. 462; *Mutual Life Assurance Society* v. *Langley* (1884), 25 Ch. D. 686; *Platt* v. *Mendel* (1884), 27 Ch. D. 246, 248; *Smithett* v. *Hesketh, supra.*

(*m*) In *Bertlin* v. *Gordon*, [1886] W.N. 31, where the mortgage was of a reversionary interest, which was likely soon to fall in, one additional period of a month was allowed; and see *Mutual Life Assurance Society* v. *Langley, supra*, where one additional period of three months was allowed; and *Smithett* v. *Hesketh, supra*, where two such additional periods were allowed.

(*n*) See *Campbell* v. *Holyland* (1877), 7 Ch. D. 166, 171, where JESSEL, M.R., observed that the final foreclosure order was "form only, just as the original deed was form only"; *Ingham* v. *Sutherland* (1890), 63 L.T. 614.

(*o*) For forms of summons, see 28 Ency. Court Forms (2nd Edn.), pp. 127 *et seq.*

(*p*) *Clay* v. —— (1745), 9 Sim. 317, n.; *Lee* v. *Heath* (1747), 9 Sim. 306, n.; *Alden* v. *Foster* (1842), 5 Beav. 592.

(*q*) See p. 577, *infra.*

(*r*) *Novosielski* v. *Wakefield* (1811), 17 Ves. 417.

(*s*) *Anon.* (1740), Barn. Ch. 221; *Edwards* v. *Cunliffe* (1816), 1 Mad. 287.

strong one is not necessary—must be given; as that the defendant has used his best endeavours to find an assignee without success, but that, if time is granted, there is a reasonable prospect of getting the money, or that negotiations for that purpose are actually pending (*t*). And the magnitude of the sum involved, and of the arrears of interest, are circumstances to which weight will be given; but not, it seems, to the latter, if the arrears have been allowed to increase (*u*). A purchaser of the equity of redemption *pendente lite* will not as a rule be granted further time (*a*).

But something more than the above excuses seems necessary upon subsequent applications; such as evidence that some steps have been actually taken, as the result of which the money is likely to be forthcoming (*b*). And a strong case of unexpected delay or difficulty must be made out to support a third or fourth application.

Where an order has been made for payment to several mortgagees who are entitled on a joint account, and one dies before the day fixed for payment, it seems that the survivors are not entitled to the benefit of the order, but a new day for payment will be appointed (*c*).

Terms of enlargement.—The order commonly directs that the time be enlarged upon payment by the mortgagor to the mortgagee, on or before the day originally fixed for payment of the principal, interest and costs, of the amount certified to be due for interest and costs on the mortgage (*d*).

But, if from the circumstances of the case, or the shortness of the interval between the time of application and of payment under the judgment, there is likely to be a difficulty in making the payment in due time, the court will direct enlargement on payment of the interest and costs in a month, or some other convenient time from the date of the order (*e*). And if there is any doubt as to the sufficiency of the security, the condition will also be imposed of immediate payment of

---

(*t*) *Nanny* v. *Edwards* (1827), 4 Russ. 124; *Eyre* v. *Hanson* (1840), 2 Beav. 478; *Quarles* v. *Knight* (1820), 8 Price 630.

Under the usual circumstances of an application by the mortgagor by reason of his being unable to raise the money in time, it is necessary to show that the estate is an ample security for the debt: *Eyre* v. *Hanson*, *supra*; *Edwards* v. *Cunliffe*, *supra*; *Nanny* v. *Edwards*, *supra*; *Anon.*, *supra*. This fact was formerly stated in the order: *Geldard* v. *Hornby* (1841), 1 Hare 251.

Where, however, a necessity for enlarging the time has arisen from the opening of the account by the act of the mortgagee, the order will be made, although the security appears on the evidence to be of doubtful sufficiency; but care will be taken that nothing is added by the delay to the amount of the debt: *ibid.*

(*u*) *Holford* v. *Yate* (1855), 1 K. & J. 677.

(*a*) *Re Parbola, Ltd.*, *Blackburn* v. *Parbola, Ltd.*, [1909] 2 Ch. 437.

(*b*) *Edwards* v. *Cunliffe*, *supra*. See *Campbell* v. *Moxhay* (1854), 18 Jur. 641, where one reason for refusing an extension was that the application was in violation of an express agreement.

(*c*) *Blackburn* v. *Caine* (1856), 22 Beav. 614; *Kingsford* v. *Poile* (1859), 8 W.R. 110; *Browell* v. *Pledge*, [1888], W.N. 166.

(*d*) *Edwards* v. *Cunliffe*, *supra*; Seton (7th Edn.), 1911 *et seq.* But where the large sum of £8,000 was due for interest, the first order was made on payment of £3,000 only on account of interest: *Holford* v. *Yate*, *supra*; and see *Forrest* v. *Shore* (1884), 32 W.R. 356. The general condition of payment of interest will not be relaxed by reason of the infancy of the person entitled to redeem: *Coombe* v. *Stewart* (1851), 13 Beav. 111.

(*e*) *Eyre* v. *Hanson*, *supra*; *Geldard* v. *Hornby*, *supra*.

the interest to accrue down to the day fixed for the ultimate payment of the mortgage debt (*f*).

If the time fixed for payment is likely to expire before the hearing of objections to the certificate which fixes the time of payment, the court will either enlarge the time on the usual application, or if the defendant omits to apply, a new day will be appointed, even after the objections have been overruled (*g*).

Where right to redeem is in dispute.—Where the right to redeem is in dispute, and time is required to prosecute an appeal, the object of the court is to make an order, which, without touching the judgment, will yet secure to the person redeeming the recovery of the money which the judgment requires him to pay. In such a case the terms imposed will be the payment into court of principal and arrears of interest, consent to a receiver and payment of interest from the commencement of the action; or of principal, interest, and costs of action and of the application (*h*). The amount paid in will be ordered to be invested at the risk of the applicant (*i*); and if the dividends or any interest are ordered to be paid to the mortgagee, it will be upon his undertaking to repay the same upon the reversal of the judgment.

Foreclosure on default at appointed time.—The order will in all cases proceed to foreclose the mortgagor upon non-payment at the appointed time of the sum upon the conditional payment of which the order is made (*k*). If the condition is not complied with, the order of foreclosure absolute may be made as of course. And its discharge has been refused with costs, though it was sworn to have been obtained by surprise during negotiations between the parties, and notwithstanding an affidavit by the tenant in possession, that he was willing to purchase the estate for more than twice as much as was due in the security (*l*).

Conditions of reopening foreclosure.—The conditions are stricter when the application is made after order absolute for foreclosure (*m*), so that, in order to grant the indulgence, the foreclosure must be reopened (*n*), and also, it seems, when the application is made after the

---

(*f*) *Geldard* v. *Hornby, supra.* The condition for payment of interest and costs will not be imposed where the foreclosure is opened by reason of the mortgagee's own acts: see *Buchanan* v. *Greenway* (1849), 12 Beav. 355.

(*g*) *Renvoize* v. *Cooper* (1823), 1 Sim. & St. 364.

(*h*) *Monkhouse* v. *Bedford Corporation* (1810), 17 Ves. 380; *Finch* v. *Shaw, Colyer* v. *Finch* (1855), 20 Beav. 555; and see *Holford* v. *Yate, supra.*

(*i*) *Finch* v. *Shaw, supra.*

(*k*) *Edwards* v. *Cunliffe, supra*; *Eyre* v. *Hanson, supra.*

(*l*) *Jones* v. *Roberts* (1827), M'Clel. & Y. 567.

(*m*) Where the plaintiffs were the public officer and the estate trustees of an insurance society, and the defendant wished to open the foreclosure after final order and the appointment of new trustees in the place of two of the trustees who had died after the final order, the proper course was for the defendant to apply to the new trustees to allow themselves to be added as plaintiffs; and if they refused, to apply under R.S.C. Ord. 15, r. 6, to have them added as defendants: *Pennington* v. *Cayley,* [1912] 2 Ch. 236.

(*n*) As to reopening the foreclosure, see *Cocker* v. *Bevis* (1665), 1 Ch. Ca. 61; *Ismoord* v. *Claypool* (1666), 9 Sim. 317, n.; *Nanfan* v. *Perkins* (1766), 9 Sim. 308, n.; *Crompton* v. *Earl of Effingham* (1782), 9 Sim. 311, n.; *Jones* v. *Creswicke* (1839), 9 Sim. 304; *Booth* v. *Creswicke* (1841), Cr. & Ph. 361. Foreclosure was opened in favour of the heir of the mortgagor where the latter had been foreclosed by his own consent: *Abney* v. *Wordsworth* (1701), 9 Sim. 317, n.

day fixed for payment has passed, but before order absolute (*o*).

The applicant must come with reasonable promptness, having regard to the nature of the property and other circumstances (*p*), and not only must he show that he will be able to redeem, if further time is given, and, if thought fit, must give security for costs in case he fails to do so (*q*), but he must also account satisfactorily for non-payment at the proper time; and he must repay all expenditure incurred by the mortgagee since the order absolute (*r*).

The foreclosure may even be opened against a purchaser if the purchase is made shortly after the order absolute, and with notice of matters which would affect the mortgagee's right to an absolute title; but not where the purchaser bought a considerable time after the date of the order absolute, and without notice of facts which would lead the court to interfere (*s*).

Circumstances under which foreclosure reopened.—The occasions upon which the court will give this relief, and the terms upon which it will be given, depend upon the circumstances of each case.

The expectation that the money will be ready, founded upon a contract for sale, or a bona fide belief from facts known to the mortgagee that a negotiation was so far complete as to make a tender of the money unnecessary; ignorance or mistake as to the state of the proceedings, or the day fixed for payment (*t*); irregularity in the proceedings before the order absolute; the illness, or accidental inability to travel, of the person charged with payment of the money; and poverty, which could be shown to be but temporary; are matters which in the various cases have been admitted as reasons for granting further time, even after the entry of the judgment for foreclosure. And the fact that the property has a special value for the mortgagor may also be taken into consideration (*u*). So, time was enlarged for redemption of a policy of life assurance where the life insured fell in after the day fixed for payment, but before foreclosure absolute (*v*). And where the mortgagor had not understood the effect of the orders nisi and absolute and there was a great discrepancy between the amount owing under the mortgage (£3,000) and the value of the mortgaged property (more than £6,000) the foreclosure was reopened (*w*). But an irregular act, done under what might have been fairly considered to be a correct view of the law,

---

The order is that the entry of the order absolute shall be vacated, and the order discharged on condition of payment on the new day appointed; but on non-payment the order absolute is to stand: *Booth* v. *Creswicke, supra; Ford* v. *Wastell* (1848), 2 Ph. 591; *Thornhill* v. *Manning* (1851), 1 Sim. N.S. 451. The foreclosure cannot be opened as to some only of the parties to the action: *Patch* v. *Ward* (1862), 4 Giff. 96.

(*o*) *Patch* v. *Ward* (1867), 3 Ch. App. 203, 212.

(*p*) *Campbell* v. *Holyland* (1877), 7 Ch. D. 166.

(*q*) *Bird* v. *Gandy* (1715), 7 Vin. Abr. 45, pl. 20; and see *Stevens* v. *Williams* (1851), 1 Sim. N.S. 545.

(*r*) *Thornhill* v. *Manning* (1851), 1 Sim. N.S. 451, 456.

(*s*) *Campbell* v. *Holyland, supra.* But an order was refused in *Re Power and Carton's Contract* (1890), 25 L.R. Ir. 459.

(*t*) *Collinson* v. *Jeffery*, [1896] 1 Ch. 644.

(*u*) See the cases cited above, and see *Joachim* v. *M'Douall* (1798), 9 Sim. 314, n.; *Ford* v. *Wastell* (1847), 6 Hare 229; *Campbell* v. *Holyland, supra.*

(*v*) *Beaton* v. *Boulton*, [1891] W.N. 30.

(*w*) *Lancashire and Yorkshire Reversionary Interest Co., Ltd.* v. *Crowe* (1970), 114 Sol. Jo. 435.

and not from fradulent motives, will not be a ground for setting aside the order absolute after it has been passed and entered (*x*).

Opening foreclosure as of right.—In the cases mentioned above the court interferes with the foreclosure as an indulgence to the mortgagor, but the mortgagor may also be entitled, either before foreclosure to have the time for redemption enlarged, or after foreclosure to have the foreclosure opened.

Thus, where the mortgagee (*y*), or the receiver appointed in the action (*z*), receives rents between the date of the certificate and the date fixed for redemption, the foreclosure will be reopened as a matter of course, and a fresh account will be taken and a new day fixed for redemption, unless in the original judgment the mortgagee submitted to be charged with a sum in respect of rents in the receiver's hands, or which might come to his hands prior to the order absolute, and the amount so received does not exceed the sum so fixed (*a*).

Where, however, rents are received between the day fixed for redemption and the date of the order absolute, the foreclosure will not be re-opened (*b*) nor will it be re-opened on the ground that the receiver appointed by the court has made a mistake in his accounts (*c*).

Suing mortgagor for payment.—And if after foreclosure the mortgagee, claiming that the property is insufficient to satisfy the mortgage debt, sues the mortgagor on his covenant for payment, this will open the foreclosure and the mortgagor will be entitled to redeem (*d*).

It is assumed, however, that the mortgagee still has the property under his control, so that upon redemption he can restore it to the mortgagor. If he has sold it to a stranger as beneficial owner then, since he cannot restore it, he cannot sue the mortgagor (*e*). The

---

(*x*) *Patch* v. *Ward* (1867), 3 Ch. App. 203.

(*y*) *Garlick* v. *Jackson* (1841), 4 Beav. 154; *Buchanan* v. *Greenway* (1849), 12 Beav. 355; *Patch* v. *Ward* (1867), 3 Ch. App. 203, 208; *Prees* v. *Coke* (1871), L.R. 6 Ch. 645; *Allen* v. *Edwards* (1873), 42 L.J. Ch. 455.

(*z*) *Jenner-Fust* v. *Needham* (1886), 32 Ch. D. 582 (C.A.); *Peat* v. *Nicholson* (1886), 54 L.T. 569; and see Seton (7th Edn.), p. 1914.

(*a*) *Barber* v. *Jeckells*, [1893] W.N. 91; *Simmons* v. *Blandy*, [1897] 1 Ch. 19. For form of such judgment, see *Lusk* v. *Sebright*, [1894] W.N. 134; and see *Ellenor* v. *Ugle*, [1895] W.N. 161, where the order absolute was allowed on certain conditions, the rents received by the receiver being insufficient to pay out-of-pocket expenses and remunera-tion. And a new day will not be fixed if the original judgment directed that any party might apply in chambers for payment or transfer to him of any money which might come to the hands of the receiver or be paid into court: *Coleman* v. *Llewellin* (1886), 34 Ch. D. 143 (C.A.). In that case the order absolute may provide for payment of the money to the mortgagee: *ibid.* It seems, however, that this latter direction will only be inserted in the judgment in special cases: *Cheston* v. *Wells*, [1893] 2 Ch. 151.

(*b*) *Prees* v. *Coke, supra*, at p. 650; *Webster* v. *Patteson* (1884), 25 Ch. D. 626; *National Permanent Building Society* v. *Raper*, [1892] 1 Ch. 54.

(*c*) *Ingham* v. *Sutherland* (1890), 63 L.T. 614.

(*d*) *Dashwood* v. *Blythway* (1729), 1 Eq. Cas. Abr. 317, pl. 3; *Perry* v. *Barker* (1803), 8 Ves. 527; *Lockhart* v. *Hardy* (1846), 9 Beav. 349. And the mortgagor has this right even though he has assigned the equity of redemption, though—under the former system of reconveyance—the reconveyance would be made subject to such equity for redemption as was vested in any person other than himself: *Kinnaird* v. *Trollope* (1888), 39 Ch. D. 636, at p. 645.

(*e*) *Lockhart* v. *Hardy, supra;* *Palmer* v. *Hendrie* (1859), 27 Beav. 349; (1860), 28 Beav. 341; *Walker* v. *Jones* (1866), L.R. 1 P.C. 50 at p. 62; *Kinnaird* v. *Trollope, supra;* *Ellis & Co.'s Trustee* v. *Dixon-Johnson*, [1924] 1 Ch. 342, at p. 351; on appeal, [1924] 2 Ch. 451 (C.A.) at p. 470; [1925] A.C. 489 (H.L.); *Rushton* v. *Industrial Development Bank* (1973), 34 D.L.R. (3d) 582.

principle does not apply if the mortgagee is prevented from restoring the estate by an act for which he is not responsible, *e.g.*, eviction by a superior landlord where the mortgagee was not liable to pay the rent or perform the covenants (*f*). Nor does it apply where the mortgagee's inability to restore the property is the result of a sale by him under his power of sale (*g*).

After foreclosure the mortgagee can still sell and make a title under his power of sale; and in this case, though the purchaser gets a good title and the property cannot be restored *in specie*, yet the foreclosure is re-opened as regards the purchase money, and the mortgagee will have to account for this to the mortgagor (*h*).

Re-opening foreclosure for fraud or collusion.—The foreclosure will also be opened in the judgment has been obtained by false evidence (*i*), or other fradulent or collusive (*j*) practice, just as other judgments are set aside under the like circumstances (*k*); but actual fraud and contrivance, and not merely constructive fraud, must be shown for the purpose (*l*).

Not usually after acquiescence.—The court is generally unwilling to open a foreclosure after long acquiescence, especially if buildings or other improvements, or settlements have been made on the faith of the order, and where the foreclosure has been by consent; and it has refused such relief after six years (*m*).

(*f*) *Re Burrell, Burrell* v. *Smith* (1869), L.R. 7 Eq. 399.
(*g*) And see p. 545, *infra.*
(*h*) *Watson* v. *Marston* (1853), 4 De G.M. & G. 230; *Re Alison, Johnson* v. *Mounsey* (1879), 11 Ch. D. 284 (C.A.); *Stevens* v. *Theatres, Ltd.*, [1903] 1 Ch. 857. (And see p. 383, *supra*, for the need for leave during the period for redemption). But apparently this is not the result of a mere agreement to sell under the power of sale; *Watson* v. *Marston, supra*, at p. 240. The fact that the mortgagee has referred to the mortgage in his will as if the debt were still subsisting, is not a ground for opening the foreclosure, but the property will pass according to his actual interest: *Took* v. *Bishop of Ely* (1705), 15 Vin. Abr. 476, note to pl. 1; *Silberschildt* v. *Schiott* (1814), 3 Ves & B. 45; *Le Gros* v. *Cockerell* (1832), 5 Sim. 384.
(*i*) *Loyd* v. *Mansell* (1722), 2 P. Wms. 73.
(*j*) *Harvey* v. *Tebbutt* (1820), 1 Jac. & W. 197.
(*k*) *Gore* v. *Stacpoole* (1813), 1 Dow. 18.
(*l*) *Patch* v. *Ward* (1867), 3 Ch. App. 203. And see *Cox* v. *Peele* (1787), 2 Bro. C.C. 334, where relief seems to have been refused merely on the ground that the remedy sought was specific performance of a parol agreement under which a decree for foreclosure had been made by consent, instead of (as it should have been) reopening of the foreclosure. See also *Morley* v. *Elways* (1668), 1 Ch. Cas. 107, where an estate was held to be redeemable, notwithstanding a release of the equity of redemption more than twenty years old, and a decree of foreclosure by consent more than five years old; because the release was made upon a secret trust to pay the mortgagor an annuity, the land being also of much greater value than the debt; and *Burgh* v. *Langton* (1724), 15 Vin. Abr. 476, where after sixteen years a decree was opened, under the concurrent circumstances of a great excess in the value of the estate, and the distressed condition of the mortgagor. The court has refused to open a decree for sale on the ground of an error in the direction as to payment of the surplus where the sale had been fairly conducted and there was in fact no surplus: *Lightburne* v. *Swift* (1812), 2 Ba. & Be. 207.
(*m*) *Took* v. *Bishop of Ely, supra*; *Lant* v. *Crisp* (1719), 15 Vin. 467; *Fleetwood* v. *Jansen* (1742), 2 Atk. 467; and see *Thornhill* v. *Manning* (1851), 1 Sim. (N.S.) 451; *Jones* v. *Kendrick* (1727), 2 Eq. Ca. Abr. 602. Acquiescence in a judgment for foreclosure does not necessarily preclude a subsequent action for redemption founded on new matter, and, notwithstanding the foreclosure, the plaintiff will have the benefit at the hearing of any equity which may arise upon his redemption action: *Fleetwood* v. *Jansen, supra.*

D—JUDGMENTS FOR SALE

Sale in lieu of foreclosure.—Where the judgment is for sale, instead of foreclosure (*n*), the direction is that, upon default in payment, the property comprised in the security shall be sold, and the proceeds applied in its discharge (*o*).

The period of six months for payment allowed by a foreclosure order is also allowed in cases of sale under the inherent jurisdiction of the court (*p*). In cases under the statutory jurisdiction, the court is not restricted as to the time for payment, but three months is usually allowed (*q*).

Security for expenses.—The order may direct the deposit in court of a reasonable sum fixed by the court to meet the expenses of the sale and secure the performance of the terms subject to which the order is made (*r*).

Where a deposit is to be made, the order will be to sell in case the deposit is paid within a short time—such as a week—from the date of the certificate of the amount to be deposited, or from the date of the order if the amount is agreed or fixed at the hearing; but in case of default in making the deposit, or in case of no sale within six months from the date of the certificate, or order, then foreclosure (*s*).

Conduct of sale.—The conduct of the sale is given to the person who has the most interest in getting the best price, *i.e.*, the mortgagor, or if he does not want it, the mortgagee lowest in priority (*t*).

(*n*) As to sale by the court in lieu of foreclosure, either under its original jurisdiction, or under the Law of Property Act 1925, s. 91, see pp. 384 *et seq.*, *supra*. As to the right of the mortgagee to the benefit of goodwill, see p. 37, *supra*; and as to his right to prevent the use by the assignee of the mortgagors of a trade name included in the security, see *Beazley* v. *Soares* (1882), 22 Ch. D. 660. If it appears that the property is deficient, foreclosure may be directed even after an order for sale: *Lloyds Bank, Ltd.* v. *Colston* (1912), 106 L.T. 420.

(*o*) For forms of order, see 28 Ency. Court Forms (2nd Edn.), pp. 110 *et seq.*, 143 *et seq.* In an action for sale by a second mortgagee, the court in Ireland refused to order the first mortgagee to lodge the deeds in court, since he was willing to produce them and let copies be taken under Conveyancing Act 1881, s. 16: *Armstrong* v. *Dickson*, [1911] 1 I.R. 435 (now Law of Property Act 1925, s. 96 (1). See p. 41, *supra*).

Where an order for sale has been made, the mortgagee will not as a rule be allowed to sell out of court under his express power: *Re Claire* (1889), 23 L.R. Ir. 281; and certainly cannot do so without leave: *Stevens* v. *Theatres, Ltd.*, [1903] 1 Ch. 857; and see footnote (*r*), p. 383, *supra*. But an order for sale obtained by a second mortgagee does not prevent a sale by a first mortgagee who is not a party to the action: *Duff* v. *Devlin*, [1924] 1 I.R. 56.

(*p*) *Lloyd* v. *Whittey* (1853), 22 L.J. Ch. 1038.

(*q*) *Supra*, p. 387. A shorter period, such as one month, may be fixed: *Staines* v. *Rudlin* (1852), 9 Hare, App. liii (margin); *Smith* v. *Robinson* (1853), 1 Sm. & G. 140; see *Lloyd* v. *Whittey*, *supra*; or an immediate sale directed. Formerly this was not done where the owner of the equity of redemption did not appear at the hearing though he had appeared in the action: *Smith* v. *Robinson*, *supra*: but under the present law the order may be made though any of the persons interested do not appear in the action: Law of Property Act 1925, s. 91 (2); *supra*, p. 385.

As to ordering an immediate sale, see cases cited, *supra*, p. 387, note (*t*).

(*r*) Law of Property Act 1925, s. 91 (2); *supra*, p. 385.

In a case in which a sale was ordered after decree for foreclosure, a sufficient amount was paid in to indemnify a later mortgagee, who had bought in several incumbrances, to the extent of his entire advances: *Laslett* v. *Cliffe* (1854), 2 Sm. & G. 278. The deposit being made for the indemnity of the mortgagee, will be applied in discharge of his costs of the sale, if it proves abortive: *Corsellis* v. *Patman* (1867), L.R. 4 Eq. 156.

(*s*) *Bellamy* v. *Cockle* (1854) 18 Jur. 465.

(*t*) See, generally, p. 386, *supra*.

Leave may be given to the mortgagee to bid at the sale (*u*). If the mortgagee becomes the purchaser, and his principal and interest exceed the purchase money, he may be let into possession as from a date earlier than that fixed by the contract (*v*).

Equitable interests bound.—The rights of equitable incumbrancers on the estate, whether they are plaintiffs or defendants, or only come in under the judgment, are bound by the order for sale, in the same manner as the equity of redemption is bound by a judgment for foreclosure (*x*). The purchaser, therefore, upon obtaining a conveyance (*y*) of the legal estate, takes the property discharged from all claims, and is not entitled to any release from the equitable incumbrancers (*z*).

E—ORDER ABSOLUTE FOR FORECLOSURE (*a*)

Affidavit of non-payment.—Upon an affidavit of non-payment of the money at the appointed time and place (*b*), or subsequently, to the person to whom it is directed to be paid, or, his agent, the order for foreclosure contained in the original judgment (*c*), whether the security is legal or equitable (*d*), will be made absolute by an order, which is obtained on an *ex parte* summons (*e*), and this whether the action was commenced by originating summons or by writ. This final order of foreclosure must be obtained, before an account is taken of subsequent

---

(*u*) *Ex parte Marsh* (1815), 1 Mad. 148; *The Wilsons* (1841), 1 W. Rob. 173. But it will be refused until other ways of selling have failed, if the mortgagee is also a trustee, and objection is made by *cestuis que trust*; *Tennant* v. *Trenchard* (1869), 4 Ch. App. 537. But if he has the conduct of the sale, some other person will be appointed for that purpose: *Domville* v. *Berrington* (1837), 2 Y. & C. Ex. 723; see *Re Laird, Ex parte M'Gregor* (1851), 4 De G. & Sm. 603.

(*v*) *Bates* v. *Bonnor* (1835), 7 Sim. 427.

(*x*) See p. 397, *supra*.

(*y*) For a vesting order, etc., in favour of the purchaser, see Law of Property Act 1925, s. 90. And see p. 386, *supra*.

(*z*) *Keatinge* v. *Keatinge* (1843), 6 Ir. Eq. R. 43; *Webber* v. *Jones* (1844), 6 Ir. Eq. R. 142. Although a sale is made by consent of all parties, yet an investment of the purchase money in court is not at the risk of the mortgagee: *Tompsett* v. *Wickens* (1855), 3 Sm. & G. 171. Neither is the investment made for his benefit, so that he cannot claim accumulations arising from the purchase moneys, unless they have been carried to his separate account: *Irby* v. *Irby* (1855), 22 Beav. 217. And see *R.* v. *De la Motte* (1857), 2 H. & N. 589. And as to distribution of a fund comprising the proceeds of the mortgaged land and other moneys, see *Taylor* v. *Waters* (1836), 1 Myl. & Cr. 266.

(*a*) For a summary of the proceedings between order nisi and order absolute, see 28 Ency. Court Forms (2nd Edn.), pp. 35 *et seq.*
There is no requirement that a foreclosure nisi certificate or a foreclosure order absolute should be served on the mortgagor: *Lancashire and Yorkshire Reversionary Interest Co., Ltd.* v. *Crowe* (1970), 114 Sol. Jo. 435. For costs, see p. 638, *infra.*

(*b*) The affidavit of non-payment must be made by all the mortgagees in the jurisdiction (if there are more than one), but the affidavit of attendance at the appointed time and place may be made by the mortgagee or his attorney if he attended by attorney: *Kinnaird* v. *Yorke* (1889), 60 L.T. 380; *Docksey* v. *Else* (1891), 64 L.T. 256; *Barrow* v. *Smith* (1885), 33 W.R. 743; and see *Frith* v. *Cooke* (1885), 52 L.T. 798. Office copies of the affidavit are not required unless the court or a judge in any particular instance otherwise directs: *Practice Directions*, [1955] 1 All E.R. 30.

(*c*) See pp. 396, 397, *supra.*

(*d*) *Lees* v. *Fisher* (1882), 22 Ch. D. 283 (C.A.).

(*e*) For form of summons, see 28 Ency. Court Forms (2nd Edn.), p. 132.

interest and costs, and a time appointed for the exercise of the next right of redemption (*f*).

Attendance by agent.—If the person entitled attends by his agent the agent ought to be authorised by a power of attorney to receive the money; and for want of such authority, the court, on the ground that it is the right of the mortgagor to have everything done with the strictest formality, has refused to make the order absolute, though no person appeared to make the payment (*g*). Orders have, however, been made both when the person entitled himself attended during a portion of the time between the hours fixed for payment; and also where he has not so attended (*h*); and also where the agent has attended, but without a power of attorney, and the mortgagor did not attend (*i*).

Effect of foreclosure of freehold mortgages.—Since freehold mortgages are now made by demise—and in the case of mortgages existing on 1 January, 1926, were converted into mortgages by demise— the mere extinguishment of the equity of redemption by the order absolute for foreclosure would not, as formerly, leave the legal estate of freehold in the mortgagee. Hence, in order that the position of the mortgagee should not be prejudiced it was necessary to provide that the foreclosure should operate automatically to vest the fee simple in the mortgagee, with the consequent merger of the mortgage term.

A similar necessity arises when the mortgagee has acquired a title under the Limitation Act 1939, free from the equity of redemption (*k*). But this is met by allowing the mortgagee to have recourse to the statutory power for enlarging the term into the fee simple (*l*), or, in the case of a legal charge, by allowing him to make a declaration vesting the fee simple in himself.

Both these cases are provided for by the Law of Property Act 1925, as follows:

88.—(2) Where any such mortgagee (*m*) obtains an order for foreclosure

---

(*f*) *Whitbread* v. *Lyall* (1856), 8 De G.M. & G. 383. And if great delay takes place in obtaining it, the court will require an explanation, and the owner of the equity of redemption must be served: *Prees* v. *Coke* (1871), 6 Ch. App. 645. No order absolute may be made where the mortgagor has died during the course of proceedings, pending a grant of probate or letters of administration: *Aylward* v. *Lewis*, [1891] 2 Ch. 81. Application should be made under R.S.C. Ord. 15, r. 7 to join the personal representative or under Ord. 15, r. 15 to appoint a person to represent the estate where there is no personal representative.

As to whether there is any need to obtain a supplementary order to give the added defendant power to redeem see (1947) 97 L.J. News 313, 328. If the mortgagor becomes bankrupt during the proceedings, his trustee must be joined.

(*g*) *Gurney* v. *Jackson* (1853), 1 Sm. & G. App. xxvi.

(*h*) *Lechmere* v. *Clamp* (1862), 31 Beav. 578; *London Monetary, etc., Society* v. *Bean* (1868), 18 L.T. 349; *Postlethwaite* v. *Tavers*, [1871], W.N. 173; *Cox* v. *Watson* (1877), 7 Ch. D. 196. In *Bernard* v. *Norton* (1864), 3 New Rep. 701; 10 L.T. N.S. 183, following *Anon.* (1844), 1 Coll. 273, an order absolute was made, though the mortgagee attended during a part only of the time fixed; and this appears to be sufficient; but in *Lechmere* v. *Clamp*, *supra*, Lord ROMILLY said that the alleged order in *Anon.*, *supra*, did not exist or could not be found.

(*i*) *Lechmere* v. *Clamp*, *supra*; *London Monetary, etc., Society* v. *Bean*, *supra*; *Cox* v. *Watson*, *supra*; *Hart* v. *Hawthorne* (1880), 42 L.T. 79; *Macrea* v. *Evans* (1875), 24 W.R. 55; *King* v. *Hough*, [1895] W.N. 60.

(*k*) *Supra*, p. 354.

(*l*) Law of Property Act 1925, s. 153.

(*m*) That is, where an estate in fee simple has been mortgaged by the creation of a term of years limited thereout, or by a charge by way of legal mortgage: s. 88 (1); see p. 377, *supra*.

absolute, the order shall operate to vest the fee simple in him (subject to any legal mortgage having priority to the mortgage in right of which the foreclosure is obtained and to any money thereby secured), and thereupon the mortgage term, if any, shall thereby be merged in the fee simple, and any subsequent mortgage term or charge by way of legal mortgage bound by the order shall thereupon be extinguished.

(3) Where any such mortgagee acquires a title under the Limitation Acts he, or the persons deriving title under him, may enlarge the mortgage term into a fee simple under the statutory power for that purpose discharged from any legal mortgage affected by the title so acquired, or in the case of a chargee by way of legal mortgage may by deed declare that the fee simple is vested in him discharged as aforesaid, and the same shall vest accordingly.

(4) Where the mortgage includes fixtures or chattels personal any statutory power of sale and any right to foreclose or take possession shall extend to the absolute or other interest therein affected by the charge.

In the case of a sub-mortgage of a freehold mortgage the same result is arrived at by providing, in effect, that the sub-mortgage term shall be extinguished, and the principal term be enlarged into the fee simple, so as to enable the sub-mortgagee to acquire the fee simple by foreclosure or enlargement (*n*).

Effect of foreclosure of leasehold mortgages.—Corresponding provision is made with regard to leasehold mortgages:

89.—(2) Where any such mortgagee (*o*) obtains an order for foreclosure absolute, the order shall, unless it otherwise provides, operate (without giving rise to a forfeiture for want of a licence to assign) to vest the leasehold reversion affected by the mortgage and any subsequent mortgage term in him, subject to any legal mortgage having priority to the mortgage in right of which the mortgage is obtained and to any money thereby secured, and thereupon the mortgage term and any subsequent mortgage term or charge by way of legal mortgage bound by the order shall, subject to any express provision to the contrary contained in the order, merge in such leasehold reversion or be extinguished.

(3) Where any such mortgagee acquires a title under the Limitation Acts, he, or the persons deriving title under him, may by deed declare that the leasehold reversion affected by the mortgage and any mortgage affected by the title so acquired shall vest in him, free from any right of redemption which is barred, and the same shall (without giving rise to a forfeiture for want of a licence to assign) vest accordingly, and thereupon the mortgage term, if any, and any other mortgage term or charge by way of legal mortgage affected by the title so acquired shall, subject to any express provision to the contrary contained in the deed, merge in such leasehold reversion or be extinguished.

(4) Where the mortgage includes fixtures or chattels personal any statutory power of sale and any right to foreclose or take possession shall extend to the absolute or other interest therein affected by the charge.

Provision is made in respect of leasehold sub-mortgages similar to that in the case of freehold sub-mortgages. In effect the sub-mortgage term and also the principal mortgage term are extinguished and the sub-mortgagee becomes entitled to the term created by the lease (*p*).

(*n*) Section 88 (5), quoted at p. 378, *supra*. For acquisition of title under the Limitation Act 1939, see p. 354, *supra*.

(*o*) That is, where a term of years absolute has been mortgaged by the creation of another term of years absolute limited thereout, or by a charge by way of legal mortgage: s. 89 (1); see p. 378, *supra*.

(*p*) Section 89 (5); quoted at p. 379, *supra*. For acquisition of title under the Limitation Act 1939, see p. 354, *supra*.

Foreclosure of registered land.—As regards registered land, the Land Registration Act 1925, provides that effect shall be given to foreclosure by the registration of the proprietor of the charge as proprietor of the land. Thus:

> **34.**—(3) An order for foreclosure shall be completed by the registration of the proprietor of the charge (or such other person as may be named in the foreclosure order absolute for that purpose) as the proprietor of the land, and by the cancellation of the charge and of all incumbrances and entries inferior (*q*) thereto; and such registration shall operate in like manner and with the same consequences as if the proprietor of the charge or other person aforesaid had been a purchaser for valuable consideration of the land under a subsisting power of sale (*r*).

Getting in legal estates.—The order for foreclosure of an equitable mortgage contains a direction for conveyance of the legal estate. Where a conveyance cannot be obtained in this way, the mortgagor will be declared to be a trustee for the mortgagee and a vesting order made under s. 44 of the Trustee Act 1925 (*s*).

Order for possession.—An order for possession may be added even where the writ or summons does not ask for it. But in the latter case the order will not be made *ex parte* (*t*). Similar orders may be made for transfer of mortgaged stock (*u*), and for the delivery (along with possession of a mortgaged public-house) of the licence (*x*).

Delivery of the deeds in foreclosure.—When the action results in foreclosure, there is in general no need to direct delivery of the deeds by the mortgagor, because the mortgagee, either by direct delivery from the mortgagor upon the making of a security, or from

---

(*q*) "For the purposes of this section an incumbrance or entry on the register shall not be deemed to be inferior to the charge in right of which title is made if the incumbrance or other interest is given the requisite priority by statute or otherwise": sub-s. (6).

(*r*) As to the extinction of the right of redemption under the Limitation Act 1939, see sub-s. (2). As to the effect of a sale under the power of sale, sub-ss. (4), (5). As to making the necessary entry in the register, see Land Registration Rules 1925, r. 147.

(*s*) *Infra*, p. 561; *Lechmere* v. *Clamp* (1861), 30 Beav. 218; (1862), 31 Beav. 578; *Re Cuming* (1869), L.R. 5 Ch. 72; *Re Crowe's Mortgage* (1871), L.R. 13 Eq. 26; *Re D. Jones & Co.'s Mortgage* (1888), 59 L.T. 859; *Jones* v. *Davies*, [1940] W.N. 174. It was held in *Smith* v. *Boucher* (1852), 1 Sm. & G. 72, that the vesting order could not be inserted in the judgment for foreclosure, but required a separate application. But there seems to be no objection to including it in the judgment under appropriate circumstances.

The former device for getting in a nominal reversion by vesting declaration is not now required: *supra*, p. 22; and see *British Empire, etc., Assurance Co.* v. *Sugden* (1878), 47 L.J. Ch. 691.

(*t*) See cases cited at p. 396, notes (*s*)–(*a*), *supra*; and see *Withall* v. *Nixon* (1885), 28 Ch. D. 413. The order for delivery of possession should contain a description of the property as in the mortgage: *Thynne* v. *Sarl*, [1891] 2 Ch. 79.

The order for foreclosure absolute does not by itself entitle the mortgagee to a writ of possession: *Wood* v. *Wheater* (1882), 22 Ch. D. 281. The order for possession is inserted for convenience in order to avoid multiplicity of proceedings. If it were omitted the mortgagee would have to take separate proceedings to recover possession, and such proceedings would be based, not on the mortgagor's default (the effect of which is exhausted by the foreclosure), but on the mortgagee's own title as owner of the land: *Wood* v. *Smallpiece*, [1942] Ch. 190 (C.A.); [1942] 1 All E.R. 252.

(*u*) *Ricketts* v. *Ricketts*, [1891] W.N. 29.

(*x*) *Crowley* v. *Fenry* (1888), 22 L.R. Ir. 96. For possession in a foreclosure action, see p. 396, *supra*.

another incumbrancer whom he has redeemed, has the deeds already in his possession. But where all the deeds are not already in the mortgagee's custody, the order, after directing the mortgagor to convey on default of payment, goes on to order the delivery of the deeds (*y*).

Deeds only affecting equity of redemption.—The mortgagee's right does not in general extend to deeds which only affect the equity of redemption of the mortgaged property. But under special circumstances (as if the possession of them by another person might affect the title), it seems that delivery of them may be ordered (*z*).

Stamp on foreclosure order.—The order absolute requires to be stamped as a conveyance on sale on the value of the property (*a*).

Effect of foreclosure order.—The order for foreclosure does not relate back to the judgment for an account, so as to make the mortgage real estate from that time; it is not until the final order that the quality of personalty is lost (*b*). In the case of trust property it is held in this case, and also where the right of redemption is extinguished under the Statutes of Limitation, on trust for sale (*c*). Thus the Law of Property Act 1925, provides:

> **31.**—(1) Where any property, vested in trustees by way of security, becomes, by virtue of the statutes of limitation, or of an order for foreclosure or otherwise, discharged from the right of redemption, it shall be held by them on trust for sale.

(*y*) *Holmes* v. *Turner* (1843), 7 Hare 367, n.

(*z*) *Greene* v. *Foster* (1882), 22 Ch. D. 566. As to delivery of the register on a sale of a ship by the Admiralty Court, see *The Tremont* (1841), 1 W. Rob. 163.

(*a*) Finance Act 1898, s. 6; Finance Act 1963, s. 55. See *Huntington* v. *Inland Revenue Commissioners*, [1896] 1 Q.B. 422, 428, n.; *Re Lovell and Collard's Contract*, [1907] 1 Ch. 249. The appropriate certificate of value should be referred to in the affidavit in support of the application and this will be put in the order. Though the order is not a transfer for value consideration, so as to confer an unimpeachable title in the case of registered land: *Re de Leeuw, Jakens* v. *Central Advance, etc., Corpn.*, [1922] 2 Ch. 540, 555 (see p. 244, *supra*).

(*b*) *Thompson* v. *Grant* (1819), 4 Mad. 438. A release after judgment of foreclosure is equivalent to an absolute foreclosure by order: *Reynoldson* v. *Perkins* (1769), Ambl. 564.

(*c*) As to disposition of the net rents where the mortgage is a trust mortgage, see *Re Horn's Estate, Public Trustee* v. *Garnett*, [1924] 2 Ch. 222.

CHAPTER 23

Bankruptcy of Mortgagor

I—SALE BY BANKRUPTCY COURT

Ordinary remedies available to mortgagee.—After the bankruptcy of the mortgagor the mortgagee may take proceedings for foreclosure or otherwise in the usual manner (a), and the bankruptcy court will not, at the request of the trustee in the mortgagor's bankruptcy, transfer such proceedings to the bankruptcy court (b). The same rule applies in the winding up of companies (c). The mortgagee is, in fact, independent of the bankruptcy or winding-up proceedings, and his action is to enforce a claim, not against the bankrupt or the company, but to his own property.

Sale of mortgaged property.—But the ordinary process in bankruptcy is by sale and the Bankruptcy Rules 1952, provide (d) that upon the application of any person claiming to be the legal or equitable mortgagee (e) of any real or leasehold property of the bankrupt the court, if it is satisfied as to the applicant's title, will direct accounts and inquiries of the principal, interest, and costs due under the mortgage, and of the rents and profits or other income received by the mortgagee, and, if satisfied that there ought to be a sale, will direct a sale to be made, and that the trustee (unless it is otherwise ordered) shall have the conduct of the sale (f). At any

---

(a) *Re Wherly, Ex parte Hirst* (1879), 11 Ch. D. 278; see *Re Hutton (A Bankrupt)*, [1969] 2 Ch. 201; [1969] 1 All E.R. 936. Where the statutory, or an express, power to sell or appoint a receiver is made exercisable by reason of the mortgagor committing an act of bankruptcy or being adjudicated a bankrupt, such power is not to be exercised only on account of the act of bankruptcy or adjudication without the leave of the court: Law of Property Act 1925, s. 110 (1).

(b) See Bankruptcy Act 1914, s. 105 (4); *Re Champagne, Ex parte Kemp*, [1893] W.N. 153. Where proceedings have been commenced before the bankruptcy, they will generally be continued in the court in which they were commenced and, unless a bankruptcy point is involved or the costs would be less in the bankruptcy court, there should not be a transfer: see *Re Hutton, supra*. In a possession action there is no need to join the trustee (see p. 324, *supra*) and the costs will be less if he is not involved.

(c) *Re David Lloyd & Co., Lloyd v. David Lloyd & Co.* (1877), 6 Ch. D. 339 (C.A.); and see *Campbell v. Compagnie Générale de Bellegarde* (1876), 2 Ch. D. 181.

(d) Rule 73.

(e) The mortgagee may waive his special power of sale, and apply to the court for an order for sale in his general character of mortgagee: *Re Cook, Ex parte Hodgson* (1821), 1 Gl. & J. 12; *Ex parte Bacon* (1832), 2 Deac. & C. 181; *Re Medley, Ex parte Barnes* (1838), 3 Deac. 223.

If the property is bought in by the trustee, the mortgagee, by applying for a second sale, waives all claims against the trustee for any difference in the amount of biddings between the first and second sales: *Ex parte Baldock* (1832), 2 Deac. & C. 60.

(f) As a general rule, where the security is sufficient, the conduct of the sale will be given to the trustee; but where the security is insufficient, to the mortgagee: *Re Jordan, Ex parte Harrison* (1884), 13 Q.B.D. 228.

such sale the mortgagee may bid and purchase. All proper parties are to join in the conveyance to the purchaser, as the court shall direct (g). The proceeds of sale must be applied first, in payment of the costs, charges, and expenses of the trustee, then in payment of what is due for principal, interest, and costs to the mortgagee; and the balance (if any) to the trustee (h). But in case of deficiency, the mortgagee can prove for the balance due to him (i).

Debt not due.—It is not a valid objection to the order for sale, that the period had not expired before which, under the terms of the mortgage, the debt could not be called in, because such a provision has reference to the mortgagee's remedies at the date of the security, when he had the responsibility of the bankrupt as well as of the estate to rely upon. He cannot be deprived both of interest and of his right to sell (k).

Other incumbrancers.—The mortgagee who applies for a sale must bring before the court all persons with whom deeds relating to the property have been deposited by the bankrupt (l). Where there are several incumbrancers, the concurrence of all is necessary, and if they do not concur, the court can only sell subject to the rights of those who dissent (m).

Charge by deposit of deeds.—A deposit of deeds is not necessary to enable the equitable mortgagee to obtain an order for sale (n), nor is a memorandum of deposit. But if the mortgagee has no memorandum, he must produce clear evidence in support of his debt, and his mere allegation will not be admitted against the affidavit of the bankrupt (o). If the deposit was made by the solicitor of the bankrupt, it must be shown that he had authority to make it (p).

Nor is the right to a sale affected either by an imperfection in the memorandum, or in the deposit, provided the intention to complete the security is shown. Freeholds and leaseholds have alike been ordered to be sold, where the deposit of the deeds relating to both was complete, but the memorandum related to one only (q), and where both were specified in the memorandum, but the deeds relating to one

---

(g) Rule 73 (2)–(5).

(h) Rule 74 (1).

(i) Rule 74 (2). The mortgagee's costs will include his costs of defending the security (*Re Hofmann, Ex parte Carr* (1879), 11 Ch. D. 62 (C.A.)), but not of negotiating the loan or preparing the mortgage deed: *Wales* v. *Carr*, [1902] 1 Ch. 860. For the better taking of inquiries and accounts, and making a title to a purchaser, all parties may be examined upon interrogatories or otherwise and must produce documents on oath: r. 75; and the court may order inquiries and accounts to be taken in like manner as in the Chancery Division: r. 76.

(k) *Re Theobald, Ex parte Bignold* (1838), 3 Mont. & A. 477.

(l) *Ex parte Burt* (1840), 1 Mont. D. & De G. 191.

(m) *Ex parte Jackson* (1800), 5 Ves. 357; *Re Watts, Ex parte Wright* (1837), 3 Mont. & A. 49.

(n) *Ex parte Jones* (1835), 4 Deac. & C. 750.

(o) Hence, where the bankrupt denied by his affidavit that the security was for past as well as for present and future advances, the order for sale was prefaced by a declaration that the deposit was for present and future advances only, and the order reserved the proceeds after payment of such advances, and gave liberty to apply for the purpose of proving the mortgagee's allegation: *Re Cowdry, Ex parte Martin* (1835), 2 Mont. & A. 243.

(p) *Re Hood, Ex parte Coleman* (1840), 4 Deac. 242.

(q) *Re Evans, Ex parte Robinson* (1832), 1 Deac. & C. 119.

only were deposited (*r*). Nor is it affected by an arrangement made subsequent to the security, between the mortgagor and a third person, under which the latter acquires an interest in the mortgaged property (*s*). And if an equitable mortgagee takes a legal mortgage with notice of the bankruptcy, his right to a sale under the equitable mortgage is only suspended, and revives when the legal security is declared to be inoperative (*t*).

Sub-mortgage.—If a mortgagee who has made a sub-mortgagee becomes bankrupt, the sub-mortgagee may obtain a sale of the bankrupt's interest in the original security (*u*); but not without a previous inquiry as to the amount due if the original security was for an uncertain sum; though leave will be given to enter a claim for the full amount due to the sub-mortgagee pending the inquiry. If after the sub-mortgage the original mortgagee has bought the equity of redemption, and the trustee rejects it, the sub-mortgagee may include it in his sale, and the trustee will be bound to convey to the purchaser (*x*).

Mortgaged leaseholds.—The right to a sale, in the case of leaseholds, is not affected by a lessee's covenant not to assign without the licence of the lessor (*y*); though it would be so if the lease were determinable on the committal of an act of bankruptcy (*z*). On an application for a sale of leaseholds, the mortgagee will not be ordered to indemnify the trustee against any breach of the covenants, since the trustee had the option of disclaiming the lease (*a*).

Where sale not ordered.—But there can be no sale where the security is inoperative for want of compliance with some legal formality (*b*); nor where there can be no proof by the mortgagee for the deficiency, as if the bankrupt is only a purchaser of the equity of redemption, whose covenant for repayment does not make him personally liable for the debt to the mortgagee (*c*) (*supra*, p. 295); nor where the title to the mortgaged property is hampered, as where it consists of a share of partnership property subject to a right of pre-emption, and the taking of partnership accounts is necessary to ascertain its value (*d*); nor where it cannot be separately sold without injury, as in the case of fixtures in a house which is not subject to the security (*e*); nor where the property is subject to other incumbrances belonging to persons not before the court, and the priorities and validity of which are disputed by the petitioner, sales in such cases

---

(*r*) *Ex parte Leathes* (1833), 3 Deac. & C. 112.
(*s*) *Re Draper, Ex parte Booth* (1832), 2 Deac. & C. 59.
(*t*) *Re Emery, Ex parte Harvey* (1839), 3 Deac. 547.
(*u*) *Re Wright, Ex parte Mackay* (1841), 1 Mont. D. & De G. 550; *Re Moore, Ex parte Powell* (1847), De G. 405.
(*x*) *Re Watts, Ex parte Tuffnell* (1834), 1 Mont. & A. 620.
(*y*) See *Doe d. Goodbehere* v. *Bevan* (1815), 3 M. & S. 353, 360.
(*z*) *Re Champney, Ex parte Sherman* (1820), Buck, 462.
(*a*) *Re Collins, Ex parte Fletcher* (1832), 1 Deac. & C. 318; see Bankruptcy Act, 1914, s. 54.
(*b*) *Re Swann, Ex parte Miller* (1849), 3 De G. & Sm. 553 (inrolment).
(*c*) *Re Stockdale, Ex parte Keightley* (1849), 3 De G. & Sm. 583.
(*d*) *Re Borron, Ex parte Broadbent* (1834), 1 Mont. & A. 635; *Ex parte Attwood* (1834), 2 Mont. & A. 24.
(*e*) *Re Clarke, Ex parte Sykes* (1849), 18 L.J. Bcy. 16.

L.M.—14

being disadvantageous to the bankrupt's estate. But in complicated cases the mortgagee may enter a claim for the whole amount of his debt, until the question of right is determined (*f*). And if part only of the property is the subject of litigated rights, the court will order sale of the other part, without prejudice to the right of the applicant against the part in respect of which the order is refused (*g*). Sale may also be ordered of the separate estate of one partner mortgaged for a partnership debt, where he alone becomes bankrupt, though there will be no proof against his estate (*h*).

There will be no order for sale if the security is open to suspicion of any taint; as (formerly) of usury (*i*); or if it is for money which cannot properly be secured by mortgage (*k*); or if the lender, having notice of a trust, lent the money to the trustee for his own purpose (*l*); or where the bankruptcy followed so close upon the deposit as to raise a presumption of fraudulent preference, unless this is rebutted by evidence (*m*). And in such cases, the court always requires satisfactory proof that the security was not made in contemplation of bankruptcy. But the application may be ordered to stand over pending an inquiry into the existence and circumstances attending the creation of the debt and deposit; and to enable the trustee to apply for a delivery of the deeds (*m*).

II—DISCLAIMER BY TRUSTEE

Vesting order in favour of mortgagee.—Under s. 54 of the Bankruptcy Act 1914, the trustee in bankruptcy can disclaim leasehold property of the bankrupt within twelve months after the first appointment of a trustee or such extended period as may be allowed by the court. But, except in such cases as may be prescribed by general rules, the leave of the court must first be obtained (*n*). Where the trustee applies for leave to disclaim, and the mortgagee does not appear at the hearing of the application, the court will order that he be excluded from all interest in, and security on, the property, unless by a short date he elects to take a vesting order (*o*). The trustee will not be allowed to disclaim to the prejudice of an equitable mortgagee, but will be ordered to assign the lease to him on having a proper indemnity (*p*).

(*f*) *Re Francis, Ex parte Bignold* (1836), 1 Deac. 515.

(*g*) *Re Price, Ex parte Wace* (1842), 2 Mont. D. & De G. 730.

(*h*) *Ex parte Lloyd* (1838), 3 Mont. & A. 601.

(*i*) *Re Jarmain, Ex parte Nunn* (1836), 1 Deac. 393.

(*k*) *Re Clark, Ex parte Wake* (1837), 2 Deac. 352.

(*l*) *Ex parte Turner* (1745), 9 Mod. 418.

(*m*) *Re Clark, Ex parte Wake, supra; Ex parte Ainsworth* (1838), 2 Deac. 563; *Re Davy, Ex parte Dewdney* (1835), 4 Deac. & C. 181; *Re Leach, Ex parte Morgan* (1840), 1 Mont. D. & De G. 116; *Re Lindon, Ex parte Clouter* (1843), 3 Mont. D. & De G. 187; but see *Re Ogbourne, Ex parte Heathcote* (1842), 2 Mont. D. & De G. 711.

(*n*) Sub-ss. (1), (3). For the cases where a lease may be disclaimed without leave, see Bankruptcy Rules 1952, r. 278.

(*o*) *Re Parker and Parker (No. 1), Ex parte Turquand* (1884), 14 Q.B.D. 405.

(*p*) *Re Müller, Ex parte Buxton* (1880), 15 Ch. D. 289 (C.A.). In *Re Clarke, Ex parte East and West India Dock Co.* (1881), 17 Ch. D. 759, the rule as to disclaimer was stated in terms which overlooked the claim of an equitable mortgagee. But see *Re Katherine et Cie, Ltd.,* [1932] 1 Ch. 70. Formerly, where the mortgagor was assignee of the lease,

The court may, on the application of the mortgagee, make an order for the vesting of the property in him, but this will not be done except upon the terms of making the mortgagee:

(a) Subject to the same liabilities and obligations as the bankrupt was subject to under the lease in respect of the property at the date when the bankruptcy petition was filed; or
(b) If the court thinks fit, subject only to the same liabilities and obligations as if the lease had been assigned to [the mortgagee] at that date (*q*).

Form and effect of order.—Thus, ordinarily the mortgagee will take the property subject, not only to future, but also to past liabilities to the lessor. But an order may be made in the alternative form, *i.e.*, limiting his liabilities to such as he would have incurred as assignee, if the court considers that he will obtain no undue advantage, and that no injustice will be done to the lessor (*r*). In either event (if the case so requires) the vesting order may be made as if the lease had comprised only the property comprised in the order; and in a proper case the order will include the whole of the property in the lease although not in the mortgage (*s*). It is open also to the lessor to take the initiative, and the court will, on the lessor's application, exclude the mortgagee from all interest in the property unless he accepts a vesting order (*t*). And where, in order to escape this liability, the mortgagees by sub-demise assigned their sub-term to a man of straw as trustee for themselves, it was nevertheless held that they must accept a vesting order or lose their security (*u*).

If, before the intervention of the mortgagee, leave has been given to the trustee in bankruptcy to disclaim, the mortgagee should apply for an order to stay proceedings pending an appeal; since, if the disclaimer is once executed, the lessor's title will be complete, and the mortgagee's remedy will be gone (*v*).

III—MORTGAGEE'S RIGHT OF PROOF

Saving of rights of secured creditors.—The Bankruptcy Act 1914, provides:

---

and not the original lessee, and the mortgage was by assignment of the entire term, the trustee could not disclaim since he was not bound by the covenants of the lease either by privity of contract, or privity of estate: *Re Gee, Ex parte Official Receiver* (1884), 24 Q.B.D. 65; but now a mortgage cannot be made by assignment: p. 22, *supra.*

(*q*) Sub-section (6).

(*r*) *Re Carter and Ellis, Ex parte Savill Brothers, Ltd.*, [1905] 1 K.B. 735 (C.A.); *Re Walker, Ex parte Mills* (1895), 64 L.J. Q.B. 783.

(*s*) *Re Holmes, Ex parte Ashworth*, [1908] 2 K.B. 812.

(*t*) *Re Finley, Ex parte Clothworkers' Co.* (1888), 21 Q.B.D. 475; *Re Baker, Ex parte Lupton*, [1901] 2 K.B. 628 (C.A.).

(*u*) *Re Smith, Ex parte Hepburn* (1884), 25 Q.B.D. 536.

(*v*) *Re Woods, Ex parte Ditton* (1876), 3 Ch. D. 459; *Re Hawes, Ex parte Sadler* (1881), 19 Ch.D. 122 (C.A.).

Where a vesting order is made in respect of registered land the order must direct the alteration of the register in favour of the person in whom the property is vested and on receipt of the order the registrar must alter the register accordingly: Land Registration Act 1925, s. 42 (2).

7.—(1) On the making of a receiving order an official receiver shall be thereby constituted receiver of the property of the debtor, and thereafter, except as directed by this Act, no creditor to whom the debtor is indebted in respect of any debt provable in the bankruptcy shall have any remedy against the property or person of the debtor in respect of the debt, or shall commence any action or other legal proceedings, unless with the leave of the court and on such terms as the court may impose.

(2) But this section shall not affect the power of any secured creditor to realise or otherwise deal with his security in the same manner as he would have been entitled to realise or deal with it if this section had not been passed.

Thus a secured creditor who does not choose to come in under the bankruptcy can use his ordinary remedies for enforcing his security (x), but he cannot at the same time retain his security and prove for the value of his debt. He can only prove for the deficiency after allowing for the security (y).

167.—"Secured creditor" means a person holding a mortgage, charge, or lien on the property of the debtor or any part thereof, as a security for a debt due to him from the debtor.

"Secured creditors".—The words "charge or lien" are not restricted to securities created by contract and they are capable of including a charge arising under process of execution (z). But as regards execution by the sheriff against the goods or lands of a debtor, s. 40 (1) of the Bankruptcy Act 1914, provides that the creditor shall not be entitled to retain the benefit of the execution against the trustee in bankruptcy of the debtor, unless he has completed the execution before the date of the receiving order, and before notice of the presentation of any bankruptcy petition, or of the commission of an available act of bankruptcy by the debtor. Under sub-s. (2) an execution against goods is completed by seizure and sale (a); and an execution against land by seizure (b); or (c) by the appointment of a receiver. Equitable execution by the appointment of a receiver of an interest other than

---

(x) *White* v. *Simmons* (1871), 6 Ch. App. 555, decided on the corresponding provision (s. 12) of the Act of 1869. If he proves, the proof is subject to the rule that there cannot be two proofs for one debt. Thus mortgagees of a policy of insurance, the mortgagor having covenanted in the mortgage to pay the premiums, cannot in the bankruptcy of the mortgagor at the same time value the policy, and prove on the value of the covenant: *Deering* v. *Bank of Ireland* (1886), 12 App. Cas. 20 (H.L.).

(y) Thus the creditor cannot retain his security and at the same time prove on a promissory note, part of the consideration for which consists of arrears of interest on the secured debt: *Re Clark, Ex parte Clark* (1841), 1 Mont. D. & De G. 622; and where a mortgagor assigns the equity of redemption and covenants to discharge the debt, and the mortgagee proves in his bankruptcy, a proof by the assignee on the covenant is a double proof and is not allowed: *Re Hoey, Ex parte Hoey* (1918), 88 L.J. K.B. 273; see *Re Oriental Commercial Bank, Ex parte European Bank* (1871), 7 Ch. App. 99, at p. 103; *Re Rushton (a Bankrupt) Ex parte National Westminster Bank, Ltd.* v. *Official Receiver,* [1972] Ch. 197; [1971] 2 All E.R. 937.

(z) But not a mere judgment creditor; nor one who has not completed the process of execution (*supra,* but see *Hall* v. *Richards* (1961), 108 C.L.R. 84); nor a garnishee order nisi; nor a charging order on land (see *Re Overseas Aviation (G.B.), Ltd.,* [1963] Ch. 24 (C.A.); [1962] 3 All E.R. 12; cf. a charging order on securities: *Re Hutchinson, Ex parte Hutchinson* (1885), 16 Q.B.D. 515. See p. 159, *supra.*

(a) The sheriff must sell within twenty-one days, otherwise his retention of possession will be an act of bankruptcy of which the creditor has notice: *Figg* v. *Moore Brothers,* [1894] 2 Q.B. 690; *Burns-Burns' Trustee* v. *Brown,* [1895] 1 Q.B. 324 (C.A.).

(b) Execution is completed by delivery of the land to the execution creditor, although the sheriff has not made a return to the writ: *Re Hobson* (1886), 33 Ch. D. 493.

(c) The words "in the case of an equitable interest" originally in this sub-section were repealed by the Administration of Justice Act 1956, s. 36 (4).

in land is not within s. 40, but since it cannot be made in such terms as to create a charge in favour of the creditor, it does not make him a secured creditor (*d*). Section 40 applies also to an attachment of debts, and it is provided that an attachment of a debt is completed by receipt of the debt. If, therefore, the judgment creditor has not received the debt before the receiving order or notice as mentioned in s. 40, he is not a secured creditor and the trustee is entitled to the debt (*e*).

In cases other than those relating to execution creditors, the question whether a creditor has a mortgage, charge, or lien will be determined in accordance with the nature of these securities (*f*).

Voting.—For the purpose of voting a secured creditor is deemed to be a creditor only in respect of the balance (if any) due to him after deducting the value of his security. And if he votes in respect of his whole debt, he will be deemed to have surrendered his security, unless the court on application is satisfied that the omission to value the security has arisen from inadvertence (*g*).

Security must be on debtor's own property.—The security which constitutes the creditor a secured creditor must be on the property of the debtor, and it is only in such a case that the creditor is within the rule that he must deduct the value of his security and prove for no more than the difference (*h*). The principle is that a man is not allowed to prove against a bankrupt's estate and to retain a security which, if given up, would go to augment the estate against which he proves (*i*). And so well is this exception to the rule as to election established that it has been said to be almost a maxim in bankruptcy, that a security is never to go in reduction of proof, unless it belongs to the estate against which the proof is tendered (*j*). Of the

---

(*d*) "An order appointing a receiver can only amount to a charge if it charges the person in whose hands the money is not to deal with it except in one way": *Re Potts, Ex parte Taylor,* [1893] 1 Q.B. 648, at p. 659; that is "except to pay it to, or hold it for, the execution creditor": *Re Pearce, Ex parte Official Receiver,* [1919] 1 K.B. 354 (C.A.), at p. 363; and no process of equitable execution could properly be granted which would have that effect: *ibid.,* at p. 364. But see now Administration of Justice Act 1956, ss. 35 and 36; R.S.C. Ord. 50; see p. 159, *supra.*

(*e*) *Re Trehearne, Ex parte Ealing Local Board* (1890), 60 L.J. Q.B. 50 (C.A.); *Re Bagley,* [1911] 1 K.B. 317 (C.A.). Payment of the amount of the debt into court by the garnishee is not a receipt by the judgment creditor so long as a third party is claiming it: *Butler* v. *Wearing* (1885), 17 Q.B.D. 182. And see also *George* v. *Tompson's Trustee,* [1949] Ch. 322; [1949] 1 All E.R. 554.

(*f*) A wife's beneficial interest in property by virtue of contributions to improvements under the Matrimonial Proceedings and Property Act 1970, s. 37 does not apply to the period after bankruptcy. The section only applies between husband and wife and does not apply between wife and a third party. *W. A. Samuels Trustee* v. *Samuels* (1973), 233 Estates Gazette 149.

(*g*) Bankruptcy Act 1914, Sched. I, r. 10. As to inadvertence, see *Re Maxson, Ex parte Trustee,* [1919] 2 K.B. 330. If the creditor votes in respect of a specific sum and does not include further liability also covered by the mortgage, and there is no inadvertence, he will be taken to have surrendered the mortgage to the extent of the whole liability: *Re Pawson,* [1917] 2 K.B. 527.

(*h*) *Re Howe, Ex parte Brett* (1871), L.R. 6 Ch. 838. "The question is whether, in substance, apart from technicality, the creditors held a security upon property of the bankrupt at the time they made their proof": *ibid.,* at p. 840.

(*i*) *Re Turner, Ex parte West Riding Union Banking Co.* (1881), 19 Ch. D. 105 (C.A.), at p. 112; *Re Dutton, Massey & Co., Ex parte Manchester and Liverpool District Banking Co.,* [1924] 2 Ch. 199.

(*j*) *Re Wyatt, Ex parte Adams* (1837), 3 Mont. & A. 157.

numerous cases in which it is applicable, a simple one is that in which the wife's estate is mortgaged to secure the debt of the husband; or where one partner mortgages his separate estate to secure a debt due from the partnership (*k*).

Joint and separate estates.—For this purpose the joint and separate estates of partners are considered as distinct estates, and a joint creditor having a security upon the separate estate of one of the partners can prove against the joint estate for the full amount of his debt without giving up his security and vice versa (*l*).

The exception from the rule against retainer and full proof does not apply where it is only in appearance that the security belongs to a separate estate. Therefore it was not admitted where the joint debt was secured by shares in a company, which, though joint property, were standing in the separate names of the joint debtors, in compliance with a rule of the company that no shares should be held jointly (*m*). Nor, where real estate bought with joint funds is used jointly, and mortgaged to secure a joint debt, can it be contended that because the conveyance was made to the partners as tenants in common, there was for the purpose of this exception to the general rule, a security upon the separate estate of each tenant in common (*n*).

Rules as to proof.—The Rules as to proof by secured creditors are contained in Schedule 2 of the Bankruptcy Act 1914. Non-compliance with the Rules excludes the creditor from all share in any dividend (*o*). The following is a summary of them (*p*):

10. If a secured creditor realises his security he may prove for the balance due to him after deducting the net amount realised.

11. If he surrenders his security for the general benefit of the creditors he may prove for his whole debt (*q*).

(*k*) *Re Hicklin, Ex parte Hedderly* (1842), 2 Mont. D. & De G. 487; *Re Hart, Ex parte Caldicott* (1884), 25 Ch. D. 716. For a case where the subject matter of the security had become vested in the creditor, so that he was not a "secured creditor", see *Re Hallett, Ex parte Cocks, Biddulph & Co.,* [1894] 2 Q.B. 256 (C.A.).

(*l*) *Re Bell, Ex parte Peacock* (1825), 2 Gl. & J. 27; *Re Brettell, Ex parte Bowden* (1832), 1 Deac. & C. 135; *Re Plummer and Wilson, Ex parte Shepherd* (1841), 2 Mont. D. & De G. 204; 1 Ph. 56; *Rolfe and Bank of Australasia* v. *Flower & Co.* (1865), L.R. 1 P.C. 27, 47; *Re Fraser, Trenholm & Co.* (1868), 4 Ch. App. 49. As to allowing amendment where a separate security has been by mistake deducted, see *Couldery* v. *Bartrum* (1881), 19 Ch. D. 394 (C.A.).

(*m*) *Re Clarke, Ex parte Connell* (1838), 3 Deac. 201; *Re Collie, Ex parte Manchester and County Bank* (1876), 3 Ch. D. 481 (C.A.); see *Re Cooksey, Ex parte Portal & Co.* (1900), 83 L.T. 435.

(*n*) *Re Burgess, Ex parte Free* (1827), 2 Gl. & J. 250.

(*o*) Rule 17.

(*p*) For the case where the petitioning creditor is himself a secured creditor the Act provides that he must in his petition either state that he is willing to give up his security for the benefit of the creditors, or give an estimate of its value. In the latter case he may be admitted as a petitioning creditor to the extent of the balance of the debt after deducting the estimated value: s. 4 (2). The surrender of the security vests the interest in it in the trustee. The security is not merged in the equity of redemption for the benefit of a subsequent mortgagee: *Cracknall* v. *Janson* (1877), 6 Ch. D. 735; and similarly where the trustee redeems: *Bell* v. *Sunderland Building Society* (1883), 24 Ch. D. 618.

(*q*) But if he does so, he cannot afterwards change his mind and rely on his security: *Re O'D, Ex parte Robinson* (1885), 15 L.R. Ir. 496. Surrender of the security and proof for the whole debt does not discharge a surety, since he is considered to contract with reference to the provisions of the Bankruptcy Act: *Rainbow* v. *Juggins* (1880), 5 Q.B.D. 138 at p. 422.

12. If he does not either realise or surrender it, he must, before ranking for dividend, state in his proof the particulars and date of his security, and the value at which he assesses it, and will be entitled to a dividend only in respect of the balance after deducting the value assessed (*r*).

13.—(a) The trustee may at any time (*s*) redeem the security on payment to the creditor of the assessed value.

(b) If the trustee is dissatisfied with the assessed value, he may require the property to be offered for sale at such times and on such terms and conditions as may be agreed upon between him and the creditor, or as, in default of agreement, the court may direct. If the sale is by auction, the creditor, or the trustee on behalf of the estate, may bid or purchase.

(c) But the creditor may at any time (*t*), by notice in writing, require the trustee to elect whether he will or not exercise his power of redeeming the security or require it to be realised (*u*); and if the trustee does not, within six months, signify in writing to the creditor his desire to exercise the power, he will not be entitled to exercise it; and the equity of redemption will vest in the creditor, whose debt will be reduced by the amount at which the security has been valued.

14. Where a creditor has so valued his security he may, at any time (*x*), amend the valuation and proof, on showing to the satisfaction of the trustee or the court, that the valuation and proof were made bona fide on a mistaken estimate, or that there has been a diminution or increase in value since the valuation (*y*).

15. Where a valuation has been amended, the creditor must repay any excess dividend he may have received over what he would be entitled to on the amended valuation, and will be entitled to be paid any deficiency; but this is not to disturb dividends already distributed.

16. If the security is realised, the net amount realised will be substituted for the valuation, and will be treated as an amended valuation (*z*).

18. Subject to the provisions of Rule 13, a creditor is not to receive more than 20*s*. in the pound and interest.

Surety.—Where a surety becomes so for the whole of the debt, but his liability is limited to a specified sum, he does not on paying

---

(*r*) This applies even where the security was given for bills of exchange which have been negotiated by the creditor, and which he has had to pay in full: *Baines* v. *Wright* (1885), 16 Q.B.D. 330 (C.A.). The estimate need not be the true estimate, but the trustee will be entitled to redeem at the amount estimated: *Re Lacey, Ex parte Taylor* (1884), 13 Q.B.D. 128. If a mortgagee has postponed his security to enable the debtor to raise more money, he will be entitled to prove for the amount which he would have received out of the security if he had not consented to postpone it: *Re Chappell, Ex parte Ford* (1885), 16 Q.B.D. 305 (C.A.).

(*s*) Before foreclosure: *Knowles* v. *Dibbs* (1889), 60 L.T. 291. Judgment for foreclosure against the trustee in bankruptcy and subsequent incumbrancers should show that the trustee was entitled to redeem at the valuation, but subsequent incumbrancers only at the full amount of the first mortgagee's debt: *ibid.*; see *Sanguinetti* v. *Stuckey's Banking Co.*, [1896] 1 Ch. 502.

(*t*) Without prejudice to his right to commence a foreclosure action: *Knowles* v. *Dibbs, supra.*

(*u*) For this purpose he may lump all his securities together; the trustee can, however, require him to value any particular security, and the creditor has a corresponding right to have any security separately valued: *Re Smith, Ex parte Logan* (1895), 72 L.T. 362.

A mortgagee whose rights are barred by the Limitation Act 1939 cannot give an effective notice under this rule: *Cotterell* v. *Price*, [1960] 3 All E.R. 315.

(*x*) Apparently the creditor cannot amend after he has by notice put the trustee to his election whether he will redeem and the trustee has elected to do so: *Re Sadler, Ex parte Norris* (1886), 17 Q.B.D. 728 (C.A.).; see *Re Fanshawe, Ex parte Le Marchant*, [1905] 1 K.B. 170; *Re Small*, [1934] Ch. 541; *Re Becher*, [1944] Ch. 78.

(*y*) The amendment will be allowed in a proper case, notwithstanding the opposition of a subsequent mortgagee: *Re Arden, Ex parte Arden* (1884), 14 Q.B.D. 121; *Baines* v. *Wright* (1885), 16 Q.B.D. 330 (C.A.).

(*z*) But the excess is applicable to the mortgagee's general costs: *Re Johnston, Millar* v. *Johnston* (1888), 23 L.R. Ir. 50; *cf. Société Générale de Paris* v. *Geen* (1883), 8 App. Cas. 606 (H.L.), as to allowance of interest on the assessed value.

that sum acquire a right of proof in priority to the creditor, and consequently the creditor can still prove for the full debt and the surety cannot prove until the creditor has received 20s. in the £. But if the surety is a surety for part of the debt and pays that part, he succeeds *pro tanto* to the right of proof of the creditor (*a*). A surety, who has not been called upon to pay is nevertheless under a contingent liability in respect of which he can prove (*b*).

Proof for interest.—The provisions of the Bankruptcy Act 1914, with regard to proof for interest are as follows:

Under s. 66 (1), where a debt proved against the estate includes interest, proof is limited to 5 per cent. per annum without prejudice to the right of the creditor to receive out of the estate any higher rate of interest to which he may be entitled after all the debts proved in the estate have been paid in full (*c*); and under sub-s. (2) the proof of the debt is subject to three rules of which the second and third direct the apportionment between principal and interest of sums realised from the security:

(b) Sums realised before the receiving order must, notwithstanding any agreement to the contrary, be appropriated to principal and interest in the proportion that the principal bears to the sum payable as interest.

(c) Where the security is realised after the receiving order or the value thereof is assessed in the proof, the amount realised or assessed is appropriated in the like proportion (*d*).

Sched. 2, r. 21, provides that on a debt whereon interest is not reserved, and which is overdue at the date of the receiving order and which is provable in the bankruptcy, the creditor may prove for interest at a rate not exceeding 4 per cent. per annum to the date of the order from the time when the debt was payable if payable by virtue of a written interest at a certain time, and if payable otherwise, then from the time when notice in writing has been given to the debtor that interest will be claimed (*e*).

And under s. 33 (8), if there is any surplus after payment of preferential debts and debts proved in the bankruptcy, it is applied in payment of interest from the date of the receiving order at 4 per cent. per annum on all debts proved in the bankruptcy (*f*).

(*a*) *Re Sass, Ex parte National Provincial Bank of England*, [1896] 2 Q.B. 12.

(*b*) *Re Paine, Ex parte Read*, [1897] 1 Q.B. 122; *Re Herepath and Delmar* (1890), 38 W.R. 752; *Re Blackpool Motor Car Co., Ltd.*, *Hamilton v. Blackpool Motor Car Co., Ltd.*, [1901] 1 Ch. 77; *Re Fenton, Ex parte Fenton Textile Association, Ltd.*, [1931] 1 Ch. 85 (C.A.). But where a surety had covenanted to keep up the premiums on a policy mortgaged by the principal debtor, and to pay interest so long as any principal remained due, and the mortgagor had agreed to indemnify him, and the mortgagee valued his security and proved for the deficiency in the bankruptcy of the mortgagor, the surety was not allowed to prove under the indemnity in respect of either head of liability, since the policy had been realised and the debt extinguished by the bankrupt: *Re Moss, Ex parte Hallett*, [1905] 2 K.B. 307. The decision was based also on the prohibition of double proof: see p. 420, note (*y*), *supra*.

(*c*) A creditor entitled to interest exceeding 5 per cent. can prove for the full interest, but, for the purpose of dividend, it cannot exceed 5 per cent.: *Re Herbert, Ex parte Jones* (1892), 8 T.L.R. 685. A creditor may by a scheme of arrangement under s. 16 of the Act of 1914, with the consent of his creditors and the approval of the court, exclude s. 66: *Re Nepean, Ex parte Ramchund*, [1903] 1 K.B. 794. As to moneylenders' loans, see Moneylenders Act 1927, s. 9.

(*d*) Rules (b) and (c) reproduce (b) and (c) of s. 22 of the Bankruptcy Act 1913. Before that Act a secured creditor, whether he had realised or assessed his security, could allocate it to interest, for which he could not prove, and prove for the principal or balance of principal: *Re Fox and Jacobs, Ex parte Discount Banking Co. of England and Wales*, [1894] 1 Q.B. 438.

(*e*) A surety who has paid a promissory note, on which he was jointly and severally liable with the bankrupt, can prove for interest from the date of payment to the date of the receiving order: *Re Evans, Ex parte Davies* (1897), 66 L.J. Q.B. 499.

(*f*) See *Re Rolls-Royce, Ltd.*, [1974] 3 All E.R. 646 (s. 317 of the Companies Act 1948, p. 425, *infra*, has no application where there is a surplus).

Principles of the bankruptcy law as to interest.—These provisions apply only to the proof of debts and they do not interfere with the right of the creditor to payment out of the seeurity of all interest which accrues due thereunder (*g*). If, however, the security is deficient and he requires to prove for any part of his debt, then the proof as regards interest must be made subject to the provisions of s. 66. A secured creditor cannot increase the amount of his proof by applying the proceeds of realisation of his security to payment of interest accruing after the date of the receiving order (*h*).

And apart from the express provisions of the Bankruptcy Act, it is a principle applicable to proof generally, that interest which accrues after the date of the receiving order cannot be proved for (*i*). If a debt is payable by instalments which include principal and interest, the rule is applied to the part which represents interest (*j*).

Administration and winding-up.—In the administration of the insolvent estates of deceased persons by the court, and in the winding up of companies, the rule formerly was that the mortgagee might prove for his whole debt, and also make what he could of his security, not receiving more than 20*s*. in the pound (*k*); but in both cases the rules in bankruptcy now apply.

Thus the Administration of Estates Act 1925 provides (*l*) that, in the administration of the estate of a deceased person which is insolvent, the funeral, testamentary, and administration expenses shall have priority and subject thereto

the same rules shall prevail and be observed as to the respective rights of secured and unsecured creditors, and as to debts and liabilities provable, and as to the valuation of annuities and future and contingent liabilities, respectively, and as to the priorities of debts and liabilities as may be in force for the time being under the law of bankruptcy with respect to the assets of persons adjudged bankrupt.

And the Companies Act 1948 provides (*m*):

317.—In the winding up of an insolvent company registered in England the same rules shall prevail and be observed with regard to the respective rights of secured and unsecured creditors, and to debts provable and to the

---

(*g*) See s. 7 (2), p. 420, *supra*.

(*h*) *Re Bonacino, Ex parte Discount Banking Co.* (1894), 10 R. 147; 1 Mans. 59; *Re Hall (William) (Contractors), Ltd. (In Liquidation)*, [1967] 2 All E.R. 1150.

(*i*) *Re Flood and Lott, Ex parte Lubbock* (1863), 4 De G.J. & S. 516; *Re Savin* (1872), 7 Ch. App. 760, at p. 764. But the creditor can set off profits realised from the security since the winding up against interest accrued during the same period: *Re London, Windsor, and Greenwich Hotels Co., Quartermaine's Case*, [1892] 1 Ch. 639.

As to the mode of proof for interest when a debt is payable at a future time, with interest meanwhile, and the bankruptcy occurs before the time of payment, see *Re Browne and Wingrove, Ex parte Ador*, [1891] 2 Q.B. 574 (C.A.); in that case the history of the law as to proof for interest in bankruptcy was considered.

(*j*) *Re Phillips, Ex parte Bath* (1882), 22 Ch. D. 450. But if the fixed instalment includes a premium, as well as principal and interest, the premium can be proved for: *Re Phillips, Ex parte Bath* (1884), 27 Ch. D. 509 (C.A.).

(*k*) *Mason v. Bogg* (1837), 2 Myl. & Cr. 443; *Kellock's Case* (1869), 3 Ch. App. 769; and see *Re Barned's Banking Co., Forwood's Claim* (1869), 5 Ch. App. 18; *Banner v. Johnston* (1871), L.R. 5 H.L. 157.

(*l*) Section 34 (1) and Sched. I, Part I. For administration of insolvent estates of deceased persons in bankruptcy, see Bankruptcy Act 1914, s. 130.

(*m*) Replacing Companies Act 1929, s. 262.

valuation of annuities and future and contingent liabilities as are in force for the time being under the law of bankruptcy in England with respect to the estates of persons adjudged bankrupt, and all persons who in any such case would be entitled to prove for and receive dividends out of the assets of the company may come in under the winding up, and make such claims against the company as they respectively are entitled to by virtue of this section.

The object of the provision of the Judicature Act 1875 which is reproduced in these enactments was to substitute for the former practice in equity, the rule of bankruptcy under which a creditor can only prove for the balance of his debt after deducting the value of his security. Hence s. 30 of the Bankruptcy Act 1914 is imported into administration (*n*) and winding up (*o*). But all the rules of bankruptcy are not imported; thus the doctrine of reputed ownership (Bankruptcy Act 1914, s. 38) is not imported into the winding up of companies (*p*); and they do not affect the rights of a secured creditor to the benefit of any securities which he might have had, either in the administration of assets or in the winding up of companies, irrespective of the rules of bankruptcy (*q*).

(*n*) *Re McMahon*, [1900] 1 Ch. 173; *Re Whitaker*, [1901] 1 Ch. 9 (C.A.), at p. 13.
(*o*) *Re Northern Counties, etc., Co.* (1880), 17 Ch. D. 337, 340.
(*p*) *Re Crumlin Viaduct Co.* (1879), 11 Ch. D. 755; *Gorringe* v. *Irwell India Rubber*, etc., *Works* (1886), 34 Ch. D. 128 (C.A.).
(*q*) *Re Withernsea Brickworks* (1880), 16 Ch. D. 337; *Re Maggi, Winehouse* v. *Winehouse* (1882), 20 Ch. D. 545. As to the mode of working out the rights of the parties under the rules in bankruptcy, see *Re Hopkins, Williams* v. *Hopkins* (1881), 18 Ch. D. 370 (C.A.). A creditor who has at first relied on his security and declined to prove, may, if the security declines in value, be allowed to come in and prove on terms: *Re McMurdo*, [1902] 2 Ch. 684 (C.A.). As to proof by an annuitant, see *Re Pink, Elvin* v. *Nightingale*, [1927] 1 Ch. 237.

PART VI

PRIORITIES OF MORTGAGES

CHAPTER 24

Priorities of Mortgages

I—PRIORITIES GENERALLY

How questions of priorities arise.—If successive advances have been made on the security of the same property by different mortgagees it may, for one reason or another, be necessary to discover the order in which the mortgages rank. A mortgagor may have contrived to borrow sums in excess of the value of the security; or the mortgaged property, though at first sufficient to support the debts of all the mortgagees, may have depreciated in value. Of course, the mortgagees have their remedy by way of the personal covenant for repayment made by the mortgagor. But the sale of the mortgaged property may be the only satisfactory method of recovering the sum lent, since the other property of the mortgagor may be of little value. Each mortgagee is then entitled to be satisfied out of the proceeds of sale in full in the order of the priority of the mortgages.

In addition to the question of order of payment, the rules as to priority also determine which one of several subsequent mortgages is entitled to the title deeds on the discharge of a prior mortgage, which one of several mortgagees can requisition a transfer instead of a reconveyance and how a mortgage will be affected in an action for redemption or foreclosure.

Possible tests of priority.—The priority of incumbrances will depend on one or more of the following considerations:

(1) Prima facie the legal estate gives priority over equitable incumbrances earlier in date, provided it has been acquired for value and without notice of the earlier incumbrance. Notice may be actual, constructive or statutory.

(2) Apart from the effect given to the legal estate, incumbrances rank in order of time in accordance with the maxim *"qui prior est tempore, potior est jure"*.

(3) The priority of an incumbrance under rules (1) and (2) may be lost by the conduct of the incumbrancer, usually in relation to the custody of the title deeds.

(4) In certain cases a mortgagee can tack further advances as against a subsequent incumbrancer.

(5) In cases governed by a system of registration of incumbrances, the priority under rules (1) and (2) may be altered in two ways:

(a) Incumbrances may rank in order of registration, and registered incumbrances may rank before those which are not registered.

(b) An unregistered incumbrance may be void as against a purchaser for value.

In addition, there are special considerations affecting the priority of judgment creditors and of shipping mortgages.

The 1925 legislation.—The legislation of 1925 had a substantial effect on the former rules which governed the priority of mortgages, but a discussion of the old law still remains necessary. Though registration has now become the most important method of determining priority, there is nothing in either the Law of Property Act 1925 (*a*), or the Land Charges Act 1925 (*b*), to repeal with regard to mortgages of the legal estate, either the rule *"qui prior est tempore, potior est jure"*, or the rule of equity giving superiority to the legal title. The statutory provisions dealing with priority assume the continuing validity of the former rules.

With regard to the modern position as to priority between mortgagees of an equitable interest in land or personalty, an understanding of the rule in *Dearle* v. *Hall* is essential.

The former classification of mortgages for the purposes of priorities—which distinguished mortgages of interests in land, and mortgages of an equitable interest in pure personalty (bills of sale being subject to statutory provisions)—was abandoned by the 1925 property legislation. Instead of the determination whether the mortgage itself is legal or equitable, the governing consideration is now whether the interest of the mortgagor which he has given as security is legal or equitable. The appropriate classification now becomes that of legal and equitable mortgages of a legal estate, and mortgages of an equitable interest, whether in land or personalty (*c*).

II—POSSESSION OF THE LEGAL ESTATE

Priority of the legal mortgagee of land.—Before 1926 it was usual in the case of a mortgage of the fee simple to convey the legal estate in fee simple to the mortgagee. Out of several possible mortgages of the property there could be only one legal mortgage. But several legal mortgages by demise of freeholds or by sub-demise of leaseholds were possible.

It was formerly the foundation of the law as to priorities of mortgages, that a mortgagee who had the legal estate should prevail over all other incumbrancers of whose securities he had no notice

---

(*a*) But see the changes in tacking, pp. 459 *et seq., infra.*
(*b*) See now Land Charges Act 1972, p. 482, *infra.*
(*c*) For a detailed discussion of the priority of legal mortgages of land after 1925, dealing particularly with the effects of registration and the relationship between the Land Charges Act 1925, and the Law of Property Act 1925, see (1941), 7 C.L.J. 243 (R. E. Megarry).

when he made his advance (*d*); and this was so, too, where a later
mortgagee had the better right to call for a conveyance of the legal
estate (*e*). And although, under the present law, the importance of
the legal estate in this respect has diminished (*f*), a consideration of
its effect still forms the necessary beginning for a statement of the law
as to priority.

The doctrine of the prevalence of the legal estate was based by
Lord HARDWICKE on the circumstance of the jurisdiction in law
and equity being administered by different courts, and it was a
consequence of the superior efficacy allowed in Equity to the Common
Law and legal titles. In his view, no such doctrine could have arisen
if law and equity had been administered in the same jurisdiction (*g*).
It might have been thought, therefore, that on the fusion of the
jurisdictions at Common Law and in Equity by the Judicature Acts
1873 and 1875, the doctrine would have disappeared and the equitable
rule would have prevailed. The distinction, however, continued (*h*),
and the doctrine of the prevalence of the legal estate remained, subject
to the changes introduced by the Law of Property Act 1925, and the
Land Charges Act 1925.

When the legal estate availed.—The legal estate was available for
the protection of a mortgagee, whether he got it in at the time of his
advance (*i*), or subsequently, provided in either case he had no notice
of a prior incumbrance when he made the advance (*j*). If an equitable
mortgagee had no notice at that time, he could protect himself by the
legal estate, although he got it in after notice (*k*).

Notice of trust.—If the mortgagee got in the legal estate at the
time of his advance, and had then no notice that it was affected by a
trust, the legal estate protected him (*j*). But he could not avail

---

(*d*) Bac. Abr. *Mortgage*, E.3. This was carried so far that a satisfied term furnished
the required legal estate, and a later equitable mortgagee, who obtained a legal title
by getting in a satisfied term and had the title deeds, was allowed to recover the land
in ejectment against an earlier equitable mortgagee: *Goodtitle d. Norris* v. *Morgan* (1787),
1 Term. Rep. 755. Subsequently it was only an unsatisfied term, or when satisfied terms
were abolished, an unsatisfied legal mortgage, which availed: *Maundrell* v. *Maundrell*
(1805), 10 Ves. 247, 270; *Taylor* v. *Russell*, [1891] 1 Ch. 8, 29.

(*e*) *Wilkes* v. *Bodington* (1707), 2 Vern. 599. Where, for instance, the legal estate
was held on trust for the later purchaser or mortgagee: *Stanhope* v. *Earl Verney* (1761),
2 Eden 81; *Taylor* v. *London and County Banking Co.*, [1901] 2 Ch. 231, 263. See *Mc-
Carthy and Stone, Ltd.* v. *Julian S. Hodge & Co., Ltd.*, [1971] 2 All E.R. 973.

(*f*) *I.e.*, in consequence of the extent to which priority is now determined by order
of registration, and of the statutory effect given to registration as constituting "actual
notice".

For the prevalence of the legal estate in another context, see *Assaf* v. *Fuwa*, [1955]
A.C. 215 (P.C.).

(*g*) "Where there is a legal title and equity on one side, this court never thought fit,
that by reason of a prior equity against a man who had a legal title, that man should
be hurt, and this by reason of that force this court necessarily and rightly allows to
the common law and to legal titles . . . for if the law and equity are administered by the
same jurisdiction the rule, *qui prior est tempore, potior est jure*, must hold": *per* Lord
HARDWICKE, C., in *Wortley* v. *Birkhead* (1754), 2 Ves. S. 571, 573.

(*h*) *Joseph* v. *Lyons* (1884), 15 Q.B.D. 280, 286.

(*i*) It is the same where the mortgagee already holds the legal estate, as in the case
of an advance by a trustee to a beneficiary: see *Huntington* v. *Greenville* (1682), 1 Vern. 49.

(*j*) *Pilcher* v. *Rawlins* (1872), 7 Ch. App. 259, 269.

(*k*) *Blackwood* v. *London Chartered Bank of Australia* (1874), L.R. 5 P.C. 92, 111;
see also *Brace* v. *Duchess of Marlborough* (1728), 2 P. Wms. 491; *Willoughby* v.
Willoughby (1756), 2 Ves. Sen. 684.

himself of it against the beneficiaries, if he got it in afterwards, and had notice of the trust when he got it in. In that case he took subject to the rights of the beneficiaries and became a trustee for them (*l*). And if, at the time of the advance, the mortgagee had notice of an equity affecting the title of the mortgagor, he took subject to that equity, since he could not claim a better title than the mortgagor (*m*).

But a trustee was entitled to the advantage of a legal estate vested in him to protect an advance made by him on the share of a beneficiary, and it would prevail over a prior incumbrance on the share of which he had no notice (*n*).

Mortgagee without, and transferee with notice.—Where a legal mortgagee had gained priority over an earlier equitable incumbrance owing to want of notice, he could transfer his security with the like advantage to a transferee with notice, for otherwise his right of disposition would be fettered (*o*). But this rule did not apply where the transfer was made voluntarily in order to avoid the effect of notice (*p*), or to a transfer in breach of a fiduciary relationship (*q*).

III—NOTICE OF PRIOR INCUMBRANCES

A—ACTUAL AND CONSTRUCTIVE NOTICE

Actual notice.—Notice is either actual or constructive: the one kind being a question of fact, the other arising from construction of law (*r*).

Knowledge may be taken to imply, and to be equivalent to, what is commonly known as actual notice. Actual notice may be oral as well as written (*s*), and may be effected as well by the delivery of a document which shows the nature and extent of the claim, as by one in the actual form of a notice (*t*). It is not necessary that it should have been given for the purpose of making a transaction valid. If it

---

(*l*) *Saunders* v. *Dehew* (1692), 2 Vern. 271; *Taylor* v. *Russell*, [1892] A.C. 244; *Taylor* v. *London and County Banking Co.*, [1901] 2 Ch. 231; *Perham* v. *Kempster*, [1907] 1 Ch. 373. See *McCarthy and Stone, Ltd.* v. *Julian S. Hodge & Co., Ltd.*, [1971] 2 All E.R. 973. *Contra*, if the mortgagees are entitled to suppose that the trusts are at an end: *Pearce* v. *Bulteel*, [1916] 2 Ch. 544. And see the statement of the doctrine by WRIGHT, J., in *Powell* v. *London and Provincial Bank*, [1893] 1 Ch. 610, at p. 615. It seems to be an open point whether, to be defeated, the mortgagee must not only know of the trust but also that the conveyance to him is in breach of trust: see Sykes, *The Law of Securities* (2nd Edn.), p. 323.

(*m*) *Cookson* v. *Lee* (1853), 23 L.J. Ch. 473, where, upon a purchase of trust property by the solicitor of the trustees being set aside, a mortgage of the property by that solicitor to a mortgagee who had notice of the relationship failed also.

(*n*) *Phipps* v. *Lovegrove* (1873),L. R. 16 Eq. 80; *Newman* v. *Newman* (1885), 28 Ch. D. 674.

(*o*) *Lowther* v. *Carlton* (1741), 2 Atk. 242; *Kettlewell* v. *Watson* (1882), 21 Ch. D. 685, 707; *Wilkes* v. *Spooner*, [1911] 2 K.B. 473 (C.A.).

(*p*) *Merry* v. *Abney* (1663), 1 Ch. Cas. 38; *Coote* v. *Mammon* (1724), 5 Bro. P.C. 355.

(*q*) *Re Stapleford Colliery Co., Barrow's Case* (1880), 14 Ch. D. 432; *Gordon* v. *Holland* (1913), 82 L.J. P.C. 81.

(*r*) Co. Litt. 309 b. The terms "actual notice" and "express notice" are both used in statutes, but probably with the same meaning; for "actual notice", see Law of Property Act 1925, ss. 197, 198; for "express notice", Fines and Recoveries Act 1833, s. 38.

(*s*) *Browne* v. *Savage* (1859), 4 Drew. 635.

(*t*) *Baille* v. *M'Kewan* (1865), 35 Beav. 177.

is actually given, the object for which it was given is not material (*u*).

But the notice must be distinct; if written notice has not been given, evidence of casual conversations, not *"ad rem"*, will not alone be sufficient. It must be shown that such an intelligent apprehension of the fact has been acquired as would induce a reasonable man or an ordinary man of business to act upon the information, and to regulate his conduct by it in the matter (*v*). And there must be clear evidence of notice, for suspicious circumstances make no notice (*w*). It seems, also, that it ought to be given by a person interested in the property (*x*); but probably a notice would be held good if given even by a self-constituted agent, provided it is on behalf of an interested person, and provided the particulars of the claim are clearly set forth.

Constructive notice.—Implied, or constructive notice, has been defined to be the knowledge which the courts impute to a person, upon a presumption so strong that it cannot be allowed to be rebutted, that the knowledge must exist, or have been communicated (*y*). It extends to matters affecting the title to property, and to circumstances which would entitle persons to equitable priorities, or change the character of rights depending upon want of notice; but not to such as relate merely to the motives and object of the parties, or to the consideration upon which the matter in hand is founded (*z*).

It is a presumption adopted for the prevention of fraud, and does not necessarily agree with, but may be contrary to, the probabilities of the particular case. A person who is proved to have known facts, from which a court, or jury, or an impartial person would properly draw a certain inference will, therefore, not be allowed to escape from notice by saying that he did not draw the natural inference from the facts (*a*).

When notice is implied.—Constructive notice of a prior incumbrance is imputed to a mortgagee, first, when, on advancing his money, he omits to make inquiries which, having regard to the state of the title known to him, are usual inquiries for a purchaser to make, and which would have led him to a knowledge of the prior incumbrance; and secondly, when he has reason to suspect a prior incumbrance, and wilfully or fraudulently avoids receiving actual notice of it. The first ground is based on the presumption of law that a purchaser has investigated the title of the property which he purchases, and has examined whatever forms a link in that title (*b*). The second is based on an obvious principle of equity. And in these circumstances, notice

---

(*u*) *Smith* v. *Smith* (1833), 2 Cr. & M. 231; *Rickards* v. *Gledstanes* (1861), 3 Giff. 298; affd. 31 L.J. Ch. 142.

(*v*) *Ford* v. *White* (1852), 16 Beav. 120; *Edwards* v. *Martin* (1865), L.R. 1 Eq. 121; *Saffron Walden, etc., Building Society* v. *Rayner* (1880), 14 Ch. D. 406.

(*w*) *Whitfield* v. *Fausset* (1750), 1 Ves. Sen. 387; *West* v. *Reid* (1843), 2 Hare, 249.

(*x*) Sugd. *V. & P.* (14th Edn.), 755.

(*y*) *Hewitt* v. *Loosemore* (1851), 9 Hare, 449; *Plumb* v. *Fluitt* (1791), 2 Anst. 432.

(*z*) Per Lord CHELMSFORD in *Eyre* v. *Burmester* (1862), 10 H.L.C. 114.

(*a*) *Re Douglas, Ex parte Snowball* (1872), 7 Ch. App. 534. And see *McCarthy and Stone, Ltd.* v. *Julian S. Hodge & Co., Ltd.*, [1971] 2 All E.R. 973.

(*b*) *Jones* v. *Smith* (1841), 1 Hare, 43; *Berwick & Co.* v. *Price*, [1905] 1 Ch. 632. And if there is anything else on the title that would put a professional man on inquiry, a mortgagee cannot set up the defence that he had no professional adviser: *Berwick & Co.* v. *Price, supra.*

may be imputed to the mortgagee although he acts in the matter, not personally, but by an agent (c).

When notice to be obtained.—To be effectual, notice must be obtained before the completion of the transaction. It will be good if given before the execution of the deed although the money has already been paid; because the payment and execution are but parts of the same transaction (d). Similarly, it will be good before payment, though security has been given for the consideration money; for perhaps after notice it will not be paid (e).

If a cheque is delivered and countermanded, notice before withdrawal of the countermand will bind the purchaser (f).

Sales by the court.—Before 1882 notice operated in a transaction under the direction of the court, just as in any other case; for the court did not warrant the validity of titles, but only employed its officer to investigate them (g). But the Law of Property Act 1925, provides as follows:

> **204** (h).—(1) An order of the court (i) under any statutory or other juris-
> diction shall not, as against a purchaser (k), be invalidated on the ground of
> want of jurisdiction, or of want of any concurrence, consent, notice or service,
> whether the purchaser has notice of any such want or not.
>
> (2) This section shall have effect with respect to any lease, sale or other
> act under the authority of the court (l), and purporting to be in pursuance
> of any statutory power notwithstanding any exception in such statute.
>
> (3) This section applies to all orders made before or after the commencement
> of this Act.

This provision does not render an order binding on any estate or interest which, having regard to the terms and scope of the order, was not intended to be bound. It does not enable the court to sell and give a title to the property of A when it supposed that it was selling the property of B (m). It seems to follow that such an order would not protect a purchaser against an incumbrance, of which he

---

(c) *Espin* v. *Pemberton* (1859), 3 De G. & J. 547. Notice to him who transacts is notice to him for whom he transacts: *Merry* v. *Abney* (1663), 1 Ch. Cas. 38. The infancy of the principal makes no difference: *Toulmin* v. *Steere* (1817), 3 Mer. 210.

At one time it appears to have been considered that a witness to a deed was affected with notice of its contents: see *Mocatta* v. *Murgatroyd* (1718), 1 P. Wms. 393; but this view was abandoned: *Welford* v. *Beezely* (1747), 1 Ves. Sen. 6; *Biddulph* v. *St. John* (1805), 2 Sch. & Lef. 521; *Rancliffe* v. *Parkyns* (1818), 6 Dow. 224, *per* Lord ELDON. And see p. 440, *infra*.

(d) *Wigg* v. *Wigg* (1739), 1 Atk. 384.

(e) *Hardingham* v. *Nicholls* (1745), 3 Atk. 304.

(f) *Tildesley* v. *Lodge* (1857), 3 Sm. & G. 543.

(g) *Toulmin* v. *Steere* (1817), 3 Mer. 210; distinguished in *Re Howard's Estate* (1892), 29 L.R. Ir. 266.

(h) The Act of 1925 reproduces s. 70 of the Conveyancing Act 1881.

(i) "Court" means the High Court and the County Courts, where those courts respectively have jurisdiction: s. 203 (3). The grant of administration by the Probate Division is an "order of court": *Hewson* v. *Shelley*, [1914] 2 Ch. 13.

(k) "Purchaser" means a purchaser in good faith for valuable consideration and includes "a . . . mortgagee": s. 205 (1) (xxi).

(l) It seems that if the court merely authorises the exercise of a statutory power out of court, the order only brings the power into force, and enables the donee of the power, *e.g.*, tenant for life, to bind the beneficiaries; it does not affect persons claiming under a paramount title: see Wolstenholme and Cherry, *Conveyancing Statutes* (13th Edn.), vol. 1, p. 335.

(m) *Jones* v. *Barnett*, [1900] 1 Ch. 370.

had notice, if the court had no notice of it, and there was nothing in the order which suggested that the incumbrancer was intended to be bound. It is also considered that it protects only completed transactions, and would not be available for a purchaser with regard to anything to be done in the future in cases where there has been fraud, although the purchaser had no notice of it (*n*). On the other hand, where the court purports to bind a third party by the order, a purchaser will be protected, even though the order is on the face of it *"ultra vires"* (*o*).

B—CONSTRUCTIVE NOTICE

1—Statutory Restriction on Constructive Notice

Statutory restriction.—The doctrines of equity concerning notice were replaced by the provisions of s. 3 of the Conveyancing Act 1882. Except as to sub-s. (1) (i), which is new, s. 199 of the Law of Property Act 1925, reproduces that section:

> **199.**—(1) A purchaser (*p*) shall not be prejudicially affected by notice of
>   (i) [*refers to instruments capable of registration under the Land Charges Act 1972 and void by reason of the non-registration thereof* (*q*)];
>   (ii) any other instrument or matter or any fact or thing unless—
>   (a) it is within his own knowledge, or would have come to his knowledge if such inquiries and inspections had been made as ought reasonably to have been made by him; or
>   (b) in the same transaction with respect to which a question of notice to the purchaser arises, it has come to the knowledge of his counsel, as such, or of his solicitor or other agent, as such, or would have come to the knowledge of his solicitor or other agent, as such, if such inquiries and inspections had been made as ought reasonably to have been made by the solicitor or other agent.
>
>   (2) Paragraph (ii) of the last subsection shall not exempt a purchaser from any liability under, or any obligation to perform or observe, any covenant, condition, provision or restriction contained in any instrument under which his title is derived, mediately or immediately; and such liability or obligation may be enforced in the same manner as to the same extent as if that paragraph had not been enacted.
>
>   (3) A purchaser shall not by reason of anything in this section be affected by notice in any case where he would not have been so affected if this section had not been enacted.
>
>   (4) This section applies to purchases made either before or after the commencement of this Act (*r*).

The provisions being of a negative character, the third subsection is unnecessary. It can be said, however, that the practical result of this provision is that the law prior to the Conveyancing Act 1882, s. 3,

---

(*n*) See *Eyre* v. *Burmester* (1862), 10 H.L.C. 90; *Heath* v. *Crealock* (1874), 10 Ch. App. 22; and *cf. Pilcher* v. *Rawlins* (1872), 7 Ch. App. 259.

(*o*) *Re Hall-Dare's Contract* (1882), 21 Ch. D. 41; *Mostyn* v. *Mostyn*, [1893] 3 Ch. 376.

(*p*) Including a mortgagee—see *supra*, note (*k*); as to the general law, see *Willoughby* v. *Willoughby* (1756), 1 Term. Rep. 763.

(*q*) See pp. 442, 482, *infra*.

(*r*) This subsection omits the proviso, now obsolete, to the Conveyancing Act 1882, s. 3, saving the rights of parties where an action was pending at the commencement of that Act, 1 January, 1883.

which this section re-enacts, can be used as a shield and not treated as going beyond the law contained in the codelike definition in this section (s).

The object of the first subsection is to get rid of some of those extensions of the law of notice which have gradually arisen out of the somewhat refined reasonings of courts of equity, and which operated with much harshness. But in applying the Act it will often be as necessary as before to consider what constitutes "knowledge", either in the person to be affected by notice, or in his agent "as such", when agency exists; whether the knowledge has been acquired in the same transaction; and what inquiries and inspections "ought reasonably to have been made" (t).

2—Constructive Notice through Non-inquiry

Inquiries which should be made.—The enactment just quoted gives as the test for constructive notice of an "instrument or matter or any fact or thing" that it would have come to the knowledge of the person against whom notice is sought to be established "if such inquiries and inspections had been made as ought reasonably to have been made by him". The inquiries which are reasonable are those which ought to have been made as a matter of prudence, having regard to what is usually done by careful men of business in similar circumstances (u). And it may be stated generally that, where a person has actual notice that the property with which he is dealing is charged or otherwise affected, it is his duty to inquire into the extent and nature of the charges; and he must not assume that the reference is only to charges which are already known to him (x).

But if there is no actual notice that the property is affected, and no turning away from the knowledge of facts which the *res gestae* would suggest to a prudent mind, there will be no constructive notice (y).

Inquiries necessary to ascertain title.—An intending mortgagee must satisfy himself that the mortgagor has at least a prima facie title. It is not sufficient for him merely to put the question "Is this your property?" (z). He will be deemed to have notice of all facts which

---

(s) See *Hunt* v. *Luck*, [1902] 1 Ch. 428, *per* VAUGHAN WILLIAMS, L.J., at p. 435.

(t) See *supra*, pp. 432 *et seq*.

(u) *Bailey* v. *Barnes*, [1894] 1 Ch. 25 (C.A.); *Berwick & Co.* v. *Price*, [1905] 1 Ch. 632. This is equivalent to the inquiries which a purchaser should make according to the practice of conveyancers. And see *Agra Bank, Ltd.* v. *Barry* (1874), L.R. 7 H.L. 135; *McCarthy and Stone, Ltd.* v. *Julian S. Hodge & Co., Ltd.*, [1971] 2 All E.R. 973; and the cases referred to in footnote (f), p. 439, *infra*.

(x) *Jones* v. *Williams* (1857), 24 Beav. 47. The omission to make inquiry so obviously tends to fraud that the purchaser is affected with notice, even though the omission does not proceed from fraudulent motives: *ibid*. On the question of constructive notice resulting from failure to make reasonable inquiries, see *Newman* v. *Real Estate Debenture Corpn., etc.*, [1940] 1 All E.R. 131.

(y) *Plumb* v. *Fluitt* (1791), 2 Anst. 432; *Evams* v. *Bicknell* (1801), 6 Ves. 174; *Jones* v. *Smith* (1841), 1 Hare, 56; affd. (1843), 1 Ph. 244. See *Agra Bank, Ltd.* v. *Barry* (1874), L.R. 7 H.L. 135; *English and Scottish Mercantile Investment Co.* v. *Brunton*, [1892] 2 Q.B. 700 (where the mortgagee's solicitor knew that the mortgaging company had issued debentures, but was told that they did not affect the property proposed to be mortgaged to his client: *Re Castell and Brown, Ltd.*, *Roper* v. *The Company*, [1898] 1 Ch. 315; *Re Valletort Sanitary Steam Laundry Co., Ltd.*, *Ward* v. *The Company*, [1903] 2 Ch. 654; *Re Bourne*, *Bourne* v. *Bourne*, [1906] 2 Ch. 427).

(z) *Mulville* v. *Munster and Leinster Bank* (1891), 27 L.R. Ir. 379.

he would have learned upon a proper investigation of the title, under a contract containing no restriction of his rights in that respect (*a*). If, therefore, he does not ask for the title deeds, he will be affected with notice of the rights of an undisclosed mortgagee in whose custody they are (*b*).

A fortiori, if knowing (*c*) that the deeds are in deposit, or that the person with whom he deals is indebted, and has given security to another, and that the title deeds are not forthcoming (*d*), he abstains from seeking information as to their actual position.

The fact that the mortgagee does not employ a solicitor, and is himself ignorant of the law, is immaterial (*e*).

But the notice will not affect the purchaser, if he afterwards purchases other lands under a title independent of the instrument of which he had notice, though that instrument may have actually related to them; he being neither presumed to take notice of, nor bound to remember, more than is necessary to make out his title (*f*).

Of whom inquiries should be made.—Where notice may depend on the result of inquiries, these should not be made of the mortgagor if there are better means of information (*g*). But while to ask those only, against whose possible fraud the inquiries are intended to be a safeguard, is in general not sufficient diligence, yet if the mortgagee has inquired honestly and to the best of his means, he will not be prejudiced because he has been misled by false information (*h*).

Notice from form of conveyance.—Notice may also be imputed from the nature or form of a conveyance. Thus, a purchaser has notice of a prior title by the concurrence in the conveyance to him of persons interested under that title (*i*). But though a peculiarity in a deed, such as the unusual position of a signature or the manner of engrossing

---

(*a*) *Re Nisbet and Potts' Contract*, [1905] 1 Ch. 391; on app., [1906] 1 Ch. 386. See also *Re Cox and Neve*, [1891] 2 Ch. 109, 117, and also Law of Property Act 1925, s. 44 (1), as amended by the Law of Property Act 1969, s. 23; also *ibid.*, s. 44 (5).

(*b*) *Berwick & Co.* v. *Price*, [1905] 1 Ch., *per* JOYCE, J., at p. 638. See *Kennedy* v. *Green* (1834), 3 Myl. & K. 699; *Jones* v. *Smith, supra*; *Hewitt* v. *Loosemore* (1851), 9 Hare, 449; *Lloyds Banking Co.* v. *Jones* (1885), 29 Ch. D. 221; *Oliver* v. *Hinton*, [1899] 2 Ch. 264.

If A claims priority over B on the ground that B took with notice of A's earlier security, the onus lies on A to prove such notice; and it is not sufficient to show that the deeds were in the hands of A if, irrespective of the security, he was the person entitled to hold them: *Re Hardy, Ex parte Hardy* (1832), 2 Deac. & C. 393. Possession of deeds by a solicitor is in the ordinary course of business and does not call for inquiry: *Bozon* v. *Williams* (1829), 3 Y. & J. 150.

(*c*) *Birch* v. *Ellames* (1794), 2 Anst. 427; *Hiern* v. *Mill* (1806), 13 Ves. 114.

(*d*) *Whitbread* v. *Jordan* (1835), 1 Y. & C. Ex. 303.

(*e*) *Berwick & Co.* v. *Price, supra*. And a person will be affected with notice of an instrument brought to his actual knowledge, though it be inartistically expressed, if the meaning is so plain, that an unprofessional person would not be misled: *Davies* v. *Davies* (1841), 4 Beav. 54.

(*f*) *Hamilton* v. *Royse* (1804), 2 Sch. & Lef. 315.

(*g*) *Taylor* v. *Baker* (1818), 5 Price, 306; *Broadbent* v. *Barlow* (1861), 3 De G.F. & J. 570.

(*h*) *Jones* v. *Smith* (1841), 1 Hare, 55; *Jones* v. *Williams* (1857), 24 Beav. 47; *Hipkins* v. *Amery* (1860), 2 Giff. 292.

(*i*) *Burgoyne* v. *Hatton* (1738), Barn. Ch. 231, where the grantor claimed as heir-at-law, but the concurrence of the devisees, the deed containing no explanation of this, gave notice of their title. And see *Stockdale* v. *South Sea Co.* (1740), Barn. Ch. 363 (inadequacy of purchase price in comparison with real value of property, notice of the existence of an incumbrance).

it, ought to cause inquiry, it will not lead to notice of a defect in the title with which it is not connected.

Notice of equities.—Nor is the rule under consideration confined to plain recitals of matters of fact. A purchaser will generally be bound by the particulars, and even sometimes by the equities, arising out of an important or peculiar transaction, recited or referred to in a deed or abstract, of which he has notice, and concerning which transaction it becomes his duty to inquire. Thus notice will be imputed of the particulars of a trust, of the existence of which there is actual notice (*k*).

But there will be no notice of an equity which the usual inquiry into title would not discover. Thus, a purchaser from a trustee will not have notice of negligence or other matter amounting to breach of trust in connection with the sale (*l*).

Notice, however, will arise where the matter depends upon the application of a clear equitable doctrine. Hence notice of the reservation of an equity of redemption is notice of the mortgage title, if the court is of opinion that the equity still subsists (*m*). Where, however, the construction of a deed is so uncertain, and the equity so doubtful, that the decision of the court could not be known, a purchaser for valuable consideration, denying actual notice, will not be affected (*n*).

Notice of deed is notice of contents.—Actual notice of an instrument which must necessarily affect the title is constructive notice of its contents and of everything to which it refers (*o*); except, it seems, that in cases of fraud, none but the parties to the deed are affected by constructive notice of the fraud (*p*). Thus, notice of a lease is notice of all covenants in it whether usual or unusual, provided the purchaser has a fair opportunity of ascertaining its provisions (*q*). And generally, he to whom an instrument is brought for the express purpose of examination in the transaction (*r*), or for whose inspection it is left open for examination in the transaction (*s*) has actual or constructive notice of its contents, though the nature of the contents may have been misrepresented. And there will be full notice of an incumbrance as against a person who takes subject to it, although in the recital of it, it is inaccurately, or not completely described (*t*).

But while a purchaser is bound by a mortgage, though not particularly specified, if the deed, subject to or under which he claims,

---

(*k*) *Malpas* v. *Ackland* (1827), 3 Russ. 273; provided, that is, the notice is clear: see *London and Canadian, etc., Co.* v. *Duggan*, [1893] A.C. 506. And see *Lacey* v. *Ingle* (1847), 2 Ph. 413 (notice imputed to mortgagee of contract for sale that prior incumbrancers had claims on the purchase money).

(*l*) *Borell* v. *Dann* (1843), 2 Hare, 440. As to receipts in deeds, see footnote 7, p. 614, *infra*.

(*m*) *Hansard* v. *Hardy* (1812), 18 Ves. 455.

(*n*) *Parker* v. *Brooke* (1804), 9 Ves. 583. See also *Bovey* v. *Smith* (1682), 1 Vern. 144.

(*o*) *Jones* v. *Smith* (1843), 1 Ph. at p. 253.

(*p*) *Read* v. *Ward* (1739), 7 Vin. Abr. 123.

(*q*) *Grosvenor* v. *Green* (1858), 28 L.J. Ch. 173; *Hyde* v. *Warden* (1877), 3 Ex. D. 72; *Re White and Smith's Contract*, [1896] 1 Ch. 637.

(*r*) *Cosser* v. *Collinge* (1832), 3 My. & K. 283.

(*s*) *Crofton* v. *Ormsby* (1806), 2 Sch. & Lef. 583.

(*t*) *Hope* v. *Liddell* (1855), 21 Beav. 183. And see *Gibson* v. *Ingo* (1847), 6 Hare, 112.

shows the existence of prior mortgages (*u*), yet there is no notice where a representation is made, concerning the mortgage deed, which is calculated to mislead, and to disarm inquiry (*v*); nor where an imperfect or erroneous statement has been made as to the contents of a deed (*x*).

Deeds not necessarily affecting title.—But while notice of a deed which must of necessity affect the title is constructive notice of its contents, this is not so with other deeds, and notice of these requires only that the person who has notice shall act honestly and shall not be guilty of gross negligence. Thus, where a settlement has been made by the proposing mortgagor which may or may not affect the land in question, a statement that the settlement does not affect it can be accepted without production of the settlement (*y*). And a purchaser is not affected with notice by matters appearing upon an abstract or a deed which merely leave room for suspicion of what the purchaser cannot know to be, and which may not be true (*z*). However, cases of this kind depend very much on their own circumstances, and that which will not affect one man will be abundantly sufficient to affect another (*a*). Moreover, circumstances which may affect a trustee with notice are not necessarily sufficient to make a person liable as a constructive trustee (*b*).

Notice by tenancy.—Notice also arises from the fact that a person other than the person with apparent title is in actual occupation or receipt of the rents of the land (*c*). Thus, where a tenant is in occupation, the purchaser is put on inquiry as to the terms of the holding and has constructive notice of the tenant's rights (*d*). Where, however, the tenant is paying rent to a person claiming adversely to the vendor, the purchaser is not, as between himself and such claimant, bound to inquire to whom the rent is paid, and has not constructive notice of his title (*e*); though it is otherwise if he inquires and finds that rent is being paid to an adverse claimant (*f*).

(*u*) *Eland* v. *Eland* (1839), 1 Beav. 235; *Farrow* v. *Rees* (1840), 4 Beav. 18.
(*v*) *Drysdale* v. *Mace* (1854), 2 Sm. & G. 255; affd. 5 De G.M. & G. 103.
(*x*) *Re Bright's Trusts* (1856), 21 Beav. 430.
(*y*) *Jones* v. *Smith* (1843), 1 Ph., pp. 254, 257. See *Finch* v. *Shaw* (1854), 18 Jur. 935; affd. *sub nom. Colyer* v. *Finch* (1856), 5 H.L.Cas. 905; *Lloyds Banking Co.* v. *Jones* (1885), 29 Ch. D. 221, 230; as to debentures, see *English and Scottish Mercantile Investment Co.* v. *Brunton*, [1892] 2 Q.B. 700; *Re Valletort Sanitary Steam Laundry Co., Ward* v. *The Company*, [1903] 2 Ch. 654; *Wilson* v. *Kelland*, [1910] 2 Ch. 306; p. 123, *supra*.
(*z*) See *M'Queen* v. *Farquhar* (1805), 11 Ves. at p. 482; *Dodds* v. *Hills* (1865), 2 Hem. & M. 424.
(*a*) *Jones* v. *Smith* (1841), 1 Hare, 43, at p. 55.
(*b*) *Williams* v. *Williams* (1881), 17 Ch. D. 437; *Karak Rubber Co., Ltd.* v. *Burden (No. 2)*, [1972] 1 All E.R. 1210.
(*c*) See *Caunce* v. *Caunce*, [1969] 1 All E.R. 722; *Hodgson* v. *Marks*, [1971] Ch. 892 (C.A.); [1971] 2 All E.R. 684; *Binions* v. *Evans*, [1972] Ch. 359 (C.A.); [1972] 2 All E.R. 70; (1973) 36 M.L.R. 25 (R. H. Maudsley).
(*d*) *Barnhart* v. *Greenshields* (1853), 9 Moo. P.C.C. 18, 32. And see *Hegeman* v. *Rogers* (1972), 21 D.L.R. (3d) 272. Where the property is in the possession of a partnership, a mortgagee from one partner has constructive notice of the title of the firm: *Cavander* v. *Bulteel* (1873), 9 Ch. App. 79.
(*e*) *Barnhart* v. *Greenshields, supra*; *Hunt* v. *Luck*, [1902] 1 Ch. 428, 432; *Green* v. *Rheinberg* (1911), 104 L.T. 149 (C.A.); and see *Smith* v. *Jones*, [1954] 2 All E.R. 823; and *Latec Investments, Ltd.* v. *Hotel Terrigal Pty., Ltd.* (1965), 113 C.L.R. 265.
(*f*) *Bailey* v. *Richardson* (1852), 9 Hare, 734; *Barnhart* v. *Greenshields, supra*; *Hunt* v. *Luck, supra*, at p. 433.

Moreover, as the principle of the doctrine is that the purchaser is not justified in assuming the possession of the occupier to be that of the apparent owner, but is bound to inquire into the nature of his interest, the notice equally arises, whether the property is described to the purchaser as occupied by the person alone who claims the interest in question, or by him and his under tenants (g).

3—Constructive Notice through Agents

Former rule in equity.—The principal may be affected by notice received through his agent (h). Originally the principal was affected by notice of such matters only as came to the knowledge of the agent at the particular time while he was actually concerned for the principal, and in the course of the very transaction which became the subject of the action (i).

It was later held, however, that where the prior transaction could be shown to have been present to the agent's mind, notice arose (k). And where an agent was employed by a person in effecting several incumbrances, and acted in those matters for the mortgagees also, the later mortgagees should be affected by notice of the earlier mortgages, notwithstanding the transactions were distinct (l).

The pre-1883 (m) rules can be summed up as follows:

(1) A mortgagee was not generally affected with notice—

   (a) of matters touching his security, by reason of knowledge acquired by his counsel, solicitor or other agent, in a different transaction; or

   (b) of matters which it was not the duty of the agent to communicate, or material for the principal to know (n).

(2) Where an agent had been employed both by the same mortgagor, and by several successive mortgagees, in effecting the mortgages, the later mortgagees had notice of the earlier mortgages. But it is questionable whether the earlier mortgagees would be taken to have notice of the later ones, even where the solicitor continued to act for them, e.g., in selling the property (o).

(3) As to securities, in which the agent was not employed by both parties, the later mortgagees would not, by employment of the same agent, be necessarily affected by notice thereof.

(g) *Bailey* v. *Richardson, supra.* And see *Crofton* v. *Ormsby* (1806), 2 Sch. & Lef. 583; *Hanbury* v. *Litchfield* (1833), 2 Myl. & K. 629; *Miles* v. *Langley* (1831), 1 R. & M. 39; affd. 2 R. & M. 626.

(h) Otherwise notice might always be avoided by employing agents: *Sheldon* v. *Cox* (1764), Ambl. 624. The doctrine is not confined to notice received through solicitors: *Merry* v. *Abney* (1663), 1 Cas. in Ch. 38.

(i) *Fitzgerald* v. *Fauconberge* (1730), Fitzgibbon, 207; *Hiern* v. *Mill* (1806), 13 Ves. 114.

(k) *Hargreaves* v. *Rothwell* (1836), 1 Keen, 154.

(l) *Brotherton* v. *Hatt* (1706), 2 Vern. 574; *Gerrard* v. *O'Reilly* (1843), 3 Dru. & War. 414.

(m) The Conveyancing Act 1882, came into operation as from 31 December, 1882.

(n) *Wyllie* v. *Pollen* (1863), 32 L.J. Ch. 782.

(o) *Thorne* v. *Heard*, [1895] A.C. 495 (H.L.).

(4) Yet they might be so affected, if it were shown that at the time of making the later mortgages, the earlier ones were known to, and at the same time were actually present to the mind of, the agent. And it seems that they might be affected inferentially also, if one transaction so closely followed the other as to afford an irresistible presumption that the earlier one was so present to his mind (*p*).

Statutory changes.—Under s. 199 of the Law of Property Act 1925, the effect of notice to the agent, whether actual or constructive, is confined to notice received in the same transaction as that with respect to which the question arises. This confirms the law as stated in Rule (1) (a), and does not affect that stated in Rule (1) (b). Rule (2) is abrogated unless the successive mortgages, from proximity of date or other circumstances, can be considered to have been made, not merely in the course of a continuous dealing with the same title, but in the course of the same transaction (*q*).

But no notice can arise under the circumstances mentioned in Rules (3) and (4) so long as the transactions are different.

Fraud of agent.—Notice to the agent is not imputed to the principal where the transaction effected by the agent is itself founded in fraud, in which the agent is so concerned that it is certain he would conceal it (*r*). And probably this rule is not altered by the statute; otherwise an agent, under its shelter, might use the knowledge which he acquired in one transaction for the purpose of committing a fraud in another. It is otherwise, however, where the matter is not necessarily fraudulent (*s*).

In all these cases the burden of proof is upon the client to show the probability of non-communication of the fact by the agent (*t*).

Relation of principal and agent.—The relation of principal and agent must subsist at the time of the transaction. But actual retainer of a person as agent seems unnecessary; for even where the person to be affected knows nothing of the matter until after its completion, if he then acts upon or adopts it, he thereby makes the agent his agent "*ab initio*".

If the agent is employed in part only of the transaction, notice arises of whatever came to his knowledge during his agency (*u*).

Solicitor as agent.—A solicitor is not an agent for the purpose of receiving notice of an incumbrance on or other dealings with the security, merely because he was employed to invest the money (*x*).

(*p*) See *Gerrard* v. *O'Reilly, supra.*

(*q*) *Re Cousins* (1886), 31 Ch. D. 671. But probably, where the agent who effected the earlier mortgage himself becomes second mortgagee, he still cannot deny notice of the earlier mortgage: see *Perkins* v. *Bradley* (1842), 1 Hare, 219.

(*r*) See *Kennedy* v. *Green* (1834), 3 Myl. & K. 699; *Cave* v. *Cave* (1880), 15 Ch. D. 639; *Rhodes* v. *Moules*, [1895] 1 Ch. 236.

(*s*) See *Le Neve* v. *Le Neve* (1747), 3 Atk. 646; *Hewitt* v. *Loosemore* (1851), 9 Hare, 449; *Bradley* v. *Riches* (1878), 9 Ch. D. 189.

(*t*) *Thompson* v. *Cartwright* (1863), 33 Beav. 178.

(*u*) *Bury* v. *Bury* (1748), Sugd. *V. & P.* (11th Edn.), App. No. 25. For the case of a bank manager, who is agent for his bank, see *Re Macnamara* (1884), 13 L.R. Ir. 158.

(*x*) *Saffron Walden, etc., Building Society* v. *Rayner* (1880), 14 Ch. D. 406.

Where both parties employ the same solicitor, the knowledge of the
mortgagor will not be notice to the mortgagee (*y*), and any notice
the solicitor acquires will not, generally, be imputed to both (*z*).

C—NOTICE BY REGISTRATION (*a*)

Actual notice.—Certain incumbrances can be registered in the
registers kept under the Land Charges Act 1972 (*b*). Under the following
provision of the Law of Property Act 1925, such registration constitutes
"actual notice":

> **198.**—(1) The registration of any instrument or matter in any register kept
> under the Land Charges Act 1972 or any local land charges register (*c*) shall be
> deemed to constitute actual notice of such instrument or matter, and of the
> fact of such registration, to all persons and for all purposes connected with the
> land affected, as from the date of registration or other prescribed date and so
> long as the registration continues in force (*d*).
>
> (2) This section operates without prejudice to the provisions of this Act
> respecting the making of further advances by a mortgagee, and applies only to
> instruments and matters required or authorised to be registered in any such
> register (*c*).

Registers under Land Charges Act.—The following registers are
kept at the Land Registry (*e*):

    (a) a register of land charges;
    (b) a register of pending actions;
    (c) a register of writs and orders affecting land;
    (d) a register of deeds of arrangement affecting land;
    (e) a register of annuities.

Under the Law of Property Act 1925, s. 198 (1), registration in any
of these registers constitutes actual notice (*f*).

Land charges.—Provision is made by the Land Charges Act 1972,

---

(*y*) *Re Cousins* (1886), 31 Ch. D. 671. And the same principle applies where the same
person acts as officer of two companies: *Re Hampshire Land Co.*, [1896] 2 Ch. 743.
It has been said that if the mortgagor, being a solicitor, himself prepares the security,
and no other solicitor is employed, the mortgagor will still be the mortgagee's solicitor;
and it makes no difference that the mortgagee pays him nothing for his services, because
it is the nature of the transaction that all the expenses should be borne by the mortgagor:
Kennedy v. *Green* (1834), 3 My. & K. 699; *Hewitt* v. *Loosemore* (1851), 9 Hare, 449; cf.
Espin v. *Pemberton* (1859), 3 De G. & J. 547; *Kettlewell* v. *Watson* (1884), 21 Ch. D. 685.
But if the mortgagee employs no solicitor, it will not be assumed, in the absence of evid-
ence, that the mortgagor's solicitor acted for him: *Atterbury* v. *Wallis* (1856), 2 Jur.
N.S. 343.

(*z*) *Dryden* v. *Frost* (1838), 3 My. & Cr. 670; *Meyer* v. *Charters* (1918), 34 T.L.R. 589;
and see *Lloyds Bank, Ltd.* v. *Marcan*, [1973] 3 All E.R. 754 (C.A.).

(*a*) For the former Middlesex Register and Yorkshire Deeds Registries, see previous
editions of this work. For registration under the Companies Act 1948, see p. 487, *infra*.

(*b*) Consolidating the Land Charges Act 1925, as amended.

(*c*) As amended by the Local Land Charges Act 1975, s. 17, Sched. 1.

(*d*) As between vendor and purchaser of unregistered land s. 198 is to be disregarded
and actual knowledge is required if the purchaser is to be affected as against the vendor
by registered land charges affecting the land the subject of contract made after the
commencement of the Law of Property Act 1969, s. 24. The commencement date for
s. 24 was 1 January 1970.

(*e*) Land Charges Act 1972, s. 1 (1).

(*f*) In the case of registered land, corresponding protection is obtained by notice,
caution, etc; see Land Registration Act 1925, s. 59.

for the registration of certain charges on, or obligations affecting unregistered land in the register of land charges (*g*).

The charges and obligations which can be registered are arranged in classes A, B, C, D, E, and F and are as follows:

A Class A land charge is—

(a) a rent or annuity or principal money payable by instalments or otherwise, with or without interest, which is not a charge created by deed but is a charge upon land (other than a rate) created pursuant to the application of some person under the provisions of any Act of Parliament, for securing to any person either the money spent by him or the costs, charges and expenses incurred by him under such Act, or the money advanced by him for repaying the money spent or the costs, charges and expenses incurred by another person under the authority of an Act of Parliament (*h*); or

(b) a rent or annuity or principal money payable as mentioned in paragraph (a) above which is not a charge created by deed but is a charge upon land (other than a rate) created pursuant to the application of some person under any of the enactments mentioned in Sched. 2 to this Act.

A Class B land charge is a charge on land (not being a local land charge (*i*)) of any of the kinds described in paragraph (a) of subsection (2) above, created otherwise than pursuant to the application of any person (*k*).

A Class C land charge is any of the following, namely—

(i) a puisne mortgage;
(ii) a limited owner's charge;
(iii) a general equitable charge;
(iv) an estate contract;

and for this purpose—

(i) a puisne mortgage is a legal mortgage which is not protected by a deposit of documents (*l*) relating to the legal estate affected;
(ii) a limited owner's charge is an equitable charge acquired by a tenant for life or statutory owner under Part III of the Finance Act 1975 (*m*) or any other statute by reason of the discharge by him of any capital transfer tax (*m*) or other liabilities and to which special priority is given by the statute;
(iii) a general equitable charge is any equitable charge which—

(*g*) Land Charges Act 1972, s. 2 (1). Land Charges affecting registered land cannot be registered under the Land Charges Act; see L.C.A. 1972, s. 14 (1). Where an instrument executed on or after 27 July 1971 conveys, grants or assigns an estate in land and creates a land charge which would otherwise require to be registered under the Land Charges Act it is not to be registered if the instrument in question gives rise to the need for compulsory registration of the land under the Land Registration Act 1925; L.C.A. 1972, s. 14 (3), repeating provisions formerly in s. 23A of the L.C.A. 1925, inserted by the Land Registration and Land Charges Act 1971, s. 9 (1).

(*h*) *E.g.*, under the Agricultural Holdings Act 1948, s. 82 (2) (see p. 164, *supra*); the Landlord and Tenant Act 1927, Sched. 1, para. (7) (see p. 164, *supra*), as amended by Land Charges Act 1972, s. 2 (2) (b), Sched. 2. The list of Class A land charges is set out in Sched. 2 to the 1972 Act. A land charge of Class A (other than a land improvement charge registered after 31 December 1969) or of Class B, when registered, takes effect as if it had been created by a deed of charge by way of legal mortgage: Land Charges Act 1972, s. 4 (1).

(*i*) Amended by Local Land Charges Act 1975, s. 19, Sched. 2.

(*k*) *E.g.*, a charge arising under the Legal Aid Act 1974 (see p. 165, *supra*). Most other statutory charges are local land charges and excluded from Class B.

(*l*) Not all the documents need have been deposited (see p. 52, *supra*). Where there are several protected mortgages priority is determined by the old rules (see p. 429, *supra*).

(*m*) As amended by the Finance Act 1975, Sched. 12, para. 18 (2).

(a) is not secured by a deposit of documents relating to the legal estate affected; and

(b) does not arise or affect an interest arising under a trust for sale or a settlement (*n*); and

(c) is not a charge given by way of indemnity against rents equitably apportioned or charged exclusively on land in exoneration of other land and against the breach or non-observance of covenants or conditions; and

(d) is not included in any other class of land charge (*o*);

(iv) an estate contract is a contract by an estate owner or by a person entitled at the date of the contract to have a legal estate conveyed to him to convey or create a legal estate, including a contract conferring either expressly or by statutory implication a valid option to purchase, a right of pre-emption or any other like right (*p*).

A Class D land charge is any of the following, namely—
   (i) an Inland Revenue charge;
   (ii) a restrictive covenant;
   (iii) an equitable easement;

and for this purpose—

(i) an Inland Revenue charge is a charge on land, being a charge acquired by the Board under Part III of the Finance Act 1975 (capital transfer tax) (*q*) . . . . .

A Class E land charge is an annuity created before 1st January, 1926, and not registered in the register of annuities.

A Class F land charge is a charge affecting any land by virtue of the Matrimonial Homes Act 1967 (*r*).

Mode of registration.—The registration of a land charge is effected in the name of the estate owner whose estate is intended to be affected (*s*).

If it is not created by an instrument, short particulars of the effect of the charge must be registered with the application to register the charge (*t*).

Although, in general, a land charge created before the commencement of the 1925 Act was not capable of registration until it had been

---

(*n*) See *Re Rayleigh Weir Stadium*, [1954] 2 All E.R. 283.

(*o*) See *Thomas* v. *Rose*, [1968] 3 All E.R. 765; *Georgiades* v. *Edward Wolfe Co., Ltd.*, [1965] Ch. 487 (C.A.); [1964] 3 All E.R. 433.

(*p*) See, *e.g.*, *First National Securities, Ltd.* v. *Chiltern District Council*, [1975] 2 All E.R. 766. An agreement to execute a legal mortgage contained in a memorandum accompanying an equitable mortgage by deposit of deeds is within this definition. But since the agreement is only subsidiary to the charge and this is not registrable under Class C (iii) the agreement does not seem to be registrable under Class C (iv). The effect would be to evade the exclusion from registration of securities accompanied by deposit of deeds. And see p. 52, *supra*.

(*q*) See Finance Act 1975, Sched. 4, paras 20 and 21, and s. 26 for the Inland Revenue charge. This part of the Land Charges Act 1972 was amended by Finance Act 1975, Sched. 12, para. 18 (3).

(*r*) See p. 217, *supra*.

(*s*) Land Charges Act 1972, s. 3 (1); Land Charges Rules 1974; see *Barrett* v. *Hilton Developments, Ltd.*, [1975] Ch. 237 (C.A.); [1974] 3 All E.R. 944. As to the name, see *Oak Co-operative Building Society* v. *Blackburn*, [1968] Ch. 730 (C.A.); [1968] 2 All E.R. 117; *Diligent Finance Co., Ltd.* v. *Alleyne* (1972), 23 P. & C.R. 346. The expenses of registration of, *inter alia*, a Class C (iii) (but not C (iv) or D (i)) land charge form part of the land charge: Land Charges Act 1972, s. 3 (4).

(*t*) Land Charges Act 1972, s. 3 (5); *e.g.*, a vendor's lien.

acquired under a conveyance made after such commencement, an exception was made in the case of puisne mortgages, and these were registrable before any transfer was made (*u*).

Vacating the registration.—Section 1 of the Land Charges Act 1972 provides:

> (6) Subject to the provisions of this Act, registration may be vacated pursuant to an order of the court (*a*).

Where there is no dispute, cancellation is effected by the registrar on the application of the person who applied for registration (*b*).

Effect of registration of statutory charges.—The Land Charges Act 1972 provides:

> 4—(1) A land charge of Class A (other than a land improvement charge registered after 31 December, 1969), or of Class B shall, when registered, take effect as if it had been created by a deed of charge by way of legal mortgage, but without prejudice to the priority of the charge.

Thus the owner of the charge has the same powers of realising the property as a legal mortgagee, and in general no application to the court is necessary (*c*).

Local land charges.—Local land charges, *e.g.*, financial charges in favour of a local authority under the Public Health Acts and Highway Acts (*d*), must be registered with the appropriate registering authority (*e*). This applies equally to registered land (*f*).

A local land charge, of the type creating a financial charge, when registered, takes effect as if it had been created by a deed of charge by way of legal mortgage, but without prejudice to the priority of the charge (*g*).

Effect of registration or non-registration.—As to the effect of registration or non-registration, see pp. 482 *et seq.*, *infra*.

(*u*) *Ibid.*, s. 3 (3); registration had an important effect as regards formal mortgages which before 1926 were equitable mortgages. The effect of the Law of Property Act 1925, Sched. 1, Pts. VII and VIII, was to turn such mortgages into legal mortgages by demise, but until registration they did not obtain the benefit of this legal estate as against a purchase in good faith without notice. In favour of such a purchaser the mortgage was deemed to remain an equitable interest; Pt. VII, para. 6; Pt. VIII, para. 5. These provisions do not apply to mortgages or charges registered or protected under the Land Registration Act 1925: *ibid.*

(*a*) The court also has an inherent power to order a registration to be vacated: *Heywood* v. *B.D.C. Properties, Ltd.* (*No.* 2), [1964] 1 All E.R. 180. And see *Price Bros. (Somerford), Ltd.* v. *Kelly Homes (Stoke-on-Trent), Ltd.*, [1975] 3 All E.R. 369 (C.A.); *Northern Developments (Holdings), Ltd.* v. *U.D.T. Securities, Ltd.*, [1977] 1 All E.R. 747.

(*b*) See Land Charges Act 1972, s. 16 (1) (b); Land Charges Rules 1974. Difficulties sometimes arise on the sale of property which is no longer subject to a mortgage but in relation to which there is an outstanding land charge registration. An entry on the register may be rebutted by the production of the mortgage in respect of which the entry was made duly discharged: see Law Society's Digest (3rd supplement), Opinion No. 136. Where the entry is removable by the vendor and cancellation is not effected before completion he should on completion hand over the charge duly discharged (unless it relates also to other property) together with the necessary forms for removal of the entry: Law Society's Digest, Opinion No. 139.

(*c*) See, *e.g.*, *Payne* v. *Cardiff Rural District Council*, [1932] 1 K.B. 241.

(*d*) Local Land Charges Act 1975, ss. 1, 2 and the Acts referred to in Sched. 1 of the 1975 Act. The 1975 Act is not in force as this goes to press.

(*e*) Local Land Charges Act 1975, ss. 5, 6.

(*f*) Land Registration Act 1925, s. 59 (2) proviso.

(*g*) Local Land Charges Act 1975, s. 7.

IV—PRIORITY BETWEEN EQUITABLE INCUMBRANCERS

Rule of priority in time.—Subject to the statutory effect of registration, equitable incumbrances rank in order of date of creation, provided the equities are otherwise equal (*h*). This is in accordance with the maxim *"qui prior est tempore, potior est jure"*, and has been justified on the ground that the first equitable incumbrancer has a vested interest which cannot be displaced except for strong reasons (*i*).

The rule is also a consequence of the principle that a mortgagor cannot grant more than he is justly entitled to. Hence, after he has diminished his ownership by the grant of an equitable charge, a second equitable charge is necessarily subject to the first (*j*).

Contemporaneous instruments.—Where several instruments have been executed on the same day, priority will follow the order of execution, subject to any contrary intention appearing on the deeds, and an inquiry may be directed to ascertain the times of execution if uncertain (*k*).

Operation of the rule.—In accordance with the above rule, the claim of an equitable mortgagee will prevail against the solicitor of the mortgagor into whose hands the deeds subsequently come, and the solicitor cannot thereby acquire any lien for his costs (*l*). Moreover, where the mortgagor made two securities by depositing part of the deeds with one person and part with another, the former had the preference (*m*). Where notice by an equitable mortgagee is not required to be given for his own protection, the omission to give notice is not a ground for postponing him, although the notice might have prevented the creation of a subsequent incumbrance (*n*).

Rule applies to equitable interests generally.—The rule is not confined to priority as between equitable incumbrances, but applies to equitable interests generally (*o*). A mere equity to set aside a deed will, however, be postponed to an actual equitable interest created for valuable consideration under the deed (*p*).

(*h*) See *Rice* v. *Rice* (1854), 2 Drew. 73, at p. 78; *Capell* v. *Winter*, [1907] 2 Ch. 376 at p. 381.

(*i*) See *Willoughby* v. *Willoughby* (1756), 1 Term. Rep. 763, at p. 773, *per* Lord HARDWICKE, C.; *Cory* v. *Eyre* (1863), 1 De G.J. & S. 149, at p. 167, *per* TURNER, L.J.

(*j*) *Phillips* v. *Phillips* (1862), 4 De G.F. & J. 208, at p. 215, *per* Lord WESTBURY, C.; *Cave* v. *Cave* (1880), 15 Ch. D. 639; *Latec Investments, Ltd.* v. *Hotel Terrigal Pty. Ltd.* (*in Liquidation*) (1965), 113 C.L.R. 265; *McCarthy and Stone, Ltd.* v. *Julian S. Hodge & Co., Ltd.*, [1971] 2 All E.R. 973.

(*k*) *Gartside* v. *Silkstone and Dodworth Coal Co.* (1882), 21 Ch. D. 762.

(*l*) *Molesworth* v. *Robbins* (1845), 2 Jo. & Lat. 358; *Smith* v. *Chichester* (1842), 2 Dr. & War. 393; *Pelly* v. *Wathen* (1851), 1 De G.M. & G. 16.

(*m*) *Roberts* v. *Croft* (1857), 24 Beav. 223; see *Dixon* v. *Mucklestone* (1872), 8 Ch. App. 155.

(*n*) *Union Bank of London* v. *Kent* (1888), 39 Ch. D. 238.

(*o*) An equitable mortgagee by deposit of deeds will be postponed to a prior purchaser, whose purchase (without negligence on his part) has not been completed: *Flinn* v. *Pountain* (1889), 58 L.J. Ch. 389; *McCarthy and Stone, Ltd.* v. *Julian S. Hodge & Co., Ltd., supra.* As to a charge upon chattels held under a hire-purchase agreement, see p. 75, *supra.*

(*p*) *Roddy* v. *Williams* (1845), 3 Jo. & Lat. 1; *Hiorns* v. *Holtom* (1852), 16 Beav. 259; *French* v. *Hope* (1887), 56 L.J. Ch. 363. But see *Latec Investments, Ltd.* v. *Hotel Terrigal Pty., Ltd., supra.*

The better equity prevails.—The rule as to priority in time is subject to the important qualification that the equities of the rival incumbrancers are in other respects equal. Equality means here the non-existence of any circumstance which affects the conduct of one of the rival claimants and makes it less meritorious than that of the other (*q*). Thus, in *Rice* v. *Rice* (*r*), a vendor conveyed without receiving the purchase money, but a receipt was indorsed on the conveyance, and the title deeds delivered to the purchaser. The purchaser then created a mortgage by deposit of the deeds and absconded. It was held that the indorsement of the receipt and the possession of the title deeds gave the mortgagee the better equity, and he had priority over the vendor's lien. However, in a case in which the first incumbrancer is postponed on the ground of negligence, the better equity of a later incumbrancer is usually founded on the negligence of the first (*s*).

Mortgages in breach of trust.—The question of the values of rival equities arises where a trustee creates a mortgage in breach of trust. The courts of this country (*t*) have held that the interest of the beneficiary is of the same quality as the interest of the equitable mortgagee, and being prior in time it prevails (*u*), provided the beneficiary has no reason to suspect want of good faith on the part of the trustee.

The fact that the beneficiary has created the trust for his own purposes, and has allowed the deeds to remain in the custody of the trustee, is not negligence so as to postpone him (*x*).

If, however, the transaction is authorised by the trust and the deed contains a proper receipt clause, the equitable title taken under the trustee will prevail (*y*).

And if trustees invest the trust fund upon property which, by the terms of the purchase, becomes subject to an obligation, the beneficiaries are bound by the obligation, though the transaction was a breach of trust, so long as they claim the benefit of the purchase (*z*).

The above principles have no application to the case of negotiable instruments, the legal interest in which passes by indorsement or

---

(*q*) *Bailey* v. *Barnes*, [1894] 1 Ch. 25, *per* LINDLEY, L.J. And see *McCarthy and Stone, Ltd.* v. *Julian S. Hodge & Co., Ltd.*, [1971] 2 All E.R. 973.

(*r*) *Supra*.

(*s*) In *Bradley* v. *Riches* (1878), 9 Ch. D. 189, FRY, J., said that priority might be displaced by showing either fraud on the part of the earlier mortgagee, or a better equity in the later. But, on another view, there appears to be no real alternative. As to postponement on the ground of negligence, see pp. 388 *et seq.*, *infra*.

(*t*) In Ireland, it has been held that the mortgagee has the better equity: see *Re Bobbett's Estate*, [1904] 1 I.R. 461; *Scott* v. *Scott*, [1924] 1 I.R. 141.

(*u*) *Cave* v. *Cave* (1880), 15 Ch. D. 639; *Coleman* v. *London County and Westminster Bank, Ltd.*, [1906] 2 Ch. 353, 361; *Walker* v. *Linom*, [1907] 2 Ch. 104, pp. 114 *et seq.* Similarly, where a personal representative charges the estate for his own purposes, the estate has priority over the mortgagee: *Re Morgan, Pillgrem* v. *Pillgrem* (1881), 18 Ch. D. 93.

(*x*) *Carritt* v. *Real and Personal Advance Co.* (1889), 42 Ch. D. 263.

(*y*) *Lloyds Bank* v. *Bullock*, [1896] 2 Ch. 192; but this will not be so when, the trustee having power to sell only, the transaction, while in form a sale, is, in substance, a mortgage: *Capell* v. *Winter*, [1907] 2 Ch. 376.

(*z*) *New London and Brazilian Bank* v. *Brocklebank* (1882), 21 Ch. D. 302.

delivery free from all equities, unless the transferee has notice (*a*).

Mortgagee from defaulting trustee.—Although the right of trustees to be indemnified out of the trust property in respect of the liabilities incurred in the exercise of their office is to be preferred to any charge created by the beneficiary (*b*), yet, since a defaulting trustee, who also has a beneficial interest, cannot share in the trust estate till his own default has been made good, a mortgagee from him is in the same position, and will be postponed to the claims of the beneficiaries (*c*).

Priorities in proceeds of sale.—The proceeds of the sale of mortgaged property are bound by the same equities and claims as bound the property itself (*d*), and if the sale is made by the first mortgagee, he will be liable to the second mortgagee if he allows the balance of the purchase money, after paying his own mortgage, to be paid to the mortgagor (*e*). And generally, any incumbrancer holding the purchase money is bound to pay it to the incumbrancers according to their priorities.

Salvage advances.—The rule that incumbrances rank in order of time is subject to an exception in favour of advances by means of which the incumbered property is saved from loss or destruction. These are payable in priority to all charges of earlier date, and rank among themselves in the inverse order of their dates. Effect will be given to this principle only where the expenditure was essential for the preservation of the property (*f*), *e.g.*, payment of head rent to prevent eviction by a superior landlord (*g*).

An incumbrancer will not lose his priority by omitting to make advances necessary for the recovery of the fund which is the subject of the security, and to answer or notice communications by the mortgagor's agent informing him of the necessity for such advances, unless distinct notice is given, that if no advances are made a new charge will be created; this will be particularly the case where the subsequent incumbrancer has taken the security without inquiry into prior rights. But the first incumbrancer will not be allowed the benefit of advances made by the other, without paying him the amount of his advances with interest (*h*).

The 1925 legislation.—The general rule as to priority in time is

---

(*a*) See *London Joint Stock Bank* v. *Simmons*, [1892] A.C. 201; *Jameson* v. *Union Bank of Scotland* (1914), 109 L.T. 850.

(*b*) *Re Exhall Coal Co.* (1866), 35 Beav. 449. But the trustee cannot set up against an assignee of the beneficiary a debt to him incurred by the beneficiary after notice: *Re Pain, Gustavson* v. *Haviland*, [1919] 1 Ch. 38.

(*c*) *Doering* v. *Doering* (1889), 42 Ch. D. 203, for the application of the same principle to derivative interests.

(*d*) *Lane* v. *Horlock* (1853), 1 Drew. 587, 616.

(*e*) *West London Commercial Bank* v. *Reliance Permanent Building Society* (1885), 29 Ch. D. 954.

(*f*) *Landowners, etc., Drainage and Inclosure Co.* v. *Ashford* (1880), 16 Ch. D. 411— a case of being wise after the event? *Network Finance, Ltd.* v. *Deposit & Investment Co., Ltd.*, [1972] Q.W.N. 19.

(*g*) *Fetherstone* v. *Mitchell* (1848), 11 Ir. Eq. R. 35; *Hill* v. *Browne* (1844), Dru. temp. Sug. 426; *Re Wadsworth, Rhodes* v. *Sugden* (1886), 34 Ch. D. 155. And see *Matzner* v. *Clyde Securities, Ltd.*, [1975] 2 N.S.W.L.R. 293. And see p. 267, *supra*, and p. 639, *infra*.

(*h*) *Myers* v. *United, etc., Assurance Co.* (1855), 7 De G.M. & G. 112.

unaffected by s. 113 of the Law of Property Act 1925 (*i*). In *Beddoes* v. *Shaw* (*j*) it was explained that that section is merely concerned with relieving persons who are investigating title to land from being affected by notice of and from making inquiries into equitable interests, of which they may have actual or constructive notice, relating to the money secured by mortgages on the land.

V—LOSS OF PRIORITY

Postponement of legal mortgagee.—A legal mortgagee may by his conduct forfeit the priority which his legal estate gives him over an equitable incumbrancer who is earlier in point of time; and he may even, despite his holding the legal estate, be postponed to a subsequent equitable incumbrancer.

Where there is an earlier equitable mortgage, the priority of the legal mortgagee depends on his taking without notice of it. When the mortgagee who is taking a legal mortgage has notice that there is a subsisting equitable charge, his title is subject to it, and if he is told that the charge has been cleared off, he must verify this; otherwise he takes his mortgage at his own risk (*k*).

The conduct which will postpone a legal mortgagee to a prior equitable incumbrance of which he had no notice may be either actual fraud or negligence.

Postponement by fraud.—Actual fraud is an obvious ground for postponement (*l*), and a mortgagee will be postponed to a subsequent incumbrance which has been created either through his own fraud or the fraud of his solicitor. In the latter case, however, it must be shown that, at the time of the fraud, the relation of solicitor and client subsisted; it is not sufficient that it had previously subsisted (*m*).

"Gross" negligence.—The negligence which will cause a legal mortgagee to be postponed usually occurs either in regard to inquiries as to the title of the mortgagor, or as to the title deeds, and in the latter case it may consist of failure to get the title deeds into the mortgagee's possession, or parting with them after they have been in his possession. Thus, a legal mortgagee will be postponed to a prior equitable incumbrancer who holds the deeds, if he has not investigated the title at all (*n*), or has not inquired for the deeds (*o*), or, having inquired, has accepted an insufficient reason for their non-production.

"Gross negligence" is an expression which is incapable of precise definition; but in *Oliver* v. *Hinton* (*p*) it was used to indicate a degree

---

(*i*) See p. 255, *supra*.
(*j*) [1937] Ch. 81; [1936] 2 All E.R. 1108.
(*k*) *Jared* v. *Clements*, [1903] 1 Ch. 428.
(*l*) See *Birch* v. *Ellames* (1794), 2 Anst. 427 (legal mortgage antedated so as to validate it in bankruptcy, and no inquiry made as to the object of a prior deposit of the deeds).
(*m*) See *Finch* v. *Shaw*, *Colyer* v. *Finch* (1854), 19 Beav. 500; affd. *sub nom. Colyer* v. *Finch* (1856), 5 H.L.C. 905. See also *Peter* v. *Russell* (1716), 1 Eq. Ca. Abr. 321.
(*n*) See *Oliver* v. *Hinton*, [1899] 2 Ch. 264.
(*o*) *Hewitt* v. *Loosemore* (1851), 9 Hare, 449; especially if the abstention from inquiry was to avoid having knowledge of a prior incumbrance: *Ratcliffe* v. *Barnard* (1871), 6 Ch. App. 652. See also *Berwick & Co.* v. *Price*, [1905] 1 Ch. 632.
(*p*) [1899] 2 Ch. 264 (C.A.). And see *Walker* v. *Linom*, [1907] 2 Ch. 104.

of negligence which made it unjust to enforce the natural order of priority. It was described in *Hudston* v. *Viney* (*q*), as follows:

"It must at least be carelessness of so aggravated a nature as to amount to the neglect of precautions which the ordinary reasonable man would have observed, and to indicate an attitude of mental indifference to obvious risks".

In a case in which, although there is no previous mortgage, the legal mortgagee leaves the deeds under the control of the mortgagor (*r*), or, having obtained possession of them, returns them to the mortgagor, with the result that a subsequent mortgage or other disposition of the estate is accepted on the faith of the deeds, the legal mortgagee will lose his priority, though, even here, it has been said (*s*) that the legal mortgagee will be postponed only if his conduct amounts to such gross negligence as to be equivalent to fraud.

In fact, however, fraud and negligence, even when it is gross negligence, are of a different nature, the one importing a design to commit the fraud, the other an omission due to carelessness or want of thought or attention (*t*), and the idea that there must be fraud has been dropped (*u*). To postpone the legal mortgagee it is sufficient that there has been gross negligence on his part (*w*). And where the equitable incumbrance precedes the legal mortgage, gross negligence is the negligence described by LINDLEY, M.R., in *Oliver* v. *Hinton* (*x*) of such a type as would render it unjust to deprive the prior incumbrancer of his priority. The rule is the same with respect to the postponement of the legal mortgagee to a subsequent equitable incumbrancer. He will be postponed if, owing to his conduct in regard to the deeds, it has been possible for the subsequent incumbrance to be created so that it would be inequitable to allow him to rely on his priority (*y*).

Negligence as to title.—As regards inquiry into title, priority will not be forfeited by the neglect of the mortgagee, or his solicitor, to obtain or inquire for an instrument recited in a deed of remote date which forms the root of title, if there was no wilful neglect on the part of the mortgagee (*z*). Nor where, from the smallness of the

---

(*q*) [1921] 1 Ch. 98, at p. 104, *per* EVE, J.

(*r*) *E.g.*, *Agra Bank, Ltd.* v. *Barry* (1874), L.R. 7 H.L. 135.

(*s*) *Evans* v. *Bicknell* (1801), 6 Ves. 174, 189, where Lord ELDON used the phrase "gross negligence that amounts to evidence of a fraudulent intention".
The onus of proving gross negligence is on the person alleging it: *Carter* v. *Carter* (1857), 3 K. & J. 617.

(*t*) *Northern Counties Fire Insurance Co.* v. *Whipp* (1884), 26 Ch. D. 482 (C.A.), at p. 494, *per* FRY, L.J.

(*u*) In *Northern Counties Fire Insurance Co.* v. *Whipp, supra*, a case in which a mortgagee had parted with the deeds, FRY, L.J., stated that fraud was required both for failing to obtain the deeds and to retain them. But it is now accepted by the text-book writers that gross negligence is sufficient; see *Coote on Mortgages* (9th Edn.), p. 1341; Waldock, *The Law of Mortgages* (2nd Edn.), pp. 395–397; Sykes, *The Law of Securities* (2nd Edn.), p. 327.

(*w*) See *Hunt* v. *Elmes* (1860), 2 De G.F. & J. 578; *Ratcliffe* v. *Barnard* (1871), 6 Ch. App. 652 (C.A.).

(*x*) [1899] 2 Ch. 264 (C.A.).

(*y*) See *Cottey* v. *National Provincial Bank of England, Ltd.* (1904), 48 Sol. Jo. 589; 20 T.L.R. 607; *Walker* v. *Linom*, [1907] 2 Ch. 104; *cf. Hudston* v. *Viney*, [1921] 1 Ch. 98. And see *Tsang Chuen* v. *Li Po Kwai*, [1932] A.C. 715 (P.C.).

(*z*) *Finch* v. *Shaw, Colyer* v. *Finch* (1854), 19 Beav. 500; affd. (1856), 5 H.L.C. 905; *Hudston* v. *Viney, supra*.

purchase money and other circumstances, the cost of investigation of title would have made it practically impossible (*a*).

Negligence as to obtaining the deeds.—As regards inquiry for the deeds and obtaining delivery of them, the legal mortgagee will not be postponed if he has made inquiry and has failed to obtain the deeds through the deceit of the mortgagor; if, for instance, the latter assures him that he has delivered to him all the deeds (*b*); or if a reasonable excuse has been given for their not being delivered (*c*). The question, what is a reasonable excuse, must always be decided in the light of the particular circumstances of the case. Where the defendant, a farmer, took a legal mortgage of a leasehold interest from a solicitor but failed to obtain possession of the lease, which in fact had already been deposited with the plaintiff, on the mortgagor's excuse that he was then busy but he would give it to him at another time, the defendant was not postponed to the plaintiff (*d*). In some cases, however, false statements as to the place or nature of the custody of the deeds have been held not to relieve the person who accepts them from notice of the real facts, when by inquiry the truth could easily have been discovered (*e*).

Mortgagee's right to the deeds.—Ordinarily, the legal owner is entitled to the deeds, and where a purchaser of land took a conveyance, but allowed the vendor to retain the deeds, and the vendor then mortgaged the land and delivered the deeds to the mortgagee, the purchaser was held to be entitled to recover the deeds from the mortgagee (*f*). Before the Judicature Acts, however, if a legal mortgagee had to come into equity to establish his priority, his suit was subject to the rule that equity would not interfere to deprive a purchaser for value without notice of any advantage he had obtained, and therefore would not order a subsequent mortgagee by deposit to give up the deeds unless he was paid off, leaving the legal mortgagee otherwise to his remedy at law (*g*). This doctrine, however, applied only as against a legal mortgagee. Where both the incumbrances were equitable, so that the matter arose solely in equity, a final order was made, and the court both declared the priority (*h*), and, if appropriate, ordered the deeds to be given up (*i*); and, since the Judicature Acts, this rule is applied whether the claim to the deeds is made by a legal or equitable mortgagee, so that if he establishes his priority, he will have an order for the delivery of the deeds (*k*).

(*a*) *Kettlewell* v. *Watson* (1882), 21 Ch. D. 685.

(*b*) *Roberts* v. *Croft* (1857), 2 De G. & J. 1; *Hunt* v. *Elmes* (1860), 2 De G.F. & J. 578; *Dixon* v. *Mucklestone* (1872), 8 Ch. App. 155.   And see *Ratcliffe* v. *Barnard, supra;* *Colyer* v. *Finch, supra.*

(*c*) *Hewitt* v. *Loosemore* (1851), 9 Hare, 449; *Espin* v. *Pemberton* (1859), 4 Drew 333.

(*d*) *Hewitt* v. *Loosemore, supra.*

(*e*) *Maxfield* v. *Burton* (1873), L.R. 17 Eq. 15; *Spencer* v. *Clarke* (1878), 9 Ch. D. 137: but see *Agra Bank* v. *Barry* (1874), L.R. 7 H.L. 135.

(*f*) *Harrington* v. *Price* (1832), 3 B. & Ad. 170; see *Smith* v. *Chichester* (1842), 2 Dr. & War. 393; and *cf. Hunt* v. *Elmes, supra* (leasehold).

(*g*) *Head* v. *Egerton* (1734), 2 P. Wms. 280; *Heath* v. *Crealock* (1874), 10 Ch. App. 22; *Waldy* v. *Gray* (1875), L.R. 20 Eq. 238.

(*h*) *Stackhouse* v. *Countess of Jersey* (1861), 1 Johns. & H. 721.

(*i*) *Newton* v. *Newton* (1868), L.R. 6 Eq. 135; reversed on the facts, 4 Ch. App. 143.

(*k*) *Manners* v. *Mew* (1885), 29 Ch. D. 725, 732; *Re Ingham, Jones* v. *Ingham,* [1893] 1 Ch. 352.

Negligence in custody of deeds.—The same principles apply in cases in which the mortgagee has had, but has afterwards given up, or otherwise lost, the possession of the title deeds. If, under the circumstances, it can be inferred that he did this fraudulently, or if "gross negligence" can be imputed to him, he will be postponed, not only in favour of the particular incumbrancer, who by the legal mortgagee's conduct has been induced to advance money on the estate, but also in favour of all later incumbrancers, who, after making proper inquiries as to the deeds, have lent their money in ignorance of the original security (*l*).

Delivery of deeds for raising money.—When the first mortgagee allows the mortgagor to have the custody of the deeds for the express purpose of creating a security up to a limited amount, which shall have precedence to his own, and the mortgagor raises a larger sum, the first mortgage will be postponed to the whole sum so raised (*m*); and the mortgagee will be postponed where he delivers the deeds to the mortgagor, in order to make a second mortgage, upon the faith that the mortgagor will disclose the first mortgage, which he omits to do (*n*).

Similarly, where the owner of property delivers the deeds to an agent in order to raise money up to a specified amount, and the agent raises money in excess of that amount and misappropriates the excess, the owner can only redeem on payment of the full amount raised (*o*). This, however, depends on the principle that an owner cannot as against an innocent purchaser or mortgagee, limit an authority which he has conferred; and the former cases depend, not strictly on negligence, but upon the estoppel arising out of the circumstance that the legal mortgagee has enabled the mortgagor to represent himself as unincumbered owner.

Statutory saving for possession of deeds.—The Law of Property Act 1925, provides:

> **13.**—This Act shall not prejudicially affect the right or interest of any person arising out of or consequent on the possession by him of any documents relating to a legal estate in land, nor affect any question arising out of or consequent upon any omission to obtain or any other absence of possession by any person of any documents relating to a legal estate in land.

Thus, questions of priority, so far as they depend on the possession of the deeds, are subject to the same considerations as before 1926 (*p*).

It should be remembered, with regard to this provision, that a first mortgagee has a right to the possession of the title deeds, whether the mortgage be by demise, sub-demise or charge by way of legal mortgage (*q*).

Where legal mortgagee not postponed.—The legal mortgagee is

(*l*) *Perry-Herrick* v. *Attwood* (1857), 2 De G. & J. 21; *Clarke* v. *Palmer* (1882), 21 Ch. D. 124.

(*m*) *Brocklesby* v. *Temperance Permanent Building Society*, [1895] A.C. 173 (H.L.).

(*n*) *Briggs* v. *Jones* (1870), L.R. 10 Eq. 92; see *Re Lambert's Estate* (1884), 13 L.R. Ir. 234.

(*o*) *Brocklesby* v. *Temperance, etc., Society, supra*; *Rimmer* v. *Webster*, [1902] 2 Ch. 163.

(*p*) See *Beddoes* v. *Shaw*, [1937] Ch. 81; [1936] 2 All E.R. 1108.

(*q*) See Law of Property Act 1925, ss. 85 (1), 86 (1).

not, however, required to guarantee the safety of the deeds, and if in spite of his having taken proper precautions for their custody, they come into the hands of the mortgagor and are used by him for creating a subsequent incumbrance, the legal mortgagee will not be postponed (*r*). Nor will he be postponed if he hands the deeds to the mortgagor upon his requesting them for a reasonable purpose (*s*); though if this purpose is only temporary, the mortgagee will be postponed if he omits to see to the return of the deeds (*t*).

The mortgagee will not be postponed if the deeds come to the mortgagor's hands by the wrongful act of a third person to whom the mortgagor had properly delivered them (*u*). Nor will he be postponed, where it cannot be discovered by what means the deeds come back into the mortgagor's possession, provided there is nothing to show that he was enabled by the first mortgagee to commit the fraud; the mere possession of the deeds by the mortgagor, without evidence that he got them through the neglect or fraud of the mortgagee, not being enough to postpone the latter (*x*). And a legal mortgagee is not guilty of negligence in omitting to give notice of his mortgage to a prior equitable mortgagee who holds the deeds, with the result that the prior equitable mortgage is paid off and a new equitable mortgage created without notice of the legal mortgage (*y*).

Postponement of equitable incumbrancer.—As between equitable incumbrancers the prima facie rule, that the incumbrancers rank in order of time (*z*), may be displaced by the fraud or negligence of the earlier incumbrancer. It has been seen that, originally, the negligence which would postpone a legal mortgagee was described as negligence so gross as to be equivalent to fraud (*a*). The negligence which will postpone an equitable incumbrancer appears never to have been described in these terms, and a distinction has been drawn between the gross negligence which will postpone a legal mortgagee and the slighter negligence which will postpone a prior equitable mortgagee to a later (*b*). The question in the latter case is, whether the earlier incumbrancer has acted in such a way that he is not justified in insisting on his prima facie priority (*c*). According to the modern view,

---

(*r*) *Northern Counties of England Fire Insurance Co.* v. *Whipp* (1884), 26 Ch. D. 482 (C.A.).

(*s*) *E.g.*, that the mortgagor wants the deeds to enable him to grant a building lease advantageous to the estate: *Peter* v. *Russell* (1716), 2 Vern. 726. And see *Martinez* v. *Cooper* (1826), 2 Russ. 198; *Hall* v. *West End Advance Co.* (1883), Cab. & El. 161. As to the suggestion that on the legal mortgagee parting with the deeds, his mortgage would become a puisne mortgage and would require to be registered as a land charge, so that if not registered it would be void as against a subsequent incumbrancer, see p. 46, *supra*.

(*t*) *Waldron* v. *Sloper* (1852), 1 Drew, 193; dist'd. in *Re Vernon* (1886), 33 Ch. D. 402; and see *Dowle* v. *Saunders* (1864), 2 Hem. & M. 242.

(*u*) *Taylor* v. *London and County Banking Co.*, [1901] 2 Ch. 231.

(*x*) *Allen* v. *Knight* (1847), 11 Jur. 527.

(*y*) *Grierson* v. *National Provincial Bank of England*, [1913] 2 Ch. 18.

(*z*) For the modern application of the same rule to things in action and equitable interests in land, see Law of Property Act 1925, s. 137 (1).

(*a*) See p. 450, *supra*.

(*b*) *Farrand* v. *Yorkshire Banking Co.* (1888), 40 Ch. D. 182.

(*c*) *Kettlewell* v. *Watson* (1882), 21 Ch. D. 685; *National Provincial Bank of England* v. *Jackson* (1886), 33 Ch. D. 1.

however, this amounts to the test for the negligence which will postpone a legal mortgagee. It is such negligence as would render it unjust to deprive the prior equitable incumbrancer of his priority (*d*). It would seem, therefore, that there is now in effect no difference between the tests for the two cases, and in each the question is, whether the conduct of the legal mortgagee or the equitable mortgagee has been such as will justifiably deprive him of the priority given to him either by the possession of the legal estate or by his being first in time (*e*).

Effect of possession of the deeds.—When two equitable interests are of the same quality, so that they furnish in themselves no ground for saying that one is superior to the other in this respect, the fact that the incumbrancer who is the later in time has possession of the deeds may give him the better equity and cause the earlier incumbrance to be postponed (*f*). This test prevails, however, only when there has been some default on the part of the prior equitable incumbrancer in respect of the deeds, and in effect he is postponed by reason of his default or negligence (*g*); or, in a case where the deeds have been left in the possession of the mortgagor, because he has thereby been enabled to deal with the property as if it were free from incumbrance (*h*). And similarly, the prior equitable incumbrancer will be postponed where, without adequate reason, he parts with the deeds after he has had them in his possession (*i*). But it is otherwise where there is no default attributable to the prior incumbrancer (*k*).

Moreover, this rule applies only where the prior equitable owner ought to have the deeds in his possession. This is usually the case with an equitable incumbrancer, but a beneficiary is not guilty of negligence if he leaves the deeds with the trustee, and is therefore not postponed to a mortgagee with whom the trustee pledges them in breach of trust; it makes no difference that the mortgaged property belongs partly to the trustee himself (*l*). This will be so, however, only where the deeds have in the first place come into the possession of the trustee. If he negligently omits to get them in, and is postponed on this ground, the beneficiary is postponed also (*m*).

(*d*) See p. 450, *supra*.

(*e*) This view was most emphatically expressed by KAY, J., in *Taylor* v. *Russell*, [1891] 1 Ch. 8, 17. His judgment was reversed by the Court of Appeal ([1891] 1 Ch. 24), but on another point, and the question of negligence as between rival equities was not discussed. In the House of Lords ([1892] A.C. 244, 262), Lord MACNAGHTEN referred to the point, but only to say that he was not convinced of the correctness of KAY, J.'s view. And see *Taylor* v. *London and County Banking Co.*, [1901] 2 Ch. 260, *per* STIRLING, L.J. Since priorities are now mainly determined by registration, the question is unlikely to be determined.

(*f*) See *Rice* v. *Rice* (1854), 2 Drew. 73, at p. 81, *per* KINDERSLEY, V.-C. Also *Nairn* v. *Prowse* (1862), 6 Ves. 752. And *McCarthy and Stone, Ltd.* v. *Julian S. Hodge & Co., Ltd.*, [1971] 2 All E.R. 973.

(*g*) *Farrand* v. *Yorkshire Banking Co.* (1888), 40 Ch. D. 182. And see *Flinn* v. *Pountain* (1889), 58 L.J. Ch. 389.

(*h*) *Layard* v. *Maud* (1867), L.R. 4 Eq. 397.

(*i*) *Waldron* v. *Sloper* (1852), 1 Drew. 193.

(*k*) *Allen* v. *Knight* (1847), 5 Hare, 272; *Re Castell and Brown, Ltd.*, [1898] 1 Ch. 315.

(*l*) *Cory* v. *Eyre* (1863), 1 De G.J. & S. 149, 169; *Bradley* v. *Riches* (1878), 9 Ch. D. 189. See p. 447, *supra*.

(*m*) *Walker* v. *Linom*, [1907] 2 Ch. 104. An equitable mortgagee by deposit of earlier title deeds will retain his priority over a mortgagee by deposit of the subsequent deeds, if he was led by the mortgagor to believe that they were the whole of the deeds: *Roberts* v. *Croft* (1857), 2 De G. & J. 1; *Dixon* v. *Muckleston* (1872), 8 Ch. App. 155.

Estoppel.—A similar principle applies where an equitable incumbrancer acts in such a way as to enable the owner of the land to represent that the incumbrance no longer exists. Where, for instance, the incumbrancer executes a conveyance containing a receipt for the money due to him, although it is not in fact paid (*n*).

This is in accordance with the doctrine of estoppel by representation, recognised both at law and in equity, namely, that where one by his words or conduct wilfully causes another to believe the existence of a certain state of things, and induces him to act on that belief, and the latter in so doing alters his own position, the former cannot aver against him the existence of a different state of things (*o*).

Misrepresentation.—Both priority in respect of possession of the legal estate and priority in time operate to the advantage of a mortgagee only if the equities are in other respects equal. Another case where the equities are not thus equal is where a mortgagee has been guilty of misrepresentation. The displacement of priority may arise from either implied or express misrepresentation. If, for instance, the first mortgagee leaves the deeds in the possession of the mortgagor, who requires them for the purpose of raising a further advance, on the understanding, however, that the existence of the prior mortgage will be disclosed, and the mortgagor conceals the prior incumbrance, the mortgagee will not, as against third parties, be able to claim that the mortgagor was acting in excess of his authority (*p*).

Conclusion.—Throughout the many and various instances of cases in which the mortgagee may lose his priority, whether it be a legal mortgagee to a prior or even subsequent equitable incumbrancer, or an equitable incumbrancer to another, and whether the grounds of such loss be actual fraud, negligence, misrepresentation or estoppel, there runs the principle that priority may be lost if the conduct of the mortgagee, who prima facie has priority, is such that it would be unjust, on the particular facts and in relation to one or more of the foregoing heads, to postpone another mortgagee whose claim is more deserving of merit.

VI—TACKING FURTHER ADVANCES

The former law of tacking.—The superiority allowed in equity to the legal estate gave rise to the doctrine of tacking. This was a particular application of the rule that a mortgagee who had the legal estate should prevail over other mortgagees of whose securities he had no notice when he made his advance.

(*n*) *Rice* v. *Rice* (1853), 2 Drew. 73; *Lloyds Bank, Ltd.* v. *Bullock*, [1896] 2 Ch. 192; *Rimmer* v. *Webster*, [1902] 2 Ch. 163, 175. See also *Jared* v. *Clements*, [1903] 1 Ch. 428.

(*o*) *Pickard* v. *Sears* (1837), 6 A. & E. 469, *per* Lord DENMAN, C.J.] For cases on estoppel in the present context, see *Kettlewell* v. *Watson* (1884), 26 Ch. D. 501; *Cannock* v. *Jauncey* (1857), 27 L.J. Ch. 57.

(*p*) *Perry-Herrick* v. *Attwood* (1857), 2 De G. & J. 21; *Northern Counties Fire Insurance Co.* v. *Whipp* (1884), 26 Ch. D. 482. See FARWELL, J., in *Rimmer* v. *Webster*, [1902] 2 Ch. 163, at p. 173: "When . . . the owner is found to have given the vendor or borrower the means of representing himself as the beneficial owner, the case forms one of actual authority apparently equivalent to absolute ownership, and involving the right to deal with the property as owner, and any limitations on this generality must be proved to have been brought to the knowledge of the purchaser or mortgagee."

Two forms of tacking.—If a legal mortgagee made a further advance on the security of the estate, and had at the time of the further advance no notice of a second mortgage, his legal estate gave priority to the further advance (*q*). If the intervening incumbrancer agreed to the further transaction, or if the prior mortgage made express provision for the extension of the security to further advances, an equitable mortgagee could also avail himself of the doctrine; in all cases, however, a mortgagee with notice, at the time of making the further advance, of a subsequent incumbrance (*i.e.*, of an intervening incumbrance) could never tack further advances against it.

The same principle applied also where, after a legal mortgage to A, and a second mortgage to B, there was a third mortgage to a different person, C, who made his advance without notice of the second mortgage. If he took a transfer of A's mortgage, he had priority, not only in respect of the first mortgage but, by virtue of the legal estate, in respect of the third as well. Consequently he could tack the third mortgage to the first and so squeeze out the second (*r*). The doctrine, applied in this form, was described as the third mortgagee's *"tabula in naufragio"* (*s*). But the effect was merely to change the order of priority, and not to alter the mode of discharging the securities by combining the debts and making the interest payable on both in the first instance, instead of the interest and principal of each in succession (*t*).

Former conditions for tacking.—But while tacking was based on the special value attached to the legal estate, it was not essential that the mortgagee claiming to tack should have the legal estate actually vested in him. It was sufficient if he had the best right to call for it (*u*). And it was sufficient if he had a partial interest in the legal estate, such as a term of years, or a security which might be used at law, such as a judgment (*x*). His claim, however, depended on the continued holding of the legal estate, and he lost the right to

---

(*q*) See (1958), 22 Conv. (N.S.) 44 (R. G. Rowley). But *quaere* whether the principle does depend on the doctrine of estates in land: see *Matzner* v. *Clyde Securities, Ltd.*, [1975] 2 N.S.W.L.R. 293.

(*r*) *Marsh* v. *Lee* (1670), 2 Ventr. 337; *Brace* v. *Duchess of Marlborough* (1728), 2 P. Wms. 491; *Wortley* v. *Birkhead* (1754), 2 Ves. Sen. 571; the court would not take from the third mortgagee the legal protection of an honest debt: *Belchier* v. *Renforth* (1764), 5 Bro. P.C. 292; *Blackwood* v. *London Chartered Bank of Australia* (1874), L.R. 5 P.C. 92, *per* Lord SELBORNE, C., at p. 111.

(*s*) This expression was attributed to HALE, C.J.; see (1728), 2 P. Wms. 491; 2 Ves. Sen. 573; but the acquisition of the legal estate in part of a security did not protect any more of the subsequent incumbrance than was charged upon that part: *Marsh* v. *Lee, supra.*

(*t*) *Latouche* v. *Dunsany* (1803), 1 Sch. & Lef. 137.

(*u*) *Wilkes* v. *Bodington* (1707), 2 Vern. 599; *Ex parte Knott* (1806), 11 Ves. 609. Thus, an incumbrancer in whose favour a declaration of trust of the legal interest had been made (*Stanhope* v. *Earl Verney* (1761), 2 Eden. 81; *Wilmot* v. *Pike* (1845), 5 Hare, 14; *Taylor* v. *London and County Banking Co.*, [1901] 2 Ch. 231, 263; but see *McCarthy and Stone, Ltd.* v. *Julian S. Hodge & Co., Ltd.*, [1971] 2 All E.R. 973), or who, having the best right to call for a transfer of that interest, had done some act short of obtaining a transfer, but equivalent to an act of ownership (*Ex parte Knott, supra*, at p. 618; *Fourth City, etc., Building Society* v. *Williams* (1879), 14 Ch. D. 140), was, for the purpose of tacking, in the same position as if he actually held the legal estate.

(*x*) *Brace* v. *Duchess of Marlborough, supra*; *Re Russell Road Purchase-Moneys* (1871), L.R. 12 Eq. 78.

tack if he parted with that estate (*y*). Further, it was necessary that he should hold both securities in his own right (*z*), and that he should have an equal equity with the mesne incumbrancer (*a*).

The legal estate might be got in either at the time of the later incumbrance which it was desired to tack, or subsequently. But while it was essential that there should be no notice of the mesne incumbrance at the time of the advance (*b*), the subsequent mortgagee could tack notwithstanding that he had notice when he got in the legal estate (*c*), that being, to use the words of Lord HARDWICKE (*d*), the very occasion that showed the necessity of taking it in. He could not, however, avail himself of a legal estate if it was got in with notice that the conveyance was a breach of trust (*e*); nor if it was got in from a satisfied mortgagee, since such a mortgagee was a trustee for the equitable incumbrancers according to their priorities (*f*). And the trustee of the mortgagor could not make use of the legal estate to alter the priorities (*g*).

It was essential to the right to tack, that the debt was either originally contracted on the credit of the estate, or, if at first it was a simple contract debt, or only a general lien upon the mortgaged property, that a specific security was taken for it without notice of the intermediate incumbrance (*h*).

Tacking against surety.—The mortgagee might also, perhaps, tack a further advance as against a surety if the contract of guarantee

---

(*y*) *Rooper* v. *Harrison* (1855), 2 K. & J. 86.

(*z*) *Morret* v. *Paske* (1740), 2 Atk. 52; *Barnett* v. *Weston* (1806), 12 Ves. 130; see *Shaw* v. *Neale* (1858), 6 H.L.C. 581.

(*a*) *Lacey* v. *Ingle* (1847), 2 Ph. 413, 419; *Rooper* v. *Harrison, supra*; as to rival equities, see pp. 446 *et seq., supra.*

(*b*) *Willoughby* v. *Willoughby* (1756), 1 Term. Rep. 763; *Brace* v. *Duchess of Marlborough, supra*; *Cooke* v. *Wilton* (1860), 29 Beav. 100. And similarly, where a prior mortgagee acquired a later incumbrance, he must have had no notice of the mesne incumbrance at the time of such acquisition: *Bedford* v. *Backhouse* (1730), 2 Eq. Cas. Abr. 615; *Morret* v. *Paske, supra.*

Where a subsequent mortgagee acquired a prior mortgage it was immaterial whether the first mortgagee, from whom the legal estate was got in, had at that time notice of the mesne incumbrance; hence a second mortgagee could not protect himself by giving notice to the first mortgagee: *Peacock* v. *Burt* (1834), 4 L.J. Ch. 33; that is, the first mortgagee could prefer which of the subsequent incumbrances he pleased; but this doctrine, though apparently accepted, was disapproved: *Bates* v. *Johnson* (1859), Johns. 304, 314; *West London Commercial Bank* v. *Reliance Building Society* (1885), 29 Ch. D. 954.

(*c*) *Blackwood* v. *London Chartered Bank of Australia* (1874), L.R. 5 P.C. 92, 111.

(*d*) *Wortley* v. *Birkhead* (1754), 2 Ves. Sen. 571, 574.

(*e*) *Saunders* v. *Dehew* (1692), 2 Vern. 271; *Taylor* v. *Russell,* [1891] 1 Ch. 8; on appeal, [1892] A.C. 244, *per* Lord MACNAGHTEN, at p. 261; *Bailey* v. *Barnes,* [1894] 1 Ch. 25; but see *Pilcher* v. *Rawlins* (1872), 7 Ch. App. 259.

(*f*) *Prosser* v. *Rice* (1859), 28 Beav. 68, 74; *Taylor* v. *Russell,* [1892] A.C. 244 (H.L.), at p. 259.

(*g*) *Ledbrook* v. *Passman* (1888), 57 L.J. Ch. 855.

(*h*) *Lacey* v. *Ingle, supra.* Hence a legal mortgagee might tack a further charge: *Lloyd* v. *Attwood* (1859), 3 De G. & J. 614. And he was allowed to tack a subsequent judgment debt: *Shepherd* v. *Titley* (1742), 2 Atk. 348; *Brace* v. *Duchess of Marlborough* (1728), 2 P. Wms. 491; *Ex parte Knott* (1806), 11 Ves. 609, since he was treated as having made a further advance on the security of the land. But a judgment creditor could not get in the first mortgage and tack his judgment debt: *Brace* v. *Duchess of Marlborough, supra*; *Ex parte Knott, supra*; *Beavan* v. *Earl of Oxford* (1856), 6 De G.M. & G. 507, 518.

did not affect his right to make further advances (*i*), and might certainly do so where he had no notice that the surety was merely a surety (*k*). But where he had notice of an intermediate charge, then, as he could not tack as against that charge, it was held that he could not in general tack as against the surety's right to the benefit of his security on payment of the first advance alone (*l*).

Tacking unsecured debts.—Although as against mesne incumbrances tacking was allowed only where the debt to be tacked was incurred on the credit of the estate, and this applied also as against the mortgagor (*m*) and persons claiming under him *inter vivos* (*n*); yet, after the death of the mortgagor, such debts could be tacked against his successors in title to the equity of redemption, so far as the land was assets in their hands for the payment of the unsecured debt (*o*). This, however, was allowed only to enable the mortgagee to recover his whole debt in one proceeding and so avoid circuity of action. It was not tacking in the full sense, so as to disturb the priorities and enable the mortgagee to exclude a mesne incumbrancer (*p*)

Mortgage to cover further advances.—As previously mentioned (*q*), a legal mortgagee who made a further advance without notice of a second mortgage could tack his further advance (*r*) by virtue of the legal estate. But there was, in addition, a form of tacking which was independent of the legal estate. This occurred when the first mortgage was expressed to cover the advance made at the time and also further advances. In such a case the mortgagee could, by virtue of the contract, tack a further advance to the original advance as against a subsequent mortgagee who had not got the legal estate, provided that, at the time of the further advance, he had no notice of the subsequent mortgage; and a mortgage to secure a current account was on the same footing (*s*). If a further advance was made either by a legal mortgagee (*t*), or by an equitable mortgagee with the best right to the legal estate, and this further advance was made without notice of the intervening mortgage, it might be tacked and priority

---

(*i*) *Williams* v. *Owen* (1843), 13 Sim. 597; *Farebrother* v. *Wodehouse* (1856), 23 Beav. 18; dissented from in *Forbes* v. *Jackson* (1882), 19 Ch. D. 615; but followed in *Nicholas* v. *Ridley*, [1904] 1 Ch. 192. This case was, however, decided by the Court of Appeal on other grounds: *ibid.*, p. 205.

(*k*) *Re Toogood* (1889), 61 L.T. 19; *Nicholas* v. *Ridley*, *supra*.

(*l*) *Drew* v. *Lockett* (1863), 32 Beav. 499; *Forbes* v. *Jackson*, *supra*; *Leicestershire Banking Co.* v. *Hawkins* (1900), 16 T.L.R. 317.

(*m*) *Challis* v. *Casborn* (1715), Prec. Ch. 407.

(*n*) *Coleman* v. *Winch* (1721), 1 P. Wms. 775; *Richardson* v. *Horton* (1843), 7 Beav. 112.

(*o*) *Heams* v. *Bance* (1748), 3 Atk. 630; *Coleman* v. *Winch*, *supra*; *Thomas* v. *Thomas* (1856), 22 Beav. 341.

(*p*) *Pile* v. *Pile* (1875), 23 W.R. 440; see *Morret* v. *Paske* (1740), 2 Atk. 52; *Irby* v. *Irby* (1855), 22 Beav. 217. As to the extension of the liability of real estate to simple contract debts, with the extension also of this right of tacking, see Administration of Estates Act 1833, now repealed and reproduced by Administration of Estates Act 1925, s. 32.

(*q*) See p. 456, *supra*.

(*r*) There may be a further advance, though no money is paid directly to the mortgagor: *Re Smith, Lawrence* v.*Kitson*, [1918] 2 Ch. 405. *E.g.*, further facilities by a bank under an overdraft, further liability for goods supplied by the mortgagee. And see footnote (*l*) to p. 461, *infra*.

(*s*) *Hopkinson* v. *Rolt* (1861), 9 H.L.C. 514; *Calisher* v. *Forbes* (1871), 7 Ch. App. 109; see *Re Weniger's Policy*, [1910] 2 Ch. 291, 295.

(*t*) *Wyllie* v. *Pollen* (1863), 3 De G.J. & S. 596.

resulted in such a case from the superiority attached to the legal estate. If, however, the contract expressly provided for the extension of the security to cover further advances, the device of tacking might be used by either a legal or an equitable mortgagee.

But notice of a subsequent mortgage prevented the first mortgagee from gaining priority for advances subsequently made, and it was decided that the same rule applied even where the first mortgage contained a covenant to make further advances (*u*).

Tacking by agreement.—It was possible, also, for the mortgagee to tack after having secured the consent of the intervening incumbrancer, and in this case it was immaterial whether the first mortgage was legal or equitable.

Abolition of tacking.—The doctrine of tacking was unjust to the mesne incumbrancer whose claim was defeated by the mere chance of the later incumbrancer's getting in the legal estate—a matter which was irrelevant to the respective merits of the claims—and it was abolished by s. 7 of the Vendor and Purchaser Act 1874. That section, however, was repealed by the Land Transfer Act 1875 (*a*), s. 129, and for the country generally (*b*) the doctrine remained in force until 1 January, 1926.

The abolition of tacking, which was unsuccessfully attempted by the Vendor and Purchaser Act 1874, is repeated, and this time, it may be presumed, finally, by the Law of Property Act 1925 (*c*), while at the same time provision is made for tacking further advances. Thus:

> **94.**—(1) After the commencement of this Act, a prior mortgagee (*d*) shall have a right to make further advances to rank in priority to subsequent mortgages (whether legal or equitable (*e*))—

(*u*) *West* v. *Williams*, [1899] 1 Ch. 132 (C.A.). The extension of the rule as to notice, via *Hopkinson* v. *Rolt, supra,* to the instant case, shows an increasing restriction by the courts of this form of tacking. Originally it was held that where the second mortgagee took with notice that the first mortgage was to cover further advances, the first mortgagee might tack advances made subsequently to the second mortgage, and it was folly of the second mortgagee with notice to take such a security: *Gordon* v. *Graham* (1716), 2 Eq. Cas. Abr. 598. This was overruled by *Hopkinson* v. *Rolt, supra*; see *London and County Banking Co.* v. *Ratcliffe* (1881), 6 App. Cas. 722 (H.L.); *Bradford Banking Co.* v. *Briggs* (1886), 12 App. Cas. 29 (H.L.); *Union Bank of Scotland* v. *National Bank of Scotland* (1886), 12 App. Cas 53 (H.L.); *Matzner* v. *Clyde Securities, Ltd.,* [1975] 2 N.S.W.L.R. 293.

The principle that notice of a subsequent incumbrance prevents a first mortgagee from gaining priority for further advances applies also to a company claiming a lien on shares of a member for debts incurred after it has received notice of an incumbrance on the shares (*Bradford Banking Co.* v. *Briggs, supra*), and applies also to mortgages of ships (*The Benwell Tower* (1895), 72 L.T. 664).

(*a*) The abolition took effect from the commencement of the former Act, namely, 7 August, 1874. The latter Act commenced on 1 January, 1876, and the repeal took effect as from 7 August, 1874, except as to anything duly done under the Act of 1874 before 1 January, 1875. Thus a legal estate acquired between those two dates seems to have given no right to tack: see *Robinson* v. *Trevor* (1883), 12 Q.B.D. 423, 432 (partly overruled on another ground by *Hosking* v. *Smith* (1888), 13 App. Cas. 582).

(*b*) There was an exception for land within the jurisdiction of the Yorkshire Registries: see Yorkshire Registers Act 1884, s. 16.

(*c*) The *tabula in naufragio* form of tacking survives where the contest is between persons other than mortgagees; see *McCarthy and Stone, Ltd.* v. *Julian S. Hodge & Co., Ltd.,* [1971] 2 All E.R. 973.

(*d*) This term includes both legal and equitable mortgagees; where it is restricted to legal mortgagees—that is, mortgagees by demise or chargees by way of legal mortgage, the term "legal mortgagee" is used: Law of Property Act 1925, s. 205 (1) (xvi).

(*e*) Thus, as regards subsequent mortgages, no distinction according as they are legal or equitable can arise. As to equitable mortgages, see *Wormald* v. *Maitland*

(a) if an arrangement has been made to that effect with the subsequent mortgagees; or

(b) if he had no notice of such subsequent mortgages at the time when the further advance was made by him; or

(c) whether or not he had such notice as aforesaid, where the mortgage imposes an obligation on him to make such further advances.

This subsection applies whether or not the prior mortgage was made expressly for securing further advances.

(2) In relation to the making of further advances after the commencement of this Act a mortgagee shall not be deemed to have notice of a mortgage merely by reason that it was registered as a land charge or in a local deeds registry, if it was not so registered at the time when the original mortgage was created (f) or when the last search (if any) by or on behalf of the mortgagee was made, whichever last happened.

This subsection only applies where the prior mortgage was made expressly for securing a current account or other further advances.

(3) Save in regard to the making of further advances as aforesaid, the right to tack is hereby abolished:

Provided that nothing in this Act shall affect any priority acquired before the commencement of this Act by tacking, or in respect of further advances made without notice of a subsequent incumbrance or by arrangement with the subsequent incumbrancer.

(4) This section applies to mortgages of land made before or after the commencement of this Act, but not to charges registered under the Land Registration Act 1925, or to any enactment replaced by that Act.

Saving for further advances.—Section 94 first prescribes the cases in which tacking is still permissible. They are confined to further advances, and there are different provisions according as the prior mortgage is made expressly for the securing of further advances or not.

In order to come within the cases mentioned in sub-s. (1), the prior mortgage may be either for a single sum or it may be a security also for further advances, and then tacking is permitted:

(a) If an arrangement has been made to that effect with the subsequent mortgagees.

Obviously the subsequent mortgagees can postpone their mortgages to further advances by the prior mortgagee, and this provision may have been inserted to avoid any question as to whether the general prohibition of tacking in sub-s. (3) precluded tacking even by consent (g).

(1866), 35 L.J. Ch. 69; *Calisher* v. *Forbes* (1871), 7 Ch. App. 109. Where a spouse's rights of occupation are by virtue of the Matrimonial Homes Act 1967, s. 2 a charge on the estate or interest of the other spouse and that estate or interest is the subject of a mortgage, the charge, if registered as a land charge after the date of the creation of the mortgage is for the purposes of s. 94, deemed to be a mortgage subsequent in date to the first mentioned mortgage: Matrimonial Homes Act 1967, s. 2 (8).

(f) Section 94 (2) originally read "date of the original advance", and the words "time when the original mortgage was created" were substituted by the Law of Property (Amendment) Act 1926, s. 7, and Sched.

(g) A transferee of mortgaged land takes subject to the state of the debt at the time of the transfer: see p. 251, *supra*. A transferee of a mortgage subsequent to an earlier mortgage under which further advances have been made steps into the shoes of the transferor and cannot stand in a better position than the transferor (see p. 251, *supra*), so if the transferor agreed to a further advance and postponement of his mortgage, the transferee is in the same position. For registered charges, in respect of which s. 94 is excluded (by sub-s. (4) thereof), see p. 462, *infra*.

(b) If [the prior mortgagee] had no notice of such subsequent
mortgages at the time when the further advance was made
by him.

Under the former law, if the prior mortgage did not cover further
advances, the further advance could only be tacked by virtue of the
legal estate. If the prior mortgage covered further advances, the
further advance could be tacked by virtue of the contract. In either
case the prior mortgagee must not have had notice of the subsequent
mortgage at the time of the further advance (*h*). This clause retains
only the requirement that there shall be no notice, and dispenses alike
with the possession of the legal estate and the necessity for the mortgage
being expressed to cover further advances. It can be said, therefore,
to introduce an extension of the doctrine of tacking. A prior mortgagee,
though he is only an equitable mortgagee—for instance a mortgagee by
deposit of deeds—and though his mortgage is not expressed to cover
further advances, may tack a further advance provided he has no
notice of the subsequent mortgage. This extension will be effective
if the subsequent mortgage is not registered, but, if it is registered,
the registration will constitute notice.

Current accounts, etc.—While, therefore, this clause appears to
retain the former law as to tacking in the case of a mortgage made to
cover further advances, and even to extend the law where the mortgage
is not so made, the practical effect, if it stood alone, would be to
abolish the former facilities for obtaining further advances; in particular where the mortgage to cover such advances is a mortgage to
secure a current account with a bank. Since registration of a subsequent
mortgage constitutes notice (*i*), no cheque drawn against the account
while it was in debit could safely be honoured, and no advance could
otherwise be made to a customer, without fresh search in the appropriate register. Accordingly, the rule that registration constitutes
notice is excluded by sub-s. (2) in cases where the prior mortgage "was
made expressly for securing a current account or other further
advances". This preserves the former law as to mortgages of this
nature. The prior mortgagee cannot tack if, at the time of the further
advance, he has notice, actual or constructive, of the subsequent
mortgage, other than the statutory notice by registration (*k*); but,
provided he searched the register at the time when the original mortgage
was created, he need not search it again on making further advances (*l*).

(*h*) *Hopkinson* v. *Rolt* (1861), 9 H.L.C. 514.
(*i*) See p. 442, *supra*.
(*k*) That is, the doctrine of *Hopkinson* v. *Rolt* (1861), 9 H.L.C. 514, is preserved.
(*l*) Under the former law, when tacking depended upon the contract in the original
mortgage, and that mortgage covered only further advances up to a specified limit,
any advance beyond the limit could be tacked only by virtue of the legal estate, if the
mortgagee had it: see *Hopkinson* v. *Rolt*, *supra*. Under s. 94 (1) tacking depends
neither on the legal estate nor on the contract, and under that sub-section an advance
beyond the limit can be tacked provided a new security is taken, and provided, of course,
there is no notice; but the benefit of sub-s. (2) can probably be obtained only where
the further advance is within the authorised limit. A mortgage "made expressly for
securing a current account or other further advances" appears to refer to the account
or advance as authorised by the mortgage. See generally (1958), 22 Conv. (N.S.) 44
(R. G. Rowley); and p. 458, *supra*.

(c)　Whether or not [the prior mortgagee] had notice as aforesaid, where the mortgage imposes an obligation on him to make such further advances.

In this case the mortgage will be made expressly for securing the further advance (*m*). The right to tack does not depend on the possession of the legal estate. Formerly it would have depended on the contract; now it depends on the statute, but the effect of notice has been altered. Formerly the prior mortgagee could not tack a further advance made after notice of a subsequent mortgage, even though he was under an obligation to make it (*n*). Now he can perform his contract and tack the further advance notwithstanding notice.

Subject to the foregoing provisions as to further advances, the right to tack is abolished. Since the right to tack further advances by virtue of the contract is preserved, this abolition in effect relates only to tacking by virtue of the legal estate (*o*). Thus, the doctrine of the "*tabula in naufragio*" is gone (*p*), and even if there had not been this express abolition, it would have ceased to operate as between successive formal mortgages, since these are now legal mortgages, although it would have remained as between legal mortgages and equitable charges.

Effect of rule in Clayton's Case.—Where a prior mortgage is made to cover a current account with a bank and notice of a subsequent mortgage is received, the rule in *Clayton's Case* (*q*) applies if the account continues to be operated upon. Subsequent payments into the account are credited to the overdraft existing at the time of the notice (*r*) and, in effect, these are for the benefit of the subsequent mortgagee. He takes subject only to the overdraft at that time, and the reduction of the overdraft correspondingly improves his security. This result can be avoided by the bank's closing the account, and, if it thinks fit, allowing the mortgagor to open a new account into which future payments will be made.

Registered charge for further advances.—Registered charges on registered land are excluded from s. 94 of the Law of Property Act 1925, and further advances on the security of such charges are subject to s. 30 of the Land Registration Act 1925:

30.—(1) Where a registered charge is made for securing further advances, the registrar shall, before making any entry on the register which would prejudicially affect the priority of any further advance thereunder, give to the proprietor of the charge, at his registered address, notice by registered post of the intended entry, and the proprietor of the charge shall not, in respect of any further advance, be affected by such entry, unless the advance is made after the date when the notice ought to have been received in due course of post.

(*m*) For the meaning of further advance, see the previous footnote.
(*n*) *West* v. *Williams*, [1899] 1 Ch. 132 (C.A.).
(*o*) But see (1957), 21 Conv. (N.S.) 195, at p. 196 (V. T. H. Delany).
(*p*) *I.e.*, in the context of mortgages at least: see *McCarthy and Stone, Ltd.* v. *Julian S. Hodge & Co., Ltd.*, [1971] 2 All E.R. 973.
(*q*) (1816), 1 Mer. 572. And see p. 544, *infra*.
(*r*) *Deeley* v. *Lloyds Bank, Ltd.*, [1912] A.C. 756 (H.L.); see *Re Chute's Estate*, [1914] 1 I.R. 180.

(2) If, by reason of any failure on the part of the registrar or the post office in reference to the notice, the proprietor of the charge suffers loss in relation to a further advance, he shall be entitled to be indemnified under this Act in like manner as if a mistake had occurred in the register; but if the loss arises by reason of an omission to register or amend the address for service, no indemnity shall be payable under this Act.

(3) Where the proprietor of a charge is under an obligation, noted on the register, to make a further advance, a subsequent registered charge shall take effect subject to any further advance made pursuant to the obligation (s).

Thus in the case of registered land, the proprietor of a charge to secure further advances, but without any obligation to do so, will receive notice of any further registered charge and can refuse to make any subsequent advance (t). If the subsequent charge is not registered, then a further advance will prevail over it by virtue of the terms of the registered charge. Where there is no obligation to make further advances and a further advance is made after registration of a subsequent charge, the further advance will not have priority, unless the subsequent chargee agrees to postpone his charge (u).

VII—PRIORITY BY NOTICE TO TRUSTEES

A—THE RULE IN DEARLE v. HALL

Priority by order of notice.—Where property is held by a trustee, or other person having the legal control of property, dispositions by the beneficial owner rank in the order in which notice of the disposition is given to the trustee. This is known as the rule in *Dearle* v. *Hall* (a).

(s) This sub-section was added by the Law of Property (Amendment) Act 1926, s. 5; *cf.* Law of Property Act 1925, s. 94 (1) (c). It is submitted that the effect is the same for a transferee from the subsequent registered chargee.

(t) The fact that the charge is to secure further advances should be shown in a prominent position on the form (so that there is no chance of the Registry overlooking the point): see (1974) 118 S.J. 889. For a proposal that the registrar should not be under an obligation to give notice, see Law Commission Working Paper No. 67, para. 117.

(u) The postponement is not, it is submitted, an alteration within s. 31 of the Land Registration Act 1925 and, therefore, does not have to be by deed in form 51 under r. 150. If s. 31 is applicable, the subsequent chargee would be bound by any postponement to which he agreed even if not by deed on the ground of estoppel, but the position of the transferee from the subsequent registered chargee would be uncertain. The section provides a means of alteration of charges by deed in form 51 and completion of the alteration by entry on the register (sub-s. (3)). If the prior chargee has failed to use the method provided it can be argued that he should lose priority for his further advance against a transferee from the subsequent chargee (whether with notice of the further advance or not), because there is no entry of the further advance on the register. Section 33 of the 1925 Act, dealing with transfer of charges, does not cover the whole ground of s. 114 of the Law of Property Act 1925 (so arguably, save in so far as s. 33 is inconsistent with s. 114, s. 114 applies and the transferee steps into the shoes of the transferor—see p. 251, *supra*). Sub-section (5) of s. 33 provides that the vesting of any term in the transferee on registration under sub-s. (4) has the same effect as if the transferee had been registered as transferee for valuable consideration of the term and this is *subject to any entry to the contrary on the register*. It can be argued that this reference to "any entry", etc., means that if there is no entry of the further advance on the register, the transferee will take with priority to it.

(a) (1828), 3 Russ. 1. For a consideration of this case and *Warner Brothers Records Inc.* v. *Rollgreen, Ltd.*, [1976] Q.B. 435; [1975] 2 All E.R. 105 (C.A.), see (1975) 39 Conv. (N.S.) 261 (Diana M. Kloss). The burden of showing absence of notice is on those who claim against an earlier security: *Re Stevens, Ex parte Stevens* (1834), 4 Deac. & C. 117. The rule in *Dearle* v. *Hall* has no application where in fact the assignor has no beneficial interest he can effectively assign: see *B. S. Lyle, Ltd.* v. *Rosher*, [1958] 3 All E.R. 597.

Thus, if a bona fide incumbrancer upon a thing in action or other property to which the rule applies (b) gives notice of his own charge to the person who has control of the property, he will generally be preferred (whether he claims under the mortgagor himself or under his personal representative (c)) to an earlier claimant who has given a later or no notice (d), unless—under the former law—the holder of the property had in some way other than by formal notice acquired notice of the earlier claim (e).

If notice of two or more assignments is received by the trustees on the same day, the assignments rank in order of their dates (f). If notice is delivered at business premises after business hours, it is treated as having been given at the time at which in the ordinary course of business, it would be opened and read, that is, on the following day (g). If two assignees rank equally in point of time, they share the fund rateably (h).

The rule applies to dispositions generally, save that a mere declaration of trust made by the beneficiary need not be notified, for this leaves the interest still in his hands, and the sub-beneficiary can assert his right only through him (i).

Where a mortgage is made to cover further advances, and notice of this mortgage has been given to the trustees, further advances probably need not be notified (k); but a further advance should not be made without inquiring of the trustees whether notice of a subsequent incumbrance has been received (k). Where the mortgage does not cover further advances, notice of any further charge must be given to the trustees (l).

Where the security is on an interest in a trust fund, part of which is in court, and part in the hands of the trustees, the assignee should obtain a stop order (m) as regards the fund in court, and give notice to the trustees as to the funds in their hands, or obtain a stop notice (n).

Origin of the rule.—The rule, when first introduced, was based on the analogy of the order and disposition clause in bankruptcy (o), which, under the Bankruptcy Law then in force, applied to things in

---

(b) For property to which the rule applies, see p. 467, infra.

(c) Re Freshfield's Trusts (1879), 11 Ch. D. 198; Montefiore v. Guedalla, [1903] 2 Ch. 26.

(d) Dearle v. Hall, supra; Meux v. Bell (1841), 1 Hare, 73; Ward v. Duncombe, [1893] A.C. 369 (H.L.); Re Dallas, [1904] 2 Ch. 385 (C.A.).

(e) Lloyd v. Banks (1868), 3 Ch. App. 488; Spencer v. Clarke (1878), 9 Ch. D. 137; Saffron Walden Building Society v. Rayner (1880), 14 Ch. D. 406.

(f) Boss v. Hopkinson (1870), 18 W.R. 725.

(g) Re Dallas, [1904] 2 Ch. 385 (C.A.), at p. 395.

(h) Re Metropolitan Rail. Co., etc., Ex parte Kent (1871), 19 W.R. 596.

(i) Hill v. Peters, [1918] 2 Ch. 273.

(k) Calisher v. Forbes (1871), 7 Ch. App. 109; Re Weniger's Policy, [1910] 2 Ch. 291. See West v. Williams, [1899] 1 Ch. 132 (C.A.). Perhaps the Law of Property Act 1925, s. 94, is confined to land, but this is not clear (see sub-s. (4)).

(l) Re Weniger's Policy, supra, at p. 296.

(m) As to stop orders, see p. 480, infra.

(n) Mutual Life Assurance Society v. Langley (1886), 32 Ch. D. 460 (C.A.).

(o) See Ryall v. Rowles (1750), 1 Ves. Sen. 348; 9 Bli. N.S. 337, upon which the judgment of PLUMER, M.R., in Dearle v. Hall was largely founded. And Re Wyatt, White v. Ellis, [1892] 1 Ch. 188 (C.A.), at p. 209.

action generally, and not, as at the present day, only to business debts (*p*). "The legal holders", it was said by PLUMER, M.R., "are converted into trustees for the new purchaser, and are charged with responsibility towards him; and the *cestui que trust* is deprived of the power of carrying the same security repeatedly into the market, and of inducing third persons to advance money on it under the erroneous belief that it continues to belong to him absolutely, free from incumbrance, and that the trustees are still trustees for him, and for no-one else." And by Lord LYNDHURST, C., "The act of giving the trustee notice is, in a certain degree, taking possession of the fund; it is going as far towards equitable possession as it is possible to go; for, after notice is given, the trustee of the fund becomes a trustee for the assignee who has given him notice" (*q*).

It has been pointed out that, in many of the subsequent cases, the facts have not been as clear or as simple as those of the leading cases, and it has become necessary to ascertain the principles on which the rule is based. In some cases, the giving of notice in respect of a chose in action has been likened to the delivery of a chose in possession. In others, courts have emphasised the necessity of preventing frauds by beneficiaries who create successive incumbrances without disclosing the earlier ones. It is said, however, that the real foundation of the judgment of PLUMER, M.R., lay in the duty of the assignee to do all that he could to obtain the possession of the subject-matter of the assignment. "He must do that which is tantamount to obtaining possession by placing every person who has an equitable or legal interest in the matter under an obligation to treat it as his property" (*r*).

The importance of the matter lay in the avoidance of the application of the rule that assignments of equitable interests rank in order of time (*s*), and this was done by treating the omission of the first assignee to give notice, so leaving the assignor free to deal with the property over again—enabling him to gain a "false and delusive credit"—as negligence sufficient to postpone him (*t*). And Lord HERSCHELL said in *Ward* v. *Duncombe* (*u*) that the leading consideration in *Dearle* v. *Hall* for laying down the rule that he who gives notice has a better equitable right than a prior incumbrancer who has given no notice was, that any other decision would facilitate fraud by the *cestui que trust* and cause loss to those who might have used every precaution before parting with their money.

It is only, however, as a protection against subsequent assignments

---

(*p*) Bankruptcy Act 1914, s. 38. See p. 91, *supra*.

(*q*) 1 Russ., pp. 13, 58. In *Ward* v. *Duncombe*, [1893] A.C. 369, Lord MACNAGHTEN took exception to the statement that notice "converts" the trustee of the fund into a trustee for the person who gives the notice: "The trustee of the fund is trustee for the persons entitled to the fund, whether he knows their names or not. The notice, no doubt, places him under a direct responsibility to the person who gives the notice . . . But before notice is given he is just as much a trustee for the persons rightfully entitled as he is after he receives the notice."

(*r*) *Dearle* v. *Hall*, *supra*, p. 23. For a full account (from which the above paragraph is taken) of the development of the rule, see (1895), L.Q.R. 337 *et seq.* (E. C. C. Firth).

(*s*) See p. 446, *supra*.

(*t*) 1 Russ., p. 22.

(*u*) [1893] A.C. 369, at p. 378.

that notice perfects the security. As between mortgagor and mortgagee the security is complete without notice (*a*).

Rule is independent of conduct.—But while in its inception the rule was an application of the general principle that a prior incumbrancer may be postponed to a subsequent incumbrancer on the ground of negligence, and was based on the consideration that, by the omission to give notice, the subsequent incumbrancer was misled, it has now ceased to depend upon the conduct of the incumbrancers, or on the subsequent incumbrancer's being in fact misled, and has become an absolute rule that, as between equitable incumbrancers, priority depends solely on notice (*b*).

It is therefore immaterial that the subsequent incumbrancer made no inquiry of the trustee before he took his security (*c*); or that the earlier incumbrancer was prevented from giving notice, because he was not aware of the assignment to himself (*d*); or that the security was such that notice could not effectually be given (*e*); or that at the date of the earlier assignment there was no trustee to whom notice could be given (*f*).

Assignees who are not within the rule.—The rule does not apply to a statutory assignee, since he cannot have been misled by the absence of notice (*g*). Hence a trustee in bankruptcy cannot, by giving notice, obtain priority over a mortgage made before the bankruptcy (*h*). He takes the property subject to all equities to which it would be liable in the hands of the bankrupt (*i*). And generally, the rule does not apply in favour of persons who are not allowed to put themselves in a better position than the assignor; such as a voluntary assignee (*k*), or a judgment creditor who has obtained a charging order (*l*), or a garnishee order (*m*), or equitable execution by the appointment of a receiver (*n*).

Effect of notice of prior incumbrance.—The subsequent assignee

---

(*a*) *Ward* v. *Duncombe, supra,* at p. 392; *Gorringe* v. *Irwell India Rubber, etc., Works* (1886), 34 Ch. D. 128 (C.A.).

(*b*) *Ward* v. *Duncombe, supra,* at p. 391; *Re Dallas,* [1904] 2 Ch. 385 (C.A.), at p. 414; see *Lloyds Bank* v. *Pearson,* [1901] 1 Ch. 865, at pp. 872–873.

(*c*) *Meux* v. *Bell* (1841), 1 Hare, 73, 84–86; *Re Brown's Trusts* (1867), L.R. 5 Eq. 88, 89.

(*d*) *Re Lake,* [1903] 1 K.B. 151.

(*e*) *English and Scottish Mercantile Investment Trust, Ltd.* v. *Brunton,* [1892] 2 Q.B. 1, 8. Of course, it makes no difference that the earlier incumbrancer has agreed not to give notice: *ibid.*

(*f*) *Re Dallas,* [1904] 2 Ch. 385, 397, 415, 417–8; as to giving notice in such a case by memorandum indorsed on the trust deed, see Law of Property Act 1925, s. 137 (4), see p. 476, *infra.*

(*g*) *Re Anderson, Ex parte New Zealand Official Assignee,* [1911] 1 K.B. 896.

(*h*) *Re Wallis, Ex parte Jenks,* [1902] 1 K.B. 719; but the trustee should give notice in order to perfect his title, and if he does so, he will have priority over a subsequent assignee from the bankrupt: *Mercer* v. *Vans Colina,* [1900] 1 Q.B. 130; *Re Beall, Ex parte Official Receiver,* [1899] 1 Q.B. 688. Otherwise he will be postponed to a subsequent assignee for value without notice of the bankruptcy, who gives notice or obtains a stop order, *e.g., Palmer* v. *Locke* (1881), 18 Ch. D. 381.

(*i*) *Re Athinson* (1852), 2 De G.M. & G. 140; see *Re Garrud, Ex parte Newitt* (1881), 16 Ch. D. 522.

(*k*) *West* v. *Williams,* [1899] 1 Ch. 132 (C.A.).

(*l*) *Scott* v. *Lord Hastings* (1858), 4 K. & J. 633.

(*m*) *Re Marquis of Anglesey, De Galve* v. *Gardner,* [1903] 2 Ch. 727, 732.

(*n*) *Arden* v. *Arden* (1885), 29 Ch. D. 702; *Re Marquis of Anglesey, etc., supra.*

cannot gain priority by giving notice to the trustees if, at the time when he took his security, he had notice of the first assignment (*o*); but if he had no notice at that time, receiving notice afterwards does not prevent him from obtaining priority by serving notice before the first assignee does so. Indeed, it is in just this situation that an incumbrancer would be moved to gain his priority by giving notice (*p*).

Bankruptcy of assignor.—But where a bankrupt creates an incumbrance on after-acquired property, the fact that the incumbrancer has notice of the bankruptcy does not prevent his acquiring priority over the trustee in bankruptcy by giving notice to the trustees of the fund before the trustee intervenes by giving such notice (*q*).

As regards business debts, to which the order and disposition clause still applies (*a*), the trustee so far stands in a higher position than the bankrupt, that whereas, under ordinary circumstances, the title of the particular assignee is complete as between him and the assignor without any notice by the assignee (*b*), the trustee, where notice has not been given by the assignee at all or until after the bankruptcy, will be entitled to the debts against the assignee (*c*).

Assignment of mortgage.—It is not necessary in order to complete the title of an assignee of a mortgage, or of a sub-mortgage, either of land or personal estate, to give notice to the original mortgagor of the assignment of the mortgage debt; because the debt is incident to the property which forms the security, and which cannot be taken from the assignee without payment (*d*). But so long as the original mortgagor has no notice of the assignment, his payments on account of the debt to his original mortgagee will discharge him (*e*).

But an equitable charge on land is an equitable interest within s. 137 of the Law of Property Act 1925, and an assignment of it requires to be protected by notice to the estate owner of the land.

B—PROPERTY TO WHICH THE RULE APPLIES

Things in action.—The application of the rule in *Dearle* v. *Hall* has been extended by the Law of Property Act 1925 (*f*), but apart from the statutory provisions the rule is confined to things in action, including equitable interests in personalty, and to such interests in real or leasehold estate as can only reach the hands of the beneficiary or assignee in the form of money (*g*).

Moreover, where the assignor of a chattel has not the legal right in

---

(*o*) *Re Holmes* (1885), 29 Ch. D. 786.

(*p*) *Mutual Life Assurance Society* v. *Langley* (1886), 32 Ch. D. 460 (C.A.). See *Wortley* v. *Birkhead* (1754), 2 Ves. Sen. 571, at p. 574, for a comparable situation in the pre-1926 law of tacking.

(*q*) *Hunt* v. *Fripp*, [1898] 1 Ch. 675; *Re Behrend's Trust, Surman* v. *Biddell*, [1911] 1 Ch. 687.

(*a*) See p. 91, *supra.*

(*b*) See p. 466, *supra.*

(*c*) *Bartlett* v. *Bartlett* (1857), 1 De G. & J. 127; see *Ex parte Richardson* (1820), Buck, 480.

(*d*) *Jones* v. *Gibbons* (1804), 9 Ves. 407; see *Re Reay, Ex parte Barnett* (1845), De G. 194.

(*e*) *Re Lord Southampton's Estate, Allen* v. *Lord Southampton* (1880), 16 Ch. D. 178.

(*f*) Section 137; see p. 469, *infra.*

(*g*) See *Ward* v. *Duncombe*, [1893] A.C., p. 390.

it, or from other circumstances cannot deliver possession, the assignee must protect himself against subsequent assignees by giving such notice as goes as far as possible towards taking possession. Otherwise the subsequent assignee, by obtaining possession, will have priority (*h*).

The rule does not apply where the security consists of a bill of exchange, promissory note payable to order, or other negotiable instrument (*i*), whether indorsed or not by the debtor (*k*). Nor does it apply to shares in a company which is precluded by its constitution from receiving notices of trusts (*l*).

Locality of fund.—The rule applies where the legal holder of the fund is in England. Thus it applies to all dealings in English trust funds settled by English trust instruments, the trustees of which are in England, although the assignor is domiciled abroad, and even though, according to his *lex domicilii*, notice to trustees is unnecessary (*m*). In the case of debts, the debtor is the person to whom notice must be given, and, if he is domiciled in England, the rule applies. If he is domiciled abroad, priority is determined by the law of his domicile, and not by the law of the domicile of either mortgagor or mortgagee (*n*).

Life policies.—Special provision with respect to life policies is made by the Policies of Assurance Act 1867. No assignment of a policy of life assurance confers on the assignee a right to sue for the policy moneys until written notice of the assignment has been given to the assurance company at their principal place, or one of their principal places of business, and the date on which the notice is received regulates the priority of all claims under any assignment (*o*). The company must, upon request in writing by the person giving notice, acknowledge in writing the receipt of the notice (*p*). But an instrument of deposit, not operating as an assignment of the policy, will not be construed as an assignment as against the company by reason of their accepting notice of it and giving a receipt; and in such a case the company may refuse payment of the policy on the death of the assured until the consent of his representatives has been obtained (*q*).

A mere agreement to execute a mortgage of a policy is not an

(*h*) *Daniel* v. *Russell* (1807), 14 Ves. 393. Cf. Sykes, *The Law of Securities* (2nd Edn.), p. 626, where it is suggested that the rule applies to all equitable interests whether in real or personal property which can reach the hands of the beneficiary or assignor only in the form of money, as well as to all types of choses in action.

(*i*) As to the effect on title where instruments are "negotiable", see *London Joint Stock Bank* v. *Simmons*, [1892] A.C. 201.

(*k*) *Re Gibbs, Ex parte Price* (1844), 3 Mont. D. & De G. 586. The incumbrancer may have an equity to have the security indorsed by the debtor or his assignees: *ibid.* But the debtor may ignore a notice given by the assignee of the consideration for the note or bill if the assignor is still the holder of the instrument itself: *Bence* v. *Shearman* [1898] 2 Ch. 582.

(*l*) *Société Générale de Paris* v. *Walker* (1885), 11 App. Cas. 20.

(*m*) *Kelly* v. *Selwyn*, [1905] 2 Ch. 117.

(*n*) *Re Queensland Mercantile and Agency Co., etc.*, [1892] 1 Ch. 219; see *Republic of Guatemala* v. *Nunez* (1926), 42 T.L.R. 625; affd., [1927] 1 K.B. 669; see Dicey and Morris, *Conflict of Laws* (9th Edn.), pp. 554–557.

(*o*) Section 3; see *English and Scottish Mercantile Investment Co.* v. *Brunton*, [1892] 2 Q.B. 700.

(*p*) Section 6. And see p. 108, *supra*.

(*q*) *Crossley* v. *City of Glasgow Life Assurance Co.* (1876), 4 Ch. D. 421; *Webster* v. *British Empire Mutual Life Assurance Co.* (1880), 15 Ch. D. 169.

assignment within the Act, and notice of it to the company will not give priority over an earlier equitable mortgagee, who has given no notice (*r*). And the benefit of a possessory lien on a policy is not lost for want of notice of it to the assurance company (*s*).

Equitable interests in land.—In accordance with the principle that the rule applies to interests in land which can only reach the beneficiary in the form of money, it applies to a sum of money raiseable by way of portion out of land (*t*); and it applies to interests in the proceeds of land which is subject to an imperative trust for sale, whether present (*u*) or future (*x*).

But until 1926 the rule did not apply to equitable interests in real (*y*) or leasehold (*z*) property, and priority could not be obtained by giving notice to the holder of the legal estate (*a*), or, where the legal mortgagee had created successive sub-mortgages, by giving notice to the mortgagor (*b*). Whether the rule applied to moneys subject to a trust for investment in land, or to capital moneys arising under the Settled Land Acts, was not clear. Since, however, land subject to a trust for sale was treated for this purpose as land, money subject to be invested in the purchase of land should have been treated as land (*c*).

Extension of rule by Law of Property Act.—But with regard to dispositions made after 31 December, 1925, the rule in *Dearle* v. *Hall* has been extended to equitable interests in land and capital money:

137.—(1) The law applicable to dealings with equitable things in action, which regulates the priority of competing interests therein, shall, as respects dealings with equitable interests in land, capital money, and securities representing capital money effected after the commencement of this Act (*d*), apply to and regulate the priority of competing interests therein.

This subsection applies whether or not the money or securities are in court (*e*).

Shares in companies.—Where the security consists of shares in a public company or undertaking, if the security is made by the directors and secretary for the purposes of the company, no further notice will be necessary (*f*).

(*r*) *Spencer* v. *Clarke* (1878), 9 Ch. D. 137.

(*s*) *West of England Bank* v. *Batchelor* (1882), 51 L.J. Ch. 199.

(*t*) *Re Hughes' Trusts* (1864), 2 H. & M. 89. And see *Malcolm* v. *Charlesworth* (1836), 1 Keen, 63.

(*u*) *Re Wyatt, White* v. *Ellis*, [1892] 1 Ch. 188, 195; on appeal, *Ward* v. *Duncombe*, [1893] A.C. 369 (H.L.), at p. 390; *Lloyds Bank* v. *Pearson*, [1901] 1 Ch. 865; *Gresham Life Assurance Society* v. *Crowther*, [1915] 1 Ch. 214.

(*x*) *Lee* v. *Howlett* (1856), 2 K. & J. 531; *Arden* v. *Arden* (1885), 29 Ch. D. 702.

(*y*) *Jones* v. *Jones* (1838), 8 Sim. 633; *Wilmot* v. *Pike* (1845), 5 Hare, 14; *Rooper* v. *Harrison* (1855), 2 K. & J. 86, 103; *Re Richards, Humber* v. *Richards* (1890), 45 Ch. D. 589; *Ward* v. *Duncombe*, [1893] A.C. 369, 390.

(*z*) *Wiltshire* v. *Rabbits* (1844), 14 Sim. 76; *Union Bank of London* v. *Kent* (1888), 39 Ch. D. 238.

(*a*) *Jones* v. *Jones, supra*; see *Taylor* v. *London and County Banking Co.*, [1901] 2 Ch. 231, 254, 255.

(*b*) *Hopkins* v. *Hemsworth*, [1898] 2 Ch. 347; see *Re Richards, supra*.

(*c*) So held in *Re Carew's Estate* (1868), 16 W.R. 1077. Cf. *Re Sandes' Trusts*, [1920] 1 I.R. 342.

(*d*) 1 January, 1926. The section does not apply until a trust has been created, and "dealing" includes a disposition by operation of law: sub-s. (10).

(*e*) As to registered land, see p. 477, *infra*.

(*f*) *Re Shelley, Ex parte Stewart* (1864), 4 De G.J. & S. 543.

If the mortgage is made by a shareholder to a third party, companies (such as banking companies) governed by the Companies Clauses Consolidation Act 1845, are not bound to recognise equities at all. As regards companies registered under the Companies Acts under s. 117 of the Companies Act 1948, no notice of a trust is to be entered in the company's register, but if directors know of circumstances showing that a transfer is fraudulent, they may be personally liable (g). But, even though notice given to the company does not affect the priority of equitable claims in respect of registered shares, such a notice is not inoperative for all purposes, and the receipt of notice by a company of a charge upon some of its shares will prevent the company from availing itself; as against those shares, of any lien under its articles of association for a debt to the company incurred subsequently to its receipt of the notice (h).

Where several persons claim shares registered in the name of another priority is governed by the rules applicable to mortgages of land before 1926 (i). Accordingly the first in time has priority unless he is postponed by his conduct in relation to the share certificate (k).

It would seem that the possession by the mortgagee of the share certificates is sufficient to take the shares out of the mortgagor's order and disposition, both for the purposes of the bankruptcy law, and probably as against subsequent incumbrancers (l).

C—GIVING NOTICE

To the legal holder of the fund.—In certain cases a trust corporation may be nominated to receive notices of dealings with real or personal property (m). Where this procedure is not appropriate or has not been used, notice must be given to the person having the legal interest in or control over the property which is the subject of the security (n). Usually this is a personal representative or trustee. In the case of a debt, or of other property depending on an obligation to pay money, such as a policy of insurance, it is the debtor or person under obligation (o).

(g) *Société Générale de Paris* v. *Tramways Union Co.* (1884), 14 Q.B.D. 424 (C.A.); affirmed without reference to this point, *sub nom. Société Générale de Paris* v. *Walker* (1885), 11 App. Cas. 20 (H.L.).

(h) *Bradford Banking Co.* v. *Briggs & Co.* (1886), 12 App. Cas. 29 (H.L.), applying the principle of *Hopkinson* v. *Rolt* (1861), 9 H.L. Cas. 514. And see p. 111, *supra*.

(i) See p. 429, *supra*.

(k) See *Moore* v. *North-Western Bank*, [1891] 2 Ch. 599.

(l) *Colonial Bank* v. *Whinney* (1886), 11 App. Cas. 426; but this case also decided that shares are "things in action", and they are not now within the "order and disposition" clause.

(m) Law of Property Act 1925, s. 138; see p. 477, *infra*.

(n) If there are prior incumbrances, notice to a prior mortgagee only affects priorities in that it prevents a prior mortgagee from tacking a further advance: *Re Weniger's Policy*, [1910] 2 Ch. 291.

(o) *Gardner* v. *Lachlan* (1838), 4 My. & Cr. 129; as to a policy of insurance, see p. 468, *supra*. If the debt is due from a company in liquidation notice should be given to the liquidator: *Re Breech-Loading Armoury Co., Wragge's Case* (1868), L.R. 5 Eq. 284. As to the effect of notice in taking a thing in action out of the order and disposition of the creditor, see *Re Seaman, Ex parte Furness Finance Co.*, [1896] 1 Q.B. 412.

In the case of a legacy, notice must be given to the executor (*p*). If the legacy is a trust legacy, then, after assent by the executor in favour of the trustees, notice must be given to the trustees. If the subject of the legacy is held by trustees under a prior instrument, and an assignment is made before assent, notice must be given to the executor, and when the assent is given, notice of the assent and of the assignment should be given to the trustees of the prior instrument. But if the assignment is made after assent, notice should be given to the trustees of the prior instrument, and not to the executor (*q*).

Derivative settlements.—Where notice is given to a trustee, this must be the trustee who is immediately responsible to the assignor. Thus in the case of a security on an interest under a derivative settlement, the notice should be given to the trustees of that settlement, and not to the trustees of the original settlement, notwithstanding that the fund is still vested in them. The trustees of the derivative settlement are bound in due course to get in the fund, and it is to them that the assignee will look for payment. In other words, there is no priority between assignees of interests under the derivative settlement and the trustees of the original settlement (*r*).

As to equitable interests in land.—In regard to the classes of property to which the rule in *Dearle* v. *Hall* was extended by the Law of Property Act 1925 (*s*), the statute prescribes the persons to whom notice is to be given as follows:

137.—(2) (i) In the case of a dealing with an equitable interest in settled land, capital money or securities representing capital money, the persons to be served with notice of the dealing shall be the trustees of the settlement; and where the equitable interest is created by a derivative or subsidiary settlement, the persons to be served with notice shall be the trustees of that settlement (*t*).

(ii) In the case of a dealing with an equitable interest in the proceeds of sale of land or in the rents and profits until sale the persons to be served with notice shall, as heretofore, be the trustees for sale.

(iii) In any other case the person to be served with notice of a dealing with an equitable interest in land shall be the estate owner of the land affected (*u*).

The persons on whom notice is served pursuant to this subsection shall be affected thereby in the same manner as if they had been trustees of personal property out of which the equitable interest was created or arose.

This subsection does not apply where the money or securities are in court (*x*).

Trustee's title.—In order that the notice may be effectual, the person to whom it is given must at the time be trustee for the assignor (*y*). This requires:

(*p*) See *Re Dallas*, [1904] 2 Ch. 385 (C.A.). But it would seem that notice to an executor who renounces is ineffective: *Re Wasdale, Brittin* v. *Partridge*, [1899] 1 Ch. 163.

(*q*) *Holt* v. *Dewell* (1845), 4 Hare, 446.

(*r*) *Stephens* v. *Green*, [1895] 2 Ch. 148 (C.A.); in accordance with *Holt* v. *Dewell*, *supra*.

(*s*) See p. 469, *supra*.

(*t*) This is in accordance with the rule stated, p. 470, *supra*.

(*u*) *I.e.*, the person in whom the legal estate in the land is vested: the fee simple in the case of freehold land; the term in the case of leasehold land: Law of Property Act 1925, ss. 1 (4), 205 (1) (v). See s. 137 (9) as to the liability of the estate owner to produce documents and furnish information to persons entitled to equitable interests.

(*x*) When the fund is in court a stop order should be obtained: p. 480, *infra*.

(*y*) *Dearle* v. *Hall* (1828), 3 Russ. 1, 58; *Meux* v. *Bell* (1841), 1 Hare, 73, 87; *Ward* v. *Duncombe*, [1893] A.C. 369 (H.L.), 387, 389, 392; *Stephens* v. *Green*, [1895] 2 Ch. 148 (C.A.), 158; *Re Dallas*, [1904] 2 Ch. 385 (C.A.).

(1) That he shall be a duly constituted trustee (*z*). Thus notice to an administrator is ineffectual unless he has obtained a grant of administration; and so, it seems, is notice to an executor who afterwards renounces without having acted, or to a trustee who disclaims (*a*).

(2) There must be under his control property in which the assignor has an actual interest, that is, the fund must be in the hands of the holder on behalf of the assignor, and priority will follow the dates of the notices after it is in his hands (*b*).

The fact, however, that at the time of the several assignments there was no trust fund and no trustee in existence does not prevent the rule in *Dearle* v. *Hall* from applying, and priorities will be regulated in accordance with notices given after the fund has come into existence, and there is a person who has legal control over it (*c*). But where notices have only been given before this time, the order in date of the incumbrances prevails (*d*).

It has been held, however, that if, before his appointment, a trustee had acquired knowledge of an incumbrance, and if this continued to operate on his mind after his appointment, it would protect the priority of the incumbrance against a subsequent incumbrance of which notice was given after his appointment (*e*), and if this was correct a formal notice given to a trustee before appointment would be good on his appointment. But the present requirement of written notice to the trustees appears to imply that it must be given after they have been appointed (*f*).

Effect of notice to one trustee.—It is the result of the rule in *Dearle* v. *Hall* that an intending mortgagee can protect himself by inquiring of the trustees whether they have received notice of any previous incumbrances (*g*). The trustee is not bound to answer (*h*),

---

(*z*) See *Webster* v. *Webster* (1862), 31 Beav. 393.

(*a*) *Re Dallas, supra*; *Re Kinahan's Trusts*, [1907] 1 I.R. 321.

(*b*) Thus in a series of Army cases it was held that notice to an Army agent of an assignment by an officer of money payable to him on retirement was only effective if at the time the agent had in his hands money either credited to the officer, or at least specifically available for him: *Somerset* v. *Cox* (1864), 33 Beav. 634; *Yates* v. *Cox* (1868), 17 W.R. 20; *Boss* v. *Hopkinson* (1870), 18 W.R. 725; *Addison* v. *Cox* (1872), 8 Ch. App. 76; *Addison* v. *Cox* (1874), 30 L.T. 253; or, perhaps, only if given after the retirement had been gazetted: *Earl of Suffolk and Berkshire* v. *Cox* (1867), 36 L.J. Ch. 591; *Johnstone* v. *Cox* (1881), 19 Ch. D. 17. As to these cases, see *Re Dallas, supra*, at p. 418. Where there were two sets of trustees, one of an annuity, and the other of a term by which the annuity was secured, notice of a prior incumbrance to one of the trustees of the annuity was held binding, although the trustees of the term had no notice: *Wise* v. *Wise* (1845), 2 Jo. & Lat. 403.

(*c*) *Re Dallas, supra*. And it was the same where, the assignor being himself the sole trustee, no effective notice could be given: *ibid.*, pp. 401–402, see *Phipps* v. *Lovegrove* (1873), L.R. 16 Eq. 80; p. 474, note (*u*), *infra*.

(*d*) *Buller* v. *Plunkett* (1860), 1 Johns. & H. 441. The rule has been applied to an attachment in the Mayor's Court, London, against a fund before it has reached the trustee's hands: *Webster* v. *Webster* (1862), 31 Beav. 393.

(*e*) *Ipswich Permanent Money Club, Ltd.* v. *Arthy*, [1920] 2 Ch. 257.

(*f*) See p. 474, *infra*.

(*g*) And it has been said to be his duty to make inquiry: *Smith* v. *Smith* (1833), 2 Cr. & M. 231; *Willes* v. *Greenhill* (1861), 4 De G.F. & J. 147, 150; but this only means that the incumbrancer cannot complain of being postponed if he omits to make this inquiry.

(*h*) *Re Wyatt, White* v. *Ellis*, [1892] 1 Ch. 188.

and if he refuses to do so, the intending mortgagee proceeds at his peril. If, however, the trustee does answer, he must answer correctly; otherwise he will be liable to indemnify the mortgagee (*i*).

But the intending mortgagee has not exhausted the means of inquiry until he has inquired of all the trustees, and hence notice to any one of them is sufficient to satisfy the rule and secure priority for the mortgagee giving the notice (*k*). If, however, the one trustee who has had notice is dead when the mortgagor negotiates a second loan, there is no chance now of making effective inquiry, the fund is once more at the disposition of the mortgagor, and a subsequent mortgagee who gives notice to the surviving trustees obtains priority (*l*).

Effect of notice to all trustees.—On the other hand, where the mortgagee has given notice to all the trustees, he has done all that is required of him to secure priority. He is not bound to watch for changes in the trusteeship and give fresh notices from time to time; and he is entitled to priority over a subsequent assignee who has taken his assignment after the death or retirement of all the first trustees, and who gives notice to the new trustees (*m*).

(*i*) *Low* v. *Bouverie*, [1891] 3 Ch. 82 (C.A.); unless, indeed, the answer has been obtained by the concealment by the inquiring party of a material fact; *e.g.*, that he had already applied to the trustees' solicitors who were considering what advice they should give: *Porter* v. *Moore*, [1904] 2 Ch. 367.

(*k*) *Smith* v. *Smith*, *supra*; *Meux* v. *Bell* (1841), 1 Hare, 73.

(*l*) *Timson* v. *Ramsbottom* (1837), 2 Keen, 35. In *Ward* v. *Duncombe*, [1893] A.C. 369, this was accepted as correct by Lord HERSCHELL, but Lord MACNAGHTEN was inclined to allow more weight to the fact that the rule had been complied with, and less to the continuing effect of the notice on the apparent control of the mortgagor. "It may be," he said, "that when an assignee or mortgagee has once discharged that duty [of giving notice] he has done all that the rule requires of him . . . and that he is not, on a change of trustees, to be deprived of his pre-existing equitable title by the diligence or by the happy thought of a subsequent incumbrancer." In *Ward* v. *Duncombe* it was not necessary to decide this point. Notice of an assignment had been given to one of two trustees, A. During his life notice of a second assignment was given to both trustees. It was held that the subsequent death of A did not deprive the first assignees of the priority they had already acquired over the second assignees in his life-time. But the doctrine of *Timson* v. *Ramsbottom* was followed in *Re Phillips' Trusts*, [1903] 1 Ch. 183, and an assignee after the death of A, who gave notice to the existing trustees, had priority over the assignee who gave notice to A alone, since the effect of his notice had ceased on A's death: see also the statement of the law by BYRNE, J., in *Freeman* v. *Laing*, [1899] 2 Ch. 355, 359.

(*m*) *Re Wasdale, Brittin* v. *Partridge*, [1899] 1 Ch. 163. Similarly, if an assignee gives notice to all the trustees and the fund is afterwards paid into court, he has priority over a subsequent assignee who takes his assignment without notice of the prior assignment after the payment into court and obtains a stop order: *Livesey* v. *Harding* (1856), 23 Beav. 141; *Re Marquis of Anglesey, De Galve* v. *Gardner*, [1903] 2 Ch. 727, 732.

The doctrine that notice given to one of several trustees secures priority only while he is living leads to complications if there are successive incumbrancers, A, B, and C, and, there being two trustees, X and Y, A gives notice to X only; B gives notice to X and Y; and C, taking his security after the death of X, gives notice to Y. Thus, while A by reason of his notice to X ranks before B, and B by reason of his notice to Y, ranks before C, yet C ranks before A because A's notice as against C is exhausted by the death of X. The solution of the difficulty is, it seems, to be found by subrogating C to A to the extent of A's charge; then comes B, his position not being disturbed; then C takes the balance, if any, of his charge; and A comes last: *Re Wyatt, White* v. *Ellis*, [1892] 1 Ch. 188, 209; see *Benham* v. *Keane* (1861), 1 J. & H. 685; argument in *Taylor* v. *London and County Banking Co.*, [1901] 2 Ch. 231, 244; *Re Weniger's Policy*, [1910] 2 Ch. 291, 296.

So, where, for any reason, out of securities in the above order, B has priority over A, and C over B, but as between A and C, A retains priority; if the fund available is not more than B's security will exhaust, it will be paid first to C, to the extent of the debt for which he has priority over B, and the balance to B. But it seems that if the

Form of notice.—Previously to the Law of Property Act 1925, notice for the purpose of the rule in *Dearle* v. *Hall* was not required to be a written or a formal notice (*n*). But in order to give priority it was necessary to show that the trustee had such knowledge of the transaction, however acquired, as an ordinary man of business would act upon (*o*). Hence, while a statement to a trustee in casual conversation was insufficient (*p*), verbal notice was effectual (*q*), provided it was brought clearly to the mind of the trustee (*r*). On this principle, if the assignee is himself one of the trustees, the knowledge which he has of his own security gives him priority over subsequent assignments made during his life (*s*). But if the assignor is a trustee, the knowledge which he has of the security does not operate as notice to him, whether he is one of several trustees (*t*), or sole trustee (*u*).

But in respect of notices after 1925 these questions cannot arise since the notice is inoperative unless in writing. Thus the Law of Property Act 1925, provides:

> **137.**—(3) A notice, otherwise than in writing, given to, or received by, a trustee after the commencement of this Act as respects any dealing with an equitable interest in real or personal property, shall not affect the priority of competing claims of purchasers in that equitable interest.

This provision does not alter the law as to the effect of notice to only one of several trustees. The only alteration in the law is as to the form of the notice. Verbal notice, or knowledge acquired

---

fund is more than enough for B all further sums received by C will be for the benefit of A: *Benham* v. *Keane* (1861), 1 J. & H. 685; affirmed, 3 De G.F. & J. 318; *Re Lord Kensington, Bacon* v. *Ford* (1885), 29 Ch. D. 527.

(*n*) *Selkrig* v. *Davies* (1814), 2 Dow, 230.

(*o*) *Lloyd* v. *Banks* (1868), 3 Ch. App. 488; *Re Worcester, Ex parte Agra Bank* (1868), 3 Ch. App. 555, 559; *Re Dallas*, [1904] 2 Ch. 385 (C.A.), at p. 399. But it was not correct to say that incumbrances ranked not in the order of notices given by the incumbrancers, but of accidental knowledge obtained by the trustees: *Arden* v. *Arden* (1885), 29 Ch. D. 702, 708.

(*p*) *Browne* v. *Savage* (1859), 4 Drew. 635; *Re Tichener* (1865), 35 Beav. 317.

(*q*) *Re Tichener, supra.*

(*r*) *Saffron Walden Second Benefit Society* v. *Rayner* (1880), 14 Ch. D. 406 (C.A.).

(*s*) *Browne* v. *Savage, supra.* It followed that if, before the fund came to the hands of the trustee, incumbrances were created in favour of A and then of the trustee, A could not secure priority. For notice by him would not operate until the trustee received the fund, and when this happened, the notice of his own security would attach and would give him priority: *Somerset* v. *Cox* (1864), 33 Beav. 634; *Roxburghe* v. *Cox* (1881), 17 Ch. D. 520; see *Re Goddard, Hooker* v. *Buckley* (1912), 57 Sol. Jo. 42 (C.A.). But notice, though ineffectual to give priority over the trustee's existing charge, prevented the trustee from acquiring any new charge or right of set-off, and he was, from that time, bound to withhold all further payments on account of the mortgagor, unless made with the mortgagee's consent: *Stephens* v. *Venables* (1862), 30 Beav. 625; *Re Pain, Gustavson* v. *Haviland*, [1919] 1 Ch. 38.

Apart from the question of notice, the priority of the holder of the fund extends not only to actual charges, but to all rights of lien, set-off, and other equities existing between him, or the estate out of which the fund is payable, and the person entitled to the fund subject to the incumbrances: *Webster* v. *Webster* (1862), 31 Beav. 393; *Stephens* v. *Venables, supra; Roxburghe* v. *Cox, supra;* see *Willes* v. *Greenhill, supra.*

(*t*) *Browne* v. *Savage, supra,* at p. 640; *Lloyds Bank* v. *Pearson*, [1901] 1 Ch. 865.

(*u*) *Re Dallas*, [1904] 2 Ch. 385 (C.A.), at pp. 401–402. Thus, where the assignor was sole trustee, no effectual notice could be given: *Phipps* v. *Lovegrove* (1873), L.R. 16 Eq. 80; and where he was one of several trustees, it was a question whether notice to him and the other trustees would be a good notice to all the existing trustees so as to survive changes in the trusteeship: see *Willes* v. *Greenhill* (1860), 29 Beav. 376 (No. 1), 387 (No. 2); on app., 4 De G.F. & J. 147. In such a case a memorandum of the assignment should now be indorsed on the trust instrument: p. 476, *infra.*

incidentally, is not enough to satisfy the rule in *Dearle* v. *Hall*. The notice must be in writing (*x*).

Notice of assignment is notice of contents.—As a general rule trustees to whom notice of an assignment is given have notice of all the contents of the deed. Thus, notice of a general charge by the deed is sufficient, and the trustees and subsequent assignees must satisfy themselves as to the extent of the charge (*y*). But it is different if, with the notice of the deed, a statement of its contents is given which is erroneous or incomplete. Thus, if the deed comprises two funds held under one settlement, and the notice specifies only one fund as being affected, there is not a sufficient notice as to the other fund (*z*); and similarly, if the notice states that only sum A is charged on the assignor's interest, while sum B is also charged, the notice is only effective as to sum A, unless the charge of sum B is merely ancillary (*a*).

Custody of the notice.—As to the custody of the notice, it is provided:

> **137.**—(8) Where a notice in writing of a dealing with an equitable interest in real or personal property has been served on a trustee under this section, the trustees from time to time of the property affected shall be entitled to the custody of the notice, and the notice shall be delivered to them by any person who for the time being may have the custody thereof; and subject to the payment of costs, any person interested in the equitable interest may require production of the notice.

In order to ensure that information as to notices received by the trustees shall always be available for intending mortgagees, the trustees on parting with the trust fund to a new trustee should inform him of such notices (*b*). Conversely, it would seem that the new trustee ought to inquire of the old trustees as to notices received, but no such obligation appears to have been judicially recognised (*c*). The practice in this latter respect is not altered, but it is now a statutory duty for the old trustees—if, as should be the case, they have the custody of the notice—to hand it over to the new trustees.

Service of the notice.—The notice must be given to the trustees personally or to an agent expressly or impliedly authorised to receive it on their behalf. Unless their solicitor has such authority, notice to him is not effectual (*d*). A notice served on an agent so authorised will be binding, though the agent, in compliance with the direction of his principal, has not forwarded the notice to him (*e*).

(*x*) And see *Smith* v. *The Owners of the Steamship "Zigurds"*, [1934] A.C. 209.

(*y*) *Re Bright's Trusts* (1856), 21 Beav. 430, 434.

(*z*) *Re Bright's Trusts, supra*; *Mutual Life Assurance Society* v. *Langley* (1886), 32 Ch. D. 460 (C.A.), at p. 474.

(*a*) *Re Bright's Trusts, supra*.

(*b*) *Re Booth's Settlement* (1853), 1 W.R. 444.

(*c*) *Phipps* v. *Lovegrove* (1873), L.R. 16 Eq. 80; and it is not the practice of the court on appointing new trustees to make such inquiry: *ibid*.

(*d*) *Saffron Walden Second Benefit Building Society* v. *Rayner* (1880), 14 Ch. D. 406; *Arden* v. *Arden* (1885), 29 Ch. D. 702, 709.

(*e*) *Re Hennessey* (1842), 2 Dru. & War. 555. As to notice to an agent who, as assignor, has an interest in withholding communication of it, see p. 441, *supra*; and as to notice to a company through an interested officer, see *Re Hennessey, supra*; *Re Sketchley Ex parte Boulton* (1857), 1 De G. & J. 163; and *cf. Bartlett* v. *Bartlett* (1857), 1 De G. & J. 127. Where it is necessary to give notice to a company or association it

The holder of, or other person having any control over, the property concerning which the notice is given, is bound to accept the notice (*f*); and if he disregards it and parts with the fund, he may be compelled to make it good to the person entitled. But he is not bound to inform the giver of the notice, that he himself has a charge upon the fund (*g*).

Indorsement on trust instrument.—In cases where there is difficulty in giving notice of an assignment, the object of the notice may be attained by indorsing a memorandum of the assignment on the trust instrument (*h*). Thus the Law of Property Act 1925, provides:

137.—(4) Where, as respects any dealing with an equitable interest in real or personal property—

    (a) the trustees are not persons to whom a valid notice of the dealing can be given: or

    (b) there are no trustees to whom a notice can be given; or

    (c) for any other reason a valid notice cannot be served, or cannot be served without unreasonable cost or delay;

a purchaser may at his own cost require that—

    (i) a memorandum of the dealing be endorsed, written on or permanently annexed to the instrument creating the trust;

    (ii) the instrument be produced to him by the person having the possession or custody thereof to prove that a sufficient memorandum has been placed thereon or annexed thereto.

Such memorandum shall, as respects priorities, operate in like manner as if notice in writing of the dealing had been given to trustees duly qualified to receive the notice at the time when the memorandum is placed on or annexed to the instrument creating the trust (*i*).

---

makes no difference that they have no rules or provisions applicable to the receipt of such notices: *Williams* v. *Thorp* (1828), 2 Sim. 257; or that they do not require notices to be given of assignments: *Re Loosemore, Ex parte Patch* (1843), 12 L.J. Bcy. 44.

(*f*) *Williams* v. *Thorp, supra*; *Re Hennessey, supra*.

(*g*) *Re Lewer, Ex parte Wilkes* (1876), 4 Ch. D. 101.

(*h*) Before this enactment it was possible to secure priority by having the incumbrance noticed in the trust instrument, where this was practicable: *Public Works Commissioners* v. *Harby* (1857), 23 Beav. 508; and before it was settled that the effect of notice to all the trustees survived changes in trusteeship (*supra*, p. 473), it was suggested that, for complete security, the assignment should be indorsed on the original deed (*Phipps* v. *Lovegrove* (1873), L.R. 16 Eq. 80), an anticipation of the present statutory provision.

Where the fund is not a fund in court and consists of any government stock, and any stock of any company registered under any general Act of Parliament, including any such stock standing in the name of the Accountant-General, and any dividend of or interest payable on such stock, and there is no trustee—if, for instance, the sole trustee is dead and there is no legal personal representative—priority can be secured by serving on the Bank of England or the company a stop notice: see R.S.C. Ord. 50, rr. 11, 12; and p. 162, *supra*.

As to giving an ordinary notice of equitable rights in shares to a limited company, see p. 469, *supra*. It may be necessary to have recourse to a stop notice, where, for instance, there is no trust instrument on which a memorandum can be indorsed.

(*i*) Presumably the memorandum will operate as if notice had been given to all the trustees; otherwise its effect would not be permanent. In the case of settled land, it is to be indorsed on the trust instrument, and not the vesting instrument; and in the case of land held on trust for sale, on the instrument whereby the equitable interest is created: sub-s. (5). Where the trust is created by statute or by operation of law, or in other cases where there is no trust instrument, the indorsement will be made on the instrument under which the equitable interest is acquired, or which is evidence of the devolution thereof; in particular, where the trust arises by reason of an intestacy, the letters of administration or probate in force when the dealing was effected are to be deemed the trust instrument: sub-s. (6). Probate will be the appropriate instrument in cases of partial intestacy.

Service on trust corporation.—In order to relieve trustees of their obligations in respect of the receipt of notices, provision is made by the Law of Property Act 1925, for the nomination of a trust corporation for this purpose:

138.—(1) By any settlement or other instrument creating a trust, a trust corporation (*k*) may be nominated to whom notices of dealings affecting real or personal property may be given, whether or not under the foregoing section, and in default of such nomination the trustees (if any) of the instrument, or the court on the application of any person interested, may make the nomination.

(2) The person having the possession or custody of any instrument on which notices under that section may be endorsed shall cause the name of the trust corporation to whom notices may be given to be endorsed upon that instrument (*l*).

(3) Notice given to any trust corporation whose name is so endorsed shall operate in the same way as a notice or endorsement under the foregoing section (*m*).

If, where a trust corporation is acting, a notice is given to a trustee, he must forthwith deliver or post it to the trust corporation, and until received by the corporation, it does not affect any priority (*n*).

It is further provided:

138.—(7) A trust corporation acting for the purposes of this section shall be bound to keep a separate register of notices of dealings in respect of each equitable interest and shall enter therein—

(a)   the date of the notice;
(b)   the name of the person giving the notice;
(c)   short particulars of the equitable interest intended to be affected; and
(d)   short particulars of the effect of the dealing if mentioned in the notice (*o*).

(9) Subject to the payment of a fee not exceeding the prescribed fee (*p*) the trust corporation shall permit any person who would, if the corporation had been the trustee of the trust instrument, have been entitled to inspect notices served on the trustee, to inspect and take copies of the register and any notices held by the corporation.

(10) Subject to the payment by the applicant of a fee not exceeding the prescribed fee, the trust corporation shall reply to all inquiries respecting notices received by the corporation in like manner and in the same circumstances as if the corporation had been the trustee of the trust instrument (*q*).

D—TRUST INTERESTS IN REGISTERED LAND

Priority cautions.—As regards dealings with trust interests in registered land, a system corresponding to the nomination of a trust

---

(*k*) As to "trust corporation", see Law of Property Act 1925, s. 205 (1) (xxviii); Law of Property (Amendment) Act 1926, s. 3; Public Trustee (Custodian Trustee) Rules 1975. And see further as to the nomination of a trust corporation, sub-ss. (5), (6) of s. 138.

(*l*) For the instrument on which notices may be endorsed, see s. 137 (4), (5), (6); p. 476, *supra.*

(*m*) See s. 137 (4).

(*n*) This does not seem to avoid the necessity of obtaining a stop order should the funds, at the time of the assignment, be in court: see p. 480, *infra.*

(*o*) The notice must be in writing (*supra*, p. 474), but no form is prescribed. As to the notice being notice of the contents of the assignment, see p. 475, *supra.*

(*p*) As to the fee for making the entry, see sub-s. (8), and Public Trustee (Fees) Order 1975. These fees in the Order apply to all trust corporations nominated for the purposes of s. 138: see sub-s. (11).

(*q*) This imposes a new obligation. A trustee is not bound to answer inquiries at all, though if he does so, he must answer correctly: see p. 472, *supra.*

corporation has been introduced, the position of the trust corporation being taken, without specific nomination, by the Land Registrar. This is by virtue of the following provision of the Land Registration Act 1925:

> **102.**—(2) Priorities as regards dealings effected after the commencement of this Act between assignees and incumbrancers of life interests, remainders, reversions and executory interests shall be regulated by the order of the priority cautions or inhibitions lodged (in a specially prescribed form) against the proprietor of the registered estate affected, but, save as aforesaid, priorities as between persons interested in minor interests shall not be affected by the lodgment of cautions or inhibitions.

The registered proprietor of registered land holds the legal estate (*r*)—in the case of freehold land the fee simple (*s*), in the case of leasehold land, the term (*t*)—and it only passes out of him by registered transfer or by devolution on death or bankruptcy (*u*). But while the legal estate is always associated with the registered title, any other interests in the land can be created by a person having a sufficient interest or power, whether he is the registered proprietor or not. These are called minor interests, and take effect in equity only. They are not entered on the register, but may be protected by entry on the register of notices, cautions, inhibitions, and restrictions. They are capable of being overridden by registered dispositions for valuable consideration, though the effect of the protection may be to restrain the proprietor from making such disposition (*x*).

The interests mentioned in s. 102 (2)—life interests, remainders, reversions, and executory interests—are therefore minor interests, and as regards them, priorities are regulated by the order of the priority cautions in the specially prescribed form, which are lodged against the registered proprietor. The form of the caution is given as Form 72 in the Schedule to the Land Registration Rules 1925 (*y*).

The Minor Interests Index.—For the entry of these cautions an Index called the Minor Interests Index is established by the following rule of the Land Registration Rules 1925:

(*r*) Land Registration Act 1925, ss. 2, 69.

(*s*) Sections 5, 20.

(*t*) Sections 9, 23.

(*u*) Sections 41, 42. And see s. 69 (4), which provides that "the estate for the time being vested in the proprietor shall only be capable of being disposed of or dealt with by him in manner authorised by this Act".

(*x*) Land Registration Act 1925, s. 101 (1), (2), (3). "Minor interests" are defined by s. 3 (xv). They are interests not capable of being disposed of or created by registered dispositions, and capable of being overridden by the proprietor unless protected as provided by the Act—*i.e.*, by notices, cautions, inhibitions, or restrictions— and they include interests under trusts for sale and settlements, whether so protected or not. The provision that they shall take effect as equitable interests corresponds to the general rule that interests which are not capable of subsisting as legal estates take effect as equitable interests: Law of Property Act 1925, s. 4 (1); but it goes further since a fee simple created off the register is a minor interest. And see *Elias* v. *Mitchell* [1972] Ch. 652; [1972] 2 All E.R. 153.

(*y*) The form of the caution is incorporated in the form of application for registration in the Minor Interests Index: Land Registration Rules 1925, Sched. Form 72. The application is made by the incumbrancer, and gives short particulars of (1) The instrument of charge; (2) The minor interest affected; (3) The nature of the dealing. For a mortgage, the appropriate protection is a caution; for an absolute assignment free from any right of redemption, it is an inhibition. See r. 229 (2), (6).

R. 11.—(1) There shall also (z) be kept an Index to be called the Minor
Interests Index in which all priority cautions and inhibitions relating to
dealings with minor interests, which do not affect the powers of disposition
of the proprietor, shall be entered.

(2) This Index shall be in such form, and contain such particulars as the
Registrar may from time to time determine. The entries therein shall not
form part of the register, nor shall any purchaser be concerned with that
Index.

The interests under consideration—life interests, etc.—do not affect
the powers of disposition of the registered proprietor (a), and consequently dealings with them can be entered in the Minor Interests
Index. That this is so is assumed by r. 229 (1), which is as follows (b):

R. 229.—(1) A priority caution, lodged under sub-s. (2) of s. 102 of the
Act, shall be entered in the Minor Interests Index, and notice of the entry
shall be given to the proprietor, and, in the case of settled land, to the trustees
of settlement (c). But a person who lodges a priority caution is not entitled
to notice of any intended registered disposition or entry in the register.

Equitable interests in registered charges.—It appears, indeed,
both from r. 11 and from the sub-rule just quoted, that this system of
entering priority cautions in respect of dealings with limited interests
in land is outside the system of registration of title (d), and exists solely
for the purpose of applying the rule in *Dearle* v. *Hall* to such dealings.
And the Act authorises similar provisions as to priorities to be applied
to minor interests in registered charges:

105.—Rules may be made for applying the provisions of this Part of this
Act (e) as to minor interests to the case of minor interests in a debt secured
by a registered charge.

The Registrar as a trust corporation.—Accordingly the following
sub-rules apply both to registered land and registered charges:

R. 229.—(4) As respects registered land, the registration of a priority caution
shall take the place of any notice or indorsed memorandum which, in the case
of unregistered land, would under s. 137 of the Law of Property Act 1925,
be given or made.

(5) As respects registered land and registered charges, the provisions of
s. 138 of the Law of Property Act 1925, shall apply as if the Registrar were
the trust corporation nominated for the purposes of that section, and the
Minor Interests Index were the register therein referred to.

Scope of priority cautions.—Although s. 102 (2) provides for
priority cautions only in respect of limited interests in the land itself,
the effect of the rules appears to be that such cautions regulate priorities
as regards all the equitable interests which may exist in respect of
registered land—both where the land is settled land and where it is
not settled land, or under a trust for sale of the land—or in a registered

---

(z) The earlier rules provide for the keeping of the Property and other Registers,
an Index Map and an Index of proprietors' names.

(a) The interest will arise under a settlement and can be overreached by the tenant
for life, who will be the registered proprietor, under his statutory powers.

(b) The rule appears to be made in pursuance of the rule-making power conferred by
r. 144 (1) (xxiii).

(c) If the system of priority cautions is confined to the equitable interests in land
mentioned in s. 102 (2), the land will, as already stated, be settled land, but the
system seems to have been extended by the rules to interests under trusts for sale:
supra.

(d) See Ruoff and Roper, *Registered Conveyancing* (3rd Edn.), pp. 135 *et seq.*

(e) Part IX, "Unregistered Dealings with Registered Land".

charge. As regards all such interests the application of the rule in *Dearle* v. *Hall* does not depend on notice to the trustees or other holders of the property, or, in the absence of trustees, on endorsed memorandum under s. 137 of the Law of Property Act 1925; or on notice to a trust corporation nominated under s. 138. But s. 138 applies as though the Registrar were the nominated trust corporation; as though priority cautions took the place of notice; and as though the Minor Interests Index were the register referred to in s. 138 (7) (*f*).

It follows that wherever an equitable interest in settled land, or in the proceeds of sale of land under a trust for sale, or in a trust fund, is offered as security it is necessary, in addition to the inquiries to be made under the rule in *Dearle* v. *Hall*, as extended or applied in ss. 137 and 138 of the Law of Property Act 1925, to inquire further whether the subject of the proposed security comprises or has at any time comprised registered land or a registered charge on registered land, and if so, inquiry must be made as to entries in the Minor Interests Index (*g*).

E—FUNDS IN COURT

Stop orders.—When a fund is in court, an incumbrancer on it can secure priority by obtaining a stop order (*h*). This will be as effectual for the purpose as notice in other cases (*i*), and will give a better right than notice to the trustees given after the payment into court (*k*); provided the mortgagor claims directly under the trustees whose trust is being administered by the court (*l*).

But the stop order will not give priority over a prior mortgagee of whose mortgage the party obtaining the stop order had notice when he made his advance, although such prior mortgagee may have omitted to obtain a stop order himself (*m*). Where, however, the

---

(*f*) Land Registration Rules 1925, r. 229 (5).

(*g*) Replies to such inquiries will be made on the principle prescribed by Law of Property Act 1925, s. 138 (9), (10); p. 477, *supra.* Land Registration Rules 1925, r. 290 (2).

(*h*) Notice to the Accountant-General of a charging order upon a fund in court is useless for the purposes of priority; for though memoranda of such orders are entered in the office of the Accountant-General, they are not considered to be any restraint upon the fund, and a doubt has been judicially expressed, whether, under such circumstances, it is proper to enter them any more than any other charge: *Warburton* v. *Hill* (1854), Kay, 470. Notice of the stop order should be given to all persons who have obtained similar orders on the fund: *Hulkes* v. *Day* (1840), 10 Sim. 41. Since the Judicature Acts, it is not necessary for a person who has recovered judgment in a Division of the High Court, other than the Chancery Division, to obtain a charging order before applying for a stop order on a fund standing to the credit of the Chancery Division: *Hopewell* v. *Barnes* (1876), 1 Ch. D. 630. A stop order cannot be obtained on a fund in court in respect of a mortgage of costs not yet ordered to be paid: *Lord* v. *Colvin* (1862), 2 Dr. & Sm. 82. See R.S.C. Ord. 50, r. 10. And see p. 163, *supra.* Where securities are not in court the procedure is by way of stop notice: see R.S.C. Ord. 50, rr. 11 *et seq.*; and see p. 162, *supra.*

(*i*) *Greening* v. *Beckford* (1832), 5 Sim. 195; *Swayne* v. *Swayne* (1848), 11 Beav. 463; *Warburton* v. *Hill, supra*; *Montefiore* v. *Guedalla,* [1903] 2 Ch. 26. Where an assignee who has obtained a stop order assigns his interest, his assignee should obtain a stop order: *Wheatley* v. *Bastow* (1855), 3 W.R. 296; on app., 7 De G.M. & G. 261 3 W.R. 540.

(*k*) *Pinnock* v. *Bailey* (1883), 23 Ch. D. 497.

(*l*) *Stephens* v. *Green,* [1895] 2 Ch. 148. And see *Re Bell* (1886), 54 L.T. 370; *Re Dallas,* [1904] 2 Ch. 385 (C.A.), at p. 403; *Re Seager Hunt,* [1906] 2 Ch. 295.

(*m*) *Re Hamilton's Windsor Ironworks, Ex parte Pitman and Edwards* (1879), 12 Ch. D. 707, 711; *Re Holmes* (1885), 29 Ch. D. 786; *Montefiore* v. *Guedalla, supra.*

second incumbrancer was ignorant of the prior mortgage when he made his advance, he will get priority by means of a stop order obtained after he is informed of the first mortgage (*n*). Like notice, also, the stop order applies only to the particular charge in respect of which it is obtained, although it is granted against the whole fund (*o*).

Apparently a stop order will not affect funds paid into court after its date unless those funds are named in the order (*p*).

Carrying share to new account.—If, after the stop order has been obtained, the share is carried over to the account of the mortgagor and his incumbrancers, a stop order obtained by a later mortgagee will not affect the priority of him who obtained the first, though, it seems, it would be otherwise if the fund were carried over to the account of the mortgagor alone (*q*).

Stop orders on same day.—When several stop orders have been obtained on the same day, a prior notice by one of the assignees will give priority to his claim (*r*); or, perhaps, the claims rank in order of their dates (*s*). And where none of the assignees has obtained a stop order, notice to the trustees may be effectual to determine priority (*t*).

Incumbrance at payment in.—When a person who has a lien upon a fund, of which he is the holder, pays it into court, he should state his claim and obtain a stop order; otherwise he may lose his priority as against a creditor without notice of the lien, who gets such an order (*u*). But if, before conversion and payment into court of the proceeds of incumbered property, an incumbrancer has completed his title by giving notice to the holder, his priority will not be affected by a stop order obtained by another claimant (*x*).

Bankruptcy of beneficiary.—If there is no fund in court which could be the subject of a stop order before the bankruptcy of the assignor, and the assignee has given notice, he will have a better right than the bankruptcy trustee to the fund when brought into court (*y*).

If the trustee himself makes the advance, the fund being in court, he should obtain a stop order, so that any other person who proposes to make an advance may ascertain if the fund is incumbered (*z*). And a trustee in bankruptcy must protect himself by a stop order (*a*).

(*n*) *Timson* v. *Ramsbottom* (1837), 2 Keen, 35.
(*o*) *Re Dallas*, [1904] 2 Ch. 385 (C.A.), at p. 395.
(*p*) *Timson* v. *Ramsbottom, ubi supra*, p. 49.
(*q*) *Mutual Life Assurance Society* v. *Langley* (1886), 32 Ch. D. 460; *Ward* v. *Royal Exchange Shipping Co., Ex parte Harrison* (1887), 58 L.T. 174.
(*r*) *Macleod* v. *Buchanan* (1864), 4 De G.J. & S. 265. The order should state whether capital or income, or both, are affected. If it does not, recourse may be had to any part of the order to ascertain its operation: *Mack* v. *Postle*, [1894] 2 Ch. 449.
(*s*) *Shaw* v. *Hudson* (1879), 48 L.J. Ch. 689.
(*t*) *Lister* v. *Tidd* (1867), L.R. 4 Eq. 462; *Mutual Life Assurance Society* v. *Langley supra.*
(*u*) *Swayne* v. *Swayne* (1848), 11 Beav. 463.
(*x*) *Brearcliff* v. *Dorrington* (1850), 4 De G. & Sm. 122; *Livesey* v. *Harding* (1856), 23 Beav. 141; see *Re Marquis of Anglesey, De Galve* v. *Gardner*, [1903] 2 Ch. 727, 732.
(*y*) *Day* v. *Day* (1857), 1 De G. & J. 144.
(*z*) *Elder* v. *Maclean* (1857), 5 W.R. 447; see *Mutual Life Assurance Society* v. *Langley supra.*
(*a*) *Stuart* v. *Cockerell* (1869), L.R. 8 Eq. 607; *Palmer* v. *Locke* (1881), 18 Ch. D. 381; and see p. 466, *supra.*

VIII—EFFECT OF REGISTRATION

A—THE LAND CHARGES REGISTER

Statutory provisions.—With regard to land charges which can be registered in the Land Charges Register, the Land Charges Act 1972, provides: (b)

4.—(2) A land charge of Class A created after the 31 December, 1888, shall be void as against a purchaser of the land charged with it or of any interest in such land, unless the land charge is registered in the register of land charges before the completion of the purchase. . . . .

(5) A land charge of Class B and a land charge of Class C (other than an estate contract) created or arising on or after 1 January, 1926, shall be void as against a purchaser of the land charged with it, or of any interest in such land, unless the land charge is registered in the appropriate register before the completion of the purchase.

(6) An estate contract and a land charge of Class D created or entered into on or after 1 January, 1926, shall be void as against a purchaser for money or money's worth of a legal estate in the land charged with it, unless the land charge is registered in the appropriate register before the completion of the purchase. . . . .

(8) A land charge of Class F shall be void as against a purchaser of the land charged with it, or of any interest in such land, unless the land charge is registered in the appropriate register before the completion of the purchase (c).

And the Law of Property Act 1925, as amended (d), provides:

97.—Every mortgage affecting a legal estate in land made after the commencement of this Act, whether legal or equitable (not being a mortgage protected by the deposit of documents relating to the legal estate affected) shall rank according to its date of registration as a land charge pursuant to the Land Charges Act 1972.

This sub-section does not apply to mortgages or charges to which the Land Charges Act 1972 does not apply by virtue of s. 14 (3) of that Act (which excludes certain land charges created by instruments necessitating registration under the Land Registration Act 1925) or to mortgages or charges of registered land (e).

This section only relates to mortgages capable of registration as land charges, namely, puisne mortgages—that is, legal mortgages not

---

(b) As to the land charges which can be registered, and as to these Classes, see p. 443, *supra*.

(c) For the section generally, "purchaser" means "any person (including a mortgagee or lessee) who, for valuable consideration, takes any interest in land or in a charge on land": s. 17 (1). And see *McCarthy and Stone, Ltd.* v. *Julian S. Hodge & Co., Ltd.,* [1971] 2 All E.R. 973; *Wroth* v. *Tyler,* [1974] Ch. 30; [1973] 1 All E.R. 897. For priority pitfalls, see (1974) 124 New L.J. 286 (D. J. Hayton).

(d) By the Land Registration and Land Charges Act 1971, s. 9 (2) and Land Charges Act 1972, s. 18 and Sched. 3, para. 1.

(e) Statutes which declare the priority between registered instruments, in effect give them priority over unregistered unstruments. Otherwise the object of registration would be defeated: see *Black* v. *Williams,* [1895] 1 Ch. 408, as to the shipping register. And see p. 489 *infra*. But registration will not give priority if the intention of the instrument is only to pass the actual interest of the grantor. Thus a deed of assignment for the benefit of creditors does not by registration acquire priority over an earlier unregistered mortgage: *Jones* v. *Barker,* [1909] 1 Ch. 321; and see *Chung Khiaw Bank, Ltd.* v. *United Overseas Bank, Ltd.,* [1970] A.C. 767 (P.C.); *Security Trust Co.* v. *Royal Bank of Canada,* [1976] A.C. 503; [1976] 1 All E.R. 381 (P.C.). Registration does not give validity to a forged deed: *Re Cooper, Cooper* v. *Vesey* (1882), 20 Ch. D. 611.

protected by a deposit of documents (Class C (i))—and equitable charges, also not secured by deposit of documents (Class C (ii), (iii), and Class D (i)), and is confined to mortgages which affect a legal estate. Thus it includes a legal and an equitable mortgage created by an estate owner (where not accompanied by deposit of deeds), but not a mortgage or charge of an equitable interest (*f*).

The Law of Property Act 1925, also provides:

> **199.**—A purchaser shall not be prejudicially affected by notice of—
> (i) any instrument or matter capable of registration under the provisions of the Land Charges Act 1925, or any enactment which it replaces, which is void or not enforceable as against him under that Act or enactment, by reason of the non-registration thereof (*g*).

Effect of registration.—Registration of puisne mortgages and equitable charges, hereinafter referred to as land charges, has, therefore, the following effect:

(i) Registered land charges rank in order of registration;

(ii) An unregistered land charge is valid as between the parties to it;

(iii) A later legal land charge does not prevail over an earlier registered equitable land charge by virtue of the legal estate (*h*);

(iv) The owner of a registered land charge (the chargee) which does not cover further advances, cannot tack a further advance made after registration of a later land charge; nor, unless he has registered a fresh land charge, can he set it up against a later land charge whether registered or not. But when the registered land charge covers further advances, the chargee can tack by virtue of the contract (i);

(v) A later land charge, whether registered or not, has priority over an earlier unregistered land charge even though it was taken with actual notice of the earlier unregistered land charge (*k*).

(vi) The Law of Property Act 1925, s. 97, enacts expressly that registered land charges rank in order of registration; s. 4 (5) of the Land Charges Act 1972, provides that a puisne mortgage or general equitable charge created or arising after 1925 shall be void as against a purchaser (*c*) of the land charged with it, or of any interest in such land, unless the land charge is registered in the appropriate register before the completion of the purchase. Difficulties may occur in reconciling these provisions where several mortgages are made before any or all are registered, and

---

(*f*) The priorities of mortgages of equitable interests in land are governed by the rules in *Dearle* v. *Hall*, as extended by s. 137 of the Law of Property Act 1925: see p. 463, *supra*.

(*g*) See *Diligent Finance Co., Ltd.* v. *Alleyne* (1972), 23 P. & C.R. 346.

(*h*) Because the later chargee has notice—by the registration—of the earlier charge, he is postponed.

(*i*) See p. 461, *supra*. This is a case where the rule that registration constitutes notice is excluded.

(*k*) See s. 4 (5), (6). This does not impose the condition that a purchaser shall himself be registered.

(*c*) For this footnote, see p. 482, *supra*.

then some or all are registered. A *circulus inextricabilis* may arise. It seems that s. 97 is to be read subject to s. 4 (5) (*l*) and the doctrine of subrogation resorted to if more than two competing mortgages are involved (*m*).

Deposit of deeds.—A mortgage, whether legal or equitable, which is accompanied by deposit of deeds, does not require registration as a land charge (*n*).

No priority is expressly conferred by statute on a mortgagee who holds the deeds (*o*), but this will usually give him priority over other mortgages, whether legal or equitable: over legal mortgages because the legal mortgagee will be postponed for negligence in not getting in or keeping the deeds (*p*); over equitable mortgagees because the possession of the deeds will give him the better equity (*q*).

Local land charges.—Failure to register a local land charge in the appropriate local land charges register does not affect the enforceability of the charge, but gives a purchaser who suffers any loss thereby, or by a defective official search certificate, a right to compensation (*r*). Where the interest is subject to a mortgage the mortgagee may claim, but no compensation is payable in respect of the mortgagee's interest as distinct from the mortgaged property (*s*).

B—THE LAND REGISTER

Registered charges.—In respect of charges on land registered under the Land Registration Act 1925, the charges rank in order of registration. Thus:

> **29.**—Subject to any entry to the contrary on the register, registered charges on the same land shall as between themselves rank according to the order in which they are entered on the Register, and not according to the order in which they are created (*t*).

(*l*) See (1943), 7 C.L.J. 243 (R. E. Megarry); for a contrary view (1950), 13 M.L.R. 534–5 (A. D. Hargreaves).
(*m*) See *Benham* v. *Keane* (1861), I John. & H. 685, at pp. 710–712; *Re Wyatt, White* v. *Ellis,* [1892] I Ch. 188, 208–209; *cf. Re Weniger's Policy,* [1910] 2 Ch. 291. And see (1961) 71 Yale L.J. 53 (G. Gilmore); (1968) 32 Conv. (N.S.) 325 (W. A. Lee). The parties may be arrangement made between themselves vary the order of priorities; see *e.g.*, p. 460, *supra.* This is done by a deed of postponement.
(*n*) Land Charges Act 1972, s. 2 (4), Class C (i), (iii). But see p. 52, *supra.*
(*o*) Section 13 of the Law of Property Act 1925 though it prevents the Act from prejudicing rights arising out of the possession of deeds, does not appear to exclude ss. 197, 198, so as to make a search unnecessary on making an advance on deposit of the deeds (see p. 452, *supra*).
(*p*) See pp. 451, 452, *supra.*
(*q*) See p. 454, *supra.* But while a mortgage by deposit, who obtains all the deeds, would prevail over an earlier unregistered mortgage—for this would be a puisne mortgage or an equitable charge and would be void against him—yet he is not safe if any material deed happens to be outstanding (see p. 45, *supra*); and this circumstance deprives this non-registrable form of security of the complete protection afforded by registration. Moreover, there is the possibility that the mortgagee by deposit may be postponed to a legal mortgagee who can account for his not holding the deeds.
(*r*) Local Land Charges Act 1975, s. 10. See note (*d*), p. 445, *supra.*
(*s*) *Ibid.*, s. 11.
(*t*) And see p. 66, *supra.* As to obtaining priority for a contemplated charge by an official search, see *Smith* v. *Morrison,* [1974] I All E.R. 957.

This, however, is subject to other arrangements, made between the parties, and the order of priority may be varied, provided the variation appears on the register. Such variation is sufficiently made by a clause in the instrument of charge providing for the charges to rank either *pari passu*, or otherwise in a manner different from the rule in s. 29 (*u*). An alternation in priorities can be made after the registration of the charge by further deed. It requires the consent of the proprietor of the registered land, and of the proprietors of all registered charges (if any) of equal or inferior priority, affected by the alteration. The alteration is completed by entry on the register (*a*).

A subsequent registered charge has priority to any prior charge not registered or protected on the register (*b*).

Lien by deposit of land certificate.—To the mortgage of unregistered land by deposit of deeds (*c*), there corresponds the lien on registered land which can be created by deposit of the land certificate (*d*). No provision is made as to priority, but protection against dealings with the land can be obtained by giving notice of the deposit to the Registrar (*e*). Further, he is protected against any subsequent registered disposition by the impossibility of effecting such disposition without production of the certificate to the Registrar (*f*). In effect, therefore, if the certificate shows no registered charge, the mortgagee by deposit obtains a first charge on the land, unless he has, at the time of his advance, notice of an unregistered charge (*g*).

Mortgages off the register.—As previously mentioned (*h*), a mortgage off the register may be created, by deed or otherwise, as if the land had not been registered, and such a mortgage should be protected by caution or notice (*i*). There is no express provision that the register constitutes notice as to registered land, corresponding to the provision that the Land Charges Register constitutes notice as to unregistered land (*k*). And this is not necessary. The title is made out, not by deeds, but by the register itself, and there is the same obligation on a mortgagee of registered land to search the register as there is on a mortgagee of unregistered land to examine the deeds. Hence the mortgagee has notice of what he would find by search of the register. Between minor interests (*l*), *e.g.*, unprotected equitable mortgages, it seems that the pre-1926 rules apply (*m*), and priority is determined,

---

(*u*) See Land Registration Rules 1925, rr. 139, 140; Form 45, Stipulations B.
(*a*) Land Registration Act 1925, s. 31; Rules, r. 150; Form 51.
(*b*) Land Registration Act 1925, ss. 20, 23: see *De Lusignan* v. *Johnson* (1973), 230 Estates Gazette 499 (where it was also held that the court had no discretion to amend the register under R.S.C. Ord. 18, r. 19 (1)).
(*c*) See p. 44, *supra*.
(*d*) Section 66; p. 66, *supra*.
(*e*) Land Registration Rules 1925, r. 239. The notice operates as a caution under s. 54 of the Act.
(*f*) *Ibid.*, s. 64.
(*g*) And see p. 67, *supra*.
(*h*) See p. 68, *supra*.
(*i*) See pp. 69, 70, *supra*.
(*k*) See p. 442, *supra*.
(*l*) See pp. 67, 69, *supra*.
(*m*) See p. 446, *supra*.

prima facie, by the order of creation rather than the date of protection (*n*).

Tacking further advances.—There has been, as regards registered land, no express abolition of the doctrine of tacking, but in effect this is abolished by the provision that registered charges rank in order of date of registration. Section 94 of the Law of Property Act 1925, which, while expressly abolishing that doctrine in general, provides for tacking in cases where the mortgage is originally made to cover further advances, does not apply to registered land, but provision to the same effect is made by s. 30 of the Land Registration Act 1925 (*o*). Apart from this, a further advance can only be safely made after searching the register, and it must be protected by a new registered charge or an alteration of the existing charge (*p*). This will then take its place in due order according to the register (*q*).

C—BILLS OF SALE (*r*)

Priority according to order of registration.—The Bills of Sale Act 1878, provides:

> **10.**—(3) In case two or more bills of sale are given, comprising in whole or in part any of the same chattels, they shall have priority in the order of the date of their registration respectively as regards such chattels.

Consequently, the holder of a later registered bill of sale does not, by taking possession of the goods, obtain priority over the holder of an earlier registered bill (*s*). And although the language of this sub-section appears to be applicable only to questions of priority between earlier and later registered bills of sale, it provides in effect that registered bills of sale shall have priority over such as are unregistered, so far as the latter have any force (*t*). And an unregistered bill of sale will be void as against an execution creditor, though the latter had notice of it when his debt was contracted (*a*). But under the Bills of Sale Act (1878) Amendment Act 1882, all unregistered bills of sale given by way of security are *ipso facto* void (*b*).

(*n*) See *Barclays Bank, Ltd.* v. *Taylor,* [1974] Ch. 137 (C.A.); [1973] 1 All E.R 752. For the confused state of priorities of mortgages of registered land see [1966] C.L.P. 26 (E. C. Ryder); (1971) 35 Conv. (N.S.) 122, 168 (S. Robinson); (1974), 124 New L.J. 634 (S. Robinson); Hayton, *Registered land;* Law Commission Working Paper No. 67 (1976). Under systems of title registration, the system of registration generally replaces the former rules of equitable priorities (see, e.g., *Farrier-Waimak, Ltd.* v. *Bank of New Zealand,* [1965] A.C. 376, (P.C.) [1964] 3 All E.R. 657; and failure to use the system's methods of protection may lead to loss of priority against a subsequent unregistered or protected equitable mortgage: see *Lapin* v. *Abigail* (1930), 44 C.L.R. 166 (on appeal *Abigail* v. *Lapin,* [1934] A.C. 491 (P.C.) and the discussion in Sykes, *The Law of Securities,* (2nd Edn.), pp. 386 *et seq.*

(*o*) See p. 462, *supra,* where the section is set out.

(*q*) See p. 485, *supra.*

(*r*) See (1969) 47 Can. Bar Rev. 420 (Dallas W. Lee).

(*s*) See *Re Middleton, Ex parte Allen* (1870), L.R. 11 Eq. 209.

(*t*) *Conelly* v. *Steer* (1881), 7 Q.B.D. 520; *Lyons* v. *Tucker* (1881), 7 Q.B.D. 523.

(*a*) *Edwards* v. *Edwards* (1876), 2 Ch. D. 291.

(*b*) See p. 93, *supra.*

D—MORTGAGES BY COMPANIES

Registration.—Mortgages and charges made by limited companies require registration with the Registrar of Companies and, if not registered, are void as regards security on the company's property, against the liquidator and creditors (*c*). In addition, company charges over unregistered land are capable of registration as land charges (*d*) and company charges of registered land capable of registration under the Land Registration Act (*e*) (in both cases, where appropriate(*f*)). The provision for registration in the Companies Register is construed strictly, and a subsequent registered incumbrancer takes free from an unregistered mortgage, even though he had express notice of it when he obtained his security (*g*).

IX—JUDGMENT CREDITORS

Effect of judgment.—The interest of the judgment creditor (whether he is with or without notice) in the property of his debtor is subject to every liability under which the debtor holds it. If the debtor has a legal estate subject to an equity effective against third parties, *e.g.*, registered, if registration is required, the judgment (if and when it becomes a charge) will be a charge upon the estate subject to the same equity; and in an equitable estate, the judgment will affect the equitable interest (*h*). A judgment creditor has, therefore, no priority by force of his judgment over persons who have prior equitable interests in the same estate (*i*); whether he claims (in an ordinary case of trust) against the estate of the *cestui que trust* (*k*) or against such an equitable interest as that of a purchaser for value who has paid his purchase money without getting a conveyance (*l*).

(*c*) See pp. 181–185, *supra*, where the requirements of registration are stated.
(*d*) See p. 52, *supra*.
(*e*) See p. 185, *supra*.
(*f*) If a prior mortgage which is capable of registration under s. 95 of the Companies Act 1948, is not so registered, but is registered under the Land Registration Act 1925, (with the appropriate note, see p. 186, *supra*) and if a subsequent charge is registered under s. 95 of the Companies Act, but not registered under the Land Registration Act, in view of the provisions of s. 60 of the Land Registration Act 1925, the subsequent charge would not by reason of its registration in the Companies Registry alone have priority; see Ruoff and Roper, *Registered Conveyancing*, (3rd Edn.), p. 532.
Where a company is registered as proprietor of land under the Land Registration Act 1925, the Registrar is not concerned with any mortgage, charge, debenture, etc., to which the land is subject, even though registered under the Companies Act 1948, unless the charge has been registered or otherwise protected under the Land Registration Act 1925: Land Registration Act 1925, s. 60.
(*g*) *Re Monolithic Building Co., Tacon* v. *Monolithic Building Co.*, [1915] 1 Ch. D. 643; see p. 182, *supra*.
(*h*) *Langton* v. *Horton* (1842), 1 Hare. 549; *Whitworth* v. *Gaugain* (1846), 1 Ph. 728; *Abbott* v. *Stratten* (1846), 3 Jo. & Lat. 603; *Hughes* v. *Williams* (1852), 3 Mac. & G. 683; *Ames* v. *Trustees of Birkenhead Docks* (1855), 20 Beav. 332.
(*i*) *Whitworth* v. *Gaugain* (1846), 3 Hare, at p. 427; affd. 1 Ph. 728; *Williams* v. *Craddock* (1831), 4 Sim 313; *Abbott* v. *Stratten, supra;* see *Lodge* v. *Lyseley* (1832), 4 Sim. 70; *Brearcliff* v. *Dorrington* (1850), 4 De G. & Sm. 122; *Eyre* v. *M'Dowell* (1861), 9 H.L. Cas. 619.
(*k*) *Newlands* v. *Paynter* (1839), 4 My. & C.R. 408.
(*l*) *Finch* v. *Earl of Winchelsea* (1715), 1 P. Wms. 277. The judgment creditor cannot, by giving notice to the trustee of a fund, put himself in any better position than the judgment debtor, and therefore cannot thereby gain priority over the mortgagees of the latter, who have omitted to give notice of their charges to the trustee: p. 466, *supra*.

Charging order (*m*).—A charging order upon stock is presumed to be a lawful charge, and therefore a charge only upon such interest as the debtor really possessed (*n*).

A judgment creditor, therefore, cannot gain priority by virtue of a charging order (whether *nisi* or absolute) over the equitable mortgagee of a chose in action who has given no notice, whether the mortgage were earlier or later than the judgment, but before the charging order; not only because the creditor gets nothing but what the debtor can dispose of, but because, before the date of the order, the debtor has ceased to be the sole owner of the fund (*o*).

The order *nisi* operates as a charge (subject to cause being shown against making it absolute) and, subject to registration of orders affecting land (*p*), it cannot be defeated by any subsequent proceeding. The priority of a creditor who has obtained judgment against the executor of his debtor, and a charging order *nisi*, will, therefore, not be affected by a decree for the administration of the debtor's estate before the charging order was made absolute (*q*). And, as a charging order has no greater effect than a charge executed by the judgment debtor (*r*), a charging order under a judgment by default for a debt which was incapable of being enforced will be inoperative (*s*).

Registration of writs and orders affecting land.—The Land Charges Act 1972 provides for the registration of writs and orders affecting land made for the purpose of enforcing a judgment or recognisance, any order appointing a receiver or sequestrator of land and any receiving order in bankruptcy, whether or not it is known to affect land (*t*). Failure to register makes such writ or order void as against a purchaser of the land (*u*). The above provision specifies the relevant priority point (*a*) for the purposes of the priority position of the judgment creditor. Until the writ or order is so registered, the judgment creditor does not have any priority.

Chattels.—Where the equitable incumbrancer of chattels has

(*m*) See pp. 159 *et seq.*, *supra*.

(*n*) See *Beavan* v. *Earl of Oxford* (1856), 6 De G. M. & G. 507; and see the judgment of ROMILLY, M. R., in *Kinderley* v. *Jervis* (1856), 22 Beav: 1; *Brearcliff* v. *Dorrington, supra; Dunster* v. *Lord Glengall* (1853), 3 Ir. Ch. R. 47; *Benham* v. *Keane* (1861), 1 John & H. 685; *Pickering* v. *Ilfracombe Rail. Co.* (1868), L.R. 3 C.P. 235; *Robinson* v. *Nesbitt* (1868), L.R. 3 C.P. 264; *Re Bell, Carter* v. *Stadden* (1886), 54 L.T. 370.

(*o*) *Scott* v. *Lord Hastings* (1858), 4 K. & J. 633; *Warburton* v. *Hill* (1854), Kay, 470. And the ground for giving a second mortgagee priority over the first, by reason of his having been led to take an incumbered as an unincumbered property, is not applicable to a judgment creditor; who has not been deceived as to the condition of the title, and as to whom the judgment debtor has been guilty of no deceit in suffering judgment: *Scott* v. *Lord Hastings*, *supra*. This view has prevailed over the opinion of the majority of the Court of Queen's Bench, who held that a judgment creditor, who, having obtained a charging order upon stock, had given notice to the trustees, was entitled to priority over a previous mortgagee of the same stock, who had given no notice of his charge. *Watts* v. *Porter* (1854), 3 E. & B. 743.

(*p*) See below.

(*q*) *Haly* v. *Barry* (1868), L.R. 3 E. & B. 743.

(*r*) See p. 159, *supra*.

(*s*) *Re Onslow's Trusts* (1875) L.R. 20 Eq. 677.

(*t*) Section 6 (1).

(*u*) Section 6 (4).

(*a*) See Sykes, *The Law of Securities* (2nd Edn.), pp. 19 *et seq.*, 28–29, 349 *et seq.* 639–640.

completed his title by giving notice (*b*), he will have priority over the subsequent judgment creditor without notice, who has sued out his *fi. fa.* It has, therefore, been held that a judgment creditor has no right to take in execution a ship and cargo, as against prior equitable mortgagees (under a security made whilst the ship was at sea), who had sent notice of the assignment to the master, and had received immediate possession of the property from him upon the termination of the voyage (*c*).

X—SHIPPING MORTGAGES

Registered mortgages.—Provision for the registration of mortgages on ships is made by the Merchant Shipping Act 1894 (*d*), and as regards priority it is enacted:

> **33.**—If there are more mortgages than one registered in respect of the same ship or share, the mortgagees shall, notwithstanding any express, implied, or constructive notice, be entitled in priority, one over the other, according to the date at which each mortgage is recorded in the register book, and not according to the date of each mortgage itself (*e*).

Although in terms this applies only to registered mortgages, yet it also gives such mortgages priority over unregistered mortgages, and a registered mortgage ranks in front of an earlier unregistered mortgage, notwithstanding that the later mortgagee had notice thereof when he advanced his money (*f*).

But the effect of s. 33 is only to substitute for the purpose of priorities the dates of registration for the dates of the instruments, and where the priorities depend, not upon the dates of the instruments, but upon matters independent of such dates, the section does not apply. A further advance made under a mortgage to secure further advances, or a further credit allowed under a current account mortgage, is such a matter. Accordingly the section does not prevent the application of the principle of *Hopkinson* v. *Rolt* (*g*), and a further advance or credit made or allowed by the holder of a first registered mortgage, when he has notice of a second registered mortgage, will not be allowed priority over the second mortgage (*h*).

(*b*) See p. 467, *supra.*
(*c*) *Langton* v. *Horton* (1842), 1 Hare, 549. It was intimated (p. 560) that if the prior equitable title was incomplete, the claim of a subsequent judgment creditor as well as that of a subsequent equitable purchaser, might prevail. But this would be contrary to the principle stated above. The judgment creditor takes subject to any prior equity.
(*d*) See p. 98, *supra.*
(*e*) See also s. 43 (5), which gives to mortgages registered on a certificate of mortgage, issued to enable a mortgage to be made abroad, priority over mortgages created subsequently to the registration of the certificate.
(*f*) *Black* v. *Williams*, [1895] 1 Ch. 408; *Barclay* v. *Poole*, [1907] 2 Ch. 284.
(*g*) (1861), 9 H.L.C. 514; see p. 458, *supra.*
(*h*) *The Benwell Tower* (1895), 8 Asp. M.C. 13. The mere fact of the second mortgage being registered does not appear to be notice so as to stop further advances by the first mortgagee. But probably a registered mortgagee cannot tack further advances by virtue of a subsequent unregistered agreement extending the mortgage to cover such advances: *Parr* v. *Applebee* (1855), 7 De G.M. & G. 585. That case was, however, decided on the ground that other persons than the first mortgagee were interested under the subsequent agreement.

Unregistered mortgages.—At first the policy of the Merchant Shipping Acts was not to allow any validity to unregistered mortgages (i); but this has been abandoned. No notice of any trust, express, implied, or constructive, can be entered in the register or received by the Registrar (k). But unregistered dealings are effective to create equitable interests, and these may be enforced by or against owners and mortgagees of ships in the same manner as in respect of any other personal property (l). Thus, an unregistered mortgage has all the ordinary incidents of a mortgage, save that it does not confer a legal title and is liable to be postponed to any registered mortgage. As between unregistered mortgages priority is determined in accordance with the principles applicable to equitable mortgages. Prima facie they rank in order of date, but a prior mortgage may be postponed for negligence or other special cause (m).

Mortgage of cargo or freight.—It is incumbent on the mortgagee of cargo which is at sea to complete his title by giving notice, if practicable, to the master (n). But if this is not practicable, or if it involves taking steps which may prove useless and burdensome, he may give notice to the shipowner and consignees. It is sufficient that he does all in his power to obtain possession, and, if he does so, he will not be postponed to an assignee of later date who has been able to give earlier notice (o). In the same way the assignee of freight must complete his title by giving notice to the persons by whom the freight is payable, though under special circumstances, notice to the owner's agent was held to be sufficient (p).

Protection against execution creditor.—Although the mortgagee is not in general deemed to be the owner of the ship, yet he is owner so far as is necessary for making the ship available as a security, and therefore he is protected against a sale of the ship by an execution creditor of the mortgagor (q).

(i) (8 & 9 Vict. c. 89), ss. 34, 45; see *McCalmont* v. *Rankin* (1852), 2 De G.M. & G. 403; Merchant Shipping Act 1854, 17 & 18 Vict. c. 104, which, though in different terms, had the same effect: *Liverpool Borough Bank* v. *Turner* (1860), 1 John. & H. 159.

(k) Merchant Shipping Act 1894, s. 56.

(l) Merchant Shipping Act 1894, s. 57, reproducing the Merchant Shipping Amendment Act 1862, s. 3. And as to the rights and liabilities of beneficial owners, see also the Act of 1894, ss. 5 (ii), 9 (v), 30, 58.

(m) See *Keith* v. *Burrows* (1876), 1 C.P.D. 722; *Liverpool Marine Credit Co.* v. *Wilson* (1872), 7 Ch. App. 507.

For a case of rivalry between a mortgagee of a ship at sea without notice that the mortgagor had given the master a power of attorney to sell, and a subsequent purchaser abroad under the power of attorney without notice of the mortgage, see *Cato* v. *Irving* (1852), 5 De G. & Sm. 210, where the title of the mortgagee was upheld, though upon the terms of his making an allowance for the expenses of fitting the ship for the home voyage.

(n) *Langton* v. *Horton* (1842), 1 Hare, 549.

(o) *Feltham* v. *Clark* (1847), 1 De G. & Sm. 307; see *Kemp* v. *Falk* (1882), 7 App. Cas. 573, at p. 585. Similarly, notice may be required to take the cargo out of the reputed ownership of the cargo owner: *Re Gwyer, Ex parte Lucas* (1858), 3 De G. & J. 113; see *Ex parte Kelsall* (1846), De G. 352.

(p) *Gardner* v. *Lachlan* (1838), 4 Myl. & Cr. 129.

(q) Merchant Shipping Act 1894, s. 34; *Dickinson* v. *Kitchen; Kitchen* v. *Irving* (1858), 8 E. & B. 789, where this was held to be the effect of the corresponding section —s. 70—of the Merchant Shipping Act 1854, notwithstanding that the mortgage postponed the mortgagee's power of sale to a date subsequent to the seizure in execution.

Contract liens and salvage.—The precedence of maritime hypothecations and liens is to be determined according to the *lex fori* (*r*). The general rule in English law is that liens arising *ex contractu*, and liens for salvage, since they are in the nature of benefits for reward, rank in the inverse order of their attachment upon the *res* (*s*). "It is almost obvious that liens [arising *ex contractu* or *quasi ex contractu*] must in general rank against the fund in the inverse order of their attachment on the *res*. They are liens in respect of claims for services rendered, and it is reasonable that services which operate for the protection of prior interests should be privileged above those interests" (*t*).

Tort liens.—Liens arising *ex delicto*, which in general occur in collision cases, take precedence over prior securities and liens arising *ex contractu*, and also salvage (*u*). A person advancing money or rendering services does so at his own will; he can exercise his discretion as to whether he will assist the ship. But an injured party has no such option, and his claim to damages must be satisfied first (*a*).

As between several damage claims in respect of collisions with the same vessel, no one claim is allowed priority. Apart from laches, the claims rank *pari passu*, and not in order of the dates of the several collisions (*b*).

Priority over mortgages.—Both contract and salvage liens, and tort liens, rank before mortgages on the ship (*c*). The mortgagee takes his security subject to such incumbrances as the law may impose upon the ship for the benefit of third persons (*d*). But a bottomry creditor will not derive any advantage over a prior incumbrancer, by reason of an advance for the necessity of the ship, beyond the actual extent of the bottomry bond. Therefore, where charterers of a ship, with notice of a mortgage, took a bottomry bond which did not cover the expenses incurred, it was held that they could not, as against the mortgagee, set off the excess against the sum which became due under the charterparty (*e*).

(*r*) *The Union* (1860), 1 Lush. 128. This is so because the matter relates to the remedy to be enforced; but questions as to the nature of the right to be enforced are determined by the law of the flag (*The Byzantion* (1922), 38 T.L.R. 744), or by the law of the place of contract: *Hill's Dry Docks Engineering Co., Ltd.* v. *Owners of S.S. "Colorado"* (1923), 39 T.L.R. 216.

(*s*) *The Sydney Cove* (1815), 2 Dods. 1; *The Hope* (1873), 1 Asp. M.L.C. 563; see *The Stream Fisher*, [1927] P. 73. See *Todd Shipyards Corporation* v. *Altema Compania Maritima SA, The Ioannis Daskalelis*, [1974] 1 Lloyd's Rep. 174 (S.C. of Can.).

(*t*) *The Veritas*, [1901] P. 304, at p. 312.

(*u*) *The Veritas, supra*, at p. 313.

(*a*) *The Aline* (1839), 1 W. Rob. 111, where it was held that the claim of a bottomry bondholder was to be postponed to a claim for damages suffered at a date subsequent to the bond. And even the lien for mariners' wages ranks after a claim for damages: *The Linda Flor* (1857), Swab. 309; *The Elin* (1883), 8 P.D. 129; *The Veritas, supra*.

If, however, a bottomry bond is bona fide granted for repairs after damage done, then, since the damage creditor derives a benefit from the repairs, he is postponed: *The Aline, supra*.

(*b*) *The Stream Fisher, supra*.

(*c*) *The Aline, supra*. In *Hope* v. *Winter* (1709), 2 Eq. Cas. Abr. 690, ransom for a captured ship ranked before a mortgage.

(*d*) *The Dowthorpe* (1843), 2 W. Rob. 73. And see *The Fairport (No. 4)*, [1967] 2 All E.R. 914.

(*e*) *Dobson* v. *Lyall* (1847), 2 Ph. 323, note.

Special priorities.—These general rules, however, are in certain cases varied, either by statute, or by consideration of the special nature of the claims to lien. Thus, the statutory lien for the salvage of human life has priority over other salvage liens (*f*); and the lien of the mariners for their wages and subsistence (which, to use the expression of Lord STOWELL, is a sacred lien, lasting as long as a plank remains) has precedence over bottomry bonds, and other securities (*g*), whether the wages were earned before or after the date of the security (*h*). And payments for wages made by the direction of the master on account of the ship, or for pilotage, towage, light dues (which are enforceable by distress and must be paid before the ship can be cleared), and dock dues, are entitled to the same priority (*i*).

Master's lien.—In like manner the master will in general have priority over other claims in respect of his wages (*k*), and in respect of advances to seamen on account of wages, and other disbursements— *e.g.* for coal (*l*)—properly made for the benefit of the ship (*m*).

But although by statute the master is put upon the same footing as to wages with the mariners, he cannot set up a lien for his own wages, or for money advanced by him for payment of the wages of the mariners, in competition with their lien; for being, by an ancient rule of law, personally liable to them for their wages, whether the security is sufficient or not, he cannot take anything from it to their detriment (*n*). Nor has the master priority over a claim for necessaries for which he has made himself personally liable (*o*) or over a bottomry bond, if, as is usually the case, he has pledged his own credit for the loan (*p*). And even though not personally liable, he cannot claim precedence over the bond holder for the wages of a previous voyage (*q*).

Similarly if the master's own shares in the ship are comprised in a mortgage, his master's lien is postponed to the mortgage (*r*).

(*f*) Merchant Shipping Act 1894, s. 544 (2): "Salvage in respect of the preservation of human life, when payable by the owners of the vessel, shall be payable in priority to all other claims for salvage": see *The Coromandel* (1857), Swab. 205; *The Eastern Monarch* (1860), Lush. 81.

(*g*) *The Sydney Cove* (1815), 2 Dods. Ad. 1; *The William F. Safford* (1860), Lush. 69.

(*h*) *The Union* (1860), 1 Lush. 128.

(*i*) *The William F. Safford* (1860), 1 Lush. 69; *The St. Lawrence* (1880), 5 P.D. 250, where it was assumed that there was a lien for towage.

(*k*) *The Salacia* (1862), 1 Lush. 545; notwithstanding he is part owner: *The Feronia* (1868), L.R. 2 A. & E. 65; *The Daring* (1868), L.R. 2 A. & E. 260; and the master's lien will have priority over execution creditors: *The James W. Elwell*, [1921] P. 351.

(*l*) *The Ripon City*, [1897] p. 226.

(*m*) *The Mary Ann* (1865), L.R. 1 A. & E. 8; *The Ripon City, supra*. In *The Ringdove* (1886), 11 P.D. 120, the master's lien for disbursements had priority over the claim of a purchaser. And the master's lien prevails over a subsequent seizure of the ship by the sheriff: *The Ile de Ceylan*, [1922] P. 256.

(*n*) *The Salacia, supra*.

(*o*) *The Jenny Lind* (1872), L.R. 3 A. &. E. 529.

(*p*) *The William* (1858), Swab. 346; *The Jonathan Goodhue* (1859), Swab. 524. Though it will be otherwise where his personal undertaking is only that he is the master, and in that character has the right to hypothecate the ship: *The Salacia, supra*. And the claim of the master may be protected by marshalling the securities, so as, for instance, to throw the claim of the bondholder on the cargo, leaving the ship and freight open to the master: *The Edward Oliver* (1867), L.R. 1 A. & E. 379; *The Daring, supra*; *The Eugénie* (1873), L.R. 4 A. & E. 123.

(*q*) *The Salacia, supra*; *The Hope* (1873), 1 Asp. M.L.C. 563.

(*r*) *The Jenny Lind, supra*, at p. 532; see *The Mary Ann, supra*; *The Daring, supra*; *The Feronia, supra*.

Bottomry bonds.—The claim for wages and other burdens, which form a lien upon the ship when she is brought into the yard of a shipwright for repairs, will be preferred to the shipwright's possessory lien, it being presumed that he received the ship subject to her existing obligations; but not to any claim for wages earned or necessaries supplied after the ship has come into the hands of the shipwright (*s*), except the usual allowance to foreign mariners for their return to their own country (*t*).

Loss of lien.—The benefit of a maritime lien may be lost by negligence or delay (*u*). On the other hand, it has been said that diligence in instituting and prosecuting the action may be rewarded with priority of claim against the fund (*a*). The court however, holds the property not only for the plaintiff who first institutes his action and obtains the arrest of the ship, but at least for all creditors of the same class who make their claims in due course (*b*).

Claims for repairs.—A mortgagee of the ship will have priority over claims for repairs or other necessities of the ship supplied in England by persons, who, not being in possession, cannot establish a lien, even though the mortgagee had notice that money had been so laid out for the use of the ship; and the rights against the ship, and against the proceeds when it has been sold, are the same (*c*).

Rights of mortgagee in possession.—A mortgagee of a ship who takes possession is entitled to freight then in course of being earned but not due (*d*); and an assignee of such freight will be postponed to an earlier mortgagee of the ship, or to a later mortgagee, who first takes, or claims from the master, possession of the ship (*e*), provided in either case the mortgagee had no notice of the assignment (*f*). But a mortgagee is not entitled to freight accrued due and payable before he took possession (although it may then remain unpaid) as against a subsequent assignee (*g*). And if the mortgagee does not actually or constructively take possession, the mortgagor or subsequent assignee can receive the freight and will not be liable to account (*h*).

The arrival of the ship in the docks is not such a completion of the voyage as will deprive a mortgagee of his right to the freight, if he does

---

(*s*) *The Gustaf* (1862), Lush. 506; *The Immacolata Concezione* (1883), 9 P.D. 37.
(*t*) *The Tergeste*, [1903] P. 26.
(*u*) *The Bold Buccleugh* (1852), 7 Moo. P.C.C. 267; *The Europa* (1863), Br. & Lush. 89; *The Fairport* (1882), 8 P.D. 48.
(*a*) *The Saracen* (1846), 4 Notes of Cases, 512; on appeal, 6 Moo. P.C. 75; *The William F. Safford* (1860), Lush. 69.
(*b*) *The Africano*, [1894] P. 141: see *The Veritas*, [1901] P. 304, 307.
(*c*) *Watkinson* v. *Bernardiston* (1726), 2 P. Wms. 367; *The New Eagle* (1846), 2 W. Rob. 441. See *The Neptune* (1835), 3 Knapp. 94; *The Scio* (1867), L.R. 1 A. & E. 353. And similarly the claim of the repairers ranks after maritime liens already accrued: *The Russland*, [1924] P. 55. As to when repairers are in possession, see *The Rellim* (1922), 39 T.L.R. 41.
(*d*) *Brown* v. *Tanner* (1868), 3 Ch. App. 597; *Keith* v. *Burrows* (1877), 2 App. Cas. 636 (H.L.); *Shillito* v. *Biggart*, [1903] 1 K.B. 683.
(*e*) *Brown* v. *Tanner*, *supra*.
(*f*) *Wilson* v. *Wilson* (1872), L.R. 14 Eq. 32, 39.
(*g*) *Shillito* v. *Biggart*, *supra*; see *Liverpool Marine Credit Co.* v. *Wilson* (1872), 7 Ch. App. 507.
(*h*) *Cato* v. *Irving* (1852), 5 De G. & Sm. 210; *Brown* v. *Tanner*, *supra*; *Liverpool Marine Credit Co.* v. *Wilson*, *supra*.

not take possession until the happening of that event. It is enough if he takes possession before the complete discharge of the cargo; for the right to freight does not accrue until the delivery of the goods, unless there is a stipulation to the contrary; and so long as they remain on board undelivered, the possession of them is as much within the reason of the rule whilst the ship is in, as whilst she is on her way to, the docks (*i*).

XI—AIRCRAFT MORTGAGES

Registered mortgages.—The Mortgaging of Aircraft Order 1972 (*k*) provides that a registered mortgage shall have priority over any other mortgage or charge on the aircraft other than another registered mortgage (*l*). Registered mortgages have priority as between themselves according to the date of entry in the register (*m*). However, where a priority notice (*n*) has been entered and the contemplated mortgage is registered within 14 days (*o*) thereafter, the mortgage is deemed to have priority from the time when the priority notice was registered (*p*). The above-mentioned provisions have effect notwithstanding any express, implied or constructive notice affecting the mortgagee (*q*), but they are not to be construed as giving a registered mortgage any priority over any possession lien in respect of work done on the aircraft (whether before or after the creation or registration of the mortgage) on the express or implied authority of any person lawfully entitled to possession of the aircraft or over any right to detain the aircraft under any Act of Parliament (*r*).

A registered mortgage of an aircraft is not affected by any act of bankruptcy committed by the mortgagor after the date on which the mortgage is registered, notwithstanding that at the commencement of his bankruptcy the mortgagor had the aircraft in his possession, order or disposition, or was reputed owner thereof, and the mortgage shall be preferred to any right, claim or interest therein of the other creditors of the bankrupt or any trustee or assignee on their behalf (*s*).

(*i*) *The John* (1849), 3 W. Rob. 179; *Brown* v. *Tanner, supra.* As to the position of the mortgagee of a part only of the ship, see *Cato* v. *Irving, supra.*
(*k*) See p. 99, *supra.*
(*l*) Art. 14 (1).
(*m*) Art. 14 (2).
(*n*) See Art. 5.
(*o*) Only days when the office of the Authority is open count: Art. 14 (3).
(*p*) Art. 14 (2) (ii).
(*q*) Art. 14 (4).
(*r*) Art. 14 (5).
(*s*) Art. 15.

PART VII

INCIDENCE OF THE MORTGAGE DEBT

CHAPTER 25

Incidence on the Death of the Mortgagor

Formerly personal estate primarily liable.—The old rule was that, as between the personal representatives of the mortgagor, and the heir or devisee of the whole or part of mortgaged land, the personalty of the mortgagor was primarily liable to the debt, and had to exonerate the mortgaged land, which was treated only as collateral security (a).

But the rule only applied to the original covenant of the mortgagor (b), and neither the covenant nor the agreement of the purchaser or devisee of the equity of redemption, in the whole or part of property mortgaged or incumbered with a charge, to pay or take upon himself the debt and interest (and, in the case of a purchase, to indemnify the vendor against it (c)), nor the covenant of one of several purchasers to take upon himself a certain part of the debt and to indemnify the purchasers of the other parts (d), subjected the personal estate of the covenantor, as between his own real and personal representatives, to the payment of the debt (e).

(a) *Pockley* v. *Pockley* (1681), 1 Vern. 36; *Cope* v. *Cope* (*circa* 1710), 2 Salk. 449; *Bartholomew* v. *May* (1737), 1 Atk. 487; *Belvedere* v. *Rochfort* (1772), 5 Bro. P.C. 299.
The rule did not apply to a transaction in which no debt was created, such as a security upon an estate for a provision under a marriage settlement, even though there was a covenant for payment: *Lanoy* v. *Athol* (1742), 2 Atk. 446; *Loosemore* v. *Knapman* (1853), Kay, 123; unless the provision was first secured by a covenant creating a debt, to which the covenant for securing the charge upon the estate was manifestly auxiliary: *Field* v. *Moore* (1855), 7 De G.M. & G. 691. Nor did the doctrine apply to a security for a loan where the security only, and not the personal ability or circumstances of the borrower, was considered; as in the case of the South Sea loans, which were raised only on the credit of the stock: *King* v. *King* (1735), 3 P. Wms. 358; nor to money raised by a tenant for life or other person who had only a limited interest under a power: *Ex parte Digby* (1821), Jac. 235.
(b) See *Lawson* v. *Hudson* (1779), 1 Bro. C.C. 58; *Cope* v. *Cope, supra; Woods* v. *Huntingford* (1796), 3 Ves. Jun. 128; *Scott* v. *Beecher* (1820), 5 Mad. 96. Where the heir or devisee of the mortgaged estate himself became entitled to the personalty and died without having discharged the mortgage, the right to exoneration out of the personal estate was not continued: *Scott* v. *Beecher, supra.*
(c) *Tweddell* v. *Tweddell* (1787), 2 Bro. C.C. 101, 152; *Hamilton* v. *Worley* (1793), 2 Ves. Jun. 62; *Butler* v. *Butler* (1800), 5 Ves. 534; *Barham* v. *Earl of Thanet* (1834), 3 Myl. & K. 607.
(d) *Forrester* v. *Leigh* (1753), Ambl. 171.
(e) *Waring* v. *Ward* (1802), 7 Ves. 332; *Adair* v. *Carden* (1892), 29 L.R. Ir. 469; *Bridgman* v. *Daw* (1891), 40 W.R. 253. Nor does such a covenant give the mortgagee a right of action against the assignee of the equity of redemption personally either for principal or interest: *Re Errington, Ex parte Mason,* [1894] 1 Q.B. 11.
On the other hand, a transaction in which the purchaser, devisee, or heir of the original mortgagor, borrowed a sum of money with which the old debt was paid off and a new mortgage made, threw the burden of the new debt on the personal estate of the purchaser, devisee, or heir in question: *Waring* v. *Ward, supra; Barham* v. *Earl of Thanet, supra; Bagot* v. *Bagot* (1864), 34 Beav. 134.

Intention to exonerate personalty.—But the old law was—as the new still is—merely a matter of presumption, capable of being rebutted by an express or implied intention to the contrary; though it was held that the intention must be so clearly expressed as to convince the mind of the judge, that the testator intended to charge the real estate with, as well as to exonerate the personalty from, the debt (*f*). The sufficiency of the expression of intention to exonerate the personalty was often difficult to determine (*g*). It was, however, well established, that the personalty was not relieved by a devise of the mortgaged estate, or of that and other property "subject to the mortgage", or "subject to the payment of the mortgage", or "subject to debts", or by any other equivalent expression not amounting to a condition or direction that the devisee should pay the debt (*h*).

The personalty was, however, exonerated by a general devise of lands for payment of the debts of the testator (*i*); also by a direction to apply a particular part of the real estate in payment of a particular debt, because, so much only of the real estate being devised as would remain after payment of the debt, the devisee could not claim more than was given him (*k*).

A specific bequest of the general personal estate was also held to show an intention to exonerate it (*l*). But where the testator specifically bequeathed the surplus of his personalty (computing it at a certain amount after payment of his debts), it was adjudged that the mortgage, as one of the debts, should be paid out of that fund, though it was thereby reduced below the amount specified (*m*).

Mortgaged property now primarily liable.—By a series of statutes, known as Locke King's Acts (*n*), now repealed, but reproduced and extended to mortgaged personal estate by the Administration of Estates Act 1925, the old rule has been reversed, and as between the persons entitled to the mortgagor's property, the mortgaged property is made the primary fund for the payment of the debt. Thus the Act last mentioned provides:

(*f*) See *Ancaster* v. *Mayer* (1785), 1 Bro. C.C. 454; *Watson* v. *Brickwood* (1804), 9 Ves. 447; *Hancox* v. *Abbey* (1805), 11 Ves. 179; *Bootle* v. *Blundell* (1815), 1 Mer. 193.

(*g*) Where exoneration was directed, it operated in favour only of the person for whose benefit the testator intended it; so that, if the gift of the personalty intended to be exonerated lapsed by the death of the legatee in the testator's lifetime, or otherwise failed, the exemption failed also, whether the personalty was vested in a subject or in the Crown: *Hale* v. *Cox* (1791), 3 Bro. C.C. 322; *Waring* v. *Ward* (1802), 5 Ves. 670; *Dacre* v. *Patrickson* (1860), 1 Dr. & Sm. 182; unless an intention could be found to apply the exonerating fund in discharge of the debt, irrespective of the benefit to the intended legatee of the fund exonerated: see *Noel* v. *Lord Henley* (1823), Dan. 322; *Noel* v. *Noel* (1823), 12 Price, 213; or unless, with an intention to exonerate, there was no particular gift of the fund exonerated. For it must then be supposed that the exoneration was meant for the benefit of whoever should take that fund: *Milnes* v. *Slater* (1803), 8 Ves. 295.

(*h*) *Serle* v. *St. Eloy* (1726), 2 P. Wms. 385; *Bickham* v. *Cruttwell* (1838), 3 My. & C. 763; *Goodwin* v. *Lee* (1853), 1 K. & J. 374; affd. 1 Jur. N.S. 948; *Jenkinson* v. *Harcourt* (1854), Kay, 688.

(*i*) *Serle* v. *St. Eloy, supra.*

(*k*) *Hancox* v. *Abbey, supra; Hale* v. *Cox, supra.*

(*l*) *Blount* v. *Hipkins* (1834), 7 Sim. 43.

(*m*) *Hawes* v. *Warner* (1704), 2 Vern. 477.

(*n*) Real Estate Charges Acts 1854, 1867, and 1877.

35.—(1) Where a person dies possessed of, or entitled to, or, under a general power of appointment (including the statutory power to dispose of entailed interests) by his will disposes of, an interest in property (*o*), which at the time of his death is charged with the payment of money, whether by way of legal mortgage, equitable charge (*p*) or otherwise (including a lien for unpaid purchase money (*q*), and the deceased has not by will, deed, or other document (*r*) signified a contrary or other intention, the interest so charged shall, as between the different persons claiming through the deceased (*s*), be primarily liable for the payment of the charge; and every part of the said interest, according to its value, shall bear a proportionate part of the charge on the whole thereof (*t*).

(2) Such contrary or other intention shall not be deemed to be signified—
(a) by a general direction for the payment of debts or of all the debts of the testator out of his personal estate, or his residuary real and personal estate, or his residuary real estate; or

---

(*o*) The Act of 1854 did not apply to leaseholds: *Re Wormsley's Estate, Hill* v. *Wormsley* (1876), 4 Ch. D. 665. This was remedied by the Act of 1877: *Re Kershaw, Drake* v. *Kershaw* (1888), 37 Ch. D. 674; and hence a rentcharge issuing out of leasehold land was within the Acts: *Re Fraser, Lowther* v. *Fraser,* [1904] 1 Ch. 726; but not land situate abroad: *Re Chantrell, Sutleffe* v. *Von Liverhoff,* [1907] W.N. 213. And since the Acts did not extend to personal estate (*Re Bourne, Martin* v. *Martin,* [1893] 1 Ch. 188, 191), they did not apply to land held on trust for sale: *Lewis* v. *Lewis* (1871), L.R. 13 Eq. 218; see *Re Bennett, Clarke* v. *White,* [1899] 1 Ch. 316, 321. But these distinctions are abolished by the present statute which applies to "property"; this includes "a thing in action and any interest in real or personal property": Administration of Estates Act 1925, s. 55 (1) (xvii).

(*p*) Including an equitable charge by deposit, whether or not accompanied by a memorandum: *Pembrooke* v. *Friend* (1860), 1 Johns. & H. 132; *Coleby* v. *Coleby* (1866), L.R. 2 Eq. 803; *Davis* v. *Davis* (1876), 24 W.R. 962. Indeed, the Act extends to every equitable charge, whether created by statute or however enforceable. Hence it applies to a charge for estate duty (*Re Bowerman, Porter* v. *Bowerman,* [1908] 2 Ch. 340; *Re Wilson,* [1916] 1 Ch. 220) and a charging order on land (*Re Anthony, Anthony* v. *Anthony,* [1892] 1 Ch. 450), but not to a general charge by the testator upon his real estate in aid of his personalty for payment of debts or legacies until the amount of the charge has become accurately defined: *Hepworth* v. *Hill* (1862), 30 Beav. 476.

(*q*) This extension was introduced by s. 2 of the Act of 1867. It includes a vendor's lien under a contract to create and sell ground rents: *Re Kidd, Brooman* v. *Withall,* [1894] 3 Ch. 558; and a lien of a company: *Re Turner, Tennant* v. *Turner,* [1938] Ch. 593; [1938] 2 All E.R. 560; *Re Birmingham,* [1959] Ch. 523; [1958] 2 All E.R. 397. The Acts did not at first apply where the purchaser died intestate: *Harding* v. *Harding* (1872), L.R. 13 Eq. 493; but under the Act of 1877 they were extended generally to intestacy; see *Re Cockcroft, Broadbent* v. *Groves* (1883), 24 Ch. D. 94, 100; and similarly, the present Act applies whether the mortgagor dies testate or intestate.

(*r*) The introduction of these words in the present consolidated enactment cures an error of drafting in the Act of 1877: see *Re Cockcroft, Broadbent* v. *Groves, supra.* For a case where a contrary intention was signified by documents other than the will, see *Re Campbell, Campbell* v. *Campbell,* [1898] 2 Ch. 206. See also *Re Nicholson, Nicholson* v. *Boulton,* [1923] W.N. 251; *Re Wakefield, Gordon* v. *Wakefield,* [1943] 2 All E.R. 29 (C.A.); *Re Birmingham, supra.*

(*s*) The provision is only intended for the benefit of the beneficiaries *inter se.* See *Re Fison's Will Trusts,* [1950] Ch. 394; [1950] 3 All E.R. 501.

(*t*) Unless the will shows a contrary intention (as to which, see *supra*), each property charged, whether real or personal estate, contributes rateably to the payment of the charge: *Lipscomb* v. *Lipscomb* (1868), L.R. 7 Eq. 501; *Trestrail* v. *Mason* (1878), 7 Ch. D. 665; *Re Newmarch, Newmarch* v. *Storr* (1878), 9 Ch. D. 12 (C.A.); *Re Major,* [1914] 1 Ch. 278. Value in this context means probate value: *Re Cohen,* [1960] Ch. 179; [1959] 3 All E.R. 740. Where several properties, each separately mortgaged, are devised to the same devisee, all the mortgages are consolidated in favour of the personal estate: *Re Baron Kensington, Earl of Longford* v. *Baron Kensington,* [1902] 1 Ch. 203. But where real estate of an intestate descended to his heir-at-law subject as to the several properties to separate mortgages, a deficiency on one property was thrown on the personal estate and not on the other mortgaged properties: *Re Holt, Holt* v. *Holt* (1916), 85 L.J. Ch. 779.

　　(b) by a charge of the debts upon any such estate;
unless such intention is further signified by words expressly or by necessary
implication referring to all or some part of the charge.
　　(3) Nothing in this section shall affect the right of a person entitled to the
charge to obtain payment or satisfaction thereof either out of the other assets
of the deceased or otherwise (*u*).

Contrary intention.—The provision in sub-s. (2) (a) that a direction
for payment of the testator's debts out of the estate there mentioned
shall not be deemed to be a signification of an intention contrary to
the statutory rule is repeated from the Act of 1867 (which referred only
to personal estate), as extended by the Act of 1877 (which added a
reference also to residuary real and personal estate or residuary real
estate (*x*)). The effect is, that a "contrary intention" is not shown by
a mere charge of, or direction for, the payment of the testator's debts
out of his personal estate, or out of his other real estate; or out of a
mixed fund, in aid of his personal estate, or in exoneration of his real
or other real estate; or by a combination of those expressions (*y*).
Where there are several properties comprised in one charge the fact
that a specific devise is made of one of the properties, while the other
passes under a residuary devise, does not indicate a contrary
intention (*z*).

　　But a contrary intention is shown by a direction to pay mortgages
out of a special fund (*a*). A direction to pay debts "except the mortgage
debts, if any, on" Blackacre, out of the residue implied that other
mortgage debts were to be paid out of residue (*b*). And a direction to
pay "trade debts" out of residuary personal estate is sufficient to
exonerate real estate, the title deeds of which were subsequently
deposited with the testator's bankers to secure an overdrawn trade
account (*c*). Where there are several properties comprised in one
charge an indication that one property was intended to form a primary
security and the other a secondary security will constitute a contrary
intention (*d*). The intention to exonerate must be signified by words
referring clearly to the mortgage debt.

　　(*u*) This provision is for the exclusive benefit of the mortgagee: *Lipscomb* v. *Lipscomb*,
supra.
　　(*x*) The provision adopts Lord CAMPBELL's construction of the Act of 1854
(*Woolstencroft* v. *Woolstencroft* (1860), 2 De G.F. & J. 347) in preference to that of
other judges: *Mellish* v. *Vallins* (1862), 2 Johns. & H. 194; *Eno* v. *Tatham* (1863),
3 De G.J. & S. 443; and other cases.
　　(*y*) *Re Newmarch, Newmarch* v. *Storr* (1878), 9 Ch. D. 12 (C.A.); *Re Rossiter, Rossiter*
v. *Rossiter* (1879), 13 Ch. D. 355; *Elliott* v. *Dearsley* (1880), 16 Ch. D. 322. Nor was it
shown even where the testator directed payment out of a specific fund of *all and every
liability* which he might have incurred during his lifetime: *Re Hooper, Ashford* v.
Brooks, [1892] W.N. 151.
　　(*z*) *Re Neeld*, [1962] Ch. 643 (C.A.); [1962] 2 All E.R. 335; overruling *Re Biss,
Heasman* v. *Biss*, [1956] Ch. 243; [1956] 1 All E.R. 89.
　　(*a*) *Allie* v. *Katah*, [1963] 1 W.L.R. 202 (P.C.).
　　(*b*) *Re Valpy, Valpy* v. *Valpy*, [1906] 1 Ch. 531.
　　(*c*) *Re Fleck, Colston* v. *Roberts* (1888), 37 Ch. D. 677; see *Re Valpy, Valpy* v. *Valpy*,
supra.
　　(*d*) *Lipscomb* v. *Lipscomb, supra*; *Leonino* v. *Leonino* (1879), 10 Ch. D. 460; *Re
Athill, Athill* v. *Athill* (1880), 16 Ch. D. 211 (C.A.).

The intention to exonerate the mortgaged estate, only extends to the value of the fund or property made liable by the testator. If that fund or property is insufficient, the residue must be borne by the mortgaged estate, though there may be other property which is liable by law to the testator's debts, *e.g.*, the general personal estate (*e*).

Where Act does not apply.—The Act does not apply to real estate of a partner mortgaged to secure a partnership debt if, at the time of the partner's death, the partnership assets are sufficient to answer all the debts of the partnership (*f*). Nor does it apply where a testator gives to a son the option of purchasing real estate at a fixed price; in such a case the price so fixed is taken to be for the land free from incumbrances (*g*). Nor where the testator was in fact a surety only for the debt and it is paid off by the principal debtor after his death (*h*).

(*e*) *Re Birch, Hunt* v. *Thorn,* [1909] 1 Ch. 787, explaining *Allen* v. *Allen* (1862), 30 Beav. 395, 403; *Re Fegan, Fegan* v. *Fegan,* [1928] Ch. 45.

(*f*) *Re Ritson, Ritson* v. *Ritson,* [1899] 1 Ch. 128 (C.A.).

(*g*) *Re Wilson, Wilson* v. *Wilson,* [1908] 1 Ch. 839; *Re Fison's Will Trusts,* [1950] Ch. 394; [1950] 1 All E.R. 501.

(*h*) *Re Hawkes, Reeve* v. *Hawkes,* [1912] 2 Ch. 251. And as to the operation of Locke King's Act where a husband had purported to mortgage property of his wife's without her knowledge, and a genuine mortgage had been created by them of their joint property, and the husband having disposed of the wife's property by will, she elected to take under his will, see *Re Williams, Cunliffe* v. *Williams,* [1915] 1 Ch. 450. The Act was held not to apply to the former property, but it applied to the latter, and the husband's estate being insufficient, the property brought in by the widow's election was liable to contribute *pari passu* with the testator's property to the discharge of his debts.

CHAPTER 26

Incidence as Between Different Properties

Liabilities of different properties.—As between the properties of different owners which are included in the same security, each property may have to contribute its share of the common burden, or one property may be entitled to be exonerated by the other. And there is a claim to exoneration where, though only a single property is mortgaged, the debt is primarily the debt of another person than the owner of the property. The incidence of the debt is also varied by marshalling.

I—CONTRIBUTION

Contribution.—The doctrine of contribution rests upon the principle that a fund, which is equally liable with another to pay the debt, shall not escape because the creditor has been paid out of that other fund alone.

If several properties, whether of one or of several owners (a), are mortgaged for, or subject equally (and not one as surety or collateral security for the other (b)), to one debt, or, if the owner of several properties, having mortgaged one of them, charges his real estate with or devises it in trust for payment of his debts (c), and the properties descend or are devised to different persons (for the rule will not hold where they come to the same person (d)), and though one of them passes by a specific and the other by a residuary devise (e), the several properties will contribute rateably to the debt, being valued for that purpose after deducting from each property any other incumbrance by which it is affected. The right of contribution between properties so charged is not affected by the Administration of Estates Act 1925, s. 35 (f), nor does this affect the liability of real and personal estate

---

(a) See *Aldrich* v. *Cooper* (1803), 8 Ves. 382; *Johnson* v. *Child* (1844), 4 Hare, 87.
(b) *Marquis of Bute* v. *Cunynghame* (1826), 2 Russ. 275; *Stringer* v. *Harper* (1858), 26 Beav. 33.
(c) *Carter* v. *Barnadiston* (1718), 1 P. Wms. 505; *Irvin* v. *Ironmonger* (1831), 2 Russ. & Myl. 531; *Middleton* v. *Middleton* (1852), 15 Beav. 450.
(d) *Stronge* v. *Hawkes* (1853), 4 De G.M. & G. 186.
(e) *Gibbins* v. *Eyden* (1869), L.R. 7 Eq. 371; *Sackville* v. *Smyth* (1873), L.R. 17 Eq. 153; *Re Smith, Hannington* v. *True* (1886), 33 Ch. D. 195, dissenting from *Brownson* v. *Lawrance* (1868), L.R. 6 Eq. 1.
(f) *Sackville* v. *Smyth, supra*; notwithstanding *Brownson* v. *Lawrance, supra*; and see *Re Smith, Hannington* v. *True, supra*. For s. 35, see p. 499, *supra*.

to contribute rateably, when both are included in the same security (*g*).

So, if one of the properties has been mortgaged for one debt and both of them for another, though the first will bear exclusively its own debt, both must contribute rateably to that which is later, the amount of the first debt being deducted from the value of the property which has paid it (*h*). But if there are successive loans, and successive securities, and nothing to show that one property was to be charged before another, all will be charged rateably (*i*), provided there is an actual specific charge upon each property, and not merely a general charge or liability upon one of them, it being necessary, in order to raise a case of rateable apportionment, that each property shall be equally liable (*k*). The right of contribution extends to sureties who are liable for the same debt, and whose liabilities are contemporaneous (*l*).

In questions of liability, the use of the word "collateral" does not imply that the security so called is secondary to another and the absence of a special provision that one property shall be resorted to before another is relevant (*m*).

Where contribution excluded.—But the right of contribution will be prevented by the right of marshalling from being applied against a property which is liable to other creditors of the debtor (*n*), or which, not being charged with his debts, and even though consisting of leasehold and other personalty, is liable under a specific or pecuniary, as distinguished from a residuary, bequest; the devisee in such cases being obliged to take the mortgaged estate as he finds it (*o*). And so, if one of several properties charged with the payment of debts is expressly made liable to the payment of a mortgage debt to which it is subject, it will not be liable to contribute with the other properties to the general charge (*p*).

(*g*) *Lipscomb* v. *Lipscomb* (1868), L.R. 7 Eq. 501; *Trestrail* v. *Mason* (1878), 7 Ch. D. 665. And see *Re Dunlop, Dunlop* v. *Dunlop* (1882), 21 Ch. D. 583 (C.A.), at p. 590. As to foreclosure where there are rights of contribution and indemnity between co-mortgagors, see *Gee* v. *Liddell*, [1913] 2 Ch. 62.

(*h*) *Lipscomb* v. *Lipscomb, supra*; *De Rochefort* v. *Dawes* (1871), L.R. 12 Eq. 540.

(*i*) *Leonino* v. *Leonino* (1879), 10 Ch. D. 460; and see *Flint* v. *Howard*, [1893] 2 Ch. 54 (C.A.).

(*k*) *Re Dunlop, Dunlop* v. *Dunlop, supra*.

(*l*) *Duncan, Fox & Co.* v. *North and South Wales Bank* (1879), 11 Ch. D. 88; and see 6 App. Cas. 1.

(*m*) *Re Athill, Athill* v. *Athill* (1880), 16 Ch. D. 211 (C.A.). Where a policy of insurance is issued subject to a condition that it will become void upon the suicide of the insured except to the extent of any interest acquired for valuable consideration or by way of security, the office holds out that the owner of such an interest will be entitled to payment; and the office, being a principal debtor in respect of the policy, has no equity in case of the suicide of an insured person who has mortgaged the policy with other property, and in the absence of fraud, to come upon that property for contribution: *Solicitors and General Life Assurance Society* v. *Lamb* (1864), 1 H. & M. 716; affirmed, 2 De G.J. & S. 251; or, if the company are themselves the principal mortgagees, to insist that the policy is void, and to throw the debt upon the other securities: *White* v. *British Empire Mutual Life Assurance Co.* (1868), L.R. 7 Eq. 394.

(*n*) *Bartholomew* v. *May* (1737), 1 Atk. 487. As to marshalling, see p. 506, *infra*.

(*o*) *Oneal* v. *Mead* (1720), 1 P. Wms. 694; *Davis* v. *Gardiner* (1723), 2 P. Wms. 187; *Wythe* v. *Henniker* (1833), 2 Myl. & K. 635; *Halliwell* v. *Tanner* (1830), 1 Russ. & Myl. 633; *Cope* v. *Cope* (*circa* 1710), 2 Salk. 449. See *Symons* v. *James* (1843), 2 Y. & Coll. C,C, 301.

(*p*) *Wisden* v. *Wisden* (1854), 2 Sm. & G. 396.

II—EXONERATION

Where one owner personally liable.—The doctrine of contribution is founded on equality. It assumes that of two properties, X and Y, comprised in the same security, both are equally liable to bear the debt. But this prima facie equality is subject to exception. Thus, if the mortgagor, being personally liable, assigns one property, X, and retains the other, Y, X is no longer treated as equally liable with Y to bear the debt, unless the assignment is expressly made subject to the mortgage (*q*). The duty of the mortgagor to discharge his own personal liability makes the property in his hands the primary fund for payment. So, too, where it has come to the hands of his personal representatives. Hence, if he or his personal representatives have paid the debt, there is no equity to compel contribution from X (*r*). On the other hand, if the mortgagee enforces the debt against X, the assignee of that property is entitled to be exonerated at the expense of Y (*s*). This is so whether the assignment of X was for valuable consideration or was voluntary (*t*).

Assignment of one property free from mortgage.—If the mortgagor has assigned both properties, each to a different assignee, the above reason fails, for neither assignee is personally liable. Where, however, the first assignment—that of X—was to a purchaser for value and contained a covenant against incumbrances, or for further assurance, this furnishes a ground for giving preferential treatment to X, and the assignee of X will be entitled to exoneration out of Y (*u*), though his claim, being only equitable, will not be enforceable against one who takes the legal estate in Y for value and without notice (*x*). It is the same where, on the assignment of X, the mortgagor represented that it was free from incumbrances (*y*). But it seems that this ground of exoneration is not available for a voluntary assignee (*z*).

Paramount mortgage.—Where properties X and Y have become vested in an owner, A, subject to a mortgage which was not created by himself, but is paramount to his title, and he assigns X, whether for value or not, here again the first ground for displacing the principle

---

(*q*) *Re Mainwaring, Mainwaring* v. *Verden*, [1937] Ch. 96 (C.A.); [1936] 3 All E.R. 840.

(*r*) *Re Darby's Estate, Rendall* v. *Darby*, [1907] 2 Ch. 465.

(*s*) *Re Best, Parker* v. *Best*, [1924] 1 Ch. 42.

(*t*) *Ker* v. *Ker* (1869), 4 Ir. R. Eq. 15.
As to an exchange, see *Kirkham* v. *Smith* (1749), 1 Ves. S. 257; and as to the effect of a sale by the court, *Lloyd* v. *Johnes* (1804), 9 Ves. 37, 64.
If a person, bound to elect between two properties, has mortgaged one of them before election, and afterwards elects to take the other, the first must be taken subject to the mortgage, but will be exonerated by the other: *Rumbold* v. *Rumbold* (1796), 3 Ves. Jun. 65.

(*u*) *Re Jones, Farrington* v. *Forrester*, [1893] 2 Ch. 461, 470; see *Averall* v. *Wade* (1835), Ll. & G. *temp.* Sugd. 252; *Hughes* v. *Williams* (1852), 3 Mac. & G. 683; *Chappell* v. *Rees* (1852), 1 De G.M. & G. 393; *Re Roddy's Estate, Ex parte Fitzgerald* (1861), 11 Ir. Ch. R. 369; *Re Roche's Estate* (1890), 25 L.R. Ir. 271.

(*x*) *Ocean Accident and Guarantee Corpn.* v. *Collum*, [1913] 1 I.R. 337.

(*y*) *M'Carthy* v. *M'Cartie*, [1904] 1 I.R. 100, 115; see *Finch* v. *Shaw, Colyer* v. *Finch* (1854), 19 Beav. 500.

(*z*) *Tighe* v. *Dolphin*, [1906] 1 I.R. 305; and see *Stronge* v. *Hawkes* (1859), 4 De G. & J. 632.

of equality fails. Hence, if A pays off the mortgage, he is entitled to contribution from X (*a*), unless he assigned X on the footing that it was free from incumbrances, so as to entitle it to exoneration on the second ground (*b*).

Mortgage by wife for husband's debt.—A person who has mortgaged his property to secure the debt of another stands only in the position of a surety and is entitled to be exonerated by the principal debtor (*c*). In this position is a wife who has mortgaged her property to secure money raised for the benefit of her husband (*d*).

Where the property of the wife, or over which she has a power of appointment (*e*), is mortgaged, and the money is paid to her and her husband, or to him, it is considered prima facie that it was borrowed for his benefit, and his property is first applied, as for payment of his own debt, unless the presumption is rebutted by proof on the part of the husband, that the whole or some part of the money did not come to his hands (*f*). And the result will be the same, where the husband has paid off the mortgage, and has taken an assignment of it in trust for himself (*g*).

Where it appears on the face of the mortgage deed that the money was paid to the husband, the court infers, subject to rebutting evidence, that the debt is the debt of the husband, and that the wife's property is a surety for it. But by way of rebuttal it may be shown that the money was in fact paid to the wife, or that it was applied by the husband for her benefit (*h*). And the wife's right to have her property indemnified depends on the circumstances of the particular case, and where it appears that the debt, though legally the debt of the husband, was contracted to pay the expenses of the extravagant joint living, no inference of her right to indemnity will be drawn (*i*).

(*a*) *Ker* v. *Ker* (1869), 4 Ir. R. Eq. 15; and see *Re Darby's Estate, Rendall* v. *Darby,* [1907] 2 Ch. 465.

(*b*) See cases in note (*u*), p. 504, *supra.*

(*c*) *Lee* v. *Rook* (1730), Mos. 318; *Evelyn* v. *Evelyn* (1731), 2 P. Wms. 659; *Peirs* v. *Peirs* (1750), 1 Ves. Sen. 521.

(*d*) *Huntington* v. *Huntington* (1702), 2 Vern. 437; *Tate* v. *Austin* (1714), 1 P. Wms. 264; *Peirs* v. *Peirs, supra; Lancaster* v. *Evors* (1846), 10 Beav. 154. And there is a similar equity in favour of a husband: *Bagot* v. *Oughton* (1717), 1 P. Wms. 347.

(*e*) *Thomas* v. *Thomas* (1855), 2 K. & J. 79.

(*f*) *Pocock* v. *Lee* (1707), 2 Vern. 604; *Tate* v. *Austin, supra; Parteriche* v. *Powlett* (1742), 2 Atk. 383; *Earl of Kinnoul* v. *Money* (1767), 3 Swans. 202, n.; *Ruscombe* v. *Hare* (1828), 6 Dow, 1. And if the debt was not originally incurred for the benefit of the husband, this equity of exoneration does not arise by reason of his giving a covenant as additional security: *Bagot* v. *Oughton, supra;* and see *Christmas* v. *Christmas* (1725), Cas. *temp.* King; *Pitt* v. *Pitt* (1823), Turn. & R. 180; *Nelson* v. *Booth* (1857), 27 L.J. Ch. 110; *Gray* v. *Dowman* (1858), 27 L.J. Ch. 702.

(*g*) *Huntington* v. *Huntington, supra.*

(*h*) *Hall* v. *Hall,* [1911] 1 Ch. 487; see *Hudson* v. *Carmichael* (1854), Kay, 613; *Parteriche* v. *Powlet, supra.* It has been said that the wife's right to exoneration of her property should be postponed to the husband's other debts: *Tate* v. *Austin, supra,* cited with approval in *Clinton* v. *Hooper* (1791), 3 Bro. C.C. 200; but this has been doubted: *Hudson* v. *Carmichael, supra;* and is inconsistent with the principle that the husband's creditors are not subrogated to the mortgagee as against the wife's property: *Robinson* v. *Gee* (1749), 1 Ves. Sen. 251.

(*i*) *Paget* v. *Paget,* [1898] 1 Ch. 470; and see further where the right to indemnify is rebutted on the ground that the debt was really the wife's: *Lewis* v. *Nangle* (1752), 1 Ambl. 150; *Clinton* v. *Hooper, supra; Earl of Kinnoul* v. *Money, supra.* The wife will also have no claim to exoneration, if, after her husband's death, she directs his

The presumption in these cases in favour of the wife may be rebutted by parol evidence, and the rule concerning the admission of such evidence appears to be that, though parol evidence is not admissible to show that a transaction purporting by the instruments themselves, or by them and by other evidence not parol, to be for the husband's benefit, was of a different kind. It may be shown that the debts of the wife were paid with the money, or that it was in fact applied to some other than the purpose for which it was raised, or that, under the circumstances, the husband's estate is not primarily liable (*k*). Hence, evidence is admissible, that the widow, in conversation with the executor, admitted an agreement that the debt should be discharged out of the estate, and disclaimed her right to exoneration.

III—MARSHALLING

Principle of marshalling.—The doctrine of marshalling rests upon the principle that a creditor who has the means of satisfying his debt out of several funds shall not, by the exercise of his right, prejudice another creditor whose security comprises only one of the funds.

Thus, if the owner of two properties, X and Y, mortgages them both to A, and then mortgages one of them, Y, to B, B may require the securities to be marshalled, that is, that A's mortgage shall be thrown upon property X so far as it will suffice, and property Y, or so much as is not required for A's mortgage, be left to satisfy B's mortgage (*l*). This principle applies to all securities, whether mortgages, charges (*m*), or liens (*n*), but it does not interfere with the right of the creditor with several securities to resort to whichever he chooses.

---

executor to apply his personalty in payment of the legacies given by his will, whether the personal estate was so applied before or after such direction: *Clinton* v. *Hooper, supra.*

And even where the money was raised for the benefit of the husband alone, the wife will have no claim, if the mortgage was made in execution of a joint power in the husband and wife to raise money by mortgage, and she took the estate subject to the power; because the estate conveyed to the mortgagee was not that of the wife alone, but was created under the power, and in conformity with the purpose of the settlement: *Scholefield* v. *Lockwood (No. 3)* (1863), 32 Beav. 439.

(*k*) *Clinton* v. *Hooper, supra*; *Thomas* v. *Thomas, supra*; *Gray* v. *Dowman, supra.*

(*l*) *Lanoy* v. *Duke of Athol* (1742), 2 Atk. 444; *Aldrich* v. *Cooper* (1803), 8 Ves. 382; *Baldwin* v. *Belcher, Re Cornwall* (1842), 3 Dru. & War. 173; *Tidd* v. *Lister* (1852), 10 Hare, 140, 157; on app. (1854), 3 De G.M. & G. 857; *Gibson* v. *Seagrim* (1855), 20 Beav. 614; *Lawrance* v. *Galsworthy* (1857), 3 Jur. N.S. 1049; *Re Roddy's Estate* (1861), 11 Ir. Ch. R. 369; *Webb* v. *Smith* (1885), 30 Ch. D. 192 (C.A.); *Victoria and Grey Trust Co.* v. *Brewer* (1971), 14 D.L.R. (3d) 28. See *Re Chute's Estate*, [1914] 1 I.R. 180, where a bank mortgage for an overdraft was treated as paid off in accordance with the rule in *Clayton's Case* (1816), 1 Mer. 572, as applied in *Deeley* v. *Lloyds Bank, Ltd.*, [1912] A.C. 756. In *Lanoy* v. *Duke of Athol, supra*, it was said that the second mortgage must be taken without notice of the first, but this does not seem to be material: *Flint* v. *Howard*, [1893] 2 Ch. 54 (C.A.), at p. 74; but *cf. Re Lawder's Estate* (1861), 11 Ir. Ch. R. 346; *Re Roddy's Estate, supra*; *Re Roche's Estate* (1890), 25 L.R. Ir. 271.

(*m*) *Lanoy* v. *Duke of Athol, supra*; *Rancliffe* v. *Parkyns* (1818), 6 Dow, 149, 214.

(*n*) *Trimmer* v. *Bayne* (1803), 9 Ves. 209; *Sproule* v. *Prior* (1826), 8 Sim. 189; but not to a right of set-off: *Webb* v. *Smith, supra*; so as, that is, to subrogate the second creditor to the first creditor's right of set-off against fund X, if he resorts to fund Y on which the second creditor's debt is charged.

The doctrine has been applied, notwithstanding Locke King's Acts, so as to entitle rentchargees under a will, whose rentcharges were to be created out of mortgaged land,

The principle only applies as against the owner of the two properties, and if A has satisfied the debt out of Y, it operates by subrogating B to his rights against X (*o*).

No marshalling to injury of third incumbrancer.—But equity will not marshal securities where in aiding one incumbrancer, it would injure another (*p*). Thus, if properties X and Y are mortgaged first to A and secondly X is mortgaged to B, and thirdly Y to C, here A may resort for his whole debt either to X or Y. Now, if A is compelled to take his debt exclusively from Y, X will be left free for B, but at the expense of C. But this would clearly be inequitable. For even if C had notice when he took his security, he had notice of no more than that A had security upon Y (*q*), and he ought not to lose the benefit of his contract in favour of B, who claims under no contract against that property. B having lent his money on property X only, and having taken no charge upon or covenant respecting Y, has no more than a potential equity, as it has been called, against that property, which by means of the subsequent security given to C was prevented from fully arising. He has no equity to prevent the mortgagor from pledging property Y to C, none to prevent A from giving up his security upon it, and so depriving B even of his chance of getting a title by redeeming A. The only equity which he has is in respect of so much as the mortgagor had not alienated for value. In such a case, therefore, the court would throw the debt of A upon both his securities, rateably according to their value, and so leave the residue of each to satisfy the subsequent incumbrancer, to whom it is specifically mortgaged (*r*). But if C takes by his contract only the

---

to have the land sold, reserving the rentcharges, and then to have any deficiency made good out of the personal estate: *Re Fry, Fry* v. *Fry*, [1912] 2 Ch. 86, following and applying *Buckley* v. *Buckley* (1887), 19 L.R. Ir. 544. It has also been applied by analogy where a broker pledged his customer's securities with his own, so that, on the broker's bankruptcy, and a sale by the pledgee of the customer's securities, the customer was entitled, as against the trustee in bankruptcy, to the benefit of the broker's securities: *Re Burge, Woodall & Co., Ex parte Skyrme*, [1912] 1 K.B. 393.

(*o*) *Mason* v. *Bogg* (1837), 2 My. & Cr. 443; *Wallis* v. *Woodyear* (1855), 2 Jur. N.S. 179; *Dolphin* v. *Aylward* (1870), L.R. 4 H.L. 486, 500–501; *The Chioggia*, [1898] P. 1, distinguishing *The Edward Oliver* (1867), L.R. 1 A. & E. 379. Observations to the contrary in *Webb* v. *Smith, supra*, are not to be relied on. As to the case where the single fund has been applied for the first creditor's debt by order of the court, see *Gwynne* v. *Edwards* (1825), 2 Russ. 289, n.
A mortgagee may resort to funds not comprised in his security, where, *e.g.*, that has been swept away by a landlord under a distress for rent: *Re Stephenson, Ex parte Stephenson* (1847), De G. 586; and see *Aldrich* v. *Cooper* (1803), 8 Ves. 382.

(*p*) *Aldrich* v. *Cooper, supra*; *Averall* v. *Wade* (1835), Ll. & G. *temp.* Sugd. 252; *Dolphin* v. *Aylward, supra*; *Victor Investment Corpn., Ltd.* v. *Fidelity Trust Co.* (1973), 41 D.L.R. (3d) 65 (S.C. of Can.).

(*q*) A purchaser is not bound to take notice of all the equities arising out of a particular deed or action: *Averall* v. *Wade, supra*; *Shalcross* v. *Dixon* (1838), 7 L.J. N.S. Ch. 180. But *cf. Webb* v. *Smith* (1885), 30 Ch. D. 192 (C.A.), at p. 202.

(*r*) *Barnes* v. *Racster* (1842), 1 Y. & C.C.C. 401; *Bugden* v. *Bignold* (1843), 2 Y. & C.C.C. 377; *Titley* v. *Davies* (1843), 2 Y. & C.C.C. 399; and see *Gibson* v. *Seagrim* (1855), 20 Beav. 614; *Liverpool Marine Credit Co.* v. *Wilson* (1872), 7 Ch. App. 507; *Flint* v. *Howard*, [1893] 2 Ch. 54 (C.A.); and *Moxon* v. *Berkeley, etc., Society* (1890), 59 L.J. Ch. 524; *Baglioni* v. *Cavalli* (1901), 49 W.R. 236. In *Re Archer's Estate*, [1914] 1 I.R. 285, under similar circumstances, marshalling of the first mortgagee's security in favour of the second mortgagee was allowed; but in *Smyth* v. *Toms*, [1918] 1 I.R. 338, this was considered to be opposed to *Barnes* v. *Racster, supra*, and the first mortgagee's debt was apportioned between his two securities.

surplus which will remain after satisfying the earlier mortgagees, the marshalling will take place between them, without regard to his interest (s).

In whose favour the doctrine applies.—The doctrine of marshalling applies in manner above stated in favour of a subsequent mortgagee of one of the properties subject to the original mortgagee's security, and it applies generally in favour of persons taking under the mortgagor by assignment, whether for value or not. Thus, if, subsequently to the mortgage, the mortgagor settles one of the mortgaged properties, the mortgage debt will be thrown as far as possible on the other (t). And a surety is entitled to the benefit of marshalling (u).

But, as in the case of the mortgagee's right to hold several securities (x), his equity of marshalling overrides the right of the surety to have the benefit of all securities for the debt which he has discharged, where he has not entered into a contract which will prevent the mortgagor from conferring upon a later mortgagee of one of the estates, the ordinary right to have the securities marshalled (y).

If a consignee or other agent pledges his principal's goods with his own for his own debt, the pledgee will be compelled to resort in the first instance to the agent's goods (z).

But the doctrine does not apply in favour of the mortgagor himself or his trustee in bankruptcy, or his personal representatives, or persons who do not take by assignment or charge or conveyance an actual interest in one of the properties. Thus, it does not apply in favour of unsecured creditors (a), or in favour of a judgment creditor (b); unless he has obtained a charge on the estate (c).

Against whom the doctrine is applied.—The doctrine applies against the mortgagor (d), and persons claiming under him otherwise than by assignment or charge. Hence it applies against his trustee in bankruptcy (e), and his personal representatives (f), and against his judgment (g) and, a fortiori, his simple contract creditors. Also as

---

(s) *Re Mower's Trusts* (1869), L.R. 8 Eq. 110.

(t) *Hales* v. *Cox* (1863), 32 Beav. 118; *Aldridge* v. *Forbes* (1840), 9 L.J. Ch. 37; *Anstey* v. *Newman* (1870), 39 L.J. Ch. 769; *Mallott* v. *Wilson*, [1903] 2 Ch. 494; but see *Re Lysaght's Estate*, [1903] 1 I.R. 235.

(u) *Heyman* v. *Dubois* (1871), L.R. 13 Eq. 158. And see *Re Westzinthus* (1833), 5 B. & Ad. 817.

(x) *Infra*, p. 514.

(y) *South* v. *Bloxam* (1865), 2 H. & M. 457.

(z) *Broadbent* v. *Barlow* (1861), 3 De G.F. & J. 570; *Re Holland, Ex parte Alston* (1868), 4 Ch. App. 168; folld. in *Re Stratton, Ex parte Salting* (1883), 25 Ch. D. 148 (C.A.).

(a) *Anstey* v. *Newman, supra.*

(b) See *Averall* v. *Wade* (1835), L. & G. *temp.* Sugd. 252, 262; *Williamson* v. *Loonstra* (1973), 34 D.L.R. (3d) 275 (B.C.S.C.).

(c) *Re Fox* (1856), 5 Ir. Ch. R. 541.

(d) *Haynes* v. *Forshaw* (1853), 11 Hare, 93.

(e) *Baldwin* v. *Belcher, Re Cornwall* (1842), 3 Dr. & War. 173; *Re Tristram, Ex parte Hartley* (1835), 1 Deac. 288; *Re Holland, Ex parte Alston* (1868), 4 Ch. App. 168; *Heyman* v. *Dubois, supra*; see *Re Stephenson, Ex parte Stephenson* (1847), De G. 586.

(f) *Flint* v. *Howard*, [1893] 2 Ch. 54 (C.A.), at p. 73. The right to marshal formerly existed against the heir: *Lanoy* v. *Duke of Athol* (1742), 2 Atk. 444, 446.

(g) *Gray* v. *Stone* (1893), 69 L.T. 282.

against the wife of the mortgagor who has charged her own property to secure the prior—that is, the double—creditor's debt (*h*).

Marshalling excluded by exoneration.—But in accordance with the rule that marshalling will not be applied to the prejudice of the rights of third persons, it will not be applied to its full extent against persons claiming part of the property by assignment or charge, whether for value (*i*), or as volunteers (*k*), unless the other part had already been disposed of with a right to exoneration against the double creditor's mortgage (*l*). Ordinarily it will be subject to apportionment of the first mortgage debt between the two parts of the property (*m*).

Maritime securities.—Maritime securities will be marshalled so far as may be consistent with the rules of maritime priority, a qualification which enables the owner of a cargo which is included in a bottomry bond, with the ship and freight, to resist a claim to throw the debt upon the cargo for the purpose of leaving the ship and freight to satisfy the debt of another bondholder, whose security was confined to them, because by the maritime law the cargo is not liable until the ship and freight are exhausted (*n*).

And demands for wages, pilotage, and towage, to which the ship and freight are liable *pro rata*, will not be thrown upon the freight, for the benefit of a bondholder on the ship only, so as to prejudice the owner of the cargo, by diminishing the residue of the freight which would otherwise be available for another incumbrancer upon the cargo (*o*). Nor will the equity be applied where both funds are not under the control of the court. Therefore, seamen will not be compelled to proceed on their personal remedy for wages against the shipowner, that the ship may be left to satisfy the bondholder (*p*).

Pleading.—It is not necessary to frame the pleadings in an action expressly for marshalling. When the court sees at any time that one class of creditors will be deprived of their debts by the claims of another class upon their fund, it will, without being called upon, direct the assets to be marshalled (*q*).

(*h*) *Tidd* v. *Lister* (1854), 3 De G.M. & G. 857.
(*i*) *Barnes* v. *Racster* (1842), 1 Y. & C.C.C. 401; *Flint* v. *Howard*, [1893] 2 Ch. 54 (C.A.), at p. 73.
(*k*) *Dolphin* v. *Aylward* (1870), L.R. 4 H.L. 486, 501.
(*l*) As to such right of exoneration, see p. 504, *supra*.
(*m*) See p. 442, *supra*. So far as *Finch* v. *Shaw* (1854), 19 Beav. 500 (affd. *sub nom. Colyer* v. *Finch* (1856), 5 H.L.C. 905, 922), and *Haynes* v. *Forshaw* (1858), 11 Hare, 93, suggest that the subsequent alienation of another part is necessarily subject to marshalling, they appear to be contrary to *Barnes* v. *Racster*, *supra*.
(*n*) *The Priscilla* (1859), 1 Lush. 1; *The Edward Oliver* (1867), L.R. 1 A. & E. 379.
(*o*) *The La Constancia* (1846), 2 W. Rob. 460.
(*p*) *The Arab* (1859), 5 Jur. N.S. 417.
(*q*) *Gibbs* v. *Ougier* (1806), 12 Ves. 413.

CHAPTER 27

Consolidation

Nature of consolidation.—A mortgagee who holds several distinct mortgages under the same mortgagor, and under which the legal dates for redemption have passed (*a*), may within certain limits, and against certain persons entitled to redeem all or some of them, consolidate them—that is, treat them as one—and decline to be redeemed as to any, unless he is redeemed as to all (*b*). The principle is that, redemption being an equitable right, the person who redeems must on his part do equity towards the mortgagee, and redeem him entirely— not taking one of his securities, and leaving him exposed to the risk of deficiency on the other (*c*). A right of consolidation may be expressly agreed between mortgagor and mortgagee in which case there will be no need to rely on the equitable doctrine. Rules or mortgages of building societies generally include a provision to the effect that the mortgagor shall not be entitled to redeem a mortgage without at the same time redeeming every other security on any other property for the time being in mortgage to the society by the mortgagor.

Where the benefit of several mortgages is in one person and the equities in another it may be convenient to treat the mortgages as one.

(*a*) Or the mortgage monies have otherwise become due; *e.g.*, in an instalment mortgage on default.

(*b*) Consolidation is an application of the rule that he who seeks equity must do equity (*Chesworth* v. *Hunt* (1880), 5 C.P.D. 266, 271), and is a condition which can only be imposed on the equitable right to redeem which arises after default in payment, not on the contractual right to redeem on the day fixed for payment: *Cummins* v. *Fletcher* (1880), 14 Ch. D. 699 (C.A.), at p. 708; *Mills* v. *Jennings* (1880), 13 Ch. D. 639 (C.A.), at p. 646; *Minter* v. *Carr*, [1894] 3 Ch. 498 (C.A.), at p. 501.

The doctrine has been applied, but probably improperly, where there were several mortgages on the same property: *Re Salmon*, [1903] 1 K.B. 147. For the conditions for consolidation, see *infra*.

(*c*) *Jennings* v. *Jordan* (1881), 6 App. Cas. 698 (H.L.), at p. 700; *Mills* v. *Jennings*, *supra*; *Griffith* v. *Pound* (1890), 45 Ch. D. 553, 560.

The mortgagee is entitled to consolidate, whether the action is by a person who is actively seeking the aid of equity to redeem, or in a foreclosure action, in which the mortgagor can redeem only upon the same terms as if he were suing for redemption; or in bankruptcy, whether the application to the court is by the mortgagee himself or not: *Tribourg* v. *Lord Pomfret* (1773), cited Ambl. 733; *Re Loosemore, Ex parte Berridge* (1843), 3 Mont. D. & De G. 464; *Watts* v. *Symes* (1851), 1 De G.M. & G. 240; *Selby* v. *Pomfret* (1861), 3 De G.F. & J. 595; notwithstanding *Holmes* v. *Turner* (1843), 7 Hare, 367, n.; *Smeathman* v. *Bray* (1851), 15 Jur. 1051.

But the mortgagor cannot insist upon consolidation as against the later mortgagee of two properties, of which there are prior mortgages to different persons. Either of such persons may be redeemed separately by the later mortgagee, notwithstanding the mortgagor's objection: *Pelly* v. *Wathen* (1849), 7 Hare, 351; affd. (1851), 1 De G.M. & G. 16.

A deed effecting such an arrangement is often called a deed of consolidation (d).

Statutory exclusion of consolidation.—In practice the doctrine of consolidation was found to cause hardship to persons dealing with estates in mortgage, and it was abolished by s. 17 of the Conveyancing Act 1881, as to securities dated after that year, unless a contrary intention was expressed in the mortgage deeds or one of them. This provision is reproduced in the following section of the Law of Property Act 1925:

93.—(1) A mortgagor seeking to redeem any one mortgage is entitled to do so without paying any money due under any separate mortgage made by him, or by any person through whom he claims, solely on property other than that comprised in the mortgage which he seeks to redeem.

This subsection applies only if and as far as a contrary intention is not expressed in the mortgage deeds or one of them (e).

(2) This section does not apply where all the mortgages were made before the first day of January, eighteen hundred and eighty-two.

(3) Save as aforesaid nothing in this Act, in reference to mortgages, affects any right of consolidation or renders inoperative a stipulation in relation to any mortgage made before or after the commencement of this Act reserving a right to consolidate.

Conditions for consolidation.—In order that the right of consolidation (where the statute is excluded) may exist it is necessary that the mortgages shall have been created by the same mortgagor, and that all the securities—with an exception as to the exercise of the power of sale—shall be in existence when the claim to consolidate is set up. But the securities need not have been originally made to the same mortgagee, nor need they be of the same nature.

Same mortgagor.—The mortgages must originally have been made by the same mortgagor (f). Thus, there can be no consolidation of a security given by a person for his own debt, with one given by him and another for their joint debt (g). And a mortgage by three cannot be consolidated with a prior mortgage by two of the same persons, though the equity of redemption belonged to all the three (g). For

---

(d) For forms, see 14 Ency. Forms are Precedents (4th Edn.), pp. 818–827. Such deeds are often made by parent and subsidiary companies in favour of banks or financial institutions and contain cross guarantees and charges.

(e) An undertaking by an equitable mortgagee to execute a legal mortgage, with all such powers and provisions and in such form as the mortgagee may require, does not entitle the latter to have the above section negatived: *Whitley* v. *Challis*, [1892] 1 Ch. 64 (C.A.); *Farmer* v. *Pitt*, [1902] 1 Ch. 954.

Where the right of consolidation is to be preserved, it is usual to provide expressly that the section shall not apply to the security: see 14 Ency. Forms and Precedents (4th Edn.), p. 97; and see proviso in Precedent 1 in the Appendix, p. 682, *infra*, but a clause providing for the preservation of the right of consolidation is equally effective: *Hughes* v. *Britannia Building Society*, [1906] 2 Ch. 606, 611. A clause excluding the statute contained in the first of several mortgages will preserve the right to consolidation, although it is not contained in the subsequent mortgages: *Re Salmon, supra*; and a clause in a subsequent mortgage is effective as to previous mortgages: *Griffith* v. *Pound* (1890), 45 Ch. D. 553.

For the purpose of determining the amount payable in respect of a mortgage on the landlord's estate the person entitled to the mortgage is not permitted to exercise any right of consolidation: Leasehold Reform Act 1967, s. 12 (3).

(f) *Cummins* v. *Fletcher* (1880), 14 Ch. D. 699 (C.A.); *Sharp* v. *Rickards*, [1909] 1 Ch. 109; notwithstanding *Beevor* v. *Luck* (1867), L.R. 4 Eq. 537; and see *Marcon* v. *Bloxam* (1856), 11 Ex. 586.

(g) *Re Raggett, Ex parte Williams* (1880), 16 Ch. D. 117 (C.A.).

the mortgagee has no right to go behind the mortgagor and inquire into equitable interests for the purpose of consolidation (*h*).

Securities in existence.—The securities must be in existence at the time when consolidation is claimed. Hence a surplus on one mortgage cannot be retained to meet a deficiency on a mortgage which has ceased to exist through the determination of its subject-matter, such as a lease (*i*), or a life interest (*k*). But this does not apply where a security has ceased to exist through realisation and hence the mortgagee's right is not affected by his selling one of the estates under his power of sale (*l*).

Different mortgagees.—The securities need not have all been made to the same mortgagee. It is sufficient that they are united in the same person when consolidation is claimed (*m*). But a mortgage to one person and a mortgage to the same person and another on a joint account cannot be consolidated (*n*).

The mortgagee has a right to the benefit of the rule, though the securities are made to trustees, and even where they are made to different sets of trustees (*o*). And if the mortgages are made to different mortgagees, one of whom takes an assignment from the other of his security, the securities may be united, whether the assignee had an interest which entitled him to require an assignment (as where he was surety for that debt (*p*)), or whether he had no such interest (*q*).

(*h*) *Sharp* v. *Rickards*, [1909] 1 Ch. 109. And a mortgagee with several securities is not entitled to the discharge of both debts against a person who happens to be engaged with another in one mortgage only, though his co-mortgagor may have pledged another property to the same mortgagee: see *Jones* v. *Smith* (1794), 2 Ves. Jun. 372; *Aldworth* v. *Robinson* (1840), 2 Beav. 287; *Higgins* v. *Frankis* (1846), 15 L.J. Ch. 329; *Bowker* v. *Bull* (1850), 1 Sim. N.S. 29.

Where a tenant for life had charged the estate in exercise of a power reserved to him, and had mortgaged the charge with other property to a second mortgagee, it was held, that the remainderman might redeem the latter without paying off the whole debt, on the ground that the burden of the whole redemption would in effect be an increase, by so much, of the charge, making the estate of no value to those in remainder. But it was intimated, that there was a distinction between the cases of the mortgagor and of the remainderman: *Lord Kensington* v. *Bouverie* (1854), 19 Beav. 39; affd. (1859), 7 H.L.C. 557. As to mortgages of different interests in the same land, see *Jones* v. *Griffith* (1845), 2 Coll. 207. For the form of an order for redemption where there were successive mortgages, first, of the entirety of land, and then of undivided shares, and the mortgages of the entirety and of one of the shares were assigned to the same person, see *Thorneycroft* v. *Crockett* (1848), 2 H.L.C. 239. The case was treated as if the securities on the undivided shares were charges on different estates. But now the entirety would be vested in trustees on trust for sale.

(*i*) *Re Raggett, Ex parte Williams* (1880), 16 Ch. D. 117 (C.A.).

(*k*) *Re Gregson, Christison* v. *Bolam* (1887), 36 Ch. D. 223. See *Brecon Corpn.* v. *Seymour* (1859), 26 Beav. 548.

(*l*) *Selby* v. *Pomfret* (1861), 1 Johns. & H. 336; *Cracknall* v. *Janson* (1879), 11 Ch. D. 1 (C.A.).

(*m*) *Tweedale* v. *Tweedale* (1857), 23 Beav. 341; *Vint* v. *Padget* (1858), 2 De G. & J. 611; *Selby* v. *Pomfret* (1861), 3 De G.F. & J. 595; *Jennings* v. *Jordan* (1881), 6 App. Cas. 698 (H.L.), at p. 700; *Pledge* v. *White*, [1896] A.C. 187 (H.L.).

(*n*) *Riley* v. *Hall* (1898), 79 L.T. 244. An assignment can be taken after the bankruptcy of the mortgagor, though the holder of an original security taken after notice of the insolvency of the mortgagor will not, in bankruptcy, be allowed to gain a preference by consolidating it with an earlier security for another debt: *Re Softley, Ex parte Hodgkin* (1875), L.R. 20 Eq. 746.

(*o*) *Tassell* v. *Smith* (1858), 2 De G. & J. 713.

(*p*) *Tweedale* v. *Tweedale*, supra.

(*q*) *Vint* v. *Padgett*, supra; folld. in *Pledge* v. *White*, supra; and see *Re Salmon, Ex parte The Trustee*, [1903] 1 K.B. 147.

A mere equitable interest in the securities will enable the mortgagee to hold them both, the right not being founded upon any principle connected with the legal estate (*r*).

Securities may be of different natures.—The incumbrancer may consolidate securities of different natures, *e.g.* an assignment of equitable personalty with a mortgage upon freeholds and leaseholds (*s*). But the surplus produce of a sale of chattels included in a bill of sale cannot be held by the grantee of the bill of sale against an execution creditor, on the ground that the former holds a mortgage of other property from the same grantor. Such a claim is considered to be inconsistent with the definition of a bill of sale, and the provision as to setting forth the consideration and other matters in the Bills of Sale Act 1878 (*t*).

Against whom consolidation can be enforced.—So long as there is no severance in the titles to the equities of redemption in the mortgaged properties, the right of consolidation is not affected by any change of ownership, whether by devolution on death, sale, mortgage, or otherwise (*u*). And provided the mortgages were all made while the properties belonged to the mortgagor (*v*), they can be consolidated notwithstanding that the union of the mortgages in one person occurs after the change of title to the equities of redemption (*w*); and with notice of such change (*x*).

No consolidation attaches after severance of equities.—But where the title to the equities of redemption has been severed, the right of consolidation cannot be enforced unless it had already attached at the time of severance. The assignee of one equity of redemption takes subject to the possibility of existing mortgages being consolidated. But the mortgagor cannot by any subsequent dealing, prejudice the rights of his assignee (*y*). The purchaser of the equity of redemption therefore takes subject only to the equities which existed at the date of the conveyance to him, and is not affected by possibilities of equities, which are dependent upon future and uncertain dealings

---

(*r*) *Watts* v. *Symes* (1851), 1 De G.M. & G. 240; *Neve* v. *Pennell* (1863), 2 H. & M. 170; and see *Re Loosemore, Ex parte Berridge* (1843), 3 Mont. D. & De G. 464, where the rule was applied in bankruptcy by directing an account of what was due upon all the securities.

(*s*) *Watts* v. *Symes*, *supra*; and see *Spalding* v. *Thompson* (1858), 26 Beav. 637; *Tassell* v. *Smith*, *supra*; *Re McDonald* (1972). 28 D.L.R. (3d) 380 (ancillary chattel mortgage).

(*t*) *Chesworth* v. *Hunt* (1880), 5 C.P.D. 266; and *a fortiori* under the Bills of Sale Act (1878) Amendment Act 1882.

(*u*) *Re Breeds, Ex parte Alsager* (1841), 2 Mont. D. & De G. 328; *Selby* v. *Pomfret*, *supra*; *Margrave* v. *Le Hooke* (1690), 2 Vern. 207.

(*v*) See *Squire* v. *Pardoe* (1891), 40 W.R. 100; p. 511, *supra*.

(*w*) Thus the right of consolidation exists where the mortgages become united after the bankruptcy of the mortgagor: *Selby* v. *Pomfret*, *supra*; *Re Salmon, Ex parte The Trustee*, [1903] 1 K.B. 147; or after the sale or further mortgage of both properties as one transaction to the same person: *Tweedale* v. *Tweedale* (1857), 23 Beav. 341; *Vint* v. *Padget* (1858), 2 De G. & J. 611; *Pledge* v. *White*, [1896] A.C. 187 (H.L.).

(*x*) *Vint* v. *Padget*, *supra*. For the suggestion that a right of consolidation should be registered as a land charge (general equitable charge, Class C (iii)), see (1948), 92 Sol. Jo. 736. But *quaere* whether the right of consolidation amounts to a charge.

(*y*) *Harter* v. *Colman* (1882), 19 Ch. D. 630; *Mutual Life Assurance Society* v. *Langley* (1886), 32 Ch. D. 460. There can be no consolidation after an assignment in bankruptcy: *Eastern Canada Savings and Loans Co.* v. *Campbell* (*No.* 2) (1971), 19 D.L.R. (3d) 231.

with the property. There is, therefore, no right of consolidation against him where the mortgage of the second property was made after the mortgagor had assigned the equity of redemption of that which was first mortgaged, nor where the securities have become united only after the separation of the equities of redemption of the several estates (z).

Extent of right of consolidation.—The mortgagee may hold both properties (subject to the above restrictions), even against the purchaser or mortgagee of the equity of redemption of one of them without notice of the other mortgage, until payment of all that is due on both (a); and though the security of such later mortgagee is earlier in date, but postponed for another consideration (b). The purchaser or other assignee may then hold until he is redeemed, both as to his own security and what he paid when he redeemed the original mortgagee (c). And if he has paid off the mortgagee who first claimed a right to consolidate, out of the purchase-money of one of the properties which he has sold, he is considered to have made the payment out of his own money to the extent to which the payment was made necessary by the original mortgagee's claim to consolidate (d).

The right of consolidation overrides the right of the surety for one of the debts, who discharges it, to have the full benefit of the security for that debt (e), unless there is a special contract that the surety's right shall have priority, or unless fraud or misrepresentation against the surety has affected the rights of the mortgagee. A contract in the surety's favour will not be inferred from the mere fact that the suretyship extends only to one of the debts, and that he refused to be bound for the other (f).

Registered charges.—By s. 25 (3) of the Land Registration Act 1925, any provision in a charge which purports to affect any registered land or charge other than that in respect of which the charge is to be expressly registered is void. Rule 154 (1) of the Land Registration

---

(z) *Jennings* v. *Jordan* (1881), 6 App. Cas. 698 (H.L.); *Hughes* v. *Britannia Permanent Benefit Building Society*, [1906] 2 Ch. 607. And see *Baker* v. *Gray* (1875), 1 Ch. D. 491; *Minter* v. *Carr*, [1894] 3 Ch. 498 (C.A.). In *Andrews* v. *City Permanent Benefit Building Society* (1881), 44 L.T. 641, a first mortgagee was allowed to consolidate against a second mortgage who had notice of an express covenant for consolidation in the first mortgage. That case was not cited in *Hughes* v. *Britannia Permanent Benefit Building Society*, *supra*, the facts of which were substantially the same, where the claim to consolidate was rejected as being contrary to the principle of *Hopkinson* v. *Rolt* (1861), 9 H.L. Cas. 514 (see p. 458, *supra*), *i.e.*, such a right of consolidation is treated as a right to tack further advances, so that the first mortgagee cannot consolidate mortgages created after he has received notice of the second mortgage.

As to the effect on consolidation of a consent by a second mortgagee to the first mortgagee making further advances in priority to himself, see *Bird* v. *Wenn* (1886), 33 Ch. D. 215. As to the effect of a voluntary settlement on consolidation, apart from the Law of Property Act 1925, s. 173 (2) (as to which, see p. 232, *supra*), see *Re Walhampton Estate* (1884), 26 Ch. D. 391.

(a) *Ireson* v. *Denn* (1796), 2 Cox, Eq. Cas. 425; *Neve* v. *Pennell* (1863), 2 H. & M. 170; *Cracknall* v. *Janson* (1879), 11 Ch. D. 1 (C.A.).

(b) *Neve* v. *Pennell*, *supra*.

(c) *Bovey* v. *Skipwich* (1671), 1 Cas. in Ch. 201; *Titley* v. *Davies* (1743), 2 Y. & C.C.C. 399, n.

(d) *Cracknall* v. *Janson*, *supra*.

(e) See p. 507, *supra*.

(f) *Farebrother* v. *Wodehouse* (1856), 23 Beav. 18; compromised on app., 26 L.J. Ch. 240. Cf. *Nicholas* v. *Ridley* (1904), 89 L.T. 234; on app., [1904] 1 Ch. 192.

Rules 1925, provides that where a charge, whether affecting the whole or a part of the land comprised in a title, reserves the right to consolidate, it shall not on that account only be registered against any other land than that expressly described in it.   Rule 154 (2) states that where the right reserved is to consolidate with a specified charge, or an application in writing is made to register the right in respect of a specified charge, the registrar shall require the production of the land certificates of all the titles affected, and, on the production thereof, shall enter in the register a notice that the specified charges are consolidated.

The Registry view of these provisions is that s. 25 of the Act does not operate to make void a clause in a charge of registered land which excludes s. 93 of the Law of Property Act, for otherwise Rule 154 would be without meaning.   Nor is a right of consolidation contained in a mortgage or charge dependent upon a notice under the Rules, although such a notice has its value (g).

(g) Ruoff and Roper, *Registered Conveyancing* (3rd Edn.), pp. 549 *et seq*, where the practice is also set out.   Note that before any entry as to consolidation can be made, all relevant charge certificates must be produced: Land Registration Rules 1925, r. 154 (2).

PART VIII

DISCHARGE OF THE MORTGAGE

CHAPTER 28

Redemption

I—THE NATURE OF THE RIGHT OF REDEMPTION

The rights of redemption.—The right to redeem a mortgage was formerly conferred on the mortgagor by a proviso or condition in the mortgage to the effect that, if the mortgagor or his representative should pay to the mortgagee the principal sum, with interest at the rate fixed, on a certain day, the mortgagee, or the person in whom the estate was vested, would, at the cost of the person redeeming, reconvey to him or as he should direct (*a*). This is still the practice in the case of a mortgage effected by an assignment of the mortgagor's interest (*b*). A proviso for reconveyance was no longer appropriate after 1925 for a legal mortgage of land (which has to be made by demise (*c*)). And it is not necessary to have a proviso for surrender of the term in such a mortgage, since the term ceases on repayment (*d*). Nevertheless, in order to define the rights of the mortgagor and the mortgagee, a proviso is inserted expressly stating that the term will cease at the date fixed (*e*).

It has been seen (*f*) that, at law, whatever form the mortgage took, upon non-payment by the appointed time, the estate of the mortgagee became absolute and irredeemable, but that equity intervened to enable the mortgagor to redeem after the date of repayment.

There are, therefore, two distinct rights of redemption—the legal or contractual right to redeem on the appointed day and the equitable right to redeem thereafter (*g*). The equitable right to redeem, which only arises after the contractual date of redemption has passed, must be distinguished from the equity of redemption, which arises when the mortgage is made (*g*).

(*a*) See pp. 6, 7, *supra*.
(*b*) *E.g.*, where the property mortgaged is a chose in action or an equitable interest in realty or personalty. For forms, see 14 Ency. Forms and Precedents (4th Edn.), pp. 121, 123.
(*c*) See p. 21, *supra*.
(*d*) Law of Property Act 1925, ss. 5, 116. See p. 550, *infra*.
(*e*) See 14 Ency. of Forms and Precedents (4th Edn.), p. 120; and see clause 3 in Precedent 1, 3 and 4 in the Appendix, *infra*. And see p. 31, *supra*. The right of redemption arises, without being expressly conferred, whenever property has been conveyed as a security for the payment of money (see p. 10, *supra*), and where the nature of the transaction is doubtful, it can be inquired into by the court: see p. 9, *supra*.
And a mortgagor of chattels can still redeem even after the mortgagee has seized the goods, so long as the goods are in the mortgagee's possession: *Johnson* v. *Diprose*, [1893] 1 Q. B. 512 (C.A.).
(*f*) See p. 7, *supra*.
(*g*) *Kreglinger* v. *New Patagonia Meat and Cold Storage Co., Ltd.*, [1914] A.C. 25 (H.L.), at p. 48.

The question has been raised whether the mortgagor can repay the mortgage debt without redeeming the mortgage. The point would only arise, in practice, in a case where the mortgagor's whole interest in the mortgaged property has been transferred to the mortgagee. Under the pre-1926 method of creating mortgages payment and reconveyance were linked and it was not possible to have the one without the other (h). On principle it would seem that the mortgagor cannot pay off his debt without redeeming. And under the old system after payment the mortgagee was trustee of the mortgaged property for the mortgagor (h). On that basis, if the mortgagor was unwilling to accept back the mortgaged property, the mortgagee could seek an order for directions, vesting order, etc., to obtain a release of the property.

The equity of redemption.—The equity of redemption has been described as an estate (i), and as an interest (k) or equitable right (l) inherent in the land. Even though the mortgagor had at law conveyed the land to the mortgagee, he was in equity considered as the owner of the land, subject only to the mortgage (m). Though strictly equitable and formerly capable of being enforced in equity alone, it was of so much consequence in the eye of the law, that the law took notice of it, and allowed it to be assigned and devised (n).

Although in legal mortgages after 1925 a legal estate remains in the mortgagor, the legal estate and the equity of redemption must still be distinguished. It has been suggested that since the mortgagor has a freehold estate he cannot have an equitable estate co-extensive with it, so that the equity of redemption subsists only as a right in equity to redeem the property, the right being attached to the mortgagor's legal estate (o). The better view, however, is that there is no such merger (p).

Assignment of equity (q).—In the absence of statutory or other express provision to the contrary, the mortgagor is free to deal with the equity of redemption. Under the Small Dwellings Acquisition Acts (r) the mortgagor is restrained from transferring the land without the lender's consent and most building society mortgages similarly expressly so provide (s). Such a restraint, which lasts only while the mortgage exists, is not objectionable as a clog on the equity (t). We have seen (u) that the burden of the covenant for payment does not

---

(h) See pp. 545, 546 *infra*.

(i) *Casborne* v. *Scarfe* (1738), 1 Atk. 603; *Re Wells, Swinburne-Hanham* v. *Howard*, [1933] Ch. 29 (C.A.).

(k) *Lloyd* v. *Lander* (1821), 5 Mad. 282.

(l) *Pawlett* v. *A.-G.* (1667), Hardres, 465, 469.

(m) *Re Wells, Swinburne-Hanham* v. *Howard, supra*.

(n) *Pawlett* v. *A.-G., supra*; *Fawcett* v. *Lowther* (1751), 2 Ves. Sen. 300 (it was subject to gavelkind and other customs which affected the ordinary legal ownership).

(o) 27 Halsbury's Laws (3rd Edn.), 231.

(p) Turner, *Equity of Redemption* (Cambridge Studies in English Legal History), pp. 186–187; Waldock, *The Law of Mortgages* (2nd Edn.), 205.

(q) See (1974) 118 S.J. 368 (Correspondence). And see p. 294, *supra*.

(r) See p. 190, *supra*.

(s) And see clause in Precedent IA in the Appendix, *infra*.

(t) See p. 524, *infra*.

(u) P. 294, *supra*.

run with the equity of redemption and there is, therefore, a danger from the lender's point of view on a long term mortgage that if the borrower could freely dispose of the property, he might disappear from the scene and the lender would be left to his security rights alone. If the value of the property had depreciated and the whereabouts of the original borrower were unknown, the lender might suffer a loss. Consent to a transfer of the equity is usually forthcoming on terms of the transferee entering into a covenant for payment with the lender (a). A transfer without consent, where such is required, does not in itself, in the case of unregistered land, invalidate the transfer, but will be a breach of the terms of the mortgage and thereby, according to the terms thereof, give the lender the right (if he so wishes) to call in the mortgage monies, etc. In the case of registered land where the restraint is protected by a restriction, this will be to the effect that without an order of the registrar no transfer is to be registered without the consent thereto of the lender, so without the prior consent there can be no registered dealing with the land. Depending on the terms of the restraint provision in the mortgage, it may be possible to avoid the restraint by a transfer of the equitable interest or interests in the property. This will not usually assist where a purchaser of the property is involved, but may be of some use where, *e.g.*, a husband wishes to transfer his interest to his wife.

II—THE TIME FOR REDEMPTION

Usual time for redemption.—Even where the principal and interest are repayable by instalments a mortgage is usually made redeemable at the expiration of six months from its date (b). The date for redemption should be the same as the date (if any) fixed by the covenant for payment (c). It should be expressed in a legal mortgage so that the time when the right to foreclosure arises can be ascertained (c). For the same reason a provision for redemption is sometimes included in a legal charge, but, in the absence of such a provision, it is generally accepted that the right of the legal chargee to foreclose arises by implication at the date fixed in the covenant for payment (d).

When a time is fixed for redemption (and such time is unobjectionable (e)) a mortgage is not redeemable until that time has arrived (f). A mortgagee may take objection to an action to redeem at an earlier day even though the mortgagor tenders interest during the whole

---

(a) See *e.g., Esso Petroleum Co., Ltd.* v. *Alstonbridge Properties, Ltd.,* [1975] 3 All E.R. 358. See Precedent 8 in the Appendix, *infra.* In *Chelsea and Walham Green Building Society* v. *Armstrong,* [1951] 1 Ch. 835; [1951] 2 All E.R. 250 where there was a registered transfer of the equity and a covenant by the transferee with the building society which was not a party to the transfer it was held that the society could sue on the covenant.

(b) See 14 Ency. Forms and Precedents (4th Edn.), pp. 120 *et seq.;* and see clause 3 in Precedent 1 and subsequent forms in the Appendix, *infra.* For the direct covenant for repayment by instalments, see p. 28, *supra.*

(c) See p. 27, *supra.*

(d) See p. 26, *supra.*

(e) See p. 522, *infra.*

(f) For regulated agreements under the Consumers Credit Act 1974, see p. 141, *supra.*

intervening period (g). But if the mortgagee has taken steps to recover payment by taking possession of the property or otherwise he cannot object (h). Where no date for redemption is specified and the debt is repayable on demand by the mortgagee, the mortgagor may, it seems, redeem at any time. And this is apparently so even where the mortgagee has covenanted not to call the mortgage in until a specified date (i).

The mortgage may expressly provide for redemption at any time, on payment of the principal together with, for example, three months' interest thereon and all costs, charges and expenses due to the mortgagee and the costs of redemption, or after a specified period of notice or upon payment of interest in lieu of notice. Building society mortgages sometimes permit redemption whenever the interest rate is varied.

For the type of mortgage where the interest is calculated for a fixed term and added to the principal as a premium (k), the mortgage should provide for an early repayment discount (l). The absence of such may result in the premium being void as an unreasonable collateral advantage (m). For regulated agreements under the Consumer Credit Act 1974, regulations will provide for a rebate on early settlement (n) and these provisions will apply equally to any security provided in relation to a regulated agreement (o).

Postponement of redemption.—The right of redemption (p), while it cannot be altogether done away with by the original contract (q), may be postponed by a covenant that during a certain time the mortgage shall remain irredeemable (r). The mere length of time of

---

(g) *Brown* v. *Cole* (1845), 14 Sim. 427; and see *Harding* v. *Tingey* (1864), 34 L.J. Ch. 13. For statutory exceptions see Ch. 34, Discharge or Modification by Statute, *infra*.

(h) *Bovill* v. *Endle*, [1896] 1 Ch. 648; *Ex parte Wickens*, [1898] 1 Q.B. 543 (C.A.), at p. 548.

(i) *G.A. Investments Pty., Ltd.* v. *Standard Insurance Co., Ltd.*, [1964] W.A.R. 264, where it was held that the only notice required was for such period as would enable the mortgagee to receive the money and bank it.

(k) See p. 30, *supra*.

(l) This is usually done by reference to a scheduled table or to the rule of 78 (a formula whereunder a sum of interest is spread over the period of a loan so that, in general terms, the interest is at a constant rate over the period and reducing: see 15 Ency. Forms and Precedents (4th Edn.), p. 126 note 16). It is not advisable to provide for a discount based simply on the proportion of the term expired, because, although the interest element will have been spread evenly over the term of the mortgage, the interest is in fact greater in the early part of the term.

(m) *Cityland and Property (Holdings), Ltd.* v. *Dabrah*, [1968] Ch. 166; [1970] 2 All E.R. 639; see p. 528, *infra*. Subject thereto there would appear to be no entitlement to a discount: see *Harvey* v. *Municipal Permanent Investment Building Society* (1884), 26 Ch. D. 273 (C.A.). The position is not like that in hire-purchase where the owner is claiming damages against the hirer on default: see Goode, *Hire-Purchase Law and Practice* (2nd Edn.), pp. 399 *et seq*.

(n) Section 95.

(o) Section 113. For a discussion on early settlement rebate in the consumer credit context, see the Crowther Report (1971), paras 5. 4. 4. and 6. 7. 6. *et seq*.

(p) Strictly the equitable right to redeem, but a restriction on the contractual right must necessarily affect the equitable right.

(q) See p. 525, *infra*.

(r) But for consumer credit agreements, see s. 94 of the Consumer Credit Act 1974 (right to complete payments ahead of time), s. 113 (which puts a security in relation to a regulated agreement in the same position) and s. 173 (contracting out forbidden): and see p. 145, *supra*.

any postponement is not in itself an objection to the enforceability of such a covenant, although it may well be an important consideration. So long as the essential requirements of a mortgage transaction are observed, and oppressive and unconscionable terms are not imposed the court will not interfere (*s*). The essential requirements of a mortgage transaction are not observed where the right of redemption is rendered illusory. The nature of the interest mortgaged is relevant in this respect. Where it is freehold or a long term of years is still outstanding, subject to the other conditions of not being oppressive or unconscionable, a long postponement may be unobjectionable (*t*). On the other hand, where the interest mortgaged is a short term of years a postponement for as long as, or nearly as long as, the remainder of the term will render the equity of redemption illusory (*a*).

As to oppressive and unconscionable terms, relevant considerations are the absence of a corresponding restraint on the mortgagee, *i.e.*, there is nothing to prevent him calling the mortgage in (*b*), the size of loan (*c*), the character and bargaining power of the parties— companies or individuals (*d*), the circumstances surrounding the

---

(*s*) *Knightsbridge Estates Trust, Ltd.* v. *Byrne*, [1938] Ch. 741; [1938] 2 All E.R. 444; LUXMOORE, J.; *reversed*, [1939] Ch. 441 (C.A.); [1938] 4 All E.R. 618; affirmed on other grounds, [1940] A.C. 613 (H.L.); [1940] 2 All E.R. 401. Note the distinction drawn by SIR WILFRED GREENE, M. R., between the equitable right to redeem and the contractual right. A direct covenant for repayment by a specified number of instalments or over a specified number of years may operate as a postponement; see *De Borman* v. *Makofaides*, [1971] Estates Gazette Digest 909; and Precedent 2 in the Appendix, *infra*.

(*t*) A postponement of 40 years in the case of freehold was considered unobjectionable in *Knightsbridge Estates Trust, Ltd.* v. *Byrne, supra* (C.A.). No opinion was expressed on this point in the House of Lords, in which the case was decided on the grounds that debentures may be irredeemable: see p. 524, footnote (*l*), *infra*.
    The following periods have been held unobjectionable: 5 or 7 years (*Teevan* v. *Smith* (1882), 20 Ch. D. 724 (C.A.), at p. 729); 5 years (*Biggs* v. *Hoddinott*, [1898] 2 Ch. 307 (C.A.); 14 years (*Williams* v. *Morgan*, [1906] 1 Ch. 804; and see *Re Fortesque's Estate*, [1916] 1 I.R. 268 (C.A.) (10 years). Such arrangements are supported on the ground that the contract is valuable to both parties—the mortgagee being sure of a continuing security and the mortgagor being freed from the expense and trouble of seeking new lenders.

(*a*) *Fairclough* v. *Swan Brewery Co., Ltd.*, [1912] A.C. 562 (P.C.) (mortgage of term of 17½ years postponing redemption until last 6 weeks of term); *Davis* v. *Symons*, [1934] Ch. 442, explained in *Knightsbridge Estates Trust, Ltd.* v. *Bryne*, [1939] Ch. at pp. 400–462; [1938] 4 All E.R., at p. 629 (mortgage of insurance policies maturing before end of postponement period); *Santley* v. *Wilde*, [1899] 2 Ch. 474 (C.A.) (mortgage of 10-year residue of term with covenant to pay one-third of net profits of rents derived from underleases—mortgage security for loan and for the payments under the said covenant) must be contrasted with these cases. It was criticised in *Noakes & Co., Ltd.* v. *Rice*, [1902] A.C. 24 (H.L.), by Lords MACNAGHTEN and DAVEY (although the criticism was on the basis that the case concerned a collateral advantage), and it seems impossible to support the decision. It has also been suggested by Dr. J. H. C. Morris that the transaction was not one of mortgage but a partnership agreement to share in the profits: Waldock, *Law of Mortgages* (2nd Edn.), 187.

(*b*) *Williams* v. *Morgan*, [1906] 1 Ch. 804; *Morgan* v. *Jeffreys*, [1910] 1 Ch. 620; *Davis* v. *Symons, supra*, at p. 448. *Quaere* whether this consideration survived the supposed rejection of the test of reasonableness by *Knightsbridge Estates Trust, Ltd.* v. *Byrne, supra*.

(*c*) *Knightsbridge Estates Trust, Ltd.* v. *Byrne*, [1939] Ch. 441 (C.A.), at p. 455; [1938] 4 All E.R. 618, at p. 625, *per* Sir WILLIAM GREEN, M.R. In that case the loan was £310,000 and the parties were a property company and the trustees of a friendly society bargaining at arm's length.

(*d*) *Samuel* v. *Jarrah Timber and Wood Paving Corpn.*, [1904] A.C. 323 (H.L.), at p. 327, *per* Lord MACNAGHTEN.

loan (e) and, perhaps, the circumstances surrounding the claim that the postponement is invalid (f).

The doctrine of restraint of trade applies to mortgages (g). A postponement which might by itself be valid may therefore be unenforceable if accompanied by an unreasonable restraint of trade during the postponement period (g).

If a provision for postponement is invalid it is invalid as much against the assign of the mortgagor as against the mortgagor himself (h).

The mortgagee is entitled to the benefit of a valid postponement provision against a subsequent mortgagee, who took his security with notice of the covenant and who will not be allowed during the stipulated period to redeem the prior mortgage (i). If he takes without notice, the equity of redemption also still seems to be bound in his hands by the covenant of the mortgagor who can give to another no better equity against the first mortgagee than he had himself.

A mortgage may be validly irredeemable for an uncertain period, when, for example, it is made to secure an annuity, or as an indemnity against future liabilities, or for any other object not capable of immediate pecuniary valuation (k). And in certain cases statute permits the postponement of redemption (l).

The rule against perpetuities does not apply to a postponement provision (m).

"Breaking" the mortgage.—In many cases where redemption is postponed the terms of the mortgage also provide that if there is any default on the part of the mortgagor in the payment of interest or instalments for a specified period the whole of the mortgage monies shall become due. Accordingly if the mortgagor has the means to redeem he has merely to default and then tender the mortgage monies. But this cannot be done, if the mortgagee has the choice of treating the default as making the mortgage monies due or not.

Once a mortgage, always a mortgage.—While redemption may

(e) See *Knightsbridge Estates Trust, Ltd.* v. *Byrne*, [1939] Ch. 441, at p. 454; [1938] 4 All E.R. 618, at p. 624, *per* GREEN, M.R.

(f) In *Knightsbridge Estates Trust, Ltd.* v. *Byrne* interest rates had generally declined below the rate specified in the mortgage. This was no doubt why the mortgagor was seeking redemption.

A restraint on redemption for 20 years and within 12 months' notice after that time, where the mortgagee was the solicitor of the mortgagor was rejected as oppressive in *Cowdry* v. *Day* (1859), 1 Giff. 316. And see *Talbot* v. *Braddill* (1683), 1 Vern. 183, 394; *Morgan* v. *Jeffreys, supra.*

(g) *Esso Petroleum Co., Ltd.* v. *Harper's Garage (Stourport), Ltd.*, [1968] A.C. 269 (H.L.); [1967] 1 All E.R. 699 (21 years unreasonable, 5 years reasonable); *Re Petrol Filling Station, Vauxhall Bridge Road, London, Rosemex Service Station* v. *Shell-Mex and B.P.* (1969), 20 P. & C.R. 1; *Texaco, Ltd.* v. *Mulberry Filling Station*, [1972] 1 All E.R. 513.

(h) *Mehrban Khan* v. *Makhna* (1930), 57 Ind. App. 168, 172.

(i) *Lawless* v. *Mansfield* (1841), 1 Dru. & War. 557.

(k) *Fleming* v. *Self* (1854), 3 De G.M. & G. 997.

(l) A company may issue perpetual debentures: Companies Act 1948, ss. 89, 455 (1); and see *Knightsbridge Estates Trust, Ltd.* v. *Byrne*, [1940] A.C. 613 (H.L.); [1940] 2 All E.R. 401. Certain agricultural mortgages and charges may be made irredeemable (see p. 128, *supra*, and the Agriculture Act 1967, s. 28 (8) (to secure loan for amalgamation, etc.).

(m) *Knightsbridge Estates Trust, Ltd.* v. *Byrne*, [1939] Ch. 441, at p. 463; [1938] 4 All E.R. 618, at p. 631.

be postponed, if the above-mentioned conditions are satisfied, it cannot be extinguished by any covenant or agreement made at the time of the mortgage (*n*) as part of the mortgage transaction. This has been summarised in the rule "once a mortgage, always a mortgage" (*o*). Hence an agreement confining the right of redemption to any given period, such as the life of the mortgagor, or to any specified class of persons, such as to the mortgagor alone, will be invalid (*p*).

Nor will an agreement made at the time of the loan not to sue for redemption or for discharge of the equity of redemption upon some event or condition be allowed (*q*); nor a separate covenant that if the mortgagee shall think fit, the mortgagor will convey to him so much of the estate as shall be of the value of the mortgage money at so many years' purchase (*r*).

An option granted to the mortgagee to purchase the mortgaged property will not be enforceable, at all events if the purchase price is a fixed one (*s*). The position is otherwise when the option relates to property other than the mortgaged property.

Where the mortgaged property is leasehold and the lease contains an option to renew or to purchase the reversion and the mortgagee exercises the option, the mortgagor is entitled on redemption to have the renewed lease or the reversion transferred to him, subject to payment of the proper expenses involved in exercising the option (*t*).

Release of equity of redemption.—Although a mortgagee cannot at the time, or as a part of the mortgage transaction, stipulate in

---

(*n*) *Fairclough* v. *Swan Brewery Co., Ltd., supra.* For the statutory exceptions, see footnote (*l*), *supra.*

(*o*) *Newcomb* v. *Bonham* (1681), 1 Vern. 7; *Spurgeon* v. *Collier* (1758), 1 Eden, 55.

(*p*) *Howard* v. *Harris* (1583), 1 Vern. 32, 191; *Salt* v. *Marquess of Northampton,* 1892] A.C. 1 (H.L.).

(*q*) *Toomes* v. *Conset* (1745), 3 Atk. 261; *Vernon* v. *Bethell* (1762), 2 Ed. 110; *Salt* v. *Marquess of Northampton, supra.*

(*r*) *Jennings* v. *Ward* (1705), 2 Vern. 520, as explained in *Biggs* v. *Hoddinott,* [1898] 2 Ch. 307 (C.A.), at pp. 315, 323.

(*s*) *Samuel* v. *Jarrah Timber and Wood Paving Corpn.,* [1904] A.C. 323 (H.L.); (1944), 60 L.Q.R. 191 (G. L. Williams); see also *Lewis* v. *Frank Love, Ltd.,* [1961] 1 All E.R. 446 (option contained in assignment of mortgage; this was not really a case of a simple transfer, but more of a new loan); *Bannerman, Brydone Folster & Co.* v. *Murray,* [1972] N.Z.L.R. 411; *Re Supreme Court Registrar to Alexander Dawson Inc.,* [1976] 1 N.Z.L.R. 615. An option granted before the mortgage was made and not part of the mortgage transaction would be enforceable: *London and Globe Finance Corpn., Ltd.* v. *Montgomery* (1902), 18 T.L.R. 661 (where it was held that the transaction was not a mortgage). Where, on a sale, part of the purchase monies are left on mortgage, a covenant for preemption is good, if part of the contract for sale: *Davies* v. *Chamberlain* (1909), 26 T.L.R. 138 (C.A.); and see *Orby* v. *Trigg* (1722), 9 Mod. Rep. 2. A right of pre-emption is not subject to the same objection as an option since the mortgagor cannot be compelled to sell. And see *Re Petrol Filling Station, Vauxhall Bridge, London, Rosemex Service Station* v. *Shell Mex and B.P., Ltd.* (1968), 20 P. & C.R. 1.
Where the mortgage and the option to purchase were part of a vendor and purchaser arrangement and where the option was given to prevent the property coming into the hands of a competitor it has been held that the option was enforceable: see *Re Moore and Texaco Canada,* [1965] C.L.Y. 2548. And so the option is, probably, valid where it is part of the sale price at the property. But a mortgagee cannot sell to himself in exercise of his power of sale in accordance with an option or right of pre-emption: see *Williams* v. *Wellingborough Borough Council,* [1975] 3 All E.R. 462 (C.A.).

(*t*) *Nelson* v. *Hannam,* [1943] Ch. 59 (C.A.); [1942] 2 All E.R. 680. Whether or not a mortgagee could stipulate to have the benefit of an option transferred to him as something collateral to a mortgage transaction was left open.

advance for the extinguishment of the equity of redemption if the debt is not paid by a certain time, yet the equity of redemption may be released under a separate transaction (*u*). The rule, which prohibits a trustee from buying the trust property from his beneficiary, does not apply to a purchase of the equity of redemption by the mortgagee from the mortgagor, since they are regarded for such a purpose as on the ordinary footing of vendor and purchaser, until the contrary is shown by the person impeaching the deed.

The right of redemption will not be defeated, however, if the release was obtained by fraud or oppression, such as would invalidate a sale between an ordinary vendor and purchaser, or, if by means of the influence of his position, the mortgagee has obtained the purchase at a nominal or insufficient price. Undervalue alone will not be sufficient to impeach the release (*x*). The validity of the release may also be impeached for other reasons (*y*).

When the release is of an interest in land it must be in writing (*z*).

Lease to mortgagee.—During the subsistence of the relation of mortgagor and mortgagee the mortgagee may not take a lease from the mortgagor upon terms which are, as regards the mortgagor, improvident (*a*). But this objection does not lie against an occupation lease for a short term at a fair rent (*b*).

Collateral advantages.—A stipulation by the mortgagor to do something in addition to repaying the loan with interest may be part of the security (*c*). A collateral advantage is a stipulation, not forming part of the security, giving the mortgagee some advantage in addition to the security. Such a stipulation may, in the circumstances, shortly to be mentioned, while being valid until redemption (*d*), become invalid upon redemption. If the provision is contained in an agreement forming a separate transaction from the mortgage (*e*) or, if, although contained in the mortgage deed, it is independent of the mortgage (*f*), the special rules relating to collateral advantages do not apply, and the validity of the stipulation must be determined on general principles. If, however, the stipulation can be construed as a term of the mortgage,

---

(*u*) *Reeve* v. *Lisle*, [1902] A.C. 461 (H.L.); but see *Lewis* v. *Frank Love, Ltd., supra*.

(*x*) *Knight* v. *Marjoribanks* (1849), 2 Mac. & G. 10; *Ford* v. *Olden* (1867), L.R. 3 Eq. 461; *Melbourne Banking Corpn.* v. *Brougham* (1882), 7 App. Cas. 307 (P.C.).

(*y*) *E.g.*, if it was made by a person without power to make it, or if there was no release of the covenant for payment of the debt.

(*z*) Law of Property Act 1925, s. 53.

(*a*) *Webb* v. *Rorke* (1806), 2 Sch. & Lef. 661; *Morony* v. *O'Dea* (1809), 1 Ba. & Be. 109; *Hickes* v. *Cooke* (1816), 4 Dow. 16.

(*b*) *Gubbins* v. *Creed* (1804), 2 Sch. & Lef. 214; *Hickes* v. *Cooke, supra*.

(*c*) *Santley* v. *Wilde*, [1899] 2 Ch. 474 (C.A.).

(*d*) Unless unconscionable in itself: *Biggs* v. *Hoddinott*, [1898] 2 Ch. 307.

(*e*) Whether or not a stipulation forms part of the mortgage is determined by the intention of the parties: *Kreglinger* v. *New Patagonia Meat and Cold Storage Co., Ltd.*, [1914] A.C. 25 (H.L.), at p. 61, *per* Lord PARKER. The question is not one of form but of substance: *ibid.*, at p. 39, *per* Lord HALDANE. But the form may be the best evidence of the intention: *ibid.*, at p. 43, per Lord HALDANE.

(*f*) The collateral advantage was independent in *De Beers Consolidated Mines, Ltd.* v. *British South Africa Co.*, [1912] A.C. 52 (H.L.); see *Kreglinger* v. *New Patagonia Meat and Cold Storage Co., Ltd., supra*, at p. 44, per Lord HALDANE; *Re Petrol Filling Station, Vauxhall Bridge Road, London, Rosemex Service Station* v. *Shell Mex and B.P.* (1968), 20 P. & C.R. 1.

the rule is that such a stipulation will not be enforceable (*g*) if it is either (1) unfair and unconscionable, or (2) in the nature of a penalty clogging the equity of redemption, or (3) is inconsistent with or repugnant to the contractual and equitable right to redeem (*h*).

Relevant considerations are the character and bargaining power of the parties—company or individual (*i*), the circumstances of the loan—commercial transaction or private loan (*i*), the nature of the security (*k*), the nature and duration of the restriction (if any) on the mortgagor's right to deal freely with the mortgaged property and other property of the mortgagor (*l*), and the terms of the collateral advantage (*m*). It is not, it seems, invalid merely because it is to endure after redemption (*n*). Stipulations making the mortgage irredeemable or postponing redemption have already been dealt with.

A provision that a land mortgage may not be redeemed without also redeeming an associated chattel mortgage has been held not to be a clog (*o*).

A collateral advantage may affect the mortgaged property (*p*), or be personal to the mortgagor (*q*).

An enforceable collateral advantage, if in substance negative, is binding not only on the mortgagor but also on his assigns and tenants who take with notice of it (*r*).

The special rules relating to collateral advantages apply to a debenture with a floating charge (*s*), but debenture holders may, if it is so provided, share in surplus assets although they have been paid off (*t*).

The doctrine of restraint of trade applies to collateral advantages (*u*).

(*g*) So long, it seems, as the mortgagor has offered to repay the mortgage: see *Esso Petroleum Co., Ltd.* v. *Harper's Garage (Stourport), Ltd.*, [1968] A.C. 269, at p. 299 (H.L.), [1967] 1 All E.R. 699, at p. 708; *Amoco Australia Pty., Ltd.* v. *Rocca Bros. Motor Engineering Co. Pty., Ltd.*, [1975] A.C. 561 (P.C.); [1975] 1 All E.R. 968.

(*h*) *Kreglinger* v. *New Patagonia Meat and Cold Storage Co., Ltd.*, *supra*, at p. 61, *per* Lord PARKER. And see *Cityland and Property (Holdings), Ltd.* v. *Dabrah*, [1968] Ch. 166; [1967] 2 All E.R. 639 (where the test appears to be one of reasonableness).

(*i*) See, *e.g.*, *Cityland and Property (Holdings), Ltd.* v. *Dabrah*, [1968] Ch., at p. 180; [1967] 2 All E.R., at p. 647.

(*k*) In *Kreglinger* v. *New Patagonia Meat and Cold Storage Co., Ltd.*, *supra*, the security was a floating charge.

(*l*) In *Bradley* v. *Carritt*, [1903] A.C. 253 (H.L.) and *Noakes & Co., Ltd.* v. *Rice*, [1902] A.C. 24 (H.L.), the restriction was perpetual. In *Kreglinger* v. *New Patagonia Meat and Cold Storage Co., Ltd.*, *supra*, it was for 5 years.

(*m*) In *Kreglinger* v. *New Patagonia Meat and Cold Storage Co., Ltd.*, *supra*, the right granted to the mortgagee to purchase the mortgagor's sheepskins was on the terms that the mortgagee should pay a price equal to the best price offered by any other person. *Quaere* whether the result would have been the same had the price not been such.

(*n*) Cf. *Noakes & Co., Ltd.* v. *Rice*, *supra*.

(*o*) *Re Macdonald & Cowtin* (1972), 28 D.L.R. (3d) 380.

(*p*) As in *Biggs* v. *Hoddinott*, *supra*.   (*q*) As in *Bradley* v. *Carritt*, *supra*.

(*r*) *John Brothers Abergarw Brewery Co.* v. *Holmes*, [1900] 1 Ch. 188; *Bradley* v. *Carritt*, *supra*; *cf. Reeve* v. *Lisle*, [1902] A.C. 461 (H.L.); *Davies* v. *Chamberlain* (1909), 26 T.L.R. 138 (C.A.).

(*s*) *De Beers Consolidated Mines, Ltd.* v. *British South Africa Co.*, [1912] A.C. 52 (H.L.).

(*t*) *Re Cuban Land and Development Co.* (1911), *Ltd.*, [1921] 2 Ch. 147.

(*u*) *Esso Petroleum Co., Ltd.* v. *Harper's Garage (Stourport), Ltd.*, [1968] A.C. 269 (H.L.); [1968] 1 All E.R. 699; (1969) 86 L.Q.R. 229 (J. D. Heydon). And see note (*g*), p. 524, *supra*.

Bonuses, premiums and costs (*a*).—A stipulation that, in case the property is sold, the mortgagee shall receive a bonus or commission has been held bad (*b*). And a stipulation in a mortgage payable by instalments making the entire debt (and not merely the balance (*c*)) recoverable in case of default being made in payment of any instalment has also been held invalid (*d*). Both these cases were decided on the principle which prevailed until after the repeal of the usury laws by the Usury Laws Repeal Act 1854, that any provision imposing on the mortgagor a liability to pay anything beyond principal, interest and costs as the price of redemption was bad (*e*). Now the validity of a provision by the mortgagee for a bonus or premium or other such sum must be determined in the same way as any other collateral advantage (*f*).

A provision that a mortgage shall be redeemable only on payment of a larger sum than that advanced is not necessarily bad (*g*). The sum may be larger than that advanced because a sum representing interest has been added to the advance (*h*). A premium may be justifiable if it is in the lieu of interest (so long as it represents interest at a reasonable rate (*i*)), or where the security is of a hazardous nature (*k*). That the premium as well as the loan (and not merely the balance of the loan) shall become payable forthwith on default is a relevant factor (*l*), as also is the fact that the premium is so large that it destroys the whole equity making it a completely deficient security (*l*).

If the provision is unreasonable it will not be payable, but interest on the principal sum advanced at a rate fixed by the court will be payable. In a recent case a rate of 7 per cent. per annum on a

---

(*a*) For the judicial control of extortionate credit bargains under ss. 137–140 of the Consumer Credit Act 1974, see pp. 152, 153, *supra*. In some jurisdictions the rate of interest is limited by statute: see, *e.g.*, the Interest Act R.S.C. 1970; *Glinert* v. *Kosztowniak* (1972), 25 D.L.R. (3d) 390; (1972) 50 Can. Bar Rev. 296 (I. Davis); and as to collateral advantages, the Unconscionable Transactions Relief Act R.S.O. 1960; *Morehouse* v. *Income Investments*, [1966] 1 O.R. 229.

(*b*) *Broad* v. *Selfe* (1863), 11 W.R. 1036; and see *Browne* v. *Ryan*, [1901] 2 I.R. 653.

(*c*) *Sterne* v. *Beck* (1863), 1 De G.J. & Sm. 595. See p. 28, *supra*.

(*d*) *Booth* v. *Salvation Army Building Association* (1897), 14 T.L.R. 3.

(*e*) Which principle did not survive *Biggs* v. *Hoddinott, supra,* and *Kreglinger* v. *New Patagonia Meat and Cold Storage Co., Ltd., supra*.

(*f*) *Kreglinger* v. *New Patagonia Meat and Cold Storage Co., Ltd., supra; Cityland Property (Holdings), Ltd.* v. *Dabrah*, [1968] Ch. 166; [1967] 2 All E.R. 639.

(*g*) *Potter* v. *Edwards* (1857), 26 L.J. Ch. 468 (loan of £700 and premium of £300 held good); *Mainland* v. *Upjohn* (1889), 41 Ch. D. 126.

(*h*) *Cityland and Property (Holdings), Ltd.* v *Dabrah, supra*. Such sums added to the advance are commonly known as premiums.

(*i*) *Cityland and Property (Holdings), Ltd.* v. *Dabrah, supra*. *Inter alia*, the nature of the security and the means of the borrower are relevant as to the reasonableness of the rate.
In *Cityland, etc.*, where the premium was held unreasonable, the premium amounted to 57 per cent. of the loan and could not be claimed to be in lieu of interest because interest was also claimed. But had it been in lieu of interest it would have represented interest at 19 per cent., or 38 per cent. taking into account that on default it became payable forthwith.

(*k*) *Potter* v. *Edwards, supra; Mainland* v. *Upjohn, supra*. See the review of these cases in *Cityland and Property (Holdings), Ltd.* v. *Dabrah, supra*.

(*l*) *Cityland and Property (Holdings), Ltd.* v. *Dabrah, supra; Wanner* v. *Caruana*, [1974] 2 N.S.W.L.R. 301. For early repayment discount, see p. 522, *supra*.

day-to-day basis has been ordered (*m*), but it was emphasised in that case that that rate was chosen on the facts of the case and that it has no bearing on what would be the proper rate in any other case.

A bonus or commission (*n*) may be deducted from the advance, the mortgagee paying only the balance. But the whole advance will be allowed as the principal debt where the bonus or commission is reasonable (*o*). If it is not deducted at the time of the advance it will be subsequently allowed in taking account of what is due to the mortgagee or under the head of just allowance (*p*).

A reasonable sum may be deducted from the advance, but be allowed in the taking of accounts, in respect of a service charge (*q*).

Interest or "commission" on unpaid instalments may be allowed if at a reasonable rate (*p*).

A solicitor-mortgagee can charge his costs, or those of the firm of which he is a member, for work done in negotiating a loan, deducing and investigating title, and preparing and completing a mortgage, against the security (*r*).

III—PERSONS ENTITLED TO REDEEM

Mortgagor and his successors in title.—The right to redeem follows the interest of the mortgagor, and is exercisable by him and also by those taking the whole of his interest, whether by assignment *inter vivos*, or by devolution on death. The right also belongs to those who have only a partial interest in the property (*s*).

Assignee of equity of redemption.—The assignee of the equity of redemption can redeem, even if a volunteer (*t*) and even if a voluntary assignment contains a power of revocation, so long as it is not acted upon. The assignee of the equity of redemption of one only of two properties comprised in the same mortgage cannot insist on redeeming

---

(*m*) *Cityland and Property (Holdings), Ltd.* v. *Dabrah, supra*. However, in that case, no evidence of prevailing market rates was filed. In fact the premium represented interest at 9½ per cent. non-reducing over six years. Non-reducing rates are common today in private mortgages and, indeed, in any but institutional mortgages, and 9½ per cent. non-reducing is far from being an exceptional rate. Hire-purchase rates are often higher. Day-to-day balances are exceptional. Even building societies lend on yearly balances. For a consideration of such mortgages, see the Report of the Committee on the Enforcement of Judgment Debts (the Payne Committee) 1969, Cmnd. 3909, paras. 1355–1358 *et seq*.

(*n*) In the case of building societies the Building Societies Act 1962, restricts bonuses and commissions: see ss. 34, 74. Premiums, however, are permitted: s. 4 (1) (g); and see *Re Phillips, Ex parte Bath* (1884), 27 Ch. D. 509 (C.A.).

(*o*) *Mainland* v. *Upjohn, supra*; *Biggs* v. *Hoddinott, supra*.

(*p*) *General Credit and Discount Co.* v. *Glegg* (1883), 22 Ch. D. 549; *Bucknell* v. *Vickery* (1891), 64 L.T. 701 (P.C.).

(*q*) *Wallingford* v. *Mutual Society* (1880), 5 App. Cas. 685 (H.L.); *Protector Endowment and Annuity Loan Co.* v. *Grice* (1880), 5 Q.B.D. 592 (C.A.). The costs of setting up the mortgage are, of course greater at the start, though the charge will usually be spread evenly over the prospective term of the mortgage.

(*r*) Solicitors Act 1974 s. 58.

(*s*) *Pearce* v. *Morris* (1869), 5 Ch. App. 227; *Tarn* v. *Turner* (1888), 39 Ch. D. 456 (C.A.). For loss of the right to redeem, see pp. 564 *et seq., infra*.

(*t*) *Rand* v. *Cartwright* (1664), 1 Cas. in Ch. 59; *Howard* v. *Harris* (1683), 1 Vern. 191, 193.

that property only, and cannot be compelled to do so, his right being to redeem the whole (*u*).

While on assignment the mortgagor ceases to be entitled to redeem, his right to do so revives if he is sued for the mortgage debt. He is then, in effect, a surety for the assignee (*a*), and he may redeem notwithstanding that the assignee has created fresh charges in favour of the mortgagee (*a*).

The right to redeem extends also to a limited interest granted by the mortgagor, such as that of a lessee under a lease which is not binding on the mortgagee and which the mortgagee refuses to recognise (*b*).

Title by adverse possession.—Where an adverse possessor has gained a title against the mortgagor, but not against the mortgagee, so that the mortgagor's title is extinguished and a new title created in the adverse possessor, there is in effect an assignment of the equity of redemption and he can redeem (*c*).

Bankrupts.—The bankruptcy of the mortgagor operates to vest the equity of redemption in the trustee, and as in the case of a voluntary assignment, the mortgagor ceases to be entitled to redeem (*d*). The right to redeem passes to the trustee, and if the mortgagee comes in under the bankruptcy, it is exercisable in accordance with the rules as to proof by secured creditors contained in the Bankruptcy Act 1914 (*e*). If the mortgagee assesses the value of his security and proves for the deficiency, the trustee can redeem on payment of the assessed value (*f*). But if the mortgagee relies on his security, and remains outside the bankruptcy, the trustee cannot redeem except on the ordinary terms (*g*).

Bona vacantia.—On the intestacy of the person entitled to the equity of redemption, in the absence of persons entitled as next-of-kin the equity of redemption passes to the Crown as *bona vacantia* (*h*). Where a corporation has executed a mortgage and later has been dissolved at a time when it was still entitled to the equity of redemption, the equity of redemption passes to the Crown as *bona vacantia* (*i*).

Subsequent incumbrancer.—A later mortgagee is entitled to

(*u*) *Mutual Life Assurance Society* v. *Langley* (1886), 32 Ch. D. 460 (C.A.); *Hall* v. *Heward* (1886), 32 Ch. D. 430 (C.A.).

(*a*) *Kinnaird* v. *Trollope* (1888), 39 Ch. D. 636, 645.

(*b*) *Tarn* v. *Turner*, *supra*, at p. 465.

(*c*) *Fletcher* v. *Bird* (1896), decided by HAWKINS, J., afterwards Lord BRAMPTON. A report of the judgment was given in the Appendix to the 6th Edn. of this work, p. 1025.

(*d*) *Spragg* v. *Binkes* (1800), 5 Ves. 583.

(*e*) Section 32; and see p. 422, *supra*.

(*f*) Bankruptcy Act 1914, Sched. 2, rr. 10–18.

(*g*) Where the mortgagee is the petitioning creditor and values his security for the purpose of the petition, it has been held that the trustee cannot claim to redeem at this value: *Re Vautin, Ex parte Saffery*, [1899] 2 Q.B. 549; *Re Lacey, Ex parte Taylor* (1884), 13 Q.B.D. 128. The point was left open by the Court of Appeal in *Re Button, Ex parte Voss*, [1905] 1 K.B. 602, where it was held that for the purpose of proof, the petitioning creditor would not, in the absence of mistake as to value, be allowed to depart from his estimate.

(*h*) Administration of Estates Act 1925, s. 46 (1) (vi); see now Intestates' Estates Act 1952, s. 4 and Sch. 1.

(*i*) *Re Wells, Swinburne-Hanham* v. *Howard*, [1933] Ch. 29 (C.A.); Companies Act 1948, s. 354.

redeem, but his right is not, as in the case of the mortgagor and the assignee of the equity of redemption, an abolute right (*k*). If it has to be asserted in an action, it is only ancillary to the later mortgagee's right to work out his remedy against the mortgaged property by foreclosure. No later incumbrancer can redeem a prior mortgagee adversely, without bringing the mortgagor before the court for the purpose of completing his remedy by foreclosure (*l*). And if by any means, as by a covenant not to foreclose till the arrival of a certain period, the later mortgagee has precluded himself from pursuing that remedy against the mortgagor, he cannot insist that, upon paying off the first mortgagee, the latter shall assign the mortgage to him, for being unable to seek relief against the mortgagor by reason of his covenant, he may not bring him forward at all, and without him the action will fail as against the prior mortgagee also (*m*).

Yet the later incumbrancer is not, in such a case, altogether without remedy, for the court will restrain the first mortgagee from depriving him of his right by a sudden sale of the property, where it appears that the sale is about to be made for that purpose (*m*). Moreover, the rule does not justify the first mortgagee in refusing to be redeemed except in an action. He should, without the necessity for judicial proceedings, accept payment from the second mortgagee, and thereupon take a transfer of the first mortgage (*n*).

Creditors.—A judgment creditor, save in the cases mentioned below, cannot redeem. A charging order in favour of a judgment creditor of a mortgagor may be made on the mortgagor's land (*o*). Such an order has the like effect as an equitable charge created by the debtor under his hand (*p*) and takes effect subject to every liability under which the debtor holds it (*q*). The chargee is therefore in the same position as the subsequent incumbrancer dealt with above.

A further mode of execution is that of the appointment by the court of a receiver by way of equitable execution against a mortgagor's estate or interest in land (*r*). A judgment creditor who has obtained such an order and registered it may redeem (*s*). The receiver holds the property subject to prior incumbrances, but the judgment creditor can obtain a sale of the interest of the debtor in the land without redeeming prior incumbrances (*t*).

(*k*) *Teevan* v. *Smith* (1882), 20 Ch. D. 724 (C.A.), at p. 729.
(*l*) *Fell* v. *Brown* (1787), 2 Bro. C.C. 276; "The natural decree is that the second mortgagee shall redeem the first mortgagee, and that the mortgagor shall redeem him or stand foreclosed": *Palk* v. *Lord Clinton* (1806), 12 Ves. 48, 58; *Farmer* v. *Curtis* (1829), 2 Sim. 466; *Teevan* v. *Smith, supra.* This is the principle known by the maxim "redeem up, foreclose down".
(*m*) *Rhodes* v. *Buckland* (1852), 16 Beav. 212.
(*n*) *Smith* v. *Green* (1844), 1 Coll. 555, 563.
(*o*) Administration of Justice Act 1956, s. 35. See p. 159, *supra.*
(*p*) Administration of Justice Act 1956, s. 35 (3). As to protection of such orders by registration, see Land Charges Act 1972, ss. 6, 20 (17), and Land Registration Act 1925, s. 59 (1).
(*q*) See p. 487, *supra.*
(*r*) Administration of Justice Act 1956, s. 36 (1). Such an appointment requires registration; see footnote (*p*), *supra.*
(*s*) *Earl of Cork* v. *Russell* (1871), L.R. 13 Eq. 210.
(*t*) *Wells* v. *Kilpin* (1874), L.R. 18 Eq. 298; *Beckett* v. *Buckley* (1874), L.R. 17 Eq. 435.

A judgment creditor has been allowed to make a payment to save an estate, where the representatives of the debtor omitted to do so (*u*).

The general creditors of the mortgagor cannot generally redeem (*a*), but under special circumstances this may be allowed, where, for instance, it is necessary for enabling them to obtain the benefit of an order of the court (*b*). If creditors can make out that the trustees to whom the mortgaged property has been assigned for their benefit are colluding with the mortgagee to prevent the recovery of their claim, or that the trustees were called on to redeem and refused to do so, or that they themselves are unsafe, it seems they may redeem (*c*). And if the bankruptcy trustee refuses to bring an action to redeem for the benefit of the estate it seems that the creditor may do so under peril of costs (*d*). But liberty to redeem will be given to the trustee first and then to the plaintiff.

Devolution on death.—On the death of the mortgagor, the equity of redemption, and with it the right to redeem, devolves on his personal representatives (*e*), and is exercisable by them until, by assent or conveyance, the equity becomes vested in the devisee or other person entitled.

Where equity is settled.—In the case of settled land the legal estate is vested in the tenant for life or statutory owners as trustee for all parties interested (*f*). Where the mortgage affects the legal estate the right of redemption is primarily in the tenant for life as estate owner. The case is within the general rule that, for the purposes of redemption, the trustees represent their beneficiaries, and the beneficiaries should not seek to redeem on their own account unless the trustees are improperly refusing to do so (*g*).

In the case of land subject to a trust for sale the legal estate is vested in the trustees and the general rule stated in the previous paragraph applies.

Where a mortgage has been made of a limited interest, such as a mortgage by the tenant for life of his life interest, this will be subject to redemption by the mortgagor and those claiming under him in the ordinary way.

Persons under disability.—Land which is limited in trust for an infant for an estate in fee simple or term of years absolute is for the purposes of the Settled Land Act 1925, settled land (*h*), and the right of redemption will be in the trustees in whom the land is vested.

(*u*) *Blagrave* v. *Clunn* (1706), 2 Vern. 576; *Frederick* v. *Aynscombe* (1739), 1 Atk. 392.

(*a*) *Beckett* v. *Buckley*, *supra*.

(*b*) *Christian* v. *Field* (1842), 2 Hare, 177.

(*c*) *Troughton* v. *Binkes* (1801), 6 Ves. 573; *White* v. *Parnther* (1829), 1 Knapp, 179, 229.

(*d*) *Francklyn* v. *Fern* (1740), Barn. Ch. 30, 32.

(*e*) Administration of Estates Act 1925, ss. 1, 3.

(*f*) Settled Land Act 1925, ss. 16, 107 (1).

(*g*) *Troughton* v. *Binkes* (1801), 6 Ves. 573, 575; *Mills* v. *Jennings* (1880), 13 Ch. D. 639 (C.A.). The old cases establish that a remainderman could not redeem without the consent of the tenant for life: *Ravald* v. *Russell* (1830), Younge 9; *Raffety* v. *King* (1836), 1 Keen, 601; *Prout* v. *Cock*, [1896] 2 Ch. 808. This is still probably so now that the tenant for life has the legal estate.

(*h*) Settled Land Act 1925, s. 1 (1) (ii) (d).

Where the right of redemption is vested in a mental patient (*i*) it is exercised by the Court of Protection on his behalf (*k*).

Co-owners.—Where, by reason of a tenancy in common, the statutory trusts have been imposed (*l*), and where there is a trust for sale arising by reason of a joint tenancy, the primary right of redemption is in the trustees. Subject thereto one co-owner may redeem the whole debt (*m*).

Sureties.—The right to redeem belongs also to a person who is under liability for the mortgage debt (*n*), or whose property is subject to the debt (*o*). Thus a surety, if he pays the debt himself, or if the mortgagor refuses to pay, is entitled to redeem (*p*). If a third person has brought property of his own into the security he is entitled to redeem in order to protect his property. Thus a wife who has mortgaged her own property for her husband's debt, and in aid of a mortgage of his property, is entitled to redeem the husband's property (*q*).

Spouse in occupation under Matrimonial Homes Act 1967.—Where a spouse becomes entitled under s. 1 of the Matrimonial Homes Act 1967, to occupy a dwelling-house or any part thereof, any payment or tender by that spouse in or towards satisfaction of any liability of the other spouse in respect of mortgage payments affecting the dwelling-house is as good as if made or done by the other spouse, but this does not affect any claim of the spouse in occupation and actually making the payment against the other spouse to an interest in the dwelling-house by virtue of the payment (*r*).

Reservation of redemption to third party.—Formerly when a legal mortgage contained a proviso for reconveyance, it sometimes happened that the reconveyance was directed to be made to persons or uses different from those to whom or to which it originally belonged, or was subject. Apart from the statutory provisions as regards mortgages by tenants in tail (Fines and Recoveries Act 1833), courts of equity were guided, in questions arising out of a variation of the rights of redemption, by the principle, that, a mortgage being nothing more than a transaction for raising a loan, there was a presumption (the strength or weakness of which depended on the circumstances of each particular case (*s*)) against an intention to alter the previous rights of the parties, further than was necessary to effect that

---

(*i*) See, generally, the Mental Health Act 1959.

(*k*) Mental Health Act 1959, s. 103.

(*l*) Law of Property Act 1925, ss. 1 (6), 34; Sched. 1, Pt. IV.

(*m*) *Marquis of Cholmondeley* v. *Lord Clinton* (1820), 2 Jac. & W. 1; *Waugh* v. *Land* (1815), Coop. G. 129; *Hall* v. *Heward* (1886), 32 Ch. D. 430 (C.A.). For partners, see *Hegeman* v. *Rogers* (1972), 21 D.L.R. (3d) 272, referring to *Re Pollard's Estate* (1863), 3 De G.J. & Sm. 541; *Cavander* v. *Bulteel* (1873), 9 Ch. App. 79.

(*n*) *Green* v. *Wynn* (1869), 4 Ch. App. 204.

(*o*) *Gedye* v. *Matson* (1858), 25 Beav. 310.

(*p*) This is by virtue of his right to avail himself of all the creditor's securities. See pp. 586–587, *infra*. The surety does not have the right to redeem, if he has given up his right to subrogation: *Royal Trust Co. Mortgage Corpn.* v. *Nudnyk Holdings, Ltd.* (1974), 4 O.R. (2d) 721.

(*q*) *Dixon* v. *Steel*, [1901] 2 Ch. 602. *Re Thompson* (1976), 8 A.L.R. 479.

(*r*) Matrimonial Homes Act 1967, s. 1 (5). See *Hastings and Thanet Building Society* v. *Goddard*, [1970] 3 All E.R. 954 (C.A.). And see p. 218, *supra*.

(*s*) *Plomley* v. *Felton* (1888), 14 App. Cas. 61, at p. 65 (P.C.).

object (*t*). Thus, if husband and wife mortgaged the wife's land, the equity of redemption would be the wife's, although, by the deed, it was reserved to the husband and his heirs, and though he kept down the interest (*u*).

To change the ownership, therefore, the court had to be satisfied that there was a purpose to do so beyond the immediate object of the mortgage, and it would not generally take the words of the deed as prima facie evidence of such purpose, though it required no express declaration of intention (*a*).

The present system of legal mortgage under which the proviso for reconveyance is replaced by a proviso for cesser is inconsistent with a change of the limitations of the land in the manner considered above, but should occasion arise for pursuing the matter reference should be made to the principles set out above (*b*).

IV—REDEMPTION OF BUILDING SOCIETY MORTGAGES

Generally.—The right of borrowers to whom advances have been made on mortgage to redeem the mortgage are the same as under any other mortgage (*c*) and will be on the terms set out in the mortgage deed and in the rules of the society. A society must set forth the conditions upon which a borrower can redeem in its rules (*d*). But an advanced member is not merely a mortgagor. He is liable to have his rights altered by an alteration of the rules, and thereby to have his right of redemption postponed (*e*).

Terminating and permanent societies.—Building societies are either terminating or permanent. A terminating society is one which by its rules is to terminate at a fixed date, or when a result specified in its rules is attained. A permanent society is a society which has not by its rules any such fixed date or specified result at which it is to terminate (*f*).

As regards redemption there is the difference that in a permanent society it is easy to ascertain how much must be paid by an advanced member who wishes to redeem. A mortgage to a permanent society generally secures the repayment of the sum advanced with interest, and possibly a premium, by a definite number of instalments in accordance with tables in the rules, and also any fines or other monies which may become payable by the member to the society under the

---

(*t*) *Fitzgerald* v. *Lord Fauconberge* (1730), Fitzgib. 207.

(*u*) *Brend* v. *Brend* (1684), 1 Vern. 213. And see *Re Duke of Marlborough, Davis* v. *Whitehead*, [1894] 2 Ch. 133.

(*a*) *Jackson* v. *Innes* (1819), 1 Bli. 104. See further the 7th Edn. of this work, at p. 594.

(*b*) See also for persons entitled to redeem, pp. 571–574, *infra.*

(*c*) *Provident Permanent Building Society* v. *Greenhill* (1878), 9 Ch. D. 122.

(*d*) Building Societies Act 1962, s. 4 (1) (g).

(*e*) *Bradbury* v. *Wild*, [1893] 1 Ch. 377. The society, if it insists that a mortgagor shall only redeem subject to his liabilities as a shareholder, must prove his membership.

(*f*) Building Societies Act 1962, s. 1 (2). For statistics of societies, see the Annual Reports of the Chief Registrar of Friendly Societies. And see p. 193, *supra.*

rules during the continuance of the security (g). In the case of a terminating society where there is no fixed date for termination, the calculation may be difficult owing to the impossibility of saying with certainty how long the society will last. Thus it has been held in the case of a terminating society that, upon the terms of the mortgage deed, and under the rules of the society, the mortgagor was entitled to redeem only upon payment of all the future subscriptions on his share until the dissolution of the society, the probable duration of the society to be ascertained by calculation, as the future payments to be treated as if immediately due (h).

Future interest and fines.—Although the mortgage provides for retention out of the proceeds of sale under the power of sale of all subscriptions, fines and other monies (i) which should then be due, or should become due, in respect of the advanced shares during the remainder of the period over which the repayment of the principal and interest was spread, this does not authorise retention in respect of interest after repayment of principal (k); and this would also apply to redemption. But an advanced member cannot redeem without paying fines which are properly due from him (l).

Effect of redemption on member's liability.—If the rules of a terminating building society expressly provide that an advanced member may redeem, on payment of his subscription to a certain period (being the period calculated for the duration of the society), the member may redeem at that period, though the failure of the funds to meet the amount of the share proposed to be realised for each member makes it necessary to continue the society for a longer period; and the society is not entitled to retain the deeds as a security for the subscriptions to become due from the redeeming member during the continued period, although he may be liable for subscriptions accruing due after redemption (m).

In the absence of special contract advanced members of permanent societies are entitled to redeem by paying up the amount remaining due on their securities and so put an end to their connection with the society. They are not bound to remain members for the purpose of sharing any loss that may have been sustained by the society (n).

(g) For forms of building society mortgages, see 3 Ency. Forms and Precedents (4th Edn.), pp. 724 *et seq.*

(h) *Mosley* v. *Baker* (1848), 6 Hare, 87; affd. (1849), 3 De G.M. & G. 1032; *Seagrave* v. *Pope* (1851), 1 De G.M. & G. 783. See *Seton* (7th Edn.), vol. 3, 2050. If the deed does not provide that the calculation is to be in accordance with the probable duration of the society or if there is no provision for calculating the probable duration of the society the mortgagor can only redeem upon payment of all dues which, according to the rules, may become due during the longest period for which the society may possibly last: *Fleming* v. *Self* (1854), 3 De G.M. & G. 997.

(i) See *Bailes* v. *Sunderland Equitable Industrial Society* (1886), 55 L.T. 808.

(k) *Re Goldsmith, Ex parte Osborne* (1874), 10 Ch. App. 41; *Matterson* v. *Elderfield* (1869), 4 Ch. App. 207.

(l) *Parker* v. *Butcher* (1867), L.R. 3 Eq. 762.

(m) *Sparrow* v. *Farmer* (1859), 26 Beav. 511; *Handley* v. *Farmer* (1861), 29 Beav. 362; but see *Harvey* v. *Municipal, etc., Building Society* (1884), 26 Ch. D. 273.

(n) *Re West Riding of Yorkshire Permanent Building Society, Ex parte Pullman* (1890), 45 Ch. D. 463 (where the members had obtained a statutory receipt before the commencement of the winding up). Where there is a special contract, advanced

Liability on dissolution of society.—Where a society is being wound up or dissolved advanced members cannot be required to pay the balance owing on their securities except in accordance with their contracts; hence they can continue to pay by instalments (o).

V—REDEMPTION ON COMPULSORY PURCHASE

The Lands Clauses Consolidation Act 1845, provides that the promoters of an undertaking to which that Act is applied by their special Act may purchase or redeem the interest of the mortgagee of any lands required for the purposes of the special Act, whether they shall have previously purchased the equity of redemption or not, and whether the mortgagee shall be entitled in his own right or in trust; and whether he be in possession by virtue of the mortgage or not, and whether the mortgage affect the lands solely or jointly with any other lands not required for the purposes of the special Act (p).

When this procedure is adopted the authority may redeem at once on payment of principal, interest, and costs, with six months' additional interest, or may give six months' notice to pay—unless there is a current notice of intention to redeem by the mortgagor— and then either immediately or at the expiration of either of such notices, the mortgagee must reconvey on payment or tender of principal, interest, and costs, the interest including any additional interest which the circumstances require (p). If the mortgagee fails to reconvey, or to adduce a good title, the authority may deposit in the Supreme Court the amount due and vest the estate and interest of the mortgagee in themselves by deed poll (r).

Where the mortgaged land is of less value than the mortgage debt, the value of the lands or compensation to be paid must be settled between the mortgagee and the person entitled to the equity of redemption on the one part and the acquiring authority on the other

---

members must on redemption pay their proper proportion of losses sustained by the society: *Re West Riding of Yorkshire Permanent Building Society* (1890), 43 Ch. D. 407.

(o) *Kemp* v. *Wright*, [1895] 1 Ch. 121; Building Societies Act 1962, s. 104.

(p) Section 108. See also the Compulsory Purchase Act 1965, Part 1. These provisions are supplementary only to the general provisions of the respective Acts and do not exclude the right of mortgagees as owners to recover compensation for severance or other injurious affection: *R.* v. *Middlesex (Clerk of the Peace)*, [1914] 3 K.B. 259.

In the absence of any express provision between the parties a mortgagee is entitled to a notice to treat even though the acquiring authority is negotiating only with the mortgagor and leaving him to discharge the mortgage: *Cooke* v. *London County Council*, [1911] 1 Ch. 604. Unless the mortgagee agrees to the acquiring authority treating only with the mortgagor, the authority must take care that his interest is provided for, otherwise it will be restrained from carrying out the works on the mortgaged land until the mortgage has been redeemed or the appropriate compensation paid to the mortgagee: *Ranken* v. *East and West India Docks and Birmingham Rail Co.* (1849), 12 Beav. 298. If the authority purchases land from the mortgagor, the mortgagor must give notice to redeem: *Re Spencer-Bell to London and South Western Rail. Co. and Metropolitan District Rail. Co.* (1885), 33 W.R. 771.

(q) Lands Clauses Consolidation Act 1845, s. 108; Compulsory Purchase Act 1965, s. 14 (2), (3).

(r) Lands Clauses Consolidation Act 1845, s. 109 (as amended by the Administration of Justice Act 1965, s. 17, Sched. 1); Compulsory Purchase Act 1965, ss. 14 (4), (5), (6), 25 (1), 28 (2).

or, failing agreement, determined by the Lands Tribunal (s). When agreed or determined, it is to be paid by the authority in settlement of the debt so far as it will extend (t) and upon payment or tender the mortgagee must reconvey all his interest in the land to the authority or as it directs (u).

Similar provisions to those mentioned above apply if the mortgagee fails to reconvey or adduce a good title (a). The payment to the mortgagee or into court must be accepted by the mortgagee in satisfaction of his debt so far as it will extend and will be a full discharge of the land from all money due thereon (b). All rights and remedies possessed by the mortgagee against the mortgagor by virtue of any bond, covenant or obligation, other than the right to the mortgaged land, remain in force in respect of so much of the debt as has not been satisfied by the payment to the mortgagee or into court (c).

Further provisions of the Acts apply where part only of the mortgaged land is required by the acquiring authority and that part is of less value than the mortgage debt and the mortgagee does not consider the remaining part of the land a sufficient security for the money charged thereon or he is not willing to release the part so required (d).

If in any of the cases mentioned above there is in the mortgage deed a time limited for payment of the principal money thereby secured, and the mortgagee is required to accept payment of his mortgage money or of part thereof at a time earlier than the time so limited, the acquiring authority must pay to the mortgagee, in addition to the sum paid off, all costs and expenses properly incurred by him in respect of, or which shall be incidental to the re-investment of, the sum paid off. If the rate of interest secured by the mortgage is higher than that which can reasonably be expected to be obtained on re-investing the money, at the time when the mortgage is paid off, regard being paid to the current rate of interest, the mortgagee will be entitled to receive from the acquiring authority, in addition to the principal and interest, compensation in respect of the loss to be sustained by him by reason of the mortgage money being prematurely paid off (e). The amount of the compensation to be ascertained, in

---

(s) Lands Clauses Consolidation Act 1845, s. 110; Compulsory Purchase Act 1965, s. 15 (1). As to the amount of compensation, *quaere* whether where the mortgagor is entitled to the gross value payment as an owner-occupier (see Land Compensation Act 1961, Sched. 2, para. 3) the compensation payable under the 1845 Act or 1965 Acts is the same as that payable under the 1961 Act. Note that the 1965 Act refers to the value of the *land*, whereas the 1961 Act refers to the relevant *interest*.

(t) Lands Clauses Consolidation Act 1845, s. 110; Compulsory Purchase Act 1965, s. 15 (2).

(u) Lands Clauses Consolidation Act 1845, s. 110; Compulsory Purchase Act 1965, s. 15 (3).

(a) Lands Clauses Consolidation Act 1845, s. 111; Compulsory Purchase Act 1965, ss. 15 (4), 28 (2).

(b) Lands Clauses Consolidation Act 1845, s. 111 (as amended by the Administration of Justice Act 1965, s. 17, Sched. 1); Compulsory Purchase Act 1965, ss. 15 (6), 25 (1).

(c) Lands Clauses Consolidation Act 1845, s. 111; Compulsory Purchase Act 1965, s. 15 (7).

(d) Lands Clauses Consolidation Act 1845, ss. 112, 113; Compulsory Purchase Act 1965, s. 16.

(e) Lands Clauses Consolidation Act 1845, s. 114; Compulsory Purchase Act 1965, s. 17 (1).

case of difference, or in other cases of disputed compensation by the Lands Tribunal (*f*). Until payment or tender of the compensation the authority is not entitled, as against the mortgagee, to possession of the mortgaged land (*g*).

VI—PAYMENT OF THE DEBT

A—NOTICE TO PAY OFF

Notice before payment.—After default by the mortgagor to repay on the appointed day, the mortgagee is generally entitled to notice before his security is discharged by payment. The reason for this was said to be that the mortgagor having lost his estate at law, and being only entitled to redeem in equity, had to do equity by allowing a reasonable opportunity for the mortgagee to find a new security for his money (*h*). Six months' notice is treated as the reasonable and proper time (*i*). But if the mortgagee demands his money, or (with the qualifications mentioned below) takes proceedings to realise his security—which amounts to a demand—notice will be unnecessary (*k*), whether the time for payment has arrived or not (*l*), and it is the same where the mortgagee has taken possession, this also being in effect a demand for payment (*m*). Where money is in court and the mortgagor applies for payment out to the mortgagee and himself, the mortgagee is entitled to six months' notice (*n*). Also, where judgment has been given in a foreclosure action appointing a specific date for redemption, the mortgagor cannot redeem before without paying interest up to that day; for the judgment has settled the rights of the parties (*o*).

Interest in lieu of notice.—By a rule of practice the mortgagee is entitled to six months' interest in lieu of notice (*p*). The mortgagee cannot claim interest in lieu of notice where he has waived the right to it by his own action (*q*).

When rule as to notice applies.—The rule, that a mortgagee, not himself taking steps to call in or realise his mortgage, is entitled to six months' notice or to six months' interest in lieu of notice, does not apply to an equitable mortgage by deposit, with or without memo-

---

(*f*) Lands Clauses Consolidation Act 1845, s. 114; Compulsory Purchase Act 1965, s. 17 (2).

(*g*) Lands Clauses Consolidation Act 1845, s. 114; Compulsory Purchase Act 1965, ss. 14 (2), (3), 16 (5).

(*h*) Now the mortgagor does not lose his estate, but will have lost his contractual right to redeem. For the position where there is no specific redemption date, see p. 522, *supra*.

(*i*) *Cromwell Property Investment Co., Ltd.* v. *Western and Toovey*, [1934] Ch. 322. For a form of notice, see Precedent 24A in the Appendix, *infra*.

(*k*) *Smith* v. *Smith*, [1891] 3 Ch. 550; *Edmondson* v. *Copland*, [1911] 2 Ch. 301.

(*l*) *Bovill* v. *Endle*, [1896] 1 Ch. 648.

(*m*) *Bovill* v. *Endle*, *supra*; for other instances where notice is unnecessary, see *Matson* v. *Swift* (1841), 5 Jur. 645; *Re Fowler, Bishop* v. *Fowler* (1922), 128 L.T. 620; *Re Moss, Levy* v. *Sewill* (1885), 31 Ch. D. 90; *Re Alcock, Prescott* v. *Phipps* (1883), 23 Ch. D. 372 (C.A.); *Hill* v. *Rowlands*, [1897] 2 Ch. 361 (C.A.).

(*n*) *Smith* v. *Smith*, *supra*.

(*o*) *Hill* v. *Rowlands*, *supra*. Cf. *Soloway* v. *Sheahan* (1972), 21 D.L.R. (3d) 388.

(*p*) *Browne* v. *Lockhart* (1840), 10 Sim. 420, 424; *Johnson* v. *Evans* (1889), 61 L.T. 18 (C.A.).

(*q*) *Banner* v. *Berridge* (1881), 18 Ch. D. 254.

randum, this being presumed to be a mere temporary security (*r*). Otherwise the rule applies not only to securities upon realty, but upon things in action and other personalty wherever the nature of the security might make it necessary for the mortgagor to take proceedings for redemption (*s*).

It applies, also, where the security is naturally discharged by an event which does not depend on the will of the debtor, or by the falling in of a policy of insurance, which constitutes the security (*t*).

A mortgagee can require fresh notice, or interest in lieu of notice, where the money is not paid on the expiration of the first notice, whether it was given by himself or the mortgagor (*u*). Six months is again the reasonable and proper period (*a*), unless, where the first notice was given by the mortgagor, there is some reasonable explanation for his failure to pay (*b*), in which case a shorter period, such as three months, will be followed.

Missing mortgagee.—Where the mortgagee is missing it will not be possible to give him notice. In such circumstances it may be possible to commence redemption proceedings seeking substituted service and asking the court to appoint a person to execute a statutory receipt or other discharge on payment of the mortgage monies into court. Alternatively if the property is to be sold the procedure under s. 50 of the Law of Property Act 1925 (*c*) may be adopted. Where all the monies have been repaid and there is evidence of that fact no further action is necessary (*d*).

B—TENDER AND PAYMENT

Effect of tender of amount due.—Upon the contractual date of redemption or upon the expiration of the notice of intention to redeem, the mortgagee is bound to know the amount due to him and if he unjustifiably refuses to accept an unconditional tender of all that is due, it will be at his own peril (*e*). A qualified refusal will be justified if an unusual form of discharge is tendered with the money; for the mortgagee is entitled to a reasonable time to be advised whether such a document is proper for him to execute and a draft should have been sent to him beforehand (*f*). The mortgagor is entitled to know how much he is liable to pay and this is provided by the mortgagee in what is now commonly called a redemption statement. The mortgagor has the

---

(*r*) *Fitzgerald's Trustee* v. *Mellersh*, (1892) 1 Ch. 385. And see p. 296, *supra*, for where the mortgage debt is repayable on demand.

(*s*) *Smith* v. *Smith, supra.*

(*t*) *Smith* v. *Smith, supra.* And where a railway company purchased land compulsorily, it was held that the mortgagee was entitled to insist on six months' interest in lieu of notice from the vendor: *Spencer-Bell to L. & S.W. Rail. Co.* (1885), 33 W.R. 771.

(*u*) *Bartlett* v. *Franklin* (1867), 38 L.J. Ch. 671; cf. *Edmondson* v. *Copland, supra.*

(*a*) *Re Moss, supra.*

(*b*) *Cromwell Property Investment Co., Ltd.* v. *Western and Toovey, supra.*

(*c*) See p. 559, *infra.*

(*d*) See pp. 550, 551, *infra.*

(*e*) *Harmer* v. *Priestly* (1853), 16 Beav. 569.

(*f*) *Webb* v. *Crosse*, [1912] 1 Ch. 323.

right to know how the redemption figure is arrived at (*g*). If the mortgagee extorts more than is due, the overpayment may be recovered by the mortgagor as money received by the mortgagee to his use (*h*), or, alternatively, money paid by mistake (*i*). If the redemption figure supplied is less than the amount actually due, the mortgagee may claim the deficiency at any time up to the discharge of the mortgage (*k*). It does not seem that there can be any place for estoppel based on the faulty statement if, as it appears, it is capable of correction until the time of discharge (*l*).

If upon tender of the sum due under a mortgage, the mortgagee refuses the tender, the mortgagor may re-enter, but the debt remains (*m*).

An action of detinue for deeds deposited by way of equitable mortgage of land cannot be supported prior to actual repayment, the proper remedy of an equitable mortgagor being an action of redemption (*n*).

Interest ceases to run upon the mortgage debt from the time at which a proper tender of the whole amount due is shown to have been made (*o*). But it ought to appear, that, from the time of the tender, the money was kept ready by the mortgagor and no profit was afterwards made from it. Upon proof to the contrary interest will still run (*p*). The money should be paid into court if there are proceedings pending in which this can be done or put on deposit, the mortgagor accounting for the interest thereon to the mortgagee (*q*). There must be an actual tender of the money due (*r*). The court will not stay the interest on proof of a proposal by the mortgagor when money is due to him from

---

(*g*) See *Cityland and Property (Holdings), Ltd.* v. *Dabrah*, [1968] Ch. 166, at pp. 172–173; [1967] 2 All E.R. 639, at pp. 641–642. For the right of the debtor under a regulated agreement under the Consumer Credit Act 1974 to know the amount and rate of the total charge for credit (s. 60 (1) (b)), the amount remaining payable (ss. 77, 78) and the settlement figure (s. 97), see pp. 139, 146, *supra*.

(*h*) *Close* v. *Phipps* (1844), 7 Mans. & G. 586; *Fraser* v. *Pendlebury* (1861), 10 W.R. 104; *Mobil Oil Canada, Ltd.* v. *Rural Municipality of Storthoaks No. 31*, [1973] 6 W.W.R. 644.

(*i*) Being a mistake of fact: see, *e.g.*, *National Westminster Bank, Ltd.* v. *Barclays Bank International, Ltd.*, [1975] Q.B. 654; [1974] 3 All E.R. 834; *Secretary of State for Employment* v. *Wellworthy Ltd. (No. 2)*, [1976] I.C.R. 13.

(*k*) See p. 553, *infra*.

(*l*) *Cf.* the bank cases, where a customer has been credited in error and would have acted differently if he had not believed he was richer than in fact he was: see *United Overseas Bank* v. *Jiwani*, [1977] 1 All E.R. 733; [1976] 1 W.L.R. 964. For the binding effect of statements given under the Consumer Credit Act 1974; see s. 172 of that Act and p. 146, *supra*.

(*m*) Co. Litt. 209 b.

(*n*) *Bank of New South Wales* v. *O'Connor* (1889), 14 App. Cas. 273 (P.C.). Under R.S.C. Ord. 29, r. 6, the party claiming to redeem personalty may pay into court the principal sum together with interest and costs and may thereupon get an order for delivery of the deeds: *ibid.*

(*o*) *Bank of New South Wales* v. *O'Connor, supra; Rourke* v. *Robinson*, [1911] 1 Ch. 480; *Edmondson* v. *Copland*, [1911] 2 Ch. 301; *Graham* v. *Seal* (1918), 88 L.J. Ch. 31 (C.A.). The tender to stop interest need not be such a tender as would be a defence to an action at law: *Webb* v. *Crosse, supra*. Executors who refuse a proper tender on the ground that they have not proved the will can demand no further interest, because they are entitled to receive the money before probate: *Austen* v. *Dodwell's Executors* (1729), 1 Eq. Cas. Abr. 318.

(*p*) *Gyles* v. *Hall* (1726), 2 P. Wms. 378.

(*q*) *Kinnaird* v. *Trollope* (1889), 42 Ch. D. 610; *Edmonson* v. *Copland, supra*. *Baratt* v. *Gough-Thomas*, [1951] 2 All E.R. 48.

(*r*) *Bishop* v. *Church* (1751), 2 Ves. Sen. 371.

the mortgagee on another account between them, to satisfy the mort-gage by deducting the sum due thereon from the other debt (s).

Where tender dispensed with.—The conduct of the creditor may amount to a dispensation with the tender. A mere claim of more than is due will not have this effect. But if claiming too much, or setting up two different claims, one of which is wrongful, he so conducts himself as to show that a tender of the amount properly due would not be accepted, it will be a dispensation (t).

Time of tender.—The payment must be tendered at a proper time and place, in sufficient money, with proper formalities, and by and to the proper person. The fixing of a special time and place for payment is unusual today. If a certain hour is fixed, an attendance before the beginning of the next hour will be sufficient (u). And to satisfy an order to pay money between certain specified hours it is not necessary to attend during the whole period (a). Where a tender was not made on time, but was properly made later, an attempted sale on the ground of default was set aside (b).

Place of tender.—Unless a particular place is agreed upon, a personal tender is generally necessary. If a particular place is fixed by the deed or by a notice by the mortgagor and there are no circum-stances making that choice of place unreasonable, an effective tender may be made there (c). The mortgaged land itself is not the place for payment, the charge being a sum in gross and not a rent issuing out of the land (d).

It may be sufficient to tender the money at the mortgagor's house, or last place of abode, though it does not appear that the tender was made to him, or even that he was within the house. This can be done, for instance, where the mortgagee is deliberately keeping out of the way to avoid the tender (e).

In the case of debentures it is usual to provide by the debenture that the principal money, and interest shall be paid at the bank or registered office of the company. In the absence of such a provision the company is bound to seek out the debenture holder in order to pay him (f).

Legal tender.—The tender must be a legal tender (g).

Production of the money.—Generally the money should be actually

---

(s) *Garforth* v. *Bradley* (1755), 2 Ves. Sen. 575. See also *Samuel Keller (Holdings), Ltd.* v. *Martins Bank, Ltd.,* [1970] 3 All E.R. 950 (C.A.).

(t) *Scarfe* v. *Morgan* (1838), 4 M. & W. 270; *Kerford* v. *Mondel* (1859), 28 L.J. Ex. 303.

(u) *Knox* v. *Simmons* (1793), 4 Bro. C.C. 433.

(a) See *Bernard* v. *Norton* (1864), 10 L.T. 183.

(b) *Camp-Wee-Gee-Wa for Boys, Ltd.* v. *Clark* (1972), 23 D.L.R. (3d) 158.

(c) *Gyles* v. *Hall* (1726), 2 P. Wms. 378.

(d) *Phipps* v. *Earl of Anglesea* (1721), 5 Vin. Abr. 209.

(e) And see *Manning* v. *Burges* (1663), 1 Cas. in Ch. 29.

(f) *Fowler* v. *Midland Electric Corpn. for Power Distribution,* [1917] 1 Ch. 656 (C.A.).

(g) As to tender generally, see Halsbury's Laws (4th Edn.), Contract, paras 520 *et seq.* When a loan is made in foreign currency, the borrower is entitled to redeem in that currency, notwithstanding that it may have depreciated in value: *British Bank for Foreign Trade, Ltd.* v. *Russian Commercial and Industrial Bank (No. 2)* (1921), 38 T.L.R. 65; *Russian Commercial and Industrial Bank* v. *British Bank for Foreign Trade,* [1921] 2 A.C. 438.

produced (*h*), but actual production may be dispensed with by the express declaration or equivalent act of the creditor if the tender is otherwise sufficient (*i*). So that if the creditor refuses to authorise his agent to take the money, or to take it himself, the tender will be good (*k*).

Tender must be unconditional.—A tender will be bad if it is clogged with a condition, as for instance, that the payment shall be taken on the balance due (*l*), unless the creditor, making no objection on account of the condition, refuses the tender on another ground, as that the amount is insufficient (*m*). But a tender is nevertheless good which reserves to the tenderer the right to tax the mortgagee's costs and to review his account (*n*).

Who may make a tender.—The persons entitled to redeem (*o*) are, of course, able to make a good tender of the mortgage money. But a good tender cannot be made by a stranger, or, generally, by anyone not entitled to the equity of redemption (*p*).

To whom the tender may be made.—The tender, to be effective, must be made to the person named for the purpose in the mortgage deed, if any, or to the person or persons legally entitled to receive the money and to reconvey the estate (*q*).

Money will be well tendered to the executors of the mortgagee, though the day fixed arrives before they have proved the will (*r*).

The mortgagor will not be discharged by payments to the agent of the mortgagee, unless the agent has authority to receive the money on the mortgagee's behalf. But where a solicitor produces a deed having in the body thereof, or endorsed thereon, a receipt for consideration money or other consideration, the deed being executed or the receipt signed by the person entitled to give a receipt, the agent has statutory authority to receive the money on the mortgagee's behalf (*s*). A trustee may authorise a solicitor to receive trust money by permitting the solicitor to have the custody of and produce a deed with a receipt in the body thereof or endorsed thereon (*t*).

Subject to the statutory exception there is no power in the mortgagee's solicitor to receive either the principal or the interest of the mortgage debt merely by virtue of his possession of the security (*u*)

(*h*) For it was said that though the creditor may at first refuse, yet the sight of the money may tempt him to take it. And see *Powney* v. *Blomberg* (1844), 8 Jur. 746 (tender by letter insufficient).

(*i*) *Dickinson* v. *Shee* (1801), 4 Esp. 67; *Thomas* v. *Evans* (1808), 10 East, 101.

(*k*) *Robarts* v. *Jefferys* (1830), 8 L.J. O.S. Ch. 137.

(*l*) *Evans* v. *Judkins* (1815), 4 Camp. 156.

(*m*) *Cole* v. *Blake* (1793), Peake, 238.

(*n*) *Greenwood* v. *Sutcliffe*, [1892] 1 Ch. 1 (C.A.).

(*o*) See pp. 529–534, *supra*.

(*p*) *Pearce* v. *Morris* (1869), 5 Ch. App. 227. An agent may, of course, pay for his principal, and if a solicitor pays off his client's mortgage, he is considered to have paid it as his agent: *Ward* v. *Carttar* (1865), 35 Beav. 171. An agent who has exceeded his authority in tendering the whole amount due will be allowed to stand by subrogation in the place of the mortgagee: *Butler* v. *Rice*, [1910] 2 Ch. 277.

(*q*) Co. Litt. 210. And see *Cliff* v. *Wadsworth* (1843), 2 Y. & C.C.C. 598.

(*r*) *Austen* v. *Dodwell Executors* (1729), 1 Eq. Cas. Abr. 318.

(*s*) Law of Property Act 1925, s. 69. A forged reconveyance will not satisfy this provision: *Jared* v. *Walke* (1902), 18 T.L.R. 569.

(*t*) Trustee Act 1925, s. 23 (3).

(*u*) *Jared* v. *Walke*, *supra*.

or to receive the principal merely by virtue of an authority to receive
the interest (*a*).

Payment to joint creditors.—Although a joint debt was discharged
at law by payment to one joint creditor (*b*), yet the receipt of one
joint creditor for a mortgage debt, without evidence of any special
authority to receive it, would not discharge the security in equity (*c*),
the interest of the creditors being then treated as a tenancy in common.
So if one of the joint creditors died, his representatives were entitled
in equity to his share of the debt (*d*). It therefore became usual to
insert in mortgages to trustees, or other persons whose interests were
intended to survive, a provision that the receipt of the survivors or
survivor should be a good discharge for the debt; and it was considered
that, if such a security had been acted upon by the mortgagees, the
clause would operate, although the deed was not actually executed by
them. Such a clause is no longer necessary, it being provided by the
Law of Property Act 1925, that where the advance is expressed to be
made by several persons out of moneys belonging to them on a joint
account, or the mortgage is made to more persons than one jointly,
the receipt in writing of the survivors or the last survivor of them, or
of the personal representative of the last survivor, is a complete discharge for the money, notwithstanding any notice to the payer of a
severance of the joint account (*e*).

C—APPROPRIATION OF PAYMENTS (*f*)

Appropriation to principal or interest.—Where the debtor
claims to be discharged by reason of payments which were not specially
made in respect either of the principal or the interest of the mortgage,
the rule is that a general payment shall be applied in the first place
to sink the interest, before any part of the principal is discharged (*g*).

Appropriation by debtor.—It is, however, the right of the debtor,
in the first instance, to declare upon what he pays the money (*h*);
and when he has so declared, the destination of the payment cannot
be changed (*i*).

Appropriation by creditor.—Where the debtor omits, at the time
of the payment, to declare upon what account the money was paid,

---

(*a*) *Withington* v. *Tate* (1869), 4 Ch. App. 288; *Bonham* v. *Maycock* (1928), 138 L.T.
736. And see *Martin* v. *Diamantikos*, [1964] V.R. 593. It may be inferred that the mortgagee treated his solicitor as his agent to receive the interest, as where, after receiving
interest by his hands, the mortgagee allowed arrears to accumulate without applying
10 the mortgagor for payment: *Kent* v. *Thomas* (1856), 1 H. & N. 473.
(*b*) *Husband* v. *Davis* (1851), 10 C.B. 645. And a release of one of several joint
debtors was at law a release of all of them: *Nicholson* v. *Revill* (1836), 4 A. & E. 675.
(*c*) *Powell* v. *Brodhurst*, [1901] 2 Ch. 160.
(*d*) *Petty* v. *Styward* (1631), 1 Eq. Cas. Abr. 290; *Vickers* v. *Cowell* (1839), 1 Beav. 529.
(*e*) Section 111, replacing s. 61 of the Conveyancing Act 1881. See p. 217, *supra*.
(*f*) For the appropriation of payments in respect of two or more regulated agreements
under the Consumer Credit Act 1974, see s. 81 of that Act.
(*g*) *Chase* v. *Box* (1702), Freem. Ch. 261; and see *Parr's Banking Co.* v. *Yates*, [1898]
2 Q.B. 460 (C.A.), at p. 466; *Wrigley* v. *Gill*, [1906] 1 Ch. 165 (C.A.).
(*h*) *Mills* v. *Fowkes* (1839), 5 Bing. N.C. 455.
(*i*) *Hammersley* v. *Knowlys* (1798), 2 Esp. 666; *Simson* v. *Ingham* (1823), 2 B. & C.
65. Entries made by the debtor in his own books are not sufficient evidence of the
particular appropriation of money paid on a general account: *Manning* v. *Westerne*
(1707), 2 Vern. 606. And see *Wrout* v. *Dawes* (1858), 25 Beav. 369.

he cannot afterwards do so (*k*). The right of appropriation is then with the creditor who may refer the payment to the debt for which he has the least available security (*l*). But when the creditor by himself or his authorised agent has accepted the payment on a particular account, he cannot afterwards change the appropriation without the debtor's consent (*m*).

The creditor may declare upon what account he receives the money at any time after payment, and before action brought or account settled between him and his debtor (*n*). The creditor's written memorandum may be used after his death as evidence of his intention (*o*), and the accounts kept by a mortgagee have been used as evidence against himself of a continuing agreement to apply rents in payment of interest, not only during the time covered by the accounts, but until the mortgagor had notice to the contrary (*p*).

When the debtor becomes bankrupt, the creditor's right of appropriation accrues to him and is fixed at the bankruptcy and must be regulated by the state of the account at that time (*q*).

The rule in Clayton's Case.—Where there is a current account, but not otherwise (*r*), and there has been no appropriation by either party, the general presumption—known as the rule in *Clayton's Case* (*s*)—is that the moneys are intended to be applied in discharge of the items of the debt consecutively (*t*). And the rule applies in favour of a purchaser or subsequent mortgagee of property mortgaged to a bank to secure a current account, unless the bank mortgage imposes an obligation on the bank to make further advances, where the bank has notice of the sale or subsequent mortgage (*u*), unless there is evidence to show that the bank did not intend to appropriate payments in discharge of the balance due at the date of the purchase or subsequent mortgage (*a*).

The presumption is liable to be rebutted by evidence of a different intention (*b*), and the rule does not apply where the interest of a surety raises an obligation against the creditor to discharge the debt for which he is liable (*c*).

(*k*) *Wilkinson* v. *Sterne* (1744), 9 Mod. Rep. 427.

(*l*) *Mackenzie* v. *Gordon* (1839), 6 Cl. & P. 875. And see *Re William Hall (Contractors), Ltd. (In Liquidation)*, [1967] 2 All E.R. 1150.

(*m*) *Kershaw* v. *Kirkpatrick* (1878), 3 App. Cas. 345.

(*n*) *Blackburn Building Society* v. *Cunliffe, Brooks & Co.* (1882), 22 Ch. D. 61 (C.A.), at p. 71; affd. *Cunliffe, Brooks & Co.* v. *Blackburn Benefit Building Society* (1884), 9 App. Cas. 857 (H.L.).

(*o*) *Wilkinson* v. *Sterne, supra*; *Simson* v. *Ingham, supra*.

(*p*) *Cockburn* v. *Edwards* (1881), 18 Ch. D. 449 (C.A.); and see *Wrigley* v. *Gill, supra*.

(*q*) *Ex parte Johnson* (1853), 3 De G.M. & G. 218.

(*r*) *Cory Brothers & Co.* v. *Mecca, Turkish S.S. (Owners), The Mecca*, [1897] A.C. 286 (H.L.).

(*s*) *Devaynes* v. *Noble, Clayton's Case* (1816), 1 Mer. 529.

(*t*) *Clayton's Case, supra*; and see *Bodenham* v. *Purchas* (1818), 2 B. & Ald. 39.

(*u*) *London and County Banking Co.* v. *Ratcliffe* (1881), 6 App. Cas. 722 (H.L.).

(*a*) *Deeley* v. *Lloyds Bank, Ltd.*, [1912] A.C. 756 (H.L.).

(*b*) *Deeley* v. *Lloyds Bank, Ltd., supra*; *Cory Brothers & Co.* v. *Mecca, Turkish S.S. (Owners), The Mecca, supra*. And see *Re Sherry, London and County Banking Co.* v. *Terry* (1884), 25 Ch. D. 692 (C.A.); *Fahy* v. *M. S. D. Spiers, Ltd.*, [1975] 1 N.Z.L.R. 240 (P.C.).

(*c*) *Pearl* v. *Deacon* (1857), 24 Beav. 186; *Kinnaird* v. *Webster* (1878), 10 Ch. D. 139.

Bank mortgages to secure overdraft facilities generally expressly exclude the operation of the rule in *Clayton's Case* by including therein a declaration that the security is to be a continuing one (*d*). And where the mortgage does not impose an obligation on the bank to make further advances the operation of the rule can be avoided in the case of a subsequent mortgage by ruling off the mortgagor's account and passing future transactions through a separate account.

VII—DISCHARGE OF THE MORTGAGE

Mortgagee's duty.—Upon the debt being paid off (*e*) the mortgagor is entitled to have the mortgaged property restored to him free from the mortgagee's security. Under the pre-1926 method of creating mortgages the mortgagor's estate or interest was conveyed to the mortgagee, and upon payment off it was the duty of the mortgagee to reconvey the property to the mortgagor (*f*). The repayment of the debt was made against the reconveyance of the property and the handing back of the deeds, and strictly these should be simultaneous transactions (*f*). As previously stated (*g*), a tender of the amount due for principal, interest and costs conditionally upon the mortgagee then and there executing a reconveyance and handing over the deeds was a good tender, so that if it was refused, interest stopped running. This assumed that the mortgagee had had a reasonable opportunity of approving the conveyance (*h*), or that for any other reason no delay was necessary (*i*). A reasonable time had to be allowed for obtaining the execution of the deed, especially when the conveying parties were not the persons to whom the tender was made (*k*).

Payment and reconveyance being thus related, it was considered, that the mortgagee's action for foreclosure implied an offer to reconvey on redemption (*l*), and he could not refuse, when the property was redeemed, to restore possession of it to the mortgagor, or those claiming under him, having no right, whether the mortgagor's title was good or bad to dispute it. Under the present system of mortgages, as was the case also under the former system, the mortgagee will not be allowed to deal with the property in such a way, that upon discharge of the debt, the property cannot be restored (*m*). This does not apply where the property has been sold by the mortgagee under his power of sale (*n*),

---

(*d*) For form, see 2 Ency. Forms and Precedents (4th Edn.), at p. 832.
(*e*) It is not enough that the borrower has a counterclaim for an equal or greater amount. See further on the relation between payment and re-conveyance *Samuel Keller (Holdings), Ltd.* v. *Martins Bank, Ltd.,* [1970] 3 All E.R. 950 (C.A.).
(*f*) *Graham* v. *Seal* (1918), 88 L.J. Ch. 31 (C.A.). As to delivery of deeds, see p. 562, *infra.*
(*g*) See p. 539, *supra.*
(*h*) *Wiltshire* v. *Smith* (1744), 3 Atk. 89; *Graham* v. *Seal, supra.*
(*i*) *Rourke* v. *Robinson,* [1911] 1 Ch. 480.
(*k*) *Webb* v. *Crosse,* [1912] 1 Ch. 323.
(*l*) *Matthews* v. *Antrobus* (1879), 49 L.J. Ch. 80.
(*m*) *Tasker* v. *Small* (1837), 3 Myl. & Cr. 63, 70; *Thornton* v. *Court* (1854), 3 De G.M. & G. 293; *Walker* v. *Jones* (1866), L.R. 1 P.C. 50; *Kinnaird* v. *Trollope* (1888), 39 Ch. D. 636.
(*n*) *Rudge* v. *Richens* (1873), L.R. 8 C.P. 358.

or where he contracted to sell it under such power (*o*), or where has been evicted by the title paramount (*p*). And the mortgagee could claim to retain the property on the ground of a future contingent claim upon it (*q*).

Under the former system of creating mortgages after payment the mortgagee became constructively a trustee for the mortgagor. There was an implied trust to surrender the estate to the person entitled to demand it (*r*). And in the meantime the mortgagor in possession was tenant at will to the mortgagee for the purposes of the limitation of actions (*s*). Now after payment the mortgage term generally becomes a satisfied term and ceases (*t*). A satisfied mortgagee is bound to take care that the security gets back to the mortgagor, or to someone to whom he authorises it to be transferred (*u*).

Mortgagee can be required to transfer mortgage.—The mortgagor is entitled to require the mortgagee to transfer the mortgage to a third party instead of taking a reconveyance to himself. The Law of Property Act 1925 (*a*), provides as follows:

95.—(1) Where the mortgagor is entitled to redeem (*b*), then, subject to compliance with the terms on compliance with which he would be entitled to require a reconveyance or surrender, he is entitled to require the mortgagee, instead of re-conveying or surrendering, to assign the mortgage debt and convey the mortgaged property to any third person, as the mortgagor directs; and the mortgagee is bound to assign and convey accordingly (*c*).

(2) The rights conferred by this section belong to and are capable of being enforced by each incumbrancer, or by the mortgagor, notwithstanding any intermediate incumbrance (*d*); but a requisition of an incumbrancer prevails over a requisition of the mortgagor, and, as between incumbrancers, a requisition of a prior incumbrancer prevails over a requisition of a subsequent incumbrancer.

(*o*) *Property and Bloodstock, Ltd.* v. *Emerton*, [1968] Ch. 94 (C.A.); [1967] 3 All E.R. 321 (even if the mortgaged property is leasehold and the landlord's consent to an assignment is required). And see *Lord Waring* v. *London and Manchester Assurance Co.*, [1935] Ch. 310; *Duke* v. *Robinson*, [1973] 1 All E.R. 481.

(*p*) *Re Burrell, Burrell* v. *Smith* (1869), L.R. 7 Eq. 399.

(*q*) See *Brecon Corpn.* v. *Seymour* (1859), 26 Beav. 548; *Chilton* v. *Carrington* (1854), 15 C.B. 95.

(*r*) *Pearce* y. *Morris* (1869), 5 Ch. App. 227. And see *Holme* v. *Fieldsend*, [1911] W.N. 111. If the mortgagee refused to reconvey after payment, the mortgagor could obtain a declaration that the mortgagee was trustee for the mortgagor and an order that the registrar convey the property to him or a vesting order: see pp. 559 *et seq., infra*.

(*s*) *Sands to Thompson* (1883), 22 Ch. D. 614.

(*t*) Law of Property Act 1925, ss. 5, 116. See pp. 550, 551 *infra*.

(*u*) *Magnus* v. *Queensland National Bank* (1888), 37 Ch. D. 466 (C.A.).

(*a*) Reproducing the Conveyancing Act 1881, s. 15 (with an addition made by the Conveyancing Act 1882, s. 12). Previously the mortgagee was bound only to reconvey to the owner of the equity of redemption: *James* v. *Biou* (1819), 3 Swans. 234.

(*b*) Every mortgagor is entitled to redeem, unless he is precluded by a special term in the mortgage from exercising his right: see p. 522, *supra*. As to a transfer so as to keep alive the rights of other persons interested in the equity of redemption, see *Alderson* v. *Elgey* (1884), 26 Ch. D. 567.

(*c*) This applies also to an equitable mortgagee or chargee and the holder of a lien: Law of Property Act 1925, s. 205 (1) (xvi); and see *Everitt* v. *Automatic Weighing Machine Co.*, [1892] 3 Ch. 506.

(*d*) This overrules *Teevan* v. *Smith* (1882), 20 Ch. D. 724 (C.A.).

(3) The foregoing provisions of this section do not apply in the case of a mortgagee being or having been in possession (*e*).

* * * * *

(5) (*f*) This section applies to mortgages made either before or after the commencement of this Act, and takes effect notwithstanding any stipulation to the contrary.

Sub-section (2), which entitles the mortgagor to call for a transfer even if there is a second mortgage (*g*), does not justify the first mortgagee in disregarding notice of the second mortgage, and where he has such notice, he should not transfer without the consent of the second mortgagee (*h*). The sub-section throws upon the mortgagee the burden, to which before the Act of 1882 he was not subject, of determining which among several other incumbrancers is entitled to priority.

Reconveyance formerly necessary.—Before the Law of Property Act 1925, the reconveyance of property which had been mortgaged by conveyance of the whole estate of the mortgagor, whether freehold or leasehold, and whether legal or equitable, was effected by a regrant or reassignment to the owner of the equity of redemption. Where the mortgage has been made by a demise for a term of years the reconveyance was effected by a surrender of the term. While in the case of equitable mortgages created by deed, the ordinary form of reconveyance was usually adopted, this was technically unnecessary since the mere receipt of the debt put an end to the mortgagee's interest (*i*). Nor was it necessary in the case of freehold (*k*) mortgages by demise, since the term ceased on payment of the debt by virtue of the Satisfied Terms Act 1845.

In the case of mortgages to unincorporated building societies s. 5 of the Building Societies Act 1836, avoided the necessity of an actual reconveyance by making a receipt endorsed on the mortgage operate to revest in the mortgagor the mortgagee's estate in the mortgaged property. And substantially the same provision was later applied to incorporated building societies (*l*).

(*e*) A mortgagee in possession is exempted from the obligation to transfer because he cannot in this way rid himself of his liability to account as mortgagee in possession: *Hall* v. *Heward* (1886), 32 Ch. D. 430 (C.A.), at p. 435; and see *Re Prytherch, Prytherch* v. *Williams* (1889), 42 Ch. D. 590; *Gaskell* v. *Gosling*, [1896] 1 Q.B. 669 (C.A.), at p. 691. He may only do so if he transfers under an order of the court.

(*f*) Sub-section (4) relates to a different matter, namely the mortgagee's right to possession, and is out of place in this section.

(*g*) Where there is a second mortgage sub-s. (1) by itself does not entitle the mortgagor to call for a transfer, for it operates only where the mortgagor is entitled to require a conveyance and if there is a second mortgage the reconveyance should be to the second mortgagee: *Teevan* v. *Smith, supra.*

(*h*) *Re Magneta Time Co., Ltd., Molden* v. *The Company* (1915), 84 L.J. Ch. 814; and see *Corbett* v. *National Provident Institution* (1900), 17 T.L.R. 5.

(*i*) And see *Firth & Sons, Ltd.* v. *Inland Revenue Commissioners*, [1904] 2 K.B. 205.

(*k*) But not leasehold mortgages: *Re Moore and Hulm's Contract*, [1912] 2 Ch. 105.

(*l*) Building Societies Act 1874, s. 42; and see now Building Societies Act 1962, s. 37. Similar provisions were later applied to friendly and industrial and provident societies: see Friendly Societies Act 1974, s. 57, Sched. 4; Industrial and Provident Societies Act 1965, s. 33.

Extension of automatic reconveyance to all mortgages.—This device of automatic reconveyance by indorsed receipt was extended to mortgages generally by the Law of Property Act 1925 (*m*), which provides:

115.—(1) A receipt endorsed on, written at the foot of, or annexed to, a mortgage (*n*) for all money thereby secured (*o*), which states the name of the person who pays the money (*p*) and is executed (*q*) by the chargee by way of legal mortgage or the person in whom the mortgaged property (*r*) is vested and who is legally entitled to give a receipt for the mortgage money (*s*), shall operate, without any reconveyance, surrender or release—

    (a) Where a mortgage takes effect by demise or subdemise, as a surrender of the term, so as to determine the term or merge the same in the reversion immediately expectant thereon;

    (b) Where the mortgage does not take effect by demise or subdemise, as a reconveyance thereof to the extent of the interest which is the subject matter of the mortgage, to the person who immediately before the execution of the receipt was entitled to the equity of redemption;

and in either case, as a discharge of the mortgaged property from all principal money and interest secured by, and from all claims under the mortgage, but without prejudice to any term or other interest which is paramount to the estate or interest of the mortgagee or other person in whom the mortgaged property was vested.

(2) Provided that where by the receipt the money appears to have been paid by a person who is not entitled to the immediate equity of redemption (*t*), the receipt shall operate as if the benefit of the mortgage had by deed been transferred to him; unless—

    (a) it is otherwise expressly provided (*u*); or

(*m*) Following the recommendation of the Royal Commission on Land Transfer 1908–1911.

(*n*) Not a transfer thereof, unless the transfer contains a further charge, when sub-s. (7) will apply. As to mortgages of personalty, see p. 556, *infra*.

(*o*) *Semble*, secured at the date of repayment. See the statutory form of receipt which refers to the balance remaining owing: Law of Property Act 1925, Third Schedule. An indorsed receipt cannot be used where only part of the mortgage money is repaid. And in such a case if no part of the security is discharged an ordinary receipt should be used. Nor can a statutory receipt be used where a mortgage deed is lost. In that case a release or surrender is necessary.

(*p*) For where the receipt does not name the payer, see *Edwards* v. *Marshall-Lee* (1975), 119 Sol. Jo. 506; p. 551, *infra*.

(*q*) It need only be under hand: (*Simpson* v. *Geoghegan*, [1934] W.N. 232; (1934), 78 Sol. Jo. 930), unless made by a building society (see p. 552, *infra*).

(*r*) *I.e.*, the property remaining subject to the mortgage at the date of the receipt: *ibid.*, sub-s. (11).

(*s*) Thus a trustee is legally entitled to give a receipt for moneys payable to him under a trust: Trustee Act 1925, s. 14. The receipt of the trustees for the time being gives a good discharge unless the mortgage expressly provides that the money is not advanced on a joint account: Law of Property Act 1925, ss. 111–113. A receipt by personal representatives of the mortgagee or a transferee should be made by all the proving personal representatives, but the fact that it was made by only one or some of the proving personal representatives does not constitute an objection to the title in the case of a mortgage by demise since on payment the mortgage term becomes satisfied: see Law of Property Act 1925, ss. 5, 116; p. 550, *infra*. Where the mortgagee is a mental patient the Court of Protection has power to make an order for the discharge of a mortgage security vested in a patient: see Mental Health Act 1959, s. 102 (1). For the practice in respect of applications for such an order, see Heywood and Massey's *Court of Protection Practice* (9th Edn.), pp. 170–172. For a form of receipt in discharge of a mortgage on behalf of a mentally disordered mortgagee, see 14 Ency. Forms and Precedents (4th Edn.), 839.

(*t*) An express statement to the effect is not necessary: *Simpson* v. *Geoghegan*, *supra*.

(*u*) See *Pyke* v. *Peters*, [1943] K.B. 242. A mortgagee cannot object to signing a receipt which includes the statement that the receipt does not operate as a transfer: *Hartley* v. *Burton* (1868), 3 Ch. App. 365, at p. 366.

(b) the mortgage is paid off out of capital money, or other money in the hands of a personal representative or trustee properly applicable for the discharge of the mortgage, and it is not expressly provided that the receipt is to operate as a transfer (*a*).

(3) Nothing in this section confers on a mortgagor a right to keep alive a mortgage paid off by him, so as to affect prejudicially any subsequent incumbrancer; and where there is no right to keep the mortgage alive, the receipt does not operate as a transfer (*b*).

This section does not affect the right of any person to require a reassignment, surrender, release, or transfer to be executed in lieu of a receipt: sub-s. (4) (*c*). The receipt may be in the form in the Third Schedule to the Act, with such variations and additions as may be deemed expedient: sub-s. (5) (*d*). Where the mortgage consists of a mortgage and a further charge or of more than one deed it is sufficient for the purposes of the section if the receipt refers either to all the deeds whereby the mortgage money is secured or to the aggregate amount of the mortgage money thereby secured and for the time being owing, and is endorsed on, written at the foot of, or annexed to, one of the mortgage deeds: sub-s. (7). The section applies to the discharge or a charge by way of legal mortgage: sub-s. (8). Building and friendly societies may employ a statutory receipt under the provisions of this section: sub-s. (9) (*e*). The section does not apply to the discharge of a charge or incumbrance registered under the Land Registration Act

---

(*a*) Where the holder of the equity of redemption is not the original mortgagor, the fact that the person paying the mortgage money is the holder of the equity of redemption should be made to appear in the receipt, where it is intended to extinguish the mortgage, unless (a) or (b) of sub-s. (2) apply: see *Cumberland Court (Brighton), Ltd.* v. *Taylor,* [1964] Ch. 29; [1963] 2 All E.R. 536. See (1971), 68 L.S. Gaz. 175 (J. E. Adams).

(*b*) Where there is a second mortgage, the second mortgagee is the person entitled to the immediate equity of redemption. Hence if the mortgagor pays off the mortgage, and takes a receipt showing that he is not so entitled, this will operate prima facie as a transfer of the mortgage to him. A mortgagor cannot, however, keep a mortgage alive in his own favour as against his own creditors: *Otter* v. *Vaux* (1856), 6 De G.M. & G. 638, see p. 594, *infra*; sub-s. (3) preserves this rule.

(*c*) In the absence of express provision therefor a mortgagor may not be able to require a re-assignment, where a statutory receipt is applicable (but see p. 551, *infra*). But in some cases a receipt will not be appropriate or sufficient: see *Nelson* v. *Hannam,* [1943] Ch. 59 (C.A.); [1942] 2 All E.R. 680 (where the mortgagee of leasehold land had exercised an option to purchase the reversion). Where there is a second mortgagee a surrender by a first mortgagee should be to the second mortgagee and not to the borrower: *Hosking* v. *Smith* (1888), 13 App. Cas. 582 (H.L.)., at p. 589. On a partial redemption a statutory receipt cannot be employed: see (*o*) p. 548, *supra.*

Quaere whether a statutory receipt may be employed where a right of consolidation exists, since the receipt will not be "for all money thereby secured".

(*d*) For the abolition of stamp duty on discharge and transfer, etc, of a mortgage, see Finance Act 1971, s. 64.

In a receipt given under the section covenants "as mortgagee" are implied, subject to any interest which is paramount to the mortgagee: sub-s. (6). These covenants include a covenant that the mortgagee has not incumbered. Accordingly, where there has been a sub-mortgage a statutory receipt may not be appropriate (see p. 263, *supra*). For forms of statutory receipt, see 14 Ency. Forms and Precedents (4th Edn.), pp. 828 *et seq*; and Precedent 24 in the Appendix, *infra.*

(*e*) As an alternative to the special forms of receipt applicable thereto, as to which, see Building Societies Act 1962, s. 37 (p. 552, *infra*), and Friendly Societies Act 1974, s. 57. It seems that the effect of the amendment made to sub-s. (9) by the Industrial and Provident Societies Act 1965, s. 77 (1), Sched. 5, is that industrial and provident societies may use only the form contained in the Industrial and Provident Societies Act 1965.

1925: sub-s. (10). In view of the words "in whom the mortgaged property is vested" in sub-s. (1) a statutory receipt is inappropriate to discharge an equitable mortgage.

Receipt operating as a transfer.—In order that the receipt may operate as a transfer (*f*) it must state the name of the person paying the mortgage money, and it must appear by the receipt that the person making the payment is not entitled to the immediate equity of redemption. A statement that the payer is not so entitled is sufficient, but such a statement is not necessary (*g*).

If the land is settled land and there is no second mortgage, the tenant for life will be entitled to the immediate equity of redemption, and if the payment is made by the trustees out of capital moneys, it is not paid by the persons entitled to the immediate equity of redemption and prima facie would operate as a transfer. In effect, however, it is on the same footing as regards the discharge of the mortgage as a payment by a mortgagor and where this fact appears it does not operate as a transfer unless expressly so provided (*h*). Where the mortgage money is paid by the tenant for life a statutory receipt would, it seems, not operate as a transfer, since the money has been paid by the person entitled to the immediate equity of redemption. Accordingly in such a case a transfer of the mortgage should be employed (*i*).

Where the land is subject to a trust for sale the legal estate therein is in the trustees who are accordingly the persons entitled to the immediate equity of redemption (if there is no second mortgage). If the mortgage money is paid by the life tenant it is not paid by the persons entitled to the immediate equity of redemption and prima facie a receipt in such circumstances would operate as a transfer.

Cessation of mortgage terms on payment.—The Law of Property Act provides:

> **5.**—(1) Where the purposes of a term of years, created or limited at any time out of freehold land, became satisfied either before or after the commencement of this Act (whether or not that term either by express declaration or by construction of law becomes attendant upon the freehold reversion), it shall merge in the reversion expectant thereon and shall cease accordingly (*k*).
>
> (2) Where the purposes of a term of years created or limited, at any time, out of leasehold land, become satisfied after the commencement of this Act, that term shall merge in the reversion expectant thereon and shall cease accordingly (*l*).

(*f*) Under s. 115, sub-s. (2). As to transfer of mortgages, see pp. 251 *et seq., supra.*

(*g*) *Simpson* v. *Geoghegan*, [1934] W.N. 232; (1934), 78 Sol. Jo. 930. And see *Pyke* v. *Peters*, [1943] K.B. 242; *Cumberland Court (Brighton), Ltd.* v. *Taylor*, [1964] Ch. 29; [1963] 2 All E.R. 536.

(*h*) See s. 115, sub-s. (2), exception (b). A note appended to the statutory form of receipt says that in such a case the receipt should state that the payers are paying the money out of a fund applicable to the discharge of the mortgage. A similar case may arise, as sub-s. (2) suggests, where payment is made by a personal representative, but usually a personal representative who pays off a mortgage is entitled to the immediate equity of redemption by devolution from the mortgagor.

(*i*) And in such circumstances prima facie merger does not follow: see p. 592, *infra.*

(*k*) This reproduces s. 2 of the Satisfied Terms Act 1845. As to satisfaction of a mortgage term, see *Anderson* v. *Pignet* (1872), L.R. 8 Ch. 180, 1889.

(*l*) This extends the same principle to sub-terms, and thus overrules *Re Moore and Hulm's Contract*, [1912] 2 Ch. 105, but only where the mortgage has been paid

(3) Where the purposes are satisfied only as respects part of the land comprised in a term, this section shall have effect as if a separate term has been created in regard to that part of the land (*m*).

116.—Without prejudice to the right of a tenant for life or other person having only a limited interest in the equity of redemption to require a mortgage to be kept alive by transfer or otherwise, a mortgage term shall, when the money secured by the mortgage has been discharged, become a satisfied term and shall cease (*n*).

Section 116 covers the same ground as s. 5. It assumes that the mortgage has been finally discharged, that is, that the term has become a satisfied term. In that case it cannot be kept on foot and so complicate the title to the land. The effect of the cessation of mortgage terms on payment is that only evidence of payment is required to discharge a mortgage by demise and this can be given as effectually by an ordinary receipt as by a statutory receipt. And a simple receipt is, apparently, sufficient to discharge a mortgage by way of legal charge (*o*). But, except in the case of registered charges (*q*), it is not the practice to discharge legal mortgages of land by an ordinary receipt. However, in certain cases, the discharging effect of a simple receipt may usefully be relied upon where, for example, there has been a reconveyance to the wrong person (and there is no question of a statutory receipt operating as a transfer) or after repayment, but before execution of a discharge, the mortgagee has disappeared.

The relationship of ss. 115 and 116 is a matter of some uncertainty. In a previous edition of this work it was stated that the provision for automatic reconveyance by endorsed receipt is not required where the mortgage term ceases on payment and that a surrender of the term in such circumstances is unnecessary and indeed is inoperative (*r*). In relation to sub-s. (4) of s. 115 it has been suggested that in the absence of express provision for reassignment, etc., a mortgagor has no right thereto when a statutory receipt is applicable (*s*). The basis for this suggestion is the automatic cesser of the term under s. 116. This suggestion cannot logically be limited to s. 115 (4), but must also apply to the right to the statutory receipt itself. Section 115 (4) assumes the existence of the right to a reassignment, etc., and in spite of the provisions of the Satisfied Terms Act 1845, on the discharge of

---

off after 31 December, 1925. Where the sub-term was already a satisfied term at that date it merged in the reversion and ceased but without prejudice to any protection which it afforded to the reversioner: Law of Property Act 1925, Sched. 1, Pt. II, para. 1.

(*m*) This is new and enables the term to be kept alive in part of the land only.

(*n*) As to the prevention of merger when a person with a limited interest in land becomes absolutely entitled to the benefit of a charge on it, see p. 592, *infra*. The effect of this automatic cessation of the mortgage term on a legal current account mortgage (such as a bank mortgage) appears to be that the mortgage would cease to be supported by a legal term as soon as, under the rule in *Clayton's Case* (see p. 544, *supra*), or otherwise, the account was in credit, but the mortgage would continue as an equitable security for further advances: see *Jones* v. *Consolidated Investment Co* (1858), 26 Beav. 256, 259; *London and County Banking Co.* v. *Ratcliffe* (1881), 6 App. Cas 722 (H.L.), 737. But this effect is in practice avoided by provision in the mortgage that the security shall be a continuing security.

(*o*) *Edwards* v. *Marshall-Lee*; see (1975) 119 Sol. Jo. 497; (1976) 40 Conv. (N.S.) 102.

(*q*) See p. 553, *infra*.   (*r*) 7th Edn., 631.

(*s*) *Key and Elphinstone* (15th Edn.), Vol. 2, 284, para. (8); 14 Ency. Forms and Precedents (4th Edn.), 69.

a mortgage by demise it was usual to effect a reconveyance by a surrender of the term. Moreover it is difficult to see the point of the detailed provisions as to statutory receipts if they are not to be employed in every case where a simple receipt would suffice. From the mortgagor's point of view the statutory receipt with its implied covenants for title (a) is the better discharge and it is submitted that no special provision for a statutory receipt is required. Nor is any special provision required for a reassignment, etc. (b).

Building society receipts.—A building society mortgage may be discharged on repayment of the mortgage debt either under the Law of Property Act 1925, or the Building Societies Act 1962 (c).

The Law of Property Act 1925, provides:

115.—(9) The provisions of this section relating to the operation of a receipt shall (in substitution for the like statutory provision relating to receipts given by or on behalf of a building, friendly, industrial or provident society) apply to the discharge of a mortgage made to any such society, provided that the receipt is executed in the manner required by the statute relating to the society, but nothing in this section shall render a receipt given by or on behalf of any such society liable to any stamp duty which would not have been otherwise payable.

And the Building Societies Act 1962, provides:

37.—(1) When all moneys intended to be secured by a mortgage (d) given to a building society have been fully paid or discharged, the society may endorse on or annex to the mortgage one or other of the following, that is to say—

(a) a receipt under the society's seal, countersigned by any person acting under the authority of the board of directors, in the form set out in the Sixth Schedule to the Act (e);

(b) a reconveyance of the mortgaged property to the mortgagor;

(c) a reconveyance of the mortgaged property to such a person of full age, and on such trusts, if any, as the mortgagor may direct.

(2) Where in pursuance of the preceding subsection such a receipt as is therein mentioned is endorsed on or annexed to a mortgage, not being a charge or incumbrance registered under the Land Registration Act 1925, the receipt shall operate in accordance with the provisions of subsection (1), (3), (6), and (8), of section 115 of the Law of Property Act 1925 (which provides for the discharge of mortgages by a receipt), in like manner as a receipt which fulfils all the requirements of subsection (1) of that section.

(3) Subsection (9) of section 115 of the Law of Property Act 1925, shall not apply to a receipt endorsed or annexed by a building society which is in the form set out in the Sixth Schedule to this Act; and in the application of that subsection to a receipt so endorsed or annexed which is not in that form, the receipt shall be taken to be executed in the manner required by the statute

---

(a) Law of Property Act 1925, s. 115 (6).

(b) In practice the statutory receipt is employed wherever appropriate, save in the case of a mortgage debenture where a simple receipt is used. If the mortgagor insists on a re-assignment, etc., where a statutory receipt would be appropriate, he must pay the costs.

(c) As to friendly societies and industrial and provident societies, see footnote (e), p. 549, *supra.*

(d) In this section "mortgage" includes a further charge, and "the mortgagor", in relation to a mortgage, means the person for the time being entitled to the equity of redemption: *ibid.*, sub-s. (5). This section does not apply to Scotland: *ibid.*, sub-s. (6).

(e) Unlike s. 115 the form cannot be varied or added to.

relating to the society if it is under the society's seal and countersigned as mentioned in paragraph (a) of subsection (1) of this section.

(4) In the case of a mortgage of registered land within the meaning of the Land Registration Act 1925, the preceding provisions of this section shall have effect without prejudice to the operation of the provisions of that Act or any rules made thereunder whether before or after the commencement of this Act (*f*).

The principal difference between the two forms of statutory receipt is that that under the Law of Property Act, but not that under the Building Societies Act, must state the name of the person who pays the money. Consequently a statutory receipt under the Building Societies Act cannot operate as a transfer. And sub-s. (7) of s. 115 which, if the appropriate references are made, allows for only one receipt where there is a mortgage and further charge or several deeds does not apply to a statutory receipt in the Building Societies Act form. Nor does sub-s. (4) of s. 115 apply.

Effect of receipt on mortgagor's liability.—The statutory receipt (*g*) precludes the mortgagee from afterwards questioning the sufficiency of the payment and releases the mortgagor from all liability in respect of the debt (*h*). But if the receipt has been delivered only as an escrow, the mortgagee may show that the mortgage has not been paid off (*i*).

Discharge of registered and noted charges, etc.—The discharge of a charge registered under the Land Registration Act 1925, is effected by notification on the register. The Land Registration Act 1925, provides:

35.—(1) The registrar shall, on the requisition of the proprietor of any charge, or on due proof of the satisfaction (whole or partial) thereof, notify on the register in the prescribed manner, by cancelling or varying the original entry or otherwise, the cessation (whole or partial) of the charge, and thereupon the charge shall be deemed to have ceased (in whole or part) accordingly.

(2) On the notification on the register of the entire cessation of a registered charge whether as to the whole or part only of the land affected thereby, the term or sub-term implied in or granted by the charge or by any deed or alteration, so far as it affects the land to which the discharge extends, shall merge and be extinguished in the registered estate in reversion without any surrender.

(*f*) Section 37 removed a number of difficulties, which previously existed, arising out of s. 115 of the Law of Property Act 1925, and s. 42 of the Building Societies Act 1874; see para. 2 of the Lord Chancellor's Memorandum on the Consolidation of Certain Enactments relating to Building Societies, dated 15 February, 1962 (H.L. 39; H.C. 117). And see previous editions of this work.

(*g*) For the effect of the redemption statement, see p. 540, *supra*.

(*h*) *Harvey* v. *Municipal Permanent Investment Building Society* (1884), 26 Ch. D. 273; *London and County United Building Society* v. *Angell* (1896), 65 L.J. Q.B. 194. The cases are all building society cases and could be said to turn on the special wording of the old Acts, under which the effect of the receipt was stated to be to vacate the mortgage or debt. Section 115 of the Law of Property Act 1925 refers merely to the discharge of the mortgaged property from the principal and interest secured thereby. But is is submitted that when the mortgage is vacated the covenant for repayment, and consequently the debt, is vacated also; see *Harvey* v. *Municipal Permanent Investment Building Society*, *supra*, at p. 286 *per* COTTON, L. J.

(*i*) *Lloyds Bank, Ltd.* v. *Bullock*, [1896] 2 Ch. 192.

As previously stated, s. 115 of the Law of Property Act 1925, does not apply to the discharge of a charge or incumbrance registered under the Land Registration Act 1925 (*k*).

The discharge of a registered charge will, in the case of a building society, a friendly society or an industrial and provident society mortgage, generally be effected by a receipt in the form allowed by the Act applicable thereto (*l*). In cases where the registered charge is a mortgage in unregistered form the discharge may be effected by statutory receipt. In other cases the discharge should be in Form 53 or 53 (Co) (*m*) of the forms set out in the Schedule to the Land Registration Rules 1925, but the registrar is at liberty to accept and act upon any other proof of satisfaction of a charge which he may deem sufficient (*n*). The same procedure applies where a person is registered as proprietor of a charge created prior to first registration (*o*) and to a registered sub-charge (*p*).

Where a mortgage existing at the time of first registration has merely been noted on the register (*q*) and has not been substantively registered, the registrar will, on proof to his satisfaction of the discharge of the incumbrance, notify such discharge, either by cancelling the original entry or by noting the fact, as he thinks fit (*r*). The appropriate proof is a statutory receipt or reconveyance. Form 53 is not applicable.

Cautions may be withdrawn (*s*) and mortgage cautions may be withdrawn in the same manner (*t*) or vacated, subject to the requisite evidence being furnished to the registrar of the discharge of the mortgage (*u*).

A notice of deposit or notice of intended deposit may be withdrawn from the register on a written request or consent signed by the person entitled to the lien created by the deposit, or notice of intended deposit, or his successor in title; accompanied in either case by the land certificate, or charge certificate (*x*).

(*k*) *Ibid.* (10).

(*l*) *I.e.*, Building Societies Act 1962, s. 37 (1); Friendly Societies Act 1974, s. 57; Industrial and Provident Societies Act 1965, s. 33. A mortgage made under the Small Dwellings Acquisition Acts may be discharged by a receipt in the form provided by s. 49 of the Housing, Town Planning, &c., Act 1919. For the discharge of building society, etc., mortgages, see Land Registration Rules 1925, r. 152.

(*m*) No fee is payable for registering the discharge of an incumbrance: Land Registration Fee Order 1976, r. 5.

(*n*) Land Registration Rules 1925, r. 151. As to other proof, and generally, see Ruoff and Roper, *Registered Conveyancing* (3rd Edn.), pp. 573 *et seq.* Where the discharge is made as to part of the land only, or as to part of the money only, the appropriate wording is set out in a note to Form 53. The application for discharge should be made under application cover A 4 (or A 5), accompanied by the charge certificate, and, where employed, Form 53.

(*o*) Land Registration Rules 1925, rr. 161, 162.

(*p*) *Ibid.*, r. 164 (1).

(*q*) Under Land Registration Act 1925, s. 49.

(*r*) Land Registration Act 1925, s. 46; Rules, rr. 201, 203.

(*s*) Land Registration Rules 1925, r. 68; in Form 16.

(*t*) *Ibid.*, r. 224 (1).

(*u*) *Ibid.*, r. 224 (2).

(*x*) *Ibid.*, r. 246. Form 86 is the relevant form.

Receipt on discharge of mortgage granted under the Small Dwellings Acquisition Acts 1899 to 1923.—A form of receipt discharging the mortgaged property under such a mortgage is contained in the Housing, Town Planning, &c., Act 1919, Sched. 4, Pt. I. Such a receipt operates as a discharge without any reconveyance, reassignment or release, and must be granted free of cost to the person paying the money, but the right of that person to require a reconveyance, reassignment, surrender, release or transfer to be executed is not affected (*y*).

Discharge of statutory mortgage.—A statutory mortgage may be surrendered or discharged by the prescribed form of receipt (*z*).

Discharge of equitable mortgages.—The statutory receipt is inapplicable (*a*). A mortgage of an equitable interest is discharged by a reassignment of the interest.

In the case of an equitable mortgage by mere deposit a simple receipt may be employed. Where the deposit is accompanied by a memorandum or deed of charge a separate receipt should be used. But a mere cancellation of the document suffices (*b*).

If the mortgage is a mortgage of an equitable interest in land, capital money, or settled funds, notice of the receipt should be given to the trust corporation, if any, nominated to receive notices, or, if none, to the trustees or estate owner (*c*).

If a priority caution has been entered in the minor interests index, this should be cancelled (*d*).

Debentures.—Where the debenture does not create a legal charge on land, it may be discharged by a simple receipt, indorsed on the debenture (*e*) or separately. A statutory vacating receipt (*f*) may be used for a debenture creating a specific legal charge, but, as indicated above (*g*), a simple receipt will be sufficient. For registered land, the appropriate method, mentioned above (*h*), should be used (*i*).

Mortgages, charges and orders registered as land charges.— The registration of a land charge may be vacated on application being made in the prescribed form and the registrar being satisfied as to discharge (*k*) or pursuant to an order of the court or a judge thereof (*l*).

Discharge of registered shipping mortgages.—The method of

(*y*) Housing, Town Planning, &c., Act 1919, s. 49 (d).
(*z*) Law of Property Act 1925, s. 120, Sched. 4, Form No. 5.
(*a*) Because the mortgagee has no legal estate which needs to be reconveyed. See (1962), 26 Conv. (N.S.), pp. 449–453 (R. G. Rowley). For a form of simple receipt, see 14 Ency. Forms and Precedents (4th Edn.), p. 839, Precedent 26 in the Appendix, *infra*.
(*b*) For partial release, see p. 582, *infra*.
(*c*) Law of Property Act 1925, ss. 137, 138.
(*d*) Land Registration Rules 1925, r. 229 (3).
(*e*) For a form, see 6 Ency. Forms and Precedents (4th Edn.), p. 1332.
(*f*) Page 548, *supra*.
(*g*) Page 551, *supra*.
(*h*) Page 553, *supra*.
(*i*) The registration at the Companies Registry will require cancellation by the official form of declaration of satisfaction and where appropriate, any land charge registration will require cancellation.
(*k*) Land Charges Act 1972, s. 18 (1), (3), Sched. 3, para. 5, Sched 4 and 5; Land Charges Rules 1974.
(*l*) Land Charges Act 1972, s. 1 (6). And see p. 445, *supra*.

automatic reconveyance by endorsed receipt is applied to shipping mortgages. Thus, the Merchant Shipping Act 1894, provides that where any registered mortgage has been discharged, the registrar shall, on the production of the mortgage deed, with a receipt for the mortgage money endorsed thereon, duly signed and attested, make an entry in the register book to the effect that such mortgage has been discharged; and upon such entry being made, the estate, if any, which passed to the mortgagee, shall vest in the same person or persons in whom the same would, having regard to intervening acts and circumstances, if any, have vested, if no such mortgage had been made (*m*). If therefore the first of two mortgages is paid off, and a receipt given for the money, and duly registered under the Act, the first mortgagee's interest vests, by virtue of the receipt, in the second mortgagee, as the person in whom it would have been vested by an intervening act, viz. the second mortgage, if the first mortgage had not been made. And the entry when made is conclusive as to the discharge of the mortgage which cannot be revived by an entry on the register that the former entry was erroneous where the priorities or other mortgagees are affected (*n*). The registrar has no power to erase entries of mortgages (*o*).

Discharge of registered aircraft mortgages.—No special form is prescribed for the discharge of such mortgages. The relevant rules (*p*) merely refer to the mortgage with a discharge or receipt for the mortgage money duly endorsed thereon or any other document which shows to the satisfaction of the Civil Aviation Authority that the mortgage has been discharged. Provision is made by the rules for notification of the Authority of the discharge and the appropriate entry in the register (*p*).

Discharge of mortgages of personalty.—It has been doubted whether the Law of Property Act 1925, s. 115, applies to mortgages of choses in action or pure personalty. It is submitted however that a statutory receipt under s. 115 is effectual to discharge such mortgages with the exception of bills of sale mentioned below. Nevertheless such mortgages are generally discharged by reassignment (*q*).

Reassignment of life policies.—A statutory receipt may be used to reassign a life policy, the subject of a legal mortgage, and in the case of a building society mortgagee the receipt under s. 37 of the Building Societies Act 1962, may be used. But a simple receipt is

---

(*m*) Section 32. And so, upon the endorsement on a certificate of mortgage (as to such a certificate, see p. 98, *supra*) of the discharge of a mortgage made under the certificate, the mortgagee's estate becomes vested in the person in whom, it would, having regard to intervening acts and circumstances (if any) have vested, if no such mortgage had been made: s. 43 (7). For a form of memorandum of discharge, see 17 Ency. Forms and Precedents (3rd Edn.), 74.

(*n*) *Bell* v. *Blyth* (1868), 4 Ch. App. 136. Where they are not so affected the court may order a receipt endorsed on a mortgage by mistake to be set aside: *The Rose* (1873), L.R. 4 A. & E. 6.

(*o*) *Chasteauneuf* v. *Capeyron* (1882), 7 App. Cas. 127 (P.C.), but he may be ordered to do so by the court, see, *e.g.*, *Burgis* v. *Constantine*, [1908] 2 K.B. 484 (C.A.).

(*p*) Mortgaging of Aircraft Order 1972, art. 9.

(*q*) For a form of reassignment, see 14 Ency. Forms and Precedents (4th Edn.), p. 857. Notice of the reassignment should be given to those to whom notice of the mortgage was given.

acceptable. However, the printed forms of a mortgage of a life policy of banks and building societies and other institutional lenders usually provide for an express reassignment (*r*). Notice of the discharge should be given to the insurance company. An equitable mortgage of a life policy may be discharged by re-delivery and the cancellation of the memorandum of deposit, if any.

Discharge of bills of sale.—A Master of the Supreme Court may order a memorandum of satisfaction to be written upon any registered copy of a bill of sale upon the prescribed evidence being given that the debt (if any), for which such bill of sale was made or given, has been satisfied or discharged (*s*). The prescribed evidence is a consent, signed by the person entitled to the benefit of the bill of sale, which must be verified by affidavit. If the consent cannot be obtained, the application is made by originating summons supported by evidence as to the satisfaction or discharge of the debt.

Discharge of consumer credit securities.—The Consumer Credit Act 1974 does not make any special provision for the discharge of securities provided in relation to a regulated agreement. The general provisions of the 1974 Act as regards early payment by the debtor, the appropriate notice, and statements apply to the agreement (*t*) and and mortgagee is required to give information to the mortgagor on request (*u*).

Discharge of collateral security.—The various types of collateral security have already been mentioned (*v*). A further charge by a mortgagor is discharged in the usual form by a statutory receipt endorsed on the principal mortgage referring to the further charge or to the aggregate amount of the mortgage money secured by both deeds (Law of Property Act 1925, s. 115 (7)). Where there is a principal debtor and a surety and payment is made by the principal debtor (there being separate mortgages) both mortgages should be discharged by statutory receipt. Where payment is made by the surety he is entitled to a discharge of his own mortgage and a transfer of the mortgage of the principal debtor (*x*). But where there are not separate mortgages, where, for example, the principal debtor does not charge any of his property but the surety does, or where both principal debtor and surety each charges his property in one deed, then, on payment by the surety he is entitled in the first case to an assignment of the personal debt of the principal debtor (the mortgage being discharged) and in the second case to a transfer of the security created by the principal debtor (the security created by the surety being released).

The mortgagor's right to policies.—The mortgagor is entitled, of course, to have back on redemption the property which is strictly comprised in the mortgage, but a question may arise whether he is

---

(*r*) For a form of receipt and reassignment, see 14 Ency. Forms and Precedents (4th Edn.), pp. 840, 841
(*s*) Bills of Sale Act 1878, s. 15; R.S.C. Ord. 95, r. 2.
(*t*) Sections 94 *et seq.*; see p. 145, *supra.*
(*u*) Section 110; see p. 148, *supra.*
(*v*) See p. 14, *supra.*
(*x*) See p. 586, *infra.*

entitled also to a policy which has been affected as a collateral security.

If the relation of debtor and creditor exists between the parties, and it has been agreed, or can be inferred, that the debtor shall be charged with the premiums, and that the policy is effected as a security or indemnity, the policy or the balance of the insurance money, after discharge of the debt, will be the debtor's. It is immaterial in such a case that the premiums were not actually paid by the debtor, if he has been charged with them in account by the creditor, and has not disputed his liability to pay them (y). The payment by the mortgagee of premiums, on the mortgagor's refusal to pay them, will not divest the latter of his right to the policy, after payment by him of the advances for the premiums with interest (z).

The circumstance that an allowance for insurance was included in the calculation of the consideration, will, however, entitle the debtor to a policy kept up by the creditor, if there was no stipulation by the debtor for an insurance. The matter is then at the option of the creditor who, whether he effects an insurance, or by retaining the money becomes his own insurer, is equally entitled to the benefit of the arrangement (a).

If the policy is not taken out under an arrangement with the debtor, but is effected entirely by the creditor for his own protection, he alone is interested in it. And the mere fact that the creditor has charged the debtor with the premiums in his accounts, if there is no evidence that the debtor was aware of the fact, or that he had agreed to pay them, will not give him a right to the policy (b).

The mortgagor will also take the benefit of the insurance if there is an agreement, express or to be inferred (c), to that effect. If there is an actual contract that the policy shall be assigned to the grantor on redemption of the security, if he shall elect to take it, then, although the grantee may be under no obligation to keep up the policy even after the grantor has elected to take it, he has clearly no right after such election (d) to dispose of it for his own benefit.

If a lessee mortgages his interest, the benefit of a fire insurance, effected in the names of himself and the lessor, with a provision that the money payable under the policy should be applied in restoring the premises, passes by, though it is not mentioned in, the mortgage, and the mortgagor will be ordered to sign a joint receipt with the lessor to the office for the money. A mere covenant by the mortgagor with the mortgagee to effect an insurance, does not imply that the mortgagee shall have the benefit of the insurance, either in discharge of the debt or in the restoration of the property, if there is no stipulation to that effect (e).

(y) *Holland* v. *Smith* (1806), 6 Esp. 11; *Lea* v. *Hinton* (1854), 5 De G.M. & G. 823; *Morland* v. *Isaac* (1855), 20 Beav. 389; *Freme* v. *Brade* (1858), 2 De G. & J. 582; *Re Storie's Will Trusts* (1859), 1 Giff. 94; *Courtenay* v. *Wright* (1860), 2 Giff. 337.

(z) *Drysdale* v. *Piggot* (1856), 8 De G.M. & G. 546; *Salt* v. *Marquess of Northampton*, [1892] A.C.1 (H.L.), at p. 16.

(a) *Freme* v. *Brade, supra.*   (b) *Bruce* v. *Garden* (1869), 5 Ch. App. 32.

(c) *Gottlieb* v. *Cranch* (1853), 4 De G.M. & G. 440.

(d) And even before election: *Hawkins* v. *Woodgate* (1844), 7 Beav. 565.

(e) *Lees* v. *Whiteley* (1866), L.R. 2 Eq. 143.

Solicitor's undertaking to discharge mortgage (*f*).—Where a mortgage is to be discharged out of the proceeds of the sale of the mortgaged property, it will often not be possible for the vendor to deliver the discharged mortgage with the remainder of the title deeds on completion (*g*). Accordingly, it is now common for completion to take place upon the undertaking of the vendor's solicitor to discharge the mortgage and to forward the discharged mortgage to the purchaser's solicitor within a specified period (*h*). The risk of liability under the undertaking ought to be considered by the maker, as he may be ordered by the court to implement his undertaking (*i*). And the liability may be greater than would at first sight appear by virtue of the reservation of a power of consolidation (*k*).

Costs of redemption.—On this topic, see pp. 653 *et seq., infra.*

Preparation of reconveyance.—The mortgagor's solicitor prepares the document of discharge (*l*).

VIII—DISCHARGE UNDER OVERREACHING POWERS

Discharge on payment into court.—Where land subject to any incumbrance, whether immediately realisable or payable or not, is sold or exchanged by the court, or out of court, the court may, if it thinks fit, on the application of any party to the sale or exchange, direct or allow payment into court of such a sum as, when invested in government securities, would in the court's view be sufficient, by means of the dividends thereof, to keep down or otherwise provide for that charge, together with any additional sum to meet further costs, expenses and interest or any other contingency (*m*). Thereupon the court may declare the land freed from the incumbrance and make any order for conveyance, or vesting order, proper for giving effect to the sale or exchange, and give directions for the retention and investment of the money in court and for the payment or application of the income thereof (*n*). The court may declare all other land, if any, affected by the incumbrance (besides the land sold or exchanged) to be freed from the incumbrance (*o*).

(*f*) See (1961), 25 Conv (N.S.), 259. For undertakings in discharge of registered charges, see (1976) 120 S.J. 406, 433, 454.

(*g*) The execution of a statutory receipt may take a number of days.

(*h*) For form, see p. 28, *infra.*

(*i*) *United Mining and Finance Corpn., Ltd.* v. *Becher,* [1910] 2 K.B. 298; *Re Mallows* (1960), 176 Estates Gazette, 1117 (undertaking to cancel entries of puisne mortgages as land charges); and see *Re a Solicitor (Lincoln),* [1966] 3 All E.R. 52; *Silver and Drake* v. *Baines,* [1971] 1 Q.B. 396 (C.A.); [1971] 1 All E.R. 473.

(*k*) There is little or no danger in the case of the private vendor and the single mortgage. But the position may be otherwise in the case of a developer vendor who may have several mortgages on foot. See further (1970) 67 L.S. Gaz. 753; (1971) 35 Conv. (N.S.) 3; (1971) 115 S.J. 684 (T. M. Aldridge); (1973) 70 L.S. Gaz. 1346, 1360 (J. E. Adams); and correspondence in (1976) 118 Sol. Jo. 406, at pp. 433, 454.

(*l*) Law Society's Digest, vol. 1, Op. 236.

(*m*) See Law of Property Act 1925, s. 50, replacing, with amendments, s. 5 of the Conveyancing Act 1881, and s. 1 of the Conveyancing Act 1911.

(*n*) *Ibid.,* s. 50 (2). *See Re Uplands,* [1948] W.N. 165.

(*o*) *Ibid.,* s. 50 (3); and see *Re Wilberforce,* [1915] 1 Ch. 104; *Lidco Investments, Ltd.* v. *Hale,* [1971] Estates Gazette Digest 669. And see footnote (*r*), p. 546, *supra.*

And payment of money into court effectually exonerates therefrom the person who makes the payment (*p*).

Discharge under overreaching conveyance.—Land can also be discharged from an equitable incumbrance (*q*) by a sale made under an overreaching trust for sale or power of sale. The trust for sale may be either a trust for sale already existing or a trust for sale created for the express purpose of overreaching the incumbrance. In either case in order that it may have the overreaching effect, the trustees must be either two or more individuals approved or appointed by the court or the successors in office of the individuals so approved or appointed; or a trust corporation (*r*). An alternative method is to create a "special settlement"; the trustees here, also, being two or more individuals approved or appointed by the court or a trust corporation. The owner of the land can then exercise the statutory powers of a tenant for life and thereby overreach the equitable incumbrance (*s*). Whether the sale is made under a trust for sale or under the statutory powers of the Settled Land Act, the land is conveyed free from the equitable incumbrance (*t*).

IX—VESTING ORDERS

Vesting orders in case of trustees and mentally disordered persons.—Since a receipt or other evidence that the mortgage money has been paid shows that the mortgage term has ceased, it should rarely be necessary to obtain a vesting order or order for conveyance on discharge of the mortgage. But a vesting order (*u*) may be required where a mortgagee is a trustee, or where he is a person mentally disordered; and there is a third case, where he is both a trustee and a person mentally disordered. Such orders can be made under the Trustee Act 1925, and the Mental Health Act 1959 (*x*), the main distinctions being that the order is made under the Mental Health Act where the mortgagee is a person mentally disordered and the mortgage belongs to him beneficially; generally, under either Act where a mental patient is a trustee; and under the Trustee Act if the mortgagee is a trustee who is not a person mentally disordered.

Mortgagee beneficially entitled to mortgage to property.— The judge (*y*) has power to make such orders and give such directions

---

(*p*) Law of Property Act 1925, s. 203 (1).

(*q*) Not being one protected by the deposit of title deeds: see Law of Property Act 1925, ss. 2 (3) and 13; Settled Land Act 1925, s. 21 (2). An unprotected equitable mortgage may be overreached even if registered as a general equitable charge.

(*r*) Law of Property Act 1925, s. 2 (2), as amended by the Law of Property (Amendment) Act 1926.

(*s*) Settled Land Act 1925, s. 21 (1).

(*t*) It is the duty of the trustees to provide for the incumbrance out of the proceeds of sale, and unless the incumbrance can be immediately paid off they must allow for a proper margin. The principle is the same as in ascertaining the amount to be paid into court, but the trustees have not the advantage of an order of the court in fixing the amount.

(*u*) As to vesting orders where an order for sale is made in reference to an equitable mortgage of land, see Law of Property Act 1925, s. 90; p. 386, *supra*.

(*x*) Replacing the Lunacy Act 1890.

(*y*) One or more judges of the Supreme Court nominated to act for the purposes of Part XIII of the Mental Health Act 1959: *ibid.*, s. 100 (1).

and authorities as he thinks fit relating to his functions with respect to the property and affairs of a patient (z), and in particular for the control (with or without the transfer or vesting of the property or the payment into or lodgment in court of money or securities) and management of any property of the patient (a).

Mortgagee-trustee.—The Trustee Act 1925, provides as follows:

41.—(1) (b) The court (c) may, whenever it is expedient to appoint a new trustee or new trustees, and it is found inexpedient, difficult, or impracticable so to do without the assistance of the court, make an order appointing a new trustee or new trustees either in substitution for or in addition to any existing trustee or trustees, or although there is no existing trustee.

In particular and without prejudice to the generality of the foregoing provision, the court may make an order appointing a new trustee in substitution for a trustee who is ... (d) incapable by reason of mental disorder within the meaning of the Mental Health Act 1959, of exercising his functions as trustee, or is a bankrupt, or is a corporation which is in liquidation or has been dissolved.

44.—In any of the following cases, namely—

(i) Where the court appoints or has appointed a trustee, or where a trustee has been appointed out of court under any statutory or express power;

(ii) Where a trustee entitled to or possessed of any land or interest therein, whether by way of mortgage or otherwise, or entitled to a contingent right therein, either solely or jointly with any other person—

(a) is under disability; or

(b) is out of the jurisdiction of the High Court; or

(c) cannot be found (e), or, being a corporation, has been dissolved;

(vii) Where any land or any interest therein is vested in a trustee whether by way of mortgage or otherwise, and it appears to the court to be expedient;

the court may make an order (in this Act called a vesting order) vesting the land or interest therein in any such person, in any such manner, and for any such estate or interest as the court may direct, or releasing or disposing of the contingent right to such person as the court may direct (f):

Provided that—

(a) Where the order is consequential on the appointment of a trustee the land or interest therein shall be vested for such estate as the court may direct in the persons who on the appointment are the trustees; and

(b) Where the order relates to a trustee entitled or formerly entitled jointly with another person, and such trustee is under disability or

---

(z) *I.e.*, under s. 102 of the Act. For the definition of patient, see s. 101.

(a) Mental Health Act 1959, s. 103 (1) (a).

(b) As amended by the Mental Health Act 1959, s. 149 (1) and Sched. 7, Pt. 1.

(c) *I.e.*, the High Court, and also the county court where the estate or fund subject to the trust does not exceed £5,000: see Trustee Act 1925, s. 67; County Courts Act 1959, s. 52 (3).

(d) The words "convicted of felony" were repealed by the Criminal Law Act 1967, Sched. 3.

(e) Since, after repayment, the mortgagee is trustee for the mortgagor, s. 44 may be used in a case where there is proof of repayment but no receipt and the mortgagee has disappeared. S. 59 of the Trustee Act 1925 enables the court to give judgment in the absence of a trustee.

(f) By s. 49 a vesting order operates as a conveyance made by the appropriate conveying parties, or, under s. 50, the court may, if it is more convenient, appoint a person to convey.

out of the jurisdiction of the High Court or cannot be found, or being a corporation has been dissolved, the land, interest, or right shall be vested in such other person who remains entitled, either alone or with any other person the court may appoint.

Section 51 provides for vesting orders as to stock and things in action being made by the court under similar circumstances (g).

54.—(1) Subject to the provisions of this section, the authorities having jurisdiction under Part VIII of the Mental Health Act 1959, shall not have power to make any order, or give any direction or authority, in relation to a patient who is a trustee if the High Court has power under this Act to make an order to the like effect.

(2) Where a patient is a trustee and a receiver appointed by the said authority is acting for him or an application for the appointment of a receiver has been made but not determined, then, except as respects a trust which is subject to an order for administration made by the High Court, the said authority shall have concurrent jurisdiction with the High Court in relation to—

(a) mortgaged property of which the patient has become a trustee merely by reason of the mortgage having been paid off;

(b) matters consequent on the making of provision of the said authority for the exercise of a power of appointing trustees or retiring from a trust (h).

X—DELIVERY OF THE DEEDS

Duty of mortgagee to have the deeds ready.—Where the mortgage is to be paid off in accordance with notice given on either side, it is the duty of the mortgagee to see that the deeds are forthcoming, so that the mortgagor may be enabled without risk to pay the money, and to take his reconveyance on the day fixed (i); and he is entitled to demand them, although by the act of the mortgagee in disposing by a single document of the property and the debt, other persons have acquired an interest in a title deed of the property (k). This right extends to previous mortgages, assignments, and reconveyances made between the same parties, or their representatives, before the redeemed mortgage (l). And where several mortgages on distinct properties have been transferred by a single deed, one of the mortgagors who

---

(g) By sub-s. (6) the provisions of the Act as to vesting orders apply to shares in ships registered under the Acts relating to merchant shipping as if they were stock. See s. 58 as to the persons who may apply under the Act.

(h) Substituted for the original s. 54 by the Mental Health Act 1959, s. 149 (1); Sched. 7.

(i) Lord Midleton v. Eliot (1847), 15 Sim. 531. And the mortgagee is not liable on account of delivering the deeds to the person not having the best right thereto, unless he has notice of the better right: Law of Property Act 1925, s. 96 (2); Corbett v. National Provident Institution (1900), 17 T.L.R. 5. To avoid the necessity of search by the mortgagee, this sub-section was amended by the Law of Property (Amendment) Act 1926, so as to exclude notice implied by registration.

(k) Dobson v. Land (1850), 4 De G. & Sm. 575, 581.

(l) Hudson v. Malcolm (1862), 10 W.R. 720. And a mortgagee or transferee of a mortgage, though he is entitled to keep a copy of the draft for his own protection until the transaction is completed, has no right to keep copies of the mortgage or transfer after he is paid off. Whatever copies he has are, as a general rule, copies paid for by the mortgagor, and must be delivered up to him when he pays off the mortgage: Re Wade and Thomas (1881), 17 Ch. D. 348.

comes to redeem singly is entitled to have the deed of transfer delivered to him, upon his covenanting to produce it (*m*).

Where the mortgagee reconveys only part of the property, and is entitled to retain the deeds by virtue of his absolute title to the greater part of the property, he ought also to covenant with the redeeming party for production (*n*).

Loss of the title deeds.—The mortgagee will not be deprived of the benefit of his security by reason of the loss of the title deeds, if the court is satisfied that a security was effected and that they have really been lost (*o*).

If the title deeds of a property have been mislaid or lost by, or stolen out of the custody of, the mortgagee or his agent, the court, either in a redemption or foreclosure action, will direct an inquiry according to the circumstances, as to what deeds or documents were delivered to the mortgagee, and whether they are or not existing or lost, or in the power of the mortgagee to produce, or what has become of them (*p*). The costs of such an action will fall on the mortgagee (*q*), and the same result follows where he has to sue a third party for them (*r*).

Indemnity and compensation by mortgagee.—If the deeds are certified to be lost, or are known to have been destroyed or fraudulently disposed of by the mortgagee or his agent, the mortgagor will be entitled to an inquiry as to what indemnity or security ought to be given in respect of the loss (*s*), and also as to what ought to be allowed as a sufficient compensation for the damage done to the estate by the loss or destruction of the deeds (*t*).

The mortgagee will also be directed to deliver, upon oath, attested copies of such of the documents destroyed of which attested copies can be made or had.

And if it is found, or appears, that the deeds were stolen, an indemnity will be ordered (*u*); but no liability arises for compensation in such a case, whether the deeds were in the possession of the mortgagee

---

(*m*) *Capper* v. *Terrington* (1844), 1 Coll. 103.

(*n*) *Yates* v. *Plumbe* (1854), 2 Sm. & G. 174.

(*o*) *Baskett* v. *Skeel* (1863), 11 W.R. 1019.

(*p*) *Smith* v. *Bicknell* (1810), cited 3 Ves. & B. 51, n.; *Stokoe* v. *Robson* (1814), 3 Ves. & B. 51; *Bentinck* v. *Willink* (1842), 2 Hare, 1.

(*q*) *James* v. *Rumsey* (1879), 11 Ch. D. 398; *Caldwell* v. *Matthews* (1890), 62 L.T. 799.

(*r*) *James* v. *Rumsey, supra.* Where the failure to produce the deeds was due to an adverse claim by an attorney, an account was ordered to be taken of the principal, interest and costs; the amount to be paid into and to remain in the bank, until the deeds could be secured and a reconveyance had: *Schoole* v. *Sall* (1803), 1 Sch. & Lef. 176.

(*s*) *Lord Midleton* v. *Eliot* (1847), 15 Sim. 531; *James* v. *Rumsey, supra*; and see as to bond of indemnity, *Caldwell* v. *Matthews, supra.*

(*t*) *Hornby* v. *Matcham* (1848), 16 Sim. 325. This compensation is given in respect of the expense to arise on future dealings with the estate in getting office copies of the order and other proceedings in the action, which must thenceforth form part of the title; and not as speculative damages for injury occasioned by the absence of the deeds at a sale; and the amount of the compensation will be set off against the principal and interest due on the security: *Brown* v. *Sewell* (1853), 11 Hare, 49; *James* v. *Rumsey. supra*; and see *Macartney* v. *Graham* (1828), 2 Russ. & Myl. 353, where the document lost was a bill of exchange, and only an indemnity was given.

(*u*) *Shelmardine* v. *Harrop* (1821), 6 Mad. 39. See form of bond of indemnity in *Stokoe* v. *Robson, supra*; and *James* v. *Rumsey, supra*, at pp. 400, 401.

himself, or of his solicitor or agent in whose custody he might properly have left them if they had been his own, if no fraud or collusion is shown (*x*).

And if the result of the inquiry is merely that the deeds are not to be found, it seems that an indemnity (*y*) only, and no compensation will be directed. For the party chargeable is then entitled to assume that which is most to his own advantage, viz. that the deeds were stolen, or are otherwise missing not by reason of any wrong or negligence on his part (*z*).

The court would formerly give compensation for the loss of deeds if the justice of the case required it, under the prayer for general relief, though indemnity only was sought by the action (*a*); and this would now be so where no general relief is claimed, by virtue of R.S.C., Ord. 18, r. 15. Such compensation is not given under any implied covenant for safe custody, but is referable to the general jurisdiction of the court in accident (*b*).

XI—LOSS OF THE RIGHT OF REDEMPTION

Generally.—The right of redemption may be lost by redemption itself, by release of the right to the mortgagee by the mortgagor (*c*), by the sale of the land by the mortgagee under his power of sale (*d*), upon foreclosure (*e*), and by extinguishment by lapse of time under the Limitation Act 1939.

EXTINGUISHMENT OF EQUITY OF REDEMPTION BY TIME (*f*)

Mortgages of land.—The Limitation Act 1939, provides:

(*x*) *Jones* v. *Lewis* (1751), 2 Ves. Sen. 240; and see *Woodman* v. *Higgins* (1850), 14 Jur. 846.

But the circumstance that the deeds were lost out of the custody of the solicitor of the mortgagee, for whose convenience they were so deposited, seems in one case to have been thought a reason (amongst others) for giving compensation: *Brown* v. *Sewell*, *supra*. But *cf. Gilligan and Nugent* v. *National Bank*, [1901] 2 I.R. 513.

(*y*) The indemnity must be given even in the absence of negligence: *James* v. *Rumsey*, *supra*.

(*z*) *Smith* v. *Bicknell*, *supra*; *Stokoe* v. *Robson*, *supra*. See *Brown* v. *Sewell*, *supra*. In *Lord Midleton* v. *Eliot*, *supra*, there was loss unexplained, but traced to the negligence of the mortgagee's agent. No compensation was directed or sought, and there was a previous correspondence on the footing of indemnity only. Where the action was against the survivors of several mortgagees, being executors, without joining the representatives of the deceased executor, who was the cause of the loss, no indemnity or compensation was given: *Smith* v. *Bicknell*, *supra*.

(*a*) *Brown* v. *Sewell*, *supra*.

(*b*) *Gilligan and Nugent* v. *National Bank*, *supra*. Where the value of the mortgaged estate was £20,000 and the amount of the mortgage debt about £9,300, the sum of £500 was proposed and approved of as a proper compensation for the loss of the title deeds and documents: *Hornby* v. *Matcham*, *supra*.

(*c*) See p. 525, *supra*

(*d*) See p. 359, *supra*.

(*e*) See p. 382, *supra*.

(*f*) See, generally, 24 Halsbury's Laws (3rd Edn.), pp. 274 *et seq.*; Preston and Newsom, *Limitation of Actions* (3rd Edn.), pp. 114 *et seq.* And see p. 354, *supra*.

12 (*g*).—When a mortgagee of land (*h*) has been in possession (*i*) of any of the mortgaged land for a period of twelve years, no action to redeem the land of which the mortgagee has been so in possession shall thereafter be brought by the mortgagor or any person claiming through him (*k*).

And further:

23.—(3) Where a mortgagee is by virtue of the mortgage in possession of any mortgaged land and either receives any sum in respect of the principal or interest of the mortgage debt or acknowledges the title of the mortgagor, or his equity of redemption, an action to redeem the land in his possession may be brought at any time before the expiration of twelve years from the date of the payment or acknowledgment.

Effect of expiration of limitation period.—At the expiration of the twelve-year period the title of the mortgagor is extinguished (*l*). If the mortgagee sells after being in possession for twelve years he may keep the whole of the proceeds of sale (*m*). In such a case he should sell as mortgagee unless the mortgage term has been enlarged (*n*).

Possession by mortgagee.—To gain the benefit of the statute, the mortgagee must enter and continue in possession solely as mortgagee. If he enters as purchaser of a life tenancy of settled land, the statute will not, during the continuance of his interest, run against the remaindermen (*o*).

Where the mortgaged property is leasehold the receipt by the mortgagee of the rent reserved thereout for twelve years amounts to adverse possession of the land (*p*).

When time begins to run.—The statute will generally begin to run from the date of the mortgagee's entry into possession (*q*), but the terms of the deed and the circumstances of the case may start the period running at another time.

Disabilities.—The provisions of the Limitation Act 1939, relating to disability apply to the disability of the mortgagor who seeks to redeem (*r*).

Acknowledgment and part payment.—As previously stated (*s*) s. 23 (3) of the Limitation Act 1939, deals with the fresh accrual of an action to redeem on acknowledgment or part payment. The formal

---

(*g*) Replacing Real Property Limitation Act 1874, s. 7.
(*g*) See *Re Midleton's Settlement, Lord Cottesloe and Lloyd* v. *A.-G. and Earl of Midleton*, [1947] 1 Ch. 583 (C.A.); [1947] 2 All E.R. 134; affd. *sub nom. Earl of Midleton* v. *Baron, Cottesloe*, [1949] A.C. 418 (H.L.); [1949] 1 All E.R. 841; *Bank of Ireland* v. *Domvile*, [1956] I.R. 37; *Smith* v. *Hill* (1878), 9 Ch. D. 143.
(*i*) See *Lord Advocate* v. *Lord Lovat* (1880), 5 App. Cas. 273 (H.L.), at p. 288; *Kirby* v. *Cowderoy*, [1912] A.C. 599 (P.C.).
(*k*) The terms of the mortgage may provide for redemption beyond the twelve-year period: *Alderson* v. *White* (1858), 2 De G. &. J. 97, 109.
(*l*) Limitation Act 1939, s. 16. As also is that of a subsequent mortgagee: *Young* v. *Clarey*, [1948] Ch. 191; [1948] 1 All E.R. 197.
(*m*) *Young* v. *Clarey*, *supra*.
(*n*) See p. 567, *infra*.
(*o*) *Hyde* v. *Dallaway* (1843), 2 Hare, 528. A life tenant holds the legal estate as trustee and cannot set up his possession against the remaindermen.
(*p*) Limitation Act 1939, s. 10 (3) (b). And see *Ward* v. *Carttar* (1865), L.R. 1 Eq. 29; *Markwick* v. *Hardingham* (1880), 15 Ch. D. 339 (C.A.).
(*q*) *Re Metropolis and Counties Permanent Investment Building Society, Gatfield's Case*, [1911] 1 Ch. 698.
(*r*) Section 22 (p. 290, *supra*). And see section 26 (fraud and mistake) (p. 290, *supra*).
(*s*) See *supra*.

provisions as to acknowledgments and part payments are set out in s. 24 (*t*).

An acknowledgment must be in writing and signed by the mortgagee or other person claiming through him, or by his agent. It must be given to the mortgagor or his successor in title or his agent (*u*). It cannot be given to the mortgagor after his title has ceased (*x*).

Where the mortgagee has entered into possession accounts of his receipt of rents are not a sufficient acknowledgment, unless kept for or communicated to the mortgagor or his agent (*y*).

Payments in respect of the mortgage debt must be made to the mortgagee or his agent (*z*). Receipt of the rents and profits by the mortgagee while in possession is not a receipt of any sum in respect of the mortgage debt and accordingly not a part payment (*a*).

Where there are first and second mortgages in favour of two sets of trustees and a member of both sets receives the rents and applies them for over twelve years in paying off the capital and interest of the first mortgage, time will not run against the second mortgagees, for when the hand to pay and the hand to receive the money due to the first mortgagees is the same, time does not run (*b*).

Acknowledgment by one of several mortgagees.—Section 25 (3) of the Limitation Act 1939, provides that where two or more mortgagees are by virtue of the mortgage in possession of the mortgaged land, an acknowledgment of the mortgagor's title or of his equity of redemption by one of the mortgagees shall only bind him and his successors in title and shall not bind any other mortgagee or his successors, and that where the mortgagee by whom the acknowledgment is given is entitled to a part of the mortgaged land and not to any ascertained part of the mortgage debt, the mortgagor shall be entitled to redeem that part of the land on payment, with interest, of the part of the mortgage debt which bears the same proportion to the whole of the debt as the value of the part of the land bears to the whole of the mortgaged land (*c*).

Acknowledgment to one of several mortgagors.—Section 25 (4) of the Limitation Act 1939, provides that where there are two or more mortgagors, and the title or right of redemption of one of the mortgagors is acknowledged as aforesaid, the acknowledgment shall be deemed to have been made to all the mortgagors.

Redemption of personalty.—There is no corresponding enactment barring actions to redeem mortgages of pure personalty (*d*), and the

---

(*t*) See pp. 285 *et seq., supra.* An acknowledgment or part payment made after the statutory period is ineffective, see p. 288, *supra.*

(*u*) *Trulock v. Robey* (1841), 12 Sim. 402; *Lucas v. Dennison* (1843), 13 Sim. 584.

(*x*) E.g., after his bankruptcy: *Markwick v. Hardingham* (1880), 15 Ch. D. 339.

(*y*) *Re Alison, Johnson v. Mounsey* (1879), 11 Ch. D. 284. And see *Wilson v. Walton and Kirkdale Permanent Building Society* (1903), 19 T.L.R. 408; *Re Metropolis and Counties Permanent Investment Building Society, Gatfield's Case,* [1911] 1 Ch. 698.

(*z*) As to part payment, see pp. 285 *et seq., supra.*

(*a*) *Harlock v. Ashberry* (1882), 19 Ch. D. 539. Payment of the rents and profits to the mortgagee by a receiver appointed by him constitutes part payment: *Berwick & Co. v. Price,* [1905] 1 Ch. 632, 642.

(*b*) *Hodgson v. Salt,* [1936] 1 All E.R. 95; *cf. Bowring-Hanbury's Trustee v. Bowring-Hanbury,* [1943] Ch. 104 (C.A.); [1943] 1 All E.R. 48.

(*b*) See Preston and Newsom, *Limitation of Actions* (3rd Edn.), pp. 237–239.

(*c*) See the 5th Interim Report of the Law Revision Committee, 1936, Cmd. 5334, p. 15.

twelve-year period is not adopted by analogy. The right of redemption is only barred upon equitable grounds, such as the acquiescence of the mortgagor in the extinction of the right of redemption, or the alteration of the position of the mortgagee (e). As in other cases of the enforcement of equitable demands after the lapse of time, it is a question of the balance of justice and injustice in granting the remedy or withholding it. Although mere length of time may bar the remedy, this is on the ground that to allow redemption would be unjust. There is no hard and fast rule that twenty years will be sufficient for the purpose, but probably there will be a difficulty in establishing a right to redeem after this period (f).

Mortgage of land and personalty.—Where a mortgage comprises both land and personalty, if the equity of redemption is barred as regards the land, it is barred as to the personalty also, because the right of redemption of the properties is indivisible (g).

Enlargement of mortgage term into fee simple.—Where a mortgagee of freehold property has acquired a title under the Limitation Acts, he, or the persons deriving title under him, may enlarge the mortgage term into a fee simple under the statutory power for that purpose (h) discharged from any legal mortgage affected by the title so acquired, or in the case of a chargee by way of legal mortgage may by deed declare that the fee simple is vested in him so discharged, and the same vests accordingly (i). Similarly, where a mortgagee of leasehold property has acquired a title under the Limitation Acts, he, or the persons deriving title under him, may by deed declare that the leasehold reversion affected by the mortgage and any term affected by the title so acquired shall vest in him, free from any right of redemption which is barred, and the same vests accordingly (without giving rise to a forefeiture for want of licence to assign), and thereupon the mortgage term, if any, and any other mortgage term or charge by way of legal mortgage affected by the title so acquired shall subject to any express provision to the contrary contained in the deed, merge in such leasehold reversion or be extinguished (k).

A long term, originating in an old mortgage by demise, the equity of redemption of which has become barred by the Limitation Acts, is not uncommonly encountered and the above provisions permit such a term to be enlarged. It must, of course, be ascertained that the conditions of s. 153 of the Law of Property Act 1925, are satisfied.

Subsequent incumbrancer.—Where a subsequent mortgagee's right of action against the mortgagor is barred (l) he cannot claim to redeem a prior incumbrancer (m).

(e) *Weld* v. *Petre*, [1929] 1 Ch. 33 (C.A.).
(f) *Weld* v. *Petre, supra, per* LAWRENCE, L.J., at pp. 54, 53.
(g) *Charter* v. *Watson*, [1899] 1 Ch. 175.
(h) Law of Property Act 1925, s. 153.
(i) *Ibid.*, s. 88 (3).
(k) *Ibid.*, s. 89 (3). For forms of enlargement of mortgage terms, see 8 Ency. Forms and Precedents (4th Edn.), pp. 570–578. As to the declaration by a registered chargee that the right of redemption is barred, see Land Registration Act 1925, s. 34 (2); p. 299, *supra.*
(l) See pp. 280 *et seq., supra.*
(m) *Cotterell* v. *Price*, [1960] 3 All E.R. 315.

CHAPTER 29

Redemption Action

I—INSTITUTION OF PROCEEDINGS (a)

High Court.—Actions for the redemption of mortgages are assigned to the Chancery Division (b). An action for redemption should be commenced by originating summons, unless there are disputed questions of fact or where questions of priority have to be determined, when the action should be commenced by writ (c). Where an action is commenced by writ which might have been commenced by originating summons, the plaintiff will only be allowed such costs as he would have been entitled to if he had commenced proceedings by summons instead of by writ (d).

The affidavit in support of the originating summons, or the statement of claim where proceedings are commenced by writ, must set out particulars of the mortgage and all the material facts showing the plaintiff's right to redeem. Any special circumstances, such as that the defendant mortgagee has been in possession, should be stated (e).

Offer to redeem.—As a general rule the mortgagor is not entitled to bring the mortgagee before the court except for the purpose of redemption (f); hence a mortgagee cannot be made a party to an action relating to the mortgage unless there is expressly or by implication an offer to redeem (g).

(a) See, generally, 28 Ency. Court Forms (2nd Edn.), Mortgages.

(b) Supreme Court of judicature (Consolidation) Act 1925, s. 56 (1) (b). And see R.S.C. Ord. 88.

(c) Re Giles, Real and Personal Advance Co. v. Michell (1890), 43 Ch. D. 391 (C.A.).

(d) Barr v. Harding (1887), 36 W.R. 216; Johnson v. Evans (1888), 60 L.T. 29.

(e) For forms, see 28 Ency. Court Forms (2nd Edn.), pp. 84 et seq.

(f) Tasker v. Small (1837), 3 My. & Cr. 63; Jefferys v. Dickson (1866), 1 Ch. App. 183; National Bank of Australasia v. United Hand-in-Hand, etc., Co. (1879), 4 App. Cas. 391 (P.C.). Redemption is the only relief to which a subsequent incumbrancer is entitled against the prior mortgagee: Gordon v. Horsfall (1846), 5 Moo. P.C. 393, 426.

(g) Troughton v. Binkes (1801), 6 Ves. 573; Balfe v. Lord (1842), 2 Dr. & War. 480; Dalton v. Hayter (1844), 7 Beav. 313; Gordon v. Horsfall, supra; Harding v. Tingey (1864), 10 Jur. (N.S.) 872; Hughes v. Cook (1865), 34 Beav. 407. See Russian Commercial, etc., Bank v. British Bank for Foreign Trade, Ltd., [1921] 2 A.C. 438. And there must be an offer to redeem though the plaintiff is a trustee, the trust having been created by the mortgagor and the mortgagee not being interested: M'Donough v. Shewbridge (1814), 2 Ba. & Be. 555; and though part of trust property has been improperly included in the mortgage, see Eaton v. Hazel (1852), 1 W.R. 87. As to the extent of the offer, see Grugeon v. Gerrard (1840), 4 Y. & C. Ex. 119. As a general rule an offer made by the pleadings cannot be recalled: Davis v. Duke of Marlborough (1819), 2 Swans., at p. 134; Bazzelgetti v. Battine (1821), 2 Swans. 156, n. And an offer to redeem made under a mistake as to the amount secured on the property was enforced in Holford v. Burnell (1687), 1 Vern. 448. But this would hardly be so now; and the court may in its discretion refuse to enforce the offer where it would be unjust to do so: Knight v.

But this rule does not apply where the object of the proceedings is to obtain the construction of the mortgage deed (*h*), or where the equity of redemption has become subject to trusts which provide for the payment of the mortgage debt and the mortgagee is made a party to an action relating to the trusts (*i*). And it does not apply where the mortgagor's claim is for sale and not redemption (*k*).

Action to impeach mortgage.—Where the action is brought to impeach the mortgage and is framed solely for this purpose so that it contains no prayer for redemption, the plaintiff cannot, upon the action failing and the validity of the mortgage being established, obtain an order for redemption; and the action will be dismissed but without prejudice to the right of redemption (*l*). But it is otherwise where the defendant has not relied solely on his title as mortgagee, but has set up an inconsistent title; for instance, that he is absolute owner (*m*); and then redemption can be ordered in the same action. And the mortgagor can claim to set aside the mortgage, or, in the alternative, if it is valid, to redeem (*n*).

Action for redemption.—It has been said that where a mortgagee is made a party to an action, the prayer for relief is the same thing as a prayer for redemption, because redemption is the proper relief (*o*); and an action may be treated as a redemption action although it involves a claim to set aside a sale by the mortgagee (*p*). But redemption will

---

Bowyer (1858), 2 De G. & J. 421; or where it is so limited in its terms as not to be strictly applicable to the state of affairs which has resulted from the hearing of the cause: *Pelly* v. *Wathen* (1849), 7 Hare, 351. And as to enforcing payment where there has been no offer to redeem, see *Hollis* v. *Bulpett* (1865), 12 L.T. 293.

Where the action was framed for redemption, an offer to redeem, if not made expressly, might be added by amendment: *Palk* v. *Lord Clinton* (1805), 12 Ves. 48. Where the action is by writ an offer to redeem should still be inserted in the statement of claim; but where it is by summons, it is, presumably, implied in the claim for redemption.

(*h*) *Re Nobbs, Nobbs* v. *Law Reversionary Interest Society*, [1896] 2 Ch. 830.

(*i*) *Jefferys* v. *Dickson, supra*; and similarly if the action relates to different property, which has been conveyed in trust to exonerate the mortgaged property, and the action cannot be effectual without the presence of the mortgagee, he may be joined without any offer to redeem him: *Dalton* v. *Hayter, supra*. And the prior mortgagee, if he is a necessary party in respect of accounts, may waive the redemption of his security, in which case the judgment should be prefaced by a statement that he consents not to be redeemed, and to allow his debt to remain a charge on the estate: *Lord Kensington* v. *Bouverie* (1854), 19 Beav. 39.

(*k*) It has been held in Ireland, where it is the practice to order sale and not foreclosure, that the action must be framed for redemption, although an order for sale, and not redemption, is sought: *M'Donough* v. *Shewbridge* (1814), 2 Ba. & Be. 555; and see *Foster* v. *Kerr* (1848), 12 Ir. Eq. R. 51, 54. But no offer to redeem appears to be necessary when a sale is asked for by the mortgagor under the Law of Property Act 1925, s. 91. And see *Murad* v. *National Provincial Bank*, footnote (*b*), p. 369, *supra*.

(*l*) *Martinez* v. *Cooper* (1826), 2 Russ. 198; *Johnson* v. *Fesenmeyer* (1858), 25 Beav. 88; *Crenver, etc., Mining Co., Ltd.* v. *Willyams* (1866), 35 Beav. 353.

(*m*) *National Bank of Australasia* v. *United Hand-in-Hand, etc., Society, supra*.

(*n*) See *Hunt* v. *Worsfold*, [1896] 2 Ch. 224. But formerly, it seems, this was not allowed: see *Ernest* v. *Partridge* (1863), 1 New Rep. 425.

(*o*) *Cholmley* v. *Countess of Oxford* (1741), 2 Atk. 267; *Palk* v. *Lord Clinton* (1805), 12 Ves. 48, 62. Consequently, if an account is taken, dismissal will be the penalty for non-payment, and this will be equivalent to foreclosure: *Cholmley* v. *Countess of Oxford, supra*; see p. 578, *infra*. But it may be that this result would only follow if there was no offer to redeem: see *Inman* v. *Wearing* (1850), 3 De G. & Sm. 729. As to amendment where the offer has been omitted, see *Palk* v. *Lord Clinton, supra*; *Balfe* v. *Lord* (1842), 2 Dr. & War. 480; *supra*.

(*p*) *Powell* v. *Roberts* (1869), L.R. 9 Eq. 169; see *Inman* v. *Wearing, supra*.

not be ordered in an action of ejectment against the purchaser unless the claim includes specifically a prayer for redemption (*q*).

In an action for redemption the plaintiff is entitled to discovery of matters required to make the action effective. Thus he can have discovery of the mortgagee's securities (*r*), of the amount claimed to be due (*s*), and of the names of incumbrancers (*t*).

Effect of foreclosure on action for redemption.—Possession under a judgment of foreclosure is a good defence to an action to redeem, where the rights of the plaintiffs or of those under whom they claim, are concluded by the judgment; but not otherwise, although the mortgagee on foreclosure had no notice of other incumbrances. The defence, therefore, will not hold against an action by subsequent incumbrancers, who were not parties to the action by which the foreclosure was effected (*u*). Under particular circumstances, however, the foreclosure will be opened, and a new right will be given to redeem (*v*).

The foreclosure cannot be pleaded until the final order has been obtained (*x*); for up to that time the estate retains the quality of a mortgage, and would not formerly pass as land, by the will of the mortgagee, made before the date of the order absolute (*y*).

Joinder of causes of action.—Since the mortgagee has an immediate right to have his accounts taken, and a time fixed for payment, and is not bound to wait the result of taking accounts and other matters in which he has no interest, a mortgagor formerly could not in the same action seek redemption of one, and foreclosure of another mortgage (*z*); and a mortgagee might demur to a bill, which, besides redemption, sought a general administration of the personal estate of

---

(*q*) *Murugaser Marimuttu* v. *De Soysa*, [1891] A.C. 69 (P.C.).

(*r*) *West of England and South Wales Bank* v. *Nickolls* (1877), 6 Ch. D. 613.

(*s*) *Bridgwater* v. *De Winton* (1863), 33 L.J. Ch. 238; *Beavan* v. *Cook* (1869), 17 W.R. 872; *Elmer* v. *Creasy* (1873), 9 Ch. App. 69.

(*t*) *Union Bank of London* v. *Manby* (1879), 13 Ch. D. 239 (C.A.). And see Law of Property Act 1925, s. 96 (1) (p. 41, *supra*). But if a trustee in whose name money is lent on mortgage is a solicitor (an ordinary part of whose duty it is to lay out money for his clients), he is not bound to discover the names of his *cestuis que trust*, or to produce documents relating to the transactions, if he cannot do it without a breach of professional confidence, notwithstanding any inconvenience which may arise to the plaintiff from want of the information: *Jones* v. *Pugh* (1842), 1 Ph. 96; *Harvey* v. *Clayton* (1675), 2 Swans. 221, n.

(*u*) *Nichols* v. *Short* (1713), 2 Eq. Cas. Abr. 608; 15 Vin. Abr. 478. A party to an action in which a judgment of foreclosure has been made is bound by it, though it was made in the absence of a person whose interest was not disclosed by the pleadings: *Bromitt* v. *Moor* (1851), 9 Hare, 374. And a mortgagor (defendant in that character to a foreclosure action) is bound by the judgment in that action in respect of his interest in another character, though the other interest did not appear upon the proceedings: *Goldsmid* v. *Stonehewer* (1852), 9 Hare, App. xxxviii. But it seems that if a person, whose interest has been foreclosed in an action to which he was a party, becomes afterwards entitled to another interest in the same estate, derived from a person who was not a party to that action, the owner of the newly-acquired interest may bring his action for redemption, notwithstanding the former judgment and foreclosure. But the pleadings ought to state the former proceedings in the foreclosure action: *Bromitt* v. *Moor, supra*.

(*v*) See p. 570, *supra*.

(*x*) *Senhouse* v. *Earl* (1752), 2 Ves. Sen. 450; see *Quarrell* v. *Beckford* (1816), 1 Mad. 269.

(*y*) *Thompson* v. *Grant* (1819), 4 Mad. 438.

(*z*) *Plumbe* v. *Plumbe* (1841), 4 Y. & C. Ex. 345.

the deceased mortgagor, and a declaration of the rights of devisees and legatees (*a*). The practice in these matters is now governed by the R.S.C., which allow a plaintiff to unite in the same action, and in the same statement of claim, several causes of action, subject to the power of the court or judge to make orders for separate trials or separate disposal of the claims (*b*).

County court.—A county court has all the jurisdiction of the High Court to hear and determine proceedings for redemption of any mortgage where the amount owing in respect of the mortgage (*c*) does not exceed the sum of £5,000 (*d*). In such proceedings the judge has, in addition to any other powers and authorities possessed by him, all the powers and authorities of a judge of the Chancery Division (*e*). The proceedings must be taken in the court within the district of which the land or any part thereof is situated (*f*).

II—PARTIES TO THE ACTION

A—PERSONS INTERESTED IN THE EQUITY OF REDEMPTION

Persons entitled to redeem.—All persons entitled to redeem (*g*) and all persons interested in the security (*h*) are necessary parties to a redemption action. The rule requiring the presence of all parties is based on the right of the mortgagee to account once and for all, which can only be done if the account is taken in the presence of all parties who could demand an account (*i*). A person entitled to redeem cannot be omitted because his interest is very small (*k*). The only exception to the rule is as regards beneficiaries under a trust and

---

(*a*) *Pearse* v. *Hewitt* (1835), 7 Sim. 471. (*b*) Order 15, rr. 1, 5.

(*c*) *I.e.*, owing at the time of the action: *Shields, etc., Building Society* v. *Richards* (1901), 84 L.T. 587.

(*d*) County Courts Act 1959, s. 52 (1). As to costs where the action is brought in the High Court, see footnote (*i*), p. 644, *infra.*

(*e*) *Ibid.*, s. 52 (2).

(*f*) C.C.R. Ord. 2, r. 2. For forms, see 28 Ency. Court Forms (2nd Edn.), pp. 148, 149.

(*g*) See also pp. 392 *et seq., supra.* The person who seeks redemption must show a good right to redeem, for the mortgagee is entitled to hold the property against everybody who has not a paramount title. If the defendant can make out a case which goes directly to show that the title is in another person than the plaintiff, the latter will not even be allowed to redeem at his peril: *Lomax* v. *Bird* (1683), 1 Vern. 182; see *Francklyn* v. *Fern* (1740), Barn. Ch. 30. But a plea in bar to redemption, on the ground of want of interest in the plaintiff, was held bad, where the mortgagor had parted with his interest in the security to an assignee for whose benefit he was seeking redemption, though the assignee must be a party to such an action: *Winterbottom* v. *Tayloe* (1854), 2 Drew. 279.

If the right to redeem is fairly dependent on the validity of an instrument, there will be no declaration as to the terms of redemption until the question of validity has been settled: *Blake* v. *Foster* (1813), 2 Ba. & Be. 387. The court will act upon a prima facie title shown by the plaintiff, however complicated, if it is supported by satisfactory evidence, and is uncontradicted, except by a mere allegation of an adverse claim, considering that the only matter determined is the right of redemption, the judgment for which will not hinder an adverse claimant from asserting his title in another proceeding: *Lloyd* v. *Wait* (1842), 1 Ph. 61.

(*h*) See pp. 574 *et seq., infra.*

(*i*) *Palk* v. *Lord Clinton* (1805), 12 Ves. 48.

(*k*) *Hunter* v. *Maclew* (1846), 5 Hare, 238. So when legal tenancy in common existed, the owners of all the undivided shares had to be parties: *Bolton* v. *Salmon*, [1891] 2 Ch. 48.

persons interested in the estate of a deceased person (*l*). But the court will not stop redemption on account of the absence of a party who cannot be found if the mortgagee runs no risk (*m*).

Owner of equity of redemption.—The mortgagor himself, or the owner for the time being of the whole, or, if the equity of redemption is held jointly, all the joint owners, must be present in every action in which the question of redemption arises between mortgagees; because after giving liberty to the later mortgagee to redeem the first, the order is, that the former in his turn may be redeemed by the mortgagor, in default of which the latter shall be foreclosed (*n*). But if he were not party to the action, his right of redemption would remain open and the first mortgagee would be exposed to another action (*o*). The mortgagor, however, need not be joined in a redemption action between the mortgagee and his derivative or sub-mortgagee.

The assignee of the equity of redemption stands in the place of the mortgagor for the purpose of this rule.

The owner of the equity of redemption of one of two properties comprised in the same mortgage cannot sue for redemption of the one property separately (*p*).

Representation of beneficiaries by trustees, etc.—As regards beneficiaries and persons interested in the estate of a deceased person it is sufficient for proceedings to be commenced by or against the trustees or personal representatives, leaving it to the court to direct beneficiaries to be joined as parties if necessary (*q*). Thus proceedings can be commenced by or against fiduciary mortgagors alone, leaving it to the court in each case to add beneficiaries if the circumstances require that they should be separately represented (*r*).

Where beneficiaries are necessary parties.—Although trustees now represent the persons beneficially interested in the mortgaged property yet where such beneficiaries are many and fluctuating, and

---

(*l*) See *infra*.

(*m*) *Faulkner* v. *Daniel* (1843), 3 Hare, 199, at p. 212. The rule that the court must have all interested parties before it is only a prima facie rule: *Re Richerson, Scales* v. *Heyhoe* (*No. 2*), [1893] 3 Ch. 146.

(*n*) The mortgagor must also be a party to an action in which the validity of the mortgage is contested: *Thompson* v. *Baskerville* (1688), 3 Rep. in Ch. 215; and see *Stackhouse* v. *Countess of Jersey* (1861), 1 Johns. & H. 721.

(*o*) *Fell* v. *Brown* (1787), 2 Bro. CC. 276; *Palk* v. *Lord Clinton, supra*; and see *Ramsbottom* v. *Wallis* (1835), 5 L.J. Ch. 92; *Caddick* v. *Cook* (1863), 9 Jur. (N.S.) 454.

(*p*) *Hall* v. *Heward* (1886), 32 Ch. D. 430 (C.A.).

(*q*) R.S.C. Ord. 15, r. 14; C.C.R. Ord. 5, r. 7.

(*r*) The practice was formerly as follows: Where trustees were suing for redemption they represented the trust estate, if, in fact they had, like executors, complete power over the estate, or had under their control funds applicable for redemption: *Mills* v. *Jennings* (1880), 13 Ch. D. 639 (C.A.); *Re Cooper, Cooper* v. *Vesey* (1882), 20 Ch. D. 611; and where the beneficiaries were infants, or the shares has been resettled, the court did not require separate representation of the infants or of persons interested under the derivative settlement: *Goldsmid* v. *Stonehewer* (1852), 9 Hare App. xxxviii. And see *Watts* v. *Lane* (1901), 84 L.T. 144.

If the trustees were also executors, it was unnecessary to join the beneficiaries: *Re Mitchell, Wavell* v. *Mitchell* (1892), 65 L.T. 851 (explaining *Wavell* v. *Mitchell* (1891), 64 L.T. 560): *Re Booth and Kettlewell's Contract* (1892), 67 L.T. 550. The former cases may still furnish guidance as to the manner in which the discretion of the court as to adding parties will be exercised, but they do not govern the initiation of proceedings.

questions arise between the trustees as to the proper mode of protecting their interests, some or all ought to be parties (*s*).

Personal representatives.—Without the assistance of the R.S.C. and C.C.R. (*t*), the executor or administrator is the proper person to sue for redemption (*u*). But where there is only an administration for the purposes of the action, *durante minore aetate*, the court will probably exercise its power to add parties if, but not unless (*v*), the beneficiaries might suffer from the limited power of the administrator (*x*).

Creditors under deed of arrangement.—Unless the trustees have some interest distinct from the creditors (*y*), they represent the creditors for the purpose of actions relating to the property comprised in the deed (*z*).

Assignment of equity during action.—In case of an assignment, creation or devolution of any estate or title *pendente lite*, the cause or matter does not become defective, but may be continued by or against the person to or upon whom such estate or title has come or devolved. And in case of a transmission of interest or liability new parties may be added if it becomes necessary or desirable (*a*). But whether an assignee is made a party to an action or not, it is a rule arising out of the maxim *"pendente lite nihil innovatur"*, that he who purchases an interest in litigated property pending the action acquires for the purposes of the action no right distinct from that of his assignor (*b*). The rule is grounded upon the reason, that any person interested in the subject-matter of an action might otherwise harass the other parties to the action by making occasions for the addition of new parties. It is therefore limited in its operation to the particular action pending which the assignment is made, and does not prevent the assignee from enforcing their rights in any other action (*c*).

If, therefore, pending an action for redemption, the equity of redemption is assigned by the mortgagor, the assignee will be bound (*d*).

(*s*) See *Minn* v. *Stant* (1851), 12 Beav. 190; and *Re De Leeuw, Jakens* v. *Central Advance and Discount Corpn.*, [1922] 2 Ch. 540.

(*t*) See p. 572, *supra*.

(*u*) See the Administration of Estates Act 1925, ss. 1 (1), 3 (1).

(*v*) *Faulkner* v. *Daniel* (1843), 3 Hare, 199, 208; *Davis* v. *Chanter* (1848), 2 Ph. 545; *Maclean* v. *Dawson* (1859), 27 Beav. 369.

(*x*) As in *Ellis* v. *Deane* (1827), Beat. 5; *Clough* v. *Dixon* (1841), 10 Sim. 564; *Groves* v. *Lane* (1852), 16 Jur. 854. The authority of an administrator *durante minore* is, while it lasts, the same as that of an ordinary administrator: *Re Cope, Cope* v. *Cope* (1880), 16 Ch. D. 49.

Where the mortgagor dies during the course of the proceedings his personal representative should seek an order under R.S.C. Ord. 15, r. 7 to carry on the proceedings.

(*y*) Though the creditors had no right of redemption apart from the trustees (*Troughton* v. *Binkes* (1801), 6 Ves. 573) they may, in this exceptional case, be parties.

(*z*) See *Morley* v. *Morley* (1858), 25 Beav. 253.

(*a*) R.S.C. Ord. 15, r. 7.

(*b*) Co. Litt. 102 b; *Metcalfe* v. *Pulvertoft* (1813), 2 Ves. & B. 200; *Bishop of Winchester* v. *Paine* (1805), 11 Ves. 194. And as to adjusting the rights of an assignee of a later mortgagee after judgment for foreclosure *nisi* by which his assignor's interest is bound, see *Booth* v. *Creswicke* (1837), 8 Sim. 352.

(*c*) *Metcalfe* v. *Pultertoft*, *supra*.

(*d*) *Garth* v. *Ward* (1741), 2 Atk. 174; *Eades* v. *Harris* (1842), 1 Y. & C.C.C. 230, 234; *Patch* v. *Ward* (1867), 3 Ch. App. 203, 208. The rule applies as well to assignments which affect the whole equitable estate or interest in question in the action as to those by which one of several parties assigns his or her separate interest: *Eades* v. *Harris*, *supra*.

But if the other party to the action desires to have the assignee *pendente lite* before the court, the latter cannot object, it being desirable that all persons interested should be present (*e*). And if a legal interest with which it is necessary to deal passes by the assignment, the assignee's presence becomes necessary; because, although the legal interest will be bound in his hands, so as to make him a trustee for the person entitled under the order, yet, unless he is joined, he cannot be compelled to reconvey (*f*).

Involuntary alienation.—The rule does not apply to cases of involuntary alienation, and, accordingly, where the mortgagor becomes bankrupt, or a judgment creditor obtains a charge on the property, the trustee in bankruptcy (*g*) or the creditor (*h*) should be joined as a party.

B—PERSONS INTERESTED IN THE SECURITY

The holder of the security.—The person in whom the legal interest in the security becomes vested, whether originally by the mortgage (*i*), or by assignment (*k*), and though he is only a trustee for the persons entitled to the mortgage money (*l*), is a necessary party to an action for redemption (*m*), so that a reconveyance may be obtained (*n*).

But one who has agreed to purchase an equity of redemption cannot make the mortgagee either of a legal (*o*), or an equitable (*p*) interest, a party to an action to compel specific performance of a contract in which he has no concern, or the performance of which will not affect his security or interfere with his remedies (*q*).

Neither the mortgagor (*r*), nor the mortgagee (*s*), is allowed to

---

(*e*) *Campbell* v. *Holyland* (1877), 7 Ch. D. 166.

(*f*) *Bishop of Winchester* v. *Paine, supra; Barry* v. *Wrey* (1827), 3 Russ. 465. In *Coles* v. *Forrest* (1847), 10 Beav. 552, the legal interest appears to have been assigned.

(*g*) *Wood* v. *Surr* (1854), 19 Beav. 551.

(*h*) *Re Parbola, Ltd., Blackburn* v. *Parbola, Ltd.,* [1909] 2 Ch. 437.

(*i*) *Wood* v. *Williams* (1819), 4 Mad. 186.

(*k*) *Wetherell* v. *Collins* (1818), 3 Mad. 255. The mortgagor will not be allowed in a redemption action to contest the mortgagee's title before redeeming: *Smith* v. *Valence* (1655), 1 Rep. in Ch. (3rd Edn.), 90.

(*l*) A person who claims to be interested in part of a mortgage debt vested in another is sufficiently represented by the latter in an action to set aside the security and should not be made a party: *Emmet* v. *Tottenham* (1864), 10 Jur. N.S. 1090. As to a trustee who has not been fully discharged from the trust by the appointment of a successor, see *Adams* v. *Paynter* (1844), 1 Coll. 530.

The trustee of the legal interest in the security having no adverse rights may properly be, and to save expense to the mortgagor ought to be, a co-plaintiff: *Smith* v. *Chichester*, (1842), 2 Dru. & War. 393; unless he refuses, or is likely to refuse, and then he should be made a defendant: *Browne* v. *Lockhart* (1840), 10 Sim. 420.

(*m*) *Wetherell* v. *Collins, supra.*

(*n*) The rule is not affected by the present automatic effect of a receipt on the discharge of the mortgage. The mortgagee is not a necessary party to an action brought by the mortgagor in possession to prevent injury to the mortgaged property: *Fairclough* v. *Marshall* (1878), 4 Ex. D. 37; *supra*, p. 336.

(*o*) *Tasker* v. *Small* (1837), 3 My. & Cr. 63.

(*p*) *Hall* v. *Laver* (1838), 3 Y. & C. Ex. 191.

(*q*) It is the same where one has agreed to purchase a property which is afterwards mortgaged: *Long* v. *Bowring* (1864), 33 Beav. 585. Both cases are based on the principle that he who claims a right to redeem must first have acquired the mortgagor's title to a reconveyance: *Franklyn* v. *Fern* (1740), Barn. Ch. 30, 32.

(*r*) *Darcy* v. *Callan* (1836), 1 Jones, Ex. Ir. 614.

(*s*) *Wroe* v. *Clayton* (1839), 9 L.J. Ch. 107; *Roberts* v. *Clayton* (1796), 3 Anst. 715.

dispute the title of the other; but if the mortgagor's title is impeached by the action, the mortgagee, having a great interest in supporting it, and being often in possession of the deeds, ought to be joined (*t*).

Purchasers from the mortgagee.—The purchaser under a power of sale in a mortgage is not a necessary party to an action by the mortgagor against the mortgagee to recover the surplus purchase money (*u*). But persons with whom the mortgagee has dealt wrongfully for the produce of the mortgaged estate are proper parties to a redemption action, as being in possession of the value of the converted part of the estate, though they no longer hold the property *in specie* (*x*).

Transferee of mortgage.—Ordinarily, where the mortgage has been assigned, and the mortgagor sues for redemption, the mortgagee need not be a party in respect of the accounts (*y*). For if the mortgagor was not a party to, or if he had not notice of the assignment, the assignee, having agreed to stand in the place of the original mortgagee, is bound by all the equities subsisting between him and the mortgagor, and cannot afterwards object to accounts which have been taken with the assignor (*z*); and where the mortgagor was a party, or had notice, because the assignor's accounts have been admitted by both parties (*a*).

But if the mortgagee had been in possession, and the mortgagor seeks an account of a surplus alleged to have been received, the mortgagee, notwithstanding his assignment, must be joined with the assignee, so that he may account for what he received in his time (*b*).

If only part of the security has been assigned to a derivative mortgagee for a less sum than the original debt, then upon an action for redemption, the original mortgagee, as well as the assignee, must be a party; for he claims an interest, *viz.* a right to redeem the assignee and prevent another account (*c*).

Personal representatives.—Both the mortgage debt and the estate or interest of the mortgagee in the mortgaged property devolve on his death upon his personal representatives, and they are the persons to represent the security in a redemption action unless by transfer or assent or other means they have divested themselves of their title (*d*).

Where a mortgagee has no legal personal representative, who (if

---

(*t*) *Copis* v. *Middleton* (1818), 2 Mad. 410. *Cf. Hitchins* v. *Lander* (1807), Coop. G. 34, where the validity of a lease was in dispute and the lessor's mortgagee was held to be a necessary party. As to pleading a paramount title to an action for redemption, see *Meder* v. *Birt* (1726), Gilb. Rep. in Eq. 185.

(*u*) *Minn* v. *Stant* (1851), 15 Beav. 49.

(*x*) *Hood* v. *Easton* (1856), 2 Jur. N.S. 917.

(*y*) *Anon.* (1680), Freem. Ch. Rep. 59; 2 Eq. Cas. Abr. 594.

(*z*) *Hill* v. *Adams* (1741), 2 Atk. 39; *Chambers* v. *Goldwin* (1804), 9 Ves. 254, 269; *Norrish* v. *Marshall* (1821), 5 Mad. 475.

(*a*) *Anon.* (1680), Freem. Ch. Rep. 59; *Car* v. *Boulter* (1697), Freem. Ch. Rep. 217.

(*b*) *Anon., supra.* It has been suggested that this case was overruled by *Chambers* v. *Goldwin, supra.* But Lord ELDON's observations in that case did not extend to the case put here, of a mortgagee in possession, and an account sought of the surplus received. Upon the principle of the case cited was decided *Lowther* v. *Carlton* (1740), as appears by the report in Barn. Ch. 358; also reported 2 Atk. 139.

(*c*) *Norrish* v. *Marshall, supra; Hobart* v. *Abbot* (1731), 2 P. Wms. 643; *Re Burrell, Burrell* v. *Smith* (1869), L.R. 7 Eq. 399. Yet if in such case the objection of the absence of the original mortgagee is not taken until the hearing, the case will be allowed to proceed without him, if being a witness, he has sworn that he is fully satisfied and retains no interest: *Norrish* v. *Marshall, supra.*

(*d*) Administration of Estates Act 1925, ss. 1 (1), 3 (1).

existing), would be a necessary defendant, the court may now proceed in his absence, or, after giving proper notices, appoint someone to represent the estate (*e*).

Mortgages to several.—If a mortgage of land is made to several persons they necessarily, under the present law, take the mortgage term jointly, since land cannot be held in undivided shares (*f*), but they may be either joint tenants or tenants in common of the mortgage money. If they are joint tenants—that is, if the money belongs to them on a joint account—then, on the death of one, the survivors or survivor are entitled to the mortgage money, and the personal representatives of the deceased mortgagee need not be joined in a redemption action. If they are tenants in common, the personal representatives should be joined, although the mortgaged estate vests in the survivors or survivor (*g*). But this will be so only if the mortgage expresses that the money is advanced by or belongs to the mortgagees in stated sums or shares. If the advance is expressed to be made out of moneys belonging to the mortgagees on a joint account, or if the mortgage is simply made to the mortgagees jointly, then they are deemed to be joint tenants (*h*).

Action to redeem by subsequent mortgagee. Redeem up, foreclose down.—In the case of successive mortgages a later mortgagee must make all mortgagees subsequent to himself, as well as the mortgagor, parties in an action to redeem the mortgage immediately prior to his mortgage (*i*). If he seeks to redeem any other prior mortgage he must make parties all mortgagees between himself and the mortgagee whom he seeks to redeem (*k*).

III—THE JUDGMENT

Order for redemption.—The common form of order for redemption directs that an account be taken of what is due to the mortgagee under the mortgage (*l*), including his taxed costs of the redemption action,

---

(*e*) R.S.C. Ord. 15, r. 15. For proceedings against estates, see R.S.C. Ord. 15, r. 6A. When the mortgagee dies during the course of the proceedings, they should be carried on against his personal representatives (R.S.C. Ord. 15, r. 7), if any, or his estate (R.S.C. Ord. 15, r. 6A (3)).

(*f*) See p. 139, *supra*.

(*g*) *Vickers* v. *Cowell* (1839), 1 Beav. 529.

(*h*) Law of Property Act 1925, s. 111; see p. 258, *supra*.

If payment is made to one joint mortgagee during the lifetime of the others, this is a good discharge of the debt at law: but the equitable rule prevails, and the security is only discharged to the extent of the payee's beneficial interest at the time (if any), although he is ultimately the last survivor in the joint account: *Matson* v. *Dennis* (1864), 4 De G.J. & S. 345; *Powell* v. *Brodhurst*, [1901] 2 Ch. 160.

(*i*) *Fell* v. *Brown* (1787), 2 Bro. C.C. 276; *Johnson* v. *Holdsworth* (1850), 1 Sim N.S. 106, at p. 109; *Farmer* v. *Curtis* (1829), 2 Sim. 466; *Rose* v. *Page* (1829), 2 Sim. 471; *Ramsbottom* v. *Wallis* (1835), 5 L.J. Ch. 92; *Richards* v. *Cooper* (1842), 5 Beav. 304; *Slade* v. *Rigg* (1843), 3 Hare, 35; *Teevan* v. *Smith* (1882), 20 Ch. D. 724 (C.A.). See p. 468, *supra*.

(*k*) *Teevan* v. *Smith*, *supra*.

(*l*) The judgment will be prefaced by a declaration that the right of redemption is subsisting, if this has been in dispute: *Holmes* v. *Turner* (1843), 7 Hare 367, note and form; *Faulkner* v. *Daniel* (1843), 3 Hare 199; *Carlon* v. *Farlar* (1845), 8 Beav. 526.

It declares, where necessary, the rights and priorities of the various incumbrancers (*Jones* v. *Griffith* (1845), 2 Coll. 207), and the order may be made without prejudice to the rights of incumbrancers between themselves.

and orders that the mortgagor pay to the mortgagee within six
months (*m*) from the date of the master's certificate the amount
certified to be due, and upon his doing so the mortgagee is ordered to
surrender or give a statutory receipt and deliver to the mortgagee
the title deeds (*n*).

Successive mortgages.—Where there are successive mortgages,
the judgment proceeds on the principle that the second mortgagee,
as the first assignee of the equity of redemption, fills the place and
acquires the rights of the mortgagor (*o*).   He has therefore the first
right to redeem, upon payment of what is due to the first mortgagee;
but, in default of payment, he is foreclosed.   This process is carried on
as to all the successive incumbrancers, until the mortgagor alone
remains, when he may in like manner redeem, or, in default, stand
foreclosed.   The judgment provides for the exercise of the rights by
directing that in case the second mortgagee shall redeem the first,
an account shall be taken of what is due to the person so redeeming on
his own security, and for what he has paid the first mortgagee with
interest thereon (*p*) and costs; and upon payment of the aggregate of
these sums the third mortgagee has liberty to redeem the second in
default of which he is foreclosed; and a further account having been
taken of what is due to the second mortgagee in respect of his own
debt, and of his payments, the next mortgagee, or, if there is none, the
mortgagor will be at liberty to redeem.   Upon non-payment to the
last person to be redeemed of what he has paid to the prior mortgagee
and of his own principal, interest and costs the owner of the mortgagor
stands absolutely foreclosed, and the property becomes that of the
mortgagee who cleared off the rest free from any mortgages (*q*).

Extension of time for payment.—The time for payment will not

Special directions may have to be given for the account.   Where the mortgagee has
been in possession the order directs as against the mortgagee an account of the rents
and profits (see p. 620, *infra*).   To the amount due to the mortgagee are added all sums
to which he may be declared to be entitled for improvements (see p. 352, *supra*), or
for payments in respect of or for the protection of his security, or the property (see
p. 351, *supra*).   If the order for redemption is made after tender, the account is directed
of what was due on the date of the tender with consequential directions to meet the
alternative results of the amount due exceeding or not exceeding the amount ordered:
Greenwood v. *Sutcliffe*, [1892] 1 Ch. 1.

The mortgagor in an action for redemption against the mortgagee and his sub-
mortgagee can have the estate discharged on payment into court of the amount found
due to the mortgagee without waiting for the settlement of the accounts and inquiries
between the mortgagee and sub-mortgagee: *Lysaght* v. *Westmacott* (1864), 33 Beav.
417.   And as to an order in a redemption action by a second mortgagee, where a later
mortgage subsequently made a sub-mortgage, see *Booth* v. *Creswicke* (1837), 8 Sim.
352.

(*m*) *I.e.*, calendar months: R.S.C. Ord. 3, r. 1.

(*n*) For forms of order, see 28 Ency. Court Forms (2nd Edn.), pp. 117 *et seq.*   And
see the judgment in Action for Foreclosure, pp. 396, *et seq. supra*.

(*o*) Thus, in taking the account the second mortgagee may assert such equity as the
mortgagor himself might have to exclude any particular item: *Mainland* v. *Upjohn*
(1889), 41 Ch. D. 126.

(*p*) See p. 631, *infra*.

(*q*) As to costs where an intermediate mortgagee redeems the first, who holds a later
mortgage, see *Mutual Life Assurance Society* v. *Langley* (1886), 32 Ch. D. 460.   As to
an action by a later mortgagee of two properties, subject to separate mortgages, see
Pelly v. *Wathen* (1849), 7 Hare, 351; on app. 1 De G.M. & G. 16; *Hallett* v. *Furze* (1885),
31 Ch. D. 312.

generally be extended in an action for redemption (r). But in special circumstances the time for payment may be extended (s).

IV—DISMISSAL OF THE ACTION FOR REDEMPTION

Affidavit of non-payment.—The action for redemption will be dismissed, on summons in chambers, upon production of the certificate of the amount due, and of an affidavit of attendance and non-payment of the money (t); even though, after the time fixed for payment, the mortgagor has tendered the principal and interest, with an additional sum for interest, to the day of tender (u).

Dismissal operates as foreclosure.—Dismissal of the action to redeem, by reason of default in payment of the money, or for any other cause than for want of prosecution, operates as a judgment of foreclosure (x); because the mortgagor admits by his action the title of the mortgagee and the debt; and if he does not discharge it, he is not allowed to harass the mortgagee by another action for the same purpose.

But if an action to redeem an equitable mortgage is dismissed by the mortgagor it has not the effect of a foreclosure, because the mortgagee does not get the relief which he would have in a foreclosure action, viz. a conveyance (y). And if the mortgagee has refused redemption, except on the terms of the discharge of another security, there is no admission by the mortgagor of the debt upon the security for which the foreclosure would operate (y); and this seems to show that the rule would not operate under such circumstances in the case of a legal mortgage.

Right to redeem refused.—The action will be dismissed at the hearing if the right to redeem is rejected by the court; and the dismissal was held upon appeal to be proper, where the plaintiff having claimed an absolute right to redeem upon certain terms, the decision was that he had no equity to redeem upon those terms (z).

So an action for redemption, by a person who is subject to the same equities as the mortgagor, will be dismissed as against a defendant,

---

(r) *Novosielski* v. *Wakefield* (1811), 17 Ves. 417; *Faulkner* v. *Bolton* (1835), 7 Sim 319.

(s) *Novosielski* v. *Wakefield, supra*; *Collinson* v. *Jeffrey*, [1896] 1 Ch. 644. As to extension of time, see pp. 403 *et seq., supra*.

(t) *Stuart* v. *Worrall* (1785), 1 Bro. C.C. 581; *Proctor* v. *Oates* (1740), 2 Atk. 140; *Newsham* v. *Gray* (1742), 2 Atk. 287.

(u) *Faulkner* v. *Bolton, supra*. For a form of order, see 28 Ency. Court Forms (2nd Edn.), p. 118.

(x) *Cholmley* v. *Countess of Oxford* (1742), 2 Atk. 267; *Bishop of Winchester* v. *Paine* (1805), 11 Ves. 194; *Hansard* v. *Hardy* (1812), 18 Ves. 455; *Inman* v. *Wearing* (1850), 3 De G. & Sm. 729. See *Garth* v. *Ward* (1741), 2 Atk. 174; *Wood* v. *Surr* (1854), 19 Beav. 551.

In the case of successive mortgages, if the mortgagor is the plaintiff, the effect of excluding his interest is that the last incumbrancer becomes quasi-mortgagor, the prior mortgagees ranking according to their priorities: *Cottingham* v. *Earl of Shrewsbury* (1843), 3 Hare 627, at p. 637.

The mortgagee may apply by motion or summons for possession: see R.S.C. Ord. 88, r. 8.

(y) *Marshall* v. *Shrewsbury* (1875), 10 Ch. 250.

(z) *Seagrave* v. *Pope* (1851), 1 De G.M. & G. 783.

who, as between himself and the mortgagor, is not liable to be foreclosed by incumbrancers on the estate, having prior rights to such
defendant (*a*).

The action for redemption will also be dismissed, if, at the hearing,
the plaintiff refuses to ask for any accounts (*b*). This may happen
when the plaintiff, being a later incumbrancer, finds that the security
is altogether insufficient.

Disclaiming defendants.—It is the practice to dismiss the action
as against defendants who disclaim all interest in the mortgaged
premises, where such defendants are able to make and do make a
complete and valid disclaimer; and provided the disclaimer is complete,
it is equally good, whether it was made before or after the commencement of the action (*c*).

But if the disclaimer is insufficient in form, as where the pleadings
admit that the property is vested in the party, and contain an entire
or partial disclaimer only of an interest therein, or is otherwise
ineffectual, the judgment will be for foreclosure (*d*).

(*a*) Thus, where A was a mortgagor, B and C, incumbrancers, and X tenant in tail
in remainder, whose estate, as between himself and A was not liable to the incumbrances
of B and C (having been exonerated therefrom by A's covenant); an action by E, a
subsequent judgment creditor of A, was dismissed against A; because E was not in the
position of a purchaser for valuable consideration without notice, but was subject to
the same equities as A, and could not compel X to pay off B and C: *Hughes* v. *Williams*
(1852), 3 Mac. & G. 683. But, *semble*, that X should first have had a permissive right
to redeem. See *Chappell* v. *Rees* (1852), 1 De G.M. & G. 393, where the same principle
was applied in an action by the assignee of the insolvent mortgagor and covenantor.

(*b*) *Gibson* v. *Nicol* (1846), 9 Beav. 403.

(*c*) *Aldworth* v. *Robinson* (1840), 2 Beav. 287; *Thompson* v. *Kendall* (1840), 9 Sim.
397; *Silcock* v. *Roynon* (1843), 2 Y. & C.C.C. 376; *Lock* v. *Lomas* (1851), 15 Jur. 162;
and *semble* also in *Ford* v. *Earl of Chesterfield* (1853), 16 Beav. 516; *Vale* v. *Merideth*
(1854), 18 Jur. 992; *Thorneycroft* v. *Crockett* (1848), 2 H.L.C. 239.

(*d*) *Appleby* v. *Duke* (1842), 1 Hare, 303; *Collins* v. *Shirley* (1830), 1 Russ. & Myl.
638, and cited in *Thompson* v. *Kendall* (1840), 9 Sim. 399, from Reg. Lib.

CHAPTER 30

The Release of the Debt or Security

Generally.—The whole or part of the debt or the security may be released, either before or after the date for repayment, upon the payment of the whole or part of the loan or without such payment.

Release of the debt.—By releasing the debt the security for the debt is released (a). To be binding a release of a debt must generally be made for consideration (b), or, if not so made, under seal. While an alleged release or forgiveness of the debt cannot be established merely by showing that the creditor had expressed an intention to release the debt (c) yet where the creditor has so acted that the debtor has done acts by which his position has been altered, the creditor will not be allowed to enforce his security (d). Moreover, a declaration of present forgiveness of the debt, though only verbal and unsupported by consideration may be effective to release the debt, if it is accompanied by the delivery of the deeds to the debtor (e). And if the mortgagee declares himself a trustee of the mortgaged premises for the mortgagor, this will be equivalent to a release (f).

A release of the debt is usually met with on the disposition of the whole of the equity of redemption, either on sale, or, for example, on its transfer to new trustees. The purchaser or other assignee of the equity of redemption is not liable on the covenant for payment (g), and the mortgagor remains liable. But the assignee will be liable to indemnify the mortgagor, even if there is no express indemnity covenant (h). On a disposition of the equity of redemption the mortgagee may release the mortgagor or his successor in title from the mortgage debt in consideration of a covenant by the purchaser or donee, or, for example, the new trustees, for payment and to observe and perform the mortgagor's covenants in the mortgage deed. The

---

(a) Shep. Touchst. Prest. 342; *Cowper* v. *Green* (1841), 7 M. & W. 633.

(b) See, *e.g.*, *Taylor* v. *Manners* (1865), L.R. 1 Ch. 48.

(c) But if the intention is there and the mortgagee cancels the mortgage this is as much a release as cancelling a bond.

(d) *Yeomans* v. *Williams* (1865), L.R. 1 Eq. 184. This will be more readily applied to the release of interest than principal, because the intention to release the latter would probably be evidenced by the giving up of the security.

(e) Or where the debtor becomes the creditor's personal representative: *Strong* v. *Bird* (1874), L.R. 18 Eq. 315. So long as the intention to forgive continued until the creditor's death: *Re Wale*, [1956] 3 All E.R. 280.

(f) *Re Hancock, Hancock* v. *Berrey* (1888), 57 L.J. Ch. 793.

(g) *Re Errington*, [1894] 1 Q.B. 11. And see p. 295, *supra*.

(h) *Waring* v. *Ward* (1802), 7 Ves. 332. And see p. 295, *supra*.

release and covenant may be included in the transfer or be affected by a separate document (*i*).

Release of the security.—As we have seen (*k*), on payment of the mortgage monies, a mortgage term becomes a satisfied term and, so it seems, a legal charge is discharged. Therefore, where the whole of the mortgage monies are paid, strictly speaking no further documentation is required though, from the practical point of view of proof of the intent to discharge, it is desirable.

In the case of a mortgage by demise, for an express release or surrender a deed is required to convey the legal estate (*l*), (but, without any formality, there may be an implied surrender, where, for example, the mortgagee hands back the mortgage deed and treats the mortgage as at an end (*m*)). So any mortgage may be discharged, informally, on proof of intent to discharge it, *e.g.*, by cancellation (*n*). But where the release is gratuitous, the appropriate formalities will be required, unless the mortgagor can rely on having altered his position on the faith of a declaration of intent to release (*o*).

The form of the release of property secured by legal mortgage depends on the circumstances (*p*). Usually it is made for value to enable the mortgagor to sell the property. In such circumstances the mortgagee may join in the conveyance rather than making a statutory receipt, where that is appropriate, or a separate deed of surrender or release followed by the conveyance. Where the mortgagee joins in the conveyance, unless the property, if any, remaining in mortgage is sufficient security for the mortgage debt, he will usually require the whole or part of the purchase money to be paid to him in discharge or reduction of the mortgage debt.

Where a sale of the property to be released is not contemplated a statutory receipt should be used, if the release is in consideration of the repayment of the monies secured by the mortgage, but otherwise a deed of surrender, where the mortgage was by demise or sub-demise, or release, in the case of charge, will be appropriate (*q*).

Release of security under equitable mortgage.—Such a mortgage does not create any legal estate or interest in favour of the mortgagee and no formal deed of release is required. A release of the whole of

---

(*i*) For release of debts by will, see Theobald on *Wills* (13th Edn.), paras 595, 596. The appointment of a debtor as executor may extinguish the cause of action in debt, but the executor may remain liable under an equitable obligation to account to those interested in the estate for the amount of the debt; see *Stamp Duties Commissioner* v. *Bone*, [1976] 2 All E.R. 354 (P.C.). For forms of surrender and release of mortgage where the debt has been released by the will of the mortgagee, see 14 Ency. Forms and Precedents (4th Edn.), pp. 853, 854, 856, 857.

(*k*) See p. 550, *supra*.

(*l*) Law of Property Act 1925, s. 52.

(*m*) *Haigh* v. *Brooks* (1839), 10 A.D. & El. 309.

(*n*) See the 7th Edn. of this work, pp. 642–644; *Coote on Mortgages*, (9th Edn.), pp. 1407 *et seq.*

(*o*) See the 7th Edn., p. 643; *Coote, ubi supra*, pp. 1408–9.

(*p*) For forms, see 14 Ency. Forms and Precedents (4th Edn.), pp. 841 *et seq.*

(*q*) Debentures are released in the appropriate manner according to what sort of charge had been created, *i.e.*, specific legal charge, equitable charge or floating charge (as to the latter, see (*r*). Application should be made to the Companies Registry on the official form for entry of release. Any land charge registration in respect of the mortgage should be cancelled (see p. 555, *supra*). For registered land, see p. 553, *supra*).

such property may be effected by the cancellation of the mortgage or a simple receipt. The release of part of equitably mortgaged property, is generally effected by a written statement or letter from the mortgagee that he has no charge on the particular property (*r*).

Partial discharge of security by trustee-mortgagees.—A trustee-mortgagee may release part of his security on receipt of the whole of the purchase money produced thereby (*s*).

Partial discharge of leasehold property.—The statutory provisions as to the realisation of leasehold mortgages (*t*) do not apply where the mortgage term does not comprise the whole of the land included in the leasehold reversion, unless the rent (if any) payable in respect of that reversion has been apportioned, either legally or informally, as respects the land affected, or the rent is of no money value or no rent is reserved, and unless the lessee's covenants and the conditions (if any) have been apportioned either expressly or by implication, as respects the land affected (*u*). Accordingly a release should never be executed as to part of mortgaged leaseholds without such apportionment.

Release of part of land affected from a judgment.—A partial release does not affect the judgment charge as respects any land not specifically released (*x*).

Lost security.—Where the mortgage deed has been lost and but for that fact a statutory receipt would have been appropriate, a release or surrender will be necessary.

Release of surety (*y*).—The fact that a creditor accepts further security from the principal debtor does not release the surety (*z*). But a surety is entitled to the benefit of collateral security (*a*). A release of the collateral security will release the surety (*b*).

Release of collateral security.—For discharge of collateral security, see p. 557, *supra*.

(*r*) But see (1962), 26 Conv. (N.S.), pp. 449–453 (R. G. Rowley). For property subject to a floating charge a letter from some officer of the company or its solicitor a letter of non-crystallisation suffices.

(*s*) *Re Morell and Chapman's Contract*, [1915] 1 Ch. 162. A purchaser of part of mortgaged lands who has notice that the mortgagees are trustees should not accept a conveyance from such trustee-mortgagees without satisfying himself that the security will not be substantially impaired, see Williams on *Vendor and Purchaser* (4th Edn.), 655, 656. But see Law of Property Act 1925, s. 113 (p. 255, *supra*).

(*t*) See Law of Property Act 1925, s. 89.

(*u*) Law of Property Act 1925, s. 89 (6) as amended.

(*x*) *Ibid.*, s. 71.

(*y*) And see pp. 584 *et seq.*, *infra*.

(*z*) *Twopenny* v. *Young* (1824), 3 B. & C. 208; *Eyre* v. *Everett* (1826), 2 Russ. 381, at p. 384.

(*a*) *Dixon* v. *Steel*, [1901] 2 Ch. 602.

(*b*) *Pearl* v. *Deacon* (1857), 1 De G. & J. 461.

CHAPTER 31

Waiver

I—WAIVER GENERALLY

Nature of waiver.—As regards the debt itself a waiver is ineffectual unless it amounts to a release (a), but the rights of the creditor under his security may be varied by waiver, provided he is cognizant of his rights (b). Waiver may be express or implied.

Express waiver.—The extent of an express waiver is governed by the language used. If the waiver is clearly limited to part of the security, the mortgagee's rights over the remainder of the security will be unaffected. Accordingly, where a mortgagee surrendered his legal interest in a leasehold security to enable the mortgagor to provide another security, but stipulated that the surrender was without prejudice to any other security he might have for his debt, he and his assignee were held to be still entitled to the benefit of the covenants in the mortgage; the legal interest only, and not the covenants, being within the operation of the surrender (c). If the waiver is on the face of it clearly a general one, it will not be restricted on the representation of one of the parties that a more limited one was intended (d).

Implied waiver.—As stated above, there can only be a waiver if the creditor is aware of his rights (b). The court will not be anxious to imply waiver from a mere omission, or other circumstances, from which the intention cannot fairly be inferred (e). Thus, where it was provided by the mortgage deed, that, as between the mortgagor and his surety, a certain part of the security given by the principal should be primarily liable to the debt, without mentioning the rest, it was held, that the surety upon paying off the debt had not lost, by the omission, the right to a transfer of the whole security (f).

Taking additional security.—If a creditor, having a security on the funds of his debtor for part of his debt, takes another security on the same funds for his whole debt, the earlier debt keeps its force and

---

(a) A mere waiver signifies nothing more than an expression of intention not to insist on the right and as such is unenforceable: *Stackhouse* v. *Barnston* (1805), 10 Ves. 453. But the plaintiff's conduct may be such as to estop him from asserting the continuance of the liability: *Yeomans* v. *Williams* (1865), L.R. 1 Eq. 184.

(b) *Vyvyan* v. *Vyvyan* (1861), 30 Beav. 65.

(c) *Greenwood* v. *Taylor* (1845), 14 Sim. 505; sub nom. *A.-G.* v. *Cox, Pearce* v. *A.-G.* (1850), 3 H.L.C. 240.

(d) *Drought* v. *Jones* (1840), 4 Dru. & War. 174.

(e) The sale by a mortgagee of mortgaged chattels discharged a collateral security of land in *Greenberg* v. *Rapoport* (1970) 10 D.L.R. (3d) 737.

(f) *Bowker* v. *Bull* (1830), 1 Sim. (N.S.) 29. See p. 586, *infra*.

may be separately dealt with (g). Similarly where a creditor, having a security upon his debtor's funds, takes afterwards, either alone (but on behalf of himself and another creditor), or jointly with such other creditor, a security for both debts on the same funds, the separate security keeps its force and may be separately dealt with. Where the surety pays off the debt or interest in arrear and his payment has been included in the security of a subsequent mortgagee, the surety having taken a note from the latter to that effect, an intention by the surety to take an additional security, and not a waiver of his old right, is to be inferred (h).

Taking substituted security.—When it is contended that the benefit of a security has been waived by the acceptance of another security in its place, it is for the owner of the estate to show that it was discharged by the taking of the new security and not for the creditor to disprove the substitution of the new security for the old. The mere acceptance of a personal security for interest in arrear, or other charge whether express or implied, is therefore not a waiver of the original security, even if a receipt is given for the amount (i). The absence of any mention of the original security, and the reservation of interest at a different rate from that which was secured by it, have been treated as evidence that the new security was taken by way of substitution (j).

II—WAIVER AGAINST SURETIES (k)

Variation of the terms of the mortgage.—The creditor may by various acts or omissions waive or lose his right against the surety for the principal debtor. This, for instance, will happen where, without the surety's consent, and without reserving his rights against him (l), the creditor gives the debtor further time for payment of the debt (m). Time is only given within this rule if there is a binding agreement arrived at for good consideration (n). The rule does not apply when time is given after judgment has been obtained against both the

---

(g) See *Miln* v. *Walton* (1843), 2 Y. & C.C.C. 354 (a case dealing with a lien on the freight of a ship which arose from the discounting of bills of exchange).

(h) *Beckett* v. *Booth* (1708), 2 Eq. Cas. Abr. 595; and see *Martin* v. *Sedgwick* (1846), 9 Beav. 333.

(i) *Barret* v. *Wells* (1700), Prec. Ch. 131; *Hardwick* v. *Mynd* (1793), 1 Anst. 111; *Curtis* v. *Rush* (1814), 2 Ves. & B. 416; *Saunders* v. *Leslie* (1814), 2 Ba. & Be. 509. *Quaere*, as against a purchaser for value of a subsequent interest in the estate on the faith of an assurance (supported by the receipt) that no interest was due: see *Kemmis* v. *Stepney* (1828), 2 Mol. 85.

(j) *Re Brettle, Brettle* v. *Burdett* (1864), 2 De G.J. & S. 244.

(k) See 18 Halsbury's Laws (3rd Edn.), pp. 502–524; Rowlatt, *The Law of Principal and Surety* (3rd Edn.).

(l) *Wyke* v. *Rogers* (1852), 1 De G.M. & G. 408. The creditor's rights can be reserved when time is given: *Re Renton, Ex parte Glendinning* (1819), Buck. 517; and this is effectual although the surety is not informed: *Webb* v. *Hewitt* (1857), 3 K. & J. 438. A general reservation is usually included in the guarantee: see footnote (w), p. 585, *infra*.

(m) *Samuell* v. *Howarth* (1817), 3 Mer. 272; *Bank of Ireland* v. *Beresford* (1818), 6 Dow. 233; *Oakeley* v. *Pasheller* (1836), 10 Bli. (N.S.) 548; *Overend, Gurney & Co.* v. *Oriental Finance Corpn.* (1874), L.R. 7 H.L. 348.

(n) *Rouse* v. *Bradford Banking Co.*, [1894] A.C. 586, 594, *per* Lord HERSCHELL, L.C.

principal debtor and the surety (*o*). A consolidation of mortgages given by the principal debtor, with the fixing of a later date for payment, operates as a giving of time and discharges the surety (*p*). The surety may also be discharged by the mortgagee consenting to the surrender of a leasehold interest which formed part of the security with the guarantor's consent (*q*)

The reason for the discharge of the surety in such a case is either that the contract for which the surety became responsible has been altered, and that he cannot be made responsible for another and different contract (*r*), or that the giving of time alters the rights of the surety against the debtor (*s*). And it is a general rule that a surety is discharged by the creditor dealing with the principal debtor or a co-surety in a manner at variance with the contract the performance of which the surety had guaranteed (*t*). The surety is also released if there has been a material alteration in his position by operation of law (*u*).

A release of the surety extends to any security he has given (*v*).

As previously stated in view of the effect of a variation of the terms of the mortgage on the obligations of the surety a guarantee usually contains a provision reserving, *inter alia*, the right of the creditor to give time to the debtor and such a provision is effective to prevent waiver (*w*).

A material change in a head contract does not discharge a guarantee of the performance of sub-contracts to which the person giving the guarantee is not a party (*x*).

Release of principal debtor.—Where the creditor gives the debtor an absolute release of the debt, the surety is discharged, and the debt

---

(*o*) *Re a Debtor*, [1913] 3 K.B. 11.

(*p*) *Bolton* v. *Buckenham*, [1891] 1 Q.B. 278 (C.A.); *Bolton* v. *Salmon*, [1891] 2 Ch. 48.

(*q*) See *Dowling* v. *Ditanda, Ltd.* (1975), 236 Estates Gazette 485.

(*r*) *The Harriett* (1842), 1 Wm. Rob. 182, *per* Dr. LUSHINGTON.

(*s*) *Browne* v. *Carr* (1831), 7 Bing. 508, *per* TINDAL, C.J. And see *Samuell* v. *Howarth*, *supra*, at p. 278, *per* Lord ELDON. The right lost is that of subrogation to the creditor's rights against the debtor upon the surety paying the creditor on the date for repayment. See also Glanville Williams, *Joint Obligations* (1949), 123, and Cardozo, *The Nature of the Judicial Process* (1932), pp. 152–4.

(*t*) *Ward* v. *National Bank of New Zealand* (1883), 8 App. Cas. 755; *Re Wolmershausen* (1890), 62 L.T. 541. And see *Lep Air Services, Ltd.* v. *Rollsowin Investments, Ltd.*, [1971] 3 All E.R. 45 (C.A.); *affd. sub nom. Moschi* v. *Lep Air Services, Ltd.*, [1973] A.C. 331 (H.L.); [1972] All E.R. 393. Sometimes the rule has been applied strictly without regard to the question whether the surety is prejudiced or not, and even though the alteration is for his benefit: *Blest* v. *Brown* (1862), 4 De G.F. & J. 367; *Polak* v. *Everett* (1876), 1 Q.B.D. 669; but there is an exception where it is evident without inquiry that the alteration is unsubstantial, or that it cannot be otherwise than beneficial to the surety, and then he is not discharged: *Holme* v. *Brunshill* (1878), 3 Q.B.D. 495, 505, *per* COTTON, L.J.; *Chatterton* v. *Maclean*, [1951] 1 All E.R. 761.

(*u*) *Mortgage Insurance Corpn., Ltd.* v. *Pound* (1895), 64 L.J. Q.B. 394, *per* WRIGHT, J.; on app., 64 L.J. Q.B. 397 (C.A.); 65 L.J. Q.B. 129 (H.L.).

(*v*) *Bolton* v. *Salmon, supra*; see *Hodgson* v. *Hodgson* (1837), 2 Keen, 704. But where a surety guaranteed the sufficiency of the principal debtor's security for part of the debt, and paid a sum of money in discharge of his guarantee, the security not being delivered up, it was not released, but remained as security for the balance: *Waugh* v. *Wren* (1862), 7 L.T. 612.

(*w*) *Cowper* v. *Smith* (1838), 4 M. & W. 519; *Union Bank of Manchester, Ltd.* v. *Beech* (1865), 3 H. & C. 672; *Perry* v. *National Provincial Bank of England*, [1910] 1 Ch. 464; *British Motor Trust Co., Ltd.* v. *Hyams* (1934), 50 T.L.R. 230. For a form, see additional proviso, p. 692, *infra*, and see footnote (*b*), p. 586, *infra*.

(*x*) *Town of Truro* v. *Toronto General Insurance Co.* (1973), 38 D.L.R. (3d) 1.

being gone at law, the creditor cannot reserve any right against the surety (y). It is the same where the creditor releases the principal debtor, and accepts another person as debtor in his stead, so that there is a novation of the contract (z). But a release by operation of law, *e.g.*, in bankruptcy, does not release the surety (a).

Again it is usual to insert in a guarantee a provision permitting the creditor to compound with the principal debtor without affecting the guarantor's liability (b).

Release of co-surety.—A discharge of one of several co-sureties, whether the liability is joint only (c), or joint and several (d), is a release of all of them, unless the creditor reserves his rights against the others (e). Where his liability is several only, he is not discharged unless his right to contribution is affected (f).

Surety's right to securities.—A surety is entitled to the benefit of every security which the creditor has against the principal debtor, the whole or any part of whose debt he has discharged (g). This right is not in abeyance until the surety is called upon to pay, but is complete throughout (h). The creditor is bound to hold and preserve the securities for the benefit of the surety, so that on payment of the debt he may receive them unimpaired (i), whether the surety was or was not aware of the existence of the securities (k), and although they were taken by the creditor after the contract of suretyship (l); and even though the surety has taken a particular indemnity upon other property, if he has done so without knowledge of the security held by the creditor, which was available for his own indemnity (m). A

(y) *Webb* v. *Hewitt* (1857), 3 K. & J. 438; *Bateson* v. *Gosling* (1871), L.R. 7 C.P. 9, *per* WILLES, J.; *Perry* v. *National Provincial Bank of England, supra. Aliter*, where, although the principal debtor is released, the debt remains: *Perry* v. *National Provincial Bank of England, supra.*

(z) *Commercial Bank of Tasmania* v. *Jones*, [1893] A.C. 313.

(a) Bankruptcy Act 1914, s. 28 (4). The surety is released by a deed of composition voluntarily entered into between the creditor and the principal debtor: *Re Renton, Ex parte Glendinning* (1819), Buck. 517, at p. 520.

(b) For forms, see Ency. Forms and Precedents (4th Edn.), vol. 2, pp. 837, 885; vol. 3, p. 752.

(c) *Re Armitage, Ex parte Good* (1877), 5 Ch. D. 46.

(d) *Nicholson* v. *Revill* (1836), 4 A. & E. 675; *Mercantile Bank of Sydney* v. *Taylor,* [1893] A.C. 317. And this applies where judgment has been obtained for the joint and several obligations: *Re E.W.A.*, [1901] 2 K.B. 642; cf. *Re a Debtor*, [1913] 3 K.B. 11.

(e) *Thompson* v. *Lack* (1846), 3 C.B. 540. But verbal negotiations prior to the release for reserving the rights against the co-sureties will not avoid the effect of the release: *Mercantile Bank of Sydney* v. *Taylor, supra.*

(f) *Ex parte Crisp* (1744), 1 Atk. 133; *Aldrich* v. *Cooper* (1803), 8 Ves. 382; *Ward* v. *National Bank of New Zealand* (1883), 8 App. Cas. 755.

(g) *Goddard* v. *Whyte* (1860), 2 Giff. 449. A surety who takes security from the principal debtor holds it not for his exclusive benefit, but for the benefit of himself and his co-sureties: *Berridge* v. *Berridge* (1890), 44 Ch. D. 168. For the effect of a voluntary payment, see (1976) 92 L.Q.R. 188 (Peter Birks and Jack Beatson); *Owen* v. *Tate*, [1976] Q.B. 402; [1975] 2 All E.R. 129 (C.A.).

(h) *Dixon* v. *Steel*, [1901] 2 Ch. 602.

(i) *Pledge* v. *Buss* (1860), Johns. 663; *Pearl* v. *Deacon* (1857), 24 Beav. 186.

(k) *Lake* v. *Brutton* (1856), 8 De G.M. & G. 440.

(l) *Forbes* v. *Jackson* (1882), 19 Ch. D. 615.

(m) *Lake* v. *Brutton, supra,* and see *Brandon* v. *Brandon* (1859), 3 De G. & J. 524. Though under different circumstances, a person who had made his own interest in the mortgaged property liable to the debt, was held to have lost his right against the principal security, by taking from the principal debtor by way of indemnity a security upon other property: *Cooper* v. *Jenkins* (1863), 32 Beav. 337.

surety for a limited sum only has, on payment of that sum, all the rights of the creditor in respect of that amount and is therefore entitled to a share in any security held by the creditor for the whole of the debt (*n*). This restriction on the creditor in dealing with his securities only applies when he has notice of the suretyship, and if he accepts the liability of two co-debtors without knowing that, while they are both principal debtors towards him, they stand in the relation of principal and surety between themselves, he is not affected by the restriction until he has notice of the rights of the surety. To these rights, subject to his own claims, he must then give effect (*o*).

The right of the surety extends to all equities which the creditor whose debt he has discharged could have enforced, not merely against the principal debtor, but against all who claim under him (*p*).

This right of the surety to the benefit of the creditor's securities was affirmed by the Mercantile Law Amendment Act 1856. A surety who pays the debt is entitled to have all the securities held by the creditor assigned to him, and to stand in the place of the creditor, and use all remedies, and, if need be, upon a proper indemnity, use his name in any proceeding in order to obtain from the principal debtor, or any co-surety, or co-debtor, indemnity for the payment he has made (*q*).

Failure of creditor to preserve securities.—The surety being thus interested in the mortgaged estate, the neglect of the creditor to preserve the securities for his benefit will cause the release of the surety, either entirely or to the extent of the lost fund (*r*). The creditor cannot, as against the surety, apply the security in payment of any other debt than that for which the surety was liable (*s*).

But the creditor is under no obligation not to assign the securities or the debt. Upon such an assignment the creditor's obligation to preserve the securities attaches upon the assignee, who also acquires the rights of the creditor against the surety; and those rights are not lost by the neglect of the assignee to give notice of the assignment to the surety; though by omitting to give notice he will risk the consequences of a payment by the surety to the assignor. But if, through the neglect of the creditor or his assignee to enforce or protect the security, the benefit of it is lost to the surety, he is discharged (*t*).

(*n*) *Goodwin* v. *Gray* (1874), 22 W.R. 312.

(*o*) *Duncan, Fox & Co.* v. *North and South Wales Bank* (1880), 6 App. Cas. 1; *Rouse* v. *Bradford Banking Co.*, [1894] A.C. 586; *Nicholas* v. *Ridley*, [1904] 1 Ch. 192.

(*p*) See *Drew* v. *Lockett* (1863), 32 Beav. 499; also *Praed* v. *Gardiner* (1788), 2 Cox Eq. Cas. 86.

(*q*) Mercantile Law Amendment Act 1856, s. 5. The statute applies to a co-debtor as well as to a surety.

(*r*) *Cf.* the absolute discharge where the terms of the principal contract are varied to the surety's disadvantage. Where securities are released the surety is released only to the extent of the loss of his security. The wasteful application of the principal debtor's estate by the creditor will release the surety: *Mutual Loan Fund Association* v. *Sudlow* (1858), 5 C.B. (N.S.) 449. Similarly if the creditor instead of proving, as he ought to do, under the bankruptcy of the debtor, without notice to the surety, releases the trustee and the bankrupt's estate in consideration of a conveyance of the equity of redemption: *Pledge* v. *Buss* (1860), Johns. 663.

(*s*) *Pearl* v. *Deacon* (1857), 24 Beav. 186.

(*t*) *Taylor* v. *Bank of New South Wales* (1886), 11 App. Cas. 596.

It is usual to insert in the guarantee a provision to prevent the release of securities discharging the surety (*u*).

III—WAIVER OF VENDOR'S LIEN

Effect of taking security.—The lien of a vendor of land for unpaid purchase-money will under certain circumstances either not arise, or, if it has arisen, will be treated as given up. In either case the lien is said to be waived. The question whether there has been a waiver usually arises when the vendor has accepted other security for the purchase-money, but the simple rule that the taking of any security shall be regarded as a substituted security and exclude the lien, has not been adopted, and it depends upon the circumstances of each case whether the proper inference is that the lien was intended to be reserved, or whether the vendor intended to rely on the other security (*x*). The burden of proof that the lien has been waived is on the purchaser (*y*).

Taking personal security.—The lien is not generally destroyed by the vendor taking a promissory note, bill of exchange, or other negotiable instrument for the purchase-money, since these are only modes of payment (*z*); nor by the vendor taking a bond (*a*) or covenant for payment of the purchase-money, even though a surety joins (*b*).

It does not matter that the conveyance contains a receipt for the purchase-money (*c*). A note may be given, not to supersede the lien, but for the purpose of ascertaining the debt, and countervailing the receipt (*d*).

Taking a mortgage.—But if it appears by direct agreement, or can be clearly inferred from the circumstances, that the vendor intended to rely upon the security only, and not upon the land, then the lien will be gone (*e*). The taking of security for part of the

---

(*u*) See footnote (*b*), p. 586, *supra*. The whole of this paragraph was quoted in *Dowling v. Ditanda, Ltd.* (1975), 236 Estates Gazette 485.

(*x*) *Mackreth v. Symmons* (1808), 15 Ves. 329, at p. 350; *Cood v. Cood and Pollard* (1822), 10 Price, 109; *Thames Iron Works Co. v. Patent Derrick Co.* (1860), 1 Johns. & H. 93. For the vendor's lien, see p. 166, *supra*.

A vendor-mortgagee may wish to rely on his lien if his mortgage is, for example, avoided for non-registration: see *Re Molton Finance, Ltd.*, [1968] Ch. 325 (C.A.); [1967] 3 All E.R. 843; *Capital Finance Co., Ltd. v. Stokes*, [1969] 1 Ch. 261 (C.A.); [1968] 3 All E.R. 625. And see *Nottingham Permanent Benefit Building Society v. Thurstan*, [1903] A.C. 6 (H.L.) (infant's mortgage void, building society given lien on property for money advanced); *Congresbury Motors, Ltd. v. Anglo-Belge Finance Co., Ltd.*, [1970] Ch. 294; [1969] 3 All E.R. 545; affd. [1971] Ch. 81 (C.A.); [1970] 3 All E.R. 385; *Coptic, Ltd. v. Bailey*, [1972] Ch. 446; [1972] 1 All E.R. 1242; cf. *Burston Finance, Ltd. v. Speirway, Ltd.*, [1974] 3 All E.R. 735 (unenforceable moneylender's mortgages).

(*y*) *Hughes v. Kearney* (1803), 1 Sch. & Lef. 132, 135; *Mackreth v. Symmons, supra*.

(*z*) *Hughes v. Kearney, supra; Grant v. Mills* (1813), 2 Ves. & B. 306; *Nairn v. Prowse* (1802), 6 Ves. 752; *Gunn v. Bolckow, Vaughan & Co.* (1875), 10 Ch. 492 (as to chattels).

(*a*) *Winter v. Anson* (1827), 3 Russ. 488; *Collins v. Collins (No. 2)* (1862), 31 Beav. 346; *Pell v. Midland Counties and South Wales Rail. Co.* (1869), 20 L.T. 288.

(*b*) *Elliott v. Edwards* (1802), 3 Bos. & P. 183; cf. *Cood v. Cood and Pollard, supra*.

(*c*) *Winter v. Lord Anson, supra*.   (*d*) *Nairn v. Prowse, supra*, at p. 759.

(*e*) *Winter v. Lord Anson, supra*, at p. 492. See *Frail v. Ellis* (1852), 16 Beav. 350. And see *Re Taylor, Stileman and Underwood*, [1891] 1 Ch. 590; *Re Molton, supra; Capital Finance Co., Ltd. v. Stokes, supra; Burston Finance, Ltd. v. Speirway, Ltd., supra; Security Trust Co. v. The Royal Bank of Canada*, [1976] A.C. 503; [1976] 1 All E.R. 381 (P.C.); and see p. 168, *supra*. For a discussion of the relationship of a lien and a mortgage see (1970) 33 M.L.R. 131 (J. H. G. Sunnucks).

purchase-money by mortgage of part of the estate and by bond (*f*), and the taking of a mortgage for part and of a note payable on demand for the residue of the purchase-money (*g*), have been held to show an intention to abandon the lien (*h*). This is apparently for the reason that a charge for part of the money shows an intention not to charge the residue.

The lien has also been decided to be lost by taking, as special security, a sum of stock, which, being sufficient or probably sufficient to cover the purchase-money, was held to have been pledged that the purchaser might have absolute dominion over the land (*i*). And, on the same principle, it has been thought that a mortgage upon another property of the purchaser would have a like effect, the obvious intention being to burden one property, so that the other might be free (*k*). But although a mortgage of another estate may not be conclusive ground for the inference that a lien was not intended (*l*), yet the doctrine which may perhaps be deduced from the cases cited is, that the taking of a distinct security is always prima facie evidence that the lien has been abandoned, but that this inference may be rebutted by proof of an agreement, or of circumstances leading to a presumption of an agreement, to the contrary.

Circumstances excluding lien.—Moreover, there is no lien where the consideration for sale is the security itself and not a sum secured; where, for example, land is granted in consideration of the purchaser's covenant to pay an annuity to the vendor (*m*); or where an express stipulation for the protection of the vendor has been substituted for the lien (*n*); or a special mode of payment has been agreed upon (*o*); or where payment was to be made within two years after a resale (*p*); or where the object of the purchase (*q*), or nature of the consideration (*r*), is inconsistent with the existence of a lien. And the vendor will lose his lien if he is a party to a subsequent mortgage which is inconsistent with it (*s*), or has enabled a resale to be made as though it did not exist (*t*).

Lien for part of consideration.—It has been held that where the unpaid purchase consideration consisted partly of a gross sum due

---

(*f*) *Capper* v. *Spottiswoode* (1829), Taml. 21.
(*g*) *Bond* v. *Kent* (1692), 2 Vern. 281.
(*h*) An inference said by Lord ELDON in *Mackreth* v. *Symmons, supra,* at p. 348, not to be conclusive. It seems that the mere retention by the vendor of the title deeds does not waive or exclude his lien: *Wreford* v. *Lethern* (1824), 2 L.J. (O.S.) Ch. 173.
(*i*) *Nairn* v. *Prowse, supra.*
(*k*) See *Mackreth* v. *Symmons, supra,* at p. 348.
(*l*) See, generally, the judgment of Lord ELDON in *Mackreth* v. *Symmons, supra;* Sugd. *Vend. & Purch.* (14th Edn.), 675; Wh. & T.C.C. in Eq. (9th Edn.), II, pp. 865 *et seq.*
(*m*) *Parrott* v. *Sweetland* (1835), 3 My. & K. 655; *cf. Dixon* v. *Gayfere, Fluker* v. *Gordon* (1857), 1 De G. & J. 655, 659.
(*n*) *Re London and Lancashire Paper Mills Co.* (1888), 58 L.T. 798.
(*o*) *Re Brentwood Brick and Coal Co.* (1876), 4 Ch. D. 562.
(*p*) *Re Parkes, Ex parte Parkes* (1822), 1 Gl. & J. 228; *cf. Re Patent Carriage Co., Gore and Durant's Case* (1866), L.R. 2 Eq. 349.
(*q*) *Earl Jersey* v. *Briton Ferry Floating Dock Co.* (1869), L.R. 7 Eq. 409.
(*r*) *Re Albert Life Assurance Co., Ex parte Western Life Assurance Society* (1870), L.R. 11 Eq. 164 (the consideration being the taking over of debts and engagements).
(*s*) *Cood* v. *Cood and Pollard, supra.*
(*t*) *Kettlewell* v. *Watson* (1884), 26 Ch. D. 501; see *Smith* v. *Evans* (1860), 28 Beav. 59.

on bonds which the purchaser had undertaken, but had failed to pay, and partly of liability for annuities, against which the purchaser had undertaken to indemnify the vendor, there was a lien as to the gross sum but not as to the annuities (*u*).

Where contract not completed.—The vendor loses his lien if by his own act or default the contract is not completed (*x*).

(*u*) *Mackreth* v. *Symmons, supra.*
(*x*) *Oxenham* v. *Esdaile* (1828), 2 Y. & J. 493; *Esdaile* v. *Oxenham* (1824), 3 B. & C. 225; *Dinn* v. *Grant* (1852), 5 De G. & Sm. 451.
For the loss of the lien of a vendor of goods, see previous editions of this work.

CHAPTER 32

Merger

I—MERGER OF CHARGES

Merger of estates (*a*).—Merger of estates took place at law when two estates in land, which were held in the same legal right (*b*), became united in the same person. The estate, which in legal valuation was the smaller estate, was then swallowed up or merged in the greater. In equity merger depended on intention and the equitable rule now prevails. There is no merger by operation of law of any estate (*c*) the beneficial interest in which would not be deemed to be merged or extinguished in equity (*d*).

Merger of charges.—Analogous to the merger of estates at law was the extinguishment, or merger, in equity of a charge on land where the absolute ownership of the charge and the land were united in the same person. Prima facie the charge was merged for the benefit of the inheritance (*e*). The court did not consider the subtleties of merger, but discharged the estate from the incumbrance; otherwise it would burden estates to no purpose (*f*). But, for example, there was no merger where the charge was subject to a prior life interest which did not determine during the life of the owner of the charge (*g*). However, the existence of liabilities which had to be satisfied out of the charge did not prevent merger (*h*).

In equity the test for merger was not the mere union of interests, but the intention of the owner, and the equitable rule now prevails (*i*).

(*a*) See, generally, as to merger, Halsbury's Laws (3rd Edn.), vol. 14, pp. 615–618; vol. 27, pp. 413–421; Preston, *Conveyancing*, vol. iii (which is devoted exclusively to the subject of merger).

(*b*) *Re Radcliffe, Radcliffe* v. *Bewes*, [1892] 1 Ch. 227 (C.A.). But see Challis, *Real Property* (3rd Edn.), 92; and *Jones* v. *Davies* (1861), 7 H. & N. 507.

(*c*) *I.e.*, a fee simple or term of years: Law of Property Act 1925, s. 1 (1).

(*d*) Law of Property Act 1925, s. 185, replacing Judicature Act 1873, s. 25 (4). This applies only to the merger of estates: *Capital and Counties Bank, Ltd.* v. *Rhodes*, [1903] 1 Ch. 631, 648 (C.A.).

(*e*) *Earl of Buckinghamshire* v. *Hobart* (1818), 3 Swanst. 186, 199.

(*f*) *Donisthorpe* v. *Porter* (1762), 2 Eden, 162.

(*g*) *Wilkes* v. *Collin* (1869), L.R. 8 Eq. 338.

(*h*) *Re French-Brewster's Settlements, Walters* v. *French-Brewster*, [1904] 1 Ch. 713. But where at the death of the owner of the land and the charge, the charge was vested in trustees and was subject to succession duty on a previous death, it was held that, since the owner could not call for an assignment by the trustees without discharging the duty, the right of the charge was not co-extensive with the title to the land, and there was no merger: *Re Simmons, Dennison* v. *Orman* (1902), 87 L.T. 594.

(*i*) Judicature Act 1925, s. 44, under which, in any conflict or variance between the rules of equity and the rules of common law, the rules of equity prevail.

The intention might be actual, evidenced by declaration (e) or by circumstances at the time of the union of interests or subsequently during the life of the owner (k); or a presumed intention, and it is presumed that the owner intends merger or not according as it is more for his benefit. When it is perfectly indifferent to him whether the charge should subsist or not, then the prima facie rule operates and the charge is extinguished (l).

The result, where an equitable mortgagee purchases the equity of redemption, may be to subject him to agreements made by the mortgagor such as an agreement to grant a lease (m).

Where limited owner acquires charge.—The rule that merger prima facie results from the union of the charge and the land in the same person applies where the interests are absolute (n). Where a tenant for life or other limited owner becomes entitled to the charge the position is reversed. Prima facie there is no merger, for it is not to be supposed that he will discharge a debt on another man's estate (o). Hence the merger only results where the tenant for life shows an intention that the charge shall be extinguished for the benefit of the remaindermen (p). The burden of proof is on those who claim to have the estate exonerated (q); and this is so even when the remainderman is the child of the tenant for life (r).

Evidence of intention.—Evidence of intention may be direct or may be inferred from the attendant circumstances, and since the intention may be formed at any time during the life of the owner, so long as his ownership both of the land and the charge continue (s), it is necessary to consider the circumstances not only at the time when the union of interests first occurs, but also subsequently. Parol evidence may be used (t).

(e) See footnote on page 591.

(k) The presumption of intention as to merger arises on the death of the person entitled both to the estate and the charge, and this intention is to be collected from all the circumstances which existed at that period, including his acts prior to his decease and all the facts affecting his position down to and at the time of his decease: *Swinfen* v. *Swinfen (No. 3)* (1860), 29 Beav. 199, 204.

(l) *Forbes* v. *Moffatt* (1811), 8 Ves. 384; *Thorne* v. *Cann*, [1895] A.C. 11 (H.L.), at p. 18.

(m) *Smith* v. *Phillips* (1837), 1 Keen, 694 (considered in *Rust* v. *Goodale*, [1957] Ch. 33; [1956] 3 All E.R. 373); *O'Loughlin* v. *Fitzgerald* (1873), 7 I.R. Eq. 483.

(n) An estate tail in possession is in general treated with regard to the extinction of charges as absolute ownership: *Ware* v. *Polhill* (1805), 11 Ves. 257, 278; *Earl of Buckinghamshire* v. *Hobart, supra,* 199; but see *Clifford* v. *Clifford* (1852), 9 Hare 675. If a tenant in tail in remainder pays off a charge it is presumed that he meant to keep the charge alive even though his interest falls into possession: *Wigsell* v. *Wigsell* (1825), 2 Sim. & St. 364; *Horton* v. *Smith* (1858), 4 K. & J. 624; *Re Chesters, Whittingham* v. *Chesters*, [1935] Ch. 77. The same principle would apply to an estate in fee simple in remainder which may never fall into possession.

(o) For the same reason, where a person entitled to the equity of redemption of an estate which is jointly mortgaged together with another pays off the mortgage, it will be kept alive in his favour: *Taws* v. *Knowles*, [1891] 2 Q.B. 564, 572 (C.A.).

(p) *Wyndham* v. *Earl of Egremont* (1775), Ambl. 753; *Williams* v. *Williams-Wynn* (1915), 84 L.J. Ch. 801.

(q) *Countess of Shrewsbury* v. *Earl of Shrewsbury* (1790), 3 Bro. C.C. 120, 127; *Burrell* v. *Earl of Egremont* (1844), 7 Beav. 205.

(r) *Re Harvey, Harvey* v. *Hobday*, [1896] 1 Ch. 137; though in such a case the smallest indication that the tenant for life meant to pay the money himself will prevent his representatives from obtaining repayment.

(s) See *supra*.

(t) *Astley* v. *Miller* (1827), 1 Sim. 298, 345.

The clearest way of causing or preventing merger is by an express declaration in the instrument which effects the union of the charge and the estate.

The assignment of the charge to the owner or to a trustee for him, while it affords some evidence of an intention against merger, is neither necessary nor sufficient for that purpose (*u*). Where it is accompanied by a declaration of trust (*x*), the intention of preventing merger should be clearly and unequivocably stated, and it will be considered that if the intention did exist, it would be expressed in such an instrument, and be accompanied by a declaration of trust of the charge (*y*).

Any dealing in relation to the property which indicates that the owner considers the charge to be existing can be used as evidence against merger (*z*). But the owner cannot set up the charge after he has disposed of the land whether by sale (*a*), mortgage (*b*), or settlement (*c*) on the footing that it is free from the charge. An intention in favour of merger may be inferred if the owner of the land disposes of it by will, making no mention of the charge (unless there are other charges to which the devise is subject and which are also not mentioned), and using language calculated to exclude the existence of any charge on the estate (*d*), or other circumstances showing that it was not treated as subject to any charge (*e*).

A charge, though merged, may be treated as existing for the purpose of liability to death duties (*f*).

Where no evidence of intention, benefit of owner prevails.— Where there is no evidence of the conduct or acts of the owner of the estate or the evidence is neutral, the course most beneficial to the owner will be considered as that which he intended to follow (*g*). The circumstances, therefore, that the estate is subject to debts and legacies, or other charges, to which the charge in question is paramount, even although from the state of the testator's assets the liability, in the case of debts and legacies, is of little apparent importance; the uncertainty whether the estate will be sufficient to bear all its burdens;

(*u*) *Hood* v. *Phillips* (1841), 3 Beav. 513, 518; *Parry* v. *Wright* (1823), 1 Sim. & St. 369; affd. (1828), 5 Russ. 142.

(*x*) See *Bailey* v. *Richardson* (1852), 9 Hare, 734.

(*y*) An intention against merger might be inferred, *e.g.*, where the owner declared a trust in favour of his personal representatives. But see *Tyrwhitt* v. *Tyrwhitt* (1863), 32 Beav. 244; *Re Gibbon, Moore* v. *Gibbon*, [1909] 1 Ch. 367.

(*z*) *Hatch* v. *Skelton* (1855), 20 Beav. 453; *Re Gibbon, Moore* v. *Gibbon*, *supra*.

(*a*) *Bulkeley* v. *Hope* (1855), 1 Kay & J. 482, 487; *Re Gibbon, Moore* v. *Gibbon*, *supra*.

(*b*) *Tyler* v. *Lake* (1831), 4 Sim. 351; *Re Gibbon, Moore* v. *Gibbon*, *supra*.

(*c*) *Gower* v. *Gower* (1783), 1 Cox Eq. Cas. 53.

(*d*) *Hood* v. *Phillips*, *supra*; *Swinfen* v. *Swinfen* (*No.* 3) (1860), 29 Beav. 199; *Re Lloyd's Estate*, [1903] 1 Ir. R. 144.

(*e*) *Pitt* v. *Pitt* (1856), 22 Beav. 294.

(*f*) *Swabey* v. *Swabey* (1846), 15 Sim. 106, 502; *Re French-Brewster's Settlements, Walters* v. *French-Brewster*, [1904] 1 Ch. 713.

(*g*) *Adams* v. *Angell* (1877), 5 Ch. D. 634 (C.A.); *Thorne* v. *Cann*, [1895] A.C. 11 (H.L.); *Liquidation Estates Purchase Co.* v. *Willoughby*, [1896] 1 Ch. 726. The owner of an estate who buys up an incumbrance at less than its full value is entitled to hold it for full value against subsequent incumbrancers: *Davis* v. *Barrett* (1851), 14 Beav. 542. And see *Ghana Commercial Bank* v. *Chandiram*, [1960] A.C. 732 (P.C.); [1960] 2 All E.R. 865.

and other matters which make it better for the owner of the estate to preserve than merge the charges, will be taken as grounds for presuming his intention to do so (h).

Circumstances affecting merger.—The intention to merge will not be imputed to a person on account of particular dealings with the estate, where those dealings are carried out in a manner, or by words, only explicable on the supposition that the person concerned was ignorant of his rights; as where a tenant for life, being also executor, paid off certain charges on the settled estate, under circumstances which showed his belief that, in the character of executor and residuary legatee of the settlor, he was bound to do so (i). On the other hand, a mortgagor who, as one of the executors and residuary legatees of the mortgagee, is treated as having in his hands the amount owing on the mortgage, will be also treated as having intended to discharge the mortgage out of his share of the residue (j).

Keeping prior mortgage on foot.—Where the owner of the land creates successive mortgages upon it he is not allowed to get in the first mortgage and set it up against the subsequent incumbrancers, because, if the mortgagor pays off a charge on the estate, he does so for the benefit of the inheritance, and of all who are entitled to subsequent charges thereon (k); and accordingly a statutory indorsed receipt cannot operate in his favour as a transfer (l). But a purchaser of the equity of redemption, not being himself liable on the mortgage, is not subject to this restriction, and he may get in the first mortgage and keep it on foot against subsequent incumbrancers; that is, he can prevent the merger of the first mortgage and, as in other cases where the question of merger arises, the result will depend upon his intention. The first mortgage will be kept on foot, if that was his intention; otherwise, it will be extinguished (m).

The doctrine of *Toulmin* v. *Steere* (n).—The judgment of Sir WILLIAM GRANT, M.R., in this case suggests that the intention necessary to keep the first mortgage on foot must be an actual intention, either expressed or evidenced by the attendant circumstances, and that, in the absence of such actual intention the purchaser of the equity of

---

(h) *Forbes* v. *Moffatt* (1811), 18 Ves. 384; *Whiteley* v. *Delaney*, [1914] A.C. 132 (H.L.).
(i) *Burrell* v. *Earl of Egremont* (1844), 7 Beav. 205; *Connolly* v. *Barter*, [1904] 1 Ir. R. 130.
(j) *Re Greg, Fordham* v. *Greg*, [1921] 2 Ch. 243.
(k) *Otter* v. *Lord Vaux* (1856), 6 De G.M. & G. 638, 642; *Re W. Tasker & Sons, Ltd., Hoare* v. *W. Tasker & Sons, Ltd.*, [1905] 2 Ch. 587 (C.A.) (a company, paying off some of its debentures, cannot keep them alive against others of the same series ranking *pari passu*; except for the purpose of re-issue: Companies Act 1948, ss. 90, 91); *Morrison* v. *Guaranty Trust Co. of Canada* (1972), 28 D.L.R. (3d) 458 (husband and wife mortgagors—wife who pays off mortgage cannot keep it alive). When a mortgagor becomes bankrupt (and so is released from the debt), and subsequently buys the first mortgage, it seems he can keep in on foot: *Re Howard's Estate* (1892), 29 L.R. Ir. 266. And it is considered that a purchase by the mortgagor, after several bona fide mesne transfers, might be set up, since the mortgagor would not then be found paying into the hand of the prior mortgagee, money which he is bound by his contract to pay in discharge of his debt: *Otter* v. *Lord Vaux, supra.*
(l) Law of Property Act 1925, s. 115 (3). See p. 549.
(m) *Adams* v. *Angell, supra; Whiteley* v. *Delaney, supra*. And see *Parkash* v. *Irani Finance, Ltd.*, [1970] Ch. 101; [1969] 1 All E.R. 930.
(n) (1817), 3 Mer. 210.

redemption is not entitled to the benefit of the presumption that he intended to keep the mortgage on foot because that would be for his benefit. This decision, however, has frequently been called in question, and the statement therein that the purchaser of an equity of redemption cannot keep up a charge for his own benefit cannot be regarded as a correct statement of the law (*o*). The intention, if it can be shown to exist, governs the case (*p*), and all that *Toulmin* v. *Steere* can be treated as deciding is, that if no intention exists, then the incumbrance which is paid off is merged, and the subsequent incumbrancers let in. While the decision stands the law does not assist the purchaser of the equity of redemption with the presumption that where he has not shown an intention, expressly or from the circumstances, he intended what was for his benefit. But the existence of mesne incumbrances is probably a circumstance indicating an intention against merger (*q*).

Cases of merger.—Sometimes, however, the circumstances show an intention that the charge which is paid off shall merge. If, for example, a mortgagee takes a conveyance of the equity of redemption, in consideration of the debts due to himself and the other mortgagees, whom he covenants to pay, prima facie the mortgagee's own debt will merge in favour of the other incumbrancers (*r*).

Effect of bankruptcy.—The giving up by a mortgagee of his security for the benefit of the creditors under the Bankruptcy Act 1914, puts the trustee in the mortgagee's place and does not destroy the security so as to let in subsequent incumbrancers (*s*). Where the trustee purchases the first mortgage, he only has the rights of a transferee as against subsequent incumbrancers (*t*). The trustees of a deed for the benefit of creditors, by which all the real and personal estate of the debtor has been conveyed to them, do not thereby become owners of the estate, so as to cause the merger of a judgment assigned to them by one of the creditors (*u*).

II—MERGER OF LOWER IN HIGHER SECURITY

General rules.—The benefit of the security will be lost by merger in a security of a higher nature; for it is a general rule of law that a party, by taking or acquiring a security of a higher nature in legal operation than the one he already possesses, merges and extinguishes his legal remedies upon the minor security. Thus a simple contract

---

(*o*) *Whiteley* v. *Delaney, supra*.

(*p*) *Adams* v. *Angell, supra*; *Minter* v. *Carr*, [1894] 3 Ch. 498.

(*q*) *Toulmin* v. *Steere* was considered in, *inter alia*, the following cases: *Watts* v. *Symes* (1851), 1 De G.M. & G. 240; *Stevens* v. *Mid-Hants Rail. Co., London Financial Association* v. *Stevens* (1873), 8 Ch. App. Cas. 1064 (C.A.); *Adams* v. *Angell, supra*; *Thorne* v. *Cann, supra*; *Liquidation Estates Purchase Co.* v. *Willoughby, supra*; *Manks* v. *Whiteley*, [1911] 2 Ch. 448; [1912] 1 Ch. 735 (C.A.); and *Whiteley* v. *Delaney, supra*.

(*r*) *Brown* v. *Stead* (1832), 5 Sim. 535. And see *Parry* v. *Wright* (1823), 5 Russ. 142, doubted in *Stevens* v. *Mid-Hants Rail. Co., supra*, at p. 1069.

(*s*) *Cracknall* v. *Janson* (1877), 6 Ch. D. 735.

(*t*) *Bell* v. *Sunderland Building Society* (1883), 24 Ch. D. 618.

(*u*) *Squire* v. *Ford* (1851), 9 Hare, 47.

debt merges in a speciality debt (*v*)—that is, a contract under seal, such as a bond or covenant—and both a simple contract debt and a speciality debt merge in a judgment (*x*).

The same principle has been applied where an informal equitable mortgage—such as a mortgage by deposit of deeds—has been followed by a formal mortgage, so that the equitable mortgage is extinguished and the formal mortgage stands as security only for the sums it is expressed to cover, although these do not include all sums which were secured by the deposit (*y*). An original mortgage will not, however, be merged in a new mortgage on the same property taken as security for the old debt and further advances (*z*).

Effect of judgment on mortgage interest.—On the above principle a covenant in a mortgage for payment of principal is merged in a judgment obtained on the covenant and the interest runs on the judgment at the rate of $7\frac{1}{2}$ per cent. per annum (*a*). If the mortgage provides for a higher rate, the right to recover the difference between the higher rate and the judgment rate depends on the form of the covenant for payment of interest, and the nature of the proceedings—whether the claim is against the mortgagor personally, or is against the mortgaged property.

If the effect of the covenant for payment of interest is that interest is to be payable so long as any principal money shall be due on the covenant for payment of principal, then it is extinguished in the judgment together with the latter covenant. On judgment being

---

(*v*) *Owen* v. *Homan* (1851), 3 Mac. & G. 378; *Price* v. *Moulton* (1851), 10 C.B. 474 (but see *Stamps Commissioners* v. *Hope*, [1891] A.C. 476 (P.C.)); *Saunders* v. *Milsome* (1867), L.R. 2 Eq. 573; *Re European Central Rail Co.*, *Ex parte Oriental Financial Corpn.* (1876), 4 Ch. D. 33 (C.A.). But a taking of a mortgage will not merge a simple contract debt if a contrary intention appears: *Bank of Victoria* v. *Looker* (1896), 21 Vict. L.R. 704. *Barclays Bank, Ltd.* v. *Beck*, [1952] 2 Q.B. 47 (C.A.); [1952] 1 All E.R. 549. For merger of the vendor's lien in a mortgage to the vendor, see the cases cited in note (*e*), p. 588, *supra*.

It is not uncommon for certain mortgages, usually second mortgages to hire-purchase and finance companies, to contain as a schedule to the deed a promissory note. In order to prevent merger of the personal remedy on the promissory note either no covenant for payment should be inserted in the mortgage, or, if inserted, it should be accompanied by a declaration against merger. For a form of mortgage to secure due payment of bills of exchange, see 14 Ency. Forms and Precedents (4th Edn.), pp. 496–498. The question as to whether there has been a merger or not is relevant in considering an action on the covenant for payment, for if the promissory note, etc., has merged in the mortgage the action must be commenced in the Chancery Division, whilst if there has not been a merger the lender can, it is submitted, sue for payment in the Queen's Bench Division on the promissory note and ignore the mortgage. Moreover if separate liability under the promissory note remains any action by the court in discharging or varying the mortgage (see pp. 600 *et seq, infra*) may not affect the liability under the promissory note.

(*x*) *Ward* v. *Liddaman* (1847), 10 L.T. (O.S.) 225. But not while the debt remains unsatisfied, so as to prevent the creditor from making the debtor bankrupt in respect of it: *Re Mostyn, Ex parte Griffiths* (1853), 3 De G.M. & G. 174. The obtaining of a judgment for the mortgage debt does not, while the judgment remains unsatisfied, prevent the mortgagee from enforcing his security: *Lloyd* v. *Mason* (1845), 4 Hare, 132.

(*y*) *Vaughan* v. *Vanderstegen* (1854), 2 Drew. 289.

(*z*) *Tenison* v. *Sweeney* (1844), 1 Jo. & Lat. 710; *Re James, Ex parte Harris* (1874), L.R. 19 Eq. 253. And see generally on the merger of an earlier equitable mortgage in a later legal mortgage, *Farrier-Waimak, Ltd.* v. *Bank of New Zealand*, [1965] A.C. 376 (P.C.); [1964] 3 All E.R. 657; see p. 43, *supra*.

(*a*) See *Sewing Machines Rentals, Ltd.* v. *Wilson*, [1975] 2 All E.R. 553 (C.A.); and note the point of there being no interest on county court judgments.

obtained no principal is any longer due on the covenant since it is gone (b). The principal is thenceforth due on the judgment. The interest covenant is considered to have this effect where it provides for payment of interest until the principal is repaid (c), or so long as the principal or any part thereof remains unpaid (d).

A covenant of this nature is said to be ancillary to the main covenant, and the excess of interest cannot be recovered in proceedings against the mortgagor personally. Where the interest covenant is not merely ancillary, but is an independent covenant, it is not extinguished in the judgment, and the excess of interest can be recovered in personal proceedings. A covenant for payment of interest so long as any principal remains due on the security is an independent covenant, since the principal is equally due on the security whether it is owing on the covenant or the judgment. Consequently under a covenant in this form the excess interest can be recovered in personal proceedings (e).

But in proceedings in which the mortgagee's claim is against the property, the full interest recovered by the mortgage is recoverable whether the interest covenant is independent or ancillary (f).

Conditions of merger of the security.—It is a necessary condition for merger of a lower in a higher security, that the remedy given by the higher shall be co-extensive with that under the inferior security. Therefore, if several persons are indebted on a joint and several note, and some only of them execute a mortgage, the liability on the note will not merge in the covenant in the mortgage (g). Nor will there be any merger unless the securities are vested in the same person (h); and the debt comprised in each security must be the same (i). There will be no merger if the higher security is ineffectual (k).

Merger prevented by intention.—Merger of a lower in a higher security may be prevented by an expressed or an implied intention to the contrary. A recital in the security that it is given by way of

---

(b) *Economic Life Assurance Society* v. *Usborne*, [1902] A.C. 147 (H.L.). The speech of Lord DAVEY in this case comments on and explains the authorities mentioned below prior to that case.

(c) *Re European Central Rail. Co., Ex parte Oriental Financial Corpn.* (1876), 4 Ch. D. 33 (C.A.).

(d) *Re Sneyd, Ex parte Fewings* (1883), 25 Ch. D. 338 (C.A.).

(e) *Popple* v. *Sylvester* (1882), 22 Ch. D. 98. For a form of independent covenant, see p. 680 in the Appendix, *infra*. Such provision is implied in a registered charge: see Land Registration Rules 1925, r. 76.

(f) *Lowry* v. *Williams*, [1895] 1 I.R. 274; *Aman* v. *Southern Rail. Co.*, [1926] 1 K.B. 59, 73. This is so in foreclosure and redemption, and also whenever an account has to be taken between mortgagee and mortgagor.

Where the mortgage allows for a higher rate than 4 per cent. up to the day fixed for payment, but there is no provision for future interest, the judgment of Lord DAVY in *Economic Life Assurance Co.* v. *Usborne* appears to assume that the full rate will run, but, in the past, only 5 per cent has been allowed: see *Wallington* v. *Cook* (1878), 47 L.J. Ch. 508.

(g) *Boaler* v. *Mayor* (1865), 19 C.B. (N.S.) 76; *Westmorland Green and Blue Slate Co.* v. *Feilden*, [1891] 3 Ch. 15.

(h) *Bell* v. *Banks* (1841), 3 Man. & Gr. 258.

(i) *Holmes* v. *Bell* (1841), 3 Man. & Gr. 213; *Norfolk Rail. Co.* v. *M'Namara* (1849), 3 Exch. 628.

(k) *Re Emery, Ex parte Harvey* (1839), Mont. & Ch. 261. *Vibart* v. *Coles* (1890), 24 Q.B.D. 364 (C.A.); cf. *Capital Finance Co., Ltd.* v. *Stokes, supra*.

further or collateral security will prevent merger both at law and in equity (*l*); and an intention against it may be sufficiently shown from the nature of the transaction, or the acts of the parties. Thus where a reversionary lease was deposited as security, and the debtor afterwards purchased the lease in possession and deposited it with the same lender as security for another sum, it was held that there was no merger (*m*).

(*l*) *Twopenny* v. *Young* (1824), 3 B. & C. 208; *Stamps Commissioners* v. *Hope*, [1891] A.C. 476 (P.C.); *Barclays Bank, Ltd.* v. *Beck, supra.*

(*m*) *Re Dix, Ex parte Whitbread* (1841), 2 Mont. D. & De G. 415. And see *Locking* v. *Parker* (1872), L.R. 8 Ch. 30.

CHAPTER 33

Destruction or Loss of the Property

Security lost with the property.—The benefit of a security may be lost by the destruction, or loss, of the property of which it is the subject (*a*). In the case of mortgaged leaseholds loss could occur through forfeiture (*b*), but not by surrender (*c*). Where the buildings on land are destroyed the rules with regard to insurance moneys will generally apply (*d*)

Though the security be lost the liability of the mortgagor under the personal covenant will remain.

Change of nature of property.—The right of the owner of property generally, and therefore of one who has a security thereon, is not destroyed by the mere transmutation of its subject-matter into a different form without his assent (*e*).

(*a*) Story on *Bailment* (9th Edn.), s. 363. As to the loss of the security in the case of mortgages of ships captured in war, see *The Marie Glaeser*, [1914] P. 218. The total loss or destruction of the ship, but nothing less, will discharge the condition of a bottomry bond: *Stephens* v. *Broomfield*, *The Great Pacific* (1869), L.R. 2 P.C. 516.

(*b*) See pp. 22, 23, *supra*.

(*c*) See p. 25, *supra*. On frustration of leases, see Cheshire and Fifoot, *Law of Contract* (9th Edn.), pp. 555–558 and 577–579.

(*d*) See p. 32, *supra*. For the effect of the impossibility of fulfilling a covenant in a mortgage, see *Moorgate Estates, Ltd.* v. *Trower*, [1940] Ch. 206; [1940] 1 All E.R. 195.

(*e*) Story on *Bailment*, s. 363.

CHAPTER 34

Discharge or Modification by Statute

I—UNDER THE HOUSING ACTS (a)

Purposes of the legislation.—The main purposes of the legislation are, *inter alia*, to provide for the removal by demolition or closing of unfit houses not capable of being made fit at reasonable expense and to provide for the clearance of areas of unfit houses (slum clearance). Provision is made for the payment of compensation and, in certain circumstances, *i.e.*, a well-maintained house or where the house has been occupied as a private dwelling, other payments.

Discharge or modification of liabilities under mortgage or instalment purchase agreement.—The Housing Act 1957, contains special provisions with regard to mortgages and such agreements where a payment falls to be made under the provisions relating to private dwellings and at the date when the house was compulsorily purchased or vacated the property was the subject of a mortgage or other charge or an agreement to purchase by instalments (b). A payment is to be made to an owner-occupier and others if the following conditions are satisfied (c):

(1) Where at any time before 13 December, 1955, the house has been purchased at site value in pursuance of a compulsory purchase order made by virtue of Part II or Part III of the Act or has been vacated in pursuance of a demolition, closing or clearance order; and

(2) If on 13 December, 1955, the house was wholly or partly occupied as a private dwelling by (or by a member of the family (d) of) a person who acquired an interest (e) in that house by purchase for value on or after 1 September, 1939, and before (a) 13 December, 1955, or (b) the date when the relevant proceedings leading to the purchase or vacation of the house were begun (f), whichever was the earlier, and at the date when the house was purchased compulsorily, or, as the case may be, vacated that person or a member of his family was entitled to an interest in the house.

If the above conditions are satisfied either party to the mortgage, charge or agreement may apply to the county court which, after giving

---

(a) See, generally, 19 Halsbury's Laws (3rd Edn.), Housing; Housing Act 1957; the Housing (Slum Clearance Compensation) Act 1965; Housing Act 1969, s. 68, Sched. 6.

(b) Housing Act 1957, Sched. 2, Pt. II, para. 5.

(c) *Ibid.*, Sched. 2, Pt. II, para. 4.

(d) *I.e.*, husband or wife, the children over 18 years of age and the parents of the person: Sched. 2, Pt. II, para. 4 (7).

(e) Interest does not include the interest of a tenant for a year or any less period than a year or of a tenant whose sole right to possession is under the Rent Act: Sched. 2, Pt. II, para. 7 (2).

(f) Sched. 2, Pt. II, para. 4 (6).

the other party to the mortgage, charge or agreement an opportunity of being heard, may, if the court thinks fit, make an order:

(a) in the case of a house which has been purchased compulsorily, discharging or modifying any outstanding liabilities of the person aforesaid by virtue of any bond, covenant or other obligation with respect to the debt secured by the mortgage or charge (*g*) or by virtue of the agreement, or

(b) in the case of a house vacated in pursuance of a demolition order, closing order or clearance order, discharging or modifying the terms of the mortgage, charge or agreement and in either case either unconditionally or subject to such terms and conditions, including conditions with respect to the payment of money, as the court may think just and equitable to impose (*h*).

In determining in any case what order, if any, to make under this provision the court must have regard to all the circumstances of the case, and in particular in the case of a mortgage or charge (a) to whether the mortgagee or person entitled to the benefit of the charge acted reasonably in advancing the principal sum on the terms of the mortgage or charge, and (b) to the extent to which the house may have become unfit for human habitation owing to any default on the part of the mortgagor or person entitled to the interest charged in carrying out any obligation under the terms of the mortgage or charge with respect to the repair of the house; and the mortgagee or person entitled to the benefit of the charge shall be deemed to have acted unreasonaby if at the time when the mortgage or the charge was made, he knew or ought to have known that in all the circumstances of the case the terms of the mortgage or charge did not afford sufficient security for the principal sum advanced (*i*).

Extension by Housing (Slum Clearance Compensation) Act 1965.—In relation to the provisions as to payments to owner-occupiers of unfit houses the conditions (referred to above) are amended by making entitlement depend not upon the date of purchase or vacation, but upon the order being made before 13 December, 1965, and extended by the provision that where the date on which the owner-occupier acquired his interest fell in the period of five years beginning with 13 December, 1950, such person will be entitled to the benefit of the provisions if any order is made within 15 years beginning with the date on which that person acquired his interest (*k*).

The 1965 Act extends the jurisdiction of the county court to modify mortgages, charges and agreements to purchase by instalments so that the provisions previously mentioned apply not only to cases where a supplementary payment is made but also where a house is purchased

---

(*g*) *Quaere* whether the court can under this provision discharge or modify liability under, for example, a promissory note which has been kept alive by a declaration against merger in the mortgage (see footnote (*u*), p. 596, *supra*). The liability under the promissory note will generally be of the same amount as the debt secured by the mortgage or charge, but it is not the same debt, and it is arguable that the covenant referred to in the section is the covenant to pay in the mortgage as opposed to the covenant to pay under the promissory note.

(*h*) Sched. 2, Pt. II, para. 5 (1). See *Plimmer* v. *Barber*, [1960] J.P.L. 269; [1960] C.L.Y. 2026.

(*i*) Sched. 2, Pt. II, para. 5 (2).

(*k*) Housing (Slum Clearance Compensation) Act 1965, s. 1.

at site value in pursuance of a compulsory purchase order made by virtue of Part II or Part III of the Housing Act 1957, or has been vacated in pursuance of a demolition order, closing order or clearance order and (a) on the date of the making of the order the whole or any part of the house is occupied as a private dwelling by a person having an interest in the house, and is so occupied in right of that interest, and (b) that person continues to own that interest until the end of the relevant period, and (c) that interest has, throughout the relevant period, been subject to a mortgage or charge or to an agreement to purchase by instalments (*l*). The relevant period means the period from the date of the making of the order to, in the case of a compulsory purchase order, the date of service of notice to treat (or deemed service of notice to treat) for purchase of the said interest, or, if the purchase is effected without service of the notice to treat the date of completion of that purchase, and in the case of any other order, the date of vacation of the house in pursuance of the order, or, if the owner of the interest died before the date of service or vacation, the date of death (*m*).

These provisions apply in relation to cases where the purchase or vacation of the house in pursuance of the compulsory purchase or other order took place at any time before, as well as after, the passing of the Act (22 December, 1965) (*n*).

The Act also adds to the matters to which the court must have regard in considering an application under these provisions, namely that the court shall have regard to whether the purchase price was excessive (*o*).

II—UNDER THE LEASEHOLD REFORM ACT 1967

Purposes of the Act.—The Act entitles tenants of houses held on long leases at low rents to acquire the freehold or an extended lease (*p*). Part I of the Act, which comprises all but two of the sections of the Act, deals with enfranchisement and extension of long leaseholds. Enfranchisement and extension may affect mortgages of both the landlord's and the tenant's estate.

Discharge of mortgages on landlord's estate.—Where a tenant has exercised his right to acquire the freehold, the landlord is bound to make to the tenant a grant of the house and premises for an estate in fee simple absolute, subject to the tenancy and to tenant's incumbrances (*q*), but otherwise free of incumbrances (*r*). Express

---

(*l*) Section 2 (2).   (*m*) Section 2 (5).   (*n*) Section 2 (4).   (*o*) Section 2 (3).
(*p*) For other Acts giving a right of enfranchisement, see Law of Property Act 1925, s. 153, and the Places of Worship (Enfranchisement) Act 1920. The latter Act is amended by the 1967 Act.
(*q*) A charge on the landlord's estate to secure the payment of money or the performance of any other obligation is not treated as a tenant's incumbrance by reason only of the grant of the tenancy being subsequent to the creation of the charge and not authorised as against the persons interested in the charge (and the mortgagee is treated as having duly concurred in the grant of the tenancy for the purpose only of validating it despite the charge on the grantor's estate). But the mortgage is treated as a tenant's incumbrance if the tenancy was granted after 1 January, 1968 (the appointed day), and it has not by the time of the conveyance become binding on the mortgagee: Leasehold Reform Act 1967, s. 12 (8).
(*r*) Leasehold Reform Act 1967, s. 8 (1).

provision is made by the Act for the automatic discharge of a mortgage affecting the landlord's interest. A conveyance made in pursuance of the landlord's obligation shall as regards any charge (s) on the landlord's estate (however created or arising) to secure the payment of money or the performance of any other obligation by the landlord or any other person, not being a charge subject to which the conveyance is required to be made or which would be overreached apart from the relevant provision (*t*), be effective to discharge the house and premises from the charge, and from the operation of any order made by a court for the enforcement of the charge, and to extinguish any term of years created for the purpose of the charge, and shall do so without the persons entitled to or interested in the charge or in any such order or term of years becoming parties to or executing the conveyance (*u*).

Where the conveyance to the tenant is effective to discharge the mortgage it is the duty of the tenant to apply (*x*) the price payable for the house and premises (*y*), in the first instance in or towards the redemption of the mortgage (and, if there are more than one, then according to their priorities), and if any amount so payable is not so paid nor paid into court in accordance with the provision in respect thereof (*z*), then, for the amount in question, the house and premises shall remain subject to the charge (*a*). For the purpose of determining the amount payable in respect of any mortgage the person entitled thereto is not permitted to exercise any right of consolidation (*b*). The mortgagee may be required to accept three months' or any longer notice of the intention to pay the whole or part of the principal secured by the mortgage, together with interest to the date of payment, notwithstanding that the terms of the mortgage make other provision

---

(*s*) A debenture holder's charge, whether a floating charge or not, in favour of trustees for such debenture holders is not a charge for this purpose. It is automatically discharged by the conveyance, the provision as to payment of the purchase price to the person (s) entitled to the benefit of the charge do not apply and the charge is to be disregarded in determining priorities. But a charge in favour of trustees for debenture holders which at the date of the conveyance is a specific and not a floating charge is a charge for this purpose: s. 12 (5). And a specific charge under a single debenture or in favour of a single debenture holder would appear to be a charge for this purpose.

(*t*) A conveyance executed under the landlord's obligation to enfranchise (a) has effect under s. 2 (1) of the Law of Property Act 1925, to overreach any incumbrance capable of being overreached under that section as if, where the interest conveyed is settled land, the conveyance were made under the powers of the Settled Land Act 1925, and as if the requirements of s. 2 (1) as to payment of the capital money allowed any part of the purchase price paid or applied in accordance with ss. 11 to 13 of the Leasehold Reform Act 1967, to be so paid or applied; (b) shall not be made subject to any incumbrance capable of being overreached by the conveyance, but shall be made subject (where they are not capable of being overreached) to rentcharges and other rents falling within s. 191 of the Law of Property Act 1925, except as otherwise provided by s. 11 of the Leasehold Reform Act 1967: Leasehold Reform Act 1967, s. 8 (4). Section 11 relates to exoneration from, or redemption of, rentcharges, etc., and s. 13 relates to payment into court in respect of mortgages, etc.: see p. 604, *infra*.

(*u*) Leasehold Reform Act 1967, s. 12 (1).

(*x*) If the tenant is himself entitled to the mortgage he can retain the appropriate amount in respect thereof: s. 12 (3).

(*y*) Less any amount paid out for the redemption of a rentcharge: s. 12 (9).

(*z*) See p. 604, *infra*.

(*a*) Leasehold Reform Act 1967, s. 12 (2).

(*b*) *Ibid.*, s. 12 (3).

or no provision as to the time and manner of payment, but the mortgagee will be entitled, if he so requires, to receive such additional payment as is reasonable in the circumstances in respect of the costs of re-investment or other incidental costs and expenses and in respect of any reduction in the rate of interest obtainable on re-investment(c).

The mortgagee need not be a party to execute the conveyance (d). But he may join in the conveyance for the purpose of discharging the house and premises from the mortgage without payment or for a less payment than that to which he would otherwise be entitled, and, if he does so, the persons to whom the price ought to be paid should be determined accordingly (e). As the mortgage is only discharged if the mortgagee is wholly, or where the purchase price is not sufficient, partially satisfied, or if payment is made into court (f), the enfranchising tenant will need to satisfy a subsequent purchaser that payment was in fact made and he should accordingly demand from the mortgagee a formal discharge, where the mortgage is paid in full, or a formal release of the security, where there is only a partial payment, or that the mortgagee join in the conveyance to acknowledge receipt of the whole amount owing to him, or the whole of the purchase money, if that is less. And if the mortgagee refuses to do so, the tenant will be entitled to pay into court the amount of the payment to be made in respect of the mortgage (g).

Where the house and premises are discharged from a mortgage (without the obligations secured thereby being satisfied by the receipt of the whole or part of the price) the discharge of the house and premises does not prejudice any right or remedy for the enforcement of these obligations against other property comprised in the same or any other security, nor prejudice any personal liability as principal or otherwise of the landlord or any other person (h).

Payment into court in respect of mortgages, etc.—The enfranchising tenant may pay into court on account of the price for the house and premises (i) the amount, if known, of the payment to be made in respect of the mortgage, or, if that amount is not known, the whole of the price or such less amount as the tenant thinks right in order to provide for that payment in the following circumstances:

(1) because for any reason difficulty arises in ascertaining how much is payable in respect of the mortgage;

(2) because a person who is or may be entitled to receive payment cannot be found or ascertained;

(3) because any such person refuses or fails to make out a title, or to accept payment and give a proper discharge, or to take any steps reasonably required of him to enable the sum payable to be ascertained or paid;

(4) because a tender of the sum payable cannot, by reason of complications in the title to it or the want of two or more trustees or for other reasons,

---

(c) Leasehold Reform Act 1967, s. 12 (4). The additional payment is presumably payable by the enfranchising tenant.

(d) *Ibid.*, s. 12 (1).

(e) *Ibid.*, s. 12 (7).

(f) *Ibid.*, s. 12 (2).

(g) Under s. 13, *supra.*

(h) Leasehold Reform Act 1967, s. 12 (6). But see s. 36 as to relief in respect of mortgages, etc., on landlord's estate, p. 605, *infra.*

(i) Less the amount for the redemption of any rentcharge: s. 13 (4).

be effected, or not without incurring or involving unreasonable costs or delay (*k*).

The tenant must pay the purchase price (*i*) into court if before execution of the conveyance written notice is given to him:

(a) that the landlord or person entitled to the benefit of a charge on the house and premises so requires for the purpose of protecting the rights of persons so entitled, or for reasons related to any application made or to be made under s. 36 of the Act (*l*), or to the bankruptcy or winding up of the landlord; or

(b) that steps have been taken to enforce any charge on the landlord's interest in the house and premises by the bringing of proceedings in any court, as by the appointment of a receiver or otherwise (*m*).

Payment into court of the correct amount automatically discharges the mortgage, but if less than the correct amount is paid in the discharge is not total (*n*). The difficulty of satisfying a subsequent purchaser as to the discharge mentioned previously (*o*) applies also in the case of payment into court.

Relief in respect of mortgages, etc., on landlord's estate.—In certain cases the landlord or a second or subsequent mortgagee will be able to apply to the court (*p*) for such order as the court thinks proper for the purpose of avoiding or mitigating any financial hardship that might otherwise be caused by the rights conferred on tenants by the Leasehold Reform Act 1967 (*q*). The jurisdiction is analogous to that under the Housing Acts dealt with in Section I of this Chapter. The mortgage must affect the estate of the immediate or a superior landlord of a house held at the passing of the Act (27 October, 1967) on a long tenancy not having more than twenty years unexpired, or on a long tenancy capable of being determined within twenty years by notice given by the landlord (*r*). The application may be made in the following circumstances:

(1) Where the landlord proposes during the tenancy (including any extension thereof under the Act) to sell or realise any property which is subject to the charge, or a tenant of the house has given notice of his desire to have the freehold (*s*);

(2) Where during the tenancy (including any such extension) the mortgagee has taken any steps to enforce the charge or demanded payment of the sum thereby secured, or, if the house or any other property subject to

---

(*i*) See footnote on page 604.

(*k*) Leasehold Reform Act 1967, s. 13 (1), (2).

(*l*) See *supra*.

(*m*) Leasehold Reform Act 1967, s. 13 (3). Where payment is to be made into court by reason only of such a notice and the notice is given with reference to proceedings in a court specified in the notice other than the county court, payment must be made into the court so specified: s. 13 (3).

(*n*) *Ibid.*, s. 12 (1), (2).

(*o*) See p. 604, *supra*.

(*p*) The county court: s. 20 (1). But where steps are taken in a court other than the county court to enforce a mortgage or recover any sum thereby secured, that other court has the like powers in relation to that or any other mortgage as the county court, or, if an application for relief is pending in the county court, the other court may suspend the proceedings for enforcement, etc., on such terms as it thinks just, or direct that the proceedings for enforcement, etc., be transferred to the county court: s. 36 (5).

(*q*) Leasehold Reform Act 1967, s. 36.

(*r*) *Ibid.*, s. 36 (1) (a), (b).

(*s*) *Ibid.*, s. 36 (2) (a).

the mortgage is subject also to another mortgage created or arising before 27 October, 1967, the person entitled to the benefit of the other mortgage has taken any steps to enforce the other mortgage or demanded payment of the sum thereby secured (*t*).

If the application is made by the landlord the court may make an order providing for all or any of the following:

(1) For discharging or modifying any liability in respect of the sum secured by the charge, whether of the landlord or of persons liable jointly with him or as surety for him;

(2) For discharging or modifying the terms of the charge whether as respects the house or any other property subject to the mortgage, or the terms of any collateral charge;

(3) For restricting the exercise of any right or remedy in respect of any such liability or charge (*u*).

If the application is made by the second or subsequent mortgagee the court may make an order providing for all or any of the following:

(1) For discharging or modifying the terms of any prior charge, whether as respects the house or any other property subject to the charge;

(2) For restricting the exercise of any right or remedy in respect of any prior charge on the house or other property subject to the charge (*x*).

In either case any order may be made either conditionally or subject to such terms and conditions, including conditions with respect to the payment of money, as the court may think just and equitable to impose (*y*).

III—UNDER THE RENT ACT 1968

Variation of the terms of regulated mortgages.—As to this, see p. 278, *supra* (*z*).

IV—UNDER THE MONEYLENDERS ACT 1927

Setting aside of security.—As to this, see p. 234, *supra* (*a*).

V—UNDER THE CONSUMER CREDIT ACT 1974

Refusal of enforcement order, etc.—As to this, see pp. 146 *et seq.*, *supra*.

VI—UNDER THE LANDS CLAUSES ACT

Redemption on compulsory purchase.—As to this, see p. 536, *supra*.

(*t*) Leasehold Reform Act 1967, s. 36 (2) (b).
(*u*) *Ibid.*, s. 36 (2).   And see footnote (*g*), p. 601, *supra*.
(*x*) *Ibid.*, s. 36 (3).
(*y*) *Ibid.*, s. 36 (4).
(*z*) And see generally, pp. 276 *et seq.*, *supra*.
(*a*) And see generally, Part III, *supra*.

PART IX

ACCOUNTS AND COSTS

CHAPTER 35

Accounts

I—ACCOUNTS GENERALLY BETWEEN MORTGAGOR AND MORTGAGEE

A—WHO IS BOUND BY THE ACCOUNTS

Accounts prima facie binding on all parties.—An account taken between the mortgagee and mortgagor, whether it is taken in or out of court, is prima facie binding not only on the parties to it, but on other persons interested in the equity of redemption. It is binding, therefore, on a subsequent incumbrancer (a). So, accounts taken in an action by a subsequent incumbrancer against the mortgagor and the prior incumbrancer, bind the mortgagor as to the amount of the debt due to the prior incumbrancer, so long as the judgment remains unimpeached (b).

And an account taken in court between the mortgagee and the tenant for life of the estate, will bind the person entitled to the vested remainder, though he was no party to the action; as well as a contingent remainderman, though not *in esse* when the accounts were taken (c).

When accounts not binding.—But the account is only binding when the parties to it represent both sides of the account. Hence the mortgagor, or a person claiming under him, is not bound by accounts taken in his absence between the mortgagee and a transferee of the mortgage (d). And accounts taken in an action are not binding upon co-defendants, as between themselves, except so far as the relief sought by the plaintiff required that such accounts should be taken as between those defendants. In the case, therefore, of a simple action to redeem against several incumbrancers, since it is unnecessary for the purposes

---

(a) *Needler* v. *Deeble* (1677), 1 Ch. Cas. 299; *Williams* v. *Day* (1680), 2 Ch. Cas. 32; *Wrixon* v. *Vize* (1842), 2 Dru. & War. 192; affd. 3 Dru. & War. 104.

(b) *Farquharson* v. *Seton* (1828), 5 Russ. 45.

(c) *Allen* v. *Papworth* (1731), 1 Ves. Sen. 163; and see *Wrixon* v. *Vize, supra.* Under the present law the tenant for life would, as estate owner, represent the remainderman.

Sureties are bound by the accounts of a receiver appointed by the court, where the accounts are regularly passed according to the course of the court: *Mead* v. *Lord Orrery* (1745), 3 Atk. 235. Where an insolvent was party to an action, he was bound by the accounts although the person who represented his estate was absent: *Byrne* v. *Lord Carew* (1849), 13 Ir. Eq. R. 1.

But a first mortgagee is under no duty to inform a second mortgagee of the true state of the account between himself and the mortgagor: *Weld-Blundell* v. *Synott*, [1940] 2 K.B. 107; [1940] 2 All E.R. 580.

(d) *Earl Macclesfield* v. *Fitton* (1683), 1 Vern. 168; *Mangles* v. *Dixon* (1852), 3 H.L.C. 702, 737.

of the judgment to take the accounts between the subsequent incumbrancers, any accounts so taken will not be binding as between them (*e*).

Interference with settled accounts.—But a settled account (*f*),
although prima facie binding on the parties to it and on other persons
interested in the equity of redemption, and although in the ordinary
course it will not be disturbed (*g*), may under special circumstances be
either reopened altogether, or may be subjected to possible alteration
in respect of particular items only. In the former case the order is
that the settled account shall be opened and set aside and a new
account taken; in the latter case, that the settled account is to stand,
but that any of the parties are to be at liberty "to surcharge and falsify
any of the items and charges therein" (*h*). Moreover, when an account
is admitted to contain an error, it can be "purged" by setting off
against that error an error shown to have been made in another account,
in favour of the person prejudiced by the first error (*i*).

Liberty to surcharge and falsify will be given merely on the ground
of error in the account (*k*); but it is essential that at least one error
shall be specifically charged and proved (*l*). This also is sufficient

---

(*e*) *Cottingham* v. *Earl of Shrewsbury* (1843), 3 Hare, 627, 638.

(*f*) A settled account is sometimes referred to as a stated account, but the meaning
is the same. The account is stated between the parties, or stated by one side and
agreed to by the other. The reservation in an account of "errors excepted" does not
prevent it from being considered as settled; and such an account will be taken to be
settled where the balance is carried over to a new account: *Johnson* v. *Curtis* (1791),
3 Bro. C.C. 266. And as to settled accounts, see *Parkinson* v. *Hanbury* (1867),
L.R. 2 H.L. 1, at p. 12; and as to when an account rendered will be deemed to have been
agreed to, see *Sherman* v. *Sherman* (1692), 2 Vern. 276; *Hunter* v. *Belcher* (1864), 2
De G.J. & Sm. 194.

(*g*) *Newen* v. *Wetten* (1862), 31 Beav. 315.

(*h*) "If any of the parties can show an omission for which credit ought to be given,
that is a surcharge; or if anything is inserted that is a wrong charge, he is at liberty
to show it, and that is falsification": *Pit* v. *Cholmondeley* (1754), 2 Ves. S. 565, 566.
It has been said that for accounts to be falsified, they must contain charges in the nature
of fraud; not merely charges which may be regarded as excessive: *Heighington* v.
Grant (1845), 1 Ph. 600, 601, *per* Lord LYNDHURST, L.C. But a charge might be so
excessive as to be improper and fraudulent in equity, though there was no actual fraud.

(*i*) *Lawless* v. *Mansfield* (1841), 1 Dr. & War. 557.

(*k*) *Vernon* v. *Vawdrey* (1740), 2 Atk. 119; *Chambers* v. *Goldwin* (1804), 9 Ves. 254
(commission on consignments improperly charged); *Langstaffe* v. *Fenwick* (1805), 10
Ves. 405 (commission on personal collection of rents by mortgagee); *Daniell* v. *Sinclair*
(1881), 6 App. Cas. 181 (compound instead of simple interest charged by common
mistake); see *Wrixon* v. *Vize* (1842), 2 Dr. & War. 192, 203.

The amount of the error, it has been said, is immaterial. The court looks at the
principle involved. Thus relief has been given upon an error of only a few shillings:
Lewes v. *Morgan* (1817), 5 Price, at p. 86; *Lawless* v. *Mansfield*, *supra*, at p. 616.

An error in the accounts not detected in, but corrected and satisfied before, the
commencement of the action, is no ground for a decree to surcharge and falsify: *Davies*
v. *Spurling* (1829), Tam. 199. On the other hand, a person whose account is impeached,
cannot deprive his opponent of the benefit arising from the existence of errors in the
account, or alter his rights, by giving him notice in the progress of the action, as he,
from time to time discovers errors, that he is willing to correct them: *Lawless* v. *Mansfield*,
supra. But perhaps it would not be safe to rely on these cases now. For overpayment
of surplus proceeds of sale by first mortgagee, see *Weld-Blundell* v. *Synott*, *supra*.

(*l*) *Parkinson* v. *Hanbury* (1867), L.R. 2 H.L. 1, at p. 12; see *Chambers* v. *Goldwin*,
supra. But particular statements of error are only necessary where the object of the
action is to impeach a settled account, and not where an account is prayed and no
settled account is proved; though the pleading suggests the existence of a settled
account. In such a case liberty will be given to surcharge and falsify, if upon inquiry
any settled account is found to exist, whether specific errors have been charged or not:

since, if one error has been proved, it may be expected that, upon investigation, others will be discovered (*m*). The error may be either of fact or of law (*n*).

It appears not to have been decided whether, where there are several distinct accounts, in some only of which errors are alleged and proved, all become liable to be surcharged and falsified (*o*).

The account will be opened altogether in case of fraud, and this notwithstanding the lapse of a great number of years (*p*). Moreover, apart from fraud, it will be reopened if the relation of the parties, or the manner in which the settlement took place, or the nature of the error proved, shows that the settlement ought not to be considered as an act binding on the parties who signed it, and that it would be inequitable for the accounting party to take advantage of it (*q*).

Thus, the account may be reopened if it contains errors of considerable extent both in number and amount; and if a fiduciary relation exists between the parties—where, for instance, the accounting party is an agent or a trustee—a less number of errors will suffice for the making of such an order (*r*). A single error of large amount has been made the ground for reopening the whole account (*s*); but ordinarily it will be sufficient to give leave to surcharge and falsify (*t*).

Where the reopening of the account is claimed, either fraud or specific error must be alleged and proved (*u*). The accounts will be more readily opened where the relationship of solicitor and client exists (*x*), "provided, that is, excessive charge or error is shown (*y*);

Kinsman v. *Barker* (1808), 14 Ves. 579; *Lawless* v. *Mansfield, supra.* If a settled account is proved, as set up by the pleadings, and no error shown by the plaintiff, the action will be dismissed: *Endo* v. *Caleham* (1831), Younge, 306; *Drew* v. *Power* (1803), 1 Sch. & Lef. 192; *Lawless* v. *Mansfield, supra.*

(*m*) *Coleman* v. *Mellersh* (1850), 2 Mac. & G. 309, 314.

(*n*) *Roberts* v. *Kuffin* (1740), 2 Atk. 112; *Langstaffe* v. *Fenwick, supra*; *Daniell* v. *Sinclair, supra,* at p. 190.

(*o*) *Lawless* v. *Mansfield, supra;* and see *Chambers* v. *Goldwin, supra,* where, however, the commission complained of extended to all the accounts.

(*p*) *Vernon* v. *Vawdrey, supra* (23 years); *Allfrey* v. *Allfrey* (1849), 1 Mac. & G. 87 (17 years). See *Drew* v. *Power* (1803), 1 Sch. & Lef. 182, 192; *Chambers* v. *Goldwin, supra,* p. 265; *Davies* v. *Spurling* (1829), Taml. 199; *Clarke* v. *Tipping* (1846), 9 Beav. 284; *Cheese* v. *Keen,* [1908] 1 Ch. 245, 252. In *Wharton* v. *May* (1799), 5 Ves. 27, the account was reopened for fraud, notwithstanding the vouchers had been destroyed by general consent.

(*q*) *Coleman* v. *Mellersh, supra,* at p. 314; *Re Webb, Lambert* v. *Still,* [1894] 1 Ch. 73, 84.

(*r*) *Williamson* v. *Barbour* (1877), 9 Ch. D. 529. But although the errors are numerous and important, yet if there has been a great lapse of time, and the books and documents have been lost, the court may decline to open the account altogether and give leave only to surcharge and falsify: *Millar* v. *Craig* (1843), 6 Beav. 433. In a foreclosure action the mortgagor can set up a claim to reopen an account by way of defence in the same way as if the claim had been made by counterclaim: *Eyre* v. *Hughes* (1876), 2 Ch. D. 148.

(*s*) *Pritt* v. *Clay* (1843), 6 Beav. 503.

(*t*) *Gething* v. *Keighley* (1878), 9 Ch. D. 547; save in case of fraud and fiduciary relationship: *Williamson* v. *Barbour, supra.*

(*u*) *Needler* v. *Deeble* (1677), 1 Ch. Cas. 299; *Knight* v. *Bampfield* (1683), 1 Vern. 179; *Dawson* v. *Dawson* (1737), West *temp.* Hard., 171; *Taylor* v. *Haylin* (1788), 2 Bro. C.C. 310; *Johnson* v. *Curtis* (1791), 3 Bro. C.C. 266.

(*x*) *Lewes* v. *Morgan* (1817), 5 Price, 42; *Morgan* v. *Evans* (1834), 3 Cl. & F. 159; *Ward* v. *Sharp* (1884), 53 L.J. Ch. 313.

(*y*) *Re Webb, Lambert* v. *Still,* [1894] 1 Ch. 73; *Cheese* v. *Keen,* [1908] 1 Ch. 245, where, however, only liberty was given to tax and to surcharge and falsify.

but unless fraud, or error amounting to evidence of fraud, in the bill of costs which forms the subject of the security, is relied on, there must be averment and proof of the specific items alleged to be erroneous (*z*).

Where the person objecting to the account was not one of the parties to it, collusion between such parties will also be a ground for opening it (*a*).

Special circumstances affecting the accounts.—Any special circumstance or fact affecting the amount due from the mortgagor to the mortgagee in a foreclosure action—such as a valuation of the security in bankruptcy—should be pleaded or brought to the attention of the court, before the usual foreclosure judgment is made, in order that a direction may be given that, in taking the accounts, regard shall be had to such special circumstance or fact. If this is not done at the trial, no such question can be subsequently raised either on taking the accounts or on the master's certificate (*b*).

When proof of accounts to be given.—In an action for an account, evidence as to the state of the accounts ought not to be allowed at the hearing, because of the inconvenience of taking an account in part which ought to be taken altogether on a subsequent proceeding (*c*). But evidence, though inadmissible to prove at the hearing the particulars of the account, may be material to show the right to an account where the defendant has not in terms conceded it; for the right is then matter of evidence (*d*).

The court may decide at the further hearing, on the certificate and merits, any question on the accounts (*e*).

B—ACCOUNTS AGAINST THE MORTGAGOR

Mortgagee's right to an account.—Whether the action is for foreclosure or redemption (*f*) the mortgagee is entitled to an immediate account (*g*) of his principal, interest, and costs, including:

(*z*) A general allegation of error will be sufficient if it is admitted by the solicitor: *Matthews* v. *Wallwyn* (1798), 4 Ves. 118, 125; but otherwise specific items must be alleged and proved to be erroneous; the account is not reopened on the mere relationship of solicitor and client: *Morgan* v. *Higgins* (1859), 1 Giff. 270, 277. See *Waters* v. *Taylor* (1837), 2 Myl. & Cr. 526; *Lewes* v. *Morgan* (1829), 3 Y. & J. 230, 394. In *Blagrave* v. *Routh* (1856), 2 K. & J. 509; on appeal (1856), 8 De G.M. & G. 620, the claim to open the account was precluded by length of time and acquiescence.

(*a*) *Sherman* v. *Cox* (1674), 3 Rep. in Chan. 83, where it was said that an account should bind, unless the plaintiff proved a great collusion.

(*b*) *Sanguinetti* v. *Stuckey's Banking Co. (No. 2)*, [1896] 1 Ch. 502.

(*c*) *Walker* v. *Woodward* (1826), 1 Russ. 107; *Law* v. *Hunter* (1826), 1 Russ. 100.

(*d*) *Tomlin* v. *Tomlin* (1841), 1 Hare, 236, 245.
In a question as to accounts which had been kept by a creditor in the position of a trustee, but which were always open to the inspection of the debtor, the books were admitted as prima facie evidence of the amount of all moneys received and paid by the creditor, with liberty to surcharge and falsify: *Ogden* v. *Battams* (1855), 1 Jur. (N.S.) 791; and an account book of a deceased mortgagee, containing entries against interest, has been admitted as evidence on behalf of his executors: *Hudson* v. *Owners of Swiftsure* (1900), 82 L.T. 389.

(*e*) *Burne* v. *Robinson* (1844), 1 Dru. & Wal. 688; *Skirrett* v. *Athy* (1811), 1 Ba. & Be. 433.

(*f*) *Du Vigier* v. *Lee* (1843), 2 Hare, 326; *Sober* v. *Kemp* (1847), 6 Hare, 155.

(*g*) *Pearse* v. *Hewitt* (1835), 7 Sim. 471.

(1)   Costs, charges, and expenses properly incurred in relation to the debt and security;

(2)   The costs of litigation properly undertaken by the mortgagee; and

(3)   The costs of the redemption or foreclosure proceedings (*h*).

He is also entitled to have a day fixed for payment or foreclosure; and all moneys for which the deed is expressly declared to be a security, or which carry interest, or are otherwise of the nature of principal, as, for instance, fines secured to a building society, may be claimed as principal (*i*).

An assignee or subsequent incumbrancer of the equity of redemption stands in the position of the mortgagor as to accounts (*k*).

Foreclosure will not be ordered without such an account if the mortgagor insists on it, even where the mortgagee swears at the hearing that the money due to him is many times more than the value of the estate.   But in that case the court will reserve the costs of the account (*l*).

Evidence of the debt.—The production of the security is prima facie evidence of the existence of the debt (*m*); and if payment is acknowledged in the usual manner by the deed, and sworn to by the mortgagee, he need not prove the payment of the consideration money by other evidence, even against a purchaser of the estate, especially after some time has elapsed (*n*).

An account stated for the purposes of a security in respect of which the debtor is entitled to the protection of the court, such as a *post obit* security, is not conclusive against him (*o*).   And where there is an uncertainty as to the amount of principal due—either because it is shown that the sum mentioned in the security was not advanced, but that only a running security was intended to be made (*p*); or by reason of the making of further advances (*q*), an inquiry may be directed to ascertain the amount lent under or on the credit of the mortgage security; and if there is no evidence of the amount really lent,

---

(*h*) See *Re Wallis, Ex parte Lickorish* (1890), 25 Q.B.D. 176; see pp. 572 *et seq.*, *infra*.

(*i*) *Blackford* v. *Davis* (1869), 4 Ch. App. 304; *Provident Permanent Building Society* v. *Greenhill* (1878), 9 Ch. D. 122.

Where the mortgage is limited to a stated sum, this means that amount of principal, exclusive of interest and costs: *White* v. *City of London Brewery Co.* (1889), 42 Ch. D. 237 (C.A.).   A current account is not necessarily closed by the appointment of a receiver: *Yourell* v. *Hibernian Bank, Ltd.*, [1918] A.C. 372 (H.L.).

(*k*) *Melbourne Banking Corpn.* v. *Brougham* (1882), 7 App. Cas. 307 (P.C.); *Mainland* v. *Upjohn* (1889), 41 Ch. D. 126.

(*l*) *Taylor* v. *Mostyn* (1883), 25 Ch. D. 48.

(*m*) *Piddock* v. *Brown* (1734), 3 P. Wms. 288.   The realisation of a surety's securities may be equivalent to a further advance to the principal debtor: *Re Smith, Lawrence* v. *Kitson*, [1918] 2 Ch. 405.

(*n*) *Goddard* v. *Complin* (1669), 1 Ch. Ca. 119; *Holt* v. *Mill* (1692), 2 Vern. 279; *Hampton* v. *Spencer* (1693), 2 Vern. 287.

(*o*) *Tottenham* v. *Green* (1863), 32 L.J. Ch. 201.   And where there are manifest signs of fraud there must be proof of actual payment: *Piddock* v. *Brown, supra*.   See as to proving consideration for a bond debt: *Whitaker* v. *Wright* (1843), 2 Hare, 310.

(*p*) *Melland* v. *Gray* (1843), 2 Y. & C.C.C. 199; and 5 Jur. 1004.

(*q*) *Gordon* v. *Graham* (1716), 2 Eq. Cas. Abr. 598; 7 Vin. Abr. 52, pl. 3.

the mortgagor will be charged to the extent of his own admissions only (*r*).

Where the debt is for costs.—In the case of a mortgage given to a solicitor by his client to secure the amount of a bill of costs, the court will assume, after several years have elapsed, that the business charged for was actually done; but the peculiar jealousy with which it watches such transactions will cause it to direct an inquiry as to the fairness of the charges, although at the time of executing the security the client had assented to the bill (*s*). And where money has been lent by the solicitor to the client, the security is not conclusive proof of the actual advance, and this must be proved by other evidence (*t*).

Payments on account of debt.—The assignee of the security will be bound to allow payments made by the mortgagor to the original mortgagee, after, but without notice of, the assignment (*u*). But payments of principal made to the mortgagee's solicitors, if the solicitors had no special authority to receive such payments, will not be allowed the mortgagor (*x*).

Accounting for rents: legal mortgage.—Subject to statutory restriction, a legal mortgagee is generally entitled to take possession immediately upon execution of the mortgage (*y*). So long as he abstains from doing so, neither the mortgagor, remaining in possession (*z*), nor his assignees in bankruptcy, nor a person holding under a mere voluntary trust for the mortgagor, and whose possession may therefore be considered to be that of the mortgagor (*a*), is bound to account to the mortgagee for the rents (*b*).

But on the legal mortgagee giving notice to the tenant to pay the

---

(*r*) *Melland* v. *Gray, supra.* Entries in the books of a deceased person, who was the solicitor of the mortgagor at the date of the mortgage, to the effect that he had received the money and had paid it over to the mortgagor, are admissible as evidence of payment of the mortgage money: *Clark* v. *Wilmot* (1841), 1 Y. & C.C.C. 53; and see *Smartle* v. *Williams* (1894), Comberbach, 247 (book of bursar of a college).

(*s*) *Wragg* v. *Denham* (1836), 2 Y. & C. Ex. 117.

(*t*) *Lewes* v. *Morgan* (1817), 3 Y. & J. 394; *Lawless* v. *Mansfield* (1841), 1 Dru. & War. 557; *Gresley* v. *Moulsey* (1861), 3 De G.F. & J. 433.

(*u*) *Williams* v. *Sorrell* (1799), 4 Ves. 389; *Re Lord Southampton's Estate, Allen* v. *Lord Southampton* (1880), 16 Ch. D. 178; *Bickerton* v. *Walker* (1885), 31 Ch. D. 151, 158; *Turner* v. *Smith*, [1901] 1 Ch. 213; *cf. Dixon* v. *Winch*, [1900] 1 Ch. 736, where there was collusion. And that a mortgagor may be debarred from claiming credit in respect of moneys realised under an earlier mortgage which he has allowed to be outstanding, see *Re Ambrose's Estate*, [1913] 1 I.R. 506; affd., [1914] 1 I.R. 123.

(*x*) *Withington* v. *Tate* (1869), 4 Ch. App. 288.

(*y*) See pp. 314 *et seq, supra.*

(*z*) *Higgins* v. *York Buildings Co.* (1740), 2 Atk. 107; *Drummond* v. *Duke of St. Albans* (1800), 5 Ves. 433; *Ex parte Wilson* (1813), 2 Ves. & B. 252; *Ex parte Calwell* (1828), 1 Mol. 259.

(*a*) *Hele* v. *Lord Bexley* (1855), 20 Beav. 127; *Flight* v. *Camac* (1856), 4 W.R. 664.

(*b*) See p. 333, *supra.* This rule applies also to the owner of an estate in possession, keeping down the interest of charges on the estate, just as to an ordinary mortgagor: *Earl of Clarendon* v. *Barham* (1842), 1 Y. & C.C.C. 688; see p. 569, *infra.* And the mortgagee of a rentcharge during the life of a tenant for life, who has not entered into possession, is not an assign of the mortgagor within the Apportionment Act, and cannot have payment of the arrears of his rentcharge out of the apportioned part of the rents to the death of the tenant for life: *Re Marquis of Anglesey's Estate, Paget* v. *Anglesey* (1874), L.R. 17 Eq. 283; *Yorkshire Banking Co.* v. *Mullan* (1887), 35 Ch. D. 125. If, however, the mortgagee is dispossessed by the mortgagor's collusion with the tenants, and his persuasion to attorn to him, he ought to account for the rents, upon coming to redeem: *Mead* v. *Lord Orrery* (1745), 3 Atk. 235; and see *Goodman* v. *Kine* (1845), 8 Beav. 379.

rent to him, he becomes entitled to rent due or in arrear at the date of the notice, as well as to rent which accrues afterwards (c); provided, in the case of a lease made after the mortgage, either that the tenant has attorned to the mortgagee (d), or that the lease is made under the mortgagor's statutory power (e).

Accounting for rents: equitable mortgage.—The right of an equitable mortgagee to rents does not arise until the time of the application upon which an order for sale is made (f). From that time he is entitled to the rent (g), even though an inquiry as to the date of his security forms part of the order (h). But if by any means he should get into lawful possession (i), he will be entitled, as a legal mortgagee under like circumstances, to the rents from the date of his possession (k), and to growing crops which he severs from the soil (l), and he will not be made to refund them upon the making of the order (m). In the same way, if rent is paid to an equitable mortgagee by a tenant who is under no mistake of fact, but knows that the rent is claimed by a mere equitable mortgagee, the tenant cannot demand it back (n).

Growing crops.—A mortgagee who has not taken possession is not entitled to growing crops which have been removed by the mortgagor between the time of demand and recovery of possession; but he has a right to all crops growing on the premises when he takes possession, unless the mortgagor can claim them as emblements under an express contract of tenancy (o). And the mortgagor and persons claiming under him will be restrained from removing them (p). This

---

(c) *Moss* v. *Gallimore* (1779), 1 Doug. K.B. 279; attornment is not necessary: Law of Property Act 1925, s. 151. ss. 9, 10.

(d) Where attornment is required, this is not conclusively shown by the tenant merely continuing in possession after receipt of the notice: *Towerson* v. *Jackson*, [1891] 2 Q.B. 484; diss. from *Underhay* v. *Read* (1887), 20 Q.B.D. 209, and *Brown* v. *Storey* (1840), 1 Man. & Gr. 117. And the attornment of the tenant will not set up the mortgagee's title by relation to the time of the notice: *Evans* v. *Elliot* (1838), 9 A. & E. 342; *Hickman* v. *Machin* (1859), 4 H. & N. 716.

(e) See p. 341, *supra*.

(f) An equitable mortgagee is not entitled to rents (which are payable to a legal reversioner), because such a mortgage creates no privity of estate between the mortgagee and the tenant entitling the mortgagee to claim the rent. Accordingly an equitable mortgagee has no right to direct a tenant of the mortgagor to pay the rent to him. In bankruptcy, where a legal mortgagee has not entered or given notice to the tenants, an order for sale is not treated as equivalent to notice, and he takes the rents only from the sale: *Ex parte Living* (1835), 1 Deac. 1; *Re Medley, Ex parte Barnes* (1838), 3 Mont. & A. 497. Payments under licence to dig brick earth, held to belong to the mortgagee as rent in arrear: *Re Brindley, Ex parte Hankey* (1829), Mont. & Mac. 247.

(g) *Re Norman, Ex parte Burrell* (1838), 3 Mont. & A. 439; *Re Birks, Ex parte Carlon* (1837), 3 Mont. & A. 328; *Re Pearson, Ex parte Scott* (1838), 3 Mont. & A. 592; *Re Postle, Ex parte Bignold* (1834), 2 Mont. & A. 16.

(h) *Re Teesdale, Ex parte Thorpe* (1838), 3 Mont. & A. 441; *Re Harvey, Ex parte Bignold* (1827), 2 Gl. & J. 273; *Re Feaver, Ex parte Smith* (1844), 3 Mont. D. & De G. 680.

(i) If, for example, the mortgage entitles him to possession.

(k) *Re Postle, Ex parte Bignold* (1835), 4 Deac. & C. 259.

(l) *Re Gordon* (1889), 61 L.T. 299.

(m) *Re Freeman, Ex parte Williams* (1865), 13 W.R. 564.

(n) *Finck* v. *Tranter*, [1905] 1 K.B. 427.

(o) *Re Skinner, Ex parte Temple* (1822), 1 Gl. & J. 216; *Re Phillips, Ex parte National Mercantile Bank* (1880), 16 Ch. D. 104.

(p) *Bagnall* v. *Villar* (1879), 12 Ch. D. 812.

applies as well to an equitable as to a legal mortgagee who has taken possession (q).

Improvements.—A mortgagor can have no allowance for money spent by him on the estate, all improvements enuring for the benefit of the mortgagee (r).

Where receiver in possession.—A receiver is entitled to rents in arrear at the time of his appointment (s); but if the mortgagor is in possession, he is liable to pay an occupation rent only from the date of the demand by the receiver (t).

If a mortgagee is restrained from taking possession, and a receiver is appointed adversely to him, on an undertaking to be answerable in damages, the receiver will be charged with an occupation rent (u). But where a receiver is in possession in an action to which the mortgagee is not a party, a mortgagee out of possession will not be entitled to the rents paid by the tenants to the receiver even after notice given them by the mortgagee; it being first necessary to apply to the court to discharge the receiver (x).

From the time of the discharge of a receiver appointed in an action to which the mortgagee is not a party, or of the application for it, the mortgagee may be considered to be in possession, and to be entitled to the rents (y).

C—ACCOUNTS AGAINST THE MORTGAGEE AND HIS ASSIGNS

Purchase of mortgage debt under par.—When the amount of the debt owing on the mortgage has been established, the mortgagor cannot claim the benefit of a purchase of the security by a transferee for less than that amount, for, as a general rule, the bona fide purchaser of an incumbrance for less than is due upon it, or than it is worth, whether he is a creditor of the mortgagor (z), or a stranger (a), is entitled, both against the mortgagor or his representatives (b) and other incumbrancers (c), to be paid all that is due on the purchased security (d). And there is no right against him for an account of what

(q) Re Gordon, supra.
(r) Norris v. Caledonian Insurance Co. (1869), L.R. 8 Eq. 127.
(s) See Re Ind, Coope & Co., Ltd., Fisher v. Ind, Coope & Co., [1911] 2 Ch. 223. But where the produce of crops was shipped to the consignees of the mortgagor, but was not converted prior to the appointment of a receiver on behalf of the mortgagee, the mortgagor was not obliged to give any account of it: Codrington v. Johnstone (1838), 1 Beav. 520.
(t) Yorkshire Banking Co. v. Mullan (1887), 35 Ch. D. 125.
(u) Re Joyce, Ex parte Warren (1875), 10 Ch. App. 222.
(x) See p. 311, supra.
(y) Thomas v. Brigstocke (1827), 4 Russ. 64. As to payments by a receiver to a first mortgagee in excess of the interest to which he is entitled, see Law v. Glenn (1867), 2 Ch. App. 634. As to payment of rents to a mortgagee by sequestrators under a sequestration for contempt, see Walker v. Bell (1816), 2 Mad. 21, and cases cited there; Tatham v. Parker (1855), 1 Jur. N.S. 992; Re Hoare, Hoare v. Owen, [1892] 3 Ch. 94.
(z) Morret v. Paske (1740), 2 Atk. 52; Darcy v. Hall (1682), 1 Vern. 49.
(a) Davis v. Barrett (1845), 14 Beav. 542; Anon. (1707), 1 Salk. 155.
(b) Phillips v. Vaughan (1685), 1 Vern. 336; Ascough v. Johnson (1688), 2 Vern. 66.
(c) Morret v. Paske, supra.
(d) So, if the reversioner in fee, not being the original mortgagor of an estate which is subject to several charges, purchases the first for less than is due upon it, he may hold it for all that is due, and the later incumbrancers will have no account against him, nor any equity to make the purchased security stand only for the price which he paid for it: Davis v. Barrett, supra.

he has paid for his purchase. This rule depends upon the principle, that the assignee stands in the place of his assignor, and as the latter might have assigned to him *gratis*, it is but just that the measure of the allowance should be what was due, and not what was paid. The assignee taking the hazard, should also have the benefit of the bargain, of which neither the mortgagor, nor any subsequent incumbrancer, can have any equity to deprive him (*e*).

The rule is, however, different, if the purchaser of the incumbrance is a person, in whom the estate charged with the incumbrance has become vested subject also to other liabilities of the former owner, as (formerly) the heir-at-law, or executor of the owner (*f*), or if he is a person standing in any confidential relation with the mortgagor, by reason of which his interest and his duty are in conflict. Such is the position of a guardian (*g*), trustee (*h*), counsel (*i*), or agent (*k*); and, it seems, that if the tenant for life buys a mortgage on the inheritance for less than is due, he does so for the benefit of the estate (*l*). And subject to the same equity is the surety of the mortgagor, who, being liable upon a contract of indemnity with his principal, is under an obligation, if he can make terms with the creditor, to treat the settlement as a payment of the debt, and to give his principal the benefit of the arrangement (*m*). To all these persons, therefore, no more will be allowed in account than they have paid for the incumbrance (*n*), with interest at the legal or current rate, if that is less than the interest reserved (*o*).

And it is the same notwithstanding the fiduciary relation has ceased, and the former trustee will be allowed no more than he has paid, unless he has entered into a fair contract with the persons interested, that he may become the purchaser, or can show that there was no fraud or concealment, nor any advantage taken of information acquired in the character of trustee (*p*).

(*e*) *Anon.* (1707), 1 Salk. 155; and see *Dobson* v. *Land* (1850), 4 De G. & Sm. 575.

(*f*) *Braithwaite* v. *Braithwaite* (1685), 1 Vern. 334; *Morret* v. *Paske, supra.* There was formerly an exception when the purchaser had bought to protect the inheritance to which he was himself entitled: *Darcy* v. *Hall, supra.*

(*g*) *Powell* v. *Glover* (1721), 3 P. Wms. 251, n.

(*h*) *Morret* v. *Paske, supra*; see also *Baskett* v. *Cafe* (1851), 4 De G. & Sm. 388.

(*i*) *Carter* v. *Palmer* (1842), 8 Cl. & Fin. 657 (H.L.).

(*k*) *Hobday* v. *Peters* (1860), 28 Beav. 349; *Morret* v. *Paske, supra.*

(*l*) See *Hill* v. *Browne* (1844), Dru. *temp.* 426.

(*m*) *Reed* v. *Norris* (1837), 2 Myl. & Cr. 361.

(*n*) But though the purchase is made by a person, who, under ordinary circumstances, would be allowed no more than he paid; yet, if it was made under the advice of a later incumbrancer, who did not disclose the fact that he, and not the purchaser, would reap the benefit of it, the full sum due will be allowed to the assignee: *Bayly* v. *Wilkins* (1846), 3 Jo. & Lat. 630.

(*o*) *Carter* v. *Palmer, supra.* The rule did not, however, extend to a tenant in common, as there was no fiduciary relation between him and his co-tenants: *Kennedy* v. *De Trafford*, [1896] 1 Ch. 762.

(*p*) *Carter* v. *Palmer, supra*; *Ex parte James* (1803), 8 Ves. 337; *Coles* v. *Trecothick* (1804), 9 Ves. at p. 247. A mortgagee, after payment of his mortgage debt, has been said (*Baldwin* v. *Banister* (1718), cited 3 P. Wms. 251; but see *Dobson* v. *Land, supra*) to be a trustee within the rule, but he hardly seems to be within the principle; unless, perhaps, he is a mortgagee in possession, holding over after payment. From the record of *Baldwin* v. *Banister*, Reg. Lib. A. 1717, 609, it would seem that the point did not arise.

Transferee takes subject to state of accounts.—Moreover, the transferee of the mortgage is bound by the state of accounts between the mortgagor and mortgagee. Hence, though the transferee may have had no notice, by indorsements on the deeds or otherwise, that part of the debt has been discharged, yet he can claim under his assignment no more than is really due as between the mortgagor and the mortgagee (*q*), without reference to what was paid on the assignment (*r*), and is subject to have the whole account taken (*s*). The mortgagee who transfers his mortgage does not thereby get rid of his liability to future accounts, but may be decreed to account, both before (*t*) and after the assignment (*u*), the reason for this being that the mortgagee must be responsible for the person to whom he assigns the mortgagor's estate. But he is not answerable if he assigns by the direction of the court (*x*).

Accounting for proceeds of sale.—On a sale of the mortgaged property by the mortgagee under his power of sale, the mortgagor is entitled to an account of the proceeds, and if, in addition to the mortgage debt, there is another account between mortgagor and mortgagee, the latter will be treated as having received the money on the mortgage account and not on the other account, provided this is in accordance with the nature of the transaction (*y*).

If the mortgagor sells, and the mortgagee adopts the contract, the mortgagee as between himself and the purchaser stands in the mortgagor's place, and must bear the loss occasioned by the insolvency of a person to whom the deposit has been paid (*z*). But as between the mortgagee and the mortgagor, if the former has consented to the sale upon the terms that he shall be paid out of the purchase-money, although his execution of the conveyance and signature of the receipt will discharge the purchaser, it will not discharge the mortgagor, if the money is misappropriated by his agent without the mortgagee's default, though the agent may have also acted for the mortgagee (*a*).

(*q*) *Porter* v. *Hubbart* (1673), 3 Rep. in Ch. 78; *Matthews* v. *Wallwyn* (1798), 4 Ves. 118; *Chambers* v. *Goldwin* (1804), 9 Ves. 254; *Mangles* v. *Dixon* (1852), 3 H.L.C. 702.

The transferee of a mortgage will not be bound by a statement in the deed as to the amount due on the security, notwithstanding a special receipt clause to the effect that part of the sum is for costs, the amount of which is to be afterwards adjusted: *Re Forsyth* (1865), 11 Jur. (N.S.) 213, 615.

(*r*) *Turner* v. *Smith*, [1901] 1 Ch. 213; *De Lisle* v. *Union Bank of Scotland*, [1914] 1 Ch. 22 (C.A.). It is assumed that the mortgagor was not a party to the assignment. If he was a witness, it should be pleaded that he knew and agreed to the contents of the deed: *Jamieson* v. *English* (1820), 2 Mol. 337.

(*s*) But it seems that if redemption is sought after a great length of time, or after the dismissal of a former action to redeem, or several assignments, the account will be taken against an assignee in possession only from the time of his purchase; prior to which the profits will be set against the interest: *Pearson* v. *Pulley* (1668), 1 Ch. Ca. 102.

(*t*) And notwithstanding the mortgagee has been in possession and has accounted with the assignee: *Venables* v. *Foyle* (1661), 1 Ch. Cas. 2.

(*u*) *Venables* v. *Foyle*, *supra*; 1 Eq. Ca. Ab. 328, pl. 2; *Hall* v. *Heward* (1886), 32 Ch. D. 430 (C.A.). See Waters, *The Constructive Trust*, pp. 197 *et seq.*

(*x*) *Hall* v. *Heward*, *supra*.

(*y*) *Young* v. *English* (1843), 7 Beav. 10; *Johnson* v. *Bourne* (1843), 2 Y. & C.C.C. 268.

(*z*) *Rowe* v. *May* (1854), 18 Beav. 613.

(*a*) *Barrow* v. *White* (1862), 2 Johns. & H. 580.

Over-payments of interest.—Where interest on the mortgage has been paid in excess of what was due, the over-payments will be treated as payments on account of principal (*b*).

Sale by mortgagee of shares.—Mortgagees of stocks or shares, who sell the securities in their hands, may apparently (contrary to the general rule) purchase themselves. But they must take them at the market price of the day and cannot credit the debtor with less than that price, on the speculation that if the securities had come together into the market, the price would have fallen (*c*).

D—ACCOUNTS AGAINST THE MORTGAGEE IN POSSESSION

Accounts extend to wilful default (*d*).—The account usually directed against the mortgagee in possession, either of tangible property or of a business (*e*), is of what he has, or without wilful default might have received from the time of his taking possession. This will include the receipts of any person whom the mortgagee has put into possession without a just title, and in derogation of the rights of the mortgagor (*f*).

If the mortgagee in possession has sold the property, the account will extend to the proceeds of sale received by him, or which without wilful default he might have received; but (if no special case is made) there will not be an inquiry into the propriety of the sale or the adequacy of the price (*g*).

Possession must be as mortgagee.—A mortgagee who is in possession of the mortgaged property will not be liable to account as mortgagee in possession unless he entered as mortgagee, and the court will not treat possession as being held by the mortgagee as such unless it is satisfied that he took possession in his capacity of mortgagee, without reasonable ground for believing himself to hold in any other capacity (*h*). Thus one who, having a lien on property, takes possession

---

(*b*) *Re Carroll's Estate*, [1901] 1 I.R. 78. But it is otherwise, where interest has been paid on money which is afterwards found not to be included in the mortgage, and this will not be taken to have been paid on account of the principal: *Blandy* v. *Kimber* (1858), 25 Beav. 537.

(*c*) *Stubbs* v. *Lister* (1841), 1 Y. & C.C.C. 81.

(*d*) For the liability of the mortgagee in possession to account, see pp. 293 *et seq.*, *supra.*

Where a mortgagee has been in possession, in any settlement of accounts between the mortgagee and mortgagor, tax payable on interest due is allowed as money received on account of interest: see *Hollis* v. *Wingfield*, [1940] Ch. 336 (C.A.); [1940] 1 All E.R. 531 (C.A.).

(*e*) *Williams* v. *Price* (1824), 1 Sim. & St. 581; see *Chaplin* v. *Young* (1864), 33 Beav. 330. As to his position, if he becomes a partner in the business, see *Rowe* v. *Wood* (1822), 2 Jac. & W. at pp. 556, 558. As to receipt of rents by mistake, see *Forster* v. *Forster*, [1918] 1 I.R. 95.

(*f*) *National Bank of Australasia* v. *United Hand-in-Hand, etc., Co.* (1879), 4 App. Cas. 391.

(*g*) *Mayer* v. *Murray* (1878), 8 Ch. D. 424; *Farrar* v. *Farrars, Ltd.* (1888), 40 Ch. D. 395. It has been said that the case of an account against a mortgagee is the only instance in which the court directs an account on the footing of wilful default without any special case made for the purpose: *Lord Kensington* v. *Bouverie* (1855), 7 De G.M. & G., 134 at p. 156; although a purchaser, whose purchase has been set aside and ordered to stand as a security, is within the rule: *Adams* v. *Sworder* (1863), 2 De G.J. & S. 44.

As to how possession is obtained, see p. 316, *supra.*

(*h*) *Gaskell* v. *Gosling*, [1896] 1 Q.B. 669, at p. 691.

thinking himself to be purchaser will not be treated as mortgagee in
possession (*i*); nor will a mortgagee who has possession as tenant (*k*);
nor one who got into possession under a forfeiture, and not as mortgagee, where his possession was acquiesced in (*l*); nor a mortgagee who
lawfully uses the property for purposes unconnected with the
mortgage (*m*). And the assignee of a tenant for life is not liable to
account to the remainderman as mortgagee in possession during the
life estate (*n*).

Attornment by mortgagor.—It has been said that the attornment
of the mortgagor, if in actual occupation, as tenant to the mortgagee—
although only by virtue of an attornment clause in the mortgage deed—
makes the mortgagee liable as mortgagee in possession to subsequent
incumbrancers (*o*); but that view has not been accepted (*p*), and the
ordinary relation of mortgagor and mortgagee continues (*q*). In any
case the mortgagee is not liable on this ground to account as mortgagee
in possession to the mortgagor (*r*).

Inquiry as to possession.—In case of doubt the court will grant
an inquiry as to the fact of possession. The inquiry will be, whether
the mortgagee has been in possession of the rents and profits as
mortgagee, and if he has, the account is directed to be taken against
him as such, including wilful default (*s*); and admission of possession,
though contrary to the fact, has been held to make him liable to account
on that footing (*t*).

Account of rents and profits.—The mortgagee who takes possession
of the mortgaged estate is required to be diligent in realising the amount
due on the mortgage, that the estate may be redelivered to the
mortgagor (*u*). He is liable to account for the rents and other profits
during his possession (*x*), and if he remains in occupation himself he

---

(*i*) *Parkinson* v. *Hanbury* (1867), L.R. 2 H.L. 1.

(*k*) *Page* v. *Linwood* (1837), 4 Cl. & F. 399.

(*l*) *Blennerhassett* v. *Day* (1812), 2 Ba. & Be. 104, 125.

(*m*) *Re Colnbrook Chemical and Explosives Co., A.-G.* v. *Colnbrook Chemical and Explosives Co.,* [1923] 2 Ch. 289. Where the creditor entered as receiver under a power of attorney and afterwards become mortgagee, he was still treated for the purpose of accounting as receiver: *Lord Trimleston* v. *Hamill* (1810), 1 Ba. & Be. 377.

(*n*) *Whitbread* v. *Smith* (1854), 3 De G.M. & G. 727, 741; *Lord Kensington* v. *Bouverie* (1855), 7 De G.M. & G. 134, 156.

(*o*) *Re Stockton Iron Furnace Co.* (1879), 10 Ch. D. 335, at pp. 356, 357. And see *Re Kitchin, Ex parte Punnett* (1880), 16 Ch. D. 226; *Re Betts, Ex parte Harrison* (1881), 18 Ch. D. 127; *Green* v. *Marsh,* [1892] 2 Q.B. 330, 336.

(*p*) *Stanley* v. *Grundy* (1883), 22 Ch. D. 478.

(*q*) *Re Knight, Ex parte Isherwood* (1882), 22 Ch. D. 384, 392.

(*r*) *Re Betts, Ex parte Harrison, supra.*

(*s*) *Dobson* v. *Lee* (1842), 1 Y. & C.C.C. 714. No special direction as to wilful default is necessary.

(*t*) *Parker* v. *Watkins* (1859), Johns. 133. As to the liability of the guardian of an infant who takes an assignment of a mortgage on the infant's estate, see *Bishop* v. *Sharp* (1704), 2 Vern. 469; but the infant's estate would now be vested in trustees.

(*u*) *Lord Kensington* v. *Bouverie* (1855), 7 De G.M. & G. 134, at p. 157; see *Langton* v. *Waite* (1869), 4 Ch. App. 402. As to the different nature of the possession of a person who holds under a receivership deed, see *Lord Kensington* v. *Bouverie, supra.*

(*x*) See *Gould* v. *Tancred* (1742), 2 Atk. 533. And he is bound, if required by the interrogatories in a redemption action, to set out in his answer such particulars as will sufficiently show the state of the account, what is due to him, and what securities he holds for the debt: *Elmer* v. *Creasy* (1873), 9 Ch. App. 69; *West of England, etc., Bank* v. *Nickolls* (1877), 6 Ch. D. 613.

In taking the account the Limitation Act is no bar where the relation of mortgagor

liable to pay an occupation rent. His liability to account extends in favour of all those who are interested in the equity of redemption, and he cannot by any dealing with the estate discharge himself of this liability (*y*). After receiving notice of a later mortgage, the mortgagee in possession becomes liable to account to the later incumbrancer for so much of the surplus rent as he has paid to the mortgagor or his representatives; but so long as the mortgagee in possession was without notice, the later mortgagee cannot call upon him or the mortgagor for an account of the bygone rents (*z*).

Equitable possession.—The action of a later incumbrancer, brought to enforce his claim (the prior incumbrancer being made a party), amounts to an equitable possession of the rents, and binds the surplus rents in the hands of the prior incumbrancer until the dismissal of the action, though it is not prosecuted (*a*). And the mortgagee must account for whatever he may receive after the order to account (*b*), though the practice is to direct the account without future words. But it is said, he is not bound to account to a later incumbrancer for the profits received after foreclosure, though he had notice of his claim before judgment (*c*).

Amount of rents to be accounted for.—Where a mortgagee enters into receipt of rents he accounts at the rate of the rent reserved (*d*). Where he enters into actual possession, it has been said that he will be charged with the utmost value the lands are proved to be worth (*e*). But his liability is limited by the circumstances of the case, and he will not usually be required to account for more than he has received, unless it is proved that, but for his gross default, mismanagement, or fraud, he might have received more (*f*).

Occupation rent.—The mortgagee, if he has been in actual occupation of the whole or some part of the property, may be charged an occupation rent, but his occupation must be stated in the

and mortgagee is subsisting; because the mortgagor having a right to get back the value of his property, every item must be brought into account: *Hood* v. *Easton* (1856), 2 Giff. 692; on appeal, 2 Jur. N.S. 917. But where the mortgagee is claiming under a tenant for life and is called to account after his death by the remainderman, there being no fiduciary relation, the account will only be carried back through the six years limited by the statute: *Hickman* v. *Upsall* (1876), 4 Ch. D. 144. And see *Forster* v. *Forster*, [1918] 1 I.R. 95.

(*y*) *Hinde* v. *Blake* (1841), 11 L.J. Ch. 26.

(*z*) *Maddocks* v. *Wren* (1680), 2 Rep. in Ch. 209; *Burney* v. *Sewell* (1820), 1 Jac. & W. 647; *Parker* v. *Calcraft* (1821), 6 Mad. 11; *Archdeacon* v. *Bowes* (1824), 13 Price, 353, 368; *Holton* v. *Lloyd* (1827), 1 Mol. 30.

After redemption, where the mortgagee has died, a claim in respect of profits during his possession, should not be made in a creditor's action, but by proceedings to correct the redemption judgment: *Shoobridge* v. *Woods* (1843), 8 Jur. 27.

(*a*) *Parker* v. *Calcraft* (1821), 6 Mad. 11.

(*b*) *Bulstrode* v. *Bradley* (1747), 3 Atk. 582.

(*c*) *Bird* v. *Gandy* (1715), 7 Vin. Abr. 45, pl. 20. A judgment creditor can obtain a charge on the property giving him a right to a sale (see p. 124, *supra*), but according to the former practice—which, it may be presumed, continues—he must submit to account as a mortgagee in possession, as the price of the relief sought: *Bull* v. *Faulkner* (1847), 1 De G. & Sm. 685; see *O'Brien* v. *Mahon* (1842), 2 Dru. & War. 306; but he will not be liable to this form of account unless he has actually obtained possession under his claim to the exclusion of the mortgagor: *Kingston* v. *Cowbridge Rail. Co.* (1871), 41 L.J. Ch. 152; see *Hele* v. *Lord Bexley* (1853), 17 Beav. 14.

(*d*) *Lord Trimleston* v. *Hamill* (1810), 1 Ba. & Be. 377, 385; *Metcalf* v. *Campion* (1828), 1 Mol. 238.

(*e*) *Lord Trimleston* v. *Hamill, supra.*   (*f*) See p. 349, *supra.*

pleadings (*g*). An inquiry as to the fact of occupation may be directed, if it is not admitted, and any necessary directions will be given for ascertaining the amount of rent to be fixed. But no rent will be charged if the property has no rental value or during such time as the property, from its ruinous state, or for any other reason, was incapable of making any return (*h*).

Where rents collected by agent.—Where the mortgagee employs an agent to collect the rents, he must account for all the rents received by that agent, and not merely for what the agent has paid to him. The death of the agent and consequent difficulty of proving what the agent received is no answer (*i*).

Accounts of mines.—The mortgagee in possession, who without special authority opens mines or quarries, will be charged with his receipts, but will not be allowed the costs of severing the produce or other expenses; for he has no right to speculate at the mortgagor's expense, and the act is a sale of part of the inheritance (*k*). But a mortgagee with an insufficient security may open new, or may lease or work abandoned mines, and will be only liable to account for the profits or royalty, and not for the value of the ore raised or the damage caused to the surface (*l*). And if he is specially authorised to work the mines, he will be allowed the expenses incurred in doing so, with interest (*m*). If the mortgagee comes into possession of open mines, he cannot be called upon to speculate by working them, however likely it may be that the mines will be improved by a large expenditure (*n*). He is not bound to advance more than a prudent owner, and cannot be charged with mismanagement if he omits to do so. But, on the other hand, a mortgage of a colliery was prima facie a mortgage of it as a going concern, and passed the right to work the mines (*o*).

(*g*) *Trulock* v. *Robey* (1846), 15 Sim. 265; *Shepard* v. *Jones* (1882), 21 Ch. D. 469 (C.A.). See *Fee* v. *Cobine* (1847), 11 Ir. Eq. R. 406.

(*h*) *Fyfe* v. *Smith*, [1975] 2 N.S.W.L.R. 408. If the mortgagee has expended money in permanent improvements, these will not increase the occupation rent, unless the expenditure is allowed him in his accounts: *Bright* v. *Campbell* (1885), 54 L.J. Ch. 1077; see p. 352; *Marshall* v. *Cave* (1824), 3 L.J. O.S. Ch. 57.

If the mortgagee has sold the estate, the admission of the purchaser into possession before the stipulated time, will not make the mortgagee liable for occupation rent, though he may have admitted him upon terms which raise a claim for wilful default: *Shepard* v. *Jones, supra.*

Where a lease by the mortgagor to the mortgagee has been set aside, the mortgagee will be charged with the rent reserved by the lease if a fair one: see *Gubbins* v. *Creed* (1804), 2 Sch. & Lef. 214; *Webb* v. *Rorke* (1806), 2 Sch. & Lef. 661.

(*i*) *Noyes* v. *Pollock* (1885), 30 Ch. D. 336.

(*k*) *Hughes* v. *Williams* (1806), 12 Ves. 493; *Thorneycroft* v. *Crockett* (1848), 16 Sim. 445. See *Taylor* v. *Mostyn* (1886), 33 Ch. D. 226; and *Hood* v. *Easton* (1856), 2 Giff. 692, where a mortgagee, without authority to work mines, authorised strangers to work them; doubted on appeal, 2 Jur. N.S. 917. As to inquiries with respect to the working of mines, see *Mulhallen* v. *Marum* (1843), 3 Dru. & War. 317; *Thorneycroft* v. *Crockett, supra.*

(*l*) *Millett* v. *Davey* (1862), 31 Beav. 470.

(*m*) *Norton* v. *Cooper* (1854), 25 L.J. Ch. 121.

(*n*) *Rowe* v. *Wood* (1820), 2 Jac. & W. 553.

(*o*) *County of Gloucester Bank* v. *Rudry Merthyr, etc., Colliery Co.*, [1895] 1 Ch. 629, distinguishing *Whitley* v. *Challis*, [1892] 1 Ch. 64. As to where the mortgagee is also a lessee of the mines with certain restrictions on working pillars, see *Taylor* v. *Mostyn, supra.* And where there is a mortgage of a business as a going concern, the mortgagee in possession is entitled to be recouped losses (not attributable to negligence) out of the proceeds of the sale of the estate: see *Bompas* v. *King* (1886), 33 Ch. D. 279 (a block of residential flats).

Repairs and improvements, etc.—For allowances to the mort-gagee for certain repairs and permanent improvements, etc., see pp. 351 *et seq., supra.*

E—TAKING ACCOUNTS WITH RESTS

Form of accounts.—The usual mode of taking accounts against the mortgagee in possession is to set the total amount of rents and profits received by, or found to be chargeable to him, against the whole amount due upon the mortgage debt; and to apply them in discharge successively of the interest of the mortgage debt, and of money advanced for costs and improvements, and then of the principal (*p*). But this is only done in arriving at the final result, when the account could, if necessary, be shown as a complete debtor and creditor account. In practice the account is taken in a series of separate accounts:

(1) An account of principal, interest and costs;
(2) An account of moneys expended by the mortgagee in repairs and permanent improvements, with interest from the date of expenditure; and
(3) An account of rents and profits.

The balance is arrived at by adding the results of accounts (1) and (2), and subtracting what the mortgagee has to account for under (3) (*q*). If, during the currency of the account, a part of the mortgaged property is sold, the net proceeds are credited to the mortgagor in account (1), first in payment of interest due, and then in reduction of principal, and the interest is correspondingly reduced; but account (2) is not further affected (*r*).

The result of taking this continuous account is that the mortgagee benefits if the rents and profits exceed the interest, since he does not apply the excess in reduction of principal, with consequent reduction of subsequent interest. He keeps it in hand paying no interest on it, while interest is running all the time on the undiminished principal. But if the rents and profits are less than the interest, the mortgagor benefits, since the deficiency is a further debt due from him, but it does not carry interest (*s*).

Accounts with rests.—Where the receipts of the mortgagee are more than sufficient to cover the interest a different method may be adopted, known as taking the account with rests. A balance in the

---

(*p*) *Webb* v. *Rorke* (1806), 2 Sch. & Lef. 661; *Union Bank of London* v. *Ingram* (1880), 16 Ch. D. 53.

(*q*) See *Thorneycroft* v. *Crockett* (1848), 2 H.L.C. 239; *Wrigley* v. *Gill*, [1905] 1 Ch. 241, at p. 253; on appeal, [1906] 1 Ch. 165 (C.A.). Account (3) includes all sums which the mortgagee has received—or, in a case of wilful default, is treated as having received (p. 620, *supra*)—by virtue of the mortgage, whether rents and profits or accidental payments, such as fines: see *Thompson* v. *Hudson* (1870), L.R. 10 Eq. 497, 498; *Union Bank of London* v. *Ingram, supra*; *Cockburn* v. *Edwards* (1881), 18 Ch. D. 449, 456 (C.A.).

(*r*) *Wrigley* v. *Gill, supra*; *Ainsworth* v. *Wilding*, [1905] 1 Ch. 435; *cf. Thompson* v. *Hudson, supra.*

(*s*) See *Union Bank of London* v. *Ingram, supra.*

account is struck at stated intervals (*t*) and the surplus to the credit of the mortgagor is applied in reduction of principal (*u*).

When accounts taken with rests.—It is not a matter of course for rests to be made against a mortgagee in possession (*v*). The order must expressly direct that the accounts shall be so taken (*x*), and special circumstances justifying the direction must be alleged and proved (*y*). The reason why rests are not the normal method of taking the accounts is said to be that the mortgagee is not bound to accept payment by driblets, but is entitled to have the account taken as whole, and not to be treated as repaid until that account has been taken (*z*). Thus, to direct the account to be with rests in a measure penalises the mortgagee (*a*), and generally this will not be done unless he went into possession where there was no arrear, or no material arrear, of interest due, or the annual rents greatly exceed the interest (*b*). Rests will also be directed where the incumbrancer denies that character, and sets up an adverse title (*c*).

(*t*) See *Montreal Trust Co.* v. *Hounslow Holdings, Ltd.* (1972), 22 D.L.R. (3d) 503.

(*u*) See *Thorneycroft* v. *Crockett, supra*. It has been said that this method applies only in the case of real estate: *Robinson* v. *Cumming* (1742), 2 Atk. 409; but there appears to be no reason for so restricting it. Under an account with rests an occupation rent for which the mortgagee is liable must be brought in: *Donovan* v. *Fricker* (1812), Jac. 165; *Wilson* v. *Metcalfe* (1826), 1 Russ. 530; but not a rent payable by the mortgagee when he is in occupation as tenant, and not as mortgagee in possession: *Page* v. *Linwood* (1837), 4 Cl. & F. 399. See p. 621, *supra*.

(*v*) *Gould* v. *Tancred* (1742), 2 Atk. 533; *Davis* v. *May* (1815), 19 Ves. 383; *Donovan* v. *Fricker* (1821), Jac. 165; *Scholefield* v. *Ingham* (1838), Coop. Pr. Cas. 477; see *Wrigley* v. *Gill, supra*.

(*x*) *Fowler* v. *Wightwick* (1810), cited 1 Mad. p. 14; *Webber* v. *Hunt* (1815), 1 Mad. 13; *Wrigley* v. *Gill, supra*. Any special matter affecting the accounts must be brought forward at the trial and dealt with in the judgment: *Sanguinetti* v. *Stuckey's Banking Co. (No. 2)*, [1896] 1 Ch. 502 (C.A.).; and see *Taylor* v. *Mostyn* (1886), 33 Ch. D. 226 (C.A.).

(*y*) The special case for rests must be made on the pleadings where the action is by writ: *Neesom* v. *Clarkson* (1845), 4 Hare, 97; see *Blackford* v. *Davis* (1869), 4 Ch. App. 304, at p. 308; otherwise, it must appear on the summons or the mortgagor's affidavit.

(*z*) *Nelson* v. *Booth* (1858), 3 De G. & J. 119, 122; *Wrigley* v. *Gill*, [1905] 1 Ch. 241, at p. 254. But this is not a sufficient ground for adopting an unnatural mode of taking the account. That mode is a tradition which the court in England has not yet had the courage to abandon. It is otherwise in Ireland, where rests are made half-yearly without special direction; but not at intermediate periods: *Graham* v. *Walker* (1847), 11 Ir. Eq. R. 415.

(*a*) See *Wrigley* v. *Gill*, [1905] 1 Ch. 241, at p. 254.

(*b*) *Uttermare* v. *Stevens* (1851), 17 L.T. O.S. 115. That rests will usually be directed if interest was not in arrear, see also *Shephard* v. *Elliot* (1819), 4 Mad. 254; *Nelson* v. *Booth* (1858), 3 De G. & J. 119; but not where it was in arrear: *Stephens* v. *Wellings* (1835), 4 L.J. Ch. 281; *Finch* v. *Brown* (1840), 3 Beav. 70; *Wilson* v. *Cluer* (1840), 3 Beav. 136. Where interest was to be paid half-yearly, and there was a half-year's interest due when the mortgagee entered, this was sufficient to save him from annual rests: *Moore* v. *Painter* (1842), 6 Jur. 903. Where the mortgagee takes possession after bills have been indorsed to him for the arrears of interest, and the bills become due and are dishonoured after possession taken, the interest is considered to be in arrear at the time of taking possession, and no rests will be made: *Dobson* v. *Land* (1851), 4 De G. & Sm. 575.

That a great excess of rents over interest will make the mortgagee liable to rests, see also *Thorneycroft* v. *Crockett* (1848), 2 H.L.C. 239; *Carter* v. *James* (1881), 29 W.R. 437. But rests will not be directed on the ground of a slight excess: *Gould* v. *Tancred, supra*; see *Baldwin* v. *Lewis* (1835), 4 L.J. Ch. 113; *Nelson* v. *Booth, supra*.

(*c*) *Incorporated Society in Dublin* v. *Richards* (1841), 1 Dru. & War. 258, 290, 334; *Montgomery* v. *Calland* (1844), 14 Sim. 79; *National Bank of Australasia* v. *United Hand-in-Hand, etc., Co.* (1879), 4 App. Cas. 391 (P.C.), at p. 409; *Wrigley* v. *Gill*, [1905] 1 Ch. 241, 254; see *Douglas* v. *Culverwell* (1862), 4 De G.F. & J. 20 (sale treated as mortgage).

But the fact that an arrear of interest is or is not due at the time of taking possession is not altogether decisive upon the question of rests, and the circumstances of the particular case will be considered. So that, if the mortgagee has been driven by the acts of others to take possession, or has been harassed by litigation, and thereby put to costs (even though the costs have afterwards been adjudged to be paid him by his opponent), and his own conduct has been free from harshness or vexation, or, if in the case of leaseholds, the security is endangered by non-payment of ground-rent or insurance, or through want of repairs, rests will not be directed against him, though as to other circumstances he might be within the general rule (*d*).

Circumstances subsequent to taking possession.—The circumstances when the mortgagee took possession usually determine his liability to rests, and if interest was in arrear, so that rests were not directed, he will not, without special reason, become liable to rests after the arrear has been paid off (*e*). But if, after the mortgagee has taken possession, there is a settled account, by which it appears that no interest is due, or that, if any is in fact due, it has been satisfied as interest by being turned into principal, and the mortgagee continues in receipt of rents more than sufficient to satisfy the interest of such principal, the settlement is considered as a rest made by the parties, and the mortgagee will henceforth be treated as a mortgagee who takes possession with no interest in arrear, and will be subject to annual rests (*f*).

Intervals of rests.—The order for accounts with rests usually directs that the rests shall be made at stated intervals—half-yearly or yearly. As long as principal remains due, the excess of rents and profits over interest and expenses at each interval is struck off the principal, and the account is then carried on upon the footing of the reduced principal (*g*).

An alternative method is to direct that rests shall be made from time to time whenever the mortgagee has an excess of rents and profits over interest in his hands. If this is combined with a direction for annual rests, a rest should be made at the date when the mortgagee has this excess in his hands, although in the interval between the annual rests, and from this date the subsequent annual rests will be computed (*h*).

(*d*) *Horlock* v. *Smith* (1844), 1 Coll. 287; *Patch* v. *Wild* (1861), 30 Beav. 99; and see *Nelson* v. *Booth*, *supra*, at p. 122.

(*e*) *Finch* v. *Brown*, *supra*; see *Davis* v. *May*, *supra*; *Latter* v. *Dashwood* (1834), 6 Sim. 462; *Scholefield* v. *Lockwood* (*No.* 3) (1863), 32 Beav. 439.

(*f*) *Wilson* v. *Cluer* (1840), 3 Beav. 136. If rests have been directed in a redemption action which is abandoned, they will also be directed in a foreclosure action afterwards commenced by the mortgagee, though no case for them is then made: *Morris* v. *Islip* (1855), 20 Beav. 654.

(*g*) This is the effect of an order substantially in the form in *Yates* v. *Hambly* (1742), 2 Atk. 360, 362: "Take an account of what shall be coming due on account of rents and profits, to be applied in the first place in payment of interest and principal, and make annual rests: and in taking such account make all just allowances": cited in *Webber* v. *Hunt* (1815), 1 Mad. 13, 14; see *Wilson* v. *Cluer*, *supra*; *Thorneycroft* v. *Crockett* (1848), 2 H.L.C. 239, 256.

(*h*) *Binnington* v. *Harwood* (1825), Turn. & R. 477.

Account when debt paid off.—As soon as no principal remains due, the effect of the order is to charge the mortgagee with compound interest on the excess of rents and profits over outgoings at each rest (*i*). And generally, when the mortgagee has been paid off his interest and principal out of rents and profits, and nevertheless continues in possession, he becomes a debtor to the mortgagor in respect of subsequent receipts and annual rests will be directed in the account against him, although no rests were directed in the original order for accounts (*k*).

Receipts after certificate.—It would seem that where money has been received after the date of the master's certificate, which represents corpus of the mortgaged property, no further account is required (*l*). But if, after that date and before the day fixed for redemption, the mortgagee varies the amount by receiving rent or other moneys in the nature of income (*m*), the accounts must be carried on and a new day (usually the expiration of a month from the date originally named) fixed for redemption (*n*). But the receipt of rent after default, and before the affidavit of default, does not make a further account necessary (*o*).

(*i*) And this is expressly stated in the order in *Cotham* v. *West*, Rolls, Nov. 15, 1839. Reg. Lib.: "Take an account, etc., and in taking the said account, make annual rests of the clear balance, and compute interest on such respective balances at £5 per cent.; and in making such annual rests, except the first, include in the balance then stated, the interest of each preceding balance, so as to charge the defendant with compound interest thereon." But the usual rate is £4 per cent.: *Ashworth* v. *Lord* (1887), 36 Ch. D. 545, 552; see *Wilson* v. *Metcalfe* (1826), 1 Russ. 530, 537; *Horlock* v. *Smith* (1844), 1 Coll. 287, 297. The order in *Cotham* v. *West* is the basis of the form now in use. See also *Raphael* v. *Boehm* (1805), 11 Ves. 92; (1807), 13 Ves. 407, 590; *Heighington* v. *Grant* (1840), 5 My. & C. 258.

(*k*) *Wilson* v. *Metcalfe* (1826), 1 Russ. 530; *Wilson* v. *Cluer*, *supra*; *Uttermare* v. *Stevens* (1851), 17 L.T. O.S. 115; *Ashworth* v. *Lord* (1887), 36 Ch. D. 545. And this may be done where the mortgagee becomes overpaid during the action, though he will not be charged with interest on the surplus received prior to the date of the certificate: *Lloyd* v. *Jones* (1842), 12 Sim. 491.
An action for an account where the mortgagee was satisfied more than six years ago is really for redemption, and therefore not barred in six years: *Ocean Accident, etc., Corpn., Ltd.* v. *Collum*, [1913] 1 Ir. R. 337.

(*l*) *Welch* v. *National Cycle Works Co.* (1886), 55 L.T. 673 (C.A.).

(*m*) Cf. *Welch* v. *National Cycle Works Co.*, *supra*; *Lacon* v. *Tyrrell* (1887), 56 L.T. 483.

(*n*) *Jenner-Fust* v. *Needham* (1886), 32 Ch. D. 582; *Garlick* v. *Jackson* (1841), 4 Beav. 154; *Alden* v. *Foster* (1842), 5 Beav. 592; *Ellis* v. *Griffiths* (1844), 7 Beav. 83; *Prees* v. *Coke* (1871), 6 Ch. App. 645. For exceptions to this rule, see p. 407, *supra*. This extension of the time for redemption is not, as in the case of an extension granted on the application of the mortgagor (see p. 404, *supra*), dependent on the mortgagor paying forthwith arrears of interest and costs: *Buchanan* v. *Greenway* (1849), 12 Beav. 355. The mortgagee accounts by affidavit for the amount received: *Oxenham* v. *Ellis* (1854), 18 Beav. 593. Where a receiver has been appointed by the court, a further account may be avoided by inserting in the order for foreclosure *nisi* liberty to apply in chambers for payment of any moneys in his hands: *Coleman* v. *Llewellin* (1886), 34 Ch. D. 143 (C.A.); and see *Smith* v. *Pearman* (1888), 36 W.R. 681. But perhaps this will only be done under special circumstances: *Cheston* v. *Wells*, [1893] 2 Ch. 151. For another form of order intended to avoid a further account where a receiver has been appointed, see *Simmons* v. *Blandy*, [1897] 1 Ch. 19, following *Barber* v. *Jeckells*, [1893] W.N. 91.

(*o*) *Constable* v. *Howick* (1858), 5 Jur. N.S. 331; *National Permanent, etc., Building Society* v. *Raper*, [1892] 1 Ch. 54.

II—ACCOUNTS OF INTEREST

A—THE RIGHT TO INTEREST

Interest on mortgage debts.—Contrary to the general rule as to loans (*p*), interest is payable upon mortgage debts, even though it is not expressly reserved, and although the mortgage is only equitable (*q*), including a charge by mere deposit of title-deeds (*r*), and generally where the principal sum is a charge on specified property (*s*). Where, however, the contract provides expressly for reconveyance upon payment of the principal, interest will not be payable (*t*), unless the deed contains elsewhere an express or implied agreement for payment of interest (*u*).

Interest arises on mortgages from day to day (*x*). Hence the person who takes the income of the security is entitled to the interest to the time of his death, or other termination of his estate.

Interest after day for redemption.—Where the security does not expressly provide for payment of interest after the time fixed for redemption, interest will still be recoverable, not on the contract, but as damages for the detention of the debt, and therefore only to the extent of the damages claimed (*y*). The mortgagor, therefore, to

---

(*p*) *Calton* v. *Bragg* (1812), 15 East, 223; *Higgins* v. *Sargent* (1823), 2 B. & C. 348; *Page* v. *Newman* (1829), 9 B. & C. 378. But see Law Reform (Miscellaneous Provisions) Act 1934, s. 3 as amended by Administration of Justice Act 1969, s. 22 (discretion in court to award interest from accrual of action until judgment); and cf. *Sewing Machines Rentals, Ltd.* v. *Wilson*, [1975] 3 All E.R. 553 (C.A.).

(*q*) *Anon.* (1813), 4 Taunt. 876; *Re Every, Ex parte Hirtzel* (1858), 3 De G. & J. 464; *Re Kerr's Policy* (1869), L.R. 8 Eq. 331.

(*r*) *Anon.*, *supra*; *Carey* v. *Doyne* (1856,) 5 Ir. Ch. R. 104; *Re Kerr's Policy*, *supra*; notwithstanding the doubt expressed in *Ashton* v. *Dalton* (1846), 2 Coll. 565.

(*s*) *Lippard* v. *Ricketts* (1872), L.R. 14 Eq. 291; *Re Drax, Saville* v. *Drax*, [1903] 1 Ch. 781 (C.A.); *Mendl* v. *Smith* (1943), 112 L.J. Ch. 279. But interest may not be allowed in addition to a premium: see *Cityland and Property (Holdings), Ltd.* v. *Dabrah*, [1968] Ch. 166, at p. 182; [1967] 2 All E.R. 639, at p. 648; see p. 528, *supra*. As to the limitation on the arrears recoverable, see p. 281, *supra*.

A power to charge land with a sum of money carries power to charge it also with interest: *Kilmurry* v. *Geery* (1713), 2 Salk. 538.

A charge of debts by will, upon real estate, does not entitle simple contract creditors to interest, unless the debtor has given to the debts the quality of specialities in his lifetime, as by making a schedule of debts and creating a trust term for payment: *Stewart* v. *Noble* (1788), Vern. & Scriv. 528; *Barwell* v. *Parker* (1751), 2 Ves. Sen. 364.

A mortgagee will be allowed no interest upon a debt which would have been satisfied but for his wrongful or inequitable act, during such time as the debt has thereby remained unsatisfied: see *Thornton* v. *Court* (1854), 3 De G.M. & G. 293, 301.

As to the right of creditors to interest under a deed of trust executed by the debtor for their benefit, see *Jenkins* v. *Perry* (1838), 3 Y. & C. Ex. 178.

For rests, see pp. 623 *et seq.*, *supra*; and p. 687, *infra*.

(*t*) *Thompson* v. *Drew* (1855), 20 Beav. 49. See *Ex parte Hodge* (1857), 26 L.J. Bkcy. 77; and cf. *Ashwell* v. *Staunton* (1861), 30 Beav. 52; *Mendl* v. *Smith* (1943), 169 L.T. 153.

(*u*) *Ashwell* v. *Staunton*, *supra*. See *Re King, Ex parte Furber* (1881), 17 Ch. D. 191.

(*x*) *Wilson* v. *Harman* (1755), 2 Ves. S. 672; *Re Rogers' Trusts* (1860), 1 Dr. & Sm. 338; Apportionment Act 1870.

(*y*) *Price* v. *Great Western Rail. Co.* (1847), 16 M. & W. 244; *Morgan* v. *Jones* (1853), 8 Ex. 620; *Cook* v. *Fowler* (1874), L.R. 7 H.L. 27; *Re European Central Rail. Co., Ex parte Oriental Financial Corpn.* (1876), 4 Ch. D. 33 (C.A.); *Re Roberts, Goodchap* v. *Roberts* (1880), 14 Ch. D. 49 (C.A.); *Goldstrom* v. *Tallerman* (1886), 18 Q.B.D. 1 (C.A.); *Mellersh* v. *Brown* (1890), 45 Ch. D. 225; see also *Re Horner, Fookes* v. *Horner*, [1896] 2 Ch. 188; *London, Chatham and Dover Rail. Co.* v. *South Eastern Rail. Co.*, [1893] A.C. 429 (H.L.), and *Mathura Das* v. *Raja Narindar Bahadur Pal* (1896), 12 T.L.R. 609 (P.C.).

avoid payment of subsequent interest, must be prepared to pay at the
day fixed, and must give notice that he will do so. And he will be liable
to pay subsequent interest, although it is only provided that interest
is to be paid until, or even that it is not to be paid after, the day of
redemption, if by the default of the mortgagor the principal was not
then paid (z).

In fixing the amount of subsequent interest the court will consider,
but will not be entirely guided by, the agreement between the parties
as to the rate payable during the time certain. And this, in the past,
it would allow, if not more than, but would be inclined to cut down if it
exceeded, 5 per cent. (a).

Interest on money retained.—The mortgagee also may be liable
to pay interest on money in his hands arising from the security; e.g.,
where, being mortgagee in possession, he holds over and receives rents
after the mortgage debt has been paid (b); or where, though not in
possession, there is a balance due from him, and he improperly resists
redemption (c); or where, after a sale under his power, he retains the
surplus (d).

Interest on expenditure.—The court allows the mortgagee interest
in certain cases upon money which he has laid out for the benefit of
the estate, or the support of his security; payments so made being
treated as further advances; and the rate is generally that which is
payable on the original loan. Thus, interest will be allowed upon fines
paid by the mortgagee for the renewal of leases upon which the estate is
held, though there is no covenant by the mortgagor for renewal (e);
upon premiums on life policies, which form part of the security (f);
upon money laid out in supporting the mortgagor's title where it has
been impeached (g); or in the redemption of land tax (h); and generally,
upon money laid out in lasting improvements or otherwise for the
benefit of the estate, where the principal so laid out is allowed (i).
But not upon costs ordered to be paid by the mortgagor, unless the
mortgagee has been given leave to add them to his security; in which

---

(z) *Price* v. *Great Western Rail. Co.*, supra; *Gordillo* v. *Weguelin* (1877), 5 Ch. D.
287 (C.A.).

(a) *Re Roberts, Goodchap* v. *Roberts*, supra; *Mellersh* v. *Brown*, supra. See *Re King,
Ex parte Furber* (1881), 17 Ch. D. 191. In *Wallington* v. *Cook* (1878), 47 L.J. Ch. 508,
the interest was cut down from 60 to 5 per cent. But a more realistic rate would now be
allowed, see *Cityland and Property (Holdings), Ltd.* v. *Dabrah*, [1968] Ch. 166; [1967]
2 All E.R. 639; and p. 633, *infra*.

(b) *Ashworth* v. *Lord* (1887), 36 Ch. D. 545. And see p. 625, *supra*.

(c) *Smith* v. *Pilkington* (1859), 1 De G.F. & J. 120.

(d) *Charles* v. *Jones* (1887), 35 Ch. D. 544 (interest allowed at 4 per cent. per annum).

(e) 5 Bac. Abr. 736; *Manlove* v. *Bale and Bruton* (1688), 2 Vern. 84; *Lacon* v. *Mertins*
(1743), 3 Atk. 4; *Woolley* v. *Drage* (1795), 2 Anst. 551.

(f) *Bellamy* v. *Brickenden* (1861), 2 Johns. & H. 137. As to interest on premiums
paid by a surety, see *Hodgson* v. *Hodgson* (1837), 2 Keen, 704.

(g) *Godfrey* v. *Watson* (1747), 3 Atk. 517.

(h) *Knowles* v. *Chapman* (1815), 3 Seton (7th Edn., 1888), 1905.

(i) *Quarrell* v. *Beckford* (1816), 1 Mad. 269; *Webb* v. *Rorke* (1806), 2 Sch. & Lef.
661. As to sums expended by the mortgagee in the working of mines, where he was
authorised by the deed to work them, see p. 622, *supra*.

It is not the practice generally to allow interest upon money expended by the
mortgagee in repairs, although it has sometimes been done: Seton (7th Edn.), 1906.

case he will be allowed to charge interest from the date of the taxing master's certificate (*k*).

Payment of interest in bankruptcy.—A mortgagee who realises his security can, notwithstanding the bankruptcy of the mortgagor, apply the proceeds in payment of principal, interest, and costs in full. But if he claims to prove in the bankruptcy (either on abandoning his security, or assessing it or realising it, and proving for the balance) he can only claim interest up to the date of the receiving order unless there is a surplus (*l*).

Neglect to claim interest.—If a prior mortgagee does not take possession and the interest falls into arrear, a subsequent mortgagee cannot redeem without paying the whole interest (*m*). And this, it is said, even though the prior mortgagee let the interest run in arrear with an ill intent, to get the estate. But if there is fraud or collusion it will be otherwise (*n*). And the neglect, without fraud, of the incumbrancer to demand interest from the tenant for life, or to require him to pay head rents, will not prejudice the right against the remainderman (*o*).

B—INTEREST ON SPECIALTY AND JUDGMENT DEBTS

Bond covering mortgage debt.—Although bond debts generally carry no interest, either at law or in equity, beyond the amount of the penalty—which is taken to represent by the agreement of the parties the ultimate amount of the debt (*p*)—yet, if there is a bond and also a mortgage to secure the same sum with all interest that may grow due thereon, interest will be carried under the mortgage beyond the penalty of the bond, for the amount of the penalty is not to prejudice the mortgage (*q*). And it matters not whether the mortgage precedes or follows the bond. Interest will also be given in such a case where the mortgagor is a surety; since the creditor may make the mortgage as available as if it were given by the principal debtor. But a trust for payment of bond debts out of the proceeds of real estate, together with the interest due and to grow due for the same to the day of

---

(*k*) *Eardley* v. *Knight* (1889), 41 Ch. D. 537. And payment of interest on costs will be directed where they have been paid under an order of the court which declared the person paying them to be entitled to an indemnity for so doing: *Wainman* v. *Bowker* (1845), 8 Beav. 363.

(*l*) *Ex parte Badger* (1798), 4 Ves. 165; *Re Lancaster, Ex parte Kensington* (1835), 2 Mont. & A. 300; *Re Savin* (1872), 7 Ch. App. 760, 764; *Re Phillips, Ex parte Bath* (1882), 22 Ch. D. 450 (C.A.).; *Re London, Windsor and Greenwich Hotels Co., Quartermaine's Case,* [1892] 1 Ch. 639. And see Bankruptcy Act 1914, s. 33 (8), 2nd Sched., para. 21; and as to payment of interest out of proceeds of mortgaged property sold by the Bankruptcy Court, see Bankruptcy Rules 1952, r. 74 (2).
Under special circumstances, as where the mortgagee at the request of the trustee has postponed the sale for the purpose of getting a better market, or has made some other special agreement with him, interest after the bankruptcy will be allowed: *Re Lancaster, Ex parte Kensington, supra*; distd. in *Re Savin, supra*, but it may be doubted whether this could be done under the present law.

(*m*) *Aston* v. *Aston* (1750), 1 Ves. Sen. 264.

(*n*) *Bentham* v. *Haincourt* (1691), Pre. Ch. 30; 1 Eq. Cas. Abr. 320, pl. 2.

(*o*) *Loftus* v. *Swift* (1806), 2 Sch. & Lef. 642; *Roe* v. *Pogson* (1816), 2 Mad. 457; *Wrixon* v. *Vize* (1842), 2 Dru. & War. 203; affd. 3 Dru. & War. 104; *Hill* v. *Browne* (1844), Dru. *temp.* 426; *Makings* v. *Makings* (1860), 1 De G.F. & J. 355.

(*p*) *Hatton* v. *Harris,* [1892] A.C. 547.

(*q*) *Clarke* v. *Lord Abingdon* (1810), 17 Ves. 106.

payment, will not carry interest beyond the penalties of the bonds; for as, by virtue of the rule under consideration, interest does not grow due beyond the penalties, the trust will be satisfied by payment of interest to the amount of the penalties (*r*).

Judgment debts.—Apart from special circumstances interest was not allowed on a judgment debt (*s*); but under the Judgments Act 1838, judgment debts bear interest at the rate of 10 per cent. per annum (*t*) from the entering up of the judgment until satisfaction (*u*), and decrees of a Court of Equity have the effect of judgments at law (*w*). And under the Rules, where a debt does not carry interest, the creditor is entitled to interest at the same rate from the date of an order for administration, but only after payment of costs, debts, and the interest of such debts as by law carry interest (*x*).

C—CAPITALISATION OF INTEREST

Interest on arrears not allowed apart from contract.—Interest upon arrears, or upon fines for non-payment of principal and interest, is not allowed by the court where there is no contract for it (*y*). Thus, in a mortgage to bankers to secure a specific sum at a fixed rate of interest, it is not open to the bank, in the absence of express contract, to charge compound interest on this sum or to include it in the general banking account (*z*). But where the mortgage is given to the bank to secure the balance of a current account, there is an implied contract for payment of compound interest with yearly or even half-yearly rests (*a*).

Before the abolition of the usury laws there could be no payment of such interest by virtue of an original stipulation in the mortgage deed, it being then essential that the interest should first be due, before any agreement to turn it into principal would hold good (*b*).

(*r*) *Hughes* v. *Wynne* (1832), 1 Myl. & K. 20; *Clowes* v. *Waters* (1852), 16 Jur. 632.

(*s*) *Lewes* v. *Morgan* (1829), 3 Y. & J. 394; *Gaunt* v. *Taylor* (1834), 3 My. & K. 302; as to the power of the court to allow interest, see *Burland* v. *Earle*, [1905] A.C. 590.

(*t*) Administration of Justice 1970, s. 44; S.I. 1977 No. 141.

(*u*) Section 17; *Fisher* v. *Dudding* (1841), 3 Man. & Gr. 238; *Parsons* v. *Mather & Platt, Ltd.* (1977) Times, 25th February (from pronouncement of the judgment). County Court judgments do not come within s. 17; see *R.* v, *Essex County Court Judge* (1887), 18 Q.B.D. 704; *Sewing Machines Rentals, Ltd.* v. *Wilson*, [1975] 3 All E.R. 553 (C.A.).

(*w*) Judgments Act 1838, s. 18. Where the amount due is to be ascertained by inquiry, interest is payable under this section only from the date when the amount is ascertained by the master's certificate: *A.-G.* v. *Lord Carrington* (1843), 6 Beav. 454.

(*x*) R.S.C. Ord. 44, r. 18; C.C.R. Ord. 29, r. 14. Where the debt accrues due after the judgment, interest runs from the due date: *Re Salvin, Worseley* v. *Marshall*, [1912] 1 Ch. 332; *cf. Lainson* v. *Lainson (No. 2)* (1853), 18 Beav. 7. As to the effect on interest of merger of the debt in the judgment, see p. 596, *supra*.

(*y*) *Procter* v. *Cooper* (1700), Prec. Ch. 116; *Thornhill* v. *Evans* (1742), 2 Atk. 330; *Parker* v. *Butcher* (1867), L.R. 3 Eq. 762; *Daniell* v. *Sinclair* (1881), 6 App. Cas. 181 (P.C.).

(*z*) *Stewart* v. *Stewart* (1891), 27 L.R. Ir. 351; and see *Mosse* v. *Salt* (1863), 32 Beav. 269; and *London Chartered Bank of Australia* v. *White* (1879), 4 App. Cas. 413, 424 (P.C.).

(*a*) *Crosskill* v. *Bower* (1863), 32 Beav. 86; *National Bank of Australasia* v. *United Hand-in-Hand, etc., Co.* (1879), 4 App. Cas. 391, 400 (P.C.).

(*b*) *Lord Ossulston* v. *Lord Yarmouth* (1707), 2 Salk. 449; *Broadway* v. *Morecraft* (1729), Mos. 247; *Re Mills, Ex parte Champion* (1792), 3 Bro. C.C. 436; *Ex parte Bevan* (1803), 9 Ves. 223; *Morgan* v. *Mather* (1792), 2 Ves. Jun. 15; *Mainland* v. *Upjohn* (1889), 41 Ch. D. 126, 136. And it was said, that interest upon interest in arrear was never allowed in equity: *Thornhill* v. *Evans* (1742), 2 Atk. 330, but this view did not persist.

Such a contract, however, is now valid where there is no question of fraud or oppression (*c*), and a provision in the mortgage for capitalisation of overdue interest will be supported (*d*).

Capitalisation after mortgage.—After the mortgage a mere notice by the mortgagee to the mortgagor is not sufficient to turn arrears of interest into principal. There must for that purpose be a distinct assent to the demand, or an agreement otherwise made. Such an agreement must be made fairly, and is generally and most properly made upon the advance of fresh money (*e*).

Capitalisation on transfer of mortgage.—Arrears of interest will be capitalised on the transfer of a mortgage, if this is made with the concurrence of the mortgagor (*f*), but not where it is transferred without his concurrence (*g*), unless, it seems, he first refuses either to pay off the debt or to join in the transfer (*h*).

The mere privity or assent of the mortgagor to the account is not sufficient to change the interest into principal, even if he signs the account, for no intent is thereby shown to alter the nature of that part of the debt which consists of interest (*i*). On the other hand conversion may take place on the mere written consent of the mortgagor or person entitled to redeem, without his being actually a party to the assignment, or even on inference of his consent arising from his acts or from his acquiescence (*k*).

Capitalisation under foreclosure order.—Interest is also in effect capitalised in working out foreclosure in an action by a first

---

(*c*) *Clarkson* v. *Henderson* (1880), 14 Ch. D. 348.

(*d*) *Wrigley* v. *Gill*, [1906] 1 Ch. 165 (C.A.). Where, however, the mortgagee goes into possession and has net rents in his hands sufficient to keep down the interest he is bound to apply them to that purpose: *ibid*. But capitalisation does not mean that the interest becomes capital for all purposes: *e.g.* for income tax: *Re Morris, Mayhew* v. *Halton*, [1922] 1 Ch. 126 (C.A.); *Inland Revenue Commrs.* v. *Oswald*, [1945] A.C. 360 (H.L.); and see p. 665, *infra*. For a form of capitalisation clause, see 14 Ency. Forms and Precedents (4th Edn.), pp. 126, 127; and form in Precedent 1A in the Appendix, *infra*. A capitalisation clause may affect the exercise of the power of sale, see p. 363, note (*u*) *supra*.

(*e*) *Tompson* v. *Leith* (1858), 4 Jur. (N.S.) 1091; *Thornhill* v. *Evans*, *supra*. But such an agreement, when made in favour of the first mortgagee, will not hold against later incumbrancers of whom he had notice: *Digby* v. *Craggs* (1762), Ambl. 612.

(*f*) *Ashenhurst* v. *James* (1745), 3 Atk. 270; *Earl of Macclesfield* v. *Fitton* (1683), 1 Vern. 168; *Matthews* v. *Wallwyn* (1798), 4 Ves. 118; *Chambers* v. *Goldwin* (1804), 9 Ves. 254; *Mangles* v. *Dixon* (1852), 3 H.L.C. 702, at p. 737.

(*g*) *Cottrell* v. *Finney* (1874), 9 Ch. App. 541. And even where the transferee of a mortgage, by payment of arrears of interest and costs, had preserved the estate from a forced sale, it appears to have been assumed that he should only have his principal without interest: *ibid.*; though apparently he should have had interest on the salvage principle: see p. 628, *supra*.

(*h*) *Anon.* (1719), Bunb. 41.

(*i*) *Brown* v. *Barkham* (1720), 1 P. Wms. 652.

(*k*) Thus, where interest had been paid for many years upon an ascertained balance of principal and interest, reported due at the date of a decree for sale, the court inferred an agreement that interest should be paid as the price of forbearance to enforce the sale: *M'Carthy* v. *Llandaff* (1810), 1 Ba. & Be. 375; and see *Ashenhurst* v. *James*, *supra*. There seems formerly to have been a practice of adding the interest to the principal, upon assignment after forfeiture by non-payment of interest, though the time for payment of the principal had not arrived: see *Gladwyn* v. *Hitchman* (1690), 2 Vern. 135. Inquiries will be directed as to what is due on the mortgage, and what has been paid by the assignee: *Smith* v. *Pemberton* (1665), 1 Cas. in Ch. 67.

As to the form of judgment where it is denied that anything was due at the time of the assignment, see *Matthews* v. *Walwyn*, *supra*, at p. 129; *Lunn* v. *St. John* (*temp.* Lord THURLOW), cited 4 Ves. 121.

mortgagee against subsequent mortgagees and the mortgagor. If successive periods of redemption are directed, the second mortgagee is first given the chance of redeeming on payment of the sum certified to be due to the first mortgagee for principal, interest and costs. If he fails to redeem, the direction is that subsequent interest shall be computed, and this computation is made, not on the principal due, or on principal and costs, but on the total amount originally certified to be due, such amount being treated as one consolidated sum (*l*). Thus, for the purpose of the further account the interest due to the first mortgagee is capitalised and made to bear interest.

Where interest runs on the whole sum found due by a certificate, it so runs only from the date when the certificate becomes binding, and up to that time on the principal only (*m*).

D—THE RATE OF INTEREST ALLOWED

Lower rate on punctual payment.—It is a well-settled, if not an intelligible rule, that if the mortgagee wishes to stipulate for a higher rate of interest in default of punctual payment, he must reserve the higher rate as the interest payable under the mortgage, and provide for its reduction in case of punctual payment (*n*). He cannot effect his object by reserving the lower rate, and making the higher the penalty for non-payment at the appointed time, because, it is said, an agreement of the latter kind, being *nomine pœnæ*, is relievable in equity (*o*).

Where the provision for reduction of interest is in a general form,

---

(*l*) *Elton* v. *Curteis* (1881), 19 Ch. D. 49, *per* FRY, J., but the learned judge did not advert to the distinction between the case in which the subsequent mortgagee, having paid the mortgagee above him, is in his turn to be redeemed by the next below him, and the case in which the subsequent mortgagee has been foreclosed for default in payment. In the former case it is clear that the subsequent interest should be on the aggregate payment; for a mortgagee who pays off a security, in the course of redemption, is always entitled to interest on what he pays as against the person who has the next right to redeem. But in the latter case nothing has happened which entitles the prior mortgagee to interest upon interest. Before *Elton* v. *Curteis, supra*, this was sometimes given to the first mortgagee, but the reason was that the mortgagor was applying for the indulgence of the court: see *Brown* v. *Barkham* (1720), 1 P. Wms. 652; *Whatton* v. *Cradock* (1836), 1 Keen, 267; *Brewin* v. *Austin* (1838), 2 Keen, 211. Thus, under the original practice, the condition for an enlargement of the time for redemption was that the applicant, whether a subsequent mortgagee or the mortgagor, should pay interest on the whole sum found due for principal, interest, and costs: *Holford* v. *Yate* (1855), 1 K. & J. 677. But afterwards it became, and still is, the practice to enlarge the time on payment within a short time of the interest in arrear and costs: *Monkhouse* v. *Bedford Corporation* (1810), 17 Ves. 380; *Edwards* v. *Cunliffe* (1816), 1 Mad. 287; *Jones* v. *Creswicke* (1839), 9 Sim. 304; and then the subsequent interest was necessarily computed on principal only: *Whatton* v. *Cradock, supra; Brewin* v. *Austin, supra*. But such considerations do not apply to the case of a subsequent mortgagee, or of the mortgagor, who does not rely on the indulgence of the court, but comes to redeem in his turn according to the terms of the judgment. However, *Elton* v. *Curteis, supra*, appears to have settled the practice.

(*m*) *Jacob* v. *Earl of Suffolk* (1728), Mos. 27.

(*n*) *Strode* v. *Parker* (1694), 2 Vern. 316; *Jory* v. *Cox* (1701), Prec. Ch. 160; *Walmesley* v. *Booth* (1741), 2 Atk. 27. As to the restriction on increasing the rate of interest under the Rent Act, see p. 277, *supra*.

(*o*) *Holles* v. *Wyse* (1693), 2 Vern. 289; *Strode* v. *Parker, supra; Nicholls* v. *Maynard* (1747), 3 Atk. 519; *Wallingford* v. *Mutual Society* (1880), 5 App. Cas. 685, 702 (H.L.). In *Brown* v. *Barkham* (1720), 1 P. Wms. 652, the higher rate was allowed as the price of the mortgagee's forbearance.

the mortgagor cannot have the benefit of it, unless he strictly performs the condition. He will have no relief after the time of payment has passed (*p*). And if the mortgagee has taken possession by reason of the mortgagor's default, he will also be entitled to the higher rate of interest reserved (*q*), even if there was no interest in arrear when he took possession, and although he did so by arrangement with the mortgagor (*r*). But if it is provided, that, as often as interest shall be paid within the limited time, the lower rate shall be accepted, or some equivalent words be used pointing to any payment of interest, the mortgagor will not, by a single breach of the condition, lose his right to the benefit of it on future payments, but only upon that particular occasion (*s*).

Commission on unpaid instalments.—A contract to pay a percentage on unpaid instalments for the interval between the time fixed for, and that of actual payment, under the name of a "commission", has been allowed as not being in the nature of a penalty (*t*); and so has a similar payment on the renewal of promissory notes (*u*). And the mortgagee of a ship may contract for a commission (2 per cent.) on any cash advance remaining unpaid for two months (*v*).

Rate of interest allowed by the court.—Where no rate of interest is fixed by the parties the court can fix it, and has in the past adopted the rate of £5 per cent. per annum (*x*). And this has also been decided to be the proper rate, where an absolute conveyance has been cut down to a security on principles analogous to those which were formerly applied in cases of usury (*y*). In the case of further advances, or of money allowed in the nature of further advances, the interest is generally given at the same rate as upon the moneys originally lent (*z*).

(*p*) *Bonafous* v. *Rybot* (1763), 3 Bur. 1370; *Jory* v. *Cox, supra; Stanhope* v. *Manners* (1763), 2 Ed. 197. There will be no relief in equity under an agreement not to call in a mortgage on punctual payment of interest, though it be but two or three days in arrear: *Hicks* v. *Gardner* (1837), 1 Jur. 541; *Leeds and Hanley Theatre of Varieties* v. *Broadbent*, [1898] 1 Ch. 343 (C.A.); *Maclaine* v. *Gatty*, [1921] 1 A.C. 376 (H.L.). A trustee is justified in accepting the lower rate, after the higher rate has become payable by the strict terms of the contract, it being the usual course to treat interest paid under such circumstances as having been paid within the time fixed: *Booth* v. *Alington* (1856), 26 L.J. Ch. 138.

(*q*) *Union Bank of London* v. *Ingram* (1880), 16 Ch. D. 53; *Cockburn* v. *Edwards* (1881), 18 Ch. D. 449, 463 (C.A.); *Bright* v. *Campbell* (1889), 41 Ch. D. 388. All explained in *Wrigley* v. *Gill*, [1906] 1 Ch. 165 (C.A.).

(*r*) *Bright* v. *Campbell, supra.*

(*s*) *Stanhope* v. *Manners, supra.* See *Burrowes* v. *Molloy* (1845), 2 Jo. & Lat. 521; *Wayne* v. *Lewis* (1855), 3 W.R. 600.

(*t*) *General Credit and Discount Co.* v. *Clegg* (1883), 22 Ch. D. 549.

(*u*) *Bucknell* v. *Vickery* (1891), 64 L.T. 701.

(*v*) *The Benwell Tower* (1895), 72 L.T. 664.

(*x*) *Ashwell* v. *Staunton* (1861), 30 Beav. 52; *Mendl* v. *Smith* (1943), 169 L.T. 153. Cf. *Re Kerr's Policy* (1869), L.R. 8 Eq. 331; *Re Drax, Savile* v. *Drax*, [1903] 1 Ch. 781 (C.A.) (4 per cent. per annum allowed); *Cityland and Property (Holdings), Ltd.* v. *Dabrah*, [1968] Ch. 166; [1967] 2 All E.R. 639 (7 per cent. per annum); *Congresbury Motors, Ltd.* v. *Anglo-Belge Finance Co., Ltd.*, [1970] Ch. 294; [1969] 3 All E.R. 545 (5 per cent.); and see p. 29, *supra.*

(*y*) See *Douglas* v. *Culverwell* (1862), 4 De G.F. & J. 20; *Re Unsworth's Trusts* (1865), 2 Dr. & Sm. 337.

(*z*) *Woolley* v. *Drag* (1795), 2 Anst. 551. It has, however, been directed to be computed after the rate current in a foreign country where the money was expended, the current rate there being less than the interest reserved by the mortgage: *Quarrell* v. *Beckford* (1816), 1 Mad. 269, at p. 281; and see *Badham* v. *Odell* (1742), 4 Bro. P.C. 349.

Variation in rate of interest.—An unwritten agreement to reduce the rate of interest on a mortgage is good; but in the absence of evidence or presumption of such an agreement, the difference between the rate reserved and that actually paid must be made good (*a*). So, if a higher rate than is reserved is paid, the excess may be deducted on discharge of the mortgage (*b*).

E—WHEN INTEREST CEASES TO RUN (c)

Notice to pay off mortgage.—The mortgagee is entitled to six months' interest from the date of the notice to him of the intended discharge of the security. If the payment is not made at the time fixed, the mortgagee is entitled to a new notice, or to six months' additional interest from the time of actual payment. But he will not be entitled to such interest if he has demanded, or taken proceedings to recover, payment, though, pending the proceedings, notice of payment has been given to and accepted by him (*e*).

If the mortgage cannot be discharged at the time fixed, by reason of the inability of the mortgagee to produce the deeds, or if in a redemption or foreclosure action he omits to attend at the time and place fixed for payment, he will be allowed no interest beyond that day. Where the omission arose from a mistake, and the mortgagor also neglected to attend, the mortgagee was not compelled to wait another six months, but a new time was fixed for payment at the end of ten days (*f*).

Interest ceases on tender.—Subject, as just mentioned, interest will cease to run upon the mortgage debt from the time at which a proper tender of the whole amount due is shown to have been made (*g*). But it ought to appear, that, from the time of the tender, the money

---

(*a*) *Lord Milton* v. *Edgworth* (1773), 5 Bro. P.C. 313; *Gregory* v. *Pilkington* (1857), 26 L.J. Ch. 177; *Re Venning* (1947), 63 T.L.R. 394 (C.A.). And note the doctrine of estoppel as enunciated in *Central London Property Trust, Ltd.* v. *High Trees House, Ltd.*, [1947] K.B. 130. For variation of mortgages, see p. 43, *supra.*

(*b*) *Tyler* v. *Manson* (1826), 5 L.J. (O.S.) Ch. 34.

(*c*) For early repayment discount, see pp. 522, 528, *supra.*

(*d*) See p. 538, *supra.*

(*e*) *Bartlett* v. *Franklin* (1867), 15 W.R. 1077; *Re Alcock, Prescott* v. *Phipps* (1883), 23 Ch. D. 372 (C.A.). Hence, if the mortgagee sells he can charge interest only up to the completion of the purchase; and it is the same if the interest is payable in advance, and the mortgagee sells before the day of payment: *Banner* v. *Berridge* (1881), 18 Ch. D. 254.

Where the mortgagee consents in an administration action to a sale of the mortgaged property, he will have interest for six months from the date of the consent, if the mortgage is discharged before the end of that time; but if it is not, interest runs to the time of payment: *Day* v. *Day* (1862), 31 Beav. 270.

(*f*) *Lord Midleton* v. *Eliot* (1847), 15 Sim. 531; *Hughes* v. *Williams* (1853), Kay, App. iv., and form of order there; *James* v. *Rumsey* (1879), 11 Ch. D. 398.

(*g*) *Lutton* v. *Rodd* (1675), 2 Cas. in Ch. 206; *Robarts* v. *Jefferys* (1830), 8 L.J. (O.S.) Ch. 137; *Cliff* v. *Wadsworth* (1843), 2 Y. & C.C.C. 598; *Kinnaird* v. *Trollope* (1889), 42 Ch. D. 610; *Bank of New South Wales* v. *O'Connor* (1889), 14 App. Cas. 273 (P.C.), at p. 284; *Rourke* v. *Robinson*, [1911] 1 Ch. 480; *Edmondson* v. *Copland*, [1911] 2 Ch. 301; *Graham* v. *Seal* (1918), 88 L.J. Ch. 31 (C.A.). As to tender, see p. 539, *supra.* The tender to stop interest need not be such a tender as would be a defence to an action at law: *Manning* v. *Burges* (1663), 1 Cas. in Ch. 29; *Webb* v. *Crosse*, [1912] 1 Ch. 323; see p. 539, *supra.*

If the right to redeem is disputed, and an inquiry becomes necessary, the mortgagee is not to lose his interest, pending the inquiry, although a tender has been made: *Sharpnell* v. *Blake* (1737), 2 Eq. Ca. Abr. 604.

was kept ready by the mortgagor, and that no profit was afterwards made of it. Upon proof to the contrary interest will still run (*h*). And it would be safer to pay the money into court (*i*).

There must be an actual tender of the money due (*j*). The court will not stay the interest on proof of a proposal by the mortgagor, where money is due to him from the mortgagee on another account between them, to satisfy the mortgage by deducting the sum due thereon from the other debt (*k*).

Purchase by mortgagee.—Upon a purchase by the mortgagee of the mortgaged estate, where the mortgagee takes possession, but completion is deferred for a long time, it may be inferred that there was a set-off of the mortgage debt against the purchase money at the time of taking possession, and interest reserved by the contract on the purchase money runs only on the balance (*l*).

F—INCIDENCE AS BETWEEN TENANT FOR LIFE AND
REMAINDERMAN

Tenant for life bound to keep down interest.—A tenant for life of a mortgaged estate is bound to keep down the interest of the charge during his life, to the extent of the rents and profits, not merely of the mortgaged property (*m*), but also of any other property comprised in the settlement under which he is life tenant (*n*). This duty subsists in favour of the reversioner and gives no right to the incumbrancer (*o*). It is for the reversioner to see that it is performed (*p*), and if it is neglected, the reversioner (*q*), or it seems the next tenant for life (*r*),

---

(*h*) *Lutton* v. *Rodd, supra*; *Gyles* v. *Hall* (1726), 2 P. Wms. 378.

(*i*) See *Kinnaird* v. *Trollope, supra*, at p. 618; *Edmondson* v. *Copland, supra*; *Barratt* v. *Gough-Thomas*, [1951] 2 All E.R. 48.

(*j*) *Bishop* v. *Church* (1751), 2 Ves. Sen. 371.

(*k*) *Garforth* v. *Bradley* (1755), 2 Ves. Sen. 675. Executors who refuse a proper tender on the ground that they have not proved the will can demand no further interest, because they are entitled to receive the money before probate: *Austen* v. *Dodwell's Executors* (1729), 1 Eq. Ca. Abr. 318.

(*l*) *Wallis* v. *Bastard* (1853), 4 De G.M. & G. 251. And as to set-off against the mortgage of sums due to persons claiming under the mortgagor, see *Pettat* v. *Ellis* (1804), 9 Ves. 563; and in bankruptcy, *Re Barker, Ex parte Penfold* (1851), 4 De G. & Sm. 282; *Re Penfold, Ex parte Ramsbottom* (1835), 4 Deac. & C. 198.

(*m*) *Revel* v. *Watkinson* (1748), 1 Ves. Sen. 93; *Amesbury* v. *Brown* (1750), 1 Ves. Sen. 477; *Faulkner* v. *Daniel* (1843), 3 Hare, 199; *Burges* v. *Mawbey* (1823), Turn. & Russ. 167 at p. 174; *Lord Kensington* v. *Bouverie* (1855), 7 De G.M. & G. 134. And in an administration action he must keep down the interest upon all debts charged upon the estate from the testator's death: *Marshall* v. *Crowther* (1874), 2 Ch. D. 199. The tenant for life is not exempted from this liability by the possession of an absolute power of appointment, by virtue whereof he is able, like the tenant in tail, to make the estate his own: *Whitbread* v. *Smith* (1854), 3 De G.M. & G. 727, 741. And a tenant in fee subject to an executory devise over is under the same liability: *Butcher* v. *Simmonds* (1876), 35 L.T. 304. So also are the assignee and judgment creditor of the tenant for life: *Scholefield* v. *Lockwood* (1863), 9 Jur. N.S. 1258.

(*n*) *Frewen* v. *Law Life Assurance Society*, [1896] 2 Ch. 511; *Honywood* v. *Honywood*, [1902] 1 Ch. 347.

(*o*) *Re Morley, Morley* v. *Saunders* (1869), L.R. 8 Eq. 594.

(*p*) *Caulfield* v. *Maguire* (1845), 2 Jo. & Lat. 141 at p. 160.

(*q*) *Lord Penrhyn* v. *Hughes* (1799), 5 Ves. 99, at p. 106; *Lord Kensington* v. *Bouverie* (1859), 7 H.L.C. 557, at p. 575; *Makings* v. *Makings* (1860), 1 De G.F. & J. 355; But *cf. Scholefield* v. *Lockwood* (1863), 4 De G.J. & Sm. 22, at p. 31: "A tenant for life has all his lifetime to pay off the arrears of interest, and he cannot be charged with neglect of duty, neither does any right arise as to the remainderman, until death or insolvency of the tenant for life." There seems to be no other authority for this view of the law.

(*r*) *Revel* v. *Watkinson, supra*.

may commence an action to make the rents available, and may compel the tenant for life to account for what has accrued; and he has an equity to have the estate recouped out of the future income accruing to the tenant for life (s).

Tenant in tail not so bound.—The adult tenant in tail of an incumbered estate is not obliged to keep down the interest on the charge; because, having—or being able by his own act to acquire—full power over the estate, neither the issue in tail nor the remainderman has any equity to call for an indemnity against the arrears of interest accrued during the possession of their predecessor (t). And on the other hand, if the tenant in tail dies without barring the entail, after keeping down the interest, or taking an assignment of the mortgage (in which case he is considered to have paid himself the interest out of the rents and profits), the issue in tail have the benefit, and the personal representatives of the tenant in tail have no equity to charge the reversion with interest accrued during his life (u).

Successive tenants for life.—Where there are successive tenants for life, each is bound to keep down the interest on incumbrances which accrues in his own time (x), and so far as the rents and profits are insufficient for this purpose, or, so far as through the insolvency of the first tenant for life the interest is not kept down, it is charged on the reversion (y).

Variation of incidence.—But the incidence of the interest may be varied by the special circumstances. Thus, if the reversioner stands by and allows the rents to be received by the tenant for life and not applied in payment of interest, the reversion will be charged, and the reversioner cannot afterwards establish a claim against the estate of the tenant for life on the ground that the rents were sufficient (z). On the other hand, the conduct of the tenant for life in keeping down out

---

(s) *Waring* v. *Coventry* (1834), 2 My. & K. 406. As to the application after a testator's death of rents in respect of separate mortgaged properties, the interest being in arrear at his death and the share in his estate settled, see *Re Coaks, Coaks* v. *Bayley*, [1911] 1 Ch. 171.

If a mortgagee who has allowed the interest to fall into arrears purchases the estate of the tenant for life, the surplus rents received after the purchase beyond the current interest of the mortgage must be applied in discharge of the arrears; and the mortgagee cannot charge the arrears upon the inheritance, for the vendor under whom he claims was bound to keep down the interest: *Lord Penrhyn* v. *Hughes, supra.* So as to a. purchaser who actually pays off the arrears: *Whitbread* v. *Smith* (1854), 3 De G.M. & G, 727, at p. 741.

(t) *Chaplin* v. *Chaplin* (1733), 3 P. Wms. 229, at p. 235; *Burges* v. *Mawbey* (1823), Turn. & Russ. 167.

(u) *Amesbury* v. *Brown* (1750), 1 Ves. Sen. 477. An infant tenant in tail, being unable to make the estate his own, was in the position of a tenant for life: *Sarjeson* v. *Cruise* (*circ.* 1750), cited in *Amesbury* v. *Brown, supra,* at p. 480; *Sergeson* v. *Sealey* (1742), 2 Atk. 412; *Burgess* v. *Mawbey, supra,* at p. 177. But now the legal estate would be vested in the trustees of the settlement as statutory owners, and ordinarily, they would keep down the interest out of rents and profits.

(x) *Caulfield* v. *Maguire* (1845), 2 Jo. & Lat. 141. The suggestion made in *Lord Penrhyn* v. *Hughes* (1799), 5 Ves. 99, 106, that the tenant for life in remainder must bear the arrears of interest which accrued in the time of a previous tenant for life, has not been accepted.

(y) *Sharshaw* v. *Gibbs* (1834), Kay, 333. And where arrears which had accrued, through insufficiency of rents, during the lifetime of one tenant for life were discharged by the trustees of a subsequent life estate, they were thrown on the reversion: *ibid.*

(z) *Lord Kensington* v. *Bouverie* (1854), 19 Beav. 39, at p. 54.

of his own moneys so much of the interest as the estate cannot pay, without informing the remainderman of the deficiency, may show that he intended to exonerate the estate so that there is no charge on the remainder (*a*).

Possession under paramount title.—The tenant for life is, it seems, not excused by the fact of a portion of the estate having been during a part of his time in the possession of another under a paramount title—*e.g.*, a jointress under a prior settlement—and he must discharge the arrears, which accrued in the time of the paramount estate, out of the additional rents received at its expiration (*b*). And to liquidate such arrears he must furnish all the rents, if necessary, during the whole of his life, but subject, it seems, to this equity, *viz.*, that if the settlor of the estate is *in loco parentis* to the tenant for life, and the tenant for life is not otherwise provided for, a reasonable maintenance shall be allowed him out of the rents and profits (*c*).

Direction to receiver to keep down interest.—The order of the court, directing a receiver to keep down the interest of incumbrances, does not amount to an appropriation of the rents and profits to that purpose, so as to make the rights of the parties where the interest has not been paid or applied for, the same as if interest had been actually paid. The order is partly made in justice to the incumbrancers, and partly for the benefit of the estate, lest the incumbrancers should proceed in respect of their unpaid interest. But if they do not apply for it, they are presumed to be content with their security for principal and interest, and the estate remains burdened with the arrears, for which there is no equity against the surplus rents paid over by the receiver (*d*).

(*a*) *Lord Kensington* v. *Bouverie* (1859), 7 H.L.C. 557.
(*b*) *Revel* v. *Watkinson* (1748), 1 Ves. Sen. 93; *Tracy* v. *Lady Hereford* (1786), 2 Bro. C.C. 128.
(*c*) *Revel* v. *Watkinson, supra*; and *Butler's Case* cited there, p. 95.
(*d*) *Bertie* v. *Earl of Abingdon* (1817), 3 Mer. 560.

CHAPTER 36

Costs

I—GENERAL RIGHT OF MORTGAGEE TO COSTS

Rule as to costs of action.—The mortgagee is entitled as of right to the costs properly incurred by him in an action of foreclosure or redemption, and this right extends to an equitable mortgagee, including a mortgagee by deposit, whether with or without a memorandum of deposit (*a*). But he may forfeit these costs by misconduct, or may even have to pay the costs of such an action in a case where he has acted vexatiously or unreasonably (*b*). The court departs from the general rule with reluctance, and seems formerly even to have doubted its power to throw costs upon the mortgagee (*c*). The jurisdiction has, however, for a long time been fully established.

After the accounts have been taken in a foreclosure action, the court will not reopen the judgment so as to include costs since incurred by the plaintiff in a different action, in respect of property mortgaged to him, which upon sale proved to be insufficient for payment of the prior incumbrancers (*d*). A mortgagee who has commenced a foreclosure action, pending an action to administer the mortgagor's estate, is entitled, after being satisfied under the latter, to dismiss his own action, and to have the costs of it (*e*).

(*a*) *R.* v. *Chambers* (1840), 4 Y. & C. Ex. 54; *Wade* v. *Ward* (1859), 4 Drew. 602; *Cotterell* v. *Stratton* (1874), L.R. 17 Eq. 543. And see *Central Mortgage and Housing Corpn.* v. *Johnson* (1971), 20 D.L.R. (3d) 622.

(*b*) *Bank of New South Wales* v. *O'Connor* (1889), 14 App. Cas. 273 (P.C.), at p. 278. For a form of order, see supplement to Ency. Court Form, Costs, p. 177. The right is treated as an implied term of the mortgage contract: *Re Wallis, Ex parte Lickorish* (1890), 25 Q.B.D. 176 (C.A.), at pp. 180, 181; or at least it rests "substantially on contract", and can only be lost or curtailed by such inequitable conduct on the part of the mortgagee as may amount to a violation or culpable neglect of his duty under the contract: *Cotterell* v. *Stratton* (1872), 8 Ch. App. 295, 302; see *M'Donnell* v. *M'Mahon* (1889), 23 L.R. Ir. 283. As regards costs, mortgagees and trustees are on the same footing: *Turner* v. *Hancock* (1882), 20 Ch. D. 303, 304. A mortgagee's costs may be postponed to an advance made for the protection of the property without notice of the mortgage: *Myers* v. *United Guarantee and Life Assurance Co.* (1855), 7 De G.M. & G. 112.

(*c*) *Francklyn* v. *Fern* (1740), Barn. Ch. 30; *Detillin* v. *Gale* (1802), 7 Ves. 583. And a claim by the mortgagor, that the mortgagee shall pay the costs, should be included in the original inquiry, for the court will not attend afterwards to evidence upon the subject: *Dunstan* v. *Patterson* (1847), 2 Ph. 341.

(*d*) *Barron* v. *Lancefield* (1853), 17 Beav. 208. But where costs of recovering possession in ejectment had not been provided for, the court, but not without hesitation, made a subsequent order, that those costs and expenses should be added to the principal: *Spurgeon* v. *Witham*, M.R., 21 December, 1855. It appeared, however, that little or no opposition was made to the order.

(*e*) *Brooksbank* v. *Higginbottom* (1862), 31 Beav. 35. And as to costs on staying proceedings in a foreclosure action, upon the offer of a later incumbrancer to pay the plaintiff's debt, see *Jones* v. *Tinney* (1845), Kay, App. xlv.

Party and party costs.—The mortgagee is entitled to party and party, not solicitor and client costs (*f*), and the scale of taxation is regulated by the amount of the original debt, and not by the amount owing when the litigation commences (*g*).

Costs, charges, and expenses.—The mortgagee is also allowed in taking the accounts all costs, charges, and expenses reasonably and properly incurred in ascertaining or defending his rights (*h*), preserving the security (*i*) or in recovering the mortgage debt (*j*). This, as well as the right to costs of foreclosure or redemption actions, is founded on the principle that the mortgagee ought to be indemnified to the extent to which he acts reasonably as mortgagee (*k*). The "costs" referred to in the rule are the costs of litigation outside the action in which the costs, charges and expenses are allowed, and properly such costs come under "charges and expenses" (*l*).

The owner of a share of an estate and his incumbrancers have but one set of costs, which is received by the first incumbrancer (*m*).

Costs are added to the debt.—Costs, whether costs of the foreclosure or redemption action or included in "costs, charges, and expenses", are not recoverable from the mortgagor personally (*n*), unless in the particular case he has become personally liable to pay them (*o*), but both as against the mortgagor and other persons interested in the equity of redemption, they are added by the mortgagee to the amount due upon his security, and must be paid as a condition of

---

(*f*) *Re Queen's Hotel Co., Cardiff, Ltd., Re Vernon Tin Plate Co., Ltd.,* [1900] 1 Ch. 792; *Re Adelphi Hotel (Brighton), Ltd., District Bank, Ltd.* v. *Adelphi Hotel (Brighton), Ltd.,* [1953] 2 All E.R. 498; *affd.* in *Central Mortgage and Housing Corporation* v. *Johnson* (1971), 20 D.L.R. (3d) 622. In *Re Griffith, Jones & Co.* (1883), 53 L.J. Ch. 303 (C.A.), it was held that, as a general rule, solicitor and client costs were given (see *Lomax* v. *Hide* (1690), 2 Vern. 185). See also *The Kestrel* (1866), L.R. 1 A. & E. 78, and *Re New Zealand Midland Rail. Co., Smith* v. *Lubbock,* [1901] 2 Ch. 357, where it was stated that a plaintiff in a debenture holder's action was, as between himself and the mortgagors, only entitled to party and party costs; but that if the assets were insufficient to pay the debentures in full, then, as between himself and the other debenture holders, he was entitled to solicitor and client costs: *Re Griffith, Jones & Co., supra.* And see note 7, p. 616, *infra.*

(*g*) *Cotterell* v. *Stratton* (1874), L.R. 17 Eq. 543.

(*h*) *Dryden* v. *Frost* (1838), 3 My. & C. 670. "A mortgagee does not in terms contract for costs, but the rule is that all costs which he, being mortgagee, properly incurs in relation to his security, are to be allowed to him": *National Provincial Bank of England* v. *Games* (1886), 31 Ch. D. 582 (C.A.), at p. 592.

(*i*) See p. 267, *supra.*

(*j*) *Ellison* v. *Wright* (1827), 3 Russ. 458.

(*k*) *Detillin* v. *Gale* (1802), 7 Ves. 583: "The owner coming to deliver the estate from that incumbrance he himself put upon it, the person having that pledge is not to be put to expense with regard to that." The basing of the right to costs on an implied term of the mortgage contract (*supra*, p. 638, note (*b*)) states this principle in another way.

(*l*) *Re Chennell, Jones* v. *Chennell* (1878), 8 Ch. D. 492; *Re Beddoe, Downes* v. *Cottam,* [1893] 1 Ch. 547.

(*m*) *Remnant* v. *Hood (No. 2)* (1860), 27 Beav. 613; *Equitable Insurance Co.* v. *Fuller* (1861), 1 Johns. & H. 379; *Ward* v. *Yates* (1860), 1 Dr. & Sm. 80.

(*n*) *Re Sneyd, Ex parte Fewings* (1883), 25 Ch.D. 338 (C.A.); *Sinfield* v. *Sweet,* [1967] 3 All E.R. 479.

(*o*) See clause 7, p. 682, *infra.* The mortgagor will be personally liable under his covenant for further assurance for costs incurred by the mortgagee under that covenant: *Langton* v. *Langton* (1854), 18 Jur. 1092; reversed, but not on this point, (1855), 7 De G.M. & G. 30.

redeeming (*p*). With the principal and interest they form a single debt and are payable in the same priority (*q*).

So, where there is a right of consolidating mortgages but not otherwise (*r*), costs incurred in respect of one estate may be added to the debt due upon another, of which redemption is ordered (*s*). And if one of two mortgagees who advanced the money in separate sums brings an action for foreclosure, the other being a defendant, the judgment will direct foreclosure on default of payment of the whole debt, and the costs of both mortgagees (*t*).

Costs in priority action.—In an action to determine priorities the costs usually follow the mortgages, but the court has a discretion, and can order one or the other of the claimants to pay the costs if a case is made for it (*u*).

Appeal as to costs.—The mortgagee's costs of a foreclosure or redemption action are not, like costs of actions in general, within the discretion of the court. Hence they are not within the provision that an appeal cannot be brought as to costs only which by law are left to the discretion of the court (*x*), and where a mortgagee has been deprived of costs on the ground of misconduct, he can appeal as of right, and, if he is successful, the costs of the appeal will be added to his security (*y*). On the other hand, if, notwithstanding the charge of improper conduct is established, the mortgagee's costs are allowed,

---

(*p*) *Frazer* v. *Jones* (1846), 5 Hare, 475, 483; *Dunstan* v. *Patterson* (1847), 2 Ph. 341; *Cotterell* v. *Stratton, supra*; *Re Sneyd, Ex parte Fewings, supra*; *Re Wallis, Ex parte Lickorish* (1890), 25 Q.B.D. 176 (C.A.). For a consideration of costs of proceedings for the recovery of possession see the Report of the Committee on the Enforcement of Judgment Debts (the Payne Committee), 1969, Cmnd. 3909, paras. 1428 *et seq.*
(*q*) *Barnes* v. *Racster* (1842), 1 Y. & C.C.C. 401; *Johnstone* v. *Cox* (1881), 19 Ch. D. 17 (C.A.); *Harpham* v. *Shacklock* (1881), 19 Ch. D. 207 (C.A.), at p. 215; *Pollock* v. *Lands Improvement Co.* (1888), 37 Ch. D. 661, 668; *Re Baldwin's Estate*, [1900] 1 I.R. 15. The mere fact that the mortgage contains a declaration that the "total amount to be recovered by the mortgages under these presents shall not exceed" so much, does not preclude the mortgagee from adding arrears of interest and costs beyond that sum, since the proviso is construed to relate exclusively to principal: *White* v. *City of London Brewery Co.* (1889), 42 Ch. D. 237 (C.A.).
(*r*) *Cotterell* v. *Stratton* (1872), 8 Ch. App. 295, 302; *Johnstone* v. *Cox, supra*; *Re Love, Hill* v. *Spurgeon* (1885), 29 Ch. D. 348 (C.A.); *De Caux* v. *Skipper* (1886), 31 Ch. D. 635 (C.A.).
(*s*) *Batchelor* v. *Middleton* (1848), 6 Hare, 75, at p. 86.
(*t*) *Davenport* v. *James* (1847), 7 Hare, 249. Costs of trustees who hold on trust to sell and pay off the mortgage may have priority over the mortgagee and his judgment creditor: *Clare* v. *Wood* (1844), 4 Hare, 81.
The mortgagee may add to his debt the costs of his trustee who is made a defendant to a foreclosure action: *Browne* v. *Lockhart* (1840), 10 Sim. 420.
(*u*) *Harpham* v. *Shacklock, supra*, at p. 215. In a case where the legal mortgagees brought a foreclosure action, and one of the defendants, an equitable mortgagee, unsuccessfully claimed priority, it was held that the plaintiffs should add their ordinary foreclosure costs to their security, and that the defendant mortgagee must pay them the residue of their costs: *Northern Counties of England Fire Insurance Co.* v. *Whipp* (1884), 26 Ch. D. 482 (C.A.), at p. 496.
(*x*) Although costs of and incidental to all proceedings are normally in the discretion of the court a mortgagee who has not acted unreasonably is entitled to the costs of proceedings to which he is a party, in so far as they are not recovered from or paid by any other person, out of the mortgaged property: R.S.C. Ord. 62, r. 6 (2).
(*y*) *Addison* v. *Cox* (1872), 8 Ch. App. 76; *Turner* v. *Hancock* (1882), 20 Ch. D. 303; *Re Knight's Will* (1884), 26 Ch. D. 82, 90; *M'Donnell* v. *M'Mahon* (1889), 23 L.R. Ir. 283.

this is done in the exercise of the discretion of the court, and the mortgagor has no right of appeal (z).

The restriction on appeals as to costs only refers to the costs of the action in which the appeal would be brought. It does not apply to an order by which the mortgagee is allowed "costs, charges, and expenses", and against this the mortgagor can appeal without leave (a).

Effect of directions for taxation and payment of costs.—A direction to tax the mortgagee's costs of the action amounts to a direction to pay him his whole costs, without exception as to any part of the cause, and will be so construed, although the mortgagee, by holding over after payment, has made the action necessary, and although he has raised an improper defence (b). But it would seem that even where the order directs costs, the taxing master may disallow costs which, having regard to the relation of the parties, ought not to be charged against the mortgagor (c).

An order for payment of costs by a mortgagee is not necessarily an order for personal payment. He may be allowed to set them off against the amount payable to him in respect of his debt (d). And where the costs of the action, or part of them, would have been thrown upon a mortgagee, being solvent, yet if he is insolvent (and, therefore, unable to pay), he will not receive any general costs (e).

Costs of bottomry bondholder.—The incumbrancer by bottomry has, in like manner, a right to the general costs of enforcing his security. But the right to the costs of a reference, to ascertain what is due on the bond, will be determined according to the circumstances of each case, though with an inclination to the bondholder. But he may be condemned in the whole costs of the reference if the result of the inquiry shows that his demand was exorbitant and extortionate (f).

II—COSTS OF ACTION

Loss of right to costs.—The jurisdiction either to deprive the mortgagee of costs, or to order him to pay costs, will be exercised where he has been guilty of gross misconduct, or even where, without improper motives, he has caused expenses to be incurred which cannot justly be thrown upon the mortgagor. The following are cases where one or the other course has been adopted (g):

(z) *Charles* v. *Jones* (1886), 33 Ch. D. 80 (C.A.).

(a) *Re Chennell, Jones* v. *Chennell, supra.* The criticism of this case by the Court of Appeal in *Bew* v. *Bew*, [1899] 2 Ch. 467, 472, applies only to costs of action and not to the other mortgagee's costs, referred to in "costs, charges, and expenses": see *Re Beddoe, Downes* v. *Cottam*, [1893] 1 Ch. 547 (C.A.), which was not referred to in the judgments in *Re Chennell, Jones* v. *Chennell, supra.*

(b) *Quarrell* v. *Beckford* (1816), 1 Mad. 269; *Wilson* v. *Metcalfe* (1826), 1 Russ. 530.

(c) *Stone* v. *Lickorish*, [1891] 2 Ch. 363.

(d) *Banks* v. *Whittall* (1847), 1 De G. & Sm. 536 at p. 541; *West* v. *Jones* (1851), 1 Sim. (N.S.) 205; see *Wheaton* v. *Graham* (1857), 24 Beav. 483. As to costs of the mortgagee's executors in a foreclosure action where the mortgagee had made himself liable to costs in a previous action, see *Long* v. *Storie* (1852), 9 Hare, 542.

(e) *Rider* v. *Jones* (1843), 2 Y. & C.C.C. 329.

(f) *The Eliza* (1842), 1 W. Rob. 328; *The Catherine* (1847), 3 W. Rob. 1; *The Kepler* (1861), Lush. 201.

(g) As to the costs of the mortgagee where the advance is made out of trust moneys, see *Allen* v. *Knight* (1847), 5 Hare, 272; *West* v. *Jones* (1851), 1 Sim. (N.S.) 205.

If the mortgagee sets up an unjust defence (*h*); or resists a claim to redeem on the ground of a foreclosure collusively obtained (*i*); or if he resists any just claim to redeem (*k*); he will be liable to so much of the costs as his improper conduct has caused, though he may be allowed the ordinary costs of redemption (*l*).

Again, if the mortgagee refuses a proper tender, even if it is made under protest (*m*); or fails on tender to execute a reconveyance which has been already approved (*n*); or proceeds after payment of all that is due; he does so on peril of paying the costs incurred after the payment or tender (*o*), whether it was made before or after the commencement of the action, and whether by the mortgagor or one representing him, or by a later incumbrancer (*p*).

When nothing due.—If the mortgagee institutes a foreclosure action, and upon taking the accounts it is shown that nothing was due at the commencement of the proceedings, or if he drives the mortgagor to institute an action under like circumstances, he must bear the whole expense of the action (*q*).

Or if, being a defendant, he denies that he is satisfied, when nothing remains due, he must pay the costs of so much of the proceedings as

---

(*h*) *Mocatta* v. *Murgatroyd* (1717), 1 P. Wms. 392; *Baker* v. *Wind* (1748), 1 Ves. Sen. 160; and see *Thornton* v. *Court* (1854), 3 De G.M. & G. 293; *England* v. *Codrington* (1758), 1 Ed. 169; *Tomlinson* v. *Gregg* (1866), 15 W.R. 51; *Tarn* v. *Turner* (1888), 39 Ch. D. 456 (C.A.). And if the contract under which the mortgagee claims is illegal: *Johnson* v. *Williamhurst* (1823), 1 L.J. (O.S.) Ch. 112; or if he has been guilty of ill conduct in attempting to deprive another of the benefit of his security by a dealing behind his back (*Taylor* v. *Baker* (1818), Dan. at p. 82); he may be refused his costs.

(*i*) *Hall* v. *Heward* (1886), 32 Ch. D. 430 (C.A.), at p. 436.

(*k*) See *Squire* v. *Pardoe* (1891), 66 L.T. 243; *Henderson* v. *Astwood*, [1894] A.C. 150 (P.C.), at p. 162.

(*l*) *Harvey* v. *Tebbutt* (1820), 1 Jac. & W. 197; *Harryman* v. *Collins* (1854), 18 Beav. 11; *Whitbread* v. *Smith* (1854), 3 De G.M. & G. 727. But where he set up an adverse title and failed, he was ordered to pay the whole costs of the action: *Roberts* v. *Williams* (1844), 4 Hare, 129; *National Bank of Australasia* v. *United Hand-in-Hand, etc., Co.* (1879), 4 App. Cas. 391 (P.C.).

And as to costs where the mortgagee makes claims which he fails to establish, see *Montgomery* v. *Calland* (1844), 14 Sim. 79; *Cockell* v. *Taylor* (1851), 15 Beav. 103, at p. 127; *Green* v. *Briggs* (1848), 6 Hare, 632; *West* v. *Jones* (1851), 1 Sim. N.S. 205, at p. 218; *Gregg* v. *Slater* (1856), 22 Beav. 314.

(*m*) *Greenwood* v. *Sutcliffe*, [1892] 1 Ch. 1 (C.A.). But if the mortgagor makes no tender, but only states in his defence that he was willing to pay so much as he considered to be due, before the institution of the action, he will not save the costs, although at the hearing he succeeds in establishing his case as to the amount due: *Hodges* v. *Croydon Canal Co.* (1840), 3 Beav. 86; *Gammon* v. *Stone* (1749), 1 Ves. Sen. 339. And see *Broad* v. *Selfe* (1863), 9 Jur. (N.S.) 885, where, under the circumstances, no costs were given on either side to the hearing. As to an offer to pay the amount found due by the certificate, see *Sentance* v. *Porter* (1849), 7 Hare, 426.

Where a tender has been made and refused, the application that the mortgagee may pay the subsequent costs, may be made at the hearing, supported by evidence of the tender and refusal: *Sentance* v. *Porter*, *supra*.

(*n*) *Graham* v. *Seal* (1918), 88 L.J. Ch. 31 (C.A.).

(*o*) *Shuttleworth* v. *Lowther*, undated, cited 7 Ves. 586; *Cliff* v. *Wadsworth* (1843), 2 Y. & C.C.C. 598; *Harmer* v. *Priestly* (1853), 16 Beav. 569; *Morley* v. *Bridges* (1846), 2 Coll. 621; *Gregg* v. *Slater* (1856), 22 Beav. 314. And to save the expense of coming to the court on further consideration, a direction that the mortgagee shall pay the costs, if the sum due does not exceed the tender, may be added to the judgment at the hearing: *Hosken* v. *Sincock* (1865), 11 Jur. N.S. 477.

(*p*) *Smith* v. *Green* (1844), 1 Coll. 555, at p. 564.

(*q*) *Binnington* v. *Harwood* (1825), Turn & Russ. 477; *Morris* v. *Islip* (1856), 23 Beav. 244; *O'Neill* v. *Innes* (1864), 15 Ir. Ch. R. 527.

have been caused by his denial or false suggestion (*r*). So where, knowing that he is already overpaid, the creditor contests the mode of taking the accounts and fails (*s*); or, having sold the mortgaged property, asserts that the surplus, after paying principal, interest, and costs, is much less than is found due from him on the master's certificate (*t*); or refuses to account and the balance is found against him (*u*); or causes subsequent proceedings by keeping money and receiving rents, long after his right to receive them as mortgagee in possession has ceased (*x*), he will be allowed such costs only as arose whilst he filled the character of a creditor, and must pay the rest.

A person who, whether his true character is that of a mortgagee or not, places himself in the position of an accounting party, and so undertakes a duty which he cannot perform by reason of the loss of vouchers for sums which he has paid, will not have the costs of taking the accounts (*y*).

Where right to costs not lost.—But in the absence of misconduct, the mortgagee will not be ordered to pay, nor will he forfeit his right to, costs by a mere bona fide extension of his claim beyond that to which the court adjudges him to be entitled (*z*), or by stipulating that the accounts required shall be furnished at the cost of the mortgagor where they are of a special nature (*a*). Nor was he made to pay the costs occasioned by a dispute as to a fact, where the court gave so much weight to the mortgagee's objection as to direct an issue, although the result was against him (*b*). But he may be deprived of costs where his claim is unfounded, although bona fide (*c*).

Costs due to loss of deeds.—If the mortgagee has lost the title deeds of the estate, he becomes liable for any costs which have been

---

(*r*) *Montgomery* v. *Calland* (1844), 14 Sim. 79; *Snagg* v. *Frizell* (1846), 3 Jo. & Lat. 383; *Ashworth* v. *Lord* (1887), 36 Ch. D. 545; *Kinnaird* v. *Trollope* (1889), 42 Ch. D. 610.

(*s*) *Skirrett* v. *Athy* (1811), 1 Ba. & Be. 433.

(*t*) *Charles* v. *Jones* (1887), 35 Ch. D. 544. As to the discretion of the court in such cases, and the mode of its exercise, see *Heath* v. *Chinn* (1908), 98 L.T. 855.

(*u*) *Tanner* v. *Heard* (1857), 23 Beav. 555; *Powell* v. *Trotter* (1861), 1 Dr. & Sm. 388.

(*x*) *Archdeacon* v. *Bowes* (1824), 13 Price, 353. Prima facie, the mortgagee in possession has a right to the costs of an action instituted to take the account, and it is not merely because there is a difficulty in taking it, not occasioned by his misconduct, or because the result is against him, that he will be deprived of his costs: *Snagg* v. *Frizell*, *supra*. Neither will this be done where he is found to have been overpaid, though he has insisted that a large sum remained due to him, if the judgment has been made to include costs in the usual form: *Gilbert* v. *Golding* (1794), 2 Anst. 442.

(*y*) *Price* v. *Price* (1845), 15 L.J. Ch. 13.

(*z*) *Loftus* v. *Swift and St. Patrick's Hospital* (1806), 2 Sch. & Lef. 642, at p. 657; *Cotterell* v. *Stratton* (1872), 8 Ch. App. 295; *Re Watts, Smith* v. *Watts* (1882), 22 Ch. D. 5 (C.A.).

(*a*) *Norton* v. *Cooper* (1854), 5 De G.M. & G. 728.

(*b*) *Wilson* v. *Metcalfe* (1818), 3 Mad. 45.

(*c*) See *Credland* v. *Potter* (1874), 10 Ch. App. 8; *Kinnaird* v. *Trollope* (1889), 42 Ch. D. 610; *Bird* v. *Wenn* (1886), 33 Ch. D. 215. In a doubtful case as to the right of foreclosure (*Teulon* v. *Curtis* (1832), Younge, 610), or to redeem (*Kirkham* v. *Smith* (1749), 1 Ves. Sen. 259), it may be that no costs will be given on either side. But the costs occasioned by an unsuccessful objection to the mortgagee's right to sue may be thrown on the defendant: *Tildesley* v. *Lodge* (1857), 3 Sm. & G. 543; and so may the costs of an action which the incumbrancer has been obliged to institute, by reason of subsequent dealings with the estate by the owner of the equity of redemption without giving notice of the charge: *Wise* v. *Wise* (1845), 2 Jo. & Lat. 403.

incurred in consequence of such loss. If, therefore, upon the mortgagor's refusal to repay the debt, by reason of the non-production of the deeds and the mortgagee's neglect to give a satisfactory indemnity, an action is brought for foreclosure (*d*) or recovery of the land (*e*), or if the mortgagor sues for redemption (*f*), and has to accept an indemnity for the loss of the deeds, the costs of any of such actions will fall upon the mortgagee. And in an action for redemption, the court will not consider whether the indemnity (*g*) (if any has been offered) should have satisfied the mortgagor, for he is entitled to institute an action, in order that any person with whom he may thereafter deal respecting the estate may be fully satisfied of the loss. But it is said that, in a foreclosure action, it will be inquired whether a proper indemnity was offered (*h*).

Unnecessary or unsuccessful proceedings.—It is the duty of the mortgagee so to pursue his remedy as not to incur unnecessary costs. Hence he must bear the cost of proceedings so far as they are mistaken or useless (*i*). And the court may except from the general costs the costs of a particular issue on which the mortgagee has failed, although the remainder of the action was justified (*j*).

And the costs incurred by an improper joinder of parties, whether as plaintiffs or defendants, must be paid by the mortgagee (*k*). Where, for instance, in an action for sale prior annuitants were joined, though the sale should have been made subject to their annuities (*l*), or where in a like action subsequent incumbrancers were needlessly made parties (*m*). But it is not a reason for depriving the mortgagee of

---

(*d*) *Stokoe* v. *Robson* (1815), 19 Ves. 385.

(*e*) *Lord Midleton* v. *Eliot* (1847), 15 Sim. 531.

(*f*) *Lord Midleton* v. *Eliot, supra*; *James* v. *Rumsey* (1879), 11 Ch. D. 398; *Caldwell* v. *Matthews* (1890), 62 L.T. 799. The mortgagee must give the indemnity at his own cost: *Lord Midleton* v. *Eliot, supra*.

(*g*) See p. 563, *supra*.

(*h*) See *Macartney* v. *Graham* (1828), 2 Russ. & Myl. 353. So, if the mortgagee has a power of sale, but by reason of the loss of the deeds he is obliged to come for a sale under a judgment, the subsequent incumbrancers are entitled to be paid their costs of the action out of the purchase money, although the amount of it is insufficient to pay the principal and interest due to the plaintiff: *Wontner* v. *Wright* (1829), 2 Sim. 543.

(*i*) Where, for instance, an action was not originally commenced as, but was turned into a foreclosure action, the costs incurred before it assumed that form were thrown on the mortgagee: *Smith* v. *Smith* (1815), Coop. G., 141; *Briant* v. *Lightfoot* (1837), 1 Jur. 20; *Philips* v. *Davies* (1843), 7 Jur. 52; *Hogan* v. *Baird* (1843), 4 Dru. & War. 296. And as to costs incurred unnecessarily, see *Marsack* v. *Reeves* (1821), 6 Mad. 108; *Ex parte Fletcher* (1832), Mont. 454; *Cocks* v. *Stanley* (1857), 4 Jur. (N.S.) 942. It has been held that where the county court has jurisdiction and both parties reside in the same circuit, only county court scale of costs will be allowed: *Crozier* v. *Dowsett* (1885), 31 Ch. D. 67. But as a rule the convenience of proceeding in mortgage cases in the High Court outweighs the saving of costs (if any), and it is believed that in practice this case is not followed. In general the plaintiff is entitled to resort to the High Court without being confined to county court costs; *Brown* v. *Rye* (1874), L.R. 17 Eq. 343; *Williams* v. *Allen*, [1889] W.N. 48.

(*j*) *Deeley* v. *Lloyds Bank (No. 2)* (1909), 53 Sol. J. 419. And a mortgagee who has neglected to attend at the appointed time and place for the completion of redemption, and has thereby created the difficulty which caused the action, has been refused his costs: *Cliff* v. *Wadsworth* (1843), 2 Y. & C.C.C. 598.

(*k*) *Pearce* v. *Watkins* (1852), 5 De G. & Sm. 315, 317.

(*l*) *Delabere* v. *Norwood* (1786), 3 Swans. 144, n.; and see *Horrocks* v. *Ledsam* (1845), 2 Coll. C.C. 208.

(*m*) *Cooke* v. *Brown* (1840), 4 Y. & C. Ex. 227.

costs, that the person, in respect of whose interest they were incurred, might have been a co-plaintiff in the action; because he might have objected to be a plaintiff (*n*).

Costs of parties added for benefit of mortgagee.—Under special circumstances the mortgagee has been ordered to pay the costs of the defendant in the first instance (even though the security is deficient), and then add them to his debt (*o*). But otherwise costs of parties whose presence is made necessary by the act of the mortgagor, are not generally paid by the mortgagee (*p*). And the mortgagee will not be ordered to pay such costs, even where he has been ordered to pay his own costs of an unsuccessful claim, the determination of which was the object of the action (*q*).

Parties added through mortgagee dealing with the estate.— The mortgagee is entitled to deal with his estate as owner so soon as the day fixed for redemption has passed and his estate has become absolute at law, and if he disposes of it so as to make other parties beside himself necessary parties to a redemption (*r*) or foreclosure (*s*) action, as trustees or otherwise, their costs will be paid by him in the first instance, and he will add them to his debt (*t*).

But the mortgagee's acts must have been so done as not to burden the estate with unnecessary expense. Therefore if he, or those who represent him, transfer mortgages on separate properties by a single deed, so as to cause a necessity for a covenant for production, either by the person redeeming (*u*), or by those interested under the assignment in case the former should waive his right to delivery (*x*), the costs of

---

(*n*) *Browne* v. *Lockhart* (1840), 10 Sim. 420; that is, to deprive the mortgagee of the costs of the party joined as a defendant it must be shown, not only that he might have been, but that he was willing to be, a plaintiff, and that the mortgagee wilfully abstained from so joining him.

(*o*) *E.g.*, costs of guardian of infant defendant. See *Harris* v. *Hamlyn* (1849), 3 De G. & Sm. 470; *Newburgh* v. *Morten* (1851), 15 Jur. 166; *Spurgeon* v. *Witham*, M.R., 21 December, 1855, on petition for costs not provided for by decree, as well as at the hearing. And as to the costs of the trustees of the equity of redemption where a judgment creditor of the mortgagees sues for the purpose of getting a charge on the mortgage debt, see *Clare* v. *Wood* (1844), 4 Hare, 81.

(*p*) *Siffken* v. *Davis* (1853), Kay, App. xxi, appears to be *contra*, but does not seem intelligible.

(*q*) *Green* v. *Briggs* (1848), 6 Hare, 632.

(*r*) *Wetherell* v. *Collins* (1818), 3 Mad. 255.

(*s*) *Bartle* v. *Wilkin* (1836), 8 Sim. 238.

(*t*) *Smith* v. *Chichester* (1842), 2 Dru. & War. 393; *Bartle* v. *Wilkin, supra.* But the costs of incumbrancers on a charge or life estate will be borne by the charge or life estate; not by the inheritance or the estate out of which the charge is raisable: *Stewart* v. *Marquis Donegal* (1845), 2 Jo. & Lat. 636. But where the mortgagee has been disallowed or ordered to pay costs, for improper conduct, the mortgagor has been ordered to pay the costs of the mortgagee's trustee and to be repaid by the mortgagee: *Montgomery* v. *Calland* (1844), 14 Sim. 79; *Cockell* v. *Taylor* (1851), 15 Beav. at p. 127. And it has been said that where an incumbrancer creates a trust for his own purposes, he gets only his own costs and pays those of his trustee; but where he devises or disposes of the charge to several, each, being made a defendant, gets his costs, because all represent but one original incumbrancer: *Galway* v. *Butler* (1819), 1 Mol. 13, n. But the former part of this proposition seems hardly consistent with the rule stated above as to the rights of the mortgagee. As to the costs of the mortgagee's trustee in bankruptcy, see *Coles* v. *Forrest* (1847), 10 Beav. 552.

(*u*) *Capper* v. *Terrington* (1844), 1 Coll. 103.

(*x*) *Dobson* v. *Land* (1850), 4 De G. & Sm. 575–581. But where the mortgagor refused an offer to deliver the deed to him upon his covenanting to produce it, the costs of his application to the court for a reconveyance were thrown upon himself: *Capper* v. *Terrington, supra.*

preparing and perfecting the covenant and attested copies, and of the redeeming parties' application to the court, will fall upon the mortgagee's estate.

And the costs of both the mortgagee himself, and of a trustee, where either of them are necessary parties by the imprudence of the mortgagee, may be thrown upon the latter (y).

If an assignment of the mortgage security is made after judgment, or, it seems, is made at all *pendente lite*, the mortgagor will not be charged with costs of the supplementary proceedings by which the assignee is brought before the court (z).

III—COSTS OF DISCLAIMING DEFENDANTS

Rules as to costs.—A defendant to a foreclosure action may be allowed costs if, having been needlessly made a party, he disclaims any interest in the subject matter of the action. His right to costs is governed by the following rules (a):

(1) Where a defendant disclaims in such a manner as to show that he never had, and never claimed, an interest at or after the commencement of the action, he is entitled to his costs against the plaintiff (b).

(2) If, having an interest, he shows that he disclaimed, or offered to disclaim before the institution of the action, under circumstances which establish actual notice of disclaimer against the plaintiff, or

---

(y) For examples of this, see *Shackleton* v. *Shackleton* (1825), 2 Sim. & St. 242; *S. C. Anon.* (1825), 3 L.J. O.S. Ch. 141; *Hickson* v. *Fitzgerald* (1826), 1 Mol. 14, n.

(z) *Barry* v. *Wrey* (1827), 3 Russ. 465; *Coles* v. *Forrest, supra.* Where an order was made in a foreclosure action to revive against an assignee after decree, it was ordered to be specified that the costs should be paid by the plaintiff: *James* v. *Harding* (1855), 24 L.J. Ch. 749. A purchaser *pendente lite* comes into court *pro bono et malo,* and may become liable for the whole costs of the action: *Anon.* (1739), 1 Atk. 89.

(a) *Ford* v. *Earl of Chesterfield* (1853), 16 Beav. 516; *Ridgway* v. *Kynnersley* (1856), 2 H. & M. 565; *Earl of Cork* v. *Russell* (1871), L.R. 13 Eq. 210; *Ward* v. *Shakeshaft* (1860), 1 Dr. & Sm. 269.

(b) *Tipping* v. *Power* (1842), 1 Hare, 405; *Gabriel* v. *Sturgis* (1846), 5 Hare, 97; *Grigg* v. *Sturgis* (1846), 5 Hare, 93; *Jones* v. *Rhind* (1869), 17 W.R. 1091. In this case he is not properly made a party: *Furber* v. *Furber* (1862), 30 Beav. 523, 524. The rule applies where he had an interest, but assigned it before action: *Glover* v. *Rogers* (1847), 11 Jur. 1000; *Hurst* v. *Hurst* (1852), 22 L.J. Ch. 546; otherwise, if he had only agreed to assign it, the actual transfer not being made till after action: *Roberts* v. *Hughes* (1868), L.R. 6 Eq. 20; see *Land* v. *Wood* (1823), 1 L.J. O.S. Ch. 89; and it applies to a trustee under a will who has never acted: *Benbow* v. *Davies* (1848), 11 Beav. 369; and to a beneficial devisee who has not accepted the devise: *Higgins* v. *Frankis* (1850), 20 L.J. Ch. 16.

The disclaimer may be either before or after the commencement of the action: *Bellamy* v. *Brickenden* (1858), 4 K. & J. 670; *Day* v. *Gudgen* (1876), 2 Ch. D. 209. If on being joined the party takes no step in the action, but states the facts to the plaintiff's solicitor and asks if he is required to appear or plead, he will have his costs incurred after that communication: *Howkins* v. *Bennet* (1863), 2 H. & M. 567, n. Cf. *Vale* v. *Merideth* (1854), 18 Jur. 992, where a formal and exact disclaimer was insisted on—that the defendant did not and never did claim and that she disclaimed; though an informal disclaimer may be effectual to prevent the personal representative of the defendant being a proper party; and if joined he will have costs: *Ridgway* v. *Kynnersley, supra.*

(c) See *Ridgway* v. *Kynnersley, supra.*

which show that with ordinary prudence he might have had such notice (*c*), he is also entitled to his costs (*d*).

(3) If, having an interest, he allows himself to be made a party to the action, and does not disclaim or offer to disclaim before action, he is not entitled to his costs (*e*).

(4) If, having been properly made a party, he disclaims during the action, and, without waiting to be asked, offers to be dismissed without costs, and is yet brought to the hearing for some special purpose of the plaintiff, he will have his costs subsequent to the disclaimer or offer (*f*).

Representative defendants.—The right of disclaiming defendants, who represent a bankrupt estate, to receive costs, is no better than that of any other defendants who disclaim; and they have no right, arising out of the office which they fill, to receive costs from the mortgagee, even upon the terms that he may add them to his debt; nor upon the ground that no assets have been received out of the estate: because they stand in the place of the bankrupt, who can give no more right than he had himself (*g*). And if the trustee litigates as a contending party, instead of disclaiming it, he will be left to take his costs out of the bankrupt's estate (*h*). The costs even of the

---

(*d*) *Ford* v. *Earl of Chesterfield, supra*; see *Thompson* v. *Kendall* (1840), 9 Sim. 397; *Lock* v. *Lomas* (1851), 15 Jur. 162. In this case he is prima facie a necessary party; see *Gibson* v. *Nicol* (1846), 9 Beav. 403; *Ohrly* v. *Jenkins* (1847), 1 De G. & Sm. 543; *Staffurth* v. *Pott* (1848), 2 De G. & Sm. 571; *Buchanan* v. *Greenway* (1848), 11 Beav. 58. But if he disclaims before action he ceases to be a necessary party, and therefore if the disclaimer is known to the plaintiff, and nevertheless he is made a defendant, this is improper. In cases where the defendant is properly made a party, the mortgagee will have the costs over against the mortgagor. Where the defendant assigns his interest before defence, see *Hawkins* v. *Gardiner* (1854), 17 Jur. 780; also *Wright* v. *Barlow* (1851), 5 De G. & Sm. 43.

(*e*) *Ford* v. *Earl of Chesterfield, supra*. To entitle a defendant who has an interest to costs there must be a disclaimer or an offer to disclaim or release: *Lock* v. *Lomas* (1851), 15 Jur. 162; *Thompson* v. *Kendall* (1840), 9 Sim. 397.

But a statement, that if he had been applied to, he would have released or disclaimed his right, but that no such application was made to him, gives no right to costs; for this shows that the right remains in the defendant; and it is not the duty of the plaintiff before action to ascertain from the defendant whether he does or does not claim an interest: *Collins* v. *Shirley* (1830), 1 Russ. & Myl. 638; *Cash* v. *Belcher* (1842), 1 Hare, 310; *Ford* v. *White* (1852), 16 Beav. 120. An untrue averment by the plaintiff that he has given the defendant an opportunity to disclaim may entitle him to costs: *Gurney* v. *Jackson* (1852), 1 Sm. & G. 97.

(*f*) *Talbot* v. *Kemshead* (1858), 4 K. & J. 93; *Dillon* v. *Ashwin* (1864), 10 Jur. (N.S.) 119; *Jones* v. *Rhind* (1869), 17 W.R. 1091; *Greene* v. *Foster* (1882), 22 Ch. D. 566, 569. The disclaimer should be made immediately on notice of the action: *Bradley* v. *Borlase* (1858), 7 W.R. 125. The offer to disclaim need not contain an offer to pay the costs of the disclaimer: *Lock* v. *Lomas, supra*. And if, while disclaiming, the defendant pleads and appears to claim his costs, he will have none: *Maxwell* v. *Wightwick* (1866), L.R. 3 Eq. 210; *Lewin* v. *Jones* (1884), 53 L.J. Ch. 1011. And he will not have costs subsequent to the disclaimer if he appears of his own accord without being required for such special purpose of the plaintiff: *Gowing* v. *Mowberry* (1863), 11 W.R. 851; *Lewin* v. *Jones, supra*; even though he is served with notice of the subsequent proceedings: *Clarke* v. *Toleman* (1872), 42 L.J. Ch. 23, disapproving *Davis* v. *Whitmore* (1860), 28 Beav. 617.

(*g*) *Cash* v. *Belcher* (1842), 1 Hare, 310; *Hunter* v. *Pugh* (1839), 1 Hare, 307, n.; *Appleby* v. *Duke* (1842), 1 Hare, 303; *Clark* v. *Wilmot* (1843), 1 Ph. 276; *Hughes* v. *Kelley* (1843), 3 Dru. & War. at p. 495. The assignee of a bankrupt mortgagor, who by his answer disclaimed all interest in the equity of redemption, and alleged a previous offer to do so, but claimed another interest in the action, was neither allowed to receive, nor ordered to pay costs: *Edwards* v. *Jones* (1844), 1 Coll. 247.

(*h*) *Rider* v. *Jones* (1843), 2 Y. & C.C.C. 329.

Attorney-General, claiming ineffectually on behalf of the Crown, have been refused, where the costs would have come out of the mortgaged property (*i*).

IV—COSTS ON SALE

Account of proceeds.—Where the mortgagee has sold the property he holds the surplus proceeds on a constructive trust (*k*) for the persons entitled to the equity of redemption. Hence an action by the second mortgagee for an account is not treated as a redemption action and is outside the rule which entitles the first mortgagee to costs; and if the action has been occasioned by his refusing to account, or if, on taking the accounts, it is found that a much larger sum is due from him than he admitted, he will either be refused costs or have to pay them (*l*).

Costs on sale by court.—The right of a mortgagee to costs extends to the case where the mortgaged property is sold under the order of the court (*m*). The order for sale does not of itself alter the rights of the parties, but the purchase money, being considered to be substituted for the property, is treated in the same manner as the property; and each incumbrancer will be paid his costs, including the costs of obtaining the direction for payment to him of the proceeds of the sale, together with his principal and interest, according to priority, the later incumbrancer taking nothing until he who is prior has been paid in full (*n*).

Expenses of the sale.—The expenses of the sale, since they are incurred as much for the benefit of the mortgagee as of other persons interested, are a first charge on the proceeds (*o*).

Waiver of mortgagee's priority.—But if the mortgagee merely consents to the sale, or is a party to the action solely with a view to the realisation of his security, his claim against the proceeds is prior to the general costs of the action (*p*). He will, however, be taken to

---

(*i*) *Perkins* v. *Bradley* (1842), 1 Hare, 219; see *Kane* v. *Reynolds* (1854), 4 De G.M. & G. 565.

(*k*) *Banner* v. *Berridge* (1881), 18 Ch. D. 254. See now Law of Property Act 1925, s. 105 (p. 373, *supra*). Though a trustee, the selling mortgagee is, it is submitted, allowed the costs involved in ascertaining any subsequent mortgagees and of payment over.

(*l*) *Tanner* v. *Heard* (1857), 23 Beav. 555; *Charles* v. *Jones* (1887), 35 Ch. D. 544; *Williams* v. *Jones* (1911), 55 Sol. Jo. 500.

(*m*) The equitable mortgagee is in the same position (though formerly he was not: see earlier editions of this work).

(*n*) *Upperton* v. *Harrison* (1835), 7 Sim. 444; *Chissum* v. *Dewes* (1828), 5 Russ. 29; *Barnes* v. *Racster* (1842), 1 Y. & C.C.C. 401; *Wild* v. *Lockhart* (1847), 10 Beav. 320; *Cook* v. *Hart* (1871), L.R. 12 Eq. 459; *Wonham* v. *Machin* (1870), L.R. 10 Eq. 447; *Leonard* v. *Kellett* (1891), 27 L.R. Ir. 418, 427.

(*o*) *Dighton* v. *Withers* (1862), 31 Beav. 423; *Re Oriental Hotels Co., Perry* v. *Oriental Hotels Co.* (1871), L.R. 12 Eq. 126; *Batten* v. *Wedgwood Coal and Iron Co.* (1884), 28 Ch. D. 317; *Lathom* v. *Greenwich Ferry Co.* (1895), 72 L.T. 790. As also are the costs of an abortive sale: *Henderson* v. *Astwood*, [1894] A.C. 150 (P.C.); *Matzner* v. *Clyde Securities, Ltd.*, [1975] 2 N.S.W.L.R. 293. Where the mortgagee is a party, he must submit to the costs of sale being paid first: *Re Regent's Canal Ironwork Co., Ex parte Grissell* (1875), 3 Ch. D. 411 (C.A.), at p. 427; and also it would seem, where, without being a party, he consents to the sale.

(*p*) *Hepworth* v. *Heslop* (1844), 3 Hare, 485; *Armstrong* v. *Storer* (1852), 14 Beav. 535; *Wonham* v. *Machin* (1870), L.R. 10 Eq. 447; *Millar* v. *Johnston* (1888), 23 L.R. Ir. 50; *Hilliard* v. *Moriarty*, [1894] 1 Ir. Rep. 316; and see *Crosse* v. *General Reversionary and Investment Co.* (1853), 3 De G.M. & G. 698.

have waived his priority over such costs if he takes advantage of an administration action in order to obtain a remedy against the mortgagor's personal estate (*q*).

Where, however, a later incumbrancer, either by an action to ascertain the priorities or by proceeding in a dormant action, is the means of securing and distributing a fund for the benefit of all the incumbrancers, his costs of the action or proceeding will be paid before the other charges on the fund, though it is no administration action (*r*).

V—COSTS, CHARGES AND EXPENSES

Costs of litigation.—The costs (other than costs of action), charges, and expenses to which the mortgagee is entitled are:

(1) Costs of litigation relating to the security; and

(2) Costs, charges, and expenses generally.

It is essential to the claim to costs of litigation that the proceedings shall have been reasonable. Hence the mortgagee will not be allowed the costs of improper, or useless, or unnecessary litigation (*s*). And he is not entitled to the costs of defending his title to the mortgage against persons other than the owner of the equity of redemption—as distinguished from defending the title to the estate (*t*); and generally he will not have the costs of litigation concerning the mortgaged property arising out of the wrongful act of a stranger (*u*).

But he will be allowed the costs of obtaining (*x*) or recovering (*y*)

(*q*) *Re Spensley's Estate, Spensley* v. *Harrison* (1872), L.R. 15 Eq. 16; also *Ford* v. *Earl of Chesterfield* (1856), 21 Beav. 426. As to an action by beneficiaries against the trustees and the mortgagees of the trust fund, see *Bryant* v. *Blackwell* (1851), 15 Beav. 44. In an action for foreclosing a mortgage of a term the mortgagee retained his priority for costs, although by agreement the reversion was included in the sale: *Cutfield* v. *Richards* (1858), 26 Beav. 241.

A mortgagee who sues for general administration of his deceased mortgagor's assets on behalf of himself and the other creditors is entitled to the usual judgment in favour of an equitable mortgagee: *Greenwood* v. *Firth* (1842), 2 Hare, 241, n.; *Skey* v. *Bennett* (1843), 2 Y. & C.C.C. 405; and also to that in favour of a general creditor: *Skey* v. *Bennett, supra.* But the modern practice is to ask for realisation of the security and payment of the deficiency from the general assets: Seton (7th Edn.), 1848.

(*r*) *White* v. *Bishop of Peterborough* (1821), Jac. 402; *Ford* v. *Earl of Chesterfield, supra; Wright* v. *Kirby* (1857), 23 Beav. 463; *Batten, Proffitt and Scott* v. *Dartmouth Harbour Commissioners* (1890), 45 Ch. D. 612; *Re Barne* (1890), 62 L.T. 922; *Carrick* v. *Wigan Tramways Co.*, [1893] W.N. 98.

(*s*) See *Dryden* v. *Frost* (1838), 3 My. & C. 670, where the mortgagee, having only a title in equity, defended an action by the legal owner for the recovery of the property: *Burke* v. *O'Connor* (1885), 4 Ir. Ch. R. 418, where the mortgagee's action for rent failed through being brought in the name of the wrong person; *Peers* v. *Ceeley* (1852), 15 Beav. 209, where the mortgagee, having sold under his power of sale, sued for specific performance, but lost the action owing to misdescription; and see *Macken* v. *Newcomen* (1844), 2 Jo. & Lat. 16.

(*t*) *Parker* v. *Watkins* (1859), Johns. 133; *Re Smith's Mortgage, Harrison* v. *Edwards*, [1931] 2 Ch. 168.

(*u*) *Doe* d. *Holt* v. *Roe* (1830), 6 Bing. 447; *Owen* v. *Crouch* (1857), 5 W.R. 545.

(*x*) *Wilkes* v. *Saunion* (1877), 7 Ch. D. 188. See *Halsall* v. *Egbunike* (1963), 107 Sol. Jo. 514 (where the mortgagor was legally aided).

(*y*) *Millar* v. *Major* (1818), Coop. *temp.* Cott. 550; *Lewis* v. *John* (1838), 9 Sim. 366; *Sandon* v. *Hooper* (1843), 6 Beav. 246, 250 (where *plaintiff* appears to be a mistake for *defendant*); on appeal, 14 L.J. Ch. 120; *Horlock* v. *Smith* (1844), 1 Coll. 287; *Owen* v. *Crouch* (1857), 5 W.R. 545.

possession of the mortgaged property; of recovering the mortgage debt, whether against the mortgagor (z), or against a surety, and although the fruits of the action are lost by the surety's insolvency (a); of taking out administration to the mortgagor, or to a person interested under his will (b) as a necessary party (c); and generally, costs incurred in asserting or defending the mortgagor's title to the property (d), or in defending the mortgage title against the mortgagor and persons claiming under him (e). And where a foreclosure action is pending when an action for redemption is brought by a later incumbrancer, the costs of the foreclosure action will be provided for in the redemption action (f).

Where party and party costs have been recovered in the litigation, the mortgagee can charge the sum required to make up solicitor and client costs (g).

Costs of preparation of mortgage not allowed.—The general costs, charges, and expenses which the mortgagee can add to his security do not include the costs of and incidental to preparing the mortgage, these being merely a simple contract debt (h); nor do they include the costs of investigating the mortgagor's title for the purpose of preparing a legal mortgage pursuant to the covenant in that behalf (i). And the solicitor of an intending mortgagee has no claim against the intending mortgagor for the cost of an unsuccessful negotiation for the security, or for the costs of investigating the title

---

(z) *National Provincial Bank of England* v. *Games* (1886), 31 Ch. D. 582 (C.A.), where *Ellison* v. *Wright*, *infra*, was preferred to *Lewis* v. *John*, *supra*, and *Merriman* v. *Bonney* (1864), 12 W.R. 461, so far as the latter two cases throw doubt on the first, on the ground that the costs are not incurred in relation to the mortgage security.

(a) *Ellison* v. *Wright* (1827), 3 Russ. 458. This is so, although the contract of suretyship is subsequent to the mortgage: *Sachs* v. *Ashby & Co.* (1903), 88 L.T. 393.

(b) *Ramsden* v. *Langley* (1705), 2 Vern. 536; but costs of administration incurred by the mortgagor's personal representative without the request of the mortgagee do not have priority over the mortgage: *Saunders* v. *Dunman* (1878), 7 Ch. D. 825.

(c) *Hunt* v. *Fownes* (1803), 9 Ves. 70.

(d) "If a mortgagee has expended any sum of money in supporting the right of the mortgagor to the estate, where his title has been impeached, the mortgagee may certainly add this to the principal of his debt, and it shall carry interest: *Godfrey* v. *Watson* (1747), 3 Atk. 517, 518; see *Sandon* v. *Hooper*, *supra*; *Sclater* v. *Cottam* (1857), 5 W.R. 744. And in estimating the value of his security in the bankruptcy of the mortgagor, the mortgagee may bring into account costs expended in properly defending an action brought against him in respect of his title to the mortgaged property after the adjudication: *Re Hofmann, Ex parte Carr* (1879), 11 Ch. D. 62.

(e) *Ramsden* v. *Langley*, *supra*; *Samuel* v. *Jones* (1862), 7 L.T. 760; see *Clark* v. *Hoskins* (1868), 37 L.J. Ch. 561, 569; *Re Baldwin's Estate*, [1900] 1 I.R. 15. This rule applied where the mortgagor sued as a poor person: *Re Leighton's Conveyance*, [1937] Ch. 149 (C.A.); [1936] 3 All E.R. 1033. And see *Sinfield* v. *Sweet*, [1967] 3 All E.R. 479 (for an unsuccessful attempt to make the mortgagor personally liable for costs to avoid the limitations imposed by s. 2 (2) (c) of the Legal Aid and Advice Act 1949); *Saunders* v. *Anglia Building Society* (*No.* 2), [1971] A.C. 1039 (H.L.); [1971] 1 All E.R. 243.

(f) *Ainsworth* v. *Roe* (1850), 14 Jur. 874.

(g) *Lomax* v. *Hide* (1690), 2 Vern. 185; *Ramsden* v. *Langley*, *supra*. For the basis of the taxation of costs other than costs of action, see *Re Adelphi Hotel* (*Brighton*), *Ltd.*, [1953] 2 All E.R. 498.

(h) *Wales* v. *Carr*, [1902] 1 Ch. 860. An agreement for the payment of the costs of an intending lender does not cover his expenses of obtaining the money: *Re Blakesley and Beswick* (1863), 32 Beav. 379; nor will an agreement to pay all costs and charges of investigating the title cover the interest of money lying idle during the negotiation of the mortgage: *Sweetland* v. *Smith* (1833), 1 Cr. & M. 585.

(i) *National Provincial Bank of England* v. *Games* (1886), 31 Ch. D. 582 (C.A.).

to the property; there being no implied contract on the part of the borrower to produce a security of any particular degree of safety, or any particular title, as in the case of a contract for sale (*k*).

Costs of completing security.—But the mortgagee will be allowed the costs of preparing a legal mortgage in pursuance of an agreement accompanying a deposit of deeds, including the expenses of such inspection of the deeds as was necessary for preparing it (*l*); and of obtaining a stop order, if the fund forming the subject of the mortgage is in court, and the mortgage authorises the application (*m*); upon a transfer of the mortgage, the transferee can add the costs of the transfer to his security if the mortgagor has been required to pay the debt, or if the interest was in arrear, but not otherwise (*n*); if the security covers a life policy, he is allowed premiums paid by him for keeping the policy on foot (*o*). And he can charge the expenses of a sale (*p*); but not the costs of such deeds as are not necessary for the security of the mortgagee, such as a declaration of trust where the mortgagee is a trustee (*q*); nor, on discharge of the mortgage, the costs of making a copy of it, though the mortgagee may at the mortgagor's cost make a fair copy of the draft security to keep until redemption (*r*).

"Just allowances."—In taking the account as between mortgagor and mortgagee, where the account has been directed by any judgment or order, all "just allowances" will be made without any direction for

---

(*k*) *Rigley* v. *Daykin* (1828), 2 Y. & J. 83; *Melbourne* v. *Cottrell* (1857), 29 L.T. (O.S.) 293; *Wilkinson* v. *Grant* (1856), 18 C.B. 319; *Re Cowburn, Ex parte Firth* (1882), 19 Ch. D. 419 (C.A.), at p. 427. For construction of an agreement on the subject, see *St. Leger* v. *Robson* (1831), 9 L.J. O.S. K.B. 184.

Where the court authorised a mortgage of an infant's estate, and the negotiation went off without any default on the part of the mortgagee, after he had incurred expenses in the examination of the title, the court allowed him his costs out of the infant's estate: *Craggs* v. *Gray* (1866), 35 Beav. 166. His costs of preparing the security, including counsel's fees, should, it has been said, be provided for by the order: *Nicholson* v. *Jeyes* (1853), 22 L.J. Ch. 833. But such a mortgage would now be made by statutory owners under the powers of the Settled Land Act 1925; *ante*, p. 199.

(*l*) *National Provincial Bank of England* v. *Games* (1886), 31 Ch. D. 582 (C.A.); and also the costs of correspondence relating to the legal mortgage: *ibid.*

(*m*) *Waddilove* v. *Taylor* (1848), 6 Hare, 307; unless the application was unnecessary: *Hoole* v. *Roberts* (1848), 12 Jur. 108.

(*n*) *Re Radcliffe* (1856), 22 Beav. 201; *Bolingbroke* v. *Hinde* (1884), 25 Ch. D. 795. See *Sewell* v. *Bishopp* (1893), 62 L.J. Ch. 985.

(*o*) *Bellamy* v. *Brickenden* (1861), 2 John. & H. 137; *Gill* v. *Downing* (1874), L.R. 17 Eq. 316. And if the insurance office is the mortgagee and the mortgage gives them power, they can themselves pay the premiums and add them to the security: *Richards* v. *Macclesford* (1841), 10 L. J. Ch. 329; *Earl Fitzwilliam* v. *Price* (1858), 4 Jur. (N.S.) 889; see *Browne* v. *Price* (1858), 4 C.B. (N.S.) 598; 4 Jur. (N.S.) 882; but an issue of a policy as between two branches of the same office will not give the right to charge the premiums: *Grey* v. *Ellison* (1856), 1 Giff. 438. The office can charge the full premiums although they have shared them with a solicitor as their agent: *Leete* v. *Wallace* (1888), 58 L.T. 577.

(*p*) *White* v. *City of London Brewery Co.* (1889), 42 Ch. D. 237 (C.A.), at p. 243; also the expenses of an attempted sale: *Sutton* v. *Rawlings* (1849), 3 Exch. 407; *Farrer* v. *Lacy, Hartland & Co.* (1885), 31 Ch. D. 42 (C.A.). The acceptance of a cheque for the deposit, which is subsequently dishonoured, is not such negligence as to deprive the mortgagee of his right to the expenses of the abortive sale: *ibid.* See also *Thompson* v. *Rumball* (1839), 3 Jur. 53; *Batten* v. *Wedgwood Coal and Iron Co.* (1884), 28 Ch. D. 317. As to expenses where there is a statutory limit, see *McHugh* v. *Union Bank of Canada,* [1913] A.C. 299, 305 (P.C.).

(*q*) *Martin* v. *Baxter* (1828), 5 Bing. 160; 2 Moo. & P. 240.

(*r*) *Re Wade and Thomas* (1881), 17 Ch. D. 348.

that purpose (s), and in general the foregoing charges are treated as just allowances (t). But where it is desired to make any unusual charge, this should be asked for at the hearing and the claim established at the hearing; and a special direction will then be inserted in the order (u).

Solicitor mortgagees.—In the absence of express agreement (x) a mortgagee cannot charge for work done by himself, although in the course of his business (y), and formerly a solicitor-mortgagee could not charge profit-costs for work done in connection with the mortgage (z), including the costs of a redemption or foreclosure action (a), but this rule was abolished by the Mortgagees Legal Costs Act 1895 (b), which is now replaced by the Solicitors Act 1974. If a mortgage is made to a solicitor either alone or jointly (c) with any other person, he, or the firm of which he is a member, shall be entitled to recover from the mortgagor in respect of all business transacted and acts done by him or them in negotiating the loan, deducing and investigating the title to the property, and preparing and completing the mortgage, such usual

---

(s) R.S.C. Ord. 43, r. 6; *Wilkes* v. *Saunion* (1877), 7 Ch. D. 188, explaining *Horlock* v. *Smith* (1844), 1 Coll. 287.

(t) *Blackford* v. *Davis* (1869), 4 Ch. App. 304.

(u) *Rees* v. *Metropolitan Board of Works* (1880), 14 Ch. D. 372; *Bolingbroke* v. *Hinde* (1884), 25 Ch. D. 795. See *Waddilove* v. *Taylor* (1848), 6 Hare, 307. If necessary, an inquiry as to the costs and charges claimed will be directed: *Merriman* v. *Bonner* (1864), 10 Jur. N.S. 534. Formerly the claim had to be made on the pleadings: *Millard* v. *Magor* (1818), 3 Mad. 433; *Ward* v. *Barton* (1841), 11 Sim. 534; and it is still advisable to do so where there are pleadings. See Seton (7th Edn.), 189. And if the judgment gives no direction, an inquiry may be directed on further consideration: *Thompson* v. *Rumball, supra.*

(x) Formerly an agreement allowing the mortgagee to charge for his personal services was void on the ground that it gave him a collateral advantage: *French* v. *Baron* (1740), 2 Atk. 120; *Scott* v. *Brest* (1788), 2 Term Rep. 238; *Chambers* v. *Goldwin* (1804), 9 Ves. 254, 271; *Leith* v. *Irvine* (1833), 1 My. & K. 277; *Broad* v. *Selfe* (1863), 11 W.R. 1036; *Comyns* v. *Comyns* (1871), 5 Ir. R. Eq. 583; *James* v. *Kerr* (1889), 40 Ch. D. 449, 459; *Field* v. *Hopkins* (1890), 44 Ch. D. 524 (C.A.), at p. 530; *The Benwell Tower* (1895), 72 L.T. 664. But this reason no longer exists, since a collateral advantage is now allowed, though it may only be enforced during the subsistence of the security: *Browne* v. *Ryan,* [1901] 2 Ir. R. 653; *supra, p.* 526; and see *Maxwell* v. *Tipping,* [1903] 1 Ir. R. 499; *Bath* v. *Standard Land Co., Ltd.,* [1911] 1 Ch. 618.

(y) *Barrett* v. *Hartley* (1866), L.R. 2 Eq. 789 (bonuses for managing business); *Matthison* v. *Clarke* (1854), 3 Drew. 3; *Furber* v. *Cobb* (1887), 18 Q.B.D. 494 (C.A.), at p. 509 (auctioneer); *Arnold* v. *Garner* (1847), 2 Ph. 231 (broker). But this rule does not now extend, as was held in *Matthison* v. *Clarke, supra,* to prevent a partner from taking remuneration, provided, if there is an agreement, that the mortgagee is excluded from sharing, or if there is no agreement, that his partnership share does not go to his partner: *Re Doody, Fisher* v. *Doody,* [1893] 1 Ch. 129, at pp. 136, 137. And see *Wellby* v. *Still,* [1893] W.N. 91; *Eyre* v. *Wynn-Mackenzie,* [1894] 1 Ch. 218 (C.A.).

(z) *Sclater* v. *Cottam* (1857), 5 W.R. 744; *Re Roberts* (1889), 43 Ch. D. 52; *Field* v. *Hopkins* (1890), 44 Ch. D. 524; *Re Wallis, Ex parte Lickorish* (1890), 25 Q.B.D. 176; *Re Doody, Fisher* v. *Doody,* [1893] 1 Ch. 129.

(a) *Stone* v. *Lickorish,* [1891] 2 Ch. 363. The rule, contrary to the exception made in favour of solicitor trustees (*Cradock* v. *Piper* (1850), 1 Mac. & G. 664), applied even where the solicitor was only one of several co-mortgagees: *Re Doody, Fisher* v. *Doody, supra.*

(b) Section 2 (1). Section 2 applied only to mortgages made after the Act: sub-s. (2). Section 3 made similar provision where a mortgage has become vested in a solicitor by transfer or transmission, and this applied to mortgages made and business done either before or after the Act; but not where judgment was given before the Act: *Eyre* v. *Wynn-Mackenzie, supra*; and a solicitor who obtained foreclosure before the Act was not allowed after the Act to recover profit costs: *Day* v. *Kelland,* [1900] 2 Ch. 745 (C.A.).

(c) *Re Norris,* [1902] 1 Ch. 741.

costs as he or they would have been entitled to receive if the mortgage had been made to a person who was not a solicitor and that person had retained and employed him or them to transact that business and do those acts (*d*)

A mortgagor who is liable to pay the bill of the mortgagee's solicitor can have it taxed under s. 70 of the Solicitors Act 1974. Where the taxation is applied for by the mortgagor under this section, items which the mortgagor would not be liable to pay as between himself and the mortgagee will be disallowed, even although the solicitor would be entitled to charge them against his client, the mortgagee (*e*).

VI—COSTS OF RECONVEYANCE

General rule.—The costs of reconveyance are borne by the mortgagor, as well in ordinary cases where the mortgage title has not been changed, or has become vested by transfer or devolution in persons from whom a reconveyance can be obtained (*f*), as where there has been a change of title or other event which necessitates special expense, such as the obtaining of a vesting order; if, for instance, the person who should reconvey is under disability or cannot be found (*g*), or if the mortgage is vested in a trustee-mortgagee who has absconded (*h*).

But there is an exception where the mortgagee is a mentally disordered person, and in that case, if he is beneficially interested in the mortgage money, the costs of any application for an order for conveyance or vesting are borne by his estate (*i*); and if he is a trustee, they are borne by the trust estate (*k*).

The mortgagor pays the ordinary costs of the reconveyance, where a reconveyance is ordered, and the stamp on the vesting order (*l*).

(*d*) Section 58 (1); replacing s. 58 of the Solicitors Act 1957. Sub-section (2) contains similar provisions to s. 2 (2) of the 1895 Act where a mortgage has become vested in a solicitor by transfer or transmission. Mortgage includes any charge on any property for securing money or money's worth: s. 58 (3).

(*e*) *Re Longbotham & Sons*, [1904] 2 Ch. 152 (C.A.), approving *Re Gray*, [1901] 1 Ch. 239; and see *Re Cohen and Cohen*, [1905] 2 Ch. 137 (C.A.). These cases seem to overrule the previous authorities, *Re Jones* (1845), 8 Beav. 479; *Re Baker* (1863), 32 Beav. 526; and *Re Kellock* (1887), 56 L.T. 887. And see *Forsinard Estates, Ltd.* v. *Dykes*, [1971] 1 All E.R. 1018.

(*f*) *King* v. *Smith* (1848), 6 Hare, 473, 475. And the mortgagor may be liable for the costs of proceedings to obtain delivery of the deeds by the mortgagee's solicitor, who claims a lien on them as against the mortgagee: *Rider* v. *Jones* (1843), 2 Y. & C.C.C. 329. As to the costs of an order for delivery of deeds where they have come into court in the course of an administration action relating to the mortgagee's estate, see *Burden* v. *Oldaker* (1844), 1 Coll. 105; *Reed* v. *Freer* (1844), 13 L.J. Ch. 417.

(*g*) *Ex parte Ommaney* (1841), 10 Sim. 298; *King* v. *Smith, supra*; *Re Stuart, Ex parte Marshall* (1859), 4 De G. & J. 317; *Webb* v. *Crosse*, [1912] 1 Ch. 323.

(*h*) *Webb* v. *Crosse, supra.*

(*i*) *Re Lewis, Ex parte Richards* (1820), 1 Jac. & W. 264; *Re Townsend* (1847), 2 Ph. 348; *Re Biddle* (1853), 23 L.J. Ch. 23; *Re Rowley* (1863), 1 De G. J. & Sm. 417. The contrary view in *Re Marrow* (1841), Cr. & Ph. 142, has not been accepted, though the exception has been admitted with reluctance: see *Re Stuart, Ex parte Marshall, supra*, at p. 319; and it did not extend to the lunacy of a person taking, on the death of the mortgagee, as formerly his heir at law: *Re Stuart, Ex parte Marshall, supra*; *Re Jones* (1860), 2 De G.F. & J. 554.

(*k*) *Re Townsend* (1850), 1 Mac. & G. 686; *Re Phillips* (1869), 4 Ch. App. 629; *Re Jones* (1876), 2 Ch. D. 70. In general a mortgage made with trust money does not disclose the trust, but it has been held that where the trust appears on the face of the mortgage, these costs fall on the mortgagor: *Re Lewes* (1849), 1 Mac. & G. 23.

(*l*) *Re Thomas* (1853), 22 L.J. Ch. 858.

Trustee for mortgagee.—A trustee for the mortgagee is bound to assign according to his direction, and if he refuses to do so, in a plain and simple case (as for instance to a purchaser under a power of sale), he will be made to pay the costs of an action rendered necessary by his refusal (*m*).

Conveyance to equitable mortgagee.—The costs of conveying to the equitable mortgagee upon the foreclosure are not generally provided for by the judgment (*n*), which simply directs the conveyance to be made. When there is no express covenant by the mortgagor to pay the costs of the conveyance, he is only bound by the terms of the judgment to execute the conveyance when tendered to him, because it is said he has only contracted to vest the estate in the mortgagee; who, according to the ordinary practice, prepares and tenders the conveyance for his execution; though since the contract, on an equitable mortgage, is a contract to transfer the legal estate to the mortgagee, the person whose duty it is to make the transfer must pay the expenses of it (*o*).

VII—COSTS UNDER LANDS CLAUSES ACT

Mortgagee's costs under Land Clauses Act.—When land which is subject to a mortgage is taken under the procedure of the Lands Clauses Consolidation Act 1845, and the purchase money deposited in court or the Bank of England, the costs of the mortgagee, upon the investment or payment out of the money, are governed by s. 80 of the Act (*p*). These provisions are now a dead letter (*q*) and in the rare cases where they should still be relevant reference should be made to the previous edition of this work.

(*m*) *Hampshire* v. *Bradley* (1845), 2 Coll. 34. As to assignment where the mortgagee has notice of an equitable claim by another person, see p. 547, *supra*.

(*n*) *Lees* v. *Fisher* (1882), 22 Ch. D. 283 (C.A.). See 28 Ency. Court Forms (2nd Edn.), 140.

(*o*) *Pryce* v. *Bury* (1853), 2 Drew. 41; affirmed L.R. 16 Eq. 153, n.

(*p*) As amended by the Administration of Justice Act 1965, Sched. 1.

(*q*) Because the reasons for payment in s. 69 of the Act have been removed and the court has a discretion as to costs under s. 50 of the Judicature Act 1925.

PART X

THE OPTION MORTGAGE SCHEME

CHAPTER 37

The Option Mortgage Scheme

The scheme.—Part II of the Housing Subsidies Act 1967, as amended, gives to those borrowing for house purchase or improvement from certain qualifying lenders a right to opt to receive Exchequer subsidy by credit towards their mortgage repayments. The object of the scheme is to give persons with modest incomes a financial benefit approximate to that obtained by persons with larger incomes who qualify, on account of correspondingly greater income tax, for greater tax relief (a). Under s. 24 of the Act the borrower may, in most cases, opt for such a subsidy in return for foregoing income tax relief in respect of mortgage interest. The loan must not be one in respect of which the Secretary of State for the Environment has made a direction under s. 24 (3A) (b), must not exceed the limit determined under s. 24A (c) and the mortgaged property must, within 12 months of the date of a repayment contract being entered into, be used wholly or partly as the residence of the borrower or as the residence of certain specified relatives of the borrower (d).

The security.—Section 24 applies to borrowing from a qualifying lender (e) on the security of a freehold or leasehold estate of the borrower or of one or more of the borrowers in land in Great Britain. The loan must relate to the amount outstanding on a previous loan for or in connection with acquiring, or acquiring a site for, or constructing, or providing by the conversion of a building on that land, or altering, enlarging, repairing or otherwise improving, a dwelling on that land (f). The repayment contract, in order to fall within the scheme, must provide for the making by the borrower to the lender of periodical payments consisting wholly or partly of payments of interest (g). When a borrower has elected to have his loan subsidised,

---

(a) The cost of the scheme for 1974–75 was 72 million: see (1974) 118 S.J. 349.

(b) Inserted by the Housing Act 1974, s. 119, Sched. 11, para 1 (4). The relevant loan is one where interest is added to capital.

(c) Section 24 (3) (c), amended by Housing Act 1974, s. 119 Sched. 11, paras. 1 (2), 2. These provisions do not apply until 6 April 1980 in respect of certain existing loans: Housing Act 1974, s. 119 (2).

(d) Section 24 (3) (c), amended by the Housing Act 1974, s. 119 and Sched, 11, para. 1 (2), and s. 24B, inserted by Sched. 11, para 2 (5). A qualifying relative is the borrower's spouse (living apart) or former spouse, the borrower's mother and the borrower's spouse's mother (if widowed, living apart from her husband or a feme sole), the borrower's parent or grandparent or (if over 16) the borrower's brother, sister or legitimate, adopted or illigitimate child or grandchild: s. 24B (2), (3).

(e) For the meaning of "qualifying lender", see p. 660, infra.

(f) Section 24 (1) (b).

(g) Section 24 (1) (c).

he will serve an option notice on the lender, and the latter must then treat the borrower as having paid certain instalments, being able to recoup himself from the Secretary of State for the Environment (h). It is provided (i) that, notwithstanding anything in the Income Tax Acts, the borrower shall not, in computing his total income, be entitled to a deduction in respect of any amount payable by way of interest under the repayment contract, shall not be entitled to relief from income tax in respect of any such interest, and shall neither be permitted nor required to make any deduction of income tax from any such payment of interest (k).

The option notice.—The borrower opts into the scheme by serving an option notice on his lender; such a notice will be of no effect unless the following conditions are satisfied:

(a) notice in writing of intention to give the option notice was given to the lender at the time when application for the loan was made or by such later time as the lender may in that particular case allow; and

(b) that the option notice was signed not later than the date when a repayment contract in respect of the loan was first entered into; and

(c) that the borrower (or each joint borrower (l)) has signed and delivered to the lender a declaration that the person signing the declaration is ordinarily resident in the United Kingdom, that the amount of the loan will not exceed the limit set under s. 24 A (m) and that the mortgaged property will within 12 months of the date a repayment contract was entered into be used wholly or partly for the purposes of a dwelling to be occupied wholly or partly as his or her residence by a specified person or persons (n) in such circumstances that the residence condition is s. 24 B of the 1967 Act is fulfilled (o). But such a declaration will not constitute notice to the lender of any interest in that land which may subsequently be acquired by any person other than the borrower (p).

In general the option notice will have effect from the date of its signing until one of the following events occurs:

(i) the satisfaction of the borrower's debt to the lender;

(ii) the realisation of the security on the interest in land in question, whether or not the borrower's debt is fully satisfied thereby;

(iii) the interest's ceasing to be security for the loan;

(iv) the vesting of the rights and obligations under the repayment contract of the borrower (or both or all joint borrowers, as the case may be) in some other person who has become beneficially entitled to the interest in land in question;

(h) The functions of the Minister of Housing and Local Government were transferred to the Secretary of State for the Environment: the Secretary of State for the Environment Order 1970, S.I. 1970 No. 1681.

(i) Section 24 (2) (b).

(k) Non-deduction of tax from interest payments is now the general rule; see p. 665, *infra.*

(l) In the case of joint borrowers, note also s. 24 (3) (d), added by Housing Act 1974, Sched. 11, para. 1 (2).

(m) See footnote (c), p. 657, *supra.*

(n) *I.e.*, qualifying relatives, see footnote (c), p. 657, *supra.*

(o) The residence condition is that the dwelling must be occupied wholly or partly as the borrower's only or main residence or in the case of joint borrowers so occupied by each of them or at any time when the borrower or any joint borrower does not so occupy the dwelling, the dwelling is so occupied by a qualifying relative of his: see Housing Act 1974, s. 119, Sched. 11, para 2 (5), inserting new s. 24B in the principal Act. Section 28A, added by the Housing Act 1974, Sched. 11, para. 6 provides for the recovery of any subsidy in the case of false declarations, etc.

(p) Section 24 (3) amended by Housing Act 1974, Sched. 11, paras. 1 and 2.

(v) the vesting of the lender's rights under the repayment contract in some other person. But if, at the expiration of the period of three months beginning with the date of that vesting, that other person is a qualifying lender, the option notice shall not cease to have effect by virtue of this provision; the provisions of Part II of the Act are to be treated as having continued to have effect during that period as if that other person were a qualifying lender, notwithstanding that at any time during that period he was not so;

(vi) if the number of the periodical payments is not fixed by or ascertainable under the repayment contract, the expiration of thirty years from the beginning of the period for which the option notice has had effect (*q*).

(vii) the taking effect of a notice under s. 26A of the Act (*r*).

The Secretary of State may direct that, in such circumstances, cases or class of case as may be specified in his direction, an option notice shall, if the qualifying lender in question so agrees, have effect notwithstanding that the conditions relating to the date of signature of an option notice and to residence and occupation (*s*) are not satisfied; but the period for which an option notice has effect by virtue of this provision shall not begin

(a) if the lender is a building society whose financial year ends on a date not earlier than 30 September, until 1 April next after the end of the financial year of the society in which the option notice is signed; or

(b) in any other case, until 1 April falling between three and fifteen months after the date of the signing of the option notice, except where the lender agrees to its beginning on an earlier 1 April falling after the date of the signing of the option notice (*t*).

Section 24 (6) of the Act provides that Part II shall have effect with respect to any loan notwithstanding any provision with respect to the making of loans by the lender in question contained in, or in any instrument made under, any other enactment.

Extension of the right to opt.—It is provided by s. 26 that, where the rights and obligations of the borrower under the repayment contract become or have become vested in some other person or persons beneficially entitled to the interest in land in question, the right to opt for subsidy is extended to such persons, the subsidy having effect from 1 April, 1968, or the date of vesting, if later. And where such rights and obligations have become vested in trustees or personal representatives and no option notice has had effect in respect of the loan they may be given option rights as the Minister may direct in exercise of his powers under s. 24 (5), and the relevant provisions of s. 24 shall apply (*u*).

Right to terminate period for which option notice has effect.— The person or persons in whom the rights and obligations under the repayment contract are for the time being vested may by notice to the

---

(*q*) Section 24 (3).

(*r*) Added by Housing Act 1969, s. 79. The Housing Act 1974, Sched. 11, para. 1 (3) adds a number of other conditions, *e.g.*, cesser of residence condition, etc.

(*s*) *Supra*.

(*t*) Section 24 (5).

(*u*) Section 26 (1), (2). For extension to housing associations and self-build societies and to purchasers from local authorities and development corporations by regulations, see sub-ss. (4), (5), (6).

lender bring the period for which the option notice has effect to an end on 31 March of any year not earlier than 1972 but only if not less than four years have then elapsed since the date of the repayment contract. The notice must be in writing and in such form as the Secretary of State may direct and must be given not less than three months before the date on which it is to take effect (x).

Qualifying lenders.—By s. 27 of the Act (y) it is provided that qualifying lenders for the purposes of any provision of Part II of the Act shall be any of the following bodies lending in pursuance of powers apart from this part of the Act:

(a) local authorities;
(b) building societies designated under section 1 of the House Purchase and Housing Act 1959;
(c) such of the following bodies as the Secretary of State may by order prescribe:
    (i) other building societies;
    (ii) insurance companies;
    (iii) friendly societies;
(d) the Housing Corporation;
(e) development corporations;
(f) the Commission for the New Towns.

The power to make orders under s. 27 (1) is exercisable by statutory instrument (z), and any such order may vary or revoke any previous order; but no such order with respect to a building society or friendly society shall be made except after consultation with the Chief Registrar of Friendly Societies, and no such order with respect to an insurance company is to be made except after consultation with the Board of Trade. Moreover, no such order removing any such society or company from the list of qualifying lenders is to be made apart from the following circumstances:

(i) on the application of the society or company; or
(ii) where the society or company has ceased to exist; or
(iii) where the removal is, in the opinion of the Minister, expedient in the public interest.

Such a removal, if it takes place, is not to affect any right or obligation of any person under Part II of the Act in connection with any loan if an option notice in respect thereof had effect immediately before the date on which the removal takes effect (a).

Amount of subsidy.—The amount of the subsidy is specified by Increase Subsidy Orders made under s. 28 (3) the principal Act (b).

Effect of option.—Since the new scheme is intended to afford tax benefits, factors to be considered by the borrower will include his present and future gross income, marital status or probable marital

---

(x) Section 26A (2), added by Housing Act 1969, s. 79 (2); as amended by Finance Act 1971, s. 66.
(y) As amended by the Local Government Act 1972, s. 272 (1), Sched. 30 and Housing Act 1974, Sched. 11, para. 4.
(z) Numerous Qualifying Lenders Orders have been made.
(a) Section 27 (2).
(b) See, *e.g.*, the Assistance for House Purchase and Improvement (Increases of Subsidy) Order 1975, S.I. 1975 No. 1240.

status, and the number, if any, of existing dependants or of probable dependants. The likelihood of a fixed or even decreasing gross income, and of the redemption occurring only after a considerable time, are factors in favour of opting for the scheme (*c*).

Guarantee of advances in excess of normal amount.—By s. 30 the housing Ministers are enabled, with Treasury approval, to enter into arrangements with insurance companies whereby, if qualifying lenders prescribed under s. 27 are willing to make loans for persons opting for subsidy under the foregoing provisions of this Part of the Act above the amount which they would normally advance without collateral security, the insurance company will guarantee the excess. The risk of loss is to be shared equally between the Minister and the insurance company and there will be an appropriate reduction in the amount of the premium payable by the borrower. In the case of building societies it is provided that the premium remaining may be added to the loan (*d*).

(*c*) For conflicting views as to the economics of the scheme, see (1967), 111 S.J. 860 (Derek A. Bate); (1968), 112 S.J. 530 (R.H.G.). For a guide to the scheme generally, see "Your Guide to the Option Mortgage Scheme" prepared by the Ministry of Housing and Local Government, etc. And see (1967) 31 Conv. (N.S.), 343 (Alec Samuels).

(*d*) There are appropriate modifications to the Building Societies Act 1962, as to which, see Housing Subsidies Act 1967, s. 30 (2).

PART XI

TAXES

TAXES

CHAPTER 38

Taxes

I—INCOME TAX

Taxation of mortgage interest.—In the case of an individual who is the recipient of mortgage interest, and who is not carrying on the business of lending money (*a*), the interest is chargeable to income tax under Case III of Sch. D (*b*). And in the case of a company it is subject to corporation tax (*c*). Premiums and discounts may be treated as interest, particularly where no interest is payable (*d*). But if interest is also payable, there is no presumption that the discount or premium is interest (*e*). Capitalised interest does not cease to be interest (*f*).

Interest paid under a guarantee.—Any sum paid by a guarantor in respect of money due from the principal debtor ranks as payment of interest and not a payment of a sum in lieu of interest (*g*).

Deduction of income tax on payment of mortgage interest.—Subject to the exceptional cases mentioned below, mortgage interest is no longer paid subject to deduction of tax by the payer. Prior to the Finance Act 1969 the provisions as to deduction of tax at source applicable to annual payments (*h*) applied to yearly interest also. Since the Finance Act 1969 (*i*) mortgage interest has, generally (*k*), been payable gross. The exceptions specified in s. 54 of the Income and Corporation Taxes Act 1970 when mortgage interest is payable under deduction of tax are where yearly interest is paid—

(a) otherwise than in a fiduciary or representative capacity, by a company or local authority, or

(b) by or on behalf of a partnership of which a company is a member, or

(c) by any person to another person whose usual place of abode is outside the United Kingdom.

But these exceptions do not apply to interest payable in the United Kingdom on an advance from a bank carrying on a *bona fide* banking

---

(*a*) A moneylender is chargeable under Case I of Sch. D.
(*b*) Income and Corporation Taxes Act 1970, s. 109.
(*c*) I.C.T.A. 1970, ss. 238 *et seq.*
(*d*) See *Inland Revenue Commissioners* v. *Thomas Nelson & Sons, Ltd.* 1938 S.C. 816; *Davies* v. *Premier Investment Co., Ltd.*, [1945] 2 All E.R. 681.
(*e*) *Lomax* v. *Peter Dixon & Sons, Ltd.*, [1943] K.B. 671 (C.A.); [1943] 2 All E.R. 255.
(*f*) *Inland Revenue Commissioners* v. *Oswald*, [1945] A.C. 360 (H.L.); [1945] 1 All E.R. 641.
(*g*) *Re Hawkins, Hawkins* v. *Hawkins*, [1972] Ch. 714; [1972] 3 All E.R. 386; (1973), 123 New L.J. 7 (F. G. Glover).
(*h*) Sections 169, 170 I.T.A. 1952; now I.C.T.A. 1970, ss. 52, 53.
(*i*) Section 26.
(*k*) For building societies, see *infra*.

business in the United Kingdom or to interest paid by such a bank in the ordinary course of that business.

Yearly interest of money.—Interest is yearly interest whenever it is paid on a loan which is in the nature of an investment, whether it is repayable on demand or not. The distinction is between a loan on mortgage and a short banker's loan (*l*).

Mortgage interest payable to building society.—Where arrangements made between the Commissioners of Inland Revenue and any building society (*m*) are in force as respects any year of assessment, income tax is not to be deducted upon payment to the society of interest on advances, being interest payable in that year (*n*).

Mortgage interest payable under the option mortgage scheme.—Where mortgage interest is paid under the option mortgage scheme (*o*), the interest must be paid without deduction of tax (*p*).

Foreign aspects.—As mentioned above, the general rule is now that tax is no longer deductible from interest payments. One of the exceptions to this general rule is for yearly interest (*q*) paid by any person to another person whose usual place of abode is outside the United Kingdom (*r*). This exception applies, between the parties, only where the proper law of the loan document is English law. There is no right of deduction for United Kingdom tax where the proper law of the document is a foreign law (*s*). Thus in the case of foreign securities where the payment of interest is made by a non-resident payer to a resident payee, tax cannot be deducted by the payer and where the payment is made by a resident payer to a non-resident payee the payer does not fulfil his obligation by deducting tax (*t*). As between the payer and the Revenue the deductibility of the tax and payment depends on the location of the debt (*u*).

Tax relief for mortgage interest (*x*).—Where appropriate, relief

---

(*l*) *Corinthian Securities, Ltd.* v. *Cato*, [1970] 1 Q.B. 377 (C.A.); [1969] 3 All E.R. 1168; (1970) B.T.R. 144. And see *Re Euro Hotel (Belgravia), Ltd.*, [1975] 3 All E.R. 1075. The distinction between annual interest and other annual payments has not hitherto had any significance (see, e.g., *Westminster Bank Executor and Trustee Co. (Channel Islands), Ltd.* v. *National Bank of Greece, S.A.*, [1970] 1 Q.B. 256 (C.A.); [1969] 3 All E.R. 504; *affd. sub nom. National Bank of Greece, S.A.* v. *Westminster Bank Executor and Trustee Co. (Channel Islands), Ltd.*, [1971] A.C. 945 (H.L.); [1971] 1 All E.R. 233). The distinction may be important in the future, see (1969) B.T.R. 230.

(*m*) Power to make such arrangements is conferred by the Income and Corporation Taxes Act 1970, s. 343.

(*n*) I.C.T.A. 1970, s. 343 (4).

(*o*) See p. 657, *supra*.

(*p*) Housing Subsidies Act 1967, s. 24 (2) (b) (iii).

(*q*) See *supra*.

(*r*) Income and Corporation Taxes Act 1970, s. 54.

(*s*) On the proper law, see p. 18, *supra*.

(*t*) *Keiner* v. *Keiner*, [1952] 1 All E.R. 643; *Bingham* v. *Inland Revenue Commissioners*, [1956] Ch. 95; [1955] 3 All E.R. 321. As to the presumption of deduction with regard to assessment on the payee, see *Stokes* v. *Bennett*, [1953] Ch. 566; [1953] 2 All E.R. 313.

(*u*) See p. 17, *supra*; *National Bank of Greece, S.A.* v. *Westminster Bank Executor and Trustee Co. (Channel Islands), Ltd.* [1971] A.C. 945 (H.L.); [1971] 1 All E.R. 233.

(*x*) Under the Income Tax Act 1952, ss. 445 (3), 524, loan interest was allowable as a deduction in estimating a person's total income. The Finance Act 1969 made major changes in the law allowing interest as a deduction in calculating a person's taxable income. The general rule became that such deduction was no longer to be allowed, except in certain specified cases, e.g., where the interest was paid under a loan for the purchase or improvement of a dwelling-house. The provisions of the 1969 Act (ss. 19 *et seq*) were

is allowed to individuals (*y*), and also to companies if the latter are not resident in the United Kingdom and the interest cannot be taken into account in computing corporation tax (*z*), in respect of—(a) annual interest chargeable to tax under Case III of Sch. D; or (b) interest which is payable in the United Kingdom on an advance from a bank, a member of a stock exchange or discount house in the United Kingdom (this includes the Republic of Ireland so long as the special double taxation agreements with that country are in force). The amount of the interest eligible for relief is to be deducted from or set off against the income of the person paying it for the year of assessment in which it is paid (*b*).

Where interest is paid at a rate in excess of a reasonable commercial rate, relief under s. 75 will not be given in respect of so much of the interest as represents the excess (*c*). It is not stated whether "reasonable commercial rate" means reasonable in the light of the rates generally prevailing or whether a higher rate might be reasonable because the borrower was a poor risk.

The cases in which relief is allowed are mentioned below. It should be noted that it is the purpose of the loan (*d*) which is the relevant factor not the nature of the security (if any).

The principal case for the relief, so far as this work is concerned, is where the loan is for the purchase or improvement of land in the United Kingdom or the Republic of Ireland. The following conditions must be satisfied (*e*)—

Firstly. The interest must have been paid by a person for the time being owning an estate or interest in land (*f*) in the United Kingdom or the Republic of Ireland.

---

replaced by ss. 57 *et seq.* of the Income and Corporation Taxes Act 1970. The Finance Act 1972, ss. 75 and 76 and Sched. 9 and 10 very largely restored the pre-1969 position. In the case of an individual, relief was not given for the first £35 of the interest paid unless the interest was protected interest: s. 75 (3). Protected interest was interest of a kind which was eligible for relief under ss. 57, 60 and 190 of the I.C.T.A. 1970 (other than interest on overdrafts), *e.g.*, interest on loans for the purchase or improvement of a dwelling-house. The Finance Act 1974 restored the position to much the same as that which prevailed before the 1969 provisions were repealed: tax relief is only available for interest on loans applied for certain specified purposes mentioned in the text, *post.* The above statement of the position as regards loans taken out after 26 March 1974 is brief, as any change of Government will probably result in a change in the relevant provisions, and the transitional provisions (the most important of which is to relieve certain obligations incurred before 26 March 1974 until 6 April 1980) are ignored here. There have been recent murmurings (see (1976) 120 S.J. 465) of the abolition of the relief but abolition would inevitably be politically unpopular. The "cost" of mortgage interest relief for 1976–77 was £1,000 million: see *Times*, 14th March.

(*y*) Including trustees and executors: see Finance Act 1974, Sched. 1, para 8.

(*z*) Finance Act 1972, Sched. 10, para. 2. For a trader or company interest may be deductible as a business expense under the general provisions as to computing profits. There are provisions excluding double relief: Finance Act 1972, Sched. 10.

(*a*) Finance Act 1972, s. 75 (1), (6).

(*b*) Finance Act 1972, s. 75 (1).

(*c*) *Ibid.*, s. 75 (2).

(*d*) The giving of credit on a sale is treated as a loan; see p. 670, *infra.* On the date of the making of the loan, see *Law* v. *Coburn*, [1972] 3 All E.R. 1115.

(*e*) Finance Act 1972, Sched. 9.

(*f*) For the difficulties which may be caused by conversion on a trust for sale and otherwise in respect of "an estate or interest in land", see (1970) 34 Conv. (N.S.) 31 (Harvey Cohen); (1970) B.T.R. 82; and see p. 160, *supra*; and Inland Revenue: Statement of practice, issued June 11 1970 (see (1970) B.T.R. 845 (Current Tax Intelligence)).

The relief does not apply to loans for the purchase or improvement of property in the Channel Islands or the Isle of Man.

Secondly. The loan on which the interest has been paid must have been applied:—

(a) in purchasing (g) the estate or interest, or one absorbed into, or given up to obtain, the estate or interest (the latter expression covers cases where money is borrowed by a landlord to buy out a sitting tenant, or where a tenant has borrowed money to buy a lease and then subsequently acquires the freehold or gives up the lease in consideration for a new lease); or

(b) in improving or developing the land or buildings on the land; or

(c) in paying off another loan, where the interest on that loan would have been protected interest had the loan not been paid off (and, if free of interest, assuming it carried interest (h)).

Interest is not eligible for relief under s. 75 unless the loan was made in connection with the application of the money as above mentioned, and either on the occasion of its application (but, it seems, the loan may be made before it is applied) or within what is, in the circumstances, a reasonable time from the application of the money. Full relief does not apply to a loan the proceeds of which are applied for some other purpose before being applied as above mentioned (i).

What constitutes a reasonable time for the above purposes will depend on the facts of the particular case. It seems that an interval not exceeding three months will be accepted as reasonable by the Revenue. It also appears that if, pending completion of a purchase, the loan is placed on deposit, relief will not be lost (see *Tax Treatment of Interest Paid* issued by the Board of Inland Revenue, booklet I.R. 11 1974).

Subject to the limit mentioned below, in the usual case of a mortgage to enable the purchaser of a dwelling-house to raise the purchase monies, relief will be allowed in respect of interest paid under the mortgage and also under any collateral mortgage. A mortgage made after the purchase transaction is only eligible for relief if the monies advanced are applied in improving or developing the property or paying off the mortgage made on the purchase (*i.e.*, the later mortgage is a substituted mortgage).

References to money applied in improving or developing land or buildings only include references to payments in respect of maintenance or repairs incurred by reason of dilapidation attributable to a period before the estate or interest was acquired. Also payments for any of the items set out in s. 72 (1) of the I.C.T.A. (deductions from rent) are excluded (k). Those items are payments in respect of maintenance, repairs, insurance, rates, etc. But expenditure incurred or defrayed

---

(g) For the tax relief problems of raising a lump sum award in favour of a former wife by a mortgage on the former matrimonial home, see (1976) 126 N.L.J. 97 (J. E. Adams).

(h) Finance Act 1972, Sched. 9, para. 1. For a criticism of the wording in para (1) " on a loan to defray money applied" for the above purposes, see (1970) B.T.R. 43 (R. Bramwell).

(i) Sched. 9, para. 2.

(k) Schedule 9, para. 3.

directly or indirectly on street works, other than works of maintenance or repair, are included (*l*). One will have to look elsewhere, *e.g.*, to the Town and Country Planning Acts and the law of landlord and tenant, as to what are "development" and "improvements" (*m*).

The Revenue booklet *Tax Treatment of Interest Paid* (I.R. 11 1974) deals with the problem in the following way:—

> "**21.**—*Improvement and development* covers every permanent alteration of the property which adds to its existing accommodation or amenities, from putting up a new building to replacing an old-fashioned central heating system with a modern one (excluding portable radiators and night storage heaters). It does not cover ordinary repairs and maintenance which do not improve the property but simply make it good or prevent deterioration. As an exception to this rule, however, if a property is bought in a dilapidated condition (which will normally result in a lower purchase price) the initial cost of repairs to put it in order is treated as part of the purchase price".

A list of some typical examples of expenditure which will be accepted by the Revenue as qualifying for improvements is set out in an Appendix to the booklet as follows:—

(a) Home extensions and loft conversions.

(b) Central heating installations (excluding portable radiators and night storage heaters).

(c) The installation of double glazing, even though it may be in a detachable form.

(d) The insulation of a roof or walls.

(e) Installation of bathrooms and other plumbing.

(f) Kitchen units, *e.g.*, sink units, which are affixed to and become part of the building; in practice, a range of matching units only some of which qualify may be treated as qualifying as a whole (other than cookers, refrigerators and similar appliances).

(g) Connection to main drainage.

(h) Garages, garden sheds, greenhouses.

(i) The construction or landscaping of gardens.

(k) Swimming pools.

(l) Reconstruction of property, *e.g.*, conversion into flats.

The above list is not exhaustive. In particular, expenditure on a number of smaller items may be met by a combined loan qualifying for relief, *e.g.*, improvements under the Clean Air Acts, fire precaution works, installation of water heating and ring mains electricity and the concreting or other improvement of driveways or paths.

Reference should be made to this very useful booklet on all questions of relief.

If the whole of the debt does not fulfil the required conditions relief is given only in respect of the proportion of any payment of interest equal to the proportion of the debt fulfilling the conditions (*n*). It will be recalled that if the interest (even if eligible for relief) is paid at a rate

---

(*l*) Schedule 9, para. 4.
(*m*) See (1970) 34 Conv. (N.S.) 38 (Harvey Cohen).
(*n*) Schedule 9, para. 15.

in excess of a reasonable commercial rate so much of any payment as represents such an excess is not eligible for relief (*o*).

Interest is not eligible for relief:—

(a) where the seller and the purchaser are a husband and his wife and either sells to the other; or

(b) where the purchaser or his or her spouse has since 15 April, 1969, disposed of an estate or interest in the land in question, and it appears that the main purpose of the purchase is to obtain relief in respect of interest on the loan; or

(c) where the purchasers are the trustees of a settlement, and the seller is the settlor, or his or her spouse, and it appears that the main purpose of the purchase is to obtain relief in respect of interest on the loan; or

(d) where the purchaser is directly or indirectly purchasing from a connected person (within the terms of s. 533 of the I.C.T.A. 1970) and the price substantially exceeds the value of what is acquired (*p*).

Where credit is given for any money due from the purchaser under any sale, that is to be treated as the making of a loan to defray money applied by the purchaser in making the purchase (*q*). This will apply, *e.g.*, where part of the purchase money remains unpaid and the purchaser pays interest to the vendor or interest becomes payable before the contractual date for completion because the purchaser has been allowed to occupy the property.

References to an estate or interest in land include references to the property in a caravan, provided it is a large caravan (*r*), or the owner or his or her spouse has paid rates as occupier of the caravan for the period in which interest has been paid (*s*), and a house boat (*t*). Yearly interest paid by a co-operative housing association is treated as paid by the tenant-members thereof (*u*). A tenant who is purchasing the property under an arrangement whereby completion is postponed (*x*), is to be treated as if he were the owner of the landlord's estate or interest (*y*). References to an estate or interest in land do not include references to a rent charge or the interest of a chargee or mortgagee (*z*). Accordingly a loan for the purchase of the benefit of a mortgage is precluded from qualifying for relief.

Thirdly. The house, land, caravan or house boat must either be (i) the main residence of the borrower (*a*) (or of a dependent relative or former

---

(*o*) Section 75 (2). See p. 667, *supra*.
(*p*) Schedule 9, para. 8.
(*q*) Schedule 9, para. 14.
(*r*) As defined by Sched. 9, para. 9.
(*s*) Schedule 9, para. 5.
(*t*) Schedule 9, para. 5A, inserted by Finance Act 1974, Sched. 1.
(*u*) Income and Corporation Taxes Act 1970, s. 341 (1) (b).
(*x*) See footnote (*u*), p. 27, *supra*.
(*y*) Schedule 9, para. 7.
(*z*) Schedule 9, para. 6.
(*a*) Where a person is required by his employment to move from his home to another place in the United Kingdom or abroad for a period not expected to exceed 4 years, a property being purchased with the aid of a mortgage which was used as his only or main

or separated spouse) or if the interest is paid less than 12 months (*b*) after the date on which the loan is made is so used within 12 months (*b*) after that date; (ii) let at a commercial rent for more than 26 weeks and when not so let either available for letting or used as in para. (i) above, or not available because of construction or repair (*c*). In the case of a dependent relative the premises must be let rent-free and without consideration (*d*).

Fourthly. Interest is only available for relief to the extent that the amount on which it is payable does not bring the total loans for a residence or residences over the relevant limit for the time being. £25,000 is the present limit (*e*). If a new loan brings the total of all loans over £25,000, only a proportion of the interest is available for relief and if the total of other loans already exceeds £25,000 no relief is available in respect of the interest on the new loan (*f*).

Any interest paid on a loan to a borrower's spouse is treated as payable on a loan made to the borrower (*g*).

Where interest is payable on a loan for the purchase or acquisition of land or of a caravan or a house boat let at a commercial rent, the interest may be relieved only against income from the rent or that of any other land, caravan or house boat, or, if the income for the current year is insufficient, carried forward to future years (*h*).

Interest paid under a bridging loan for up to 12 months, or longer if the Board directs (*i*), is eligible for relief. Interest paid in respect of the loan on the property to be disposed of continues to be eligible for relief whether or not used as an only or main residence and the benefit of the interest relief is granted in respect of the loan for the new property as if there had been no former loan (*k*).

The other cases where interest is eligible for relief are:—

(a) Loan applied in acquiring an interest in a close company (*l*).
(b) Loan applied in acquiring an interest in a partnership (*m*).
(c) Loan by specified persons to purchase machinery or plant (*n*).

---

residence before he went away will still be treated as his only or main residence, provided it can reasonably be expected to be used again as such on his return. The relief is limited to 4 years: Inland Revenue Notice 16 July 1976.

(*b*) The Board may extend the period of 12 months: Finance Act 1974, Sched. 1, para 4 (2).

(*c*) Finance Act 1974, Sched. 1, para. 4 (1).

(*d*) Finance Act 1974, Sched. 1, para. 4 (3). This requirement is the same as for the capital gains tax exemption for a residence: see Finance Act 1965, s. 29 (10); Wheatcroft and Whiteman, *Capital Gains Tax* (2nd Edn.), pp. 204 *et seq.*

(*e*) Finance Act 1974, Sched. 1, para. 5 (1). Finance Act 1976, s. 25 maintains the same amount for the year 1976–77.

(*f*) Finance Act 1974, Sched. 1, para. 5 (1). The loans to be taken into account are any made after 26 March 1974 in respect of a main residence, any made before 26 March 1974 in respect of any residence and any mortgage option loan: para. 5 (2). For joint loans other than those to husband and wife, see para. 5 (3).

(*g*) *Ibid.*, para. 5 (4).

(*h*) Finance Act 1974, Sched. 1, para. 7.

(*i*) A longer period might be appropriate if the property market was exceptionally depressed.

(*k*) Finance Act 1974, Sched. 1, para. 6.

(*l*) Finance Act 1974, Sched. 1, paras. 9, 10, 13–16.

(*m*) *Ibid.*, paras. 11, 12, 13–16.

(*n*) Finance Act 1972, Sched. 9, Pt. II.

(d) Loan to pay capital transfer tax (*o*).
(e) Loan to purchase life annuity (*p*).

II—SOME OTHER TAXES

Capital gains tax.—The conveyance or transfer by way of security of an asset or of an interest or right in or over it or transfer of a subsisting interest or right by way of security in or over an asset (including a re-transfer on redemption of the security) is not treated as involving any acquisition or disposal of the asset for capital gains tax purposes (*q*). It is further provided that, where a person entitled to an asset by way of security or to the benefit of a charge or incumbrance on an asset deals with it for the purpose of enforcing or giving effect to the security, charge or incumbrance, his dealings with it are treated as if they were done through him as nominee by the person entitled to it, subject to the security, charge or incumbrance (*r*).

Capital transfer tax (*s*).—Capital transfer tax is payable on any non-exempt disposition whereby the value of a person's estate is reduced. So, *e.g.*, a gratuitous discharge or transfer of a mortgage or a discharge or transfer for less than full value will give rise to a charge (*t*). Furthermore, the Finance Act 1975, as amended, makes specific provision for interest free or cheap loans charging such to capital transfer tax as transfers for value made out of the transferor's income (*u*).

Value added tax.—Mortgages as such are exempt from V.A.T. (*x*), but a solicitor's services in connection with the mortgage are subject to the tax (*y*).

Development land tax.—This is a tax on disposals of land in respect of the realised development value. The creation and vacation of mortgages are not treated as disposals (*z*), so there is then no charge to the tax. Where the mortgagee or other person enforcing the mortgage sells the mortgaged property, he sells as bare trustee for the defaulting

---

(*o*) *Ibid.*, paras. 17–22, as amended by Finance Act 1975, Sched. 12, para. 19, Sched. 13.

(*p*) *Ibid.*, para. 24. See generally on the 1972 Act (1972) B.T.R. 189; (1972) 36 Conv. (N.S.) 303 (G. R. Bretten);

(*q*) Finance Act 1965, s. 22 (6).

(*r*) Finance Act 1965, s. 22 (7). This applies to dealings of any person appointed to enforce or give effect to the security, charge or incumbrance as receiver and manager. See *Re McMeekin* (1973), 48 T.C. 725 (N.I.). For liability to the tax on the satisfaction of a debt on payment to an assignee of the benefit of the debt, see Finance Act 1965, Sched. 7, para. 11.

Note schemes involving a mortgage have been devised to avoid the effect of capital gains on a disposal (see *e.g.*, (1970) 120 New L.J. 936 (B. Morcom)). These have not proved successful: see *Thompson* v. *Salah*, [1972] 1 All E.R. 530. See also *Coren* v. *Keighley*, [1972] 1 W.L.R. 1556.

(*s*) See generally, Morcom and Parry, *Capital Transfer Tax*.

(*t*) So the exemption for normal expenditure out of income may apply: Finance Act 1975, Sched. 6, para. 5.

(*u*) S. 41, as amended by Finance Act 1976, ss. 115–117.

(*x*) Under the exemption in the Finance Act 1972, Sched. 5, Group 5 (Finance), as substituted by the Value Added Tax (Consolidation) Order 1974, S.I. 1974 No. 1146.

(*y*) Services of a legal nature are not within the exemption. For the liability of money-brokers to V.A.T. on commission, see *Customs and Excise Commissioners* v. *Guy Butler (International), Ltd.* [1976] 2 All E.R. 700.

(*z*) Development Land Tax 1976, s. 46 (3).

mortgagor (*a*), so that, for the purposes of the tax, it is the mortgagor who makes the disposal and is liable to the tax (*b*). However, where the mortgagor's usual place of abode is outside the United Kingdom, the general rule (*c*) is that the purchaser must account to the Revenue for the tax (otherwise payable by the mortgagor) by way of deduction from the purchase monies (*d*).

III—STAMP DUTIES

Generally.—The *ad valorem* duties under the head "Mortgage, Bond, etc.," Sched. I, Stamp Act 1891, were abolished by the Finance Act 1971, s. 64. Instruments formerly subject to these duties are now exempt. A mortgage deed may, where appropriate, require stamping as a voluntary disposition, *e.g.*, a gratuitous transfer of a mortgage (*e*). Mortgages of stock, formerly falling within the provisions of s. 23 of the Stamp Act 1891, ceased to be subject to stamp duty by virtue of the Finance Act 1972, Sched. 7, para. 1 (3) (a). Loan capital duty under s. 8 of the Finance Act 1899 and the duty on marketable securities under Sched. 1 of the Stamp Act 1891 were abolished by s. 49 of the Finance Act 1973, and a stamp duty on a chargeable transaction of a capital company, in place of the former share capital duty, was introduced by s. 47 of the Finance Act 1973 (*f*).

(*a*) *Ibid.*, s. 32.
(*b*) *Ibid.*, s. 28.
(*c*) For the exceptions, see s. 40 (2), (3), (6).
(*d*) Development Land Tax 1976, s. 40 (1). And see (1976) 40 Conv. 392.
(*e*) *Anderson* v. *Inland Revenue Commissioners.*, [1939] 1 K.B. 341; [1938] 4 All E.R. 491.
(*f*) For the former duties, see the previous edition of this work. On the capital duty, see Sergeant and Sims' *Stamp Duties and Capital Duty* (7th Edn.).

APPENDIX

BASIC
CONVEYANCING
AND COURT FORMS

See further, for conveyancing forms
14 (Mortgages) and 19 (Sale of Land)
Ency. Forms and Precedents, *Precedents for
the Conveyancer* and Hallett's *Conveyancing
Precedents*; for court forms, see 28 Ency.
Court Forms (2nd Edn.), Mortgages.

SUMMARY OF PRECEDENTS

CHARGES AND MORTGAGES

1. Legal charge. One borrower to one lender

THIS LEGAL CHARGE is made the ... day of ... BETWEEN [*the borrower*] of [*address and description*] (hereinafter called "the Borrower"[1] which expression shall where the context admits include persons deriving title under the Borrower[2] or entitled to redeem this security[3]) of the one part and [*the lender*] of [*address and description*] (hereinafter called "the Lender" which expression shall where the context admits include persons deriving title under the Lender[2]) of the other part

WHEREAS:[4]

(1) The Borrower is the estate owner in respect of the fee simple absolute in possession of the property described in the Schedule hereto[5] (hereinafter called "the mortgaged property") [subject as mentioned in the said Schedule but otherwise] free from incumbrances

Or

(1) The Borrower is possessed of the property described in the Schedule hereto (hereinafter called "the mortgaged property") for a legal estate for the residue of the term of years granted by the Lease short particulars of which are set out in the said Schedule subject to the rent thereby reserved and to the covenants and conditions therein contained but otherwise free from incumbrances

(2) The Lender has agreed to lend to the Borrower the sum of £ ... upon having the repayment thereof with interest thereon at the rate hereinafter mentioned secured in manner hereinafter appearing

---

[1] "Mortgagor" and "mortgagee" should not be used as they may lead to confusion and transposition.

[2] By the Law of Property Act 1925, s. 205 (1) (xvi) such persons are included within the definitions of "mortgagor" and "mortgagee". The reference to such persons is therefore unnecessary as far as the statutory powers are concerned. But if, as is usually the case, additional powers are included in the deed the reference is necessary.

Some draftsmen prefer an interpretation clause as the first or last clause of the deed. This is often convenient where a standard printed form is to be used.

[3] A person may be entitled to redeem, although he has not derived title under the borrower, *i.e.*, an assignor of the equity of redemption, if sued for the mortgage debt (see p. 529, *supra*); or a surety who has paid the debt (see p. 533, *supra*).

[4] The omission of recitals in modern conveyancing forms is to be deplored. They are useful because statements contained in a deed 20 years old may be taken as accurate, unless and except so far as they may be proved to be inaccurate (Law of Property Act 1925, s. 45 (6)), they may be necessary for a mortgage to qualify as a good root of title (at any rate they make it a better root of title), and they may operate by estoppel to the benefit of the mortgagee.

[5] See the Schedule and note 9 thereto, *infra*.

For a form of warranty that the borrower is in personal occupation of the mortgaged property and has not let or agreed to let it or any part as an attempt to deal with the tenancy by estoppel situation (as to which see p. 340, *supra*), see Hallett's *Conveyancing Precedents*, 608.

NOW[6] in pursuance of the said agreement and in consideration of the sum of £ ... paid by the Lender to the Borrower (the receipt whereof the Borrower hereby acknowledges)[7] THIS DEED WITNESSETH as follows:

1. The Borrower HEREBY COVENANTS with the Lender to pay to the Lender on ... day of ... next[8] the sum of £ ... [*the amount advanced*][9] with interest thereon from the date hereof at the rate of ... per cent. per annum[10] And also if the said sum of £ ... shall not be so paid to the Lender (as well after as before any judgment)[11] interest at the rate aforesaid by equal half yearly [quarterly] payments on the ... day of ... [*state dates of payment*] in each year on the principal moneys or such part thereof as shall from time to time remain owing[12].

2. The Borrower as beneficial owner[13] HEREBY CHARGES BY WAY OF LEGAL MORTGAGE[14] All That the mortgaged property [subject as mentioned in the said Schedule] with the payment to the Lender of the principal moneys interest and other money hereby covenanted to be paid by the Borrower or otherwise hereby secured.

[3. If the Borrower shall on the ... day of ... next[15] pay to the Lender the said sum of £ ... with interest thereon from the date hereof at the said rate the Lender will at the request and cost of the Borrower duly discharge this security[16]].

4. The Borrower HEREBY COVENANTS with the Lender:

(1) To pay all outgoings and keep the mortgaged property free from any charges taking priority over the money hereby secured[17];

(2) To observe and perform all covenants provisions and regulations affecting the mortgaged property;

---

[6] It is convenient to interpose the receipt clause here to avoid having a separate receipt clause at the beginning of the operative part of the deed or a reference to the consideration in both the covenant for payment and the charge clauses.

[7] Apart from the statutory effect of a receipt clause contained in a mortgage deed (see the Law of Property Act 1925, s. 68, which makes it unnecessary for a transferee for value of the mortgage to inquire whether the money was in fact paid), a transferee for value of the mortgage is not affected with notice of non-payment unless this would appear by investigation of title (*Powell* v. *Browne* (1907), 97 L.T. 854 (C.A.)).

[8] This date is generally 6 months from the date of the deed. As to payment on demand see p. 296, *supra*.

[9] For a form of covenant to pay present and future advances, see p. 696, *infra*.

[10] As to the rate of interest, see p. 29, *supra*. For a form of proviso for reduction of the rate of interest, see p. 683, *infra*. For a clause providing for interest to vary with bank rate, see 14 Ency. Forms and Precedents (4th Edn)., p. 118. For forms providing against decrease in value of pound sterling, see 14 Ency. Forms and Precedents (4th Edn.), p. 124; *Precedents for the Conveyancer* 7–9.

[11] This avoids the mortgage debt being merged in the judgment and the consequent reduction of interest; see pp. 596, 597, *supra*.

[12] For qualified covenants by personal representatives and trustees, see p. 27, *supra*.

[13] As to the covenants implied by the use of the words "beneficial owner", see the Law of Property Act 1925, s. 76 (1) (C), (D), Sched. 2, Pts. III, IV.

[14] It is considered that the fact that the charge is by way of legal mortgage must be expressed somewhere in the deed if it is to take effect as such, but the whole expression need not appear together, *e.g.*, an introductory clause might state that "this deed is by way of legal mortgage" and in the charge clause the borrower may simply charge the property: see footnote (*k*), p. 25, *supra*.

[15] This should be the same date as is fixed by the covenant for payment of principal; see p. 521, *supra*.

[16] As to the proviso for cesser, see p. 31, *supra*. For the assignment of the benefit of covenants, etc., see p. 38, *supra*.

[17] See Statutory Charges, pp. 164 *et seq.*, *supra*.

(3) To keep the buildings for the time being comprised in or subject to this security insured against loss or damage by fire[18] [in the name of the Lender[19]] to the full value thereof with some insurance office or underwriters approved by the Lender and duly and punctually to pay all premiums and other payments required for effecting and keeping up such insurance as and when the same shall become due and when required by the Lender to produce to him the policy or policies of such insurance and the receipt for each such payment[20];

(4) That all moneys received by the Borrower under any insurance on the buildings for the time being comprised in or subject to this security not effected or maintained under the foregoing covenant shall if the Lender so requires be applied in making good the loss or damage in respect of which the moneys shall have been received or be paid to the Lender and be applied by him in or towards the discharge of the money for the time being owing hereunder[1];

(5) To keep all buildings for the time being comprised in or subject to this security in repair and to permit the Lender and his agents with or without workmen or others to enter and inspect the said buildings at all reasonable times for the purpose of ascertaining the state of repair thereof (without the Lender being thereby rendered liable to account as mortgagee in possession[2]) and to make good all defects and wants of repair of which notice in writing shall be given by the Lender to the Borrower And if the Borrower shall fail to keep the said buildings in repair or if default shall be made by the Borrower in making good for one month after receipt of such notice as aforesaid the Lender and his agents with or without workmen or others shall thereupon be entitled to enter upon the mortgaged property or any part thereof and execute such repairs as in the opinion of the Lender may be necessary (without the Lender thereby becoming liable to account as mortgagee in possession)[2];

(6) Not to commit any waste upon or injure or in any manner or by any means lessen the value of the mortgaged property or any part thereof.

---

[18] As to the statutory power, see Law of Property Act 1925, ss. 101 (1) (ii), 108 (1). As to the application of insurance moneys, see Law of Property Act 1925, s. 108 (3). (p. 32, *supra*).

[19] Or "in the joint names of the Borrower and of the Lender" or omit altogether.

[20] In the case of a charge of leaseholds where the lease contains a covenant to insure it will be sufficient to provide that "the Borrower will on demand produce to the Lender the policy or policies of any insurance effected in accordance with the covenant in that behalf contained in the Lease and the receipt for each premium paid in respect thereof".

For a general covenant for payment and charge of costs, charges and expenses incurred by the Lender by the Borrower's breach of covenant or otherwise, see Clause 7, *infra*.

[1] If this clause is not included such moneys need not be applied in making good or in discharge and such other policy may, by reason of the average clause, prejudice the rights of the mortgagee; see footnote (g), p. 33, *supra*.

[2] For the purpose of this provision, see p. 352, *supra*.

In the case of a charge of leaseholds where the lease contains a covenant to repair it will be sufficient to provide that "the Borrower will keep the property in repair in accordance with the covenant in that behalf contained in the Lease".

5. PROVIDED ALWAYS:

(1) The statutory power of sale shall be exercisable at any time after the principal money hereby secured shall have become due and Section 103 of the Law of Property Act 1925 shall not apply to this security[3];

(2) The Borrower shall not be entitled (without the consent in writing of the Lender) to exercise any powers of leasing or accepting surrenders of leases conferred on a mortgagor in possession by the Law of Property Act 1925[4] [nor shall he confer on any person or persons a contractual licence or any other right or interest to occupy the property or any part thereof];

(3) Section 93 of the Law of Property Act 1925 (restricting the Lender's right of consolidation) shall not apply to this security[5];

(4) On entering into possession of the mortgaged property or any part thereof in exercise of his powers in that behalf the Lender may as agent for and on behalf of the Borrower and at the Borrower's expense remove store sell or otherwise deal with in such manner as the Lender may in his discretion think fit any furniture and effects of the Borrower which he shall have refused or omitted to remove from the mortgaged property within 7 days after such entry into possession Provided Always that the Lender shall not have any right in equity to any such furniture or effects or any charge or security thereon or otherwise as to constitute this security a bill of sale[6].

6. The present use of the mortgaged property is a permitted use thereof under the provisions of the Town and Country Planning Acts and orders and regulations made thereunder and the Borrower will not use the mortgaged property for any other purpose except with the consent in writing of the Lender and the relevant planning authority and will deliver any such consent of the relevant planning authority to the Lender but shall be entitled to a copy thereof If the Borrower persists in such use after a refusal of consent on the part of the Lender all and every or any of the powers and remedies conferred on mortgagees by the Law of Property Act 1925 (as hereby varied and extended) shall become immediately exercisable by the Lender
And the Borrower will forthwith produce to the Lender any order or notice or other matter whatsoever affecting the mortgaged property and served on the Borrower but the Borrower shall be entitled to a copy thereof.

7. The Borrower will on demand repay to the Lender all money properly paid and all costs charges and expenses properly incurred hereunder by the Lender (as to such costs charges and expenses on a full indemnity basis)[7] together with interest thereon from the time of paying or incurring the same until repayment at the rate aforesaid and until so repaid such costs charges and expenses shall be charged upon the property for the time being subject to this security and shall be added to the principal money hereby secured and interest thereon as aforesaid shall be charged upon the same property and shall be payable by equal [half yearly] payments on the respective

---

[3] For modification of the statutory power of sale, see p. 360, *supra.*
[4] For modification of the statutory powers of leasing, see p. 344, *supra.*
[5] For consolidation, see Ch. 27, *supra.* For registering the right reserved by this provision, see footnote (x), p. 513, *supra.*
[6] For the purpose of this provision, see p. 331, *supra.*
[7] See pp. 638, 639, *supra*; and (1954) 18 Conv. (N.S.) 149 (E. H. Bodkin).

dates hereinbefore appointed for payment of interest on the said principal money[8].

IN WITNESS, etc.

THE SCHEDULE above referred to

[*Description of the mortgaged property*[9] *with particulars of Lease (if leasehold) and of other matters, e.g., adverse rights, restrictive covenants, and underleases (if leasehold), to which the mortgaged property is subject*].

1A. Some additional clauses

Covenant against registration[10]

No person or persons shall be registered under the Land Registration Acts 1925 to 1971 or any Act amending or re-enacting the same as proprietor or proprietors of the mortgaged property or any part thereof without the consent in writing of the Lender and the costs incurred by the Lender of entering any caution against registration of the mortgaged property shall be deemed to be costs properly incurred by the Lender hereunder[11]

Proviso for reduction of the rate of interest on punctual payment

The Lender will accept interest at the rate of ... per cent. per annum in lieu of the higher rate hereinbefore mentioned[12] if the Borrower shall pay interest at such reduced rate on any [13] day hereinbefore appointed for payment or within [30] days thereafter and if and so long as the Borrower shall perform all his covenants and obligations hereunder (other than that relating to the payment of the said principal money and interest)

Proviso for capitalisation of interest

If any interest payable hereunder shall not be paid within [30] days after the date hereby appointed for payment thereof then as from such last mentioned date but without prejudice to the Borrower's right at any time to enforce payment thereof as interest in arrear under the covenant or provision under which the same shall have become due the interest so in arrear shall be capitalised by way of compound interest and added to the principal sum hereby secured so as to form one aggregate sum and shall be charged on the mortgaged property and until payment shall thenceforth shall carry compound interest at the rate and be payable on the days aforesaid PROVIDED

---

[8] Without this clause a mortgagee is only entitled to add his costs, charges and expenses to his security, and they do not form a debt for which the mortgagor may be sued; see p. 639, *supra*.

No attornment clause is included in this precedent. For attornment clauses and their use (if any), see pp. 34, 35, *supra*. For form, see Precedent 1A, *supra*.

[9] The description should either be in full or by reference to another deed, *e.g.*, the conveyance to the borrower.

[10] This covenant is commonly found but rarely necessary. If the land is already registered, it is inappropriate. It is not necessary if the mortgage is contemporaneous with a deed leading to first registration. The usual procedure in that case (see p. 62, *supra*) is that the application is prepared by the borrower's solicitors and lodged by the lender's solicitors. In other cases the borrower's position is usually safeguarded by reason of his possession of the title deeds.

[11] See Clause 7, Precedent 1, *supra*.

[12] See Clause 1, Precedent 1, *supra*.

[13] If the borrower is more than [30] days in arrear with any payments of interest he loses the benefit of the reduced rate in respect of that payment, but not for any subsequent payment, unless he again defaults. If one default is permanently to deprive him of the reduced rate, substitute "every" for "any".

that the Borrower may on any of the days hereby appointed for payment of interest pay to the Lender in addition to the interest then due on the principal moneys for the time being owing on this security all or any part of the principal moneys then representing interest capitalised hereunder[14]

Proviso for variation of rate of interest

The Lender shall have power from time to time to vary (whether by way of increase or reduction) the current rate of interest payable hereunder and the dates on and the periods for which such interest shall be calculated Notice in writing of any such variation shall be given by the Lender to the Borrower and any varied rate of interest shall take effect from the date specified in such notice which shall not be less than two months after the date of such notice[15]

[Provided always that any increase shall not exceed . . . per cent. per annum[16]]

Proviso that debt shall not be called in for term certain

If the Borrower shall comply with all his obligations hereunder the Lender shall not before the . . . day of . . . call in the said principal money hereby secured or any part thereof or take any other steps to enforce this security[17] PROVIDED nevertheless that the statutory power of sale shall as aforesaid be exercisable at any time after the said principal money shall have become due[18]

Proviso restricting redemption for term certain

The Borrower shall not be entitled to redeem this security during the period of . . . years[19] from the date thereof unless the Lender shall have gone into possession or appointed a receiver of the mortgaged property or taken any other steps to enforce this security

Proviso restricting dealings with equity

Not without the previous written consent of the Lender to convey assign transfer mortgage or otherwise howsoever dispose of the mortgaged property[20]

Extension of lender's leasing power

The statutory powers of leasing conferred on the Lender shall be extended so as to authorise the Lender to grant leases and make agreements for leases for any term and at any rent with or without payment of a fine or premium (provided that any such fine or premium paid to the Lender shall be applied

---

[14] As to capitalisation of interest, see p. 630, *supra*. A capitalisation clause may prevent exercise of the power of sale on the ground that interest is two months in arrears; see *Davy* v. *Turner* (1970), 114 Sol. Jo. 884.

[15] Where the mortgage does not provide for variation it may be possible for the mortgagee to call in the mortgage debt and then agree a new mortgage at a new rate of interest. A mere threat to call in may force the mortgagor to agree a variation.

[16] Some upper limit is advisable, see p. 29, *supra*.

[17] This proviso does not prevent the mortgagor redeeming on six months' notice: *Cromwell Property Investment Co., Ltd.* v. *Western and Toovey*, [1934] Ch. 322; see p. 538, *supra*, and generally, p. 28, *supra*. Trustees lending money on mortgage are expressly authorised to contract that the principal shall not be called in for a period not exceeding 7 years: Trustee Act 1925, s. 10 (2).

[18] See Proviso (1), Precedent 1, *supra*.

[19] See generally, p. 522, *supra*.

[20] See p. 520, *supra*.

by the Lender as if it were money paid to the Lender on the exercise of the power of sale conferred or implied by this deed).[1]

Power to lease or sub-demise on sale of mortgaged property

The statutory power of sale conferred on the Lender shall be extended so as to authorise the Lender to carry such sale into effect either (a) in the case of such of the mortgaged property as is freehold by a demise thereof or by demises of parts thereof or (b) in the case of such of the mortgaged property as is leasehold by a sub-demise thereof or sub-demises of parts thereof for such term or terms and at such rent or rents with or without payment of a fine or premium as the Lender shall think fit and also to sell the freehold or leasehold reversion or reversions so created.[2]

Power to sell by instalment sale, etc.

The statutory power of sale is hereby modified so that any sale by the Lender may be in such form as to the manner thereof as to the method of payment of the purchase price and otherwise as the Lender may think fit.[3]

Proviso as to compulsory purchase of mortgaged property

If before the whole of the moneys hereby secured shall have been repaid the mortgaged property shall be compulsorily acquired by or be the subject of a compulsory purchase demolition clearance or a redevelopment order made by the local authority or by any other competent authority then any compensation paid to the Borrower by such local or other authority in respect of the mortgaged property shall be applied by the Borrower in the first place in discharge of the moneys hereby secured (including the costs of the Lender incurred in discharging this security or otherwise) and subject thereto shall belong to the Borrower PROVIDED that if the amount of such compensation shall be insufficient to discharge the whole of the moneys hereby secured [after payment by the Borrower of the instalments of principal or a proportionate part thereof and interest thereon (if any) down to the date when the Borrower shall be required to vacate the mortgaged property] then (i) the whole of such compensation shall be paid to the Lender and (ii) if the site of the mortgaged property shall not be acquired by such authority the Borrower will at the request and expense of the Lender transfer the site of the mortgaged property to or at the direction of the Lender and upon payment of the instalments of principal or a proportionate part thereof and interest thereon (if any) and compensation money and on the execution of such transfer the Lender shall sign a memorandum (to be prepared at the cost of the Lender) endorsed hereon acknowledging that he has received payment from the Borrower of all moneys intended to be hereby secured

Attornment clause[4]

The Borrower hereby attorns tenant to the Lender of the mortgaged property during the continuance of this security at the yearly rent of a peppercorn if demanded but nothing in this clause shall prevent the Lender from at any time entering on and taking possession of the mortgaged property and so determining the tenancy hereby created[5]

---

[1] See p. 360, *supra*.
[2] See p. 360, *supra*. And 14 Ency. Forms and Precedents (4th Edn.), 139.
[3] See p. 361, footnote (s) *supra*.
[4] See generally, p. 34, *supra*.
[5] For notice determining the tenancy, see p. 35, *supra*.

1B. Legal charge by co-owners[6]

THIS LEGAL CHARGE is made the ... day of ... BETWEEN [*a borrower*] of [*address and description*] and [*the other borrower*] of [*address and description*] (hereinafter called "the Borrowers" which expression shall where the context admits include persons deriving title under the Borrowers or entitled to redeem this security) of the one part and [*the lender*] of [*address and description*] (hereinafter called "the Lender" which expression shall where the context admits include persons deriving title under the Lender) of the other part

WHEREAS:

(1) The Borrowers are the estate owners in respect of the fee simple absolute in possession of the property described in the Schedule hereto (hereinafter called "the mortgaged property") [subject as mentioned in the said Schedule but otherwise] free from incumbrances upon trust for sale for themselves beneficially as joint tenants [*or* tenants in common in equal shares]

Or

(1) The Borrowers are possessed of the property described in the Schedule hereto (hereinafter called "the mortgaged property") for a legal estate for the residue of the term of years granted by the Lease short particulars of which are set out in the said Schedule subject to the rent thereby reserved and to the covenants and conditions therein contained but otherwise free from incumbrances upon trust for sale for themselves beneficially as joint tenants [*or* tenants in common in equal shares]

Continue as in Precedent 1, *substituting* "*Borrowers*" *for* "*Borrower*"

NOW in pursuance, *etc.,* as in Precedent 1, *substituting* "*Borrowers*" *for* "*Borrower*" THIS DEED WITNESSETH as follows:

1. The Borrowers HEREBY JOINTLY AND SEVERALLY COVENANT with the Lender [*continue covenant for payment of principal and interest; see Clause* 1, *Precedent* 1].

Continue as in Precedent 1 *substituting* "*Borrowers*" *for* "*Borrower*"[7] *and varying Borrower's covenants as follows;*

4. The Borrowers HEREBY JOINTLY AND SEVERALLY COVENANT with the Lender:

Continue as in Precedent 1, *substituting* "*Borrowers*" *for* "*Borrower*".

1C. Legal charge to several lenders[8]

THIS LEGAL CHARGE is made the ... day of ... BETWEEN [*the borrower*] of [*address and description*] (hereinafter called "the Borrower" which expression shall where the context admits include persons deriving title under the Borrower or entitled to redeem this security) of the one part and [*a lender*] of

---

[6] The usual case will be where husband and wife are the co-owners. The legal estate cannot be vested in more than four persons (see p. 175, *supra*). Where there are more than four co-owners the trustees of the legal estate, all the co-owners and the lender will be parties; for a form, see 14 Ency. Forms and Precedents (4th Edn.), pp. 214–217.

[7] The Borrowers will generally charge as beneficial owners. For the covenants implied thereby, see note 13, Precedent 1, *supra*.

[8] See p. 175, *supra*.

[*address and description*] and [*another lender*] of [*address and description*] (hereinafter called "the Lenders" which expression shall where the context admits include persons deriving title under the Lenders) of the other part

WHEREAS:

(1) [*Recital of title; as recital* (1), *Precedent* 1]

(2) The Lenders have agreed to lend to the Borrower the sum of £ ... out of moneys belonging to them upon a joint account[9] upon having the repayment thereof with interest thereon at the rate hereinafter mentioned secured in manner hereinafter appearing.

Continue as in Precedent 1, *substituting* "*Lenders*"[10] *for* "*Lender*".

2. Charge by way of legal mortgage. Repayment by instalments[11]

THIS LEGAL CHARGE is made the ... day of ... BETWEEN [*parties and recitals as in Precedent* 1]
NOW in pursuance, *etc., as in Precedent* 1 THIS DEED WITNESSETH as follows:

1. [*Covenant for payment of principal and interest; see Clause* 1, *Precedent* 1][12]

2. [*Charge; as Clause* 2, *Precedent* 1].

[3. [*Proviso for redemption; as Clause* 3, *Precedent* 1]].

4. If the Borrower shall pay to the Lender on the ... day of ... next and thereafter every ... week [month] instalments of combined principal and interest of £ ... each the Lender will apply the balance if any of the total of such payments made in each period of ... months[13] after deduction therefrom of such an amount as is required to discharge all interest due for the time being on this security at the commencement of each such period of ... months[10] in reduction of the said principal sum hereby secured[14]

[*Or* 4. If the Borrower shall pay to the Lender on the ... day of ...next and thereafter for the next subsequent [*number of instalments*] week [month] instalments of combined principal and interest of £ ... each (apportioned as to £ ... to principal and as to the balance to interest)][15]

[*Or* 4. If the Borrower shall pay to the Lender on the ... day of ... next and thereafter every ... [month] the sum of £ ... on account of the principal

---

[9] Even without an express statement that the money is advanced on a joint account, persons dealing in good faith with mortgagees may assume, unless the contrary is expressly stated in the instruments relating to the mortgage, that they are entitled to the mortgage debt on a joint account: Law of Property Act 1925, s. 113 (1) (a); see pp. 175, 255, *supra*.
[10] As to contributory mortgages, see footnote (*k*), p. 176, *supra*. As to the effect of covenants with two or more persons jointly, see the Law of Property Act 1925, s. 81.
[11] As to payment by instalments, see p. 28, *supra*.
[12] For the direct method of drafting an instalment mortgage, see p. 28, *supra*. The disadvantage of a direct covenant for the mortgagee is that if he exercises his power of sale he will have to prove that the instalments are in arrears (see p. 360, *supra*), and for the mortgagor that the form of the covenant may postpone redemption (see footnote (*s*), p. 523, *supra*).
[13] Quarterly, six- or twelve-monthly rests are appropriate.
[14] This is the flat rate method; see p. 30, *supra*.
[15] This is suitable for cases where a lump sum representing interest at the agreed rate and non-reducing over the period of the mortgage is added to the advance to form one sum.

sum due hereunder and also shall pay to the Lender on the ... day of ... next and thereafter every ... [month] interest at the rate aforesaid on the principal money for the time being unpaid][16]

And if the Borrower shall in all respects comply with the conditions of this deed then the Lender shall accept payment of the said principal sum hereby secured and the interest thereon by the instalments at the times and in manner aforesaid.

5. Notwithstanding that any instalments may have been paid pursuant to Clause 4 hereof the balance of the principal sum hereby secured shall continue to be due for all the purposes of the exercise of statutory or other powers on [*the date mentioned in Clause* 1].[17]

[6. (In addition to any other powers he may have in this respect)[18] the Borrower may upon giving to the Lender at least one calendar month's previous notice in writing or upon payment of one month's interest in lieu of notice repay the whole or any part of the moneys hereby secured PROVIDED that no such repayment may be made unless all the said instalments payable under Clause 4 hereof shall have been duly paid and that any sum so paid shall not be less than £[100].]

7. The statutory power of sale shall be exercisable at any time after the principal money hereby secured shall have become due and Section 103 of the Law of Property Act 1925 shall not apply to this security [PROVIDED that if at the date mentioned in Clause 1 hereof the Borrower shall have paid regularly to the Lender all the said instalments mentioned in Clause 4 hereof payable up to that date then the Lender will not exercise any of the powers conferred on mortgagees by the said Act unless and until:

(1) a subsequent instalment (or some interest) payable hereunder is in arrear and unpaid for [28] days after becoming due; or

(2) there has been a breach of some provision herein contained or implied and on the part of the Borrower to be observed or performed (other than the covenant for payment of the principal money and interest aforesaid) in respect of which written notice has been given to the Borrower requiring him to remedy such breach and which notice has not been complied with by him within [one calendar month] after service thereof.]

8. [*Borrower's covenants; as Clause* 4, *Precedent* 1].

9. [*Provisos; as Clause* 5, *Precedent* 1, *omitting* (1)].

10. [*Planning matters; as Clause* 6, *Precedent* 1].

11. [*Covenant for payment and charge of costs, charges and expenses; as Clause* 7, *Precedent* 1].

IN WITNESS, etc.

THE SCHEDULE above referred to
[*As in Precedent* 1]

---

[16] This is the fixed instalment method; see p. 30, *supra*.

[17] Without this clause it may be that the mortgage money cannot be called in or the mortgagee's powers exercised until default. See *De Borman* v. *Makkofaides*, [1971] Estates Gazette Digest 909.

[18] The borrower may redeem on the legal date for redemption (see p. 521, *supra*), and after that date on due notice (see p. 538, *supra*). Where there is a direct covenant to pay instalments these powers may not be available unless this clause is included (see footnote 12, *supra*).

3. Mortgage by demise of freeholds

THIS MORTGAGE is made the ... day of ... BETWEEN [*parties and recitals as in Precedent* 1]

NOW in pursuance, *etc., as in Precedent* 1 THIS DEED WITNESSETH as follows:

    1. [*Covenant for payment of principal and interest; as Clause* 1, *Precedent* 1].

    2. The Borrower as beneficial owner[19] HEREBY DEMISES unto the Lender ALL That the mortgaged property To HOLD the same unto the Lender for the term of [3,000] years[20] from the date hereof without impeachment of waste[1] [subject as mentioned in the said Schedule] and subject also to the proviso for cesser[2] hereinafter contained.

    [3. PROVIDED that if the Borrower shall on the said ... day of ... next[3] pay to the Lender the said principal sum of £ ... with interest thereon from the date hereof at the said rate then the term hereby created shall cease].

    [4. *Provision for repayment by instalments, if desired; as Clause* 4, *Precedent* 2].

    5. [*Borrower's covenants and other clauses; as in Precedents* 1 *and* 2, *as appropriate*].

IN WITNESS, etc.

THE SCHEDULE above referred to

[*As in Precedent* 1]

---

[19] See footnote 13 in Precedent 1.

[20] The term is usually 3,000 or 1,000 years. A legal charge of freeholds takes effect as if a term of 3,000 years had been created in favour of the mortgagee: Law of Property Act 1925, s. 87 (1) (see p. 25, *supra*). Pre-1926 freehold mortgages were converted into mortgages by demise for a term of 3,000 years, second or subsequent mortgages each being for a term one day longer than each prior mortgage: Law of Property Act 1925, Sched. 1, Pt. VII, paras. 1 and 2 (see p. 53, *supra*). A similar term is taken by mortgagees in converted post-1925 mortgages by conveyance; Law of Property Act 1925, s. 85 (2) (see p. 20, *supra*). And see Law of Property Act 1925, Sched. 6, Specimen Abstract 1 (Mortgage for a term of 1,000 years).

[1] Legal charges and converted mortgages (see footnote (19), *supra*) are without impeachment for waste and it is usual to so provide where the mortgage is expressly made by demise.

[2] As to the proviso for cesser, see p. 31, *supra*.

[3] The same date as is fixed by the covenant for payment of principal.

4. Mortgage by sub-demise of leaseholds

THIS MORTGAGE is made the ... day of ... BETWEEN [*parties and recitals as in Precedent* 1]

And also (where appropriate)

(3) The lessor's consent hereto has been duly obtained

NOW in pursuance *etc., as in Precedent* 1 THIS DEED WITNESSETH as follows:

1. [*Covenant for payment of principal and interest; as Clause* 1, *Precedent* 1].

2. The Borrower as beneficial owner[4] HEREBY DEMISES unto the Lender ALL That the mortgaged property TO HOLD the same unto the Lender for the residue now unexpired of the term created by the said Lease except the last [10] days thereof[5] [subject as mentioned in the said Schedule] and subject also to the proviso for cesser[6] hereinafter contained.

[3. PROVIDED that if the Borrower shall on the said ... day of ... next pay to the Lender the said principal sum of £ ... with interest thereon from the date ... hereof at the said rate the sub-term hereby created shall cease].

[4. *Provision for repayment by instalments, if desired; as Clause* 4, *Precedent* 2].

5. [*Borrower's covenants and other clauses; as Precedent* 1 *and* 2 (*as appropriate*)].

IN WITNESS, etc.

THE SCHEDULE above referred to
[*As in Precedent* 1]

---

[4] See footnote 13 in Precedent 1.
[5] Or "the last day thereof". The "10 days" allows for several mortgages of the property each being for one day longer than the previous one. But it is not essential to so provide as there can be successive legal mortgages by sub-demise for the same or varying sub-terms (Law of Property Act 1925, s. 149 (5)).
[6] As to the proviso for cesser, see p. 31, *supra.*

5. Charge of registered land[7]

H.M. LAND REGISTRY

LAND REGISTRATION ACTS 1925 TO 1971

County, County borough } · · ·
or London borough

Title Number ...[8]

Property...

Date...

In consideration of ... pounds (£ ...) (the receipt whereof is hereby acknowledged) I, [*the borrower*] of [*address and description*] (hereinafter called "the Borrower" which expression, *etc., as in Precedent* 1) as beneficial owner hereby charge[9] the land comprised in the above title[10] with the payment to [*the lender*] of [*address and description*] (hereinafter called "the Lender" which expression, *etc., as in Precedent* 1) of the principal sum of £ ... with interest thereon at the rate of ... per cent. per annum payable [half yearly] on the [*state dates of payment*] in every year

[*Add provisions for payments by instalments* (*see Precedent* 2), *if appropriate*]

[The following provisions shall have effect in respect of this charge:

1.[11] The Borrower hereby covenants with the Lender:[12]

[*Continue with Borrower's covenants, as Clause* 4, *Precedent* 1]

[*Provisos, etc., as in Precedent* 1]

Signed, sealed and delivered

by the said [*the borrower*] in the

presence of   [*Signature and seal of borrower*]

---

[7] As to charges of registered land generally, see Ch. 3, *supra*. This form can be used in simple cases for land already registered or for a charge contemporaneous with a deed inducing registration (see p. 59, *supra*) with the modifications mentioned below. For forms of charge, see Land Registration Rules 1925, Forms 45 *et seq*. If a more complicated form is required use unregistered form with Registry heading. And see the special stipulations in the notes to Form 45. For the covenants on the part of the borrower implied in a registered charge, see p. 63, *supra*.

[8] Leave blank if the land is not already registered.

[9] The words "by way of legal mortgage" are not required: *Cityland and Property (Holdings), Ltd.* v. *Dabrah*, [1968] Ch. 166; [1967] 2 All E.R. 639.

[10] Or "the land edged red on the accompanying plan being part of the land comprised in the above title", or, if the land is not yet registered, describe the land by reference to the deed inducing registration.

[11] The lay-out of the printed forms generally requires these to be placed on the reverse side of the form or on a separate sheet.

[12] A covenant for payment is sometimes included as the implied covenant is "on the part of the person being proprietor of such land at the time of the creation of the charge": Land Registration Act 1925, s. 28 (1). If a surety is a party there should be an express covenant for payment (use Clause 1, Precedent 6).

6. Legal charge. Surety joining in to covenant for payment of principal and interest[13]

THIS LEGAL CHARGE is made the ... day of ... BETWEEN [the borrower] of [address and description] (hereinafter called "the Borrower" which expression, etc., as in Precedent 1) of the first part [the surety] of [address and description] (hereinafter called "the Surety") of the second part and [the lender] of [address and description] (hereinafter called "the Lender" which expression, etc., as in Precedent 1)

WHEREAS:

(1) [Recital of title as in Precedent 1]

(2) [Recital of agreement for loan as in Precedent 1]

(3) The Surety has agreed to join in this deed as surety for the Borrower in manner hereinafter appearing

NOW in pursuance of the said agreement and in consideration of the sum of £ ... paid by the Lender to the Borrower [at the request of the Surety] (the receipt whereof the Borrower [and the payment whereof as aforesaid the Surety] hereby [respectively] acknowledge[s]) THIS DEED WITNESSETH as follows:

1. The Borrower and the Surety HEREBY JOINTLY AND SEVERALLY COVENANT with the Lender [continue as in Clause 1, Precedent 1].

2. [Charge; as Clause 2, Precedent 1].

[3. Proviso for redemption; as Clause 3, Precedent 1].

4. The Borrower and the Surety HEREBY JOINTLY AND SEVERALLY FURTHER COVENANT with the Lender [continue with covenants as Clause 4, Precedent 1]

Continue as in Precedent 1 and add to provisos:

As between the Borrower and the Surety the Borrower and the mortgaged property shall be primarily liable for the payment of the moneys hereby secured but this provision shall not prejudice the Lender in the exercise of any of his rights and remedies for enforcing this security[14]

[Or

As between the Borrower and the Surety the Borrower and the mortgaged property shall be primarily liable for the payment of the moneys hereby secured but as between the Surety and the Lender the Surety shall be treated as principal debtor for the moneys hereby secured[15]]

And the Surety shall not be released from liability hereunder by time given to the Borrower or any other variation of the provisions of this deed or by anything by reason of which but for this provision the Surety would as surety only have been released[16]

Continue as in Precedent 1.

---

[13] For collateral security, see pp. 14, 15, supra.

[14] This part of the proviso merely states the general law that as between the borrower and the surety the borrower is primarily liable.

[15] The effect of this paragraph together with the last paragraph of the clause is that, as between the surety and the lender, the surety is not a surety but a principal debtor.

[16] This provision prevents the surety being released by the giving of time, etc., to the borrower by the lender. For release of sureties, see pp. 584 et seq., supra.

7. Legal charge. Spouse entitled to charge under Matrimonial Homes Act 1967 joining in to postpone charge[17]

THIS LEGAL CHARGE is made the ... day of ... BETWEEN [*the borrower*] of [*address and description*] (hereinafter called "the Borrower" which expression, *etc.*, [*as in Precedent* 1] of the first part [*the lender*] of [*address and description*] (hereinafter called "the Lender" which expression, *etc.*, [*as in Precedent* 1] of the second part and [*the spouse*] of [*address and description*] (hereinafter called "the Wife [the Husband]") of the third part

WHEREAS:

(1) By a Conveyance dated the ... day of ... and made between ... of the one part and the Borrower of the other part the property described in the Schedule hereto (hereinafter called "the property") was conveyed to the Borrower in fee simple [subject as mentioned in the said Schedule but otherwise] free from incumbrances

Or if leasehold recite Assignment to Borrower for residue of term mentioned in the Schedule [*as in Precedent* 1]

(2) The Wife[18] is entitled to a charge (hereinafter called "the Wife's Charge") on the property by virtue of the Matrimonial Homes Act 1967 and such charge is registered under the Land Charges Act 1925 as a land charge Class F under registration No. L.C. ...

(3) The Lender has agreed to lend to the Borrower the sum of £ ... upon having the repayment thereof with interest thereon at the rate hereinafter mentioned secured in manner hereinafter appearing such security to have priority to the Wife's Charge

(4) The Wife has agreed to join herein for the purpose of postponing the Wife's Charge to the security hereby created in manner hereinafter appearing NOW in pursuance, *etc.*, *as in Precedent* 1 THIS DEED WITNESSETH as follows:

1. [*Covenant for payment of principal and interest; see Clause* 1 *Precedent* 1].

2. For the purpose of postponing the Wife's Charge to the security hereby created but not furtherwise or otherwise the Wife as mortgagee HEREBY RELEASES and the Borrower as beneficial owner HEREBY CHARGES BY WAY OF LEGAL MORTGAGE All That the property [*continue as in Precedents* 1 *or* 2 *adding in Proviso*]

Nothing herein contained shall as between the Borrower and the Wife affect or prejudice any of the rights or remedies of the Wife under the Wife's Charge which shall remain in force subject to this Legal Charge and the postponement of the Wife's Charge shall be deemed to relate only to the moneys expressed secured by this deed and shall not in respect of any further moneys advanced by the Lender be deemed to confer on the Lender any like right of priority over the Wife's Charge[19]

THE SCHEDULE above referred to
[*Description of property*]

---

[17] For the Matrimonial Homes Act 1967, see generally pp. 216 *et seq., supra.*
[18] It is assumed for the remainder of this form that the wife has the charge.
[19] This form can be adapted for the postponement of other types of charge or of a prior mortgage.

8. Conveyance by former husband to former wife of his interest in mortgaged property

THIS CONVEYANCE is made the . . . day of . . . BETWEEN *the husband* of *address and description* (hereinafter called "the Husband") of the first part *the lender*[20] of *address and description* (hereinafter called "the Lender") of the second part and *the wife* of *address and description* (hereinafter called "the Wife") of the third part

WHEREAS:

(1) By a Conveyance (hereinafter called "the Conveyance") dated the . . . day of . . . and made between *the vendor* of the one part and the Husband and the Wife of the other part the property hereinafter described and expressed to be hereby conveyed (hereinafter called "the Property") was conveyed to the Husband and the Wife upon trust to sell the same and to hold the net proceeds of any such sale after payment of costs and the net rents and profits until sale after payment of all outgoings in trust for themselves as beneficial joint tenants *or* tenants in common in equal shares

(2) By a Legal Charge (hereinafter called "the Legal Charge") dated the . . . day of . . . and made between the Husband and the Wife of the one part and the Lender of the other part the Property was charged by way of legal mortgage to the Lender with the payment of the principal sum interest and other monies therein mentioned

(3) By order of the [*court*] dated the . . . day of . . . the Husband was ordered to transfer to the Wife all his estate and interest in the Property

(4) The principal sum of £. . . remains owing on the security of the Legal Charge but all interest thereon has been paid up to the date hereof

(5) The Lender has agreed to join herein to show its consent to the conveyance hereby made and for the purposes hereinafter appearing

NOW THIS DEED made in pursuance of the said Order WITNESSETH as follows:

1. The Husband as beneficial owner HEREBY ASSIGNS to the Wife ALL THAT his beneficial share or interest in the Property and the net rents and proceeds of sale thereof TO HOLD the same unto the Wife absolutely[1]

2. The Husband and the Wife as trustees[2] HEREBY CONVEY to the Wife ALL THAT the Property TO HOLD the same unto the Wife in fee simple SUBJECT to the Legal Charge

---

[20] The lender is joined in to show his consent to the assignment of the equity (see p. 520, *supra*) and for the purposes of the release of the husband from the mortgage liability. Each case will depend upon its own facts.

[1] Where the husband and wife are beneficial joint tenants the appropriate form of conveyance is usually a release, but the above form can also be used.

[2] Or as beneficial owners, if so desired.

3. In consideration of the covenant on the part of the Wife with the Lender hereinafter contained³ the Lender HEREBY RELEASES the Husband from the sum of £. . . now owing in respect of the principal money interest and other monies on the security of the Legal Charge and the covenants by him therein contained and from all claims and demands thereunder

4. The Wife HEREBY COVENANTS with the Lender at all times hereafter to pay to the Lender in accordance with the provisions of the Legal Charge the principal money interest and all other monies thereby secured and due or at any time hereafter to become due thereunder and to observe and perform all the covenants and obligations on the part of the Husband and Wife contained or implied in the Legal Charge³

5. Save as aforesaid all covenants powers provisions and agreements contained in the Legal Charge shall continue in force

[Certificate of value where appropriate]

IN WITNESS, etc.

8A.   Indemnity clause for inclusion in conveyance to former spouse when mortgagee not party

The Wife HEREBY COVENANTS with the Husband that she and the persons deriving title under her will duly and punctually pay all principal money and interest and other monies secured by and henceforth to become payable under the Legal Charge⁴ and will observe and perform the covenants by the Borrowers therein contained and will at all times hereafter keep the Husband and his estate and effects indemnified from all actions proceedings costs claims and demands in respect of any omission to pay the said monies or any breach or non-observance of the said covenants

---

³ The wife would remain bound by the covenants in the legal charge, if, as is usually the case, they were made jointly and severally. However, lenders generally like fresh covenants.
⁴ If the mortgaged property is leasehold the indemnity covenant should relate also to the rent and covenants in the lease.

9. Legal charge to secure present and future advances to finance building[5]

THIS LEGAL CHARGE is made the ... day of ... BETWEEN [*parties as in Precedent* 1]

WHEREAS:

(1) [*Recital of title as in Precedent* 1]

(2) The Borrower has requested the Lender to lend him the sum of £ ... [*total amount of advance*] for the purpose of completing [commencing] the erection of the said dwelling house

(3) The Lender has agreed to lend to the Borrower the sum of £ ... [*initial advance*] and to make the further advances hereinafter mentioned upon having the repayment thereof with interest thereon at the rate hereinafter mentioned secured in manner hereinafter appearing

NOW in pursuance of the said agreement and in consideration of the sum of £ ... [*initial advance*] paid by the Lender to the Borrower (the receipt whereof the Borrower hereby acknowledges) and of the covenant by the Lender hereinafter contained THIS DEED WITNESSETH as follows:

1. The Borrower HEREBY COVENANTS with the Lender to pay the Lender on the ... day of ... next the sum of £ ... [*the initial advance*] with interest thereon from the date hereof at the rate of ... per cent. per annum AND ALSO on the ... day of ... or the ... day of ... whichever shall next happen after every such advance respectively every sum advanced by the Lender pursuant to the covenant by the Lender hereinafter contained[6] or otherwise[7] with interest thereon at the rate aforesaid from the date of such further advance AND FURTHER if the said sums shall not be so paid to the Lender (as well after as before any judgment) interest at the rate aforesaid by equal half yearly [quarterly] payments on the ... day of ... [*state dates of payments*] in each year on the principal moneys or such part thereof as shall from time to time remain owing.

2. [*Charge; as Clause* 2, *Precedent* 1].

[3. If the Borrower shall on the ... day of ... next pay to the Lender the said sum of £ ... [*the initial advance*] and shall likewise pay to him on the days on which the same respectively ought to be paid under the foregoing covenant in that behalf any such further advances and all other moneys hereby secured with interest thereon as hereinbefore provided the Lender will at the request and cost of the Borrower duly discharge this security].

4. This Legal Charge shall be a security to the Lender not only for the sums hereinbefore covenanted to be paid by the Borrower but also for any further advances which may be made to the Borrower on the security of the same.

---

[5] This form is suitable for cases where the borrower has acquired a building plot and entered into a building contract for the erection of a house.

[6] Any further advances made under the covenant by the lender rank in priority to any subsequent mortgages made prior to the further advances; see further pp. 461 *et seq., supra.*

[7] The lender is obliged to make further advances up to the limit specified in his covenant, but, without obligation, may make further advances beyond that limit.

Continue as in Precedent 1

Add to Borrower's covenants

At his own cost and before the ... day of ... to construct and complete the said dwelling house in a proper and workmanlike manner fit for immediate habitation with proper drains sewers and conveniences and in accordance with the plans and specifications therefor and the bye-laws and regulations applicable thereto.

To expend in the erection of the said dwelling house not less than a sum of £ ... [8],[9].

If the Borrower shall fail to construct and complete the said dwelling house as aforesaid in accordance with the covenant by him hereinbefore contained the Lender may at any time thereafter enter upon the mortgaged property and complete the same and all expenses incurred by the Lender under this power shall be deemed to have been properly incurred under this security.

Continue as in Precedent 1[10]

Including proviso that debt shall not be called in for term certain[11] and proviso restricting redemption for term certain[12] and extension of Lender's leasing powers, etc. from additional clauses Precedent 1A And add Lender's covenant

The Lender HEREBY COVENANTS with the Borrower that he will from time to time advance to the Borrower[13] within [10] days after being so requested such further sums as the Borrower shall by notice in writing to the Lender request to be advanced not exceeding in the whole the sum of £ ... [total amount of further advances] (making with the sum of £ ... [the initial advance] now advanced the said sum of £ ... [total amount to be advanced])[14]

PROVIDED ALWAYS that :

(1) the obligation of the Lender to make further advances shall only apply if and so long as the Borrower shall pay all interest payabe hereunder within [14] days from the time hereby appointed for payment thereof and shall perform all his obligations under the covenants on his behalf herein contained or implied by statute (other than in regard to the payment of principal and interest);

(2) no request shall be made as aforesaid for the payment of a larger sum than £ ... or a smaller sum than £ ... and the sum so requested shall be a multiple of £ [100];

---

[8] The sum payable by the borrower under the building contract.

[9] If the borrower is obliged to insure under the building contract he should covenant to produce the policy and receipts pending completion of the building and the covenant to insure as in Precedent 1 should be expressed to become effective on completion.

[10] In proviso (1) the statutory power of sale should be expressed to be exercisable at any time after the said sum of £ ... [initial advance] shall have become due.

[11] Until at least the estimated date of completion of the building. In the proviso the power of sale should be made exercisable at any time after the said sum of £ ... [the initial advance] shall have become due.

[12] The period of restriction should be the same as in the proviso that the debt should not be called in.

[13] And it may be desired that the benefit of the covenant should be personal to the borrower. If so, an appropriate proviso adapted from that in the previous note should be included; see further Hallett's *Conveyancing Precedents*, pp. 624–626.

[14] It may be desired to add to the clause the following proviso:

"The obligation to make further advances under this covenant shall not be binding on the personal representatives of or on any other person or persons deriving title under the Lender".

For several other alternatives see Hallett, *ubi, supra*.

(3) the aggregate amount of such advances shall not at any time exceed [three quarters] of the sum for the time being certified in writing by a surveyor to be approved by the Lender and whose charges shall be paid by the Borrower as having been expended in material and labour for the construction of the said dwelling house or works incidental thereto[15]

Continue as in Precedent 1.

THE SCHEDULE above referred to

[*The mortgaged property will be the building plot described in the terms of the conveyance thereof together with the dwelling house in the course of erection or to be erected thereon*].

10. Legal charge by trader of business premises goodwill and book debts[16]

THIS LEGAL CHARGE is made the ... day of ... BETWEEN [*parties and recital of title as in Precedent* 1]

(2) The Borrower is now carrying on and has for some time past carried on upon the mortgaged property the trade or business of...

(3) The Borrower is indebted to the Lender in the sum of £ ... in respect of goods supplied and the Lender has agreed to forego the immediate payment thereof upon having such repayment and the repayment of all sums payable in respect of goods which may hereafter be supplied and the repayment of all moneys which may hereafter be advanced by him to the Borrower[17] secured in manner hereinafter appearing

[*Or (as appropriate) recital* (2) *in Precedent* 1 *then continue as in Precedent* 1]

NOW in pursuance of the said agreement and in consideration of the premises THIS DEED WITNESSETH as follows:

1. The Borrower HEREBY COVENANTS with the Lender to pay to the Lender on the ... day of ... next the sum of £ ... [*the amount owing*] with interest thereon from the date hereof at the rate of ... per cent. per annum AND ALSO all such further sums as may from time to time be owing by the Borrower to the Lender in respect of goods supplied or money advanced as aforesaid with interest thereon at the rate aforesaid from the expiration of [one] month from date of delivery of such goods or the date of such advance respectively AND FURTHER if the said sums shall not be paid to the Lender (as well after as before any judgment) interest at the rate aforesaid by equal half yearly [quarterly] payments on the ... day of ... [*state dates of payment*] in each year on the principal moneys or such part thereof as shall from time to time remain owing.

2. [*Charge; as Clause* 2, *Precedent* 1][18].

---

[15] The times and amounts of advances will vary depending on the circumstances.
[16] As to mortgages of choses in action, Ch. 6, *supra*.
[17] In this precedent there is no obligation to make further advances.
[18] Fixtures attached to the property pass without express mention; see pp. 36, 74 *et seq.*, *supra*. As to fixed trade machinery, see p. 83, *supra*. It is unnecessary and better not to expressly include fixtures in the security.

3. The Borrower as beneficial owner HEREBY ASSIGNS unto the Lender FIRST ALL the goodwill of the said trade or business carried on by the Borrower[19] SECONDLY the full benefit of all contracts entered into by or with the Borrower in respect of the said trade or business THIRDLY ALL those the book debts and other moneys which now are or may hereafter become owing to the Borrower in connection with the said trade or business[20] AND FOURTHLY ALL capital profits and other moneys received by the Borrower in respect of the said trade or business To HOLD the same unto the Lender subject only to the proviso for redemption hereinafter contained.

4. If the Borrower shall on the ... day of ... next pay to the Lender the said sum of £ ... [*the amount owing*] and shall likewise pay to him on the day on which the same respectively ought to be paid under the foregoing covenant in that behalf any such sums or advances and all other moneys hereby secured with interest thereon as hereinbefore provided the Lender will at the request and cost of the Borrower duly re-assign to the Borrower the property hereby mortgaged or otherwise discharge this security.

Continue as in Precedent 1

Adding to Borrower's covenants

( ) To insure and keep insured with some office or underwriters approved by the Lender against loss or damage by fire to the full value thereof all fixtures and fittings upon the mortgaged property and also the stock-in-trade on the said property and on demand to produce to the Lender the policy or policies of such insurance and the receipt for each premium paid in respect thereof;

( ) To keep the said fixtures and fittings in repair and replace any which have become worn out or otherwise unfit for use by others of a like nature and equal value;

( ) To devote himself actively to the conduct of the said business;

( ) To keep proper books of account of the said business and duly enter therein particulars of all dealings and transactions of the said business and keep such books and all correspondence and other documents belonging or relating to the said business upon the mortgaged property and to permit the Lender or any person appointed by him for that purpose to examine such books and documents at all reasonable times and make copies or extracts therefrom and give to the Lender all information with regard to the said business which he may reasonably require;

( ) Not to receive compound or release any of the said book debts or do anything whereby the recovery of the same may be impeded delayed or prevented without the consent of the Lender.

Continue as in Precedent 1

Include the following provisos

---

[19] As to goodwill, see p. 37, *supra*. As to the use of the mortgagor's trade name, see *Beazley* v. *Soares* (1882), 22 Ch. D. 660.

[20] As to book debts, a mortgage in this form will be merely equitable until notice is given to the debtors; Law of Property Act 1925, s. 136 (1); and see p. 113, *supra*. The giving of notice will inevitably impair the mortgagor's credit; see p. 113, *supra*. A provision that the lender will not give notice of the mortgage to the debtors until default may be included. The power of attorney which is included in this precedent (see p. 700, *infra*) is intended to secure the lender's position in the absence of notice to the debtors. But in the event of the borrower's bankruptcy such form may be useless; see p. 113, *supra*.

( ) It shall not be incumbent on the Lender to take any steps or institute any proceedings for the recovery of the several debts and moneys hereby mortgaged or any of them nor shall the Lender be answerable for any loss arising from his having neglected to take such steps or institute such proceedings.[1]

( ) It shall be lawful for the Lender after the statutory power of sale has become exercisable to enter into any arrangement or accept any composition in relation to the debt hereby assigned without the concurrence of the Borrower and any such arrangement or composition shall be binding on the Borrower[2].

And add the following clause

The BORROWER HEREBY APPOINTS the Lender and the persons deriving title under the Lender his attorney or attorneys in his name and on his behalf to demand sue for receive and give effectual discharges for all or any of the book or other debts or other moneys hereby mortgaged.

Continue as in Precedent 1.

11. Mortgage and general charge by limited company

THIS MORTGAGE AND GENERAL CHARGE[3] is made the ... day of ... BETWEEN [*the company*] whose registered office is situate at [*address*] (hereinafter called "the Company") of the first part [*the lender*] of [*address and description*] (hereinafter called "the Lender") of the second part and [*the sureties*] of [*addresses and descriptions*] (hereinafter called "the Sureties")[4] of the third part

WHEREAS:

(1) The Company is the estate owner, *etc., continue as in Precedent* 1

(2) The Lender has agreed to lend to the Company the sum of £ ... upon having the repayment thereof with interest thereon at the rate hereinafter mentioned secured in manner hereinafter appearing

(3) The Sureties have agreed to join in this deed as sureties for the Company in manner hereinafter appearing

NOW, *etc., as in Precedent* 1, *substituting "Company" for "Borrower"* THIS DEED WITNESSETH as follows:

1. The Company and the Sureties HEREBY JOINTLY AND SEVERALLY COVENANT with the Lender [*continue as in Precedent* 1].

2. [*Charge; as Clause* 2, *Precedent* 1].

3. [*Proviso for redemption; as Clause* 3, *Precedent* 1].

---

[1] The lender should be protected against any liability in this respect: see *Ex parte Mure* (1778), 2 Cox Eq. Cas. 63; *Williams* v. *Price* (1824), 1 Sim. & St. 581.

[2] In this form the power conferred is not unreasonable, but a clause in general terms, conferring this power on the lender at any time can rarely be reasonably required by the lender.

[3] Or "THIS DEBENTURE". For debentures generally, see Ch. 7, *supra*.

[4] It is usual in the case of smaller private companies, to require some or all of the director/shareholders to join in the deed as guarantors.

4. For further securing the payment of the principal moneys interest and other moneys hereby covenanted to be paid the Company as beneficial owner HEREBY:

(1) CHARGES with the payment to the Lender of the said moneys:

    (*a*) by way of specific charge all its uncalled capital[5] for the time being and all other the freehold and leasehold property[6] now or at any time during the continuance of this security belonging to the Company; and

    (*b*) by way of floating security[7] all the undertaking and goodwill of the Company and all its property (other than the property hereinbefore charge by way of legal mortgage or specifically mortgaged or charged or specifically hereinafter assigned) assets and rights whatsoever and wheresoever both present and future but so that the Company shall not be at liberty save with the written consent of the Lender to create any mortgage or charge in priority to or *pari passu* with this security or to sell the undertaking of the Company or any portion thereof or to deal with its book or other debts or securities for money otherwise than by getting in and realising the same in the ordinary course of business

(2) ASSIGNS to the Lender the goodwill and connection of the business or businesses now or at any time during the continuance of this security carried on by or for the account of the Company upon any of the said properties hereinbefore charged by way of legal mortgage or specifically as aforesaid[8].

5. Notwithstanding anything hereinbefore contained the principal money hereby secured and all unpaid interest which has accrued hereunder shall become immediately payable:

(1) if the Company makes default for [30] days in the payment of any interest hereunder; or

(2) if a distress or execution is levied or issued against any of the property of the Company and is not paid within [14] days; or

(3) if an order is made or an effective resolution passed for winding up the Company; or

(4) if the Company ceases or threatens to cease to carry on its business or substantially the whole of its business; or

(5) if an incumbrancer takes possession or a receiver is appointed of any part of the assets of the Company; or

(6) if the Company is unable to pay its debts within the meaning of Section 223 of the Companies Act 1948 or any statutory modification or re-enactment thereof; or

(7) if the Company makes any default in observing or fulfilling any of its obligations hereunder (other than in regard to the payment of the said principal moneys or interest thereon).

---

[5] As to a mortgage of uncalled capital, see p. 124, *supra*.
[6] This creates a fixed equitable charge on such property. As to mortgages of future-acquired property, see p. 12, *supra*.
[7] For floating charges, see pp. 121 *et seq.*, *supra*.
[8] For mortgage of goodwill, see p. 37, *supra*. And see Precedent 10, note 19.

6. As regards the property hereinbefore charged by way of legal mortgage and specifically charged the Company and the Sureties HEREBY JOINTLY AND SEVERALLY FURTHER COVENANT with the Lender [*continue with covenants in Clause 4, Precedent 1, substituting "the said property" for "the mortgaged property" and "Company" for "Borrower"*] and adding

( ) That the company will carry on its business in a proper and efficient manner.

( ) That the Company will not without the written consent of the Lender sell or otherwise dispose of the whole or any substantial part of its undertaking or assets.

7. *Provisos as Clause 5, Precedent 1, and adding additional proviso from Precedent 6.*

8. *Clause 6, Precedent 1.*

9. *Clause 7, Precedent 1.*

10. (1) In this deed any reference to a receiver shall be deemed to include a reference to a receiver and manager;

(2) At any time after the principal moneys hereby secured shall have become payable the Lender may appoint by writing a receiver or receivers of the property hereby charged or any part thereof upon such terms as to remuneration and otherwise as he shall think fit provided that such remuneration shall not exceed a commission at the rate of £ [5] per cent. on the gross amount of all moneys received by such receiver and may from time to time remove any receiver so appointed and appoint another in his stead[9];

(3) A receiver so appointed shall be the agent of the Company and the Company shall be responsible for such receiver's acts and defaults and for his remuneration costs charges and expenses to the exclusion of liability on the part of the Lender;

(4) A receiver so appointed shall be entitled to exercise all powers conferred on a receiver by the Law of Property Act 1925[10] and by way of addition to and without limiting those powers such receiver shall have power:

(a) To take possession of and get in the property hereby charged;

(b) To carry on or concur in carrying on the business of the Company;

(c) To sell or concur in selling any of the property hereby charged or otherwise deal therewith on such terms in the interest of the Lender as he shall think fit provided always that section 103 of of the Law of Property Act 1925 shall not apply;

(d) To make any arrangement or compromise which he shall think fit expedient in the interests of the Lender;

(e) To do all such other acts and things as may be considered to be incidental or conducive to any of the matters and powers aforesaid and which the receiver may or can lawfully do as agent for the Company;

(5) The Company hereby irrevocably appoints any and every receiver appointed as aforesaid the attorney and attorneys of the Company

---

[9] As to the appointment of a receiver, see pp. 126, 300 *et seq.*, *supra.*
[10] S. 109: see pp. 301, 302, *supra.*

and in its name and on its behalf and as its act and deed to execute seal and deliver any deed assurance agreement instrument or act which may be required or may be deemed proper for the purposes aforesaid;

(6) The net profits of carrying on the said business of the Company and the net profits of any sale and all other money received by the receiver or receivers shall be applied by him or them after provision for all matters specified in paragraphs (i) (ii) and (iii) of sub-section (8) of section 109 of the Law of Property Act 1925[11] and sections 94 and 319 of the Companies Act 1948[12] in or towards satisfaction of all principal moneys and interest due to the Lender provided that any payment made by the receiver or receivers to the Lender may be made on account of principal moneys so due or on account of interest so due or partly in one way and partly in the other as the receiver or the receivers shall deem expedient. Any surplus shall be paid to the Company.

In Witness, etc.[13]

THE SCHEDULE

[Particulars of presently owned freehold or leasehold property subject to Legal Charge]

EQUITABLE MORTGAGES[14]

12. Memorandum under hand[15] to accompany deposit of title deeds

To [*the lender*] of [*address and description*]
[In consideration[16] of your forbearing to press for immediate repayment of the sum of £ ... now owing to you by me] I, [*the borrower*], of [*address and description*] HEREBY DECLARE that I have this day deposited with you the documents of title[17] specified in the Schedule hereunder to secure the repayment to you on demand of the [said] sum of £ ... [advanced by you to me (the receipt whereof I hereby acknowledge)] [and of every further sum which you may hereafter advance me] with interest[18] thereon at the rate of ... per cent. per annum [as to the said sum of £ ... from the date hereof and as to every further sum advanced from the date of such advance] payable by equal

---

[11] See p. 302, *supra*.
[12] These sections deal with the payment of preferential debts.
[13] For registration of company charges, see p. 184, *supra*. For registration otherwise than under the Companies Act, see p. 183, *supra*. As to registered land, see p. 185, *supra*.
[14] See, generally, pp. 11 *et seq.* and 44 *et seq.*, *supra*. As to equitable mortgages of registered land, see pp. 66 *et seq.*, *supra*.
[15] This mortgage not being under seal the power of sale and other powers conferred by the Law of Property Act 1925, s. 101, will not apply. The lender will have to apply to the Court for relief.
[16] Consideration (or forbearance) is necessary for an agreement to create a mortgage (see p. 48, *supra*), but not where there has been a deposit.
[17] Not all documents of title to the mortgaged property need be deposited (see p. 45, *supra*), but the lender's interest may be prejudiced if all the documents are not deposited (by being overreached; see p. 560, *supra*).
[18] Interest will be payable even if not mentioned, see p. 627, *supra*.

[quarterly] payments on the [*state days of payment*] in each year [AND I HEREBY UNDERTAKE when so required by you at my own cost to execute a legal mortgage of the property to which the said documents of title relate in your favour in such form and containing such covenants and provisions as you may reasonably require including provisions excluding Section 93 (relating to consolidation)[19] and Section 99 (1) (relating to mortgagor's power of leasing)[20] of the Law of Property Act 1925 for further securing repayment of the money secured by the said deposit][21,22].

Dated the ... day of ...

THE SCHEDULE

[*List of documents deposited*]

13. Memorandum under seal[1] to accompany deposit of title deeds

As in Precedent 12 *and add*

AND I FURTHER HEREBY DECLARE that I shall henceforth hold the said property as trustee[2] for executing such charge or mortgage as aforesaid and the statutory power of appointing a new trustee in my place shall be exercisable by you and the persons deriving title under you who shall have full power to make such appointment and to remove me from such trusteeship at your or their sole and unfettered will and pleasure notwithstanding that none of the events referred to in the said statutory power as conditions precedent to its exercise shall have occurred and further that on any such exercise of the said statutory power the party or parties exercising the same may appoint himself or themselves to be the new trustee or trustees.

AND I HEREBY IRREVOCABLY APPOINT you and the persons deriving title under you to be the attorney and attorneys[3] of me and the persons deriving title under me and in my or their names and on my or their behalf and as my or their act and deed or otherwise to sign seal and deliver and otherwise perfect any such legal or formal mortgage or registered charge as aforesaid or (without executing any such mortgage) any deed assurance or act which may be required or may be deemed proper on any sale by you of the said property or of any part thereof under the power of sale conferred by this security in

---

[19] See *Farmer* v. *Pitt*, [1902] 1 Ch. 954, and pp. 50, 511, *supra*.

[20] See pp. 342 *et seq.*, *supra*.

[21] An equitable mortgagee by deposit is entitled to call for a legal mortgage even in the absence of express agreement: see p. 49, *supra*. This undertaking should be registered as an estate contract under Class C (iv) of the Land Charges Act 1925, s. 10 (1): see pp. 52, 444, *supra*.

[22] For registration as a land charge, see pp. 51 *et seq.* and pp. 442 *et seq.*, *supra*. For registration of company charges, see pp. 181, *et seq.*, *supra*. For notice of (intended) deposit of land certificate, see pp. 66, 67, *supra*.

[1] The memorandum being under seal the power of sale and other powers conferred by the Law of Property Act 1925, s. 101, apply. As to the extent of the power of sale of an equitable mortgagee, see p. 379, *supra*.

[2] For the purpose of the declaration of trust, see p. 49, *supra*.

[3] For the purpose of the power of attorney, see p. 50, *supra*. A power of attorney may usefully be employed by way of security to receive the income of land where it is desired that the creditor shall not have any right to dispose of the land; see, *e.g.*, 1 Ency. Forms and Precedents (4th Edn.), 349.

order to vest in the purchaser the legal estate and all other my or their estate and interest in the said property or such part thereof as the case may be. This power of attorney is given by way of security.[4]

IN WITNESS, etc.

THE SCHEDULE

14. Equitable charge of land[5]

To [*the lender*] of [*address and description*]

I, [*the borrower*], of [*address and description*] HEREBY CHARGE the freehold [leasehold] property described in the Schedule hereto with the payment to you on the . . . day of . . . of the sum of £ . . . now advanced by you to me (the receipt whereof I hereby acknowledge) with interest thereon at the rate of . . . per cent. per annum from the date hereof and also if the said sum of £ . . . shall not be so repaid on the day aforesaid with the payment on the . . . day of . . . and the . . . day of . .. in every year of interest at the rate aforesaid on the principal money for the time being secured.

Dated the . . . day of . . .

THE SCHEDULE
[*Particulars of property charged*][6]

15. Memorandum[7] to accompany deposit of securities[8]

MEMORANDUM

To [*the lender*] of [*address and description*]

[In consideration of your forbearing to press for immediate repayment of the sum of £ . . . now owing to you by me] I, [*the borrower*] of [*address and description*] HEREBY DECLARE that I have this day deposited with you the securities listed in the Schedule hereto to the intent that they may be security for and charged with the repayment of the [said] sum of £ . . . [advanced by you to me (the receipt whereof I hereby acknowledge)]

I AGREE that I will on the . . . day of . . . next pay to you the said sum of £ . . . with interest thereon from the date hereof until repayment at the rate of . . . per cent. per annum

---

[4] See p. 50, *supra*.

[5] For equitable charges generally, see pp. 156 *et seq., supra*. The primary remedies of an equitable chargee are sale or the appointment of a receiver; see p. 158, *supra*.

[6] For registration of an equitable charge not secured by deposit of title deeds as a land charge under Class C (iii), Land Charges Act 1925, s. 10 (1), see pp. 52, 443, *supra*; for where the land charged is registered, see p. 70, *supra*. If the land is unregistered in a compulsory area a caution should be entered on the register against first registration (Land Registration Act 1925, s. 53; Land Registration Rules 1925, r. 64).

[7] In the case of a mortgage by deposit of shares, etc., there is an implied power of sale exercisable on reasonable notice: *Stubbs* v. *Slater*, [1910] 1 Ch. 632 (C.A.), and see p. 359, *supra*. If the memorandum is under seal the statutory power of sale under the Law of Property Act 1925, s. 101, will apply; see pp. 360 *et seq., supra*.

[8] For mortgages of shares generally, see pp. 109 *et seq., supra*.

PROVIDED that if I shall on the ... day of ... next pay to you the said sum of £ ... with interest thereon as from the date hereof at the rate aforesaid you will redeliver the said securities to me or as I shall direct.

I UNDERTAKE for myself and my personal representatives from time to time to execute all transfers powers of attorney and other documents (including a proper legal mortgage of the said securities) which you may require for perfecting your title to any securities subject hereto or for vesting or enabling you to vest the same in yourself or your nominee or in any purchaser.

The charge hereby created shall affect and the securities subject hereto shall include in addition to the securities mentioned in the Schedule hereto any securities substituted therefor and all stocks shares rights moneys or property accruing or offered at any time by way of redemption bonus preference option or otherwise to or in respect of any securities hereby charged and I UNDER-TAKE to deposit with or pay the same to you immediately upon the receipt thereof[9].

Dated the ... day of ...

or

IN WITNESS, etc.[10]

THE SCHEDULE

[List of securities deposited]

SECOND MORTGAGES[11]

16. Second or subsequent legal charge

THIS LEGAL CHARGE is made the ... day of ... BETWEEN [*parties as in Precedent* 1]

WHEREAS:

(1) The Borrower is seised of the property described in the First Schedule hereto (hereinafter called "the mortgaged property") for a legal estate in fee simple in possession subject [as mentioned in the said Schedule and] to the Legal Charge[s] [Mortgage[s] particulars of which are set out in the Second Schedule hereto (hereinafter called "the prior Mortgage[s]") but otherwise free from incumbrances

Or

(1) The Borrower is possessed of the property described in the First Schedule hereto (hereinafter called "the mortgaged property" for a legal estate for the residue of the term of years mentioned in the said Schedule subject to the rent covenants and conditions thereby reserved and contained

---

[9] A mortgage of shares probably does not extend, in the absence of express provision therefor, to a bonus issue, etc.: see p. 110, *supra*. The only real sanction for the enforcement of this provision is to make the loan repayable on demand.

[10] For notice to the company, see p. 111, *supra*. For stop notice, see p. 112, *supra*.

[11] For second and subsequent mortgages generally, see Ch. 11, *supra*. For the disadvantages of second mortgages, see pp. 171, 172, *supra*. For second mortgages of registered land, see pp. 70, 71, *supra*.

and subject also [as further mentioned in the said Schedule and] to the [Legal Charge[s] [Mortgage[s] particulars of which are set out in the Second Schedule hereto (hereinafter called "the prior Mortgage[s]") but otherwise free from incumbrances

(2) The principal sum of £ . . . remains owing on the security of the prior Mortgage but all interest thereon has been paid up to the date hereof [*or* together with the sum of £ . . . for interest thereon]

[*Or*

(2) There is now owing upon the security of the prior Mortgages the sums specified in the said particulars set out in the Second Schedule hereto but all interest thereon has been paid up to the date hereof [*or* together with the sums also specified in the said particulars for interest thereon]][12]

(3) [*Agreement for loan; as recital* (2), *Precedent* 1]

NOW in pursuance, *etc., as in Precedent* 1 THIS DEED WITNESSETH as follows:

1. [*Covenant for payment of principal and interest; See Clause* 1, *Precedent* 1].

2. The Borrower as beneficial owner HEREBY CHARGES BY WAY OF LEGAL MORTGAGE ALL That the mortgaged property [subject as mentioned in the First Schedule hereto and] subject to the prior Mortgage[s] and to the principal moneys and interest thereby secured with the payment to the Lender of the principal moneys interest and other money hereby covenanted to be paid by the Borrower or otherwise hereby secured.

[3. *Proviso for redemption as Clause* 3, *Precedent* 1].

Continue as in Precedent 1[13].

Add to Borrower's covenants (*if desired*)

( ) Duly and punctually to pay all interest payable in respect of the prior Mortgage[s] and from time to time to produce to the Lender on demand the receipts for every such payment

And continue

PROVIDED ALWAYS

(1) The statutory power of sale shall apply hereto with the following extension namely that the same shall become immediately exercisable by the Lender without notice to the Borrower

   (i) If the Borrower shall be adjudicated bankrupt have a receiving order made against him or enter into any arrangement or composition with his creditors; or

   (ii) If the interest secured by the prior Mortgage[s] shall be in arrear and unpaid for [14] days after the same shall have become due; or

---

[12] It is desirable to recite the state of the prior mortgage to give the lender a remedy under the covenants for title implied by the mortgagor mortgaging as beneficial owner (should a larger sum than that recited be owing), and to bind the mortgagor in case of a sale by the second mortgagee.

[13] The covenants to insure and repair may be in the form appropriate to mortgaged leasehold property; see notes 20 and 2, p. 681, *supra*.

(iii) If the Borrower shall fail on demand to produce to the Lender any receipts for the payment of interest under the prior Mortgage[s]; or

(iv) If any step shall be taken or proceedings instituted by way of sale or otherwise for the purpose of enforcing the prior Mortgage[s]

Continue as in Precedent 1

And add to provisos.

( ) The Lender may settle and pass the accounts of any person in whom the prior Mortgage[s] may for the time being be vested and all accounts so settled and passed shall as between the Lender and Borrower be conclusive and binding on the Borrower.

Continue as in Precedent 1[14].

THE FIRST SCHEDULE above referred to

[*Particulars of mortgaged property*]

THE SECOND SCHEDULE above referred to

[*Particulars of prior mortgage[s]*]

17. Second or subsequent mortgage of freeholds by demise[15]

THIS MORTGAGE is made the ... day of ... BETWEEN [*parties and recitals as in Precedent 16*]

NOW in pursuance, *etc., as in Precedent 1* THIS DEED WITNESSETH as follows:

1. [*Covenant for payment of principal and interest as in Precedent 1*].

2. The Borrower as beneficial owner HEREBY DEMISES unto the Lender ALL That the mortgaged property TO HOLD the same unto the Lender for the term of [3,000[16]] years and [one[17]] day[s] from the date hereof without impeachment of waste [subject as mentioned in the First Schedule and] subject to the prior Mortgage[s] and to the principal moneys and interest thereby secured and also subject to the proviso for cesser hereinafter contained.

[3. *Proviso for cesser; see Clause 3, Precedent 3*].
Continue as in Precedent 16[18].

---

[14] Notice of the subsequent mortgage should be given to the first mortgagee; see Precedent 19, *infra*. The subsequent mortgagee should either obtain the title deeds (but these will usually be held by the first mortgagee) or register his mortgage as a land charge of Class C (i) under Land Charges Act 1925, s. 10 (1); see pp. 51, 52, 443, *supra*. For second or subsequent mortgages of registered land, see pp. 70–71, 171, *supra*.

[15] See generally, p. 170, *supra*. See also the notes to Precedent 16, *supra*.

[16] Or whatever is the term under the prior mortgage. Where the prior mortgage is a legal charge it takes effect as though a term of 3,000 years had been granted: Law of Property Act 1925, s. 87 (1).

[17] Each subsequent mortgage should be for a term one day longer than the prior mortgage. But this is not essential: Law of Property Act 1925, s. 149 (5).

[18] For notice to the first mortgagee and registration, see note 14 to Precedent 16, *supra*.

18. Second or subsequent mortgage of leaseholds by sub-demise[19]

THIS MORTGAGE is made the ... day of ... BETWEEN [*parties and recitals as in Precedent* 16]

And also (*where appropriate*)

(4) The lessor's consent hereto has been duly obtained

NOW in pursuance, *etc.*, *as in Precedent* 1 THIS DEED WITNESSETH as follows:

1. [*Covenant for payment of principal and interest as in Precedent* 1].

2. The Borrower as beneficial owner HEREBY DEMISES unto the Lender ALL That the mortgaged property To HOLD the same unto the Lender for the residue now unexpired of the term created by the said Lease except the last [9][20] days thereof [subject as mentioned in the First Schedule and] subject to the prior Mortgage[s] and to the principal moneys and interest thereby secured and also subject to the proviso for cesser hereinafter contained.

[3. *Proviso for cesser; See Clause* 3, *Precedent* 4].

Continue as in Precedent 16[1].

19. Notice of second mortgage from second to first mortgagee[2]

To [*the first mortgagee*][3]

[*Address*]

As solicitors for [*the second mortgagee*] of [*address*] we hereby give you notice that by a [Mortgage] [Legal Charge] dated the ... day of ... and made between [*the borrower*] of the one part and [*the second mortgagee*] of the other part the property comprised in the [Mortgage] [Legal Charge] dated the ... day of ... and made between the said [*the borrower*] of the one part and yourself [*or the original mortgagee*] of the other part has been mortgaged [charged] to [*the second mortgagee*] to secure the sum of £ ... and interest at the rate of ... per cent. per annum.

Dated ...

[*Signature and address of Solicitors*]

---

[19] See generally, p. 170, *supra*. See also the notes to Precedent 16, *supra*.

[20] This assumes the prior mortgage was for the term of the lease less the last 10 days thereof. Each subsequent mortgage should be for a term one day longer than the previous one. But this is not essential: Law of Property Act 1925, s. 149 (5).

[1] See note 18, p. 708, *supra*.

[2] See generally, p. 171, *supra*. Although registration of a mortgage as a land charge constitutes actual notice (Law of Property Act 1925, ss. 197, 198) this notice should be given.

[3] As to service of notices, see p. 365, *supra*.

TRANSFERS[4]

20. Transfer of mortgage. Mortgagor not a party[5]

THIS TRANSFER OF MORTGAGE is made the ... day of ... BETWEEN [*the transferor*] of [*address and description*] (hereinafter called "the Mortgagee") of the one part and [*the transferee*][6] of [*address and description*] (hereinafter called "the Transferee") of the other part

SUPPLEMENTAL to a Legal Charge [Mortgage] dated the ... day of ... and made between ... of the one part and [*the original mortgagee*] [the Mortgagee] of the other part

WHEREAS:

(1) The said [*the original mortgagee*] died on the ... day of ... and Probate of his Will dated the ... day of ... was [*or* Letters of Administration to his estate were] granted to the Mortgagee out of the Principal [...District] Probate Registry on the ... day of ...

[*Or*

(1) By a Transfer of Mortgage dated the ... day of ... and made between the said [*the original mortgagee*] of the one part and the Mortgagee of the other part the benefit of the said Legal Charge [Mortgage] was transferred to the Mortgagee as therein stated]

[*Or*

(1) The benefit of the said Legal Charge [Mortgage] is now [or remains] vested in the Mortgagee]

(2) The principal sum of £ ... remains owing upon the security of the said Legal Charge [Mortgage] but all interest thereon has been paid up to the date hereof [*or* together with the sum of £ ... for interest thereon]

(3) The Transferee has agreed to pay to the Mortgagee the sum of £ ... upon having such transfer of the benefit of the said Legal Charge [Mortgage] as is hereinafter contained

NOW in pursuance of the said agreement and in consideration of the sum of £ ... now paid by the Transferee to the Mortgagee (the receipt whereof the Mortgagee hereby acknowledges) THIS DEED WITNESSETH that the

---

[4] For transfers generally, see Ch. 14, *supra*. For transfers of registered charges use printed form of Form 54, Land Registration Rules 1925; application form A4 with fee as per Land Registration Fee Order 1976, para. V. And see p. 65, *supra*. For the statutory form, see Law of Property Act 1925, Sched. 3, Form No. 1.

[5] The mortgagor will usually only be a party where the transfer is made under the Law of Property Act 1925, s. 95 (transfer in lieu of discharge; see p. 546, *supra*). For the advantages of the mortgagor being a party, see p. 251, *supra*. Where it is not possible to join the mortgagor, inquiry should be made as to the state of the mortgage debt.

[6] Where there are several transferees use the above form, substituting "Transferees" for "Transferee", and otherwise modify as required, and add before the acknowledgement of receipt after "the sum of £ ... now paid by the Transferees" the words "out of money belonging to them on a joint account". These words are not strictly necessary, but are usually included (see Precedent 1C, p. 687, *supra*, footnote 9).

Mortgagee as mortgagee[7] [*or* as personal representative of the said [*the original mortgagee*] deceased] HEREBY CONVEYS AND TRANSFERS to the Transferee the benefit of the said Legal Charge [Mortgage]

[*Where the transfer is by a personal representative add*

And HEREBY DECLARES that he has not previously hereto given or made any conveyance or assent in respect of any legal estate in the mortgaged property or any part thereof

And HEREBY ACKNOWLEDGES the right of the Transferee to the production of the Probate of the Will [*or* the Letters of Administration to the estate] of the said [*the original mortgagee*] deceased (the possession of which is retained by the Mortgagee) and to delivery of copies thereof]

IN WITNESS, etc.[8]

21. Transfer by personal representative to beneficiary[9]

THIS TRANSFER OF MORTGAGE is made the ... day of ... BETWEEN [*the personal representative[s]*] of [*address[es] and description[s]*] (hereinafter called "the Personal Representative[s]") of the one part and [*the beneficiary*] of [*address and description*] (hereinafter called "the Beneficiary") of the other part

SUPPLEMENTAL to a Legal Charge [Mortgage] dated the ... day of ... and made between [*the original mortgagor*] of the one part [*the original mortgagee*] of the other part

WHEREAS:

(1) The said [*the original mortgagee*] died on the ... day of ... and Probate of his Will dated the ... day of ... was [*or* Letters of Administration to his estate were] granted to the Personal Representative[s] out of the Principal [... District] Probate Registry on the ... day of ...

Or

(1) [*The deceased*] was at the date of his death hereinafter recited entitled to the benefit of the said Legal Charge [Mortgage]

(2) The said [*the deceased*] died on the ... day of ... and Probate of his Will dated the ... day of ... was [*or* Letters of Administration to his estate were] granted to the Personal Representative[s] out of the Principal [... District] Probate Registry on the ... day of ...].

( ) The Personal Representative[s] has [have] duly paid and discharged all debts funeral and testamentary expenses and death duties payable out of the estate of the said [*the original mortgagee*] [*the deceased*]

---

[7] This implies a covenant that the mortgagee has not incumbered: Law of Property Act 1925, s. 76 (1) (F), Sched. 2, Pt. VI. Accordingly a mortgagee should not transfer as such where a sub-mortgage has been made.

[8] Notice of the transfer should be given to the mortgagor; see Precedent 23, *infra*. The transferor should hand over the title deeds (if he has them).

[9] For the use of a transfer rather than an assent, see footnote (g) p. 257, *supra*. A registered charge may be transferred by transfer (in Form 54) or by assent (in Forms 56 or 57); Land Registration Act 1925, s. 43, automatically passes the mortgage debt, so that the difficulties that arise in unregistered conveyancing do not apply.

( ) In the administration of the said estate the Beneficiary is entitled to have the Legal Charge [Mortgage] transferred to him and the Personal Representative[s] has [have] agreed to make this transfer accordingly.

NOW in consideration of the premises THIS DEED WITNESSETH as follows:

1. The Personal Representative[s] as personal representative[s] of the said [*the deceased*] deceased HEREBY CONVEY[S] AND TRANSFER[S] to the Beneficiary the benefit of the said Legal Charge [Mortgage].

2. The Personal Representative[s] HEREBY DECLARE[S] that he [they] has [have] not previously hereto given or made any conveyance, *etc., continue as in Precedent* 20.

3. The Personal Representative[s] HEREBY ACKNOWLEDGE[S] the right of the Beneficiary to the production of the Probate of the Will, *etc., continue as in Precedent* 20.

IN WITNESS, etc.[10]

22. Transfer of mortgage on appointment of new trustees[11]

THIS TRANSFER OF MORTGAGE is made the ... day of ... BETWEEN [*the continuing* [*and retiring*] *trustees*] of [*addresses and descriptions*] (hereinafter called "the Mortgagees") of the one part and [*the continuing* [*and new*] *trustees*] of [*addresses and descriptions*] (hereinafter called "the Transferees") of the other part

SUPPLEMENTAL to a Legal Charge [Mortgage] dated the ... day of ... and made between [*the mortgagor*] of the one part and [*the original mortgagee*] [*or* the Mortgagees] of the other part

WHEREAS:

(1) [*State of mortgage debt; as recital* (2), *Precedent* 20]

[*If transferors not original mortgagees*

(2) The benefit of the said Legal Charge [Mortgage] is now vested in the Mortgagees]

(3) The Transferees have become jointly entitled in equity to the benefit of the said Legal Charge [Mortgage] and accordingly the Mortgagees have agreed at the request of the Transferees to execute such transfer of the benefit thereof as is hereinafter contained

NOW in consideration of the premises THIS DEED WITNESSETH that the Mortgagees as mortgagees HEREBY CONVEY AND TRANSFER to the Transferees the benefit of the said Legal Charge [Mortgage].

IN WITNESS, etc.

---

[10] Notice of the transfer should be endorsed on the Probate or Letters of Administration; see Administration of Estates Act 1925, s. 36 (5).
See further note 8, Precedent 20, *supra*.
[11] See, generally, pp. 255, 256, *supra*. Land mortgaged to secure trust moneys (other than land conveyed on trust for securing debentures or debenture stock) cannot be vested in new trustees by a vesting declaration: Trustee Act 1925, s. 40 (4) (a). Notice of the transfer should be given to the mortgagor; see Precedent 23, p. 713, *infra*.

23. Notice of transfer by transferee to mortgagor[12]

To [*the mortgagor or person entitled to equity of redemption*]

[*Address*]

As Solicitors for [*the transferee*] of [*address*] we hereby give you notice that by a Transfer of Mortgage dated the ... day of ... and made between [*the original mortgagee or other transferor*] of the one part and the said [*the transferee*] of the other part the benefit of a Legal Charge [Mortgage] dated the ... day of ... and made between yourself [*or the original mortgagor*] of the one part and [*the original mortgagee*] of the other part for securing the sum of £ ... and interest at the rate of ... per cent. per annum has been transferred to the said [*the transferee*] to whom all payments of principal and interest must in future be made.

Dated ...   [*Signature and address of Solicitors*]

DISCHARGES[13]

24. Statutory receipt on discharge of mortgage[14]

I, [*the original mortgagee*[15] *or transferee*] of [*address and description*] HEREBY ACKNOWLEDGE that I have this ... day of ... received the sum of £ ... representing the [balance remaining owing in respect of] principal money[16] secured by the [annexed] within [above] written Legal Charge [Mortgage] together with all interest and costs the payment having been made by [the ... within [above] named [the said] [*original mortgagor*]] [*or present mortgagor*][17] of [*address and description*] [This receipt does not operate as a transfer][18].

As WITNESS, etc.[19]

---

[12] For notice of transfer generally, see p. 256, *supra*.
[13] See generally Part VIII, *supra*.
[14] See generally pp. 548, *et seq.*, *supra*. For form see Law of Property Act 1925, Sched. 3, Form No. 2. For discharge of registered charge see p. 553, *supra*.
[15] Where the payment is made to the personal representative(s) of the mortgagee the acknowledgement may, but need not, be made by the personal representative(s) expressly stated to be such and include a declaration that there has been no previous assent or conveyance in addition to an acknowledgement for production (see Precedent 20, *supra*).
     As regards receipts by the survivor(s) of joint beneficial mortgages, see Law of Property Act 1925, s. 111 (p. 258, *supra*) and s. 113 (p. 255, *supra*).
[16] An endorsed receipt only effects an automatic reconveyance when it is for the whole of the moneys secured at the date of repayment. See further p. 548, *supra*.
[17] Where the payment is made by the personal representatives of the mortgagor the receipt may, but need not, state their capacity and after their names may be added "out of a fund properly applicable for the discharge of the said Legal Charge [Mortgage]" (see Law of Property Act 1925, s. 115 (2) (b), p. 549, *supra*).
     Where the payment is made by other persons entitled to the immediate equity of redemption there may be added after their names "the persons entitled to the immediate equity of redemption."
[18] The statement that the receipt does not operate as a transfer prevents the receipt operating as a transfer where the money appears to have been paid by a person who is not entitled to the immediate equity of redemption; see Law of Property Act 1925, s. 115 (2) (a), p. 548, *supra*.
[19] The receipt may be under hand, unless made by a building society under the Building Societies Act 1962, see p. 552, *supra*.

24A. Notice of intention to pay off mortgage money by mortgagor to mortgagee[20]

To [*the mortgagee*]

[*Address*]

As Solicitors for [*the mortgagor*] of [*address*] we hereby give you notice that the said [*the mortgagor*] will at the expiration of [six][1] months from the service of this notice pay to you the principal money interest and other moneys (if any) then owing on the security of the Legal Charge [Mortgage] dated the ... day of ... and made between [the said [*the mortgagor*] or [*the original mortgagor*] of the one part and yourself [*or the original mortgagee*] of the other part.

Dated   [*Signature and address of Solicitors*]

25. Release or surrender of part of mortgaged property[2]

THIS SURRENDER[3] AND RELEASE is made the ... day of ...
BETWEEN [*the mortgagee*] of [*address and description*] (hereinafter called "the Mortgagee")[4] of the one part and [*the mortgagor*] of [*address and description*] (hereinafter called "the Borrower") of the other part

SUPPLEMENTAL to a Legal Charge [Mortgage] dated the ... day of ... and made between the Borrower of the one part and the Mortgagee of the other part[5]

WHEREAS:

(1) [*State of mortgage debt; as recital* (2), *Precedent* 20]

(2) The Mortgagee has agreed with the Borrower that in consideration of the payment by the Borrower to the Mortgagee of the sum of £ ... in part discharge of the said sum of £ ... [*amount owing for principal and interest (if any)*] the Mortgagee shall surrender and release to the Borrower such part of the mortgaged property as is described in the First Schedule hereto

---

[20] See generally, p. 538, *supra*. No notice is required for an equitable mortgage by deposit with or without a memorandum.

[1] Or the period specified in the mortgage.

[2] Where the whole of the mortgaged property is to be released to enable the mortgagor to sell free from mortgage either the mortgage should be discharged by a statutory receipt before the conveyance or the mortgagee should join in the conveyance to surrender and release the property sold. Where a sale is not contemplated a statutory receipt should be used if the release is in consideration of the repayment of all the moneys secured by the mortgage, but otherwise this deed should be used; see p. 581, *supra*. For partial discharge of registered charge use printed form of Form 53 adding (where the discharge is to part of the land only) "as to the land shown and edged with red on the accompanying plan, signed by me, being part of the land charged by the said charge", or (where as to part of the money only) "to the extent of £ ... "; see note to Form 53, Land Registration Rules 1925. As to partial discharge of leasehold property, see p. 582, *supra*. As to release of part of equitably mortgaged property, see p. 581, *supra*.

[3] "Surrender" is appropriate in the case of a mortgage by demise. "Release" is more appropriate for a legal charge. But the expression "Surrender and Release" is commonly used in both cases and sometimes the deed is called a "Reconveyance".

[4] Or "Lender" if the original mortgagee, and so called in the mortgage.

[5] Or as appropriate.

NOW in pursuance of the said agreement and in consideration of the sum of
£ ... paid by the Borrower to the Mortgagee (the receipt whereof the
Mortgagee hereby acknowledges) in reduction of the said mortgage debt[6]
THIS DEED WITNESSETH as follows:

1. The Mortgagee as mortgagee HEREBY SURRENDERS AND RELEASES
unto the Borrower ALL That the property described in the First Schedule
hereto To HOLD the same unto the Borrower discharged from all principal
moneys and interest secured by and from all claims and liability under the
said Legal Charge [Mortgage] [*add if mortgage by demise* and to the intent
that so far as regards the property hereby surrendered and released the term
created by the said Mortgage shall merge and be extinguished in the reversion
immediately expectant thereon] PROVIDED ALWAYS that nothing herein
contained shall operate to prejudice or affect the security of the Mortgagee
under the said Legal Charge [Mortgage] in respect of so much of the property
comprised therein as is not hereby surrendered and released for the payment
to the Mortgagee of so much of the said principal moneys as remains owing
thereunder and the interest thereon.

2. The Mortgagee HEREBY ACKNOWLEDGES the right of the Borrower to
the production of the documents mentioned in the Second Schedule hereto
(the possession of which is retained by the Mortgagee) and to delivery of
copies thereof[7].

IN WITNESS, etc.

THE FIRST SCHEDULE above referred to
[*Particulars of property released*]

THE SECOND SCHEDULE above referred to
[*Documents retained by mortgagee*]

26. Receipt endorsed on memorandum of deposit of title deeds[8]

I, the within named [*the mortgagee*[9]], HEREBY ACKNOWLEDGE that I have
this day of ... received from the within named [*the mortgagor*] the sum of
£ ... representing the principal moneys and interest referred to within.

27. Release of rights of occupation under Matrimonial Homes Act 1967[10]

THIS DEED[11] OF RELEASE is made the ... day of ... BETWEEN [*the
spouse entitled to the charge*] of [*address and description*] (hereinafter called

---

[6] For appropriation of payments to principal or interest, see pp. 543–545, *supra*.
[7] See *Yates* v. *Plumbe* (1854), 2 Sm. & G. 174, and p. 563, *supra*, for the mortgagor's
right to such acknowledgement.
[8] Or other equitable mortgages (save those by assignment) and charges. See generally,
p. 555, *supra*.
[9] Adapt Precedent 24, *supra*, if there has been a transfer of the mortgage. For
transfer of equitable mortgages, see p. 253, *supra*.
[10] See generally, pp. 216 *et seq.*, *supra*. And see Precedent 7, *supra*.
[11] The release may simply be in writing: Matrimonial Homes Act 1967, s. 6 (1).

"the Wife [Husband]") of the one part and [*the other spouse*] of [*address and description*] (hereinafter called "the Husband [Wife]") of the other part

WHEREAS:

[*Recitals* (1) *and* (2), *Precedent* 7]

(3) The Wife[12] has agreed with the Husband to release the property from the Wife's Charge

(4) In the negotiations leading to the said agreement the Wife (as she hereby admits) has been advised by Messrs. [*name*] Solicitors, of [*address*] as to the effect of this release

NOW in pursuance of the said agreement the Wife as mortgagee HEREBY RELEASES the property from the Wife's Charge and all rights remedies claims and demands thereunder to the intent that the Husband shall hold the property freed and discharged from the Wife's Charge[13] [and UNDERTAKES with the Husband to apply to H.M. Land Registry for the cancellation of the registration thereof].

IN WITNESS, etc.

THE SCHEDULE above referred to

28. Solicitor's undertaking to discharge mortgage[14]

To [*the purchaser of the mortgaged property or his Solicitors*]

Re: [*description of mortgaged property*]

In consideration of your today completing the purchase of [*description of the property*] we hereby undertake forthwith to pay over to [*the mortgagee*] the money required to redeem the Mortgage [Legal Charge] dated and to forward the receipted Mortgage [Legal Charge] to you as soon as it is received by us from [*the mortgagee*]

[*Signature and address of vendor's Solicitors*]

29. Appointment of receiver[15]

THIS APPOINTMENT is made the ... day of ... BETWEEN [*the mortgagee*] of [*address and description*] (hereinafter called "the Mortgagee") of the one part and [*the receiver*] of [*address and description*] (hereinafter called "the Receiver") of the other part

WHEREAS:

(1) By a Legal Charge [Mortgage] dated the ... day of ... and made between [*the mortgagor*] of the one part and [*the original mortgagee*] [*or* the Mortgagee] of the other part the freehold [leasehold] property described in

---

[12] It is assumed for the remainder of this form that the wife has the charge.
[13] This form may be adapted for a release of a mortgage or charge in other circumstances.
[14] See generally, p. 559, *supra*.
[15] For receivers generally, see Ch. 18, *supra*. For provisions as to receivers for inclusion in mortgage, see p. 701, *supra*. As to when the power of appointment arises and is exercisable, see pp. 300 *et seq.*, *supra*.

the Schedule hereto was charged by the said [*the mortgagor*] in favour of the [said [*the original mortgagee*]] [Mortgagee] [*or* was demised by the said [*the mortgagor*] to the said [*the original mortgagee*] [Mortgagee]] for the term of ... years from the date thereof] to secure the sum of £ ... with interest thereon at the rate of ... per cent. per annum

(2) The said Legal Charge [Mortgage] provides, *inter alia*, as follows:

"[*Set out receiver clause and/or any provision the breach of which has given rise to the power to appoint a receiver*]"

(3) On the ... day of ... notice was served by the Mortgagee on the said [*the mortgagor*] requiring payment of the said principal sum of £ ... but no part thereof has been paid by the said [*the mortgagor*] *or recite what other circumstances have given rise to the power to appoint the receiver*

NOW THIS DEED WITNESSETH as follows:

1. In exercise of his statutory power in that behalf[16] [*or* in pursuance of the said provisions contained in the said Legal Charge [Mortgage]] the Mortgagee HEREBY APPOINTS the Receiver to be the receiver of the [rents profits and] income of the mortgaged property.

2. The Mortgagee hereby delegates to the Receiver the power of leasing and accepting surrenders of leases conferred on him by the Law of Property Act 1925 [17,18].

3. The Receiver shall be entitled for his remuneration and in satisfaction of all costs charges and expenses incurred by him as receiver to retain out of any money received by him a commission at the rate of 5 per cent. on the gross amount of all money received[19].

[4. The Mortgagee hereby directs the Receiver out of the money received by him to insure to the extent which the Mortgagee might have insured and keep insured against loss or damage by fire all buildings effects or property of an insurable nature comprised in the said Legal Charge [Mortgage][20]].

[5. The Mortgagee further directs the Receiver to apply the residue (if any) of the money received by him after providing for the matters specified in the first four paragraphs of sub-section (8) of Section 109 of the Law of Property Act 1925 and subject to the provisions of that Act as to the application of insurance money in or towards discharge of the principal money secured by the said Legal Charge [Mortgage][1]].

IN WITNESS, etc.[2]

THE SCHEDULE above referred to

[*Description of mortgaged property*]

---

[16] Law of Property Act 1925, ss. 101 (1) (iii), 109.

[17] Law of Property Act 1925, ss. 99 (13), 100 (13).

[18] Where the appointment is pursuant to provisions contained in the mortgage deed these should be set out in the appointment in the same manner.

[19] See Law of Property Act 1925, s. 109 (6). The maximum is 5 per cent. Accordingly where property is mortgaged in respect of which the appointment of a receiver would be an appropriate remedy express provision as to the receiver and his remuneration should be included on the mortgage; see, *e.g.*, p. 702, *supra*.

[20] See Law of Property Act 1925, s. 109 (7).

[1] For section 109, see p. 301, *supra*.

[2] The Law of Property Act 1925, s. 109 (1), requires writing only but the appointment is usually made under seal. Stamp 50p. as a letter or power of attorney whether under seal or not.

29A. Notice of appointment of receiver by mortgagee to tenant[3]

To [*the tenant*]

[*Address*]

As Solicitors for [*the mortgagee*] of [*address*] the mortgagee under a Legal Charge [Mortgage] dated the ... day of ... and made between [*the original mortgagor*] of the one part and [*the original mortgagee*] [*or* the said [*the mortgagee*]] of the other part of [amongst other properties] the property [*description*] now occupied by you we hereby give you notice that by an Appointment dated the ... day of ... and made between the said [*the mortgagee*] as mortgagee of the one part and [*the receiver*] of the other part the said [*the receiver*] was duly appointed receiver of the income of the mortgaged property. And we require you to pay to the said [*the receiver*] as agent of the said ... [*the mortgagor*] at [*address*] and to no other person all rent now due and henceforth to become due in respect of the property now occupied by you until you receive further notice. This notice is not a recognition that your tenancy is binding on the said ... [*the mortgagee*].

Dated ...   [*Signature and address of Solicitors*]

30. Notice requiring payment of mortgage moneys prior to issue of summons for possession[4]

To [*the mortgagor*][5]

[*Address*]

As Solicitors for [*the mortgagee*] we hereby require you to pay to us forthwith the moneys now owing under the [Legal Charge] [Mortgage] dated the ... day of ... and made between yourself [*or the original mortgagor*] of the one part and [the said [*the mortgagee*] [*or the original mortgagee*]] of the other part namely £ ... made up as to £ ... in respect of the [balance of the] principal money and as to £ ... in respect of interest together with interest accruing at the rate of ... per day from the date hereof[6].

Dated ...   [*Signature and address of Solicitors*]

---

[3] Or the notice may be given by the receiver himself.
[4] See *Chatsworth Properties, Ltd.* v. *Effiom*, [1971] 1 All E.R. 604 (C.A.).
[5] As to service of notices, see p. 365, *supra*. As to notice to second and subsequent mortgages, see p. 364, *supra*.
[6] Notice of intention to sell on default of payment may be added. The statutory power of sale becomes exercisable, *inter alia*, where notice requiring payment of the mortgage money has been given and default has been made for three months after service of the notice: Law of Property Act 1925, s. 103 (i) (see p. 363, *supra*). In practice s. 103 is usually modified by the terms of the mortgage; see, *e.g.*, Clause 5 (1) Precedent 1, *supra*; Clause 7, Precedent 2, *supra*. In any case, the mortgagee will usually be relying on s. 103 (ii), *i.e.*, arrears of interest.
   If the mortgage money is not repaid within a short while (say 14 days) after receipt of the notice, or, if, after the mortgagor has requested time, it becomes apparent that the money will not be forthcoming, proceedings for possession should be commenced. By the time the order is effective the power of sale will be exercisable.
   It is not the practice to give a notice demanding delivery up of possession before action. Mortgagors are unlikely to take any point on this since in many cases they are only too willing for an order for possession to be made against them so that they can obtain alternative accommodation from the local authority.

31. Originating Summons by mortgagee of land for possession[7]

19 ... [8] No.

IN THE HIGH COURT OF JUSTICE

CHANCERY DIVISION

DISTRICT REGISTRY[9]

GROUP

BETWEEN   Plaintiff

and

Defendant

TO [*the Defendant*] of [*address*]

LET the Defendant, who is the mortgagor under the Legal Charge hereinafter mentioned, within 14 days after service of this Summons on him, inclusive of the day of service, cause an appearance to be entered to this Summons which is issued on the application of the Plaintiff [*name*] of [*address*] who is the mortgagee under the said Legal Charge.

By this Summons the Plaintiff claims[10]:

(1) Payment of all money due to the Plaintiff under the Legal Charge dated ... and made between the Defendant of the one part and the Plaintiff[11] of the other part and such costs as would be payable if this claim were the only relief granted[12];

(2) In default of the parties agreeing the amount so due all necessary accounts and inquiries;

(3) Foreclosure or sale;

(4) The appointment of a receiver of the mortgaged property;

(5) Delivery by the Defendant to the Plaintiff of vacant[13] possession of [*description of mortgaged property*[14]] charged by the Defendant to the Plaintiff by the Legal Charge;

(6) Further or other relief;

(7) Costs.

If the Defendant does not enter an appearance, etc.

DATED, etc.

---

[7] For the exclusive jurisdiction of the county court in most possession actions relating to dwelling-houses, see pp. 319 *et seq.*, *supra*.

[8] The letter to be included here is the initial of the (first) plaintiff's surname, or in the case of an application by a bank or building society the initial of the (first) defendant's surname; see *Practice Direction*, [1950] W.N. 513.

[9] An originating summons by which a mortgage action is begun may not issue out of any district registry, other than Liverpool or Manchester, unless the mortgaged property is situated in the district of the registry: R.S.C. Ord. 88, r. 3.

[10] Various relief is claimed although it is only possession which will be sought at the hearing. The inclusion of other relief adds little or nothing to the costs and has the advantage that if difficulties arise before, on or after the hearing, *e.g.*, with regard to the amount due under the mortgage, they can be dealt with under the summons. If possession only had been sought a fresh summons would be required.

[11] Or as the case may be.

[12] All costs, charges and expenses recoverable on foreclosure or sale are not necessarily recoverable under the covenant alone.

[13] It is to be doubted whether the inclusion of the word "vacant" adds anything; see p. 331, *supra*.

[14] The property should be adequately described, in order that a writ of possession may be completed as to enable the sheriff to identify the property; see p. 324, *supra*.

32. Affidavit in support of Originating Summons for possession
[*Heading as in Summons*]

I, [*Plaintiff*] of [*address and description*] make oath and say as follows:

1. I am the Plaintiff herein [*or* I am one of the Plaintiffs herein and I am authorised by my co-Plaintiff[s] to make this affidavit on [his] [her] [their] behalf]. I am able to depose to the facts and matters hereinafter mentioned from my own knowledge and from information supplied to me by the Solicitors acting for me [us] herein, Messrs. [*name*] of [*address*].

2. By a Legal Charge dated the . . . and made between the Defendant of the one part and myself this deponent [and my co-Plaintiffs *or the original mortgagee(s) as appropriate*] of the other part the freehold [leasehold] property known as [*description of property*] was charged by the Defendant by way of legal mortgage in [my] [our] favour [of the said *original mortgagee(s)* to secure the repayment to me [us] [the said *original mortgagee(s)*] of the sum of £ . . . together with interest thereon as therein mentioned. A true copy of the said Legal Charge[15] is now produced and shown to me marked " . . .[16]1".

3. The said Legal Charge contains the following provisions which are material to these proceedings:

   "[*Set out relevant clauses of Legal Charge*]".

If the Plaintiff is not original mortgagee show title to mortgage and exhibit transfer.

4. The Defendant is in default of payment of the [interest] [*or* instalments] payable under the said Legal Charge.

5. None of the said instalments [no interest] has been paid [since [*the date of last payment (if any)*]]].

6. The state of account between the Defendant and myself[17] is as follows:
   (i) Advance .. .. £
   (ii) Repayments .. .. £
   (iii) Amount of interest [instalments] in arrear at the date of summons and at the date hereof .. .. .. £
   (iv) The amount remaining due under the Legal Charge:
   In respect of principal .. .. £
   In respect of interest .. .. £
   Total amount remaining due .. .. .. £

[There is now produced and shown to me marked " . . .[16]2" a Schedule of payments containing particulars of the repayments made by the Defendant].

[7. By registered letter dated . . . my Solicitors gave the Defendant formal notice requiring payment of the principal and interest then due under the Legal Charge.[18]]

---

[15] The affidavit must exhibit a true copy of the mortgage and the original mortgage, or, in the case of a registered charge, the charge certificate must be produced at the hearing: R.S.C. Ord. 88, r. 6 (2).   [16] Insert initials of deponent.
[17] R.S.C. Ord. 88, r. 6 (3) requires these particulars. Where the plaintiff's claim includes a claim for interest to judgment, the affidavit must state the amount of a day's interest: R.S.C. Ord. 88, r. 6 (7). In practice, the plaintiff's solicitor is directed to bring a computation of interest into chambers.   [18] See Precedent 30, *supra.*

A true copy of that letter is now produced and shown to me marked " ...¹3". There is also now produced and shown to me marked " ...¹64" the original Advice of Delivery of the said registered letter signed by .....

8. Neither I nor my Solicitors have received any reply to this notice.

9. The Defendant has failed to pay to me or my Solicitors the said principal and interest or any part thereof.

10. The Defendant is in possession of the mortgaged property as mortgagor[19]. No other person is to the best of my knowledge in possession of the mortgaged property.

SWORN[20] at [*address*] this ... day of ...

before me

[*Commissioner's signature*]   [*Deponent's signature*]

A Commissioner for Oaths.

33. Particulars of Claim by mortgagee of land for possession[1]

IN THE   COUNTY COURT[2]

Plaint No.

BETWEEN

Plaintiff

and

Defendant

PARTICULARS OF CLAIM[3]

1. By a Legal Charge dated   and made between the Defendant of the one part and the Plaintiff of the other part the freehold [leasehold] property known as [*short description of property*] was charged by the Defendant by way of legal mortgage in favour of the Plaintiff to secure the repayment to the Plaintiff of the sum of £   together with interest thereon as therein mentioned.

2. The said Legal Charge contains the following provisions which are material to these proceedings:

[*Set out relevant clauses of the Legal Charge*]

---

[19] Where the plaintiff claims delivery of possession the affidavit must give particulars of every person who to the best of the plaintiff's knowledge is in a possession of the mortgage property: R.S.C. Ord. 88, r. 6 (4). If the mortgage creates a tenancy other than a tenancy at will between the mortgagor and mortgagee, the affidavit must show how and when the tenancy was determined and if by service of notice when the notice was duly served. Although possession is sought it is not the practice to give notice requiring delivery up of possession before action. See note 6, at end, Precedent 30, *supra*.

[20] It no longer matters that the affidavit is sworn before the issue of the summons: see *Practice Direction*, [1969] 2 All E.R. 639.

[1] See generally pp. 319, *et seq.* For forms of order, see County Court Practice 1976, pp. 856,857.

[2] The appropriate court is the one for the district in which the mortgaged property is situate: C.C.R. Ord. 2, r. 2.

[3] See, generally, as to the matters to be stated in the Particulars of Claim, C.C.R. Ord. 7, r. 7.

3. The mortgaged property consists of [*or* includes] a dwelling-house within the meaning of Part IV of the Administration of Justice Act 1970.

4. The net annual value for rating of the mortgaged property is £   [*or* does not exceed £1,000].

5. The Defendant is in default of payment of the interest [instalments] payable under the Legal Charge. None of the said instalments [no interest] has been paid [since *the date of the last payment (if any)*].

6. The state of account between the parties is as follows:

    (i) the amount of advance   £

   (ii) the sum payable from time to time under or in connection with the Legal Charge   £   (per week)

 (iii) the amount of such sums in arrear   £

 (iv) the amount remaining due under the Legal Charge   £

Interest is accruing on the said sum of £ ... at ... *per diem.*

7. By letter dated   the Plaintiff's Solicitors Messrs. of   gave the Defendant notice[4] requiring payment of the principal and interest then due under the Legal Charge. The said letter was duly delivered[5].

8. Neither the Plaintiff nor his Solicitors have received any reply to the said letter nor received payment of the said principal or interest nor any part thereof.

9. The Defendant is in possession of the mortgaged property as mortgagor.

10. The Plaintiff has not before the commencement of these proceedings taken any proceedings against the Defendant in respect of the mortgaged property and has not obtained possession thereof nor has he taken any proceedings against the Defendant in respect of the principal money or interest.

And the Plaintiff claims[6]:

  (1) Payment of all money due to the Plaintiff under the said Legal Charge and such costs as would be payable if this claim were the only relief granted;

  (2) In default of the parties agreeing the amount so due all necessary accounts and inquiries;

  (3) Foreclosure or sale;

  (4) Possession of the mortgaged property [*description*];

  (5) Further or other relief;

  (6) Costs.

[*Signature*]

Plaintiff's Solicitors, of [*address*] where they will accept service of proceedings on behalf of the Plaintiff

To the Registrar of the ...
County Court and to the Defendant

---

4 See Precedent 30, *supra.*
5 Delivery will be proved at the hearing by the Advice of Delivery.
6 See note 10, Precedent 31, *supra.*

34. Affidavit in support of Particulars of Claim[7]

[Heading as for Particulars of Claim]

I *[name]* of *[address and description]* make oath as follows:

1. I am the Plaintiff herein [*or* I am one of the Plaintiffs herein and I am authorised by my co-Plaintiff(s) to make this affidavit on behalf] [*or* I am the [Secretary] of the Plaintiff Company [Society] and I am authorised to make this affidavit on its behalf].

2. I crave leave to refer to the Particulars of Claim herein.

3. The said Legal Charge is now produced and shown to me marked *[initials of deponent* 1].

4. As to the state of account between the Defendant and myself [the parties] there is now produced and shown to me marked [2] a mortgage repayment book [card] [*or* a schedule of payments] containing particulars of the repayments made by the Defendant.

5. A true copy of the said letter dated the   is now produced and shown to me marked [3]. There is also now produced and shown to me marked [4] the original Advice of Delivery of the said letter.

6. The bundle of correspondence now produced and shown to me marked [5] contains true copies of letters from my Solicitors [the Plaintiff's Solicitors] to the Defendant [and the Defendant's replies thereto].

7. There is now produced and shown to me marked [6] a report by Mr. *[name]* [enquiry agent], of *[address]* in which he states what he had been able to discover with regard to the Defendant's means[8].

8. My means of knowledge I respectfully submit sufficiently herein appear.

SWORN at *[address]* this   day of

before me   *[Deponent's Signature]*

[Commissioner's signature]

A Commissioner for Oaths

---

[7] Unless the court otherwise orders, evidence in support of or in opposition to the plaintiff's claim may be given by affidavit: County Court (Amendment No. 5) Rules 1970. Building society officers, etc., will no doubt take advantage of this method which avoids having to be present in court. In some cases it may be appropriate to include some of the matters in this affidavit in the Particulars of Claim.

[8] Such a paragraph may be required to forestall the exercise by the court of the additional powers conferred by the Administration of Justice Act 1970, e.g., to adjourn, etc., either on the defendant's application therefor or on the court's own initiative. The plaintiff's own financial position may be relevant in considering the length and terms of the adjournment, etc. See, generally, pp. 326–330, *supra*.

Index

NOTE: Numbers in square brackets, thus [206], refer to footnotes

A

ABROAD
property situated, registration of charge
on, 183
mortgage of, 16–17

ABSOLUTE OWNER
powers to mortgage, 175

ACCOUNTS
consumer credit transaction, 153
errors, setting off and correcting,
610–612
foreclosure proceedings, in, 383, 396–397
interest, of. *See* INTEREST
mortgagee and assigns, against—
interest, over-payment of, 619
proceeds of sale, 618
purchase of mortgage debt under par,
616
shares, sale and purchase of, 619
transferee takes subject to, 618
mortgagee in possession, against—
allowances for repairs and improvements, 623
attornment by mortgagor, whether
affecting, 620
duty to render, 348–349
equitable possession, 621
form of, 623
inquiry as to possession, order for,
620
later incumbrancer, to, 349
mines and quarries, in case of, 351,
622
possession must be as mortgagee, 619
proceeds of sale, 349
rent, amount to be accounted for,
621
occupation, when chargeable,
349, 621
where collected by agent, 622
rents and profits, of, 620
rates at which charged, 349
rests, with—
debt paid off, after, 626
form of, 623
grounds for, 624
intervals of, 625
liability to, 625
order for, 624
receipts after master's certificate,
626
transfer of mortgage, liability after,
349
wilful default, on footing of, 619
mortgagor, against—
costs, for, 612–613
evidence of debt, 613
growing crops, position as to, 615

ACCOUNTS—*continued*
mortgagor, against—*continued*
improvements, whether allowance
for, 616
mortgagee's right to, 612
payments on account, allowance for,
614
receiver in possession, where, 616
rents, equitable mortgage, under, 615
legal mortgage, under, 614
solicitor—mortgagee, in case of, 614
mortgagor and mortgagee, between—
error in, charging and proving, 610
reopening for, 611
surcharge and falsification
for, 610
foreclosure action, in, 612
fraud, reopening for, 611
"just allowances", meaning, 651
new account, when ordered, 610
parties bound by, 609
proof in action for, 512
remainderman, when bound by, 609
reopening, order for, 610
solicitor—mortgagee, in case of, 611
special circumstances, pleading, 612
order for taking, in action for foreclosure, 396–397
order for taking, in action for redemption, 576
surcharge and falsification, 610–612

ACCRETIONS TO SECURITY
compensation for compulsory acquisition, 38
enfranchisement of leaseholds, by, 37
enlargement of long lease by, 36
equitable mortgage by deposit, in case
of, 47
goodwill of business, 37
leaseholds, to, 36, 37
mortgagor, improvements by, 36
substituted interest
acquired by 36
new lease, benefit of, to whom accruing,
36

ACKNOWLEDGMENT. *See also*
LIMITATION OF ACTIONS
extension of limitation period, 285–290,
566

ACQUIESCENCE
opening of foreclosure, as bar to, 408

ACTION
foreclosure. *See* FORECLOSURE
limitation period. *See* LIMITATION OF
ACTIONS
marshalling, pleadings in, 509
possession, for. *See* POSSESSION

D

FORECLOSURE—*continued*
proceedings—*continued*
parties to—*continued*
collateral security, mortgagor of, 392
co-mortgagees, 391
equity of redemption, owner of, 392
settlement of, 393
holder of the security, 390
judgment creditors, 394
personal representatives, 391, 393
subsequent incumbrancers, 391, 394
transferee of mortgage, 391
trustee in bankruptcy, 393
trustees, 393
pleadings, 395
registered land, in case of, 395
relief sought in, 395
security made in excess of power, validity in, 177
statement of claim, matters to be included in, 396
stay by bankruptcy court, 274–275
subsequent incumbrances, proof of, 293
redemption by incumbrancer, effect of, 399
proceedings after, 570
registered land, in case of, 388
right to—
equitable chargee, whether having, 384
mortgagee by deposit, of, 382, 384
legal mortgagee, 384
non-payment of debt when due, on, 382
proprietor of registered charge, 384
reversion, mortgagee of, 385
successive mortgagees, 384
sale in lieu of—
agreement to execute legal mortgage subsisting, where, 385
conduct of, 387, 409–410
discretionary remedy, as, 386
equitable charges, to realise, 386
interests bound by, 410
grounds for refusing, 387
interlocutory application, on, 386
judgment creditor, at instance of, 388
for, 409
jurisdiction to order, 385
mortgagee's consent, when required, 388
order for, 382
proceeds, payment into court, 387
registered land, in case of, 388
reserve price, fixing, 387
security for expenses, 409
ship, in case of, 389
terms on which ordered, 387
time allowed for payment before, 409
when ordered, 382
severance of title to property, effect of, 394
things in action, mortgage of, 383

FOREIGN SECURITY
enforcement by English court, 17
floating charge over, effect of, 17

FOREIGN SECURITY—*continued*
land abroad, mortgage of, 16
lex situs, application of, 16

FORFEITURE
leasehold, of, loss of security by, 599
mortgagor of leaseholds, incurred by, relief against, 23

FORGERY
mortgage, of, 244
husband and wife cases, 244
transfer, 252

FRAUD
constructive notice, effect on, 438
deceit of mortgagor, whether mortgagee postponed by, 450
equity of redemption, release obtained by, 526
foreclosure, opening by reason of, 395, 408
limitation of actions, effect on, 290–291
negligence, distinguished from, 450
prior incumbrancer, of, postponement for, 453
priority, loss by, 449, 453

FRAUDULENT PREFERENCE
burden of proof of, 229
debenture issue, setting aside as, 125
when deemed to be, 125
dispositions constituting, avoidance of, 228–229
solicitor being creditor, whether implied from, 229
what constitutes, 229

FREEHOLDS
legal mortgage of, 21
conversion to mortgage by demise, 53

FREIGHT
mortgage of, notices to be given, 490
mortgagee in possession, rights to, 493

FRIENDLY SOCIETIES
borrowing powers, 198
consumer credit agreement not regulated, 134
discharge of mortgage to, 199
loans by—
directed securities, upon, 198
members, to, 198
moneylenders, whether, 235
option mortgage scheme, qualified lenders under, 660

FUND IN COURT
incumbrancers on, priority between, 480
stop order. *See* STOP ORDER

FURNITURE
removal of mortgagor's, 331–332

FURTHER ADVANCES. *See* TACKING

FUTURE PROPERTY
equitable mortgage of, 12

G

GAMING
contracts, avoidance of, 245
money paid under, whether
recoverable, 245–246
loans for payment of bets, 246
losses paid by agent, whether recoverable from principal, 246
securities, illegal consideration, as, 245

GARAGE
estate development, separate disposition under, 40

GARNISHEE ORDER
proceeds of sale by mortgagee, when bound by, 375

GARNISHEE PROCEEDINGS
nature and effect of, 163

GOODWILL
benefit of, accretion to security, as, 37
compensation for, on compulsory purchase, 37
mortgage of, profit-sharing loan, by, 113
receiver for debenture holders, duty to preserve, 305

GUARANTEE. See also SURETY
contract of, 3
interest, tax relief, 665
security under Consumer Credit Act, 1974...136

H

HIRE
agreement, powers of court as to, 152

HIRE PURCHASE
Consumer Credit Act, 1974, application of, 132
regulated agreement—
courts, powers as to, 152
repossession of goods on default under, 144–145
termination of, 145

HIRE-PURCHASE AGREEMENT
bill of sale, distinguished, 80
fixtures, 75
legal effects of, 80

HOUSING
loans by local authorities. See LOCAL AUTHORITIES

HOUSING ACTS
discharge or modification of liabilities by, 600
purposes of, 600

HOUSING ASSOCIATION
assistance by local authorities to, 188
company, may be, 192
co-operative, mortgage interest, tax relief, 670
industrial and provident society, may be, 192
loans by Housing Corporation to, 192
local authorities to, 188
meaning, 191–192

HOUSING ASSOCIATION—continued
registered, 192
unregistered, 192

HOUSING CORPORATION
body corporate, 192
establishment of, 192
housing associations, functions as to, register of, 192
loans by, 192
advances by building society subsequent to, 192
objects of, 192
unregistered self-build associations, functions as to, 192

HOUSING SOCIETIES
building society advances to, 192
housing associations include, [191]. See also HOUSING ASSOCIATION
Housing Corporation, functions as to, 192

HOUSING SUBSIDIES ACT, 1967
option mortgage scheme under. See OPTION MORTGAGE SCHEME

HUSBAND AND WIFE. See also MARRIED WOMAN
action for possession, spouse, whether to be joined, 323, 324
co-owners, mortgage by husband forging wife's signature, 244
former husband, conveyance of interest to former wife—
form, 694
indemnity clause, 695
lease by mortgagor to wife with intent to defraud, 231
undue influence not presumed between, 241

HYPOTHECATION
bottomry. See BOTTOMRY
meaning, 4
respondentia, by way of, 4

I

IMPERFECT SECURITY. See VOID OR IMPERFECT SECURITIES

IMPROVEMENTS
Agricultural Mortgage Corporation, loans by, 207
authorised, what are 205–206
charge on land for—
effect of, 206
Minister of Agriculture, Fisheries and Food, to, 206
mode of creation, 206
priority of, 206
public improvements, [206]
registration, 206
rentcharge, by way of, 206
settled land, in case of, 199, 205
land or buildings, of, interest, tax relief, 668–669
repairs by mortgagee incorporating, 351, 352
tenant for life, powers to mortgage for, 199, 205

PRINTED IN GREAT BRITAIN BY THE WHITEFRIARS PRESS LTD.
LONDON AND TONBRIDGE